African Paleoecology and Human Evolution

Humans evolved in the dynamic landscapes of Africa under conditions of pronounced climatic, geological, and environmental change during the past 7 million years. This book brings together detailed records of the paleontological and archeological sites in Africa that provide the basic evidence for understanding the environments in which we evolved. Chapters cover specific sites, with comprehensive accounts of their geology, paleontology, paleobotany, and their ecological significance for our evolution. Other chapters provide important regional syntheses of past ecological conditions. This book is unique in merging a broad geographic scope (all of Africa) and deep time framework (the past 7 million years) in discussing the geological context and paleontological records of our evolution and that of organisms that evolved alongside our ancestors. It will offer important insights to anyone interested in human evolution, including researchers and graduate students in paleontology, archeology, anthropology, and geology.

Sally C. Reynolds is Principal Academic in Hominin Palaeoecology and Head of the Institute for Studies of Landscape and Human Evolution at Bournemouth University, UK. She has over 20 years of research experience in the study of African mammalian fauna, past environments, and landscapes. She previously co-edited *African Genesis: Perspectives on Hominin Evolution* (Cambridge University Press, 2012).

René Bobe is Head Paleontologist with the Paleo-Primate Project at Gorongosa National Park, Sofala, Mozambique, and a Research Affiliate at the Primate Models for Behavioural Evolution Laboratory, School of Anthropology, University of Oxford, UK. He has been studying early hominin paleoecology in eastern Africa for the past 30 years, with fieldwork in Ethiopia, Kenya, and Mozambique. His research focuses on fossil mammals that provide long-term records of ecological change.

African Paleoecology and Human Evolution

Edited by

Sally C. Reynolds
Bournemouth University

René Bobe
University of Oxford

CAMBRIDGE
UNIVERSITY PRESS

University Printing House, Cambridge CB2 8BS, United Kingdom

One Liberty Plaza, 20th Floor, New York, NY 10006, USA

477 Williamstown Road, Port Melbourne, VIC 3207, Australia

314–321, 3rd Floor, Plot 3, Splendor Forum, Jasola District Centre, New Delhi – 110025, India

103 Penang Road, #05–06/07, Visioncrest Commercial, Singapore 238467

Cambridge University Press is part of the University of Cambridge.

It furthers the University's mission by disseminating knowledge in the pursuit of education, learning, and research at the highest international levels of excellence.

www.cambridge.org
Information on this title: www.cambridge.org/9781107074033
DOI: 10.1017/9781139696470

© Cambridge University Press 2022

This publication is in copyright. Subject to statutory exception and to the provisions of relevant collective licensing agreements, no reproduction of any part may take place without the written permission of Cambridge University Press.

First published 2022

Printed in the United Kingdom by TJ Books Limited, Padstow Cornwall

A catalogue record for this publication is available from the British Library.

Library of Congress Cataloging-in-Publication Data
Names: Reynolds, Sally C., editor. | Bobe, René, 1960- editor.
Title: African paleoecology and human evolution / edited by Sally C. Reynolds, Bournemouth University, René Bobe, University of Oxford.
Description: Cambridge, United Kingdom ; New York, NY : Cambridge University Press, 2022. | Includes index.
Identifiers: LCCN 2021050165 (print) | LCCN 2021050166 (ebook) | ISBN 9781107074033 (hardback) | ISBN 9781139696470 (ebook)
Subjects: LCSH: Evolutionary paleoecology. | Human evolution — Africa. | BISAC: SOCIAL SCIENCE / Anthropology / Physical
Classification: LCC QE721.2.E87 A37 2022 (print) | LCC QE721.2.E87 (ebook) | DDC 560/.45096—dc23/eng/20211216
LC record available at https://lccn.loc.gov/2021050165
LC ebook record available at https://lccn.loc.gov/2021050166

ISBN 978-1-107-07403-3 Hardback

Additional resources for this publication at www.cambridge.org/africanpaleoecology.

Cambridge University Press has no responsibility for the persistence or accuracy of URLs for external or third-party internet websites referred to in this publication and does not guarantee that any content on such websites is, or will remain, accurate or appropriate.

We dedicate this volume to generations of fieldworkers and researchers who, by virtue of their tireless efforts under African skies, have revealed the evidence with which to understand our origins.

Contents

List of Contributors ix
Acknowledgments xiii

Part I Modern Africa and Overview of Late Cenozoic Paleoenvironments

1 **Introduction: African Paleoecology and Human Evolution** 1
René Bobe and Sally C. Reynolds

2 **Approaches to the Study of Past Environments** 7
Peter Andrews, Sally C. Reynolds, and René Bobe

3 **Environmental and Stratigraphic Bias in the Hominin Fossil Record: Implications for Theories of the Climatic Forcing of Human Evolution** 15
Philip J. Hopley and Simon J. Maxwell

4 **Late Miocene and Earliest Pliocene Paleoecology of Africa: A Synthesis** 24
Jessamy H. Doman and Emily Goble Early

5 **The Middle Pleistocene Through the Holocene of Africa: A Synthesis** 33
J. Tyler Faith

Part II Southern Africa

6 **The Southern African Sites: Paleoenvironmental Syntheses and Future Research Prospects** 49
Sally C. Reynolds

7 **Geology, Fauna, and Paleoenvironmental Reconstructions of the Makapansgat Limeworks *Australopithecus africanus*-Bearing Paleo-Cave** 66
Kaye E. Reed, Kevin L. Kuykendall, Andy I.R. Herries, Philip J. Hopley, Matt Sponheimer, and Lars Werdelin

8 **Paleoenvironments and the Context of Plio-Pleistocene Hominins at Kromdraai, South Africa** 82
Jean-Baptiste Fourvel and J. Francis Thackeray

9 **Using the Faunal Community to Determine the Local Ecology for Early Hominins at Cooper's Cave at 1.5 Ma** 86
Darryl de Ruiter

10 **The Paleoenvironments of Sterkfontein: Old Questions, New Approaches** 92
Lauren C. Sewell, Job M. Kibii, and Sally C. Reynolds

11 **Swartkrans: A Record of Paleoenvironmental Change in the Cradle of Humankind** 102
Darryl de Ruiter

12 **Cornelia-Uitzoek: Paleoecology, Archeology and Geochronology** 120
James S. Brink†, John A.J. Gowlett, Andy I.R. Herries, John Hancox, Jacopo Moggi-Cecchi, Daryl Codron, Lloyd Rossouw, Gary Trower, Olivia M.L. Stone, Britt Bousman, Rainer Grün, and Antoine Souron

13 **The Paleoecology of the *Australopithecus africanus* Type Site at Taung, South Africa** 135
Philip J. Hopley and Brian F. Kuhn

14 **Wonderwerk Cave, Northern Cape Province: An Early–Middle Pleistocene Paleoenvironmental Sequence for the Interior of South Africa** 142
Liora Kolska Horwitz, Margaret D. Avery, Marion K. Bamford, Francesco Berna, James S. Brink†, Michaela Ecker, Yolanda Fernandez-Jalvo, Paul Goldberg, Sharon Holt, Julia Lee-Thorp, Ari Matmon, Robyn Pickering, Naomi Porat, Lloyd Rossouw, Louis Scott, Ron Shaar, and Michael Chazan

Part III Eastern and Central Africa

15 **Hominid Paleoenvironments in Tropical Africa from the Late Miocene to the Early Pleistocene** 161
René Bobe and Sally C. Reynolds

16 **Mammal Paleoecology from the Late Early Pleistocene Sites of the Dandiero Basin (Eritrea), With Emphasis on the Suid Record** 187
Tsegai Medin, Bienvenido Martínez-Navarro, Marco P. Ferretti, Massimiliano Ghinassi, Mauro Papini, Yosief Libsekal, and Lorenzo Rook

17 **The 6-Million-Year Record of Ecological and Environmental Change at Gona, Afar Region, Ethiopia** 197
Naomi E. Levin, Scott W. Simpson, Jay Quade, Melanie A. Everett, Stephen R. Frost, Michael J. Rogers, and Sileshi Semaw

Contents

18 **The Hadar Formation, Afar Regional State, Ethiopia: Geology, Fauna, and Paleoenvironmental Reconstructions** 214
Christopher J. Campisano, John Rowan, and Kaye E. Reed

19 **Fossil Vertebrates and Paleoenvironments of the Pliocene Hadar Formation at Dikika, Ethiopia** 229
René Bobe, Denis Geraads, Jonathan G. Wynn, Denné Reed, W. Andrew Barr, and Zeresenay Alemseged

20 **Miocene to Pliocene Stratigraphy and Paleoecology of Galili, Ethiopia** 242
Ottmar Kullmer, Oliver Sandrock, Thomas Bence Viola, Wolfgang Hujer, Zelalem Bedaso, Doris Nagel, Andrea Stadlmayr, Fritz Popp, Robert Scholger, Gerhard W. Weber, and Horst Seidler

21 **Melka Kunture, Ethiopia: Early Pleistocene Faunas of the Ethiopian Highlands** 256
Denis Geraads, Rosalia Gallotti, Jean-Paul Raynal, Raymonde Bonnefille, and Margherita Mussi

22 **Early Pleistocene Fauna and Paleoenvironments at Konso, Ethiopia** 269
Gen Suwa, Berhane Asfaw, Hideo Nakaya, Shigehiro Katoh, and Yonas Beyene

23 **Paleontology and Geology of the Mursi Formation** 278
Michelle S.M. Drapeau, Jonathan G. Wynn, Denis Geraads, Laurence Dumouchel, Christopher J. Campisano, and René Bobe

24 **Mammalian Diversity Patterns and Paleoecology in the Lower Omo Valley, Ethiopia** 289
Enquye W. Negash, René Bobe, Zeresenay Alemseged, and Jonathan Wynn

25 **Paleoecology and Paleoenvironments of Early Quaternary Faunal Assemblages from the Nachukui Formation in Kenya: Insights from the West Turkana Archeological Project** 298
Jean-Philip Brugal and Hélène Roche

26 **Early Hominins and Paleoecology of the Koobi Fora Formation, Lake Turkana Basin, Kenya** 311
René Bobe, João d'Oliveira Coelho, Susana Carvalho, and Meave Leakey

27 **Early Pliocene Faunal Assemblages from the Tugen Hills, Kenya: A Comparison of Field Collection Methods and Some Implications for Paleoenvironmental Reconstruction** 332
Katie M. Binetti, Andrew Hill†, and Joseph V. Ferarro

28 **The Southern Chemeron Formation, Tugen Hills, Kenya: A Review and a Paleoecological Analysis of the Bovid Fauna** 343
Emily Goble Early

29 **Fauna and Paleoenvironments of the Homa Peninsula, Western Kenya** 360
Laura C. Bishop, Thomas W. Plummer, David R. Braun, Peter W. Ditchfield, Emily Goble Early, Fritz Hertel, Cristina Lemorini, James S. Oliver, Richard Potts, Thomas Vincent, Elizabeth Whitfield, and Rahab N. Kinyanjui

30 **Mammalian Fauna of the Olorgesailie Basin and Southern Kenya Rift** 376
Richard Potts and J. Tyler Faith

31 **Context and Environments of the Lower Pleistocene Hominins of Peninj, Tanzania** 384
Denis Geraads, Ignacio de la Torre, and Christiane Denys

32 **Paleoecology and Vertebrate Taphonomy of DK Site (Bed I), Olduvai Gorge, Tanzania** 394
Paul Farrugia and Jackson K. Njau

33 **Lower Bed II Olduvai Basin, Tanzania: Wetland Sedge Taphonomy, Seasonal Pasture, and Implications for Hominin Scavenging** 413
Charles R. Peters, Marion K. Bamford, and John P. Shields

34 **Paleoecology of Laetoli, Tanzania** 435
Terry Harrison, Amandus Kwekason, and Denise F. Su

35 **The Paleoenvironment of the Plio-Pleistocene Chiwondo Beds of Northern Malawi** 453
Ottmar Kullmer, Oliver Sandrock, Harrison Simfukwe, Timothy G. Bromage, and Friedemann Schrenk

Part IV   Northern Africa

36 **The Northern African Sites: Paleoenvironmental Syntheses** 461
Denis Geraads

37 **Ahl al Oughlam, Morocco: The Richest Fossil Site in North Africa at the Pliocene/Pleistocene Boundary** 468
Denis Geraads, David Lefèvre, and Jean-Paul Raynal

38 **Tighennif (Ternifine), Algeria: Environments of the Earliest Human Fossils of North Africa in the late Early Pleistocene** 475
Denis Geraads

39 **Early *Homo* on the Atlantic Shore: The Thomas I and Oulad Hamida 1 Quarries, Morocco** 481
Denis Geraads, Camille Daujeard, David Lefèvre, Rosalia Gallotti, Abderrahim Mohib, and Jean-Paul Raynal

Volume References   492
Index   576
Color plates can be found between pages 306 and 307

Contributors

Zeresenay Alemseged
Department of Organismal Biology and Anatomy, University of Chicago

Peter Andrews
Natural History Museum, London

Berhane Asfaw
Rift Valley Research Service

Margaret A. Avery
Iziko Museums of South Africa

Marion K. Bamford
Evolutionary Studies Institute, University of the Witwatersrand

W. Andrew Barr
George Washington University

Zelalem Bedaso
College of Arts and Sciences: Geology, University of Dayton

Francesco Berna
Department of Archaeology, Simon Fraser University

Yonas Beyene
Association for Research and Conservation of Culture

Katie M. Binetti
Department of Anthropology, Baylor University

Laura C. Bishop
Research Centre in Evolutionary Anthropology and Palaeoecology, School of Biological and Environmental Sciences Liverpool John Moores University and The Sino-British College, University of Shanghai for Science and Technology

René Bobe
School of Anthropology, University of Oxford; Gorongosa National Park, Sofala, Mozambique; Interdisciplinary Center for Archaeology and Evolution of Human Behavior (ICArEHB), Universidade do Algarve

Raymonde Bonnefille
CNRS, CEREGE UMR Europole Méditerranéen de l'Arbois Aix-en-Provence

Britt Bousman
Center for Archaeological Studies, Department of Anthropology, Texas State University

David R. Braun
Center for the Advanced Study of Human Paleobiology, Department of Anthropology, The George Washington University

James S. Brink†
Florisbad Research Station, National Museum, Bloemfontein

Timothy G. Bromage
Department of Molecular Pathobiology, New York University College of Dentistry

Jean-Philip Brugal
LAMPEA (UMR 7269) MMSH BP 647

Christopher J. Campisano
Institute of Human Origins, School of Human Evolution and Social Change, Arizona State University

Susana Carvalho
Primate Models for Behavioural Evolution Laboratory, School of Anthropology, University of Oxford

Michael Chazan
Anthropology Department, University of Toronto

Daryl Codron
Department of Zoology & Entomology, University of the Free State

Camille Daujeard
Département de Préhistoire, UMR 7194 du CNRS, Muséum National d'Histoire Naturelle

Ignacio de la Torre
Instituto de Historia, CSIC

Darryl de Ruiter
Department of Anthropology, Texas A&M University

Christiane Denys
Muséum National d'Histoire Naturelle

Peter W. Ditchfield
Research Laboratory for Archaeology and the History of Art, University of Oxford

João d'Oliveira Coelho
Primate Models for Behavioural Evolution Laboratory, School of Anthropology, University of Oxford

List of Contributors

Jessamy H. Doman
Department of Anthropology, Yale University

Michelle S.M. Drapeau
Département d'Antropologie, Université de Montréal

Laurence Dumouchel
Department of Anthropology, Wichita State University

Michaela Ecker
Anthropology Department, University of Toronto

Melanie A. Everett
Chevron Energy Technology Co., Houston

J. Tyler Faith
Natural History Museum of Utah & Department of Anthropology, University of Utah

Paul Farrugia
Indiana University, Department of Earth and Atmospheric Sciences

Joseph V. Ferarro
Department of Anthropology, Baylor University

Yolanda Fernandez-Jalvo
Departamento de Palaeobiologia, Museo de Nacional de Ciencias Naturales

Marco P. Ferretti
Scuola di Scienze e Tecnologia (Sezione di Geologia), Università degli Studi di Camerino, Camerino

Jean-Baptiste Fourvel
Laboratoire TRACES UMR 5608 Université Toulouse Jean Jaurès Maison de la Recherche

Stephen R. Frost
Department of Anthropology, University of Oregon

Rosalia Gallotti
Université Paul-Valéry Montpellier 3, Archéologie des sociétés méditerranéennes - LabEx Archimede, Montpellier

Denis Geraads
CR2P, Muséum National d'Histoire Naturelle, CNRS, Sorbonne Université

Massimiliano Ghinassi
Dipartimento di Geoscienze, Università degli Studi di Padova, Padova

Emily Goble Early
Anthropology Section, Arizona Museum of Natural History

Paul Goldberg
Archeology Department, Boston University

John A.J. Gowlett
Department of Archaeology, Classics and Egyptology, University of Liverpool

Rainer Grün
Research School of Earth Sciences, The Australian National University

John Hancox
CCIC Coal (Pty) Limited, South Africa

Terry Harrison
Department of Anthropology, New York University

Andy I.R. Herries
Department of Archaeology, and History La Trobe University

Fritz Hertel
Biology, California State University, Northridge

Andrew Hill†
Department of Anthropology, Yale University

Sharon Holt
Florisbad Quaternary Research Department, National Museum, Bloemfontein

Philip J. Hopley
Department of Earth and Planetary Sciences, Birkbeck, University of London

Liora Kolska Horwitz
National Natural History Collections, Faculty of Life Sciences, The Hebrew University

Wolfgang Hujer
OMV Exploration & Production GmbH

Shigehiro Katoh
Division of Natural History, Hyogo Museum of Nature and Human Activities, Sanda

Job M. Kibii
Division of Palaeontology, National Museums of Kenya

Rahab N. Kinyanjui
Palynology & Paleobotany section, Earth Sciences Department, National Museums of Kenya

Brian F. Kuhn
Department of Geology, University of Johannesburg

Ottmar Kullmer
Division of Paleoanthropology, Research Institute and Natural History Museum Frankfurt

Kevin L. Kuykendall
Department of Archaeology, University of Sheffield

Amandus Kwekason
Museum and House of Culture, National Museum of Tanzania

Meave Leakey
Turkana Basin Institute, Stony Brook University, USA

Julia Lee-Thorp
Research Laboratory for Archaeology, University of Oxford

David Lefèvre
Université Paul-Valéry Montpellier 3, Archéologie des sociétés méditerranéennes - LabEx Archimede, Montpellier

Cristina Lemorini
Dipartimento di Scienze dell'Antichità, Università di Roma La Sapienza

Naomi E. Levin
Department of Earth & Environmental Sciences, University of Michigan

Yosief Libsekal
National Museum of Eritrea

Bienvenido Martínez-Navarro
ICREA, IPHES-CERCA, URV, Insitut Català de Paleoecologia Humana i Evolució Social, Tarragona

Ari Matmon
Institute of Earth Sciences, The Hebrew University

Simon J. Maxwell
Department of Earth and Planetary Sciences, Birkbeck, University of London

Tsegai Medin
IPHES-CERCA, Institut Català de Paleoecologia Humana i Evolució Social, Tarragona Commission of Culture and Sports of Eritrea

Jacopo Moggi-Cecchi
Laboratori di Antropologia, Dipartimento di Biologia, Università' di Firenze

Abderrahim Mohib
Moroccan Ministry of Culture

Margherita Mussi
Università di Roma Sapienza, Dipartimento di Scienze dell'Antichità

Doris Nagel
Department of Paleontology, University of Vienna

Hideo Nakaya
Department of Earth and Environmental Sciences, Kagoshima University

Enquye W. Negash
Center for the Advanced Study of Human Paleobiology, George Washington University

Jackson K. Njau
Indiana University, Department of Earth and Atmospheric Sciences

James S. Oliver
Anthropology Section, Research and Collections Center, Illinois State Museum

Mauro Papini
Dipartimento di Scienze della Terra, Università degli Studi di Firenze, Firenze

Charles R. Peters
Department of Anthropology, University of Georgia

Robyn Pickering
Department of Geological Sciences, University of Cape Town

Thomas W. Plummer
Department of Anthropology, Queen's College, City University of New York and NYCEP

Fritz Popp
Department for Geodynamics and Sedimentology, University of Vienna

Naomi Porat
Geological Survey of Israel

Richard Potts
Human Origins Program, National Museum of Natural History, Smithsonian Institution and Department of Earth Sciences, National Museums of Kenya

Jay Quade
Department of Geosciences, University of Arizona

Jean-Paul Raynal
PACEA, CNRS, Université de Bordeaux, and INSAP, Rabat

Denné Reed
Department of Anthropology, University of Texas at Austin

Kaye E. Reed
Institute of Human Origins and School of Human Evolution and Social Change, Arizona State University

Sally C. Reynolds
Faculty of Science and Technology, Bournemouth University,

Hélène Roche
CNRS, Paris-Nanterre University

Michael J. Rogers
Department of Anthropology, Southern Connecticut State University

Lorenzo Rook
Dipartimento di Scienze della Terra, Paleo[Fab]Lab, Università degli Studi di Firenze

Lloyd Rossouw
Florisbad Quaternary Research Department, National Museum, Bloemfontein & Department of Plant Sciences, University of the Free State, Bloemfontein

John Rowan
Department of Anthropology, University of Albany, SUNY

List of Contributors

Oliver Sandrock
Departmemt of Earth- and Life History, Hesse State Museum Darmstadt

Robert Scholger
Lehrstuhl für Angewandte Geophysik, Montanuniversität Loeben

Friedemann Schrenk
Division of Paleoanthropology, Senckenberg Research Institute and Natural History Museum Frankfurt

Louis Scott
Department of Plant Sciences, University of the Free State

Horst Seidler
Department of Evolutionary Anthropology, University of Vienna

Sileshi Semaw
Centro Nacional de Investigación sobre la Evolución Humana

Lauren C. Sewell
Faculty of Science and Technology, Bournemouth University

Ron Shaar
Institute of Earth Sciences, The Hebrew University

John P. Shields
Georgia Electron Microscopy, University of Georgia

Harrison Simfukwe
Cultural & Museum Centre Karonga, Malawi

Scott W. Simpson
Department of Anatomy, Case Western Reserve University School of Medicine

Antoine Souron
PACEA, UMR CNRS 5199, Université de Bordeaux

Matt Sponheimer
Department of Anthropology, University of Colorado, Boulder

Andrea Stadlmayr
Department of Evolutionary Anthropology, University of Vienna

Olivia M.L. Stone
School of Biological, Earth and Environmental Sciences, University of New South Wales

Denise F. Su
Institute of Human Origins, School of Human Evolution and Social Change, Arizona State University

Gen Suwa
Department of Biological Sciences, University of Tokyo

J. Francis Thackeray
Evolutionary Studies Institute, University of the Witwatersrand

Gary Trower
Evolutionary Studies Institute, University of the Witwatersrand

Thomas Vincent
Research Centre in Evolutionary Anthropology and Palaeoecology, School of Biological and Environmental Sciences, Liverpool John Moores University

Thomas Bence Viola
Department of Anthropology, University of Toronto

Gerhard W. Weber
Department of Evolutionary Anthropology, University of Vienna

Lars Werdelin
Department of Palaeobiology, Swedish Museum of Natural History

Elizabeth Whitfield
Research Centre in Evolutionary Anthropology and Palaeoecology, School of Biological and Environmental Sciences Liverpool John Moores University

Jonathan G. Wynn
Division of Earth Sciences, National Science Foundation

Acknowledgments

This book has been a communal effort and we could not have achieved this without the assistance of a multitude of generous colleagues. The task of synthesizing large parts of the fossil record of an entire continent was a considerable challenge, one which would never have been possible without the support and patience of over 120 contributing authors.

Firstly, we would like to thank all our colleagues who have contributed to this volume as authors or co-authors. All chapters were peer-reviewed and we are very grateful to our many colleagues who kindly offered their time and expertise in the review process: Jordi Agusti, Peter Andrews, Margaret Avery, Andrew Barr, Anna K. Behrensmeyer, Miriam Belmaker, Matthew Bennett, Faysal Bibi, Scott Blumenthal, the late James Brink, Jean-Philip Brugal, João Coelho, Lucile Crètè; Andrew Du, Laurence Dumouchel, Tyler Faith, Joe Ferraro, Denis Geraads, John Harris, Terry Harrison, Phil Hopley, Liora Horwitz, Kris Kovarovic, Carles Martín-Closas, Bienvenido Martínez-Navarro, Jackson Njau, David Patterson, Martin Pickford, Tom Plummer, Amy Rector, Darryl de Ruiter, Denné Reed, Kaye Reed, Oliver Sandrock, Lauren Sewell, Gen Suwa, Amelia Villaseñor, and Tim White.

Secondly, we would like to thank the staff at Cambridge University Press, especially Jenny van der Meijden for her expert help during the production process. Bruno Matos created the regional and continental maps that are a key part of this volume. Matthew Bennett modified the figure for the African biome map.

Finally, we would like to give heartfelt thanks to our families for their support and patience while we produced this book.

Sally C. Reynolds
Poole

René Bobe
Oxford

Part I Modern Africa and Overview of Late Cenozoic Paleoenvironments

Introduction: African Paleoecology and Human Evolution

René Bobe and Sally C. Reynolds

Early hominins were not limited to particular sites or localities in a paleontological or archeological sense, but lived and died in complex and dynamic landscapes and ecosystems of which we have partial, incomplete records. The fossil evidence of early hominin paleoenvironments is always limited, sometimes providing brief snapshots of small areas, other times affording very coarse chronological and spatial resolution over large distances. Taphonomic conditions typically vary within any one locality over time, and from one locality to another. And yet, it is these partial and biased records that we use to build an understanding of the forces that have shaped our evolution.

We think that to gain a better understanding of our evolution and its ecological context it is necessary to take a broad view. As in the pioneering volume by Clark Howell and François Bourlière, *African Ecology and Human Evolution* (1963), here we aim to consider the whole continent of Africa during the time when our lineage emerged and dispersed across the continent. The focus of this volume is on the paleoenvironmental conditions and paleoecological relationships that are likely to have shaped the evolution of our ancestors as well as closely related species during the past 7 million years. We aim to discuss regions with a rich fossil record as well as regions with a sparse record, from north to south and from east to west (Figure 1.1).

This volume bears witness to decades of painstaking work by numerous researchers at hundreds of different sites. The research presented in the following chapters is necessarily interdisciplinary and builds on the efforts of scholars like Jean de Heinzelin, Bill Bishop, Maurice Taieb, Frank Brown, and Richard Hay, who, among others, laid a solid geological foundation for studies of hominin paleoenvironments. Likewise, the taphonomic approaches of Kay Behrensmeyer in East Africa, among others, continue to shape paleoecological studies across the continent.

This volume is organized into four main parts. In Part I, we present a review of key methods of paleoecological reconstruction, discuss biases in the hominin fossil record, and provide two synthetic chapters on the paleoenvironments of the continent. Part II is focused on southern Africa (Figure 1.2), with an overview chapter followed by site-specific contributions on Makapansgat, Kromdraai, Cooper's Cave, Sterkfontein, Swartkrans, Cornelia-Uitzoek, Taung, and Wonderwerk Cave.

Part III begins with an overview of eastern, central, and western African paleoenvironments during the late Miocene to the early Pleistocene, followed by site-specific chapters on Buia, Gona, Hadar, Dikika, Galili, Melka Kunture, Konso, the lower Omo Valley, West Turkana, East Turkana, Tugen Hills, the Homa Peninsula, Olorgesailie, Peninj, Olduvai, Laetoli, and the Karonga Basin (Figure 1.3a, 1.3b). Part IV provides a discussion of North African paleoenvironments in the Pliocene and Pleistocene, with site-specific contributions on Ahl al Oughlam, Tighenif, Thomas Quarry, and Oulad Hamida Quarry (Figure 1.4).

As currently understood, hominin evolution spans the period from nearly 7 Ma (million years) to the present (Figure 1.5). This time frame is based on the earliest records of possible hominins, including the species *Ardipithecus kadabba* (Haile-Selassie, 2001; Haile-Selassie et al., 2004a, 2009a), *Orrorin tugenensis* (Senut et al., 2001), and *Sahelanthropus tchadensis* (Brunet et al., 2002). Thus, current evidence indicates that the earliest hominins lived in eastern and central Africa. The earliest evidence of the genus *Australopithecus* dates to about 4.2 Ma, and by about 3.4 Ma there is some evidence of phylogenetic diversification with a few species of *Australopithecus* occurring in eastern, central, and possibly southern Africa (Haile-Selassie et al., 2016a). *Homo* and *Paranthropus* appear in the fossil records of eastern Africa toward the end of the Pliocene, about 2.8–2.7 Ma (Wood and Leakey, 2011; Villmoare et al., 2015), and diversify during the early Pleistocene (Antón et al., 2014). By the end of the early Pleistocene, ~0.8 Ma, only species of the genus *Homo* remain in Africa and elsewhere (Rightmire, 2013; Schroeder et al., 2017).

Hominid evolution takes place in the late Cenozoic during a time of important climatic, tectonic, and environmental changes. After the Mid-Miocene Climatic Optimum, 17–15 Ma, high-latitude global temperatures as measured by oxygen isotopes in marine Foraminifera began to decline (Figure 1.6; Zachos et al., 2001). This cooling trend resulted in the establishment of the East Antarctica ice sheets in the middle Miocene (Lewis et al., 2007) and the West Antarctic ice sheets in the late Miocene (Zachos et al., 2001). The late Miocene climatic cooling culminated in ephemeral glaciation in the northern hemisphere between 6 and 5.5 Ma (Holbourn et al., 2018) coincident with the Messinian salinity crisis (Krijgsman et al., 1999; Garcia-Castellanos and Villaseñor, 2011). The early Pliocene (4.5–3.0 Ma) saw a return to warmer temperatures (Wara et al., 2005; Ravelo et al., 2006; Fedorov et al., 2013) with generally wetter conditions in much of Africa (Feakins and deMenocal, 2010;

Supplementary resources for this chapter are available on www.cambridge.org/africanpaleoecology

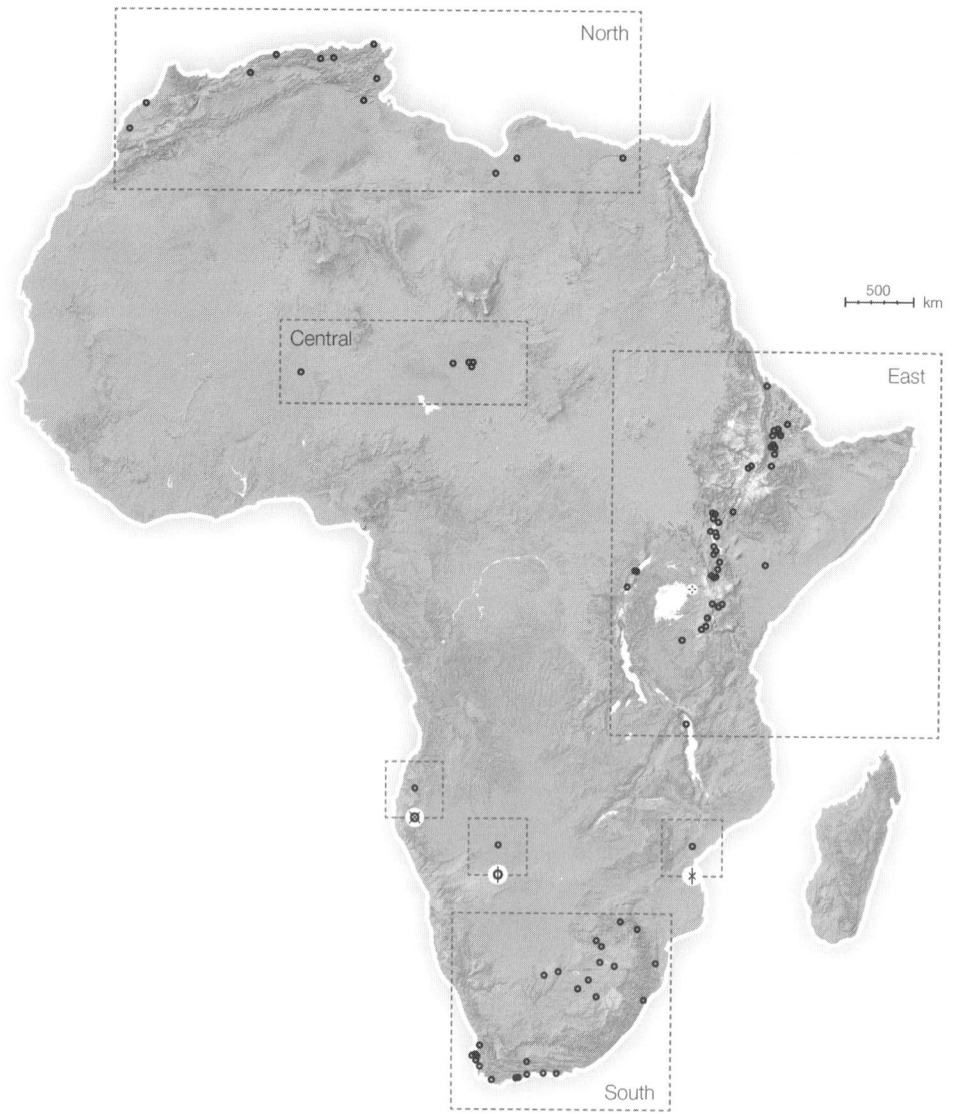

Figure 1.1 Continental map of Africa, with dashed boxes showing the geographic extent of the smaller regional maps. Individual sites (or site regions) are indicated with open circles and are labelled in the regional maps and discussed in the text.

Salzmann et al., 2011). The late Pliocene and Pleistocene was a time of further global cooling, with the onset of Northern Hemisphere glaciation between 3 and 2.6 Ma (Ravelo et al., 2004), and increasing amplitude of climatic oscillations during the Pleistocene ice ages (Raymo and Huybers, 2008). The mid-Pleistocene transition at ~0.95 Ma was marked by increased ice volume in northern latitudes and an increase in the amplitude of climatic oscillations (Larrasoaña et al., 2003). Dust records off the coast of Africa indicate that there were peaks of aridity at 2.8, 1.7, and 1.0 Ma (deMenocal, 1995). Alongside these major trends, climate cycles resulting from orbital forcing, i.e., changes in the Earth's orbital precession, axial obliquity, and orbital eccentricity (Milankovitch cycles; Hays et al., 1976; Shackleton, 2000; Philander and Fedorov, 2003; Lisiecki and Raymo, 2007; Bajo et al., 2020), may have played an important role in environmental and ecological changes in Africa (Kingston et al., 2007; Lupien et al., 2019). Cycles of ~21 ky (orbital precession) were dominant during the Miocene and most of the Pliocene, shifting to 41 ky (obliquity) dominant cyclicity at ~2.8 Ma, and 100–400 ky cycles (eccentricity modulating orbital precession) after 1 Ma (Tiedemann et al., 1994; deMenocal, 1995). Orbital forcing interacts with monsoon cycles to modulate levels and distribution of precipitation across eastern Africa, where the Intertropical Convergence Zone plays a key role (Feakins and deMenocal, 2010). Some of the high-eccentricity intervals coincided with periods of high precipitation in eastern Africa and expansion of rift valley lakes (Trauth et al., 2005, 2009). However, it remains a major challenge to relate the fine-scale resolution of many climatic records from the oceans to the coarser and more discontinuous records of hominins and their environments on land (Behrensmeyer, 2006).

The climatic changes discussed above are manifested in Africa through their influence on precipitation and vegetation. In modern African savannas, the proportion of woody vs. grassy

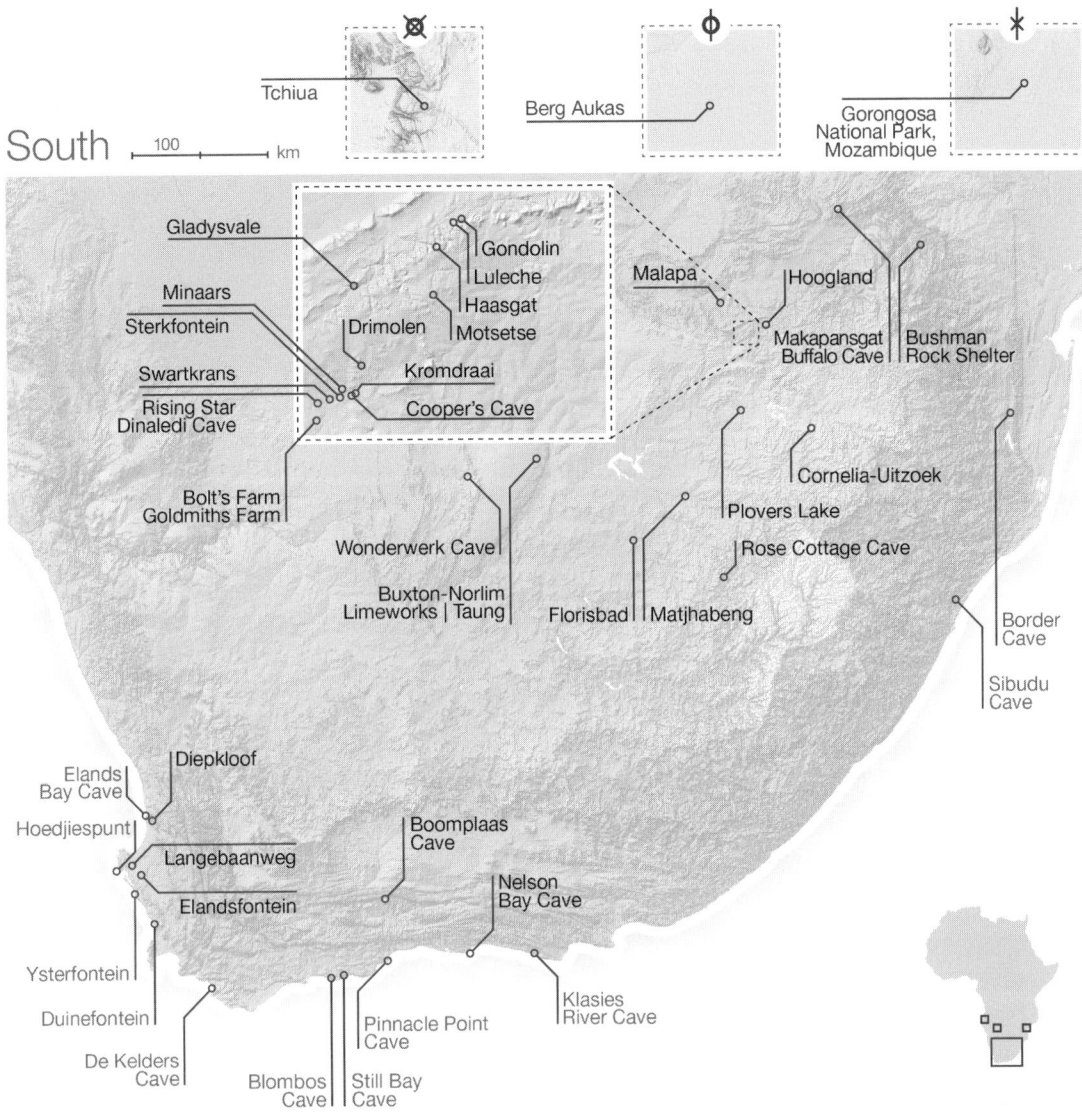

Figure 1.2 Regional map of southern Africa, including site regions in Angola, Namibia, and Mozambique. The very dense cluster of sites in the Cradle of Humankind World Heritage Site are indicated in the dashed inset box.

vegetation is primarily determined by mean annual precipitation. Regions which receive <650 mm of rain per year tend to have constrained woody cover but with significant grasses (Sankaran et al., 2005). Regions with more than 650 mm of rainfall have woody cover that tends to become dominant, unless constrained by fires or herbivores, with megaherbivores playing an important role in opening up wooded areas (Western, 1989). It is not only the amount of rainfall that's important in structuring vegetation: the seasonal distribution of rainfall and the severity and length of dry seasons also play a key role (Shorrocks, 2007). Furthermore, topography and soil types modify the effects of rainfall.

In our environmental descriptions, we rely on Frank White's African main vegetation types (White, 1983). *Forests* consist of continuous stands of trees with interdigitating crowns in multiple layers, frequently with lianas. Canopy height ranges from 10 to 50 m or more. The ground layer may include shrubs, bryophytes, and localized grasses. Rainforests are most widespread in the Guineo-Congolian region, with drier forests in this region classified as semi-evergreen. Dry forests, which may experience several months of dry season, are most common in the Zambezian and Sudanian regions. Riparian or gallery forests bordering fluvial channels and floodplains provide shade, refuge, and arboreal resources in areas that may otherwise have sparse arboreal vegetation. Afromontane forests typically occur at elevations above 1500 m and are composed of shorter trees than in lowland rainforests. *Woodlands* consist of widely spaced stands of trees with canopies covering at least 40 percent of the ground surface. Canopy height ranges from 8 to 20 m, and heliophilous grasses dominate the ground layer. Deciduous and semideciduous woodlands are common in the Sudanian and Zambezian regions. *Bushland* consists of areas dominated by woody plants usually 3–7 m in height, and covering at least 40 percent of the ground surface. Bushland is

Modern Africa and Overview of Late Cenozoic Paleoenvironments

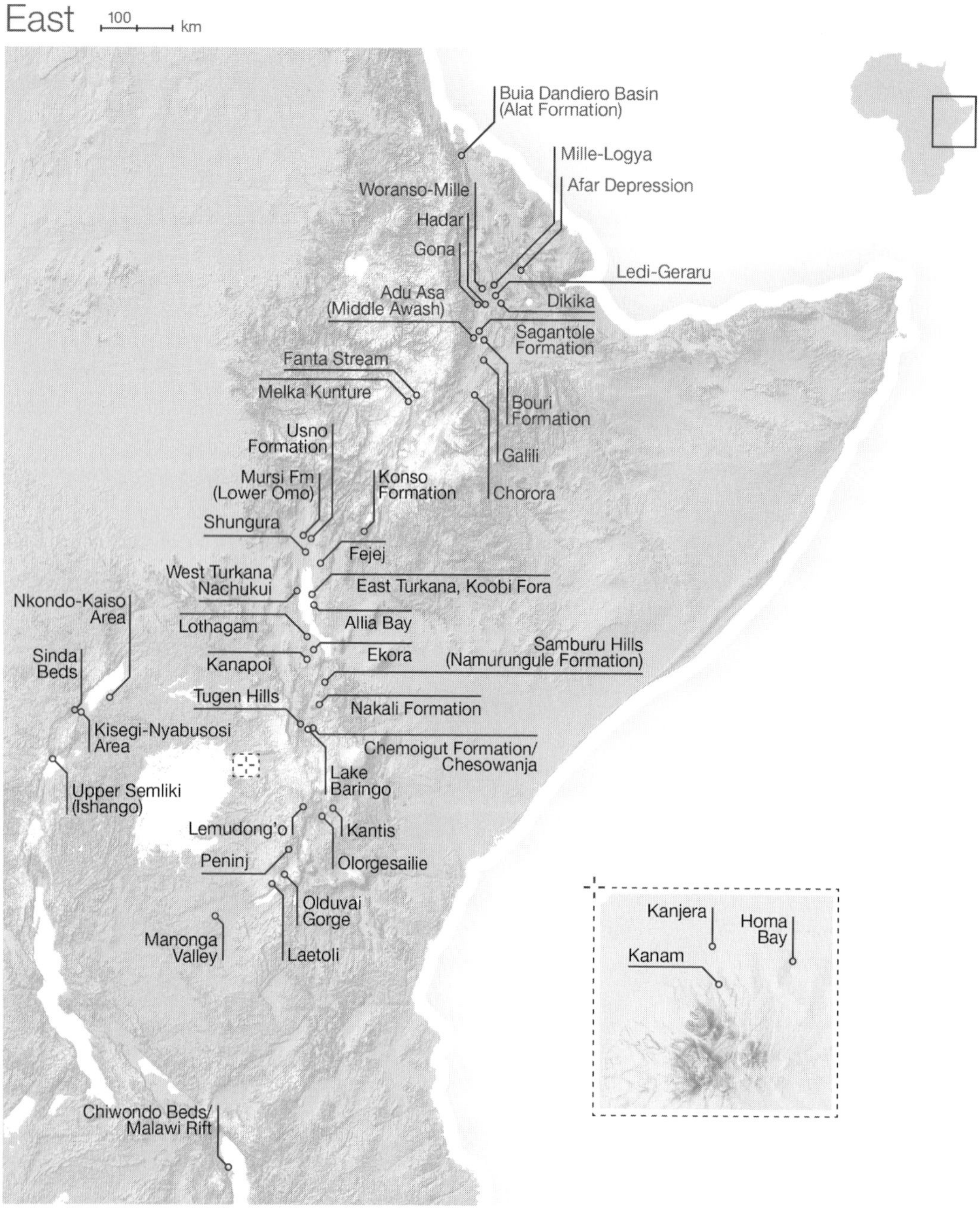

Figure 1.3a The dense clustering of sites in eastern Africa is closely associated with the East African Rift System, which contains two main rift branches: the Eastern (Gregory) Branch, which extends from the Afar region in Ethiopia through Kenya and Tanzania, and the Western (Albertine) Branch from Uganda and the DRC to Malawi and Mozambique.

Figure 1.3b The central African region comprises few sites but includes the oldest hominin material currently known from Africa, namely *Sahelanthropus tchadensis* (Vignaud et al., 2002).

Introduction

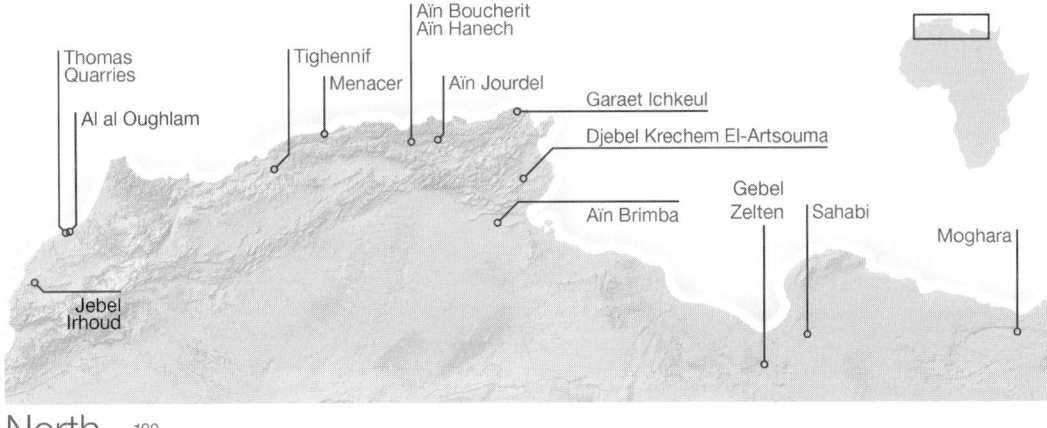

Figure 1.4 The important sites of northern Africa, including Jebel Irhoud, which has yielded the oldest remains of *Homo sapiens* (Hublin et al., 2017).

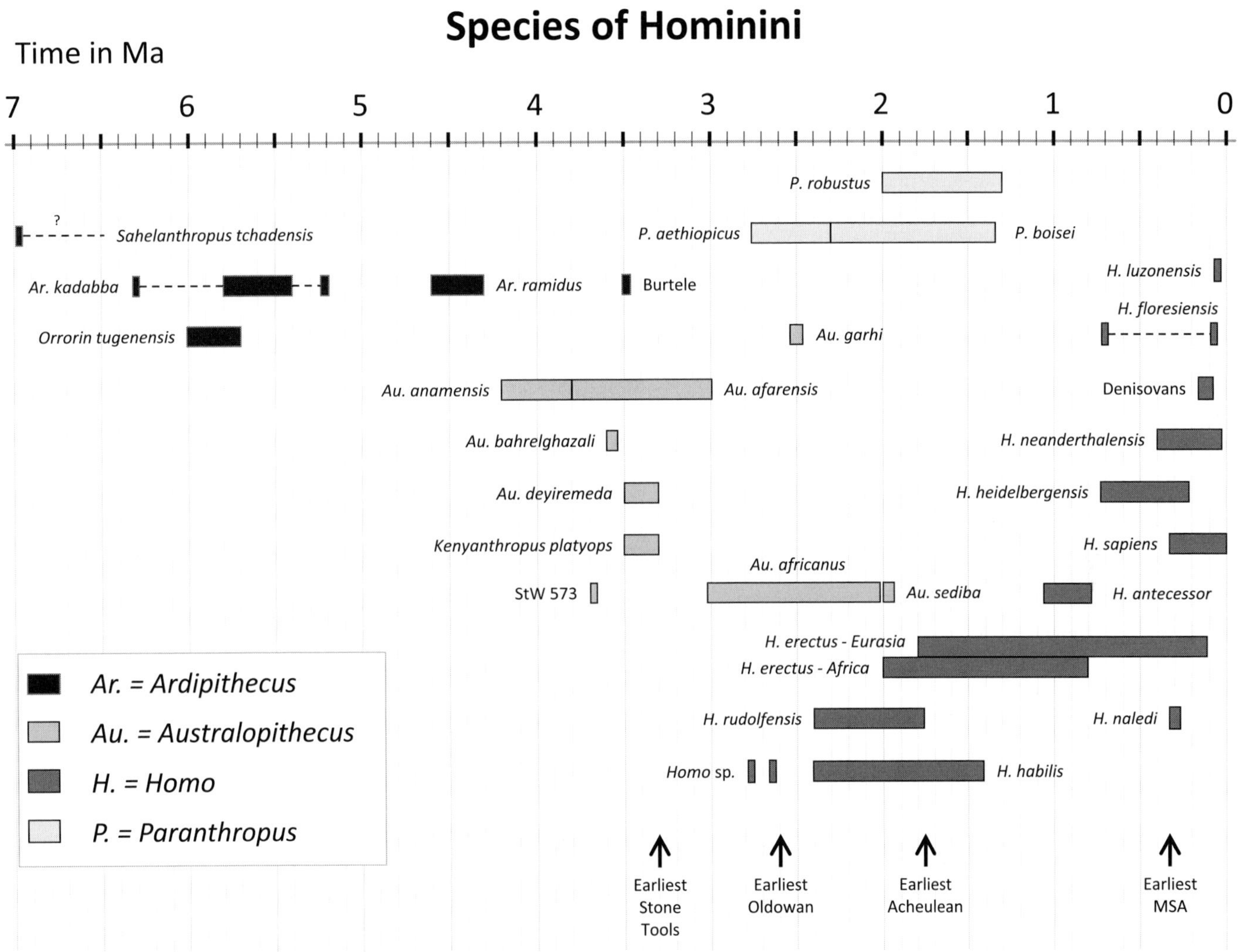

Figure 1.5 Chronology of hominin species. There are alternative interpretations to the hominin taxa depicted here. (A black and white version of this figure will appear in some formats. For the color version, please refer to the plate section.)

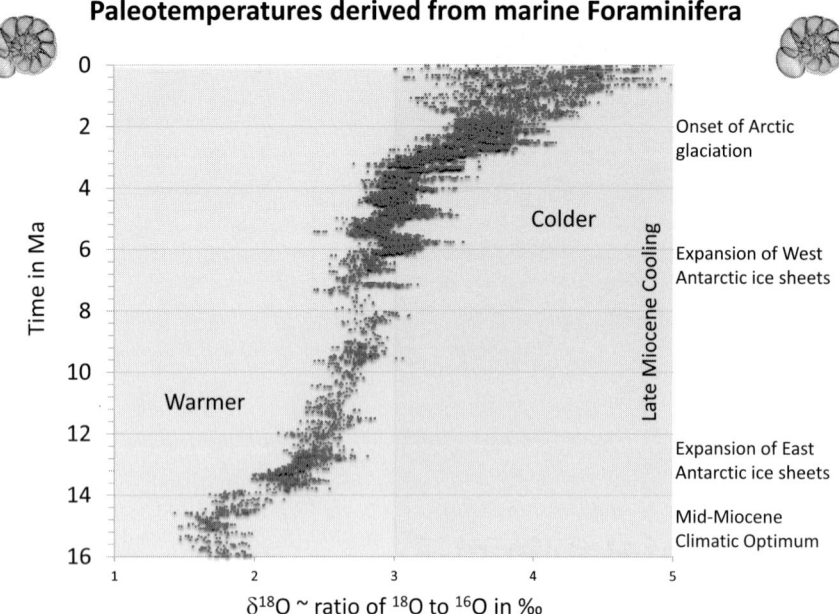

Figure 1.6 Paleotemperatures derived from benthic Foraminifera with $\delta^{18}O$ values in ‰ on the horizontal axis and time in Ma (million years) on the vertical axis. Graph drawn with data from the Deep Sea Drilling Project and the Ocean Drilling Project summarized in Zachos et al. (2001). This graph provides a view of global temperatures during the past 16 million years as a general background to understanding evolution in Africa. (A black and white version of this figure will appear in some formats. For the color version, please refer to the plate section.)

common in the Somalia–Masai region. *Wooded grasslands* are areas in which woody plants cover from 10 percent to 40 percent of the surface area, with grasses predominating. *Grasslands* are areas covered primarily by grasses with up to 10 percent cover of woody plants. Sedges (Cyperaceae) may be very common in edaphic grasslands associated with waterlogged conditions, which are widespread in the Sudanian, Zambezian, Somalia–Masai, and coastal regions. The term *savanna* refers to tropical and subtropical grasslands with scattered bushes and trees where the dominant grasses tend to be C_4 plants (Shorrocks, 2007). These vegetation types usually grade into one another and may be interdigitated in complex ways depending on various factors (topography, hydrology, and soils).

We use the term *environment* to refer broadly to the supporting matrices of life that surround living organisms (Calow, 1999). An environment may be more or less heterogeneous depending on the organism sensing it (Begon et al., 2006). Paleoenvironments are the inferred matrices of life surrounding organisms in the past. The term *habitat* refers to the place where a species or population lives. Species favor some habitats over others, evidenced by their abundance and distribution. An assemblage of species that interact with one another in a given area is called a *community* (Levin et al., 2009). Fossil assemblages rarely constitute past communities in an ecological sense. Time-averaging, bone durability, and transport tend to mix individuals from different communities at different times (Behrensmeyer et al., 2000). On a broader scale, the term *ecosystem* refers to the integrated biological and physical components of a landscape with a range of community types (Levin et al., 2009).

The chapters that follow provide a rich source of primary and synthetic data on hominin paleoenvironments and paleoecology in Africa, with most contributions focusing on the Pliocene and early Pleistocene, but also with contributions spanning from the late Miocene to the late Pleistocene and Holocene. Several chapters present primary data on the mammalian fauna, but also discuss other available paleoenvironmental and paleoecological sources of evidence. We hope that these contributions will generate further synthetic work, exploration of unknown areas, and generate new ideas and approaches to the study of our African origins.

2 Approaches to the Study of Past Environments

Peter Andrews, Sally C. Reynolds, and René Bobe

Introduction

In a book on African paleoecology and human evolution, it is important to define several key themes, including biomes, vegetation formations and associations, as well as plant physiognomy. We first define these terms, before examining the sources of data employed in paleoenvironmental reconstructions. Finally, we provide an overview of the approaches used to understand past habitats, which underpin the chapters on the specific sites which make use of these approaches to refine our understanding of African paleoenvironments and the place of hominins within them.

Biome – A major regional ecological community of plants and animals extending over large natural areas, for example, tropical forest, or subtropical grassland (Figure 2.1). The plants of terrestrial biomes consist of Formations. We are concerned here with the forest, savanna, grassland, and desert biomes, particularly with the first two, which are key habitats associated with early hominin activity.

Vegetation Formation – A climax community of plants extending over large areas and their nature determined by climate, for example, tropical rainforest. Plant formations form the main natural vegetation types of the world.

Vegetation Association – These are the natural units of vegetation within a Vegetation Formation. There might be many plant associations in a single forest, savanna, or grassland, the variations resulting from variations in soil, topography, and altitude. Soil catenas have a succession of plant associations dependent on the different soils.

Plant physiognomy – This term covers all aspects of the structure of vegetation, for example, height, density, thorniness, evergreen, or deciduous plants.

Catena – A grouping of soil–vegetation types in relation to topography (Milne, 1935). Catenas form when soils change along a gradient, usually down a slope, and this relationship is repeated wherever the same topographic and geological conditions occur. They form within single rainfall, temperature, and altitudinal zones and the nature of the vegetation associations is affected by the combination of soil types and topography (Milne, 1935). Several catenas have been described for Laetoli (Tanzania) environments (Andrews and Bamford, 2008; see also Harrison et al., Chapter 34), e.g., downslope from broad-leaved woodland association on hill slopes with shallow soil → low *Acacia* woodland association on lower slopes with deep clay soils and impeded drainage → riverine woodland association where erosion has cut through the deep soils. Milne (1947) gives another example from the Uyansi plateau, Tanzania: upper slopes, deciduous thicket → middle to lower slopes, open woodland → lowest slopes, transition open woodland → bottom flats, hard pan vegetation of low trees and grass.

Mosaic vegetation – A soil–vegetation patchwork following topography and relief (modified from Morison et al., 1948). Landscape heterogeneity leading to heterogeneous habitats promotes the coexistence of a wide range of species and greater biodiversity (Reynolds et al., 2015). Fossil faunal assemblages may accumulate over enough time for climate changes between wetter and drier habitats to give the appearance of mosaic habitats. Mosaic vegetation associations follow topography within a single climatic zone, in which case it is based on catenas, or it may be related to altitude, with precipitation and temperature varying with altitude. Variations in climate occur over a minimum distance of 100 km (Griffiths, 1976), i.e., within areas of at least 10,000 km^2, and mosaic vegetation would normally occur within these distances. It is, therefore, a local effect at the landscape level, rather than a regional effect.

Habitat heterogeneity is assumed to be the major driving force behind continental and global biodiversity (Kerr and Packer, 1997), but within Africa the correlation between mammal species richness and variations in topography has low significance. Multiple regression models of 17 climate and topography variables in southern Africa showed that the one-variable and two-variable models most highly correlated with mammal species richness were measures of seasonality (temperature and precipitation), and only with the three-variable model did topography play a part (Andrews and O'Brien, 2000). Habitat heterogeneity is important at the local and landscape level and therefore also for fossil faunas.

Spatial mosaics are common wherever there are variations in soil, topographic relief, or water availability. Several recent soil/vegetation catenas have been described for the Laetoli region (Andrews et al., 2011) and their presence has been inferred for the Pliocene deposits based on the geomorphology of the region (Hay, 1987). Modern vegetation mosaics are typically transient stages in a vegetation succession, both spatial and temporal. For example, there is evidence for temporal mosaic variation

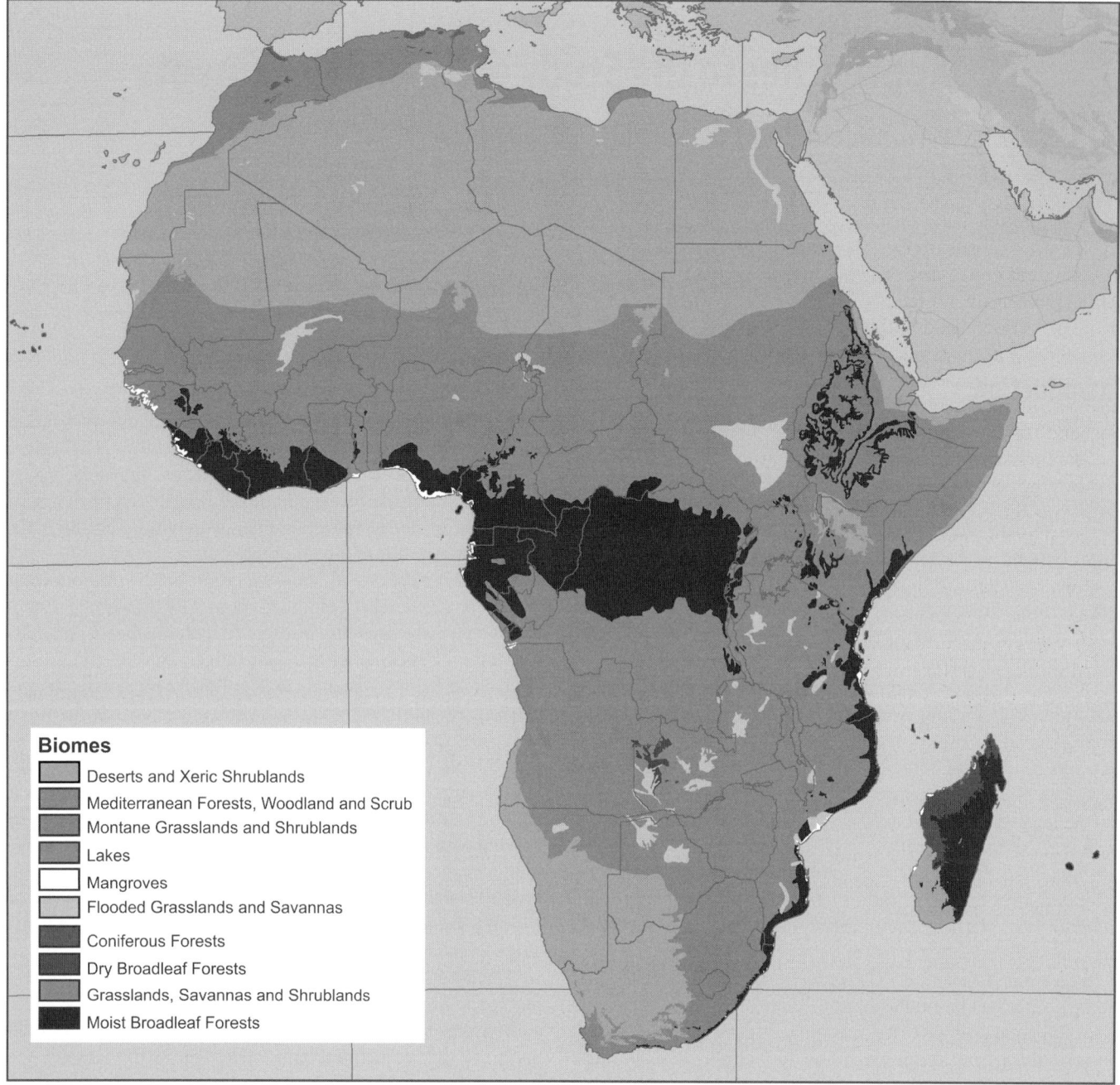

Figure 2.1 Simplified biome map of Africa, with emphasis on the major biomes of interest in the fossil record, namely forest, savanna, grassland, and desert. (*Source*: Modified from https://sedac.ciesin.columbia.edu/data/set/nagdc-population-landscape-climate-estimates-v3/maps based on WWF (2006) World Biomes Data set, www.worldwildlife.org/biome-categories/terrestrial-ecoregions). (A black and white version of this figure will appear in some formats. For the color version, please refer to the plate section.)

for the Masai Mara: it was observed to be open grassland in the nineteenth century (White, 1915) and was heavily grazed by wild and domestic livestock, but it reverted to dense woodland thicket during the rinderpest outbreak in the late nineteen century when there was ~95 percent mortality of large mammals, including almost all domestic stock (Sinclair, 1979a, 1979b). With European expansion into the region, much of the area was mechanically cleared to eradicate the tsetse fly, and bush-clearing was facilitated by the reintroduction of elephants in the 1970s, so that the area is now once again open grassland.

Sources of Evidence

In this section we describe several sources of evidence and analytical methods to infer past environments.

Sediments and Soils

Soils may be formed in the past and preserved as paleosols, and may be regarded as trace fossils representing past ecosystems (Retallack, 1991; Retallack et al., 1995). The different stages of soil formation can often be identified in preserved paleosols, indicating how mature the soil was, and soil horizons may still be identifiable. In exceptional cases, the uppermost layer, the humus horizon may still be preserved. Paleosols are a key feature found at many hominin-bearing sites in Africa, such as Taung, South Africa (Parker et al., 2016; Hopley and Kuhn, Chapter 13). Fossil sand dunes, for example, are key ancient features associated with the other southern African sites of Langebaanweg, Elandsfontein, and Still Bay (Reynolds, Chapter 6). There is a close relationship between aeolian processes and climatic aridity, and at its most extreme this may be seen in the formation of fossil sand dunes. The presence of tropical forest in Central Africa growing on old sand dunes shows the existence of a former arid period affecting the region, and the structure of the aeolian deposits may indicate wind strength and direction. The formation of soil calcretes is another indicator of aridity, coupled with highly seasonal rainfall, for both are requisites for the formation of calcareous nodules in soil and calcretes.

The presence of lakes and their expansion and contraction is shown by past shorelines and the formation of shoreline terraces, providing information on changes in past rainfall. The chemical composition of the sediments themselves may indicate if the lakes had drainage outlets or were closed systems with consequent build-up of minerals. The taxonomic distribution of aquatic organisms such as diatoms or ostracods can indicate water temperature or salinity. Many key hominin sites were based around paleo-lakes, such as Olduvai Gorge, Tanzania (see Peters et al., Chapter 33; Farrugia and Njau, Chapter 32), Hadar, Ethiopia (Campisano et al., Chapter 18), Konso, Ethiopia (Suwa et al., Chapter 22), Olorgesailie, Kenya (Potts and Faith, Chapter 30), and the Chad Basin, Chad (Vignaud et al., 2002; Bobe and Reynolds, Chapter 15).

Structures in the immediate vicinity of fossil sites provide evidence on the local environment. For example, evidence of rivers or channels may be present, or there may be drainage features in the sediments, outflow or spring deposits. Both the soil formation processes and the nature of weathering processes in the soils provide evidence on past climates. Well-aerated soils may have a reddish color indicating the presence of oxidized iron compounds, or waterlogged soils may be deprived of oxygen and be gleyed, giving a gray color. Lignites and black clays may form in waterlogged soils, and calcareous horizons in the soil profiles may form under conditions of seasonal drying of the soil. As the rain penetrates the soil, it carries down dissolved minerals from the upper part of the soil, and if the rain is heavy and prolonged, these minerals may be carried to great depths through the soil, but when it is sparse and seasonal, the minerals may only be carried down a few tens of centimeters. When the rain stops and no more water is passing down the soil, the soil dries out and the minerals in the water are deposited at the lowest point the water has reached. Repetitions of this process over hundreds or thousands of years result in calcretes or hard pans in the soil, sometimes so thick that they impede further drainage of water through them, resulting in local flooding.

The integration of local and regional sedimentary features is therefore a primary source of evidence on past environments. Landscape reconstruction at Olduvai Gorge showed that the sediments at FLK 22 accumulated as a 100 m wide and half-meter high peninsula between a river to the south and a freshwater marsh to the north (Blumenschine et al., 2012b). Recent minor uplift of the FLK Fault appears to have played a role in deflecting the river channel and containing the wetland's flood basin. Good drainage on the peninsula permitted the establishment of woody vegetation. Short mixed sedge/grassland occurred in open areas on the peninsula and lower-lying channel (Bamford et al., 2006, 2008; Peters et al., Chapter 33), while mixed-species marshland occurred in the wetland. The trees on the peninsula within this landscape mosaic provided repeated activity foci for hominins and carnivores, and arboreal refuge in the vicinity that allowed hominins to acquire resources at the more open ecotone between the peninsula and wetland. In this way, the dense and diverse paleoanthropological assemblages from FLK 22 and elsewhere on and immediately north of the peninsula are predicted by a model of Oldowan hominin land use (Blumenschine et al., 2012b). This example shows just how valuable the landscape approach is and how much it adds to interpretations based on single sites.

Geomorphology on the landscape level may also provide insights into habitat variability (Bailey et al., 2011; Reynolds et al., 2011). This is a function of variations in geology, soils, and topography rather than climate, and if these features can be reconstructed for a fossil site it may then be possible to reconstruct the structure of plant communities that were present in the past. For example, the geomorphology of the Laetoli area in northern Tanzania (Hay, 1987) showed that the Pliocene sediments at Laetoli were deposited on an uplifted peneplain of basement rocks that had an uneven surface with low relief, dissected by shallow valleys for the most part and with drainage to the west and southwest. Compared with today, there was less topographic relief over most of the area during the Pliocene. The development of paleosols on the surfaces of the sediment and the presence of fossilized termite nests, which have been found in some abundance in some levels, indicate stable land surfaces with good drainage and well-established vegetation over several thousands of years (Leakey and Harris, 1987; Harrison et al., Chapter 34).

Relating present-day vegetation to existing geomorphological structures showed great variability of woodland types related to different topographical and edaphic features (Andrews and Bamford, 2008; Andrews et al., 2011): several types of riverine woodlands and gallery forest, broad-leaved deciduous woodlands on thin, well-drained soils, *Acacia* woodlands on valley bottoms with impeded drainage; limited areas of grassland on soils with well-developed calcretes; and increasing forest elements in the flora to the east with increasing altitude (and rainfall). All these associations exist today under one climatic regime, semi-arid with rainfall 500–700 mm. Comparing this distribution of existing vegetation to geomorphology and then extending this comparison to the Pliocene geomorphology of the Laetoli area, it was possible to reconstruct the distributions of past mixed woodlands at the site. For some levels it was possible to check predictions against fossil plant remains; for example, fossil wood, grass and sedges, and pollen (Bamford, 2011a, 2011b).

Stable Isotopes

The analysis of stable isotopes in soil carbonates and organic matter measures proportions of C_3 to C_4 plants present. In tropical environments, C_3 plants include nearly all trees, shrubs, and herbs, together with grasses where there is a cool growing season, while C_4 grasses grow in open, unshaded places. The carbon isotope composition of carbonates in fossil soils shows that C_4 vegetation was present in Africa by about 9 Ma, but it began to expand only after about 7 Ma (Cerling, 1992). In other words, Miocene vegetation was mainly trees and shrubs, with little evidence of open grassland until the Pleistocene, after the emergence of *Homo*.

The paleogeographic reconstruction mentioned previously for landscape analysis of Olduvai Bed I has also been tested for carbon isotopes, and this confirms the existence of open wooded grassland for upper Bed I, the level associated with the earliest member of the genus *Homo*, *H. habilis*. Analyses of micromammals confirms this, and it contrasts with the results for middle Bed I, for which the small mammals indicate the presence of dense closed woodland (Fernandez-Jalvo et al., 1998; Harrison et al., Chapter 34).

The carbon isotope proportions can also be investigated in the enamel of herbivorous mammals, which provides an indication of the vegetation the animals were eating while the tooth enamel was forming. For example, 500 specimens from the Pliocene deposits at Laetoli had a mix of C_3 and C_4 signals on the teeth from 23 large mammal species (Kingston and Harrison, 2007; Kingston, 2011; Harrison et al., Chapter 34): suids had mixed and C_4 diets; giraffes had only C_3 diets; equids had mainly C_4 diets; different bovid tribes ranged from C_3 to C_4; and monkeys, proboscideans, and rhinos had mixed diets. Ostrich eggshells had an exclusively C_3 signal. The results indicate environmental variability at Laetoli, with vegetation varied enough to support both grazers and browsers. Oxygen isotopes were used to calculate an aridity index for the site derived from the water deficit (WD) calculated for different groups of mammals, and the range of values for WD at Laetoli indicated mean annual precipitation nearly the same as it is today.

Isotopic analysis of herbivore teeth from Dikika, Ethiopia (Bedaso et al., 2013; see also Bobe et al., Chapter 19) show that a range of wooded savanna habitats was present at the site, but there was no indication of forest or closed canopy woodland and C_4 grasses made up nearly 75% of herbivore diets. The relative proportions of wooded versus grassed habitats changed through time, and the oxygen isotope values suggest that the climate was wetter than earlier in the Pliocene and at present. In a similar vein, Wynn and colleagues (2020) have used hominin stable carbon isotope values to reconstruct changing diets of *Paranthropus* within the Shungura and Usno Formations (Ethiopia), which complements the findings of Negash and colleagues (2020; Chapter 24) on the herbivore isotopes of the same deposits.

The oxygen isotope composition of bone is largely determined by the $\delta^{18}O$ value of environmental water, although this is affected by the different species' metabolic processes. Plant foliage can be enriched in ^{18}O by evaporation from the leaves, so that an animal feeding on leaves exposed to the sun has enriched $\delta^{18}O$ values. This is the case with giraffes, which feed high up on the tree canopies, and for arboreal monkeys such as the seven arboreal monkeys living in closed canopy forest in the Taï Forest, Côte d'Ivoire (Krigbaum et al., 2013). Differences in $\delta^{18}O$ values between species correlated with the different canopy levels and suggest that it might be possible to identify the canopy levels occupied by fossil species.

Nitrogen isotopes are used to investigate differences in trophic level, which may indicate the presence of meat in the diets of fossil animals or the consumption by herbivores of aquatic plants (Palmqvist et al., 2008). The $\delta^{15}N$ levels distinguish meat-eaters and herbivores, but as many carnivorous species also eat vegetation, the evidence can be debatable, and meat-eating populations of chimpanzees show no difference in isotope values between males and females although males have been observed to eat six or seven times more meat (Smith et al., 2010). The explanation may be that the tooth enamel is formed during infancy, when infants and juveniles have little access to meat, or that adults do not eat enough meat to influence their isotopic signal.

Trace Fossils and Taphonomy

Trace fossils are the imprint left by living organisms in sediment where the organisms themselves have disappeared, such as footprints. Commonly found trace fossils are burrows in the sediment that have later been infilled with sediment of different colors or textures. Rarely, the organism is found in association with the burrow. Also trace fossils are the impressions made by plant roots, which form both in the sediment and on the surfaces of bones preserved in the sediment, which are visible as branching grooves with rounded profiles on the surfaces of the bones. Occasionally, whole trees are preserved as infilled cavities, for example the fossil ape site of Rusinga Island, Kenya (Walker and Teaford, 1988).

The presence of footprints preserved in the Footprint Tuff at Laetoli, described by Mary Leakey (Leakey and Harris, 1987), was the first and earliest unequivocal evidence for hominin bipedalism just over 3.6 Ma. Tracks, trails and footprints of many species of mammals and birds preserve evidence of the movements of animals across the Pliocene land surface (Bennett and Reynolds, 2021).

Traces of carnivore activity such as chew marks or digested bones and teeth may show the presence of a predator species even if body fossils are absent (Brain, 1981; Andrews, 1990; Su and Harrison, 2008). Other traces may be present, such as rodent gnawing, weathering, and rounding by water or wind abrasion. These traces are considered as the focus of taphonomic studies, but can also be environmental indicators.

Trace fossils also include pellets and scats left by all types of animals, which are referred to as coprolites if preserved (Andrews, 1990). In some cases, it is possible to infer the presence of a specific predator in a fossil assemblage even without body fossils. If the actual pellet or scat is present, this may be informative, but even in their absence the degrees of breakage and digestion of the prey remains is often enough to identify the predator. At Laetoli, many coprolites retain enough of their original shape for them to be identified at least to family (Harrison, 2011i).

Taxonomic Evidence of Paleoecology

Paleoenvironmental reconstructions relying on indicator species (and their inferred ecologies) employ either a few "significant" species or larger sections of the faunal assemblage (Avery, 1987a, 1987b, 1990, 1991). This approach assumes ecological equivalence between fossil organisms and their living relatives, and the same representation of habitats between past and present. This may be justified for plants or for recent fossil faunas, since the species may still be alive today, in which case there is direct evidence as to their ecological attributes. Bamford and colleagues (2008; see also Peters et al., Chapter 33) documented an area of grassland at Olduvai dated to 1.8 Ma, with similar fossil species and floral composition to the present day.

Ecological assessments using mammal species can be more problematic and are based on intuitive knowledge of the adaptations of the species concerned. Previous assessments of the specialist grazing diet of *Antidorcas bondi*, using dental morphology (specifically hypsodonty) and isotopic studies for example, have been shown to underestimate the degree of dietary variability observed using other dietary proxies (Brink and Lee-Thorp, 1992; Ecker and Lee-Thorp, 2018; Sewell et al., 2019). This method has some application along a continuous stratigraphic sequence, for example of small mammals in the study by Van der Meulen and Daams (1992) on the Miocene small mammal faunas from Spain.

Pollen is widely used for habitat reconstruction, but it is rarely preserved in association with mammal fauna. While the floral species composition may be well-documented by pollen analysis, the structure of the vegetation may still be ambiguous, especially if there is some indication that the pollen (which is wind-dispersed) comes from many different locations and has been time-averaged, as has been shown for Olduvai Gorge floral fossils (Bonnefille, 1984a).

Fossil leaf morphology may provide rainfall estimates, for in tropical Africa the physiognomy of leaves (independent of plant species identification) is related linearly to moisture variables, providing evidence both of seasonality and total rainfall. Regression models of the relationship between leaf area and annual precipitation as calculated for living floras have been applied to sites in the Tugen Hills (Kenya) generating rainfall predictions for comparison with independent identifications of fossil vegetation (Jacobs, 1999, 2001).

Invertebrates and lower vertebrates, where preserved, are a valuable source of paleoenvironmental evidence. Land gastropods are ecologically conservative and many have highly specific habitat requirements, and because they are small and not very mobile they can be found in microenvironments which are informative of edaphic or topographic features. A high diversity of carnivorous snails in East African fossil faunal assemblages may indicate forest environments, for example (Verdcourt, 1963).

Taxonomic analysis is still generally used for small mammal Pleistocene faunas. Taxonomic composition of successive faunas in a sedimentary sequence may be due to differences in vegetation and climate, but also indicates the predator behavior of the accumulating agents (owls, versus hyaenas). The taxonomic composition of large rodent assemblages from the Miocene of Spain has been used to make inferences about climatic change during the mid- to late Miocene (Van der Meulen and Daams, 1992). The strength of this technique is that it is based on a consistent approach to large faunal assemblages, where the pattern of the taxonomic change in the rodent faunas over a 10-million-year period appears to coincide with temperature curves from other environmental sources, indicating temperature increase during the first part of the middle Miocene followed by a sharp decrease about 15 Ma.

A similar approach has been used for the species abundances and species numbers of the large mammals in the long Omo sequence by Bobe and colleagues (2002) spanning the end of the Pliocene and into the early Pleistocene (from 4 to 2 Ma). Changes in abundances in suids, monkeys, and bovids were related to vegetation changes from more forested environments to more open woodland environments and have been shown to be coincident with marine isotope evidence of climate change.

Vrba (1980) developed a taxonomic index based on the proportions of bovid tribes in fossil faunas: alcelaphines and antilopines (grazers such as wildebeest and gazelles) compared with tragelaphines and reduncines (mainly browsers such as bushbuck and waterbuck). The index of one to the other, known as the alcelaphini and antilopini criterion, or AAC, shows the relative proportions of grazers to browsers, leading to inferences about vegetation cover and climate and habitats. The link with vegetation and climate is tenuous at best, for grass is the dominant ground vegetation in all phases of savanna, and closed woodland and open grassland can exist side by side within the same climatic regime based on differences in soil, topography and altitude. Many studies use alcelaphines as indicators of open grassland, as in the open plains of Serengeti, but modern ecology shows that alcelaphines live equally in wooded or bushed environments.

Small and large-bodied bovids may coexist because their feeding strategies are so different. The dominant bovids in the later Pliocene deposits at Laetoli were alcelaphines, which are grass-eaters like wildebeest, and neotragines, which browse on leaves (Su and Harrison, 2008): the latter is a small antelope, like dik-diks today, and they frequent and feed in dense thickets, hence their browsing diet, but the thickets are often found scattered in more open wooded areas occupied by the alcelaphines.

Carnivore diversity during the late African Miocene (Werdelin and Lewis, 2013) showed major changes through time: between 7 and 8 Ma, there were sabre-toothed cats, long-limbed hyaenas, giant bear dogs with many smaller carnivores as well. Three million years later there were members of the cat family (modern lions and leopards), modern-looking hyaenas, several dog species, and a giant civet present. Carnivore diversity peaked between 3 and 4 Ma, but after 2 Ma numbers of species declined steeply, with the loss of the sabre-toothed species and other giant forms and the modern carnivoran guild emerged. Functional adaptations of the carnivores at these different stages indicate that hypercarnivores decline, while modern faunas fill fewer ecological niches than their Miocene counterparts. Climate cooling during this period may explain this, but carnivore biodiversity in southern Africa appears not to correlate with climatic factors (Andrews and O'Brien, 2000), but may indicate the effects of the emergence of the genus *Homo*, with a greater reliance on hunting.

Numbers of species per unit area may provide climatic or habitat information, but also present several confounding issues. Different types of mammal have different relationships with climate and habitat variables, as suggested by Andrews and O'Brien (2000). Arboreal frugivore species richness is most highly correlated with presence of forests, whereas terrestrial herbivores are more highly correlated with habitat heterogeneity; similarly, small mammal species richness is correlated with rainfall, whereas large mammals are most highly correlated with minimum monthly temperature. Another issue is that the greatest species richness in Africa is found where topographic relief is greatest, in contrast to plant species richness, which is highest in high temperature/rainfall conditions, that is in tropical forests. In the absence of climatic and habitat context, the interpretation of paleoecology from species richness can be problematic.

Two attempts to reconstruct past communities through analysis of species lists were habitat spectra and the taxonomic habitat index by Van Couvering (1980) and Evans and colleagues (1981), respectively. These both weight fossil species according to their degree of relationship to living species. For habitat spectra, living species were given a weight of six, and their habitat preferences were weighted by this amount. Extinct species were given weights of five if their genus was still extant and four if it was not and decreasing still further to subfamily and family relationships. Habitat preferences modified by this weighting was calculated for all species in a fossil assemblage and a spectrum constructed for the sum of the habitat weightings (Van Couvering, 1980).

The taxonomic habitat index is based on weightings derived from habitat ranges for all living species in Africa, and the weighted averages for all species in recent faunal assemblages are added together and divided by the number of species to give an average ordination score for the fauna (Evans et al., 1981). For fossil faunas, further calculations consider degrees of relationship of the fossil species with living taxa: extant species in the fossil fauna keep their habitat ranges unchanged, but extinct species are given scores averaged for all species in the genus; extinct genera have scores averaged for all species and genera in a subfamily, and so on. For example, an extant monkey species such as the red-tailed monkey (*Cercopithecus ascanius*) is scored 1 for forest habitats; an extinct species of *Cercopithecus* is weighted for the genus, which averages 0.9 for forest and 0.1 for woodland; and an extinct cercopithecine genus has a score based on all extant cercopithecine genera.

Regarding all types of paleoecological reconstructions being attempted, there remains the issue that past environments, ecosystems, or habitats may have no modern counterparts. It may be possible to interpolate evidence within and between modern habitats to try and reconstruct what the nature of the habitats was like, for example the Olduvai Gorge woodland in middle Bed I (Fernandez-Jalvo et al., 1998). The structure of the woodland faunal community at three levels in middle Bed I had no match in any of the modern woodland communities compared with it, and it seemed to be intermediate between deciduous woodland and semideciduous forest.

The study by Andrews (2006) explores the mix of species found in fossil assemblages by creating artificially reconstructed faunal assemblages composed of different modern habitats. Mixed faunas produced greater variability in habitat representation, and when experimental habitat mixtures were compared with the Pliocene deposits at Laetoli, which did not resemble any single fauna, it showed a mixture of semideciduous forest and woodland faunas, while the Ndolanya Beds fauna was most like the three to one mixture of faunal assemblages from bushland and grassland sites (Andrews, 2006). This may suggest that dense woodland with patches of forest were present for the Laetoli Beds and bushland with patches of grassland for the Ndolanya Beds.

The effects of faunal impoverishment can be approached by deliberately introducing known biases into recent faunas representing different habitats (Andrews, 2006). These biased faunas can then be used for comparison with fossil faunas to see if they match better than unbiased assemblages. Removal of small species produced no change in the ecological signal of the faunas until over half of the species had been removed, so that tropical forest faunas retained their forest signal with only 40 percent of the species remaining. Removing large mammals progressively, starting from the largest, produced even less of a change in the habitat signal.

Ecomorphology

Mammal ecomorphology considers the functional morphology of species environmentally, rather than taxonomically. By comparing the pattern of morphologies obtained for fossil species with those of modern species of known habitats, inferences are drawn about the range of fossil adaptations. The basic assumption is that similar morphologies suggest similar habitats, and that this method is to some degree taxon-free, that is, independent of the taxonomic identification of the species used, in contrast to the use of indicator species, as discussed previously.

There are several qualifications that must be considered to these assumptions: (1) present-day species may occupy habitats that are less than optimal, making them less informative about previous habitat adaptations; (2) species do not always adapt in identical morphological patterns, even in response to the same environmental stimulus (e.g., Rein, 2010); and (3) animals with similar morphologies do not always use it in the same way. For example, hawks, shrikes, and Australian shrike tits have similar hooked beaks, but use these for different diets (Harvey and Pagel, 1991).

The strength of ecomorphology is that it is quantifiable and repeatable. Most studies target specific skeletal elements, such as skulls and teeth, or long bones and phalanges, and they generally are restricted to single taxonomic groups. For example, within the family Bovidae, the morphology of the femur differentiates bovids associated with grassland, forest, and mixed habitats (Kappelman, 1991). Likewise, Meike Köhler (1993) defined three ruminant morphological types based on analyses of body profile, horn types, upper and lower jaws, morphology of the limb extremities, and proportions of the limb bones, and these three types are related to a finely graduated habitat change from closed to open habitats. Habitat change has likewise been detected at Laetoli, using bovid ecomorphology (Kovarovic et al., 2002; Kovarovic and Andrews, 2011), which indicates continuous regional woodland cover in the older Laetolil beds and decreasing cover in the younger upper Ndolanya Beds deposits, although the area was still wooded.

Molar hypsodonty is an important ecomorphological character, with higher crowns facilitating the longer effective life of the tooth (Janis, 1988; Jernvall and Fortelius, 2002; Damuth and Janis, 2011). Grazing herbivores in open habitats have significantly more hypsodont teeth (regardless of food preference) compared with those living in closed habitats, due to the presence of abrasive foods and grit in their diets. The amount of soil ingested during feeding is likely greater for animals feeding close to the ground in open habitats, but this does not necessarily imply grass. Browsing herbivores, by contrast, feed on leaves of trees or bushes well above ground level (Madden, 2014).

Measures of hypsodonty combined with stable isotopes from an early Pleistocene site at Venta Micena in Spain have been effective in reconstructing past diet and trophic patterns within large mammal communities (Palmqvist et al., 2008). Within the herbivore species, 7 had grazing adaptations, 2 were mixed feeders, and 2 were browsers, despite carbon isotopes indicating that all 11 species consumed exclusively C_3 vegetation. Oxygen and nitrogen isotopes revealed further differences in their uptake of water or consumption of aquatic plants and lichens, indicating different dietary niches.

Analysis of mesowear and microwear is highly useful and complementary for assessing dietary signals (Hunter and Fortelius, 1994; Fortelius and Solounias, 2000; Kaiser and Fortelius, 2003; Sewell et al., 2019). Mesowear, specifically the relative heights of the cusps, indicates the lifetime dietary signals and can be used to distinguish between grazers and browsers, while microwear provides dietary information specific to the weeks prior to death.

Incisor morphology in primates is also related to diet, with frugivorous species having relatively larger incisors than leaf-eating species, particularly marked when colobine monkeys are compared with cercopithecines, or gorillas to chimpanzees and orangutans (Deane, 2009). Frugivores and hard-object fruit-eaters possess more strongly curved incisors, both side to side and from top to bottom, while soft-object fruit-eaters have less-curved incisors and leaf-eating primates have the flattest incisors. This spectrum observed in extant primates appears like that seen in Miocene apes (Deane, 2009).

The relationship between primate microwear and food is based on the jaw mechanics and the angle of the upper and lower teeth, although microwear patterns for primates with a known diet of large hard objects are not diagnostic (Butler, 1952; Grine, 1981; Walker, 1981; Gordon, 1982, 1988; Teaford, 1994; Ungar, 1994, 2005, 2007). Numerous pits and scratches may reflect the ingestion of grit with the food, which in the case of herbivores is easily explained because their food is at ground level, but primate diets (fruits and seeds) are unlikely to be contaminated with grit. The heavy wear, thick enamel and abundance of pits on the teeth of some Miocene apes have been explained by their feeding on hard objects, but a study by Lucas and colleagues (2013) suggests primate enamel wear shows minimal input from plant remains, even hard shells and seeds. However, microscopic dust particles ingested with food could cause, and alter, existing microwear features on primate teeth.

Community Paleoecology

Community measures of paleoecology take all species in the fauna into account, and measure their functional attributes across size, diet, and locomotion. These have been invaluable in African hominin paleohabitat studies (Reed, 1997; Bobe and Eck, 2001; de Ruiter et al., 2008a; Negash et al., Chapter 24, and references therein).

Species richness for a specific assemblage is referred to as alpha diversity (α-diversity), which is simply the number of species in an assemblage for a given time and place, while beta diversity is specific to the differences between fauna or floral species between sites, and gamma diversity refers to the species differences that can be observed when looking across geographic regions (Whittaker, 1960, 1972; Peet, 1974; Sepkowski, 1988). These diversity measures are dependent on several specific factors, such as time, surface area, and sampling strategies.

Beta diversity is important in fossil faunas that accumulate over time and from several disparate sources but is harder to measure. High turnover, which characterizes tropical savannas, could theoretically lead to disproportionately high diversity levels for time-averaged faunas. Fossil assemblages from sediments accumulating over thousands of years may be drawn from different parts of the environment, or the environment itself may have changed over time as a result of climatic or physical change. In all these cases, the level of species richness in a fossil assemblage may not be an accurate representation of any one environment in the past, and it may be difficult to compare with present-day richness figures, which are based on specific time and place data.

Levels of species richness are also directly related to area: for example, α-diversity scales to (area) 0.25 (Mares, 1992). South American present-day mammalian α-diversity appears to be lower in tropical lowland forests than in dryland habitats because they contain fewer species than dryland habitats (434 species against 509). However, the area occupied by the dryland habitats is almost double that of lowland forest, so that species richness per unit area is greater in the forest environments (Mares, 1992). For fossil faunas, however, there is often little information about the size of the area being sampled.

Fourth, the distribution of species within a fauna is another aspect of diversity, and is referred to as evenness (Tuomisto, 2012; Daly et al., 2018). This is a measure of equitability and it distinguishes between forest faunas, which have many mammal species all more or less abundant (more equable), and open grassland faunas, which are dominated by few species. The present-day mass herds of reindeer in the arctic tundra, bison in the American prairies, and wildebeest in the Serengeti plains are cases in point. Some living and fossil faunas are dominated by one or two species, while others have more or less equal numbers of individuals for most species.

Finally, estimates of species richness are also affected by sampling problems, both for modern ecological communities and for fossil assemblages (e.g., Andrews, 1990). Ideally, the representation of animals or plants in a site is best shown both by the species present and by their abundances, but assessing abundances is affected by sample size, with larger samples showing higher numbers of species present. However, in fossil assemblages, sample size is often limited, and can affect how these patterns are interpreted within rare taxonomic groups, such as hominins (Hopley and Maxwell, Chapter 3; Maxwell et al., 2018).

Selective destruction of bones may occur both before and after fossilization. For example, at Laetoli, the rarity of hominin fossil remains has partly been attributed to taphonomic destruction by scavengers and slow accumulation rates of sediments, with bones left exposed on the ground surface (Harrison et al., Chapter 34; Su and Harrison, 2008). Bones from large-bodied species were exposed on the surface for longer and were therefore relatively rarely preserved in the sediments, while smaller mammal bones appear relatively more abundant due to quicker burial.

Most animal and plant taxa show diversity gradients, that is, changing numbers of species across space (and time in the case of fossil biota), and these have been interpreted in terms either of physico-chemical factors, such as latitude or climate, the heterogeneity of the habitat, or as a result of biological interactions such as competition or predation (Simpson, 1964; Kerr and Packer, 1997; Andrews and O'Brien, 2000, 2010; Willig et al., 2003).

Ecological diversity is based on convergence of adaptation in unrelated faunas and has been recognized since the time of Charles Darwin (1859). Convergent evolution results in the production of similar adaptations in phylogenetically distantly related organisms subject to similar agents of natural selection, although convergence is constrained by availability of genetic variability in the converging lineages and sufficient time for it to act (Harrison, 1962; Andrews et al., 1979; Dawkins, 1986). For example, in lowland tropical forests in Asia, America, and Africa, there are rodents with gliding (flying) adaptations belonging to different families, and anteaters in South America with similar adaptations to African anteaters (Myrmecophagidae and Tubulidentata, respectively) due to convergent evolution. Extending this to whole mammalian communities living in similar habitats, these tend to show similar adaptations despite having no species in common. Similarities in the fossil teeth morphology across communities can therefore be employed to reconstruct the community structure based on them, even if these groups are extinct, as in the case of Eocene adapiform primates (Seiffert et al., 2009). Interactions between flora and fauna can also be inferred, such as fruit production by plants and the radiations of rodents (hard fruits) and primates (soft fruits; Collinson and Hooker, 1991, 2003), or the relationships between spiny plants, and mammalian browsing (Charles-Dominique et al., 2016). Finally, Barr (2017) examined the relationship between bovid postcranial traits and vegetation in sub-Saharan Africa, which may be employed to infer environmental variables based on bovid fossils within an assemblage.

Some of the most informative studies have attempted to examine broader aspects of modern mammalian faunal communities and associate these to specific habitat types in the past (e.g., Reed, 1997, 1998, 2013; Faith, 2013; Andrews and Hixson, 2014 and references therein).

Conclusions

We have defined some key terms related to vegetation structure and presented a broad-brush review of approaches to past environments and paleoecology (e.g., Damuth et al., 1992; Bobe et al., 2007a; Reed, 2013). The chapters that follow make extensive use of these approaches and provide valuable examples of their application to our understanding of African paleoenvironments.

Acknowledgments

We would like to thank Laurence Dumouchel for useful comments and suggestions to this chapter.

3

Environmental and Stratigraphic Bias in the Hominin Fossil Record
Implications for Theories of the Climatic Forcing of Human Evolution

Philip J. Hopley and Simon J. Maxwell

Introduction

Comparisons between the hominin or Neogene mammal fossil record and contemporaneous paleoclimate proxies have been commonplace since the pioneering studies of Elisabeth Vrba (1980, 1992, 1995a, 1995b). Vrba combined the new macroevolutionary theories of punctuated equilibrium and species selection (e.g., Eldredge and Gould, 1972; Vrba, 1985b) with emerging evidence for global climate change in the Plio-Pleistocene (e.g., Shackleton et al., 1990) to produce testable hypotheses of faunal turnover pulses in the Neogene fossil record. Vrba focused her analyses on the speciose Neogene bovids, rather than hominins, to ensure statistically robust results. Periods of bovid, and by inference hominin, turnover (origination, extinction and migration) between 2.8 and 2.5 Ma and at ~1.8 Ma were linked to episodes of global cooling seen in the global stable isotope records (Vrba, 1995b). Behrensmeyer et al. (1997) argued that Vrba's turnover pulses were predominantly a product of sampling bias, by showing that bovid diversity and the number of bovid-bearing localities covaried. A study by deMenocal (1995) was the first to take Vrba's hypothesis a step further by replacing the bovid fossil record with the hominin fossil record and suggesting that African aridity was behind the evolution of early *Homo* at approximately 2.0 Ma. This study took the hominin fossil record at face value despite its far greater incompleteness relative to the bovids, paving the way for a new wave of paleoclimatic theories. Potts (1996, 1998a, 1998b) took the debate further from Vrba's original approach by dispensing with the notion of a shared climatic forcing between hominins and other mammals and proposed the Variability Selection (VS) hypothesis. The VS hypothesis is formulated around the idea that early hominins evolved unique adaptions for ecological versatility in response to climatic variability, so the fossil record of other mammal groups cannot be used to falsify the hypothesis. More recent iterations of the VS hypothesis (such as Maslin and Trauth, 2009; Shultz and Maslin, 2013; Maslin et al., 2014) also rely exclusively on the hominin fossil record as the explicit test case for their hypothesis.

This leads to the pertinent question of whether the hominin fossil record is of suitable quality to make sound inferences about the timing of speciation, extinction, and migration events; and in turn, whether these patterns can be explained by external factors, such as climatic change. The fossil record of any plant or animal group is an incomplete representation of the evolutionary history of that group (Tarver et al., 2011), and given this incompleteness, we need to assess how incomplete the fossil record is, what specific biases dominate, and how this might affect our ability to make comparisons with other data sets, such the paleoclimate record (Figure 3.1). While there is an extensive literature on this subject for the more plentiful marine invertebrates (such as Bush et al., 2002, 2004; Goodwin et al., 2004; Bennington et al., 2009) and Mesozoic terrestrial vertebrates (Signor and Lipps, 1982; Upchurch et al., 2011; Brocklehurst et al., 2012; Tennent et al., 2016; Varnham et al., 2021), this topic is rarely discussed within the specific context of human evolution. One reason for the lack of debate on this subject may be a perception that the hominin fossil record is so patchy that it is unlikely to pass a rigorous analysis of its completeness. While this may be the case, it is important to look at the biases that prevail within the hominin fossil record and to make recommendations for future research approaches. This chapter reviews the nature of the hominin fossil record and investigates what can, and cannot, be inferred about the climatic forcing of human evolution.

Comparison of Paleoclimate Archives with the Hominin Fossil Record

Studies of hominin evolution and climate universally depend on a comparison between geological records of climatic or ecological change with one or more aspects of the hominin fossil record. The geological dataset can be a local record of African vegetation or rainfall (Cerling, 1992; Wynn, 2004; Cerling et al., 2011b) or a global record of climate change, such as an oxygen isotope time series from deep sea foraminifera (Vrba, 1995b; deMenocal, 1995, 2004). It is clear that African paleoclimate can be distinct in many aspects (e.g., period and amplitude of climate variability, direction and timing of stepwise changes) from a globally averaged record (Maslin and Christensen, 2007), and it is therefore the preferred choice for studies of hominin–climate interactions. Unfortunately, Africa is one of the least well-understood climatic regions on Earth because of its short instrumental record (approximately 100 years) and a historical shortage of climatic research. Climatic variability in Africa occurs at all scales from seasonal to multi-millennial (Nicholson, 2000), and these timescales of variability can be nested (for example, millennial-scale changes in seasonality).

Modern Africa and Overview of Late Cenozoic Paleoenvironments

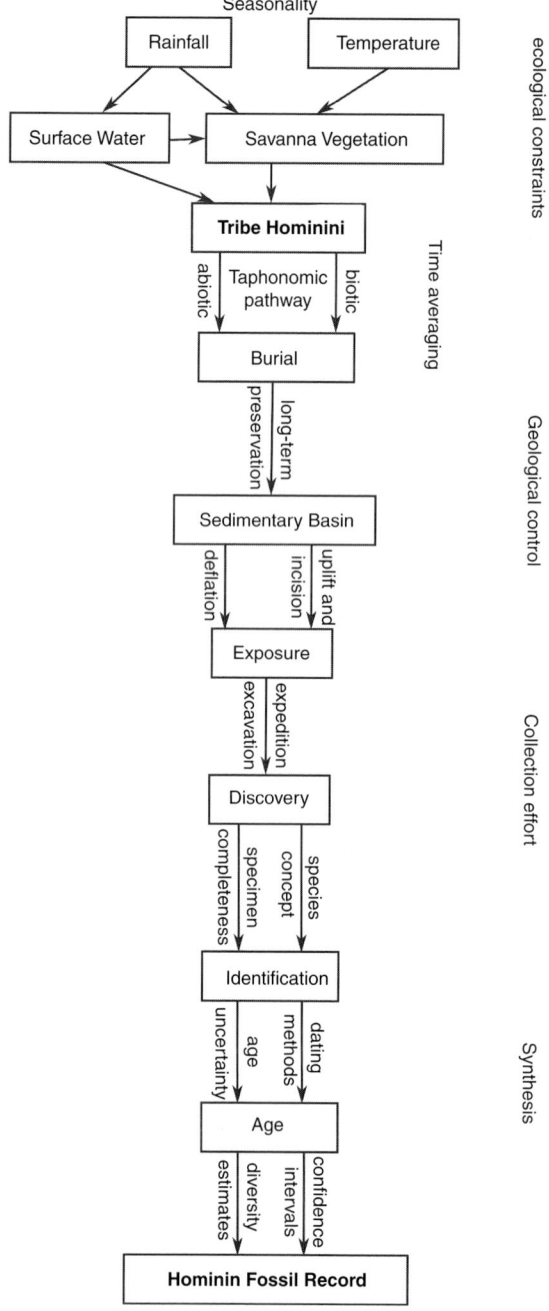

Figure 3.1 A schematic representation of the ecological, geological, and anthropological factors that combine to produce the observed hominin fossil record. The ecological constraints on hominin distribution are of interest for comparison with paleoclimate proxies, but the confounding geological and anthropological controls are rarely considered.

proxies to represent one or more aspects of the climate system. Proxies are calibrated to modern-day climatic processes via the instrumental record, but for the geological past uniformitarian assumptions are often required. Multi-proxy approaches and comparisons with external forcings (e.g., orbital parameters) are key to ensuring fidelity between paleoclimate proxies and climatic parameters. Reconstructing the Plio-Pleistocene climate history of Africa is an active, and vibrant field of research, with many new studies contributing to improved understanding (Campisano et al., 2017; Caley et al., 2018).

Several African Plio-Pleistocene paleo-environmental records are derived from the same sedimentary basins or geological sequences as the mammal/hominin fossil record to which they are being compared; these data sets are also likely to share a stratigraphic and chronological framework. In such circumstances it is important to ensure that any correlations are not related to common-cause effects (Dunhill et al., 2014). For example, suggestions of links between the frequency of volcanic activity and mammal diversity (Bobe and Carvalho, 2019), or links between lake levels and hominin diversity (Shultz and Maslin, 2013), may be driven by confounding variables such as depositional rate or facies associations (Holland, 2016).

Before paleo-climatic and -environmental proxies can be meaningfully compared to events in the hominin fossil record (speciation, extinction, migration), we here consider the fossil record and rock record biases that are routinely documented in other fields of vertebrate paleobiology (Marshall, 1990, 1997; Tarver et al., 2011; Butler et al., 2011), but which have not received as much attention within the environmental context of human evolution.

Geological Biases

Eastern Africa is the only region in Africa to have a fossil record spanning the entirety of hominin evolution (the last 9.3–6.5 million years ago; Moorjani et al., 2016; see Figure 3.2). This is because the East African Rift Valley is fortunate enough to combine layer-cake stratigraphy with fluvio-lacustrine depocenters and exposure of sediments through rifting and incision (e.g., Feibel, 2011). The sedimentary succession is interspersed with volcanic ashes that can be correlated over hundreds of kilometers and dated precisely with radiometric methods, such as potassium–argon dating. Age estimates for the intervening sediments are obtained via interpolation, enabling new fossil finds to be incorporated within an existing chronometric framework. While this geological setting is favorable, there are some geological biases that warrant consideration. Depositional environments within the Miocene to Pleistocene of Eastern Africa can be broadly characterized as volcanic, lacustrine, or terrestrial, each of which has a distinctive fossil preservation potential. Volcanic rocks such as lavas cannot yield fossils, and deep lacustrine environments are unlikely to yield fossils of terrestrial mammals, except in rare circumstances, due to the transport of bloat-and-float carcasses (e.g., Mallon et al., 2018). Therefore, most Eastern African terrestrial mammal fossils, including hominins, are found in paleosol, fluvial, deltaic or shallow lacustrine environments. However, basin-scale sedimentary environments are rarely considered when collating hominin-bearing horizons or

Paleoclimate records from early hominin sites are typically of low resolution (10,000s to 100,000s of years; Passey et al., 2010; Cerling et al., 2011b; Uno et al., 2016b), meaning higher-frequency climatic information is not preserved. This picture may improve soon through the targeting of high-resolution climate archives (often via continental drilling) that can resolve the Plio-Pleistocene climate of Africa down to millennial, centennial, or even annual timescales (Scholz et al., 2011; Campisano et al., 2017; Hopley et al., 2018; Deino et al., 2019). Paleoclimate archives can be well resolved, but by necessity they are dependent on chemical, sedimentological, or biological

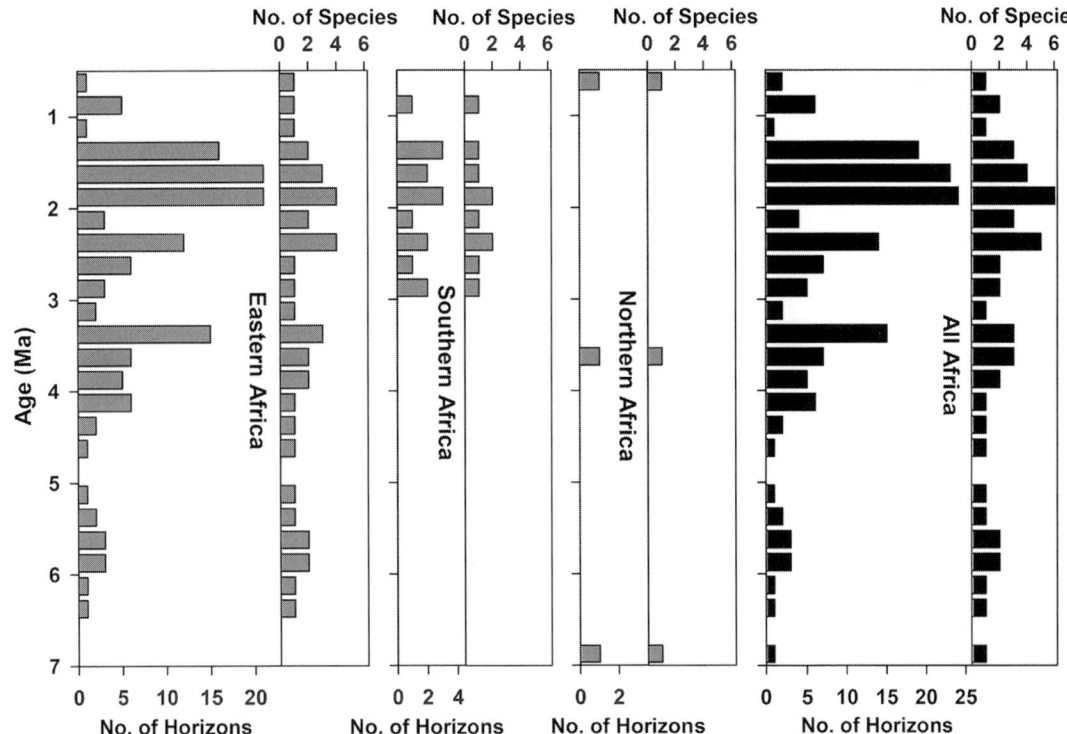

Figure 3.2 Hominin species (taxic) diversity and the number of hominin-bearing horizons for the geographical provinces of eastern, southern, and northern Africa. Data from Maxwell (2018); last updated December 2017.

First (FAD) and Last (LAD) Appearance Dates (see Figure 3.3). There are clearly instances when a FAD/LAD coincides with a facies change (for example, from a fluvial to a deep lacustrine environment) and the absence of hominin fossils from prior/subsequent layers has been given an evolutionary, rather than a geological, explanation. To address this shortfall, independent assessments of Fossil Recovery Potential (Marshall, 1997; Holland, 2003), that is, the probability of recovering a fossil at a particular time, should be explicitly incorporated into assessments of hominin stratigraphic ranges.

The geological setting of the southern African fossil record is very different to that of the Eastern African Rift Valley, and comes with its own set of geological biases. The distribution of Miocene to Recent fossils in this region is limited to the outcrop of the karstic rocks, predominantly Proterozoic dolomites, that host the cave deposits. Most fossil mammals are discovered among mined or excavated cave sediments and assigned an approximate age using biostratigraphic principles (Avery, 2019). Each paleo-cave has a unique sequence of clastic sediments and speleothems (cave carbonates), equivalent to a mini sedimentary basin, so correlation between cave sequences is not practical. If the age or faunal content is considered interesting (perhaps if primates or hominins are among the initial faunal remains) then further excavation and/or dating follows. As the establishment of cave chronologies is both laborious and expensive, temporal frameworks are applied *post hoc* and are typically focused on hominin-bearing caves. This often results in more dating effort being applied to cave sequences that have yielded particular taxa (such as hominins), and a lack of secure dating beyond the known stratigraphic range of southern African hominins (Avery, 2019). This has implications for our understanding of localities where early hominins have yet to be discovered and accentuates the bonanza effect (distortion of the fossil record through repeated collection of fossils from rich fossil-bearing localities) within southern Africa (Maxwell, 2018).

The southern African hominin fossil record currently spans ~3 Ma to ~1 Ma, with a concentration of cave breccias (and hominin fossils) dated between 2.5 Ma and 1.5 Ma (Figure 3.2; Herries et al., 2009; Pickering et al., 2010, 2011, 2019). Dirks and Berger (2013) and Herries et al. (2019) have outlined geological controls that may be responsible for the restricted age range of cave sediments in southern Africa: post-Miocene uplift of the African erosion surface and subsequent cave inception along reactivated faults. In this scenario, the lack of southern African late-Miocene and early-Pliocene cave deposits, and by extension early hominins of this age, is explained by the destruction of older deposits through surface erosion (Herries et al., 2019). However, it is also worth considering the analytical constraints on the principal method of age determination in southern African caves – uranium-series dating of speleothems. Uranium–thorium (U–Th) methods can be applied to speleothems from the Recent (a few decades old) to ~600 ka (Dorale et al., 2004); uranium–lead (U–Pb) methods can theoretically be applied to speleothems of any age (Woodhead et al., 2006), although given the relatively low U concentrations in southern African karst waters (typically <1 ppm), ages younger than 1 Ma are beyond current analytical capabilities. Therefore, there is a "dating gap" between ~1.0 Ma and ~0.6 Ma, meaning the likelihood of obtaining uranium-series ages from this time window is very low. Speleothem U–Pb ages require correction for initial $^{234}U/^{238}U$ disequilibrium (Engel et al., 2019), usually via measurement of the $^{234}U/^{238}U$ ratio in the sample. However, for

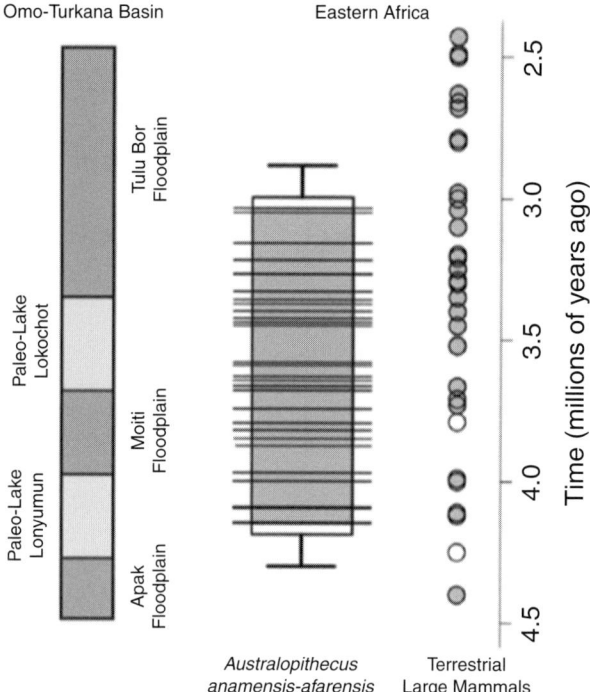

Figure 3.3 Comparison of hominin-bearing horizons and observed stratigraphic range with sedimentary facies and fossil occurrence data. Deep lake phases are less likely to yield hominin fossils, influencing the distribution of hominin-bearing horizons and the observed stratigraphic range (see section on geological biases). Observed temporal range of *Australopithecus anamensis-afarensis* (gray rectangle) along with estimated origination and extinction ages (white rectangle extensions) and their 95% confidence intervals (error bars); modified from Du et al. (2020). The horizontal lines (n = 30) inside the gray rectangle show the observed temporal distribution of *Au. anamensis-afarensis* fossil horizons; 7 of the 30 hominin fossil horizons are from the Omo-Turkana Basin, 15 are from the Awash Basin and 6 from the Olduvai Basin. The circles to the right indicate midpoint ages of sites where terrestrial large mammals are preserved in Eastern Africa (Omo-Turkana, Awash, and Olduvai Basins); gray-filled circles represent those sites where large-bodied primates are found. The ages for deep lake phases (shading) within the Turkana Basin, Paleo-lake Lokochot (3.7 to ~3.4 Ma) and Paleo-lake Lonyumun (~4.3 to ~4.0 Ma) are from Feibel (2011) and McDougall et al. (2012).

speleothems with true ages of approximately 3 Ma or older, the measured $^{234}U/^{238}U$ ratio is so close to equilibrium that a meaningful correction cannot be made, and the sample cannot be accurately dated. It is likely that these constraints are, at least in part, responsible for the current distribution of southern African U–Pb ages (Pickering et al., 2019; Hopley et al., 2021). Use of the ^{235}U–^{207}Pb chronometer may offer a solution for dating older speleothem samples, as disequilibrium correction is not required (Engel et al., 2019); an initial study using this method has produced a late Miocene age for a speleothem from the Cradle of Humankind, South Africa (Hopley et al., 2018).

The northern African fossil record is currently characterized by just a few late Miocene and Plio-Pleistocene fossiliferous localities on the margins of paleo-lakes and modern dunes (Lebatard et al., 2008) and a highly discontinuous record of hominin fossils (see Figure 3.2). Beyond the Rift Valley, and outside of karstic or river terrace environments, the exhumation and discovery of mammal fossils is extremely rare; in addition, the acidic soils of modern and ancient rainforest environments are not conducive to the preservation of bioapatite fossils.

Anthropogenic and Collection Biases

Anthropogenic biases can be derived from several sources relating to the discovery, collection, and interpretation of fossils (Figure 3.1). The discovery of fossils from the Miocene to Recent of Africa is rarely the product of chance or amateur discovery; instead, large-scale funded scientific expeditions are the norm. Choice of expedition locality is driven by geological age and sediment exposure, but also by expectations for the discovery of hominin (and perhaps other mammal) fossils. This is known as the bonanza effect (Raup, 1977; Dunhill et al., 2012), through which research intensity is focused on geographical regions and fossil-bearing formations/localities that have already proven to yield fossils of interest. For example, long-term excavation efforts at a small number of key research areas or localities (e.g., Sterkfontein, Swartkrans, Omo-Turkana Basin, Afar Triangle) results in elevated hominin skeletal completeness scores (Maxwell, 2018), but may not increase the likelihood of recognizing hominin diversity (Maxwell et al., 2018). Conservative research strategies that focus on proven and abundant hominin-bearing deposits are understandable within the context of limiting research risk and obtaining research funding. Once an expedition has commenced, and new fossils start to be discovered, collection biases come to the fore.

A rare opportunity to investigate collection biases was provided by research expeditions to the Shungura Formation undertaken by independent French and American teams between 1967 and 1976 (Alemseged et al., 2007; Eck, 2007). With largely equivalent sedimentary sequences exposed in the two adjacent field areas, the differences in abundance and diversity between the two collections was attributed to different approaches to fossil collection (Alemseged et al., 2007; Eck, 2007). The American team had an implicit sampling protocol of cranial–dental elements only (except for hominins and other primates), whereas the French team collected cranio-dental and postcranial elements (Eck, 2007). The differences in fossil abundance and taxic diversity between the two collections are best explained by differences in collection strategy, effort (field hours), and how this effort was focused toward different geological units. Clearly, collection strategies will influence paleoecological interpretations if not taken into account. A fuller understanding of collection biases requires explicit collection protocols (Thompson et al., 2015) and detailed records of research and collection effort. Unfortunately, for most hominin-bearing localities these records are rarely available.

Taphonomic Bias and Time-Averaging

Taphonomic bias is often the first bias considered within the context of hominin evolution, and it is a subject that has received a great deal of attention (Brain, 1981; Behrensmeyer 1982; Cutler et al., 1999; de Ruiter and Berger, 2000; Alemseged, 2003; Soligo and Andrews, 2005). Taphonomic bias can explain the presence or absence of different taxa or skeletal elements within a fossil assemblage in relation to specific taphonomic pathways, e.g., carnivore accumulation, river transport, death-traps, etc. This can have implications for the relative abundance of hominins and other mammal taxa within a fossil assemblage and needs to be taken into account when comparing fossil assemblages with distinctly different taphonomic histories (such as southern African cave deposits versus Eastern African fluvio-lacustrine deposits). An additional aspect of the taphonomy of faunal assemblages is the temporal resolution, or time-averaging, over which the deposit was accumulated (see Figure 3.1). Time-averaging of hominin-bearing fossil assemblages is usually considered to be on the time frame of 100s to 10,000s of years (Behrensmeyer, 1982; Stern, 1994; Cutler et al., 1999; Behrensmeyer et al., 2007a; Hopley and Maslin, 2010). This has little impact on the absolute ages of fossil assemblages (given the typical uncertainty of ~100,000 years), or on comparison with large-scale perturbations in the paleoclimatic record (typical uncertainty of ~100,000 years). However, time-averaging does have the potential to obscure faunal change across orbital cycles, particularly over the dominant and shortest period cycle: precession (see Figure 3.4). As discussed by Hopley and Maslin (2010), there is little evidence to show that African mammal assemblages can resolve the orbital cycles in rainfall and vegetation that are so apparent in paleoclimate archives from across Africa (e.g., Caley et al., 2018; Yost et al., 2021). The vast majority of African hominin-bearing fossil assemblages are reconstructed as mosaic environments (Reynolds et al., 2015); Kanjera South, Kenya, is a notable exception, being composed principally of savanna-dwelling taxa (Plummer et al., 2009b). Plio-Pleistocene savanna mosaics are often envisaged as patches of woodland, savanna, and wetland all coexisting during a discrete and stable snapshot of time (Reed, 1998; Andrews et al., Chapter 2, this volume). While it can be argued that there are genuine savanna mosaic environments in Africa today, and in the past (Reynolds et al., 2015), it is important to consider the changes to the floral and faunal composition that occur over time, and how this could contribute to the observed environmental heterogeneity of fossil assemblages (see Figure 3.4).

Herbivorous mammals tend to have specific dietary niches (browsers or grazers or mixed feeders), and this is reflected in the distinct carbon isotopic composition of their skeletal remains (Cerling, 2003). They are physiologically bound to their dietary specialism, so in a changing environment they will continue to consume their preferred diet through selective feeding or migration and will have a relatively constant carbon isotope signature. In contrast, carnivores and omnivores are not restricted solely to C_3- or C_4- derived foodstuffs in the way that herbivorous grazers and browsers are (Codron et al., 2007). Carnivores can be selective over their preferred prey species and are likely to consume more browsing herbivores during wooded intervals and more grazing herbivores during grassy intervals (Hayward, 2006). Similarly, mixed feeders and omnivores have a degree of dietary flexibility that can change with available resources, leading to a broad range of carbon isotope values over time or between localities (Copeland et al., 2009; Cerling et al., 2013). Therefore, in a series of time-averaged faunal assemblages that accumulate under an oscillating climate, we would expect to see a broad isotopic range for the carnivores and omnivores from each assemblage and an invariant mean isotopic value (see Figure 3.4C). This concept can be evaluated by looking at the $\delta^{13}C$ data for *Australopithecus afarensis* from Hadar,

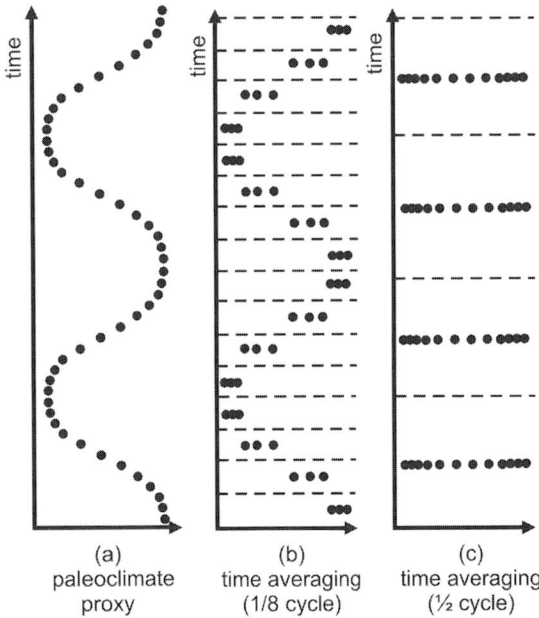

Figure 3.4 Assessment of the environmental fidelity of time-averaged faunal deposits under an oscillating climate (from Hopley and Maslin, 2010). A hypothetical paleoclimate curve shows oscillations typical of orbitally forced climate change (A). Time averaging at intervals of an eighth of a cycle preserves the key paleoclimatic information (B), whereas time averaging at intervals of half a cycle obscures the oscillatory nature of the paleoclimate proxy (C). In this scenario, inter-assemblage variability is minimal and intra-assemblage variability is high. Scenario (C) is typical of Plio-Pleistocene faunal assemblages from African hominin sites and is indicative of a climatically mixed assemblage (see Hopley and Maslin [2010] for more details).

Ethiopia (Wynn et al., 2013). The Hadar Formation provides a large hominin sample of 22 $\delta^{13}C$ measurements (see Figure 3.5) derived from six faunal assemblages (submembers) within a high-resolution stratigraphic sequence (Campisano and Feibel, 2007). Comparison with the insolation record (Laskar et al., 2004) for this time interval, indicates that each faunal assemblage accumulated over more than one precessional cycle, and that the broad range and invariant mean of the *Au. afarensis* data fits with the climate-averaging predictions shown in Figure 3.5. At least some of the dietary variability observed within each submember must reflect dietary change over time. Additional proxies for time-averaging (such as carnivore $\delta^{13}C$; Hopley and Maslin, 2010) should be produced for African localities to help quantify the effects of climate-averaging on paleoenvironmental reconstructions.

Uncertainty in the Timing of Speciation and Extinction

First and Last Appearance Dates (FADs and LADs, respectively) define the known stratigraphic range of taxa, but due to the vagaries of preservation, this is always an underestimation of the true species duration. It is not appropriate to use a FAD or LAD to infer the timing of an origination or extinction event because, by definition, an origination or extinction event must have occurred before the FAD and after the LAD of that taxon, respectively. Bobe and Leakey (2009) addressed this problem by attaching 95 percent confidence intervals to the FAD of early

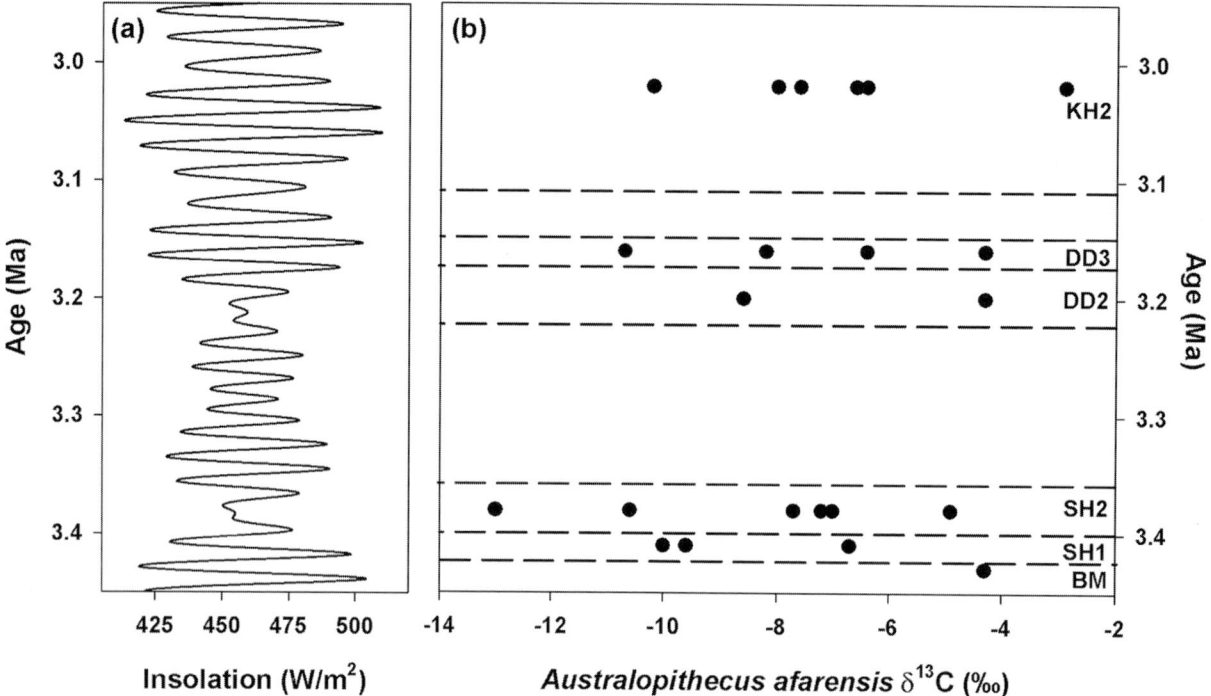

Figure 3.5 Assessment of climate-averaging for a high-resolution hominin-bearing sequence from Hadar, Ethiopia. (a) July Insolation at 15° North between 3.45 and 2.95 Ma (from Laskar et al., 2004). The ~21 ka precessional cycle is responsible for most of the calculated changes in insolation. (b) *Australopithecus afarensis* carbon isotope ($\delta^{13}C$) values from the Hadar Formation, Ethiopia (redrawn from Wynn et al., 2013). Submember names are recorded adjacent to the right y-axis, and their duration (Campisano and Feibel, 2007) is marked by the dashed lines. All submembers show more than 20,000 years of time averaging and represent more than one precessional cycle. The wide range of *Au. afarensis* $\delta^{13}C$ values and invariant mean values across submembers is consistent with that expected for a sequence of climatically mixed faunal assemblages (see Figure 3.4C).

Homo and other mammal taxa from the Omo-Turkana Basin based on the sample-size correction method of Koch (1987). This method requires a large multi-taxon data set from a well-sampled stratigraphic sequence, so cannot be applied to the diverse geographic and stratigraphic settings of the entire hominin fossil record. An alternative approach is to attach confidence intervals to both ends of the observed stratigraphic range, using the method first developed by Strauss and Sadler (1989) and routinely used in marine and terrestrial paleontology (e.g., Strauss and Sadler, 1989; Marshall, 1990, 1994, 1997; Weiss and Marshall, 1999). Confidence intervals are calculated using the number of stratigraphic horizons from which a taxon has been found and the time range between the oldest and youngest representative of the taxon to estimate the true stratigraphic range at the 50 percent or 95 percent confidence level:

$$CI = 1 - 2(1+\alpha)^{-(H-1)} + (1+2\alpha)^{-(H-1)}, \qquad (1)$$

where α is the confidence interval expressed as a fraction of the total known stratigraphic range, CI is the confidence level, and H is the number of known fossiliferous horizons (Marshall, 1990). The value of α can be found by trial and error using Equation (1).

This approach has been applied to selected fossil hominin taxa (e.g., Bobe and Carvalho, 2019; Du et al., 2020) where the number of fossil-bearing horizons is high enough to draw reliable conclusions. Using a database of hominin-bearing horizons (last updated December 2017), Maxwell (2018) applied confidence intervals to all early hominin species represented by three or more horizons (see Table 3.1). The two species with the most complete fossil record are *Paranthropus boisei* and *P. aethiopicus* (Table 3.1), due principally to the fact that isolated molar teeth can be assigned to these taxa with confidence. *Paranthropus boisei* has been found at 31 distinct stratigraphic horizons within a stratigraphic range lasting 1.0 Ma. This produces well-constrained upper and lower confidence intervals of approximately 130,000 years, which represents less time than the uncertainties associated with the radiometric age determinations for most fossil localities (see Wood and Constantino, 2007). *Australopithecus afarensis*, *P. aethiopicus*, and African *Homo erectus* have equivalent confidence intervals on their stratigraphic ranges. However, several early hominins have a sparse fossil record (collected from between three and eight stratigraphic horizons), representing between 680,000 years (*P. robustus*), 1,010,000 years (*Ardipithecus ramidus*), and 1,380,000 years (*Au. africanus*) of uncertainty at both ends of their stratigraphic range (see Table 3.1). There are an additional four early hominin species *Au. sediba* (Malapa, South Africa), *Au. garhi* (Bouri, Ethiopia), *Au. bahrelghazali* (Koro Toro, Chad), and *Sahelanthropus tchadensis* (Toros-Menalla, Chad), which to date have been found at just one stratigraphic horizon each. Because such taxa do not have a stratigraphic range, meaningful confidence intervals cannot be assigned to these taxa.

Total-Evidence Dating (TED) approaches the timing of speciation by combining morphological and stratigraphic data from the fossil record with morphological and molecular sequence data from extant species to both estimate phylogenetic relationships and divergence dates. Püschel et al. (2021) used TED methods to estimate the age and uncertainties of

Table 3.1 Stratigraphic range and confidence interval data for early African hominin taxa. First and Last Appearance Dates were taken from Wood and Boyle (2016) and updated by Maxwell (2018). Upper and lower 95% confidence intervals (CIs) were calculated using Equation 1 (Marshall, 1990) from a database of horizon counts (Maxwell, 2018). Fossil discoveries after 2018 have not been included in this database or analysis. Those taxa for which a meaningful CI cannot be calculated (i.e., $H \leq 2$) are represented by a dash (–).

Species	FAD (Ma)	LAD (Ma)	Stratigraphic range (Ma)	H	CI (Ma)
Sahelanthropus tchadensis	7.00	7.00	0.00	1	–
Orrorrin tugenensis	6.10	5.70	0.40	4	0.92
Ardipithecus kadabba	6.30	5.20	1.10	7	0.92
Ardipithecus ramidus	4.51	4.30	0.21	3	1.01
Kenyanthropus platyops	3.54	3.35	0.19	4	0.44
Australopithecus anamensis	4.20	3.90	0.30	8	0.20
Australopithecus afarensis	3.70	3.00	0.70	22	0.13
Australopithecus bahrelghazali	3.58	3.58	0.00	1	–
Australopithecus deyiremeda	3.50	3.30	0.20	2	–
Australopithecus africanus	3.00	2.40	0.60	4	1.38
Australopithecus garhi	2.50	2.50	0.00	1	–
Australopithecus sediba	1.98	1.98	0.00	1	–
Paranthropus aethiopicus	2.66	2.30	0.36	13	0.13
Paranthropus boisei	2.30	1.30	1.00	31	0.13
Paranthropus robustus	2.00	1.00	1.00	8	0.68
Homo habilis	2.33	1.65	0.68	13	0.24
Homo rudolfensis	2.00	1.78	0.22	4	0.51
African Homo erectus	1.90	0.78	1.12	26	0.18

divergence dates within Hominini. Using this method, uncertainty in divergence date is typically 1.5 Myr for hominins older than 3 Ma and approximately 1.0 Myr for hominins younger than 3 Ma. These uncertainties are similar to those proposed using the confidence interval approach outlined above. TED represents a welcome methodological advancement to the quantification of divergence date estimates. Whether CI or TED methods are used, the pattern of poorly constrained lineages is the same: all time intervals throughout the last 7 million years are associated, given current uncertainties, with hominin speciation or extinction events. As an unwanted consequence, any known or inferred global or regional climatic event that has occurred over the last 7 million years can be invoked as a causal mechanism for an individual hominin origination or extinction event. While these myriad climate-evolution links are attractive associations for authors to make (e.g., Caley et al., 2018; Püschel et al. 2021; Shultz and Maslin, 2013), they currently cannot be justified beyond "just-so" stories (Smith, 2016).

Hominin Diversity and Sampling Bias

Species diversity is an important part of our understanding of human evolutionary history (Wood and Boyle, 2016). Are there trends in hominin diversity through time, and can they be explained by ecological or climatic processes (e.g., deMenocal, 1995; Shultz and Maslin, 2013; Maslin et al., 2014)? Before the evolutionary implications of observed hominin diversity can be assessed, it is essential to consider the taxonomic (Wood and Boyle, 2016), geological, and anthropogenic (Maxwell et al., 2018) influences that obscure the evolutionary picture. Among other terrestrial mammal groups there are several studies that have shown a strong correlation between taxic diversity and sampling intensity (e.g., Bush et al., 2004; Butler et al., 2011; Mannion et al., 2011; Newham et al., 2014; Tennent et al., 2016). This is because time periods with more fossil localities or larger faunal assemblages will have a greater diversity due to their closer approximation to the true biological diversity, as demonstrated for Neogene bovids (Behrensmeyer et al., 1997). Maxwell et al. (2018) investigated the geological and anthropological influences on early African hominin diversity by comparing hominin diversity (both taxic and phylogenetic diversity estimates) with sampling metrics such as geological formation counts. The number of primate-bearing formations per time bin was shown to be a reliable predictor of hominin taxic diversity. Hominin phylogenetic diversity, which has been partially corrected for sampling bias (Smith, 1994), varied independently of the sampling metrics tested.

Hominin taxic diversity is influenced by the number of horizons, geological formations, and sedimentary basins that have yielded identifiable hominin remains (Figure 3.2). The brief time period between 2.0 Ma and 1.25 Ma contains the greatest number of fossil-bearing horizons in both the Eastern and southern African regions and is also the time interval with the highest overall hominin taxic diversity (up to six species, see Wood and Boyle, 2016). The presence/absence of southern African hominin localities accounts for approximately one third of total hominin diversity. Total observed hominin diversity drops from the peak of six species between 2 Ma and 1.75 Ma down to an average of two species prior to 3 Ma when the southern African record is absent. True hominin diversity is likely to be underrepresented by the small number of hominin-bearing basins and formations, especially during the earlier stages of hominin evolution. Further investigation is required to determine what other geological and anthropological factors may underlie the observed pattern of hominin diversity through time.

Sampling Proxies and Future Directions

Most of the above approaches to the hominin fossil record assume a constant Fossil Recovery Potential (FRP) through geological time (Du et al., 2020). This assumption is unlikely to be met by the patchy record of terrestrial mammals, such as hominins (Holland, 2016), and needs to be addressed explicitly. FRP can be investigated using independent sampling proxies, such as sedimentary facies changes (Marshall, 1997; Holland, 2003) or geological age distributions. Future work should look to integrate assessments of FRP with estimates for the timing of origination and extinction and hominin diversity.

Sampling proxies or metrics are used to compare the hominin fossil record with independent measures of geological processes or anthropological activities and offer alternative lines of inquiry to the ubiquitous comparisons with paleoclimate proxies. For example, Maxwell et al. (2018) used hominin-, primate-, and mammal-bearing formation counts, and collection counts (specifically counts of discovery years), as a proxy for sampling intensity through time. Correlation between primate-bearing formations and early African hominin taxic diversity indicated that the number (and geographical extent; Maxwell, 2018) of available fossiliferous formations was a major control on hominin diversity during any time interval. Development of more specific sampling proxies based on depositional environments, dating frequency or fieldwork intensity, has the potential to provide a more nuanced understanding of the observed hominin fossil record.

New fossil discoveries repeatedly reshape our understanding of evolutionary history (Tarver et al., 2011) and the hominin fossil record is itself changing through research time. After almost 100 years of hominin discoveries in Africa, the hominin fossil record is still relatively sparse and immature. Through comparison with other fossil groups, this maturity can be quantified, and improvements can be monitored (e.g., Benton and Storrs, 1994). Studies that track the development of the hominin fossil record through research time are rare (e.g., Foley 2005; Maxwell et al., 2018; Maxwell 2018) but valuable (Figure 3.6). For this type of research to progress, data sets on the broader pursuits of paleoanthroplogy, including logs of fieldwork time, dating effort, sedimentary facies, and publications per locality, should be collected and shared – irrespective of whether these research efforts result in the discovery of new hominin fossils.

Discussion and Conclusion

Assessments of hominin diversity through geological time are affected by uncertainty in the stratigraphic range of each taxon as well as by geological, anthropological, and geographical collection biases. The three biogeographic regions of Africa that hosted early hominins have endemic faunas, including hominin species. However, the relative contribution of these three regions varies with time; for example, the rarity of southern African cave deposits prior to 3 Ma artificially reduces hominin diversity between 6 Ma and 3 Ma. The number of hominin-bearing formations and basins is low during earlier time intervals, with large consequences for observed hominin diversity (Maxwell et al., 2018). At a finer temporal and geographic scale, fluctuations in sedimentary facies determine the preservation potential of mammal, including hominin, fossils.

This review underlines the necessary caution required when comparing the hominin fossil record with paleoclimate proxies. The commonly employed FADs and LADs rarely take the inherent uncertainties associated with stratigraphic ranges into account, although this situation is improving (see Du et al., 2020; Püschel et al., 2021). The stratigraphic range of each early hominin has a large associated uncertainty, at best 120,000 years at the 95 percent confidence level (Du et al., 2020), and often in excess of 1 Myr (Püschel et al., 2021). The hominin fossil record is gradually expanding and improving, but it will take decades of new discoveries to see a significant improvement in the confidence intervals on the stratigraphic ranges of most hominin species. In

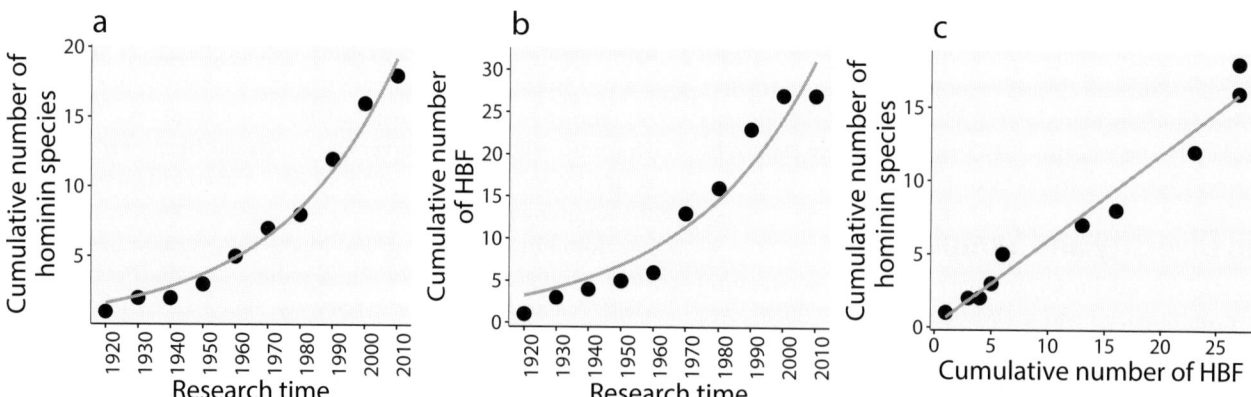

Figure 3.6 Exponential increase in hominin diversity (a) and hominin-bearing formations (HBF; b) in Africa since 1920 (from Maxwell et al., 2018). Based on these curves and the strong association between hominin diversity and fossil-bearing formations (c), it seems likely that hominin diversity will continue to increase in the future as more fossiliferous formations are explored. Data up to date to 2017.

the meantime, proxies for the hominin fossil record, such as the more complete record of fossil bovids or cercopithecids, or stone tool industries, can provide more reliable and fruitful comparisons with temporally constrained climatic events. By acknowledging current deficiencies in the hominin fossil record, we aim to bring attention to the new approaches being developed and employed throughout the broader discipline of paleobiology to openly identify, discuss, and correct fossil sampling biases.

Climatic variability has been a strong focus of the hominin–climate debate in recent years, although tests of these hypotheses have been elusive (e.g., Will et al., 2021). The variability selection hypothesis (Potts, 1996, 1998a, 1998b) does not explicitly define the timescale of climate variability to which hominin versatility is an adaptive response, but the most likely time frame is that of orbital variability. As demonstrated above, hominin-bearing fossil assemblages do not have sufficient temporal resolution to investigate the evolutionary response to orbital forcing. Without evidence to the contrary, most African faunal assemblages should be viewed as mixed assemblages incorporating individuals from the entire range of orbital-scale variations in rainfall intensity and vegetation composition. Shorter time frames of variability, such as annual or inter-annual variability, can be resolved from isotopic analysis of individual teeth, and this could provide a means of investigating variability selection, although comparing these short and mixed records with suitable paleoclimatic data is a significant challenge.

In addition to the above recommendations, it is clear that improvements to the African paleoclimate record are required. An improved understanding of the causes and characteristics of apparent climate transitions, for example at 2.5 Ma or 1.8 Ma, would be beneficial. Specifically, do these transitions represent an increase in mean aridity across multiple orbital cycles or are the aridity changes expressed as seasonal or inter-annual changes in rainfall? It is important to understand the climatic mechanisms involved before predicting the appropriate evolutionary responses or looking for validation from the fossil record. Given the vagaries of the fossil record, and an evolving climatic history of Africa, the various hypotheses of human evolution and climate change are set to remain hypothetical for some time yet.

Acknowledgments

Thanks to Sally Reynolds, René Bobe, and Matthew Bennett for providing insightful reviews and comments.

Late Miocene and Earliest Pliocene Paleoecology of Africa
A Synthesis

Jessamy H. Doman and Emily Goble Early

Background

While the Plio-Pleistocene saw the radiation of multiple hominin species adapted to a variety of environments across Africa and beyond, the origin of our clade is firmly rooted in the Miocene. In fact, the distribution and composition of the living African fauna today owe much to the events of the late Miocene and earliest Pliocene. This period featured momentous climatic, glacial, and eustatic shifts on a global scale, in contrast to the preceding warm and relatively stable, middle Miocene (Zachos et al., 2001). Decades of paleoclimatic research – primarily based on ocean, ice, and lake cores (e.g., Hodell et al., 1986; deMenocal, 2004; Cohen et al., 2009; Bonnefille, 2010; Feakins et al., 2013) have enabled the reconstruction of the major changes that occurred during this period. We know that the Earth's temperature fell precipitously, and that escalation of Antarctic glaciation created knock-on effects in ocean water temperatures, dramatic sea-level drops, and atmospheric circulation changes leading to widespread aridification. Estimated divergence dates for west-central and east African rainforest tree taxa suggest that through the effects of these climatic changes, combined with continued movement, uplift, and rifting of tectonic plates, Africa was modified to such an extent that regions previously characterized by flat and homogeneously forested landscapes were replaced by a topographically diverse terrain ranging from desert to montane forest (Couvreur et al., 2008; Maslin et al., 2015).

The impact of these shifts at the regional and local scales is still not fully understood, but, without question, this was a crucial period for human evolution and African fauna and flora as a whole. Biotic turnover led to the replacement of more archaic forms by those that might not look out of place on African landscapes today (Hill, 1995; Kingston et al., 2002). At the same time, the first bipedal apes – members of our tribe, Hominini – diverged from those that would evolve into chimpanzees (Figure 4.1).

The movement of the earliest hominins out of the trees and onto the plains on two legs was theorized for many years to have been directly caused by the shift to cooler, drier conditions (e.g. Wheeler, 1991), yet the increasing body of paleontological data demonstrates a much more complex series of events, and the questions of when, why, or even where the hominin lineage diverged from other hominines still exist. Molecular data have in part helped to identify *when* to look – the majority of analyses place the *Pan–Homo* divergence at 8–4 Ma (Bradley, 2008), but the continued lack of consensus and variety of divergence estimates ranging from 14 to 3 Ma (Table 4.1) is problematic for the

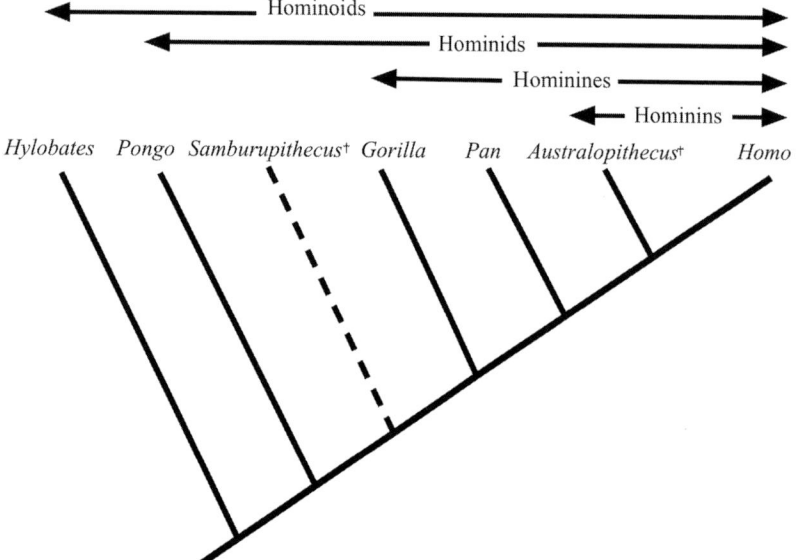

Figure 4.1 Simplified cladogram depicting relationships of the hominoid primates following the nomenclature of Harrison (2010b). Dashed line signifies uncertain phylogenetic placement.

Supplementary resources for this chapter are available on www.cambridge.org/africanpaleoecology

interpretation of putative fossil hominid remains. Some explanation for this lack of consensus may come from the recent suggestion that the ancestors of humans and chimpanzees diverged early, but continued to exchange genes for millions of years after (Disotell, 2006; Patterson et al., 2006; Rieux et al., 2014).

Promisingly, concerted fossil recovery in sediments spanning the period in question has greatly increased our understanding of this part of our phylogenetic tree. In fact, in the last two decades the number of known late Miocene hominoids has grown considerably (e.g., Brunet et al., 2002; Haile-Selassie, 2001; Pickford & Senut, 2001a; Kunimatsu et al., 2007; Suwa et al., 2007b). As the hominid hypodigm grows, in combination with molecular data, paleoanthropologists and paleoecologists are closer to the goal of refining time estimates of major phylogenetic events and correlating these with environmental change. Human evolution, via natural selection, took the course it did as adaptations arose to counter the variety of external pressures – such as food and water availability, predation, etc. – that our hominin ancestors faced. Thus, it is the field of paleoecology that can help to answer the question of *why* hominins adopted their peculiar suite of traits – including upright posture and bipedal locomotion – by isolating the increments of morphological change in human evolution, via a high-resolution understanding of their paleo-landscapes both temporally and spatially. Site-specific paleoecological studies based on floral, geochemical, and faunal analysis have in recent years allowed climate reconstruction at local and regional scales, complementing those at the continental and global scales (e.g., Tsujikawa, 2005a, 2005b; Le Fur et al., 2009; Su et al., 2009; White et al., 2009a, 2009b; Coutros, 2016). Often these reconstructions at differing levels are in conflict with one another, demonstrating that even within relatively close regions, hominin sites had localized climates – primarily as a result of divergent topography (e.g., Cerling et al., 2010, and references therein; Coutros, 2016).

In approaching the question of *where*, some paleoanthropologists have shifted their gaze to more far-reaching parts of the African continent and beyond (Hill, 2007; Begun, 2015).

Table 4.1 *Pan–Homo* divergence dates published since 2000.

Estimated time of *Pan–Homo* split (Ma)	References
12.0–10.0	Arnason and Janke (2002)
9–7.1	Hasegawa et al. (2003)
7–5.5	Kumar et al. (2005)
	Raaum et al. (2005)
	Glazko and Nei (2003)
	Wildman et al. (2003)
	Steiper and Young (2006)
<5.5	Rieux et al. (2014)
	Eizirik et al. (2004)
	Hobolth et al. (2007)
	Chen and Li (2001)
	Yoder and Yang (2000)
	Stauffer et al. (2001)

Paleoanthropology has in the past focused almost exclusively upon the east African rift valleys and South Africa. Yet paleobiogeographical studies have shown us that, at certain times in the past, inter- and intracontinental migrations, rather than *in situ* biotic evolution, were a significant factor in the differentiation of African faunal communities. This fact, combined with the relatively recent realization that early hominins were not restricted to eastern and southern Africa (Brunet, 2010), demonstrates that biogeography is an essential consideration in the realm of paleoanthropology.

Through the detailed study of paleontological records, we are now more aware of short-term climatic events and the existence of refugia that otherwise do not reconcile with the broader trends that have long been documented (e.g., Brunet et al., 2005). Therefore, this chapter takes the form of a review of the climatic, tectonic, and biotic events surrounding the *Pan–Homo* divergence and subsequent hominin radiation, broken down into their respective temporal and spatial contexts across the entire continent (Figure 4.2). Data for the figure are available in Supplementary Information.

Global Climatic Deterioration and the Hominines *Nakalipithecus*, *Samburupithecus*, and *Chororapithecus*: 12–8 Ma

To better understand the adaptations that set our tribe, Hominini, apart, it is helpful to view them in the context of our hominid ancestors and the challenges that they faced in the early part of the Late Miocene. Two potential stem hominines *Nakalipithecus nakayamai* (Kunimatsu et al., 2007) and *Samburupithecus kiptalami* (Tsujikawa, 2005a, 2005b) were present during a time of significant climatic upheaval. In contrast with the relatively warm and climatically stable middle Miocene, the globe entered into periods of significant cooling and drying after 12.5 Ma (Bakker and Mercer, 1986; Kingston and Hill, 1999). As the Earth cooled, positive feedback in the form of the albedo effect further escalated the cooling of the Earth's climate system, and a 4–5°C drop in ocean temperature, a world-wide drop of 7°C, and growth of the Antarctic ice is indicated by a major shift in the foraminiferal $\delta^{18}O$ sheet (Shackleton and Kennett, 1975; Zachos et al., 2001; Figure 4.3). This in turn led to a dramatic drop in sea level – variably quoted as 90–140 m (Haq et al., 1987; Hardenbol, 1998; Moore et al., 1987).

Paleoenvironmental data from across Africa demonstrate the different ways local climates manifest in response to global and regional climatic events. A strong contrast developed between eastern and western South Africa, for example. As increasingly cold Antarctic water enhanced upwelling in the Benguela Current and the subtropical anticyclone strengthened off the coast of southwestern Africa, the Namib Desert became hyperarid, while there continued to exist extensive Malagasy-like forests on the eastern side (Bakker and Mercer, 1986; Hoetzel et al., 2015). An unfortunate lack of time-successive vertebrate fossil localities from Namibia hampers paleoclimatic reconstructions of this area, but mid–late Miocene fossiliferous localities in the Otavi Mountains provide an intriguing insight. Fauna retrieved from cave breccias at the mining sites of Berg

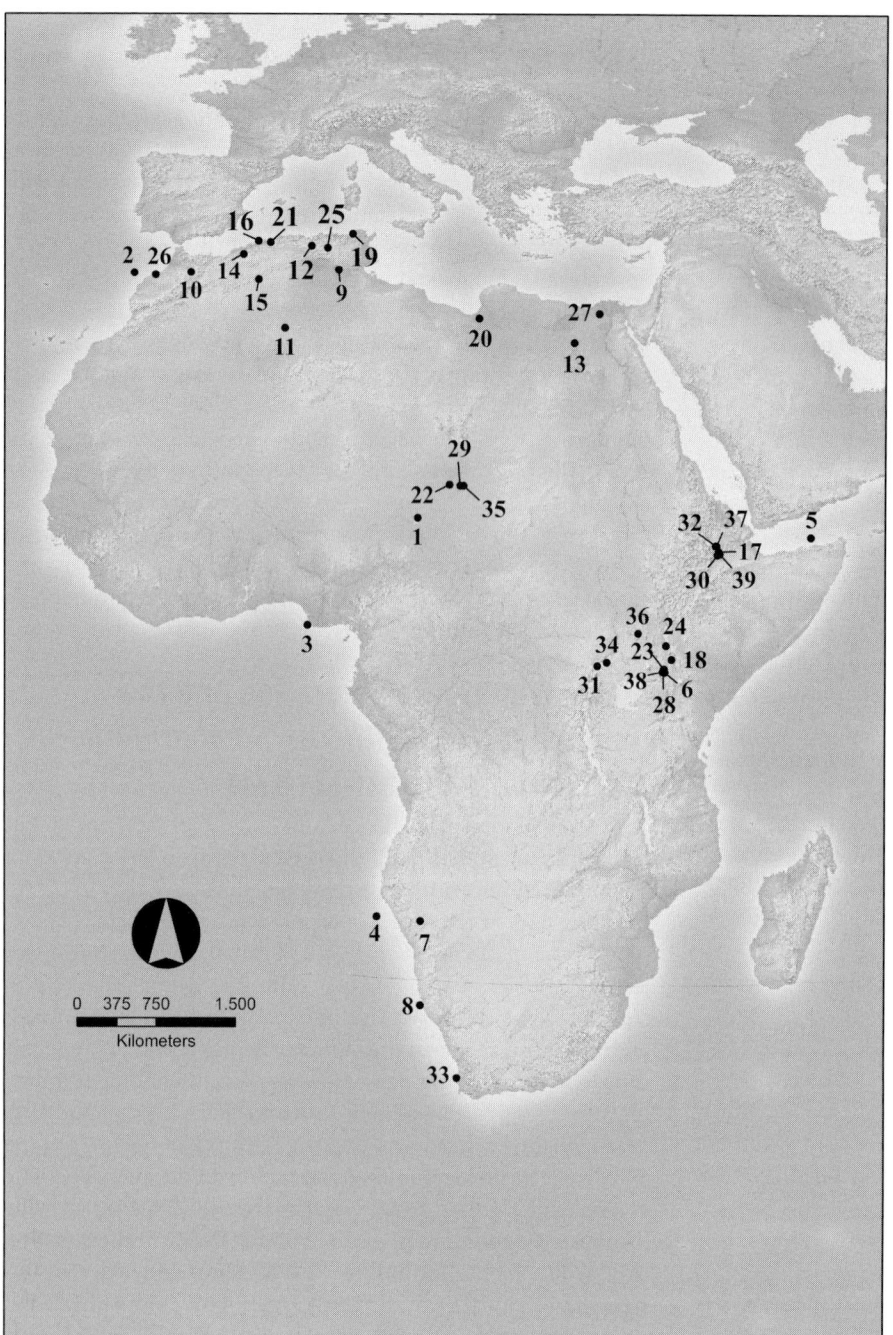

Figure 4.2 Map of Africa with sites mentioned in the text. Numbers refer to localities as listed in the online supplementary material for this chapter.

Aukas and Harasib are suggestive of a riparian forest refugium within an otherwise arid landscape, supporting lorisoids, cercopithecoids, and the proconsulid-like hominoid *Otavipithecus namibiensis* in the same environs as desert-adapted rodents (Conroy et al., 1992; Senut and Gommery, 1997). Thus, while found within the developing Namibian desert, *Otavipithecus* was likely exploiting a quickly shrinking but tolerable refugium.

Widespread aridity also penetrated northwest and equatorial Africa into what is now the Sahara, and previously forested lowlands became colder and drier, with relict forests surviving in mountainous regions (Sarnthein et al., 1982). The prevalence of subtropical forest along the Mediterranean coastline is also suggested by large and diverse faunal communities at the sites of Bled Douarah (Tunisia) and Bou Hanifia and Oued Mya 1 (Algeria) (Arambourg, 1963a; Robinson et al., 1969; Sudre and Hartenberger, 1992). Faunal observations of these sites initially supported an early spread of grasslands in northern Africa, heralded by the first appearance of the three-toed hipparion horses in Africa and hypsodont bovids, including the caprine, *Protoryx* (Robinson, 1972, 1986). However, reinterpretations of early late Miocene hipparions as mixed feeders (Bernor et al., 2004) alongside the description of several tropical tree macrofossils and crocodilians in the Beglia Fm of Tunisia (Pickford, 2000) indicate that these sites were more humid and heavily wooded than previously thought. In fact, they suggest that extensive river systems crossed what is now the Sahara, and the faunal record from the

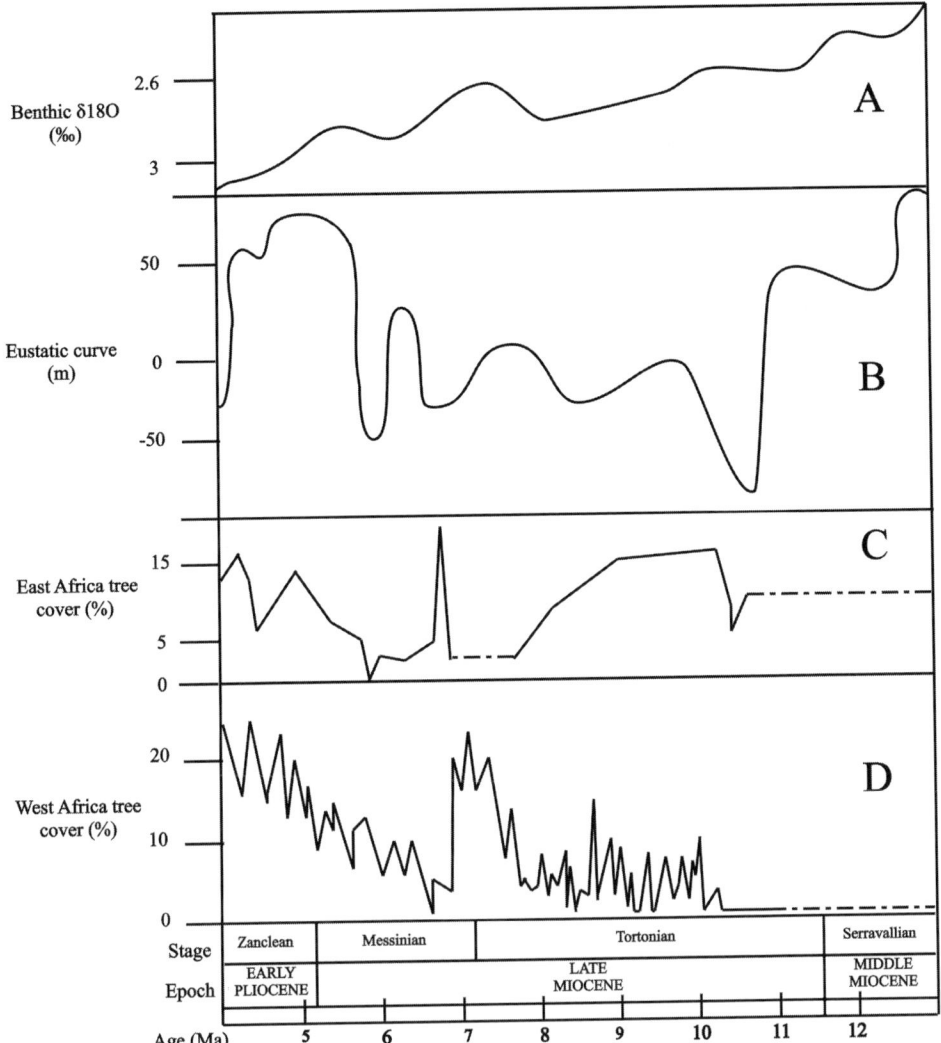

Figure 4.3 Comparison of selected climatic and paleoenvironmental proxies for the time period discussed. (A) Benthic $\delta^{18}O$ (‰) values as an indicator of long-term deep-sea cooling and ice sheet formation from Zachos et al. (2001). (B) Eustatic curve relative to modern day sea level from Haq et al. (1987). (C,D) Tree density as calculated by Bonnefille (2010) utilizing proportion of tree/shrub in pollen profiles from the Gulf of Aden (east) and Niger Delta (west) cores.

Western Desert of Egypt supports this view. Mean annual rainfall at the locality of Sheikh Abdallah (also known as Gebel Bellorat) was calculated at 750–1200 mm based on the faunal assemblage – which includes the arboreal porcupine *Atherurus* and a galagid – modern equivalents of which today are only found in the forests some 10° further south (Pickford et al., 2006). The biogeographic patterns of mammals closely tied to water sources also offer clues relating to hydrological connections – the distribution of the hippopotamid *Kenyapotamus* and the anthracothere *Libycosaurus anisae* in both east Africa and Tunisia ~10 Ma indicate faunal exchange via paleodrainages connecting east and north Africa, perhaps via western Egypt (Lihoreau et al., 2006).

The spread of arid environments appears to have occurred more gradually in east Africa than the rest of the continent (Hoetzel et al., 2015; Senut et al., 2009). While this may in part reflect the dearth of fossil sites in east Africa relative to north Africa during this time, it is also evident that differing forcing mechanisms were at play. Superimposed upon the global climatic disturbances were important tectonic factors, and it appears that these were particularly felt in east Africa. Africa may have been moving as much as 5 cm per year for the bulk of the Neogene and the effects of this latitudinal change upon African environments would not have been minor – northward movement of the continent would have changed precipitation patterns of the equatorial Hadley cells, resulting in the observed trend of aridification and southward displacement of tropical forests, as indicated by offshore pollen profiles (Brown, 1995; Bonnefille, 2010). In the east, increasing evidence suggests that regional and local tectonic uplift associated with the Rift formation had greater impact on regional climates than previously thought (Sepulchre et al., 2006). The late Miocene saw dramatic rifting and extension of the Ethiopian rift into Kenya, creating the Afar junction and causing the interior and east African plateaus to rise, blocking moisture from the Atlantic and creating a rain shadow effect over much of eastern Africa (Sepulchre et al., 2006).

As a result, reduced annual rainfall and accentuated seasonality of precipitation caused significant change and diversification in vegetation in the east African region. This has been captured as a shift in pollen abundance in the Gulf of Aden ~10.4 Ma, with a significant spike in Poaceae (grasses) followed by a more gradual increase in the arid-adapted shrubs of the Amaranthaceae (amaranth and goosefoot) family (Bonnefille, 2010; Figure 4.3).

The pollen signature is supported by fauna and flora of the terrestrial hominid-bearing sediments in the Tugen and Samburu Hills, Kenya. A shift from tropical rainforest at Kabasero in the Ngorora Formation, Tugen Hills (12.6 Ma) to a seasonally dry woodland nearby at Waril (10 Ma) reflects the replacement of denser forest by more deciduous, open woodland and a 50 percent decrease in summer precipitation, indicated by fossil leaf physiognomy (Jacobs and Deino, 1996). The Ngorora rainforest provided habitation for primates such as victoriapithecids and at least one small-bodied hominoid, neither of which are documented in the later sediments (Hill et al., 2002).

Viewing the changing nature of regions that were populated with hominoids may help us understand their morphological adaptations. *Samburupithecus kiptalami* – another relatively primitive hominoid sharing traits with the proconsulids – makes its earliest appearance in the Namurungule Formation in the Samburu Hills, following a sharp shift in local climate at ~ 9.6 Ma (Ishida and Pickford, 1997). Lithology and both vertebrate and invertebrate records (Pickford et al., 1987; Tsujikawa, 2005a, 2005b) suggest that the dry, wooded vegetation of the underlying upper Aka Aiteputh Formation was replaced by a more open-wooded environment bordering savanna, but one that experienced *increased* precipitation (Sakai et al., 2010). The juxtaposition of increased precipitation yet more open country during a time of increasing regional aridity may be explained by enhanced seasonality – with a wetter wet season and a drier dry season – brought on by the combined effects of global cooling, Himalayan uplift, and northern hemisphere glaciation intensifying the Indian monsoon and increasing moisture transport by the Intertropical Convergence Zone (Betzler et al., 2016; Sakai et al., 2010). The dental evidence from *Samburupithecus* – specifically thick enamel and rounded cusps of the upper molars – may indicate increasing adaptations for the processing of more fibrous plant matter during dry seasons (Harrison, 2010b).

The complex, rift-dominated, and volcanic topography of east Africa enabled the development of a variety of environments within short distances from one another, creating highly heterogeneous habitats or a "patch-work quilt effect" (Bonnefille, 2010: 405). The possible hominine *Nakalipithecus nakayamai* is known from the 9.8 Ma Nakali Formation – reconstructed as a wetter habitat than that suggested at the temporally contemporaneous Ngorora and upper Aka Aiteputh formations 80 km and 300 km away, respectively (Kunimatsu et al., 2007). The differing paleoenvironments at Nakali, Samburu Hills, and Tugen Hills demonstrate the influence of topography upon local habitat response to global and regional climate change, and warn against extrapolating ecological implications from single fossil sites or cores to a broader temporal or spatial scale (Kingston, 2007). Perhaps more importantly, these sites offer important case studies in the non-linear relationship between rainfall and vegetation and the different types of seasonality that can arise under different circumstances, particularly in the presence of highly localized, tectonically active rift basins, such as can be seen in the Okavango today (e.g., Reynolds et al., 2016).

The combination of sea-level change and climatic deterioration caused substantial reshuffling of faunal communities during this period, culminating with the Vallesian Crisis at 9.7 Ma (Eronen et al., 2009; Agustí et al., 2013). Lower sea levels enabled the movement of hipparionine equids from North America across the Bering Strait and eventually into Africa (Steininger et al., 1985; Sen, 1990). Other immigrants into Africa included hyaenids (represented by *Hyaenictis*, *Protictitherium*, and *Lycyaena* at Beni Mellal and Bled Douarah), the felid *Machairodus*, the gomphothere *Anancus*, the chalicothere *Ancylotherium*, and tetraconodontine suids (first represented in Africa by *Nyanzachoerus* – also identified on the Arabian subcontinent; (van der Made, 1998; Bishop and Hill, 1999; Bobe, 2006; Bernor et al., 2009; Werdelin and Peigné, 2010; Agustí et al., 2013). In response to shifting oceanic and atmospheric circulation patterns, the tropical vegetation zone shifted south and the evergreen forests of Europe were replaced by deciduous environments (Agustí et al., 2013). The climatic crisis at 9.7 Ma was significant enough that the biodiversity that characterized early Vallesian European ecosystems dwindled and many elements adapted to the warm, wet, subtropical environments – including hominoids – disappeared in Europe either through extinction or southward migration to Africa (Fortelius et al., 1996).

Such immigration significantly shaped the Namurungule and Nakali fauna, which share affinities with similarly aged sites in Greece (Samos and Pikermi), Iran (Maragheh), and India (Siwaliks; Nakaya et al., 1987; Turner and O'Regan, 2015). It has been posited, in fact, that *Nakalipithecus* appears closely related to *Ouranopithecus* from Greece (Harrison, 2010b). It is not out of the realm of possibility that faunal movement into Africa in the late Miocene included hominoids from which hominins evolved (Begun, 2015). However, *Nakalipithecus* is slightly older and more primitive dentally than its Greek cousin, and the discovery of several new hominoids in Africa in this time period have strengthened the case for an African origin for the hominin clade (Haile-Selassie, 2001; Brunet et al., 2002; Pickford and Senut, 2001a; Cote, 2004; Pickford & Senut, 2005; Kunimatsu et al., 2007; Suwa et al., 2007b; Harrison, 2010a).

The trend of increased precipitation and seasonality captured in the Samburu Hills faunal record heralded the beginning of a period of increasingly intense climatic fluctuations featuring wet and warm punctuations within an otherwise global cooling period. Multiple proxies from the Namibian, Moroccan, and Gulf of Aden cores (Figure 4.2) indicate warm, humid conditions came to prevail across the entire continent 9 Ma ago (Bonnefille, 2010; Hoetzel et al., 2015; Stein and Sarnthein, 1984). However, this humid period was relatively short-lived, documented by a swift replacement of woodland pollen in the Namibian core with grass pollen and charcoal at 8.3 Ma, in response to another decrease in global temperature and the expansion of the Antarctic ice sheets (Hoetzel et al., 2015). The southwestern core data have helped to elucidate the evolution of savanna grasslands, whereby the spread of grassy habitats provided fuel for bushfires, which in turn favored pioneer plant regrowth of predominantly C_4 (tropical grass) vegetation (Hoetzel et al., 2015).

It was during this return to cooler, drier conditions that a large hominoid was living in what may have remained a forest refugium in present-day Ethiopia (Suwa et al., 2007b). Dental elements attributed to *Chororapithecus abyssinicus* were recovered from ~8 Ma sediments at Beticha in the Chorora Formation, a site that has been reconstructed as a closed, humid habitat – perhaps a lake margin – based on the presence of colobine primates, browsing ungulates, and near-pure C_3 (non-tropical grass, trees or shrub) signals from hippopotamus tooth enamel (Katoh et al., 2016; Suwa et al., 2007b). Like *Samburupithecus*, *Chororapithecus* has been argued to represent a stem member of Gorillini based on its large size and dental morphology (Suwa et al., 2007b) – with improvement of the sample, which chiefly consists of dental elements, it may be synonymized (Harrison, 2010b). The molecular evidence for a gorilla–chimpanzee/human split at 10.5 Ma (Disotell, 2013) certainly supports this time frame, and the position of *Nakalipithecus* at 9.6 Ma as an even more primitive member of the gorilla clade (Katoh et al., 2016). Importantly, all known purported gorilla relatives appear to have been living in wetter environments or those that experienced high seasonal rainfall, suggesting that, as today, these large apes were less ecologically flexible than other hominid species, and restricted to more humid habitats (Kingdon, 2013).

The Development of the Sahara and the First Hominin, *Sahelanthropus*: 8–6.5 Ma

While savanna and desert biomes were becoming more widespread across Africa from 8 Ma onwards – aeolian sand deposits in the Djurab Desert, Chad, signify the genesis of the Sahara Desert 8–7 Ma (Schuster et al., 2006) – continued humid periods featuring dramatic expansion of forest and woodlands were not insignificant either. Weakening of the summer monsoon allowed the spread of desert conditions across Africa, but also caused greater sensitivity to orbital forcing – a probable explanation for the Sahara's subsequent fluctuations in extent (Zhang et al., 2014). Over 100 wet–dry cycles have been suggested to have occurred in the ancient Lake Chad basin between the Messinian and early Pliocene, documented as sequences of lacustrine, perilacustrine, and aeolian deposits and remote sensing evidence of numerous lake level stands (Griffin, 2006; Leblanc et al., 2007). These fluctuations are mirrored in alternating rainforest–Gramineae pollen in the Niger delta core, indicating periodic expansion of grasslands into rainforest areas and vice versa (Morley, 2000). During the "Niger Forest Phase" noted by Bonnefille (2010) ~7.5–7 Ma, humid habitats may have stretched continuously across the continent. This is supported in the east by a tree pollen peak evident in the Gulf of Aden at 6.8 Ma, and the existence of a seasonal woodland at Kapturo in the Mpesida Beds, Tugen Hills at 7.2–6.7 Ma (Jacobs and Deino, 1996). While these pollen fluctuations have been said to "closely parallel" sea-level fluctuations (Morley and Kingdon, 2013: 51), it is clear from the Bol core sediments that lakes in the ancient Lake Chad basin fluctuated in size in response to the precessional cycle (Griffin, 2006; Moussa et al., 2016).

Consequently, the earliest plausible hominin appeared in relatively wet circumstances during otherwise increasingly arid conditions in the Djurab Desert of northern Chad. Cranial and mandibular remains of *Sahelanthropus tchadensis* were retrieved from perilacustrine deposits immediately overlying the aeolian deposits, in the lowermost Anthracotheriid Unit (7.3–7.1 Ma) at Toros-Menalla (Brunet et al., 2002). The date of these deposits place *Sahelanthropus* very close to the likely *Pan–Homo* divergence date, supported morphologically by reconstruction of the basicranium, which appears to feature an anteriorly positioned foramen magnum – traditionally interpreted as an indicator of orthograde posture (although see Ruth et al., 2016). Additional derived features in the anterior dental morphology – including the lack of a canine honing complex – support a basal hominin status (Brunet et al., 2002). The combination of autapomorphic features (such as a very thick supraorbital region), primitive features relative to African apes, and derived features relative to *Australopithecus* demonstrate the diversity of adaptations and complex nature of early hominin evolution. Perhaps more importantly, the discovery highlights the need for further paleoanthropological research outside of east and South Africa.

Toros-Menalla also offers important clues as to the changing nature of faunal guilds and their habitats. In addition to the possible emergence of the first hominins, the assemblage reflects a period of significant turnover in flora and fauna across the entire continent (Brunet et al., 2002; Douady et al., 2003; Feakins et al., 2013). Greater proportions of animals suited to grazing are documented – including the first leporids in Africa ~7 Ma (Winkler, 2002; Lopez-Martínez et al., 2007; Suwa et al., 2015). This African radiation of leporids occurred alongside a decline in fossil pikas (Ochotonidae), perhaps due to the former's greater ability to exploit C_4 resources (Ge et al., 2012). This is in accordance with a shift in east Africa 8–7 Ma within the diets of equids and proboscideans to primarily C_4 vegetation (Cerling et al., 1997).

In contrast with the Vallesian, intercontinental movement was dwindling by 7 Ma and distinct faunal provinces developed within Africa (Bibi, 2011b). The exchange of mammals via hydrological connections between east and north Africa discontinued – by the time of *Sahelanthropus*, a Chado-Libyan biogeographical province to the exclusion of east Africa developed. This is evidenced by distinct hippopotamid lineages at Toros-Menalla and Lothagam, and the confinement, among other taxa, of the anthracothere *Libycosaurus petrocchi* to Toros-Menalla and Sahabi in Libya, while the family disappeared in east Africa entirely (Boisserie et al., 2005b; Lihoreau et al., 2006). Thus, while east and north African faunal assemblages were diverging, wet environments continued to connect the ancient Lake Chad basin to the Libyan Sirt basin across what is now 2000 km of hyperarid land (Lihoreau et al., 2006) and perhaps beyond – it is of note that the Toros-Menalla assemblage includes fauna – e.g., the equid *Hipparion* cf. *abudhabiense* – shared with the Baynunah fauna of the Arabian subcontinent (Bibi et al., 2008).

The reconstruction of hydrological gateways on the paleolandscape has vital significance for understanding the potential range of early hominins, which would also have been highly reliant on permanent water bodies. The local faunal community at Toros-Menalla included grassland-adapted mammals such as hamsters, leporids, and grazing bovids; forest-dwelling primates; and aquatic crocodiles, hippos, and anthracotheres (Le Fur et al., 2009). In combination with mesowear analysis, the evidence suggests they inhabited a grassland habitat with open woodland on a lakeshore that featured swamps and open fresh waters (Otero et al., 2011). By offering a more buffered, permanent water source able to survive wet–dry oscillations, the ancient Lake Chad basin would have had important implications for biotic – including hominin – evolution. Comparison has been made to today's Okavango Delta, in Botswana (Brunet et al., 2005), which also offers a mesic refugium under otherwise arid and fluctuating conditions – it is likely that similar environments were a key factor in early hominin diversification. In addition to the refugium hypothesis, it has also been suggested that the cyclical shifts in local environment may have favored the development of animal species with high adaptability to variable habitats (Griffin, 2006). Thus, the existence of *Sahelanthropus* at the crossroads, both temporally and spatially, of such diverse environments may help to explain the combination of features seen in the earliest hominins – i.e., their early form of bipedalism and orthograde posture in conjunction with continued arboreal adaptations – and the subsequent adaptive flexibility that characterizes the hominin lineage.

Extreme Aridification and the First East African Hominins, *Ardipithecus kadabba* and *Orrorin tugenensis*: 6.5–5.5 Ma

The Miocene drying trend culminated at ~6 Ma with one of the driest phases affecting the African continent in the last 10 Ma (Bonnefille, 2010; Figure 4.3) at the same time as the hominin lineage diversified in east Africa. Pronounced cooling coincided with drastic vegetation change, manifesting in offshore cores as an appreciable enrichment in $\delta^{18}O$ and the spread of widespread steppe and minimum tree cover across the entire longitude of the continent (Miller et al., 1987; Bonnefille, 2010). Yet, pockets of established forest existed in east Africa. Tropical vegetation reminiscent of central African rainforest is documented in the Mpesida Beds, Tugen Hills, Kenya, by tree stumps preserved in a 6.37 Ma ash flow (Doman and Coutros, 2015; Kingston et al., 2002). A deciduous forest or woodland existed at the nearby site of Kapcharar in the Lukeino Formation, ~6 Ma (Bamford et al., 2013), while the contemporaneous deposits of the Nkondo Formation west of Lake Albert in Uganda have yielded fossil fruits and wood indicative of mixed evergreen and deciduous forest (Dechamps et al., 1992; Bonnefille, 2010). The latter environment has been likened to that of Cameroon today, probably receiving an annual rainfall of ~1000 mm/year. The macrofloral assemblages are complemented by some of the earliest modern-type colobine fossils in the Tugen Hills and at Nkondo (Gundling and Hill, 2000; Gilbert et al., 2010).

How should we reconcile the terrestrial macroflora, fauna, and pedogenic $\delta^{13}C$ evidence – in the Tugen Hills indicating continued C_3/C_4 heterogeneity throughout this period (Kingston et al., 1994) – with the abrupt and severe drying trend indicated by offshore records? Obvious considerations are that we continue to lack the temporal resolution to identify short and temporary forest periods, or that we must better appreciate the potential for considerable spatial heterogeneity in vegetation. Topographic heterogeneity likely explains in part the isotopic signals of mixed vegetation throughout the Tugen Hills succession. On the other hand, the late Miocene–Pliocene sequence at Lothagam, Kenya more closely replicates the Gulf of Aden pattern of aridification at ~6 Ma, in terms of both faunal assemblage and isotopic data. Taxa from the lower Nawata Formation (7.4–6.5 Ma) indicate a well-vegetated environment; whereas the large mammals from the upper Nawata Formation (6.54 to >4.2 Ma) are indicative of drier, open habitats (McDougall and Feibel, 1999; Cerling et al., 2003b; Leakey and Harris, 2003a). A putative hominin represented only by teeth is first recorded in the upper member (Leakey and Walker, 2003). A left upper third molar (KNM-LT 22930), and right lower incisor (KNM-LT 25935) are similar in morphology and size to some *Australopithecus* specimens, albeit with lower crowns and thinner enamel. Barring further associated specimens, their taxonomic affinity remains unclear.

The earliest evidence for hominins in east Africa thus occurs during this drying phase in the form of *Orrorin tugenensis* from the Lukeino Formation (Pickford and Senut, 2001a), and *Ardipithecus kadabba* from Gona and the Middle and Central Awash in Ethiopia, 6.3–5.2 Ma (Haile-Selassie, 2001; Simpson et al., 2015). The *Orrorin* hypodigm is widely accepted to reflect a bipedal hominin, although the implications for this and its style of bipedality have been debated (Richmond and Jungers, 2008; Almécija et al., 2013). Associated fauna from four different sites (namely Kapsomin, Kapcheberek, Cheboit, and Aragai) suggest *Orrorin* inhabited more thickly forested environments than that at Toros-Menalla. The presence of species such as *Colobus* and impala, in association with oncolites (spherical, stromatolite-like structures formed by carbonate-secreting microbes in shallow water), have been used to reconstruct an open woodland habitat with dense tree clumps near a lake and open-country nearby, but the different sites from which *Orrorin* has been recovered represent a range of environments, indicating the species may have exhibited flexibility in habitat and diet (Pickford and Senut, 2001b). As *Orrorin* remains are mostly postcranial, it is near impossible to compare to the morphology of *Sahelanthropus* and it has been suggested that with expansion of the hypodigm, the two will come to be lumped (Haile-Selassie et al., 2004a). However, further anatomical comparisons of the *Orrorin* humerus that indicate strongly developed elbow flexor muscles, and observations of canine morphology, suggest a more primitive placement for *Orrorin* compared to *Sahelanthropus* and younger hominins, comparing more favorably with female *Pan* (Senut et al., 2001; MacLatchy et al., 2010).

The sample of *Ar. kadabba* remains is similarly restricted to few specimens providing even fewer overlapping elements, complicating taxonomic comparisons. Similarities between what is known of *Ar. kadabba*, *Sahelanthropus* and *Orrorin*, however, have been used to suggest that they are in fact the same species, or at least genus (Haile-Selassie et al., 2004a). Habitual bipedalism has been inferred based on a single pedal phalanx (AME-VP-1/71, a left fourth proximal phalanx), although other postcranial aspects indicate *Ar. kadabba* retained some degree of arboreality (Haile-Selassie, 2001). Primitive dental morphology including a slight canine honing complex – although more derived than *Pan* – and *Pan*-like canine dimorphism have been used to suggest a *Ar. kadabba*'s position as a basal hominin (MacLatchy et al., 2010).

Fauna from the Adu-Asa Formation and Gona demonstrate *Ar. kadabba* lived – or at least died – in a locally forested environment (Haile-Selassie et al., 2004b). The dominance in the faunal record of reduncines, and presence of tragelaphines and bovines, support the evidence for woodland habitat bordering a permanent water source (Su et al., 2009). It is also hypothesized that the sites were once at a much higher elevation than today – supported by the occurrence of a number of small mammals that today are generally restricted to highlands – including the root rat *Tachyoryctes* – as well as *Lophiomys*, *Crocidura*, *Procavia*, and *Atherurus* (WoldeGabriel et al., 2001; Wesselman et al., 2009; Kingdon et al., 2013). The closed-environment hypothesis for *Ar. kadabba* has been questioned by findings that carbon isotopes from fossil herbivore enamel show these animals had a mixed diet of C_3 and C_4 vegetation, as found in African bushlands today (Levin et al., 2008).

Faunal turnover during this period was likely a function of both *in situ* evolution and migration events, as once again many African fossil sites came to include Eurasian elements (Benammi et al., 1996). The dramatic cooling during this period manifested in the largest build-up thus far of the Antarctic ice sheet and consequently an appreciable drop in global sea level (Figure 4.3). An apparent African–Iberian mammal exchange event occurred at >6.2 Ma, caused by a significant restriction between the Mediterranean and Atlantic flow (Hodell et al., 2001). The African murid, *Paraethomys*, appeared for the first time in southern Spain, while the emigration of European *Apodemus* cf. *jeanteti*, *Stephanomys numidicus*, and *Castillomys crusafonti* to North Africa is documented at sites such as Argoub Kemmellal, Algeria at around 6 Ma (Benammi et al., 1996). The Eurasian bovid *Kobus porrecticornis* is first recorded in Africa in the Mpesida beds of the Tugen Hills (Bibi, 2011b).

The culmination of late Miocene climate change – combined with tectonic closure of the Straits of Gibraltar – was the Messinian Salinity Crisis (MSC), wherein the Mediterranean Sea dried up entirely between 5.96 and 5.33 Ma. The eustatic fall and subsequent rise has been estimated to have been between 1000 and 1500 m – massive deposits of evaporates in the Mediterranean basin have been suggested to be the result of repeated desiccation events during this period (Gargani and Rigollet, 2007; Bache et al., 2012). In what has been coined the "Gerbil Event" – for the influx of African rodents adapted to subdesertic, arid environments – African immigrants crossed the desiccated Mediterranean basin (Moyà-Solà et al., 1984; Agustí et al., 2006; De Bruijn, 1973; Jaeger, 1975). Evidence of the hippopotamid *Hexaprotodon* and camelid *Paracamelus*, an eastern immigrant, in the Iberian Peninsula at this time suggests they may have formed part of the dispersal from North Africa (Lacomba et al., 1986; Pickford and Morales, 1994). This period also observes the first entrance into Europe of the African cercopithecoid, *Macaca*, which inhabited the warm, humid, and densely forested site of Moncucco Torinese in Italy (5.4–5.33 Ma; Alba et al., 2014). The utility of genetic evidence to reconstruct evolutionary and biogeographic events is also demonstrated by the conclusion that it was during this time interval, based on molecular divergence estimates, that the first modern African proboscidean emigration out of Africa occurred, with *Stegodon* dispersing into Asia (Kalb, 1995).

It is interesting to note that the complete desiccation of the Mediterranean and Red Seas occurred alongside the peak of the "Zeit Wet" phase in North Africa, as monsoonal activity displaced the desert zone northwards to be over the Mediterranean (Griffin, 2002). In an important example of how extremely localized climates can be under certain atmospheric and topographic conditions, a marked humid phase is recorded in the sedimentological and pollen records at ~5.5 Ma in northern Africa. (Bonnefille, 2010; Van Damme and Van Bocxlaer, 2009). High rainfall, expanded lakes, and increased runoff from the Eonile and Eosahabi rivers carved massive ravines – in some places as deep as 2500 m – as they emptied into the parched Mediterranean (Griffin, 2002).

Early Pliocene Humidity, Formation of the Rift Valley Lakes, and *Ardipithecus ramidus*: 5.5–4.4 Ma

The MSC ended – by some accounts rather dramatically – with the Zanclean Deluge, when the Mediterranean refilled through a combination of eustatic and tectonic processes, marking the end of the Miocene at 5.33 Ma (Clauzon et al., 1996; Hodell et al., 2001; Loget et al., 2005). This heralded a warm, humid phase featuring rapid warming of the world's oceans, significantly impacting global marine and terrestrial biodiversity including a number of extinctions and originations within Rodentia, Bovidae, Hippopotamidae, Proboscidea, Rhinocerotidae, and Carnivora (Cerdeño, 1998; van der Made et al., 2006; Hilgen et al., 2007; Hull and Norris, 2009; Leakey and Werdelin, 2010; Morales et al., 2015; Vrba, 2015). The replacement of arid landscapes with grasslands and forest is documented in multiple offshore cores, and by 4.5–4 Ma, relatively homogeneous, tropical forest vegetation once again extended from the east to the west coasts of Africa (Bonnefille, 2010). In South Africa, C_3 vegetation persisted, but pollen, microwear, and stable isotope records capture the transition from more temperate, woodland vegetation to sclerophyllous shrub-, grass-, and sedge-land similar to the subtropical Cape fynbos today (Coetzee, 1993; Cowling et al., 2005).

During the midst of this African forest phase, an intriguing hominin inhabited the Tugen Hills, sites in Ethiopia, and possibly Lothagam (Apak Member) – all at roughly 4.4 Ma (Ward & Hill, 1987; Hill and Ward, 1988; WoldeGabriel et al., 1994; Semaw et al., 2005; Binetti, Chapter 27, this volume). This species demonstrates a peculiar suite of characters including an abducted, grasping hallux and long, ape-like forelimbs. The ulna exhibits a short olecranon process, which allowed full extension, yet the metacarpals are shorter than those of extant hominoids and, for these reasons, it has been suggested that the forelimbs were adapted to arboreal foraging rather than dedicated climbing (Lovejoy, 2009). Not all authors agree *Ar. ramidus* should be placed within the hominin clade (Harrison, 2010a), but there is no question that it has vital significance for interpreting hominid evolution and reconstructing the last common ancestors of human and non-human apes. A greater understanding of morphological differentiation among hominin species will come with further paleoanthropological fieldwork, and it is likely that the continued discovery of surprising amalgams of traits – for example, the unique mix of primitive and derived traits observed in some early hominins – will add further support that human evolution was not linear, and there was greater diversity within the initial radiation as hominins adapted to the multitude of environments in Africa at that time.

Isotopic, botanical, and faunal evidence suggests *Ar. ramidus* lived in a humid but cool woodland (Ambrose et al., 2011; Louchart et al., 2009; Semaw et al., 2005; White et al., 2009a; WoldeGabriel et al., 2009a), although isotopic evidence indicates more open environments and the presence of fossil papionins suggests grasslands were available near the type site of Aramis (Cerling et al., 2010; Levin et al., 2008). Here, and at the ~4.9 Ma Haradaso Member of the Sagantole Formation, endemic African clades dominate the faunal assemblage, indicating that the Ethiopian faunal realm was fully established by this time, having been cut off from the North African–Eurasian – or Palearctic – realm (Bibi, 2011). Aramis supported a richer flora and fauna than seen in the region today, thanks to its higher water budget, due to either more continuous Pliocene El Niño effects (Fedorov et al., 2006), or higher elevation at that time (Pik et al., 2003). The latter hypothesis is supported by a thorough ecovariable analysis of the fauna at Tabarin in the Tugen Hills that implies *Ar. ramidus* there inhabited an Afro-montane niche (Binetti, Chapter 27). The debate over the paleoenvironment of *Ar. ramidus* has been heated and is ongoing, perhaps because while multiple proxies have found evidence for a variety of habitats including woodland, forest, and grasslands, it is not known whether the species had a particular preference within this mosaic. Certainly, open grasslands existed in east Africa by 4.4 Ma, but there is no definite evidence that any of the known early hominins exploited them (Kingston et al., 1994; White et al., 2006). Continued collection of high-resolution spatial analysis of their paleo-landscapes will perhaps lead to the identification of possible restrictions of hominin species to certain environments and the ability to test hypotheses such as that regarding *Ardipithecus* in high-elevation forest biomes at multiple localities.

Conclusion

Via close comparison of environmental proxies, climatic events, and biotic events it is clear that the evolution of hominoids, alongside their faunal cohabitants, occurred against a backdrop of increasingly strong seasonality with highly contrasting wet–dry seasons. Furthermore, it has become apparent that the period of pronounced global cooling and drying that led to shrinking forests and biotic change in Africa was interrupted by warm, humid punctuations that had equally critical consequences for flora and fauna. Further detailed work will eventually tell us more about the periodicity and spatial extent of the influence of these events.

Continued paleontological and paleobotanical research, including an increasing compendium of paleoenvironmental reconstructions of terrestrial sites from across Africa, have done much in recent years to uncover highly detailed African ecological change and heterogeneity in the late Miocene and early Pliocene. Furthermore, refinement of absolute dating methods has enabled the linkage of paleoclimatic signals drawn from ocean and lake cores to the terrestrial evidence, with promising consequences for the generation and testing of new hypotheses for biotic community response to environmental change (Cohen et al., 2009). Such hypotheses might include consideration that the exploitation of open-country landscapes by hominin species in the Plio-Pleistocene was made possible by the acquisition of bipedalism, but was not the reason for it. Another might invoke adaptive flexibility – or eurytopy – in itself a reaction to late Miocene climatic instability and the development of seasonal dry seasons when hominins were forced to venture further for food resources (Parravicini and Pievani, 2016).

Paleoenvironmental reconstructions of the places in which the earliest hominins lived and adopted terrestrial bipedalism overwhelmingly represent woodland, forest, or mosaic habitats, and the combined evidence tells us that the hominin radiation involved diverse morphological adaptations across a heterogeneously vegetated landscape. The different and complex ways localized biomes respond to broader climatic shifts are important lessons in avoiding the extrapolation of environmental information derived from one site to another based on temporal or geographic proximity, because small differences in topography or sudden shifts in climate on relatively short timescales may have occurred. The presence of the earliest hominins at apparently heterogeneous, mosaic landscapes is not surprising – many African mammals inhabit areas at the intersection of multiple ecological niches today, such as in our example of the Okavango Delta. Whether the implication of this for human evolution is that the earliest hominins were in the process of adapting to a wide range of ecological conditions, or were, conversely, becoming confined to mesic refugia under increasingly fluctuating climatic conditions remains to be supported by the discovery of more fossil evidence. It makes sense that the ability to adjust to open-country life, which we certainly see in Pleistocene hominins, could have been built upon previous modifications that allowed exploitation of varying habitats from earlier in human evolution. As such, adaptive flexibility may have been the first reaction to the clearly documented late Miocene climatic instability.

A Note From the Authors

This chapter would not have been possible without the extraordinary influence of our friend and mentor, the late Andrew Hill. His passion for paleontology, knowledge, and life itself inspired and supported our work and that of all his students, wherever they have found themselves.

5 The Middle Pleistocene Through the Holocene of Africa
A Synthesis

J. Tyler Faith

Introduction

The last 780,000 years in Africa, the Middle Pleistocene through the Holocene, witnessed several crucial events in hominin evolutionary history. These include: (1) the dissolution of the Acheulean (1.6 Ma to 160 ka) and development of the Middle Stone Age (MSA: ~285 to 50 ka) and Later Stone Age (LSA: from ~50 ka) archaeological industries (Ambrose, 1998; Villa et al., 2012; Tryon and Faith, 2013), (2) the appearance of both archaic and anatomically modern *Homo sapiens* (reviewed in McBrearty and Brooks, 2000; Wood and Richmond, 2000), and (3) the dispersal of modern humans within and out of Africa (Soares et al., 2012; Rito et al., 2013). These events are thought by many to be mediated by climate-driven environmental change (e.g., Compton, 2011; Potts, 2013; Jones and Stewart, 2016; Timmerman and Friedrich, 2016), although a lack of empirical paleoanthropological evidence (e.g., well-dated hominin remains or archaeological sites) directly associated with paleoenvironmental records obscures our understanding of these relationships. In the absence of such evidence, the faunal record, in addition to being a crucial source of paleoenvironmental data, provides essential ecological and evolutionary context for evaluating climate's potential role in the more recent phases of human evolution.

This chapter reviews the African large mammal record from the Middle Pleistocene through the Holocene. For this time period the multitude of sites, strong geographic coverage for some regions (e.g., southern Africa), and enhanced temporal resolution – especially over the last ~100 ka – provides a superb opportunity to explore evolutionary and ecological trends. Rather than attempting to review the many sites that have been documented, this chapter focuses on the broad patterns of faunal turnover since the Middle Pleistocene.

Climatic Context

At the global scale, the last 780 ka represents a continuation of the longer-term trend toward cooler (particularly at high latitudes) and increasingly variable climate, with high-amplitude 100-ka glacial cycles being established between 1.2 and 0.8 Ma (Shackleton et al., 1984; Tiedemann et al., 1994; Zachos et al., 2001). Marine records of African climate variability from off the coasts of West and East Africa document shifts in eolian sediment flux, a proxy for moisture availability, that are broadly consistent with global records, documenting wet–dry cycles that correspond to high-latitude glacial (dry) and interglacial (wet) phases (deMenocal, 1995, 2004; but see Trauth et al., 2009). This general relationship between cold and dry and warm and wet is frequently used as a framework to explore the relationship between Quaternary African climate and the evolution of its biota (e.g., Klein, 1983; Lahr and Foley, 1998; Marean and Assefa, 2005; Cowling et al., 2008; Rector and Verrelli, 2010; Lorenzen et al., 2012).

Despite the coherence of these broad-scale patterns, at regional spatial scales there is overwhelming evidence that the nature and timing of climatic change varied across Africa as a result of numerous mechanisms, including the complex interplay between orbital forcing, the position of the Intertropical Convergence Zone (ITCZ) and the westerlies, high-latitude climate events (e.g., Heinrich Events), and ocean temperature gradients (e.g., deMenocal, 1995; Trauth et al., 2003, 2005; deMenocal, 2004; Stuut et al., 2004; Chase and Meadows, 2007; Verschuren et al., 2009; Blome et al., 2012; Ziegler et al., 2013). For example, climate proxies from southeastern portion of southern Africa indicate dry conditions during the Last Glacial Maximum (LGM), consistent with the continental-scale pattern (deMenocal, 1995, 2004), whereas records from the southwestern portion of southern Africa indicate increased moisture availability (Chase and Meadows, 2007). The former in part reflects the weakening of summer rainfall systems derived from the Indian Ocean (in addition to local processes) and the latter relates to the expansion of Antarctic sea ice and subsequent equatorward shift of the southern hemisphere westerlies (van Zinderen Bakker, 1976; Stuut et al., 2004), bringing more winter rainfall to the region. In equatorial Africa, there is evidence that late Quaternary precipitation tracks ~23 ka precessional cycles (and ~11.5 ka half-precessional cycles) rather than 100 ka glacial cycles (Rossignol-Strick, 1985; Trauth et al., 2003; Kingston, 2007; Verschuren et al., 2009). This reflects the influence of precession on the timing and intensity of tropical insolation, which in turn is a major determinant of the intensity of the tropical monsoon. The same mechanism is also thought to be important in the precipitation history of the Sahara and Sahel of North Africa (deMenocal et al., 2000), but it also appears that variation in the strength of the Atlantic meridional overturning circulation (AMOC) – currents that bring warm surface waters north and send cool, deep waters south – may play a more important role in the precipitation history here (Castañeda et al., 2009).

The complexity of late Quaternary climate across Africa translates to complexity in the dynamics of past environments and habitats that played a central role in driving evolutionary change (Vrba, 1985b, 1992, 1993; Behrensmeyer et al., 1992; Barnosky, 2001; Blois and Hadly, 2009; Faith and Behrensmeyer, 2013). However, despite these challenges, broad-scale climate phenomena remain important in developing and testing hypotheses of the influence of climate on terrestrial ecosystems and evolutionary process (Vrba, 1995; Potts, 1998a, 1998b, 2013; Kingston, 2007; Cowling et al., 2008; Compton, 2011; Lorenzen et al., 2012). The patterns emphasized in this chapter are almost certainly mediated by a combination of continental-scale, regional, and local climate changes.

The Fossil Record

Table 5.1 reports a selection of large mammal fossil sites from the Middle Pleistocene through the Holocene, with sites assigned to North Africa, East Africa, and southern Africa to facilitate regional comparisons (Figure 5.1). This list is far from comprehensive, but it does include key sites that are well-reported in the literature or feature prominently in our understanding of the past. Our knowledge of the late Quaternary faunas of West and Central Africa is so poor that these regions are not included here. As is also the case with African mammal assemblages from earlier time periods, the sites yielding faunal remains from the Middle Pleistocene through the Holocene are primarily the focus of paleoanthropological and archaeological research addressing the behavioral, ecological, and environmental context of hominin evolution. The majority of these, especially from southern Africa and North Africa, are MSA and LSA cave sites, where the faunal remains represent discarded food refuse, although carnivores and large raptors are also known to be important bone accumulators at archaeological sites (e.g., Faith, 2013).

Table 5.2 summarizes the temporal distribution of 173 terrestrial mammalian taxa during the early Middle Pleistocene (780–500 ka), late Middle Pleistocene (500–126 ka), Late

Table 5.1 Select large mammal fossil localities from the Middle Pleistocene through the Holocene. This list is not comprehensive but includes sites that feature prominently in our understanding of the past or that are sufficiently well-reported in the literature.

Locality	Large mammal references
North Africa	
Aïn Bahya, Morocco	Michel, 1992
Aïn Maarouf, Morocco	Geraads et al., 1992
Abu Ballas Mudpans, Egypt	Van Neer and Uerpmann, 1989
Bir Hmairiya, Tunisia	Aouadi et al., 2014
Bir Tarfawi, Egypt	Gautier, 1993; Wendorf et al., 1993
Bizmoune, Morocco	Fernandez et al., 2015
Bouknadel, Morocco	Michel, 1992
Dakhleh Oasis, Egypt	Churcher et al., 1999; Churcher et al., 2008
Doukkala I, Morocco	Michel, 1992
Doukkala II, Morocco	Michel, 1992; Michel and Wengler, 1993
El Harhoura 1, Morocco	Aouraghe, 2000, 2004; Monchot and Aouraghe, 2009
El Harhoura 2, Morocco	Michel et al., 2009; Michel et al., 2010
El-Kilh, Egypt	Wendorf and Schild, 1976
El Mnasra, Morocco	Nespoulet et al., 2008
Fayum Oasis, Egypt	Gautier, 1976; Linseele et al., 2014
Felids Cave, Morocco	Raynal et al., 2008
Grotte des Contrebandiers, Morocco	Dibble et al., 2012; Hallett-Desguez, 2012
Grotte des Gazelles, Morocco	Bougariane et al., 2010
Grotte des Hominidés, Morocco	Geraads, 1980a; Raynal et al., 2010
Grotte des Rhinocéros, Morocco	Raynal et al., 1993
Haua Fteah, Libya	Higgs, 1967; Klein and Scott, 1986
Ifri n'Ammar, Morocco	Hutterer, 2010
Isna, Egypt	Wendorf and Schild, 1976
Jebel Irhoud, Morocco	Thomas, 1981a; Amani and Geraads, 1993, 1998
Khashm el Girba, Sudan	Marks et al., 1987; Abbate et al., 2010
Kom Ombo, Egypt	Peters, 1990a
Makhadma, Egypt	Vermeersch, 2000
Mugharet el 'Aliya, Morocco	Arambourg, 1967; Steele, 2012
Oued el Akarit, Tunisia	Brun et al., 1988
Phacochères, Algeria	Bagtache et al., 1984; Hadjouis, 1985, 1990, 2002
Rhafas Cave, Morocco	Michel, 1992
Salé, Morocco	Jaeger, 1973
SHM-1, Tunisia	Aouadi et al., 2014
Tamar Hat, Algeria	Merzoug and Sari, 2008
Tighenif (Ternifine), Algeria	Geraads et al., 1986
Wadi Assaka, Morocco	Wengler et al., 2002
Wadi Kubbaniya, Egypt	Gautier et al., 1980; Gautier and Van Neer, 1989
Wadi Sarrat, Tunisia	Martínez-Navarro et al., 2014
East Africa	
Amboseli, Kenya	Behrensmeyer and Boaz, 1981
Asbole, Ethiopia	Alemseged and Geraads, 2000; Geraads et al., 2004c; Frost and Alemseged, 2007
Bodo, Ethiopia	Kalb et al., 1982a, 1982b; Clark et al., 1994; Geraads et al., 2004c
Bulbula, Ethiopia	Lesur et al. 2016
Ele Bor, Kenya	Gifford-Gonzalez, 2003
Enkapune Ya Muto, Kenya	Marean, 1992a
Gol Kopjes, Tanzania	Marean and Gifford-Gonzalez, 1991
Homa Peninsula, Kenya	Ditchfield et al., 1999; O'Regan et al., 2005
Isenya, Kenya	Brugal and Denys, 1989
Kapthurin Formation, Kenya	Cornelissen et al., 1990; McBrearty et al., 1996; McBrearty and Jablonski, 2005; O'Regan et al., 2005

Locality	Large mammal references
Karungu, Kenya	Faith et al., 2013; Faith et al., 2015
Kibish Formation, Ethiopia	Assefa et al., 2008; Rowan et al., 2015
Kisese II, Tanzania	Marean and Gifford-Gonzalez, 1991
Lainyamok, Kenya	Shipman et al., 1983; Potts et al., 1988; Potts and Deino, 1995; Faith et al., 2012
Lake Eyasi, Tanzania	Mehlman, 1987; Domínguez-Rodrigo et al., 2008
Lukenya Hill, Kenya	Marean and Gifford-Gonzalez, 1991; Marean, 1992b, 1997; Faith et al., 2012
Manonga Valley, Tanzania	Harrison and Baker, 1997
Manyara Beds, Tanzania	Kaiser et al., 2010; Frost et al., 2012
Mfangano Island, Kenya	Tryon et al., 2012
Mochena Borago, Ethiopia	Lesur et al., 2007
Mumba Rock Shelter, Tanzania	Mehlman, 1989; Prendergast et al., 2007
Nasera Rock Shelter, Tanzania	Mehlman, 1989
Olorgesailie, Kenya	Isaac, 1977; O'Regan et al., 2005; Haradon, 2010
Porc Epic Cave, Ethiopia	Assefa, 2006
Rusinga Island, Kenya	Tryon et al., 2010; Faith et al., 2011; Tryon et al., 2012
Wakrita, Djibouti	Gutherz et al., 2015
Southern Africa	
Apollo 11 Cave, Namibia	Thackeray, 1979
Blombos Cave, South Africa	Henshilwood et al., 2001
Boomplaas Cave, South Africa	Klein, 1978a, 1983; Deacon, 1984; Brink, 1999; Faith, 2013
Border Cave, South Africa	Klein, 1977
Byneskranskop 1, South Africa	Schweitzer and Wilson, 1982; Faith, 2012a
Buffelskloof Rock Shelter, South Africa	Opperman, 1978
Bushman Rock Shelter, South Africa	Brain, 1969b; Badenhorst and Plug, 2012
Cave of Hearths, South Africa	Cooke, 1988; Haradon, 2010
Chelmer Farm, Zimbabwe	Cooke and Wells, 1951
Die Kelders Cave, South Africa	Klein and Cruz-Uribe, 2000
Diepkloof Rock Shelter, South Africa	Steele and Klein, 2013
Duinefontein 2, South Africa	Cruz-Uribe et al., 2003
Elands Bay Cave, South Africa	Klein and Cruz-Uribe, 1987
Elandsfontein, South Africa	Klein and Cruz-Uribe, 1991; Klein et al., 2007
Equus Cave, South Africa	Klein et al., 1991
Florisbad, South Africa	Brink, 1987, 1994, 2005
Gladysvale Cave, South Africa	Lacruz et al., 2002
≠Gi, Botswana	Helgren and Brooks, 1983; Brooks and Yellen, 1987
Herolds Bay Cave, South Africa	Brink and Deacon, 1982
Heuningneskrans Shelter, South Africa	Klein, 1984a
Hoedjiespunt, South Africa	Klein, 1983
Kabwe, Zambia	Clark et al., 1947; Klein, 1973
Kalkbank, South Africa	Mason, 1988a; Hutson, 2012
Kathu Pan, South Africa	Klein, 1988; Porat et al., 2010
Klasies River, South Africa	Klein, 1976, 1983
Kruger Cave, South Africa	Brown and Verhagen, 1985
Leopards Hill Cave, Zambia	Klein, 1984a
Lincoln Cave, South Africa	Reynolds et al., 2007
Melkbos, South Africa	Hendey, 1968
Nelson Bay Cave, South Africa	Klein, 1972, 1983; Deacon, 1984; Faith, 2012a
Pinnacle Point, South Africa	Rector and Reed, 2010
Plovers Lake, South Africa	Thackeray and Watson, 1994; de Ruiter et al., 2008b
Redcliff Cave, Zimbabwe	Cruz-Uribe, 1983
Rose Cottage Cave, South Africa	Plug and Engela, 1992; Plug, 1997
Sea Harvest, South Africa	Klein, 1983
Sibudu Cave, South Africa	Plug, 2004; Clark and Plug, 2008
Swartklip 1, South Africa	Hendey and Hendey, 1968; Klein, 1975, 1983
Twin Rivers, Zambia	Bishop and Reynolds, 2000
Vlakkraal, South Africa	Wells et al., 1942; Brink, 1994
Wonderwerk Cave, South Africa	Thackeray et al., 1981; Thackeray, 1984; Klein, 1988; Thackeray and Brink, 2004
Ysterfontein, South Africa	Halkett et al., 2003

Pleistocene (126–12 ka), Holocene (<12 ka), and present (extant) from North Africa, East Africa, and southern Africa. The division of the Middle Pleistocene at 500 ka has no formal stratigraphic basis, but it does correspond to the approximate age (± 100 ka) of important faunal transitions previously reported across parts of Africa (Potts, 1998a, 1998b Brink, 2005; Codron et al., 2008; Geraads, 2010b; Faith et al., 2012). The data reported in this list are derived from sources reported in Table 5.1, supplemented by consultation of several additional reviews (Plug and Badenhorst, 2001; O'Regan et al., 2005; Werdelin and Sanders, 2010; Geraads, 2011). The following taxonomic orders are included: Carnivora, Tubulidentata, Proboscidea, Artiodactyla, Perissodactyla, and Primates. Taxa from orders that include mostly smaller mammals (e.g., Rodentia, Lagomorpha, Hyracoidea, Chiroptera) or that are exceptionally rare in the fossil record (e.g., Pholidota) are not considered here because they are not systematically reported in the literature, which tends to emphasize the large mammals. Question marks in Table 5.2 indicate species occurrences that are equivocal either because of taxonomic or chronological uncertainty. For example, the possible presence of impala (*Aepyceros melampus*) in the southern African Middle Pleistocene reflects the fact that no southern African specimens of *Aepyceros* from this time (Lacruz et al., 2002; Haradon, 2010) or earlier (Reed, 1996) are firmly identified beyond the genus level, although the extant species is unquestionably present by the Late Pleistocene (Clark and Plug, 2008). Likewise, the first appearance of the chimpanzee genus *Pan* from the Kapthurin Formation in Kenya is dated to between 545 and 284 ka (McBrearty and Jablonski, 2005); it is unquestionably present by the late Middle Pleistocene, but only possibly present in the early Middle Pleistocene.

Faunal Turnover

Faunal turnover is defined here as a difference in taxonomic composition through space or time. Late Cenozoic paleontological research in Africa is largely concerned with turnover through time (Behrensmeyer et al., 1997; Reed, 1997; Bobe and Eck, 2001; McKee, 2001; Bobe et al., 2002; Frost, 2007; Faith and Behrensmeyer, 2013), motivated to a large extent by Vrba's turnover–pulse hypothesis (Vrba, 1985b, 1988, 1993, 1995). Temporal patterns of faunal turnover arise from speciation, extinction, or range shifts that cause species to appear or disappear from the fossil record of a given area. These evolutionary processes are thought to be mediated by climate-driven environmental change (Vrba, 1985b; Barnosky, 2001; van Dam et al., 2006; Blois and Hadly, 2009; Faith and Behrensmeyer, 2013), which alters or fragments the composition and distribution of a species' habitat. This in turn translates to range shifts as a species tracks its preferred habitat or to the division of populations into geographically and genetically isolated groups (i.e., vicariance), an important precursor to extinction and speciation (Mayr, 1942, 1963, 1970).

Faunal turnover through space can be mediated by a combination of climatic and environmental gradients, which limit the distribution of species' habitat, and biogeographic barriers (e.g., rivers, mountain ranges, oceans, deserts) that prevent a species from extending its range into areas of suitable habitat. Two prominent biogeographic barriers to the dispersal of large mammal species within Africa include the Sahara Desert and the equatorial forest belt. Spanning more than 9 million km^2 from the Red Sea to the Atlantic coast of North Africa, the Sahara Desert is for most mammalian species an impenetrable dispersal barrier isolating Mediterranean North Africa from sub-Saharan Africa today. However, proxies for paleoenvironment and paleoclimate (Lézine, 1989; Lézine et al., 1990; deMenocal et al., 2000; Kröpelin et al., 2008; Larrasoaña et al., 2013), in addition to the archaeological record (Kuper and Kröpelin, 2006), attest to wetter "Green Sahara" phases that supported diverse biota and human populations. The most recent and best documented of these occurred from ~10 to 6 ka (Larrasoaña et al., 2013) within the African Humid Period (~14.5–5.5 ka; deMenocal et al., 2000). This is linked to increased summer insolation and a strengthened AMOC, which caused an intensified African monsoon to bring increased precipitation to the Sahara. The associated expansion of mesic vegetation communities (e.g., grasslands, shrublands, and woodlands) likely facilitated faunal interchange between North Africa and sub-Saharan Africa.

The equatorial forest belt includes the tropical forests of Central and Western Africa and the fragmented Afromontane and coastal forests of East Africa. Although not continuous across East Africa today, it is likely to have expanded relative to the present under conditions of high rainfall and elevated CO_2 concentrations – both of which favor woody vegetation – possibly forming an important dispersal barrier between the savannas of East and southern Africa (Cowling et al. 2008; Lorenzen et al., 2012; Morley and Kingdon, 2013). Pollen archives from equatorial East Africa document an expansion of forest vegetation during the African Humid Period (Maitima, 1991; Street-Perrot and Perrot, 1993), which may reflect the most recent phase of forest belt expansion. The expansion and contraction of the forest belt across East Africa during the Quaternary is further suggested by simulations of glacial and interglacial vegetation cover (Cowling et al., 2008) and the geographic distribution of plant and animal species (White, 1983; Kingdon, 1990; Wronski and Hausdorf, 2008; Morley and Kingdon, 2013). Perhaps the best support for the periodic presence of a dispersal barrier across the equator is provided by the phylogeography of savanna vertebrates. Genetic evidence from numerous widely distributed species, including wildebeest (*Connochaetes taurinus*), hartebeest (*Alcelaphus buselaphus*), eland (*Taurotragus oryx*), giraffe (*Giraffa camelopardalis*), ostrich (*Struthio camelus*), and white-tailed mongoose (*Ichneumia albicauda*), among many others, indicates distinct lineages north and south of the equator (e.g., Dehghani et al., 2008; Miller et al., 2011; Lorenzen et al., 2012). This attests to previous phases of allopatry that potentially resulted from an expanded forest belt.

While difficult to document in the fossil record, it is important to recognize that faunal turnover through space or time may also be driven by biotic factors, especially competition between species (Van Valen, 1973; Masters and Rayner, 1993). Several paleontological and paleoanthropological studies have invoked competition as an explanation for turnover in cases where climatic effects on turnover are not readily apparent (Foley, 1994; Alroy, 1998, 2000; Grove, 2012), although this may reflect problems of temporal and spatial scale (Barnosky, 2001; Raia et al., 2005; Faith and Behrensmeyer, 2013). In the absence of robust methods for empirically documenting competition in the fossil record, this potentially important mechanism of turnover is not considered here.

Continental-Scale Temporal and Spatial Trends

To explore continental-scale patterns of faunal turnover, a Principal Coordinates Analysis (PCoA) is conducted on the presence/absence matrix in Table 5.2. The PCoA is conducted on a similarity matrix obtained using the Dice Coefficient for presence/absence data using the Paleontological Statistics (PAST) software package (Hammer et al., 2001). For a given pair of regional time bins (columns in Table 5.2), the Dice Coefficient is calculated as $2j/(a+b)$, where j is the number of species that co-occur at bin A and B, a is the number of species in bin A, and b is the number of species in bin B. The PCoA arranges assemblages in multidimensional space so that similar bins cluster together and dissimilar bins farther apart.

Figure 5.2A illustrates PCoA Axes 1 and 2, which account for 53.1 percent and 18.5 percent of the variation in species composition, respectively. PCoA Axis 1 distinguishes North Africa (negative values) from East and southern Africa (positive values), while Axis 2 distinguishes East (positive values) from southern Africa (negative values). The tight clustering by region

Table 5.2 The presence of large mammal species in North, East, and southern Africa since the Middle Pleistocene (early Middle Pleistocene: 780–500 ka; late Middle Pleistocene: 500–126 ka; Late Pleistocene: 126–12 ka; Holocene: <12).

Taxon	North Africa					East Africa					Southern Africa				
	Early Middle Pleistocene	Late Middle Pleistocene	Late Pleistocene	Holocene	Extant	Early Middle Pleistocene	Late Middle Pleistocene	Late Pleistocene	Holocene	Extant	Early Middle Pleistocene	Late Middle Pleistocene	Late Pleistocene	Holocene	Extant
Canidae															
Canis adustus	–	–	–	–	–	–	X	X	X	X	–	–	–	X	X
Canis aureus	–	X	X	X	X	X	X	X	X	X	–	–	–	–	–
Canis mesomelas	–	–	–	–	–	?	X	X	X	X	X	X	X	X	X
Canis mohibi[†]	X	X	–	–	–	–	–	–	–	–	–	–	–	–	–
Lycaon pictus	–	X	X	X	X	–	X	X	X	X	X	X	X	X	X
Lycaon magnus[†]	X	–	–	–	–	–	–	–	–	–	–	–	–	–	–
Otocyon megalotis	–	–	–	–	–	–	X	X	X	X	–	–	–	–	–
Vulpes chama	–	–	–	–	–	–	–	–	–	–	X	X	X	X	X
Vulpes vulpes	X	X	X	X	X	–	–	–	–	–	–	–	–	–	–
Vulpes rueppelli	X	X	X	X	–	–	–	–	–	–	–	–	–	–	–
Vulpes zerda	–	–	–	X	X	–	–	–	–	–	–	–	–	–	–
Mustelidae															
Aonyx capensis	–	–	–	–	–	–	–	–	–	–	X	X	X	X	X
Ictonyx lybica	X	X	X	X	X	–	–	–	–	–	–	–	–	–	–
Ictonyx striatus	–	–	–	–	–	–	–	–	–	–	X	X	X	X	X
Lutra sp.	X	X	X	X	–	–	–	–	–	–	–	–	–	–	–
Mellivora capensis	?	X	X	X	X	X	X	X	X	X	X	X	X	X	X
Mustela putorius	–	–	X	X	X	–	–	–	–	–	–	–	–	–	–
Viverridae															
Civettictis civetta	–	–	–	–	–	–	–	–	X	X	X	X	X	X	X
Genetta tigrina	–	–	–	–	–	–	–	–	–	–	X	X	X	X	X
Genetta sp. (probably *Genetta genetta*)	X	X	X	X	X	X	X	X	X	X	X	X	X	X	X
Herpestidae															
Atilax paludinosis	–	–	–	–	–	–	–	–	–	X	X	X	X	X	X
Cynictus penicillata	–	–	–	–	–	–	–	–	–	–	X	X	X	X	X
Galerella pulverulenta	–	–	–	–	–	–	–	–	–	–	–	X	X	X	X
Galerella sanguinea	–	–	–	–	–	–	–	–	–	–	–	–	X	X	X
Helogale parvula	–	–	–	–	–	–	–	–	–	–	–	–	–	X	X
Herpestes ichneumon	X	X	X	X	X	X	X	X	X	X	X	X	X	X	X
Ichneumia albicauda	–	–	–	–	X	–	–	–	X	X	–	–	X	X	X
Mungos mungo	–	–	–	–	–	–	–	–	–	X	–	–	X	X	X
Rhynchogale melleri	–	–	–	–	–	–	–	–	–	X	–	–	–	X	X
Suricata suricatta	–	–	–	–	–	–	–	–	?	–	–	X	X	X	X
Hyaenidae															
Crocuta crocuta	X	X	X	X	–	X	X	X	X	X	X	X	X	X	X
Hyaena hyaena	X	X	X	X	X	X	X	X	X	X	–	–	–	–	–
Parahyaena brunnea	–	–	–	–	–	–	–	–	–	–	X	X	X	X	X
Proteles sp.	–	–	–	–	–	–	–	–	X	X	X	X	X	X	X

Table 5.2 (cont.)

Taxon	North Africa					East Africa					Southern Africa				
	Early Middle Pleistocene	Late Middle Pleistocene	Late Pleistocene	Holocene	Extant	Early Middle Pleistocene	Late Middle Pleistocene	Late Pleistocene	Holocene	Extant	Early Middle Pleistocene	Late Middle Pleistocene	Late Pleistocene	Holocene	Extant
Felidae															
Acinonyx jubatus	–	–	x	x	x	?	?	?	?	x	x	x	x	x	x
Caracal caracal	–	–	x	x	x	?	x	x	x	x	x	x	x	x	x
Felis margarita	–	–	x	x	x	–	–	–	–	–	–	–	–	–	–
Felis nigripes	–	–	–	–	–	–	–	–	–	–	–	–	x	x	x
Felis sylvestris	x	x	x	x	x	x	x	x	x	x	x	x	x	x	x
Homotherium sp.[†]	x	–	–	–	–	–	–	–	–	–	–	–	–	–	–
Leptailurus serval	–	–	–	–	–	?	?	?	?	x	x	x	x	x	x
Megantereon whitei[†]	–	–	–	–	–	–	–	–	–	–	–	x	–	–	–
Panthera leo	x	x	x	x	–	x	x	x	x	x	x	x	x	x	x
Panthera pardus	x	x	x	x	–	x	x	x	x	x	x	x	x	x	x
Ursidae															
Ursus arctos[†]	x	x	x	x	–	–	–	–	–	–	–	–	–	–	–
Orycteropodidae															
Orycteropus afer	–	–	–	–	–	–	x	x	x	x	x	x	x	x	x
Orycteropus crassidens[†]	–	–	–	–	–	?	?	x	–	–	–	–	–	–	–
Elephantidae															
Elephas recki[†]	–	–	–	–	–	x	–	–	–	–	x	–	–	–	–
Elephas iolensis[†]	x	x	x	–	–	–	–	–	–	–	–	–	–	–	–
Loxodonta atlantica[†]	x	x	?	–	–	–	–	–	–	–	x	–	–	–	–
Loxodonta africana	–	x	x	x	–	x	x	x	x	x	–	x	x	x	x
Camelidae															
Camelus thomasi[†]	x	x	x	–	–	–	–	–	–	–	–	–	–	–	–
Hippopotamidae															
Hippopotamus amphibius	x	x	x	x	–	x	x	x	x	x	x	x	x	x	x
Hippopotamus gorgops[†]	–	–	–	–	–	x	–	–	–	–	–	–	–	–	–
Suidae															
Hylochoerus meinertzhageni	–	–	–	–	–	–	–	x	x	x	–	–	–	–	–
Kolpochoerus paiceae[†]	–	–	–	–	–	–	–	–	–	–	–	x	–	–	–
Kolpochoerus limnetes[†]	–	–	–	–	–	x	–	–	–	–	–	–	–	–	–
Kolpochoerus majus[†]	–	–	–	–	–	x	–	–	–	–	–	–	–	–	–
Kolpochoerus sp.[†]	x	–	–	–	–	–	–	x	–	–	–	–	–	–	–
Metridiochoerus andrewsi[†]	–	–	–	–	–	–	–	–	–	–	–	x	–	–	–
Metridiochoerus modestus[†]	–	–	–	–	–	x	–	–	–	–	–	–	–	–	–
Metridiochoerus compactus[†]	x	–	–	–	–	–	–	–	–	–	–	–	–	–	–
Phacochoerus sp.[1]	x	x	x	x	–	?	x	x	x	x	?	x	x	x	x
Potamochoerus sp.[2]	–	–	–	–	–	x	x	x	x	x	–	–	–	x	x
Sus scrofa	–	x	x	x	x	–	–	–	–	–	–	–	–	–	–
Giraffidae															
Giraffa camelopardalis	–	–	x	x	–	x	x	x	x	x	x	x	x	x	x
Giraffa cf. *pomeli*[†]	x	–	–	–	–	–	–	–	–	–	–	–	–	–	–
Sivatherium maurusium[†]	–	–	–	–	–	–	–	–	–	–	–	x	–	–	–

Table 5.2 (cont.)

Taxon	North Africa					East Africa					Southern Africa				
	Early Middle Pleistocene	Late Middle Pleistocene	Late Pleistocene	Holocene	Extant	Early Middle Pleistocene	Late Middle Pleistocene	Late Pleistocene	Holocene	Extant	Early Middle Pleistocene	Late Middle Pleistocene	Late Pleistocene	Holocene	Extant
Bovidae: Tragelaphini															
Taurotragus oryx	–	–	–	–	–	?	x	x	x	x	x	x	x	x	x
Taurotragus sp.	–	?	x	–	–	–	–	–	–	–	–	–	–	–	–
Tragelaphus algericus[†]	x	–	–	–	–	–	–	–	–	–	–	–	–	–	–
Tragelaphus angasi	–	–	–	–	–	–	–	–	–	–	–	–	x	x	x
Tragelaphus imberbis	–	–	–	–	–	–	?	?	x	x	–	–	–	–	–
Tragelaphus scriptus	–	–	–	–	–	?	x	x	x	x	x	x	x	x	x
Tragelaphus spekei	–	–	–	–	–	–	–	–	x	x	–	–	–	x	x
Tragelaphus strepsiceros	–	–	–	–	–	x	x	x	x	x	x	x	x	x	x
Tragelaphus sp.	x	x	x	–	–	–	–	–	–	–	–	–	–	–	–
Bovidae: Hippotragini															
Addax nasomaculatus	–	–	–	x	x	–	–	–	–	–	–	–	–	–	–
Hippotragus equinus	–	?	x	–	–	–	x	x	x	x	x	x	x	x	x
Hippotragus niger	–	–	–	–	–	–	–	–	–	–	x	x	x	x	x
Hippotragus gigas[†]	?	–	–	–	–	–	–	–	–	–	x	–	–	–	–
Hippotragus leucophaeus[†]	–	–	–	–	–	–	–	–	–	–	x	x	x	x	–
Oryx spp.[3]	x	x	x	x	–	x	x	x	x	x	x	x	x	x	x
Bovidae: Reduncini															
Kobus ellipsiprymnus	–	–	?	–	–	x	x	x	x	x	x	x	x	x	x
Kobus kob	?	?	?	–	–	x	x	x	x	–	–	–	–	–	–
Kobus leche	–	–	–	–	–	–	–	–	–	–	x	x	x	x	x
Redunca arundinum	–	–	–	–	–	–	–	x	x	x	x	x	x	x	x
Redunca fulvorufula	–	–	–	–	–	–	–	x	x	x	x	x	x	x	x
Redunca redunca	–	?	x	x	–	–	–	x	x	x	–	–	–	–	–
Bovidae: Alcelaphini															
Alcelaphus buselaphus	–	?	x	x	–	x	x	x	x	x	–	x	x	x	x
Beatragus hunteri	–	–	–	–	–	–	x	x	x	x	–	–	–	–	–
Connochaetes gnou	–	–	–	–	–	–	–	–	–	–	x	x	x	x	x
Connochaetes taurinus	x	x	x	?	–	x	x	x	x	x	x	x	x	x	x
Damaliscus dorcas	–	–	–	–	–	–	–	–	–	–	x	x	x	x	x
Damaliscus hypsodon[†]	–	–	–	–	–	–	x	x	–	–	–	–	–	–	–
Damaliscus lunatus	–	–	–	–	–	–	x	x	x	–	–	–	–	x	x
Damaliscus aff. *lunatus*[†]	–	–	–	–	–	–	–	–	–	–	x	–	–	–	–
Damaliscus niro[†]	–	–	–	–	–	x	–	–	–	–	x	x	x	–	–
Damaliscus sp. nov.[†]	–	–	–	–	–	–	–	–	–	–	x	–	–	–	–
Megalotragus priscus[†]	–	–	–	–	–	–	–	–	–	–	x	x	x	x	–
Megalotragus sp.[†]	–	–	–	–	–	x	x	x	–	–	–	–	–	–	–
Rabaticeras arambourgi[†]	x	–	–	–	–	–	–	–	–	–	x	–	–	–	–
Parmularius ambiguus[†]	x	–	–	–	–	–	–	–	–	–	–	–	–	–	–
Parmularius sp. nov.[†]	–	–	–	–	–	–	–	–	–	–	x	–	–	–	–
Rusingoryx atopocranion[†]	–	–	–	–	–	–	x	–	–	–	–	–	–	–	–

Table 5.2 (cont.)

Taxon	North Africa					East Africa					Southern Africa				
	Early Middle Pleistocene	Late Middle Pleistocene	Late Pleistocene	Holocene	Extant	Early Middle Pleistocene	Late Middle Pleistocene	Late Pleistocene	Holocene	Extant	Early Middle Pleistocene	Late Middle Pleistocene	Late Pleistocene	Holocene	Extant
Bovidae: Aepycerotini															
Aepyceros melampus	–	–	–	–	–	x	x	x	x	x	?	?	x	x	x
Aepyceros sp. nov.[†]	–	–	–	–	–	–	–	x	–	–	–	–	–	–	–
Bovidae: Caprini															
Ammotragus lervia	–	?	x	x	x	–	–	–	–	–	–	–	–	–	–
Capra nubiana	–	–	–	x	x	–	–	–	–	–	–	–	–	–	–
Unnamed caprine[†]	–	–	–	–	–	–	–	–	–	–	x	x	x	x	–
Bovidae: Cephalophini															
Cephalophus natalensis	–	–	–	–	–	–	–	–	x	x	–	–	–	x	x
Cephalophus sp.	–	–	–	–	–	x	x	x	x	x	–	–	–	–	–
Philantomba monticola	–	–	–	–	–	–	–	–	–	–	–	–	–	x	x
Sylvicapra grimmia	–	–	–	–	–	?	?	x	x	x	x	x	x	x	x
Bovidae: Madoquini															
Madoqua sp.	–	–	–	–	–	x	x	x	x	x	–	–	–	x	x
Bovidae: Peleini															
Pelea capreolus	–	–	–	–	–	–	–	–	–	–	x	x	x	x	x
Bovidae: Antilopini															
Gazella atlantica[†]	?	?	x	–	–	–	–	–	–	–	–	–	–	–	–
Gazella cuvieri	–	–	x	x	x	–	–	–	–	–	–	–	–	–	–
Gazella dama[4]	–	–	x	x	x	–	–	–	–	–	–	–	–	–	–
Gazella dorcas	–	–	x	x	x	–	–	x	x	x	–	–	–	–	–
Gazella dracula[†]	x	x	–	–	–	–	–	–	–	–	–	–	–	–	–
Gazella granti[4]	–	–	–	–	–	?	x	x	x	x	–	–	–	–	–
Gazella aff. *granti*[†]	–	–	–	–	–	x	–	–	–	–	–	–	–	–	–
Gazella leptoceros	–	–	x	x	x	–	–	–	–	–	–	–	–	–	–
Gazella rufifrons[4]	–	x	x	x	x	–	–	–	–	–	–	–	–	–	–
Gazella soemmerringii[4]	–	–	–	–	–	–	–	–	?	x	–	–	–	–	–
Gazella thomsonii[4]	–	–	–	–	–	?	x	x	x	x	–	–	–	–	–
Gazella tingitana[†]	–	x	x	–	–	–	–	–	–	–	–	–	–	–	–
Gazella sp.[†]	–	–	–	–	–	–	–	–	–	–	x	–	–	–	–
Antidorcas australis[†]	–	–	–	–	–	–	–	–	–	–	x	x	x	–	–
Antidorcas bondi[†]	–	–	–	–	–	–	–	–	–	–	x	x	x	x	–
Antidorcas recki[†]	–	–	–	–	–	–	–	–	–	–	x	–	–	–	–
Antidorcas marsupialis	–	–	–	–	–	–	–	–	–	–	?	x	x	x	x
Antidorcas sp.	–	–	–	–	–	x	x	–	–	–	–	–	–	–	–
Litocranius walleri	–	–	–	–	–	–	–	x	x	x	–	–	–	–	–
Bovidae: Neotragini															
Nesotragus moschatus	–	–	–	–	–	–	–	–	x	x	–	–	–	x	x
Bovidae: Oreotragini															
Oreotragus oreotragus	–	–	–	–	–	–	–	x	x	x	x	x	x	x	x
Bovidae: Raphicerini															
Raphicerus campestris	–	–	–	–	–	–	–	x	x	x	x	x	x	x	x

Table 5.2 (cont.)

Taxon	North Africa					East Africa					Southern Africa				
	Early Middle Pleistocene	Late Middle Pleistocene	Late Pleistocene	Holocene	Extant	Early Middle Pleistocene	Late Middle Pleistocene	Late Pleistocene	Holocene	Extant	Early Middle Pleistocene	Late Middle Pleistocene	Late Pleistocene	Holocene	Extant
Raphicerus melanotis	–	–	–	–	–	–	–	–	–	–	x	x	x	x	x
Raphicerus sharpei	–	–	–	–	–	–	–	–	x	–	–	–	–	x	x
Bovidae: Ourebiini															
Ourebia ourebi	–	–	–	–	–	?	?	x	x	x	x	x	x	x	x
Bovidae: Bovini															
Bos primigenius[†]	x	x	x	x	–	–	–	–	–	–	–	–	–	–	–
Bos sp.[†]	–	–	–	–	–	x	–	–	–	–	–	–	–	–	–
Syncerus acoelotus[†]	–	–	–	–	–	x	–	–	–	–	–	–	–	–	–
Syncerus antiquus[†]	–	–	x	x	–	x	x	x	–	–	x	x	x	–	–
Syncerus caffer	–	x	x	x	–	?	?	x	x	x	x	x	x	x	x
Bovidae: Tribe Unknown															
Spiral horn[†]	–	–	–	–	–	–	–	–	–	–	x	–	–	–	–
Cervidae															
Cervus elaphus	–	–	x	x	x	–	–	–	–	–	–	–	–	–	–
Megaceroides algericus[†]	–	–	x	x	–	–	–	–	–	–	–	–	–	–	–
Equidae															
Equus africanus	–	–	x	x	x	x	x	x	x	x	–	–	–	–	–
Equus algericus[†]	?	?	x	x	–	–	–	–	–	–	–	–	–	–	–
Equus capensis[†5]	–	–	–	–	–	–	–	–	–	–	x	x	x	x	–
Equus grevyi	–	–	–	–	–	–	x	x	x	x	–	–	–	–	–
Equus lylei[†]	–	–	–	–	–	–	–	–	–	–	–	x	?	–	–
Equus mauritanicus[†]	x	x	x	x	–	–	–	–	–	–	–	–	–	–	–
Equus melkiensis[†]	?	?	x	–	–	–	–	–	–	–	–	–	–	–	–
Equus quagga	–	–	–	–	–	x	x	x	x	x	x	x	x	x	x
Equus zebra	–	–	–	–	–	–	–	–	–	–	–	–	x	x	x
Rhinocerotidae															
Ceratotherium simum	x	x	x	x	–	x	x	x	x	x	x	x	x	x	x
Diceros bicornis	–	–	–	–	–	x	x	x	x	x	x	x	x	x	x
Stephanorhinus hemitoechus[†]	–	?	x	–	–	–	–	–	–	–	–	–	–	–	–
Cercopithecidae															
Theropithecus oswaldi[†]	x	–	–	–	–	x	–	–	–	–	x	–	–	–	–
Papio ursinus	–	–	–	–	–	–	–	–	–	–	x	x	x	x	x
Papio sp.	–	–	–	–	–	x	x	x	x	x	–	–	–	–	–
Colobus sp.	–	–	–	–	–	x	x	x	x	x	–	–	–	–	–
Cercopithecus albogularis	–	–	–	–	–	–	–	–	–	x	–	–	–	x	x
Chlorocebus sp. (vervet)	–	–	–	–	–	–	–	–	x	x	–	–	–	x	x
Macaca sylvanus	?	?	x	x	x	–	–	–	–	–	–	–	–	–	–
Galagidae															
Galago senegalensis	–	–	–	–	–	–	–	–	x	x	–	–	–	–	–
Galago moholi	–	–	–	–	–	–	–	–	–	x	–	–	–	x	x

Table 5.2 (cont.)

Taxon	North Africa					East Africa					Southern Africa				
	Early Middle Pleistocene	Late Middle Pleistocene	Late Pleistocene	Holocene	Extant	Early Middle Pleistocene	Late Middle Pleistocene	Late Pleistocene	Holocene	Extant	Early Middle Pleistocene	Late Middle Pleistocene	Late Pleistocene	Holocene	Extant
Hominidae															
Pan sp.	–	–	–	–	–	?	x	x	x	x	–	–	–	–	–
Homo erectus†	x	–	–	–	–	–	–	–	–	–	–	–	–	–	–
Archaic *Homo sapiens*†	x	–	–	–	–	x	x	?	–	–	x	x	–	–	–
Homo sapiens	–	x	x	x	x	–	x	x	x	x	–	–	x	x	x

† = Extinct.
[1] The two species of warthog (*Phacochoerus aethiopicus* and *P. africanus*) are inconsistently recognized as separate in published faunal lists.
[2] The bushpig (*Potamochoerus larvatus*) and red river hog (*P. porcus*) are inconsistently recognized as separate in published faunal lists.
[3] *Oryx* spp. includes *Oryx beisa* (East Africa), *O. gazella* (South Africa), and *O. dammah* (North Africa). Fossil specimens are frequently identified to genus only and the East and South African species are often considered in published lists to be the same species and assigned to *O. gazella*.
[4] Among the gazelles assigned to *Gazella*, the genus *Nanger* is now often used for *dama*, *granti*, and *soemmerringi*, and the genus *Eudorcas* for *rufifrons* and *thomsonii*. All gazelles are assigned to *Gazella* here because it is uncertain which genus applies to the extinct species if *Gazella*, *Eudorcas*, and *Nanger* are recognized.
[5] Churcher et al. (1999; Churcher, 2006) report **Equus capensis** from the Middle Pleistocene through the Holocene of Egypt. The taxonomic attribution of these specimens is equivocal and they may belong to Grevy's zebra or to an extinct North African equid such as *Equus mauritanicus* (Faith, 2014).

is apparent irrespective of time, implying that – at the continental scale – geography, rather than time, is the primary source of variation in faunal composition across Africa since the Middle Pleistocene. These results parallel those provided by O'Regan et al. (2005) for African faunas from 1.0 to 0.5 Ma and imply a deep history to the regional zonation of African faunas.

Temporal variation is apparent in Figure 5.2B, which plots PCoA Axes 1 and 3 (15.1 percent of variation). Axis 3 accounts for the shift in faunal composition from the early Middle Pleistocene to the present. Although all three regions show a parallel pattern with Axis 3 values increasing through time, North Africa shows a far greater spread of values, indicating a greater magnitude of turnover. This is also evident in Table 5.3, which quantifies turnover across successive time bins for each region as 1 – Dice Coefficient, such that greater values indicate less similarity and greater turnover. In addition to high levels of turnover, North Africa is also unique in that there is marked faunal change between those species documented in the Holocene compared to the present, the result of numerous extirpations (12) and global extinctions (5) (Table 5.2).

For all three regions, the highest degree of faunal turnover occurs across the transition from the early Middle Pleistocene to the late Middle Pleistocene at ~500 ka (Table 5.3). This transition is characterized by the loss of many archaic species that are typical of the Early Pleistocene. These include the saber-toothed cats *Megantereon whitei* and *Homotherium*, the giant baboon *Theropithecus oswaldi*, several suid species belonging to the genera *Kolpochoerus* and *Metridiochoerus*, a sivathere (*Sivatherium maurusium*), and numerous bovids, including *Rabaticeras arambourgi*, *Hippotragus gigas*, and *Antidorcas recki*, among others. Although the analytical boundary between early Middle Pleistocene faunas and late Middle Pleistocene faunas is (arbitrarily) established here as 500 ka, the temporal resolution in the fossil record is too coarse and the number of relevant sites too few to determine the precise temporal boundary of this turnover event and whether it occurred in a geological instant or was drawn out over tens of thousands of years. However, in East Africa, the large mammal assemblage from Lainyamok (Kenya) dated to between 339 and 392 ka is very similar in taxonomic composition to Late Pleistocene sites in the region (Potts and Deino, 1995; Faith et al., 2012), suggesting that this phase of turnover was probably complete by ~400 ka.

Range Shifts

The North African record attests to remarkable range shifts, a factor that plays a key role in explaining the high degree of turnover through time compared to sub-Saharan Africa (Table 5.3). This includes the immigration of Eurasian species, such as wild boar (*Sus scrofa*), red deer (*Cervus elaphus*), giant deer (*Megaceroides algericus*), narrow-nosed rhinoceros

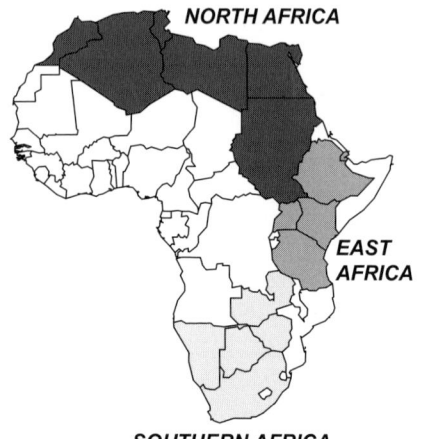

Figure 5.1 The countries in North, East, and southern Africa providing the late Quaternary fossil assemblages considered here (Table 5.1).

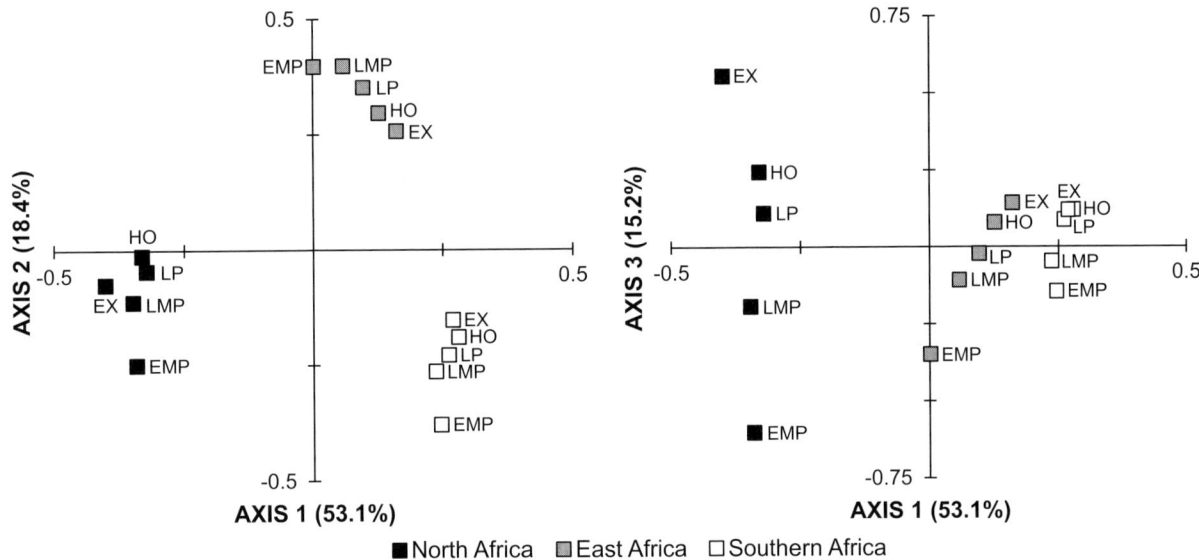

Figure 5.2 Principal Coordinates Analysis of large mammal occurrences in Table 5.2. (A) Axes 1 and 2, (B) Axes 1 and 3. EMP = early Middle Pleistocene (780–500 ka); LMP = late Middle Pleistocene (500–126 ka); LP = Late Pleistocene (126–12 ka); HO = Holocene (<12 ka); EX = Extant.

(*Stephanorhinus hemitoechus*), and European pole-cat (*Mustela putorius*). Some of these species may have entered Africa by swimming the Gibraltar Straits during marine regressions (glacial phases of the Pleistocene), while others, particularly *Stephanorhinus*, likely came from the east, following the Mediterranean shore (Geraads, 2010) during humid phases that promoted more hospitable environments across the Sahara and the Levant. The presence of species typical of sub-Saharan Africa is also well documented, with fossil sites including elephant (*Loxodonta africana*), white rhinoceros (*Ceratotherium simum*), warthog (*Phacochoerus* sp.), eland (*Taurotragus* sp.), roan antelope (*Hippotragus equinus*), Bohor reedbuck (*Redunca redunca*), waterbuck (*Kobus ellipsiprymnus*), kob (*Kobus kob*), hartebeest (*Alcelaphus buselaphus*), blue wildebeest (*Connochaetes taurinus*), buffalo (*Syncerus caffer*), giant long-horn buffalo (*Syncerus antiquus*), and giraffe (*Giraffa camelopardalis*). These species almost certainly expanded into North Africa during moist Green Sahara phases that would have allowed dispersal from sub-Saharan Africa, and they may have done so repeatedly during the Quaternary as dispersal corridors opened and closed. Their last appearances in North Africa occur during the Late Pleistocene and Holocene (Table 5.2). For at least some of these species, extirpation from North Africa may have been driven by increased aridity after the African Humid Period (Klein, 1984b; Faith, 2014). These extirpations, in addition to four global extinctions during the Holocene (*Bos primigenius*, *Equus algericus*, *Equus mauritanicus*, *Megaceroides algericus*) contribute to the exceptionally high degree of turnover observed between Holocene faunas and the present (Table 5.3).

There are only rare examples of such dramatic range shifts documented in the East African fossil record. Klipspringer fossils (*Oreotragus oreotragus*) are not known in East Africa until the end of the Pleistocene (Marean, 1992b). However, the genus has a long history in South Africa, with fossils of the extant species potentially present by the earliest Pleistocene (Gentry, 2010). This suggests dispersal from the south. A similar situation may also be true for southern reedbuck (*Redunca arundinum*) and mountain reedbuck (*R. fulvorufula*), although this is complicated by the uncertain taxonomic assignment of specimens attributed to *Redunca* sp. at earlier East African localities (Bobe and Eck, 2001; Geraads et al., 2004a, 2004c; Reed, 2008). While not evident in the fossil record, genetic data attest to the extirpation of blue wildebeest (*Connochaetes taurinus*) and common warthog (*Phacochoerus africanus*) from East Africa and subsequent recolonization from a southern African refugium (Lorenzen et al., 2012).

A small number of Middle-to-Late Pleistocene sites document marked range shifts within East Africa (Marean and Gifford-Gonzalez, 1991; Marean, 1992b; Potts and Deino, 1995; Tryon et al., 2010; Faith et al., 2013, 2015, 2016; Rowan et al., 2015). For example, arid-adapted Grevy's zebra (*Equus grevyi*), which historically ranged through arid to semi-arid grasslands and shrublands in the Horn of Africa, is known from fossils in southern Kenya and northern Tanzania, ~500 km south of its historical range. Grevy's zebra is consistently associated with other arid-adapted species, including *Oryx beisa* and extinct *Damaliscus hypsodon*, which suggests that its southward expansion was permitted by expansion of dry grassland habitats and contraction of the equatorial forest belt (Faith et al., 2013, 2016). Removal of this dispersal barrier may have also facilitated the northward expansion of southern reedbuck (*Redunca*

Table 5.3 Faunal turnover (1 − Dice Coefficient) across successive time bins for North, East, and southern Africa. Values can range from 0 to 1 with higher values indicating greater turnover. EMP, early Middle Pleistocene (780–500 ka); LMP, late Middle Pleistocene (500–126 ka); LP, Late Pleistocene (126–12 ka); HO, Holocene (<12 ka); EX, extant.

	EMP to LMP	LMP to LP	LP to HO	HO to EX
North Africa	0.28	0.19	0.23	0.22
East Africa	0.25	0.09	0.11	0.06
Southern Africa	0.15	0.11	0.08	0.03

arundinum) into northeast Lake Victoria (Faith et al., 2015, 2016) and the westward excursion of the extinct long-horn buffalo (*Syncerus antiquus*) into the eastern Democratic Republic of the Congo (Peters, 1990b).

Conversely, the more mesic-adapted blue wildebeest (*Connochaetes taurinus*) is found in Members I and III of the Kibish Formation in southern Ethiopia, ~770 km north of its present range (Rowan et al., 2015). Its northward expansion likely reflects the presence of environments that were more humid than at present. This is supported by the associated faunas, which include numerous specimens of *Kobus* and *Tragelaphus*, and by the relationship between deposition of Kibish Formation sediments and the development of Mediterranean sapropels (McDougall et al., 2008), which form during periods of increased rainfall in East Africa. Together with Grevy's zebra, the fossil record of blue wildebeest indicates that the ranges of arid- and mesic-adapted species were alternately expanding and contracting in response to changes in moisture availability.

The southern African record lacks strong evidence for major range expansions from East or North Africa over the last 780 ka. Reynolds (2007b) proposes that, compared to East Africa, the environments of southern Africa were more stable across the Quaternary, translating to more stable faunal communities. This scenario is consistent with genetic evidence (Lorenzen et al., 2012) and with the relatively low degree of faunal turnover observed here for southern Africa (Table 5.3). Whereas dramatic environmental variability in North Africa, which ranged from humid Green Sahara phases to extreme aridity, contributed to the immigration and extirpation of sub-Saharan African species, relative stability in southern Africa may have reduced opportunities for East (or Central) African species to expand their ranges southwards.

Extinction and Speciation

There are at least 49 large mammal species that made their first appearance on continental Africa over the last 780 ka years, although seven of these are now extinct (*Damaliscus hypsodon, Rusingoryx atopocranion, Aepyceros* sp. nov., *Gazella tingitana, Megaceroides algericus, Equus lylei,* and *Stephanorhinus hemitoechus*; Table 5.2). These gains are offset by at least 54 extinctions. Of the extinct species, 47 are globally extinct and 6 probably or certainly evolved into other forms (*Lycaon magnus, Antidorcas recki, Homo erectus,* Archaic *Homo sapiens, Damaliscus* aff. *lunatus, Rabaticeras arambourgi*). The brown bear (*Ursus arctos*), known from North Africa until the mid-nineteenth century (Hamdine et al., 1998), survives outside of Africa in Eurasia and North America.

Faith (2014) summarizes evidence indicating that the majority of species known to have disappeared since the Late Pleistocene were grazers or preferred open grassland habitats, a pattern that can be extended here to the last 780 ka. This is especially clear among the Bovidae, which accounts for the majority of large mammal species and almost half the extinctions. The tribes Alcelaphini and Antilopini, which include species characterized by hypsodont teeth and cursorially adapted limbs, are considered the archetypal open grassland lineages. Species of these tribes account for 64 percent (= 16/25) of the bovid extinctions, whereas they today account for only 25 percent (= 20/81) of extant African bovids recognized by Kingdon and Hoffmann (2013; Fisher's exact test: $p < 0.001$). Extinctions across other tribes are also dominated by grazers, some of which were massive in size, including three species of the Bovini (*Bos primigenius, Syncerus acoelotus,* and *S. antiquus*), two of the Hippotragini (*Hippotragus gigas* and *H. leucophaeus*), and an unnamed caprine antelope. Conversely, there is only a single extinction among the Tragelaphini (*Tragelaphus algericus*), which includes browsers and mixed feeders that prefer wooded habitats; none among the Reduncini, which includes grazers that prefer well-watered habitats; and none among the lineages of small-bodied browsing species that prefer closed habitats, including the Cephalophini, Neotragini, and Madoquini.

The loss of grassland species is also evident across other ungulate families. For example, the number of African equids, which are today represented by four bulk grazers (*Equus africanus, E. grevyi, E. quagga, E. zebra*) that inhabit a continuum of open habitats from arid scrublands to mesic grasslands, was more than halved (Table 5.2), following the loss of *E. algericus, E. capensis, E. lylei, E. mauritanicus,* and *E. melkiensis*. Two of the surviving equids, *E. grevyi* and *E. africanus*, are now endangered and critically endangered, respectively (Moehlman et al., 2015; Rubenstein et al. 2016), suggesting that these long-term losses may continue through the present (e.g., Faith et al., 2013). African suids suffered major losses, with the extinction of three species of *Metridiochoerus* and three species of *Kolpochoerus*. Species of the former are known to have been large-bodied specialized grazers and the latter included substantial amounts of grass in the diet (from mixed feeding to grass-dominated; Harris and Cerling, 2002; Bishop et al., 2006a; Codron et al., 2008; Bishop, 2010). Among the Primates, the only extinct species that did not leave any descendants is the massive terrestrial grazer *Theropithecus oswaldi* (Jablonski and Frost, 2010), the last record of which dates to the early Middle Pleistocene (~509 ka) in the Kapthurin Formation of Kenya (Cornelissen et al., 1990; Deino and McBrearty, 2002). The genus to which it belongs is today represented by the gelada (*T. gelada*), a species that is morphologically too primitive to have likely descended from the specialized *T. oswaldi* (Jablonski, 1993).

While the chronology and environmental context of extinctions during the Middle Pleistocene is poorly resolved, those losses that took place since the Late Pleistocene are better understood. Among those extinct species documented in more than just a handful of sites (typically >6 sites) and for which secure extinction chronologies are available, the losses are known to have occurred between ~13 and 6 ka (Faith, 2014). Where paleoenvironmental records are also available, the timing of these extinctions coincide with climate-driven environmental change. The South African record in particular – especially paleoenvironmental inferences derived from large mammal and micromammal fossil sequences – shows that the loss of open grassland species, including *Equus capensis, Syncerus antiquus, Megalotragus priscus, Antidorcas australis, A. bondi,* and an unnamed caprine, was associated with decline in the availability or productivity of grassland habitats since the LGM (Klein, 1972, 1980, 1983, 1984b; Brink and Lee-Thorp, 1992;

Brink, 1999; Faith, 2011, 2013, 2014; Figure 5.3). At Lukenya Hill in Kenya, the last appearances of *S. antiquus* and *Damaliscus hypsodon* are dated to between the LGM and the onset of the Holocene and coincide with a loss of arid grasslands and scrublands (Marean and Gifford-Gonzalez, 1991; Marean, 1992b). Several other grassland species, including *Damaliscus niro*, *Rusingoryx atopocranion*, and (possibly) *Equus lylei*, disappear from East or southern Africa at some point during the Late Pleistocene, potentially for similar reasons. The North African extinctions are poorly understood, but the disappearance of the large-bodied grazers *Bos primigenius*, *Synercus antiquus*, *Equus mauritanicus*, and *E. melkiensis* and one browser (*Megaceroides algericus*) during the middle Holocene are associated with an abrupt shift toward severe aridity following the African Humid Period (Faith, 2014; Fernandez et al., 2015).

With the exception of an apparent radiation of North African *Gazella* (*G. cuvieri*, *G. dama*, *G. dorcas*, *G. leptoceros*, and *G. soemmerringii*) during the late Middle Pleistocene and Late Pleistocene (Table 5.2), the ecology of those species with first appearances over the last 780 ka is distinct from those that become extinct. While there are no extinctions among browsing bovids, four small-bodied browsers that prefer dense vegetation cover make their first appearances, including blue duiker (*Philantomba monticola*), red forest duiker (*Cephalophus natalensis*), suni (*Nesotragus moschatus*), and gerenuk (*Litocranius walleri*). The presence of four browsers among the 16 extant bovids with FADs compared to none among the 25 extinct species is significant (Fisher's exact test: $p = 0.033$). Excluding the gerenuk, a member of the Antilopini, these browsers are representatives of the Cephalophini and Neotragini, tribes for which there are no known extinctions (tribal designations follow Kingdon and Hoffmann, 2013). FADs are also documented among other bovid tribes for which there are few or no extinctions, including three species of Tragelaphini (*Tragelaphus angasi*, *T. imberbis*, and *T. spekei*), one of the Reduncini (*Redunca redunca*), and one of the Raphicerini (*Raphicerus sharpei*).

Several arboreal primates that subsist on fruit, insects, and leaves make their first appearance since the Middle Pleistocene, including Syke's monkey (*Cercopithecus albogularis*), vervets (*Chorocebus*), lesser galago (*Galago senegalensis*), mohol galago (*Galago moholi*), and greater galago (*Otolemur crassicaudatus*); their ecology contrasts starkly with that of the massive terrestrial grazer *Theropithecus oswaldi*. Whereas many of the extinct suids are grazers – especially those of the genus *Metridiochoerus* – the only suid to appear in Africa since the Middle Pleistocene is the giant forest hog (*Hylochoerus meinertzhageni*), a mixed feeder that prefers dense forest cover and is first known from the Late Pleistocene of the Kibish Formation in Ethiopia (Assefa et al., 2008). The omnivorous wild boar (*Sus scrofa*) appears in North Africa during the late Middle Pleistocene (Michel, 1992), but it represents a Eurasian immigrant.

There are substantial gains in the diversity of the Carnivora. The handful of extinctions (*Canis mohibi*, *Lycaon magnus*, *Homotherium* sp., *Megantereon whitei*) and extirpation of *Ursus arctos* are more than offset by the first appearance of 12 species. These include side-striped jackal (*Canis adustus*), bat-eared fox (*Otocyon megalotis*), fennec fox (*Vulpes zerda*), European polecat (*Mustela putorius*), Cape gray mongoose (*Galerella pulverulenta*), slender mongoose (*Galerella sanguinea*), common dwarf mongoose (*Helogale parvula*), white-tailed mongoose (*Ichneumia albicauda*), banded mongoose (*Mungos mungo*), Meller's mongoose (*Rhynchogale melleri*), sand cat (*Felis margarita*), and black-footed cat (*F. nigripes*). However, with the exception of the extinct jackal *C. mohibi*, the losses primarily affected large-bodied species (>20 kg), whereas the gains are restricted to small-bodied species, particularly mongooses (Herpestidae). The ecological niches of *U. arctos* and the saber-toothed cats *Homotherium* and *Megantereon* are vacant in contemporary African ecosystems.

Evolutionary Process or Sampling Bias?

While there are broad ecological contrasts in body size, diet, or habitat preference that distinguish the set of species with first appearances from their extinct counterparts, the underlying cause of this contrast is uncertain. The tendency for those species with first appearances to be smaller-bodied, associated with moderate-to-dense tree cover, or to include substantial amounts of browse in the diet could reflect one of two processes: (1) higher speciation rates among lineages with these traits (i.e., an evolutionary explanation), or (2) better representation of fossil sites that sample the environments inhabited by species with these traits (i.e., a taphonomic explanation). At present, the latter cannot be ruled out. In their examination of Quaternary East and southern African mammals, Patterson et al. (2014) show that the Late Pleistocene and Holocene are far better sampled than earlier times, a pattern consistent with expectations of taphonomic bias in site preservation (Surovell et al., 2009). Such a bias explains why a relatively large number of FADs (32/49 = 65 percent) and LADs (24/54 = 44 percent) occur during the Late Pleistocene or Holocene, despite this time representing only

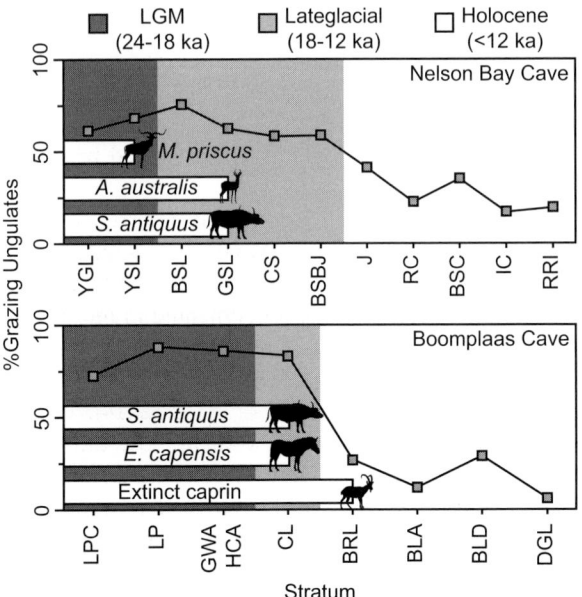

Figure 5.3 The last appearances of extinct ungulates in the stratified sequences from Nelson Bay Cave and Boomplaas Cave in South Africa arrayed against the abundance of ungulate grazers. At both sites, extinctions coincide with a long-term decline of grazers since the Last Glacial Maximum (LGM). Modified from Faith (2014).

126 ka of the last 780 ka (16 percent). In terms of global climate dynamics, this time period encompasses the full range of glacial and interglacial conditions, in addition to shorter-term climate cycles, meaning that diverse environments should be recorded. To the extent that interglacials can be equated to more mesic conditions that favor dense vegetation cover, better representation of interglacial sites (or at least sites from humid climate phases) could explain the tendency for FADs favoring browsing bovids or arboreal primates. A large number of Late Pleistocene and Holocene cave sites (e.g., Plug and Badenhorst, 2001) could also account for the many FADs among small-bodied carnivores, which may be less likely to preserve in open-air contexts (Behrensmeyer and Boaz, 1980). Taken together, these biases allow for the possibility that the emergence of many species occurred long before the Middle Pleistocene, but because of sampling error we only find evidence of them in the more recent fossil record.

The same cannot be said for extinctions. Unlike the case of FADs, a species with a LAD in the last 780 ka must have undergone extinction in this time frame; better sampling of the fossil record will only shift LADs closer to the present. The preponderance of large-bodied grassland species among the extinct species is not readily explained by taphonomic bias. For example, had there been substantial extinctions among small-bodied forest species, we would expect to find evidence of those extinctions at the same sites documenting FADs for blue duiker, red forest duiker, or suni and arboreal primates. We do not.

It follows that the loss of species that are grazers or prefer grassland habitats over the last 780 ka may be rooted in long-term ecological and evolutionary processes (Faith and Behrensmeyer, 2013; Faith, 2014). Expansion of C_4 grasslands since the late Miocene contributed to the diversification of grassland mammals (e.g., the bovid tribes Alcelaphini and Antilopini) and morphological adaptations to grazing in open habitats, including an increase in hypsodonty, body size, and cursoriality (Potts and Behrensmeyer, 1992; Bobe, 2006). The extinctions across this grazing niche since the Middle Pleistocene represent a clear reversal of this trend. For example, the extinct species *Antidorcas bondi*, *Damaliscus hypsodon*, and *Rusingoryx atopocranion* were more hypsodont than any extant African bovid (Figure 5.4). Likewise, *Theropithecus oswaldi*, *Syncerus antiquus*, *Megalotragus priscus*, *Hippotragus gigas*, *Equus capensis*, *Hippopotamus gorgops*, and *Metridiochoerus andrewsi* were among the largest of their respective lineages. A possible explanation for this reversal is increasingly variable climates associated with the establishment of 100 ka glacial–interglacial cycles by the Middle Pleistocene (Faith, 2014). This heightened global-scale variation may have operated in conjunction with regional-scale climate processes to create increasingly unstable grassland habitats. As grasslands contracted or fragmented in response to high-amplitude late Quaternary climate changes – presumably of a higher magnitude than had occurred since grasslands expanded in Africa – those species that depended on those habitats would have been more prone to extinction. This is best illustrated for Late Pleistocene and Holocene extinctions across Africa and may very well have played a role in extinctions during the Middle Pleistocene.

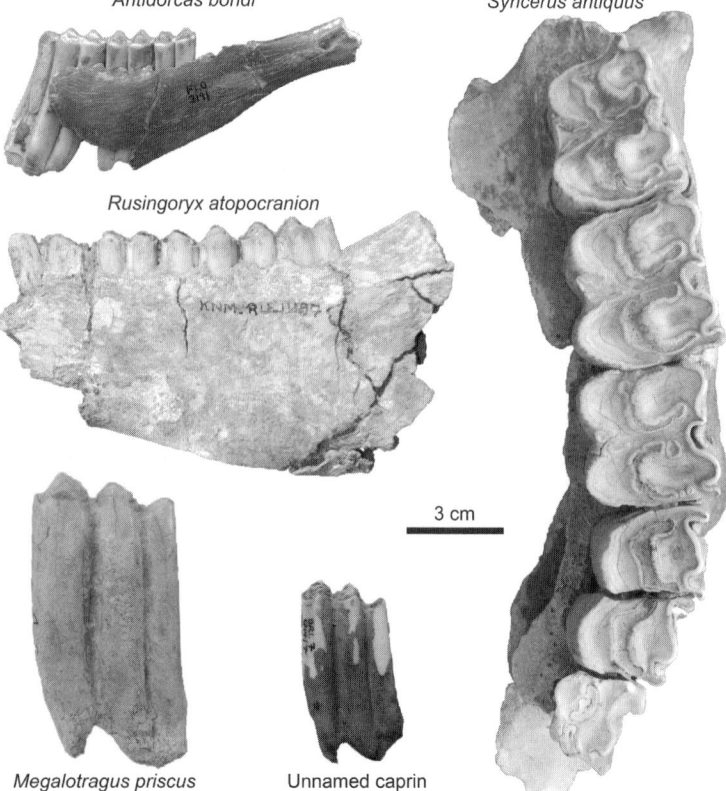

Figure 5.4 Select examples of exceptionally hypsodont or large-bodied bovids that became extinct during the Late Pleistocene and Holocene. *Antidorcas bondi*: right mandible with m1-m3 from Florisbad, South Africa (FLO3191); *Syncerus antiquus*: right maxilla with P2-M3 from Florisbad, South Africa (FLO2263); *Rusingoryx atopocranion*: left mandible with p3-m3 from Wakondo, Rusinga Island, Kenya (KNM-RU 11197); *Megalotragus priscus*: left m3 from Nelson Bay Cave, South Africa (YSL/3Δ5); unnamed caprin: left m3 from Boomplaas Cave, South Africa (BRL7 Q14/7).

Implications for Hominin Evolution

Modern Human Origins

Morphological evidence indicates substantial diversity among early modern human populations (Crevecoeur et al., 2009; Gunz et al., 2009; Harvati et al., 2013; Tryon et al., 2015). Likewise, molecular data indicate deep roots of multiple genetically distinct lineages potentially predating the earliest fossil evidence of *Homo sapiens* (Harding and McVean, 2004; Blum and Jakobsson, 2010; Campbell and Tishkoff, 2010; Rito et al., 2013). Together, both lines of evidence suggest long-term persistence of geographically and genetically isolated populations of archaic *Homo sapiens* within Africa, leading some to suggest the emergence of modern humans took place through a form of multiregional evolution within Africa involving phases of both isolation and dispersal (Harding and McVean, 2004; Rito et al., 2013).

Such a scenario is fully consistent with the faunal record. Since the Middle Pleistocene, if not earlier (O'Regan et al., 2005), we see evidence for strong regional zonation of African faunal communities (Figure 5.2). While inter-regional species dispersals did occur, especially from sub-Saharan Africa to North Africa, these were never of sufficient magnitude to blur taxonomic distinction between regions. As seems to have been the case with the associated large mammals, it is reasonable to envision that the history of early modern humans was characterized by long-term phases of population isolation punctuated by episodes of exchange and admixture during environmental windows that facilitated dispersals. Identifying those windows remains an important challenge to future research on the biogeography of modern human origins. While others have relied on paleoclimate records to infer potential dispersal windows (e.g., Vaks et al., 2007), refining the chronology of African large mammal dispersals may also provide valuable insight into identifying those times where dispersals would have been possible.

Ecological Flexibility

Potts (1998a, 1998b, 2013; Potts and Faith, 2015) proposes that environmental variability played a central role in driving hominin behavioral innovation and evolutionary change, leading to the emergence of increasingly adaptable, or ecologically flexible, hominin species. To provide paleontological support from other lineages, he notes that fossil evidence spanning 1 Ma to ~330 ka at Olorgesailie and Lainyamok in southern Kenya documents the extinction of large-bodied grassland specialists (e.g., *Equus oldowayensis*, *Theropithecus oswaldi*, *Elephas recki*, and *Metridiochoerus* spp.) and replacement by less-specialized (in terms of body mass and hypsodonty) species found today (e.g., *Equus grevyi*, *Papio anubis*, *Loxodonta africana*, and *Phacochoerus africanus*; Potts, 1998a, 1998b). This chapter shows that the taxonomic winnowing of grassland specialists was not just restricted to a handful of species in southern Kenya, but rather affected numerous species throughout the continent.

Thus, the emergence of *Homo sapiens* and development of both the MSA and LSA industries occurred while less-versatile grassland mammals were disappearing across the continent. Behavioral innovations of the MSA, such as improved control of fire (Brown et al., 2009), development of compound tools and projectile weaponry (Brooks et al., 2006; Wadley et al., 2009; Wilkinson et al., 2012), and use of traps and snares (Wadley, 2010) are likely to have allowed early modern humans to more effectively forage across a more diverse range of habitats. When considered in the context of other African mammals, the ability to exploit multiple habitats could have potentially spelled the difference between survival and extinction among populations of early modern humans.

Conclusions

The fossil record of large African mammals of the last 780 ka is dynamic. In addition to recording remarkable cases of range expansion and contraction, it documents the first appearance of at least 42 species that persist to the present and the extinction of at least 54. Counts for the former may diminish as continued sampling pushes FADs earlier into the Pleistocene, whereas the latter has increased substantially in the last several decades (Faith, 2014) and is likely to continue to do so in the future. The net result is a long-term decline in large mammal richness, with a substantial number of losses occurring since the Late Pleistocene. While some have invoked human impacts in the more recent extinctions (e.g., Klein 1980, 1984b), I have argued here that these losses are embedded in long-term evolutionary processes set in motion long before the emergence of *Homo sapiens* (see also Faith, 2014).

However, there is little question that humans today are dramatically influencing ecosystems in Africa and beyond (Barnosky et al., 2011). Coupled with the effects of climate change in the near future, increasingly rapid declines in richness seem likely. Considering the long-term patterns evident in the fossil record, it may come as little surprise that numerous species threatened with extinction today are large-bodied or hypsodont open habitat specialists such as Grevy's zebra (*Equus grevyi*), wild ass (*Equus africanus*), addax (*Addax nasomaculatus*), scimitar-horned oryx (*Oryx dammah*), hirola (*Beatragus hunteri*), Cuvier's gazelle (*Gazella cuvieri*), slender-horned gazelle (*G. leptoceros*), Speke's gazelle (*G. spekei*), and Dama gazella (*G. dama*). While conservationists routinely focus on identifying regions that are priorities for wildlife conservation (Myers et al., 2000; Brooks et al., 2001), there is untapped potential to turn to the fossil record to identify ecological or morphological variables associated with extinction risk. As paleontological evidence becomes increasingly accepted as a valuable source of insight into contemporary conservation challenges (Grayson, 2005; Lyman, 2006; Dietl and Flessa, 2009; Faith, 2012b; Louys, 2012; Wolverton and Lyman, 2012; Faith et al., 2013), this should become an important priority for continued paleontological research in Africa.

Acknowledgments

I am grateful to Sally Reynolds and René Bobe for inviting me to contribute to this volume and to the late James Brink, René Bobe, Amy Rector and Sally Reynolds for their useful comments on a previous draft of this chapter. Many of the ideas presented here stem from discussions and collaborations with my friends and colleagues, including Kay Behrensmeyer, Don Grayson, Dan Peppe, Rick Potts, John Rowan, and Christian Tryon.

Part II Southern Africa

6 The Southern African Sites
Paleoenvironmental Syntheses and Future Research Prospects
Sally C. Reynolds

Introduction

This volume provides an overview of paleoenvironmental reconstructions of hundreds of different sites, using dozens of different analytical methods. The intention of this chapter is to bring together some of those data relevant to the sites of southern Africa to highlight future research directions.

There is a well-developed framework and a broad understanding of large-scale patterns of climate change at both regional and global scales (e.g., deMenocal, 1995, 2004, 2011; Partridge et al., 1997; Sepulcre et al., 2006; Maslin et al., 2014, 2015). The main climate question is the degree to which shifts in climate drove faunal turnover and, ultimately, homin evolution. This question is typically approached via a combination of continental-scale summaries focused on key indicator species, timing of hominin technological advances or paleoenvironmental proxies (e.g., Vrba, 1993, 1995b; Bobe et al., 2002; Ecker et al., 2018a, 2018b; Smith et al., 2019 and many others). Because this reasoning relies on establishing correlative associations, it is constantly challenged by issues of causality versus coincidence. Moreover, because such studies usually rely on continental-scale data, regional and local discrepancies are rarely explored.

Kingston (2007) and Marean et al. (2015: 62) argued for an alternative approach and framework that "moves beyond the strict correlative research that continues to dominate the field." An alternative is to focus on a "bottom-up" strategy, focused on local and regional ecological processes. Hominins and other fauna did not passively "adapt to changes in rainfall and temperature," but rather their behavior sought to meet their resource requirements, namely finding water, food, mates, and predator refuge on a landscape that met those needs to different degrees, both spatially and through time (Reynolds et al., 2011; Marean et al, 2015: 63). Water is the key element in virtually all the sites discussed in this volume, and it may be that understanding the relationship of hydrology to specific landscapes in driving hominin and faunal movements is a more explicit way of understanding the relationship between climate, geology, and hominins (Cuthbert et al., 2017; Caley et al., 2018).

In such an approach, local variation, often subsumed and lost in continental-scale synthesis, matters a great deal. There is a growing consensus that large-scale climate shifts, together with the local environmental context, both play important roles in how site habitats change through time, and this volume is a first step toward creating a more synthetic understanding of the site habitats available to hominins in specific places and times. In looking at the habitat evidence on a site-by-site basis, this chapter presents an overview of the general characteristics of these habitats, along with an indication of what paleoevironmental data have been used to reconstruct these past habitats.

I discuss the sites of Angola and Namibia first, before moving on to the southern African interior, after which I provide a brief summary of the paleoenvironments of the coastal sites. The coastal sites are not associated with hominins such as *Australopithecus* and *Paranthropus*, and tend to sample later time periods and warmer, wetter paleohabitats. A series of excellent paleoenvironmental syntheses such as Meadows and Baxter (1999) provide a detailed discussion of the uniqueness of the Southern Cape as a region, and how climatic changes in the area were not paralleled by shifts in other regions within southern Africa. Similarly, Ecker and colleagues (2018a, 2018b) argued for a unique trajectory for central southern Africa.

This overview is not intended to be exhaustive, but merely to serve to convey an overall impression of the sites and the types of habitats represented at a given time interval. Most of the sites in the southern African interior within the area now designated as the Cradle of Humankind UNESCO World Heritage Site derive from breccia deposits within karstic cavities in the Malmani Dolomite, within the Eccles Formation (Partridge, 1978, 1979; Dirks and Berger, 2013). These sites were initially discovered, prospected, and later mined for lime deposits, leaving lime-miners' dumps of *ex-situ* brecciated material associated with each site. The history of the prospecting and paleontological investigations in these is summarized by Thackeray (2016), while a good review of the stone tool industries across southern Africa can be found in Dusseldorp et al. (2013). Avery (2019) has published detailed species lists per fossil locality and Scott and Neumann (2018) provide a pollen-based overview of the vegetation context for specific time intervals.

As in any review chapter of this nature, it is impossible to do justice to each site, and so priority has been given to sites containing clear signals of paleoenvironments via various proxies, specifically omitting sites with only stone tools and/or human remains or sites that are too recent (Holocene). There are numerous fossiliferous sites too small to have formal names, but preliminary details and species lists exist (see Berger and Brink, 2007; Avery, 2019).

49

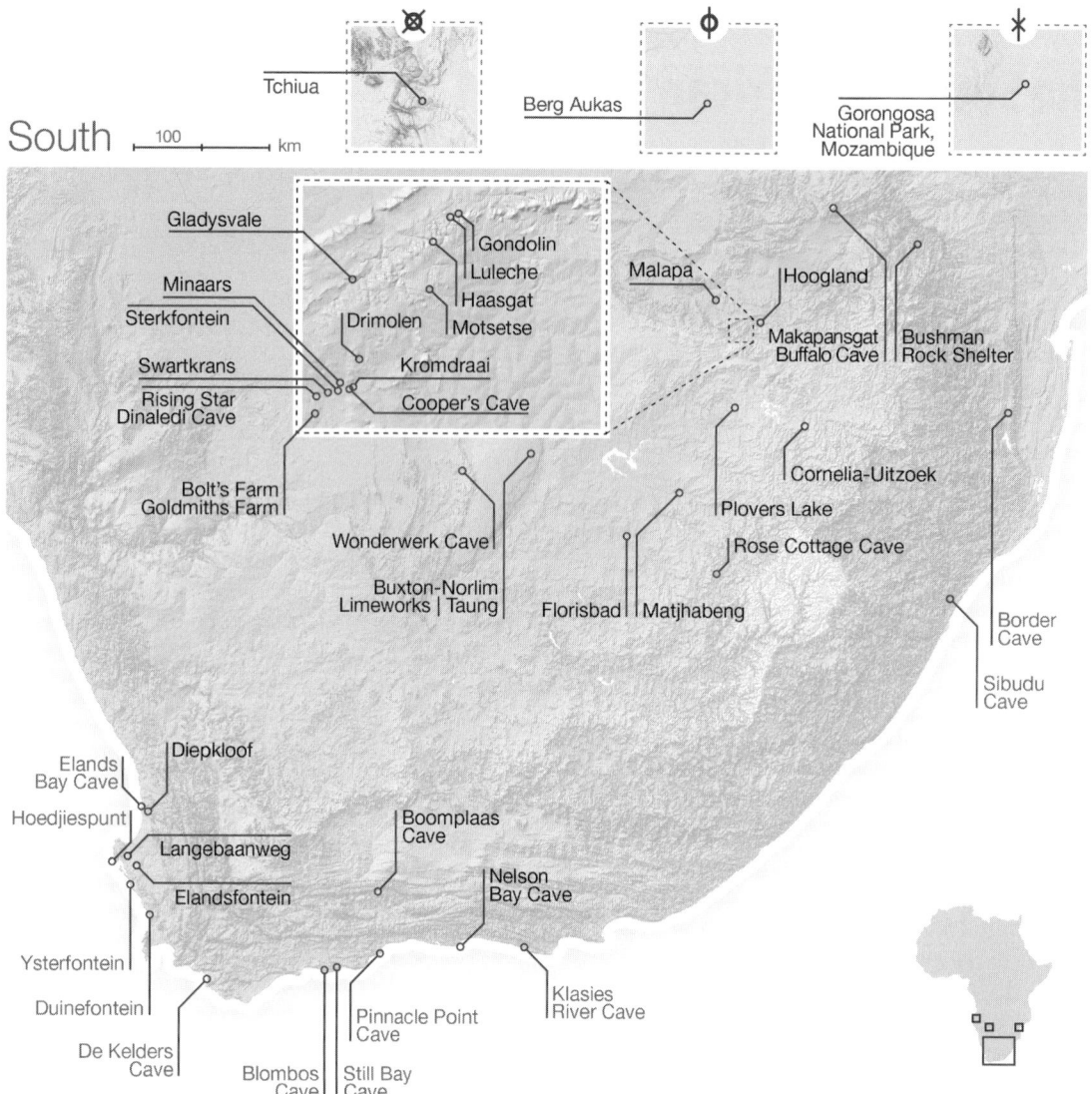

Figure 6.1 Fossil localities discussed in the text. Note that the Gorongosa site in Mozambique is shown on this figure, but is discussed in the text of Bobe and Reynolds, Chapter 15 (this volume).

In contrast to traditional frameworks that stress the chronological or alphabetical order of the sites, I have chosen to arrange the localities in latitudinal order (i.e., by spatial proximity, rather than by date order) within their geographic regions. The rationale for this framework is that sites occur in zones with geographic coherence, which is lost when clustering sites by ages only (e.g., Ashley 2020). Therefore, I will first look at the sites in southwestern Africa, before moving to the interior and those of the UNESCO World Heritage Site, the Cradle of Humankind. Subsequently, I cover the other sites of the interior before finally reviewing the coastal sites of the Cape and southern coast more generally. These coastal sites are ordered from west coast to east coast (Figure 6.1). Sites that receive in-depth treatment elsewhere in the volume are covered here in brief only.

Southwestern Africa

I discuss southern Angola and northern Namibia as a southwestern African region (Figure 6.1). This region has extensive dolomites that have undergone karstic processes and contain fossiliferous breccias dating from the middle Miocene to the Recent (Pickford et al., 1994a). These occur in different taphonomic contexts from localities in the East African Rift System.

Humpata Plateau, Angola

The Humpata Plateau (Huíla Province, southern Angola) has a series of karstic deposits with Early Pleistocene fossils, including abundant cercopithecids (Dart, 1950; Jablonski, 1994). Fossil localities include Tchiua, Malola, Ufefua, and Cangalongue (Pickford et al., 1994a). Tchiua is dominated by cercopithecids and micromammals, with termite tunnels in some breccias (Pickford et al., 1992). The Humpata primate fauna includes *Theropithecus*, *Soromandrillus*, and one colobine (Gilbert, 2013). Many of the cercopithecid cranial specimens from the Humpata Plateau are subadult individuals with damage consistent with predation by a large avian raptor (Gilbert et al., 2009). Humpata Plateau paleoenvironments resembled those in the region today, but with somewhat wetter/drier fluctuations (Pickford et al., 1994a; Pickford and Senut, 1997).

Otavi Region, Namibia

The karstic system in the Otavi region of northern Namibia has yielded abundant breccias with fossils spanning the Miocene to Holocene. The Berg Aukas vanadium mine has a series of caves and fissure-filling breccias dating from the Middle Miocene, Pleistocene, and Holocene (Pickford et al., 1994a). The Berg Aukas hominoid mandible of *Otavipithecus namibiensis*, with an estimated age of 13 Ma, is associated with mostly nocturnal micromammal taxa (rodents, macroscelideans, bats; Conroy et al., 1992, 1993). A hominin femur of uncertain provenience but probably of Pleistocene age came from deep in the Berg Aukas mine (Grine et al., 1995).

The paleoenvironmental signal from the Berg Aukas Middle Miocene micromammals indicates wooded environments associated with *Otavipithecus* (Conroy, 1996). The Late Miocene fossiliferous locality of Harasib 3a includes cercopithecids (at least one colobine species) and galagos (Conroy et al., 1996). Hyracoids of the family Pliohyracidae are present in the Middle Miocene breccias (Pickford, 1994c), while Late Miocene Berg Aukas contains the family Procaviidae (Rasmussen et al., 1996). Other localities in the Otavi region, e.g., Jägersquelle, Nosib, and Uisib, date to the Pleistocene (Pickford et al., 1994a).

The late Miocene blocks from Berg Aukas and Harasib 3 indicate environments ranging from grasslands to wooded savanna, and the Plio-Pleistocene blocks contain micromammals that indicate arid conditions (Conroy et al., 1993). The extreme aridity of southwestern Africa today, with its most pronounced expression in the Namib Desert, was influenced by the Late Miocene Benguela upwelling system (Heinrich et al., 2011; Hoetzel et al., 2015).

Sites Within the UNESCO Cradle of Humankind

Makapansgat

The Makapan Valley which lies 19 km east-northeast of the city of Mokopane (Limpopo Province, South Africa), contains caves with deposits of differing ages, including Buffalo Cave, Cave of Hearths, and Cold Air Cave (Reed, 1997; Tobias, 2000; Hopley et al., 2007b; Reed et al., Chapter 7, this volume). Makapansgat was first discovered by Raymond Dart and announced by Clarence van Riet Lowe in 1938. Excavation commenced in 1946, and Limeworks Members 3 (also called the "Grey Breccia") and 4 yielded a sample of 27 hominin specimens, representing a minimum number of 10 individuals, which were later assigned to *Australopithecus prometheus* (Dart, 1948). The hominin-bearing Member 3 is approximately 3.0 Ma in age. The australopithecine-bearing deposits do not contain stone tools (however, see the Makapansgat pebble described by Dart, 1955), but other deposits do. During an early survey, stone tools were discovered in an abandoned mine adjacent to the Historic Cave and this became known as Cave of Hearths and was excavated from 1947 to 1954 (Mason, 1962; Tobias, 1971). This excavation, first led by van Riet Lowe (1954; Brain et al., 1955) and then by Revil Mason (1962, 1988a), uncovered the longest archaeological sequence in southern Africa, spanning the Earlier Stone Age (late Acheulian) to the Iron Age and historic periods (Tobias, 1971).

Reed and colleagues (Chapter 7, this volume) synthesize a range of paleoenvironmental evidence and conclude that the Makapansgat *Australopithecus* paleoenvironments were somewhat more wooded than today. The fossil fauna is highly diverse and includes extinct species such as the browsing chalicothere (*Ancylotherium hennigi*; Sponheimer et al., 2001). Stable carbon isotope studies on the chalicothere, as well as other perissodactyl fossils (e.g., *Hipparion lybicum*), indicate that the habitat hosted a high percentage of browsing taxa, suggesting that the site had woodland, riverine forest, and grasslands in close proximity (Sponheimer et al., 2001).

For the micromammal-derived habitat signal, Leichliter (2018) indicates that Makapansgat habitat possessed the highest percentage of woody vegetation (45 percent) of all hominin sites examined. Stable carbon isotopes of the micromammal species from Rodent Corner and the Exit Quarry localities also indicate browsing micromammals and a lack of grazing specialists (Hopley et al., 2006). Reptiles are preserved, specifically tortoises from the Grey Breccia (Broadley, 1962; de Lapparent de Broin, 2000).

Pollen analysis suggests that the Member 2 temporal period prior to the deposition of Member 3 was forested, but shifting to grasslands (Cadman and Rayner, 1989). Environments during Member 3 times were again more forested, but were characterized by more woodland than forest (Cadman and Rayner, 1989; Reed et al., Chapter 7, this volume).

Buffalo Cave

Buffalo Cave, in the Makapan Valley, has been known since the 1940s but was only excavated after 1993 (Kuykendall et al., 1995). There are no hominins reported from this site. The *in-situ* fossil deposits appear to date to between 1.07 and 0.78 Ma based on paleomagnetic and biostratigraphic correlations with eastern African fauna (Herries et al., 2006a).

Identified fossil material (*ex situ*, from miners' dumps) includes Bovidae, Suidae, Felidae, Hyaenidae, Equidae, and Cercopithecidae, with some extinct species, such as *Hipparion* and the enigmatic ovibovin *Bos makapani*, first published by Robert Broom (1937), for which the cave is named. This combination of extant and extinct species suggests that some temporal mixing of these faunal elements might have occurred. Preservation of micromammals and some reptile fossils has been documented (Kuykendall et al., 1995). The types of species represented in the Buffalo Cave faunal assemblage suggest savanna or grassland environments, dominated by alcelaphin species, such as the bontebok (*Damaliscus*) and the wildebeest (*Connochaetes*), as well as the presence of equids (*Equus* and *Hipparion*). The Cape Buffalo (*Syncerus*) and two other bovid species (*Redunca* and *Tragelaphus*) suggest a forested, wetter habitat at some time during fossil deposition. Either this suggests a mosaic habitat with gallery forest or the presence of several different breccia types at Buffalo Cave, which may suggest that the material derives from different climatic phases (Kuykendall et al., 1995).

Hopley and colleagues (2007a, 2007b, 2018) propose that, based on the speleothem records of this cave, southern Africa experienced a sudden reduction in rainfall with an increase in grasslands at *ca.* 1.7 Ma, like eastern Africa (Trauth et al., 2005), and which may reflect the onset of the Walker Circulation.

Malapa

Malapa site lies in a steep-sided valley, roughly 15 km north-northwest of the Sterkfontein site, and close to Johannesburg in the Gauteng Province. This is the Type Site for *Australopithecus sediba*. The 2008 discovery of the site yielded three partial *Australopithecus sediba* skeletons (Berger et al., 2010; L'Abbé et al., 2015). This deposit has been dated to 1.977 Ma, and the fossils are encased in water-laid sediments (Dirks et al., 2010).

The Malapa bovid fossils include common grazers such as *Megalotragus* and *Equus*, which are consistent with the presence of grasslands, but also the klipspringer (*Oreotragus* sp.), which indicates rocky outcrops (Dirks et al., 2010). The presence of two tragelaphins, namely the bushbuck (*Tragelaphus* cf. *scriptus*) and the kudu (*Tragelaphus* cf. *strepsiceros*), indicate woodland in the vicinity. Inferences made from carnivorans from the site suggest a mix of open and wooded habitats (Kuhn et al., 2011). Non-hominin primate remains are rare, and only a partial cranium of a baboon, assigned to *Papio angusticeps*, is presently known (Gilbert et al., 2015). A well-preserved *Metridiochoerus* partial cranium has been described (Lazagabaster et al., 2018a).

Micromammal preservation appears to be good, with at least one elephant shrew (*Elephantulus* sp.) hemi-mandible specimen being subject to 3D scanning and digital reconstruction (Val et al., 2011). Insect evidence, specifically of termites and necrophagous insects, has been identified on the *A. sediba* fossils (Backwell et al., 2020). Phytoliths associated with the dentitions of the Malapa hominins have revealed a high diversity of plant types, suggesting a diet of C_4 grasses and C_3 dicotyledonous plants (Henry et al., 2012). Botanical remains from a carnivore coprolite indicate the presence of conifer plants (*Podocarpus*), suggesting that habitats were cooler and moister than at present (Bamford et al., 2010). Overall, the paleoenvironmental studies suggest areas with abundant grass and woody vegetation around the time of fossil deposition.

Hoogland

This site is located on the Hennops River and lies 22.5 km west of Pretoria in the Schurveberg mountains. Robert Broom prospected the region in 1936 and collected fossils referred to as the "Schurveberg collection" (Adams et al., 2010). Among these were several important specimens, including the type specimen of *Papio* (*Dinopithecus*) *ingens* and a mandible that was originally attributed to "*Felis whitei*" (now *Megantereon cultridens*). Later excavations produced a modest sample of fossils, but no hominins or archaeological material. Paleomagnetic analyses combined with biochronological indicators suggest that fossil deposition occurred over an extended temporal period, between 2.5 and 3.0 Ma.

Recent stable isotope studies show that Hoogland contains a speleothem record that dates to the Late Miocene (7.25–5.33 Ma) and records a predominantly C_3-dominated vegetation signal based on carbon isotope values (Hopley et al., 2019). This older date therefore represents the maximum age for the Hoogland breccias and material contained within them.

Browsing and grazing bovids, equids, a small sample of carnivores, and hyraxes have been recovered (Adams et al., 2010). Two isolated primate dental specimens have been identified, one of which is assigned to the extinct gelada, *Theropithecus oswaldi*. Indeterminate birds and a snake fossil, assigned provisionally to the Subfamily Pythoninae, have been documented (Adams et al., 2010). The fauna suggests a mix of grassland and woodland during the Hoogland fossil deposition (Adams et al., 2010).

Gondolin

This site lies near the small town of Broederstroom, in the foothills of the Magaliesberg mountains (North West Province). The site, previously quarried for deposits of calcium carbonate speleothem (called limestone), was first excavated in 1979 by Elisabeth Vrba. In 1999, Colin Menter and colleagues published two isolated hominin molars from the Gondolin sediments (Menter et al., 1999). One of these is a robust molar assigned to *Paranthropus* (Kuykendall, 2012). No lithic or bone tools have been recovered from the site to date. There are three fossil-bearing deposits at Gondolin. These are the *ex-situ* GDA deposit and the two *in-situ* deposits, referred to as GD1 and GD2 (Herries and Adams, 2013). Dating analyses using magnetostratigraphy have shown that the main faunal layers of GD2 are slightly older than 1.78 Ma (Herries et al., 2006b).

Fossils include large species less commonly encountered at cave sites, such as hippopotamus and rhinoceros, but with a remarkable dearth of primate material (Watson, 1993b). Of the macromammalian taxa, these are dominated by small-sized bovids, particularly the reedbuck (*Redunca arundinum*) and the fossil klipspringer (*Oreotragus major*). Extinct species, including *Metridiochoerus andrewsi*, *Hipparion steytleri*, and *Equus capensis*, are recorded. A detailed study of the *Metridiochoerus* material was made by Pickford (2013b), who suggested a derived Stage III morphology, and thus a young age of 1.6–1.5 Ma for the deposits, as well as confirming the open grassland aspect of the paleoenvironments. As well as small mammal species, such as rock hares (genus *Pronolagus*), Watson (1993b) reports the reasonably large sample of a large, extinct porcupine (*Hystrix makapansensis*), which is formally described by Adams (2012c). A species list of micromammals by Sénégas and colleagues (2005), shows that the micromammals can be used to reconstruct the post-quarrying deposition of the *ex-situ* material. Fossils of frogs and birds have also been identified (Watson, 1993b).

No evidence for fossil pollen or insects has been published to date. Based on the types of faunal species present, the paleoenvironment is described as being dominated by grassland, rocky outcrops, and close to a source of permanent water near the entrance to the dolomitic cave (Watson, 1993b). This paleoenvironmental reconstruction was subsequently confirmed by stable carbon isotope analyses of enamel from the GD2 fauna (Adams, 2012b).

Luleche

The recently discovered site lies close to Gondolin in the Skurweberg Mountains in the North-West Province. All fossil material studied to date derives from faunal collection from *ex-situ* breccia dumped after quarrying for calcium carbonate speleothem deposits by miners. No archeological material or hominins have been recovered from the site, which has little *in-situ* breccia (Adams et al., 2007).

The absence of temporal indicators means that there is little idea about how old the site and deposits may be, but the faunal composition is consistence with others of known late Pliocene/early Pleistocene age (Adams et al., 2007). The bovid-dominated fossil assemblage suggests rocky, mostly grassland habitats, with a wooded component, specifically with the presence of the klipspringer (*Oreotragus oreotragus*), various alcelaphins, and a single individual attributed to the nyala (*Tragelaphus angasi*; Adams et al., 2007). There are no indications of reptiles, birds or micromammals, invertebrates, or pollen preservation from the site to date.

Haasgat

Haasgat lies on a steep slope of the Skurweberg range in the upper reaches of the Witwatersrand Spruit (Plug and Keyser, 1994). As with many sites in the region, the locality was heavily mined, resulting in two breccia accumulations: the *ex-situ* dump-derived, and the *in-situ* deposits. The site was first studied in 1987 (Keyser and Martini, 1991), with dates of >1.95 Ma, which have been published using a combination of biochronology and paleomagnetic dating (Herries et al., 2014). A more recent date suggests that the sediments are 1.6 Ma for the middle flowstone (Pickering et al., 2019). There are no records of stone tools, and only a single fragment of unidentifiable hominin molar has been found (Leece et al., 2016), but primate specimens of *Papio angusticeps* have been recovered (McKee and Keyser, 1994). A new species of cercopithecoid monkey has been named from the site, *Cercopithecoides haasgati* (McKee, et al., 2011). In total, three extinct species of primate are known from the site (Adams and Rovinsky, 2018). Plug and Keyser (1994) state that the site is also the oldest known occurrence of the gray duiker (*Sylvicapra grimmia*) in Africa.

A diverse macromammalian species list by Plug and Keyser (1994; also Adams, 2012a), shows a mix of extinct and extant forms of the same genera, for example springbok (*Antidorcas bondi* and *A. marsupialis*) and equids (*Equus quagga* and extinct *E. capensis*). Based on the presence of indicator taxa, such as the two species of klipspringer (*Oreotragus major* and *O. oreotragus*), rock hyraxes, both extinct and extant (*Procavia transvaalensis* and *P. capensis*, respectively), indicate that there were rocky outcrops, and high numbers of grazing taxa indicate extensive grasslands nearby (*Equus* and alcelaphins). The presence of giraffe (*Giraffe camelopardalis*) and kudu (*Tragelaphus strepsiceros*) listed by Plug and Keyser (1994) suggest woodland, although Adams (2012a) suggests that giraffe is absent. Finally, species associated with swamps and wetland (e.g., waterbuck, *Kobus ellipsiprymnus*) and lechwe (*Kobus leche*) suggest that water was present during bone accumulation (Plug and Keyser, 1994). This suggests that, although the topography has remained similar, the site catchment area became drier over time (Plug and Keyser, 1994; but see Adams, 2012a). Stable isotope analyses of the herbivore fauna suggest that diets were relatively more C_3-dominated but with a C_4 grazing signal too (Adams et al., 2013). Micromammals and reptiles have been recovered (Adams et al., 2015).

Gladysvale

This Middle Pleistocene site lies 13 km east of Sterkfontein and has been known since the 1990s and excavated between 1991 and 1992 (Berger et al., 1993). This site was originally mined for bat guano and calcium carbonate during the early 1900s (Berger and Tobias, 1994). There are fossil deposits of various ages present and the Gladysvale Internal Deposit has been dated with uranium series methods to between the Late–Mid-Pleistocene (~570 ka) and the Holocene (~7 ka; Pickering et al., 2007). Hominin fossils include dental specimens assigned to *Australopithecus* cf. *africanus* and a single subadult proximal hominin phalanx (Schmid and Berger, 1997). An Acheulean handaxe has been recovered from decalcified material at the site (Berger et al., 2006).

The vertebrate species include extinct genera such as *Pachycrocuta*, *Dinofelis*, and *Makapania*, as well as a diverse range of micromammal and bat species (Berger et al., 1993; Lacruz et al., 2002). The presence of the black rhinoceros (*Diceros bicornis*) and extinct elephant, *Elephas* sp., suggest that woodland and tree cover was present. The presence of grazers (equids and alcelaphins) indicates a predominantly savanna grassland habitat during the fossil accumulation (Berger et al., 1993). A new species of ancestral wild dog, named *Lycaon sekowei*, was described from the site by Hartstone-Rose and colleagues (2010).

An abundant micromammal assemblage of 29 species, including insectivores, bats, and rodents is documented (Avery, 1995b). A fossil *in-situ* brown hyena (*Parahyaena brunnea*) latrine has been recovered and one of the hyena coprolites preserves ancient human hair (Backwell et al., 2009; Berger et al., 2009). Microscopic fossil snails (*Rophidophora insularis*) suggest arboreal vegetation existed in the vicinity (Pickering et al., 2007).

Floral fossils include rare seeds of the wild date palm (*Phoenix reclinata*) and date to approximately 6 ka (Bamford, 2000). Overall, evidence from flowstone stable isotopes suggest a high proportion of C_3 plants (40–75 percent) but with consistent presence of C_4 plants over the same time interval (Pickering et al., 2007). Given that the deposition was episodic, it is likely that the fauna accumulated during different climatic phases.

Motsetse

The site lies roughly 16 km to the northeast of Sterkfontein. Known since 1999, the site was briefly excavated in the early 2000s (Berger and Lacruz, 2003). There are three main fossil-bearing members identified, referred to as Upper, Middle, and Lower deposits. Successful radiometric dating has not been done on the site or the material, but biochronological estimates have been used to date the deposition to between 1.64 and 1.0 Ma (Berger and Lacruz, 2003). Although hominin and primate fossils have not been recovered from the site to date, there is a fossil assemblage from decalcified deposits.

The mammalian species list includes extinct species, such as the saber-toothed *Dinofelis piveteaui*, but most of the assemblage is extant, grassland genera and species, such as *Equus*, *Connochaetes*, *Damaliscus*, and *Antidorcas* (Berger and Lacruz, 2003). In contrast, the presence of gray rhebok (*Pelea capreolus*) indicates montane grasslands with some woodland suggested by the presence of the kudu (*Tragelaphus strepsiceros*). The abundance of rock hyrax specimens (*Procavia capensis*) and the klipspringer (*Oreotragus oreotragus*) together indicate rocky outcrops.

Little is currently known as far as micromammal and non-mammalian faunal evidence (reptiles, birds) is concerned. Preliminary mentions of fossilized pupae exposed in the Lower deposit suggest that insect preservation is likely (Berger and Lacruz, 2003). Overall, the mammal species indicate paleoenvironments with mainly grassland with some woodland and rocky outcrops in the vicinity.

Drimolen

This site, lying 7 km north of Sterkfontein, was first excavated in 1992. Two separate accumulations, referred to as the Main Quarry and the Makondo site, are identified. The Main Quarry has yielded an impressive assemblage of hominin fossils of primarily *Paranthropus robustus* but also some early *Homo* (Keyser et al., 2000). A juvenile hominin cranium assigned to *Homo erectus* has been recovered (Herries et al., 2020). The Main Quarry sediments were deposited over a brief period between 2.04 and 1.95 Ma, and the Makondo deposits have been dated to approximately 2.61 Ma (Herries et al., 2018, 2020). A small number of stone tools (*n* = 6) are known from the Main Quarry site (Kuman, 2003; Stammers et al., 2018), while a slightly larger assemblage of bone tools (*n* = 22) has been recovered (Backwell and d'Errico, 2008). The site has produced an abundance of hominin remains, and hominin age-at-death studies show natural mortality patterns, such as those observed in wild ape populations (Riga et al., 2019). This indicates different accumulation scenarios for this site relative to Swartkrans, where the "young adult" age category is poorly represented at Drimolen compared with Swartkrans (Riga et al., 2019).

Although many of the associated fauna listed in Keyser et al. (2000) do not provide any biochronological signal, the overall paleoenvironmental signal is one of dry grasslands, dominated by grazing bovids such as wildebeest (*Connochaetes*) and the extinct giant hartebeest (*Megalotragus*). Subsequent research has revealed a faunal assemblage representing 14 mammalian families including suids (*Metridiochoerus* sp.) and equids (cf. *Eurygnathohippus cornelianus*), but has further consolidated the picture of grassland habitats between 1.5 and 2.0 Ma (Adams et al., 2016). Recent discoveries of *in-situ* primate and carnivore material from the Makondo site show similar faunal compositions to the Main Quarry (Rovinsky et al., 2015).

A detailed, diverse micromammal species list was published by Sénégas and colleagues (2005). Broadley (1997) described a new species of fossil tortoise, *Psammobates antiquorum*, based on a well-preserved carapace from the site. Overall, the evidence points to open grassland habitats during the time of hominin presence in the site region.

Plovers Lake

This site lies in the Blaaubank river valley, roughly 6 km northeast of Swartkrans and Sterkfontein, and contains one of the youngest fossil deposits currently known from the Cradle of Humankind. Two separate fossiliferous deposits, FBU1 and PDU, are identified. The Late Pleistocene deposits have been dated using uranium series of the flowstone to between ~62.9 and ~88.7 ka (de Ruiter et al., 2008b). An assemblage of Middle Stone Age-like tools, cut-marked bones, and human skeletal remains have been recovered, which Lombard et al. (2019) suggest may be more recent Iron Age humans.

Macromammalian and microfaunal remains, as well as isolated remains of birds, reptiles, and fish have been recovered. The presence of species like the forest buffalo (*Syncerus caffer*) suggests a greater degree of tree cover in the past than is present today. Water-dependant taxa (e.g., water mongoose, Cape clawless otter, and hippopotamus) indicate that the area was moister than today. Finally, antilopin species like *Antidorcas bondi* indicate the presence of grassland.

Birds are well represented in the PDU, although they are rarer in the FBU1. The avifauna preserved at the site includes a species of lovebird, which suggests a degree of tree cover (Stidham, 2010). Reptile fossils, including tortoises and monitor lizards, are known from both deposits (de Ruiter et al., 2008b). The FBU1 sample contains a virtually complete vertebral column of a small snake. A single fish vertebra has been recorded from the FBU1 assemblage (de Ruiter et al., 2008b). Although no insect remains have been recorded, insect damage (likely termite in origin) has been identified on Plovers Lake fossils (Backwell et al., 2012). The overall paleoenvironmental reconstruction is of a permanent surface water body, with a mix of grasslands and greater woodland than at present (de Ruiter, et al., 2008b).

Minaars

This site lies close to Sterkfontein and was initially prospected by Robert Broom, but the exact location was subsequently lost. Gommery et al. (2012b) have identified the likely location of the site and provide an account for the faunal species and depositional context of this lesser-known Pleistocene cave sequence. The site is best known for the jackal cranium initially assigned to *Thos antiquus* by Broom, now referred to as *Canis mesomelas* (Broom and Schepers, 1946; Ewer, 1956). Apart from this, a male *Papio angusticeps* is known from dental and postcranial material. Preliminary records of indeterminate alcelaphins, springbok (cf. *Antidorcas* sp.), the extinct Cape horse (*Equus capensis*), and other equids (*Equus* sp.) suggest a grassland-dominated environment of uncertain age. Very little is known regarding preservation of various vertebrate and invertebrate taxonomic groups at present (Gommery et al., 2012b).

Kromdraai

Kromdraai, lying roughly 2 km east of Sterkfontein, was discovered by Robert Broom in 1936 and is the Type Site for *Paranthropus robustus* (Broom, 1938a; Fourvel and Thackeray, Chapter 8, this volume). There are two brecciated fossil-bearing deposits, designated Kromdraai A (KA) and B (KB). Kromdraai A lacks hominin fossils and is sometimes referred to as the "Faunal site". A substantial stone tool assemblage has been recovered from Kromdraai (n = 100 stone tools and manuports; Kuman, 2003). Kromdraai B, divided into five Members, has yielded fossils of *Paranthropus robustus* and a small number of specimens more like early *Homo* (Braga and Thackeray, 2003). These two sites and their faunal assemblages were previously considered to be two separate deposits, but now are considered as one cave complex (Braga and Thackeray, 2016).

An abundance of taxonomic groups, including six families of carnivores and several primate species, is represented (Heaton, 2006; Fourvel and Thackeray, Chapter 8, this volume). Several new and rare species have been described from the site, including a rare fossil honeybadger (genus *Mellivora*; Gommery, et al., 2008) and a new viverrid, *Civettictis braini* (Fourvel, 2018).

Abundant reptiles and bird species have been reported, including a lovebird (Brain, 1975b; Stidham, 2009) and a new species of ibis, *Geronticus thackerayi* (Pavia, 2019). The bird species indicate a grassy environment with some tree cover, set among rocky cliffs (Fourvel et al., 2016).

The majority of the paleoenvironmental work relies on the presence of indicator herbivore species (Fourvel and Thackeray, Chapter 8, this volume). The presence of savanna grassland is inferred from alcelaphins (*Alcelaphus*, *Damaliscus*) and antilopins (*Antidorcas*), as well as other grazing species (e.g., *Equus*). Despite the strong grassland signal, there are wetland-dwelling taxa present, like the Cape clawless otter, (*Aonyx capensis*) and species more closely linked to the presence of more wooded habitats (such as tragelaphins, *Parapapio*, and *Cercopithecoides*).

Isotopic analysis of preserved micromammals indicates grassland habitats (Thackeray et al., 1999). Overall, the paleoenvironmental reconstructions all point to a similar mix of grassland, with some woodland in the proximity to water and associated wetlands.

Cooper's Cave

Cooper's Cave is located between the sites of Sterkfontein and Kromdraai and was discovered in 1938 when the first hominin was identified by J.C. Middleton Shaw (Berger et al., 2003). De Ruiter (Chapter 9) provides a brief site overview. The hominins, the majority of which are assigned to *Paranthropus robustus*, are dated to between 1.5 and 1.4 Ma, and are associated with primates, carnivores, suids, bovids, and an unusually high number of mongoose species (Cohen et al., 2019). A sample of Early Pleistocene stone tools has been recently been recovered from Cooper's D (Sutton et al., 2017).

Most of the faunal assemblage appears to have been accumulated by carnivores, with hyaenids, including *Chasmaporthetes*, *Crocuta ultra*, and *Parahyaena brunnea*, all represented (Kuhn et al., 2017). The fauna at the site preserve traces of insect boring into the cortical bone surfaces (Parkinson, 2016). Preliminary research at the site indicates the presence of several frog species, including *Amietia*, and the burrowing frog species *Tomopterna* and *Breviceps* (Matthews, pers. comm.). The overall paleoenvironmental signal suggests grasslands, with some woodland and a nearby permanent water source (de Ruiter, Chapter 9).

Sterkfontein

Sterkfontein is arguably one of the most important sites in southern Africa and is the only site with a series of chronologically successive Members from roughly 3.67 ± 0.16 Ma (Granger et al., 2015) to the mid-Pleistocene, with the Lincoln Cave deposits, dating to between 252,600 ± 35,600 and 115,300 ± 7,700 years (Reynolds et al., 2003, 2007).

Several species of hominins have been discovered from this site, as well as stone tools of the Earlier Stone Age (Oldowan, Early Acheulean), and Middle Stone Age (reviewed in Reynolds and Kibii, 2011). The oldest and most complete *Australopithecus* skeleton derives from the Silberberg Grotto at this site (Clarke and Kuman, 2019), as well as important crania, such as *Australopithecus africanus* (Sts 5) and *Homo habilis* (StW 53), which features possible defleshing marks made by stone tools, like those observed from Bodo and Herto in Ethiopia (White, 1986; Pickering et al., 2000; Clark et al., 2003).

The majority of the paleoenvironmental and habitat reconstruction work was initially done by Elisabeth Vrba (1975, 1976), who considered the habitats of the Bovidae species present, specifically the AAC (Alcelaphini and Antilopini Criterion) as a key indicator of open, arid, grassland habitats. More recently, this framework has been complemented by a deeper understanding of the stable carbon isotope signals from fossil enamel (Sponheimer and Lee-Thorp, 1999; Luyt and Lee-Thorp, 2003; van der Merwe et al., 2003; Lee-Thorp et al., 2007; Sewell et al., Chapter 10, this volume), as well as the habitat preferences of the micromammal species represented (Avery, 2001; Avery et al., 2010). Several species of birds have bene identified from deposits such as the Name Chamber (Val and Stratford, 2015). Rare fossil remains, such as fragments of fossilized wood (Bamford, 1999), provide important insights to the habitats. Various pollen types have been recovered from the speleothems of Members 4 and 5 (Carrión and Scott, 1999).

Re-examination of previously excavated material, such as the hominin skeleton StW 431 (from Member 4) with high-resolution microcomputed tomography, has revealed traces of postmortem boring damage by insects (Odes et al., 2017). Frogs, reptiles, and birds have all been recovered from the site (Pocock, 1969; Tobias and Hughes, 1969).

Given the proximity to the Blaaubank stream, the paleoenvironments sampled appear to show heterogeneous habitats through time, with grassland, woodland, and gallery forest all well-represented throughout the sequence, with the relative proportions varying from more wooded pre-Member 5 to less wooded after the beginning of Member 5, so approximately 1.7 Ma (Luyt and Lee-Thorp, 2003; Sewell et al., Chapter 10, this volume). The site provides context regarding key climatic and habitat shifts, in association with faunal changes and hominin behavioral changes.

Swartkrans

This site lies close to Sterkfontein and was discovered by Robert Broom and John Robinson in 1948 (Figure 6.1). Charles "Bob" Brain excavated the site from 1965 onwards, making invaluable contributions to the understanding of the site itself, but also more widely to issues of fossil taphonomy (Brain, 1981; Brain et al., 1988; Brain, 1993a, 1993b, 1993c; de RuiterChapter 11). Swartkrans contains five Members of varying ages. The Swartkrans Formation ranges from ~2.19 to 1.80 Ma for Member 1, to the younger deposit, Member 3 ~0.96 Ma (reviewed in Gibbon et al., 2014; de Ruiter, Chapter 11). Members 4 and 5 are younger deposits, with ages of ~110 ka and ~12–9 ka, respectively (Brain, 1993b; Watson, 1993a; Sutton et al., 2009). Swartkrans was the first site to reveal evidence of two coexisting hominin genera and is one of the largest repositories of *Paranthropus robustus*, as well as the last appearance datum (LAD) for this species.

Swartkrans contains a sample of burnt bones that potentially documents the earliest hominin-controlled use of fire (Brain and Sillen, 1988). A recently identified burnt primate cuboid bone from Member 3 (Pickering et al., 2017) enlarges this sample of earliest burnt bones. Strontium isotopes (reflecting the influence of hydrology) have been used to reconstruct the likely hominin use of the landscape around Swartkrans, specifically examining evidence for use of riparian and non-riparian plants (Sillen et al., 1998; see also Copeland et al., 2011). Overall, hominin mortality patterns suggest predation by carnivores, such as the leopard (*Panthera pardus*; Brain, 1993a, 1993b, 1993c; Riga et al., 2019).

This site shows paleoenvironmental change through time, via several different paleoenvironmental proxies as outlined by de Ruiter (Chapter 11; Sewell, et al., 2019). The majority of paleoecological work derives from the presence of herbivore species and inferences about their paleoecology (e.g., Vrba 1974, 1975). Later work by Reed (1997) and Reed and Rector (2006) found evidence for forested areas and edaphic grasslands within this open habitat.

The macromammalian fossil record is extensive and comprises mainly grazing faunas, such as three species of equids (*Equus quagga*, *E. capensis*, and *Eurygnathohippus lybicum*) while springbok and several alcelaphins are abundantly represented (de Ruiter, 2003, Chapter 11). In contrast, the lechwe (*Kobus* cf. *leche*) and the southern reedbuck (*Redunca arundinum*) suggest the presence of closed, wetter habitats, and the Cape clawless otter (*Aonyx capensis*), marsh mongoose (*Atilax* sp.) and hippopotamus suggest the presence of water.

Microfaunal species comprise 29 species, including insectivores, bats, elephant-shrews, and other rodent species. The habitat reconstructions based on microfauna identified from across the Swartkrans Members indicates grasslands in the presence of surface water and with slightly higher temperatures than today (Avery, 1998, 2001). In summary, the evidence suggests that the Swartkrans habitat was not very different to today, with an open habitat comprised of significant grasslands, a large, permanent river (the paleo-Bloubank River), and the likely presence of edaphic grasslands.

Rising Star/Dinaledi Cave

Rising Star Cave lies 2.2 km west of the Sterkfontein Caves and is the Type site of a new hominin species, *Homo naledi* (Berger et al., 2015). The site was excavated between 2013 and 2014. In total, 1500 fossils representing at least 15 hominin individuals have been recovered, including a juvenile (Dirks et al., 2017; Bolter et al., 2020). Staining and erosion of the hominin fossils suggest that reworking has taken place (Dirks et al., 2015, 2017). Three separate groups of sediments have been identified, namely, Units 1, 2, and 3, with all hominins deriving from a narrow (20–30 cm) horizon, referred to as Sub-unit 3b.

Dating of the hominin-bearing sediments via a variety of methods (paleomagnetic analyses, uranium series, and electron spin resonance) has provided dates of between 236 ka and 414 ka (Dirks et al., 2017). The cavern context suggests that these individuals may have been deliberately placed within the cavern after death (Dirks et al., 2015).

These hominin fossils are not associated with a macromammalian faunal assemblage, and the exception appears to be the preservation of a juvenile baboon tooth (Dirks et al., 2017) and the remains of barn owl (*Tyto alba*) that has been identified (Kruger and Badenhorst, 2018). Future work will offer greater insight into the nature of the paleoenvironments of this hominin species.

Bolt's Farm Deposits

This site lies 3 km southwest of Sterkfontein. It is composed of 23 separate breccia-filled cavities within the dolomite, with no direct association between the fossils of these pits, the coordinates of which are published by Sénégas et al. (2002). Robert Broom first examined the fossil material in detail, and no hominins, bone tools, or stone tools have been recovered from the Bolt's Farm sites to date (Broom, 1937). Reviews of the site excavation history are published elsewhere (Gommery et al., 2008, 2012a; Thackeray et al., 2008). Detailed early excavation was done by researchers from the University of California Africa Expeditions (Camp, 1948). The Bolt's Farm fossils that remain housed in various collections in the University of California Berkeley campus have been identified and published by Monson et al. (2015).

Biochrononology was first used to establish the deposit ages; however, recent uranium–lead flowstone dates for some of the pits by Pickering et al. (2019) indicate a more recent range of dates from 2.6 Ma (Pit 14) and 1.3 Ma (Pit 7). One of these breccia localities, Waypoint 160, was previously suggested to be as old as 4.5–4.0 Ma, based on biochronology alone; however, Pickering et al. (2019) suggest a range of dates of 2.2–1.7 Ma for the Waypoint 160 flowstones.

The Bolts Farm material is clearly rich in a diversity of vertebrate species. Most of the pits contain fossils that represent both grazing and browsing ungulate species (e.g., Badenhorst, et al., 2011). Several species of extinct primates have been identified, including *Parapapio* sp. and *Theropithecus* (Gilbert, 2007b;

Gommery et al., 2008; 2019), as well as suid species which suggest that the oldest suid material may be of similar age as that found at Makapansgat (Pickford and Gommery, 2016, 2020). The springbok horncores from Pit 3 represent several species of fossil *Antidorcas*, which indicates that grassland with some browse was present between 1.5 and 1.0 Ma (Reynolds, 2007a). Pit 4, also known as Garage Ravine Cave (estimated to date anywhere from 2.0 to 0.1 Ma), preserves the Cape zebra (*Equus capensis*), as well as large alcelaphin (*Alcelaphus/Connochaetes*) and eland (*Tragelaphus oryx*) and a jackal (*Canis mesomelas*; Badenhorst et al., 2011). Habitat preferences of the browsing and grazing bovid fauna from X Cave (thought to be younger than 2.5 Ma), including the klipspringer (*Oreotragus oreotragus*), suggest rocky outcrops, grassland, woodland, and a permanent water source, much like the present-day site (van Zyl et al., 2016).

Several bird species are present, including a bird of prey (Falconiformes; Badenhorst et al., 2011) and a bald ibis (*Geronticus* cf. *calvus*; Pavia et al., 2017). A range of fossil traces (mammal coprolites) and small vertebrate species such as amphibians, micromammals (including hedgehogs, shrews, and bats), birds, and reptile fossils have been identified in the University of California, Berkeley collections (Monson et al., 2015). Taken together, the habitat associations of these identified species suggest a heterogeneous habitat with abundant grass in close association with a source of permanent water (Pickford and Gommery, 2016).

Goldsmith's Farm

This site lies close to Sterkfontein and fossils from a small-scale excavation have been analyzed and published by W.D. Mokokwe (2006). No hominins, artifacts, or radiometric dating have yet been published from the site, although isolated stone tools are present. Over 68 percent of the identifiable fossil material represents carnivores, including the extinct saber-toothed cat, *Dinofelis barlowi*, which is taken as the chief indicator that the material is older than 1.4 Ma, which is the LAD of this species (Lewis, 1997; Mokokwe, 2006).

Despite the higher proportion of carnivores, any evidence that the site was a den is absent, with no evidence of chewed bone, juvenile carnivore individuals, or coprolites (Mokokwe, 2006). Some primates (representing either *Papio* or *Parapapio*) are preserved. The bovids, representing a tragelaphin and medium-sized alcelaphin (*Damaliscus*), are also present.

There is a modest collection of bird fossils known from the site, as well as other mammalian fossils (such as hare). The presence of *Dinofelis* and baboons is considered indicative of some woodland, while the alcelaphin suggests grassland in the area (Mokokwe, 2006). Little is known of insects or plant fossil preservation, but there is scope for more detailed paleoenvironmental work at this site.

Buxton-Norlim Limeworks/Taung

This is the Type site of *Australopithecus africanus* and the first hominin site discovered in Africa (Dart, 1925a). This site consists of 17 identified fossil-bearing localities, revealed by prospection and quarrying for calcium carbonate speleothem deposits (Dart, 1925a; Kuhn et al., 2016). Despite intensive excavations during the early years after the discovery, the juvenile Taung child remains the only hominin recovered to date (Dart, 1925a; Hopley and Kuhn, Chapter 13, this volume) and dating of the fossils has proven complex. Earlier faunal dating suggested an age of 2.6–2.8 Ma (McKee, 1993a), with recent estimates lying between 3.03 and 2.58 Ma (Kuhn et al., 2016). Younger deposits are also present: another previously undescribed locality, named Tunnel Wall, preserves Middle Stone Age and Later Stone Age tools in association with an assemblage of ostrich eggshell fragments (Monson et al., 2015).

Early excavations in 1947 by the U.C. Africa Expedition aimed to recover more hominin specimens (Camp, 1948; summarized in Monson et al., 2015), while recent fieldwork has focused on increasing the paleoenvironmental data and gaining a greater understanding of the stratigraphy and site formation processes (Kuhn et al., 2016; Hopley and Kuhn, Chapter 13, this volume).

Macromammalian fauna associated with the hominin include numerous primate species, and one extinct suid, *Notochoerus* cf. *capensis*. Of the bovids, the nyala (*Tragelaphus* cf. *angasii*) and buffalo (*Syncerus* cf. *acoelotus*) suggest a somewhat more wooded component in contrast to the grasslands suggested by the gazelles (*Gazella* sp.). There are numerous fossils of smaller vertebrate fauna, such as bats, reptiles, birds, and amphibians, and micromammals that have been identified in the California-held collections (Monson et al., 2015). Fossil terrapin (Pelomedusidae) and freshwater crab (*Potamonautes* sp.) remains have also been recorded from the pink deposits (Hrdlička, 1925; Kuhn et al., 2016; Hopley and Kuhn, Chapter 13, this volume), indicating aquatic habitats, specifically with the presence of a well-oxygenated ephemeral or seasonal river or stream close to the site.

Pieces of fossilized eggshell represent several bird species, probably a raptor (possibly a species of black eagle), an owl species, and a helmeted guineafowl (Kuhn et al., 2015; Hopley and Kuhn, Chapter 13, this volume). The hominin and other primate material were accumulated by a bird of prey, such as the Crowned Eagle (*Stephanoaetus coronatus*; Berger and Clarke, 1995; Berger, 2006).

A recovered fossil carder bee nest (ichnogenus *Celliforma*) suggests that angiosperms (flowering plants) were present (Parker et al., 2016), in addition to an abundance of other insects and insect traces identified in the deposits. The presence of ground-nesting insects is significant as an indicator of the preservation of paleosols at the site, rather than sedimentary deposition within a cave (Hopley et al., 2013; Parker et al., 2016). Leaf impressions in the tufa of the site are described by Bamford (2000).

Overall, the insects, eggshell, and faunal evidence suggest a dry grassland habitat, with a significant wetland and riverine wooded component, like the mix of habitat types found at the site today.

Younger Sites in the Southern African Interior

These sites fall within the interior of South Africa, in a wide arc from Bushman Rock Shelter in the North to Rose Cottage Cave in the south (Figure 6.1).

Bushman Rock Shelter

The Bushman Rock Shelter (BRS) is situated in the district of Ohrigstad (Limpopo Province, South Africa). The deposits contain Middle Stone Age, Later Stone Age, and Iron Age artifacts. Previous excavations carried out in the 1960s and 1970s are reviewed in Porraz et al. (2015). The oldest deposits are Pleistocene, and the younger deposits sample the terminal Pleistocene/Holocene transition.

The macromammalian faunal assemblage is dominated by grazing bovids and equids, suggestive of a mix of woodland and rocky outcrops. Rare species, namely the pangolin (*Smutsia temminckii*) and the aardvark (*Orycteropus afer*), are represented (Badenhorst and Plug, 2012). The species list includes birds, reptiles, fish, amphibians, and land snails (Badenhorst and Plug, 2012). Ostrich eggshell is preserved in the deposits, and seeds and other botanical remains have been recovered. The sediments preserve plant food items, such as marula (*Sclerocarya birrea*) fruits and African potato (genus *Hypoxis*) corms (Plug, 1981; Wadley, 1987; Mitchell, 2002). Unusually, the giant land snails (*Achatina* sp.) and tortoises are common in the assemblages, followed by ungulates and monitor lizards (*Varanus* sp.; Porraz et al., 2015). Based on proportions of grazing species versus browsing species, the overall environmental signal appears to indicate a savanna woodland environment (Badenhorst and Plug, 2012).

Border Cave

This cave lies on the border with South Africa's KwaZulu Natal Province and Swaziland (Klein, 1977). Excavations were begun by Raymond Dart in 1934. Field seasons conducted in 1941–1942 (University of the Witwatersrand and the Bureau of Archaeology) revealed an infant skeleton, whose grave was cut into older sediments (Cooke et al., 1945; Grün and Beaumont, 2001). As such, the cave contains some of the earliest material assigned to anatomically modern humans, but in a secondary context (Grün et al., 1990). Evidence of hearths has been recovered (Butzer et al., 1978). The oldest sediments have been dated to 200 ka using electron spin resonance (Grün and Beaumont, 2001).

The species list indicates extant fauna, but also with extinct Cape zebra (*Equus capensis*) and extinct springbok (*Antidorcas bondi*), contrasting with the appearance of early domesticates in later levels (sheep/goat). The mammalian diversity appears quite limited, probably due to the high levels of bone fragmentation (Klein, 1977).

Based on the types of micromammal species represented, early phases (130 ka), were dominated by miombo (*Brachystegia*) woodland with 25–100 percent higher rainfall than the present day. Drier winters with greater seasonality may have prevailed at this time. In later periods (around 96 ka) vegetation and, consequently, rainfall reflect conditions more like the present-day bush savanna with forest patches (Avery, 1982b, 1992). Overall, the Border Cave Pleistocene paleohabitat resembled "a persistent mosaic of dense, low thickets, particularly along watercourses, and large expanses of grassland and savannah" Klein (1977: 19).

Matjhabeng

The site of Matjhabeng (formerly called Virginia) fills a unique geographic and temporal gap in the fossil records of southern Africa, because it represents a little-sampled Pliocene interval of 4.0–3.5 Ma (de Ruiter et al., 2010b). Excavations conducted between 2007 and 2009 have yielded a diverse fauna that includes fish, amphibians, reptiles, birds, and rodents together with 29 macromammalian taxa. The site contains species common to the older Langebaanweg and the younger Makapansgat. Extinct species represented include *Mammuthus subplanifrons*, *Eurygnathohippus*, chalicotheres (*Ancylotherium*), and sivatheres (*Sivatherium*). Isotopic analysis suggests that the paleoenvironment comprised grasslands with wetland and woodland components. The presence of several aquatic and amphibious species (e.g., hippopotamus and crocodile) suggests a riverine setting (de Ruiter et al., 2010b).

Cornelia-Uitzoek

This open-air site is close to the town of Cornelia in the eastern Free State of South Africa (Figure 6.1). It is located 115 km south of Johannesburg and is the Type locality of the Cornelian Land Mammal Age (Cooke, 1974). The background to the site and excavation history are covered in Brink and colleagues (Chapter 12, this volume). The central plains location of the site, combined with the early *Homo* upper molar and the bone bed in which it has been found, have been dated by paleomagnetism to between 1.07 and 0.99 Ma (Brink et al., 2012; Chapter 12, this volume) and serves to highlight the large geographic area that hominins were ranging over at that time. A sample of 13 Acheulean bifaces and biface-flakes have been recovered, despite which the bones were likely accumulated by hyenas (Brink, 2004; Brink et al., 2012).

The overall paleoenvironmental reconstruction is of surface water and swamps, suggested by hippo (*Hippopotamus gorgops*) and ungulates such as giant long-horned buffalo (*Syncerus antiquus*; Brink, 2004; Brink et al., 2012; Toffolo et al., 2019). Stable carbon isotope data suggest that these habitats were C_4-grassland dominated (Codron et al., 2008). The fossils indicate a combination of freshwater, and largely to semi-arid C_4-grassland conditions, based on a high proportion of equids, alcelaphins, and antilopins, with some bush cover. The mix of extinct and modern forms suggests a transitional phase in the faunal composition, with the former deriving from an East African biogeographic connection but the latter reflecting southern endemism, especially the first appearances of *Connochaetes gnou laticornutus*, *Damaliscus niro*, and the extinct springbok, *Antidorcas bondi* (Brink et al., 2012; Chapter 12, this volume).

Wonderwerk Cave

Wonderwerk Cave lies 45 km south of the town of Kuruman in the Northern Cape Province of South Africa. B.D. Malan first excavated the site in 1943 (Malan and Wells, 1943). The cave is a large dolomitic cavity, with Pleistocene and the Holocene deposits containing Earlier, Middle, and Later Stone Age stone tools (Horwitz and Chazan, 2015; Horwitz et al., Chapter 14, this volume). Paleomagnetic methods have been used to date the deposits to between ~0.78 and 1.96 Ma (Chazan et al., 2008), with evidence that fire was made within the cave at approximately 1.0 Ma ago (Berna et al., 2012).

The plant and faunal preservation are excellent, and a diverse faunal assemblage includes extinct species, such as the equid *Eurygnathohippus* sp. and the giant hyrax *Procavia antiquus*, which suggest the faunal community samples older periods, suggesting habitats were much like the present (Brink et al., 2016). The extreme aridity of the cave has contributed to the exceptional preservation of keratin-sheathed horncore with degraded DNA of an extinct alcelaphin, *Damaliscus niro*, dating to *ca.* 800 ka (Thackeray and Brink, 2004).

The diverse vertebrate fauna includes numerous fragments of ostrich eggshell (*Struthio camelus*) from deposits of varying ages, especially the layers dating to the Early Mid-Pleistocene (Ecker et al., 2015). Fossil leopard tortoise (*Stigmochelys pardalis*) from the deposits has also been analyzed for structural properties and taphonomic inferences (Holt et al., 2019). Micromammals were likely accumulated by an owl, such as the Western barn owl (*Tyto alba*; Fernandez-Jalvo and Avery, 2015).

From the wealth of data available, including pollen evidence, it appears that prior to 1.0 Ma, the environment was generally arid, becoming more so after 1.0 Ma (Scott and Thackeray, 2015; Ecker et al., 2015a, 2015b; Chazan et al., 2020; Horwitz et al., Chapter 14, this volume).

Florisbad

This site, known since 1912, lies 45 km north-northwest of the city of Bloemfontein (Free State Province) and features a spring on the edge of a large pan (playa). The site gives its name to the Florisian Land Mammal Age and is known for the 1936 discovery of the Florisbad cranium (Broom, 1913; Dreyer, 1938; Hendey, 1974; Grün et al., 1996). Dating showed ages of 279 ka for the oldest sediments (electron spin resonance and optically stimulated luminescence), while the hominin was dated to around 259 ka (Grün et al., 1996). The site shows excellent preservation of fauna, pollen, insects, wood, as well as abundant stone tools (Brink, 1987, 1988; Kuman et al., 1999).

Kuman and Clarke (1986) report a mix of extinct and extant mammalian fauna, including *Megalotragus priscus*, *Syncerus* (*Pelorovis*) *antiquus*, *Damaliscus niro*, *Equus capensis*, *Sivatherium maurusium*, and *Antidorcas bondi*. Some of the modern species are strongly associated with aquatic habitats, such as *Hippopotamus amphibius* (hippo), *Aonyx capensis* (the clawless otter), and *Atilax paludinosus* (the water-mongoose). Stable carbon isotope studies suggest that the extinct springbok (*Antidorcas recki*) formed part of an ancient grazing succession, like the present-day Serengeti (Brink and Lee-Thorp, 1992).

Insect traces, specifically of mites, have been identified (Coetzee and Brink, 2003). Wood fragments from the site have been identified by Bamford and Henderson (2003) as a non-local wood species, *Zanthoxylum chalybeum* (Engl.), the kundanyoka knobwood (Rutaceae), which is today found in Zimbabwe. The botanical evidence is presented by Scott and Nyakale (2002) and Scott and Rossouw (2005), and the pollen samples preserved in hyena coprolites analyzed by Scott and colleagues (2003) contain halophytes (Chenopodiaceae) from local salt pans, as well as spring sedges. This in turn suggests hyena activity near the spring and saltpan. The overall paleoenvironmental signal is of grasslands with some woodland in proximity to the spring.

Rose Cottage Cave

This cave is situated on the Platberg in the Free State Province (Wadley, 1997). The site was first excavated by B.D. Malan in the 1940s and has yielded both Middle and Later Stone Age artifacts. The climatic effects of the Maloti-Drakensberg on the surrounding sites, such as Rose Cottage Cave, have been summarized by Stewart and Mitchell (2018). Radiocarbon dating shows that human habitation starting at around 31.3 ka, within the context of changing site conditions (Wadley, 1997). The diverse range of preserved macromammalian species may indicate the hunting proficiency of the humans (Plug and Engela, 1992). Several species recovered from the site are absent from the region today, such as the leopard (*Panthera pardus*) and vervet monkey (*Chlorocebus aethiops*), suggesting that terminal Pleistocene and Early Holocene habitats may have been more wooded.

A mix of extant and extinct herbivore species is evident, with the blue antelope (*Hippotragus leucophaeus*) being represented as well as *Megalotragus priscus*, *Antidorcas bondi*, and *Equus capensis* (Plug and Engela, 1992; Faith and Thompson, 2013).

Several bird species are preserved, including helmeted guineafowl (*Numida melagris*; Plug and Engela, 1992). Micromammal species indicate that a smaller temperature range may have existed during the fossil accumulation, specifically lower summer and higher winter temperatures Avery (1997). The overall signal from the mammal species is that some form of grassland would have prevailed throughout the sequence (Plug and Engela, 1992; Avery, 1997).

Sites of the Southern African Coastal Regions

Many of the sites in this section are coastal; however, some of these sites, such as Boomplaas Cave, are also included in this section, because on the scale of the southern Africa subregion, such sites cluster more naturally with the coastal sites (Figure 6.1).

Elands Bay Cave

Elands Bay Cave (also known as EBC) lies on the Cape Deseada headland. The cave has been excavated since the 1970s and contains a rich cultural and environmental record of the Holocene but includes older occupations (Parkington, 1972, 1976, 1980, 1981; Porraz et al., 2016). This cave was occupied over short, repeated occupation periods between 40 ka and 300 BP (Cartwright and Parkington, 1997). It is considered one of the key sites in the Late Pleistocene/Early Holocene temporal period (Porraz et al., 2016). So called "megamiddens" at the site suggest rising population levels and changing foraging strategies (e.g., Jerardino, 2012, 2016).

The terrestrial mammalian species include one of the very latest occurrences of the giant Cape zebra (*Equus capensis*) dated between 12 ka and 10 ka (Klein and Cruz-Uribe, 2016). The species suggest that the temporal period prior to 10 ka included several grazers such as the springbok (*Antidorcas marsupialis*) in addition to two equids (including the extinct Cape Zebra) and a suid (*Potamachoerus porcus*). However, the presence of the hedgehog, *Erinaceus frontalis*, in these levels indicate wetter conditions than today (Parkington et al., 2000).

Marine mammals include a higher frequency of Cape fur seals (*Arctocephalus pusillus*) at this site relative to neighboring sites like Diepkloof. The average fur seal age suggests people were present mainly in the August–October interval (Steele and Klein, 2013; Klein and Cruz-Uribe, 2016).

Microfauna is present in younger levels (~13 ka to 300 BP) and appears to have been accumulated by owls, rather than humans (Matthews, 1999). The body sizes of the abundant remains of Dune rat (*Bathyergus suillus*) have been used to infer changing rainfall levels (Klein, 1991).

Abundant tortoise remains suggest that humans foraged for naturally occurring tortoise carcasses after wildfires, and median tortoise size suggests that this collection occurred around 10,000 years ago (Avery et al., 2004).

Preserved wood and charcoal fragments, as well as pollen, have been used to infer the past habitats from the Elands Bay Cave (see floral species lists in Cowling et al., 1999, and Parkington et al., 2000). These remains indicate trends in vegetation change, from Afromontane forest and riverine woodland communities after about 18 ka, through mesic thicket and fynbos vegetation in the terminal Pleistocene, and finally moving to the more open, xeric vegetation which is present today. These trends suggest declining regional rainfall over the last 40 ka (Cowling et al., 1999).

Diepkloof Rock Shelter

Diepkloof Rock Shelter lies 180 km north of Cape Town in the Western Cape Province. Excavations first began in 1973 (Parkington and Poggenpoel, 1987). Early evidence of symbolic engraving on a sample of 270 fragments of ostrich eggshells at around 60 ka as well as some human remains have been recovered (Texier et al., 2010; Verna et al., 2013). Sediment dating via optically stimulated luminescence (OSL) and thermoluminescence (TL) methods indicates that the oldest deposits date to ~107 ka and the youngest deposits to ~52 ka (Tribolo et al., 2013). Currently, the shelter is 14 km from the sea and this distance would have been greater during the Middle and Later Stone Age (Steele and Klein, 2013).

A wide range of mammalian species include the extinct long-horned buffalo (*Syncerus capensis*) and the blue antelope (*Hippotragus leucophaeus*) with several species of duiker and hippopotamus (Steele and Klein, 2013). Extreme fragmentation has hampered precise species identifications, but general environmental inferences based on the broad taxonomic groups are possible. The site has small sample of ostrich eggshell, Cape fur seal, and dolphin bones represented, and snake vertebrae are recorded, as well as several species of mussels and limpets exploited by humans on the rocky shores. The Middle Stone Age levels of this site indicate that humans were exploiting birds, especially coastal bird species (Val, 2019). Exploitation of coastal and marine vertebrate resources is indicated by the remains of dolphins and Cape fur seals (*Arctocephalus pusillus*).

Micromammalian remains include small rodents, insectivores, lizards, frogs, and small passerine birds (Avery in Parkington, 1987).

Charcoal preserved within the sediments has been analyzed and identified to species (Cartwright, 2013). Collins and colleagues (2017) obtained the first leaf-wax isotopic data in a terrestrial context of this antiquity in South Africa. These data indicate an increasing proportion of arid-adapted vegetation brought to the site during the Late Howiesons Poort. This trend may reflect habitat change in the site region, but also may reflect changing vegetation selection strategies on the part of the inhabitants. The water-dependent species, such as hippopotamus, in the Diepkloof assemblage highlights the role of the nearby vlei through time as part of the paleoenvironment.

Elandsfontein

Elandsfontein is located on the West Coast approximately 100 km north-northwest of Cape Town (Klein, 1978b). Initial excavation began in the 1950s, and a decade later the Saldanha cranium was found (also referred to as the Hopefield cranium; Singer and Wymer, 1968). This cranium has been assigned to *Homo heidelbergensis* and is associated with Acheulean bifacial stone tools (Rightmire, 1998). There is a recent new excavation of a Mid-Pleistocene fossil deposit at this site (Braun et al., 2013). Hominins appear to have played a very small role in the bone accumulations relative to the carnivores (Klein et al., 2007). Dating for the site rests in biochronology with eastern African deposits and suggests an age of between 1.0 and 0.6 Ma.

The species from Elandsfontein Main Excavation shows a mix of extinct and extant faunas, including *Megantereon whitei*, *Equus capensis*, *Syncerus antiquus*, *Hippotragus gigas*, *Antidorcas recki*, and *Sivatherium* (Klein et al., 2007; Braun et al., 2013). Several different megafaunal taxa, such as elephants, hippopotamus, and white and black rhinoceros, have been recovered from this site (Klein et al., 2007; Forrest, 2017). The presence of grazing taxa (such as equids and alcelaphins, and antelopes such as *Antidorcas*) suggests a significant grassy component to the Elandsfontein habitat, while a lesser number of browsers (such as the Cape buffalo, *Syncerus caffer*) indicate that woody and/or shrubby vegetation was also present (Klein et al., 2007). Recent stable isotopic analysis of macromammal teeth suggests that ancient spring activity at the site may have buffered Elandsfontein from regional Mid-Pleistocene aridification (Lehmann et al., 2016).

Studies of stable carbon isotopes from Cape mole-rats (*Bathyergus suillus*) suggest a positive relationship with both the presence of hominins and C_4 vegetation on the landscape (Patterson et al., 2016).

Early palynological analyses by Singer and Wymer (1968) suggest that plant taxa such as yellowwood (*Podocarpus* sp.), smalblad (*Metrosideros* sp.), acacia (*Acacia* sp.), marula (*Schlerocarya* sp.), and plumbago (*Plumbago* sp.) were present at the site. Pollen analysis from preserved hyena coprolites indicates the presence of a marshy pool at the site (Scott et al., 2003). The current fynbos biome of the region would not have been sufficient to support resident grazing species, so it can be inferred that these animals were migratory (Klein et al., 2007). Mesowear analysis of 15 bovid species suggests that a wooded component (trees, broad-leaved bush, and fynbos) may have been more significant (Stynder, 2009).

Hoedjiespunt

This site, designated HDP1, lies on the shores of Saldanha Bay, on the southern African West coast. The locality was discovered in 1993, when several isolated teeth attributed to *Homo sapiens* were found (Berger and Parkington, 1995). A Middle Pleistocene human tibia is also known from the site (Churchill et al., 2000b). Despite the presence of humans, taphonomic work done by Stynder (1997) suggests that the macromammalian faunal assemblage was accumulated by the brown hyena (*Parahyaena brunnea*).

The macromammal species represent both extinct and extant species, with rare species like the extinct blue antelope (*Hippotragus leucophaeus*) and the extinct southern springbok (*Antidorcas australis*) as well as the Cape zebra (*Equus capensis*) represented (Stynder, 1997; Hare and Sealy, 2013). Given the coastal nature of the site, it is expected that species such as the Cape fur seal (*Arctocephalus pusillus*) and dolphins (Dephinidae indet.) would be represented. Several bird species have also been identified; these include the jackass penguin (*Spheniscus demersus*) and the ostrich (*Struthio camelus*). There is also a tortoise species, namely the angulate tortoise (*Chersina angulata*), identified (Stynder 1997).

Micromammals from Hoedjiespunt 1 and the inferred taphonomic agents suggest that, unlike the macromammalian fauna, these microfauna were accumulated by a bird of prey, probably a barn owl (*Tyto alba*; Matthews et al., 2006a). The desert rat (*Zelotomys woosnami*) was an unexpected species to be identified from this site, because this species currently has a limited distribution, several hundred kilometers to the north (Matthews, pers. comm.).

Stable carbon isotopes suggest that large grazing species, mainly feeding on C_3 grasses but with some C_4 grasses also, were resident during a glacial period with lower sea levels and widespread grasslands present with the ecosystem (Hare and Sealy, 2013).

Langebaanweg

Langebaanweg lies on the western coast of South Africa, approximately 110 km north of Cape Town (Hendey, 1970, 1977, 1981a, 1981b; Brumfitt et al., 2013; Figure 6.1). The locality contains several deposits of varying ages, of which the oldest is the Varswater Formation, with the Quartzose and Pelletal Phosphate Members dating to ~ 5.1 Ma (Roberts et al., 2011). The region contains Earlier Stone Age material at a neighboring site called Anyskop (Kandel and Conard, 2012). *Homo sapiens* footprints are recorded from the Langebaan Lagoon at 117 ka years (Lee and Roberts, 1997).

The Varswater Formation preserves Pliocene faunas with no known relatives in either northern or eastern Africa. There are similarities to fauna from the Late Miocene from the Middle Awash, Ethiopia, specifically the localities of Asa Koma and Digba Dora (Haile-Selassie et al., 2004b). Megafaunal taxa are well-represented, including three species of proboscideans, and hippopotamids (Sanders, 2007; Boisserie and Merceron, 2011). The gomphothere is recognized as a new, endemic taxon, *Anacus capensis* (Sanders, 2007). Several important and rare faunas, including the African bear (*Agriotherium africanum*), a wolverine (*Plesiogulo monspessulanus*), the only African peccary species (*Pecarichoerus*), and several species of hyena are represented. The oldest specimens assigned to the aardvark (*Orycteropus*) have been found at this site (Lehmann, 2004) and the earliest example of a Pliocene equid, *Eurygnathohippus hooijeri* (Bernor and Kaiser, 2006). Although well-known from other, later sites, the short-necked giraffid *Sivatherium hendeyi* is represented by more than 500 individuals (Roberts et al., 2011).

Apart from the diverse mammalian fauna, there are also sharks, bony fishes, snakes, lizards, and turtles, and a great many numbers of birds, including marine birds, such as penguins (Hendey, 1977, Rich, 1980; Ksepka and Thomas, 2011; Roberts et al., 2011; Manegold, 2013; Manegold and Louchart, 2012; Manegold et al., 2014). Two new species of parrots from these deposits are the oldest geological record of the Psittaciformes in Africa (Manegold, 2013). The presence of the oldest true woodpeckers assigned to a new species (*Australopicus nelsonmandelai*) suggest the presence of riverine forest during the early Pliocene (Manegold and Louchart, 2012). Several marine species are represented, including seals, as well as cetacean fossils with evidence of postmortem feeding damage from marine predators (Govender et al., 2012; Govender and Chinsamy, 2013; Govender, 2015).

Of the preserved reptiles, chameleons have been studied in detail (Dollion et al., 2015). Anuran fossil diversity is also very high at this site (Van Dijk, 2003, 2006a; Matthews et al., 2015). Matthews et al. (2015, 2016) illustrate that anurans can be informative of different types of water bodies or specific seasonal rainfall zones. Their study of the frog community from 5.1 Ma indicates relatively high rainfall around that time (Matthews et al., 2015).

The dietary proxies, including stable carbon isotopes, dental textural microwear analysis, and phytoliths, have been used to reconstruct the vegetation of the herbivores at 5.1 Ma. The diets of hippos indicate that grass and suitable water bodies were present at the site during the Early Pliocene (Boisserie and Merceron, 2011). Bovid taxa, including grazers, appear to have been consuming more C_3 than C_4 grasses, according to stable carbon isotope, mesowear studies, and phytolith evidence (Franz-Odendaal et al., 2002; Rossouw et al., 2009; Stynder, 2011; Lehmann et al., 2016).

Dental textural microwear analysis conducted on the fossil bovids of the Varswater Formation indicates the presence of mosaic habitats, including fynbos vegetation, some grasses, and woodland elements (Merceron and Ungar, 2005; Ungar et al., 2007). This mosaic of woodland, C_3 grasses, and fynbos in association with a surface body of water characterize the habitats at 5.1 Ma.

Ysterfontein

This rock shelter lying approximately 70 km north-northwest of Cape Town contains deeply stratified Middle Stone Age sediments (Figure 6.1). Accelerator radiocarbon dating of ostrich eggshell suggests an age of older than 33,400 years ago, while stone tools suggest an older date of 70 ka (Halkett et al., 2003). Human and cultural remains from the site suggest that inhabitants did not fish routinely before 50 ka (Klein et al., 2004). The site also shows fewer tortoise remains compared with other sites, but a far higher proportion of ostrich eggshell fragments preserved within the deposits (Klein et al., 2004).

The faunal remains were predominantly accumulated by humans (Klein et al., 2004). Some of the mammalian taxa represented have been absent from the region since the Holocene. These include the zebra (*Equus* sp.), blue antelope (*Hippotragus leucophaeus*), southern reedbuck (*Redunca arundinum*), black wildebeest (*Connochaetes gnou*), eland (*Taurotragus oryx*), and long-horned buffalo (*Syncerus antiquus*). These are thought to have migrated through the area, due to the lack of permanent grazing in the sclerophyllous fynbos present at the time. A body of fresh water must have been present at the site, based on the presence of the wetland-dwelling spur-winged goose (*Plectopterus gambensis*) and the red knobbed coot (*Fulica cristata*). Shellfish, snakes, tortoises, birds, and hyena coprolites have been recovered (Klein et al., 2004). Overall, Klein et al. (2004) suggest that the prehistoric inhabitants of the shelter were living in a diverse terrestrial setting where grasslands, woodland, and fresh water were available.

Duinefontein 2

The site of Duinefontein 2 lies 35 km north of Cape Town (Figure 6.1). The site was first discovered in the 1970s and excavated in 1973 by R.G. Klein. It is an open-air site, which contains two buried paleosurfaces dated with luminescence dating to approximately 270 ka (discussed in Feathers, 2002). The geological setting of the dune field is reviewed in Roberts et al. (2009). Despite the preservation of Late Acheulean artifact scatters and mammalian fossil bone, a relative lack of cut-marks together with higher proportions of carnivore tooth marks on the bones suggests that the hominins did not accumulate most of the fauna (Klein et al., 1999; Cruz-Uribe et al., 2003).

Large grazing species, including the extinct Cape zebra (*Equus capensis*), the extinct long-horned buffalo (*Syncerus antiquus*), and the long-horned ancestral black wildebeest (*Connochaetes gnou laticornutus*) are abundant, suggesting a greater proportion of grasslands and broad-leafed bush cover during hominin activity in the environment. Several megafaunal species, such as elephant (*Loxodonta africana*) and both white and black rhinoceros (*Ceratotherium simum* and *Diceros bicornis*) and hippopotamus (*Hippopotamus amphibius*), are represented. Mammals and micromammal species from the two horizons show a mix of extinct and extant species and suggest the presence of a pond or marsh, such as southern reedbuck (*Redunca arundinum*) and Saunder's vlei rat and swamp rat (*Otomys saundersiae* and *O. irroratus*, respectively; Cruz-Uribe et al., 2003).

Hyena coprolites are abundant (Klein et al., 1999; Cruz-Uribe et al., 2003). Amphibian bones are identified as the African clawed toad, or platanna (*Xenopus*), which comprises 40 percent of the bones represented (Sampson, 2003). Rarer species include the toad (*Bufo* sp.), the rain frog (*Breviceps* sp.), and the sand frog (*Tomopterna* sp.), which may be the earliest occurrence of this genus in the fossil record (Sampson, 2003). The spatial patterning of the amphibian fossils suggests a fluctuating edge of an ancient pond, without much tree cover (Sampson, 2003). The reconstruction of the paleoenvironment indicates the presence of a pond or marsh around which animals were congregating and would have differed from the local fynbos vegetation in historic times and the present day (Klein et al., 1999; Cruz-Uribe et al., 2003).

Die Kelders

Die Kelders comprises two contiguous caves (named DK1 and DK2) with an MSA sequence that has been dated to between 71 and 57 ka (Grine et al., 1991; Feathers and Bush, 2000; Klein and Cruz-Uribe, 2000). Luminescence dates average about 60–70 ka (Feathers and Bush, 2000).

The MSA faunal sample from DK1 includes extinct long-horned buffalo (*Syncerus antiquus*), and Cape zebra (*Equus capensis*), in association with extant species that are no longer present in the local region, such as black wildebeest (*Connochaetes gnou*), springbok (*Antidorcas marsupialis*), and southern reedbuck (*Redunca arundinum*; Klein and Cruz-Uribe, 2000). A mix of grassland and woodland is suggested by the presence of both grazing and browsing rhinoceros (*Ceratotherium simum* and *Diceros bicornis*, respectively). These species suggest that relatively moist, cool, grassy conditions with marshy, swampy grass was available during the MSA. The faunal assemblage also preserves marine mammals, such as Cape fur seal (*Arctocephalus pusillus*), as well as indeterminate dolphins and whales (Klein and Cruz-Uribe, 2000).

Small mammal preservation is good, and the body size comparisons of dune mole-rats (*Bathyergus suillus*) and Cape gray mongooses (*Galerella pulverulenta*) imply cooler temperatures at the time of deposition (Klein and Cruz-Uribe, 2000). Reptile bones, from species such as the mole-snake (*Pseudoapsis cana*) and the angulate tortoise (*Chersina angulata*), are abundant in the DK1 Middle Stone Age assemblage (Klein and Cruz-Uribe, 2000). Bird bones are well distributed within the DK1 sediments, with jackass penguins (*Spheniscus demersus*) being more common in the older levels. Both eagle owls (genus *Bubo*) and humans accumulated the fauna, with penguins, larger ungulates, and seals being associated with human hunting. In contrast, species like the Cape gannet (*Morus capensis*) and Cape cormorant (*Phalacrocorax capensis*) are more common in the later deposits. Fish bones occur only in the LSA deposits, including eight coastal species. Klein and Cruz-Uribe (2000) infer that LSA fishing practices used both lines and nets, because fish remains represent a range of individual sizes. The assemblages clearly indicate that humans were exploiting a range of marine and terrestrial food sources during the MSA and LSA against a backdrop of cooler, grassier environs.

Blombos Cave

Blombos Cave lies 300 km east of Cape Town and has been excavated and studied since 1991 (Henshilwood et al., 2001). The site deposits span the Middle Stone Age and the Later Stone Age and have been dated to around 120 ka via OSL (Jacobs et al., 2006).

Evidence of advanced human behaviors, such as the engraved ochre dating to 77 ka and ochre-processing as early as 100 ka, have been recovered (Henshilwood et al., 2002, 2011). The site was inhabited by humans during times of high sea levels, but abandoned during lower sea levels, when the formation of large dunes blocked the cave entrance (Jacobs et al., 2006).

The fauna sheds light on what species humans were exploiting for food, as well as more general indicators of climatic and environmental conditions (Henshilwood et al., 2001). A mix of terrestrial and marine species, including dolphins (Delphinidae indet.) and Cape fur seals (*Arctocephalus pusillus*), along with more typical indicators of both closed and wooded environments, such as black rhinoceros (*Diceros bicornis*), Cape buffalo (*Syncerus caffer*), and African elephant (*Loxodonta africana*), are represented. Alcelaphins (*Connochaetes gnou* and/or *Alcelaphus buselaphus*) reflect the presence of grassland within relative proximity to the site. The large mammal assemblage is dominated by small, size 1 antelopes, such as grysbok (*Raphicerus melanotis*) and steenbok (*Raphicerus campestris*), the common duiker (*Sylvicapra grimmia*), and the klipspringer (*Oreotragus oreotragus*; Thompson and Henshilwood, 2011). The presence of freshwater is indicated by hippopotamus (*Hippopotamus amphibius*) and the Cape clawless otter (*Aonyx capensis*) within the deposits.

Charred remains of the Cape dune mole-rat (*Bathygerus suillus*) and high numbers of rock hyraxes (*Procavia capensis*) and angulate tortoise (*Chersina angulata*) suggest intensive human exploitation of these species for food (Henshilwood, 1997; Badenhorst et al., 2014; Thompson and Henshilwood, 2014). The small mammals represented suggest that the transition from MIS 5a to 4 was accompanied by a less-diverse micromammal assemblage (Nel and Henshilwood, 2016). Recovered species of shellfish and fish species largely reflect those found in the region today (Hensilwood et al., 2001).

The vegetation around the cave was likely to have been a variant of fynbos, which was widely encountered across the region, and which likely hosted larger migratory mammal species, especially grazers. Extinct grazers such as *Equus capensis* suggests that grassland may have been a more important component of the site vegetation than was present in later, historic, periods (Henshilwood et al., 2001).

Still Bay

The Still Bay coast, to the east of Blombos Cave, preserves a series of ichnological sites that feature Pleistocene aeolian exposures of a wide range of fossil trackways including antelope, reptile, and carnivores (Roberts, 2003; Helm et al., 2019a, 2019b). OSL and amino acid racemization (AAR) have been employed to create a chronological framework for these trackways (Roberts et al., 2008). Elephant (*Loxodonta africana*) tracks have been dated to ~143 ka to 8 ka with OSL dating (Roberts et al. 2008). Giraffe tracks from the Still Bay area extend the known geographic range of this species (Helm et al., 2018). Helm et al. (2018) infer that the Pleistocene glacial conditions and exposed southern coastal plain would have provided a migration route for these species. The trackways are a significant data set to complement the body fossils and other regional climatic proxies (Quick, 2013; Quick et al., 2015).

Pinnacle Point

Pinnacle Point lies 10 km west of Mossel Bay town and contains numerous fossil localities and caves of varying ages within the late Pleistocene (Marean et al., 2004, 2007; Bar-Matthews et al., 2010; Marean, 2010). Human presence has been established within periods dating to ~162 ka, ~125 ka, ~110 ka, and ~99–91 ka, which corresponds to during Marine Isotope Stage (MIS) 6, 5e, 5d, and 5c, respectively, using OSL methods (Jacobs, 2010).

Large terrestrial mammals are more common than small mammals, tortoises, and marine mammals, which is an unusual pattern for coastal sites; however, fragmentation complicates precise taxonomic identifications (Thompson, 2010). Multivariate analyses of the mammalian community structures suggest complex climatic changes during MIS 6 (Rector and Reed, 2010). The micromammal fossil assemblages from Cave 9 at Pinnacle Point, which date to the transition between MIS 6 and 5, were likely collected by owls (either spotted eagle owl or barn owl) and suggest that the period during which the fossils were accumulated was warm and wet, with relatively dense vegetation, but in the older assemblages there is some indication that the vegetation was relatively open, fynbos-dominated vegetation (Matthews et al., 2011, 2019). Marine invertebrates, especially shellfish, were accumulated by humans for food (Jerardino and Marean, 2010). Although complex climate changes are indicated, micromammal species suggest a fynbos component was prevalent throughout much of the periods represented (Matthews et al. 2019), until a large dune ~90 ka made the cave inaccessible until the Late Pleistocene (Jacobs, 2010).

Boomplaas Cave

Boomplaas Cave lies 4 km to the west of the Cango Caves and contains Late Pleistocene and Holocene sediments that were excavated by Hilary Deacon in the 1970s and document paleoenvironmental change in South Africa (Deacon, 1979, 1995; Deacon et al., 1984; Mitchell, 2002). The site sediments have yielded ostrich eggshell remains as well as charcoal.

The macromammalian fauna show that large grazing ungulates were much more common during the late Pleistocene than they were during the Holocene, indicating more grassland than today (Klein, 1978b; Faith, 2013). However, the modern vegetation in the vicinity of Boomplaas cave today is unable to support an abundant grazing community (e.g., Boshoff and Kerley, 2001), and this suggests that vegetation has shifted significantly from what is reported for past habitats (Faith, 2013). The micromammalian evidence is in broad agreement, indicating fluctuations between open vegetation and changes in precipitation (Avery, 1982a).

Nelson Bay Cave

This site lies close to the town of Plettenberg Bay. Ray Inskeep first excavated this cave in the 1960s, followed by Richard Klein in the 1970s (Inskeep, 1987; Klein, 1972). The oldest sediments date to at least 60 ka while most of the faunal remains date to 23.5 ka (Sealy et al., 2020).

The diverse species represented are mainly those species that have been recorded in the Plettenburg Bay region in historical times, apart from several extinct species, such as *Megalotragus* sp. and *Syncerus antiquus*, as well as possible bloubok (*Hippotragus leucophaeus*; Klein, 1972).

Microfauna is recorded from the site, as are avifauna and fish (Klein, 1972; Faith et al., 2019b). Several species of marine mammals are also recorded, such as dolphin and Cape fur seal (*Arctocephalus pusillus*). Stable carbon isotopes from herbivore enamel indicate the presence of more C_3 grasses but with fewer C_4 grasses at the time of the Last Glacial Maximum (Sealy et al., 2020), when sea levels were far lower than today (by as much as 120 m). Later periods (12 to 7 ka) are marked by the disappearance of grazing herbivores and an increase in browsers, which by the later Holocene levels (after 5 ka) indicate similar environments to those of the present day (Sealy et al., 2020; Mucina et al., 2006).

Klasies River Cave

The sites of the Klasies River lie on the Eastern Cape coast, South Africa (Figure 6.1), and comprise five caves forming three archaeological sites along 5 km of the coastline (Singer and Wymer, 1982; Wurz et al., 2018). Initially the Main Site was excavated by Ronald Singer and John Wymer in 1967 and 1968 and subsequently by Hilary Deacon in 1984 (Singer and Wymer, 1982; Deacon and Geleijnse, 1988).

Electron spin resonance dating of the human tooth enamel (Grün et al., 1990) and paleomagnetic dating (Nami et al., 2016) has been used to date the deposits. Human occupation of the site is evidenced by abundant MSA and LSA stone tools and a modest sample of human bones (Rightmire and Deacon, 1991; Grine, 2012), as well as cooking residues of starchy foods (Larbey et al., 2019) and engraved ochres pieces (d'Errico et al., 2012b). The Main Site contains MSA tools and is dated to between 100 ka and ~70.9 ka (Wurz, 1999, 2002; Wurz et al., 2018).

Large mammal faunal are dominated by rock hyraxes (*Procavia capensis*), as well as small bovids such as the Cape grysbok (*Raphicerus melanotis*), and marine fauna such as Cape fur seal (*Arctocephalus pusillus*; Van Pletzen, 2000). Grazers, browsers, and aquatic species (*Hippopotamus amphibius*) suggest a mix of woodland and grassland around freshwater was present during human occupation. A high diversity of grazers, including the extinct long-horned buffalo (*Syncerus antiquus*) and blue antelope (*Hippotragus leucophaeus*), indicate the presence of grasslands through which these grazers migrated seasonally (Wurz et al., 2018; Reynard and Wurz, 2020).

Skeletal part representation differs between small- and large-bodied bovids and this may suggest possible selective transport by humans (e.g., Klein, 1989, Turner, 1989; Van Pletzen, 2000). The micromammal species suggest a vegetation mosaic like the present, but with grassier, more open vegetation at the time of the deposition of the central part of the sequence (Avery, 1987b; Nel et al., 2018).

A rich and diverse fish species list is dominated by estuarine and intertidal species (von den Dreisch, 2004). A diverse frog assemblage is similar in composition to the present-day anurans in the region, namely *Bufo*, *Breviceps*, and *Tomopterna*, and are similar to those species recovered from Duinefontein 2 (Sampson, 2003; Van Dijk, 2006b).

A small sample of woody taxa charcoal remains of beech (*Protorhus longifolia*) and the coastal hibiscus (*Hibiscus* cf. *tiliaceus*) have been used to reconstruct warmer conditions in the Late Holocene relative to the present (Zwane, 2018).

Sibudu

Sibudu Cave (KwaZulu-Natal) lies north of Durban and overlooks the Tongati River (Figure 6.1; Wadley and Jacobs, 2006). The deposits represent three distinct age clusters within the Middle Stone Age (~37 ka, ~50 ka, and ~60 ka) and the Iron Age and span the transitions from the industries of the Still Bay, Howieson's Poort, and post-Howieson's Poort, but these appear unassociated with habitat changes identified at the site (Robinson and Wadley, 2018). The site has excellent preservation with an especially well-preserved seed assemblage, which has enabled reconstruction of vegetation and animal communities in the past (Wadley, 2004, 2006; Sievers, 2006; Bruch et al., 2012; Lennox and Wadley, 2019). Sedges are well presented in the deposits, and these have been inferred to be due to human harvesting and introduction into the cave, probably as bedding material (Sievers, 2011). Also represented is the poisonous tamboti tree (*Spirostachys africana*), which is a woodland tree found near water (Lennox and Bamford, 2015).

Terrestrial mammals as well as marine vertebrates and invertebrates, and freshwater species, such as frogs, birds, fish, snakes, crocodile, and crab have been identified (Plug, 2004, 2006). Among the terrestrial fauna, extinct species include the Cape zebra (*Equus capensis*), the giant hartebeest (*Megalotragus priscus*), and the giant buffalo (*Syncerus antiquus*). Juveniles and old individuals are rare, suggesting that humans were competent hunters concentrating on prime adult prey animals (Plug, 2004). Several extant, but rare, fauna, such as the scaly anteater (*Manis temminckii*), have also been identified. The presence of primate species, including bushbaby (*Galago* sp.) and vervet monkey (*Chlorocebus aethiops*), and also the presence of giraffe (*Giraffa camelopardalis*), indicates the presence of woodland and forest, but with a significant component of grassland. Microfaunal species including bats, shrews, and rodents have been identified (Plug, 2004). The avifauna suggests that Sibudu inhabitants exploited various bird species as prey throughout the sequence (Plug and Clark, 2008; Val et al., 2016).

Correspondence analysis of temporal patterns in seeds and macromammalian species indicated a mix of forest, riverine, and open grassland habitats present (Reynolds, 2006). Floral species indicate that late MSA paleoenvironments had higher temperatures, especially in winter (Bruch et al., 2012). Stable carbon isotope studies of tooth enamel indicate that major habitat transitions are visible at Sibudu, with the oldest MSA levels representing warm, wooded, and mesic conditions, followed by increasingly cooler, drier, and grassier habitats in the late MSA and final MSA stages (Robinson and Wadley, 2018).

Discussion and Conclusion

These sites demonstrate the rich paleontological record that can used to reconstruct the habitats in which hominins lived and evolved. The previous decades have seen numerous new discoveries and, crucially, the application of new analytical techniques. In particular, the application of stable carbon isotope analysis to the fossil fauna has offered powerful insights into general dietary signals (e.g., Lee-Thorp et al., 2007) while recently offering more detailed insights into the seasonality of the diets in the early life of the individual concerned (e.g., Hodgkins et al., 2020). There is also further scope for investigation of vegetation temporal changes from multi-proxy analyses using fossil herbivore teeth, for example (e.g., Sewell et al., 2019). Detailed microhabitat signals from smaller faunas such as birds, reptiles and insects are producing new insights (e.g., Avery, 2001; Matthews et al., 2016; Parker et al., 2016; Manegold, 2013; Stidham, 2009; 2010; Leichliter et al., 2016, 2017; Vilakazi et al., 2018). New techniques mean that even the smallest fossils can now be visualized and identified without destruction (Val et al., 2011).

Creating detailed databases of micromammal fauna has enabled researchers such as Leichliter (2018) to quantify the degree of woody and non-woody affiliated taxa for fossil sites across southern Africa. Another area showing promise is the use of phytoliths to identify the plants associated with hominin and faunal diets, such as that of *Australopithecus sediba* (Henry et al., 2012; Cordova and Avery, 2017). Increased use of pollen has been a powerful means to examine past vegetation cover associated with human dispersal throughout southern Africa (Scott and Neumann, 2018).

There are some questions requiring more focus, such as how well do these fossil assemblages represent the range of past living ecosystems accurately (Hopley and Maslin, 2010; Du et al; 2019; Faith et al., 2019a; Pickering et al., 2019, Stratford et al., 2020)? Furthermore, do bones and teeth preserve accurate biogenic signals over millions of years (Lee-Thorp and Sponheimer, 2003)?

This overview should convince the reader that we do not lack data – far from it. The challenge for the coming decades is to integrate existing and new data sets in a way that allows the discipline to test for robust links between hominin habitats at specific sites within a framework of large-scale climate shifts that may, or may not, have been a causal factor in key transitions in hominin evolution.

Acknowledgments

Many thanks to Margaret Avery, Philip Hopley, Matthew Bennett, Thalassa Matthews, and René Bobe for helpful feedback on this chapter. Any oversights or errors are my sole responsibility. I would like to dedicate this contribution to James Brink.

7 Geology, Fauna, and Paleoenvironmental Reconstructions of the Makapansgat Limeworks *Australopithecus africanus*-Bearing Paleo-Cave

Kaye E. Reed, Kevin L. Kuykendall, Andy I.R. Herries, Philip J. Hopley, Matt Sponheimer, and Lars Werdelin

Introduction

The Makapansgat Valley is located in Limpopo Province, South Africa (Figure 7.1), and is the northernmost of the South African australopithecine fossil sites. Hominin fossils were first recovered there in 1947, but the history and significance of the valley dates to the nineteenth century. The name of the site and valley derives from the Historic, or Gwasa, Cave at the head of the valley, which was the location of a siege in 1854 (Naidoo, 1987; Esterhuysen et al., 2008) on local Ndebele tribespeople by a Boer Commando in retaliation for two massacres – themselves retaliation for raids for ivory and slave labor by the Boer on Ndebele villages. The chief was Mokopane, and the cave became known as "Makapan's Cave" or -*gat* in Afrikaans.

In 1925, following the news stories about Raymond Dart's discovery of the Taung fossil (Dart, 1925a) from the Buxton-Norlim Limeworks, a schoolmaster in Pietersburg named Wilfrid Eitzman visited the then-active limeworks in the Makapansgat Valley and arranged for the shipment of a box of fossils to Raymond Dart at the University of the Witwatersrand Medical School, setting off a chain of events that lasted several decades (Tobias, 1979). The fossils in the box were mostly those of the Family Bovidae, and some of them appeared to have been burned. Dart arranged for chemical testing of some of these fossil fragments (Dart and Craig, 1959); when carbon was noted as one of the components, Dart concluded that the bones had been burned, and thus that a human type of hunter had accumulated the material in the relatively recent past. On this basis, Dart published a report about the Makapansgat Limeworks locality (Dart, 1925b), identifying it as a site of hominin occupation.

Because of the national significance of the siege at Historic Cave, the South African archeologist Clarence van Riet Lowe visited the site in 1937 for the South African Archeological Survey to establish its status as a national monument (van Riet Lowe, 1938). During this survey, he discovered stone tools in an abandoned mine adjacent to the Historic Cave, and determined that they derived from a different cave deposit than the historic materials. This became known as the Cave of Hearths and was the focus of systematic excavations from 1947 to 1954 (Mason, 1962; Tobias, 1971). These excavations, first led by van Riet Lowe (1954; Brain et al., 1955) and then by Revil Mason (1962, 1988b), resulted in the longest archaeological sequence in Southern Africa, spanning the Earlier Stone Age (late Acheulian) to the Iron Age and

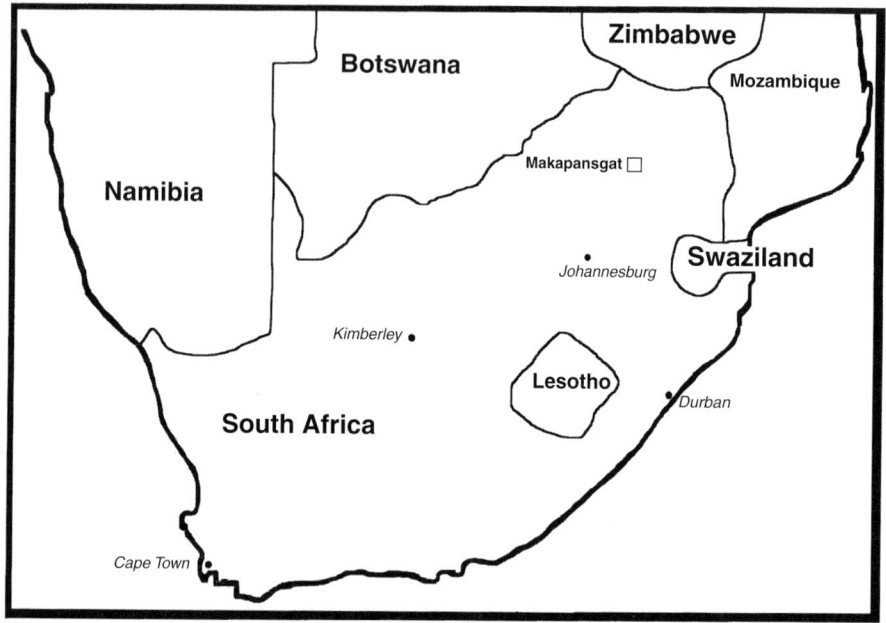

Figure 7.1 Location of the Makapansgat Valley in South Africa.

Supplementary resources for this chapter are available on www.cambridge.org/africanpaleoecology

historic periods (Tobias, 1971), and produced the first extensive framework for archeological interpretation in the region. Work in the late 1990s and early 2000s showed that this deposit — with its rare occurrence of Acheulian in a cave setting — is <780 ka, but the suggested early evidence for hearths is not supported (Herries and Latham, 2009).

When the materials from the Cave of Hearths were publicized, Dart assumed that the bovid fossils previously recovered by Eitzman at the Limeworks had likely been butchered by the humans whose tools were found in the Cave of Hearths (Dart and Craig, 1959; P.V. Tobias, pers. comm., 1997). In 1945, Phillip Tobias, leading a student expedition at the request of Dart, discovered that the cave from which the bovid remains had been recovered was about a kilometer from the Cave of Hearths. There was no trace of tools at this second cave, dubbed the "Limeworks Cave." In the absence of stone tools in the Limeworks deposits, Dart developed the elaborate Osteodontokeratic Culture model (or ODK) to explain the cultural behavior of the australopiths and the immense fossilized bone beds at the Makapansgat Limeworks and other South African hominid sites (Dart, 1956, 1957, 1960). Brain (1981), in his complex research on cave taphonomy, discarded the ODK model. Tobias' expedition also resulted in the discovery of small papionins, which suggested to Tobias and Dart that the Makapansgat Limeworks fossil deposits might be contemporaneous with the Sterkfontein deposits (now defined as Sterkfontein Member 4 and dated to slightly younger, between ~2.6 and ~2.1 Ma; Herries et al., 2013). In 1946, Dart's anatomy students collected large *ex-situ* blocks of breccia left by lime mining in the cave and transported them to the University of the Witwatersrand. Thus began the removal of the thousands of fossils embedded in the breccia blocks.

In 1947, James Kitching recovered an australopithecine occiput (MLD-1) in the *ex-situ* breccia dumps at the Limeworks, and Dart, recalling the "burnt" bones that had been analyzed in 1925, called the hominin *Australopithecus prometheus* (Dart, 1948). Between 1947 and 1993, 46 specimens of what is now referred to *Au. africanus* were recovered from mostly *ex-situ* Limeworks breccia blocks (Boné and Dart, 1955; Oakley et al., 1975). A few exceptions, such as the partial skull MLD37/38, were recovered *in-situ* (Dart, 1959, 1962a) from what is now Member 4 (Partridge, 2000) but was formerly Member 4a (Partridge, 1979). Over 25,000 other fossil specimens were also retrieved from about 20 tons of breccia (Dart, 1957; Kitching, pers. comm., 1994). Numerous researchers through the years have described various mammalian specimens, groups of mammals, and the community of mammals recovered from the Limeworks (Dart, 1948, 1957; George, 1950; Kitching, 1951, 1963, 1965, 1980; Toerien, 1952, 1955; Greenwood, 1955, 1958; Churcher, 1956; Wells and Cooke, 1956; Ewer, 1957b, 1958, 1967; Freedman, 1957, 1960, 1976; Hooijer, 1958; Robinson, 1963; Gentry, 1970; Maier, 1970, 1972; Randall, 1972, 1981; Eisenhart, 1974; Brickhill, 1976; Cooke, 1978c, 1988, 1994; Gentry and Gentry, 1978a, 1978b; Maguire, 1979; Vrba, 1987a, 1987b; Bender, 1990, 1992; Reed, 1996, 1998).

Removal of other *in-situ* breccia blocks directly from the limeworks was accomplished under the auspices of Tobias and Kitching (Member 4, MLD 37–38–34), and research between 1993 and 2005 by McKee. Crawford et al. (2004) focused on *in-situ* fossil extraction from Members 2 and 4, and although no substantive hominin fossils were recovered, they added important information on the stratigraphy and dating of the site.

Geology

The Makapansgat Limeworks consists of a mixture of underground and open-cast mine workings into one of the largest paleokarst deposits yet discovered in South Africa (Figure 7.2). The paleokarst consists of a single larger paleo-cave deposit consisting of a large cavern with small side passages (Latham et al., 1999, 2003). The sediments of this ancient cave have become cemented, and in many areas deroofed due to erosion. The lime miners targeted a massive basal speleothem deposit which undermined the fossil-bearing paleo-cave sediments. As a result, if you visit the site today you stand in large mined passages where the speleothem once existed, and the walls of the mined passages consist of the cavern and cave passages that were filled with fossil-bearing sediments (Figure 7.2).

Dart (1952) originally described the sediments within the paleo-cave from which the lime workers had extracted the fossils. He identified 11 "layers," with the color of each being mentioned, and inferred the climatic conditions under which deposition occurred. Several others reviewed the cave stratigraphy (Barbour, 1949a, 1949b; King, 1951; Brain et al., 1955) before Wells and Cooke (1956) described the sequence of six separate levels, of which the "grey marl" (aka Member 3 or Grey Breccia) was the most fossiliferous. They noted that both the stratified pink/red breccia (Member 2) and the coarse pink breccia (Member 4 and Central Debris Pile of Partridge, 2000) also contained some fossils. In their description, they noted the main fossil-bearing units that would form the basis of Partridge's (1975, 2000) well-known Member System (defining five Members) representing Member 3, Member 2, and Member 4. Despite extra subdivisions, Wells and Cooke's (1956) stratigraphy and Partridge's (1979) stratigraphy are identical with the exception of an additional layer defined by Wells and Cooke (1956) between Member 1 and Member 2 (a manganese-rich layer of pink sand and travertine). These deposits represent part of the Original Ancient Entrance deposits (or Member X, as defined by Latham et al., 2003, 2007) representing an earlier entrance to the site that was later sealed. In contrast, Brain (1958) simplified the stratigraphy by defining four units and including the gray marl in his Lower Phase 1, with Member 4 representing Upper Phase 1 and Member 5 Phase II.

Maier (1970) first referred to the deposits as the "Makapansgat Formation," and within this "formation" Partridge (1979) developed his first attempt at a Member system, defining five Members with subdivisions in Member 4 (a–b) and Member 5 (a–e) based on their sedimentological character. In this classic Member system, Member 1 was represented by a basal flowstone floor (often incorrectly termed a travertine) that had large ridges of speleothem that once filled the open-cast quarries of the Main Quarry and East (or Exit) Quarry. This Member formed a number of different depositional basins in the Limeworks paleo-cavern. On the western side of the Main Quarry Ridge and Eastern Side of the East Quarry Ridge, well-laminated red siltstone and

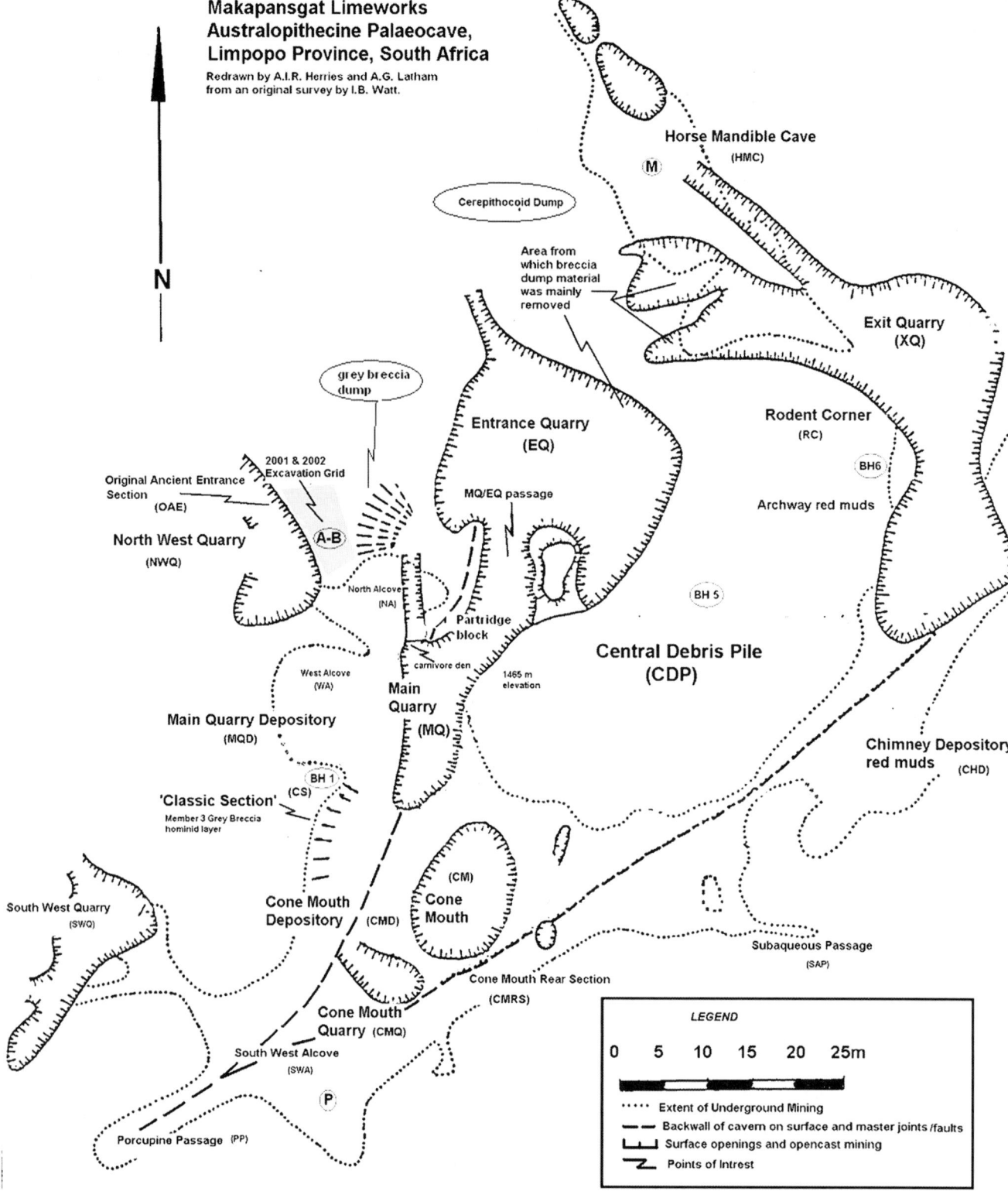

Figure 7.2 Schematic showing the distribution of deposits in the Limeworks cave. Redrawn by A.I.R. Herries and A. Latham from an original by I.B. Watt.

sandstone deposits were defined as Member 2, despite there being no stratigraphic connection between the Eastern and Western occurrences of Member 2. This unit is often incorrectly termed a breccia, but is instead a sequence of laminated calcareous sandstones, siltstones, and mudstones. In the western area between what is known as the Classic Section and the Collapsed Cone, a gray bone breccia cemented and capped by speleothem occurs, defined as Member 3. This is the source of almost all the *Au. africanus*, as well as most other mammal fossils. Between the two speleothem ridges in the center of the paleo-cavern a pink breccia was deposited with generally large clasts, and this was defined as Member 4b (Partridge, 1979). Member 4a is a clast-less deposit at the northern end of the Main Quarry in an area termed the Partridge block, and is the source for the *Au. africanus* fossil MLD37/38 (Dart, 1959, 1962a). Member 5 (a–e) consisted of unconsolidated sand/silt stone with rounded to subrounded cobbles that occurred around the Collapsed Cone and, in the case of Member 5e, in other isolated pockets. Based on this Member system, Brock et al. (1977) and then McFadden et al. (1979) undertook the first paleomagnetic work, and suggested an age of between 3.3 and 2.8 Ma for Member 2 and then 3.32 and 2.90 Ma, respectively, the latter noting Member 2 was likely between 3.32 and 3.06 Ma. It should be noted, however, that the ages for the reversals used for these estimates has changed significantly since that time (see Cande and Kent, 1995 and Singer, 2014).

Maguire et al. (1985) suggested that the strict adherence to the law of superposition implicit in the Member system was not appropriate in a cave deposit. Maguire (1985) suggested that various "Members" from the Makapansgat Cave site could have been deposited contemporaneously, but by different accumulating agents. Moreover, Maguire et al. (1980) and Maguire (1985) proposed naming the sediments after the depositional basin in which they were deposited (i.e., North West Quarry, etc.). Pocock (1985) and Maguire et al. (1985) further noted that "red cave silts" defined as part of Partridge's (1979) Member 2 seemed to contain fossils of vastly different ages in different parts of the cave.

Latham et al. (1999, 2003, 2004) revisited the stratigraphic issues at the Limeworks and further noted issues with Partridge's (1979) concept of a Member sequence, also noting that parts of Member 4b and Member 2 and 3 would have formed at the same time, and that in fact Member 2 would have been derived from the winnowing of fine grains from Member 4b, which itself would have formed throughout the entire life history of the Limeworks paleo-cavern's deposition. As they note, this would make the magnetostratigraphic interpretation and thus age of McFadden et al (1979) incorrect. Latham et al. (1999, 2003, 2004) also noted there was no reason to suggest that the deposits in the eastern part of the site that have been defined as Member 2 were contemporary with those in the western part of the site from where the *Au. africanus* remains were recovered. Latham et al. (1999, 2003, 2004) also defined a previously unrecognized deposit between Partridge's (1979) Member 1 and Member 2. In these earlier publications, Latham et al. (1999, 2003, 2004) define these deposit as the Ancient Original Entrance (AOE) deposits, while Latham et al. (2007) define it as "Member X."

Partly in response to these suggestions, Partridge (2000) redefined his Member system, and Member 4a that is found just in the Main Quarry area of the site became Member 4. In turn, his Member 4b that consists of the bulk of clast-supported breccia between the western and eastern quarries became known as the Central Debris Pile (CDP). He did not, however, include the newly described AOE in this re-evaluation. Thus, much of the fauna that was once described as being from "Member 4" actually comes from Partridge's (2000) CDP unit. Moreover, as Herries et al. (2013) pointed out in their review of *Australopithecus* sites in South Africa, it is also possible that much of the fauna that is defined as deriving from Member 2 does not come from the red siltstone in the western part of the site, which underlies the Member 3 *Australopithecus africanus*-bearing Grey Breccia, but may instead originate from an area where bone-bearing red siltstone has been excavated above Horse Mandible Cave in the North-West Quarry (James Kitching, pers. comm., 1994). Because deposits of a similar sedimentological character are seen throughout the cave complex it is hard to confidently determine the provenance of much of the fauna recovered from *ex-situ* blocks. The exception is fossil material from the Member 3 *Au. Africanus*-bearing Grey Breccia itself, which is highly distinctive and unique to one confined area of the site against the ceiling and walls of the western edge of the Main Quarry, at the top of what is known as the Classic Section.

As such, more work needs to be undertaken on the site to fully understand its stratigraphic complexity and the age of the various deposits and fossils throughout the paleo-cavern. However, a continuous stratigraphic sequence of deposits can be defined from the western part of the paleo-cave system and this has been used to re-date the site by paleomagnetic analysis (Hopley et al., 2007a; Herries et al., 2013). While a range of radiometric methods has been attempted at the site, none have been successful to date (Herries et al., 2013). This well-defined western sequence starts with the Basal Flowstone (Member 1), which consists of multiple interlocking flows and was likely formed over a vast period of time. Member 1 is thus potentially very old (early Pliocene at least, but potentially late Miocene) with a complex formational history (Figure 7.2). The massive nature of the speleothem is unlike anything seen at other, younger paleo-cave sites in Gauteng and points to its formation under a very different climate. The survival of such potentially old deposits at the Makapansgat Limeworks is also not seen in the Gauteng region and likely relates to the nature of the cave and subsequent erosion of the landscape in the two regions (Herries et al., 2018).

The Member 1 basal flowstone transitions to interlayered siltstone, sandstones, and flowstone in the North West Quarry that forms the first opening to the cave and the deposition of the inclined Original Ancient Entrance deposits (OAE as termed by Latham et al., 2003; Latham and Warr, 2008; Herries et al., 2013) based on the name painted on the wall of the North West quarry [Orig. (Ancient) Opening]; rather than AOE as in Latham et al. (2003). The base of the OAE records a reversed magnetic polarity, like much of the underlying basal flowstone, but toward its top it shows mixed polarity that Herries (2003; see also Hopley et al., 2007a) interpreted as the Kaena and Mammoth events between 3.33 and 3.03 Ma. Thus, if fossil material were recovered from the OAE this would likely be the oldest from the site at >3 Ma. However, as noted by Herries et al. (2013), the mixed signals from the top of the OAE and the instability of remanence in some samples makes confirmation of this sequence of reversals, and thus age, difficult. Work is ongoing to clarify this.

The OAE sequence is capped by a thick flowstone (The Fantastic Flowstone) that is then overlain by the well-stratified red siltstone and sandstone of the Main Quarry – Member 2 West (M2 w; Herries et al., 2013). M2 w has a normal polarity, except perhaps at its very base, and this has been interpreted as being between 3.03 and 2.561 Ma (ages recalculated from Herries et al., 2013 based on the new age for the Gauss–Matuyama Boundary at 2.61 Ma; Singer, 2014). Rather than infilling the cave from a westerly direction like the OAE, M2 w is formed from the winnowing of fine-grained material from the northern part of the CDP (Member 4b) to the northwest of the Main Quarry. M2 w eventually filled up most of the basin formed in the basal siltstone on the western side of the cave between a large speleothem ridge and the western wall of the cavern, although deposition still occurred at the very northern end of the Main Quarry with the deposition of pink siltstone deposits that show an intermediate polarity (Member 4a; Partridge, 1979; Member 4; Partridge, 2000; Herries et al., 2013). This has been used to suggest that these deposits formed close to the 2.61 Ma Gauss–Matuyama magnetic reversal. This is significant because this is the area known as the "Partridge Block," from which the *Au. africanus* fossil MLD37/38 was recovered, and it would thus be the youngest hominin from the Makapansgat Limeworks. Material from M2 w in this western sequence is thus dated to between 3.03 and 2.61 Ma, but there is uncertainty as to whether any other significant fossil material has come from this deposit as it was not extensively mined, unlike other areas of red siltstone and sandstone at the site.

In the southern area of the Main Quarry, known as the Classic Section, the red siltstone and sandstone of M2 w almost completely filled the roof of the cave, making it impossible for animals to have accessed this area. This is significant because the M2 w deposits are directly overlain at their most southerly extent by the *Au. africanus*-bearing Member 3 (M3) Grey Breccia, which would have been deepest around the western edge of the Collapsed Cone. It is thus likely that the animals that accumulated the bones in M3 entered the cave from a southerly direction down the talus cone formed by the CDP, rather than from the Main Quarry. Despite this difference in deposition, there is little evidence for a major hiatus between the end of deposition of M2 w and M3.

Member 3 caps the Classic Section area of the site and is directly overlain by two phases of speleothem growth that contain a magnetic reversal correlated to the 2.61 Ma Gauss–Matuyma reversal (and also the Pliocene–Pleistocene Boundary) that may also occur in the Partridge Block and also seems to occur in the Collapsed Cone deposits at the very southern end of the western part of the cavern. Member 5 then overlies these deposits. Based on this sequence the only fossil material that can be given any form of temporal constraint is the material from Member 3, which is likely between 3.03 and 2.61 Ma. The fossils from the CDP (Member 4b) could actually derive from any period of deposition at the site.

Paleoenvironmental Proxies

Analyses of the fossil fauna and hominins from the Makapansgat Limeworks have included dental microwear (Hopley et al., 2006; Schubert et al., 2006), dental microwear texture (Williams, 2013), mesowear (Schubert, 2007), enamel isotopes (Sponheimer et al., 1999; Fourie et al., 2002; Hopley et al., 2006), ecomorphology (Reed, 2008), community structure (Reed, 1997, 1998), and palynology (Cadman and Rayner, 1989; Zavada and Cadman, 1993). Numerous geological studies have provided paleoenvironmental inferences (e.g., King, 1951; Butzer, 1980; Turner, 1980; Rayner et al., 1993; Partridge, 2000; Hopley et al., 2007a), but many of these are not quantitative proxies and have produced a wide range of rainfall reconstructions (see summary by Rayner et al.,1993).

Palynology

Pollen samples were recovered from the M2 w red siltstone and sandstone of the Classic Section (Cadman and Rayner, 1989). They indicate that the environment during the M2 w period just prior to the deposition of M3 was forested transitioning to grasslands, and that during M3 times were again more forested but were characterized by more woodland than forest. This difference in environment may reflect some form of hiatus between the deposition of M2 w and M3 that would be consistent with the Herries et al. (2013) interpretation of the different directions of deposition of these two deposits. Rodent Corner and two areas either side of the Collapsed Cone (Cone Mouth, Figure 7.2) were analyzed by Zavada and Cadman (1993). Cone B came from the west side of the Collapsed Cone and consists of laminated red siltstone that is equivalent to M2 w. The samples from this unit contained high proportions of arboreal pollen except at the very base and at the top of the sequence, which consists of coarse breccia equivalent to the CDP (Member 4b). They attributed this to bushveld trees, while the non-arboreal pollen was attributed to/grasses. Cone C came from the Classic Section side of the Collapsed Cone and consisted of pink breccia at the base followed by red breccia and then red breccia with bones. This section was relatively constant in its distribution of pollen with the arboreal taxa representing plants from riverine, or other relatively wet, habitats. The Rodent Corner sample is shown as being taken from the area of the site known as the Archway and may not be directly related to the actual Rodent Corner fossil bed. It consisted of pink breccia consistent with the CDP (Member 4b). It contained high proportions of grass pollen and the tree pollen came from vegetation that existed in drier habitats, but the age of this deposit is unknown. Based on the known stratigraphy of the site, the pollen sequence would seem to suggest greater wetland and arboreal pollen, and thus a mixture or trend from wetland to closed environments in the pre 2.61 Ma deposits of M2 w and more open environments during the post 2.58 Ma deposits of the Upper Collapsed Cone and parts of the CDP (Member 4b).

Isotopic Analyses

Carbon isotope data were obtained from the tooth enamel of many mammalian species from Member 3 (Sponheimer et al., 1999, 2001), including hominins (Sponheimer and Lee-Thorp, 1999), and Hopley et al. (2006) analyzed rodent samples from the Rodent Corner bone bed and the East (Exit) Quarry (Figure 7.2). These data reveal that the M3 bovids were dominated by browsers, including animals that were morphologically mixed feeders, e.g., *Aepyceros*. Equids were predominately grazers, but other perissodactyls showed interesting results. *Ceratotherium* was in the range of mixed feeders, and *Ancylotherium* and *Diceros* were in the browser range. Sponheimer et al. (1999) differentiated between grazers, which focus on plains grasses, and fresh grass grazers, which focus on grasses found in wetland habitats. *Australopithecus africanus* is in the range of mixed feeders, as is *Hyaena makapani* (Sponheimer and Lee-Thorp, 1999). The conclusion overall was that the diets of the fauna suggested a wooded but mosaic habitat in which there were open wetland habitats available, an interpretation that is in part consistent with the pollen signature from the pre-2.61 Ma deposits (Cadman and Rayner, 1989). Fourie et al. (2002) analyzed the *Parapapio* species from Makapansgat and suggested two dietary patterns – one in *P. broomi* (mixed C_3 diet with abundant rootstocks) and the other represented in *P. jonesi/P. whitei* (mixed C_4 diet with fewer roots). Hopley et al. (2006) analyzed the microfauna from Rodent Corner and from the Exit Quarry and concluded that because of the lack of any grazing specialist rodents, the habitat was more wooded than it is today. Based on the species present in this sample that show some similarity to the ~5.2 Ma Langebaanweg fauna (Pocock, 1985; Roberts et al., 2011), it may be that the rodents sampled in this area of the cave were deposited earlier than Member 3 (3.03–2.61 Ma), which could indicate a slight change from more closed to open environments through time at the Limeworks. However, it may also indicate that rodents, having been accumulated differently from larger-bodied M3 fauna, represent a part of the habitat in which a predator hunted.

Dental Wear

Schubert (2007) analyzed mesowear of seven bovid taxa from Member 3. Mesowear examines attrition–abrasion wear patterns in the diet, and the results were better aligned with the carbon isotope data than with taxonomic assumptions regarding diet. The browsers demonstrated higher attrition-based wear, whereas the mixed feeders and grazers showed higher abrasion-based wear. Schubert et al. (2006) used microwear of Bovidae from the Limeworks to compare dietary results based on mesowear to carbon isotopes. The results suggest, as do the other analyses, that there are a greater number of browsing species than would be expected using taxonomic uniformitarianism. Williams (2013) analyzed several specimens of *Parapapio whitei* from Makapansgat (stratigraphic placement not identified), and concluded that *P. whitei* consumed some underground storage organs and other terrestrial resources with heavy grit.

Taphonomy and Cave Morphology

Cave taphonomy was studied in detail by Brain (1958, 1981, 1994) and others (Berger and Clarke, 1995; de Ruiter and Berger, 2000; McKee, 2010) and their work is used here to examine possible accumulating agents for each deposit. There are many unknowns regarding the accumulations of the various deposits in the Limeworks paleo-cave. Reed (1996) suggested that the fossils from Member 2 deposits were accumulated as a result of a death trap in the cave. However, based on the newest geological findings, it is unclear from where the limited fauna derived (see above). Maguire et al. (1980) and Maguire (1985) suggested that the Member 3 deposit was accumulated by hyenas (with possible contributions from porcupines and hillwash), while the CDP deposit was accumulated *at the same time* by leopards, although in reality it depends on where in the CDP deposit the fossils were recovered as to whether they are contemporary with Member 3. Indeed, part of Member 2 is also contemporary with the CDP. While Members 3 and CDP share much of the same fauna, the abundances of the animals are quite different and this likely reflects different accumulating agents in different parts of the cave. The CDP deposits represent the retreat of a horizontal cave entrance, whereas the M2 w red siltstone and sandstones represent material winnowed further back into the cave. The nature of the entrance to the cave would have permitted access by a variety of animals that is very different to the often more vertical entrances to paleo-caves in the Gauteng area like Sterkfontein. However, given that these fossils derive from dump material, sampling effects may also be responsible for the differences. Because the CDP is a talus cone formed by the retreat of the entrance through time, the fossils found in that deposit were accumulated in association with a large cave entrance.

The fossils in Member 3 were deposited in a low recess against the wall and ceiling at the western side of the paleo-cavern. Access to this region was likely via the talus cone entrance associated with the CDP. The recess was unlikely to have been in a dark zone of the cave but rather on the edge of a large, well-lit cavern. In contrast, the deposits of M2 w would have been located in a dark part of the cavern prior to the entrance retreating. The OAE deposits represent infill from a completely different entrance that may have been more vertical. These geomorphological differences during deposition, as well as their varying ages, are likely to account – at least in part – for differences observed in the assemblages in taxonomy and abundances of taxa in each collection area.

Summary

Based on the history and geology of the fossil site described above, in the next section we will integrate the various geologic, isotopic, microwear, and habitat reconstruction data for each collection zone of the cave. We will also utilize new modern community data to reconstruct the habitat for the various accumulations for the paleo-cave.

Materials and Methods

Fossils from the Limeworks were mostly taken from the sediment blocks removed by the miners. Most of the fossils from the Grey Breccia (Member 3) and Member 2 were removed and cleaned with a blunt punch; there was no acid preparation involved (James Kitching, pers. comm., 1994). Craniodental fossils were identified to species level by various researchers (Dart, 1948, 1957; George, 1950; Kitching, 1951, 1963, 1965, 1980; Toerien, 1952, 1955; Greenwood, 1955, 1958; Churcher, 1956, 2000; Wells and Cooke, 1956; Ewer, 1957b, 1958, 1967; Freedman, 1957, 1960, 1976; Hooijer, 1958; Robinson, 1963; Gentry, 1970; Maier, 1970, 1972; Randall, 1972, 1981; Eisenhart, 1974; Brickhill, 1976; Cooke, 1978c, 1988, 1994; Gentry and Gentry, 1978a, 1978b; Maguire, 1979; Vrba, 1987a, 1987b; Bender, 1990, 1992; Reed, 1996; Cooke, 2005). Postcranial elements were stored by family (or species, if known) and by element in wooden boxes (KER; KLK, personal obs.).

Ecomorphology and Community Structure

In order to reevaluate the habitat reconstructions derived from the fauna, we performed new analyses that involved analyzing the distribution of mammalian functional traits in the fossil collection for comparison with the distribution of mammalian functional traits in modern game parks, game reserves, and nature reserves throughout Africa. We used categories of diet and substrate use for the functional traits of the mammals (Table 7.1). Allocation of the fossil material to functional traits was based on previously developed methodologies (Janis, 1988; Van Valkenburgh, 1988; Spencer, 1995a; Reed, 2008; DiMaggio et al., 2015a). Mandibular measurements of modern and fossil bovid taxa, as well as isotopic information, predicts feeding behavior (Sponheimer et al., 1999). Data from Benefit and McCrossin (1990) on shearing crests was used to reconstruct primate diets. Some of the fossil animals, such as the aardvark (*Orycteropus* cf. *afer*), were assigned trophic and substrate traits based on their similarity to their modern congeners.

We totalled the number of species greater than 500 g that possessed each of the functional traits for each modern locality; we did the same for each assemblage at Makapansgat. This provides a taxon-free method of understanding the assemblages and communities so that the fossil sites can be comparable to the modern localities (Reed, 2008). Rather than categorizing the 202 modern localities by vegetation physiognomy (e.g., forest, grassland, etc.), we present them in the figures in categories of mean annual rainfall (MAR) derived from WorldClim. Correspondence analysis (CA) is an exploratory ordination technique that allows both the functional traits and the localities to be analyzed in the same ordination, suggesting possible driving forces for the placement of the localities. We only used the six functional traits that gave us the highest separation among the localities in the CA: arboreal, aquatic, terrestrial, frugivory, fresh grass grazing, and grazing. After performing the CA, we plotted the first two dimensions and the first and third dimensions in bivariate space, to observe the distribution of the fossil assemblages within the overall ecological space defined by the functional traits of the modern communities. The first

Table 7.1 List of functional traits assigned to extant and fossil species.

Trophic code (TR)	Meaning
B	Browser/leaves
C	Meat
CB	Meat/bone
CI	Meat/insects
F	Fruit
FG	Fresh grass
FL	Fruit/leaves
G	Grass
I	Insects
MF	Mixed feeder – leaves/grass
OM	No reference
R	Roots/tubers
Substrate code (SS)	
A	Arboreal
AQ	Aquatic
F	Fossorial
TA	Terrestrial/arboreal
T	Terrestrial

dimension accounted for 75 percent, the second for 11 percent, and the third for 7 percent of the variation among the localities. The fossil assemblages were placed within these plots as supplementary points so that their position among the modern localities could be visualized.

Results

Member 1 (Basal Flowstone) Summary

The Member 1 basal flowstone is a thick sequence of pure white flowstone that was extensive across much of the Makapansgat Limeworks prior to its extraction by mining. Only a few exposures of the flowstone remain, the largest being in the Collapsed Cone area of the limeworks. The Member 1b flowstone has uranium concentrations that are too low for U–Pb dating, but has an age estimate of approximately 4.2–3.6 Ma for its most recent layers based on magnetostratigraphy and faunal correlation (Hopley et al., 2007b). The older parts of the flowstone could be early Pliocene or late Miocene in age. Carbon isotope values of the flowstone are low and invariant (−8.8 ‰ to −7.1 ‰), indicating a stable vegetation structure dominated by C_3 vegetation. Five stable isotope samples taken from other sections of the Makapansgat Limeworks Member 1b flowstones (North Alcove of the Original Ancient Entrance and the Entrance Quarry) also show the characteristic low $\delta^{13}C$ values of the Member 1b flowstones (Hopley et al., 2009), indicating C_3 vegetation throughout the up to 20-m thick (Latham et al., 2003) Member 1b sequence. This contrasts with all the younger Makapansgat Limeworks faunal localities that show clear evidence for a mixed C_3 and C_4 vegetation, as occurs in the valley today. Younger speleothems from elsewhere in the Makapansgat Valley, such as the early Pleistocene Buffalo Cave Flowstone (Hopley et al., 2007a, 2018) and the late Holocene stalagmites from Cold Air Cave (Holmgren et al., 2003), all show the higher carbon isotope values indicative of mixed C_3 and C_4 vegetation and systematic changes in vegetation structure across orbital (precession) cycles.

Table 7.2 lists the species found in the various breccia blocks, classified on the basis of sedimentological type (akin to Members 2–5). As mentioned above, it is likely unknown where all of the "Member 2" material derived, but we include it for comparison. We also list fauna for assemblages considered M3 and CDP (previously M4b), as well as the microfauna from Rodent Corner and the Exit Quarry Basal Red Mud Collection (Member 2 East). Abundances are from Reed (1996), and are based on craniodental remains unless a taxon was known only from identifiable postcrania, e.g., fossil humeri of *Orycteropus* species. Species lists were updated to new nomenclature as of 2016. Table 7.3 lists a composite result of isotope values and micro-/mesowear for various mammals.

Member 2 (Red Siltstone and Sandstone) Summary

As can be seen in Table 7.2, the fossil material assumed to be associated with this deposit is quite limited, and this is not surprising given that the red siltstones have been winnowed from an entrance talus cone breccia. As such, only the smaller bones would have been reworked from these entrance deposits by

Table 7.2 Species list from the Makapansgat Members and Rodent Corner (RC).

Order	Class	Family/Tribe	Species	M2	M3	M4	M5	RC
Mammalia	Afrosoricida	Chrysochloridae	*Calcochloris hamiltoni*	0	2	0	0	1
	Carnivora	Canidae	aff. *Canis brevoristris*	0	1	0	0	0
			Canis sp.	1	5	0	0	0
			Canis cf. *L. adustus*	0	6	0	1	0
			Canis cf. *L. mesomelas*	0	7	1	0	0
			Vulpes cf. *V. chama*	0	5	1	0	0
		Felidae	*Acinonyx* cf. *A. jubatus*	0	3	0	0	0
			Caracal sp.	0	17	0	0	0
			Dinofelis sp.	2	9	1	0	0
			Dinofelis darti	0	9	1	0	0
			Felis sp.	1	8	0	0	0
			Felis "brickhilli" nov. sp.	2	2	0	0	0
			Felis cf. *F. lybica*	0	9	0	0	0
			Homotherium sp.	2	0	0	0	0
			Homotherium problematicum	0	1	0	0	0
			Leptailurus cf. *L. serval*	0	2	0	0	0
			Panthera sp.	1	0	0	0	0
			Panthera cf. *P. pardus*	0	9	0	0	0
		Hyaenidae	*Crocuta* cf *C. crocuta*	0	0	1	0	0
			Hyaena makapani	0	259	2	0	0
			Pachycrocuta sp.	1	0	0	0	0
			Pachycrocuta brevirostris	0	12	0	0	0
		Herpestidae	*Crossarchus* sp.	0	0	1	0	0
			Galerella sp.	1	1	0	0	0
		Mustelidae	Large sp.	0	1	0	0	0
	Certartiodactyla	Aepycerotini	*Aepyceros* sp. 1	0	34	0	0	0
			aff. *Aepyceros*	0	11	0	0	0
			Aepyceros cf. *A. melampus*	0	0	0	3	0
		Alcelaphini	Alcelaphini indet.	0	332	12	0	0
			Damaliscus gentryi	0	0	0	1	0
			Megalotragus sp.	0	3	0	0	0
			Parmularius sp. nov.	0	24	0	0	0
			Parmularius braini	0	26	0	0	0

Table 7.2 (cont.)

Order	Class	Family/Tribe	Species	M2	M3	M4	M5	RC
		Antilopini	Gazella vanhoepeni	3	506	2	0	0
		Bovini	Simatherium cf. kohllarseni	0	54	8	0	0
			Syncerus cf. S. acoeloutus	0	0	0	3	0
		Boselaphini	?Boselaphus sp.	0	128	0	0	0
		Cephalophini	Cephalophus sp.	0	20	0	0	0
		Hippotragini	?Hippotragini	0	1	0	0	0
			Wellsiana torticornuta	0	1	0	0	0
			Hippotragus cookei	0	7	0	0	0
			Hippotragus gigas	0	0	0	1	0
		Neotragini	Neotragini sp.	1	157	1	6	0
			Oreotragus cf. oreotragus	0	15	0	0	0
			Oreotragus major	0	0	0	1	0
		Ovibovini	Makapania broomi	0	401	3	3	0
		Reduncini	Redunca darti	0	552	4	0	0
			Kobus I	0	0	0	1	0

Table 7.3 Previously published dietary isotope values from Makapansgat fauna. Carbon and oxygen isotope data are presented in the conventional delta (δ) notation in parts per thousand (‰) relative to V-PDB.

Guild	Member/locality	Species	Specimen no.	$\delta^{13}C$	$\delta^{18}O$	Source
Browser	3	Aepyceros sp.	M7504	−11	2.1	Sponheimer et al. (1999)
Browser	3	Aepyceros sp.	M9178	−8.6	−2.9	Sponheimer et al. (1999)
Browser	3	Aepyceros sp.	M9177	−8.6	−1.4	Sponheimer et al. (1999)
Browser	3	Gazella vanhoepeni	M7805	−12.4	2.3	Sponheimer et al. (1999)
Browser	3	Gazella vanhoepeni	M7811	−12.8	1.7	Sponheimer et al. (1999)
Browser	3	Gazella vanhoepeni	M8823	−10.9	3.2	Sponheimer et al. (1999)
Browser	3	Gazella vanhoepeni	M9014	−11.5	1.9	Sponheimer et al. (1999)
Browser	3	Gazella vanhoepeni	M529	−10.3	−0.2	2004
Browser	3	Gazella vanhoepeni	M1188	−10.6	0.8	2004
Browser	3	Tragelaphus sp. aff. T. angasi	M6325	−12.7	2	Sponheimer et al. (1999)
Browser	3	Tragelaphus sp. aff. T. angasi	M7689	−11.8	0.4	Sponheimer et al. (1999)
Browser	3	Tragelaphus sp. aff. T. angasi	M9053	−12.6	1.1	Sponheimer et al. (1999)
Browser	3	Tragelaphus sp. aff. T. angasi	M183	−9.5	1.7	Sponheimer et al. (1999)
Browser	3	Tragelaphus sp. aff. T. angasi	M760	−10	0.8	2004
Browser	3	Tragelaphus pricei	M6769	−12.5	−0.2	Sponheimer et al. (1999)
Browser	3	Tragelaphus pricei	M19	−12.0	1.4	Sponheimer et al. (1999)
Browser	3	Tragelaphus pricei	M6477	−10.9	1.4	Sponheimer et al. (1999)
Browser	3	Ancylotherium hennigi	M2143	−10.6	−1.1	Sponheimer and Lee-Thorp (1999)
Browser	3	Ancylotherium hennigi	M140	−10.1	−0.5	Sponheimer and Lee-Thorp (1999)
Browser	3	Ancylotherium hennigi	M2428	−10	−0.9	Sponheimer and Lee-Thorp (1999)
Browser	3	Cephalophus sp.	M6518	−11.4	1.8	Sponheimer and Lee-Thorp (1999)
Browser	3	Cephalophus sp.	M6281	−11.6	3.2	Sponheimer and Lee-Thorp (1999)
Browser	3	Diceros bicomis	M642/2106	−13.1	−5.6	Sponheimer and Lee-Thorp (1999)
Browser	3	Diceros bicomis	M2108	−11	−1.1	Sponheimer and Lee-Thorp (1999)

Table 7.3 (cont.)

Guild	Member/locality	Species	Specimen no.	δ¹³C	δ¹⁸O	Source
Browser	3	Diceros bicornis	M2109	−10.8	−3.5	Sponheimer and Lee-Thorp (1999)
Browser	3	Gazella gracilior	M766	−12.4	3.9	Sponheimer and Lee-Thorp (1999)
Browser	3	Gazella gracilior	M767	−10.7	3.1	Sponheimer and Lee-Thorp (1999)
Browser	3	Giraffa jumae	M2085	−12.6	4.4	Sponheimer and Lee-Thorp (1999)
Browser	3	Giraffa jumae	M936	−11.9	5.4	Sponheimer and Lee-Thorp (1999)
Browser	3	Giraffa jumae	M938	−11	2.4	Sponheimer and Lee-Thorp (1999)
Browser	3	Giraffa jumae	M1113	−10.8	0.6	Sponheimer and Lee-Thorp (1999)
Browser	3	Giraffa jumae	M528	−10.5	3.2	Sponheimer and Lee-Thorp (1999)
Browser	3	Giraffa jumae	M8853	−10.5	1.6	Sponheimer and Lee-Thorp (1999)
Browser	3	Giraffa jumae	M1798	−9.6	1.1	2004
Browser	3	Neotragini sp.	M1209	−12.4	0.7	Sponheimer and Lee-Thorp (1999)
Browser	3	Neotragini sp.	M9172	−11.6	1.6	Sponheimer and Lee-Thorp (1999)
Browser	3	Neotragini sp.	M1177	−11.3	−0.5	Sponheimer and Lee-Thorp (1999)
Browser	3	Neotragini sp.	M9173	−11.2	1.8	Sponheimer and Lee-Thorp (1999)
Browser	3	Oreotragus cf. oreotragus	M6293	−11.7	2	Sponheimer and Lee-Thorp (1999)
Browser	3	Oreotragus cf. oreotragus	M997	−11.4	−1.2	Sponheimer and Lee-Thorp (1999)
Mixed feeder	3	Simatherium cf. kohllarseni	M7319	−4.4	0.8	Sponheimer and Lee-Thorp (1999)
Mixed feeder	3	Simatherium cf. kohllarseni	M8163	−4.3	0.2	Sponheimer and Lee-Thorp (1999)
Mixed feeder	3	Simatherium cf. kohllarseni	M388	−3.9	0.4	Sponheimer and Lee-Thorp (1999)
Mixed feeder	3	Simatherium cf. kohllarseni	M8161	−3.4	−1.1	Sponheimer and Lee-Thorp (1999)
Mixed feeder	3	Makapania broomi	M1398	−3.6	−0.8	Sponheimer et al. (1999)
Mixed feeder	3	Makapania broomi	M6274	−1.0	2.4	Sponheimer et al. (1999)
Mixed feeder	3	Makapania broomi	M6528	−3.5	1	Sponheimer et al. (1999)
Mixed feeder	3	Makapania broomi	M978	−5.3	−1.7	Sponheimer et al. (1999)
Mixed feeder	3	Makapania broomi	M7685	−0.3	0	2004
Mixed feeder	3	Boselaphini	M591	−8.8	−2.6	2004
Mixed feeder	3	Boselaphini	M7243	−5.2	−0.6	2004
Grazer	3	Parmularius braini	M6272	−1.2	1.3	Sponheimer et al. (1999)
Grazer	3	Parmularius braini	M774	−1.2	−0.6	Sponheimer et al. (1999)
Grazer	3	Parmularius braini	M8351	−0.2	−0.9	Sponheimer et al. (1999)
Grazer	3	Parmularius braini	M8835	−0.6	−0.7	Sponheimer et al. (1999)
Grazer	3	Redunca darti	M6269	−4.5	0.1	Sponheimer et al. (1999)
Grazer	3	Redunca darti	M8897	−1.4	−2.1	Sponheimer et al. (1999)
Grazer	3	Redunca darti	M6609	−0.6	1	Sponheimer et al. (1999)
Grazer	3	Redunca darti	M6305	−0.5	−0.8	Sponheimer et al. (1999)
Grazer	3	Redunca darti	M387	0.4	0.4	2004
Grazer	3	Redunca darti	M6280	1.3	0.2	1997
Grazer	3	Parmularius sp. nov.	M6963	−0.2	2.1	Sponheimer and Lee-Thorp (1999)
Grazer	3	Parmularius sp. nov.	M6669	0.9	−0.9	Sponheimer and Lee-Thorp (1999)
Grazer	3	Parmularius sp. nov.	M6308	1.3	3.1	Sponheimer and Lee-Thorp (1999)
Grazer	3	Ceratotherium simum	M8939	−4.3	−2.2	1997
Grazer	3	Ceratotherium simum	M8940	−3.6	−1.6	1997
Grazer	3	Ceratotherium simum	M167	−3.3	−2.3	1997
Grazer	3	Ceratotherium simum	M2088	−2.7	−1.7	1997
Grazer	3	Eurygnathohippus lybicum	M2505	−2	−3.4	Sponheimer and Lee-Thorp (1999)

Table 7.3 (cont.)

Guild	Member/locality	Species	Specimen no.	$\delta^{13}C$	$\delta^{18}O$	Source
Grazer	3	Eurygnathohhippus lybicum	M2480	−1.3	−1.3	Sponheimer and Lee-Thorp (1999)
Grazer	3	Eurygnathohhippus lybicum	M2476	0	−1.5	Sponheimer and Lee-Thorp (1999)
Grazer	3	Eurygnathohhippus lybicum	M193	0.2	−2.4	Sponheimer and Lee-Thorp (1999)
Grazer	3	Notochoerus capensis	M2025	−1	−2	Sponheimer and Lee-Thorp (1999)
Grazer	3	Notochoerus capensis	M8913	−0.6	−1.2	Sponheimer and Lee-Thorp (1999)
Grazer	3	Potamochoeroides shawi	M1826/1890	−2.3	−4.9	1998
Grazer	3	Potamochoeroides shawi	M1859	−2.2	−2.4	1998
Grazer	3	Potamochoeroides shawi	M1886	−1.8	−6	1998
Carnivore	3	Hyaena makapani	M6909	−9.3	−2.2	Sponheimer and Lee-Thorp (1999)
Carnivore	3	Hyaena makapani	M8347	−8.1	−3	Sponheimer and Lee-Thorp (1999)
Carnivore	3	Hyaena makapani	M8314	−7	−3.9	Sponheimer and Lee-Thorp (1999)
Mixed feeder	3	Xenohystrix crassidens	M1809	−8.2	−2	1997
Mixed feeder	3	Xenohystrix crassidens	M2510	−4.9	−5.6	1997
Primate	Lime Dump	Australopithecus africanus	MLD 12	−7.7	−1.7	Sponheimer et al. (2013)
Primate	Lime Dump	Australopithecus africanus	MLD 28	−8.1	−3.5	Sponheimer et al. (2013)
Primate	Lime Dump	Australopithecus africanus	MLD 30	−5.6	−3.9	Sponheimer et al. (2013)
Primate	Lime Dump	Australopithecus africanus	MLD 41	−11.3	−3.9	Sponheimer et al. (2013)
Micromammals	MRCIS	Otomys cf. gracilis	n/a	−7	0.9	Hopley et al. (2006)
Micromammals	MRCIS	Otomys cf. gracilis	n/a	−5.8	−1	Hopley et al. (2006)
Micromammals	MRCIS	Otomys cf. gracilis	n/a	−8.1	−1	Hopley et al. (2006)
Micromammals	MRCIS	Otomys cf. gracilis	n/a	−4.5	−3	Hopley et al. (2006)
Micromammals	MRCIS	Otomys cf. gracilis	n/a	−5.6	−4.4	Hopley et al. (2006)
Micromammals	MRCIS	Mystromys cf. hausleitneri	n/a	−7.7	−1.1	Hopley et al. (2006)
Micromammals	MRCIS	Mystromys cf. hausleitneri	n/a	−8.9	−2.3	Hopley et al. (2006)
Micromammals	MRCIS	Mystromys cf. hausleitneri	n/a	−10	−4.2	Hopley et al. (2006)
Micromammals	MRCIS	Mystromys cf. hausleitneri	n/a	−7.9	−2.3	Hopley et al. (2006)
Micromammals	MRCIS	Myosorex cf. varius	n/a	−5.5	−2.7	Hopley et al. (2006)
Micromammals	MRCIS	Myosorex cf. varius	n/a	−8.4	−3.7	Hopley et al. (2006)
Micromammals	EXQRM	Otomys cf. gracilis	n/a	−3.6	−1.1	Hopley et al. (2006)
Micromammals	EXQRM	Otomys cf. gracilis	n/a	−9.6	0.6	Hopley et al. (2006)
Micromammals	EXQRM	Otomys cf. gracilis	n/a	−5.6	−3	Hopley et al. (2006)
Micromammals	EXQRM	Otomys cf. gracilis	n/a	−4.3	−2.7	Hopley et al. (2006)
Micromammals	EXQRM	Otomys cf. gracilis	n/a	−4.5	−1.6	Hopley et al. (2006)
Micromammals	EXQRM	Otomys cf. gracilis	n/a	−4.9	−2.2	Hopley et al. (2006)
Micromammals	EXQRM	Mystromys cf. hausleitneri	n/a	−6.3	−0.4	Hopley et al. (2006)
Micromammals	EXQRM	Mystromys cf. hausleitneri	n/a	−6.7	−1.1	Hopley et al. (2006)
Micromammals	EXQRM	Mystromys cf. hausleitneri	n/a	−7.6	−1.1	Hopley et al. (2006)
Micromammals	EXQRM	Mystromys cf. hausleitneri	n/a	−6.6	−1.4	Hopley et al. (2006)
Micromammals	EXQRM	Mystromys cf. hausleitneri	n/a	−5.6	−2.6	Hopley et al. (2006)
Micromammals	EXQRM	Myosorex cf. varius	n/a	−5.5	−1.5	Hopley et al. (2006)
Micromammals	EXQRM	Myosorex cf. varius	n/a	−6.4	−1.1	Hopley et al. (2006)
Micromammals	EXQRM	Myosorex cf. varius	n/a	−6.5	−3	Hopley et al. (2006)

Dates with no citation publication from Sponheimer collection data.

water flow. If any bones larger than the clasts exist then these must have either been brought in by carnivores or have entered the cave via death traps. None of this material possesses any bone modification, such as weathering, carnivore chewing, or gnaw marks, and as such it is compatible with a death trap or natural death scenario. While the main entrance to the cave is reconstructed as being horizontal, there were no doubt small vertical entrances in the ceiling of the cave. This is fairly consistent with the types of animals that are found, that is, mostly felids (42.86 percent), bovids (28.57 percent), and primates (28.57 percent). There is no pattern in the ratio of cranial to postcranial material as animals increase in body size (Klein and Cruz-Uribe, 1984), which would suggest a carnivore accumulation. In fact, there appears to be no identifiable pattern other than random accumulation of fauna.

As there are only 13 species identified in this collection, reconstructing the habitat seems pointless, especially because it is not clear that all of the red siltstone and sandstone deposits from the *ex-situ* blocks represent the same "Member 2," and thus the same time period. Interestingly, however, 36 percent of the species attributed to these deposits are either arboreal or semi-arboreal. Cadman and Rayner (1989), based on the pollen that they recovered, suggested that Member 2 w (as represented in the Classic Section) was a forest that changed to open grassland consistent with the isotopic change from Member 1 to Member 3. Should this collection actually derive from the same place in the cave, it could be fairly closed with MAR ranging from 700 to 900 mm per year based on the pollen; however with limited fauna, we cannot say anything definitively.

Member 3

The fauna that derives from Member 3 was likely deposited as one unit, although there may be some limited time-averaging involved. There are 7420 craniodental specimens from this member that have been identified to represent 62 species (Table 7.2). There are an additional 22,652 postcranial specimens from this Member, but only 15,604 are identifiable to element. Distal and proximal ends of long bones are present, but most of the shafts have been broken into flakes or long, thin fragments. The most abundant element (2028 specimens, 13.12 percent) is humeral shaft fragments between 2 and 6 cm in length; this is followed by metacarpal shaft fragments (1090 specimens, 6.99 percent), and distal humeri (1016 specimens, 6.51 percent). Metacarpals and humeri are some of the densest bones of the body in artiodactyls (Lyman, 1994); therefore, their high representation is expected simply on the basis of bone density variation.

There are 259 specimens of *Hyaena makapani* that were divided into age classes using the wear of the p3, with Age Class I representing very young individuals with deciduous teeth and Age Class V representing very old individuals. There were 95 specimens (minimum number of individuals (MNI) = 18) that could not be aged as they were missing p3. There are also 271 specimens of hyena coprolites, which also provide evidence that the hyenas lived in the cave, at least part-time. Puncture marks that are typical of carnivore crushing and additional carnivore tooth marks, occur frequently on many bones. Most of the mammals represented are in the same size range, i.e., there are adults of smaller mammals, but juvenile representatives of the larger ones. In fact, of the equids, giraffids, rhinocerotids, and large bovids, 73 percent are juvenile individuals. The equids especially appear to range in age from birth to 2 months old, based on tooth eruption patterns of modern horses. Most of the giraffids are also young individuals, although there are more adult individuals represented in the long bones of these species. This pattern is consistent with hyenas hunting small or juvenile animals some of the time, and scavenging and/or hunting larger or adult animals and transporting less of the carcass. This results in pieces of the larger animals being brought back to the cave together with complete skeletons of animals under about 80 kg. There are adult cranial specimens of "Neotragini," Cephalophini, Reduncini, Antilopini, and Suidae, but very few adult cranial specimens of animals over 120 kg. We assume that the heads of larger adult mammals may have been too large or bulky for hyenas to transport. In the postcranial material, the situation is reversed. Bovid Size Class III (85–296 kg) is more highly represented than the smaller size classes (<85 kg). This is due to two factors: (1) hyenas were able to move limbs of larger animals because they weighed less than the whole carcass, and (2) it is probable that the bones of smaller animals were consumed and thus eliminated elsewhere (Marean, 1991; Lyman, 1994).

Finally, we would like to note that there was a large number of teeth that Vrba (classified in boxes in storage at the University of the Witwatersrand) has labeled "?*Boselaphus*" (Table 7.2). These teeth share characteristics with boselaphins and tragelaphins – the crenulated enamel of the former and the shape of the lobes of the latter – and probably could be placed in either. However, if the teeth belong to Boselaphini, then they should be compared with the *Miotragocerus* (Gentry, 2010) from Langabaanweg for possible further identification.

Many of the smaller carpals, tarsals, and astragali in the M3 collection have been acid-etched or eroded, i.e., they have been through an animal's stomach. Of the total postcranial material, only 4.66 percent are these small, hard bones and this pattern suggests that many of the rest of them were eliminated outside of the cave. Marean (1991) has shown that hyenas swallow the carpal and tarsal complexes whole, and these smaller bones are eliminated elsewhere. All of these facts suggest that the majority of this fossil assemblage was accumulated by *Hyaena makapani*.

Additional accumulation may have been from porcupines, as there are three species that are present in the collection. Many of the bovid metapodials (37 percent) are weathered, although most of the other long bones show no weathering. The weathered metapodials were also gnawed by porcupines, who likely contributed to the assemblage by dragging these bones into the cave. The unweathered bones, presumably deposited inside the cave, show no evidence of being gnawed.

Maguire et al. (1985) suggested that the M3 material was concentrated in the back parts of the cave by water. This seems quite unlikely, as Latham et al. (1999) suggest ample evidence against flooding to deposit fossils further into the cave. Moreover, the bone and speleothem clasts of the Grey Bone Breccia have a manganese coating derived from the weathering of dolomite by meteoric waters. The paucity of clastic material in the deposit does not support the interpretation of water accumulation. The most plausible explanation for the accumulator of the M3 deposit is as the result of action by hyenas with a little help from porcupines. These fossils, which were deposited in a speleothem grotto, were then encased and capped by a speleothem dated to ~2.61 Ma.

Habitat reconstructions for this member range from closed forested environment (Cadman and Rayner, 1989) to open, arid savanna (Benefit and McCrossin, 1990). Most of the other habitat reconstructions lie between those extremes (Wells and Cooke, 1956; de Graaff, 1957; Ewer, 1958; Maier, 1970; Klein, 1977; Cooke, 1978c; Howell, 1978b; Kitching, 1980; Levinson, 1985; Vrba, 1985b, 1987a, 1987b; Reed, 1997). The CA plotting the first and second dimensions (Figure 7.3) suggests that the habitat was similar to the Siniaka-Minia Nature Reserve, Chad (MAR = 817 mm) and Matobo National Park (NP), Zimbabwe (MAR = 517 mm). Interestingly, Matobo NP looks much like the Makapansgat region of today, with rocky outcrops and wooded valleys. The first and third dimensions of the CA (Figure 7.4) positions Member 3 near Kruger NP, South Africa (MAR = 502 mm) and Mahango NP, Namibia (MAR = 562 mm), both of which have seasonally flooded areas. Large numbers of reduncin specimens from the deposit also suggest that there was a wetland habitat nearby. The hippopotamus indicates a river, lake, or other water source. The small tragelaphins suggest more wooded habitat as they appear to be similar to the modern bushbuck, while the larger tragelaphins indicate some patchy environments – similar to that of extant nyala and kudu. The pollen recovered from the Classic Section indicates the presence of both open and closed habitats (Cadman and Rayner, 1989), as does most of the dietary data from mesowear, microwear,

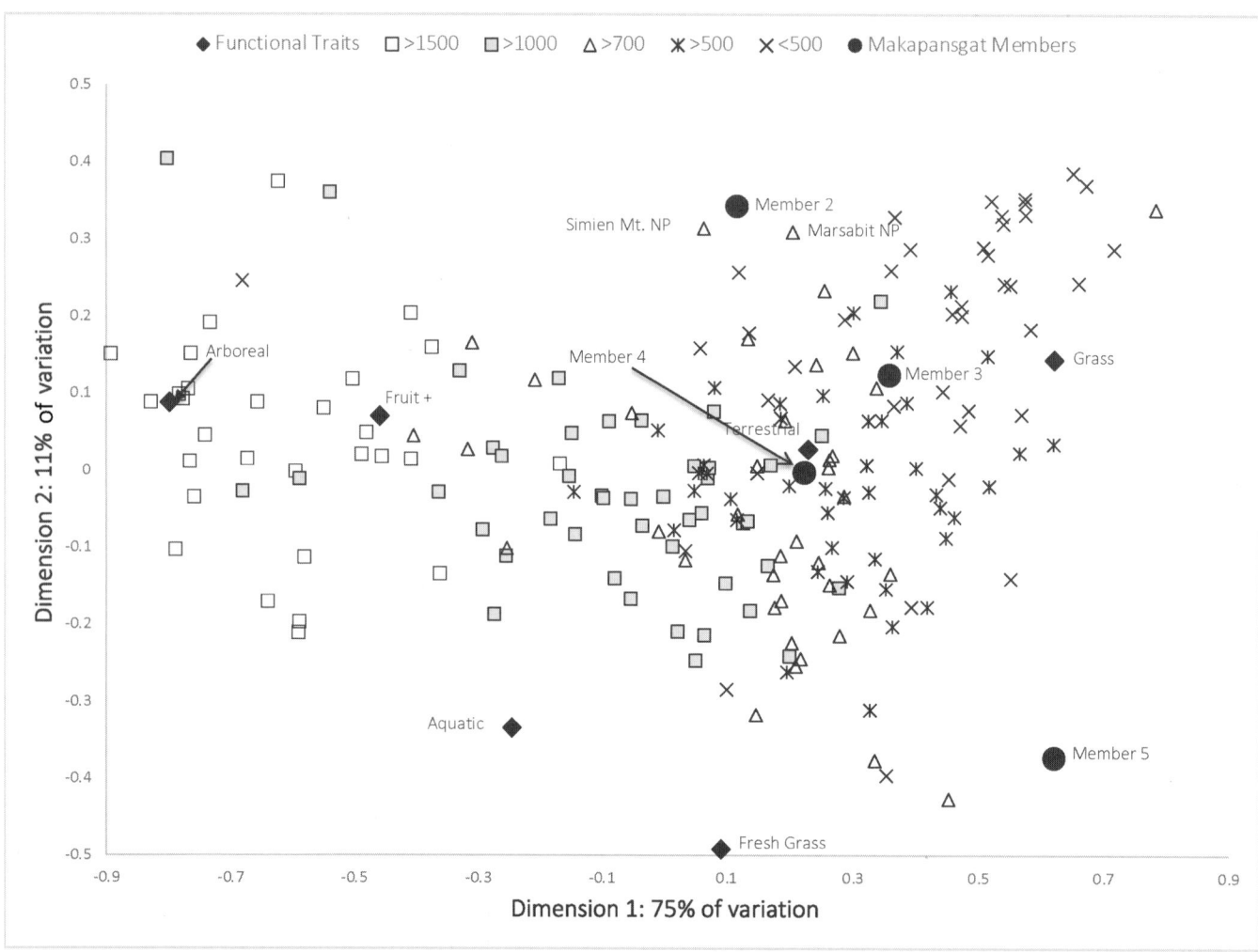

Figure 7.3 Correspondence analysis bivariate plot of the first two dimensions. The first dimension is ordinated such that the functional traits of arboreality and fruit- and leaf-eating are toward the left of the graph, while grazing is to the far right. Therefore, the left side of the graph has localities that tend to come from habitats with higher rainfall and more trees – more arboreal and frugivorous mammals. In contrast, localities with high numbers of grazing animals are to the right of the graph and these tend to be sites with lower mean annual rainfall and more open habitat. This dimension accounts for 75 percent of the variation among the modern localities. The second dimension is ordinated by functional traits that indicate the presence of rivers, lakes, or wetlands (aquatic and fresh grass grazing), which are at the bottom and contrasted with the lack of this type of taxa at the top. On the right side of the graph there is a larger distribution along the second axis because there are many modern localities that have these water sources, but do not have high annual rainfall (i.e., the Okavango Delta). This dimension accounts for 11 percent of the variation among the modern localities, and therefore the CA accounts for 86 percent of the variation among the localities. See text for comments on positioning of Makapansgat deposits.

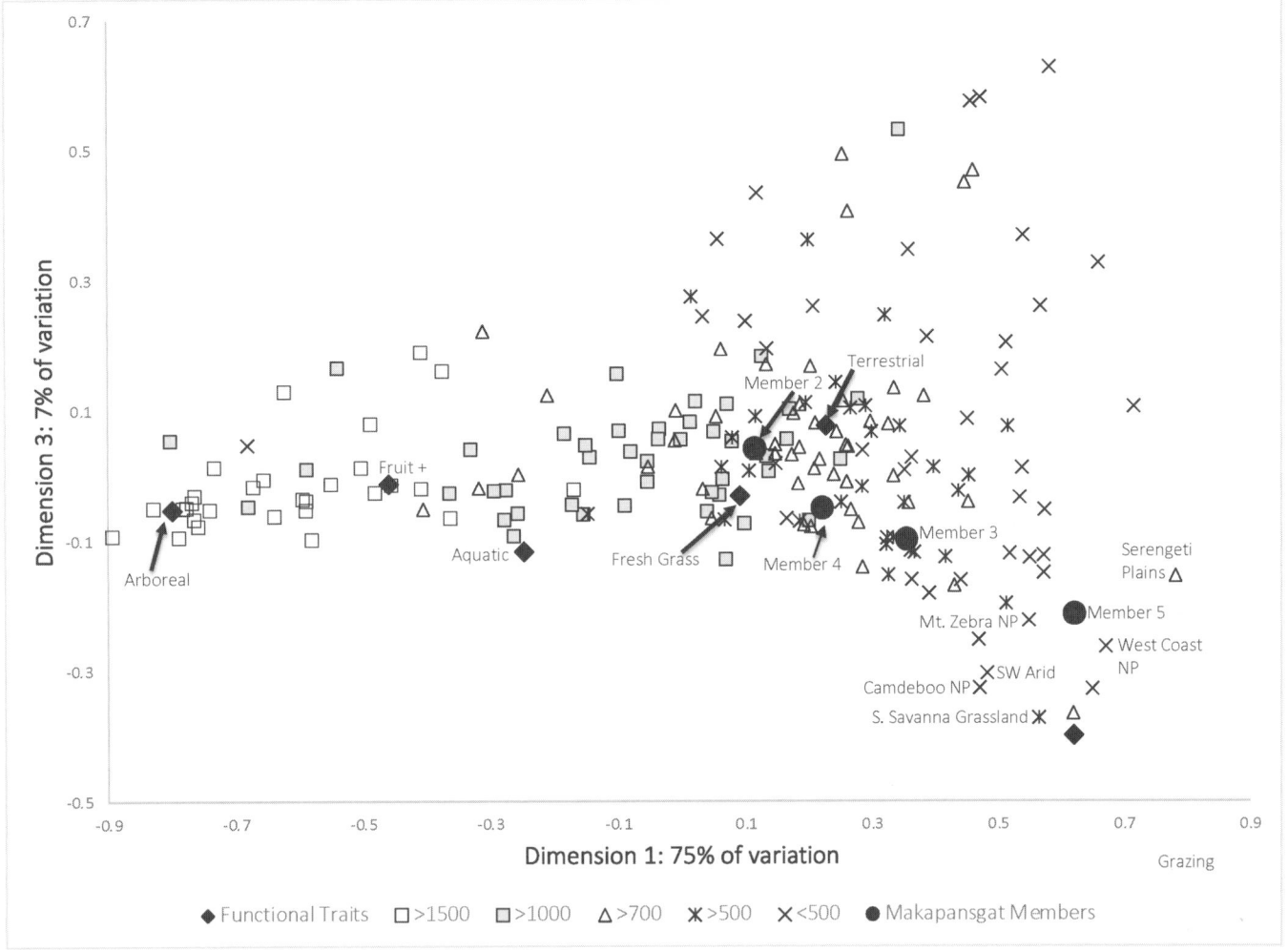

Figure 7.4 Correspondence analysis bivariate plot of the first and third dimensions. The first dimension has the same properties as those described in Figure 7.3. Dimension 3, accounting for 7 percent of the variation among the localities, is ordinated from the top with sites that are extremely unlike the others, with few numbers of taxa with the functional traits. Interestingly, these sites are all in North Africa and represent a likely extreme in community composition. See text for comments on positioning of Makapansgat deposits.

and isotopes. Macromammal carbon isotope values range from −13.1‰ to +1.3‰ (Sponheimer and Lee-Thorp, 1999), indicating the full range of browsing to grazing diets, similar to other South African faunas such as Swartkrans M1 and Sterkfontein M4 (e.g., Lee-Thorp et al., 2003). The Makapansgat Member 3 fauna lacks any low carbon isotope values indicative of the closed canopy effect (<−15‰), which are seen in the ~2.3–1.9 Ma Haasgat HGD assemblage from the northern hills of the Cradle of Humankind (Adams et al., 2013; Herries et al., 2014); however, direct comparison with the closed-canopy component of the Haasgat assemblage is hampered by the lack of isotopic data from shared species. Taken at face value, all of the Makapansgat Member 3 data indicate a mosaic habitat consisting of bushland, woodland, and wetlands with rainfall in the range of 500–800 mm per annum.

The accumulation of the Makapansgat Member 3 assemblage by a single carnivore species, *Hyaena makapani*, is unusual among South African Plio-Pleistocene cave assemblages (e.g. Pickering et al., 2004). Most Cradle of Humankind assemblages contain multiple large carnivore accumulators and, by inference, were deposited over a protracted period of time (O'Regan and Reynolds, 2009; Kuhn et al., 2017). As shown by Hopley and Maslin (2010), these multi-carnivore assemblages are characterized by a broad carbon isotope range across the carnivorous guild, suggesting that they accumulated under more than one climatic state (i.e., time- and climate-averaging). In contrast, Makapansgat Member 3 may have accumulated over a relatively brief period of time (between a few hundred and a few thousand years) and may represent a much less time-averaged data set. While there are currently only three carnivore $\delta^{13}C$ measurements from Makapansgat Member 3, they are closely clustered, between −9.3‰ and −8.1‰ (Sponheimer and Lee-Thorp, 1999; see Table 7.3). These values are in strong contrast to the single $\delta^{13}C$ measurement from a Hyaenidae cf. *Crocuta* individual (+0.8‰) from the grassland-dominated paleo-environment of Kanjera South, Kenya. Like Makapansgat Member 3, the Kanjera South assemblage shows an unusually high temporal resolution, but unlike Makapansgat Member 3 it is characterized by a dominant vegetation type – C_4 grasses (Plummer et al., 2009b). This leads to the pertinent question of whether the mixed vegetation of Makapansgat Member 3 represents a genuine savanna mosaic environment or a time-averaged accumulation of various habitats. While more research is required to produce a definitive answer to this question, on the strength of the current evidence we would suggest that Member 3 represents a genuine savanna–woodland mosaic from a relatively brief snapshot of Plio-Pleistocene time. It is also worth stressing that we have no indication of how this Member 3 environment fits within the longer-term Plio-Pleistocene climate of the Makapansgat Valley. The reconstructed "mixed environment" may by chance approximate the long-term mean vegetation for the Makapansgat Valley (i.e., accumulated during an intermediate phase of a precession cycle). Clearly, more work is required if we are to produce a firm understanding of the climate/vegetation history of this and other localities from faunal analysis.

Member 4/Central Debris Pile

This assemblage contains many of the same species as Member 3. Hyraxes are the only new mammals; the assemblage has only half the number of the bovid species (9 versus 19) that were recovered from Member 3. There are 258 craniodental specimens from 32 species. For the most part, these specimens are well preserved, but fragile. There are only 129 total postcranial specimens, which are poorly preserved. Postcranial elements are mostly complete shafts without ends, but there are several specimens that are proximal or distal parts of bones or are complete.

It is possible that the accumulating agent caused the difference in representation between Members 3 and 4, or that selective sampling of the blocks has taken place due to the lower density of fossils in the breccia blocks from these units. The accumulation pattern suggests that carnivores, but not hyenas, collected the assemblage. First, there are only two hyenid remains from the deposit; this represents 1.86 percent of the total MNI, whereas in Member 3 the percentage of hyenids to total MNIs was 6.26 percent. The carnivore to ungulate plus carnivore ratio is 17.9 percent, which is not enough for a hyenid accumulation (Klein and Cruz-Uribe, 1984).

There are two interesting points about the fauna from this assemblage: (1) the ratio of cranial material to total postcranial material is 1.57, whereas in M3 it is 0.261 (many more cranial specimens than postcranial specimens); and (2) the distribution of mammalian orders appears to show prey bias rather than reflecting community structure: 29.9 percent ungulates, 6.5 percent carnivores, 5.6 percent hyraxes, 2.8 percent rodents, and 55.14 percent primates. In extant African communities, primates range from 0 percent to 35 percent, and of course the percentage is highest in rainforest habitats. While mammalian communities of the terminal Pliocene to early Pleistocene could have been different from those of today, this is still an extremely high number of primates. Many of the primate skulls are missing the occipital region, and on four of the skulls, not only is the occiput missing, but there are four crush marks on the top of the skull. The four crush marks are in the correct position and number to have been made by bird talons (Berger and Clarke, 1995).

Studies of black eagles have shown that they specialize today on hyraxes, but will also eat baboons and small ungulates (Berger and Clarke, 1995; Sanders et al., 2003; Berger and McGraw, 2007). These prey animals range in size from 4 to 14 kg. These birds often break open the skull at the back to eat the brain, and then discard the rest of the cranium. They consume the other bones of the animal. These other bones are often regurgitated, but not necessarily where they were eaten. Consequently, we suggest that birds of prey contributed to the mostly primate and hyrax component of this assemblage. The portion of the deposit that consists of larger ungulates could have been accumulated by a leopard-like felid, or simply be random hillwash. The preservation of long bones from this member is very poor and thus it is almost impossible to see if the bones have been chewed or gnawed. There were likely two (or more) accumulators for the M4/CDP deposit, and it is highly likely that M3 and at least parts of M4 (CDP) were deposited penecontemporaneously, although fossils from the CDP could have accumulated over almost the entire life history of the cave and as such it may not be a temporally distinct unit like Member 3.

Previous habitat reconstructions for this member suggest cool, open savanna (Cadman and Rayner, 1989), and wooded, moderately open, mesic habitat (Vrba, 1988). The CA of the first and second dimensions (Figure 7.3) positions M4/CDP near Matusadona NP (MAR=762 mm), near Lake Karibe in Zimbabwe. The CA of the first and third dimensions (Figure 7.4) positions M4 near Mago National Park, Ethiopia (MAR=575). The CA plots indicate that M4/CDP had substantial available water from either lakes or rivers, with woodland and grasslands, in agreement with Vrba (1988). Again, however, if this is a time-averaged assemblage, an accurate habitat reconstruction is not possible.

Member 5

This assemblage is derived from the "Collapsed Cone" and the Horse Mandible Cave, which are quite different deposits from the other assemblages and also from each other. The Collapsed Cone deposits of M5 have been dated to younger than 2.61 Ma and so are younger than M3, perhaps significantly younger given the presence of erosional channels into the underlying deposits (Herries et al., 2013). There are 155 identified craniodental specimens, as well as 59 postcranial specimens, all of which are bovids. Sixty percent of this assemblage is cranial material and 25.8 percent of that is *Tragelaphus strepciceros*, the extant kudu. The total carnivore to ungulate ratio is 2.94, possibly indicating that carnivores did not accumulate the deposit.

These assemblages (if contemporaneous) were likely deposited during a much more open and drier environmental regime than the Pliocene and Early Pleistocene deposits. The CA of the first and second dimensions (Figure 7.3) place M5 off by itself in the lower right quadrant, with the nearest locality being the Kafue Flats portion of Kafue Flats NP, Zambia (MAR = 861). However, the CA of the first and third dimensions (Figure 7.4) place M5 in roughly the same region, but with other very open national parks, such as the Serengeti Plains, Tanzania, and Golden Gate NP, South Africa. The closest modern locality in this two-dimensional space is Mountain Zebra NP, South Africa (MAR = 356), which is exceptionally dry and open. Species identified in the M5 assemblages that reflect this more open environment include *Hippotragus gigas*,

Damaliscus gentryi, and *Equus capensis*. It may be, as suggested by Reynolds et al. (2011), that tectonic activity allowed dry open grasslands and wetlands to co-exist across the environment. However, the presence of bushbuck and kudu in the assemblage still suggests that there was some woody cover, although probably patchy in distribution, and *Kobus*, *Syncerus*, and *Hippopotamus* indicate a nearby water source and fresh grass for feeding. It is possible that the more grassland-adapted species were recovered from Horse Mandible Cave, whereas the more woodland-adapted taxa were recovered from the Collapsed Cone, or that the environment featured high levels of habitat heterogeneity.

Rodent Corner and Exit Quarry

The Makapansgat Limeworks has yielded two distinct micromammal assemblages (Pocock, 1987), one from the Makapansgat Rodent Corner *in-situ* pink breccia (MRCIS), and one from the Exit Quarry basal Red Mud (EXQRM). These two assemblages are independent of the macromammal M3 and M4 deposits and are best viewed as temporally distinct units (Maguire et al., 1985; Latham et al., 1999, 2003). Based on biostratigraphic correlation with other South African micromammal assemblages, the two assemblages have been assigned a mid-Pliocene age of *ca.* 3.3–3.5 Ma (Pocock, 1987; Denys, 1999). The three most abundant micromammal species at Makapansgat Limeworks, the extinct *Otomys* cf. *gracilis* and *Mystromys* cf. *hausleitneri* and the extant *Myosorex* cf. *varius*, were subjected to paleodietary analysis using a combined stable isotope and dental microwear approach (Hopley et al., 2006). Carbon isotopes indicate the presence of a C_4 component to the diet of each of the mid-Pliocene species and a broadly similar diet to modern-day micromammals living in the Makapansgat Valley (Hopley et al., 2006). Thus, a woodland and/or bushland region with grass ground cover was present. This is slightly different from M3 times, which appear to have been deposited during a wetter environment.

Discussion and Conclusion

The paleoenvironments reconstructed for the collection units for which we have suggested habitats are similar to the ones that exist in the Makapansgat Valley today. There may have been lesser or greater rainfall in the past, but other than M5, the habitat reconstructions fall well within the modern analogs for woodland to grassland/wetland environs. Most of the assemblages likely have mammalian taxa from different parts of the cave system and, as such, paleoenvironmental reconstructions are at best broad generalizations.

M3 is an exception regarding paleoenvironment, as the retrodicted accumulating agent (hyenas) fits well with the geomorphology known within the cave – the collection is in a space that was likely used for denning. Other than possible time-averaging, the fauna from this unit seems to form a cohesive unit (Vrba, 1988; Reed, 1998) and the other proxies for M3 also support the type of habitat seen in the valley today, albeit wetter.

While a variety of environmental proxies have been produced for M3, there have not been similar kinds of analyses (involving dental wear, isotopes, etc.) for material recovered from M2, M4 (CPD), or M5. Again, it may only tell us that the species that are the same from all these units ate the same things or wore their teeth in the same way. Subject to their availability, further research on the micromammals from M3 would be informative. The main issue for further research is to understand, if possible, which fauna came from which deposit for the depositional units outside of M3.

Acknowledgments

AIRH acknowledges funding from the Australian Research Council as part of Future Fellowship grant FT120100399. The authors would like to thank Sally Reynolds and René Bobe for inviting them to contribute to this volume. KER would like to thank David Feary for help with figures.

Paleoenvironments and the Context of Plio-Pleistocene Hominins at Kromdraai, South Africa

Jean-Baptiste Fourvel and J. Francis Thackeray

Introduction

The Plio-Pleistocene site of Kromdraai (Gauteng province, South Africa) is a dolomitic cave situated approximately 2 km east of Sterkfontein, on the southern side of the Bloubank (or Blaubank) stream. It has long been considered as two distinct localities of relatively limited spatial extent. One locality yielded the type specimen of *Paranthropus robustus* (TM 1517; the only partial skeleton of this species known thus far; Broom 1938a, 1938b, 1941, 1942, 1943) and is referred to as "Kromdraai B" (KB), or the "hominin site." The younger "Kromdraai A" (KA) site is situated about 30 m to the west of KB. KA has not yet yielded hominin fossils and is therefore called the "faunal site." KB yielded an Oldowan stone tool (a polyhedral core). Stone artifacts associated with the early Acheulean or Oldowan were found at KA (Kuman et al., 1997) and therefore also indicate a hominin presence. It is now recognized that KA and KB are part of the same cave complex (Braga and Thackeray, 2016).

Recent fieldwork undertaken at Kromdraai since 2002 by the Kromdraai Research Project (KRP) has established stratigraphical relationships between KA and KB, and has demonstrated the much larger size of this site than previously thought, through the exposure of extensive (previously unexplored) fossiliferous deposits (Braga and Thackeray, 2016). In particular, a new excavation area, called the KB extension site, is situated to the north of the previous excavation at Kromdraai undertaken by Broom (1938–1943), Vrba (1977–1978), and Thackeray (since 1993), but relatively close to the exploratory excavation by Brain in 1955 and 1956.

There has been a diversity of opinion on the chronology and paleoenvironments of the KB site, as well as on the taxonomy and phylogenetic status of its fossil hominins (Grine, 1982, 1988; Vrba and Panagos, 1982; Tobias, 1988; Thackeray et al., 2001; Kaszycka, 2002; Braga and Thackeray, 2003; Lacruz, 2007; Braga et al., 2013; Braga and Thackeray, 2016). An age estimate for the oldest KB fossil assemblage was set via biochronological dating (Vrba, 1976, 1981; Vrba and Panagos, 1982, McKee et al., 1995) and paleomagnetism (Thackeray et al., 2002) to postdate the 2.6 million years (Ma) boundary between the Pliocene and Pleistocene (Gibbard and Head, 2009). It is now recognized that the KB hominins found *in situ* are spread across the succession of at least three time periods, as represented by three distinct depositional cycles separated by major unconformities (Braga et al., 2013). The temporal depth represented by the KB fossil-bearing sediments is still unknown, but may be substantially older than 2 Ma.

The lithostratigraphy, chronology, paleobiology, and paleoenvironments at the KB site represent central elements to obtain a broader picture of the earliest southern African hominin evolutionary contexts. Several *P. robustus* specimens from KB present a less-derived morphology than other conspecifics sampled thus far in other sites and may represent the oldest occurrence of this species in southern Africa (Grine, 1988; Braga et al., 2013; Braga and Thackeray, 2016). The scope of this chapter is to briefly review the latest observations on paleoenvironmental research of the KB deposits and to present our current knowledge within an integrated regional context.

The Kromdraai Fossil Assemblages and Excavations

The KB fossil assemblage comprises more than 6200 specimens in total, stored at the Ditsong National Museum of Natural History (formerly Transvaal Museum) in Pretoria, supplemented by additional specimens obtained by the new Kromdraai Research Project (more than 2000 specimens catalogued with KW prefixes, curated at the University of the Witwatersrand in Johannesburg).

The KB fossils were recovered during five distinct periods: 1938–44 (Broom, 1938a, 1938b, 1941, 1942, 1943; Broom and Schepers, 1946), 1955–56 (Brain, 1958, 1975b, 1978, 1981), 1977–80 (Vrba, 1981; Partridge, 1982; Grine, 1982, 1988; Vrba and Panagos, 1982), and 1993 onwards (Thackeray et al., 2001, 2002, 2003, 2005; Braga and Thackeray, 2003, Braga et al., 2013; Braga and Thackeray, 2016). The KA fossil assemblage includes more than 1800 faunal remains, curated at the Ditsong National Museum of Natural History (Brain, 1981).

The Kromdraai Lithostratigraphy and Biostratigraphy: The Context for Paleoenvironmental Reconstructions

The site of Kromdraai corresponds to an unroofed cave that is part of a huge network of galleries formed during the Miocene–Pliocene period and partially cut by the erosional surface, due to the deepening of the valley. Surface deposits accumulated as colluvia. The fossil bone remains were introduced into the cave either by carnivores or by natural pitfall trapping (Vrba, 1976; Brain, 1981). The newly discovered fossil sample has been studied by one of us (JBF). The various taphonomical features observed on the paleontological sample for the newly excavated Member 2 (or Unit P) support the hypothesis of a bone accumulation resulting from carnivore activities (felid and hyenid).

The detailed lithostratigraphy of KB indicates successions of deposits, mineralizations, demineralizations, and declogging by the karst and subsumes a complex succession of more than one time period. Only a minority of the KB fossils can be assigned to the single and relatively homogeneous period represented by the calcified Member 3 deposits (Brain, 1981; Vrba, 1981; Vrba and Panagos, 1982; Thackeray et al., 2005). Because the KB fossil assemblage was not recovered from a single stratigraphic unit, it is confusing that it is still often considered as a homogeneous sample (e.g., Skinner et al., 2013). A few KB hominin specimens and the majority of the KB faunal sample were found during Brain's excavation (1955–1956) mainly from decalcified deposits (Brain, 1975, 1981). As already emphasized by others (Brain, 1981; Vrba, 1981; Vrba and Panagos, 1982), these deposits potentially included fossils from Members 1–4 defined by Partridge (1982). Previous biochronological assessments of the KB faunal assemblage (e.g., McKee et al., 1995; Heaton, 2006) did not distinguish between the sample from the calcified Member 3 breccia (from Vrba's excavation) and Brain's sample from decalcified deposits with probable mixing of specimens from Members 1–4. These interpretations should be considered with caution and several KB fossil samples need to be considered separately because they were gathered from distinct geological contexts (i.e., solid vs decalcified breccias), from different lithostratigraphic provenience (i.e., Member 2 vs Member 3), or from various circumstances of discovery not known precisely (i.e., *ex situ* vs *in situ*).

As yet, most of the KB fossil sample is from Member 3. The faunal remains now found in the northernmost part of KB that is currently being excavated (Kromdraai extension site) is interpreted as Member 2 (or Unit P). A detailed account of the new stratigraphic interpretation of the Kromdraai A and B sites and the new faunal and hominin discoveries has been published elsewhere (Braga and Thackeray, 2016; Braga et al, 2017; Fourvel, 2018).

Paleoenvironments

A summary of fauna from Kromdraai, including updated data from the excavations undertaken by Brain and Vrba, is given in Table 8.1.

Table 8.1 Faunal spectrum (Minimal Number of Individuals) from Kromdraai localities, Kromdraai A from Brain's excavations and Kromdraai B from Brain's and Vrba's excavations. Data from Brain (1981), Vrba (1981), Gommery et al. (2008b), and Pickford (2013a, 2013b).

				Brain's excavations				Vrba's excavations	
Order	Family	Genera	Species	KA	KB L1	KB L2	KB L3	KB 3E	Total
Primates	Cercopithecoidea	*Gorgopithecus*	*Gorgopithecus major*	8					8
Primates	Cercopithecoidea	*Gorgopithecus*	? *Gorgopithecus major*					2	2
Primates	Cercopithecoidea	*Parapapio*	*Parapapio jonesi*	2					2
Primates	Cercopithecoidea	*Papio*	*Papio* cf. *hamadryas robinsoni*					5	5
Primates	Cercopithecoidea	*Papio*	*Papio robinsoni*	1	11	4	3		19
Primates	Cercopithecoidea	*Papio*	*Papio* cf. *angusticeps*					4	4
Primates	Cercopithecoidea	*Papio*	*Papio angusticeps*	11	9	1	4		25
Primates	Cercopithecoidea	*Cercopithecoides*	*Cercopithecoides williamsi*		2		3	6	11
Carnivora	Felidae	*Megantereon*	*Megantereon* cf. *gracile*					2	2
Carnivora	Felidae	*Megantereon*	*Megantereon eurynodon*	1					1
Carnivora	Felidae	*Megantereon*	? *Megantereon* sp.				1		1
Carnivora	Felidae	*Dinofelis*	*Dinofelis piveteaui*	1					1
Carnivora	Felidae	*Dinofelis*	? *Dinofelis*				1		1
Carnivora	Felidae	*Homotherium*	*Homotherium* sp.	1					1
Carnivora	Felidae	*Panthera*	*Panthera leo*	1					1
Carnivora	Felidae	*Panthera*	*Panthera pardus*	1	1		1	1	4
Carnivora	Hyaenidae	*Pachycrocuta*	*Pachycrocuta bellax*	1					1
Carnivora	Hyaenidae	*Crocuta*	*Crocuta crocuta*	3					3
Carnivora	Hyaenidae	*Parahyaena*	*Parahyaena* cf. *brunnea*		1	1	1		3
Carnivora	Hyaenidae	*Proteles*	*Proteles* sp.				1		1
Carnivora	Canidae	*Canis*	*Canis atrox*	1					1
Carnivora	Canidae	*Canis*	*Canis mesomelas*	8					8

Table 8.1 (cont.)

Order	Family	Genera	Species	KA	Brain's excavations KB L1	KB L2	KB L3	Vrba's excavations KB 3E	Total
Carnivora	Canidae	Canis	Canis sp.		1	1	2		4
Carnivora	Canidae	Nyctereutes	Nyctereutes terblanchei	1					1
Carnivora	Canidae	Vulpes	Vulpes pulcher	1					1
Carnivora	Herpestidae	Atilax	Atilax mesotes	1					1
Carnivora	Herpestidae	Crossarchus	Crossarchus transvaalensis	1					1
Carnivora	Herpestidae	Herpestes	Herpestes sp.		1	1			2
Carnivora	Mustelidae	Mellivora	Mellivora capensis				1		1
Artiodactyla	Bovidae	Syncerus	Syncerus cf. acoelotus					1	1
Artiodactyla	Bovidae	Syncerus	Syncerus sp.	2					2
Artiodactyla	Bovidae	Damaliscus	Damaliscus sp.	32					32
Artiodactyla	Bovidae	Connochaetes	cf. Connochaetes sp.	5	1	1	1		8
Artiodactyla	Bovidae	Megalotragus	cf. Megalotragus sp.	2					2
Artiodactyla	Bovidae	Hippotragus	Hippotragus cf. equinus	1					1
Artiodactyla	Bovidae	Redunca	Redunca cf. arundinum	1					1
Artiodactyla	Bovidae	Pelea	Pelea cf. capreolus	3					3
Artiodactyla	Bovidae	Antidorcas	Antidorcas recki	13	1	1	1		16
Artiodactyla	Bovidae	Antidorcas	Antidorcas bondi	6	1		1		8
Artiodactyla	Bovidae	Gazella	Gazella sp.		1				1
Artiodactyla	Bovidae	Raphicerus	Raphicerus sp.	1					1
Artiodactyla	Bovidae	Tragelaphus	Tragelaphus cf. scriptus	1					1
Artiodactyla	Bovidae	Tragelaphus	Tragelaphus cf. strepsiceros	5					5
Artiodactyla	Bovidae	Taurotragus	Taurotragus cf. oryx	2					2
Artiodactyla	Hippoptamidae	Hippopotamus	Hippopotamus sp. aff. Protamphibius				1	1	
Artiodactyla	Suidae	Phacochoerus	Phacochoerus modestus	1					1
Artiodactyla	Suidae	Metridiochoerus	Metridiochoerus andrewsi	2					2
Artiodactyla	Suidae	Potamochoeroides	Potamochoeroides hypsodon				1		1
Perissodactyla	Equidae	Hipparion	Hipparion steyleri	1					1
Perissodactyla	Equidae	Equus	Equus burchelli	5					5
Perissodactyla	Equidae	Equus	Equus capensis	23					23
Hyracoidea	Procaviidae	Procavia	Procavia antiqua	10					10
Hyracoidea	Procaviidae	Procavia	Procavia transvaalensis	6					6
Hyracoidea	Procaviidae	Procavia	Procavia sp.		1				1
Rodentia	Hystricidae	Hystrix	Hystrix africaeaustralis	3					3
Rodentia	Hystricidae	Hystrix	Hystrix cf. makapanensis	1					1

The bovids are dominated by *Alcelaphus*, *Damaliscus*, and *Antidorcas*, which, together with an abundance of *Equus* (only in KA while *Equus* is absent fro KB), indicate savanna grassland. Tragelaphines are present but not common. Primates include *Parapapio* and Cercopithecoidea.

Within the newly excavated Member 2, the faunal spectrum has been widely extended. Numerous bird remains have been collected and studied. These remains and their identifications have ecological implications, suggesting a grassy environment with scattered trees, and rocky cliffs (Fourvel et al., in Braga and Thackeray, 2016).

The carnivore spectrum from Kromdraai B, which was previously represented by 8 taxa (Brain, 1981; Turner and Wood, 1993), is now composed of at least 24 species belonging to 6 families (Braga and Thackeray, 2016; Fourvel, 2018). A new viverrid species (*Civettictis braini* n. sp.) has been identified, supplementing the high faunal richness at Kromdraai (Fourvel, 2018). The identification of cursorial predators such as large canids (which was previously refered to cf. *Lycaon* sp. and now defined as a new *Canis* species, *Canis hewitti* n.sp.) as well as the small-sized felid caracal and serval are indicative of an open environment. The

Cape clawless otter *Aonyx capensis* is indicative of a wetland (potentially a riverine habitat) in the vicinity of the site within the Blaubank valley.

The KB animal bones collected from *in-situ* breccias include a predominance of cercopithecoid monkeys, notably leaf-eating forms (Colobinae) whose presence suggest relatively wooded and moist surroundings. The KB Cercopithecinae sample is taxonomically diverse and includes several papionins, which suggest woodland mosaic or savanna environments. Along with an extinct and large-bodied subspecies of the contemporaneous *Papio hamadryas* (*P. h. robinsoni*), this sample includes two other extinct papionin species: the large and unusual *Gorgopithecus major* and the smaller *Papio angusticeps* (or *P. izodi angusticeps*), either regarded as indistinguishable from *P. izodi* (Werdelin and Sanders, 2010) or considered as endemic to Kromdraai (Heaton, 2006).

Isotopic Evidence

Indications of paleoenvironmental changes have been obtained from stable carbon isotope ratios ($\Delta^{13}C$ values) in fossil tooth enamel based on samples from Kromdraai (Thackeray et al., 1999; Sponheimer et al., 2005b; Kirsanow, 2009). Regarding fossil hominins, a single *P. robustus* tooth (the lower second permanent molar of TM 1600) has been measured for its $\Delta^{13}C$ value (−7.9‰; Sponheimer et al., 2005b). The result would suggest a paleodiet of C_3 leaves and fruits with some degree of the consumption of C_4-related protein (perhaps insects such as termites, or the meat of ungulates that consumed C_4 grasses). Thackeray et al. (1999) analyzed stable carbon isotopes in tooth enamel from a fossil rodent (*Aethomys namaquensis*) at KB, and noted that it related to predominantly C_4 grassland environments, although in modern contexts this species has the potential to occupy a diversity of habitats.

Biochronology

When compared to other faunal assemblages from the Plio-Pleistocene in South Africa, the representation of fauna for Kromdraai Member 2 (or Unit P) suggests an age older than 2.0 Ma. The carnivores are particularly of interest. Among them, the best available biochronological indicator is the unique pattern of association of five felid (*Dinofelis barlowi*), hyenid (*Chasmaporthetes silberbergi*), canid (*Prototocyon recki* and *Canis hewitti*) and mustelid (*Prepoecilogale bolti*) taxa. Thus, *D. barlowi* is a machairodont considered to occur in this region between 3.5 and 2 Ma (Werdelin and Lewis, 2001). Likely after 2 Ma, *D. barlowi* is replaced by a specialized and more widely distributed form, *D. piveteaui*. *D. barlowi* has been reported from Sterkfontein (Members 2 and 4), Bolt's Farm, Swartkrans Member 1, Drimolen Main Quarry and possibly Drimolen Makondo and Malapa. The occurrence of this species in Member 2 (Minimum number of Individuals, MNI=2) and the absence of *D. piveteaui* suggests an age of > 2 Ma for this deposit. Among the hyenids, *C. silberbergi* is also represented in Member 2, and has been identified only in Sterkfontein Members 2 and 4 (Werdelin and Peigné, 2010). Two canid taxa from Kromdraai are biochronologically relevant. In the first instance, this assemblage contains the first documentation of *P. recki* which occurs in East Africa at Olduvai (c. 2Ma) and Laetoli (c. 3.5 Ma). Secondly, the presence or absence of large canid taxa appears to indicate a separation between pre- and post- 2Ma fossil assemblages from the "Cradle of Humankind," where larger canids are represented in some post-2 Ma sites (e.g., Swartkrans, Kromdraai A and Cooper's D) but they do not occur before 2 Ma. Interestingly, no large canid is reported from Unit P. Instead, this ecological niche is occupied by the newly described *C. hewitti* (NMI=6). Among the mustelids, the occurrence of the extinct weasel *P. bolti* also represents an important biochronological marker of Member 2 (Fourvel et al., 2016). This rare species is widely distributed from South Africa (Bolt's Farm) to Tanzania (Laetoli) and Morocco (Ahl al Oughlam) (for more details, see Geraads, 2016). This species is suggested to have evolved during a relatively short period, between 3.7 and 2.6 Ma (Geraads, 2016). The skull recovered from Kromdraai is morphologically and metrically aligned with late Pliocene *P. bolti* from Bolt's Farm, Laetoli and Ahl al Oughlam, as opposed to the early Pleistocene specimen from Cooper's D, and which is considered to be derived toward the modern zorilla (O'Regan et al., 2013).

References

Geraads, D., 2016. Pleistocene Carnivora (Mammalia) from Tighennif (Ternifine), Algeria. *Geobios* 49, 445–458

Werdelin, L., Lewis, M.E., 2001. A revision of the genus *Dinofelis* (Mammalia, Felidae). *Zoological Journal of the Linnean Society* 132, 147–258.

Conclusion

Taken together, the Plio-Pleistocene fauna from Kromdraai (associated with early *Homo* and *Paranthropus robustus*) would suggest a mosaic woodland savanna, adjacent wetland, or riverine habitats.

Acknowledgments

This work was supported by the South African National Research Foundation, the French Ministry of Foreign Affairs, and the French Embassy in South Africa through the Cultural and Cooperation Services.

Using the Faunal Community to Determine the Local Ecology for Early Hominins at Cooper's Cave at 1.5 Ma

Darryl de Ruiter

Introduction

Cooper's Cave has been known as a hominin-bearing locality since 1938, when J.C. Middleton Shaw discovered the first hominin tooth there while exploring for fossils on the farm of a Mr. Cooper (Shaw, 1939, 1940). The site was described being about midway between Sterkfontein and Kromdraai, and had been extensively mined for lime, resulting in large dumps of breccia. Shaw's senior assistant, Dr. Julius Staz, was searching through breccia dumps outside of what is today referred to as Cooper's B using hammers and chisels to break up the rock when he discovered an upper third molar of some type of hominin. The obvious comparisons at the time were with *Australopithecus africanus* and *Paranthropus robustus*, although Shaw (1939) felt his tooth was more human-like than either of these taxa. In a later, more detailed discussion of the tooth, Shaw (1940) concluded that it did not belong to either australopith taxon, but was otherwise unwilling to allocate it taxonomically. Broom (1946) and Robinson (1956) later examined Cooper's tooth, and concluded that it was probably an *Australopithecus africanus* upper left third molar. Unfortunately, the original tooth has been lost, leaving only a cast of the specimen behind. Berger et al. (1995) re-examined this cast, and agreed with Broom's and Robinson's conclusion that the tooth was likely *Australopithecus* cf. *africanus*. However, given the poor quality of the available cast, the taxonomic affinity of the specimen might be best considered unconfirmed.

In 1954, C.K. (Bob) Brain undertook work at Cooper's B and extracted a sample of mammalian fossils, although no hominin fossils were recognized at the time (Brain, 1958). An isolated incisor that was collected during the period of either Shaw's or Brain's activities was later recognized as hominin, attributable to either *A. africanus* or early *Homo* (Berger et al., 1995). This incisor was recovered from a box labeled Cooper's A, although it is unclear how Cooper's A and B relate to each other, and it is possible that they actually represent different components of the same deposit (Berger et al., 1995). Subsequently, a partial cranium and face collected during Brain's operations at Cooper's B was recognized as belonging to *P. robustus* (Steininger et al., 2008). Under the aegis of the Duke Paleoanthropology Field School excavations were recommenced in 2001 in a previously unexplored area of the Cooper's deposits, designated Cooper's D, and almost immediately additional hominin fossils were recovered (Berger et al., 2003; de Ruiter et al., 2009). Hominin craniodental fossils from Cooper's D include mandibular fragments and isolated teeth from juvenile individuals, and all are attributable to *P. robustus*. One adult is represented by a thoracic vertebra, which can be tentatively ascribed to *P. robustus*.

Geology and Stratigraphy of Cooper's D

The site of Cooper's Cave is comprised of three fossiliferous deposits (Cooper's A, B, D). However, as mentioned above, it is unclear precisely how the Cooper's A and B deposits relate to each other, and it is possible that they represent different components of the same deposit. Cooper's D, on the other hand, is a spatially distinct deposit comprised of both heavily calcified and decalcified components. Cooper's Cave is housed in the dolomites of the Monte Christo Formation of the Malmani Subgroup and the Transvaal Supergroup (Berger et al., 2003; de Ruiter et al., 2009). Because the Cooper's A and B faunal assemblages are less well known than that of Cooper's D, I focus on the latter here. The area of excavation at Cooper's D extends along an east–west-trending, 3 m wide × 20 m long de-roofed cavern (see de Ruiter et al., 2009 for complete description of the geology of Cooper's D). The deposit is divided into two distinct components, labeled Cooper's D East and West, with the western deposit representing the older of the two (Figure 9.1). The fossil-bearing sediments of Cooper's D East rest on the dolomite cave floor, above a flowstone or stalagmite layer. On the northern side of the deposit, a pocket of internally derived (non-fossiliferous) dolomite residuum represents a time before the cave was open to external infilling. The fossil-bearing sediments found in the middle of Cooper's D East form two superimposed units that are separated by an erosional contact. Although the lower unit fines upwards toward this boundary, and the upper unit coarsens upward away from this contact, the two units are essentially the same: massive sediment with a reddish brown sandy matrix, dolomite clasts, and fossil bone, referred to as Facies A (Figure 9.1).

The sediments typical of the Cooper's D West deposits are comprised of basal stalagmites overlain by erosive sediments consisting of dolomite blocks concentrated in a reddish brown sandy matrix in the southeastern corner of the "breccia" pinnacle. Above this unit, a series of small flowstones, including a small stalagmite, form a break in clastic sedimentation. The

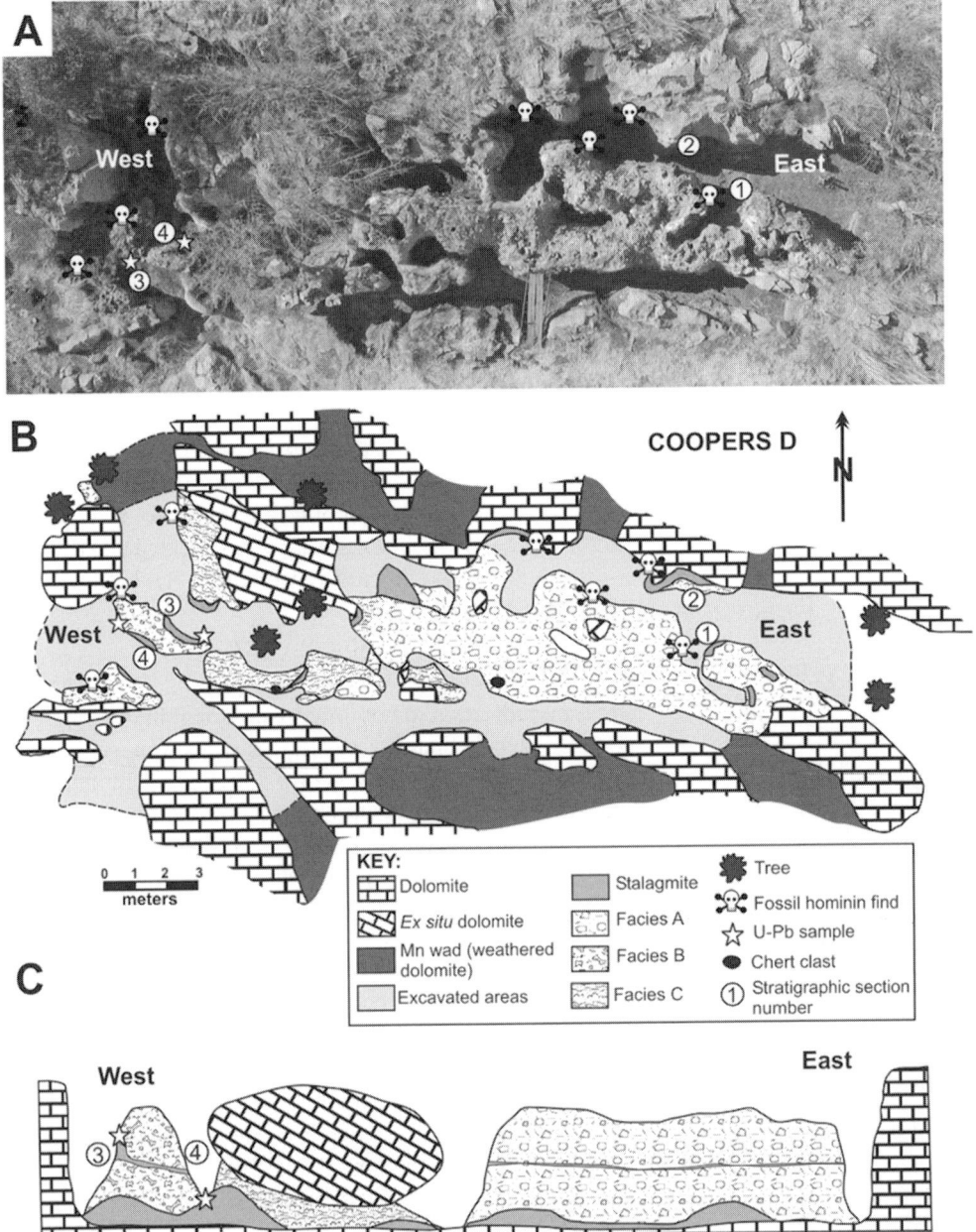

Figure 9.1 The Cooper's D locality. A, aerial photograph; B, plane-table geological map; C, simplified cross-section, facing north. All to same scale. Locations of hominin specimens are indicated in A and B. Stratigraphic section numbers indicate where sections were drawn; see de Ruiter et al. (2009) for full details regarding stratigraphic sections, lithofacies descriptions, and U–Pb samples. Figure from de Ruiter et al. (2009) with permission.

next sedimentary unit is essentially similar in that it is a blocky, bone-rich, reddish brown sandy sediment. Once again a series of small, laterally non-persistent flowstones separate this sedimentary unit from the final unit, the latter which also consists of dolomite roof blocks in a reddish brown, bone-rich sandy matrix. This suite of units is here defined as Facies B. They are distinct from Facies A in that they contain more, smaller, dolomite clasts and many more fossil bones and teeth. In the northwest part of the Cooper's D deposit, and in between the East and West sections described here, a third type of sediment is observed. This is a brownish red, sandy sediment with distinct layering that is extremely rich in microfaunal fossils. Very few other clasts are present, with none of the dolomite blocks which characterize Facies A and B. This is termed Facies C.

The dips on the clasts in the Cooper's D eastern deposit form a centripetal pattern, indicating they were deposited as a cone beneath a vertical to subvertical roof opening. The sediments in the western part of the deposit form a similar cone. The differences between these accumulations are subtle, but Facies A in the east is in general coarser-grained and less fossil-rich than Facies B in the west. The coarser-grained material (the dolomite blocks) accumulated directly under or close to the two entrances, while the finer-grained, more mobile material was washed further into the cave, forming the layered Facies C deposits. This hydrodynamic sorting that separated the finer-grained sediments had a similar, and in fact stronger, effect on the small and buoyant microfaunal bone, which is concentrated in Facies C. It is also possible that owls were using the cave at around this time, perhaps even perching on the fallen roof block, which could account for the density of microfaunal bones (de Ruiter et al., 2009). All the microfaunal bone appears to be reworked, and this distribution pattern is also true for the other fossil bone. In general, the macrofossils are found in the finer-grained portions of the both Facies A and B.

Dating of Cooper's D

As with most other fossil deposits in South Africa, Cooper's was initially faunally dated. Suid specimens including *Metridiochoerus andrewsi* and *M. modestus* from Cooper's correlated with the KBS Member at Koobi Fora, suggesting an age of 1.88–1.64 Ma (Harris and White, 1979). Delson (1984, 1988) constructed a series of biozones based on the longer, stratigraphically controlled sequences of east Africa, and concluded that Cooper's A and B were approximately 1.9–1.65 Ma. The diverse fauna from Cooper's D led Berger et al. (2003) to conclude that the site likely spanned an age of 1.9–1.6 Ma. However, the advent of U–Pb dating in South Africa allowed more precise chronological control for the Cooper's D deposit. Well-stratified flowstones embedded in the calcified clastic sediments of Cooper's D West allow us to bracket the fossils contained within these clastic sediments (de Ruiter et al., 2009). The U–Pb ages for these flowstones, coupled with the detailed stratigraphy of the site, were used to suggest a series of events in the formation, infilling, and final erosion of the cave into the present state (Figure 9.2). Prior to the cave opening up to externally derived sediments and fossils, drip waters formed the stalagmites and flowstones found at the base of all the sections dated to 1.526 (± 0.088) Ma. More arid conditions lead to the cessation of speleothem growth and surface weathering opened up fissures in the cave roof, through which sediments and fossils were deposited into the eastern and western sides of the cave. The collapse of large dolomite roof blocks separated the two deposits. A break in sediment accumulation is marked by a second episode of flowstone formation at around 1.4 Ma. Clastic sedimentation continued after this, ending in the complete collapse of the cave roof and present-day levels of erosion.

Materials and Methods

The combined faunal assemblage recovered from Cooper's D East and West is large and well preserved, with well over 50,000 catalogued specimens, all of which are curated at the Evolutionary Studies Institute at the University of the Witwatersrand. Although Cooper's D East and West deposits can be distinguished on geological grounds, the relationship between lithofacies and recovered fossils is not as clear. Most of the faunal material is derived from decalcified sediments that have undergone unknown levels of sediment compaction, bioturbation, and hydroturbation resulting from the decalcification process. Given that there is no discernable difference between fauna recovered from the Cooper's D East and West deposits, they are considered as a single entity. To date, a subset of the fauna has been thoroughly analyzed, amounting to 8488 specimens identifiable to skeletal element and taxonomic family, forming the basis of our understanding of the Cooper's D fauna (de Ruiter et al., 2009). From this subset a minimum of 203 individual mammals have been identified, including primates, carnivores, hyracoids, perissodactyls, artiodactyls, rodents and lagomorphs (Table 9.1).

Each specimen included in this study was visually examined using a 10× magnification hand-held lens, and all instances of possible taphonomic alteration were examined under a low-power microscope. Fossils were identified using comparative collections held at the University of the Witwatersrand, the Transvaal (now Ditsong) Museum, and the Florisbad Quaternary Research Department at the National Museum in Bloemfontein. Paleoenvironmental proxies examined in this study include faunal assemblage composition, microwear texture analysis, and stable light isotopes (de Ruiter et al., 2009; Steininger, 2011).

Results

Taphonomy of Cooper's D

There is no indication of hominin involvement in the Cooper's D accumulation, as there are no cut marks or hammerstone percussion marks on any of the specimens studied (de Ruiter et al., 2009). Of the 8488 specimens examined, 90 exhibit carnivore punctate depressions, including one of the hominins (CD 6807); this latter fossil shows a linear series of three small punctate depressions that compare favorably with those left by a small canid such as the jackal *Canis mesomelas*, which is known from the site. A further 26 specimens show gastric etching, while there do not appear to be any specimens showing porcupine gnawing. At the same time, only three coprolites were recovered, probably produced by *Parahyaena brunnea* (Val et al., 2014). Bone breakage patterns (Villa and Mahieu, 1991) are equivocal, and thus do not aid in resolving the mode of accumulation. A ratio of carnivores to carnivores + ungulates that exceeds 20 percent has been cited as evidence of carnivore involvement in a fossil accumulation, specifically hyenas (Cruz-Uribe, 1991; Pickering, 2002; Kuhn et al., 2008). At 26 percent, the carnivores to carnivores + ungulates ratio indicates that hyenas were likely to have been significant contributing agents in Cooper's D. The relatively high representation of small carnivores such as viverrids, mustelids, and canids point to a probable contribution by the brown hyena *P. brunnea* (Brain, 1980, 1981). These combined factors implicate hyenas as an important, although likely not exclusive, bone-accumulating agent of the Cooper's D assemblage (de Ruiter et al., 2009). Other accumulators such as felids and perhaps a natural death trap are also likely, and the bones probably arrived in the cave by a variety of means over time (Brain, 1980). In addition, it has been suggested that the cave was occupied by large-bodied primates who might have succumbed within the cave (Val et al., 2014), although the evidence supporting this hypothesis (mortality profile of primates, limited indication of carnivore damage to primate bones, hypothesized appearance of original cave entrance) is circumstantial.

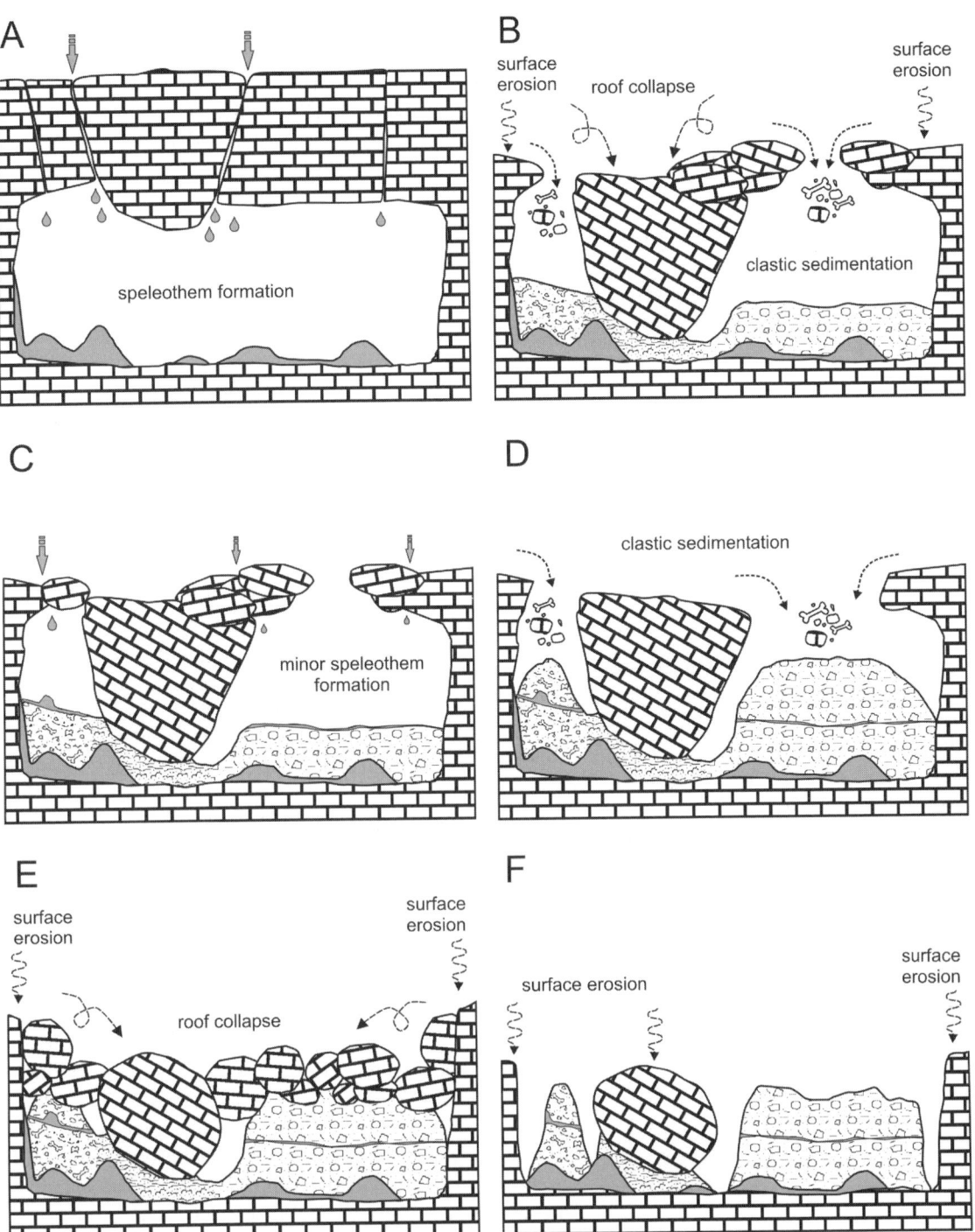

Figure 9.2 Hypothesized formation, infilling and erosion of the Cooper's D deposit. A, vadose cave forms, with subsequent speleothem formation (1.526 ± 0.088 Ma); B, surface weathering allows for clastic sedimentation, ultimately leading to partial roof collapse; C, cave briefly closed to external sedimentation, allowing additional speleothem formation (ca. 1.4 Ma); D, cave reopens to surface, once again allowing clastic sedimentation; E, cave infills almost to the roof, and final roof collapse terminates clastic sedimentation; F, subsequent surface erosion and decalcification remove much of the collapsed roof, resulting in the modern paleo-cave. Figure from de Ruiter et al. (2009) with permission.

Faunal Assemblage Composition of Cooper's D

The primates of Cooper's D include the hominins *P. robustus*, while among the non-human primates are specimens attributed to *Papio hamadryas robinsoni* and *Theropithecus oswaldi oswaldi* (Berger et al., 2003; de Ruiter et al., 2009; DeSilva et al., 2013; Folinsbee and Reisz, 2013), the latter of which is especially numerous at Cooper's D (Folinsbee and Reisz, 2013). In addition, the genus *Gorgopithecus* has been provisionally identified at Cooper's D (DeSilva et al., 2013). Carnivores are abundant at Cooper's D, comprising mustelids and viverrids (de Ruiter et

Table 9.1 Faunal material recovered from Cooper's D with estimates of minimum numbers of individuals (MNI). Data from de Ruiter et al. (2009), DeSilva et al. (2013), Folinsbee and Reisz (2013), Hartstone-Rose et al. (2007, 2010), and O'Regan et al. (2013).

Order	Family	Tribe	Genus and species	MNI
Primates	Hominidae		*Paranthropus robustus*	6
	Cercopithecidae			12
			Theropithecus oswaldi oswaldi	8
			Gorgopithecus sp.	1
Carnivora	Felidae		*Panthera leo*	1
			Panthera pardus	4
			Acinonyx jubatus	1
			Felis caracal	2
			Felis lybica	3
			Megantereon whitei	1
			Dinofelis sp.	2
	Hyaenidae		*Crocuta crocuta*	4
			Parahyaena brunnea	1
			Chasmaporthetes sp.	1
			Proteles cristatus	1
	Canidae		*Canis mesomelas*	5
			Lycaon sekowei	2
	Viverridae		*Herpestes ichneumon*	2
			Suricata sp.	3
			Cynictis penicillata	2
			Civettictus cf. *civetta*	1
	Mustelidae		*Propoecilogale bolti*	1
			Mellivora capensis	1
Hyracoidea	Procaviidae		*Procavia antiqua*	5
			Procavia transvaalensis	1
Perissodactyla	Equidae		*Equus quagga*	1
			Equus capensis	1
Artiodactyla	Suidae		*Metridiochoerus andrewsi*	9
			Metridiochoerus modestus	1
	Giraffidae		*Sivatherium maurusium*	2
	Bovidae	Neotragini	*Neotragini* sp. indet.	1
			Raphicerus sp.	2
		Alcelaphini	*Megalotragus* sp.	5
			Connochaetes sp.	15
			Medium-sized *alcelaphine*	19
			Damaliscus sp.	7
		Antilopini	*Antidorcas marsupialis*	18
			Antidorcas bondi	12
		Hippotragini	*Hippotragus* sp.	5
		Reduncini	*Redunca* cf. *fulvorufula*	2
		Tragelaphini	*Tragelaphus strepsiceros*	7
			Tragelaphus cf. *scriptus*	2
		Bovini	*Syncerus* sp.	2
		Peleini	*Pelea* sp.	3

Table 9.1 (cont.)

Order	Family	Tribe	Genus and species	MNI
Rodentia	Hystricidae		*Hystrix africaeaustralis*	4
	Pedetidae		*Pedetes* sp.	2
Lagomorpha	Leporidae		cf. *Lepus* sp.	12
Total				203

al., 2009; O'Regan et al., 2013), felids including a well-preserved *Megantereon whitei* mandible (Hartstone-Rose et al., 2007), hyaenids (de Ruiter et al., 2009), and canids including the novel taxon *Lycaon sekowei* (Hartstone-Rose et al., 2010). Hyraxes are relatively rare, as are equids, although at least two species of each group are represented (de Ruiter et al., 2009). Among the artiodactyls, suids are relatively common compared to other hominin bearing localities in the area, and two individuals of the giraffid *Sivatherium* are known. As is typical of the cave infills of the Bloubank Valley, bovids numerically dominate the assemblage, including a preponderance of alcelaphines and antilopines. To date only the larger rodents have been studied (de Ruiter et al., 2009), with a small number of porcupines and springhares known. Interestingly, a large number of lagomorphs are known as well (de Ruiter et al., 2009). A single turtle carapace fragment was recovered.

Paleoenvironment of Cooper's D

The majority of the ungulate fauna from Cooper's D indicate a heterogeneous environment consisting of both grasslands and woodlands, and are comprised of large numbers of individuals of Alcelaphini, Antilopini, *Equus*, and *Metridiochoerus* (de Ruiter et al., 2009; Rector et al., 2016). The Cercopithecidae, Giraffidae, Bovini, and Tragelaphini also point to the presence of a relatively wooded component, with at least a localized existence of dense riverine underbrush. A nearby, permanent water source is indicated, likely in the form of the paleo-Bloubank River. It is difficult to determine precisely which component of the reconstructed habitat mosaic was preferred by the hominins, although a recent study has indicated that *P. robustus*-bearing assemblages tend to show an inverse relationship between the hominins and grassland-adapted taxa (de Ruiter et al., 2008a; see also Chapter 11 in this volume). In other words, the more grassland-adapted taxa there are in a given assemblage, the fewer hominins there tend to be. This suggests that although the Cooper's D hominins are associated with a grassland environment at some level, it is possible that they favored a more closed portion of the habitat mosaic. Such a suggestion is supported by isotopic studies indicating a diet of both C_4 grassland and C_3 woodland based foods for *P. robustus* (Sponheimer et al., 2005a, 2005b, 2006b; Ungar and Sponheimer, 2011). In addition, among the bovids of Swartkrans and Cooper's D, Steininger (2011) noted a relative paucity of C_4 grazing specialists (even within bovid Tribes such as the Alcelaphini), alongside an increase in the proportion of mixed feeders, that did not support the existence of extensive open grasslands associated with *P. robustus*. Steininger (2011) also attempted microwear texture analysis of the Cooper's bovid teeth, although extensive manganese encrustation on the majority of teeth resulted in very low sample sizes.

Discussion and Conclusions

The large and well-documented faunal assemblage from Cooper's D reveals a diverse animal community that is especially rich in primates, carnivores, suids, and bovids (de Ruiter et al., 2009). The Cooper's D deposit has been radiometrically dated to *ca.* 1.5–1.4 Ma, making it one of the younger *P. robustus* localities known. The paleoenvironment comprised a grassland component, a woodland component, and a nearby permanent water source. However, although grasslands are indicated, a C_4-dominated ecosystem might not have been present, suggesting a more heterogeneous environment than is typically associated with *P. robustus* (Steininger, 2011). Taphonomic indicators suggest a variety of accumulating agents in operation over time. *Paranthropus robustus* is definitively known from Cooper's B and Cooper's D (Steininger et al., 2008; de Ruiter et al., 2009). Either *Australopithecus* or *Homo* is known from Cooper's A and B, although the distinction between these two deposits remains uncertain (Berger et al., 1995). If the isolated teeth from Cooper's A and B are indeed *Australopithecus*, in particular the original molar from Cooper's B, this would have important biogeographical implications. Combined with the *Paranthropus* partial cranium from Cooper's B, these fossils would be the first potential evidence of the coexistence of *Australopithecus* and *Paranthropus* in South Africa. Alternatively, if these teeth represent *Homo*, then we have another site demonstrating the coexistence of *Homo* and *Paranthropus*. Additional research into the hominin teeth from Cooper's Cave, and additional excavations in these deposits will likely be profitable.

Acknowledgments

Thanks to Lee Berger, Steve Churchill, and the Duke Paleoanthropology Field School for all their efforts at Coopers. Thanks also go to Sally Reynolds and René Bobe for organizing this important volume. This research was funded by the Cornerstone Faculty Fellowship of the College of Liberal Arts at Texas A&M University.

10 The Paleoenvironments of Sterkfontein
Old Questions, New Approaches

Lauren C. Sewell, Job M. Kibii, and Sally C. Reynolds

Introduction to the Site

Sterkfontein, in the Cradle of Humankind World Heritage Site (Gauteng Province, South Africa), lies on a low hill overlooking the Blaaubank River, close to numerous other fossil-rich hominin-bearing sites (including Swartkrans, Kromdraai, Drimolen, Malapa, and Cooper's Cave; Figure 10.1). Lying within the narrow pre-Cambrian Malmani dolomite formation, the caves contain deposits that record the paleoenvironmental context related to hominin evolution from roughly 3.7 million years until the Upper Pleistocene, as well as the hominins themselves (Broom, 1936; Brain, 1981; Kuman, 1994a; Reynolds and Kibii, 2011; Granger et al., 2015; Val and Stratford, 2015; Stratford, 2017).

Sterkfontein remains one of the most important fossil hominin and Earlier Stone Age (ESA) sites globally. It is one of the very few South African sites that spans important climatic and technological transitions, namely the Pliocene–Pleistocene transition and the Oldowan–Early Acheulean transition, along with other sites like Wonderwerk Cave (Horwitz et al., Chapter 14) and Olduvai Gorge, Tanzania (Farrugia and Njau, Chapter 32, and Peters et al., Chapter 33). It also overlaps in age with fossil localities in other parts of Africa and with key events, such as

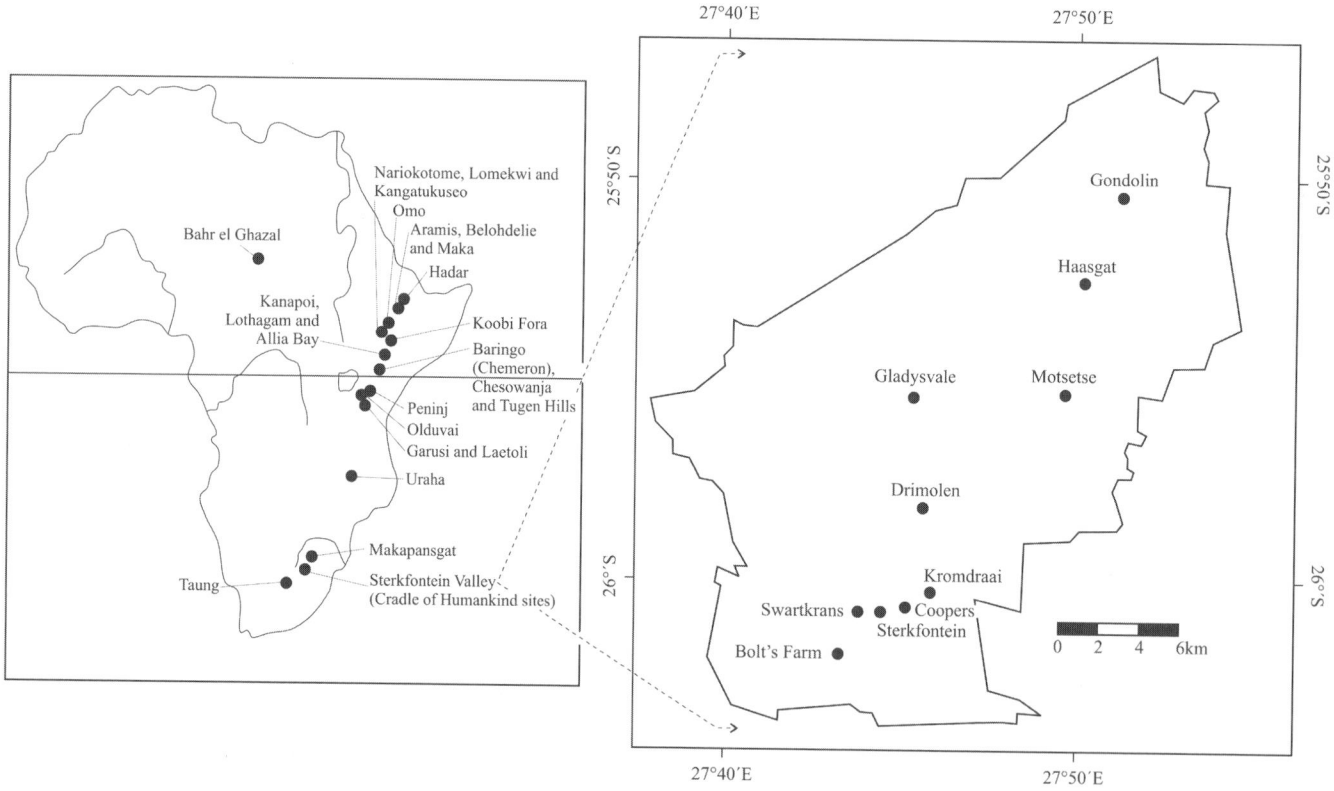

Figure 10.1 A map of the major hominin sites in Africa on the left (Tobias, 2000), with the South African Cradle of Humankind hominin sites on the right (edited from Reynolds and Kibii, 2011) to show the proximity of Sterkfontein to other fossil-bearing sites.

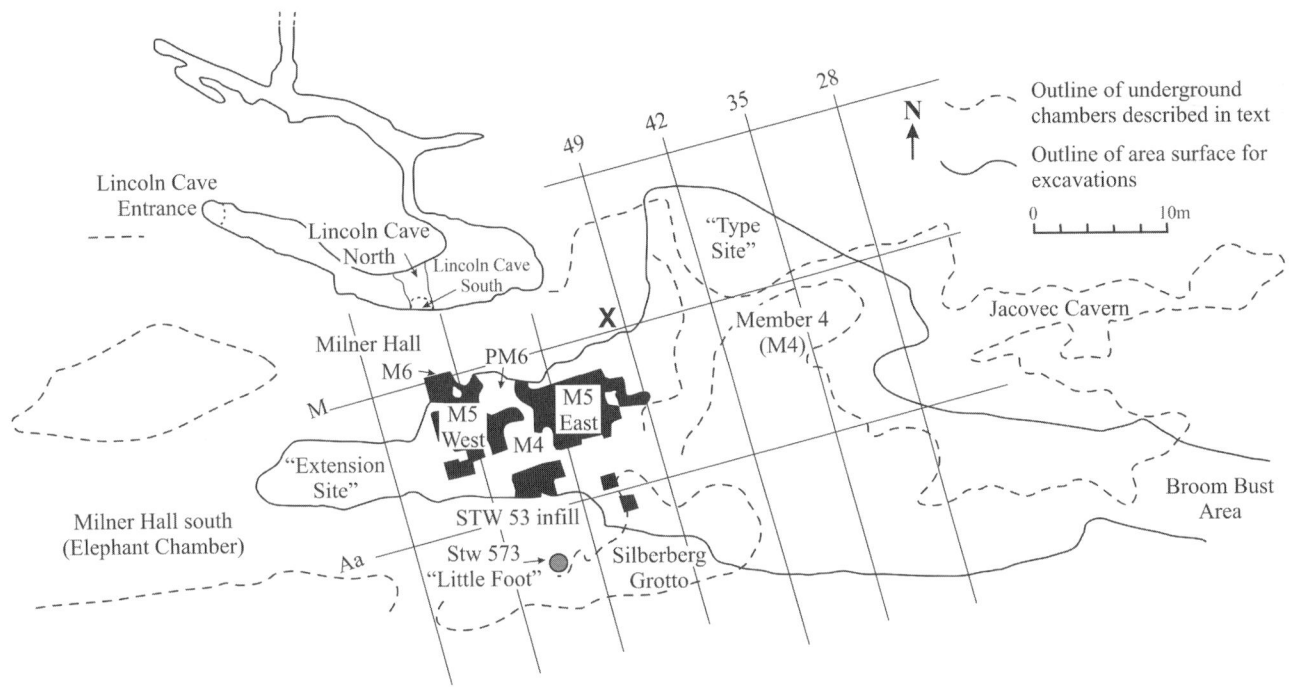

Figure 10.2 Composite plan view of Sterkfontein deposits, showing the exposed deposits of the Sterkfontein excavation (Member 4 and Member 5), the underground deposits (Silberberg Grotto and Jacovec Cavern) and the approximate spatial relationship of the Lincoln Cave to the main Sterkfontein cave system (Reynolds and Kibii, 2011). The Name Chamber lies directly under Member 5 (Clarke, 1994). Please note: Lincoln Cave and Sterkfontein cave systems are not shown to exactly the same scales. There are approximately 7 m between the northernmost limit of the main excavation and the deposit in Lincoln Cave South (Reynolds and Kibii, 2011).

the earliest appearance of *Homo* at Ledi-Geraru, Ethiopia at 2.8 Ma (Villmoare et al., 2015). The sequence, therefore, is ideal for addressing and testing evolutionary questions about the role of climate change in hominin evolution and behavioral adaptations over millions of years (e.g., Vrba, 1993, 1995b).

Sterkfontein consists of an extensive underground cave network containing numerous fossiliferous deposits of varying ages, as well as de-roofed cave deposits exposed at the surface (Figure 10.2). The site enjoyed renewed interest with the discovery of the near-complete StW 573 *Australopithecus prometheus* skeleton by Ronald Clarke in 1997, which led to numerous studies on Sterkfontein Member 2, chiefly focused on the dating and taphonomy of this important hominin skeleton (Clarke, 1998, 1999, 2002a, 2002b; Berger et al., 2002; Partridge et al., 2003; Pickering et al., 2004a; Pickering and Kramers, 2010, Herries and Shaw, 2011; Clarke and Kuman, 2019).

Several other deposits, including the *Australopithecus*-bearing Jacovec Cavern and the mid-Pleistocene Lincoln Cave deposits, continue to provide important insights into the prevailing habitat conditions associated with the fauna and hominins during various temporal periods. Ongoing investigations by Dominic Stratford and colleagues aim to further understand these deposits, particularly in the Name Chamber (Stratford, 2011, 2015; Val and Stratford, 2015). For the sake of brevity here, we direct the interested reader to a wealth of papers about the history of the site and the discovery of the earliest stone tools and hominins (Robinson, 1962; Kuman, 1994a, 1994b; Clarke, 1994; Kuman and Clarke, 2000; Clarke, 2006, 2012; Stratford, 2018, among others).

Sterkfontein Stratigraphy and Overview of Deposit Dating

The Sterkfontein Members have been dated using a range of methods (see the summary of these in Table 10.1). Despite the complexity of karst stratigraphy, it remains vital in understanding the depositional sequences of these cave deposits and their ages. Initially interpreted as a "layer-cake" model (e.g., Robinson, 1952, 1962), subsequent stratigraphic interpretations over decades of research since the early work by Tim Partridge (1978) indicate that Sterkfontein stratigraphy is more complex than the initial models suggested. Subsequent studies, such as those by Partridge (2000), Herries et al. (2009), Pickering et al. (2010), and Pickering and Kramers (2010), have proposed alternative models, for example that of successive layers of talus cone infills, or even the infilling of disconnected but contemporaneous caverns. In addition, numerous studies revealed that the reworking of older artifacts and fauna into younger deposits is a common process within karstic caves (e.g., for the Lincoln Cave, see Reynolds et al., 2007).

Therefore, the site formation processes and the contents of the deposits (artifacts, fauna, hominins) must be interpreted in combination as part of a complete picture of site formation (deposition, collapse, reworking, erosion, redeposition); this is particularly pertinent when dates for these deposits are being assessed (e.g., Herries and Shaw, 2011). Full discussion of geomorphological processes and sedimentary features of the Sterkfontein formation is available elsewhere (see Clarke, 1994; Pickering and Kramers, 2010; Stratford, 2011, 2015,

Table 10.1 Date ranges for each Sterkfontein Member, references and dating method.

Deposit	Published dates for deposits	Additional information
Jacovec Cavern	4.0 Ma, Cosmogenic nuclides (Partridge et al., 2003)	Orange and brown breccias dated (cosmogenic nucleotides ^{26}Al and ^{10}Be). Orange breccia is older, ca. 4.02 ± 0.270 (0.41) Ma; brown dated to ca. 3.76 ± 0.26 (0.41) Ma
		Presence of an equid suggests younger than 2.36 Ma (Kibii, 2000, 2004), but possibility of mixed material in this deposit
Member 2	4.0 Ma, Cosmogenic nuclides (Partridge et al., 2003)	Paleomagnetic dating placed M2 between the Mammoth–Gauss and the Gilbert–Gauss magnetic polarities, ca. 3.22–3.58 Ma (Partridge et al., 1999)
	3.67 ±0.16 Ma Cosmogenic nuclides (Granger et al., 2015)	Cosmogenic nuclides (^{26}Al and ^{10}Be) burial dates of ca. 4.17 Ma sparked debate (Berger et al., 2002; Clarke, 2002)
	3.30–3.33 Ma, Paleomagnetism (Partridge et al., 1999)	U–Pb isotopic dating ca. 2.2 Ma (Walker et al., 2006) and ca. 2.6–2.8 with an error of 2.01 ± 0.06 (Pickering and Kramers, 2010) for the capping flowstone associated with hominin StW 573 confirms the reproducibility of these dates
	2.2 Ma, Uranium–lead isotopes (Walker et al., 2006)	
	2.6–2.8 Ma, Uranium–lead and uranium–thorium isotopes (Pickering and Kramers, 2010)	
Member 4	2.8–2.4 Ma, Bovid biochronology (Vrba, 1974, 1975, 1976, 1982b)	Initial dating was relative to radiometrically dated eastern African sites
	~ 2.5 Ma, Primate biochronology (Delson, 1984, 1988)	Electron spin resonance was conducted on bovid teeth (2.1 ± 0.5 Ma) (Schwarcz et al., 1994)
	2.8–2.6 Ma, Faunal seriation (McKee, 1996)	The presence of *Equus* suggests an upper age limit of <2.36 Ma (Herries and Shaw, 2011)
	~ 2.1 Ma, Electron spin resonance (Schwarcz et al., 1994)	Paleomagnetic dates position Member 4 within the younger Reunion event at 2.15–2.14 Ma (Partridge, 2005; Herries and Shaw, 2011). The Sts 5 fossil dates yielded are between 2.16 and 2.05 Ma
	2.15–2.14 Ma Paleomagnetism (Partridge, 2005)	Herries and Shaw (2011) revised the stratigraphic layers within Member 4 as M4A: 2.8–2.2 Ma, M4B: 2.6–2.2 Ma, and M4C 2.2–2.0 Ma
	2.65–2.01, Uranium–lead and uranium–thorium isotopes (Pickering and Kramers, 2010)	
	2.58~2.16 Ma, Paleomagnetism (Herries and Shaw, 2011)	
Member 5: STW 53 Infill	2.6–2.0 Ma, Fauna (Kuman and Clarke, 2000)	Younger than M4 but older than M5 East (Oldowan) Infill (Kuman and Clarke, 2000)
	1.8–1.4 Ma, dating seriation (Herries et al., 2009)	Presence of *Theropithecus oswaldi* (not present in Member 4), associated with grassland. Earliest appearance of this species is ca. 3.7–3.5 Ma in Kenya (Leakey et al., 1996) and last appearance is 0.4 Ma in South Africa (Pickford, 1993)
	1.8–1.5 Ma, revised dating seriation (paleomagnetism and electron spin resonance) (Herries and Shaw, 2011)	Absence of stone tools also indicates StW 53 pre-dates M5 East Oldowan
Member 5: East Infill	2.0–1.7 Ma, Biochronology and archeology (Kuman and Clarke, 2000)	Biochronological dates based on the presence of *Phacochoerus modestus*, *Struthio* (giant ostrich,) and *Equus* sp. which are morphologically similar to those known from Olduvai Bed I and II (Kuman and Clarke, 2000)
	1.4–1.1 Ma dating seriation (Herries et al., 2009)	
	2.18 ± 0.21 Ma, cosmogenic nuclides (Granger et al., 2015)	
Member 5: West Infill	1.7–1.4 Ma, Biochronology and archeology (Kuman and Clarke, 2000)	Acheulean stone tool typology and associated hominin remains ca. 1.7–1.4 Ma (Kuman and Clarke, 2000)
	1.3–0.8 Ma, dating seriation (Herries et al., 2009)	
	1.3–1.1 Ma, Paleomagnetism and electron spin resonance (Herries and Shaw, 2011)	
Post Member 6: L/63 Infill	Mid–late Pleistocene age, faunal correlations, and archeology (Reynolds et al., 2007)	Correspondence analysis of fauna against M5 W fauna shows fauna and hominin species in L/63 Infill are more similar to those in the Upper Pleistocene deposits (Reynolds et al., 2007)
	684–251 Ka, electron spin resonance (Herries and Shaw, 2011)	

Table 10.1 (cont.)

Deposit	Published dates for deposits	Additional information
Lincoln Cave North	**0.253–0.115 Ma**, Uranium series (Reynolds et al., 2003, 2007)	Uranium series dating of the capping and lower flowstones ca. 252,600 ± 35,600–115,300 ± 7700 (Reynolds et al., 2003, 2007)
Lincoln Cave South	**Mid–late Pleistocene**, age, archeology (Reynolds et al., 2007)	

2017; Stratford et al., 2012, 2014; Bruxelles et al., 2014; Val and Stratford, 2015).

Regional Climatic Context for the Sterkfontein Fossil Deposits

Sterkfontein is one of the few African sites that sample the Plio-Pleistocene transition, at ca. 2.58 Ma (Cohen and Gibbard, 2011). Large-scale climate change studies, such as that by deMenocal (2004: 3), suggest that step-wise drying trends led to the appearance of "more varied and open habitats at 2.9–2.4 Ma and after 1.8 Ma" in eastern Africa. Hopley and Maslin (2010) caution that southern African cave deposits, such as those at Sterkfontein, sample more than one precessional cycle (~7000 years) and are therefore likely to be "climate-averaged," showing a mix of species characteristic of both open, grassland-dominated periods of the climate cycle as well as woodland-dominated extremes. In contrast, Pickering and colleagues (2019) have suggested that only drier temporal periods are sampled within the Sterkfontein Valley deposits; however, the range of habitats represented at all the sites argues against any such interpretation.

Wonderwerk is the one of the few broadly contemporary sites located in the central southern African region. This site has yielded some of the only direct floral evidence of past vegetation (from which climate can be directly inferred). The Wonderwerk evidence shows that C_3 and C_4 grasses and wetlands remained major components of the Early Pleistocene environments, at least in the central interior of South Africa (Ecker et al., 2018). Recent studies (Ecker et al., 2018) suggest climate across the Oldowan–Acheulean transition is driven by a combination of global carbon dioxide levels and regional rainfall, producing regionally distinct vegetation ecosystems, which cannot necessarily be transposed to penicontemporanous deposits members at Sterkfontein.

At a regional scale, Makapansgat speleothem studies by Hopley et al. (2007b) indicate an expansion of the C_4 (grass) plants at approximately 1.7 Ma, which Hopley et al. (2007b) have related to the onset of the Walker Circulation. Additionally, increasing aridity in southern Africa after 2.1 Ma (Weigelt et al., 2008) would also have favored the development of grasslands. The climate data from the Makapansgat Valley suggest that the region, including Sterkfontein, would have experienced similar aridification and increase in C_4 grasses over the period represented. While the Makapansgat Collapsed Cone pre-dates the earliest Sterkfontein deposits, it appears likely that similar climatic trends would have been experienced by *Australopithecus* in Sterkfontein Member 2 through to the younger Member 4 deposits and finally by the *Paranthropus* and early *Homo* represented in the Member 5 infills (Kuman and Clarke, 2000; Hopley et al., 2007b).

Overview of Site Taphonomic Processes

Several modes of bone accumulation are represented within the Sterkfontein deposits, and the majority of fossil deposits indicate the action of both biotic (e.g., hyenas and porcupines) and abiotic (e.g., slopewash) factors in accumulating the fauna. These include death traps, where animals have fallen into a steep shaft or aven from which they could not escape. Examples of this include the Member 2 StW 573 hominin (Pickering et al., 2004a; Clarke and Kuman, 2019). Another well-represented mode of accumulation, particularly in the Member 4 hominin assemblage, is the action of carnivores that accumulated a wealth of fossils as part of their denning activities. Member 4 contains the largest number of *Australopithecus* specimens, co-occurring with a speciose carnivore guild, totaling 14 species in 5 families (Table 10.2a). An overrepresentation of female and juvenile hominins in this member was suggested by Lockwood and Tobias (1999) to be the result of the prey selection of large carnivores. Natural death-trap accumulations and slopewash played a lesser part in the accumulation of the Member 4 material (e.g., Brain, 1981; Kibii, 2004). These various processes may have been active at different times and there may have been several points of ingress for fossil material (e.g., Pickering and Kramers, 2010).

The fossils preserved in the Member 5 infills appear to have been carnivore-accumulated, at least in part (Pickering, 1999). The StW 53 infill has yielded quite a small bone sample, with relatively low numbers of biotically modified bones. Pickering (1999) suggests that leopards (*Panthera pardus*) may have played a role in the bone damage. However, possible cut marks on the StW 53 hominin cranium led Pickering et al. (2000) to propose that hominin butchery activities accumulated part of the material. However, recently these cut marks have been reinterpreted as representing trampling damage (Hanon et al., 2018), although Oldowan and Acheulean stone tools from Member 5 East and West infills do point to hominin activity during the formation of these deposits (Kuman and Clarke, 2000). Slopewash and winnowing modified the Oldowan stone tool assemblage, leaving a lack of small debitage (Kuman 1994a, 1994b). As well as these stone tools, Member 5 has also yielded the only bone tool documented thus far at Sterkfontein (Val and Stratford, 2015).

Pickering (1999) proposed a serial-denning scenario for Member 5 West, in which hyenas are considered to be one of the main bone accumulators. Brown hyenas (*Parahyaena brunnea*) appear to have been responsible, but also with lesser contributions from spotted hyenas (*Crocuta crocuta*), as part of a serial denning scenario (Pickering, 1999). Some porcupine involvement is also suggested. The lack of direct evidence for hominin butchery activity on the bones (e.g., cut marks, chop marks, or hammerstone percussion) suggests the animal bones were accumulated by different agents than the Early Acheulean archaeological assemblage found in this deposit.

Other important deposits, such as the Name Chamber faunal assemblage, suggest a mixed origin of sediments accumulated by both abiotic and biotic agents (Val and Stratford, 2015). The younger deposits, namely those from the Lincoln Cave and the L/63 infill, indicate some denning activity by jackals (*Canis* cf. *mesomelas*) and some degree of porcupine gnawing damage is also observed on the bones of the L/63 assemblage (Reynolds, 2010; O'Regan et al., 2011a). Neither of these younger deposits appear to contain faunal elements bearing signs of hominin or human activities, such as chop marks, cut marks or burnt bones (Reynolds et al., 2007).

Sterkfontein Paleoenvironmental Reconstructions

Brief Overview of Entire Sterkfontein Sequence

The recognition of possible links between hominin evolution (especially of the genus *Australopithecus*) and savanna grasslands in Africa dates back to Raymond Dart (1925a). The earliest studies attempting reconstructions of Sterkfontein habitat conditions were based largely on the presence/absence of macromammalian indicator fauna (e.g., Broom, 1938a; Cooke, 1963; Robinson, 1963; Vrba, 1980, 1985c, 1995b; Brain et al., 1988; Watson, 1993a). These studies suggested more closed, forested conditions associated with *Australopithecus africanus* (specifically in Member 4) transitioning to more open, grassland-dominated habitats in Member 5 with giant gelada (*Theropithecus*), zebras (*Equus*), and ostrich (*Struthio* sp.) considered key faunal indicators associated with the appearance of stone tools and early *Homo* at Sterkfontein (Hughes and Tobias, 1977; Kuman and Clarke, 2000). By today's standards analysis of the presence/absence of key species may seem relatively unsophisticated, but it was a useful way of assessing the grassland versus woodland component of the environment. Later, statistical analysis of the bovid composition of modern game parks enabled Vrba (1980) to define her Alcelaphini–Antilopini Criterion (AAC) which, in turn, provided a useful benchmark for assessing the general paleovegetation signal associated within a specific fossil assemblage and/or site.

In the intervening years, several new methods have been used to assess the validity of another of Vrba's influential hypotheses, namely the Turnover Pulse Hypothesis (Vrba, 1985b). Important advances, such as examining the stable isotopic composition of the mammalian enamel (e.g., Lee-Thorp et al., 2007) have revolutionized our approach to faunal diets and reconstructing habitats of the past. Other, more recent, developments have produced methods aimed at identifying specific dietary preferences such as dental use–wear (mesowear and microwear) studies. Such techniques are now routinely employed to gain greater insight into the diets and environments of the herbivores at various stages of their life cycles (e.g., Sewell et al., 2019). In the case of antelopes with flexible diets, such as the springbok and impala (genera *Antidorcas* and *Aepyceros*, respectively), these diets have been shown to be reliable indicators of prevailing vegetation conditions (Sewell et al., 2019; Sewell, 2019). While certain recent studies suggest that the breccias in the Cradle of Humankind may only sample temporal periods of drier climates and associated faunal communities (Pickering et al., 2019), we argue that the observed degree of flexibility (between grazing and browsing signals) in the diets of these animals from Sterkfontein and Swartkrans does not support this assertion (Sewell et al., 2019). The faunal species identified from the various Members are reported in Reynolds and Kibii (2011) and we present a summary of these data in Table 10.2a and 10.2b.

Building on this more detailed work on past diets, it is clear that seasonal changes in diets are becoming the new focus of paleoenvironmental research. The recognition of dietary variability in hominins such as *Australopithecus africanus* (van der Merwe et al., 2003) and *Paranthropus robustus* (e.g., Sponheimer et al., 2006b) indicates a need to understand the seasonal degree of change experienced by hominins and fauna living around the Sterkfontein site region. It is, of course, possible that these species were not full-time residents, but instead migrated through the region during specific seasons. This has been inferred for some of the carnivore species and for hominins (Reynolds, 2010; Copeland et al., 2011).

While seasonal changes are important, there is also the need to understand the proportions of each habitat type available more generally at sites like Sterkfontein. Here, the use of smaller mammals as microscale habitat indicators (such as the analysis of micromammals by Avery, 2001) has an invaluable contribution to make. Processes that promote the stability of heterogeneous habitats have also aided our understanding of the long-term drivers of habitat change and vegetation cover. A greater awareness of the role of landscape dynamics, such as tectonic processes (Reynolds et al., 2011), that may promote habitat heterogeneity at smaller spatial scales has led to a fundamental shift in our approach to reconstructing paleohabitats. Instead of simple habitat categories such as "closed" versus "open," the more recent paleoenvironmental reconstructions for Sterkfontein point strongly toward habitat heterogeneity, also known as "mosaic" habitats, which appear to be associated with many hominin sites through time and across Africa (e.g., Avery, 2001; Reed, 1997; de Ruiter et al., 2008a; Brophy, 2011; Reynolds and Kibii, 2011; Reynolds et al., 2011, 2015).

Techniques Employed to Reconstruct Paleoenvironments

Paleoenvironmental reconstructions have traditionally concentrated on various types of faunal analyses, ranging from the

Table 10.2a Number of mammalian species of each Family found in each member at Sterkfontein. "1+" is stated where the fossil species is identified above species level only, e.g., "*Antidorcas* sp." where one or more species may be represented within this category (subject to further taxonomic investigation). References for species: Avery, 2001; Avery et al., 2010; Brain, 1981; Kuman and Clarke, 2000; Reynolds and Kibii, 2011; Val and Stratford, 2015; Sewell et al., 2019.

Taxonomic group	Family	JC	M2	M4	Stw 53	M5 E	M5 W	L/63	LC	NC
Primates and Carnivora	Hominidae	1+	2+	2+	1+	1	1	1+	1	
	Cercopithecidae	5+	4	7+	3+	2+	1+	1	1	2+
	Felidae	5+	6	6+	1	2+	2	1+	1+	2+
	Canidae	2		3+	1	1+	1	1	4+	1+
	Viverridae	2			1+	3+	2+	2+	1+	1+
	Hyaenidae	4+	3+	7+	1+	2+	4+		1+	2+
Other fauna	Equidae	1+		2+	1+	1+	1+	1	1	1+
	Elephantidae		1							
	Hippopotamidae							1		
	Suidae	1		2+		1	1		1	2+
	Procaviidae		2	2	2	1	1	1	2	
	Hystricidae		1			1	1	1	1	
	Pedetidae	1		x		1		1	1	1
	Leporidae	1		1+				2+	1	1+
	Aves	1+				1				
	Chelonia	1								
Micromammals	Chrysochloridae					4+	1	3+		3+
	Soricidae			2		2	2	2		2
	Muridae			7+		10+	9+	10+		10+
	Nesomyidae			3		5	4	6+		6+
	Myoxidae					1	1	1		1
	Bathyergidae					1	2+	2+		1
	Rhinolophidae					1+		1+		1+
	Vespertilionidae					1+		1+		3+
	Macroscelididae			2		2	1	2		1

Table 10.2b Number of mammalian species of Family Bovidae are separated to distinguish between differing tribes with contrasting paleoenvironmental associations. References for species: Avery, 2001; Avery et al., 2010; Brain, 1981; Kuman and Clarke, 2000; Reynolds and Kibii, 2011; Val and Stratford, 2015; Sewell et al., 2019.

Family	Tribe	JC	M2	M4	Stw 53	M5 E	M5 W	L/63	LC	NC
Bovidae	Alcelaphini	2+	1+	3+	2+	2+	2+	2+	2+	3+
	Hippotragini	1+		3+					1+	
	Bovini	1+		1+						
	Ovibovini		1	2+	1					
	Aepycerotini			2+			1+			
	Tragelaphini	1+		2		1	1+		1	1
	Reduncini	1+		2		1+	1+	1+	1+	
	Antilopini			4+	1	1+	1+	1+	1+	1+
	Neotragini	1+				1		1	1+	
	Peleini			1				1	1	
	Boselaphini			1+	1+					

presence/absence of habitat indicator species (typically herbivores) such as Elisabeth Vrba's AAC criterion (Vrba, 1974, 1975, 1976) to more complex analysis of whole assemblages (e.g., Reynolds et al., 2007; de Ruiter et al., 2008a) or in-depth analyses of dental aspects of specific taxa, using isotopes or microwear to examine habitat at the scale of the diet of the individual animal (e.g., Sewell et al., 2019). Recently, some new alternative methods have been developed. For example, Caruana (2017) inferred micro-paleoenvironmental signals from archeological (lithic) material from Sterkfontein Member 5 and compared this to material from Swartkrans Member 1 (which is considered to be roughly contemporaneous). The position of the Blaaubank may have been closer to the Swartkrans site, and thus hominins' access to the river gravels would have been somewhat easier. This, in turn, implies that Swartkrans Member 1 may have experienced slightly wetter conditions than at Sterkfontein Member 5 over the same temporal period (Caruana, 2017).

Floral preservation is rare in the Cradle of Humankind sites, but where botanical data exist, they can vastly improve reconstructions of vegetation cover in the past. Studies of fossil wood and other botanical remains by Bamford (1999; Sterkfontein Member 4) and Bamford et al. (2010; Malapa – ca. 15 km NNE from Sterkfontein, dated 1.95–1.78 Ma (Dirks et al., 2010)) suggest cooler, moister forest vegetation was relatively widespread during Sterkfontein Member 4, and in Member 5 accumulations. The extensive assemblages of pieces of fossilized wood of a liana species (*Dichapetalum* cf. *mombuttense*) and shrub (*Anastrabe integerrima*) from Member 4 supported conclusions from faunal analysis of a dominance of woodland paleoenvironments, supporting forest-fringe type habitats (Bamford, 1999) relative to later members. Microbotanical remains of conifer (aff. *Podocarpus*) are present in the Malapa coprolite and also found, although in very low concentrations (0.4%), in Sterkfontein Member 5 travertine samples. These show at least some wetter, forest-type habitats existed and to a greater extent than previously assumed at that interval (Bamford et al., 2010).

Specific Reconstructions for Paleoenvironments by Individual Members

The general paleoenvironmental signal, obtained in light of new evidence (e.g., Avery, 2010; Sewell et al., 2019; Sewell, 2019), supports the presence of heterogeneous habitats at Sterkfontein. The question remains how to accurately identify the dominant paleovegetation elements within these heterogeneous habitats, knowing that the full picture is complicated by issues such as climate-averaging (Hopley and Maslin, 2010) and possible erosion and reworking of fossils within the karst sediments. Here we present a Member by Member summary of the current paleoenvironmental evidence and interpretations, from oldest to youngest deposits.

(1) Jacovec Cavern

Analyses of the faunal composition of the Jacovec Cavern deposit by Kibii (2004) suggest a habitat mosaic consisting of riverine gallery forest, with bushland and open country present at the site. The carnivores and bovids present indicate a wide range of habitat types, from more closed deposits (e.g., the small duikers and the tragelaphines) to those indicating mixed habitats of grassland and savanna woodland, and finally, those which may indicate more open, grassland habitats (e.g., alcelaphins, hippotragins, reduncins). The presence of large non-hominin primates, especially of arboreal colobine species within the Jacovec Cavern, is highly indicative of substantial tree cover probably equivalent to Africa's tropical and montane forests.

(2) Member 2

The latest dates for deposit indicate an age of approximately 3.67 ± 0.16 million years for the specimen identified as *Australopithecus prometheus* and the other fauna contained within this Member (Granger et al., 2015). As far as paleoenvironmental reconstructions are concerned, Pickering et al. (2004a) suggest that a degree of open grassland and rocky outcrops are indicated during the accumulation of the Member 2 fauna. A gallery forest with a close permanent source of water is indicated by the co-association of obligate drinkers, such as the alcelaphins, leopards (*Panthera pardus*), and cercopithecoids (Pickering et al., 2004a).

(3) Member 3

This Member is an unexcavated exposed Member in the Silberberg Grotto that contains fossils, but about which little is currently known. Certain authors have suggested that Sterkfontein Members 3 and 4 may, in fact, represent a single Member (e.g., Pickering and Kramers, 2010).

(4) Member 4

Sterkfontein Member 4 is an important deposit, due mainly to the large sample of *Au. africanus* specimens recovered from this member, possibly indicating the preferred habitats of *Au. africanus* (and possibly also of the proposed *Australopithecus* "Second Species"; Clarke, 1988; and see Clarke, 2012; Kimbel and White, 1988; Moggi-Cecchi, 2003 and references therein). The earliest detailed reconstructions for Member 4 paleoenvironments centered on the interpretation of presence and absence of fossil fauna, specifically Bovidae (e.g., Vrba, 1975, 1985c, 1995b), which suggested a wooded environment with close proximity to open grassland. Specifically, the presence of ovibovines (*Makapania broomi*) and hippotragins were interpreted as suggesting wooded environments, along with open grassland indicator Bovidae tribes, such as the Alcelaphini and Antilopini. Later work by Reed (1997), using the relative proportions of all species present (rather than only ungulates or herbivores), showed a high percentage of terrestrial animals (23.3 percent), combined with a significant proportion of frugivorous mammals (16.7 percent), but a significantly low percentage of arboreal animals (3.3 percent). These proportions supported the scenario of open woodland with bushland and thicket.

Stable carbon isotope work by Luyt and colleagues (Luyt, 2001; Luyt and Lee-Thorp, 2003) on herbivore and carnivore enamel has identified the full spectrum of browsers, grazers, and mixed feeders within Member 4. Further, the extent of woodland was shown to have been larger than originally proposed by Vrba (Luyt, 2001). The extinct C_3 feeders (consuming trees, shrubs, and herbs, or their consumers) include *Hippotragus* cf. sp. aff. *gigas* and the carnivore *Homotherium latidens*. The extinct C_4 consumers (grazers) include *Redunca darti* while the mixed feeders include *Antidorcas* sp. and *Tragelaphus* sp. aff. *angasi* for bovids, and the extinct hyena *Chasmaporthetes nitidula* (Luyt, 2001). Recent bovid dietary studies in springbok (*Antidorcas*) underscore the likely habitat heterogeneity of Member 4 habitats. An increase in browse consumption by antelopes such as *Antidorcas recki* suggests the greater presence of mixed woodland (Sewell et al., 2019; Sewell, 2019). Studies of cercopithecoid postcranial morphology indicate the presence of a range of several distinct habitat types: forest, open woodland/bushland, and grassland (Elton, 2001; Williams and Geissler, 2014). Individuals falling into the "open terrestrial" habitat category dominate the cercopithecoid sample, signaling the presence of a significant open component during Member 4 times (e.g., Williams and Geissler, 2014).

Unusually for any fossil deposit in the southern African region, Member 4 also yielded fossil wood specimens (Bamford, 1999). The presence of liana vines (most similar to the extant species equatorial forest vine species *Dichapetalum mombuttense*) and the Pambati tree (*Anastrabe integerrima*) in the fossil wood sample along with the presence of the extinct colobine monkey (*Cercopithecoides williamsi*) suggested a forest-fringe environment (Bamford, 1999; Kuman and Clarke, 2000). Furthermore, australopithecine locomotor behavior has been interpreted as having a strong arboreal component (Wood and Richmond, 2000), suggesting that a mosaic of woodland and grassland areas would have suited the habitat requirements of *Au. africanus*.

Micromammal species analyzed by Avery (2001) lend a different perspective to the debate regarding the Member 4 paleoenvironments. Micromammal species are represented by 12 identified species, which occur across other deposits at the site (Avery, 2001). This suggests that, from the perspective of the predators (owls), there existed a similar range of environments in Member 4 times to those of subsequent Member 5 infills and Post Member 6. A single extinct species of unknown habitat preference (*Proodontomys cookei*) is represented, which also occurs in Member 5 East, Member 5 West, and at Swartkrans (Members 1–3; Avery, 2001). However, the short-snouted elephant shrew (*Elephantulus fuscus*) is found only in Member 4 and Member 5 East, and this species is known to prefer moist woodland environments. Taken together, Avery's (2001: 127) reconstruction was that the classic mosaic habitat of "grass with trees along river, bush with grass on the hillsides and grass with some trees and bushes on the plains" prevailed during Member 4 times.

Evidence for the diets and preferred habitat of the abundant hominin, *Au. africanus*, from stable carbon isotope studies reveal a significant proportion of C_4 foods, and that their diets were highly variable during Member 4 (Sponheimer and Lee-Thorp, 1999; van der Merwe et al., 2003, Sponheimer et al., 2005a). Analyses using ratios of strontium and calcium (Sr/Ca) in hominin enamel indicate that the *Australopithecus* diets from Sterkfontein Member 4 show higher Sr/Ca ratios relative to *Paranthropus robustus* from Swartkrans Member 1 (Sponheimer et al., 2005b). The authors suggest that these results may indicate either high levels of grazing, or insectivory, in the diets of *Australopithecus* from Sterkfontein (Sponheimer et al., 2005b). Both studies indicate that *Australopithecus* exploited grassland and woodland food resources regularly, or ate animals (termites, other fauna) that had eaten significant quantities of C_4 foods.

This revised paleoenvironmental reconstruction has bearing on the occurrence of *Equus* in Sterkfontein Member 4, fossils of which have previously thought to be intrusive from a later Member 5 infill (Kuman and Clarke, 2000). The first appearance of *Equus* in the African fossil record is at 2.33 ± 0.03 Ma (lower Member G of the Shungura Formation, Ethiopia; Churcher and Hooijer, 1980). Recent isotopic work on the diets of *Equus* from eastern Africa (specifically the Turkana Basin, Kenya) indicates that *Equus* is associated with almost exclusively grazing diets across sites in eastern Africa (Cerling et al., 2015a; Uno et al., 2018). If one considers the relatively younger age estimates for Member 4 suggested by combined paleomagnetic, uranium–lead, and electron spin resonance (ESR) studies (Schwarcz et al., 1994; Pickering and Kramers, 2010; Herries and Shaw, 2011), there is no *a priori* reason why *Equus*, and the grasslands likely to be closely associated with the presence of this genus, could not occur in the later, upper beds of Sterkfontein Member 4, which date to less than 2.36 Ma. The ESR ages in particular, supported by paleomagnetism and U–Pb, suggest that Member 4 formed over a very long time period, perhaps as long as 600 kyr (2.6–2.0 Ma). Two species of the family Equidae are present at the neighboring but younger site of Coopers D, specifically *Equus capensis* and *Eurygnathohippus* cf. *cornelianus*, which date to 1.38 ± 0.11 Ma (Badenhorst and Steininger, 2019).

Taken together, the stable carbon isotope data from the hominins, as well as the high numbers of mammal species present, appears to suggest that Member 4 had a high degree of habitat heterogeneity. Does this indicate the possible effects of time- and climate-averaging during Member 4 deposit accumulation? High habitat variability over the same time period has been reported from Laetoli in East Africa, based on vegetation evidence (Andrews and Bamford, 2008; Harrison and colleagues, Chapter 34). However, there are indications that Member 4 is a time-averaged accumulation that does not reflect a single faunal community or habitat state (e.g., O'Regan and Reynolds, 2009; Hopley and Maslin, 2010). Future work is needed to understand the role of time-averaging of wet–dry periods versus relatively constant levels of high habitat heterogeneity in the creation of these observed levels of species diversity in Member 4.

(5) Name Chamber

The Name Chamber's mixed faunal assemblage (dominated by bovids) is consistent with open and dry conditions (e.g., *Equus* sp. and *Pedetes capensis*), alongside woodland and humid-associated taxa (e.g., *Tragelaphus strepsiceros*; Val and Stratford, 2015). This is to be expected as the likely time-averaged Name Chamber deposit is largely a mix of Member 4 and Member 5 material (Stratford et al., 2012; Stratford, 2017).

(6) Member 5

Member 5 is separated into three distinct infills, which likely reflect similar paleoenvironments. The extinct giant gelada baboon (*Theropithecus oswaldi*) is present in StW 53 and Oldowan Infills, but is absent in Member 4, suggesting that Member 4 and Member 5 deposits sample slightly different environmental conditions and so are of different ages (Kuman and Clarke, 2000). Closely associated with grassland environments, *T. oswaldi* is argued to have appeared within the Sterkfontein region after a shift in the environment toward drier conditions at 2.1 Ma (Weigelt et al., 2008). The earliest record of this genus is dated to around 3.7–3.5 Ma, from the Kalochoro Member at Lothagam, in Kenya (Leakey et al., 1996). The last appearance of *T. oswaldi* in South Africa is at Hopefield (Western Cape Province, South Africa), which dates to about 0.4 Ma (Pickford, 1993).

(6.1) Member 5: Stw53

The Stw53 paleoenvironments of open, drier, grassland conditions are suggested by the presence of the extinct species of gelada, *Theropithecus oswaldi*, and an equid in the StW 53 infill (Kuman and Clarke, 2000). This marks a shift from largely closed, wetter conditions present in Member 4 to drier, more grassland conditions in Member 5.

(6.2) Member 5: East (Oldowan)

Faunal composition from the Oldowan infill, including the equids (*Equus* sp.), springhare (*Pedetes capensis*), ostrich (*Struthio* sp.), and lion (*Panthera leo*), as well as the various species of Antilopini and Alcelaphini, have been interpreted as indicating a drier and more open environment (Pickering, 1999). The tibia of the giant ostrich (*Struthio* sp.) from this infill is similar to specimens from Olduvai (Clarke, 1994; Bibi et al., 2017). Likewise, Cooke (1994) suggested a similarity between extinct giant warthog (*Metridiochoerus/Phacochoerus modestus*) specimens with those identified from Olduvai Bed I. However, an ecomorphological analysis of all bovids from this infill indicates that a significant amount of tree cover was available in the vicinity (Bishop et al., 1999b).

(6.3) Member 5: West (Acheulean)

Fauna from the Member 5 West (Early Acheulean) appears to indicate open or wooded grassland or open savanna (Vrba, 1975; McKee, 1991; Reed, 1997; Kuman and Clarke, 2000) relative to Member 4 times (Luyt, 2001; Luyt and Lee-Thorp, 2003), and this is in keeping with drier conditions after 1.7 Ma and the onset of the Walker Circulation, as has been proposed by Hopley et al. (2007b). Consistent with this are new data from bovid diets: *Antidorcas* (springbok), one of the most abundant fossil antelopes in many African fossil assemblages and a habitually employed paleohabitat indicator within faunal assemblages, suggests mixed habitats were present from the late Pliocene, with indications of increased environmental instability and habitat heterogeneity around Sterkfontein Member 5 West temporal period. This is inferred from increased *Antidorcas* intra- and interspecific dental variation and lifetime dietary signals from fossils deriving from the Member 5 West deposit (Sewell et al., 2019; Sewell, 2019).

(7) Lincoln Cave

Lincoln Cave North's faunal assemblage uniquely contains a single incisor of the hippopotamus (*H. amphibius*; Reynolds et al., 2003) and bushbuck (*Tragelaphus scriptus*), which prefers "riparian thicket" (du Toit and Owen-Smith, 1989). Therefore, on the basis of these species, the paleoenvironment of Lincoln Cave North is inferred as slightly wetter than Member 5 West and later post-Member 6 L/63 Infill as well as than the Lincoln Cave South paleoenvironment (Reynolds et al., 2007).

Lincoln Cave South and the post-Member 6 L/63 Infill are dominated by extant fauna that are common in the area today. In contrast with the Member 5 West assemblage, the younger deposits are dominated by small carnivore species, signifying either that taphonomic processes influenced the deposit or that larger carnivores (such as lions, leopards, and hyenas) moved out of the Sterkfontein site catchment area during the Upper Pleistocene (Reynolds et al., 2007; Reynolds, 2010). An overview of the environments is provided in Table 10.3.

Table 10.3 Summary of published paleoenvironmental reconstructions by Sterkfontein Member. References: [1] Kibii, 2004; [2] Pickering et al., 2004a; [3] Mokokwe, 2016; [4] O'Regan and Reynolds, 2009 [5] Reynolds et al., 2007; [6] Ogola, 2009.

Sterkfontein deposit	Summary of published paleoenvironmental reconstructions for deposits
Jacovec Cavern	A mosaic of both open and closed habitats, comprised of a riverine gallery forest, with bushland and open country.[1] Relatively open with a permanent water supply in the vicinity[2]
Member 2	Open grassland and rocky outcrops.[2] Riverine gallery forest with surrounding bushland and occasional open areas with the possibility of standing local source of water
Member 4	Mosaic habitats with the greatest variety of habitats available.[3] Mosaic but with more dominant woodland component than later members. Wetter (faunal remains and woody plants – Bamford, 1999; Kuman and Clarke, 2000). Presence of arboreal primates suggests at least some tree cover.[3] Forest fringe environment with both open and wooded plains.[4] A continuum of forested, open woodland and grassland habitats.[1]
Member 5: StW 53 Infill	Open, drier (than Member 4), grassland
Member 5: East Infill	Moderately wooded areas.[3] More open grassland than Member 4
Member 5: West Infill	Mosaic but with greater grassland presence than Member 4. Open/woodland grassland or open savanna. A marked shift to drier, more open grassland environments
Post Member 6: L/63 Infill	Savanna mosaic environments; savanna woodland and grassland habitats near a permanent water source (such as a swamp or perennial stream).[6] Changing environment[3]
Lincoln Cave North	Slightly wetter than the earlier Member 5 West and later, Lincoln Cave South and L/63[5]
Lincoln Cave South	Similar to modern environments in region today
	Drier, more open grassland environments, similar to Member 5 West[5,6] and modern analogs[5]

Conclusions

Sterkfontein remains one of the richest *Australopithecus*-bearing sites in the world, and one of less than a handful of African sites that can inform us of the habitats directly associated with the *Australopithecus* to *Homo* transition, and second, the Oldowan–Acheulean transition (see Horwitz et al., Chapter 14 for Wonderwerk Cave's perspective on the latter transition). The sequence, therefore, is ideal for addressing questions about the role of climate change in hominin evolution and the habitat conditions accompanying key behavioral adaptations.

For Sterkfontein, indications drawn mainly from the habitat associations of the mammal species present, but also taking stable carbon isotope studies into account, indicate gradual, but directional, change from closed, wetter, woodland-dominated habitats pre-Member 4 (namely Member 2, Silberberg Grotto, Milner Hall, and Jacovec Cavern) and during Member 4 times, toward more open, arid grassland-dominated habitats from the uppermost beds of Member 4 and Member 5 onwards (Lee-Thorp et al., 2007). A slightly wetter environment is suggested for Lincoln Cave North, also based on the types of fauna present (Reynolds et al., 2007).

While there is an observable shift from closed to open habitats, there is also a significant degree of habitat heterogeneity present throughout the temporal sequence, suggested by the types of fauna preserved. This indicates that, rather than dramatic sweeping changes accompanying the appearance of early *Homo* and the Early Acheulean, the situation is one of subtle shifts on a continuum between habitats much like the area today (quite dry), versus a slightly wetter and more wooded version of the same landscape. This may partly explain why animals that were mixed feeders in the past have remained well-represented in the deposits (e.g., springbok, see Sewell et al., 2019 and Sewell, 2019). Other proxies of habitat change (such as cercopithecoid postcranial evidence and *Antidorcas* dietary evidence) likewise indicate gradual changes (Mokokwe, 2016; Sewell et al., 2019; Sewell, 2019).

Yet there are still gaps in our understanding of the record of Sterkfontein. Future avenues for research include establishing the degree of seasonality present in the Sterkfontein Valley at specific times in the past; the degree to which bovid species present in the deposits were resident or migratory through the region; and greater targeted prospection for little-studied faunal groups such as birds, reptiles, micromammals, and insects (see Parker et al., 2016 and Leichliter et al., 2017; Genise and Harrison, 2018; Leichliter, 2018). Future paleoenvironmental data are unlikely to entirely rewrite our understanding of these habitats, but will certainly provide more detailed and site-specific data on past habitat types and the hominins' place within them.

Acknowledgments

The authors would like to thank Ronald J. Clarke and Kathleen A. Kuman for their support and encouragement of our work. We dedicate this work to our late colleagues, Charles Lockwood, Tim Partridge, and especially to Phillip V. Tobias, who supported research at Sterkfontein for so many years. We would like to thank an anonymous reviewer whose comments greatly improved this manuscript. Thank you also to Fiona Coward for her kind proof-reading, and to Wendy Voorvelt for her assistance with the figures.

11 Swartkrans: A Record of Paleoenvironmental Change in the Cradle of Humankind

Darryl de Ruiter

Introduction

The first hominin fossils were recovered from Swartkrans by Robert Broom and John Robinson of the Transvaal Museum, working at the site at the behest of Wendell Phillips of the University of California's Africa Expedition, in September of 1948. Broom considered the Swartkrans fossils to represent a new species of robust australopith that he named *Paranthropus crassidens* (Broom, 1949), although the material was later transferred to *P. robustus* (Robinson, 1954, 1956). Excavations continued through 1949, when a shortage of funds brought work to an end in November of that year. During the succeeding Christmas holiday, a local lime miner by the name of Fourie moved into Swartkrans and began blasting operations to remove a recently exposed seam of limestone for use by the gold-mining industry in nearby Krugersdorp. Broom and Robinson occasionally returned to the site to inspect the breccia that was also being loosened during the course of Fourie's limestone blasting, which resulted in the recovery of several spectacular australopith specimens such as SK 23 and SK 48. In addition, Broom and Robinson recovered several specimens that could be attributed to early *Homo*, such as SK 15 and SK 45 (Broom and Robinson, 1949, 1952). Because SK 15 was derived from the "brown breccia" (Member 2, see below), Broom and Robinson initially held it to be considerably younger than the australopith fossils recovered from the "pink breccia" (Hanging Remnant of Member 1, see below). However, SK 45 was derived from the same "pink breccia" that had produced so many *P. robustus* fossils, and thus demonstrated for the first time the coexistence of multiple species of early hominin (Broom and Robinson, 1952). Broom died in 1951, but Robinson continued to conduct paleontological research at the site until 1953, unearthing numerous additional hominin fossils.

After 12 years of dormancy, in 1965 C.K. Brain of the Transvaal Museum recommenced operations at the site, beginning with cleaning the rubble left behind from Fourie's activities. Brain soon realized that Fourie's mining episode of the early 1950s was not the first time that Swartkrans had been scoured for limestone. In the early 1930s the site had been partially blasted out, and the resulting quarry refilled with loosened breccia to allow for a cocopan track to be laid. From 1965 until 1972 Brain sorted through this miner's rubble and was rewarded with numerous hominin fossils (Brain, 1970).

In 1968 the property was purchased by the University of the Witwatersrand, allowing Brain to continue his excavations undisturbed. Beginning in 1972 and continuing until 1979, Brain undertook excavation of the natural overburden in the cave, which allowed him to decipher the complex geology of the system, and source most of the previously recovered fossils back to their original geological Members (Brain, 1976). Initially it was thought that two main Members could be recognized, Members 1 and 2 (Butzer, 1976), although Brain's later *in situ* excavations revealed additional units (Brain, 1993a). During the 1972–1979 phase of activity, Brain discovered that the Member 1 deposit was actually an isolated mass of bone-bearing breccia adhering to the north wall of the cave that had been undercut by erosion, the cavity being filled by later sediments. He termed this heavily calcified mass the Hanging Remnant of Member 1, and hypothesized the existence of a lower and slightly older deposit upon which the Hanging Remnant had originally rested, which he termed the Lower Bank of Member 1. This Lower Bank was eventually located in the form of an uncalcified deposit stretching across much of the site, and together these two components comprise Member 1, the oldest of the Swartkrans sediments. After clearing the overburden, between 1979 and 1986 Brain conducted *in situ* excavations at the site, recovering tens of thousands of bones from the Lower Bank of Member 1, Member 2 (comprised of a more heavily calcified component and a decalcified component), and the then newly recognized Member 3. Two additional younger Members, 4 and 5, were recorded at Swartkrans, but are not discussed further here; materials recovered from Member 4 are comprised almost entirely of MSA tools, while Member 5 dates to approximately 11,000 BP (Brain, 1993b).

In 2005 new excavations at Swartkrans were begun by the Swartkrans Palaeoanthropological Research Project, recovering additional hominin fossils and slightly revising Brain's stratigraphic interpretations of the site (Sutton et al., 2009; Pickering et al., 2012, 2016, 2017).

Geology and Stratigraphy of Swartkrans

As is the case in most fossiliferous cave systems in South Africa, the geology and stratigraphy of Swartkrans is complex. Repeated cycles of erosion and deposition are evident, resulting in the recognition of five geological members that comprise a

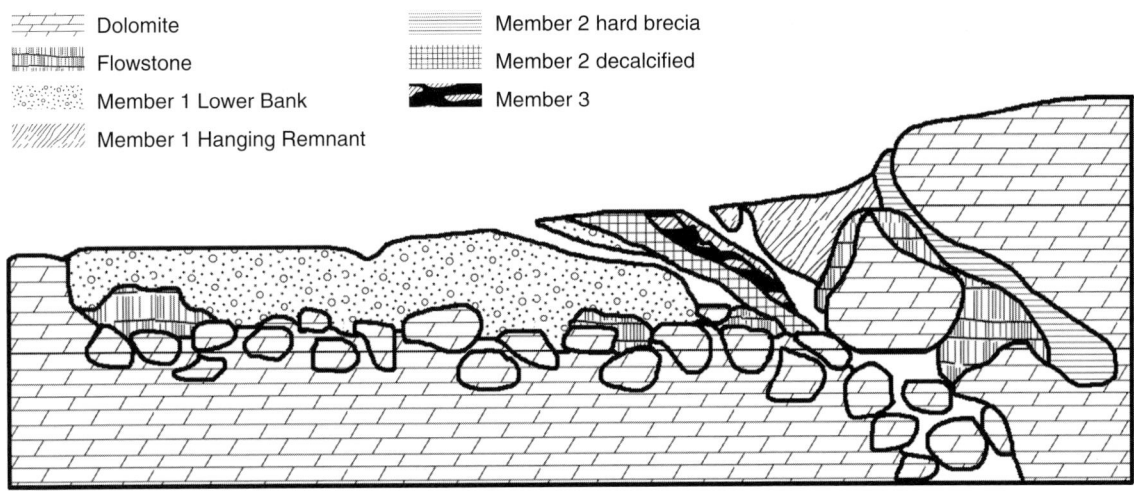

Figure 11.1 Generalized cross-section of the Swartkrans Cave reconstructed as it appeared prior to excavation. Modified from Brain (1993a).

depositional mosaic; in this chapter we will focus on Members 1–3, as these are the early hominin-bearing deposits. The geological situation summarized below is more fully documented and illustrated in Brain (1993a) and Pickering et al. (2016). For detailed maps of the excavations and stratigraphy of the site, the reader is referred to Brain (1976, 1993a) and to Pickering et al. (2012, 2016). A simplified reconstruction of the stratigraphy of the cave as it would have appeared prior to Broom and Robinson's excavations is presented in Figure 11.1, modified from Brain (1993a).

Swartkrans is a karstic cave housed in the late Archaean bedrock of the Monte Christo Formation of the Malmani Subgroup of the Chuniespoort Group. The cavern initially dissolved in water far below the ground surface (phreatic). Valley incision lowered the water table, leaving an air-filled cavern wherein stalactites and stalagmites began to form through the evaporation of lime-rich water percolating through the overlying dolomite. Joints began to form in the dolomite, and over the southeast wall one joint in particular enlarged and opened to the outer surface. This shaft-like opening admitted sediments that formed an uncalcified, fossiliferous talus cone that has been designated the Lower Bank of Member 1 (Figure 11.1). Eventually this opening became choked off by sediment while other shaft-like openings formed, one of which opened over the north wall and allowed ingress of fossil rich sediments that formed the Hanging Remnant of Member 1 (originally called the "pink breccia"). The Hanging Remnant is much more heavily calcified than the Lower Bank, indicating that a good deal of lime-rich water was available during its formation. After some amount of time, deposition of the Hanging Remnant ceased and a period of erosion commenced. Flowing water entered the system through a new shaft-like opening between the south and north walls, eroding an irregular channel between the Hanging Remnant and the Lower Bank. This channel later filled up with fossiliferous sediment that formed Member 2, which itself became solidified by lime rich water dripping from the roof of the cave. A later erosional cycle formed a gully along the western wall of the cave, removing parts of Members 1 and 2, afterwards filling up with fossiliferous sediment that formed Member 3, the latter which also became solidified by lime rich water. Subsequent exposure to the elements decalcified part of the Member 2 and virtually all of the Member 3 sediments, serendipitously facilitating later fossil extraction. Subsequent hillside erosion removed most of the dolomite roof of the cave, forming additional eroded pockets within the older sediments that later became filled with sediments that formed Members 4 and 5 (not discussed further). Most recently Pickering et al. (2016) have recognized two additional fossiliferous deposits (the "Talus Cone Deposit" and the "Underground North Extension"), which are not yet assigned to a particular member.

Dating

Until relatively recently, dating of the fossil-bearing cave infills of South Africa was based on biostratigraphic comparisons with radiometrically dated sites in East Africa. Vrba (1975) initially suggested that the Member 1 bovid fauna she examined (now recognized as being from the Hanging Remnant of Member 1) indicated an age of between 1 and 2 million years (Ma). Data from other faunal correlations were used to refine the age of the Hanging Remnant of Member 1 to approximately between 2.0 and 1.5 Ma for Members 1 and 2 (White and Harris, 1977; Cooke, 1983; Delson, 1984; Vrba, 1985a). Brain (1993b) subsequently considered the entirety of the Swartkrans assemblages from Members 1–3 to fall between 1.8 and 1.0 Ma. Using a combination of biochronology, paleomagnetic dating, and electron spin resonance (ESR) dating, Herries et al. (2009) suggested that Member 1 was *ca.* 2.0 Ma, Member 2 *ca.* 1.7–1.1 Ma, and Member 3 *ca.* 1.0–0.6 Ma. Robyn Pickering et al. (2011) utilized U–Pb radiometric dating to produce an age estimate of *ca.* 1.9–1.8 Ma for Member 1, and a maximum possible age of 1.706 ± 0.069 Ma for Member 2. These U–Pb dates accord closely with a cosmogenic nuclide burial dating estimate of 1.99 ± 0.19 Ma for Member 1 (Gibbon et al., 2014), while the latter dating method has produced an estimate of 0.96 ± 0.09 Ma for Member 3

(Gibbon et al., 2014). In sum, Member 1 (including the Hanging Remnant and Lower Bank) likely dates to just under 2.0 Ma based on both U–Pb and cosmogenic nuclide dating, Member 2 is younger than 1.7 Ma via U–Pb and possibly about 1.5 Ma based on faunal correlations, and Member 3 is likely around 1.0 Ma based on cosmogenic nuclide dating.

Paleoenvironments at Swartkrans

The site of Swartkrans has produced a wealth of (sometimes contradictory) information regarding the paleoenvironments of the hominins (Table 11.1). The majority of these studies are based on the associated faunal assemblages recovered from the respective members, while some insight has been achieved through study of the geology of the cave and the isotope chemistry of the fossils. Most studies have highlighted the high proportion of grasslands reconstructed (but see Benefit and McCrossin, 1990, for a contrasting view), although de Ruiter et al. (2008a) have cautioned that such reconstructed paleoenvironments do not necessarily correspond to habitat preferences of the hominins.

Perceptions regarding the paleoenvironment of Swartkrans have changed over time. Early investigations held that the environment at the time of deposition was similar to that of today (Brain, 1958; Cooke, 1963), although the stratigraphy and geology of the cave system was only rudimentarily understood. To correct this, Butzer (1971, 1976) undertook a lithostratigraphic analysis of the Swartkrans Formation, identifying two distinct units, Member 1 (later recognized as the Hanging Remnant of Member 1) and Member 2. He saw the paleoenvironment as a predominantly open grassland or parkland, although by his estimation the amount of moisture and

Table 11.1 Paleoenvironmental proxies at Swartkrans over the years.

Paleoenvironmental proxy	Analysis employed	Member(s)	Paleoenvironment indicated	Citations
Geology	Sand grain angularity; breccia color, chert-quartz ratios	1HR, 2	Conditions comparable to the present day; 1HR deposited under drier conditions	Brain, 1958
Macrofauna	Species presence/absence	1HR	Similar to modern climate	Cooke, 1963
Geology	Sediment geomorphology	1HR, 2	Dry, open grassland, with moister and drier intervals	Butzer, 1971, 1976
Bovids	Proportions of bovid tribes	1HR	Open, arid grassland	Vrba, 1975, 1976, 1980, 1985a, 1985b, 1988, 1995b
Hominins	Deciduous molar microwear pattern	1HR	Drier, more open and xeric, with possible edaphic grasslands	Grine, 1981
Bovids	proportions of bovid tribes	1HR, 2	open, arid grassland	Shipman and Harris, 1988
Macrofauna	Species presence/absence, relative abundance of individuals	1LB, 2, 3	Open grassland with nearby woods and rocky habitats, with fairly extensive water	Brain et al., 1988
Papionins	Molar shear crest lengths	1HR	Wetter with moderate degree of tree cover	Benefit and McCrossin, 1990
Macrofauna	Sspecies presence/absence	1LB, 2, 3	Open savanna with rocky habitats, a fairly extensive riparian woodland, and permanent water	Brain, 1993a; Watson, 1993a
Microfauna	Relative abundance of individuals	1LB, 2, 3	Arid, open grassland/savanna, with some bushland/woodland, near a river	Avery, 1995a, 2001
Macrofauna	Functional morphology, ecological structure analysis	1LB, 2, 3	Open habitat, with nearby woodland or forest, and patches of edaphic grassland; becoming drier and less wooded over time	Reed, 1997
Cercopithecoids	Functional morphology	1HR, 2	open grassland/woodland	Elton, 2001
Macrofauna	Species presence/absence	1HR, 1LB, 2, 3	Open grasslands, with extensive woodlands, and nearby permanent water	de Ruiter, 2003
Macrofauna	Functional morphology; ecological structure analysis	1LB, 2, 3	Open, arid grassland/shrubland	Reed and Rector, 2006
Isotopes	Relative abundance of C_3 vs. C_4 feeding herbivores	1HR, 2	Dominated by C_4 grasslands; more C_3 wooded component in 1HR	Lee-Thorp et al., 2007
Macrofauna	Relative abundance of individuals; correspondence analysis	1HR, 1LB, 2, 3	Open grasslands, with extensive woodlands, and nearby permanent water	de Ruiter et al., 2008a

associated vegetation would have fluctuated over time; accumulation of parts of the deposits would have occurred during periods that were moister than current conditions, while accumulation of other parts would have occurred during periods that were drier than today.

Beginning in the 1970s, Elisabeth Vrba studied the associated bovid fauna at Swartkrans, effectively setting the stage for our current understanding of the paleoenvironment. In particular, she considered the bovid tribes Alcelaphini and Antilopini to reflect open grassland environments; thus the high proportions of these animals in the Swartkrans assemblages marked the environments at the time of deposition as particularly open and arid (Vrba, 1975, 1976, 1980, 1985a, 1985b, 1988). In contrast, the environment she reconstructed for Sterkfontein Member 4 was moister and more vegetated, thus a distinct transition could be recognized between the two. This environmental change was hypothesized to be the direct cause of the evolutionary appearance of both early *Homo* and of *P. robustus* (Vrba, 1995b). Following this, it was suggested that the open, arid paleoenvironment of Swartkrans would have resulted in the presence of more fibrous and/or harder foods that would, in turn, have resulted in evolutionary changes observed in the dentition of *P. robustus* (Grine, 1981). Using the proportions of a slightly modified set of bovid tribes relative to Vrba, Shipman and Harris (1988) agreed that the paleoenvironment at Swartkrans reflected an open, arid habitat, although they also concluded that a limited range of potential comparative habitats had so far been sampled in South Africa.

With the advent of *in situ* efforts in 1979, Brain's meticulous excavations revealed large faunal assemblages from Members 1 (Lower Bank), 2, and 3 (Brain et al., 1988; Brain, 1993a, 1993b; Watson, 1993). Within these assemblages, a much wider diversity of animals was recorded, owing in part to the lightly calcified or decalcified nature of the deposits, which greatly facilitated fossil recovery. In addition to the ubiquitous alcelaphines and antilopines, Brain also recovered bovids that were indicative of rocky habitats and of more wooded habitats. An extensive, permanent water source was signaled by the presence of otter, water mongoose, and hippopotamus, and the environment was thought to be not unlike that of today, although perhaps more watered (Brain, 1993b; Watson, 1993a). Subsequent investigation of enlarged samples, and inclusion of the Hanging Remnant of Member 1 into the analysis, did not alter this conclusion significantly, although perhaps even more extensive woodlands were indicated (de Ruiter, 2003). The overall similarity of the macrofaunal assemblages across the various Members at Swartkrans suggested that paleoenvironmental conditions were broadly similar over time (Brain et al., 1988; Watson, 1993a; de Ruiter, 2003). In contrast, a comprehensive analysis of the functional morphology and ecological structure of the fauna from these deposits suggested that although the environments were typically open habitats, there was nonetheless evidence of environmental change over time, and additional potential habitats were recognized in the form of forests and edaphic grasslands (Reed, 1997; Reed and Rector, 2006).

Similar to the macrofauna, microfaunal remains from across the Swartkrans Members indicated a predominantly open, arid environment, with slightly higher temperatures than today, and slightly more extensive water availability (Avery, 1995, 1998, 2001). In contrast to this open reconstructed environment, data from the dentition of papionins from Swartkrans suggested a wetter environment with a moderate degree of tree cover (Benefit and McCrossin, 1990). However, analysis of the postcrania of the papionins from Swartkrans indicated a more open grassland to perhaps woodland component (Elton, 2001).

Evidence from isotopic studies is more limited, because moving from ^{13}C values in fossils to paleovegetation is complex. Factors such as diagenesis and the uncertainty regarding the relationship between dietary and enamel $\delta^{13}C$ obscure the issue (Sponheimer et al., 2007). That being said, the relative abundance of C_3 versus C_4 feeding herbivores indicates the paleoenvironment was likely dominated by C_4 grasslands, with a somewhat more C_3 wooded component evident in the Hanging Remnant of Member 1 (Lee-Thorp et al., 2007). In addition to paleoenvironmental studies, investigation into the isotopic composition of the teeth of the hominins themselves was first undertaken at Swartkrans, demonstrating a considerable C_4 (tropical grasses) component to the diet of the hominins that must have been somehow derived from the surrounding grasslands (Lee-Thorp et al., 1989, 1994; Lee-Thorp and van der Merwe, 1993; Sponheimer et al., 2005a). Whether the hominins ate grasses, or ate animals that consumed these grasses, is difficult to determine at present. However, it was also demonstrated that the hominins were capable of altering their diets on both seasonal and interannual scales, suggesting that they did not necessarily specialize on these grassland resources (Sponheimer et al., 2006b).

One thing that all of these studies share is the reasonable assumption that the environment reconstructed reflects the habitat preference of the hominins, in particular *P. robustus*; thus the association between *P. robustus* and open grasslands is a persistent factor in our understanding of their paleoecology. However, de Ruiter et al. (2008a) demonstrated an unexpected pattern in the faunal assemblages from Swartkrans, Sterkfontein, Cooper's Cave, and Kromdraai: the more grassland-adapted animals that were recovered from a particular faunal assemblage, the fewer *P. robustus* individuals there tended to be. Testing for isotaphonomic conditions (de Ruiter et al., 2008a; and see below) did not reveal a significant bias in the taxonomic composition of any of the assemblages. Data on a selection of carnivore lairs were combined with modern carnivore kill data to demonstrate that carnivore predation patterns are strongly representative of their surrounding animal communities (de Ruiter et al., 2008a). Data on animal abundances were recorded for a series of modern game parks to assess habitat preferences for a series of large-bodied (>500 g) mammals. These combined data sets showed that the taxonomic composition of a given faunal assemblage reflected its surrounding animal community, and that in turn, the animal community reflected the habitat from which it was drawn, reinforcing the conclusions being drawn from fossil assemblages. The modern game park data were also used to assign fossil taxa from the *P. robustus*-bearing sites to broad habitat groups (grassland, woodland, closed/wet), which were then evaluated via correspondence analysis (de Ruiter et al., 2008a). Not surprisingly, the hominin sites, including the assemblages from Swartkrans, clustered with animals assigned to the "grassland" category. However, when relative abundance values for the australopiths themselves were inserted into the analysis, they plotted closer to the "woodland" category, indicating that the hominins shared the most comparable abundance profile with woodland-adapted taxa. Correlating the proportional representation of australopiths to that of the other fauna, de Ruiter et al. (2008a) encountered a strong, statistically significant, negative association between *P. robustus* and grassland-adapted taxa. Although the proportional representation of australopiths relative to woodland- or closed/wet-adapted taxa was not significant, the strong negative association with grassland-adapted animals indicated that the more of these grassland-adapted animals there were in an assemblage, the fewer hominins there tended to be. Because of this, they concluded that although the australopiths are consistently associated with grasslands, this does not necessarily reflect their habitat preference (de Ruiter et al., 2008a). In fact, the australopiths appeared to be somewhat averse to grasslands, suggesting that although they occupied a predominantly grassland environment, they might have either preferred a different habitat, or perhaps they were habitat generalists capable of tolerating, if not favoring, a grassland environment.

Taphonomy

Swartkrans is one of the most intensively taphonomically studied fossil sites in Africa. Following Dart (1957, 1962; Dart and Craig, 1959) it was initially assumed that the hominins were the occupants of the cave, and that the bones recovered were the remains of their hunted meals. However, in a series of groundbreaking papers comprising decades of research, Brain (1967, 1969a, 1970, 1972, 1974, 1975a, 1975b, 1976, 1978, 1980, 1981, 1993b; Brain et al., 1988) demonstrated that, rather than representing the food remains of the hominins, the hominins, in fact, were themselves the victims of the hunters and scavengers of Africa. In particular, in his volume *The Hunters or the Hunted*, Brain (1981) presents a thorough and meticulously documented compendium of his taphonomic research. The cast of potential agents that Brain (1981) identified includes spotted hyena (*Crocuta crocuta*), brown hyena (*Parahyaena brunnea*), striped hyena (*Hyaena hyaena*), leopard (*Panthera pardus*), black eagle (*Aquila verreauxi*), porcupine (*Hystrix africaeaustralis*), and an assortment of owls among extant taxa. Also large, extinct carnivores such as *Dinofelis, Megantereon, Machairodus, Homotherium, Chasmaporthetes*, and *Pachycrocuta* potentially contributed to the assemblage.

The role of leopards was most clearly demonstrated by tooth marks preserved on a hominin cranium (SK 54), which Brain (1970) showed had been damaged by the canines of a leopard. Brain (1970, 1981, 1993b) and Vrba (1976) both considered leopards to be the predominant bone-accumulating agent at Swartkrans, while hyenas, porcupines, and other contributors were also implicated. Brain and Vrba both also hypothesized the possible involvement of extinct saber-tooth and false saber-tooth cats, possibly as a specialized predator of primates, which would account for the high proportion of primates found in the assemblages. Brain (1993b) raised an additional hypothesis that, at times, Swartkrans served as a primate sleeping site, where predation near or within the cave would result in the high proportion of primates recovered. Conversely, de Ruiter (2004) recomputed the relative abundance of large-bodied animals at Swartkrans, and reported a lower proportion of primates than previously indicated. He concluded that while either a specialized predator of primates or a sleeping site situation might have occurred, they were not necessary to explain the relative abundance of primates.

Examining modern leopard cave caching behavior, de Ruiter and Berger (2000) concluded that leopards were predominantly responsible for the felid-derived components of the Swartkrans assemblages. Extinct saber-tooth cats were considered to be potential contributors, although their involvement was not necessarily inferred, while hyenas were also considered to be probable contributing agents (de Ruiter and Berger, 2000). Medium-sized carnivores such as leopards and hyenas, along with other agents such as extinct saber-tooth cats, raptors, owls, and porcupines, are thus the principal contributors to the Swartkrans assemblages (de Ruiter, 2003, 2004; de Ruiter and Berger, 2000; de Ruiter et al., 2010a). As Brain (1980: 107) has pointed out, "any cave which has been opened for thousands of years is likely to have had bones brought to it in a variety of different ways."

In addition to carnivores and rodents, there is evidence that the hominins themselves produced some part of the Swartkrans assemblages. Stone tools have been recovered in some abundance from all of the *in situ* Members (Lower Bank of Member 1, Members 2 and 3), which can be considered part of a core/chopper/flake tradition (Clark, 1993). Because associated flaking debitage is generally lacking, the tools appear to have either fallen in from the surrounding catchment area or were carried in by hominins (alive or dead), although there is some indication that the tools were used inside the cave itself in the Member 3 assemblage (Clark, 1993). Hominin-modified bone is rare, although both cut marks and hammerstone fractures have been recorded, typically at low frequencies equaling less than 1 percent of a given assemblage (Pickering et al., 2005, 2007). A small number of bone tools have also been identified, which were possibly used for digging termite mounds (Brain and Shipman, 1993; Backwell and d'Errico, 2001, 2004). Of especial interest is the appearance of some 270 bones from Member 3 that bear indications of having been burned, possibly representing the oldest evidence for the controlled use of fire on earth (Brain and Sillen, 1988; Brain, 1993c; Sillen and Hoering, 1993). Given that both *P. robustus* and *H. erectus* are known from Swartkrans, it remains unclear as to which hominin might have produced the tools and marks. Even the fact that only *P. robustus* fossils are associated with the burnt bones in Member 3 cannot reliably identify them, nor rule them out, as the hominin actor. Notwithstanding, some level of hominin activity both within and around the cave can be confirmed, even if the majority of hominins were ultimately entombed in the cave as a result of carnivore activities.

Fluctuations in $^{87}Sr/^{86}Sr$ ratios represent a useful tool for documenting movements in ancient animals in the Swartkrans area (Copeland et al., 2010, 2011). By looking at biologically available Sr in different geological substrates and in fossil enamel we can determine if individual animals were born and died in the immediate vicinity of the cave, or if they moved or were transported to Swartkrans prior to becoming interred there. A significant number of small australopith teeth, possibly representing females, are from non-local individuals, potentially indicating that females were more likely than males to disperse from their natal groups (Copeland et al., 2011). $^{87}Sr/^{86}Sr$ ratios were used to determine that eagles were unlikely to be a significant source of primates in the Swartkrans assemblages, a conclusion supported by skeletal part representation in all assemblages with the possible exception of the Hanging Remnant of Member 1 (de Ruiter et al., 2010a). In this latter assemblage there is some indication from skeletal part representation that eagles might have contributed some of the primates and procaviids, although potentially biased fossil-collecting procedures in the 1950s render such a conclusion tentative.

To investigate the potential habitat preferences of *P. robustus*, de Ruiter et al. (2008a) tested for conditions of isotaphonomy to assess whether any of the Swartkrans faunal assemblages might be especially taphonomically biased, or if they all showed similar patterns of bone surface modification and/or faunal and skeletal part representation. As noted above, a variety of taphonomic agents can be detected in the Swartkrans assemblages, although there does not appear to be a bias relating to accumulating agent (de Ruiter et al., 2008a). A potential bias was noted relating to depositional matrix, as fossils recovered from hard breccia appear less fragmented, and show a relative overabundance of craniodental remains. This bias almost certainly relates to the difficulty one encounters when removing fossils from hard matrix. Because the process is long and labor-intensive, a premium is placed on the more identifiable craniodental remains and the more complete postcranial elements. In addition, Broom was principally interested in collecting hominins, and less so in non-hominin fossils (Broom, 1950). Fortunately, because taxonomic identification is based primarily on abundant isolated teeth, and as these teeth are relatively evenly distributed across all of the Swartkrans assemblages, it is unlikely that this particular taphonomic bias has irretrievably masked the underlying taxonomic signal (de Ruiter et al., 2008a). As a result, comparison of the various faunal assemblages from Members 1 (Hanging Remnant and Lower Bank), 2, and 3 is possible.

Materials and Methods

Recovery methods have changed dramatically over time at Swartkrans. In the earliest years, Robert Broom and John Robinson employed a particularly hominin-centric search model (Broom, 1950), discarding the majority of non-hominin-bearing blocks of breccia that were loosened by Fourie. For example, between 1948 and 1951 they collected approximately 100 hominin fossils, while only 14 bovid fossils were recovered during this same time period. In addition, visitors to the site in those early years would often remove discarded blocks of breccia with fossils in them as souvenirs, thus biasing these early collections to an unknown extent (Brain, 1993b). After Broom's death, Robinson was more meticulous in collecting fossils and breccia, although he did not engage in complete recovery of all available material. While the Hanging Remnant assemblage was biased by Broom's procedures, Brain's meticulous sorting of discarded breccia between 1965 and 1972, and his excavations through the overburden from 1972 to 1979, largely mitigated this bias. With the advent of Brain's 1979–1986 *in situ* excavations, complete recovery of all fossil material became a reality.

Because of the different collection procedures that have been employed in the past at Swartkrans, we must assess the potential influence of taphonomic biasing on the composition of the Swartkrans assemblages to confirm that they are reflective of the original deposited bone assemblages. de Ruiter et al. (2008a) examined a series of taphonomic indicators at Swartkrans and other sites to assess the relative contribution of particular bone-accumulating agents. de Ruiter et al. (2008a) also studied skeletal part representation as a proxy to investigate the potential taphonomic overprint that might exist owing to depositional matrix and/or bone accumulator. Chord distances were computed to compare both the taphonomic and taxonomic composition of the assemblages. Chord distances are measures of assemblage dissimilarity, focusing on the relative proportions of categories over absolute abundances; thus they are effective for analyzing assemblages comprised of varying sample sizes (Ludwig and Reynolds, 1988). Chord distance values are computed between assemblage *j* and assemblage *k* by the formula:

$CRDjk = SQRT[2(1 - ccos_{jk})]$

with $ccos_{jk} = \Sigma^S(Xij*Xik)/SQRT[\Sigma^S X^2ij \Sigma^S X^2ik]$

where *Xij* represents the abundance of the *i*th taxon or skeletal element in the *j*th assemblage, *Xik* represents the abundance of the *i*th taxon or skeletal element in the *k*th assemblage, and S is the total number of taxa or skeletal elements common to the two assemblages. Chord distance values range from zero for assemblages with identical composition, to the square root of 2 (≈1.414) for assemblages with nothing in common. These taphonomic analyses are replicated here, although focusing strictly on the Swartkrans assemblages. This present study further differs from de Ruiter et al. (2008a) in that the skeletal elements studied are drawn from all macromammals larger than 1 kg in body size instead of just the larger animals greater than 23 kg in body size; hominin proportions are based on the higher numbers of *P. robustus* individuals recorded by Brain (1981) and Grine (1989); and proportions of Antilopines are corrected relative to those of de Ruiter et al. (2008a) (see below).

The fauna recovered from the earlier excavations (1948–1979) of the Hanging Remnant of Member 1 and Member 2 have been investigated by a number of specialists over the years (see Brain, 1981 and de Ruiter, 2001 for detailed bibliographies). Watson (1993) initially identified the macrovertebrate faunas from the *in situ* excavations of 1979–1986. Converting Brain's detailed excavation records into a workable geographical information system (GIS) model (Nigro et al., 2003), de Ruiter (2001,

2003, 2004) was able to incorporate a large amount of material previously considered of uncertain provenience, which in turn allowed him to assess the entirety of the Swartkrans faunal assemblages in a single research program. In addition, postcranial remains were also included in the analysis, facilitated by the documentation of the taxonomically diagnostic morphology of a selection of postcranial remains of bovids (de Ruiter, 2001). Inclusion of postcranial remains resulted in the recognition of several additional taxa not previously recorded in the Swartkrans assemblages (de Ruiter, 2003).

Relative abundance data have been demonstrated to be effective for signaling environmental or climatic changes, as responses of animal communities to external fluctuations are more likely to be reflected in proportions of animals than in speciation or extinction events (Bobe and Eck, 2001; Bobe et al., 2002; Alemseged, 2003; de Ruiter et al., 2008a). To assess relative abundance, numbers of identified specimens (NISP) and minimum numbers of individuals (MNI) were computed (de Ruiter, 2001, 2003, 2004). MNIs for large mammals (>1 kg) were computed using a manual overlap approach developed by Bunn (1982). Fossils are identified first to skeletal part and then to taxon, and then are simultaneously inspected by laying them out on a large table or floor to determine potential inter-individual associations. Factors such as size and developmental age are considered, while other factors such as surface preservation and spatial positioning (apart from member attributions) are not considered. When large numbers of teeth are considered, for instance bovid dentitions, they are first sorted into broad, non-overlapping wear stages to reduce the number of potential comparisons. This specimen-by-specimen approach, although labor-intensive, provides the best estimates possible for numbers of individuals in a given taxon (de Ruiter, 2001, 2004). Data on smaller animals (<500 g) such as rodents, insectivores, reptiles, amphibians, and avians are taken from published sources (Brain, 1981; Watson, 1991, 1993; Avery, 1998, 2001).

Correspondence analysis was conducted to assess the association between *P. robustus* and a subset of ecologically sensitive taxa drawn from the larger Swartkrans assemblages. These include the Cercopithecidae, Equidae, Suidae, and Bovidae, while other groups such as carnivores and rare animals are excluded (see de Ruiter et al., 2008a for details). Each taxon included, with the exception of the hominins, was assigned to a particular habitat category as documented in de Ruiter et al. (2008a), and the analysis was run. Correspondence analysis is a visual ordination technique designed to graphically display relationships between variables. Utilizing data arranged in bivariate contingency tables, correspondence analysis visually displays clusters of points representing similar, closely related variables, while dissimilar variables appear farther apart from each other (Greenacre and Vrba, 1984; Greenacre, 2007). For instance, when applied to faunal assemblages, taxa are grouped with the habitats in which they are well represented, while at the same time each habitat is grouped with the taxa which are prominent in it. The resulting clusters of similar variables are interpreted by examining their spread across each axis in search of the underlying features that unite them. Because there are no probabilities associated with correspondence analysis, it is especially useful for examining proportional data that might not be normally distributed.

Results

Taphonomy

Data on taphonomic indicators relating to bone-accumulating agents are presented in Table 11.2. Stone tools and hominin-modified bones are effectively absent from the Hanging Remnant of Member 1, although the likelihood is strong that depositional matrix is influencing this. Removing fossils and stone tools from hard breccia is difficult, and the probability is high that human modifications of bones and stones might be obscured during the extraction process. The relatively high proportion of hominin-modified bone in Member 3 includes the burnt bones described by Brain and Sillen (1988). Carnivore- and rodent-modified

Table 11.2 Taphonomic indicators diagnostic of bone accumulating agents.

	SKLB	SKHR	SKM2	SKM3
Stone tools	62	1	132	73
Hominin-modified bone	13 (0.22)	0	31 (0.37)	375 (5.96)
Carnivore-modified bone	131 (2.17)	45 (0.47)	72 (0.86)	197 (3.13)
Rodent gnawed bone	22 (0.36)	6 (0.06)	24 (0.29)	41 (0.65)
Coprolites	59 (0.98)	0	8 (0.10)	0
Carnivore: carnivore + ungulate ratio	0.21	0.18	0.20	0.23
Total NISP of taxonomically identifiable fossils	6040	9583	8416	6293

Note: The stone tool category excludes debitage and naturally occurring stone. Hominin-modified bone includes cut- and hammerstone percussion-marked bones and bones with probable traces of burning, regardless of the potential author(s) of these traces. Numbers in parentheses indicate percentage of total NISP of taxonomically identifiable fossils recovered from each deposit. Carnivore-modified bone includes bones with tooth markings and with evidence of gastric etching. Carnivore coprolites are considered to be highly diagnostic of hyena activity (Pickering, 2002). A carnivore:carnivore+ungulate ratio of 0.20 or greater is generally considered to be indicative of carnivore, probably hyena, activity (Cruz-Uribe, 1991; Pickering, 2002), although lower values do not necessarily exclude hyenas as accumulating agents (Lacruz and Maude, 2005). Data on hominin-modified bones for SKLB, SKM2 and SKM3 from Pickering et al. (2007).

bones are typically rare. Carnivore coprolites are also rare, and the possibility of specimen disintegration subsequent to fossilization likely influenced the numbers of coprolites ultimately recovered. The carnivore to ungulate ratio is relatively high in all assemblages, highlighting carnivore activity in the accumulations. In sum, there are indications of both hominin and carnivore activity, although no single accumulating agent can be demonstrated as being dominant. It is therefore apparent that a variety of accumulating agents were responsible for the Swartkrans assemblages, mitigating the potential biases that might be introduced by individual agents.

Skeletal part representation is a useful indicator of taphonomic overprinting in an assemblage (Bobe and Eck, 2001; Bobe et al., 2002; de Ruiter et al., 2008a), as changes in proportional representation of elements will likely signal the existence of biasing. Minimum numbers of elements (MNE) for a selection of skeletal elements are presented in Table 11.3. These particular elements include both cranial and postcranial elements that represent a variety of shapes and structural densities. Chord distance values computed between assemblages indicate that they are generally quite similar in composition, although some differences are evident, in particular relating to the Hanging Remnant of Member 1 (Table 11.4). The taphonomic chord distances between the Hanging Remnant (heavily calcified) and the other assemblages (uncalcified/decalcified) are the highest, while the chord distance between the decalcified Members 2 and 3 is very low, indicating near equivalence. If we expand our taphonomic chord distance comparisons to include the Lower Bank of Member 1 versus Member 2 and Member 3, respectively (all of which are uncalcified or decalcified) we again see low values, indicating that the assemblages are very similar in composition. In sum, there is some evidence of a slight bias relating to depositional matrix. However, when we compare the taphonomic chord distances in Table 11.4 to chord distances generated using taxonomic data from the animal communities represented in the respective assemblages (also in Table 11.4, which uses taxonomic data from Table 11.5, more details below) we see that no significant correlation is evident (Spearman's $r_s = 0.657, p = 0.156$). In other words, the taphonomic conditions vary independent of the taxonomic makeup of the assemblages. Because the majority of taxonomic identifications are based on dental remains, which do not appear to be biased in composition (de Ruiter et al., 2008a), taxonomic abundance data from the assemblages represent reasonable reflections of the original animal paleocommunities. Because of this, fluctuations in taxonomic abundance across the Swartkrans assemblages can be interpreted as the responses of animal communities to changing environmental conditions.

Table 11.3 Abundance of skeletal elements (MNE) for all animals greater than 1 kg in body weight in each of the faunal assemblages.

	SKLB	SKHR	SKM2	SKM3	Total
Maxilla	30	189	42	75	336
Mandible	68	285	83	195	631
Isolated teeth	583	707	361	811	2462
Humerus	66	43	73	139	321
Radius	36	30	35	82	183
Metacarpal	30	30	35	80	175
Femur	36	39	28	51	154
Tibia	31	28	21	50	130
Metatarsal	49	33	20	107	209
Astragalus	47	33	27	58	165
Total	976	1417	725	1648	4766

Table 11.4 Taphonomic versus taxonomic chord distance matrix for the Swartkrans macromammal (mammals >1 kg) assemblages, with micromammal (rodents and insectivores <1 kg) taxonomic chord distances in parentheses. Taphonomic chord distances for macromammals from Table 11.3; taxonomic chord distances for macromammals from Table 11.5. Taxonomic data on micromammals are unavailable for SKHR and taphonomic data are not available for any of the micromammal assemblages. Values in bold represent temporally adjacent assemblages.

	SKLB	SKHR	SKM2	SKM3
SKLB	–	**0.481**	0.348 (0.125)	0.471 (0.029)
SKHR	**0.332**	–	**0.613**	0.855
SKM2	0.159	**0.256**	–	**0.448 (0.125)**
SKM3	0.150	0.262	**0.082**	–

Taphonomic / Taxonomic

Table 11.5 Macromammalian and micromammalian fauna recovered from Swartkrans.

	Member 1				Member 2		Member 3	
	Lower Bank		Hanging Remnant					
	NISP	MNI	NISP	MNI	NISP	MNI	NISP	MNI
Class Mammalia								
Order Primates								
Family Hominidae								
Homo erectus	1	1	8	4	15	5		
Paranthropus robustus	46	13	264	85	31	17	16	9
Family Cercopithecidae								

Table 11.5 (cont.)

	Member 1				Member 2		Member 3	
	Lower Bank		Hanging Remnant					
	NISP	MNI	NISP	MNI	NISP	MNI	NISP	MNI
Papio hamadryas	72	12	159	30	83	20	117	23
Papio (Dinopithecus) ingens	2	1	65	17	8	1		
Theropithecus oswaldi	11	4	36	16	6	2	18	7
Cercocebus sp.			35	7				
Cercopithecoides williamsi	1	1			4	4		
Cercopithecidae indet.	157		152		129		242	
Order Carnivora								
Family Felidae								
Panthera leo	3	1	2	2	15	1	1	1
Panthera pardus	51	4	76	14	72	5	67	5
Acinonyx jubatus					2	1	2	1
Felis caracal	1	1						
Felis serval	1	1						
Felis lybica	1	1					2	1
Dinofelis sp.			7	1				
Homotherium sp.					1	1		
Megantereon whitei			1	1	3	1	2	1
Felidae indet.	3		5		4		16	
Family Hyaenidae								
Crocuta crocuta	1	1	25	5	6	1	6	2
Parahyaena brunnea	1	1	14	5	21	6	16	4
Chasmaporthetes nitidula	3	2	18	6	4	1	5	2
Proteles sp.	5	1	2	1	4	1	3	1
Hyaenidae indet.	34		22		32		83	
Family Canidae								
Canis mesomelas	71	4	31	5	127	7	141	10
Canis sp.					4	1	14	1
Vulpes sp.	8	1	2	2			22	3
Otocyon recki					1	1		
Canidae indet.	5		3		5		5	
Family Mustelidae								
Aonyx capensis	7	3			1	1	5	2
Mellivora sivalensis					2	1		
Family Viverridae								
Atilax sp.					2	1	3	1
Cynictis penicillata					2	1	1	1
Herpestes ichneumon	5	1						

Table 11.5 (cont.)

| | Member 1 | | | | Member 2 | | Member 3 | |
| | Lower Bank | | Hanging Remnant | | | | | |
	NISP	MNI	NISP	MNI	NISP	MNI	NISP	MNI
Herpestes sanguineus					1	1		
Suricata suricatta			1	1	3	2	18	3
Genetta tigrina							1	1
Viverridae indet.	6				2		6	
Order Tubulidentata								
Family Orycteropodidae								
Orycteropus afer	1	1			4	1	3	1
Order Pholidota								
Family Manidae								
Manis sp.	1	1					1	1
Order Proboscidea								
Family Elephantidae								
cf. *Elephas* sp.	5	2	2	1			2	1
Order Hyracoidea								
Family Procaviidae								
Procavia transvaalensis	44	3	24	8	82	16	33	5
Procavia antiqua	212	17	38	16	304	34	221	14
Order Perissodactyla								
Family Equidae								
Eurygnathohippus lybicum	8	1	5	2	7	1	18	1
Equus capensis	18	3	22	6	31	7	40	7
Equus quagga					26	9	7	1
Equidae indet.	14		16		5		21	
Order Artiodactyla								
Family Suidae								
Phacochoerus antiquus	3	1			25	7	12	1
Metridiochoerus andrewsi	1	1	13	7	1	1	6	1
Suidae indet.	4		12		4		28	
Family Hippopotamidae								
Hippopotamus sp.	16	1	2	1	2	1	1	1
Family Giraffidae								
Gen. et sp. indet.	2	1	1	1	4	1	5	1
Family Bovidae								
Megalotragus sp.	11	3	22	7	18	4	26	4
Connochaetes sp.	88	23	168	48	97	19	238	33
Medium Alcelaphine	78	11	220	37	204	24	102	19
Damaliscus sp.	39	7	63	20	233	29	132	17
Alcelaphini indet.	57		93		95		70	

Table 11.5 (cont.)

	Member 1				Member 2		Member 3	
	Lower Bank		Hanging Remnant					
	NISP	MNI	NISP	MNI	NISP	MNI	NISP	MNI
Makapania sp.	8	1	12	3	2	1	5	1
Ovibovini indet.	2				2		1	
Antidorcas sp.	43	16	117	45	570	124	138	33
Gazella sp.	11	5	12	7	19	5	35	14
Antilopini indet.	35		53		426		91	
Oreotragus oreotragus	3	1	1	1	3	3	8	1
Raphicerus campestris	4	1	3	1	37	7	20	4
Ourebia ourebia					11	3		
Neotragini indet.	14		1		6		40	
Syncerus sp.	6	2	22	2	14	2	14	3
Pelorovis sp.					3	1		
Taurotragus oryx					5	1	11	2
Tragelaphus strepsiceros			18	7	17	6	5	2
Tragelaphus scriptus					7	4		
Tragelaphini indet.					2		2	
Hippotragus sp.			9	3	32	9	8	4
Hippotragini indet.	1	1	2		1		5	
Pelea sp.	1	1	3	3	34	10	8	2
Peleini indet.					1			
Redunca arundinum			1	1				
Kobus leche					1	1	3	1
Reduncini indet.			1					
Bovidae indet.	957		692		3171		1655	
Order Lagomorpha								
Family Leporidae								
Gen. et sp. indet.	74	10			28	7	72	9
Order Rodentia								
Family Pedetidae								
Pedetes sp.	5	2	2	1	2	1	3	1
Family Hystricidae								
Hystrix africaeaustralis	14	2	6	3	8	1	5	2
Family Muridae								
Dendromus melanotis			12				4	3
Malacothrix typica			21				12	11
Steatomys pratenesis			36				28	4
Desmodillus auricularis			3				2	1
Tatera leucogaster			76				15	33

Table 11.5 (cont.)

| | Member 1 | | | | Member 2 | | Member 3 | |
| | Lower Bank | | Hanging Remnant | | | | | |
	NISP	MNI	NISP	MNI	NISP	MNI	NISP	MNI
Acomys spinosissimus		3				2		1
Aethomys chrysophilus		91				64		68
Dasymys sp.		140				53		73
Mastomys sp.		160				78		57
Mus sp.		24				19		6
Rhabdomys pumilio		27				18		5
Thallomys sp.		13				2		5
Mystromys albicaudata		3288				1133		1637
Proodontomys cookei		155				52		57
Otomys saundersiae		685				288		366
Family Myoxidae								
Graphiurus murinus		58				33		30
Family Bathyergidae								
Cryptomys damarensis		536				308		263
Georychus capensis		83				25		49
Family Macroscelididae								
Elephantulus fuscus		6				1		4
Elephantulus intufi		484				237		244
Macroscelides proboscideus		22				6		18
Order Insectivora								
Family Chrysochloridae								
Amblysomus julianae		43				29		24
Chrysospalax villosus		28				20		9
Family Soricidae								
Myosorex tenuis		109				44		33
Suncus varilla		4				1		1
Order Chiroptera								
Family Rhinolophidae								
Rhinolophus capensis			+					
Rhinolophus blasii	1	1						
Family Vespertilionidae								
Myotis tricolor	1	1					1	1
Eptesicus hottentotus		+				+		
Class Reptilia								
Chelonia indet.	26	1			32	2	57	2
Reptile indet.	11	1			11	1	26	2

Table 11.5 (cont.)

| | Member 1 | | | | Member 2 | | Member 3 | |
| | Lower Bank | | Hanging Remnant | | | | | |
	NISP	MNI	NISP	MNI	NISP	MNI	NISP	MNI
Class Amphibia								
Amphibian indet.	75	29			9	5	9	2
Class Aves								
Phasianidae	3	2						12
Sturnidae								9
Accipitridae								9
Corvidae								4
Tytonidae								3
Threskiornithidae	2	1						3
Falconidae								3
Columbidae								2
Anatidae								2
Ardeidae								2
Podicepididae								1
Aves indet.	214	10	1	1	187	10		
Class Gastropoda								
cf. *Achatina* sp.			15	15				

Data from: Brain, 1981; Watson, 1991, 1993a; Avery, 1998, 2001; de Ruiter, 2001, 2003, 2004. Plus signs indicate a taxon is present although MNI data are unavailable. NISP data are unavailable for the micromammals examined by Avery (1998, 2001) and for the avians examined by Watson (1991).

Vertebrate Fauna

A comprehensive list of all identifiable fauna from each of the hominin-bearing members of Swartkrans is presented in Table 11.5. The lists are compiled from Brain (1981), Watson (1993), de Ruiter (2001, 2003, 2004), and this study for the macromammalian components, and from Watson (1991) and Avery (1998, 2019) for the micromammalian, reptilian, amphibian, and avian components. It should be noted that hominin fossils have been more exhaustively examined and counted than any other taxon (e.g., Grine, 1989); therefore, the numbers presented in Table 11.5 are likely to overestimate the numbers of hominins relative to other taxa such as bovids. Every effort was made to count non-hominin individuals in a similar fashion as the hominins, although sorting through the volumes of non-hominin material recovered over the years at Swartkrans rendered an identical level of precision virtually impossible. A total of 30,332 macromammalian fossils were examined in this study, 15,592 of which were identifiable to Family, and 8102 of which were identifiable to genus or species (Table 11.5); of these 8102, only 381 are hominins, while 4034 are bovids. Because of this, proportions of hominins in individual assemblages must be interpreted cautiously. Below are details on the taxa presented in Table 11.5, arranged according to taxonomic order.

Primates. The precise taxonomic allocation of the early *Homo* specimens from Swartkrans has been the subject of considerable debate. Initially diagnosed as *Telanthropus capensis* (Broom and Robinson, 1949; Robinson, 1953), specimens such as SK 15, SK 45, and SK 80 were ultimately sunk into *H. erectus* (Robinson, 1961). Ronald Clarke (Clarke et al., 1970; Clarke and Howell, 1972) was able to refit a subsequently recovered cranial fragment (SK 847) to SK 80, producing a relatively complete cranium that he later tentatively assigned to *H. erectus* (Clarke, 1977, 1985). These specimens have since been regarded by some as *H. habilis*, and by others as *H. erectus* (see Grine, 2005 for a thorough review). Recent claims that the Swartkrans early *Homo* materials might represent a novel taxon (Grine et al., 1996; Schwartz and Tattersall, 2003; Curnoe, 2010) are unsubstantiated (Berger et al., 2010; de Ruiter et al., 2013; Grine, 2005), and the early *Homo* specimens from Swartkrans remain most closely aligned with *H. erectus* (Antón, 2012; Antón et al., 2014). Swartkrans presents the largest collection of *P. robustus* fossils in Africa. Although often attributed to the genus *Australopithecus*, a recent Bayesian analysis of hominin phylogeny has demonstrated that the "robust" australopiths represent a distinct monophylum (Dembo et al., 2015); thus, *Paranthropus robustus* represents a valid taxonomic designation.

Several species of baboons are known from Swartkrans, as well as one species of Colobine monkey. Freedman (1957) named a new species of the genus *Papio*, *P. robinsoni*, for a large number of fossil baboons from Swartkrans. It was later referred to a subspecies of Hamadryas baboon, *P. hamadryas robinsoni* (Szalay and Delson, 1979), a move supported by Watson (1993). *P. h. robinsoni* is found in all Members at Swartkrans. *Dinopithecus ingens* was recovered from Swartkrans, although Watson (1993) referred to specimens recovered in the SKX assemblage as *Papio (Dinopithecus) ingens*, following the suggestion by Szalay and Delson (1979). It was recovered from all stratigraphic levels. Freedman (1957) named a new species, *Simopithecus danieli*, from Swartkrans, although it was later transferred to *Theropithecus (Simopithecus) oswaldi danieli*, which was recovered from all Members, including the later *in situ* excavations (Watson, 1993). A number of small primate specimens from the Hanging Remnant of Member 1 have been referred to *Parapapio jonesi*, although Eisenhart (1974) considers them better positioned in *Cercocebus*. Finally, the colobine monkey *Cercopithecoides molletti* was erected for several fossils recovered from Swartkrans (Freedman, 1957). Freedman later sank *Cercopithecoides molletti* into *C. williamsi*, a move Szalay and Delson (1979) agreed with. *Cercopithecoides williamsi* is probably found in 1LB, M2, and M3, although Watson (1993) referred to the specimens from 1LB as *Cercopithecoides* sp.

Carnivora. *Panthera leo* is recorded in all of the Swartkrans assemblages, although its presence in the Lower Bank of Member 1 and in Member 3 is tentative because only postcranial remains have been recovered. *Homotherium* is recognized in Member 2 based on a metacarpal that is incompatible with any other large-bodied felid (Werdelin and Lewis, 2001). A single species of *Megantereon*, *M. whitei*, is known throughout Africa (Hartstone-Rose et al., 2007). It is recorded in the Hanging Remnant of Member 1, Member 2, and Member 3 at Swartkrans, while its identification in Member 2 is based on two postcranial specimens. Hyaenids at Swartkrans include the extant *Hyaena brunnea* and *Crocuta crocuta*, as well as the extinct *Chasmaporthetes nitidula* in all of the Members. The aardwolf *Proteles* is also recognized throughout the Swartkrans assemblages. *Canis mesomelas* is well represented in all assemblages, while a second type of large canid that cannot be attributed to *C. mesomelas* is recorded in Members 2 and 3 (Watson, 1993). *Vulpes* is recognized in the Lower Bank of Member 1 from several canid postcranial elements that are too small to be attributed to *Canis*. *Atilax*, the water mongoose, is known in Members 2 and 3 from diagnostic postcranial remains. *Genetta tigrina* is likewise known from a single, diagnostic radius in Member 3.

Tubulidentata and Pholidota. Aardvarks (*Orycteropus*) are found in all assemblages, identified by their diagnostic postcranial remains. Pangolins (*Manis*) are recognized in the Lower Bank of Member 1 and in Member 3 based on their diagnostic bifurcated terminal phalanges.

Proboscidea. The elephant fossils in the Hanging Remnant of Member 1 are postcranial elements, and although their extreme large size identifies them as elephantid, they are assigned to the genus *Elephas* as that is the only Proboscidean found elsewhere at Swartkrans. The remainder of the elephants, from the Lower Bank of Member 1 and from Member 3, are tooth fragments that can be reasonably assigned to this genus.

Hyracoidea. Hyraxes, also known as dassies or rock rabbits, are well represented in all assemblages. Two distinct species can be recognized on both size and morphological grounds. Large samples sizes are found in all of the *in situ* assemblages, while a smaller sample is available from the Hanging Remnant of Member 1. Despite the small number of identified specimens in the Hanging Remnant, there are a large number of individuals, represented by relatively well preserved and complete crania and mandibles. This is partly because Broom had a particular affinity for the hyraxes of Swartkrans, and went out of his way to collect their remains during the 1949–1951 phase of operations at the site.

Perissodactyla. Although rare, *Eurygnathohippus* is known from all assemblages. Two species of *Equus* are recognized, *E. quagga* and the larger *E. capensis*. *Equus capensis* is known from all Members, while *E. quagga* is recorded only in Members 2 and 3.

Artiodactyla. Two suid taxa are identified at Swartkrans, *Metridiochoerus andrewsi* and *Phacochoerus antiquus*. de Ruiter (2003) reported *M. modestus* from Member 2, although this no longer seems likely. Watson (1993) referred to the *M. andrewsi* material as *Tapinochoerus meadowsi*, although the taxonomic groupings of Harris and White (1979) are followed here. Fossils of giraffes are rare, including mostly postcranial elements. One tooth in Member 2 is most likely *Sivatherium maurusium*, although such an identification must be considered tentative.

Bovids comprise the majority of the assemblages, and are universally the most common family encountered. Unfortunately, the vast majority of bovid fossils are isolated teeth, making identification difficult. More complete horn cores are vanishingly rare, while relatively complete crania are unknown, further complicating efforts to identify bovids to species. Within the Bovidae the Alcelaphini tend to be the most commonly encountered animal, although in Member 2 there is a preponderance of Antilopini individuals. The category "Medium Alcelaphine" (Table 11.5) potentially encompasses a range of genera that are similar in size and dental morphology, including *Connochaetes* (*gnou*), *Damaliscus* (*lunatus*), *Alcelaphus*, and *Beatragus* among extant genera, as well as the extinct genera *Rabaticeras* and *Parmularius*. Because these taxa are so difficult to discriminate based on isolated teeth, they are grouped here on the understanding that such a lumping likely underestimates the true number of individuals present (see Brophy, 2011; Brophy et al., 2014). The specific attributions of the alcelaphines is also uncertain, again because the majority of specimens are represented by isolated teeth. The Antilopini are well represented in the Swartkrans assemblages, appearing in all of the deposits. As many as four species of *Antidorcas* (*A. marsupialis*, *A. australis*, *A. recki*, and *A. bondi*) have been varyingly described in the Swartkrans assemblages (Vrba, 1976; Brain, 1981; Watson, 1993; de Ruiter, 2003). However, owing to the difficulty encountered when trying to distinguish these species based on isolated teeth, in this study they are all combined into one taxon, *Antidorcas* sp., on the understanding that such collapsing will almost certainly underestimate numbers of individuals. More detailed analysis of the antilopines of Swartkrans is needed. de Ruiter et al. (2008a: table 11.7) incorrectly recorded a combined 22 individuals of *Antidorcas* sp. in the Member 2 assemblage of Swartkrans, when in fact there are 124 individuals; this discrepancy has been rectified in this study (Table 11.5). Although rare, specimens of *Gazella* are known from all of the Swartkrans assemblages, and are the only bovid taxon for which some numbers of horn cores can be identified.

The Neotragini are represented by several species, the most common being the steenbok (*Raphicerus campestris*). Of the Bovini, the Cape Buffalo *Syncerus* is recognized in all of the Swartkrans assemblages. Its larger cousin, *Pelorovis*, is also identified in Member 2. The Tragelaphini are known from all of the Swartkrans assemblages save the Lower Bank of Member 1, although they are best represented in Member 2 where kudu (*T. strepsiceros*) and bushbuck (*Tragelaphus scriptus*) are found alongside eland (*Taurotragus oryx*). The Hippotragini are rare, and generally cannot be identified beyond the level of the genus, while a single hippotragine specimen from the Hanging Remnant of Member 1 remains poorly identified only to the level of the tribe. The Peleini are known from all members, being most abundant in Member 2. The Reduncini are poorly represented, with *Redunca arundinum* found in the Hanging Remnant of Member 1, and *Kobus leche* in Members 2 and 3.

Small mammals. Smaller mammals such as lagomorphs are well represented, although the precise genus and species represented are unknown at present. Larger rodents such as the springhare (*Pedetes* sp.) and porcupine (*Hystrix africaeaustralis*) are known in all of the deposits. Data for small rodents, insectivores, and bats are taken from Avery (1998, 2001).

Non-mammals. Reptiles and amphibians are documented in all of the assemblages except for the Hanging Remnant of Member 1, although this is likely an artifact of the difficulty of extracting such small and fragile remains from hard breccia. They are present in the residue of acid preparation of Hanging Remnant breccia, although they have not yet been studied in any detail. Avians are also well represented, although they have also not been studied in any detail. Watson (1991) undertook a pilot study of avian remains from Member 3, but otherwise they are only very poorly understood. As was the case with reptiles and amphibians, the absence of avians in the Hanging Remnant assemblage is likely an artifact of the extraction process. Finally, gastropods are known from the Hanging Remnant, probably in the form of *Achatina*, a rather large form of land snail. Their absence from the other assemblages probably relates more to preservational environment and lack of study than it does to an actual absence in the past.

Summary of Paleoenvironments in the Swartkrans Faunal Assemblages

Chord distances between the macromammal component of the Swartkrans assemblages (Table 11.4) show that the assemblages are broadly similar overall, although the moderately high values reveal a degree of variation in faunal composition. While the highest chord distances are found between the Hanging Remnant of Member 1 and other assemblages, relatively high values are also encountered between the non-hard breccia assemblages (e.g., Members 2 and 3). As a result, despite their broad similarity, it would appear that some level of faunal change is evident between the Swartkrans macromammal assemblages. Turning to the micromammal assemblages (in parentheses in Table 11.4), however, we see that there is very little difference between them. This indicates that at this smaller scale of mammals, relatively little faunal change occurred. This discrepancy between large and small mammals might relate to the differing taphonomic histories of the two faunal components, or it might relate to some other factor, such as differential impact of forces driving the faunal changes. Further research into the micromammalian assemblages is clearly warranted to test for similar results as are seen in macromammals.

A subset of the faunas presented in Table 11.5 was used to assess the similarity of the assemblages via correspondence analysis (Table 11.6). Ecologically sensitive taxa including the Cercopithecidae, Equidae, Suidae, and Bovidae were chosen, and were assigned to a series of three broad habitat categories (grassland, woodland, closed/wet) as in de Ruiter et al. (2008a), and a correspondence analysis performed (Figure 11.2). The three habitat categories were analyzed first, and values for *P. robustus* and *H. erectus* were inserted as supplementary points so that they would not influence the outcome of the habitat separation. The assemblages from Members 2 and 3 align most closely with the "grassland" category, while the Hanging Remnant of Member 1 makes its closest approach to the "woodland" category. This latter result relates to the relatively high number of primates (in particular *Papio* and *Cercocebus*) recovered in this assemblage, otherwise the proportions of grassland-adapted taxa are relatively high and similar to that of the other Members. In other words, although the high numbers of primates are pulling the Hanging Remnant of Member 1 closest to the "woodland" category, it must be remembered that the predominant faunal signal indicates a largely grassland environment (Figure 11.3). The Lower Bank is positioned between "grassland" and "woodland" along the first axis (which accounts for almost 85 percent of the inertia). Again, it is worth noting that the preponderance of faunal evidence indicates a largely grassland-dominated environment, so this correspondence analysis must be approached with caution. *Paranthropus robustus* plots as an outlier, although its position to the far right of the figure (i.e., along axis 1 in particular) indicates that its relative representation is most similar to the "woodland" category along the first axis, while it is farthest from the "closed/wet" category along this same axis. *Homo erectus* on the other hand plots closest to the "grassland" category along axis 1, although the small sample sizes of early *Homo* require that we treat any interpretations with caution. What these limited data indicate is that although grassland-adapted taxa predominate across the deposits, the abundance profile of *P. robustus* is more similar to that of woodland-adapted taxa than it is to grassland-adapted taxa.

Correlating proportions of *P. robustus* with proportions of taxa assigned to the three habitat categories, we see a strong, effectively statistically significant negative association between

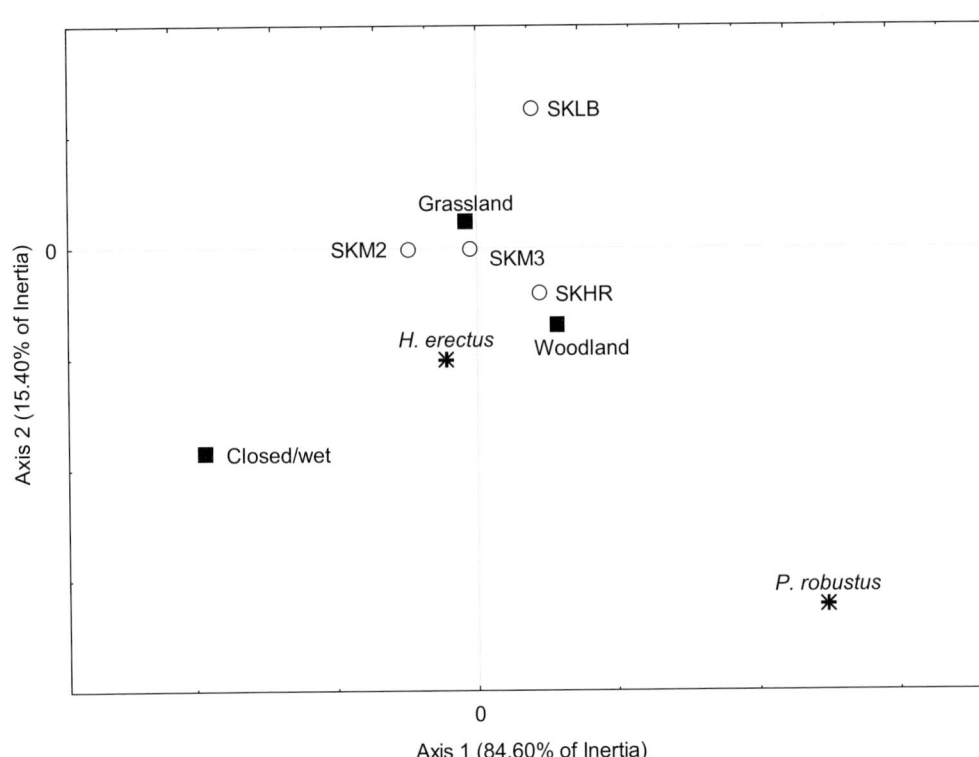

Figure 11.2 Correspondence analysis of a subset of ecologically sensitive macromammals from Swartkrans. Abbreviations are as follows: SKLB, Member 1 Lower Bank; SKHR, Member 1 Hanging Remnant; SKM2, Member 2; SKM3, Member 3. Data from Table 11.6.

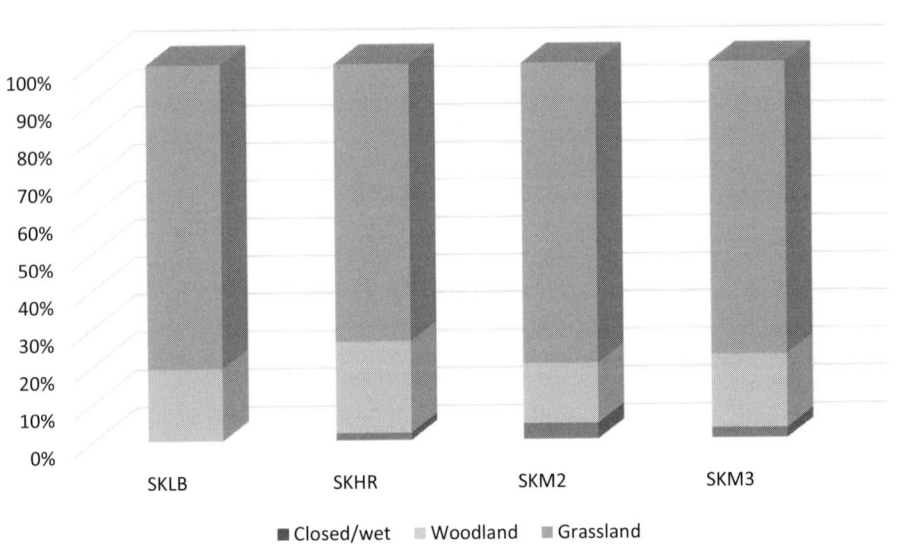

Figure 11.3 Proportions of ecologically sensitive macromammals attributed to the three habitat categories. Data from Table 11.6.

the robust australopiths and the "grassland" category ($r_s = -0.95$, $p = 0.05$), while correlations with the other two categories are weak and statistically insignificant. As was seen with the wider sample of *P. robustus* assemblages in de Ruiter et al. (2008a), the more grassland-adapted animals there are in a given assemblage at Swartkrans, the fewer *P. robustus* individuals there tend to be. In other words, although these hominins are consistently found associated with grasslands, this does not necessarily reflect a habitat preference. Turning to the smaller number of *H. erectus* individuals, there appears to be a strong and statistically significant negative correlation with the "woodland" category ($r_s = -0.95$, $p = 0.05$). This would appear to indicate that the more woodland-adapted animals there are in an assemblage, the fewer *H. erectus* there appear to be, although this would require confirmation with larger sample sizes before any firm conclusions could be drawn.

Summary of Reconstructions for Each Site Member

The oldest deposit at Swartkrans, the Lower Bank of Member 1, reflects an open habitat comprised of significant grasslands. A relatively large, permanent river is indicated (the paleo-Bloubank River), which likely supported patches of edaphic grasslands. Some form of woodland or forest was present, as well as

Table 11.6 Comprehensive minimum numbers of individuals (cMNI) of the select subset of macromammalian taxa from the Bloubank Valley cave infills with reconstructed habitat associations. These data form the basis of the correspondence analysis presented in Figure 11.2.

	SKLB	SKHR	SKM2	SKM3	Associated habitat
Paranthropus robustus	13	85	17	9	–
Papio hamadryas robinsoni	12	30	20	23	Woodland
Papio (Dinopithecus) ingens	1	17	1	0	Woodland
Theropithecus oswaldi	4	16	2	7	Grassland
Cercocebus sp.	0	7	0	0	Woodland
Cercopithecoides williamsi	1	0	4	0	Woodland
Equus quagga	0	0	9	1	Grassland
Equus capensis	3	6	7	7	Grassland
Eurygnathohippus lybicum	1	2	1	1	Grassland
Phacochoerus sp.	1	0	7	1	Grassland
Metridiochoerus andrewsi	1	7	1	1	Grassland
Megalotragus sp.	3	7	4	4	Grassland
Connochaetes cf. *taurinus*	23	48	19	33	Grassland
Medium-sized alcelaphine	11	37	24	19	Grassland
Damaliscus sp.	7	20	29	17	Grassland
Antidorcas sp.	16	45	124	33	Grassland
Gazella sp.	5	7	5	14	Grassland
Oreotragus oreotragus	1	1	3	1	Woodland
Raphicerus campestris	1	1	7	4	Woodland
Ourebia ourebi	0	0	3	0	Closed/wet
Syncerus sp.	2	2	2	3	Woodland
Pelorovis sp.	0	0	1	0	Woodland
Taurotragus oryx	0	0	1	2	Woodland
Tragelaphus strepsiceros	0	7	6	2	Woodland
Tragelaphus scriptus	0	0	4	0	Woodland
Hippotragus sp.	0	3	9	4	Closed/wet
Kobus cf. *leche*	0	0	1	1	Closed/wet
Redunca arundinum	0	1	0	0	Closed/wet
Pelea sp.	1	3	10	2	Grassland
Total	107	352	321	189	

areas with rocky outcrops. A similar paleoenvironment is indicated for the Hanging Remnant of Member 1, although a more extensive wooded component is suggested. Likewise, a relatively open grassland with a nearby permanent water source and some degree of wooded or forested land is indicated in Members 2 and 3. The overall picture that arises from all of the Swartkrans assemblages is of an environment similar to that of today, although with a larger river supporting a more extensive woodland and with some form of edaphic grassland. In other words, the area was wetter than today, and more wooded or forested. Although there is evidence of faunal change over time, likely reflecting some level of environmental change, it does not appear to be patterned. For instance, along axis 1 of Figure 11.1 the Member 1 assemblages plot near the "woodland" category, the Member 2 assemblage plots between the "grassland" and "closed/wet" categories, and the Member 3 assemblage plots very close to the "grassland" category. This does not support a directional interpretation that the paleoenvironment became more open and arid over time. Rather, the changes appear to reflect fluctuations in animal community responses to prevailing environmental conditions, instead of some form of directional alteration in the environment. More importantly, we must keep in mind that whatever the prevailing environmental conditions were, they were not necessarily the preferred habitat for the hominins. Conditions were sufficient for the hominins to survive, although we must continue to search for more fossils from additional deposits reflecting a wider range of potential paleohabitats if we wish to better understand the precise habitat preferences of the hominins.

Discussion and Conclusions

As has been noted for decades, the Swartkrans assemblages are dominated by grassland-adapted faunas, for instance the alcelaphines and antilopines of the Bovidae. This is the case whether one examines macrofauna or microfauna. However, with further excavations it has become clear that in addition to these grassland-adapted animals, a variety of woodland-, wetland-, and rocky outcrop-adapted animals were also present in the environment in the past. Fluctuations in conditions over time are reflected in the composition of the assemblages, although there does not appear to be any directionality to this change. The greatest likelihood is that environmental conditions changed at both smaller (i.e., tectonic) and larger (i.e., climatic) scales over time. This, combined with the varying impact of multiple bone-accumulating agents over time, influenced the composition of the surrounding animal communities, and in turn the composition of the recovered faunal assemblages. The hominins themselves were impacted by the changes, varying in their proportional representation in response to alterations in prevailing environmental conditions (de Ruiter, 2004; Reed, 1997).

The important point to be stressed here, however, is that the prevailing habitat reflected in each of the Swartkrans assemblages, the open grassland, would not necessarily have been the habitat preference of *P. robustus*. Rather, they appear to have been a type of habitat generalist. On the other hand, *H. erectus* appears to have been less common in woodland habitats, perhaps showing a greater affinity for grasslands than *P. robustus*. But, given the small sample sizes available from Swartkrans, we must approach these data with caution. However, these results do accord with the conclusions of Bobe and Behrensmeyer (2004) when they noted that the appearance of *H. erectus* was coupled with an episode of significant grassland expansion, further highlighting the importance of grasslands to the early evolution of *Homo*. In addition, these results might also provide support for the importance of endurance running in open grasslands as an adaptive strategy for *H. erectus* (Bramble and Lieberman, 2004), although again, such a conclusion must be approached very cautiously.

Several areas of future research can be identified. The discord between macrofauna and microfauna requires resolution, because fluctuations in taxonomic composition across the macrofaunal assemblages are not mirrored in microfaunal assemblages. As the taphonomic composition of the microfaunal assemblages is unknown, a good place to begin would be a comprehensive reanalysis of the Swartkrans microfauna, focusing in particular on the postcranial remains. The difficulties inherent in identifying bovids based mainly on isolated teeth can be surmounted, although a great deal of research is needed into the diagnostic dental morphologies of the different extant and extinct bovids (e.g., Brophy, 2011; Brophy et al., 2014). Improved identification of bovids would likely allow for more precise diagnoses of habitats, allowing us to move beyond the simple tripartite breakdown of "grassland," "woodland," and "closed/wet," and to develop a much more nuanced understanding of habitat utilization. Finally, additional research with more sites and with expanded faunal data sets are required to further test the associations between particular hominin species and their surrounding animal paleocommunities. Specimens representing early *Homo*, possibly *H. erectus* (*ergaster* to some), are recorded from Sterkfontein (Kuman and Clarke, 2000), Drimolen (Moggi-Cecchi et al., 2010), and Cooper's Cave (Berger et al., 1995); thus, more detailed documentation of these hominins and their associated faunal assemblages might prove profitable in this regard.

Acknowledgments

Special thanks must go to Bob Brain for all his years of tireless effort at Swartkrans. Without his pioneering work, we would know so little about cave formation and cave taphonomy. This entire chapter is only possible because of the research that he did at Swartkrans. I thank Stephany Potze and Teresa Kearny of the Ditsong National Museum for allowing access to the Swartkrans fossils and the modern comparative faunal materials. Thanks also go to Sally Reynolds and René Bobe for organizing this important volume. This research was funded by the Cornerstone Faculty Fellowship of the College of Liberal Arts at Texas A&M University. As I was revising the final draft of this paper, I learned with sadness of the passing of Laura Brain, Bob Brain's partner and confidante of more than 50 years. Laura was the heart and soul of Swartkrans, and she was fond of describing the peace and happiness she felt any time that she was at the site. I dedicate this chapter to her memory, because without her efforts, we would know so little of the site. She will be sadly missed.

12 Cornelia-Uitzoek: Paleoecology, Archeology, and Geochronology

James S. Brink†, John A.J. Gowlett, Andy I.R. Herries, John Hancox, Jacopo Moggi-Cecchi, Daryl Codron, Lloyd Rossouw, Gary Trower, Olivia M.L. Stone, Britt Bousman, Rainer Grün, and Antoine Souron

Introduction

Brief History of Research at Uitzoek

The fossil locality is situated on the farm "Uitzoek" in the Schoonspruit valley, near the town of Cornelia in the northeastern Free State Province of South Africa (Figures 12.1 and 12.2). The site consists of fossil-bearing valley-fill deposits within the Schoonspruit Valley. The hominin fossil and bulk of the fossil and artifact-bearing deposits of the site are dated by paleomagnetism to between 1.07 and 1.01 Ma (ages updated with respect to reversal ages of Singer, 2014), with other fossil and archeological deposits occurring to less than 780 ka (Brink et al., 2012). In older literature the Uitzoek site is referred to only as "Cornelia," but it is in reality one of several fossil vertebrate and Stone Age archeological sites in the Schoonspruit valley and in the nearby Venterspruit drainage. These drainages fall within the northeastern part of the Vaal River catchment and flow northward into the Vaal River (Tooth et al., 2004; Figure 12.1).

Fossils were discovered in the 1920s by schoolchildren who showed them to the local school master, a Mr. Louw. Some of these specimens were sent to Dr. E.C.N. van Hoepen, then director of the National Museum in Bloemfontein. The site was investigated by van Hoepen during the 1920s and 1930s and he produced substantial samples of fossil bones and Acheulean artifacts (Van Hoepen, 1930, 1932a, 1932b, 1947). He identified and described an archaic fossil fauna, which ultimately became the type assemblage of the Cornelian Land Mammal Age (LMA) of southern Africa (Cooke, 1974; Hendey, 1974; Klein, 1984c). Van Hoepen's work on the suids and equids from Uitzoek was of particular importance, as it served as reference for later work on eastern African materials, showing a previous biogeographic connection between southern and eastern Africa. Later, in 1953, A.C. Hoffman, who succeeded van Hoepen as director of the National Museum, and A.W. Crompton conducted new excavations, while R.J. Mason collected stone artifacts in 1960 (Clark, 1974). In the early 1970s, J.J. Oberholzer, who succeeded Hoffman as director of the National Museum, commissioned studies of the geology, archeology, and paleontology of the site, and the results of these studies were published in a summary volume (Butzer, 1974; Clark, 1974; Cooke, 1974). Butzer identified a number of nearby sedimentary sequences in the Schoonspruit and adjacent drainages. One of these on the farm "Mara," about 5 km upstream from Uitzoek, has produced mammalian fossils and Acheulean artifacts, similar to those found at Uitzoek, but in less abundance.

Following the summary studies by Butzer, Cooke, and Clark, a common opinion developed in the second half of the twentieth century that Uitzoek was mostly eroded away and that it ceased to be productive. However, during the early 1990s surveying by members of the Florisbad Quaternary Research Department of the National Museum showed that the site still had the potential for further fossil discoveries (Bender and Brink, 1992). New systematic excavations began in 1998 (Brink and Rossouw, 2000), which exposed a densely packed fossil bone bed, interpreted as a hyena accumulation that was minimally modified by postdepositional sediment movement and compaction, but essentially in primary context (Brink, 2004). After more than a decade of systematic excavation, the bone bed has yielded an enlarged collection of mammal fossils, Acheulean artifacts, and the first human fossil material, a first upper molar attributed to early *Homo* (Brink et al., 2012).

Foot surveys were conducted in the Schoonspruit and in nearby drainages as part of the Cornelia project. Acheulean artifacts were documented at Thomasvlei in the lower Venterspruit. Tortoise cores with early Levallois preparation were found at Johanna, which is the farm immediately upstream of Uitzoek, while MSA materials and geologically younger fossil mammal remains of the Florisian LMA were recorded in the upper reaches of the Venterspruit (Figure 12.2).

Geological Setting

The valley fill deposits at Uitzoek are illustrated in Figure 12.3 (see also Butzer, 1974; Brink and Rossouw, 2000; Brink, 2004). The sedimentary fill has been cut through and eroded by the Schoonspruit. The erosion is caused by the lowering of the flow level of the Schoonspruit as it cuts down into its own deposits and into the underlying bedrock, in the process exposing the fossil content of the Quaternary deposits. Locally the Ecca Group is extensively intruded by Mid-Jurassic-aged dolerite, which creates aureoles of hornfels with the surrounding mudrocks. A local source of hornfels is found to the southeast of the site, where there is a dolerite intrusion. Hornfels has been

Supplementary resources for this chapter are available on www.cambridge.org/africanpaleoecology

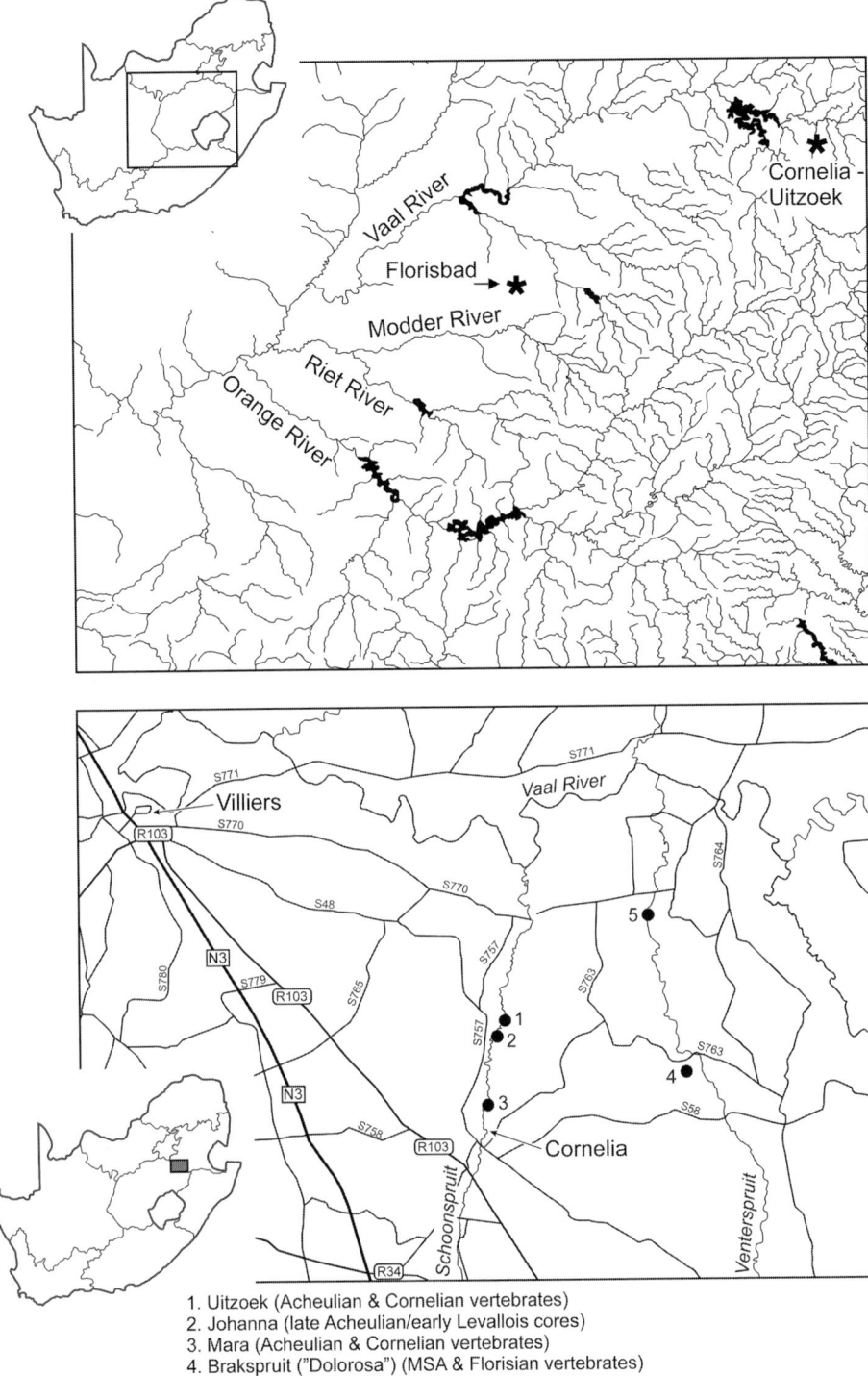

Figure 12.1 The Vaal River drainage system and the positions of Cornelia-Uitzoek and Florisbad, respectively, the name localities of the Cornelian and the Florisian Land Mammal Ages, with a topographic map showing the Uitzoek locality (1) and selection of stone artifact occurrences and fossil vertebrate localities (2–5) as found in the northward-flowing drainages of the Schoonspruit and the Venterspruit. Locality no. 4, "Dolorosa," is in the Brakspruit, a side stream within the Venterspruit drainage.

observed on the surface and in animal burrows, although there is no present-day exposure, but the blocks of hornfels on the surface are a good visual match for the artifacts from the bone bed (see below).

The Quaternary sedimentary exposures at Uitzoek were originally described by Van Hoepen (1930) and Butzer (1974), who identified a series of stratigraphic horizons, Beds 1–6. The new work led to identification of the stratigraphic sequence shown

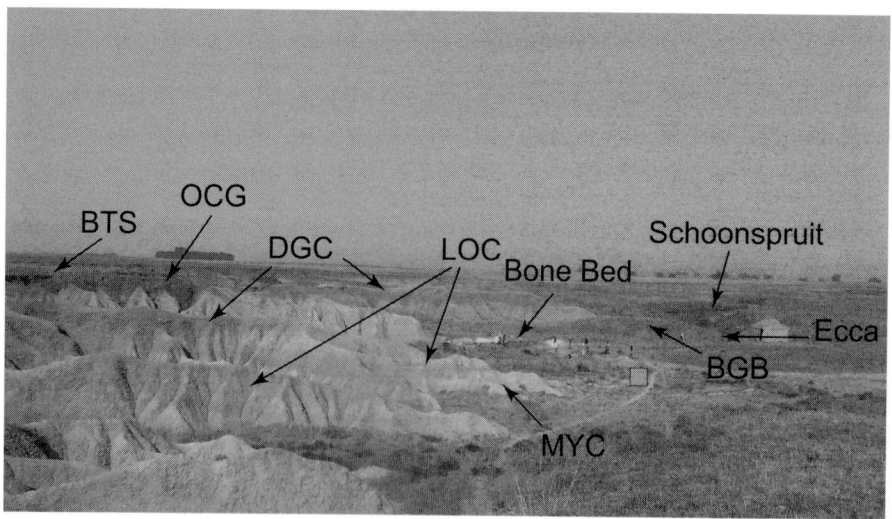

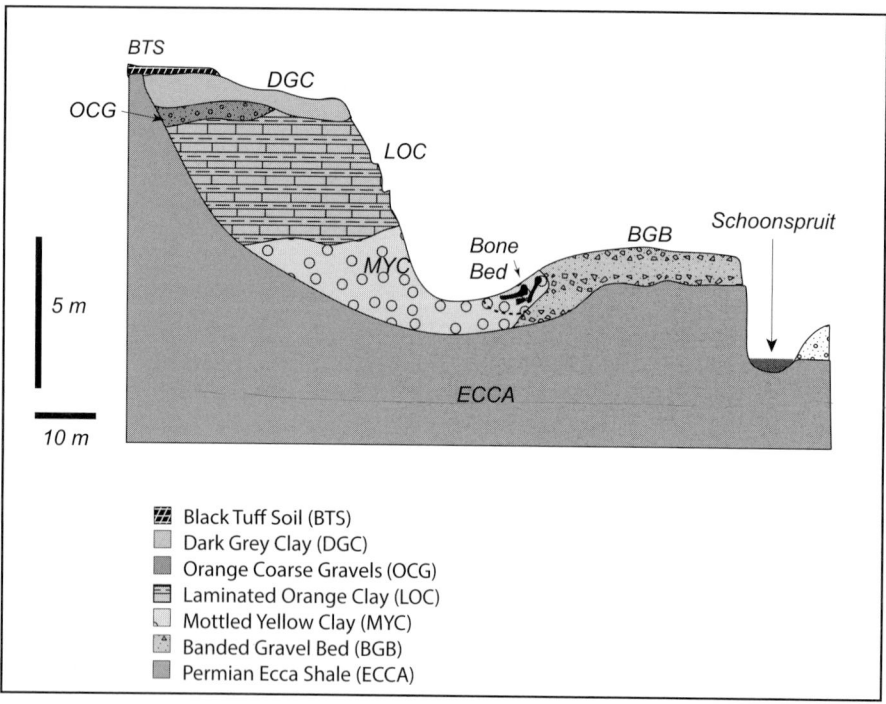

Figure 12.2 A south-facing panoramic view of the sedimentary exposures at Uitzoek (A) and a diagram of the sedimentary sequence (B).

in Figures 12.3 and 12.4. The base of the succession is formed by a poorly sorted gravel layer termed the Banded Gravel Bed (BGB, Butzer's Bed 1), which overlies the eroded Ecca Group bedrock. Fossil bone is rarely preserved in the BGB, and where present, it is usually rolled and abraded. Occasional Acheulean artifacts are found in the BGB, sometimes rolled and abraded and sometimes less so. The BGB forms a point bar toward the east, where it has been exposed by excavation of the bone bed. The BGB grades into the Mottled Yellow Clay (MYC, Butzer's Bed 2). This unit contains the richest fossil horizon, a densely packed bone bed interpreted as a collapsed hyena accumulation, essentially in primary context (Brink, 2004). The matrix of the bone bed can be distinguished from the MYC basin, in which it was accumulated, by its softer consistency and more intense mottling. Acheulean bifaces are found among the fossil bones, often in unusual orientations, sometimes tilted or on end, as if tumbled in from an overlying surface. The hominin tooth (see below) was also recovered from the bone bed, along with Acheulean artifacts. The bone bed occurs part way through the MYC, which grades into the Laminated Orange Clay unit (LOC, Butzer's Bed 3). The LOC is in turn overlain by the Orange Coarse Gravels (OCG) and the Dark Gray Clay (DGC). The top of the succession has been pedogenically altered to form the Black Turf Soil (BTS). Younger Acheulean material occurs within the LOC and in the strata above it, within the OCG and DGC.

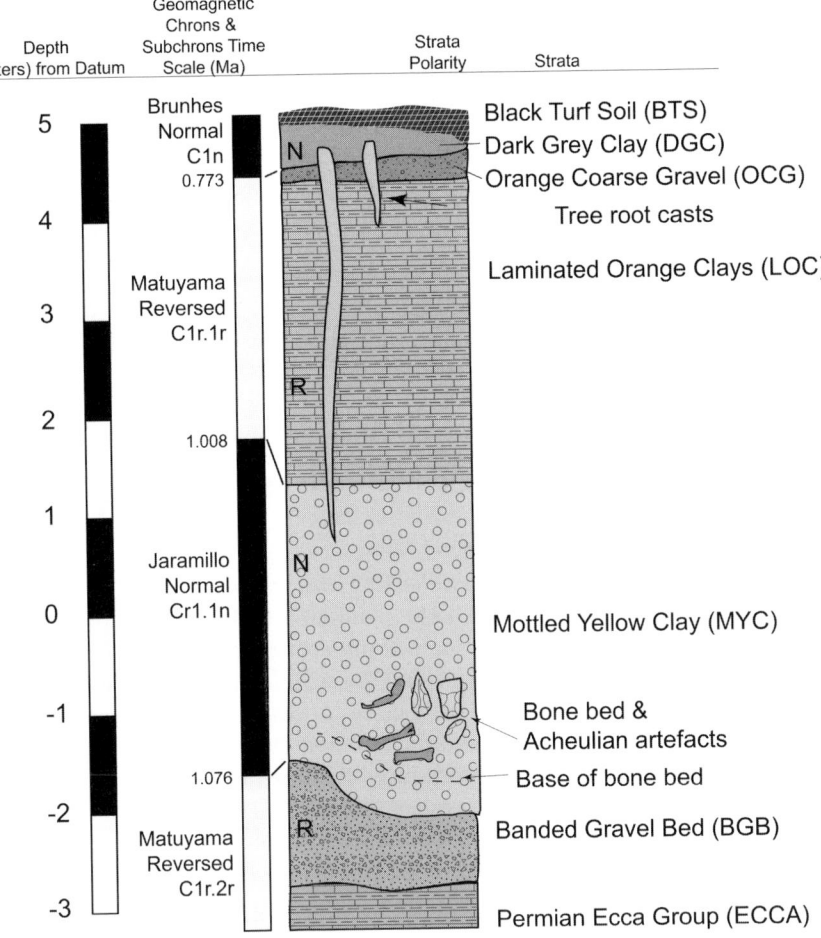

Figure 12.3 A stratigraphic profile of the sedimentary deposits at Uitzoek, showing their correlation with the geomagnetic timescale.

Dating

Attempts at applying electron spin resonance (ESR) dating at Uitzoek were unsuccessful because of the high uranium content of the sediments. The uranium derives from Karoo-aged sedimentary rocks upstream in the Schoonspruit catchment. We were able to date the depositional sequence at Uitzoek, including the bone bed, by means of magnetostratigraphy. A pilot study was undertaken in 2006. Ten samples from the MYC, LOC, and DGC indicated a sequence of normal (N), reversed (R), and normal (N). In 2008 we expanded the study and sampled from 23 levels in the sedimentary profile at the site of the excavation of the bone bed. These results confirmed the pilot study and the bone bed could be bracketed within the Jaramillo Sub-Chron between 1.07 and 0.99 Ma (Brink et al., 2012; Figure 12.4). Changes in the age for the upper Jaramillo Sub-Chron reversal now make this age 1.076 to 1.008 Ma (Singer, 2014).

The distribution of characteristic stone artifacts through the depositional sequence at Uitzoek added to our understanding of the chronology. Acheulean bifaces occur throughout the sedimentary sequence, in the BGB, within the MYC bone bed, as sparse occurrences on ephemeral paleo-landsurfaces together with fossils in the LOC deposits, and as occasional finds in the OCG and DGC. The LOC is bracketed by paleomagnetism to between 1.01 Ma and 780 ka, while the OCG and the DGC are younger than 780 ka. Artifact occurrences in the OCG and DGC are particularly well developed in the southern portion of the site and suggest only evidence for the Acheulean and no evidence for artifacts showing Levallois technology. Thus, the sedimentary package at Uitzoek as a whole probably pre-dates ca. 0.5 Ma (Herries and Shaw, 2011). Late Middle Stone Age (MSA) or Later Stone Age (LSA) artifacts are found as surface scatters in the southern exposures at Uitzoek, but these have not been found in sedimentary context.

Paleoenvironmental Proxies Recovered

Fossil Vertebrates

We recovered a rich vertebrate fossil assemblage from the bone bed in the MYC, most of which have 3D coordinates. This assemblage includes the hominin tooth and occasional hyena coprolites. In addition, we recovered a small assemblage of vertebrate fossils from the LOC. The LOC occurrences derive from old land surfaces that were briefly exposed. Such a surface in the LOC was excavated and exposed and produced evidence for ephemeral human occupation. In addition, a fissure filling within the LOC was exposed and sampled. It contained an accumulation of mainly smaller fragmented vertebrate remains. We tested the bone bed deposits for microvertebrates by water sieving, but without success.

The old collection, recovered mainly by van Hoepen in the 1920s and 1930s and by Hoffman and Crompton in the 1950s, consists of 1030 specimens, with most of these being identifiable (Table 12.1).

Stable Isotopes from Tooth Enamel

Stable carbon and oxygen isotope analysis of tooth enamel carbonate has been completed from 61 specimens, representing 12 large mammal herbivore taxa (Codron et al., 2008), and tooth enamel isotopic series were extracted for two specimens of *Antidorcas bondi* (Brink and Codron, unpublished data; Table 12.2).

Fossil Pollen

Several blocks of sediment from the MYC bone bed were tested for fossil pollen, but were sterile (L. Scott, pers. comm.).

Grass Phytoliths

Blocks of sediment from the MYC bone bed were sampled and abundant grass phytoliths were recovered (see below).

Micromorphology

In 2014 and in 2016 the deposits at Uitzoek were sampled for micro-sedimentary analysis. This work is in progress (M.B. Toffolo, pers. comm.).

Materials and Methods

Previous Excavations

Early phases of collecting and excavation at Uitzoek by van Hoepen (1920s/1930s) and later by Hoffman and Crompton (1950s) were done without spatial recording. From old photographs it is clear that the sedimentary exposures at Uitzoek extended previously close to the present-day channel of the Schoonspruit and that erosion during the second half of the twentieth century caused the face of the exposed and eroded deposits (locally called "dongas") to recede by about 30–50 m. Therefore, much sediment had been eroded away and the early excavations were done in bodies of sediment that no longer exist. However, from unpublished records in the National Museum, and from published descriptions by van Hoepen (1930, 1932a, 1932b, 1947) and Butzer (1974), it is evident that these deposits were similar to those that remain today. Also, the old collection does not differ much in taxonomic composition or proportions of frequencies from the MYC bone bed (Table 12.2).

Table 12.1 Taxonomic lists and frequencies of vertebrates from the MYC bone bed (1998–2015) and the old collection at Uitzoek, according to number of identified specimens (NISP). †, extinct.

	1998–2015	Old collection
Primates		
Homo sp.	1	–
Carnivora		
Panthera leo	3	5
Indet.	1	–
Proboscidea		
Indet.	5	2
Perissodactyla		
Eurygnathohippus cornelianus†	2	6
Equus sp. cf. *E. capensis*†	25	69
Equus sp. cf. *E. quagga*	25	125
Rhinocerotidae indet.	1	2
Artiodactyla		
Hippopotamus gorgops†	2	49
Phacochoerus sp.	3	–
Metridiochoerus modestus†	3	11
Metridiochoerus compactus†	3	2
Kolpochoerus paiceae†	1	4
Sivatherium maurusium†	2	4
Syncerus antiquus†	11	54
Damaliscus niro†	209	237
Megalotragus eucornutus†	12	24
Connochaetes gnou laticornutus	79	150
Antidorcas recki†	4	–
Antidorcas bondi†	197	257
Aepyceros helmoedi†	12	1
Sylvicapra grimmia	8	2
Raphicerus sp.	1	–
Total	610	1004

Table 12.2 Large mammal herbivore taxa from Cornelia-Uitzoek that have been sampled and analyzed for stable carbon and oxygen isotope compositions of tooth enamel carbonate, including the number of individuals studied (*n*) and their accession numbers (data from Codron et al., 2008).

Taxon	*n*	Accession numbers
Perissodactyla		
Equus sp. cf *E. capensis*	5	COR1244, COR18, COR641, COR683, COR930
Equus sp. cf. *E. quagga*	5	COR11, COR2736, COR2784, COR2837, COR71
Eurygnathohippus cornelianus	5	COR612, COR614, COR615, COR618, COR620
Artiodactyla		
Hippopotamus gorgops	5	COR1118, COR1152/6, COR1154/6, COR1165/6, COR1304
Kolpochoerus paiceae	4	C200, COR275, COR289, CORnonum
Metridiochoerus compactus	5	COR101, COR1102, COR1113, COR1287, COR267
Phacochoerus sp.	2	C1047, COR285

Taxon	n	Accession numbers
Antidorcas bondi	12	COR1665A, COR1665B, COR1665C, COR2072, COR901, COR902, COR903, COR904, COR907, COR909, COR901,* COR902*
Sycerus antiquus	5	COR141, COR35, COR36, COR498, COR502
Connochaetes gnou laticornutus	5	COR2314, COR554, COR557, COR84, COR86
Damaliscus niro	5	COR2615, COR2649, COR2729, COR2788, COR2808
Megalotragus eucornutus	5	COR2717, COR551, COR632, COR944, CORnonum

*Specimens sampled in series along the enamel growth axis (previously unpublished data).

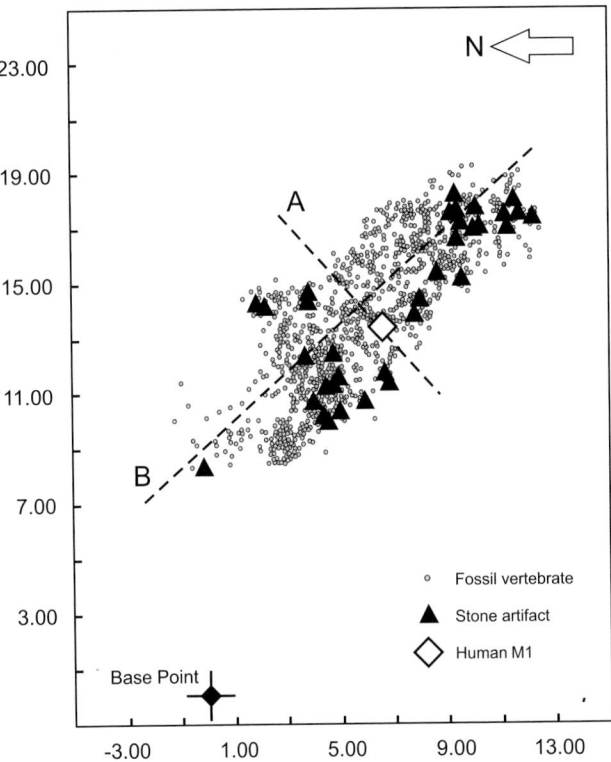

Figure 12.4 A two-dimensional plan view of the MYC bone bed, showing vertebrate finds, the position of the human M¹ and stone artifacts. The bone bed has a NW/SE orientation.

In 1998 the new excavations by the Florisbad Quaternary Research Department started with a 2 × 2 m² test cutting, which exposed the northern end of the MYC bone bed. Systematic excavations continued at Uitzoek in yearly field seasons from 2000 onwards, with the exception of 2003. All finds, including vertebrate fossils, stone artifacts, and sediment samples, have been recorded in three dimensions with reference to an arbitrary grid system (Figures 12.4 and 12.5).

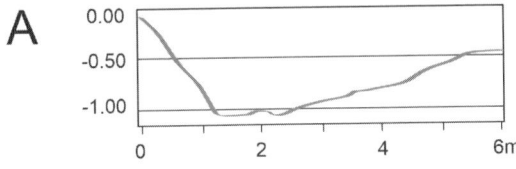

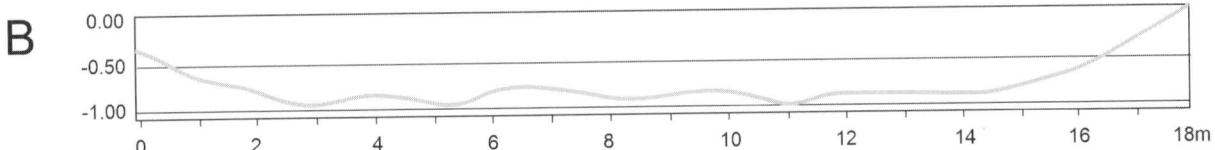

Figure 12.5 The cross-sectional profiles of the MYC bone bed.

Analytical Techniques

Paleomagnetic Dating

The paleomagnetic methods employed at Cornelia-Uitzoek are referred to in Brink et al. (2012), which we summarize here. In 2006 we analyzed 10 paleomagnetic samples at the Geomagnetic Laboratory of the University of Texas at Austin using the methods outlined in Gose (2000). The samples derived from five superimposed positions within the MYC, LOC, and DGC. In 2008 we sampled an additional 23 levels from the Uitzoek type section at the site of the excavation. We took three to six subsamples per level, using standard sample cubes in less consolidated sediments, and oriented block samples where possible.

The plastic cubes were subject to alternating field (AF) demagnetization and the block samples to thermal demagnetization at the University of Liverpool Geomagnetism Laboratory and subsequently at The Australian Archeomagnetism Laboratory at La Trobe University.

Fossil Vertebrates and Stone Artifacts

All vertebrate remains and stone artifacts were prepared *in situ* where possible and mapped in three dimensions by means of a Sokkia SET-3 total station. Because of the relatively poor quality of the local hornfels and because of the soil moisture that is maintained in the clay matrix of the MYC bone bed, some stone artifacts were in poor condition and had to be prepared *in situ*. In many cases vertebrate fossils were further prepared at the

Florisbad Quaternary Research Station. The vertebrate remains were identified to skeletal element and taxon. Routine osteological measurements were taken where specimens were complete enough.

Two-dimenstional spatial plots were created to produce projections of the specimens in plan (Figure 12.5). In addition, preliminary 3D rendering was done of the MYC bone bed using ArcGIS version 10.2 and cross-sectional profiles were created along the long and short axes of the occurrence (Figure 12.6). A preliminary taphonomic analysis of the bone bed materials was undertaken by Brink (2004).

The stone artifacts were studied on site and at the Florisbad Quaternary Research Station. Artifacts were photographed within a graduated frame. All bifaces were measured in plan and side view following the scheme of Isaac (1977) and Gowlett and Crompton (1994).

Isotopic Sampling of Tooth Enamel

Tooth specimens of individual large mammal herbivores were sampled from the Cornelia-Uitzoek collections at the Florisbad Quaternary Research Station. Only adult molars were used for the analysis, to ensure that the sample would not be biased by changes in isotope composition that occur at younger ages due to suckling and weaning. Enamel powder was removed using a diamond-tipped microdrill attached to a 1-mm burr. Two specimens of *Antidorcas bondi* were also sampled serially, starting from the dentino-enamel junction and thereafter removing powder samples at increments 2 mm apart toward the tip of the crown. Individual powder samples were treated with a 1.0 M glacial acetic acid solution, rinsed, and freeze-dried at −40°C for 24 hours. Stable isotope analysis was carried out at the stable light isotope laboratory of the Department of Archaeology, University of Cape Town, South Africa. Samples were loaded into a Thermo Corporation Gas Bench II in vacutainers, flushed with helium, and reacted at 72°C for a minimum 1 hour in 100 percent phosphoric acid (H_3PO_4). Resultant CO_2 headspace gas was sampled, dried, and separated before being introduced to a Finnigan MAT 252 Mass Spectrometer (Finnigan, Bremen). $^{13}C/^{12}C$ and $^{18}O/^{16}O$ ratios are reported in conventional δ notation in parts per thousand (‰) relative to the Vienna PeeDee belemnite (VPDB) standard. Standard deviations (sd) of 10 repeated measurements per specimen were below 0.2‰ for $δ^{13}C$, and for $δ^{18}O$ only samples that yielded sd < 0.3‰ were retained in the data set.

All taxa included in the sample are predicted to have been primarily grazers, based on ecomorphological and stable isotope studies of other assemblages (e.g., Brink and Lee-Thorp, 1992; Lee-Thorp et al., 1994; Sponheimer et al., 1999; Cerling et al., 2015a), and on feeding behavior of their closest living relatives (Skinner and Smithers, 1990; Gagnon and Chew, 2000). The distribution of taxa in isotope space is examined visually using bi-plots of $δ^{13}C$ and $δ^{18}O$ values for each taxon, with standard ellipse areas (corrected for small sample sizes, SEAc) delineating specific isotopic niche breadths (Jackson et al., 2011). Isotopic niches of taxa are compared using one-way ANOVAs and Tukey's HSD for multiple comparisons, with each isotope in turn as the dependent variable. Despite the relatively small sample, statistical assumptions for parametric hypothesis testing are satisfied (Shapiro Wilk's test for normality of residuals: $W = 0.977$, $p = 0.351$ and $W = 0.962$, $p = 0.063$, respectively; Levene's test for homogeneity of residual variances: $F_{10,61} = 0.000$, $p = 1.000$ for both isotopes). Because of the small sample size of each taxon ($n = 2$–10), however, averages are presented with non-parametric descriptives (medians with first and third quartiles). Isotopic niche breadths of taxa are compared based on Monte Carlo comparisons of Bayesian posterior distributions over 10^4 simulations of predicted SEAc scores. The genus *Phacochoerus* is omitted from hypothesis testing as it is represented by only two specimens. All analyses are conducted using R2.14 (R Development Core Team, 2011), including the SIBER package within SIAR (Jackson et al., 2011).

Phytolith Analysis

The samples were analyzed using standardized protocols established for the extraction of grass phytoliths from fossil soils, as described in Rossouw (2016), but summarized here. Essential steps included deflocculation and the elimination of carbonates using HCl in low concentrations (10 percent). The resultant residue was transferred into a 50-ml centrifuge tube and centrifuged at 3000 rpm for 3 minutes. The supernatant liquid was decanted and the residue washed with distilled water. The same process was repeated three times. Clays were removed by means of sedimentation over a period of 12 hours. Extraction of phytolith involved mineral separation with a heavy liquid solution of sodium polytungstate with a density of 2.35 g/cm³. Fractions were mounted in glycerin jelly on glass slides and examined microscopically under transmitted light using Nikon 50i polarizing light microscope at ×400 and ×1000 magnifications. Phytolith counts were based on systematic scanning following standardized transects for each slide. The counts were normalized as percentages of the short-cell sum for each sample, based on the total count of all the morphotypes per slide.

The phytolith results obtained from the bone bed samples were analyzed using principal component analysis (PCA) by comparing the percentages of the total sum of the saddle and trapezoid morphotypes that were counted in the modern and fossil phytolith data sets.

Results

Paleomagnetic Dating

The results of the pilot study showed normal polarity for the MYC, reversed for the LOC, and normal for the DGC. This sequence was confirmed in a follow-up study. In addition, a single sample with reversed polarity direction was identified from the BGB, so the polarity of this unit was not conclusive. Samples taken subsequently from a clay lens in the BGB were not successful, so work is continuing in this regard. The matrix of the MYC bone bed records mostly intermediate directions of polarity, which we argue is a reflection of mixing of the sediments within the bone bed due to postdepositional processes, including the collapse of an old land surface within the bone bed. Samples from the edge of the bone occurrence record a stable normal polarity as do the surrounding MYC samples, both at the same stratigraphic level and above the bone accumulation. The overlying LOC and OCG recorded reversed polarity, and the capping beds (DGC) normal polarity.

The paleomagnetic results suggest that the DGC falls within the Brunhes normal Chron (–0.78 Ma to present); that the OCG and LOC fall within the Matuyama reversed Chron between 1.01 and 0.78 Ma; and that the MYC, including the bone bed, is constrained within the Jaramillo normal SubChron between 1.076-1.008 Ma. The taxonomic similarity between the MYC bone bed and the upper part of the Olduvai sequence (Upper Bed II, Beds III and IV) supports this interpretation.

Fossil Vertebrates

Taxonomy and Biogeography

Fossil vertebrates are found sparsely in the BGB, but the densely packed bone bed from the MYC has produced the bulk of the vertebrate remains and Acheulean stone artifacts from Uitzoek (Brink et al., 2012). In the LOC, occasional vertebrate fossils and stone artifacts are found as ephemeral occurrences on short-lived paleo-landsurfaces. We do not see any difference in taxonomic composition between the vertebrate finds from the MYC bone bed and the sparse occurrences in the LOC. It is of note that the hipparion *Eurygnathohippus cornelianus* is found in the LOC. This provides the youngest dated occurrence for hipparions in southern Africa at *ca.* 0.99–0.78 Ma. Fossil vertebrates are not preserved in the overlying strata (OCG and DGC). It is likely that the early work at Uitzoek mostly sampled bone occurrences similar to that of the MYC bone bed, given the similarity of the taxonomic composition and frequencies (Table 12.1).

Van Hoepen's early work demonstrated an archaic component in the Uitzoek fauna, which includes the hipparion *E. cornelianus*, and the suids *Metridiochoerus compactus*, *Kolpochoerus paiceae*, and shows a biogeographic link with eastern Africa (Reynolds, 2007b; Bernor et al., 2010; Bishop, 2010). Braun et al. (2013) noted that South African dental specimens of *K. paiceae* are similar in size and shape to specimens of *Kolpochoerus* found in Beds III and IV of Olduvai Gorge, Tanzania. An ongoing extensive revision of the genus similarly indicates that *K. paiceae* is likely conspecific with at least part of the eastern African samples usually assigned to *K. olduvaiensis* (Souron et al., 2015; Bibi et al., 2018). Further support for an eastern African connection is provided by the extinct hippo, *Hippopotamus gorgops*, which occurs at Olduvai and in the deposits of the Turkana Basin (Hooijer, 1958; Weston and Boisserie, 2010). More recently we demonstrated the presence of an archaic human, *Homo* sp., which compares well with early *Homo* specimens from Olduvai and Ethiopia, and the extinct springbok, *Antidorcas recki*, which is also commonly recorded in early Pleistocene contexts in eastern Africa (Gentry and Gentry, 1978a, 1978b; Harris et al., 1988a; Gentry, 2010; Brink et al., 2012). These archaic forms reflect a lingering biogeographic link with eastern Africa. They disappeared from the fossil record in the south before the Florisian LMA, which is dated to sometime between *ca.* 0.78–0.56 Ma and 0.001 Ma (Lacruz et al., 2002; Brink, 2005; Brink et al., 2016). In contrast, southern endemics, reflecting a derived grazing component in the fauna, include an early morphotype of the South African endemic black wildebeest, *Connochaetes gnou laticornutus*, as well as a derived temporal form of *Damaliscus niro* and an early form of Bond's springbok, *Antidorcas bondi* (Brink and Lee-Thorp, 1992; Thackeray and Brink, 2004; Brink, 2005; Brink et al., 2016). The evolution of the black wildebeest in particular marks the appearance of southern endemism, reflecting the typical open, Highveld-type grasslands becoming a permanent feature of the landscape of the central plains of southern Africa (Brink, 2005; Brink et al., 2016). The dual character of the Uitzoek fauna, i.e., the archaic component suggesting a previous biogeographic connection with eastern Africa, and the derived southern endemic component, points to an age equal to or younger than the upper levels of Olduvai, which is consistent with the interpretation of the paleomagnetic results.

Site Formation and Taphonomy

The lower parts of the sedimentary package at Uitzoek (BGB, MYC, and LOC) appear to have accumulated relatively rapidly in a time just prior to 1.01 Ma (given only the 1.01 Ma and not the 1.08 Ma reversal is identified in the sequence) and younger. The BGB is a fluvial gravel that grades into the clays of the MYC and represents a fluvial cycle (Figure 12.4). Preliminary taphonomic interpretation of the MYC bone bed suggests that it was accumulated on a paleo-surface in an abandoned channel, or donga, within the MYC and that the primary agent of accumulation was a large bone-gathering predator, possibly spotted hyenas *Crocuta crocuta*, given the prey composition, the degree of fragmentation, and the presence of hyena coprolites in the bone bed (Brink, 2004). The bone bed has a NW/SE linear orientation that is virtually horizontal, but inclined at both ends, presumably toward the paleo-landsurface (Figures 12.5 and 12.6). In 2D plan view Acheulean artifacts occur more or less evenly in the MYC bone bed as occasional inclusions, apparently tumbled in postdepositionally from a collapsed paleo-landsurface. The artifacts are unabraded, but show evidence of *in situ* weathering. The local concentration of handaxes and flakes indicates a substantial if intermittent hominin presence in the area. The hominin tooth, which was found in the central part of the bone bed (Figure 12.4), confirms the presence of humans on the ancient landscape (Brink et al., 2012).

Paleoecology

The fossil vertebrate assemblages from the MYC bone bed and the old collection (Table 12.1) are dominated by equids and the bovid tribes Alcelaphini and Antilopini (Figure 12.6). This is typical of semi-arid sub-Saharan grassland/savannas (Kruuk and Turner, 1967) and this, in the absence of members of the tribes Reduncini and Hippotragini in the faunal lists, points to a relatively dry savanna/grassland in the paleo-environment. The absence of Reduncini is significant in the light of the presence of the Schoonspruit, which one would imagine may have provided some suitable habitat for wetland or water-loving forms.

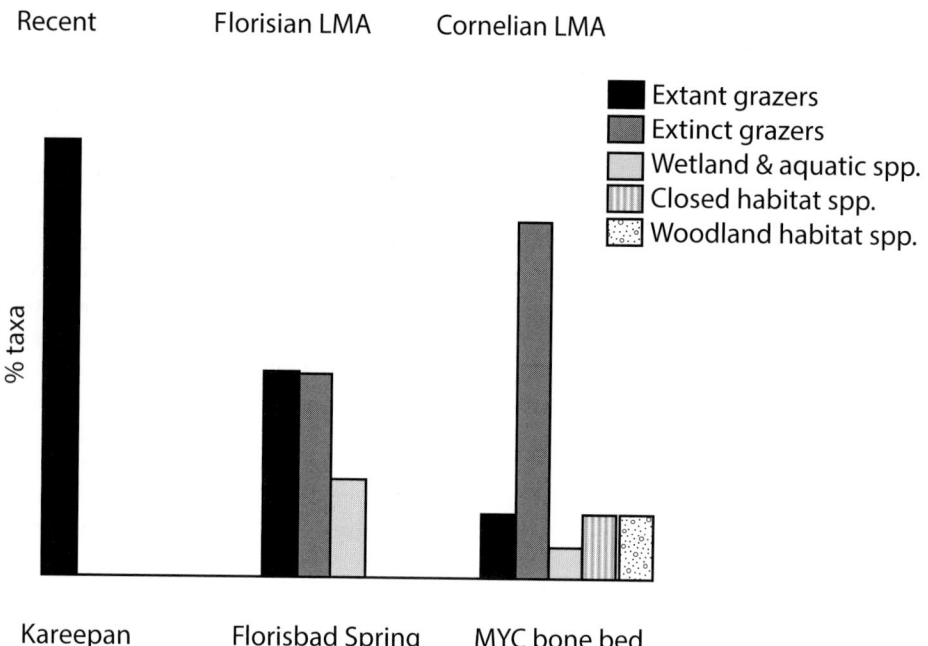

Figure 12.6 A comparison of the taxonomic composition of the MYC bone bed (Cornelian LMA) with that of the Florisbad Spring (Florisian LMA) and a Holocene brown hyena assemblage from Kareepan. The MYC bone bed taxonomic composition reflects a dry grassland environment with some closed and woodland habitat. The closed habitat and woodland components became extinct by the time of the Florisian LMA and reflect a temporal trend and shift in central southern Africa toward open habitat and wetlands in the mid-Quaternary (Brink, 2016).

This is in sharp contrast to mid- and later Quaternary times of the Florisian LMA, when wetland and aquatic forms, such as reduncins and hippos, became an important and very visible component in the landscape of the central interior (Brink et al., 2016).

The Hominin

The hominin specimen (COR 2011) is identified as a RM^1, because of its overall morphology, the lack of hypocone and metacone reduction, and the straight roots (not tilted distally). It comprises a worn but complete crown with roots damaged during excavation. Most of the root system was recovered and glued back in their original position. The crown is well preserved, but the texture and color of the occlusal surface have been altered postdepositionally to the extent that some of the morphological features are better visible on a cast.

The morphological features (a relative mesio-distal (MD) elongation, rather steep buccal and lingual faces, lack of any bucco-lingual (BL) expansion) suggest attribution to the genus *Homo*. The MD length versus the BL width dimensions fall within the range of the early *Homo* specimens (including *Homo habilis sensu lato*, and *Homo* sp. from southern Africa and Ethiopia), very close to OH 24 and SK 27, and are larger than *H. ergaster*, *H. antecessor*, and European *H. heidelbergensis* specimens (see also Brink et al., 2012, for more details). If correct, then this tooth is the youngest occurrence of such an archaic form of *Homo* in southern Africa as well as the oldest hominin specimen outside of the hominin bearing paleo-caves formed in the Malmani dolomite of northern South Africa (Herries and Shaw, 2011; Herries et al., 2013; Herries and Adams, 2013).

Archeology

Cornelia stands in the context of a southern African Acheulean record which embraces a numbers of sites, including Sterkfontein Member 5, Wonderwerk Cave, Rietpuits, Cave of Hearths, Montagu Cave, Sundays River sites (Penhill Farm and others), Kathu Pan, Canteen Kopje, and Amanzi Springs (Deacon, 1970; Kuman, 1994a, 1994b; Gibbon et al., 2009; Herries and Shaw, 2011; Berna et al., 2012; Chazan, 2015a, 2015b; Pickering, 2015; Chazan et al., 2017; Lotter and Kuman, 2018). While great advances have been made at some sites, many remain undated or poorly dated (Porat et al., 2010; Herries and Shaw, 2011; Pickering, 2015). Clark (1974) already had enough evidence to propose a basic picture of the Acheulean characteristics at Cornelia, which we now know is one of the oldest dated Acheulean localities in southern Africa (Brink et al., 2012). At around 1 Ma for the bone bed occurrence, it belongs in approximately the same time range as Eastern African sites such as Olorgesailie, Isinya, Kariandusi, and Kilombe (Durkee and Brown, 2014; Gowlett et al., 2015). At the time of study by Clark (1974) most bifaces came from the basal gravel levels, lower than the bone bed occurrence.

The presence of artifacts including bifaces in the basal gravels (BGB) was reconfirmed in 2012 when two hand axes were found. Earlier, Clark (1974) had reported numerous specimens. One of the new specimens is abraded, the other very fresh. A 2014 specimen is large and very well finished. Together they make the important point that in this catchment both relatively small and highly finished bifaces can occur at an early date – in the oldest sediments – so that "early" need not equate with "large" or "crude."

Small numbers of quartzite flakes have also been found from the basal levels, mainly from the area of a small cutting made at the north of the site. Gray hornfels was also in use for flake production. Hominins thus used the two main raw materials available to them, and maintained their interest in them over a long period.

The MYC bone bed occurrence is striking for the concentration of its archeological assemblage, as well as of the bones. The artifacts are consistently made from a pale yellowish hornfels (it is darker below the patinated surface). Hand axes and cleavers are the dominant tools, made from large flake blanks up to 24 cm long (Figure 12.7). The makers were clearly confident in the use of this material, which must have been plentifully available at just this limited moment in time. The free use implies a local source – most likely on the rise to the southeast of the site, where there is a dolerite intrusion. Hornfels that is a good visual match for that on the site has been observed on the surface and in animal burrows, although there is no present-day exposure. Two features – the large size of the bifaces, and the presence of large intermediate flakes not worked into bifaces – are consistent with the idea that the source was close, so that there was no need for hominins to economize in the amount of material that they transported. More generally across the African Acheulean the presence of large intermediate flakes seems to provide a good index to closeness of raw material, as these flakes appear to be by-products of biface manufacture, transported for potential usefulness. A similar picture is seen at STIC Casablanca, at Peninj, and at Kariandusi (Biberson, 1961a, 1961b; Gowlett and Crompton, 1994; Raynal et al., 1995; de la Torre, 2009).

Overall, the bone bed assemblage is very complete, representing most Acheulean forms of the typical Acheulean procedural template (see Gowlett, 1996; Goren-Inbar et al., 2018: 400), minus just the large cores and many of the small trimming flakes. These features argue for a "working toolkit" not far from its manufacturing position.

In the larger picture, the bone bed assemblage represents an "event" on the landscape, a punctuation probably arising from a favorable conjunction of several factors which together produced an exceptional circumstance. These were perhaps a place where game crossed the valley, and were vulnerable to predation by animals or humans; a time when a rich raw material source was exposed locally; and a context where relatively rapid sedimentation would preserve the evidence. The artifacts may well have been used in butchery, but there is no direct evidence for this, the most suggestive indication being a case where a bone was found touching a cleaver flake.

Following deposition of the bone bed, the pattern reverts to a sporadic discard of artifacts, which are found thinly dispersed

Figure 12.7 Dorsal, ventral, and side views of COR3363, a hand axe (A), and COR3195, a cleaver (B). Scale in cm.

throughout the higher layers. Individual Acheulean bifaces were discarded here and there, but evidence for the flaking of quartzite cobbles is much more widespread, especially in the higher-level channels that cross the southern gullies. The preserved cores, and the flake size distributions, both indicate that quartzite cobbles, generally of ca. 10–12 cm diameter, were being worked down into a polyhedral or roughly discoidal form. The flakes produced had a modal value of ca. 50–70 mm long, suitable for many general cutting and scraping tasks, but there is also strong evidence that some cores were worked down with the aim of yielding smaller flakes in the range of 20–40 mm long. In addition to small quartzite discoid cores, there are small cores of a gray hornfels, which would have yielded sharper flakes.

Several features pick these industries out as part of the broad Acheulean technocomplex as it operated from about one million to 500,000 years ago. The first is the actual presence of hand axes: although they are not closely associated with the other elements, they are similarly dispersed throughout the sediments. Next there is the casual but somewhat standardized nature of the cores, with an alternate striking approach often leading to a discoid form. Particular shapes of flake are recurrent, notably long divergent forms that curved around the base of the core. Then despite the consistent patterns of flaking, there are very few formal small tools. Last, there is a complete lack of Levallois cores or pointed or elongate flakes which might point to a development toward the early MSA. Only at the very south end of the Cornelia exposures does material occur that appears to belong to the late MSA or LSA (see below).

The main points of interest in the Acheulean levels are the repeating, longstanding, patterns of competent reduction of quartzite cores for the production of flakes; and the consistent accompanying emphasis on production of small-sized flakes that must have been used for delicate tasks.

The biface forms from the higher levels are highly varied. The dispersed nature of deposition would suggest that these were specimens carried by individuals, and their moderate size may tally with this – most are in the size range 10–18 cm long, and weights are also moderate. A scarcity of cleavers may also fit with this generalized use. They form a prominent part of the bone bed assemblage, but otherwise are rare or atypical. This bias may also reflect partly the use of quartzite and smaller hornfels blanks, which were less suitable for the construction of a classic cleaver edge.

Other sites in the area cast some further light on the patterns of Acheulean choice of materials in relation to tasks and landscape. The Thomasvlei site lies a few kilometers away toward the Vaal, in the adjacent Venterspruit catchment. Unlike Cornelia, the 18 bifaces from a gravel lag deposit include dolerite specimens. This rock was used for some massive compact cleavers, while a dark hornfels seems to have been preferred for hand axes. A vesicular rock was used for both. This other window into the Acheulean provided by the Thomasvlei site confirms that cleavers were part of the regional repertoire – as elsewhere along the Vaal – but suggests that raw material availability constrained their production by the tool makers rather more than in the case of hand axes.

A shift of technology, of the kind often found in the late Acheulean, can be seen at Johanna, just 2 km south of Cornelia. Here, three tortoise cores have been found, resembling smallish, thick bifaces. One of them has been struck, but the flake failed. They show a specific Levallois preparation pattern entirely absent at Cornelia, even in the upper levels. The general chronology of Levallois technique elsewhere would suggest that these fall clearly within the last half million years (Wilkins et al., 2010, 2012; Johnson and McBrearty, 2010; Potts et al., 2018). They were geared to the production of somewhat oval flakes, about 70 × 50 mm.

The latest archeology at Cornelia comes from gullies at the southern edge of the exposures. Here a gravel is visible in section. Artifacts have been found as a surface scatter over an area of exposures about 30 × 20 m. The emphasis is on the production of small flakes of 20–30 mm and even smaller. Some cores of black hornfels are almost randomly struck, but two large quartzite cores about 30–40 mm thick were struck across the end in a systematic pattern. This industry uses a wider range of raw materials, including black hornfels, translucent quartzite, and a brown chert. There are examples of small scrapers and notches. Three small pieces from the exposures show evidence of bifacial working; however, not to a common pattern. For the moment, this material has a poor context, but it does seem to be reasonably consistent in content. It is likely to represent late MSA/early LSA activities in the area. MSA material is more plentiful in the adjacent Venterspruit catchment. Altogether, the research at and around Cornelia has demonstrated human presence through much of the last million years in a variety of contexts and expressions. The Cornelia-Uitzoek occurrence is significant as one of the best exemplars in southern Africa of a moderate-sized Acheulean site at a key location in landscape.

Isotopic Results from Fossil Tooth Enamel

$\delta^{13}C$ and $\delta^{18}O$ values in tooth enamel carbonate of 61 large mammal herbivores from Cornelia-Uitzoek range from −8.0‰ to +2.1‰ and −4.7‰ to +3.8‰, respectively. $\delta^{13}C$ values reflect largely C_4-based diets (median = −2.2‰; Table 12.3), but vary between taxa (medians from −5.6‰ in *Hippopotamus gorgops* to +0.6‰ in *Megalotragus eucornutus*). Some of this variation can be attributed to differences across taxa (one-way ANOVA, $F_{10,61} = 7.598$, $p < 0.0001$) insofar as *A. bondi* and *H. gorgops* have lower $\delta^{13}C$ values than *Eurygnathohippus cornelianus*, the smaller-bodied *Equus* sp. cf *E. quagga*, *Damaliscus niro*, and the bovine in the sample (Tukey HSD $p < 0.0001$–0.019). No other taxa differ significantly from each other in $\delta^{13}C$ values ($p = 0.201$ to 1.000), evident in the substantially overlapping niches in isotopic bi-space (Figure 12.8). Similarly, the isotopic niche breadths (measured as the SEAc for each species) were similar for all taxa (median SEAc ranged from 2.54 in *H. gorgops* to 7.63 in *M. eucornutus*), except that *A. bondi* had a significantly wider ($p < 0.05$) niche than other species in 5 of 10 cases.

Smaller interspecies differences in $\delta^{18}O$ values (medians range from −2.4‰ in *Hippopotamus gorgops* to +2.2‰ in *Kolpochoerus*) mean that even fewer species differ significantly

Table 12.3 Descriptive statistics for stable isotope analysis of Cornelian fauna, and isotopic niche breadths (SEAc) of each taxon analyzed.

Taxon	n	$\delta^{13}C_{VPDB}$ (‰) Median	Q25–75	n_Mixed	$\delta^{18}O_{VPDB}$ (‰) Median	Q25–75	SEA_c Median	Q25–75	Q5–95
Equus sp. E. capensis	5	−3.8	−5.7 to −1.4	3	−0.4	−1.2 to 0.1	6.1	4.7 to 8.2	6.1 to 13.2
Equus sp. cf. quagga	5	−0.6	−0.9 to 0.1	1	0.5	−1 to 0.6	7.1	5.4 to 9.4	7.1 to 15.4
Eurygnathohippus cornelianus	5	−1.6	−2 to −0.5	2	−1.2	−1.3 to −0.6	2.5	2.7 to 4.8	3.6 to 7.6
Hippopotamus gorgops	5	−5.6	−5.7 to −5.5	5	−2.4	−3.2 to −2	3.6	2 to 3.4	2.5 to 5.4
Kolpochoerus paiceae	4	−2.5	−2.8 to −2.2	4	2.2	1.2 to 3.2	3.1	2.3 to 4.4	3.1 to 7.4
Metridiochoerus compactus	5	−2.7	−3.6 to −1.2	3	0.9	0.2 to 1.3	5.9	4.6 to 8	5.9 to 12.9
Phacochoerus sp.	2	−2.1	−2.9 to −1.4	1	−1.2	−1.4 to −1	–		
Antidorcas bondi	10	−4.7	−6.6 to −3.3	10	0.7	−0.4 to 1.6	11.0	9 to 13.6	11 to 19
Syncerus antiquus	5	−0.3	−0.3 to 0	1	−1.2	−1.8 to 0.1	4.1	3.1 to 5.5	4.1 to 8.7
Connochaetes gnou laticornutus	5	−2.8	−4.1 to −2.3	4	−0.4	−1.8 to 0.1	5.1	3.9 to 6.9	5.1 to 11
Damaliscus niro	5	0.1	0 to 1.3	0	0.4	0.2 to 0.7	3.5	2.7 to 4.6	3.5 to 7.6
Megalotragus eucornutus	5	0.6	−0.8 to 0.9	1	1.4	0.5 to 1.7	7.6	5.8 to 10.3	7.6 to 16.3
All taxa	61	−2.2	−4.4 to −0.6	35	0.1	−1.8 to 0.9			

from others in oxygen isotope compositions. Only *H. gorgops* shows any deviation from the average $\delta^{18}O$ values across the sample, being significantly ^{18}O-depleted relative to *Kolpochoerus*, *Metridiochoerus compactus*, and *Megalotragus eucornutus*; Tukey $p < 0.001$–0.043). The relatively low $\delta^{18}O$ values for *H. gorgops* likely reflect an aquatic lifestyle (cf. Bocherens et al., 1996; MacFadden, 1998, 2005; Clementz and Koch, 2001; Clementz et al., 2008; Harris et al., 2008).

Two specimens of *A. bondi* analyzed serially along the enamel growth axis show within-individual shifts in $\delta^{13}C$ values of 2.6‰ and 3.6‰, respectively (Figure 12.9a), and in $\delta^{18}O$ values of 2.6‰ and 3.4‰, respectively (Figure 12.9b). These ranges are consistent with a temporally dynamic feeding behavior, likely a response to phenological changes through time (e.g., seasonal or annual). The ranges for these two individuals are within the ranges observed across the 10 individual *A. bondi* specimens analyzed as bulk samples, indicating that varied feeding behavior was probably common in this taxon. The variability in feeding behavior of *A. bondi* from Uitzoek is in contrast to geologically younger specimens from Florisian contexts, which show a more specialized grazing behavior (Brink and Lee-Thorp, 1992; Codron et al., 2008). This reflects a temporal shift in feeding behavior and records the process of *A. bondi* becoming a specialized small-bodied ruminant grazer in the mid and late Quaternary during the Florisian LMA. This can be seen in its dental morphology, with molars becoming more hypsodont and enamel walls thickening in Florisian samples (Brink et al., 2013).

Phytolith Analysis

It has been shown that the morphology of grass silica short-cell (GSSC) phytoliths consistently follows meaningful environmental trends due to the relationship between phytolith shape and certain ecological niches occupied by grasses in southern Africa (Rossouw, 2009; Cordova and Scott, 2010). Several persistent morphologies have been recognized (Twiss et al., 1969; Ellis, 1987; Mulholland, 1989; Madella et al., 2005). Three major grass phytolith complexes or classes, namely the lobate-, saddle-, and trapeziform-shaped varieties, represent a range of 11 morphologically different GSSC morphotypes. Although they are not mutually exclusive, it is recognized that the overall predominance in production of certain types can be linked to prevailing growing season temperatures and consequently photosynthetic pathway (Rossouw, 2009). The relationship between these morphotypes can therefore be utilized to distinguish between C_3 and C_4 grasses as well as between grasses favoring one of the three different biochemical subtypes present within the C_4 pathway (NADP-me, NAD-me, and PCK).

The predominance of saddle morphotypes in the samples from the MYC bone bed is interpreted as an indication of warmer, summer-rainfall growing conditions (C_4). Drier C_4 conditions (NADP-me grass types versus NAD-me grass types) are indicated. Figure 12.10 provides a summary of this analysis, illustrating the similarity of the Uitzoek bone bed phytoliths with C_4 conditions, as found in the present-day Nama Karoo Biome of South Africa.

Summary and Conclusions

Cornelia-Uitzoek has particular importance as it contains the oldest hominin fossil in southern Africa in an open context (outside of the Malamni dolomite of northern South Africa), as well as a rare example of multiple open air Pleistocene localities in well-defined geological context, with directly associated fauna and Acheulean archaeology in a dated sequence. The co-occurrence of vertebrate fauna, including the youngest specimen attributed to early *Homo* in South Africa, Acheulean

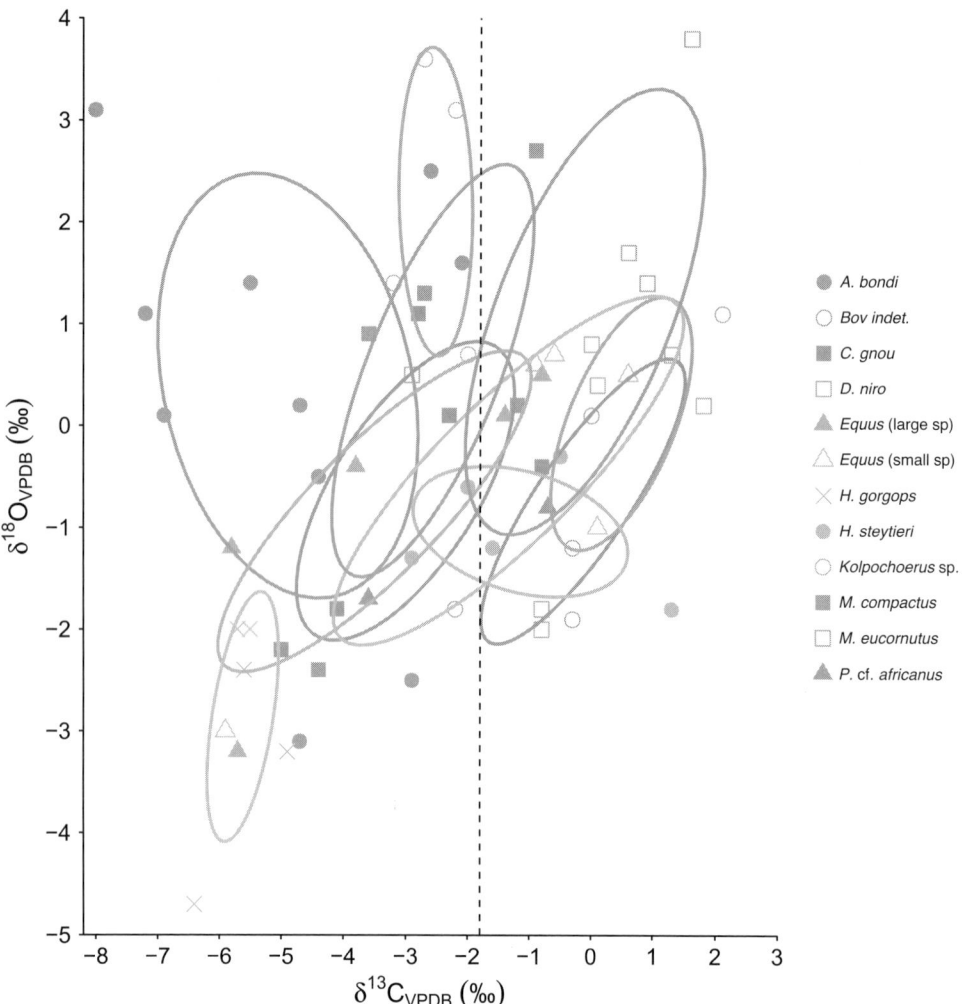

Figure 12.8 Stable carbon and oxygen isotope compositions of Cornelian grazer fauna. Ellipses for each taxon are standard ellipse areas (SEAc) used to depict isotopic niche breadths. The vertical dashed line represents a threshold for interpreting herbivore diets: to the right of the vertical, i.e., higher $\delta^{13}C$ values, individuals' diets are expected to be entirely C_4-derived, whereas lower values depict diets comprising a mixture of C_3/C_4 foods (see Discussion text for details). Note that a similar vertical delineating pure C_3 diets would be positioned at approximately –12.3‰ along the $\delta^{13}C$ axis. Data are from Codron et al. (2008). (A black and white version of this figure will appear in some formats. For the color version, please refer to the plate section.)

industries, and other paleoecological evidence has allowed multidisciplinary studies to an unusual degree. The site also holds future potential for understanding changes in the Acheulian from prior to 1 Ma to less than 0.78 Ma.

The fossil and archeological record of the Schoonspruit and Venterspruit drainages span approximately the last million years. The fossil- and artifact-bearing deposits at Uitzoek fall in the time between *ca.* 1.08 Ma to less than 0.78 Ma, but the MYC bone bed, which produced the main fossil and artifact occurrences, is constrained in geological time by paleomagnetism to between 1.08 and 1.01 Ma, although perhaps closer in age to 1.01 Ma. At Uitzoek Acheulean artifacts occur in the basal gravels (BGB), within the MYC bone bed, and in overlying deposits, the LOC, OCG, and DGC. Scatters of hornfels flakes, possibly late MSA or LSA, occur on the southern exposures at Uitzoek, but these have not been found in sedimentary context. In the LOC there is evidence for ephemeral human occupation on short-lived paleo-landsurfaces. At Mara, a few kilometers upstream in the Schoonspruit drainage, fluvial gravels very similar to the BGB at Uitzoek have produced Acheulean bifaces and Cornelian fossil vertebrates. In the nearby Venterspruit drainage at Thomasvlei, Acheulean bifaces are found in a lag deposit. Further upstream in the Venterspruit abundant MSA occurrences and Florisian-aged fossil vertebrates are found eroding from the deposits as surface scatters. At Johanna, the farm immediately upstream from Uitzoek, late ESA tortoise cores are found showing Levallois preparation, but no fossil vertebrates are found.

The MYC bone bed at Uitzoek has been the focus of recent fieldwork. The fossils and stone artifacts of the MYC bone bed occur in the same matrix, but the occurrence is interpreted as a postdepositionally displaced hyena bone accumulation. It seems to have accumulated on an exposed surface within the MYC, possibly in a tunnel or a channel that was eroded into the MYC. An overlying landsurface containing the Acheulean artifacts appears to have collapsed into it. The MYC bone bed

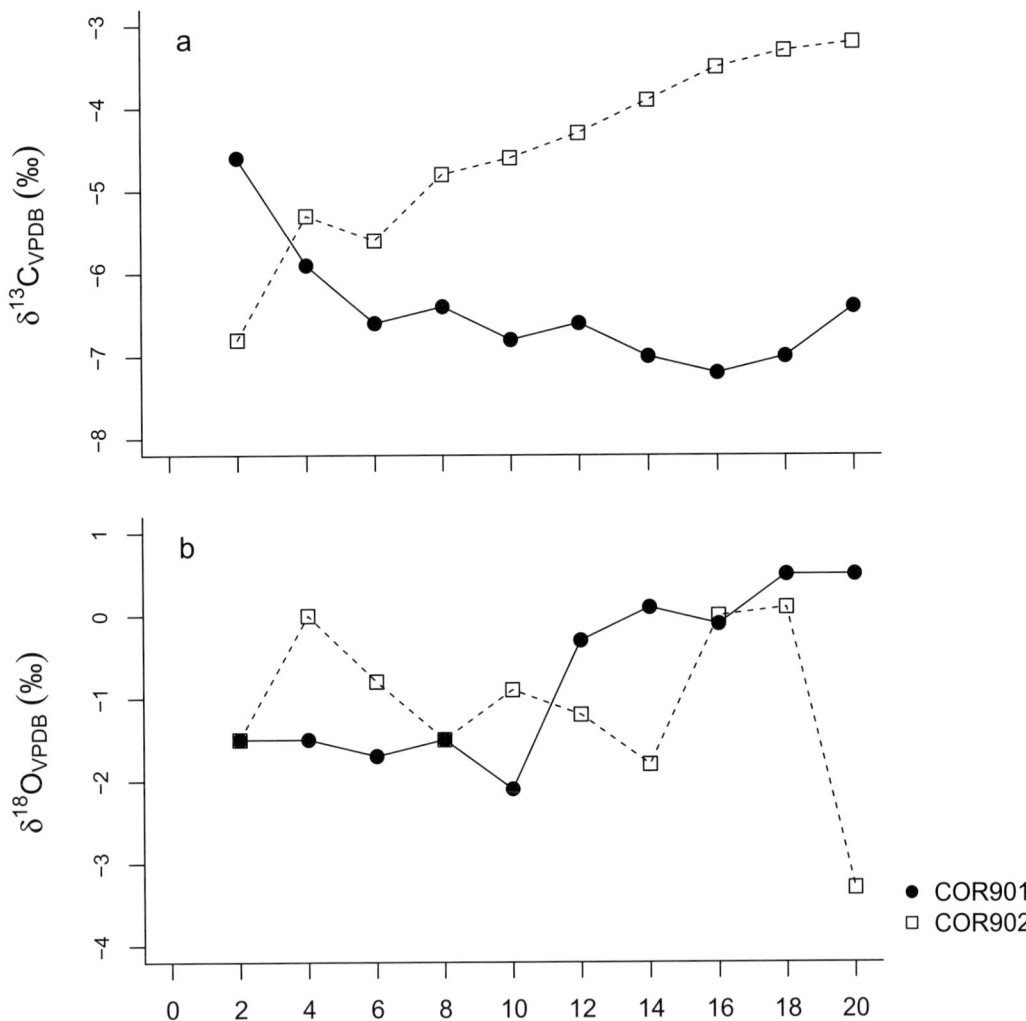

Figure 12.9 Isotopic time series for two specimens of *Antidorcas bondi* from Cornelia-Uitzoek, derived from microsamples removed at 2 mm increments along the enamel growth (longitudinal) axis.

fossil vertebrate assemblage indicates a paleofauna adapted largely to semi-arid C_4 grassland conditions, being dominated by equids, alcelaphins, and antilopins, with a minor element suggesting some bush cover. However, the absence of reduncins and hippotragins is particularly striking, given the presence of the Schoonspruit and their visibility in geologically younger fossil occurrences of the Florisian LMA. Fossil phytoliths recovered from the MYC bone bed matrix indicate a predominance of saddle morphotypes, which supports the interpretation of the vertebrate assemblage as reflecting mainly a semi-arid C_4 grassland. It is noteworthy that some distance away in the western interior of southern Africa, at Wonderwerk Cave, a similar paleoenvironmental signature is recorded (Rossouw, 2016). Given the uniformity of the southern African landscape, in contrast to that of eastern Africa (Bobe, 2006), and given the first appearance in the fossil record of ancestral black wildebeest at Uitzoek, and its need for the uniform open habitat (Brink et al., 2016), the phytolith evidence may suggest that relatively semi-arid C_4 grasslands were becoming a common feature of the southern African landscape by the Cornelian LMA.

We were able to extract stable isotope data from the fossil teeth of the MYC bone bed. The data largely support the morphological and phytolith interpretation, but indicate a substantial element of C_3 food in the diets of grazing bovids, such as the alcelaphins. This is particularly clear for *Antidorcas bondi*, which is in contrast to Florisian samples that consistently show a specialized C_4 diet. This suggests that the species was in the process of evolving into its eventual feeding niche as a specialized C_4 grazer, which is in support of the dental morphology of Cornelian *A. bondi* that indicates a transitional stage in the process of evolving a specialized grazing morphology (Brink et al., 2013). Actually, many of the large mammal herbivore species present at Cornelia may have been in a similar "early" phase of evolution toward later specialized feeding niches (Codron et al., 2008).

An eastern African biogeographic link is suggested by the extinct grazing suids, *Kolpochoerus paiceae* and *Metridiochoerus compactus*, the sivathere, *Sivatherium maurusium*, and the impala, *Aepyceros helmoedi* (see also Reynolds, 2007b). Other forms that may be considered to reflect an eastern African biogeographic link are the hipparion, *Eurygnathohippus cornelianus*, and the hippo, *Hippopotamus gorgops*. The evolutionary

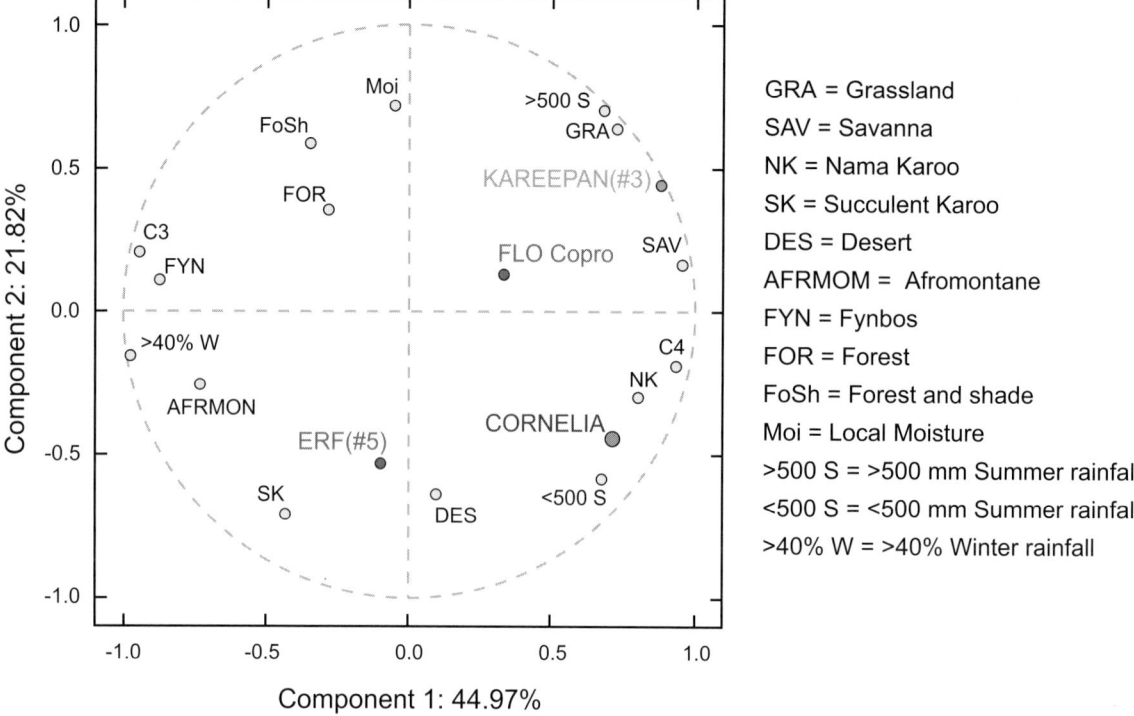

Figure 12.10 A visual representation of a principal component analysis of the phytoliths from the MYC bone bed, based on of 11 GSC morphotypes represented by the distribution of 271 grass species in South Africa. The results suggest that the paleoenvironment reflected by the MYC bone bed compares best with the modern-day Nama Karoo Biome, i.e., a semi-arid grassland with some bush cover. Other plotted samples are Florisbad coprolite (FLO Copro), Erfkroom (ERF(#5)) and Kareepan (KAREEPAN(#3)).

and biogeographic position of the giant wildebeest *Megalotragus eucornutus* is not yet clear, because it may not be ancestral to the Florisian form, *M. priscus* (Brink et al., 2015a). The human molar is similar to early *Homo* from eastern and southern Africa and represents another archaic element in the fauna, possibly in support of an earlier eastern African biogeographic link. The evolutionary trajectory at Uitzoek is evidently toward the establishment of open-habitat grazing faunas, as seen in the Florisian localities in the local drainages and elsewhere in the central interior. In this sense the Cornelian LMA represents a time of transition, when the southern endemic faunas of the Florisian and recent times became established.

Acknowledgments

The co-authors wish to express their deep appreciation and thanks for James Brink's efforts in initiating and carrying through this paper. James had almost entirely completed his work so that the chapter appears in the form that he had envisaged. We have all greatly benefited from working with James: time and again all his colleagues have noted his thoughtfulness, consideration, and kindness as a collaborator. The shared campfires, wines, and brandies are also in our memory. We are greatly saddened by his loss, but it was our privilege to help with James' work in exploring the Cornelia-Uitzoek sites, research recorded here for always.

Excavations at Cornelia-Uitzoek were funded initially by a grant of the French Department of Foreign Affairs, through a French–South African paleontological agreement, to JSB and by the National Museum, Bloemfontein, but later through a grant of the National Research Foundation, African Origins Platform, User ID 65245, to JSB. Paleomagnetic sampling undertaken by BB in 2006 was supported by the Leakey Foundation and Texas State University–San Marcos. The 2006 samples were measured and analyzed by Holly Meier, Deidra Aery, and BB at the Geomagnetic Laboratory of the University of Texas at Austin in collaboration with Wulf Gose. All subsequent paleomagnetic analysis was conducted by AIRH at the University of Liverpool Geomagnetism Laboratory with the support of Mimi Hill and Florian Stark, and the Australian Archaeomagnetism Laboratory. This analysis was supported by an Australian Future Fellowship as part of ARC Grant FT120100399. The study of fossil suids by AS was funded by a postdoctoral grant of the Fyssen Foundation and the LaScArBx, a research program supported by the ANR (ANR-10-LABX-52).

Without the help of the Florisbad team this research would not have been possible. We acknowledge in particular the assistance of Mr. Abel Dichakane, Ms. Sharon Holt, Mr. Peter Mdala (who uncovered the hominin molar), Mr. Jacob Maine, Mr. Bonny Nduma, Mr. Isaac Thapo, and Mr. Adam Thibeletsa. We are grateful to Mr. Johan van Heerden, owner of Uitzoek farm, for access to the Uitzoek site. JSB wishes to thank the Council and the Director of the National Museum, Bloemfontein, for support. Finally, we thank Wendy Voorvelt for her redrafting of Figure 12.1.

13 The Paleoecology of the *Australopithecus africanus* Type Site at Taung, South Africa

Philip J. Hopley and Brian F. Kuhn

Introduction

In November of 1924, Robert Young delivered a "cercopithecid" skull from the Buxton-Norlim Limeworks, near Taung, in what is now the North West Province of South Africa, for description to Australian anatomist Raymond Dart, of the University of the Witwatersrand Medical School (Dart, 1925a; Tobias, 1985). This primate specimen turned out to be the first early hominin fossil ever recovered from Africa and the juvenile type specimen for *Australopithecus africanus* (Dart, 1925a). Since this discovery a number of adult specimens have been found at cave sites in the Cradle of Humankind (e.g., Broom and Schepers, 1946; Dart, 1948; Broom et al., 1950), but no other hominin fossils have been recovered from the Type Site at Taung. As a direct result of Dart's 1925a *Nature* paper, a number of researchers made exploratory trips to the Limeworks that resulted in a slew of early publications by Aleš Hrdlička (1925), Robert Young (1925), Lidio Cipriani (1928), Raymond Dart (1926, 1929), and Robert Broom (1925a, 1925b, 1929, 1930, 1934, 1938a, 1939, 1943, 1945, 1946, 1948a, 1948b). While these early investigations into the type locality of *Au. africanus* garnered a wide body of publications, a proper exploratory foray into the region only occurred in 1947–48 with the University of California Africa Expedition (Camp, 1948; Peabody, 1954). Twenty years later, Karl Butzer published his geological work (Butzer, 1974), and 11 years after that Timothy Partridge published his geological interpretations (Partridge, 1985). Prior to the renewed research in 2010, the last concerted effort into the region was from 1988 to 1994 under the direction of Phillip Tobias, of the University of the Witwatersrand School of Anatomical Sciences. The Tobias years were jointly run by Michel Toussaint and Jeffrey McKee in 1988; and solely by McKee thereafter (McKee and Tobias, 1990, 1994; McKee, 1993a, 1993b, 1994). During this time McKee mapped many of the previously discovered deposits along with a number of new fossil deposits (McKee, 1994). Of the 17 fossil deposits documented by McKee (1994), it is only the fossils collected from the Hrdlička and Dart Pinnacles (now known collectively as the Type Site; Kuhn et al., 2016) that are currently known to be of late Pliocene and Early Pleistocene age and as such are of relevance to early southern African hominin evolution. A new phase of geological and paleoecological research at the Type Site commenced in 2010 (Herries et al., 2013; Hopley et al., 2013; Doran et al., 2015; Kuhn et al., 2015, 2016; Parker et al., 2016).

Geological and Biogeographical Setting

At the southeast margin of the Kalahari Desert, in the North West and Northern Cape Provinces of South Africa, the dolomitic Ghaap Plateau forms an east–west trending escarpment at the boundary with quartzites and shales of the Proterozoic Transvaal Supergroup. Groundwater exits the dolomite in a series of springs along the Ghaap escarpment, forming complex sequences of tufa deposits including waterfall tufas and carapaces that accumulate over the underlying bedrock and surficial deposits (Butzer et al., 1978b) which often contain fossils (Peabody, 1954; Curnoe et al., 2006). Such deposits include the area now known as the Buxton-Norlim Limeworks, which is located on the northeast escarpment edge of the Ghaap Plateau, 15 km SW of the small town of Taung (Figure 13.1) in the North West Province (Reynolds et al., 2011).

The Buxton-Norlim Limeworks consists of a 50-m thick (Tobias et al., 1993) sequence of carbonates consisting predominantly tufa, but also with breccia (Butzer et al., 1978b) and calcrete (Hopley et al., 2013) horizons. The Cenozoic carbonates of the Ghaap Plateau overlie the shales of the Late Carboniferous Dwyka Group and post-date the uplift of the southern African interior (Butzer et al., 1978b). Initial studies of the history of the southern African landsurface suggested substantial Neogene uplift (Partridge and Maud, 1987; Dirks and Berger, 2013); however, recent work suggests that uplift has been minimal since the Late Cretaceous (Flowers and Schoene, 2010; Erlanger et al., 2012). The implication of this revised uplift history is that the earliest Ghaap Plateau tufas could be Paleogene in age; further chronological work is required to establish this. Younger parts of the tufa sequence (and incorporated fossils) have produced ages ranging from late Pliocene to Holocene (McKee, 1994; Hopley et al., 2013; Doran et al., 2015).

The Cenozoic carbonate rocks of the Ghaap Plateau are highly susceptible to dissolution by surface waters and this can lead to the development of caves (Curnoe et al., 2006) or karstic fissures (e.g., Dirks and Berger, 2013) and *in situ* karstification, known as ghost-rock karstification (Dubois et al., 2014), as seen along the northern wall of the Buxton-Norlim Limeworks today.

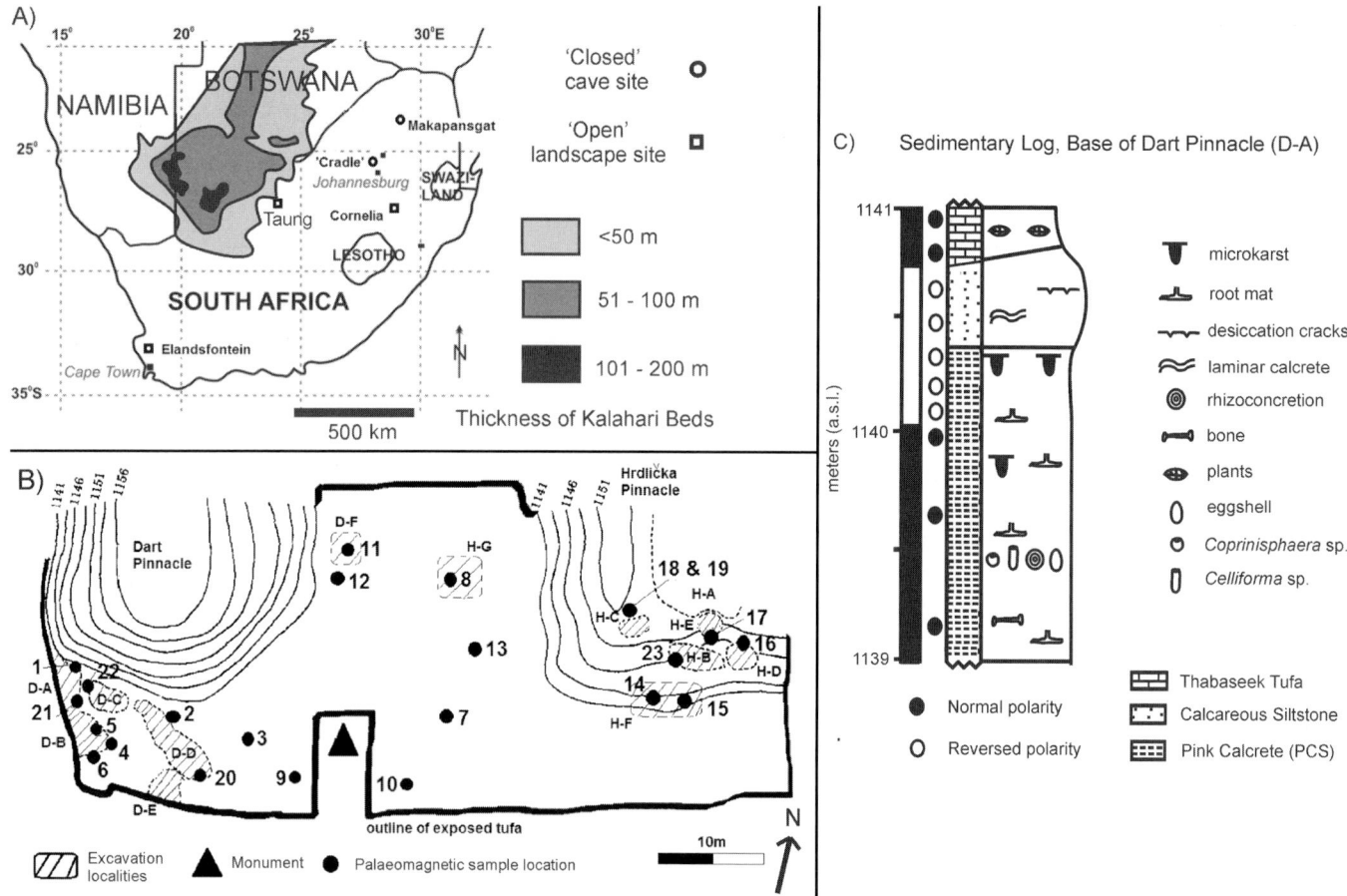

Figure 13.1 (A) Location of the Buxton-Norlim Limeworks (Taung) in relation to other hominin-bearing localities in South Africa. The thickness and extent of the Tertiary Kalahari Group sediments are indicated. (B) The location of outcrops (dotted lines) and sampling localities around the Dart and Hrdlička Pinnacles. (C) Sedimentological log and magnetostratigraphy of the Plio-Pleistocene sediments exposed at the base of the Dart Pinnacle (excavation locality D-A). From Hopley et al. (2013).

These subsequent phases of karstic erosion have provided the accommodation space for the accumulation of cave sediments and fossil and archeological assemblages, as seen throughout the Ghaap Plateau (Humphreys and Thackeray, 1983; Curnoe et al., 2006). The fossil assemblages of the Type Site have historically been interpreted as cave fills (e.g., Peabody, 1954; Butzer, 1974; Tobias et al., 1993; McKee, 2010) and comparisons have been made with the dolomitic caves of Gauteng Province, such as Sterkfonteim, Swartkrans, and Malapa (Partridge, 2000). It is clear that karstic processes will differ significantly between the Precambrian Dolomites of Gauteng and the Cenozoic carbonates of the Ghaap Plateau, including speleogenesis, cave/fissure morphology, and karstic sedimentation.

Situated on the southern margin of the Kalahari Desert, the area of Taung is semi-arid, receiving on average <500 mm of rainfall per year (Thomas and Shaw, 1991). The majority (>80 percent) of this rainfall falls in the summer months (October–April) in association with the southward migration of the Inter-Tropical Convergence Zone (ITCZ) and Zaïre Air Boundary (ZAB) across southern Africa. Mean Annual Temperature (MAT) is approximately 19°C, with warmer temperatures in the summer months. Diurnal temperature ranges are high with occasional winter ground frost (Thomas and Shaw, 1991). The low humidity and warm to hot temperatures of the Kalahari lead to high potential evapotranspiration rates and low amounts of surface runoff (Nicholson et al., 1997). With short instrumental records, climate variability in the Kalahari is poorly understood (Zinke et al., 2004); however, significant interannual and interdecadal southern African rainfall variability can be explained by teleconnections with the El Niño Southern Oscillation (ENSO) and the Indian Ocean Dipole (IOD; e.g., Woodborne et al., 2015). Longer-term changes in rainfall and vegetation are controlled by orbital changes, predominantly the ~23,000-year precession cycle (e.g., Partridge et al., 1997; Holmgren et al., 2003; Hopley et al., 2007b, 2018).

Soil development in the southern Kalahari is generally restricted and has low fertility, due principally to the sandy nature of the underlying Kalahari Group sediments and to the low rainfall; greater soil development occurs around pans and in dry (or seasonal) river valleys (Thomas and Shaw, 1991), such as the Thabasikwa River valley to the north and east of the Buxton Limeworks site. The vegetation in the vicinity of Taung is composed of Mopane scrub and woodland savanna, although the impact of farming and grazing animals is difficult to quantify

(Thomas and Shaw, 1991). Pollen records indicate similar vegetation structure in the region throughout the Holocene (Klein et al., 1991; Scott et al., 2012).

Stratigraphy

Designations such as "Dart Cave," "Hrdlička Cave," "*Australopithecus* Cave," and "Spiers' Cave" were used by Broom as early as 1946. Peabody speculated on the presence of three distinct fossil deposits within the Hrdlička Pinnacle and went as far as to say the pink deposits were from a wet phase (Peabody, 1954). McKee and Tobias (1994) reported on five distinct depositional units within the Hrdlička Pinnacle and five separate units within the Dart Pinnacle (or *Australopithecus* Pinnacle; Partridge, 2000). The underlying consistency has always been the site designations of the Dart Pinnacle and the Hrdlička Pinnacle as being two separate deposits (McKee, 2016; McKee and Kuykendall, 2016). These "pinnacles" are the result of human activity and were left as witness sections by the miners; geologically, they are not distinct deposits and prior to mining were one continuous unit. This fact is supported by both paleomagnetic analysis and sedimentological studies indicating that the pink (PCS) deposits and red (YRSS) infills occur in both Pinnacles (Partridge et al., 1991; Hopley et al., 2013), as well as early observations by Young (1925). The PCS deposits and the Thabaseek Tufa (first described by Peabody, 1954) of both pinnacles share the same normal magnetic polarity (see Figure 13.1), while the red infill (YRSS) has a reversed polarity wherever it occurs and is clearly a younger deposit (Herries et al., 2013; Hopley et al., 2013). Thus, it should be recognized that the Dart and Hrdlička Pinnacles are a single site containing at least two distinct fossil deposits, as pointed out by Hopley et al. (2013), and should now collectively be referred to as the Type Site (Kuhn et al., 2016). It is clear from sedimentological and geochemical observations on the matrix of the "Taung Child" skull (Partridge et al., 1991; Tobias et al., 1993) that the fossil comes from the distinctive PCS Calcrete deposit. This provenance work means that the paleoecology and geochronology of the PCS deposit is of direct relevance to the age and environment of *Au. africanus* at Taung.

Dating

The dating of the sediments at the Type Site and of the "Taung Child" itself has a long and inconclusive history. Initial age estimates following the discovery of the "Taung Child" were based entirely on biostratigraphic inferences. With few comparative fossil sites from Africa, these early age estimates were based on the recognition of extinct faunal species from Taung Type Site and the belief that a human ancestor such as *Australopithecus* should be of Miocene or Pliocene age (Young, 1925; Dart, 1926, 1929; Broom, 1929, 1930). By the 1950s, further australopiths and their associated faunal assemblages had been described from cave deposits to the north, enabling Taung Type Site, Makapansgat, and Sterkfontein to be identified as older than the fossil assemblages of Kromdraai and Swartkrans (Ewer, 1956, 1957a; Cooke, 1963).

A change in thinking came when Wells (1967, 1969) suggested on the basis of similarities between the fossil baboons of Taung Type Site and Swartkrans that the Taung deposit was the youngest of the *Au. africanus* sites. This seemed to be confirmed by the young geomorphological age estimates of <0.83 Ma (Partridge, 1973; later discounted by Butzer, 1974), the ionium (thorium) dating of the Thabaseek Tufa to <1.2 Ma (Vogel and Partridge, 1983; falsified by Tobias et al., 1993), and thermoluminescence dating (Vogel, 1985). In the 1980s Delson (1984, 1988) conducted a review of the primates and concluded that the site was around 2.3 Ma and intermediate in age between Sterkfontein and Swartkrans. In the 1990s, Cooke (1990a) published a revised list of the Taung fauna (based on previously undescribed specimens housed at the University of California) and McKee (1993a) and McKee et al. (1995) updated the biostratigraphy to suggest that the PCS deposits of the Dart Pinnacle were likely around 2.8–2.6 Ma (the "younger" Hrdlička Pinnacle deposits were assigned an age of around 2.3 Ma). It should be noted that as these are biochronological age estimates, they need to be revised following the recent paleomagnetic and radiometric dating of many of the South African sites, and the refined ages of East African fossil assemblages (Herries et al., 2006a, 2006b, 2009, 2013; Herries and Shaw, 2011; Herries and Adams, 2013).

A new era of radiometric dating was ushered in by Walker et al. (2006), who combined uranium–lead ages on flowstones with magnetostratigraphy at Sterkfontein, and this was followed by U–Pb ages for the other South African cave deposits (e.g., Pickering et al., 2011). A paleomagnetic study at Taung has been undertaken (Herries et al., 2013; Hopley et al., 2013), and U–Pb dating is underway. The paleomagnetic work suggests that the PCS deposits have Normal polarity and dates to the end of the Gauss Chron between 3.03 and 2.58 Ma, making the "Taung Child" contemporary with the Makapansgat Limeworks *Au. africanus* specimens. The younger YRSS karstic sediments have a reversed polarity and are dated to the Matuyama Chron between 2.58 and 1.95 Ma (Kuhn et al., 2016), making it contemporary with Sterkfontein Member 4.

Taphonomy

Brain (1981) was the first author to assess the taphonomy of the Taung faunal assemblage. He suggested that, while the majority of Taung faunal materials were most likely collected by leopards (*Panthera pardus*), many smaller mammal specimens could have been collected by an avian predator. Brain (1981) speculated that the eggshells recovered at Taung were most likely derived from Cape eagle owls (*Bubo capensis*). Brain based his assumptions on modern nesting practices of Cape eagle owls in direct association with the twilight zones of caves combined with the long-held presumption that the Taung fossil-bearing deposits were cave infills. McKee (2010) explored the taphonomy of water-borne carcasses within a tufa cave, and concluded that this taphonomic pathway could be relevant to the low-density bone accumulations of the PCS deposits. However, subsequent sedimentological analysis (Hopley et al., 2013; Parker et al., 2016) indicated that the fossiliferous PCS deposits are palustrine calcretes, and do not contain tufas formed within a river channel.

Berger and Clarke (1995) compared the Type Site assemblages (Cooke 1990a; McKee, unpublished) with published faunal assemblages accumulated by three extant eagles found in South Africa: the martial eagle (*Polemaetus bellicosus*), the black eagle (*Aquila verreauxii*), and the crowned eagle (*Stephanoaetus coronatus*). They concluded that the majority of the faunal remains from Taung, including the "Taung Child," were probably collected by a large raptor, but did not specify the species. Each of the eagles in question are capable of carrying prey that are equivalent in body sizes to most of the fauna identified at the Type Site, including the "Taung Child" (Berger and Clarke, 1995). Recent studies of crowned eagle hunting behavior (Sanders et al., 2003; McGraw et al., 2006; Trapani et al., 2006) corroborate the possibility that a raptor may have contributed to the faunal accumulation at Taung. Taphonomic damage to the hominin cranium (i.e., talon puncture marks and scratches) further supported the possibility that a large raptor may have acted as the agent of accumulation (Berger, 2006; Berger and McGraw, 2007). A study of Plio-Pleistocene cercopithecid fossils from sites on Angola's Humpata Plateau demonstrates that Taung is not an isolated case of raptor predation on primates in the fossil record. It appears that researchers often dismiss raptor predation as a selective force operating during primate evolution (Gilbert et al., 2009). Furthermore, specific alarm calls and antipredator behavior in the presence of aerial predators by multiple primates (Struhsaker, 1967; Cheney and Seyfarth, 1981; Goodman, 1994; Csermely, 1996; Zuberbühler et al., 1997; Zuberbühler, 2001; Fichtel et al., 2005) suggests that aerial predators continue to exert selective pressures on primate populations today.

Materials and Methods

(1) Collection Methods and/or Brief Overview of Excavation History

After 90 years of sporadic excavation, the Taung fossil collections are spread around the world. The Ditsong National Museum of Natural History (DNMNH), Pretoria, South Africa curates the materials collected by Broom (S. Potze, pers. comm. 2012). The majority of Peabody's (1954) collections are in the care of the University of California Museum of Paleontology, Berkeley, California, USA (Cooke, 1990a), while some were sent to the School of Anatomical Sciences at the University of the Witwatersrand and other specimens were repatriated and are now in the care of DNMNH. In 1954 Peabody stated that material excavated by Hrdlička (1925) was located in the British Museum; however, to the authors' knowledge no such material has been located. The material Hrdlička is thought to have excavated is not extensive, consisting of a single well-preserved primate skull and a few fragments of others, the rest of which he left in the wall of the pinnacles (Hrdlička, 1925). It is assumed that Peabody excavated this material in 1947–48. With the exception of Peabody and McKee, all previous excavations appear to have concentrated on the Hrdlička Pinnacle. Other material excavated by McKee, under the directorship of Tobias, in the late 1980s and early 1990s were relocated from the University of the Witwatersrand School of Anatomical Sciences to the Evolutionary Studies Institute and subsequently to the DNMNH for further study. Additional unstudied material also appears to have remained at the site (Kuhn et al., 2016) and this material is now at the DNMNH for further study. The faunal material discussed here is from previously published or documented material, i.e., Cooke (1990a), McKee (unpublished; as cited in Berger and Clarke, 1995) and Kuhn et al., 2015. A single faunal assemblage is reported, as geological provenance (i.e., PCS vs. YRSS) of specimens is often uncertain; taxonomy was updated using Werdelin and Sanders (2010).

(2) Stable Isotope Paleoecology

Taung is unusual among South African hominin localities for not having been subjected to a study of hominin or faunal stable isotope paleoecology. This may be because the most common faunal groups to be studied isotopically, the bovids and suids, are only represented by a small number of identifiable specimens. There is, however, scope for a study of primate isotope ecology. Initial stable isotope work has been undertaken on the avian eggshell fragments and sediment present in the hominin-bearing PCS calcrete (Kuhn et al., 2015) and on the overlying Thabaseek Tufa deposits exposed in the area between the two pinnacles (Doran et al., 2015).

Results

Table 13.1 shows a total of 49 species recorded from the Taung Type Site. Twenty-two species (45 percent) are extinct and 10 of these extinct species are unique to the Type Site. The majority of these unique species are micromammals (Eulipotyphla and Rodentia) from the karstic infills of the Hrdlička YRSS deposits (de Graaff, 1960). The taxonomy of these micromammal groups are in flux (Werdelin and Sanders, 2010; Winkler et al., 2010), and it is likely that not all of these taxa are valid (e.g., *Prototomys cambelli*). Of the extinct macromammals from the Taung Type Site, the primate *Procercocebus antiquus* and bovid *Cephalophus parvus* have uncertain provenance, and could be from the older PCS, the younger Hrdlička cave fill (YRSS), or both.

The documented Taung collection is composed predominantly of primates (Table 13.1). It seems likely that this represents either a taphonomic bias or collection bias; taphonomically this may relate to the position of the PCS calcrete beneath a bird of prey nest. This is supported by talon marks on the primate remains, the abundance of primate cranial elements (Berger and Clarke, 1995), and the presence of possible Aquilinae eggshells within the PCS deposit (Kuhn et al., 2015). For the YRSS deposits the relevant taphonomic pathway may be a natural death assemblage, as baboons inhabit caves and crevices within the tufa along the edge of the escarpment today and primates are known to use caves for thermoregulation (Barrett et al., 2004; Pruetz, 2007). Of the cercopithecoid species, the extinct mandrill (Gilbert, 2007a) *Procercocebus antiquus* (unique to Taung) and the extinct baboon *Papio izodi* have been collected from the hominin-bearing PCS calcrete (Cooke, 1990a; Gilbert, 2007a; McKee and Kuykendall, 2016). An assessment of the dental

Table 13.1 List of fauna comprised from Cooke (1990a), McKee (unpublished, as cited in Berger and Clarke, 1995), Kuhn et al. (2015), Gilbert (2007a), Dart (1925a), and Werdelin and Sanders (2010).

Order	Species
Eulipotyphla	*Crocidura taungsensis**†
	Macroscelides sp.
	Elephantulus antiquus†
	Elephantulus (*Nasilio*) sp. (large)†
	Crocidura cf. *bicolor*
	Suncus varilla
Chiroptera	*Rhinolophus* cf. *darlingi*
Lagomorpha	*Lepus* sp. or *Pronolagus* sp.
Hyracoidea	*Procavia antiqua**
	Procavia transvaalensis*
Rodentia	*Gypsorhychus darti**†
	Gypsorhychus minor*†
	Petromus minor*†
	Pedetes gracilis*†
	Mystromys antiquus†
	Thallomys debruyni†
	Prototomys cambelli*†
	Cryptomys robertsi†
	Gerbilliscus cf. *brantsi*
	Mastomys cf. *natalensis*
	Malacothrix cf. *typica*
	Proodontomys cookei†
	Desmodillus auricularis
	Dasymys sp. nov.†
	Rhabdomys cf. *pumilio*
	Acomys cf. *cahirinus*
	Malacothrix cf. *typica*
	Hystrix cf. *africaeaustralis*
	Dendromus sp.
	Otomys gracilis†
Primates	*Australopithecus africanus*†
	Procercocebus antiquus* †
	Parapapio broomi†
	Papio izodi†
	Cercopithecoides williamsi†
Carnivora	*Panthera* cf. *pardus*
	Canis cf. *mesomelas*
	Herpestes cf. *sanguineus*
Artiodactyla (Suidae)	*Notochoerus* cf. *capensis*†
Artiodactyla (Bovidae)	*Gazella* sp.
	Oreotragus oreotragus
	Syncerus cf. *acoelotus*†
	Tragelaphus cf. *angasii*
	Cephalophus parvus (small spp.)*†
Testudines	*Pelomedusa* cf. *subrufa*
Strigiformes	cf. *Athene noctua*
Galliformes	*Numida meleagris*
Accipitriformes	*Aquila* sp.
Decapoda	*Potamonautes* sp.

* Species unique to the Taung Type Site. † Extinct species.

microwear of these two species indicates that *P. izodi* overlaps with the microwear patterns of the omnivorous chacma baboon *P. ursinus* and that *Pr. antiquus* microwear patterns cluster with other Plio-Pleistocene papionins. The conclusion of this study was that the Taung primates were living in a savanna–woodland environment that may have been marginally wetter (closed) than it is today.

The bovid and suid assemblage from the Type Site is very small compared to other South African hominin localities; this in part may reflect the genuine rarity of bovids and suids from Taung; however, as discussed by Kuhn et al. (2016) this may be related to the biased interests of previous collectors. Of the five identified bovid species (Table 13.2), only one, *Oreotragus oreotragus*, can be confidently assigned to the PCS deposits beneath the Dart Pinnacle (McKee and Kuykendall, 2016); the other four bovid species are from the younger YRSS deposits within the Hrdlička Pinnacle. *Oreotragus oreotragus* (klipspringer) is predominantly a browser today, and most likely in the past, as determined from ethological and isotopic observations (Sponheimer and Lee-Thorp, 2003). Bovid species from the Hrdlička Pinnacle include the extant nyala, *Tragelaphus angasii*, known to be a mixed feeder with a preference for browsing (Sponheimer and Lee-Thorp, 2003), and the extinct species *Syncerus* cf. *acoelotus* and *Cephalophus parvus*, which can be assumed to be grazers and browsers, respectively, based on the diets of their extant and extinct cogeners (Sponheimer et al., 1999; Sponheimer and Lee-Thorp, 1999; Cerling et al., 2003c). The only documented suid from the Type Site is the extinct species *Notochoerus* cf. *capensis* (see Table 13.2), which is known from carbon isotope studies to have had a grazing (C_4) diet (Sponheimer and Lee-Thorp, 1999; Sponheimer et al., 2006a).

Like all other hominin localities from the Plio-Pleistocene of Africa, with the notable exception of Kanjera South, Kenya (Plummer et al., 2009b), the Taung Type Site contains a mixture of grazing, browsing, and mixed-feeding species. In summary, the primates and ungulates of Taung indicate that unknown proportions of both grassland and woodland were to be found in the vicinity of the Type Site during the accumulation of the older PCS and younger YRSS mammalian assemblages. In this

Table 13.2 Summary of paleoclimatic/paleoenvironmental proxies recovered from the Taung Type Site. The Thabaseek Tufa paleoenvironment is not discussed in detail in the text, as it a younger lithology that has not yielded hominin or faunal remains.

Paleoenvironmental proxy	Locality/lithology	Source	Paleoecology
Faunal analysis (vertebrates)	Dart and Hrdlička	Cooke (1990a); McKee and Kuykendall (2016)	Primates, bovids and chelonia, aves. Typical of mixed savanna
Sediment analysis	PCS calcrete	Peabody (1954); Butzer (1974)	Wetter and possibly cooler than today
Dental microwear (papionins)	Dart and Hrdlička	Williams and Patterson (2010)	Open woodland
Stable isotopes (eggshells)	PCS calcrete	Kuhn et al. (2015)	C_3 woodland and C_4 grassland present
Insect traces (carder bee cells)	PCS calcrete	Parker et al. (2016)	Dry soil in proximity of angiosperms
Stable isotopes (tufa)	Thabaseek Tufa	Doran et al. (2015)	Shallow tufa lakes and riverine tufa
Plant fossils	Thabaseek Tufa	Bamford (pers. comm.); Doran et al. (2015); McKee and Kuykendall (2016)	Angiosperms, macrophytes and algae typical of shallow rivers and lakes

respect the paleoecology of Taung is both similar and indistinguishable from most other Plio-Pleistocene African hominin localities. It is expected that future work on the faunal IDs and geological provenance (via sedimentological analysis) of fossils within existing collections will help to refine this broad-brush picture of the paleoecology of the Taung Type site.

In addition to the mammalian assemblage, avian remains have been identified via eggshells. Most of the analyzed eggshell fragments have a predominant C_4 signal, indicating the presence of a graminivorous species such as the helmeted guineafowl, *Numida meleagris*. One fossil eggshell (T93-17) has morphological similarities with those of Verreaux's eagles (*Aquila verreauxii*), and a C_3 isotopic signal consistent with a primate-consuming bird of prey (Kuhn et al., 2015). The stable isotope analysis of fossil eggshells from the hominin-bearing PCS calcrete indicates that there were both C_3 and C_4 plants present in the vicinity of the site, as observed in all other Plio-Pleistocene assemblages from South Africa (e.g., Sponheimer et al., 1999; Lee-Thorp et al., 2000; van der Merwe et al., 2003). Further work on avian fossil remains is ongoing.

Discussion and Conclusion

Paleoenvironmental evidence for the hominin-bearing calcrete (PCS) at Taung comes principally from sedimentology and stable isotope ecology (see Table 13.2) as well as limited faunal analysis. The comprehensive faunal list from the Type Site (Table 13.1) is composed of specimens from both the older PCS calcrete and the younger YRSS cave infill. These distinct assemblages may have formed 100,000s of years apart, making meaningful paleoenvironmental inferences difficult. Most specimens have a preserved sedimentological matrix adhering to the fossil, making it possible to assign specimens and species to the PCS or YRSS fossil assemblage. Work to assign specimens to either assemblage is underway, and is likely to produce a more nuanced reconstruction of the paleoecology of Taung. Preliminary data indicate that the taxic differences between the two faunal assemblages are small and that both are typical of a woodland–savanna mosaic environment, as has been reconstructed for other South African hominin localities (e.g., Sponheimer et al., 1999; Lee-Thorp et al., 2000; van der Merwe et al., 2003). As discussed in Hopley and Maxwell (Chapter 3), a distinction must be made between a single snapshot of time preserving a true woodland–savanna mosaic and the changing proportions of woodland and savanna vegetation that occurred during the substantial time interval during which either the PCS calcrete or YRSS cave infill at Taung was formed. Further investigation into the time interval represented by the two fossil assemblages at the Type Site is required before any quantitative assessment of the Plio-Pleistocene vegetation structure of Taung can be made.

Previous reconstructions of a wetter environment than today (e.g., Peabody, 1954; Butzer, 1974) have been influenced by the presence of the extensive tufa deposits at Taung and the assumption that the accumulation of the PCS fossil assemblage was contemporaneous with tufa deposition (e.g., McKee, 2010). However, Hopley et al. (2013) demonstrate that the PCS is a calcrete interbedded within the Thabaseek Tufa and is therefore temporally distinct from the tufa deposits outcropping at the Type Site. Further sedimentological work is required to determine whether the PCS calcrete was deposited close to the margins of a tufa lake or whether it formed during a relatively arid period in which the Thabaseek River and its associated lakes were of minimal extent. Paleoecological indictors from the PCS calcrete itself show a relatively moist soil (Parker et al., 2016) in the proximity of both savanna grassland and woody cover (Kuhn et al., 2015; Parker et al., 2016), frequented by baboons, bovids, and birds (Cooke, 1990).

It has often been reported that the faunal assemblage at Taung has a freshwater component (e.g., McKee, 1993a), specifically the freshwater turtle (terrapin), *Pelomedusa* cf. *subrufa*, and the crab, *Potamonautes* sp. (Cooke, 1990a). Both of these freshwater species have been found at other Plio-Pleistocene hominin localities such as the Chiwondo Beds of Malawi (Karl, 2012), Laetoli in Tanzania (Harrison, 2011h), Lothagam in Kenya (Martin and Trautwein, 2003; Wood, 2003), and the Lower Aramis Member, Ethiopia (WoldeGabriel et al., 2009a). An important question to discuss is the degree to which these species are dependent on a freshwater habitat. *Pelomedusa subrufa* is the single extant species of its genus and is distributed across sub-Saharan Africa. It has a habitat preference for swamps and seasonal wetlands as opposed to the fully lacustrine conditions typical of other African turtles (Luiselli et al., 2000). During the dry season the turtles will forage on land (Miller,

1979; Luiselli et al., 2011), and if conditions become too arid they will burrow into the soil and aestivate (Luiselli et al., 2000). Wood (1973) suggests that the relative rarity of *Pelomedusa* sp. in the Plio-Pleistocene of Africa, relative to other lacustrine turtle species, is due to its preference for seasonal wetlands. The presence of *Pelomedusa* cf. *subrufa* in the PCS calcrete at Taung may be indicative of aestivation during the dry season in the proximity of a marginal wetland associated with the Paleo-Thabaseek River.

The freshwater crab *Potamonautes* sp. is endemic to Africa (Dobson, 2004) and the fossil record of this genus extends back to the Late Miocene of eastern Africa (Morris, 1976; Martin and Trautwein, 2003). There are a number of *Potamonautes* species found in the rivers and wetlands of the summer rainfall region of South Africa in the present day (e.g., *P. sidneyi* and *P. perlatus*; Gouws and Stewart, 2001). Crabs such as *P. sidneyi* shelter in burrows dug into the side of muddy river banks and leave their burrows at night or after rain. As they mature they spend more time on land; they also mate on land. Although the species assignment of *Potamonautes* sp. from Taung is uncertain, it is likely that the fossil crabs would have exhibited some degree of terrestriality, especially during the dry season. The presence of these crabs at Taung suggests proximity to a well-oxygenated ephemeral or seasonal river or stream.

Other Crustacea represented in the PCS calcrete at Taung are the Ostracoda, as fragments of their calcareous tests are occasionally observed in thin section (Sombroek, pers. comm.). Freshwater ostracods can live in lakes, temporary water bodies, or even in moist soils, so without species- or genus-level identification they are not environmentally diagnostic. Other freshwater taxa such as fish, crocodiles, waterfowl, and aquatic gastropods are common in east African fluvio-lacustrine deposits (e.g., Leakey and Harris, 2003a) and are indicative of extensive and perennial water bodies. The absence of these taxa from Taung is further evidence for the marginal or ephemeral nature of the freshwater water body present during the deposition of the PCS calcrete.

Areas of Interest for Future Work

There are a number of research avenues that may lead to an improved understanding of the paleo-ecology of Taung. It is apparent from this study that further work is required (and underway) to identify the stratigraphic/sedimentological provenance of faunal specimens excavated during the 1988–1994 seasons, from the University of California, the material rescued from the site itself (Kuhn et al., 2016), and the Ditsong Museum collections; only then can a comprehensive list of fauna from the PCS calcrete (where the Taung Child most likely comes from) be produced. Work to improve the stratigraphy and dating of the site is underway with a particular focus on sedimentology, paleomagnetism, and uranium–lead dating. Stable isotope analysis of the primate assemblage would be particularly informative because the extinct species *Procercocebus antiquus* and *Papio idozi* are found at Taung and their dietary preferences are poorly understood. Additional techniques such as clumped isotope paleo-temperature estimates (e.g., Passey et al., 2010) may also be fruitful. As the centenary of the discovery of the Taung Child draws closer, we expect that this often overlooked and misunderstood locality will once again become central to the understanding of early hominin evolution.

Acknowledgments

Our thanks to Stephen Frost and Christopher Gilbert for their help in the identification of specific primate specimens. We are also grateful to Stephanie Caruana and Andy Herries for comments and contributions to early versions of this chapter. We thank Alexandra Bountalis, Matthew Caruana, Taylor Doran, Thomas Wigley, and Colin Menter for aid in the field. Fieldwork was supported by National Geographic Grants (#8774–10 and #3212) to PJH, and a Palaeontological Scientific Trust grant to BFK. Research conducted under SAHRA permit 80/09/10/028/51. We thank the MEC for Environment in the North West Province for their continued support and access to the site.

14 Wonderwerk Cave, Northern Cape Province: An Early–Middle Pleistocene Paleoenvironmental Sequence for the Interior of South Africa

Liora Kolska Horwitz, Margaret D. Avery, Marion K. Bamford, Francesco Berna, James S. Brink†, Michaela Ecker, Yolanda Fernandez-Jalvo, Paul Goldberg, Sharon Holt, Julia Lee-Thorp, Ari Matmon, Robyn Pickering, Naomi Porat, Lloyd Rossouw, Louis Scott, Ron Shaar, and Michael Chazan

Introduction

Localities in the interior of South Africa, such as Taung and Vaal River sites, were intensively researched after hominins were discovered in the early 1900's (Péringuey, 1911; Dart, 1925a; Goodwin, 1928), but then neglected for the fossil-rich, dolomitic breccia sites in Gauteng Province (e.g., Cooke, 1963, 1967; Vrba, 1976; Brain, 1981; Brain and Sillen, 1988; Bamford, 1999; Pickering and Kramers, 2010; Herries and Shaw, 2011; Reynolds et al., 2011; Lee-Thorp and Sponheimer, 2013). Recently, knowledge of the interior region has increased, following excavations at Florisbad (Brink, 1988; Kuman et al., 1999; Toffolo et al., 2015), Taung, including Equus Cave (Scott, 1987; Klein et al., 1991; McKee and Tobias, 1994; Lee-Thorp and Beaumont, 1995; Johnson et al., 1997; Hopley et al., 2013; McKee, 2016), Canteen Kopje (Beaumont, 1990, 2004; McNabb and Beaumont, 2011; Smith et al., 2012; Lotter et al., 2016), Pniel (Beaumont, 1990; Kunneriath and Gaillard, 2010; Hutson, 2018), Erfkroon (Churchill et al., 2000a; Brink et al., 2015a), Bundu Farm (Kiberd, 2006; Hutson, 2018), Cornelia (Brink et al., 2012; Toffolo et al., 2019) and the Kathu Complex (Porat et al., 2010; Wilkins and Chazan, 2012; Wilkins et al., 2012; Walker et al., 2014; Lukich et al., 2019, 2020).

Wonderwerk Cave preserves a rich, multiproxy paleoenvironmental sequence for the interior spanning the last ~2 million years (Beaumont and Vogel, 2006; Chazan et al., 2008, 2012; Chazan and Horwitz, 2015; Horwitz and Chazan, 2015). The cave lies at 1665 m.a.s.l. on the eastern flank of the Kuruman Hills, in the Northern Cape Province at the base of a small 122-m high conical hill (Figure 14.1; Figure14.2a,b). The cave is *ca.* 140 m long with a floor area of *ca.* 2400 m² (Figure 14.3). This chapter summarizes the paleoenvironmental record at Wonderwerk including the ecological setting, site formation process, the dating of the sequence, and fossil data sets relevant to changing Pleistocene climate.

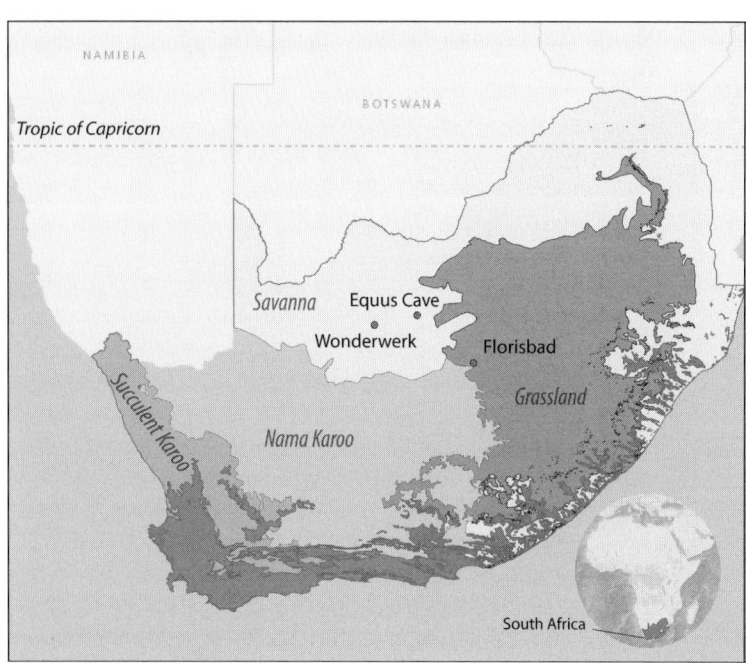

Figure 14.1 (a) Map showing location of Wonderwerk Cave and vegetation biomes of South Africa.

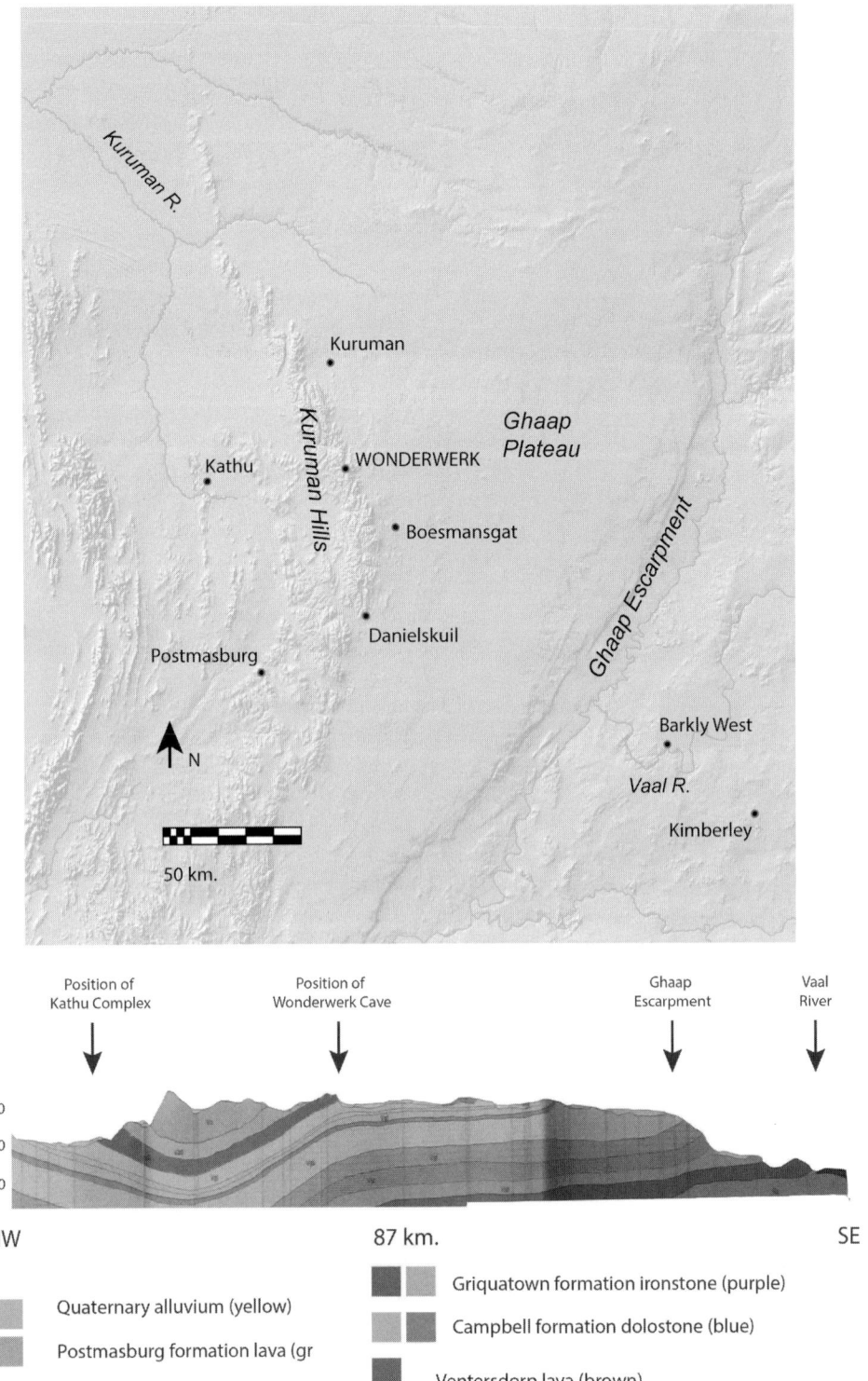

Figure 14.1 (b) Detailed map showing site location and landscape features (A black and white version of this figure will appear in some formats. For the color version, please refer to the plate section.)

Ecological Setting

Wonderwerk Cave lies in the semi-arid to arid zone, in a summer rainfall region with mean annual precipitation of *ca.* 480 mm and high interannual rainfall variability with years of flooding and drought (Nash and Endfield, 2002; Tfwala et al., 2017). Winters are very dry (less than 5 percent of the annual rainfall), with frequent frosts (Schulze, 1997). The region is classified as falling within the Savanna Biome, with a mosaic of vegetation around the cave (Mucina and Rutherford, 2006; Brink et al., 2016). Vegetation falls into several categories: (1) grassy woodland of the

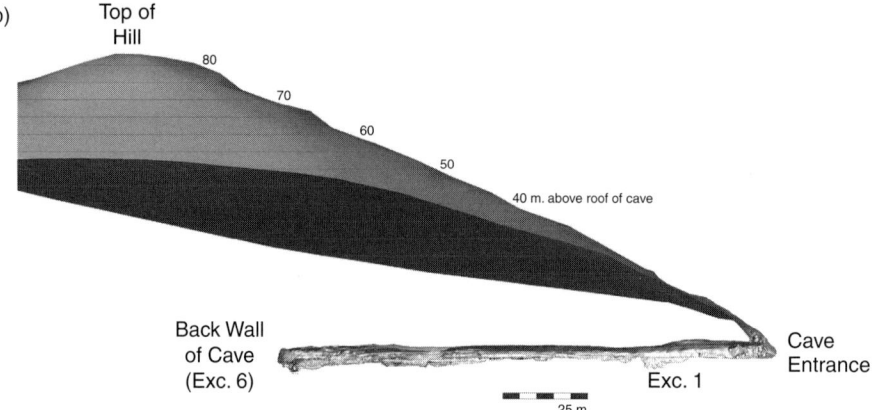

Figure 14.2 (a) Historical photograph from *ca.* 1940s showing location of cave at the base of the hill. Note the gentle slope of the talus outside. (b) Section through the hillside showing the location of the cave relative to the hill (figure generated from a 3D scan of the cave – see Rüther et al., 2009).

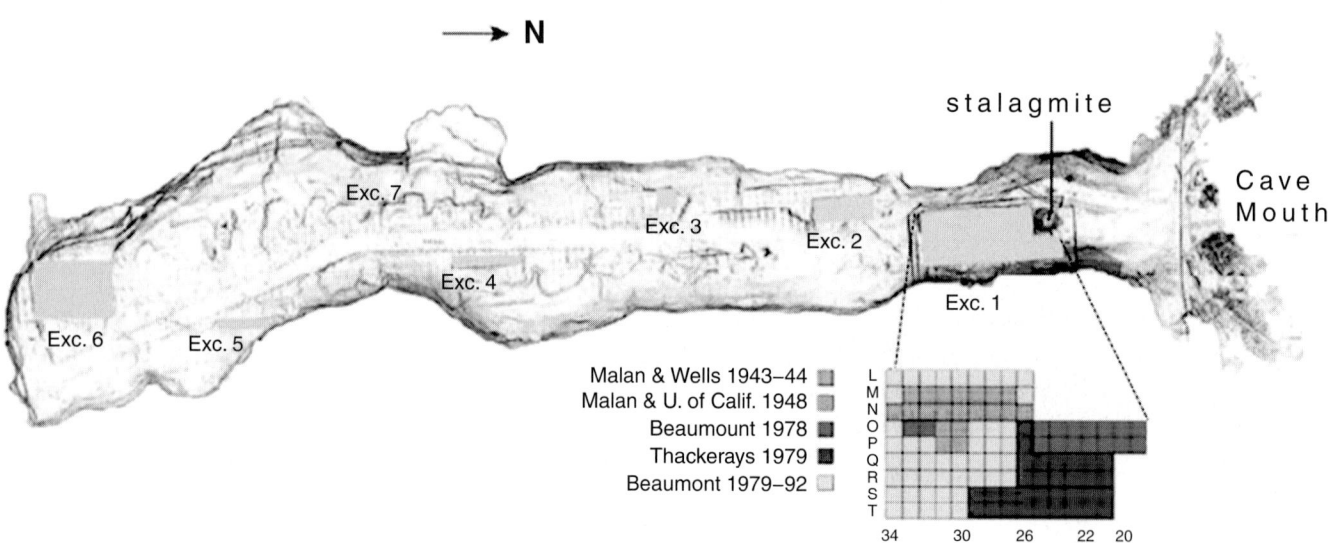

Figure 14.3 Plan of the interior of cave showing the location of the different areas excavated by P.B. Beaumont (figure generated from a 3D scan of the cave – see Rüther et al., 2009). Enlarged view of excavation grid from Beaumont and Vogel (2006). Grid scale is in yards (1 yard = 91.44 cm). (A black and white version of this figure will appear in some formats. For the color version, please refer to the plate section.)

Kuruman Mountain Bushveld subdivision, SVk1; (2) Kuruman Vaalbosveld subdivision (SVk8); (3) Kuruman Thornveld (SKv9) vegetation; (4) Kathu Bushveld (SKv12); and (5) the transition zone to the Nama Karoo Biome to the south (Rutherford and Westfall, 1986; Mucina and Rutherford, 2006). Today large mammals are rare, but include warthog, eland, springbok, dik-dik, aardwolf, and anteaters (Brink et al., 2016). Hyena, caracal, small felids, black-backed jackal, and foxes are quite common, with reptiles and numerous rodent species present (Brink et al., 2016). Historically, a rich spectrum of mammals inhabited the region (Roche, 2004; Boshoff et al., 2016).

Karst formations within the Ghaap Group dolomites include Bushmansgat (Bushmanshole) – a 290-m deep sinkhole 12 km south of Wonderwerk, and the spring that emerges at the Eye of Kuruman ~40 km to the north (Figure 14.1b). Several springs occur on the Ghaap Plateau; however, the closest water sources are at Bushmanshole and a seep and pool located on the eastern side of Gakorosa Hill around 5 km away (Humphreys and Thackeray 1983: 20; Beaumont, 1990).

History of Excavation

During the Second World War, the organic-rich guano deposits inside the cave were removed and sold as fertilizer by the farm owners, the Bosman family, thereby uncovering artifacts and fossils. These finds were sent to the Bureau of Archaeology (Pretoria), resulting in a visit by B.D. Malan in 1940, who in January 1943 and November 1944 directed excavations near the front of the cave (now called Excavation 1). Test excavations were dug in an area adjacent to the east cave wall – in front of a large stalagmite ca. 30 m in from the cave entrance (Figure 14.4) and ca. 60 m in from the cave entrance (Figure 14.3; Malan and Wells, 1943). Malan and Cooke (1941) gave a preliminary account of the fauna from guano-diggers' dumps and described the extinct fauna and Later Stone Age (LSA), Middle Stone Age (MSA) and Fauresmith, artifacts (Malan and Wells, 1943). Frank Peabody of the University of California African Expedition southern section expanded Malan's excavation in 1948, and "produced evidence of cultures as far back as Early Stone Age" (Camp, 1948: 551). Following a hiatus, K.W. Butzer undertook a geochemical and sedimentological study of the exposed sections between 1974 and 1977 (Butzer et al., 1979; Butzer, 1984a, 1984b).

Extensive excavations were conducted by Peter Beaumont between 1978 and 1996. Seven different areas inside the cave were excavated (Figure 14.3; Beaumont and Vogel, 2006). In 1979, Anne and J. Francis Thackeray joined Beaumont and excavated the LSA occupations in Excavation 1. Together, the Beaumont and Thackeray excavations yielded ~5 m of stratified deposits, spanning the Acheulean to the historic period (Avery, 1981; Thackeray et al., 1981; Humphreys and Thackeray, 1983; Thackeray, 1983, 2015). The LSA palynology was published by Van Zinderen Bakker (1982), revised by Scott (Scott and Thackeray, 2015), while Beaumont published several articles (Beaumont, 1982, 1990, 2004, 2011; Beaumont and Vogel, 2006).

Beaumont identified 12 archeological strata (Str.) in Excavation 1 (Table 14.1). Strata 1 through 4 represent a series of LSA industries (Ceramic LSA, Wilton, Oakhurst, and possibly Robberg). Stratum 5 is a mix of Acheulean and LSA, but how they articulate in this layer is currently unclear. Underlying Str. 5, with a clear chronological hiatus, are Strata 6–12 with 2 m of deposit, containing an Oldowan industry at the base overlain by Acheulean industries (Figure 14.5). No Middle Stone Age was identified here, although it occurs in the adjacent Excavation 2 (Beaumont and Vogel, 2006; Chazan et al., 2020). Fauresmith industries, transitional between the Earlier Stone Age (ESA) and MSA, are found in Excavation 6 at the back of the cave.

Wonderwerk Cave contains perhaps the longest record of hominin occupation in southern Africa, from the Oldowan through to the LSA. Moreover, the cave has yielded a rich corpus of finds – including organic remains – from even the earliest levels. Given the potential of this site, an interdisciplinary project led by M. Chazan and L.K. Horwitz has, since 2004, studied the excavated finds (lithic, fauna, and botanical remains) from the Beaumont excavations and dated these levels using several radiometric methods (Chazan et al., 2008, 2012; Chazan and Horwitz, 2015; Shaar et al., 2021), as well as 3D laser-scanner surveys (Rüther et al., 2009). Excavations in historic Excavation 1 were re-initiated in 2012 (Chazan et al., 2017).

Figure 14.4 (a) Photograph toward the cave interior showing extent of Excavation 1 constrained by railing. Note the large stalagmite on the right. (b) Photograph taken from in front of Excavation 1 toward the back of the cave. Note the rounded ceiling and smooth, parallel cave walls.

Table 14.1 Paleoenvironmental sources for the ESA strata at Wonderwerk Cave.

Material	Presence	Exc 1, ESA strata examined	Status	Published
Sediment micromorphology and geology	Present	Str. 12–6	Published	Chazan et al., 2008, 2012; Matmon et al., 2012; Goldberg et al., 2015
Micromammals	Present	Str. 12–6	Str. 12–11 taxonomy and taphonomy analyzed and published; Str. 10–6 taxonomy partially analyzed and published; Str. 10, 6, and 7 taphonomy analyzed and published	Avery, 2022; Birkenfeld et al., 2015; Fernández-Jalvo and Avery, 2015; Fernández-Jalvo et al., 2018; Marin-Monfort et al., 2022
Macrofauna	Present	Str. 12–6	Str. 12–11 fully analyzed and published	Brink et al., 2015b, 2016
Stable light isotopes ($\delta^{18}O$ and $\delta^{13}C$) – ostrich eggshell	Done	Str. 12–6	Str. 12–6 fully analyzed and published	Ecker et al., 2015a
Stable light isotopes ($\delta^{18}O$ and $\delta^{13}C$) – tooth enamel	Done	Str. 12–6	Str. 12–6 fully analyzed and published	Ecker et al., 2018b
Macrobotanicals	Present	Str. 12–6	Str. 12–5 fully analyzed and published	Berna et al., 2012; Bamford, 2015a, 2015b
Phytoliths	Present	Str. 12–6	Str. 12–7 fully analyzed and published	Rossouw, 2016
Pollen	Very rare to absent	Str. 12–6	Strata 12–7 examined; insufficient to publish	L. Scott, pers. comm., 2017

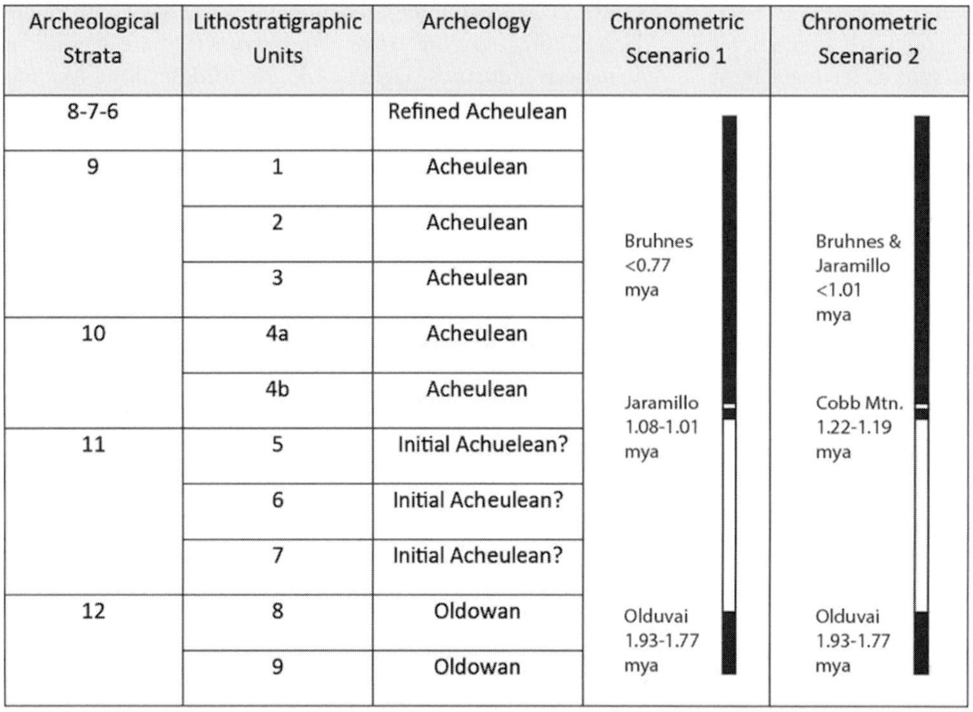

Archeological Strata	Lithostratigraphic Units	Archeology	Chronometric Scenario 1	Chronometric Scenario 2
8-7-6		Refined Acheulean		
9	1	Acheulean	Bruhnes <0.77 mya	Bruhnes & Jaramillo <1.01 mya
	2	Acheulean		
	3	Acheulean		
10	4a	Acheulean		
	4b	Acheulean	Jaramillo 1.08-1.01 mya	Cobb Mtn. 1.22-1.19 mya
11	5	Initial Achuelean?		
	6	Initial Acheulean?		
	7	Initial Acheulean?		
12	8	Oldowan	Olduvai 1.93-1.77 mya	Olduvai 1.93-1.77 mya
	9	Oldowan		

Figure 14.5 Schema showing Beaumont's archeological strata, their equivalent lithostratigraphic units (after Goldberg et al., 2015) and archeological industries, as well as their associated chronometric ages outlining two possible dating scenarios (after Shaar et al., 2021).

Site Formation

Pleistocene localities in southern Africa occur in river terraces (i.e., the Vaal Gravels), spring mounds (i.e., Florisbad), and karst infill (i.e., sites in the Cradle of Humankind). Karst occurs along the margins of the subcontinent as caves and rockshelters (Marker and Gamble, 1987). Wonderwerk Cave has a wide entrance that opens onto a gently sloping talus, and so is actually a continuum of the landscape outside. Wonderwerk was a site of primary hominin occupation, rather than hosting secondarily deposited materials deriving from outside of the cave. Mapping of the interior of Wonderwerk Cave and the surrounding landscape (Figure 14.2; Rüther et al., 2009) indicates that the cave extends through the center of the hill and the current opening admitted the hominins, animals, and sediment.

Wonderwerk Cave is a phreatic tube that extends *ca.* 140 m into the eastern flank of the Kuruman Hills, formed in dolomites of the Late Archean–Early Proterozoic Ghaap Group, immediately below the contact with the overlying Banded Iron Formation (Eriksson et al., 1993). Matmon et al. (2012) suggested that the cavity opened only in the mid- to late Pliocene. Sediments underlying basal archaeological layer, Str. 12, are interpreted as phreatic sediments predating cave opening. The source of sediments is primarily derived from the Kalahari, which may have been brought in by wind transport and biotic agents. Overall, the rate of sedimentation within the cave was remarkably slow, with an estimated accumulation of *ca.* 1–1.3 mm/kyr.

Beaumont's excavations provide a series of discontinuous windows into the sedimentary sequence throughout the cave. Our detailed sedimentological analysis has been limited to Excavations 1 and 2. In Excavation 1 the sediments form a clearly stratified sequence and levels can be traced across the entire excavation area (Chazan et al., 2017) and the extent of the cave, as proposed previously (Beaumont and Vogel, 2006). Excavation 1 is located just behind the large stalagmite, approximately 15 m in from the cave entrance (Figure 14.3), and comprises archaeological Strata 12–9, made up of 10 lithostratigraphic units (Figure 14.5, Table 14.1; Chazan et al., 2008; Goldberg et al., 2015). It has not been possible to directly correlate these units with Butzer's (1984a) sediment stratigraphy. Archaeological Strata 8–6, which are ESA, appear only to be represented in the southern profile in Excavation 1 (Shaar et al., 2021).

The ESA sediments are soft, powdery, reddish, bedded silt and sand with localized accumulations of roof spall, and with certain layers highly diagenetically altered. The lowermost archeological deposits (Str. 12, Unit 9) consist of finely bedded to laminated very fine sand deposited by low-energy sheet flow, which is overlain by whitish gray sediments with dark mottles of manganese and greenish stringers of dahllite (carbonate-hydroxylapatite). Unit 9 provides the only evidence in the ESA sequence for water transport of sediment but even in this context there was not adequate energy to transport the fauna and lithic remains found in this unit as secondary deposition from outside the cave. Evidence of abrasion or water-sorting is absent on tools and fossils.

Above Unit 9, the sediments are silts and aeolian sands of varying thickness. The sedimentology of the ESA sequence has granular silty aggregates in all strata above the Oldowan in Str 12. These aggregates suggest a pan close to the cave (Goldberg et al., 2015, Figure 14.6). The Kalahari is the source of the sands, although these were resident in the valleys around the cave for a before being deposited (Matmon et al., 2012). The sedimentary cycles are complex and include periods of low deposition, in which surfaces are identifiable, as well as erosional events, deformation due to saturation by water, and cementation. Although remains of bats occur in small numbers throughout the Wonderwerk Cave sequence (Avery, 2007, 2022), the only deposit that might be guano-related is the dahllite at the top of Unit 9.

Dating and Archaeology

The dating of the ESA sequence is complex and relies on paleomagnetism and cosmogenic burial dating (Chazan et al., 2008, 2012; Matmon et al., 2012; Shaar et al., 2021). There is potential

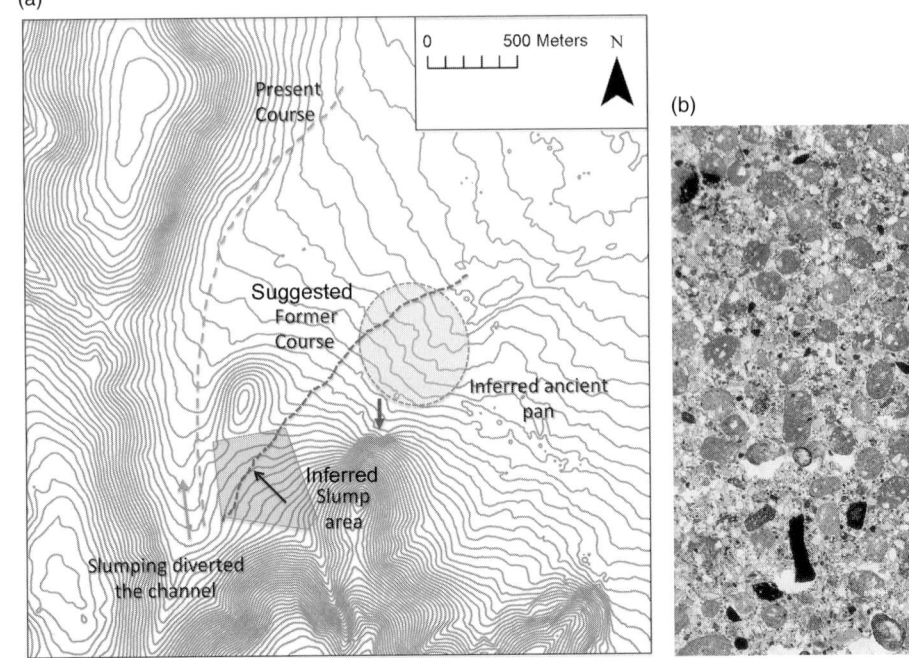
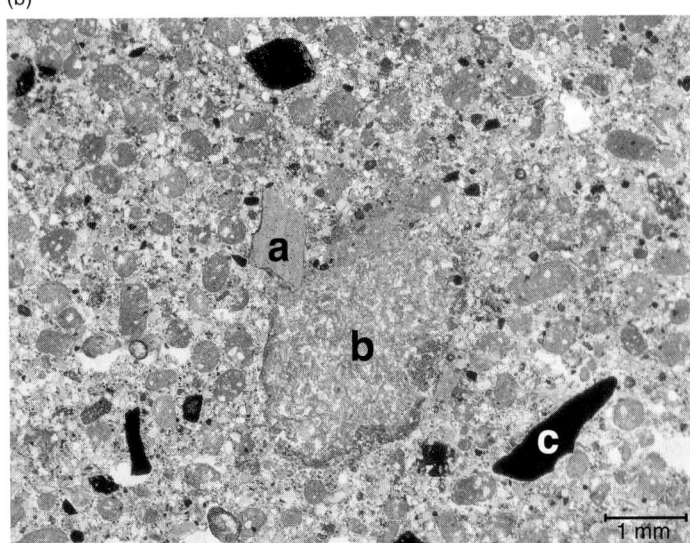

Figure 14.6 (a) Topographic map of area surrounding Wonderwerk. Shown here are the location of the site (blue arrow), the present-day water course, an inferred former course diverted by slump or fan aggradation, and the approximate position of an inferred ephemeral pan that furnished the silty clay aggregates that occur in some strata of the cave.
(b) Photomicrography of sample WW-05-03 from Stratigraphic Unit 4a (Archeological Stratum 10). Visible here are a number of round, silty aggregates containing quartz silt. The other, generally coarser grains are derived from the Banded Iron Formation cropping out above the cave. They consist of angular to subrounded opaque, black, iron-rich clasts and gray pale brown ones composed of silt. Plane-polarized light; scale is 1 mm.

for U-Th and U-Pb speleothem dating (e.g., Beaumont and Vogel, 2006; Pickering, 2015). Optically stimulated luminescence (OSL) has dated the MSA in Excavation 2 (Chazan et al., 2020), but has not yielded meaningful results for the uppermost ESA. The cosmogenic sequence ($n = 14$ samples) suggests that sediment entered the cave over a 100-ky long period before settling (Shaar et al., 2021). Currently, the most securely dated component is the basal deposit of Str. 12, which can be attributed to the Olduvai subchron (1.93–1.77 Ma; Figure 14.5). This age finds further support in the cultural record, with a small-tool industry attributed to the Oldowan at the base of the sequence (Str. 12) as well as faunal biochronology (Chazan et al., 2012). The onset of the Acheulean in Str. 11 is dated to ~1.77–1.22 Ma and is associated with a reversal that postdates the Olduvai event.

Recent high-density resampling in Excavation 1 of the paleomagnetic sequence revealed a previously undetected brief normal event near the top of Str. 11. This may relate to the Cobb Mountain normal geomagnetic polarity event or the Jaramillo Subchron; therefore, the age of the overlying upper part of Strata 10 through 6 remains unclear. All paleomagnetic samples from these levels are normal, thus representing either the Jaramillo and the Bruhnes Subchrons with the intervening reversal missing due to erosion or lack of sedimentation. Alternately, these layers could all fall within the Bruhnes, thus postdating 0.77 Ma (Figure 14.5). Strata 10 through 6 are associated with a series of Acheulean industries of increasing refinement (Chazan, 2015a, 2015b; Chazan et al., 2008, 2012), but lack chronological markers. The TT-OSL date for the onset of the early MSA in Excavation 2 of 238 ± 13 kyr provides an absolute minimum age for the end of the ESA. However, dated Fauresmith localities in the Northern Cape, including Bestwood 1, Kathu Pan 1, and Canteen Kopje, suggest that the end of the ESA is probably much earlier (Chazan et al., 2013; Lukich et al., 2019; Richard et al., 2022).

Pleistocene Paleoclimate

Wonderwerk Cave preserves a paleoclimate record over almost 2 million years, and Table 14.1 presents the spectrum of paleoenvironmental proxies currently used, including macrofauna (both taxonomy and isotope analysis), micromammals, macrobotanicals, grass phytoliths, and ostrich eggshell (isotope analysis and biometry). Micromorphology of the sedimentary sequence and related geological research at Kathu Pan and the Mamatwan mine (Matmon et al., 2015; Lukich et al., 2020), both located to the west of the Kuruman hills, provides a broader perspective on hydrological changes through the Pleistocene. Speleothem and pollen data are currently limited to the Holocene deposits.

Macrofauna

H.B. Cooke first identified the fauna from the guano diggers' pit, which were found with MSA and LSA lithics (Malan and Cooke, 1941). Cooke reported extinct species [*Equus quagga* (today referred to as *E. quagga quagga*), *E. capensis* (*E. kuhni* and *E. cawoodi* = synonymous with *E. capensis*), a large alcelaphine *Peloroceras helmei* (synonymous with *Megalotragus priscus*)] as well as extant ones [*Hystrix africaeaustralis*, *E. burchellii* (now *E. quagga burchellii*), *Syncerus caffer*, *Connochaetes* sp. (subsequently identified by Cooke, 1963 as *C. taurinus*), *Damaliscus* cf. *pygargus*, *Alcelaphus buselaphus caama*, *Antidorcas marsupialis*, *Hippotragus* sp. cf. *H. niger* (confirmed by Cooke, 1963 as *H. equinus*), *Taurotragus oryx*, *Phacochoerus* cf. *aethiopicus* (confirmed by Cooke, 1963) and *Ceratotherium simum*]. Cooke (1963) listed several additional species: *Papio ursinus*, *Mellivora capensis*, cf. *Hyaena brunnea*, *Equus plicatus*, *Diceros bicornis*, *Phacochoerus africanus*, *Tragelaphus angasi*, "*Homoioceras*" *bainii* (= *Syncerus antiquus*), cf. *Sylvicapra grimmia*, *Kobus ellipsiprymnus*, *Oryx gazella*, *Alcelaphus helmei* (which is equivalent to the previously identified *Peloroceras helmei*, both currently included in *Megalotragus priscus*), and *Raphicerus campestris*.

The guano pit fossils were assigned to the Middle and Upper Pleistocene, and so equivalent or earlier than the MSA. This was based on the presence of extinct taxa – a large buffalo ("*Homoioceras*" *bainii*), a large alcelaphine (*Alcelaphus helmei*) and a large zebra (*E. capensis*) that were subsequently assigned by Klein (1988) to *Pelorovis antiquus* (currently *Syncerus antiquus*), *Megalotragus priscus*, and *E. capensis*, respectively. Malan reported finding only one unidentified large bovid tooth in the *in situ* Fauresmith or earlier layers (Malan and Wells, 1943).

Malan and Wells (1943) noted the presence of an "ibex horn" in the guano diggers' collection. This horn and a few other horn fragments, which still retain a keratinous sheath, were subsequently identified as the extinct alcelaphine, *Damaliscus niro* (Thackeray and Brink, 2004), and likely dating to the Middle Pleistocene, intermediate between Florisbad (ca. 400,000–100,000 years BP) and Cornelia-Uitzoek (ca. 1 Ma years BP; Brink et al., 2012; Chapter 12).

The macrofauna from the LSA strata excavated in Excavation 1 by the Thackerays and Beaumont were published by J.F. Thackeray (1983, 2015), while a small sample of MSA and a possible Acheulean faunal assemblage excavated in 1978 by Beaumont was published by Klein (1988: Table 14.1). Eight species were identified: Leporidae, *Pedetes capensis*, *Hystrix africaeaustralis*, *Procavia capensis*, *Canis mesomelas*, Viverridae, *Equus* cf. *burchellii*, and ?*Connochaetes gnou*. Klein noted a complete overlap in the spectrum of species represented in both MSA and Acheulean layers, and suggested that they represent reworked deposits. A similar doubt was expressed by Beaumont in his 1990 report where he only tentatively identified the ESA collection studied by Klein as Acheulean.

Since 2006, we have concentrated on the fauna from the Beaumont excavations in Excavation 1, in ESA Strata 7 through 11 and Oldowan Str. 12. This material has been supplemented by a limited 2007 excavation in Str. 12. Taphonomic analyses are ongoing and extensive carnivore damage (tooth puncture holes, pits, and gnawed bone edges) and rodent (especially porcupine) gnawing are evident with extreme breakage and fragmentation (Figure 14.7), which has been exacerbated by burning, especially in Strata 12, 11, and 10. Most remains are partial bones/teeth and fragments. For example, in Str. 11, the 253 bones identified to skeletal element had an average bone length of 23.4 mm, SD 13.4 and breadth 12.7 mm, SD 7.5; and in Str. 12, in a sample of

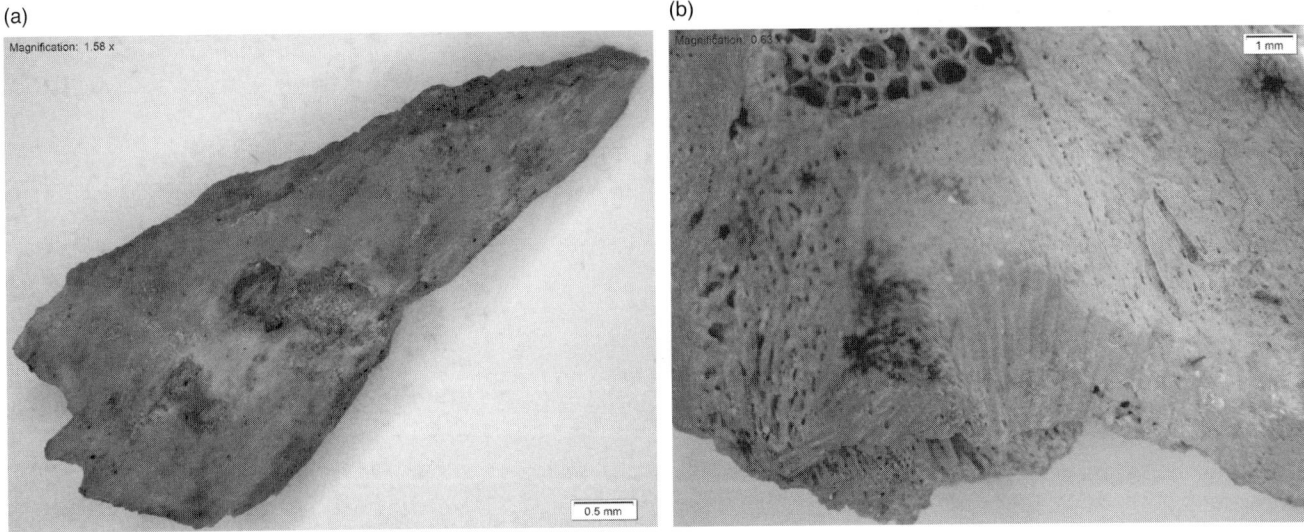

Figure 14.7 Photographs of taphonomic specimens from Wonderwerk Cave. (a) Mammalian bone fragment with carnivore puncture marks (specimen WW1382). (b) Mammalian bone fragment showing porcupine gnawing (specimen WW413).

345 identified bones, mean bone length was 14.5 mm, SD 7.6 and breadth 7.9 mm, SD 4.2 (Brink et al., 2016). These taphonomic issues have clearly limited the identification of remains to lower taxonomic levels with most placed in size-classes.

The identifiable macrofaunal assemblage from Str. 12 and 11, totals just 490 mammalian remains. A detailed species list is currently available only for Strata 12 and 11 (Table 14.2; Brink et al., 2016), complemented by a preliminary list of ungulates based primarily on dental remains from Strata 7 through 12 (Table 14.3). Strata 12 and 11 show similar taxonomic diversity (Brink et al., 2015b, 2016). Medium-sized bovids and equids dominate, but with few carnivores, which is surprising given the extensive carnivore bone damage and cave setting. Hyracoidea are also common, represented by two species (the smaller *Procavia antiqua* and the larger *P. transvalensis*) and two genera of Lagomorpha (*Lepus* and *Pronolagus*). In addition, there are two species of large rodents – *Pedetes* and *Hystrix* (Table 14.3). The Strata 11 and 12 faunal assemblages have a mid-Makapanian (Land Mammal Age; LMA) character due to the archaic faunal components (e.g., an unnamed large extinct caprine resembling *Makapania broomi* and *Procavia transvaalensis*), which is corroborated by the radiometric ages.

The ESA strata ungulate assemblage shows a substantial proportion of equids, including a member of the Hipparionini in Str. 12, and *E. quagga quagga* in Strata 10 and 7 (Table 14.3). *E. capensis* might also be represented, but the material is fragmentary. Apart from a single rhino tooth in Str. 8, megafauna are absent throughout the ESA sequence (although identified as present at the cave by Cooke – see above), while medium-sized bovids, such as *Damaliscus* and *Tragelaphus*, predominate. Likewise, suids are absent, although previously noted by Cooke. Small-sized bovids (e.g., *Antidorcas, Sylvicapra, Raphicerus*) that are the most common ungulates in subrecent surveys for the region are scarce.

Although data are limited, some general trends are evident. Both Str. 12 and 11 reflect a generally semi-arid grassland–savanna environment, given the prominence of equids and the absence of wetland indicators. In contrast, in Str. 10, there are more browsing species (e.g., *Taurotragus, Tragelaphus*) or mixed feeders (*Pelea, Antidorcas*) than grazers. Mesic conditions in Str. 10 are indicated by the presence of wetland-dwelling *Kobus leche*, a species that to date has not been identified in any other ESA layers. In the overlying Strata 9–7, aside from one browser – the black rhino in Str. 8 – all species are grazers characteristic of a semi-arid plains/grassland–savanna. Equids and medium-sized ungulates continue to predominate in Str. 9 through 7, accompanied by small-sized bovids (*Antidorcas, Redunca*). The Holocene strata show an increase in grazers (Thackeray, 2015), as in the present-day taxa (Table 14.4), suggesting expansion of the grasslands.

To conclude, apart from Str. 10, the ESA faunal data reflect the presence of a typical semi-arid plains/grassland–savanna, a biome currently found to the east of the site. In contrast, Str. 10 reflects more mesic conditions, and closely resembles that documented for other, mainly later Mid-Pleistocene mammalian faunas in the southern African interior (Brink, 2016).

Micromammals

Wonderwerk Cave sediments host thousands of micromammal remains. Two Pleistocene assemblages have been published: (1) from Beaumont's original excavation in 1978 (Sq. P32-33), comprised 2966 individuals representing a minimum of 28 species (Avery, 1995a); and (2) from Beaumont's 1979 excavations, which is abundant, but fragmented (Avery, 2007, 2022; Fernández-Jalvo and Avery, 2015; Marin-Montfort et al., 2022). These factors limited initial identifications to genus level (Avery, 2007, 2022). To date, this series has produced >71,000 individuals belonging to a minimum of 36 genera in at least 5 Orders, and as many as 48 species, but not all are identified (Table 14.4). Micromammals were identified using dental and jaw

Table 14.2 Large vertebrate remains recovered from Wonderwerk Cave, Strata 12 and 11, according to number of identified specimens (NISP). Note, the numbers for Stratum 12 presented here differ slightly from those given in Chazan et al. (2012, table S1). We consider these data to be the most reliable

Order	Family	Tribe	Genus and species	Totals	Str 12 NISP	Str. 11 NISP
Rodentia			Pedetes sp.		6	2
			Hystrix sp.		12	–
				Rodentia total	18	2
Lagomorpha			Lepus sp.		5	–
			Pronoloagus sp.		7	1
			Indet.		5	2
				Lagomorpha total	17	3
Primates	Cercopithecidae		Indet.		1	–
				Primates total	1	–
Carnivora	Hyaenidae		Indet.		–	1
	Canidae		Indet.		2	1
	Indet.		Medium		5	1
			Small		3	–
				Carnivora total	10	3
Hyracoidea			Procavia transvaalensis		9	1
			Procavia antiqua		10	v
			Indet.		22	5
				Hyracoidea total	41	10
Perissodactyla	Equidae	Hipparionini	?Eurygnathohippus sp.		2	–
		Indet.			28	15
				Perissodactyla total	30	15
Artiodactyla	Bovidae	Caprini	Indet.		4	4
		Alcelaphini	Indet.		12	17
		Antilopini	Gazella sp.		–	1
			Indet.		1	5
		Tragelaphini	Indet.		–	1
		Indet.	Large		–	7
			Large–medium		46	67
			Small–medium		79	75
			Small		14	9
				Artiodactyla total	156	185
				Grand total	272	218

morphology and Rodentia is by far the best-represented order, while other taxa such as Chrysochloridae (golden moles) and Chiroptera (bats) were poorly represented (Avery, 2007). The low frequency of bats is consistent with the absence of guano deposits, apart from the top of Str. 12.

Avery's 1995 stratigraphy differs slightly from Beaumont's stratigraphy of a shorter chrono-stratigraphic framework comprising only 12 strata, which is the system presently in use for Excavation 1.

For paleoenvironmental reconstructions, each micromammal genus was characterized by: (1) the three types of vegetation forms they inhabit (grass, scrub, trees/bushes); (2) the two types of habitats in which this vegetation form occurs (closed or open); (3) landscape topography (flats, hillside, waterside);

Table 14.3 Preliminary identifications of ungulates found in ESA strata at Wonderwerk Cave compared to their subrecent occurrence

Species	Kuruman Hills area today* %	N teeth in Wonderwerk Cave					
		Str. 7	Str. 8	Str. 9	Str. 10	Str. 11	Str. 12
Diceros bicornis	–	–	1	–	–	–	–
Hipparionini indet.	–	–	–	–	–	–	2
Equus quagga quagga	–	1	–	–	1	–	–
Equus sp.	–	3	1	3	8	15	28
Caprinae, extinct	–	–	–	–	–	4	4
Hartebeest, *Alcelaphus buselaphus*	8.3	–	–	–	–	–	–
Blesbok, *Damaliscus pygargus*	1.9	–	–	–	–	1	1
Alcelaphus/Damaliscus	–	3	–	–	–	–	–
Alcelaphini indet.	–	5	3	2	2	17	12
Gazella sp.	–	–	–	–	–	1	–
Bond's springbok, *Antidorcas bondi*	–	1	–	–	–	–	–
Springbok, *Antidorcas marsupialis*	36.1	1	–	–	1	–	–
Antilopini indet.	–	1	–	–	–	5	1
Reedbuck, *Redunca arundinum*	0.9	–	–	–	1	–	–
Gray rhebok, *Pelea capreolus*	5.6	–	–	–	1	–	–
Gemsbok, *Oryx gazella*	5.7	–	–	–	–	–	–
Kobus leche	–	–	–	–	2	–	–
Duiker, *Sylvicapra grimmia*	99.1	–	–	–	–	–	–
Steenbok, *Raphicerus campestris*	100	–	–	–	–	–	–
Klipspringer, *Oreotragus oreotragus*	2.8	–	–	–	–	–	–
Kudu, *Tragelaphus strepsiceros*	0.9	–	–	1	3	–	–
Eland, *Taurotragus oryx*	2.8	–	–	–	2	–	–
Tragelaphini	–	1	1	–	1	1	–
Total N teeth		16	6	6	22	44	48

Counts include some post-cranial material but mainly teeth.
* Data from Humphreys and Thackeray (1983:Table 1).

and (4) dryness of vegetation (xeric versus mesic) (Avery, 1995a). Avery's 1995 analysis confirms that all taxa identified still occur regionally. When the ESA micromammals data were analyzed to model the relationship between the ecological variables using multiple linear regressions and t-tests (Hammer et al., 2001), three of the ecological variables were found to be negatively correlated – "closed," "trees," and "mesic" – while the "open" variable was significant and positively correlated, indicating that the majority of micromammals represented in the ESA were open-habitat species. This is supported by Avery's finding that all ESA strata were mainly dominated by micromammals that primarily inhabit grassy, flat topography (25 percent). The other vegetation forms represented were some scrub, with a relatively high percentage of trees and bush (Avery, 1995a).

The habitats present in the lower ESA occupation (old Str. 16–14 = new upper part of Str. 12 through 11) appear closed and wetter, with subtropical, mesic micromammals consistently represented. In the later ESA layers (*ca.* Str. 9 upward), increasing desiccation led to open vegetation and a drier habitat. The latter resembled an extremely open savanna except along the rivers and near the ranges of hills where bush savanna predominated.

Figure 14.8 presents relative proportions of genera in the two lowest ESA strata (new Str. 11 and 12). The data demonstrate that Str. 12 had a relatively drier, more open environment (with high frequencies of Gerbillinae and Chrysochloridae) trending to moister, cooler conditions, with higher frequencies of Soricidae in Str. 11. Based on Avery (1995a), the uppermost ESA levels (such as Str. 7 and 6) are more xeric with the most open vegetation.

Microfaunal taphonomic analysis of Str. 11 and 12 shows signs of digestion and, therefore, predation. The agent has been identified as the barn owl (*Tyto alba*) (Marin-Montfort et al., 2022). This is due to the very particular taphonomic traits, including very low percentage of digestion, low grades of damage, and high skeletal survival (Andrews, 1990). Other owls or

Table 14.4. Micromammals identified (Avery 1995a, 2007, 2022) in Pleistocene levels at Wonderwerk Cave (WW). Taxa present in all strata unless specified. All taxa currently in the Northern Cape Province (NC), except where stated (after Avery and Avery, 2011).

Order	Family: Sub-family	Common Name	% Total Sample	Stratum	Genus & Species	NC Genus & Species	Notes
Afrosoricida	Chrysochloridae	Golden Moles (*Chlorotalpa, Chrysochhloris*)	0.14				
					Chlorotalpa sp.	*Chlorotalpa* sp.	
					Chrysospalax villosus (Rough-Haired Golden Mole)	*Chrysospalax villosus*	not currently found in NC
Macroscelidea	Macroscelididae	Elephant shrews (*Elephantulus, Macroscelides*)	10.44				
					Elephantulus myurus (Eastern Rock Elephant Shrew)	*Elephantulus myurus*	
					Elephantulus pilicaudus (Karoo Rock Elephant Shrew)		new species (Smit et al. 2008) possibly represented
					Elephantulus rupestris (Western Rock Elephant Shrew)		possibly represented
					Macroscelides proboscideus (Short-eared Elephant Shrew)	*Macroscelides proboscideus*	
Soricomorpha	Soricidae: Crocidurinae	Shrews (*Crocidura, Suncus*)	7.86				
					Crocidura cyanea (Reddish-Gray Musk Shrew)	*Crocidura cyanea*	
					Crocidura flavescens (Greater Red Musk Shrew)	*Crocidura flavescens*	
					Crocidura fuscomurina (Bicolored Musk Shrew)	*Crocidura fuscomurina*	
					Crocidura hirta (Lesser Red Musk Shrew)	*Crocidura hirta*	
					Suncus varilla (Lesser Dwarf Shrew)	*Suncus varilla*	
Soricomorpha	Soricidae: Myosoricinae	Mouse & Forest Shrews	1.29				
					Myosorex varius (Forest Shrew)	*Myosorex varius*	
		Shrews Indet.	7.50				
Rodentia	Gliridae: Graphiurinae	Dormice (*Graphiurus*)	0.04		*Graphiurus microtis* (Large Savanna African Dormouse)	*Graphiurus microtis*	
Rodentia	Nesomyidae: Cricetomyinae	Pouched Mouse (*Saccostomus*)	2.32		*Saccostomus campestris* (Southern African Pouched Mouse)	*Saccostomus campestris*	
	Nesomyidae: Dendromurinae	Climbing Mice (*Dendromus*)	3.47		*Dendromus melanotis* (Gray African Climbing Mouse)	*Dendromus melanotis*	
	Nesomyidae: Dendromurinae	Large-eared Mice (*Malacothrix*)	0.99		*Malacothrix typica* Large-eared African Desert Mouse	*Malacothrix typica*	
	Nesomyidae: Dendromurinae	Fat Mice (*Steatomys*)	2.89		*Steatomys krebsii* (Kreb's African Fat Mouse)	*Steatomys krebsii*	

Order	Family: Sub-family	Common Name	% Total Sample	Stratum	Genus & Species	NC Genus & Species	Notes
	Nesomyidae: Mystromyinae	White-tailed Rats (*Mystromys*)	9.52		*Mystromys albicaudatus* (African White-tailed Rat)	*Mystromys albicaudatus*	
	Nesomyidae: Petromyscinae	Pygmy Rock Mice (*Petromyscus*)	0.95		*Petromyscus collinus* (Pygmy Rock Mouse)	*Petromyscus collinus*	
Rodentia	Muridae: Deomyinae					*Acomys* sp. (Spiny mouse)	not certainly present
	Muridae: Gerbillinae	Short-tailed Gerbil (*Desmodillus*)	0.58		*Desmodillus auricularis* (Cape Short-tailed Gerbil)	*Desmodillus auricularis*	
	Muridae: Gerbillinae	Gerbils (*Gerbilliscus*)	12.32				
					Gerbilliscus brantsii (Highveld Gerbil)	*Gerbilliscus brantsii*	
					Gerbilliscus leucogaster (Bushveld Gerbil)	*Gerbilliscus leucogaster*	
						Gerbilliscus brantsii et/aut leucogaster	previously *Tatera*. probably both *brantsii* and *lecugaster* represented
	Muridae: Gerbillurus	Hairy-footed Gerbils (*Gerbillurus*)	9.68				
					Gerbillurus paeba (Paeba Hairy-footed Gerbil)	*Gerbillurus paeba*	
						Gerbillurus vallinus (Brush-tailed Hairy-footed Gerbil)	probably represented
	Muridae: Murinae					*Aethomys ineptus* (Tete Veld Rat)	previously *Aethomys chrysophilus*
						Aethomys sp.	previously included *Micaelamys* spp.
Rodentia	Muridae: Murinae	Dasymys (*Dasymys*)	0.04	7,8,9,10,11	*Dasymys incomtus s.l.* (Common Dasymys)	*Dasymys incomtus s.l.*	either *D. incomtus* or *D. capensis* as currently understood (Mullin et al. 2005)
	Muridae: Murinae	Lemniscomys (*Lemniscomys*)	0.19	6,7,9,10,11,12	*Lemniscomys rosalia* (Single-Striped Lemniscomys)	*Lemniscomys rosalia*	
	Muridae: Murinae	Mastomys (*Mastomys*)	4.42				
					Mastomys coucha Southern (African Mastomys)	*Mastomys coucha*	previously *M. natalensis*
						Mastomys coucha et/aut natalensis	
		Micaelamys (*Micaelamys*)	6.89		*Micaelamys namaquensis* Namaqua Micaelamys	*Micaelamys namaquensis*	previously *Aethomys namaquensis*
		Pygmy Mice (*Mus*)	0.42		*Mus indutus* (desert pygmy mouse)	*Mus indutus*	
					Mus minutoides (African pygmy mouse)	*Mus minutoides*	
		Four-striped Grass Rat (*Rhabdomys*)	0.64		*Rhabdomys pumilio* (Xeric Four-striped Grass Rat)	*Rhabdomys pumilio*	more likely that *R. pumilio* is represented at WWK not the mesic form *R. dilectus*

Table 14.4 (cont.)

Order	Family: Sub-family	Common Name	% Total Sample	Stratum	Genus & Species	NC Genus & Species	Notes
		Thallomys (*Thallomys*)	0.04	10,12	*Thallomys nigricauda* (Black-tailed Thallomys)	*Thallomys nigricauda*	
		Zelotomys (*Zelotomys*)	1.46		*Zelotomys woosnami* (Woosnam's Zelotomys)	*Zelotomys woosnami*	
	Muridae: Otomyinae	Karoo and Vlei Rats	12.53			indet.	previously *Myotomys* was a subgenus of *Otomys*
						Myotomys sloggetti (Rock Karroo Rat)	
						Myotomys unisulcatus (Bush Karroo Rat)	
					Otomys angoniensis (Angoni Vlei Rat)	*Otomys angoniensis*	
					Otomys irroratus (Southern African Vlei Rat)	*Otomys irroratus*	
Rodentia	Bathyergidae	Mole-rats (*Cryptomys, Georychus*)	2.81				
		Southern African Mole-rat			*Cryptomys hottentotus*	*Cryptomys hottentotus*	
		Cape Mole-rat			*Georychus capensis*?	*Georychus capensis*	not certainly present
Chiroptera	Rhinolophidae	Horseshoe bats (*Rhinolophus*)	0.46				
					Rhinolophus capensis (Cape Horseshoe Bat)	*Rhinolophus capensis*	
					Rhinolophus clivosus (Geoffroy's Horseshoe Bat)	*Rhinolophus clivosus*	
						Rhinolophus darlingi (Darling's Horseshoe Bat)	
						Rhinolophus denti (Dent's Horseshoe Bat)	
Chiroptera	Nycteridae	Slit-faced Bats (*Nycteris*)	0.003	9		*Nycteris thebaica* (Egyptian Slit-faced Bat)	
Chiroptera	Molossidae	Free-tailed Bats (*Tadarida*)	0.02	6,7,10,12	*Tadarida aegyptiaca* (Egyptian Free-tailed Bat)	*Tadarida aegyptiaca*	
						Sauromys petrophilus (Roberts's Flat-headed Bat)	
Chiroptera	Vespertilionidae: Vespertilioninae	Serotines (*Eptesicus*)	0.01	6,10,12	*Eptesicus hottentotus* (Long-tailed Serotine)	*Eptesicus hottentotus*	
		Myotis? (*Myotis*)	0.001	7			
		Serotines, Pipistrelles (*Neoromicia*)	0.01	6,7,9,10	*Neoromicia capensis* (Cape Serotine)	*Neoromicia capensis*	previously *Eptesicus capensis*
Chiroptera	Cistugidae				*Cistugo seabrae* (Angolan Wing-gland Bat)	*Cistugo seabrae*	
Chiroptera	Miniopterinae	Natal Long-fingered Bat (*Miniopterus*)	0.05		*Miniopterus natalensis*	*Miniopterus natalensis*	previously *M. schreibersii*
		Bats indet.	0.01	8,9,10,11,12			

mammalian carnivores may produce taphonomic traits that overlap, but this is not the case with *T. alba* (Fernández-Jalvo and Andrews, 2016). Moreover, this species may reside in the same locality for long periods. They may nest relatively close together and develop communal roosting in well-suited areas, thereby accumulating many small mammals as suggested for Excavation 1 due to the spatial distribution of the micromammals (Birkenfeld et al., 2015; Fernández-Jalvo and Avery, 2015). Barn owls give an accurate representation of prey species for the

habitats within which they hunt, i.e., more open environments. There is, therefore, a possible bias toward a higher abundance of open-habitat species. This does not preclude the possibility that the owls nested and/or roosted in more closed environments, where other prey species are found that were less frequently hunted.

No signs of water abrasion were observed on the Str. 12 and 11 fossils (Fernández-Jalvo and Andrews, 2003), so water transport of these assemblages is discounted. Ongoing research focused on signs of burning, including calcined bones (high temperatures) and two separate focal areas containing burnt micromammal remains, do not fit the scenario of wildfires (Fernández-Jalvo et al., 2018).

Macrobotanicals

Charcoal fragments were studied microscopically and for identification used the features of the tissues and cells, compared with reference collections at the University of the Witwatersrand, complemented by InsideWood, a software identification program (Bamford, 2015a, 2015b). Samples of calcified macrobotanical remains were disaggregated, but the resulting fragments were too small to contain sufficient diagnostic features for identification (Table 14.5 indicates identified species).

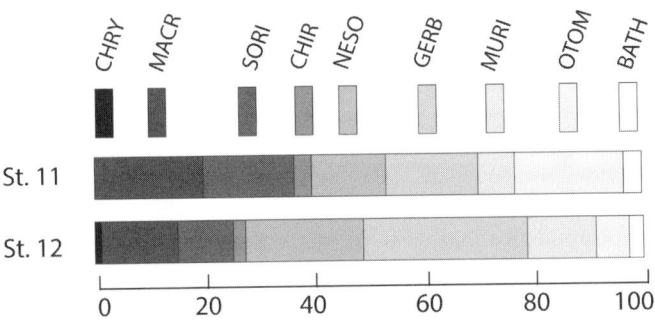

Figure 14.8 Proportional representation based on MNI counts of micromammal Orders in samples from Wonderwerk Cave Excavation 1, Strata 12 and 11. Key: CHRY, Chrysochloridae; MACR, Macroscelididae; SORI, Soricidae; CHIR, Chiroptera; NESO, Nesomyidae; GLIR, Gliridae; GERB, Gerbillinae; MURI, Murinae; OTOM, Otomyinae; BATH, Bathyergidae.

Table 14.5 Macrobotanical remains from the ESA strata at Wonderwerk Cave

Archeological stratum	Macrobotanicals (1)			Plant material from micromorphology (2)	Phytolith presence (3)
	Size	Quantity	Identification	Identification	
6			No material		Not checked
7	5–10 cm	1	Bean-like seed (Fabaceae)		Not checked
		1	Similar to but longer than *Phoenix reclinata* (Arecaceae)		
		1	*Berchemia*-like seed		
8			Loose calcified grass litter		Not checked
9		–	No material	Plant tissues cf. derived from roots, bird nests, guano, and phytoliths (Lithostratigraphic Unit 3, Sample 11–6)	X
10				Ashed plant remains (Lithostratigraphic Unit 4a, sample 11–7)	X
	0–5 cm	Lots	Calcified grass litter and leaf fragments	Fragments of micritic pseudomorphs of plant tissues (Lithostratigraphic Unit 4a, sample 11–7)	X
	5–10 cm	Lots	Calcified grass litter and leaf fragments	Seed coats (Lithostratigraphic Unit 4a, sample 11–7)	
		2	Sedge culm (possibly *Eleocharis* spp.)		
11	15–20 cm	11	Root casts		X
	25–30 cm	7	Root casts		
12	40–45 cm	1	Piece of very poor charcoal	Siliceous phytoliths (Lithostratigraphic Unit 9, sample 05–09)	X

(1) see also Bamford (2015a)
(2) seen in thin sections described by Berna et al. (2010); Goldberg et al. (2015)
(3) X = present, see this paper

Root casts: Str. 11 contained 18 root casts lacking internal structure. The root casts from the lowest spits (square R28, depth 25–30 cm; 7 pieces) are larger than those from the upper spits (square R29, depth 15–20 cm; 11 pieces); lower spits maximum size 11 × 70 mm (diameter × length) and minimum size 4 × 15 mm; upper level has a maximum size of 2.5 × 23 mm, and a minimum size of 1 × 5 mm. The difference in root cast size may indicate different vegetation being brought into the cave, i.e., larger root casts from larger plants. It could, however, also be a taphonomic effect, where the larger root casts were formed when there were more dissolved minerals in the embedding medium and/or better conditions for precipitation.

Calcified plant remains: These were found in Str. 11, 10, and 8 and comprised calcified roots and plant litter comprising dicot twigs, leaves, grass and sedge culms, all less than 2 mm in diameter and 5 mm in length. The larger calcified fragments are dicotyledonous and monocotyledonous leaf fragments, pieces of narrow diameter dicot stems, grass and sedge culms (Table 14.4). The sedge culms have a diameter of 0.7 mm with a very thin epidermis surrounding an aerenchymatous cortex. Unfortunately, most of the fragments are too small to be diagnostic; for example, to identify leaves one needs at least half the leaf to indicate the leaf shape (apex, base, width) and primary, secondary, and tertiary venation. To identify monocot culms, the type and distribution of the vascular bundles, pith, and epidermal features are required, none of which are preserved.

Seeds: Three probably calcified, or silicified, seeds were recovered from Str. 7. The first seed resembles *Phoenix reclinata* (Arecaceae) but is slightly longer; the second resembles a bean (Fabaceae), but further identification is not possible; the third seed (12 × 8 × 3 mm) is oval in outline, flattened, and has a rough texture.

Charcoal: In Str. 10, there was evidence for low-temperature fire (wood ash, burnt sediment, burnt bone, pot-lid fractures on stone: Berna et al., 2012), implying that the calcified plant remains recovered in this layer served as light plant fuel. In Str. 12 one piece of poorly preserved, unidentifiable charcoal was found.

Grass Phytoliths

Phytoliths were extracted from 16 sediment samples that were taken at 10–15 cm intervals from ESA Str. 12 through 9 (Rossouw, 2016). The same samples did not yield any pollen, suggesting unfavorable preservation. Phytolith counts were made by systematic scanning under a polarizing microscope at 500× magnification following standardized transects. Counts were normalized as percentages of the short-cell sum for each sample, based on the total count of all the morphotypes per slide. Interpretation was made by assigning ecological meaning to phytoliths by comparing a range of ecological preferences in modern grasses with the phytoliths that they produce, rather than just using phytoliths to discriminate between grass subfamilies, tribes, or genera.

A model of proportional representation was created based on the relative occurrence and rate of production of 11 grass silica short-cell phytolith morphotypes produced in 309 modern grass species (National Museum Bloemfontein Phytolith Database). Two groupings were identified: (1) saddle-shaped and variant 1 bilobate morphotypes correlate with the exclusively to predominantly C_4 subfamilies and with warm, locally mesic to dry and arid summer rainfall conditions (<500 mm per annum) characteristic of Nama-Karoo or Savanna grass communities; (2) trapeziform-shaped morphotypes (including trapezoid, rondel, oblong, and reniform-shaped morphotypes, collectively called pooid morphotypes) are significantly correlated with C_3 subfamilies that are affiliated with cooler, winter rainfall growing conditions associated with Succulent Karoo and Fynbos grass communities (see note 1 in Henderson et al., 2006; supplementary data in Chazan et al., 2012; Rossouw, 2016).

Grass phytoliths were generally well-represented throughout the ESA sequence. The relative frequencies of the different phytolith types are shown in Figure 14.9a. Ordination through correspondence analysis (CA) was performed to aid interpretation, which is presented in Figure 14.9b. Based on comparison with modern morphotype ecology, the phytolith composition of the lower-most part of Str. 12 (Lithostratigraphic Unit 9) correlates with a warm Savanna to Nama-Karoo C_4 grassland, while the top of Str. 12 (Lithostratigraphic Unit 8) shows a slight shift toward cooler growing conditions analogous to Succulent Karoo communities characterized by C_3 subfamilies. This cooling trend becomes more pronounced in overlying Str. 11. Internal fluctuations, from cooler to warmer conditions, are observed in Str. 10, with a general shift back to a warm Savanna in Str. 9.

Stable Light Isotope Analysis

Stable light isotope analysis has been widely applied in southern Africa for reconstructing Quaternary paleo-environments (e.g., Lee-Thorp and Talma, 2000; Loftus et al., 2016). Isotope studies have been undertaken for carbon ($\delta^{13}C$) and nitrogen ($\delta^{15}N$) stable isotope analysis of Holocene equid tooth dentine (Thackeray and Lee-Thorp, 1992). Subsequently, $\delta^{18}O$ and $\delta^{13}C$ of Holocene ostrich eggshell (OES) fragments with $\delta^{18}O$ values of ostrich eggshell highly correlated with relative humidity and mean annual precipitation (Lee-Thorp and Ecker, 2015). However, the $\delta^{13}C$ values obtained for ostrich eggshell do not necessarily represent the full spectrum of vegetation available, because ostriches are opportunistic feeders. Consequently, the $\delta^{13}C$ isotopic composition of eggshell reflects only those plants which ostriches consumed. Today, most grasses in the Savanna Biome, in which Wonderwerk Cave lies, use the C_4 photosynthetic pathway (Vogel et al., 1978), while the tree, shrub, and herbaceous cover use the C_3 photosynthetic pathway. Crassulacean Acid Metabolism (CAM) pathway plants are generally rare in this region.

For the ESA strata at the cave, this method was applied to the analysis of 88 OES fragments spanning Str. 12 through 6 in Excavation 1 (Ecker et al., 2015a). The $\delta^{18}O$ and $\delta^{13}C$ values obtained on OES from the ESA sequence at Wonderwerk Cave were used to track relative humidity and local ecology throughout the sequence (Figure 14.10a). The carbon isotope data show that ostrich diet throughout the sequence was primarily

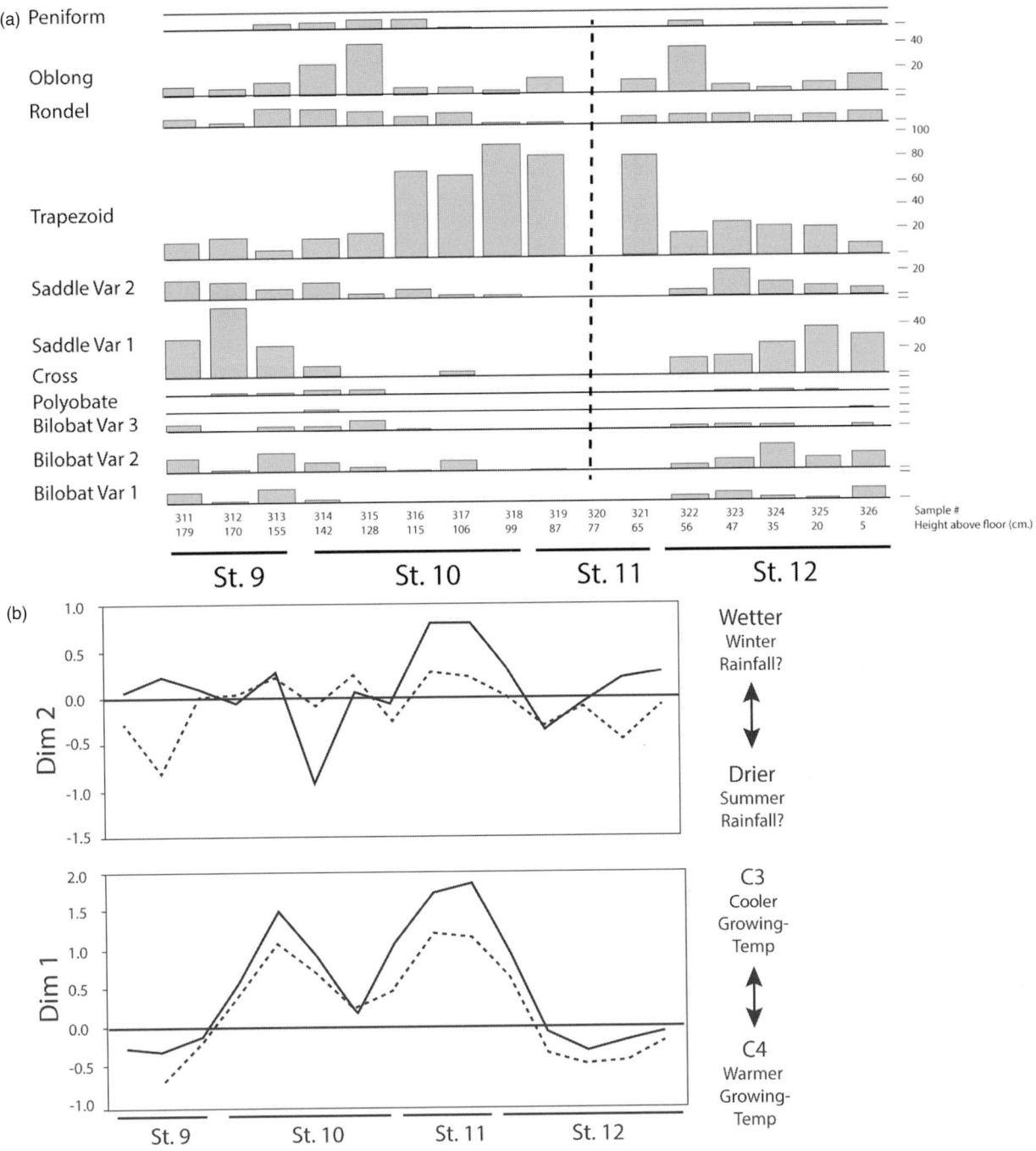

Figure 14.9 (a) Percentage diagram of grass silica short-cell phytolith retrieved from Str. 12 through 9. Counts were normalized as percentages of the short-cell sum for each sample, based on the total count of all the morphotypes per slide. (b) Interpretation of phytolith data based on ordination.

C_3 plants, with some C_4 (or possibly CAM) plants. There is a marked shift in $\delta^{13}C$ values between Strata 12–11 and Str. 10, the latter having the widest distribution of carbon isotope values ranging from a predominantly C_3 to a predominantly C_4 diet. The extreme C_4 values may represent short spells within the long-time span covered by Str. 10.

Overall, $\delta^{18}O$ values for the early/mid-Pleistocene sequence denote a generally arid setting for the cave. The Oldowan level Str. 12 shows generally high, ^{18}O-enriched values, indicating xeric conditions. Low values for the overlying Str. 11 indicate moister conditions, though sample size for this stratum is low. Statistical tests (Mann–Whitney U-tests) indicate that Str. 10 differed from all other ESA strata, with a cluster of the lowest $\delta^{18}O$ values in the series, indicating moister conditions. From Str. 9 upwards, mean $\delta^{18}O$ values are similar and indicative of drier conditions, or at least more frequent dry spells.

The biometry of OES fragments from the same ESA strata at the cave are useful indicators of paleoenvironmental conditions, due to relationships between nesting environment (temperature and humidity) and eggshell pore density and thickness (Ecker et al., 2015a). Results obtained corroborated those for light stable isotopes, with eggshell thickness increasing over

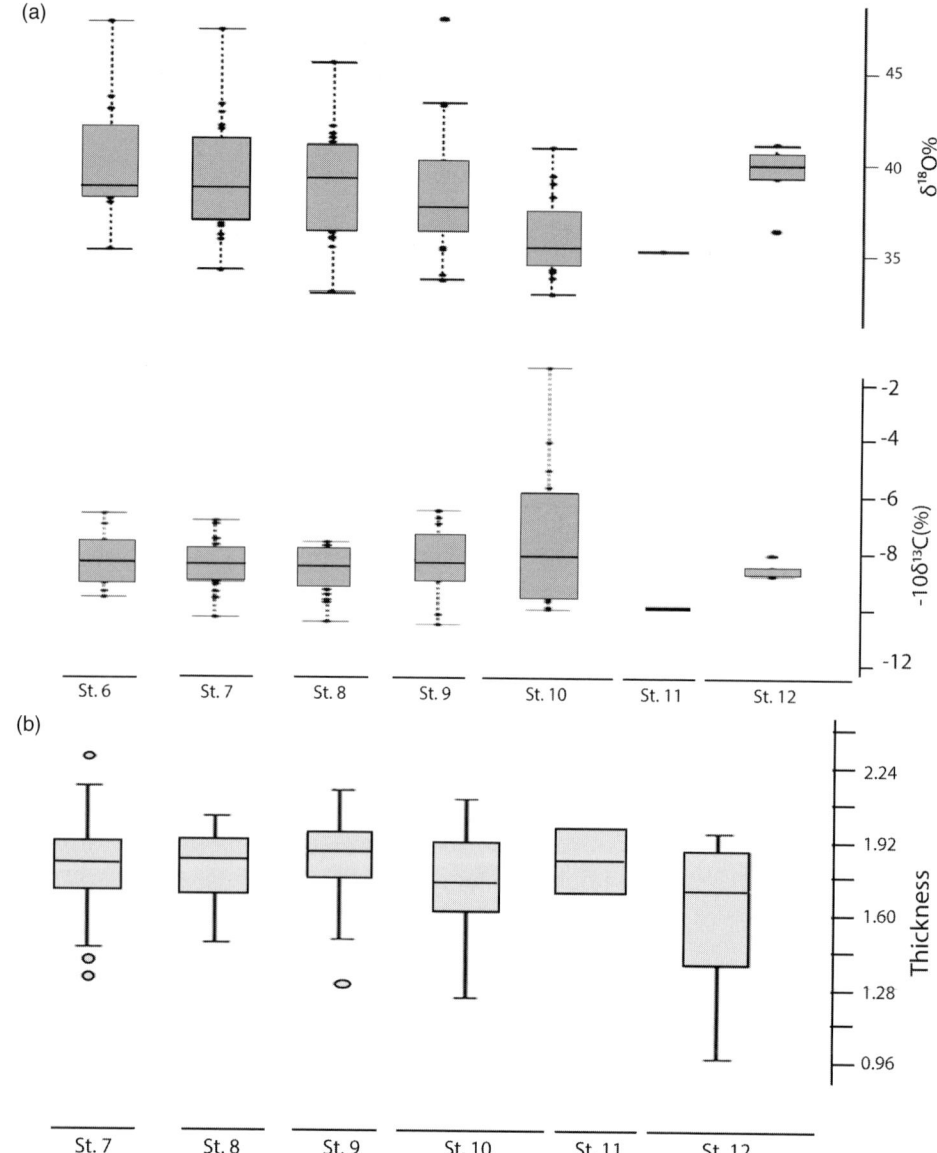

Figure 14.10 Boxplots showing the distribution of (a) carbon and oxygen isotope data for ostrich eggshell from Wonderwerk Cave Str. 12–6. The $\delta^{13}C$ values are expressed relative to VPDB, while $\delta^{18}O$ values are expressed relative to VSMOW. (b) Box plot showing ostrich eggshell thickness (in mm) for early/mid-Pleistocene strata. Note the shift in the lower size range in samples from Str. 12–10 versus Str. 9–7.

time (Figure 14.10b), associated with an increase in pore density (i.e., the number of pores per mm^2) and pore size (width; Ecker et al., 2015a); specifically, statistically significant differences were found in eggshell thickness and pore density ($P < 0.035$) between Str. 10 and 9. This suggests a shift toward drier/warmer conditions in the later ESA.

Stable light isotopes on ESA and Holocene herbivore teeth (18 species; $n = 438$ specimens) corroborate the OES trends, with both carbon and oxygen isotope results showing significant shifts indicating fluctuations in proportions of C_4 plants and moisture availability (Ecker et al., 2015b, 2018b; Ecker, 2016). Data for the Oldowan Str. 12 at Wonderwerk point to a dry, open savanna with predominantly C_3 vegetation with some C_4 grasses. In the overlying Str. 11 and base of Str. 10, there is a trend towards more mesic conditions. However, marked climatic oscillations are evident at the Mid-Pleistocene transition (Str. 10). Low pCO_2 mean values from the overlying Str. 9 onwards (Hönisch et al., 2009), correlate with a rise in $\delta^{13}C$ values of grazers (Alcelaphini, Equids, and Rodentia), indicating more C_4 plants in their diet. At the same time, oxygen isotopes in OES show increased aridity, suggesting shifts toward ecosystems dominated by C_4 grasses.

Sedimentology and Geology

Recent investigations by Matmon et al. (2015) at the Mamatwan Mine have demonstrated that a shallow water body persisted for at least 450 kyr in the region spanning the period 1.5–1.2 Ma or even earlier, providing further evidence of moister climates. Geochemical analysis of the Mamatwan sediments suggests that the Trans-Tswana drainage system, which transected the Kalahari Basin from north to south, was still active during this period (Vainer et al., 2018).

Reconstruction of Paleoclimatic Conditions

Research on isotopic values and ecology of southern African hominin-bearing sites is predominantly centered on the dolomitic breccias of Gauteng Province (primarily sites in the Cradle of Humankind), or in the Fynbos biome (e.g., Klein, 1983, 1984a, 1984b, 1984c, 1988; Reed, 1997; Sponheimer and Lee-Thorp, 2009; Herries et al., 2010; Reynolds and Kibii, 2011), and have provided general overviews of paleoenvironment and paleoclimatic conditions prevailing in southern African sites for the period 2–1 Ma. However, these sites are located in markedly different biomes far to the south-east or north of this site. Moreover, these deposits represent time-averaged complexes, for which consensus on the chronology of these sites has been elusive (e.g., Reed, 1997; de Ruiter, 2003; Berger et al., 2002; Partridge et al., 2003; Herries et al., 2010; Pickering et al., 2019). As such, they are less suitable as proxies for paleoenvironmental reconstruction of the southern African arid interior.

As outlined above, the Wonderwerk Cave sequence provides a unique archive of early Quaternary environmental information particularly for the arid interior of southern Africa from several different paleoenvironmental proxies of varying resolutions (Table 14.1), partly influenced by differences in sampling methods during excavation and fieldwork. Thus, microfauna and faunal and OES isotopic signatures provide information on general paleoenvironmental and paleoclimatic trends by stratum, which often do not tally precisely with the lithostratigraphic units. In contrast, the phytolith data, which were sampled in concert with the lithostratigraphy, provide fine-grained data. Despite the inherent limitations of the different data sets, it has been possible to reconstruct the ESA paleoenvironmental sequence at the cave, constrained by a robust chronological framework.

Trends indicated within paleoclimatic proxies, from basal strata upwards, are summarized below and in Table 14.6. The base of the sequence, from the base to the upper two thirds of Str. 12, are securely dated by cosmogenic burial dating and paleomagnetism to the Olduvai Subchron, 1.93–1.77 Ma. The macro- and micromammals and isotopic signatures of OES and herbivores point to a semi-arid, warm and open savanna environment with predominantly C_3 vegetation and a small component of C_4 plants. The phytolith results suggest a Nama-Karoo grassland.

From the top of Str. 12 through to the top of the overlying Str. 11, moister and cooler conditions set in with a shift to grasses resembling those in the current Succulent Karoo vegetation cover. The timing of the onset of this shift is obscured in the macro- and micromammalian assemblages and associated isotopic signatures, due to our inability to attribute material within a stratum to a particular phase, i.e., top of Str. 12, and the relatively small sample sizes. This shift falls toward the end of the Olduvai SubChron *ca.* 1.77 Ma through to *ca.* 1.0 Ma, as evidenced by the corrected cosmogenic burial ages and associated reversed paleomagnetic signal that characterizes most, if not all, of Str. 11 (Shaar et al., 2021).

Currently the cave lies in the Savanna Biome, with the Nama Karoo Biome slightly to the south and west, a biome which is characterized by deciduous shrubs and grasses due to the irregular rainfall it experiences. The Succulent Karoo biome presently lies far to the west along the coast and is a harsh environment; extremely dry and hot summers with winter rainfall varying from 20 to 290 mm per year (Figure 14.1a).

Table 14.6 Summary of paleoclimatic data for the different proxies from the ESA levels at Wonderwerk Cave

Lithostratigraphic units	Archaeological strata	Macrofauna	Micromammals	Phytoliths	Isotopes OES	Biometry OES
	6, 7, 8	Semi-arid grassland/savanna	Most xeric and most open	?	Xeric or more frequent dry spells	Xeric
1–3	9		Trending to xeric	Warm savanna to Nama-Karoo grassland	Xeric or more frequent dry spells	Xeric
4	10	Overall more mesic		Fluctuating between warm and cool	Fluctuating between very moist to very dry (very C_3 to very C_4)	Moist
Base of 4	Base of 10		Trending to moist and cool			
5–6	11	Semi-arid grassland/savanna		Cooler, shifts to Succulent Karoo	Moist	?Moist
7						
8	12	Semi-arid grassland/savanna	Dry, open environment			
9				Warm savanna to Nama-Karoo grassland	Xeric C_3, small C_4 component	

The main difference between the Succulent Karoo biome and the Nama Karoo biome is that the former receives its rain from cyclonic rainfall in winter, while the Nama Karoo obtains its rain from summer thunderstorms. As documented in this study, grasses like those in the Succulent Karoo biome shifted eastward to encompass the region of Wonderwerk Cave, probably facilitated by moister and cooler conditions resulting from the encroachment of the winter rainfall regime. The presence of a shallow Early–Middle Pleistocene water body at Mamatwan (Matmon et al., 2015) is further evidence of moister climatic conditions at the time.

Unstable conditions are documented within Str. 10 (likely the Jaramillo and onset of the Bruhnes, *ca.* 1.0 Ma–*ca.* 0.7 Ma), specifically extremes of moist, xeric conditions, associated with swings from a C_3 environment to one dominated by C_4 species, reflected by grass phytolith and isotopic data sets. Stratum 10 overlaps with the rapid infilling of the body of water detected at Mamatwan (Matmon et al., 2015). It is probable that this period of instability reflects the onset of the mid-Pleistocene transition, which marks the shift in glacial–interglacial climates, from relatively low-amplitude, high-frequency cycles (41-kyr period) to higher-amplitude, low-frequency cycles (100-kyr period; Pisias and Moore, 1981; Head and Gibbard, 2005).

From Str. 9 onwards, there is a return to more xeric conditions or more frequent dry spells, supported by the phytolith data that denote a shift back to drier and warmer conditions, associated with a warm Nama Karoo grassland. The isotope record from the fauna indicates grazing specializations, and few mixed-feeding species, a pattern that continues in the region today (Codron et al., 2008).

The top layers of the ESA sequence in the cave, Str. 8 through 6, exhibit the most xeric and most open environments of all layers, based on macro- and micromammalian data as well as isotopic values from ostrich eggshell. Conditions probably most closely resembled those in the cave's vicinity today.

Conclusions

First, paleoenvironmental conditions during the Oldowan and early Acheulean at Wonderwerk Cave indicate open, dry savanna environments, comprised mainly of C_3 vegetation with some C_4 plants. Second, climatic oscillations are evident at the Mid-Pleistocene transition significant changes in faunal and floral communities, as well as erosional transport and depositional capacities of drainage systems (e.g., Diekmann and Kuhn, 2002; Schefuß et al., 2003; deMenocal, 2004; Lee-Thorp et al., 2007). Third, the Wonderwerk phytolith sequence indicates C_4 grass expansion from *ca.* 1.77 Ma with the eastward spread of the Nama Karoo biome. This continues throughout the Pleistocene resulting in the establishment of semi-arid conditions post-1.0 Ma (Cornelian fauna; Codron et al., 2008; Brink et al., 2012, 2015b). Hopley et al. (2007a) have suggested that C_4 plant expansion was a response to aridity caused by the onset of the Walker Circulation in the Pacific Ocean. Finally, the end portion of the ESA sequence suggests a long-term drier climatic trend.

Ongoing research on the ESA sequence at Wonderwerk Cave, including isotopic analyses of mammalian fauna, rodent taxonomy, and geomorphology, will aid further paleoenvironmental reconstructions.

To date, this sequence demonstrated key events: (i) that Wonderwerk Cave was first used by hominins during the Olduvai Subchron (1.93–1.77 Ma), making it the earliest documented intentional cave-use worldwide (Chazan et al., 2012; Shaar et al., 2021); (ii) the earliest use of fire at Wonderwerk Cave, which is dated to *ca.* 1.0 Ma (Berna et al. 2012), based on the presence of *in situ* ash, burnt bones, burnt sediment, and pot-lid fractures on lithics, in addition to calcified twigs which could have served as kindling; (iii) the Wonderwerk ESA sequence provides the first comprehensive radiometric framework within a single depositional sequence for the arid interior of South Africa for comparisons with other regions in southern and eastern Africa.

Acknowledgments

Liora Kolska Horwitz and Michael Chazan thank all members of the Wonderwerk Cave team for their contributions and their friendship which has made this an enjoyable and intellectually stimulating project. Team members: P. Goldberg and F. Berna (micromorphology); A. Matmon (cosmogenic burial dating); N. Porat (OSL); R. Pickering (U/Pb); R. Shaar and the late H. Ron (paleomagnetism); M. Bamford (macrobotanicals); L. Scott (palynology); L. Rossouw (phytoliths); L.K. Horwitz, S. Holt, and the late J. Brink (macrofauna); M.D. Avery and Y. Fernandez-Jalvo (micromammals); J. Lee-Thorp and M. Ecker (isotopes); M. Chazan (lithics). This research builds on the work of the late Peter Beaumont. Fieldwork is conducted under SAHRA permit to M. Chazan and museum analysis under agreement with the McGregor Museum (whose Director, S. Swanepoel, and Head of Archaeology, D. Morris, are warmly thanked). This research has been supported by the Canadian SSHRC and the Wenner Gren Foundation grants to M. Chazan.

Part III Eastern and Central Africa

15 Hominid Paleoenvironments in Tropical Africa from the Late Miocene to the Early Pleistocene

René Bobe and Sally C. Reynolds

Introduction

In this chapter we review the evidence for hominid paleoenvironments in tropical Africa from the late Miocene to the early Pleistocene (Figure 15.1). Here we use the term *hominid* to refer to the family of the great apes and humans (family Hominidae, superfamily Hominoidea), and *hominin* (tribe Hominini) for the clade on the human side of the divergence from our last common ancestor with the genus *Pan* (Figure 15.2). This review is intended to complement the other regional reviews (northern African and southern African sites, see Chapters 6 and 36, respectively) and the overviews of Miocene to Holocene faunas (late Miocene and early Pliocene by Doman and Goble Early, this volume and Middle Pleistocene to Holocene by Faith, Chapter 5). The methods used in the reconstruction of past environments, e.g., stable isotopes, ecomorphology, community paleoecology, are summarized in Andrews and colleagues (Chapter 2).

Tectonics and the East African Rift System

The context of active tectonics, uplift, rifting and volcanism in eastern Africa began with the development of the East African Rift System (EARS) starting in the late Oligocene, first along the Eastern Branch (~24 Ma), and then along Western Branch (~10 Ma; Figure 15.3; Ebinger, 1989; Ring et al., 2018). The Eastern Branch runs from the Afar through the Main Ethiopian Rift, the Omo-Turkana Basin, the Kenya Rift, and ends in the North Tanzanian Divergence Zone. The Western Branch runs from Lake Albert in the north through Lake Edward, Lake Kivu, Lake Tanganyika, Lake Rukwa, Lake Malawi, and the Urema Graben to south of Beira, Mozambique (MacGregor, 2015). There is an offshore Southeastern Branch that runs parallel to the coast of Tanzania and Mozambique (Chorowicz, 2005). Regional uplift has been caused by mantle flow of the African Superplume (Ebinger and Scholz, 2012; Bagley and Nyblade, 2013) beginning about 30 Ma in the Lake Tana region of Ethiopia, with rifting propagating from the Afar to the south after major uplift (Chorowicz, 2005). At the northernmost end of the EARS, the Afar triangle is a triple junction at the intersection of the African, Arabian, and Somali plates.

Topographic uplift and rifting processes created a series of sedimentary basins with highly heterogeneous environments across eastern Africa, with highlands that captured moisture and precipitation from the Indian Ocean and gave rise to rivers that flowed into the succession of graben basins of the rift, forming lakes and wetlands. Today, these Great Lakes are among the largest and most speciose freshwater bodies on Earth (Salzburger et al., 2014). Most of these lakes are on the Rift Valley floor, with the notable exception of Lake Victoria, located between the Eastern and Western branches of the rift. Tectonic uplift also contributed to increased aridity in parts of eastern Africa (Sepulchre et al., 2006). Along with rifting, volcanism has played a major role in the geologic history of the EARS, especially in the northern sectors and along the Eastern Branch (Chorowicz, 2005). Tectonic processes beyond Africa also influenced the environments of eastern Africa during the late Cenozoic, such as the uplift of the Tibetan Plateau about 8 Ma (Molnar et al., 1993, 2010), and the closing of the Indonesian seaway through changes in Indian Ocean circulation patterns (Cane and Molnar, 2001).

Chronologic and Geographic Scope

We review evidence and interpretations of how early hominins and their immediate ancestors or close relatives fit into the landscapes of tropical Africa. We consider it important to take a broad view across space and time, to consider areas where early hominins have been found, as well as those where they have not, areas where early hominins are abundant and areas where they are rare. We also consider some key late Miocene sites that precede the earliest appearance of hominins in Africa (Figure 15.4). Each area presents a limited window into the evolutionary history of the continent, but vast areas of Africa remain paleontologically unknown. For most of this chapter we focus on the EARS from Eritrea in the north to Mozambique in the south (first along the Eastern Branch, then along the Western Branch), but we also discuss sites in central and western Africa. The evidence that we briefly review here serves as the empirical framework for the formulation and testing of environmental hypotheses and models that seek to explain various aspects of hominin evolution, including the savanna hypothesis (with deep historical roots; Dart, 1925a; Domínguez-Rodrigo, 2014; Howell and Bourlière, 1963), the turnover pulse hypothesis (Vrba, 1988, 1995b), the variability section hypothesis (Potts, 1996, 1998a), or the amplifier lakes hypothesis (Trauth et al., 2010), among others.

Paleontologically speaking, we use the term locality to refer to a relatively discrete "patch" of fossils or artifacts deriving from a relatively restricted stratigraphic horizon. Although this definition

Eastern and Central Africa

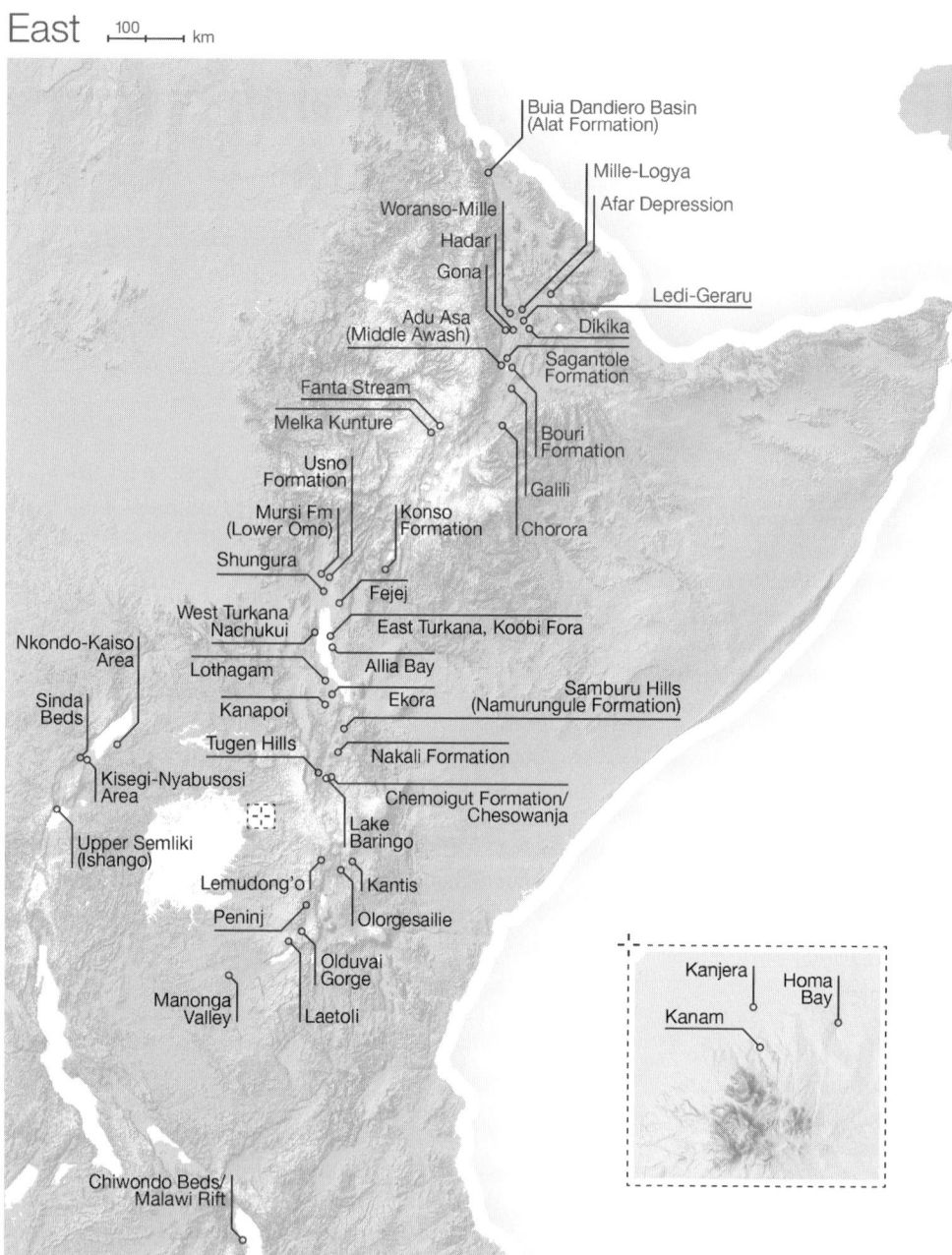

Figure 15.1 Fossil sites discussed in the text. Please note that although Gorongosa site in Mozambique is discussed in this chapter, the site location is shown in Figure 6.1.

is broad and flexible, it is based on the use of this term by the International Omo Research Expedition (de Heinzelin, 1983a), the International Afar Research Expedition (Taieb et al., 1976), and the Middle Awash research project (de Heinzelin et al., 2000; Haile-Selassie and WoldeGabriel, 2009b). However, paleontological localities often consist of surface fossil collections that may derive from multiple horizons, i.e., they may be time-averaged and represent multiple ecological communities and ecosystems.

Afar Rift

The Afar paleontological record was first recognized by Maurice Taieb, who began working in the Afar region in 1966 (Taieb, 1974). In the late 1960s and early 1970s, Taieb documented several areas that remain the focus of active research, including the Woranso-Mille, Leadu, Ledi-Geraru, Hadar, and the Middle Awash (Taieb et al., 1972).

Buia, Dandiero Basin, Eritrea

Buia, which lies in the Dandiero Basin (Danakil Depression, Eritrea), has been investigated since 1994 and records Pleistocene fossils, including a *Homo erectus* cranium (UA 31) from the **Alat Formation**, dating to about 1 Ma (Figure 15.5; Abbate et al., 1998). This Formation consists of lacustrine deposits and a complex deltaic system that reaches 90 m in thickness and contains ichnofossils, gastropods, fishes, chelonians, crocodiles, and mammals, as well as Acheulean and Oldowan artifacts (Abbate et al., 2004, 2012; Martínez-Navarro et al., 2004; Rook et al., 2010, 2013). There is a single primate specimen, assigned to

Hominid Paleoenvironments in Tropical Africa

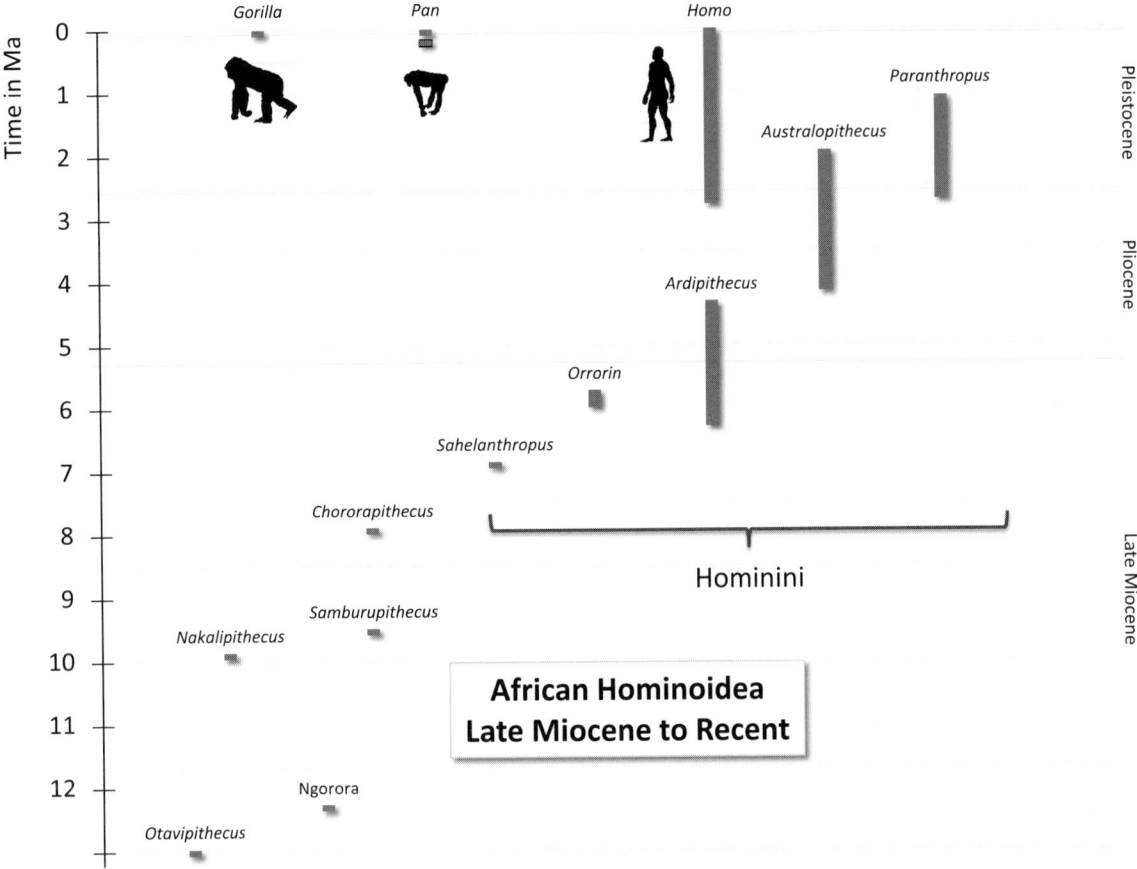

Figure 15.2 Chronology of African hominoid genera from the late Miocene to the present.

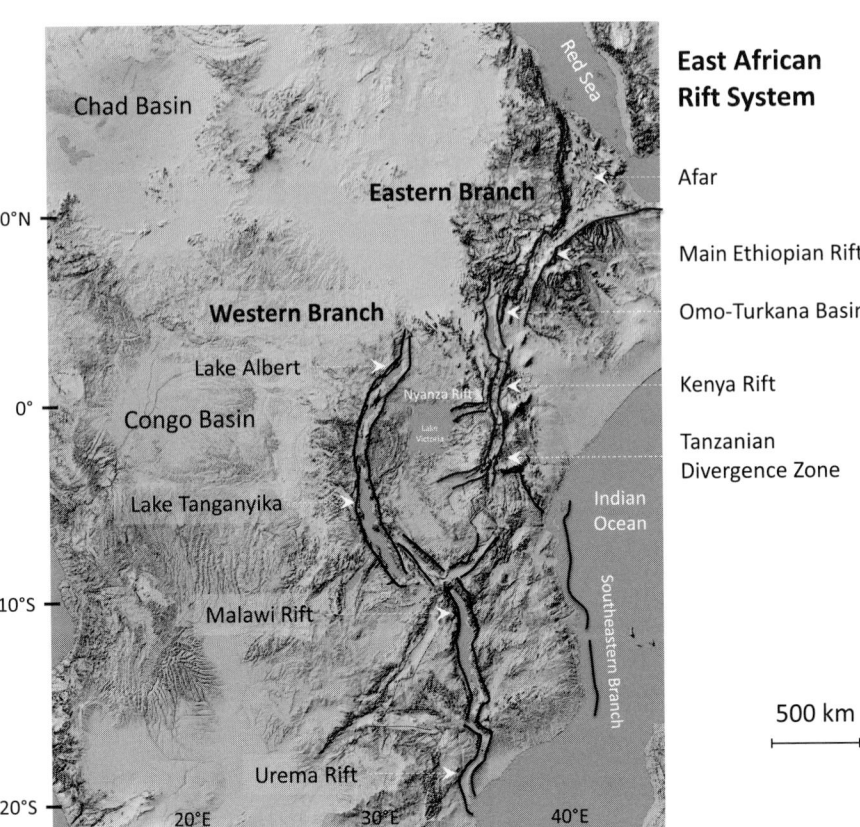

Figure 15.3 The East African Rift System with the Eastern Branch, the Western Branch, and some of the major basins and rifts. The development of the East African Rift System since the Miocene has played a major role in shaping the physical environments and modifying the conditions under which which plants and animals have been evolving in eastern Africa. Base map from NASA Shuttle Radar Topography Mission (www2.jpl.nasa.gov/srtm/). (A black and white version of this figure will appear in some formats. For the color version, please refer to the plate section.)

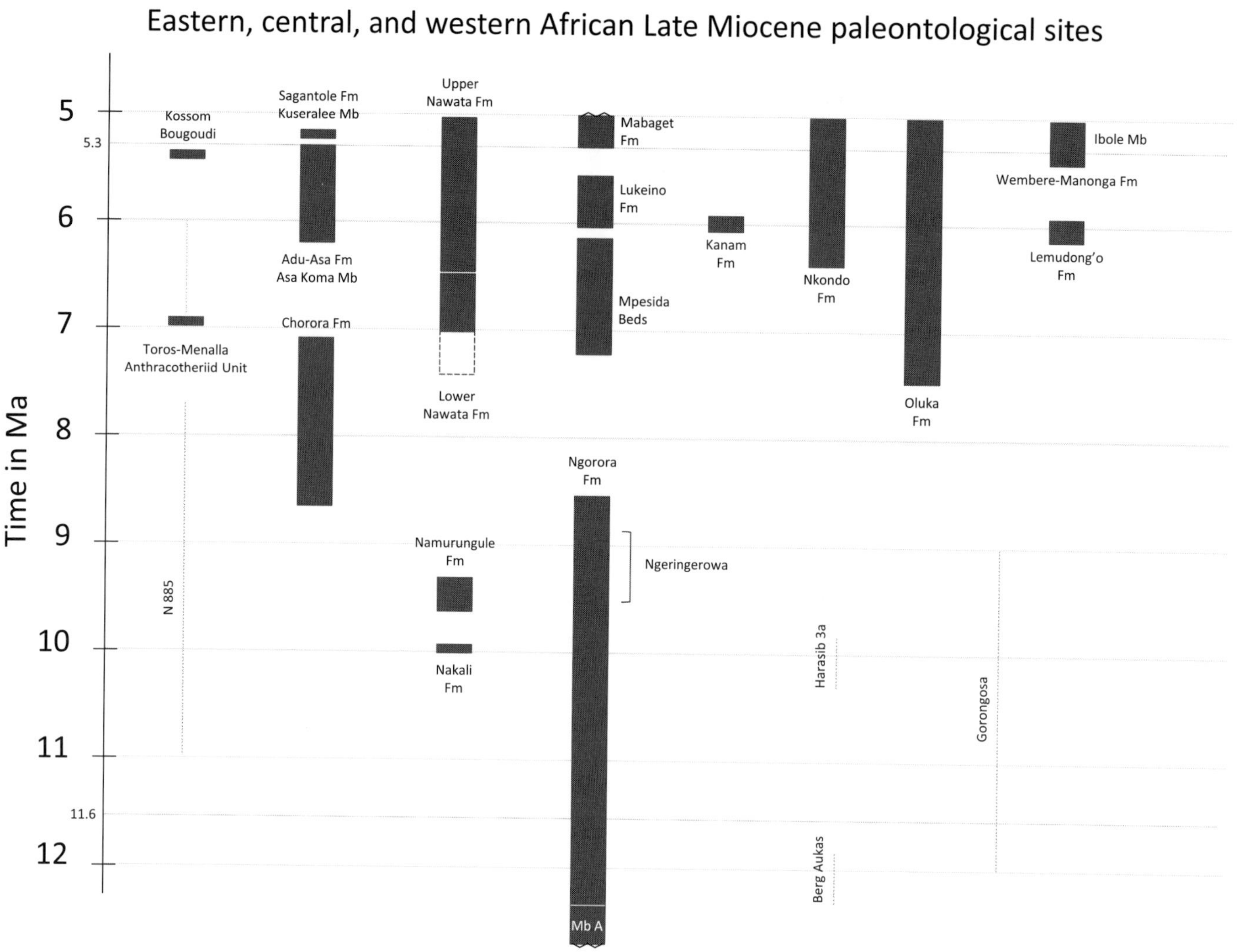

Figure 15.4 Chronology of late Miocene geological formation and fossiliferous deposits in eastern, central, and western Africa. Vertical dashed bars indicate dating uncertainties of some sedimentary sequences.

Theropithecus cf. *oswaldi* (Rook et al., 2010). Bovid genera include *Bos*, *Pelorovis*, *Tragelaphus*, *Kobus*, *Hippotragus*, and *Gazella* (Martínez-Navarro et al., 2004, 2010), and three species of suids are known, namely *Kolpochoerus olduvaiensis*, *Kolpochoerus majus*, and *Metridiochoerus modestus*. The ecological characteristics of these suids are described by Medin and colleagues (Medin et al., 2015; Chapter 16). *Equus* cf. *grevyi* is also present. The megafauna consists of *Giraffa* cf. *jumae*, *Hippopotamus gorgops*, *Ceratotherium simum*, and *Elephas recki* (Ferretti et al., 2003a). The hominin-bearing deposits have an abundance of water-dependent fauna (e.g., *Hippopotamus*, *Kobus*, *Tragelaphus spekei*, *Crocodylus*) as well as grassland taxa (e.g., *Equus*, *Metridiochoerus*, *Theropithecus*; Martínez-Navarro et al., 2004), suggesting that *H. erectus* occurred in grassy habitats close to a major lake.

Mille-Logya

This project research area in the Afar has newly discovered paleontological localities radiometrically and magnetostratigraphically dated from 2.9 to 2.4 Ma (Figure 15.5; Alemseged et al., 2020). The Mille-Logya Project, initiated by Z. Alemseged in 2012, has recovered specimens of early *Homo* and more than 2000 vertebrate fossils. The fossiliferous sequence, up to 60 m in thickness, represents the northward migration of the Hadar Basin. The sequence is divided into three informal units: Gafura, Seraitu, and Uraitele. The Gafura sediments contain abundant gastropods and vertebrate fossils underlying a diatomaceous unit. The Seraitu lake beds contain ostracods, gastropods, bivalves, and vertebrates, as well as several air-fall tuffs. Uraitele includes some fluvial channels in a predominantly lacustrine setting. For most of this time, *Aulacoseira* diatoms suggest the presence of a deep and well-mixed lake (Alemseged et al., 2020). The most abundant mammals are Bovidae (944 specimens), Equidae (218 specimens), Suidae (165 specimens), Hippopotamidae (135 specimens), and Cercopithecidae (62 specimens). Remarkably, there are 10 specimens of Camelidae, usually very rare elsewhere in Africa (Geraads et al., 2021). Alemseged and colleagues (2020) provide a full faunal list for each of the three units. The fauna from the older unit is similar to that from the upper Hadar Formation and the fauna from the two younger units indicates the presence of more open conditions in the area. The *Homo* specimen derives from Uraitele, the youngest unit, broadly associated with a fauna that indicates a prevalence of grassy vegetation. No *in situ* archeological artifacts have yet been found.

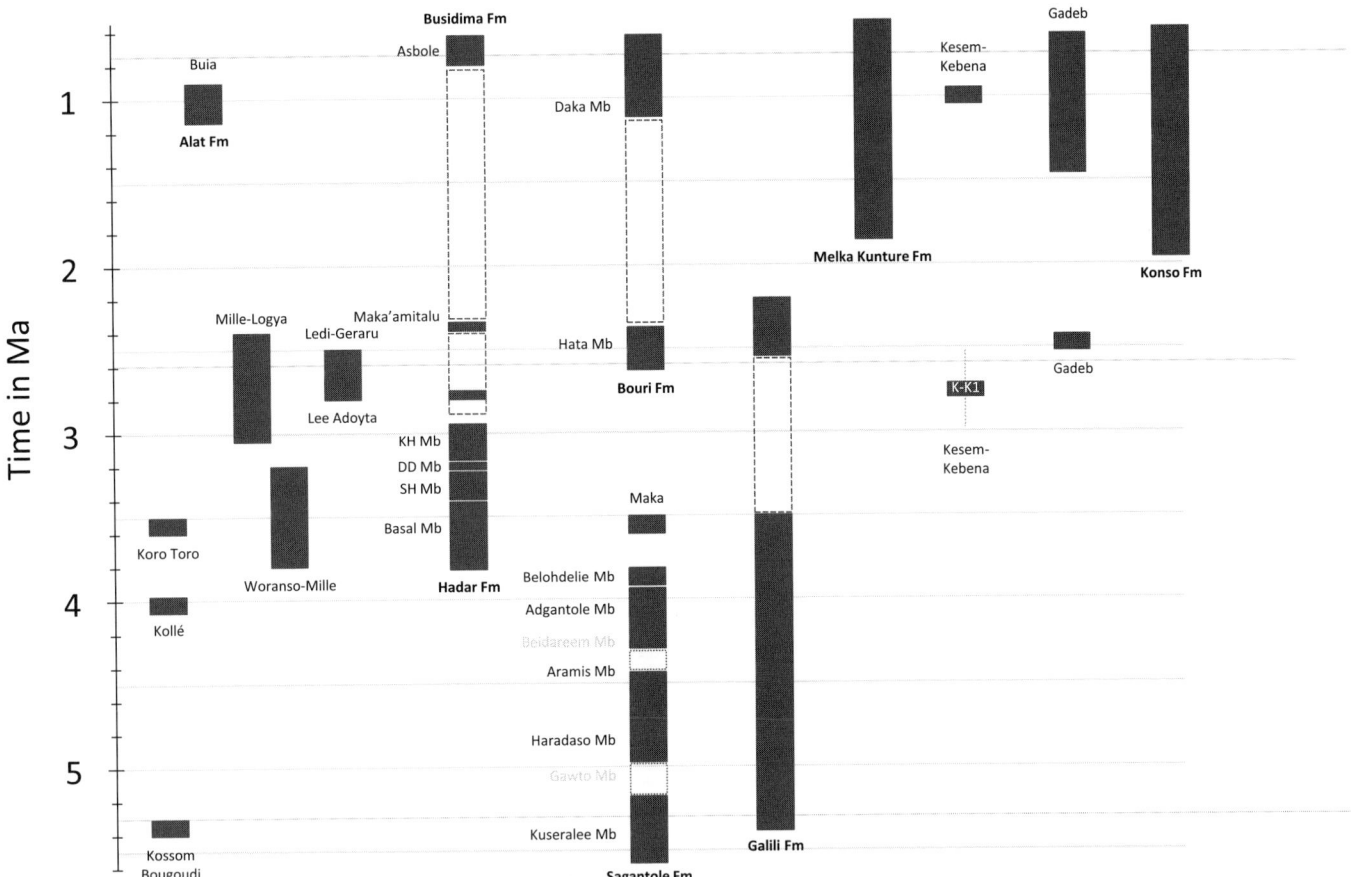

Figure 15.5 Chronology of key fossil sequences in the Afar, Main Ethiopian Rift, and Chad Basin dating from the early Pliocene to the early Pleistocene.

Woranso-Mille

Woranso-Mille has fossiliferous deposits aged 3.8 to 3.2 Ma (Figure 15.5; Deino et al., 2010; Saylor et al., 2016). This area has been systematically studied by Y. Haile-Selassie and colleagues since 2002 (Haile-Selassie et al., 2007). Remarkable hominins have been discovered at Woranso-Mille, including a partial skeleton of a large *Australopithecus afarensis* individual (Haile-Selassie et al., 2010b); a partial foot with grasping adaptations (Haile-Selassie et al., 2012); another species of *Australopithecus*, *Au. deyiremeda* (Haile-Selassie et al., 2015); and the first *Au. anamensis* cranium (Haile-Selassie et al., 2019). Cercopithecids are abundant at Woranso-Mille, comprising 40 percent of the mammalian fauna, and *Theropithecus oswaldi* cf. *darti* represents about 90 percent of the monkey specimens (Frost et al., 2014). This dominance of a presumed terrestrial grazer, *Theropithecus oswaldi* (Frost and Delson, 2002; Cerling et al., 2013b), indicates that grasslands were common. The carnivoran fauna includes *Eucyon*, *Enhydriodon*, *Torolutra*, *Hydrictis*, *Civetticis*, *Genetta*, *Sahelictis*, *Galerella*, *Ichneumia*, *Crocuta*, *Chasmaporthetes*, *Homotherium*, *Dinofelis*, *Panthera*, and *Felis* (Werdelin et al., 2014). The bovid fauna is dominated by Aepycerotini and Tragelaphini, followed by Alcelaphini (Geraads et al., 2009b), and indicates that wooded or bushy areas were also present. Suids are abundant, and include *Cainochoerus*, *Nyanzachoerus*, *Notochoerus*, and *Kolpochoerus* (Curran and Haile-Selassie, 2016; Reda et al., 2019). Other mammalian taxa include hippopotamids, giraffids (both *Giraffa* and *Sivatherium*), equids, and rhinocerotids. Proboscideans in the Woranso-Mille assemblage include *Anancus*, cf. *Mammuthus*, *Elephas* (*E. ekorensis* and *E. recki brumpti*), and *Loxodonta* (Sanders and Haile-Selassie, 2012). The paleoenvironments were composed of riparian woodlands and grasslands along a river draining into a lake (Curran and Haile-Selassie, 2016).

Ledi-Geraru

This research area encompasses sediments of the Hadar Formation (see below; Dupont-Nivet et al., 2008; DiMaggio et al., 2008, 2015a), as well as younger deposits from 2.9 to 2.5 Ma in the Lee Adoyta basin (DiMaggio et al., 2015b) and the Ali Toyta river drainage (Figure 15.5; Braun et al., 2019b). Within the Ledi-Geraru area, the Hadar Formation consists of ~230 m of lacustrine and near-shore sediments. The bovids and giraffids have been described by D. Geraads and colleagues (Geraads et al., 2012a, 2013b), while the giraffids from the younger Lee Adoyta basin were described by J. Rowan and colleagues (2017). Ledi-Geraru has produced the earliest *Homo*: a partial mandible from the Lee Adoyta region, locality LD 350, dated to nearly 2.8 Ma (Villmoare et al., 2015). The *Homo* specimen, LD 350–1, derives from fine silts underlain by the Gurumaha Tuff, dated to *ca.* 2.82 Ma (DiMaggio et al., 2015b). The Lee Adoyta faunal sample consists of 614 mammals in the interval from ~2.8 to 2.6 Ma. The *Homo* specimen appears associated with a high relative abundance of Alcelaphini (Bibi et al., 2017) and a turnover in the suid fauna (Lazagabaster et al., 2018b) indicating the presence of more open C_4 grasslands relative to the earlier Hadar Formation (Robinson et al., 2017). Also, the site of Bokol Dora 1 (BD 1) in the Ali Toyta area contains the earliest Oldowan tools dating to *ca.* 2.6 Ma (Braun et al., 2019b). The BD 1 archeological horizon was deposited near the edge of a receding lake and buried by a subsequent lake transgression.

Hadar

The fossiliferous deposits of Hadar were first identified by M. Taieb, and in 1973 fieldwork focused on the deposits of Hadar north of the Awash River (Taieb et al., 1972). Since the early 1970s, paleoanthropological work produced a rich record of Pliocene vertebrates. The **Hadar Formation** is divided into the Basal, Sidi Hakoma, Denen Dora, and Kada Hadar Members, and dates from about 3.8 Ma to 2.9 Ma (Figure 15.5). The fossiliferous deposits are primarily fluvio-deltaic, with several lacustrine transgressions from paleo-lake Hadar (Campisano and Feibel, 2007). The Hadar Formation has produced the largest sample of *Australopithecus afarensis* in eastern Africa (Johanson et al., 1978, 1982a, 1982b, 1982c; Kimbel et al., 1982, 1994; Kimbel and Delezene, 2009). The history of research at Hadar and the rich literature on the Hadar Formation environmental reconstructions are reviewed in detail by C. Campisano and colleagues (Chapter 18), who conclude that the main environments between 3.4 and 3 Ma were woodlands with varying proportions of grasslands. The Hadar area also has younger deposits of the **Busidima Formation** (Campisano, 2012). A maxilla of an early species of *Homo* (*H.* cf. *habilis*) was found in deposits of the Busidima Formation in the Maka'amitalu Basin in 1994 (Kimbel et al., 1997). This specimen, A.L. 666-1, and associated Oldowan tools, derives from sediments just below the BKT-3 tephra, dated to 2.35 Ma. The vertebrate fauna associated with the A.L. 666-1 hominin indicates that the Hadar paleoenvironments had become more open by 2.35 Ma than those of the earlier Hadar Formation (Kimbel et al., 1996).

Dikika

In 1999, Z. Alemseged launched the Dikika Research Project to study sediments of the Hadar Formation south of the Awash River (Alemseged et al., 2005). At Dikika, exposures of the Hadar Formation date from nearly 3.8 Ma to about 2.9 Ma (Figure 15.5; Wynn et al., 2006, 2008). Dikika has provided evidence relevant to *Australopithecus afarensis* ontogeny (Alemseged et al., 2006; Gunz et al., 2020), locomotor adaptations (Green and Alemseged, 2012; DeSilva et al., 2018), and paleoenvironments (Wynn et al., 2008). Locality DIK-55 is of especial archeological interest as it provides evidence of the earliest stone-tool modified bones at *ca.* 3.4 Ma (McPherron et al., 2010). This early evidence of stone tool use has proved controversial (Domínguez-Rodrigo et al., 2010b; Njau, 2012b; Sahle et al., 2017), but has triggered new research on bone surface modification (Thompson et al., 2015). The sedimentological record indicates that most of the Hadar Formation formed under lacustrine deposition near the basin's depocenter to the northeast, with periodic transgressions of the lake's shoreline across low-gradient topographic conditions toward the southwest, with deltaic and braided fluvial systems flowing into the lake. The fossil mammal record has been described by D. Geraads and colleagues (Geraads, 2005; Geraads et al., 2010b, 2011, 2015b), and a synthesis of Dikika's paleoenvironments is provided elsewhere (Bobe et al., Chapter 19). Analyses of stable isotopes (Bedaso et al., 2013) and faunal abundance data indicate that Dikika *Au. afarensis* occurred in extensive woodlands and wooded grasslands near streams flowing to the ancient Lake Hadar.

Asbole

The Asbole area west of the Awash River was surveyed by Z. Alemseged in 1999 (Alemseged and Geraads, 2000), followed by extensive fieldwork in 2000 and 2002 (Geraads et al., 2004c). Here, deposits of the Busidima Formation are dominated by fluvial sedimentation in a half-graben. The fauna and artifacts are bracketed by a conglomerate aged *ca.* 0.8 Ma and the Bironita Tuff with a date of 0.64 Ma (Wynn et al., 2008; Bedaso et al., 2010). Colobines are abundant among five species of primates (Frost and Alemseged, 2007), as is the marsh cane-rat *Thryonomys*. The bovid *Kobus* and the suid *Kolpochoerus* dominate the artiodactyls, while hippopotamids are rare (Geraads et al., 2004c). Stable isotopes from dental enamel show that both C_3 and C_4 resources were available, but most mammals have a C_4 signature (Bedaso et al., 2010). Thus, the sedimentological and faunal data suggest gallery woodlands with extensive grassy floodplains.

Gona

Gona has fossiliferous deposits from the late Miocene to the Pleistocene, which encompass outcrops of the Adu-Asa Formation (*ca.* 6.4–5.2 Ma), Sagantole Formation (5.2–3.9 Ma), Hadar Formation (3.8–2.9 Ma), and Busidima Formation (2.7–0.15 Ma) (Figure 15.5; Kleinsasser et al., 2008; Quade et al., 2008; Levin et al., Chapter 17). The site is known for Oldowan tools dated to 2.6 Ma (Semaw et al., 1997, 2003), but Gona also has late Miocene hominin specimens of *Ardipithecus kadabba* (Simpson et al., 2015), early Pliocene *Ardipithecus ramidus* (Semaw et al., 2005; Simpson et al., 2019), and early Pleistocene *Homo erectus* (Simpson et al., 2008; Semaw et al., 2020). In Chapter 17, Levin and colleagues provide a synthesis of paleoenvironmental change in this region during the last 6 million years. In the late Miocene, *Ar. kadabba* occurred in environments consisting of well-watered wooded habitats near lakes and rivers, and in the proximity of volcanic centers. These environments became more open when *Ar. ramidus* inhabited the Afar region. During the deposition of the Hadar Formation, the Gona area had a range of environments from woodlands to grasslands, with river deltas draining into paleo-Lake Hadar. The Busidima Formation represents a different depositional system with a dominant meandering river. In this formation, the earliest stone-tool makers are associated with the axial paleo-Awash River, where river cobbles were tool raw materials (Quade et al., 2004). *Homo erectus* inhabited a region with gallery forests near the river and grasses dominating the floodplains. These environments became increasingly open through the Pleistocene (Quade et al., 2004; Levin et al., Chapter 17).

Middle Awash

These deposits were explored in the early 1970s by M. Taieb, who mapped geological sections and collected fossils and artifacts along the Awash River (Taieb et al., 1972; Taieb, 1974). From 1975 to 1978, the Rift Valley Research Mission in Ethiopia (RVRME) led by J. Kalb carried out research in the area (Kalb et al., 1980, 1982a, 1982b, 1982c), and in 1981, J. Desmond Clark and Tim White launched the Middle Awash research project (Clark et al., 1984; White, 1984). Since then, the Middle Awash has been established as a key area for hominin evolution during the last 6 million years. Middle Awash hominins include *Ardipithecus kadabba* (Haile-Selassie, 2001, 2004a), *Ardipithecus ramidus* (White et al., 1994, 2009b; White, 1995), *Australopithecus anamensis* (White et al., 2006), *Australopithecus afarensis* (White, 1984; White et al., 1993), *Australopithecus garhi* (Asfaw et al., 1999; de Heinzelin et al., 1999), *Homo erectus* (Asfaw et al., 2002), *Homo heidelbergensis* (or *rhodesiensis*; Conroy et al., 1978; Kalb et al., 1980), and *Homo sapiens idaltu* (White et al., 2003). The Middle Awash fossiliferous areas on both sides of the Awash River are patchy and separated by large distances.

Historically, several hominin localities on the east side of the modern Awash River were among the first to be discovered. The **Bodo** hominin cranium, discovered in 1976, was associated with Acheulean artifacts, and with a fauna including *Hippopotamus*, *Theropithecus*, *Kobus*, *Equus*, *Elephas*, and *Crocodylus* (Conroy et al., 1978; Kalb et al., 1980). The site of Bodo is dated to about *ca.* 600 ka. The first Pliocene hominin was the **Maka** proximal femur, found by T. White in 1981 (Clark et al., 1984; White, 1984). The Maka fossils derive from sands and gravels with intercalated tephra dating to about 3.4 Ma. The Maka femur and subsequently discovered specimens at the site (e.g., humerus, mandible) are assigned to *Australopithecus afarensis*, with the femur showing clear evidence of bipedal locomotion (White et al., 1993, 2000; Lovejoy et al., 2002). The fauna is similar to that from the Denen Dora Member at Hadar, and includes the mammalian taxa *Nyanzachoerus kanamensis*, *Notochoerus euilus*, *Praedamalis howelli*, *Ugandax*, *Diceros praecox*, *Theropithecus*, and *Elephas recki brumpti* (Clark et al., 1984; Vrba and Gatesy, 1994); the paleoenvironments are reconstructed as seasonally dry grassy woodlands. After finding the Maka hominin femur in 1981, about 700 m from the femur site, the team found the **Belohdelie** hominin frontal bone, now dated to nearly 3.9 Ma (White, 1984; Asfaw, 1987). In 1990, hominin specimens dating to ~2.5 Ma were found east of the Awash River at Matabaietu and Gamedah (White et al., 2005). Below we provide a brief description of the Late Miocene to Early Pleistocene geological formations in this area.

The **Adu-Asa Formation** (*ca.* 6.3–5.2 Ma; Figure 15.4) is exposed along the western rift margin of the Middle Awash region, and also in the Gona research area (see above; Kalb, 1993; WoldeGabriel et al., 2001; Kleinsasser et al., 2008; Haile-Selassie and WoldeGabriel, 2009a). This formation is divided into four members (WoldeGabriel et al., 2009b). The oldest is the Saraitu Member, which is underlain by basaltic lavas dated to *ca.* 6.33 Ma. Sediments consist of fluvial deposits with some aquatic vertebrate fossils (WoldeGabriel et al., 2001). The overlying Adu Dora Member consists primarily of lacustrine deposits. The Asa Koma Member, dating from 5.77 to 5.54 Ma, consists of fluvial deposits with abundant fossil vertebrates, including most of the specimens attributed to *Ardipithecus kadabba* (Haile-Selassie, 2001; Haile-Selassie et al., 2004a; WoldeGabriel et al., 2009b). No fossils have been collected from the Rawa Member above the Adu-Asa Formation (Haile-Selassie et al., 2004b). There are more than 2000 fossil vertebrates in the fluvial deposits of the Asa Koma Member (WoldeGabriel et al., 2001). Monkeys are represented by the genus *Pliopapio* and by two species of colobines (Frost et al., 2009; Haile-Selassie and WoldeGabriel, 2009a; Haile-Selassie et al., 2004b). Among bovids, Reduncini and Tragelaphini are abundant, while Alcelaphini are absent (Haile-Selassie et al., 2009b). There is a diverse fauna of megaherbivores, including the proboscideans *Anancus*, *Primelephas*, *Mammuthus*, and *Deinotherium* (Saegusa and Haile-Selassie, 2009), the rhinocerotid *Diceros*, the giraffids *Palaeotragus* and *Giraffa*, and a hippopotamid (Haile-Selassie et al., 2004b). The large mammalian predators include the felids *Machairodus* and *Dinofelis*, as well as the hyaenids *Hyaenictitherium* and *Hyaenictis*. The ursid *Agriotherium* is also present (Haile-Selassie and Howell, 2009). Stable carbon isotopes indicate the presence of woodlands and grassy woodlands, and oxygen isotope ratios indicate cool and humid habitats associated with *Ar. kadabba*. This interpretation is supported by the ecological characteristics of the fauna (Haile-Selassie et al., 2004b; Su et al., 2009).

The **Sagantole Formation** (5.6–3.9 Ma; Figure 15.5) consists of lacustrine, fluvial, and volcaniclastic sediments exposed in the Central Awash Complex, and comprises seven members; from oldest to youngest these are the Kuseralee, Gawto, Haradaso, Aramis, Beidareem, Adgantole, and Belohdelie Members (Kalb, 1993; Renne et al., 1999; WoldeGabriel et al., 2013). An additional member is identified in the Gona research area: the Segala Noumou Member (Quade et al., 2008). The fluvio-lacustrine sediments of the Kuseralee Member (5.6–5.2 Ma) yielded a hominin pedal phalanx from the Amba East locality described alongside earlier specimens of *Ardipithecus kadabba* (Haile-Selassie, 2001; WoldeGabriel et al., 2001). The Gawto Member (5.2–5.0 Ma) is composed primarily of basaltic lavas, and the Haradaso Member (4.98–4.4 Ma) contains mostly aquatic fossils (Renne et al., 1999). The Aramis Member (4.4–4.3 Ma) has a rich fossil record including at least 36 individuals of *Ar. ramidus* as well as 40 vertebrate species (White et al., 2009a). White and colleagues employ a range of faunal, paleobotanical, and geochemical evidence (Louchart et al., 2009; White et al., 2009a; WoldeGabriel et al., 2009a) to describe the ancient *Ardipithecus* environment as a cool and humid woodland setting with small patches of forest, with more distant areas grading into open habitats, with *Ardipithecus* occupying the closed part of the habitat. The colobine monkeys and tragelaphin bovids, and their postcranial ecomorphology, suggest closed habitats, as does the stable isotopic composition of *Ardipithecus* and other fauna. In contrast, T. Cerling and colleagues argue that the same isotopic data presented as evidence of woodlands and forests could be interpreted as evidence of riparian forest to grassland habitats associated with *Ar. ramidus* (Cerling et al., 2010, 2014). The Aramis paleontological and geochemical evidence was collected across a 9-km transect of sediments and it is likely that several types of vegetation occurred at this scale, and that *Ar. ramidus* occurred in the wooded parts of the landscape. Fluvial deposits of the Adgantole Member (4.1–3.89 Ma) at Aramis have yielded an *Australopithecus anamensis* maxilla dated to ~4.1 Ma (White et al., 2006). About 10 km west of Aramis, the site of Asa Issie yielded additional specimens of *Au. anamensis* associated with >500 fossil vertebrates. The Asa Issie fauna is dominated by colobine monkeys and tragelaphin bovids, with a lack of Alcelaphini and Reduncini and only rare aquatic taxa (fish, crocodiles, hippopotamids). Pedogenic carbonates suggest humid, grassy woodlands (White et al., 2006).

The **Bouri Formation** consists of the Hata (Hatayae), Daka (Dakanihylo), and Herto Members, with the Herto Member divided into an Upper/Lower Member, separated by a major stratigraphic division (Clark et al., 2003). This sequence crops out in the Bouri Horst. The Hata Member of the Bouri Formation dates from *ca.* 2.5 to >1.0 Ma (Figure 15.5) and contains *Australopithecus garhi* (Asfaw et al., 1999; de Heinzelin et al., 1999). The *Au. garhi* specimens and faunal remains with evidence of butchery date to the early part of the Hata Member, 2.5 Ma. However, a taphonomic reevaluation of these butchery marks indicates that some of the marks may have been crocodile-made (Sahle et al., 2017). More than 400 fossil vertebrates were collected from the Hata Member. The holotype of hippopotamid *Hexaprotodon bruneti* derives from this member (Boisserie and White, 2004). The evidence from Bouri Hata indicates that *Au. garhi* and the stone-modified bones occurred within open grassy floodplains alongside riverine forests and a nearby shallow lake (de Heinzelin et al., 1999).

The Daka Member of the Bouri Formation consists of alluvial sediments related to lakeside beaches and distributary channels. A *Homo erectus* partial cranium was found at locality BOU-VP-2 in 1997 (Asfaw et al., 2002). The member dates from about 1 Ma to 0.8 Ma and contains abundant early Acheulean artifacts and fossils with butchery marks (WoldeGabriel et al., 2008). The Bouri Daka vertebrate fauna includes more than 700 specimens, with bovids as the most abundant mammals. Alcelaphin bovids are particularly abundant and diverse and indicate the presence of open grasslands. Diverse Reduncini and abundant *Hippopotamus* indicate that water-margin habitats were common (Asfaw et al., 2002; Gilbert and Asfaw, 2008).

The youngest member of the Bouri Formation is the Herto Member (0.26–0.16 Ma), composed of fluvial and lake margin sandstones exposed in the southwest parts of the Bouri Horst (de Heinzelin et al., 1999; Clark et al., 2003). In the Upper Herto Member, bracketed between 160 ka and 154 ka, fossils of *Homo sapiens idaltu* occur with Acheulean and Middle Stone Age artifacts, and with butchered hippopotamus carcasses (Clark et al., 2003; White et al., 2003). The Herto mammal fauna includes *Connochaetes*, *Kobus*, *Hippopotamus*, and *Equus*, among other taxa. Along with the sedimentological evidence, the fauna indicates grassland habitats around a freshwater lake (Clark et al., 2003).

Galili

This site is located in the southern Afar Rift, where the fluvio-lacustrine sedimentary sequence of the **Galili Formation** dates from 5.37 Ma to 2.15 Ma (Figure 15.5; Hujer et al., 2015). The Formation consists of several sedimentary cycles divided into the Lasdanan, Dhidinley, Godiray, Shabey Laag, Dhagax, and Caashacado Members. The first fossils from this region were found in 1997 by Y. Haile-Selassie and colleagues (Haile-Selassie and Asfaw, 2000), and subsequent work has documented over 2000 fossil vertebrates (Kullmer et al., 2008). The stratigraphy and paleoecological context of the Galili hominins are well described by O. Kullmer and colleagues (Chapter 20). Stable isotopes from dental enamel indicate that mammals had a range of dietary resources available, but in the time from ~4.4 to 3.9 Ma most taxa had a mixed C_3/C_4 to C_3-dominated diet (Bedaso, 2011). Hominins and other vertebrates inhabited landscapes that fluctuated between wooded and grassy conditions during the Pliocene (Macchiarelli et al., 2004a; Kullmer et al., 2008).

Main Ethiopian Rift

Kesem-Kebena

The Paleoanthropological Inventory of Ethiopia (established 1988) documented potential sites in new areas along the Ethiopian Rift and adjacent highlands. One of these was Kesem-Kebena, at the junction between the southern Afar and the northern end of the Main Ethiopian Rift, with a Plio-Pleistocene sedimentary sequence composed of fluvial and lacustrine deposits, including vertebrates and Acheulean artifacts (WoldeGabriel et al., 1992). The richest locality, K-K1, with a radiometric age of >2.23 Ma, has fish, turtles, crocodiles, hippopotamids, bovids, and cercopithecids (*Theropithecus*). The bovids include Aepycerotini, cf. Reduncini, Alcelaphini, Tragelaphini, and Bovini. The mammalian fauna provides a biochronological estimate of 3–2.5 Ma. The fauna and sedimentology indicate that the late Pliocene beds were deposited in a freshwater environment. There are also younger localities of Middle Pleistocene age: the K-K4 faunal assemblage includes *Theropithecus*, *Colobus*, viverrids, Tragelaphini, Alcelaphini, Antilopini, *Metridiochoerus*, and *Equus* (WoldeGabriel et al., 1992). Aquatic vertebrates are absent. Other middle Pleistocene localities with fauna and artifacts are K-K3, K-K6 (with Acheulean bifaces), and K-K7.

Chorora

The **Chorora Formation** is composed of Late Miocene fluvial and lacustrine sediments that crop out at the transition between the Afar Rift and the Main Ethiopian Rift. The Type Locality fossils date to ~8.5 Ma (Katoh et al., 2016). The hominoid *Chororapithecus abyssinicus* (Suwa et al., 2007b) derives from the Beticha locality sediments dated to ~8 Ma (Figures 15.2 and 15.4). The localities Teso Tadecho, Odakora North, and Gutosadeen date to ~7.2 Ma. The youngest Chorora fossils derive from Chifara, dated to between 7.15 and 7.0 Ma (Katoh et al., 2016). The cercopithecid fauna includes three species of Colobinae and the earliest record of Cercopithecinae (possibly a small Papionini; Suwa et al., 2015). Other mammals include rodents (Geraads, 2001), two species of Hippopotamidae (Boisserie et al., 2017), *Nyanzachoerus*, Sivatheriini, *Palaeotragus*, boselaphin bovids, hipparionins (Bernor et al., 2004), rhinocerotids, *Ancylotherium*, the proboscidean *Stegotetrabelodon*, *Deinotherium*, and several carnivores (Suwa et al., 2015). The Beticha locality has an abundance of primates and rare hipparionins and is interpreted as a forested lake margin paleoenvironment (Suwa et al., 2007b).

Melka Kunture

The site in the Ethiopian highlands, at an elevation of over 2000 m (on the shoulder of the Main Ethiopian Rift), has a fossil record that goes back to 1.8 Ma (Figure 15.5). Lithic industries from the Oldowan to the Late Stone Age are documented (Bailloud, 1965; Gallotti and Mussi, 2018). A volume edited by J. Chavaillon and D. Piperno (2004b) provides details on the archaeology and paleontology. D. Geraads and colleagues (Chapter 21) provide a review of current and past research at the site with an emphasis on the early Pleistocene faunas and paleoecology. The **Melka Kunture Formation** (~1.8–0.7 Ma) consists of alluvial and volcanic sediments deposited by the paleo-Awash River, with episodes of direct tephra deposition. Pollen samples indicate mixed vegetation types including forests, high-elevation scrubland, and grasslands (Bonnefille et al., 2018). The most abundant fossil mammals are hippopotamids, alcelaphin bovids, and equids (Geraads et al., Chapter 21). The paleoenvironments can be characterized as open grasslands near the paleo-Awash River.

Fanta Stream

Fanta Stream is an Early Pleistocene archaeological and paleontological site within Addis Ababa in the Ethiopian highlands at an elevation of 2150 m (Lanzarone et al., 2016). The Fanta Stream is a tributary of the upper Awash River in an area of agricultural and urban development (Akaki Subregion). The fluvial sediments of the site rest on rock units dated from 5.1 to 2.0 Ma (Morton et al., 1979; Chernet et al., 1998), providing a maximum age for fossils and Acheulean artifacts. Mammalian fossils, many of them found *in situ*, include Alcelaphini, Bovini, *Equus*, and *Hippopotamus*, suggest highland grasslands in the proximity of a body of permanent water. The surface of the site is rich in Acheulean artifacts (handaxes, cleavers), but the relationship between the stone tools and *in situ* fauna remains to be determined (Bobe et al., 2009). Fanta Stream and other sites in the region provide evidence of hominin occupation of highland areas in the early Pleistocene. The fauna and environmental context may resemble that of Melka Kunture, and the site merits further investigation. Being within the city limits of Addis Ababa, the site presents unique opportunities for public education, tourism, and outreach, but also the challenges associated with expanding agriculture and urban development.

Gadeb

The site of Gadeb near the headwaters of the Webi Shebele River was first excavated by J.D. Clark in 1975 and 1977 (Clark, 1979). Along with Melka-Kunture and the Fanta Stream site, Gadeb lies at an elevation of ~2400 m and provides evidence of Early Pleistocene hominin highland occupation. The Gadeb deposits consist of lacustrine claystones and diatomites, interbedded with volcanic ashes, measuring up to 70 m in thickness (Williams et al., 1979; Eberz et al., 1988). Several volcanic ashes have been correlated to tephra layers in the Turkana Basin, including the Black Pumice Tuff (1.55 Ma), the Lower Nariokotome Tuff (1.33 Ma), and Silbo Tuff (0.74 Ma; Haileab and Brown, 1994). Lake Gadeb formed in the region about 2.7 Ma, but the archeological levels date from 1.45 to 0.7 Ma and are associated with fluvial deposition (Williams et al., 1979). The archeology includes Oldowan and Acheulean artifacts (Kurashina, 1987; de la Torre, 2011), and a *Hippopotamus* partial skeleton at locality Gadeb 8F contains evidence of hominin butchery (Clark, 1987). Pollen records from Lake Gadeb at about 2.5 Ma suggest grasslands and heath moorland under cooler climatic conditions than today (Bonnefille, 1983).

Konso

The Konso-Gardula site at the southern end of the Main Ethiopian Rift was discovered in 1991 by the Paleoanthropological Inventory of Ethiopia (Asfaw et al., 1992). The **Konso Formation** is composed of ~200 m of lacustrine, lake-margin, and channel facies spanning the period 1.95–0.85 Ma (Figure 15.5), with 27 tephra units providing chronostratigraphic control (Katoh et al., 2000; Suwa et al., Chapter 22). The Konso sediments accumulated in a basin with fluctuating lake levels spanning several regression and transgression cycles. The fossiliferous exposures occur at 21 sites at elevations between 1150 and 1400 m (Suwa et al., 2003, 2014a). Depositional gaps show that the Konso faunal record falls into six time intervals (Nagaoka et al., 2005). Hominins are rare, but important specimens include a *Homo erectus* mandible and cranial fragments (Suwa et al., 2007a) and a partial skull of *Paranthropus boisei* (Suwa et al., 1997). The Konso archaeological record includes Oldowan artifacts in the early part of the sequence, and a rich record of Acheulean artifacts from 1.75 Ma to the top of the formation. The Acheulean record shows remarkable refinement in the elaboration of handaxes over time (Beyene et al., 2013). The paleontological record consists of 8000 fossil vertebrates.

Bovids, followed by hippopotamids, suids, and equids, are the most abundant mammalian family throughout the formation. Monkeys are rare, but *Theropithecus oswaldi* is present (Frost, 2014). Megaherbivores (proboscideans, giraffids, rhinocerotids) are rare. Hyaenids are the most abundant carnivore at most localities. Mammalian relative abundances fluctuate significantly through the Konso Formation. In some levels, Alcelaphini and Antilopini reach 86 percent of the fauna; in other levels only 8 percent (Suwa et al., Chapter 22). Fish fossils are fragmentary, while crocodiles and turtles are abundant in some localities. Fossil birds indicate streams and freshwater bodies (Louchart, 2014). Overall, the fauna indicates that there were open grasslands bordering the lake up until ~1.4 Ma, while the upper levels show a more complex pattern of wet and dry grasslands with woodlands surrounded by a lake.

Omo-Turkana Basin
Lower Omo Valley

The lower Omo Valley of southern Ethiopia has one of the richest and longest Plio-Pleistocene fossiliferous sequences in this region. Three major geological formations of the Omo Group deposits are exposed in the lower Omo Valley: the Mursi, Usno, and Shungura Formations (Figure 15.6). Previous work on the Mursi Formation, with deposits dating to about 4 Ma, is reviewed by Drapeau and colleagues (Chapter 23). The **Mursi Formation** appears to sample one of the most wooded (perhaps forest) and humid environments in eastern Africa during the Pliocene (Drapeau et al., 2014). The fact that no hominins have been found in the Formation, despite a large sample of fossil mammals, may indicate that they were uncommon in wet and wooded environments, but further taphonomic work is needed to test this idea.

The **Usno Formation** has a sample of about 2500 fossil vertebrates, including 21 hominins from unit U-12, dated to about 3.3 Ma (Suwa, 1990; Bobe, 1997). Most of these specimens are isolated teeth classified as Hominini indet., but a few are referred to *Australopithecus* cf. *afarensis* (Kimbel and Delezene, 2009). Most of the Usno fossil vertebrates derive from sediments that correlate with lower Member B of the Shungura Formation (de Heinzelin and Haesaerts, 1983b).

The **Shungura Formation** has a sedimentary sequence with an aggregate thickness of ~760 m, consisting of 12 members dating from >3.6 to about 1.0 Ma, with a fossil record of over 50,000 vertebrates (Brown et al., 1970; Coppens, 1978; Howell, 1978a; de Heinzelin, 1983b; Bobe, 1997; Alemseged, 1998; Eck, 2007). At the base of the sequence, the Basal Member (>3.6 Ma) has a sparse fossil record. Member A (3.6–3.4 Ma) to Member L (1.38–1.0 Ma; there is no "member I" in the sequence) have yielded a rich record of fossil vertebrates, including 282 hominins and their paleoenvironmental context (Alemseged et al., 2007). E. Negash and colleagues present an analysis of diversity patterns and faunal similarity across members of the Shungura Formation in Chapter 24, and recently published a comprehensive study of stable isotopes in all major mammals (Negash et al., 2020), including hominins (Wynn et al., 2020).

Member A (3.6–3.4 Ma) through the middle of Member G (2.1 Ma) was dominated by a large meandering river (de Heinzelin

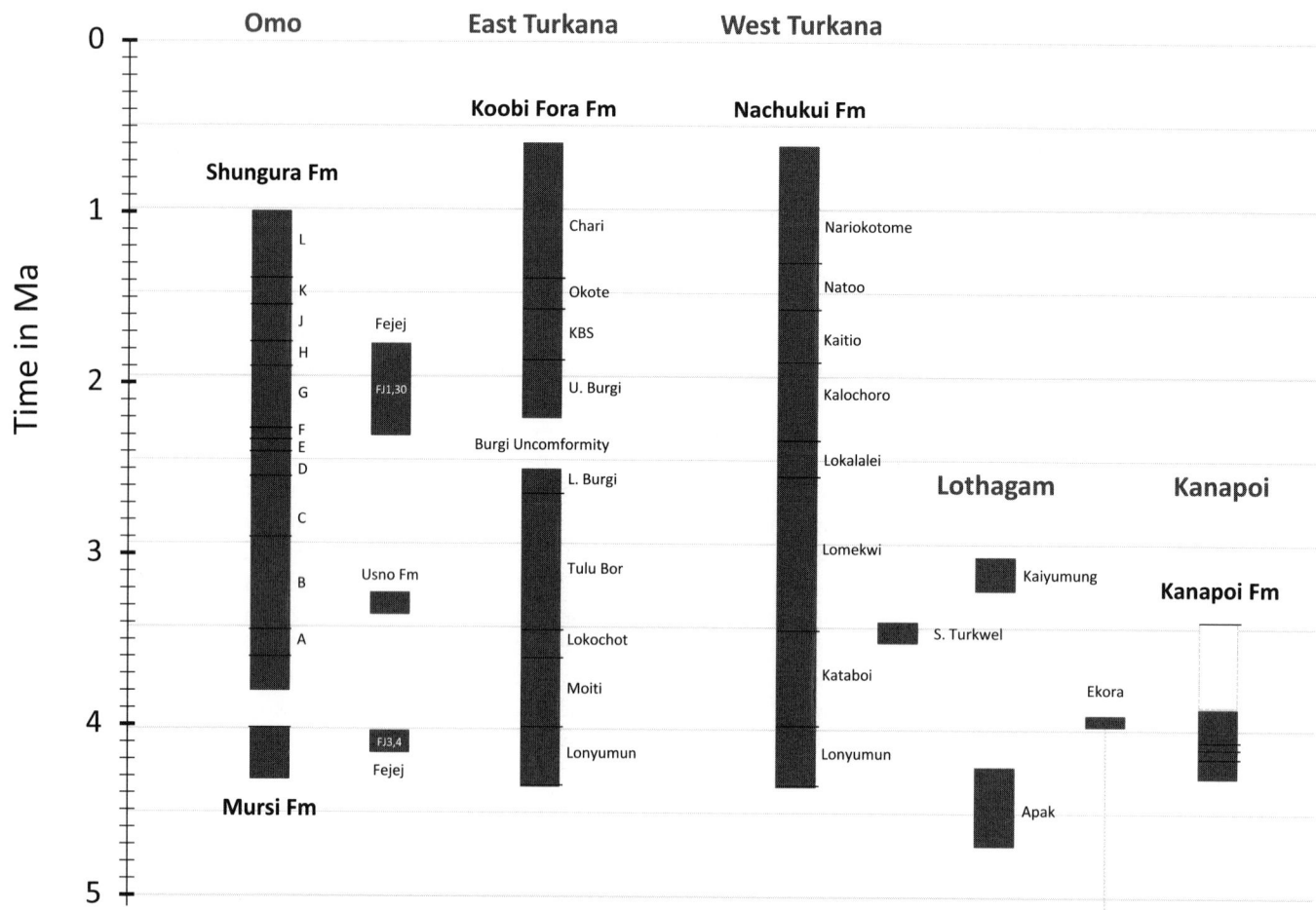

Figure 15.6 Chronology of the Omo Group deposits in Ethiopia and Kenya, including the lower Omo Valley (Mursi, Usno, and Shungura Formations), East Turkana (Koobi Fora Formation), West Turkana (Nachukui Formation), and Kanapoi (Kanapoi Formation).

et al., 1976), with a shift to lacustrine conditions in middle/upper Member G (2.1–1.9 Ma), and a return to fluvial conditions in Members H–L (1.9–1.0 Ma; de Heinzelin and Haesaerts, 1983a). Paleosols in the lower Formation (Members A and B) indicate relatively high precipitation, with reduced precipitation in Member C and above (Haesaerts et al., 1983). Stable isotopes from pedogenic carbonates show that Members B through G formed in extensive woodlands, with a shift to wooded grasslands above Member G, i.e., after 2 Ma (Levin et al., 2011). The evidence of paleobotanical remains (wood, fruits, and pollen; Bonnefille and Letouzey, 1976; Bonnefille and Dechamps, 1983; Dechamps and Maes, 1985) and micromammals (Wesselman, 1984, 1995) support the more extensive woodlands and forests in Members A and B relative to later members, with more open conditions from Member G onwards. Analyses of larger mammals likewise suggest shifts in faunal taxonomic abundances between Members B and C, at about 2.9–2.8 Ma, and higher proportions of grazing species first in Members D, E, and F, 2.5–2.4 Ma (Bobe and Eck, 2001; Negash et al., 2015), then at the base of Member G at 2.3 Ma (Alemseged, 2003; Negash et al., 2015), and more markedly after 2 Ma (Bobe and Behrensmeyer, 2004).

Even though these environmental changes are well documented in the Shungura Formation from 3.6 to 2 Ma, the lower Omo Valley remained more wooded than other parts of the Omo-Turkana Basin, such as West and East Turkana, and acted as a woodland refugium (Bobe, 2011; Levin et al., 2011; Plummer et al., 2015). In summary, the lower Omo Valley was characterized by extensive riverine forests and woodlands under relatively mesic conditions (Members A and B), followed by a transition to less-forested conditions (Member B to Member C, at about 2.9–2.8 Ma), then an increase in grasslands in Members D, E, and F, i.e., from about 2.5 Ma to 2.3 Ma. Profound changes in the Omo paleoenvironments occurred above Member G, after 2 Ma, when grasslands became more prevalent like the East and West Turkana regions.

Fejej

The Plio-Pleistocene site of Fejej is located in the Omo Basin very close to the Ethiopia–Kenya border, with sediments of the Koobi Fora Formation just to the south. It was identified by the Paleoanthropological Inventory of the Ethiopian Ministry of Culture in 1989 (Asfaw et al., 1991). Geological surveys have established that Oligocene deposits have abundant fossil wood associated with the Fejej Basalt (Davidson, 1983). Pliocene localities (FJ-3, FJ-4) with fossil vertebrates, including hominins (in locality FJ-4), date to ~4.1 Ma (Figure 15.6; Asfaw et al., 1991; Fleagle et al., 1991; Kappelman et al., 1996). A reanalysis of the Fejej material by C. Ward assigned the hominin teeth to *Australopithecus anamensis* (Ward, 2014). Archeological sites are documented at locality FJ-1 with Oldowan artifacts, stratigraphically below a tuff dated to ~1.9 Ma (Asfaw et al., 1991, 1993; Haileab and Feibel, 1993; Chapon et al., 2005, 2011). There is a small sample of fossil hominins from FJ-1, including a cf. *Paranthropus boisei* distal humerus, and a few *Homo* cf. *habilis* teeth (de Lumley and Marchal, 2004). The fauna from FJ-1 includes *Theropithecus*, *Paracolobus*, *Deinotherium*, *Elephas*, *Ceratotherium*, *Diceros*, *Equus*, *Notochoerus*, *Metridiochoerus*, *Kolpochoerus*, *Pelorovis*, *Aepyceros*, *Tragelaphus*, and alcelaphin and reduncin bovids, among other mammals (Barsky et al., 2011; Echassoux et al., 2004). *Aepyceros* is particularly abundant (Echassoux et al., 2004). There are also species of turtle, crocodile, and fish. The faunal evidence indicates an environment with woodlands and grasslands with a river and/or lake during hominin occupation.

East Turkana

The **Koobi Fora Formation** on the east side of Lake Turkana (East Turkana) consists of 565 m of fluvio-lacustrine deposits dating from ~4.3 Ma to 0.7 Ma (Figure 15.6), and is divided into eight members: the Lonyumun, Moiti, Lokochot, Tulu Bor, Burgi, KBS, Okote, and Chari Members (Brown and Feibel, 1986; Feibel et al., 1991). The chronological framework of the Formation is well-constrained by frequent deposition of volcanic ashes, many of them with radiometric dates, or correlated with other well-dated tephra (Brown, 1982; Brown et al., 2006; Brown and McDougall, 2011; McDougall et al., 2012). This formation has a rich record of fossil hominins, including the species *Australopithecus anamensis*, *Au. afarensis*, *Paranthropus boisei*, *Homo rudolfensis*, *H. habilis*, and *H. erectus* (*ergaster*; Leakey and Leakey, 1978; Wood, 1991; Leakey et al., 1995; Spoor et al., 2007; Wood and Leakey, 2011; Leakey et al., 2012; Grine et al., 2019).

Artifacts are present in the upper Burgi, KBS, and Okote Members (~2–1.4 Ma), specifically of Oldowan and Acheulean technologies (Harris and Isaac, 1976; Isaac, 1997; Braun and Harris, 2009; Braun et al., 2010; Presnyakova et al., 2018). The paleontological record is abundant, currently with ~12,000 accessioned mammals, which represent only a portion of the specimens that have been excavated and collected (Bobe et al., Chapter 26). Although nearly all major groups of mammals have been published, some in great detail (Harris, 1983a, 1991c; Jablonski and Leakey, 2008; Werdelin and Lewis, 2013a), the Koobi Fora fossil record continues to increase and some taxa require taxonomic revision. Taphonomy and paleoecology have been a key component of research at Koobi Fora (Behrensmeyer, 1975, 1985), and these fields continue to provide fresh perspectives on the early hominin environments (Behrensmeyer et al., 2007b; Patterson et al., 2017a, 2017b, 2019; Bobe and Carvalho, 2019). The Koobi Fora Formation provides evidence of significant environmental and evolutionary changes through time, and of significant heterogeneity across space (Bobe et al., Chapter 26). Paleosol analysis has detected three episodes of increased aridity and expansion of C_4 grasses in East and West Turkana between: (1) *ca*. 3.6 and 3.4 Ma, (2) 2.5 and 2.0 Ma, and (3) *ca*. 1.8 and 1.6 Ma (Wynn, 2004). The East Turkana vegetation changed from woodlands and wooded grasslands to increasing grasslands after 2 Ma, but with evidence of continuous landscape heterogeneity.

West Turkana

The **Nachukui Formation** consists of ~730 m of lacustrine and fluvial sediments exposed along the western margin of the Lake Turkana Basin in Kenya (Harris et al., 1988b). Numerous tuffs in the sequence provide chronological control and correlations with other sites (Brown and McDougall, 2011; McDougall et al., 2012). The formation is divided into eight members: the Lonyumun (4.3–3.97 Ma), Kataboi (3.97–3.42 Ma), Lomekwi (3.42–2.53 Ma), Lokalalei (2.53–2.33 Ma), Kalochoro (2.33–1.87 Ma), Kaitio (1.87–1.56 Ma), Natoo (1.56–1.30 Ma), and Nariokotome (1.30–0.7 Ma) Members (Figure 15.6). At Lothagam, three other members are contemporaneous with parts of the main Nachukui Formation farther north: the Apak (4.3–4.2 Ma), Moruongori (~4.1–4 Ma), and Kaiyumung Members (~3.6–3.2 Ma; McDougall and Feibel, 1999). Fluvial deposits are interrupted by several lacustrine intervals, including the Lonyumun Lake (4.1–4.0 Ma), the Lokochot Lake (~3.5 Ma), and the Lorenyang Lake (~2–1.5 Ma) prior to the formation of modern Lake Turkana in the Late Pleistocene (Feibel, 2011). The current version of the PaleoTurkana Database has 2031 records of fossil vertebrates from the Nachukui Formation (Bobe and Carvalho, 2019). Hominin taxa include *Australopithecus* indet. (Ward et al., 1999b; Wood and Leakey, 2011), *Kenyanthropus platyops* (Leakey et al., 2001), *Paranthropus aethiopicus* (Walker et al., 1986), *Paranthropus boisei* (Brown et al., 2001; Prat et al., 2003), and *Homo erectus* (Walker and Leakey, 1993). The Nachukui Formation archeological sites include the earliest records of lithic artifacts (Harmand et al., 2015), but see (Archer et al., 2020), several Oldowan sites (Roche et al., 2003; Tiercelin et al., 2010), and the earliest Acheulian (Lepre et al., 2011).

J.P. Brugal and H. Roche provide a paleoenvironmental analysis of the fauna from the Kalochoro and Kaitio Members (Chapter 25). The distribution of bovid taxa across sites suggests significant environmental heterogeneity at West Turkana during the Plio-Pleistocene (Harris et al., 1988), but environments were typically more open than those in the Omo and East Turkana (Bobe, 2011). Carbon isotope data from paleosols shows that woodlands and wooded grasslands dominated from 4 to ~2.5 Ma, and that after 2 Ma C_4 grasslands became more prominent (Levin et al., 2011). Carbon isotopes from plant wax biomarkers show that in the interval from 2.3 to 1.7 Ma the vegetation structure varied from 5 percent C_4 to 100 percent C_4, but with an overall shift toward a greater proportion of C_4 habitats after 2.1 Ma (Uno et al., 2016a). Various studies indicate persistent environmental differences between West and East Turkana during the Plio-Pleistocene (Bobe et al., 2007b; Bobe, 2011; Fortelius et al., 2016), likely due to the half-graben basin configuration (Feibel, 2011).

Lothagam

The Lothagam area lies west of Lake Turkana and preserves an abundance of Late Miocene vertebrates from the **Nawata Formation** (Patterson et al., 1970; Behrensmeyer, 1976; Leakey et al., 1996; Leakey and Harris, 2003). Most specimens derive from fluvial sediments of the Lower Member of the Nawata Formation (7.4–6.5 Ma), but some also derive from the Upper Member (6.5–5 Ma; Figure 15.4; McDougall and Feibel, 1999).

Bovidae are the most common family of mammals (Harris, 2003), with Suidae (Harris and Leakey, 2003b), Hippopotamidae (Weston, 2003), Cercopithecidae (Leakey et al., 2003), and Equidae present (Bernor and Harris, 2003). These five families constitute 81 percent of the Lothagam mammals. At the genus level, the most common taxa are *Nyanzachoerus*, *Archaeopotamus*, *Aepyceros*, *Parapapio*, and *Eurygnathohippus* (Bobe, 2011). Lothagam has a number of holotype specimens, including that of *Nyanzachoerus tulotos* (KNM-LT 316) from the lower Nawata Formation (Cooke and Ewer, 1972). Stable carbon isotopes from dental enamel indicate that both *Nyanzachoerus* and *Archaeopotamus* shifted their diet from predominantly C_3 resources in the Lower Member to a mix of C_3 and C_4 resources in the Upper Member of the Nawata Formation. *Aepyceros* at Lothagam had a C_3 diet, and *Eurygnathohippus* underwent a rapid transition from a mixed diet to a purely C_4 diet at ~7 Ma (Cerling et al., 2003b).

Fish specimens are abundant and provide key information about regional water bodies (Stewart, 2003). The fossil vertebrates indicate that late Miocene environments were heterogeneous, including elements of forests, woodlands, and grasslands in the vicinity of a broad river, but these environments became more open in the transition from the Lower to the Upper Member ~6.5 Ma. Lothagam also has younger fossils of Pliocene age within exposures of the Apak and Kaiyumung Members of the Nachukui Formation (Figure 15.6; McDougall and Feibel, 1999).

Lothagam hominins are noteworthy for their rarity. There are two hominin teeth from the Upper Member of the Nawata Formation, and a mandible fragment (KNM-LT 329) from the Apak Member of the Nachukui Formation (Leakey and Walker, 2003). The isolated teeth date to between 6.5 and 5 Ma, and the Lothagam mandible dates between 5 and 4.3 Ma (McDougall and Feibel, 1999). Establishing the ecological or taphonomic reasons for hominin rarity in the late Miocene remains an intriguing research problem.

Ekora

Located between Lothagam and Kanapoi, the site of Ekora has produced a limited but important Early Pliocene fauna including mollusks, fishes, turtles, crocodiles, and mammals (Patterson et al., 1970). The sediments are fluvio-lacustrine in origin and are dominated by mudstones, siltstones, and fine-grained sandstones (Powers, 1980). The Ekora sedimentary sequence partly overlaps in age with that of Kanapoi (Figure 15.6; Behrensmeyer, 1976). Among mammals, there are species of *Nyanzachoerus* (Geraads and Bobe, 2020b), *Ceratotherium*, *Eurygnathohippus* (Hooijer and Maglio, 1974), *Anancus*, *Elephas*, and *Loxodonta*. The holotype of *Elephas ekorensis* derives from this site (Maglio, 1970). This species is the earliest known representative of the genus *Elephas* (Sanders et al., 2010; Sanders, 2020).

Kanapoi

Between 1964 and 1967, Bryan Patterson led surveys in the Kanapoi area, making important discoveries, including that of a hominin humerus among other Pliocene vertebrates (Patterson and Howells, 1967; Cooke and Ewer, 1972; Hooijer and Patterson, 1972; Maglio, 1973; Hooijer and Maglio, 1974). Patterson also provided an initial description of the Pliocene sequence known as the **Kanapoi Formation** (Patterson et al., 1970), later elaborated by Powers (1980). After a long hiatus in research, a team led by Meave Leakey and the National Museums of Kenya (NMK) conducted extensive surveys and excavations from 1994 to 1997, which led to the discovery and description of a new hominin species, *Australopithecus anamensis* (Leakey et al., 1995, 1998). This work led to the documentation of hundreds of fossil vertebrates, as described in a volume edited by J.M. Harris and M. Leakey (2003a). Further work at Kanapoi was led by F.K. Manthi and the NMK, with excavations in 2003, and then with field seasons from 2007 to 2008, and from 2012 to 2015 (Manthi et al., 2020b). The Kanapoi Formation consists of up to 60 m of fluvial, deltaic, and lacustrine sediments resting on Mio-Pliocene basalts. At the base there is a lower fluvial sequence, followed by a lacustrine interval of the Lonyumun Lake, and then an upper fluvial sequence (Powers, 1980; Feibel, 2003, 2011). Chronologic control is provided by several tuffs with radiometric dates, indicating that most of the Kanapoi fossils date to the interval from 4.2 to 4.1 Ma (Figure 15.6; McDougall and Brown, 2008).

The Kanapoi fossil record comprises 69 mammal species representing 29 Families from 11 Orders. Hominins are abundant, with a sample of 74 specimens of *Au. anamensis* (Ward et al., 2020). There is also a large sample of monkeys, with *Parapapio* the most abundant primate (Frost et al., 2020). The most common mammal in the Kanapoi collections is *Nyanzachoerus* (Geraads and Bobe, 2020b), and the second most common mammal is *Tragelaphus* (Geraads and Bobe, 2020a). There are nine genera of megaherbivores (body mass > 1000 kg): aff. *Hippopotamus*, *Elephas*, *Loxodonta*, *Anancus*, *Deinotherium*, *Giraffa*, *Sivatherium*, *Ceratotherium*, and *Diceros* (Boisserie, 2020; Geraads, 2020; Geraads and Bobe, 2020a; Sanders, 2020). Micromammals are abundant and diverse but very patchy in distribution (Manthi and Winkler, 2020).

There are three species of crocodilians (Brochu, 2020), and fish are particularly abundant in the lacustrine sequence (Stewart and Rufolo, 2020). There are also significant collections of birds, including 10 families (Field, 2020), squamates (Head and Müller, 2020), anurans (about half of them belonging to the genus *Hemisus*; Delfino, 2020), and gastropods (Van Bocxlaer, 2020). Stable carbon isotopes from pedogenic carbonates indicate that Pliocene Kanapoi had a range of environments dominated by woodlands and wooded grasslands (Quinn and Lepre, 2020; Wynn, 2000), but that many mammals had significant C_4 diets (Manthi et al., 2020a). The geological, sedimentological, isotopic, and paleontological evidence indicates that Kanapoi environments between 4.2 and 4.1 Ma were highly seasonal and heterogeneous, with an ample supply of fresh water in streams and the Lonyumun Lake. The fact that *Au. anamensis* is relatively abundant in the Kanapoi Formation, even after considering collecting and taphonomic factors (Bobe et al., 2020a), may indicate that the Pliocene habitats in the region were favorable to this species. It appears that *Au. anamensis* may have been absent or rare in other eastern African sites with differing paleoenvironments.

Kenya Rift Valley

Samburu Hills

The Samburu Hills area, west of Baragoi and east of the Suguta Valley, has a succession of Neogene sedimentary rocks, with the Nachola Formation at the base, followed by the Aka Aiteputh Formation and the Namurungule Formation, with the latter as the most relevant to our discussion of Late Miocene paleoenvironments (Sawada et al., 2006). Since 1980, the area has been studied by the Japan–Kenya Paleoanthropological Expedition. The **Namurungule Formation** consists of ~200 m of lacustrine, delta, and pyroclastic sediments with a rich vertebrate fossil record (Saneyoshi et al., 2006). The large hominoid *Samburupithecus kiptalami* (Ishida and Pickford, 1997), radioisotopically dated to between 9.6 and 9.5 Ma (Figure 15.2), derives from pyroclastic flow deposits of the Namurungule Formation (Figure 15.4; Sawada et al., 1998). The formation is divided into a lower member and an upper member separated by a lahar, with *Samburupithecus* and most of the mammalian fauna deriving from the lower member (Tsujikawa, 2005a). Hipparionin equids are the most abundant mammal in both members, followed by the giraffid *Palaeotragus*. Boselaphini are very abundant in the lower member but absent from the upper member (Tsujikawa, 2005b). $\delta^{13}C$ values indicate that the Namurungule equids had a mixed feeding diet but with a preference for C_4 resources, while other taxa, e.g., bovids, hippopotamids, suids, and rhinocerotids, had mixed feeding strategies. Deinotheres were C_3 browsers (Uno et al., 2011). The environments associated with *Samburupithecus* would have included trees and grasses close to a lake. We may speculate that *Samburupithecus* was adapted to the wooded parts of the Namurungule environments, but open habitats occurred in close proximity.

Nakali

The fossiliferous exposures at Nakali were first explored by E. Aguirre in 1969, who identified several taxa of Miocene fossils, with *Hipparion* as the most common (Aguirre and Leakey, 1974). Since 2002 a team from Kyoto University and the NMK has been conducting systematic research in the area. This site has gained great paleoanthropological importance since the description of the large hominoid *Nakalipithecus nakayamai* as a possible ancestor of the African apes and humans (Figure 15.2; Kunimatsu et al., 2007). The holotype of this species, KNM-NA 46400, is a mandible fragment with m1–m3 similar in size to that of a female gorilla. A second hominoid species based on an upper premolar was later reported from the same site (Kunimatsu et al., 2016). The **Nakali Formation** is a sequence of 340 m in thickness exposed over an area of 16 km² east of the Suguta Valley. The formation is divided into Lower, Middle, and Upper Members, and it is underlain by the Alengerr Tuffs, dated to 10.6 Ma, and overlain by the Nasorut sequence, dated to 7.74 Ma. The lower part of the formation consists of lacustrine sediments, and the upper part is fluvio-lacustrine. The hominoid *Nakalipithecus* and most of the mammalian fauna derive from the fluvio-lacustrine deposits of the Upper Member, bracketed between 9.9 and 9.8 Ma (Figure 15.4; Kunimatsu et al., 2007).

More than 4000 fossil vertebrates, and plants, have been collected from the Nakali sites (Kunimatsu et al., 2016). The primate fauna includes one of the earliest records of colobines in Africa (Nakatsukasa et al., 2010), the latest record of nyanzapithecines (Kunimatsu et al., 2017b), and a galagid (Kunimatsu et al., 2017a). Other mammals include rodents (Flynn and Maurice, 1984), carnivorans (Morales and Pickford, 2006), artiodactyls (Tsubamoto et al., 2015, 2017, 2020), perissodactyls (Handa et al., 2015, 2017, 2019), and proboscideans. $\delta^{13}C$ values from dental enamel indicate that nearly all Nakali mammals were C_3 browsers or mixed feeders, with the exception of a few equid teeth that indicate a significant component of C_4 grasses in the diet of some animals (Uno et al., 2011). Thus, at nearly 10 Ma, Nakali has the earliest evidence in eastern Africa of mammals beginning to shift from primarily C_3 dietary resources to diets with a significant component of C_4 resources.

Tugen Hills – Baringo Basin

The Tugen Hills area, extending for about 100 km along a north–south axis west of Lake Baringo in the Central Kenya Rift, exposes fossiliferous sediments spanning from the Middle Miocene to recent times. The area has undergone significant uplift since the Pliocene and today reaches an elevation of 2400 m (Pickford, 1994a). Geological formations defined in the Tugen Hills include, from oldest to youngest, the Muruyur Beds (16–13.3 Ma), the Ngorora Formation (13.3–8.5 Ma), the Mpesida Beds (7.29–6.2 Ma), the Lukeino Formation (6.06–5.6 Ma), the Chemeron Formation (5.3–1.6 Ma), and the Kapthurin Formation (0.7–0.2 Ma; Bishop et al., 1971; Bishop and Pickford, 1975; Deino and Hill, 2002; Deino and McBrearty, 2002; Deino et al., 2002; Hill, 2002; Doman, 2017; Rasmussen et al., 2017). Some researchers recognize the Mabaget Formation (5.3–4.5 Ma) as corresponding to the early deposits of the Chemeron Formation. One of the first fossil hominins from Kenya was found in the Chemeron Formation during the course of geological mapping in 1965 (Martyn, 1967). In this volume, there are two chapters dedicated to the Chemeron Formation (Binetti et al., Chapter 27; Goble, Chapter 28). Here we briefly review the paleoenvironments in the Ngorora Formation, the Mpesida beds, the Lukeino Formation, and the Chemeron Formation.

The **Ngorora Formation** (13.3–8.5 Ma; Figure 15.4) has an aggregate thickness of ~365 m of fluvio-lacustrine volcaniclastic and tuffaceous deposits at the type locality of Kabarsero (Bishop and Chapman, 1970). The sequence – bracketed by the Tiim Phonolites below and the Ewalel Phonolites above – is divided into five members, with Member A at the base and Member E at the top, and has produced abundant fossils, including plants, mollusks, insect traces, fishes, and mammals (Bishop and Pickford, 1975). The Ngeringerowa area, south of the main Ngorora deposits, has fossils that date from 9.5 to 8.8 Ma and correlate with the upper part of the Ngorora Formation (Hill et al., 2002). Lacustrine sediments predominate in the Ngorora sequence, but there are also fluvially reworked pyroclastic deposits (Pickford, 1978). Freshwater conditions in Member A gave way to an alkaline lake in Member C, with abrupt and significant fluctuations in lake levels during Members C and D times (Rasmussen et al., 2017).

Ngorora primates include the latest occurrences of *Victoriapithecus* in sediments overlying the Kabarsero forest, and the earliest occurrences of Colobinae in the Ngeringerowa area (Benefit and Pickford, 1986; Hill et al., 2002). There are two specimens of Hominoidea: an upper molar (KNM-BN 1378) found in 1968 (Bishop and Pickford, 1975) and a lower premolar (KNM-BN 10489) found in 1983 derive from member C (~12 Ma; Figure 15.2). The carnivore fauna includes a large creodont of the family Hyaenodontidae, with a date of 13–12 Ma (Morales and Pickford, 2005). There is also the amphicyonid *Agnotherium*, the mustelids *Vishnuonyx* and *Eomellivora*, the viverrid *Tugenictis*, a small herpestid, and the percrocutid *Percrocuta* (Morales and Pickford, 2005). Among bovids, boselaphins of the genus *Protragocerus* are most abundant, especially in Members B–D (Thomas, 1981b). Among suids, *Listriodon* occurs in Member A and *Lopholistriodon* in Members B–D (Pickford, 2001b). One of the earliest records of hipparionin equids in Africa dates to between 11 and 10.5 Ma (Pickford, 2001a). The giant hyrax *Parapliohyrax* derives from Members B–E (Pickford and Fischer, 1987). Megaherbivores include rhinocerotids, giraffids, hippopotamids, deinotheriids, and gomphotheriids (Pickford, 1978).

Abundant and remarkably preserved fishes, mostly of the family Cichlidae, were recovered from several layers in Members C and D (Rasmussen et al., 2017). Turtles and crocodiles are common, and there are also remains of a marabou stork, an ostrich, and *Anhinga* (Pickford, 1978).

Palynological samples from Member C consist of *Juniperus*, *Podocarpus*, Euphorbiaceae, Poaceae, and Astaraceae, and indicate wooded grasslands and grassy woodlands (Rasmussen et al., 2017). A locality near Kabarsero dated to 12.6 Ma has produced fossil leaves that indicate wet forests with West African affinities (Jacobs and Kabuye, 1987; Jacobs and Deino, 1996). Leaf physiognomy indicates that mean annual temperature would have been ~22°C. At the site of Waril, dated to ~10 Ma, the paleobotanical evidence indicates seasonally dry woodlands or wooded savannas (Jacobs, 1999; Jacobs et al., 2010).

During the long span of the Ngorora Formation, local environments shifted considerably with an expanding and contracting lake under frequent volcanism and tectonic movements. At times there was a tropical forest in the region as indicated by the fossil leaves, but also open woodlands and grasslands as suggested by the diverse mammalian fauna.

The **Mpesida Beds** (7.29–6.2 Ma; Figure 15.4) consist of ~100 m of lacustrine deposits and pyroclastic debris with surrounding lava flows (Doman, 2017). The locality of Kapturo (7.2–6.7 Ma) in the lower Mpesida Beds preserves fossil leaves indicative of deciduous woodlands, and leaf physiognomy indicates a mean annual temperature of 21.7°C for this region in the late Miocene (Jacobs and Deino, 1996). In the upper Mpesida Beds, the Rormuch area has well-preserved fossil wood indicative of tropical rain forest at 6.4 Ma (Kingston et al., 2002), and fossil wood from the site of Cheparain provides evidence of a seasonal, semi-evergreen forest at 6.3 Ma (De Franceschi et al., 2016). The sample of fossil vertebrates consists of ~350 specimens including fishes, turtles, crocodiles, and mammals (Doman, 2017). Among mammals, the fauna includes colobine primates, leporids, hyaenids, bovids, suids, hippopotamids, giraffids, equids, rhinocerotids, chalicotheriids, gomphotheriids, stegodontids, and elephantids. A full taxonomic list is provided by Doman (2017).

The **Lukeino Formation** (6.06–5.6 Ma; Figure 15.4) consists of ~130 m of lacustrine sediments near the base, clastic deposits, and volcanic tuffs toward the top (Sawada et al., 2002). The holotype of *Orrorin tugenensis* was recovered from the Kapsomin locality, and other *Orrorin* specimens were found at Cheboit, Kapcheberek, and Aragai (Senut et al., 2001). The hominins derive from both lacustrine and fluvial floodplain deposits, and they were found in a sample of 1275 fossil vertebrates, including abundant fishes, crocodiles, and hippopotamids (Doman, 2017; Pickford and Senut, 2001b). Stable isotopes from dental enamel indicate that the mammals had a range of dietary resources available, from C_3 plants to C_4 tropical grasses (Roche et al., 2013). Impalas (*Aepyceros*) are the most abundant bovid tribe at the hominin locality of Kapsomin. The cercopithecid fauna includes cf. *Parapapio lothagamensis* and a colobine (Gilbert et al., 2010). Based on the habitat preferences of the mammalian species preserved, the paleoenvironments appears to have been open woodland, with denser stands of trees that fringed the lakeshore and nearby streams. A comprehensive and multi-proxy analysis of the Mpesida Beds and the Lukeino Formation paleoecology by Doman (2017) shows that the Tugen Hills area in the late Miocene had significant environmental heterogeneity, with areas of forest and heavy tree cover, and areas of grasses. However, compared to other sites of similar age elsewhere in eastern Africa (e.g., Lothagam), the Tugen Hills area retained faunal elements more common in earlier sites (e.g., the Chorora Formation). In this regard, the Tugen Hills area may be seen as a relict or refugium where some species persisted longer than elsewhere in Africa (Doman, 2017).

The **Chemeron Formation** (5.3–1.6 Ma; Figure 15.7) is underlain by the Late Miocene Kaparaina Basalts and overlain by the Middle Pleistocene Kapthurin Formation (Deino and Hill, 2002; Deino et al., 2002). Pickford refers to the Mabaget Formation (5.3–4.5 Ma) as the sequence elsewhere called Chemeron Formation – Northern Extension (Pickford et al., 2004). The Chemeron sequence is composed of fluvial and lacustrine sediments with intercalated tuffs and paleosols. There are more than 100 distinct paleontological localities, with most fossil specimens deriving from lacustrine silts (Goble, 2011). Some key hominins derive from the Chemeron Formation, including an early hominin mandible fragment (KNM-TH 13150) from Tabarin dated to 4.42 Ma and assigned to *Ardipithecus ramidus* (Binetti et al., Chapter 27), and a temporal bone considered to be one of the earliest specimens of *Homo* (KNM-BC 1; Martyn, 1967; Hill et al., 1992). A partial skeleton of *Theropithecus brumpti* dates to 2.63 Ma (Gilbert et al., 2011). Early records of *Heliosciurus* and *Paraxerus* derive from ~4.4 Ma deposits (Winkler, 2002). The largest faunal sample comes from locality BPRP #1 (Baringo Paleontological Research Project #1), dated to 5.14 Ma. At this locality, Hippopotamidae are the most abundant family of mammals, followed by Suidae, Deinotheriidae, Bovidae, Gomphotheriidae, Rhinocerotidae, and Elephantidae, in that order (Goble, 2011).

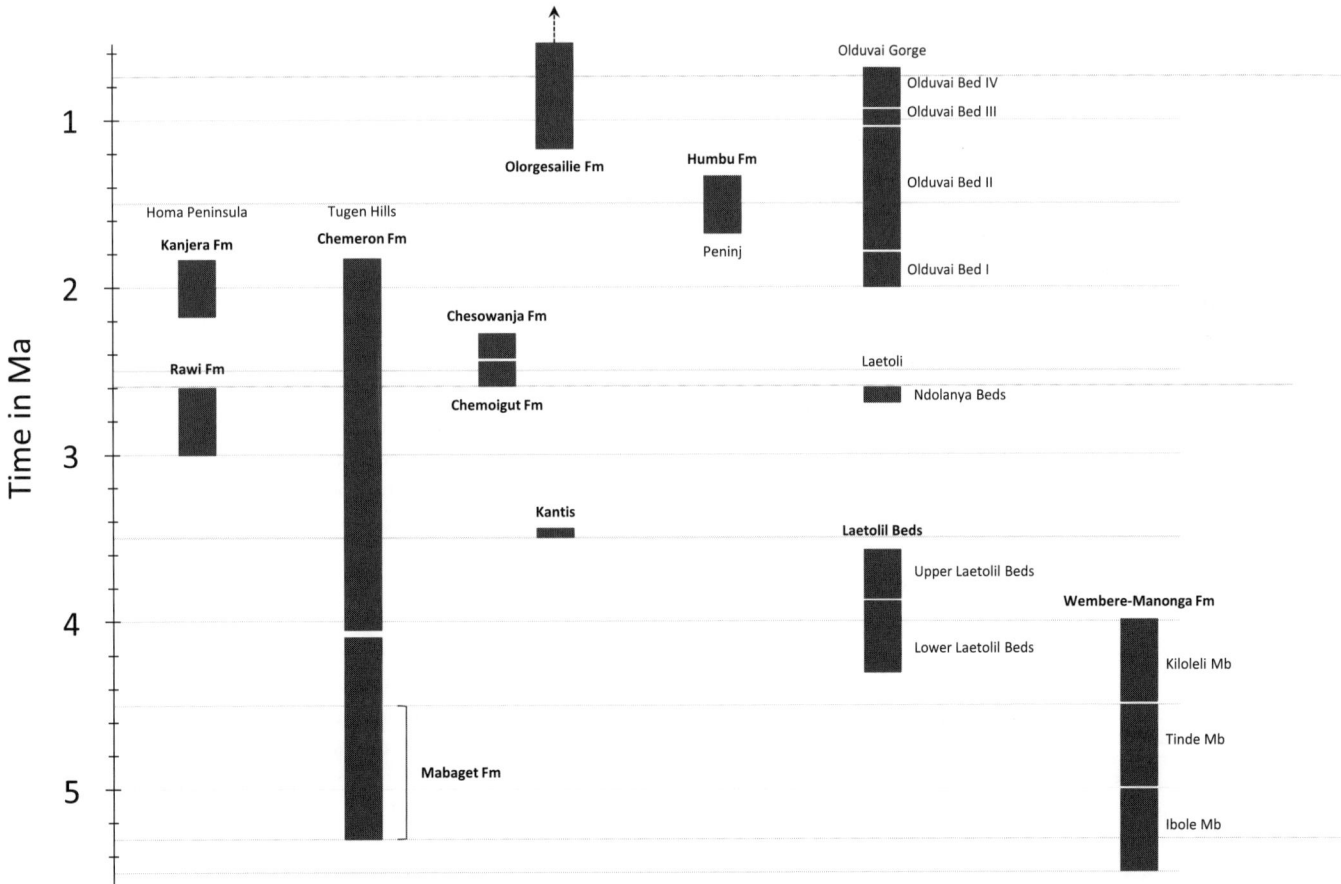

Figure 15.7 Chronology of key fossil sequences in the Homa Peninsula, Kenya Rift, and Tanzania Divergence zone dating from the early Pliocene to the early Pleistocene.

Faunal and isotopic evidence indicates that this site had wooded environments, with a smaller component of grasslands. The hominin KNM-TH 13150, *Ar. ramidus*, is associated with forest species at 4.4 Ma (Pickford et al., 2004). Stable isotopes from pedogenic carbonates show a persistent mix of C_3 and C_4 habitats over time, with no trend toward a greater proportion of C_4 grasslands (Kingston et al., 1994). More recent work on stable isotopes from plant wax biomarkers indicates an increase in C_4 vegetation at ~3 Ma (Lupien et al., 2019). In the middle part of the Chemeron Formation, a series of diatomites at the Pliocene/Pleistocene boundary (2.7–2.55 Ma) indicates the presence of large fresh water lakes that fluctuated with a periodicity of 23 kyr, i.e., precession-driven cycles amplified by changes in the eccentricity of the Earth's orbit (Deino et al., 2006a; Kingston et al., 2007). These fluctuations demonstrate the direct effects that broader climatic cycles had on local environments of eastern Africa during the Pliocene and Pleistocene.

Overlying the Chemeron Formation, the 125-m thick **Kapthurin Formation** dates from about 0.6 to 0.2 Ma (Deino and McBrearty, 2002). The archeological record of the Kapthurin Formation spans the transition from Acheulean to Middle Stone Age technologies (McBrearty and Tryon, 2006; Tryon and McBrearty, 2002). The sequence is divided into five members, with K1 at the base and K5 at the top. Members K1, K3, and K5 are fluvio-lacustrine; members K2 and K4 are composed primarily of tephra deposits (Deino and McBrearty, 2002). Member K3, dated to 0.5 Ma, is of particular interest here as it has yielded specimens of *Homo* as well as the only known fossils of the genus *Pan* (McBrearty and Jablonski, 2005). The *Homo* specimens derive from fluvial sediments of member K3, and the chimpanzee fossils derive from lacustrine sediments in K3'. The stratigraphic level of the chimpanzee fossils consists of clays and sands deposited in a shallow body of water with localized streams and a fossil spring. Other fossils from this member include gastropods, fishes, turtles, crocodiles, bovids, hippopotamids, suids, proboscideans, rodents, and a colobine monkey. The K3' fauna is consistent with the presence of permanent water, localized marshy conditions, and woodland (McBrearty and Jablonski, 2005). Vertebrate fossils from the fluvial deposits are similar to those from K3' and suggest that *Homo* and *Pan* may have occurred in broadly similar environments at this time.

Chesowanja

The **Chemoigut Formation** at Chesowanja, east of Lake Baringo, has a record of vertebrates that includes one of the latest occurrences of *Paranthropus boisei*, as well as Oldowan tools (Carney et al., 1971; Gowlett et al., 1981). The ~50-m thick Chemoigut Formation is composed primarily of lacustrine silts. The Chesowanja basalt dated to 1.42 Ma separates the Chemoigut Formation below the basalt from the Chesowanja Formation above (Figure 15.7; Gowlett et al., 1981; Hooker and Miller, 1979). At the Chesowanja archeological sites, pieces of burned clay intermingled with bones and tools suggest the presence of small, controlled fires. This, along with evidence from the site FxJj20 in Kenya (Hlubik et al., 2019), provides evidence of early hominin use of fire. Among mammals, there is *Paranthropus*, *Theropithecus*, *Equus*, *Ceratotherium*, *Metridiochoerus*, *Kolpochoerus*, *Hippopotamus*, *Tragelaphus*, *Kobus*, *Megalotragus*, *Connochaetes*, *Antidorcas*, *Elephas*, and *Deinotherium* (Bishop et al., 1978). The Chemoigut Formation fossil record includes gastropods, bivalves, fishes, turtles, and crocodiles. Ecologically, the fauna indicates varied vegetation types close to a large body of water.

Kantis

The Kantis Fossil Site is located on the shoulders of the Gregory Rift, on the outskirts of Nairobi (Figure 15.1) at an elevation of 1746 m (Mbua et al., 2016). Since 2009, E. Mbua of the National Museums of Kenya has led excavations at the site, where she has documented 740 specimens of hominins, cercopithecids, hippopotamids, suids, bovids, giraffids, rhinocerotids, equids, elephantids, and a few carnivorans from a dense bone bed dated to 3.45 Ma (Figure 15.7). Overlaying basalt, the Kantis sediments consist of poorly sorted "high-viscosity gravity flows," volcanic mudflows (lahar), and sandy layers of fluvial origin (Mbua et al., 2016). The hominin sample consists of two deciduous premolars, an upper canine, and a proximal ulna; all specimens are attributed to *Australopithecus afarensis*.

Hippopotamids (mostly aff. *Hippopotamus*) are the most common mammals. Among bovids, Alcelaphini are the most abundant tribe, and *Aepyceros* is also common, while Tragelaphini and Reduncini are rare. Other abundant taxa include *Notochoerus euilus*, a papionin primate, and the equid *Eurygnathohippus*. Among rhinocerotids, both *Ceratotherium* and *Diceros* are present, but *Ceratotherium* is common whereas *Diceros* is rare. The carnivoran fauna includes *Homotherium*, *Crocuta*, and *Enhydriodon*. The high abundance of hippopotamids in the Kantis sample indicates that presence of a large body of water in the area during the Pliocene.

Stable carbon isotopes from dental enamel indicate a mixed C_3/C_4 diet but with preference for C_4 resources in hippopotamids ($\delta^{13}C$ values of –2.2‰, $n = 30$), a C_4-dominated diet in Alcelaphini ($\delta^{13}C$ values of –1.1‰, $n = 8$), and a C_4-dominated diet in *Notochoerus* ($\delta^{13}C$ values of –0.9‰, $n = 22$). Giraffids are the only mammalian family with a C_3-dominated diet ($\delta^{13}C$ values of –11.3‰, $n = 6$; Mbua et al., 2016). Although the faunal, sedimentary, and isotopic data indicate that Kantis had mixed environments during the Pliocene, including woodland, bushland, and grassland near a river, this high-elevation Kenyan site appears to have been more open, with a greater proportion of grasslands than the contemporaneous Hadar Formation sites in Ethiopia (Hadar and Dikika), where *Au. afarensis* is common.

Lemudong'o

The late Miocene site of Lemudong'o lies on the western shoulder of the southern Kenya Rift at an elevation of 1593 m (Ambrose et al., 2003). The **Lemudong'o Formation** consists of 135 m of primarily lacustrine and lake margin deposits with interstratified tuffs, a sedimentary sequence interpreted to have formed in a shallow lake and its surroundings fed by streams, and subject to desiccation (Ambrose et al., 2007b). Although several paleontological localities have been identified, the most productive locality is LEM 1 (Lemudong'o 1), where L. Hlusko and colleagues carried out a 100% collection strategy (Ambrose et al., 2007a). LEM 1 has two fossiliferous horizons, from which a total of 1268 specimens have been accessioned at the National Museums of Kenya. Most of the fossils come from the upper of these two horizons, which consists of mudstones and the speckled tuff, dated to 6.084 Ma (Figure 15.4; Deino and Ambrose, 2007). This upper sequence represents a narrow temporal period within which the fossils were deposited. Although the deposits are lacustrine in origin, no fish fossils have been found, and crocodiles are rare. Also, large mammals such as hippopotamids and proboscideans are scarce.

Taphonomic considerations suggest that small and medium-sized carnivores played a major role in bone accumulation (Ambrose et al., 2007a). Carnivora are presented by a diverse set of 12 species (Howell and Garcia, 2007). Mongoose species are represented by four genera including *Helogale*, *Herpestes*, *Ichneumia*, and *Genetta*. Canid remains have been identified as *Eucyon*, a genus known from Langebaanweg in southern Africa (Reynolds, Chapter 6).

Cercopithecids are abundant, making up ~31 percent of the fauna. All identified cercopithecid specimens belong to the subfamily Colobinae, and they include the species *Paracolobus enkorikae*, a small colobine with an estimated mass of 7–8 kg with arboreal postcranial adaptations (Hlusko, 2007b). Two other unnamed colobine species are also present. Only four hipparionine cheek teeth have been recovered from this locality, and these are referred to *Eurygnathohippus* (Bernor, 2007). The scarcity of equids suggests that open environments were not widespread at Lemudong'o.

Small mammals include a relatively large sample of lagomorphs attributed to the extinct genus, *Alilepus*, which is also known from the Lower Nawata Formation at Lothagam (Darwent, 2007). Other small mammals include three genera of porcupines: *Xenohystrix*, *Hystrix*, and *Atherurus*, of which the *Xenohystrix* and *Atherurus* are the earliest records for these genera in Africa (Hlusko, 2007a). The diversity of porcupines led Hlusko to infer a predominately forested environment, but with wooded grassland areas nearby.

The non-mammalian fauna includes two snake taxa, similar to the African python, and to vipers or cobras (Head and Bell, 2007). Both are commonly recovered as fossil taxa and known from other Miocene sites from Africa, such as Toros-Menalla and Koro Toro (Brunet et al., 2000; Vignaud et al., 2002). Avifaunal remains include an owl species, a large eagle, and a pheasant (cf. *Phasianus*; Stidham, 2007). Some of the avian predators are likely to have accumulated part of the fossils recovered at the site, such as the small mammal faunas.

Overall, the geological, sedimentological, paleobotanical, and paleontological evidence indicates that at Lemudong'o there was a shallow, fluctuating lake in a rift valley basin with woodlands and gallery forests around the lake margin, with wooded grasslands nearby. These environments appear to have been more wooded than other parts of eastern and central Africa from the time around 6 Ma, such as Lothagam and Toros-Menalla.

Olorgesailie

The Olorgesailie Basin with an area of about 65 km² in the southern Kenya Rift has a rich record of Pleistocene fossil vertebrates and lithic artifacts (Brooks et al., 2018; Potts et al., 2018). The **Olorgesailie Formation** consists of fluvial, lacustrine, floodplain, and volcanic sediments divided into 14 members, dating from 1.2 Ma to 0.499 Ma (Figure 15.7; Behrensmeyer et al., 2002; Deino and Potts, 1990; Potts and Faith, Chapter 30). Although hominin presence is well established through the rich archeological record of Acheulean artifacts, only one hominin specimen has been described (Potts et al., 2004). In the earliest intervals, diatomaceous sediments in Member 1 (~1 Ma) show significant lake fluctuations, from shallow to deep lakes (Owen et al., 2008), and pedogenic carbon isotopes show that the surrounding vegetation was composed of C_4 grassland (Sikes et al., 1999). Equids are abundant in this member. Member 7, dated to ~0.9 Ma, has a high concentration of the cercopithecid *Theropithecus oswaldi* in braided stream and floodplain deposits (Potts et al., 1999). Members 10 and 11 preserve sands and gravels with high concentrations of animal bones, particularly hippopotamids and suids. This relay of taxonomic dominance in the Olorgesailie Formation provides an example of faunal changes mediated by shifts in environments (Potts, 2007). Above the Olorgesailie Formation, the Oltulelei Formation deposits date from 320 to 36 ka and preserve evidence of Middle Stone Age artifacts (Brooks et al., 2018). The transition from the Olorgesailie to the Oltulelei Formation records marked environmental changes and faunal turnover (Potts et al., 2018).

Nyanza Rift

Homa Peninsula

The Homa Peninsula in western Kenya has a long history of paleoanthropological research (Boswell, 1935; Leakey, 1936), with localities spanning the Late Miocene to the Recent (Bishop et al., Chapter 29; Pickford, 1987), and an excellent record of lithic technologies (Bishop et al., 2006b). These sites are located in the Nyanza Rift and consist of fluvio-lacustrine sediments with interspersed tephra. The main geological formations are the Kanam, Homa, Rawi, Abundu, Kasibos, and Kanjera Formations. The oldest sediments are the clays and silts with tuffaceous deposits of the **Kanam Formation** (Figure 15.4), with exposures at Kanam West, Kanam Central, and Kanam East.

The Kanam Formation dates to the latest Miocene, ~6 Ma, with a diverse mammalian fauna that includes six genera of megaherbivores: *Elephas*, *Stegotetrabelodon*, *Anancus*, *Deinotherium*, *Ceratotherium*, and *Hexaprotodon* (Pickford, 1987). Although there may be some temporal overlap, the fauna from the **Homa Formation** is generally younger than the Kanam Formation, and includes *Theropithecus*, *Nyanzachoerus*, *Notochoerus*, *Kolpochoerus*, *Metridiochoerus*, *Tragelaphus*, as well as the megaherbivores *Elephas*, *Loxodonta*, *Deinotherium*, *Diceros*, *Sivatherium*, and *Hippopotamus* (Bishop et al., Chapter 29). The holotype of *Nyanzachoerus kanamensis* derives from the Kanam West locality (Leakey, 1958). The younger **Rawi Formation** (Figure 15.7) includes the holotype of *Giraffa jumae*, Leakey 1967. Faunal correlations suggest a latest Pliocene age for this formation.

Recent work has focused on the **Kanjera Formation**, where stable isotope evidence from pedogenic carbonates and mammalian enamel shows strong evidence of hominins in a grassland ecosystem at ~2 Ma (Plummer and Bishop, 2016; Plummer et al., 2009b). This evidence from Kanjera South provides the earliest evidence in eastern Africa of an ecosystem dominated by C_4 grasslands (>75 percent). Grazing mammals inhabiting this landscape included *Theropithecus, Metridiochoerus, Kobus, Parmularius, Antidorcas*, and *Equus*, but there were also a few C_3 browsers like *Giraffa* and *Deinotherium*, and mixed-feeders like *Cercopithecus* and *Tragelaphus* (Plummer et al., 2009b). Hippopotamids, crocodiles, and cormorants indicate proximity to water. Bovids are by far the most abundant family of mammals at Kanjera South, and among bovids Alcelaphini and Antilopini make up 92 percent of the sample. Abundant lithic artifacts and stone-tool modified bones demonstrate that hominins were actively accessing animal resources in a lake margin setting (Behrensmeyer et al., 1995; Ferraro et al., 2013; Ditchfield et al., 2019).

Southern Gregory Rift, Tanzania

Peninj

The site of Peninj lies close to the northwestern shores of Lake Natron in Tanzania, near the Peninj river, and has been known since prospection by Mary Leakey in 1959 (Geraads et al., Chapter 31). A mandible of *Paranthropus boisei* was found here in 1964 (Leakey and Leakey, 1964) in sediments of the **Humbu Formation** that also yielded an extensive Acheulean assemblage dating to *ca.* 1.5 Ma (Figure 15.7; Isaac and Curtis, 1974). The archeological record of Peninj has been well described (Domínguez-Rodrigo et al., 2002; de la Torre et al., 2003, 2008), and is summarized by D. Geraads and colleagues (Geraads et al., Chapter 31). The Peninj Group deposits include the Humbu and Moinik Formations, characterized by alkaline lacustrine environments (Foster et al., 1997; Isaac, 1967).

The most common mammals are *Hippopotamus* and at least four species of Alcelaphini (Geraads, 1987a; Ndessokia, 1987). The mammalian fauna is dominated by grazing taxa (e.g., Alcelaphini), but there are also browsing taxa (e.g., *Giraffa, Tragelaphus*). Micromammals are dominated by family Muridae, and, among these, by *Thallomys* (Denys, 1987b). A palynological sample from the Humbu Formation indicates a dominance of grasslands, with local fresh water taxa also present (*Typha*, Cyperaceae) (Barboni, 2014). Thus, by 1.5 Ma the Peninj hominins inhabited complex environments close to a lake surrounded by grasslands.

Olduvai Gorge

Olduvai Gorge in Tanzania is central to the development of hominin studies (L.S.B. Leakey, 1928, 1959; L.S.B. Leakey et al., 1931, 1961, 1964; Tobias and von Koenigswald, 1964; Tobias et al., 1965; M.D. Leakey, 1966, 1971, 1994). The gorge is located on the western platform of the East African Rift, where it cuts into the Serengeti plains. The geology of the Olduvai beds was first studied by H. Reck in 1913, and in 1931 L.S.B. Leakey led the first of many field seasons to study the paleontology and archeology of Olduvai (L.S.B. Leakey, 1951). The geology, vertebrate paleontology (L.S.B. Leakey, 1965), archeology (M.D. Leakey, 1971, 1994), and hominins (Tobias, 1967a, 1991) have been described in a series of monographs. Additional publications have further focused on specific taxonomic groups, like the cercopithecids (Gilbert et al., 2016) and bovids (Gentry and Gentry, 1978a, 1978b).

Olduvai has played a central role in studies of hominin subsistence strategies and procurement of animal resources (Bunn, 1981; Potts and Shipman, 1981; Bunn and Kroll, 1986; Shipman, 1986; Binford et al., 1988a, 1988b; Potts, 1988; Blumenschine, 1995; Domínguez-Rodrigo, 1997; Domínguez-Rodrigo et al., 2007). Special issues of the *Journal of Human Evolution* (Blumenschine et al., 2012a; de la Torre et al., 2018), *Palaeogeography, Palaeoclimatology, Palaeoecology* (Domínguez-Rodrigo et al., 2017), and *Quaternary Research* (Domínguez-Rodrigo et al., 2010a) synthesize recent advances in the archeology and paleoecology of Olduvai. In this volume there are two chapters dedicated to the paleoecology of Olduvai Gorge (Farrugia and Njau, Chapter 32; Peters et al., Chapter 33).

Sediments began to accumulate about 2 Ma in the Olduvai Basin (Figure 15.7), which was a rather shallow depression (<100 m) of about 50 km in diameter (Ashley and Hay, 2002). Several volcanoes in the region (Lemagrut, Sadiman, Oldeani, Olmoti, and the Ngorongoro caldera) have produced large amounts of ash and lavas deposited in the basin (Hay, 1976; Ashley and Hay, 2002). The sedimentary sequence is divided, from oldest to youngest, into Bed I, Bed II, Bed III, Bed IV, the Masek Beds, and the Ndutu and Naisiusiu Beds (Hay, 1976). **Bed I** consists of ~40 m of primarily tephra deposits spanning from above the Naabi Ignimbrite at 2.038 Ma to Tuff IF at 1.803 Ma (Deino, 2012). During Bed I times there was a closed, saline lake at the center of the basin, the Olduvai Lake, which fluctuated seasonally and through climatic cycles, reaching about 15 km in diameter at its maximum (Hay, 1990; Deino, 2012). Locally, springs and wetlands provided fresh water, especially during drier intervals (Ashley et al., 2010, 2014, 2017). Estimates of annual precipitation indicate that the region received from 250 mm during arid intervals to 750 mm during wet intervals (Magill et al., 2013). Pedogenic carbon isotopes and biomarkers indicate that the vegetation during Bed I times varied between grassy woodlands and wooded grasslands (Cerling and Hay, 1986; Sikes, 1994; Magill et al., 2013a). Complex, seasonal, and dynamic mosaics of vegetation that include woodlands and grasslands are inferred from phytoliths (Ashley et al., 2010; Barboni et al., 2010; Albert and Bamford, 2012), and plant macrofossils (Bamford et al., 2008; Habermann et al., 2016). Key hominins from Bed I include the OH 5 cranium, holotype of *Paranthropus boisei* (Zinj) (Leakey, 1959), the OH 7 holotype of *Homo habilis* (L.S.B. Leakey et al., 1964), and the OH 8 foot (Day and Napier, 1964). Other Bed I specimens of *H. habilis* include the OH 24 cranium (M.D. Leakey et al., 1971), the OH 62 partial skeleton (Johanson et al., 1987), and the OH 65 maxilla (Blumenschine et al., 2003). The main Bed I archeological localities are DK I, FLK I, FLK N I, FLK NN I, and HWK I. Bovids are the most common mammals in Bed I, and among bovids Alcelaphini is the most common and diverse tribe in most localities (with the exception of FLK NN I; Gentry and Gentry, 1978a, 1978b). Ichnological evidence from a tuff layer reported by Plint and Magill (2021) confirm the presence of large artiodactyls on the landscape at this time. Faunal evidence indicates that Bed I paleoenvironments changed from closed and wooded conditions in the lower levels to open grasslands in the upper levels (Kappelman, 1984; Plummer and Bishop, 1994; Fernandez-Jalvo et al., 1998).

Bed II consists of fluvial, eolian, pyroclastic, and lacustrine sediments (Hay, 1976) dating from 1.803 to ~1.1 Ma (Deino, 2012; McHenry, 2012; McHenry and Stanistreet, 2018). This part of the sequence is usually divided into lower Bed II, middle Bed II, and upper Bed II, with a faunal break between lower Bed II and the upper levels. Bed II archeological sites include VEK, HWK, and HWK E. The transition from Oldowan technologies to Acheulean technologies at Olduvai occurs in Bed II at 1.66 Ma (de la Torre et al., 2018). Key hominins from Bed II include the OH 9 cranium of *Homo erectus* (Rightmire, 1979) and the OH 80 partial arm of *Paranthropus boisei* (Domínguez-Rodrigo et al., 2013). Isotopic (Sikes, 1994), paleobotanical (Bamford, 2005), and faunal evidence (Kovarovic et al., 2013) indicates that lower Bed II paleoenvironments were locally variable and dynamic with mix of vegetation types that included woodland and grassland (Peters and Blumenschine, 1995), but the increasing relative abundance of Alcelaphini throughout Bed II times indicates that environments were becoming more open (Gentry and Gentry, 1978b). A re-evaluation of the faunal evidence (fishes and mammals) indicates that middle Bed II paleoenvironments were dominated by seasonal grasslands at the margins of an alkaline lake (Bibi et al., 2018). The mammalian fauna was dominated by C_4 grazing bovids and equids (Uno et al., 2018). Ichnological evidence confirms the paleo-wetland, which was trampled by large mammal taxa, specifically hippopotamus (Ashley and Liutkus, 2002), and this complements fossil plant studies done for lower Bed II which indicate a seasonal wetland (Peters et al., Chapter 33).

Excavations of Acheulean sites in **Bed III** (1.15–0.95 Ma) and **Bed IV** (0.95–0.78 Ma), and in the overlying Masek Beds (0.78–ca. 0.5 Ma), were carried out from 1968 to 1973 by Mary Leakey (Leakey, 1994; Stanistreet, 2012). Bed III has a lower concentration of fauna and artifacts than other parts of the sequence, but Bed IV has abundant archeological sites, and abundant fish, crocodiles, and hippos (Hay, 1990). Hominins from Bed IV include the *Homo erectus* braincase OH 12 (Rightmire, 1979). Isotopic evidence shows increasingly prevalent C_4 grasslands from Bed III to Bed IV and the Masek Beds (Cerling and Hay, 1986).

Laetoli

The geological context and fauna of Laetoli have been well described in a series of volumes, first by Mary Leakey and colleagues (Leakey and Harris, 1987), and later by Terry Harrison and colleagues (Harrison, 2011a, 2011b). In this volume, Harrison and colleagues provide an up-to-date synthesis of research (Chapter 34). Laetoli is well-known in paleoanthropology as the site of the *Australopithecus afarensis* holotype (Johanson et al., 1978b), and the Laetoli footprints (Leakey and Hay, 1979). Laetoli has been markedly influenced by the action of nearby volcanic centers, including Lemagurut, Satiman, Ngorongoro, Olmoti, and Oldeani, which would have produced extensive tuffaceous deposits (Harrison et al., Chapter 34).

The Pliocene fossiliferous sequence is divided into the **Lower Laetolil Beds** (4.3–3.85 Ma), the **Upper Laeolil Beds** (3.85–3.6 Ma), and the **Ndolanya Beds** (2.66 Ma; Figure 15.7; Harrison, 2011a). The Ngaloba Beds at the top of the sequence produced a hominin cranium dating to >200 ka (Day et al., 1980).

Extensive paleoecological work in the Upper Laetolil Beds indicates that there were no large or permanent bodies of water in the region during the Pliocene, and that the vegetation of Laetoli was overall more open and less wooded than other parts of the East African Rift at the time (Andrews, 1989; Kingston and Harrison, 2007; Musiba et al., 2007; Su and Harrison, 2007). Nevertheless, areas of woodland were also present, especially along seasonal watercourses (Andrews and Bamford, 2008).

Manonga Valley

Systematic paleontological collections of the Manonga Valley were carried out beginning in 1990 by the Wembere–Manonga Paleontological Expedition (WMPE) organized by T. Harrison. In 1997, a full volume dedicated to the geology, paleontology, and paleoecology of the fossiliferous deposits of the Manonga Valley was published (Harrison, 1997a).

The **Wembere–Manonga Formation** spans from the late Miocene to the early Pliocene, ~5.5–4.0 Ma (Figures 15.4 and 15.7; Harrison, 1997a). This formation consists of up to 66 m of lacustrine and lake shore deposits divided into three members: the Ibole (~5.5–5.0 Ma), Tinde (~5.0–4.5 Ma), and Kiloleli Members (~4.5–4.0 Ma; Verniers, 1997). At the end of the Miocene, regional rifting produced a shallow depression that led to the Wembere–Manonga paleolake, which would have covered over 10,000 km² during its maximum extent in the early Pliocene.

Fossil vertebrates occur in at least 30 paleontological localities at a modern elevation of 1000–1160 m (Harrison and Mbago, 1997). Paleoenvironments were dominated by a shallow lake undergoing transgression–regression cycles (Verniers, 1997). The Ibole Member has abundant fish and crocodile fossils. The mammalian fauna is dominated by proboscideans (*Anancus*, *Primelephas*; Sanders, 1997) and suids (*Nyanzachoerus*; Bishop, 1997), but hippopotamids are very common. Alcelaphini are the most abundant bovids. The most abundant mammals in the Tinde Member are Reduncini and hippopotamids, which together make up 82 percent of the mammalian fauna (Harrison, 1997b). Fossil fish are also abundant (Stewart, 1997), as are crocodiles and turtles. The Kiloleli Member has abundant fossil fish, turtles, and crocodiles, but the extent of the lake had diminished considerably relative to the earlier interval.

The mammalian fauna is dominated by Alcelaphini, which make up 61 percent of all bovids (Gentry, 1997; Harrison, 1997b). The Kiloleli Member would have been drier, with more open environments than the earlier Tinde Member. Overall, paleoenvironments were centered on a paleolake that expanded and contracted during the Late Miocene and Early Pliocene. The environments surrounding the lake were complex, with woody and grassy vegetation, but relatively open environments predominated. It is interesting that no hominins have been found, and only a single specimen of cercopithecid derives from this formation (Harrison and Baker, 1997).

Western Rift Valley

The onset of sedimentation in the Western Branch, or Albertine Rift Valley, occurred in the late part of the Middle Miocene (Pickford et al., 1993), and resulted in one of the longest records of lacustrine sedimentation in Africa (Senut and Pickford, 1994). In this region, Paleolake Obweruka occupied the basin from ~7.5 to 2.5 Ma. At its maximum extent this was a large and deep lake, more than 500 km long and 50 km wide (Brachert et al., 2010; Van Damme and Pickford, 1999). With the rise of the Ruwenzori Horst during the Pliocene/Pleistocene transition, the lake was divided into the northern Paleolake Kaiso and the southern Paleolake Lusso (Van Damme and Pickford, 1999). The Miocene to Recent deposits reach 4 km in thickness, with mollusks as the most abundant fossils (Van Damme and Pickford, 2003). Today Lakes Albert and Edward drain to the Nile basin but in the past, they formed part of the Congo River drainage.

Nkondo-Kaiso Area, Uganda

Along the eastern shores of modern Lake Albert in Uganda, the Nkondo-Kaiso area holds ~200 m of fluvio-lacustrine sediments with an important fossil record (Schneider et al., 2017). Fossil vertebrates derive mostly from lacustrine deposits of the Nkondo, Warwire, Kyeoro, and Kaiso Village Formations (Pickford et al., 1993; Schneider et al., 2017). The holotype specimens of *Notochoerus euilus* and "*Sus*" *limnetes* derive from the Kaiso area (Harris and White, 1979).

The **Nkondo Formation** (~6.5–5 Ma; Figure 15.4) is about 70 m thick (Schneider et al., 2017) and includes samples of fossil wood and fruits that indicate the presence of forest and wooded savanna in the region (Bonnefille, 2010). There is an abundant mammalian fauna that includes the rare ursid *Agriotherium*, the mustelid *Torolutra* (Petter et al., 1994), hyaenids, machairodontines, the giraffids *Sivatherium* and *?Palaeotragus* (Geraads, 1994c), the bovids *Tragelaphus*, *Simatherium*, *?Menelikia*, *Kobus*, Alcelaphini, and *Aepyceros* (Geraads and Thomas, 1994), hippopotamids, and *Nyanzachoerus*. Rhinocerotids and equids are also present, and chalicotheres, possibly *Ancylotherium*, are represented by two fragmentary elements (Pickford and Senut, 1994). Proboscideans include *Stegodon*, *Loxodonta*, *Anancus*, and *Mammuthus* (Tassy, 1994). Mollusks, fishes, and hippopotamids are common in most levels (Pickford and Senut, 1994). Overall, the Nkondo Formation samples lacustrine and terrestrial faunas that indicate closed habitats surrounding a large lake.

The ~80 m thick **Warwire Formation** (~4.5–3.5 Ma; Figure 15.8) is rich in mollusk fossils (Schneider et al., 2017), and the mammalian fauna includes *Torolutra*, *Tragelaphus*, *Simatherium*, *Aepyceros*, *Menelikia*, *Kobus* (Geraads and Thomas, 1994), *Giraffa* (Geraads, 1994c), *Nyanzachoerus*, and the proboscideans *Deinotherium*, *Stegodon*, and *Loxodonta* (Tassy, 1994). It is noteworthy that the proboscidean *Stegodon* is common in the Nkondo and Warwire Formations, while it is rare or absent in contemporaneous sites in the eastern branch of the Rift. *Stegodon* and other mammals indicate a certain degree of endemism in the Albertine Rift.

The **Kyeoro Formation** (3.5–2.6 Ma; Figure 15.8) is about 8-m thick and has a sparse fossil record (Schneider et al., 2017). There are three horn core fragments, one of which may be identified as *Kobus*. There are also hippopotamids, suids, equids, and proboscideans (Pickford and Senut, 1994). The **Kaiso Village Formation** (~2.6–2.0 Ma; Figure 15.8) is about 23-m thick (Schneider et al., 2017), and its fauna includes *Pelorovis*, *Aepyceros*, *Kobus*, *Menelikia*, *Megalotragus*, *Antidorcas*, *Notochoerus*, *Kolpochoerus*, *Equus*, *Ancylotherium*, and *Elephas* (Pickford and Senut, 1994). The first appearance of *Equus* in the Albertine Rift is in the Kaiso Village Formation, roughly contemporaneous with its earliest record in the Omo Shungura Formation of Ethiopia at ~2.3 Ma (Eisenmann, 1994).

Kisegi-Nyabusosi Area, Uganda

This area located south of Lake Albert in Uganda has exposures of the Oluka, Nyaburogo, Nyakabingo, and Nyabusosi Formations (Pickford et al., 1993). Fishes are abundant and diverse in most levels (Pickford and Senut, 1994). In the **Oluka Formation** (8–5 Ma; Figure 15.4), proboscideans are common and include *Stegotetrabelodon*, *Primelephas*, and a primitive elephantid. *Hipparion* and *Libycosaurus* are also present, as is *Nyanzachoerus* (Senut and Pickford, 1994).

The **Nyaburogo Formation** (~4.5–3.6 Ma; Figure 15.8) has abundant fishes, and also the mammals *Torolutra*, *Hipparion*, and *Nyanzachoerus* (Pickford and Senut, 1994). The **Nyakabingo Formation** (~3 Ma) has a smaller fossil sample, but fishes, suids, and proboscideans are present. In the **Nyabusosi Formation** (2–1.5 Ma) *Kolpochoerus* is common. There are three species of hippopotamid, including *Hippopotamus gorgops* (Pickford and Senut, 1994). As in the Nkondo-Kaiso area, the Kisegi-Nyabusosi area indicates relatively wooded environments in the late Miocene and Pliocene, with increasingly open habitats in the Pleistocene. The late Miocene–Pliocene faunas show greater endemism than those of the Pleistocene, when the mammalian fauna becomes more similar to that of the eastern branch of the rift valley.

Sinda, Democratic Republic of Congo (DRC)

The Mio-Pliocene **Sinda Beds** (Figures 15.1 and 15.8) are located west of the Semliki River, in the Sinda-Mohari region of the DRC and consist of 150 m of deposits with a fauna that is rich in mollusks, fishes, and aquatic reptiles, but few mammals (Makinouchi et al., 1992; Yasui et al., 1992). The mammalian fauna is composed of a possible *Agriotherium*, a deinotheriid, *Anancus*, *Mammuthus*, *Stegodon*, *Brachypotherium*, *Aceratherium*, a small hippopotamid, a possible *Sivatherium*, and a bovid (Yasui et al., 1992). Among turtles, there is *Erymnochelys*. There are four genera of crocodiles: *Crocodylus*, *Euthecodon*, *Mecistops*, and *Osteolaemus*. Fishes include the genera *Gymnarchus*, *Sindacharax*, *Synodontis*, *Bagrus*, *Auchenoglanis*, *Hydrocynus*, *Clarias*, and *Lates*. Overall the fauna has similarities to the Nkondo Formation in Uganda, and dates from the Late Miocene to the Early Pliocene. The paleoenvironments appear more humid and forested than in the eastern branch of the East African Rift Valley.

Upper Semliki, DRC

Several Early Pleistocene sites are exposed along the upper Semliki River near Lake Edward (DRC). Fossiliferous deposits north of Lake Edward had long been known (Fuchs, 1934; de Heinzelin, 1962), and systematic research was carried out by the Semliki Research Expedition, which from 1982 to 1988 documented a diverse record of fossil vertebrates, invertebrates, plants, and archeological sites from the **Lusso Beds** (Figure 15.8; Harris et al., 1987, 1990; Boaz, 1990). Most of these sites are within Virunga National Park. The Lusso Beds are primarily lacustrine in origin, and more than 60 taxa of woody plants are documented including *Acacia*, *Brachystegia*, *Canthium*, *Combretum*, *Dichapetalum*, *Phoenix*, *Podocarpus*, *Sapium*, and *Tessmannia*, among others (Dechamps and Maes, 1990). The fossil wood indicates a range of environments including lowland forest, swamp forest, gallery forest, woodlands, but also open and even steppe vegetation, with pronounced wet/dry seasons. This might indicate that the Pliocene comprised an association of hydrophytic and xerophytic communities (Dechamps and Maes, 1990), but it is possible that some degree of time-averaging contributed to this mix of vegetation types.

The Lusso Beds fossil record also includes about 27 species of mollusks (Williamson, 1990), a diverse sample of fish species (Stewart, 1990), anurans, four species of chelonians (Meylan, 1990), crocodiles, and at least 22 species of mammals. The site of Senga 5A has two specimens of *Theropithecus*, and the site Lu2 has an isolated molar of Colobinae. Bovids are the most abundant family of mammals, with species of *Tragelaphus*, *Kobus*, and *Menelikia* resembling equivalent taxa in the Shungura Formation Members F and G (2.3–2.0 Ma; Gentry, 1990). Among bovids, Alcelaphini are most abundant, followed by Tragelaphini and Reduncini. Hippopotamids are the second most abundant family, with two species, one large and one small (Pavlakis, 1990), while elephantids are the third most abundant group (Sanders, 1990). Suids are represented by *Notochoerus*, *Kolpochoerus*, and *Metridiochoerus*, and the Lusso Beds specimens are similar in morphology to these taxa in Shungura Members F to G (2.4–2.0 Ma; Cooke, 1990b). Both *Eurygnathohippus* and *Equus* are also present (Bernor and Sanders, 1990). The sedimentological, faunal, and paleobotanical evidence indicates that the upper Semliki region from about 2.4 to 2.0 Ma had a range of environments near the shores of a lake, in close proximity to lowland

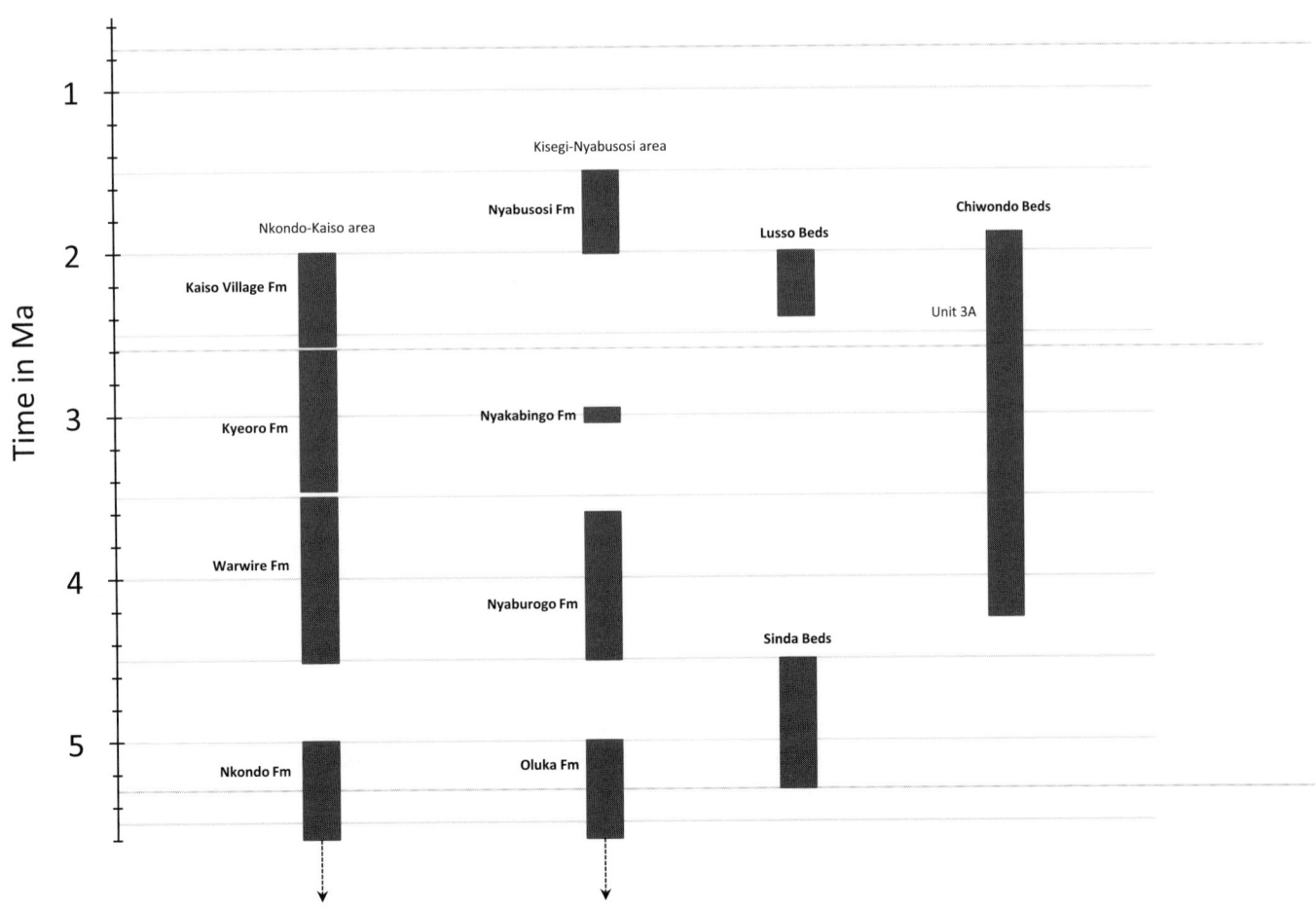

Figure 15.8 Chronology of key fossil sequences in the Western Branch of the EARS dating from the early Pliocene to the early Pleistocene.

tropical rainforest, but with extensive woodlands and grasslands that included mammals similar to those found in the eastern branch of the Rift Valley. Although no Early Pleistocene hominins were identified by the Semliki Research Expedition, a re-evaluation of a hominin upper molar from Ishango 11 and its geological context indicates that the tooth likely derives from the Lusso Beds and belongs to a species of *Australopithecus* or early *Homo* (Crevecoeur et al., 2014). This hominin tooth and the archeological sites indicate that hominins had expanded their geographical range into the Western Rift by ~2 Ma, if not earlier.

Malawi Rift
Chiwondo Beds

The Hominid Corridor Research Project has been conducting paleontological research in the Malawi Rift since 1983, and has collected over 1200 fossil vertebrates of Plio-Pleistocene age from the **Chiwondo Beds**, Karonga Basin (Kullmer et al., Chapter 35). The Chiwondo Beds include fluvio-lacustrine sediments and paleosols from which three hominin specimens derive: a mandible fragment of *Homo rudolfensis* (UR 501) from Uraha (Schrenk et al., 1993), a maxillary fragment of *Paranthropus boisei* (RC 911) from Malema (Kullmer et al., 1999b), and an isolated molar of *Homo rudolfensis* (MR-1106) from Mwenirondo (Kullmer et al., 2011). Faunal correlations and biostratigraphy indicate that the hominins, all from stratigraphic Unit 3A, date to ~2.4 Ma (Figures 15.1 and 15.8; Kullmer, 2008). Other primates include *Theropithecus* and *Parapapio* (Frost and Kullmer, 2008), but primates overall constitute a very small proportion of the total faunal sample (less than 1 percent).

The vertebrate fauna preserved at these localities is biased toward medium-sized and large terrestrial ungulates (Sandrock et al., 2007; Kullmer et al., 2008). In stratigraphic Unit 3A the most abundant family of mammals are the Bovidae, followed by Equidae, Suidae, Hippopotamidae, Elephantidae, and Giraffidae. Rhinocerotidae, Deinotheriidae, and Camelidae are also present. Among Bovidae, the most abundant tribes are Alcelaphini, Hippotragini, and Antilopini, indicating grassy, open environments (Kullmer et al., Chapter 35).

Fish species have been assigned to extant taxa, such as lungfish (genus *Protopterus*), catfishes (Families Bagridae, Clarotidae and Clariidae), cichlids, and a single tooth referred to tigerfish (genus *Hydrocynus*; Stewart and Murray, 2013). Stewart and Murray argue that the Chiwondo Beds fishes originated from the coastal rivers of eastern Africa, whereas the modern Lake Malawi fishes have affinities with the Zambezian hydrological system.

Stable carbon isotopes from pedogenic carbonates in the Chiwondo Beds and the overlying Chitimwe Beds provide a record of persistent C_3 vegetation, with a smaller component of C_4 grasslands in the Karonga Basin from 4.3 to 1.8 Ma, and then from the Middle to Late Pleistocene (Lüdecke et al., 2016a). This dominance of C_3 vegetation in the Malawi Rift contrasts with the greater proportion of C_4 vegetation in eastern African sites like the Omo-Turkana Basin and the Afar Rift during this time. This pattern is reflected in $\delta^{13}C$ values from dental enamel in suids and hominins, which show lower values (more C_3 vegetation in the diet) than contemporaneous taxa in the Omo-Turkana Basin and the Afar (Lüdecke et al., 2016b; Lüdecke et al., 2018).

Urema Rift
Gorongosa National Park

The southernmost paleontological sites in the East African Rift System (EARS) have recently been discovered in Gorongosa National Park, Mozambique. The map of this site region is provided in Reynolds (Chapter 6; see also Figure 15.1). In a brief report, Pickford documented the presence of fossil wood and mammal bone of Miocene age (Pickford, 2013c). Beginning in 2016, the Paleo-Primate Project Gorongosa has discovered more than a dozen fossil sites, some with an abundant mammalian fauna including complete teeth and mandibles (Habermann et al., 2019; Bobe et al., 2020b). The Gorongosa sites derive from the **Mazamba Formation**, a ~130-m thick sequence exposed on the eastern shoulder of the Urema Graben, at an elevation of ~100 m. The Gorongosa paleontological record now includes fossil wood, invertebrates, fish, crocodiles, and mammals. Dating efforts are currently underway, but the geological evidence indicates a Late Miocene age (Figure 15.4). Gorongosa is distinct from other EARS sites in its coastal plain and estuarine depositional environments (Habermann et al., 2019).

Chad Basin

The Chad Basin has become one of the key regions of Africa for Neogene vertebrate evolution and biogeography (Figure 15.9). Fossil vertebrates, including hominins, have been known from Chad since the early 1960s (Coppens, 1966). Lacustrine, perilacustrine, and aeolian sedimentary sequences accumulated during the Late Miocene and Pliocene in the intracratonic sag depression of Lake Chad (Moussa et al., 2016). A large lake with hydrological connections to North Africa occupied the basin during the Zeit Wet Phase of the Late Miocene (7.5–5.5 Ma), but contracted during the Pliocene (Griffin, 2002).

There are four main fossiliferous areas dating from the late Miocene to the Pliocene: Toros-Menalla, Kossom Bougoudi, Kollé, and Koro Toro. The hominin *Sahelanthropus tchadensis* was found in the late Miocene deposits of TM 266 in the Toros-Menalla area (Brunet et al., 2002, 2005; Zollikofer et al., 2005), and specimens of *Australopithecus bahrelghazali* were found in the Pliocene deposits of Koro Toro (Brunet et al., 1995, 1996). There has been controversy regarding the context and taxonomy of the Chad hominins (Wolpoff et al., 2002; Beauvilain and Le Guellec, 2004; Beauvilain, 2008; Callaway, 2018), but, as discussed below, there are several lines of evidence to support the general paleoenvironmental context of the region. The fossiliferous areas of Kossom Bougoudi (Brunet et al., 2000) and Kollé (Brunet et al., 1998) have not yielded hominins, but they contribute to Mio-Pliocene African environments and biogeography. These sites in the Mio-Pliocene Chad Basin formed along the ancient shores of paleo-lake Chad, which had strong biogeographic connections with the Sirte Basin of Libya during the Late Miocene (Lihoreau et al., 2006; Viriot et al., 2008).

Figure 15.9 Fossil localities in Niger and Central Africa, as discussed in the text.

Toros-Menalla

The Toros-Menalla area, where the hominoid *Sahelanthropus tchadensis* was found (Brunet et al., 2002), dates to the Late Miocene, between 7 and 6 Ma based on faunal correlations (Figure 15.4; Vignaud et al., 2002). Cosmogenic nuclides have provided dates of *ca.* 7 Ma (Lebatard et al., 2008; Lebatard et al., 2010). *Sahelanthropus* and other vertebrate specimens derive from sandstones of the Anthracotheriid Unit (AU), named after the abundant fossils of the anthracotheriid *Libycosaurus* (Lihoreau et al., 2006). The AU is underlain by aeolian facies and overlain by lacustrine facies. At the hominin site, locality TM 266, sediments of the AU indicate perilacustrine environments, ranging from a shallow lake to semi-desert conditions farther away.

Anthracotheriids (Lihoreau et al., 2014), hippopotamids (Boisserie et al., 2005b), giraffids, and proboscideans dominate the large mammal fauna (Le Fur et al., 2009). The holotype of the hippopotamid *Hexaprotodon garyam* derives from this site (Boisserie et al., 2005). Suids are represented by the genus *Nyanzachoerus*, including the holotype of *Nyanzachoerus khinzir* (Boisserie et al., 2014). There are at least eight species of bovids, with the tribe Reduncini the most common but also with new species of Hippotragini: *Tchadotragus sudrei* and *Saheloryx solidus* (Geraads et al., 2008, 2009a). Mesowear in bovid teeth indicates a diet based primarily on grasses (Blondel et al., 2010). Among mammalian predators, hyaenids are the most abundant, but there are also sabre-toothed felids (Peigné et al., 2005b; de Bonis et al., 2010), the earliest African mongoose (Peigné et al., 2005a, 2008), and the earliest African foxes (de Bonis et al., 2007). Primates other than *Sahelanthropus* include the colobine *Cercopithecoides bruneti* (Pallas et al., 2019).

Fish, turtles, and crocodiles are abundant, as are water birds (Louchart et al., 2005a, 2005b, 2008). Ancient trace fossils of dung beetle brood balls and the remains of termitaria have been identified within the sediments of both Toros-Menalla and Koro Toro (Vignaud et al., 2002; Viriot et al., 2008), along with preserved fossil nests and fungus comb structures associated with termite fungiculture (Duringer et al., 2006, 2007).

Phytoliths from TM 266 provide evidence of palm groves and woody vegetation cover of at least 40% (Novello et al., 2017). Overall, the paleoecological evidence indicates that the Toros-Menalla localities formed in lacustrine and perilacustrine environments with some swampy areas; bordering the lake, there would have been gallery forests and extensive grasslands (Vignaud et al., 2002; Le Fur et al., 2009). *Sahelanthropus* probably occupied the wooded areas among the range of environments available in the Chad Basin during the Late Miocene.

Kossom Bougoudi

The Kossom Bougoudi area has a vertebrate fossil record dating to the Mio-Pliocene boundary, *ca.* 5.3 Ma (Figure 15.4; Brunet et al., 2000; Lebatard et al., 2008). No hominins have been found at Kossom Bougoudi, but there is a diverse fauna that includes fish and crocodilians, aquatic birds, and a range of mammalian predators (de Bonis et al., 2008), four species of proboscideans, the aardvark *Orycteropus abundulafus* (Lehmann et al., 2005), abundant hippopotamids, suids, a camelid (one of the oldest in Africa), and a bovid fauna dominated by Reduncini and Hippotragini (as at Toros-Menalla). It is noteworthy that no specimens of Tragelaphini have been found at Kossom Bougoudi, or at the other Mio-Pliocene sites in the Chad Basin (Geraads et al., 2009a). The hippopotamids may be ancestral to the species described at the site of Kollé, *Hexaprotodon mingoz*, and may represent a lineage endemic to this region of Africa (Boisserie et al., 2003). The suid *Kolpochoerus deheinzelini* (likely ancestral to *K. afarensis*) occurs both at Kossom Bougoudi and in the Aramis Member of the Sagantole Formation in the Middle Awash (Brunet and White, 2001). The occurrence of *K. deheinzelini* at Kossom Bougoudi demonstrates that *Kolpochoerus* goes at least as far back as the Miocene/Pliocene boundary in Africa, and also that there were biogeographical connections between the Chad Basin and the Afar during this time. Overall, the fauna suggest extensive aquatic habitats, with grasslands and wooded areas in the form of gallery forests (Fara et al., 2005). Stable isotopes from dental enamel indicate that Kossom Bougoudi mammals had a full range of diets from C_3 browsing giraffids to C_4 grazing Reduncini and Hippotragini (Zazzo et al., 2000).

Kollé

Kollé is an important site in Chad of early Pliocene age, with a cosmogenic nuclide age of *ca.* 4 Ma (Figure 15.5; Lebatard et al., 2008, 2010). No hominins have been found at Kollé, but there is a fauna that includes three genera of crocodiles, proboscideans as the most common mammals, hippopotamids, suids, and giraffids; bovids are represented primarily by specimens of Reduncini and Hippotragini, followed by Alcelaphini (Brunet et al., 1998; Geraads et al., 2009a). The holotype of the hippopotamid *Hexaprotodon mingoz* derives from this site, and this species along with earlier hippos from the Chad Basin suggest some degree of endemism (Boisserie et al., 2003). In this regard, by the Pliocene the Chad Basin may have been relatively isolated from the hydrological networks of the East African Rift. There is also a species of aardvark, *Orycteropus djourabensis* (Lehmann et al., 2004). Stable carbon isotopes indicate that the mammalian fauna was dominated by mixed feeders and C_4 grazers (Zazzo et al., 2000). As with the other Pliocene sites in the Chad Basin, Kollé was dominated by perilacustrine environments including gallery forest, woodland, and extensive open grasslands (Fara et al., 2005).

Koro Toro

Koro Toro in the Chad Basin is the type site of *Australopithecus bahrelghazali* (Brunet et al., 1995, 1996) and dated to *ca.* 3.6 Ma (Figures 15.5 and 15.9; Lebatard et al., 2008). Although some researchers consider this species to be a geographic variant of *Au. afarensis* (White, 2002; Haile-Selassie et al., 2016a), *Australopithecus* in the Chad Basin was found 2500 km west of the rich sites in the East African Rift System, and indicates that the genus may have been widely distributed in Africa at this time.

Some of the bovid species, e.g., *Kobus korotorensis* and *Kobus tchadensis*, indicate a certain degree of endemism (Geraads et al., 2001), while others, *Parmularius pachyceras*, may be shared with the Hadar Basin (Geraads et al., 2012a). The bovid fauna is dominated by Reduncini, Alcelaphini, and Antilopini, indicating relatively grassy and open environments, with some extent of bush cover (Geraads et al., 2001). Hippopotamids are rarer than in the earliest sites of the Chad Basin, and might indicate greater aridity (Boisserie et al., 2003). Stable carbon isotopes indicate that the mammalian fauna was dominated by C_4 grazers (Zazzo et al., 2000). The *Australopithecus* specimens from Koro Toro have $\delta^{13}C$ values from dental enamel that indicate a significant component of C_4 resources in their diet (Lee-Thorp et al., 2012).

Abundant preservation of freshwater fish indicates open waters in paleo-lake Chad during the Pliocene (Otero et al., 2009, 2010). Phytoliths provide evidence of more open vegetation during the Pliocene than in the Late Miocene of the Chad Basin (Novello et al., 2017), but taphonomic issues with phytoliths need to be carefully assessed (Cabanes and Shahack-Gross, 2015). Taphonomic studies to establish the context of *Australopithecus* in relation to the faunal and geochemical evidence remain to be done, but in the Pliocene of Chad *Australopithecus* may have lived in relatively open environments dominated by C_4 vegetation around a large lake.

The Congo Basin

The immense Congo Basin straddles the equator near the center of the African plate where it captures most of the precipitation in Africa, which drains through the Congo River into the Atlantic Ocean (Livingston and Kingdon, 2013). The Congo is the largest African river in terms of discharge, and its 4000-km length passes through savannas, marshes and forests, and crosses the equator twice (Goudie, 2005; Flügel et al., 2015). Extensive areas of rainforest dominate the basin, especially along the central course of the river (Plana, 2004; Happold and Lock, 2013). Given its position at the heart of the continent, the large amount of moisture that it captures, and the barrier to terrestrial species dispersal posed by the river, the Congo basin plays a central role in African biogeography (Plana, 2004). In the Paleogene the Congo Basin may have drained into the Indian Ocean (Stankiewicz and de Wit, 2006), and in the Neogene a very large lake may have flooded large areas of the basin (Beadle, 1974; Peters and O'Brien, 2001). The Congo Basin played a central role in the evolution of gorillas, chimpanzees and bonobos (Takemoto et al., 2015), but fossils of their evolutionary history within the basin are not known. Paleontological sites are sparse, but some aspects of the basin's history can be reconstructed with geomorphological and phylogenetic data (Giresse, 2005; Kadima et al., 2011; Guillocheau et al., 2015).

West Africa

Fossil deposits of Late Miocene to Early Pleistocene age are very rare in West Africa. There is, however, extensive paleoenvironmental information derived from offshore and coastal sediments of the Niger Delta (Morley and Richards, 1993) and from the Ocean Drilling Program (ODP) cores in northwest Africa (Vallé et al., 2014). In the Niger Delta cores, grass pollen and charred grass cuticles (due to savanna fires) are rare or absent in Early Miocene deposits, but appear in the Middle Miocene, and are abundant in Late Miocene deposits (Morley and Richards, 1993). Pollen records of woody plants including forest taxa indicate that there was a forest phase in West Africa between 7.5 and 7.0 Ma (Bonnefille, 2010). The data indicate that grass-dominated communities became more extensive and fires more frequent after 6.5 Ma, but there were significant fluctuations in the types of vegetation throughout the late Cenozoic (Morley and Richards, 1993; Bonnefille, 2010). At about 2.7 Ma, there is a reduction in tree cover in West Africa reflected in the Niger Delta sediments (Morley, 2000). Palynological records from the ODP Sites 658 and 659 off the coast of Mauritania show that there was savanna vegetation in West Africa from 3.6 to 3.0 Ma, with wet conditions between 3.24 and 3.2 Ma, followed by incursions of desert conditions between 3.0 and 2.5 Ma, and a decline in woodland thereafter (Leroy and Dupont, 1994). NE Trade Winds intensified in the region after about 2.5 Ma in correspondence with the intensification of Northern Hemisphere glaciations (Vallé et al., 2014).

N 885, Niger

A faunal sample of Late Miocene age that included an anthropoid mandible fragment was collected in southwestern Niger during 1960s petroleum exploration (Pickford, 2008). The site, N 885, provides a small but important window on Late Miocene fauna, but its stratigraphic context remains uncertain (Figure 15.4). The fauna includes fossil fish (Nile perch), crocodiles, anthracotheres (*Libycosaurus*), a reduncin bovid, and a possible hominoid about the size of a chimpanzee (Pickford et al., 2009). The presence of the aquatic species points to well-watered environments (lake, swamp, river, or a combination of these), in contrast to present conditions. The detailed context of these fauna remains unknown.

Tobène, Senegal

This is one of the rare Neogene paleontological sites in West Africa. Only recently described by Lihoreau and colleagues (2021), Tobène has yielded fossil vertebrates in continental deposits intercalated between Eocene phosphate ore and Quaternary sands. Pliocene vertebrates include crocodilians, *Deinotherium*, *Nyanzachoerus*, *Giraffa*, *Simatherium*, Antilopini, Caprini, *Homotherium*, *Genetta*, and two species of Mustelidae (Lihoreau et al., 2021). Tobène shows that there is the potential for further paleontological discoveries in this poorly known region of Africa.

Discussion and Conclusions

The late Cenozoic paleoenvironmental context of eastern, central, and western Africa (late Miocene to early Pleistocene) saw multiple climatic, tectonic, and environmental changes influence complex patterns of floral and faunal evolution. Some of these changes occurred at macroscales, i.e., continental or regional scales, while other changes were on the scale of sedimentary basins. For hominins, the mesoscale changes might have been most relevant, i.e., scales that are consistent with the home ranges of large terrestrial primates.

Paleobotanical records indicate that African environments in the late Miocene were diverse and heterogeneous, ranging from tropical forests to open grasslands (Bonnefille, 2010). C_3 woodlands and grasses dominated eastern Africa until about 10 Ma, when there is evidence from the site of Nakali of the first herbivorous mammals to begin shifting their diet from C_3 to C_4 resources (Uno et al., 2011). Between 8 and 6 Ma, C_4 grasses began to expand across parts of eastern Africa (Cerling et al., 1993, 1997, 1999), but the expansion of grasses was complex and uneven across tropical Africa, occurring first in some regions, and much later in other regions (Feakins et al., 2005; Bonnefille, 2010; Cerling et al., 2011b, 2015a; Levin, 2015; Lüdecke et al., 2016a). All known species of Late Miocene hominoids (Figure 15.2) appear to have been broadly associated with wooded environments. However, it remains a major challenge to integrate the data of environmental heterogeneity from across Africa to the specific habitats of Miocene hominoids.

Hominins began to appear in the Late Miocene, during a time of major climatic, tectonic, environmental, and faunal changes. The earliest records of hominins derive from the Chad Basin, the Afar Rift, and the Kenya Rift (Figure 15.3). The Chad Basin in the Late Miocene had a large lake surrounded by grasslands and woodlands along water courses (Vignaud et al., 2002). It is likely that *Sahelanthropus* occupied the woodlands and gallery forests in this landscape. During the Late Miocene the Chad Basin was well-watered, and had biogeographical connections with North Africa (Lihoreau et al., 2006) as well as the Western Rift (Pickford and Senut, 1994). However, there are also indications of aridity with the accumulation of aeolian deposits that portend the origins of the Sahara Desert (Schuster et al., 2006). Other early hominins derive from the EARS. *Ardipithecus kadabba* in the Afar Rift is associated with woodland habitats during the late Miocene (Su et al., 2009), as is *Orrorin tugenensis* in the Kenya Rift (Pickford and Senut, 2001b). In the Early Pliocene, *Ardipithecus ramidus* occurred in an area that had woodlands and grasslands, but this hominin was more closely associated with the wooded end of the habitat spectrum (White et al., 2009a). Major chronologic and geographic gaps remain (Cote, 2018) and limit our understanding of hominin origins.

The earliest species of *Australopithecus*, *Au. anamensis*, first occurs at 4.2 Ma, but its origination may have been significantly earlier (Bobe et al., 2020a). At Kanapoi, *Au. anamensis* inhabited a rich ecosystem with woodlands and grasslands, with a diverse fauna in a basin that had abundant fresh water. Its descendant, *Au. afarensis*, appears to have inhabited similar environments in the Afar (Campisano et al., Chapter 18), but, with the incorporation of some C_4 foods, this species shows a shift in its diet relative to earlier hominins (Wynn et al., 2013, 2016; Levin et al., 2015). Contemporaneously with *Au. afarensis*, *Au. bahrelghazali* in Chad lived in more open environments and had a predominantly C_4 diet (Lee-Thorp et al., 2012). *Australopithecus* is the first genus known to have ranged from the Chad Basin to the East African Rift and southern Africa. However, comparisons of *Australopithecus* paleoenvironments across Africa are complicated by varying collection methods and taphonomic conditions (Behrensmeyer and Reed, 2013).

In the Afar, the earliest species of *Homo* occurred in more open environments relative to *Australopithecus* (DiMaggio et al., 2015b). Analysis of $\delta^{13}C$ values indicates that the earliest species of *Homo* resembled those of *Au. afarensis*, but *Homo* moved toward greater reliance on C_4 dietary resources by ~1.65 Ma (Patterson et al., 2019). By this time, East African *Paranthropus* had a mostly C_4 diet (van der Merwe et al., 2008; Cerling et al., 2011a). In the Turkana Basin where early Pleistocene *Homo* and *Paranthropus* co-occur, hominins lived in complex and dynamic environments with abundant fresh water (Bobe and Carvalho, 2019). At about 1.5 Ma, there is a significant increase in the number of archeological sites, including those well documented in the Turkana Basin (Isaac, 1997). Hominin–environment interactions underwent a profound transformation during this time, with increasing reliance on lithics and animal resources. *Homo* species began to disperse from Africa in the Early Pleistocene, while the causes of the extinction of *Paranthropus* around 1.2 Ma remains a key research question.

Significant knowledge gaps remain for sites in tropical Africa where West Africa and the Congo Basin are key regions for modern biodiversity but are paleontologically largely unknown. New sites to fill such gaps could greatly advance our evolutionary knowledge. Better conceptual integration of paleoecological data is needed, particularly of different, apparently contradictory, proxies. Although there is a wealth of paleoenvironmental information from most sites, it remains a challenge to relate these signals to hominin fossils themselves, especially the highly dynamic East African Rift settings (Kingston, 2007). Taphonomic studies at particular sites have provided a strong foundation upon which to build paleoecological analyses, e.g., Behrensmeyer at Koobi Fora (Behrensmeyer, 1975, 1978a, 1985; Behrensmeyer and Cooke, 1985) or the Middle Awash team at

Aramis (Louchart et al., 2009; White et al., 2009a; WoldeGabriel et al., 2009a). However, at most research areas it remains a problem to relate broad paleoenvironmental signals from isotopes or fauna specifically to the hominins. Comparison of fossil sites with different taphonomic histories and different collection protocols remains difficult. Nevertheless, environmental heterogeneity and rapid changes over time emerge as a common theme.

Acknowledgments

We would like to thank Susana Carvalho, Zeresenay Alemseged, Marion Bamford, João d'Oliveira Coelho, Martin Pickford, and Tim White for suggestions and corrections, which helped improve this chapter. Any remaining errors and omissions remain our responsibility.

16 Mammal Paleoecology from the Late Early Pleistocene Sites of the Dandiero Basin (Eritrea), With Emphasis on the Suid Record

Tsegai Medin, Bienvenido Martínez-Navarro, Marco P. Ferretti, Massimiliano Ghinassi, Mauro Papini, Yosief Libsekal, and Lorenzo Rook

Introduction

In the East African Rift System, Plio-Pleistocene environmental instability triggered major environmental changes, which in turn influenced patterns of mammal diversification, dispersal, and turnover (Bobe and Eck, 2001; O'Regan et al., 2005, 2011b; Hernández-Fernández and Vrba, 2006; Martínez-Navarro, 2010; Patterson et al., 2014), including hominin evolution (Behrensmeyer, 2006; Bailey and King, 2011; Potts, 2013; Antón et al., 2014).

While environmental and faunal variations during the Pliocene and Early Pleistocene are well-known from continental successions of Ethiopia and Kenya (Behrensmeyer et al., 1997; Trauth et al., 2007; Ashley et al., 2009, among many others), the Early–Middle Pleistocene transition is a discontinuous record. The latter time span is crucial, because it included a series of significant abiotic and biotic events, such as the onset of 100-ka glacial cycles (Kingston, 2007) and the increase of the geographic range of *Homo erectus sensu lato* (Antón, 2013).

The most studied Early to Middle Pleistocene continental deposits of eastern Africa include Olduvai Beds II and IV of the Olduvai Gorge succession (Domínguez-Rodrigo et al., 2013) in Tanzania, the Olorgesailie Formation (Owen et al., 2009) in Kenya, and the Daka Member of the Bouri Formation (Gilbert and Asfaw, 2008) in Ethiopia.

In the northernmost sector of the African Rift Valley, the only major continental succession of the Early–Middle Pleistocene transition that provides abundant vertebrate and hominin remains is located in the Buia-Dandiero Basin (northern Danakil Depression; south of the Gulf of Zula, see Figure 16.1), an area well known for the 1-million-year-old *Homo* cranium from the Buia site (Abbate et al., 1998; Macchiarelli et al., 2004b; Ghinassi et al., 2015). Since its discovery in 1994, the area has been the subject of research and has yielded a number of hominin remains (Abbate et al., 1998; Macchiarelli et al., 2004b; Bondioli et al., 2006; Zanolli et al., 2014), abundant fossil vertebrates (Ferretti et al., 2003a; Delfino et al., 2004; Martínez-Navarro et al., 2004; Martínez-Navarro et al., 2010; Rook et al., 2010, 2013; Medin et al., 2015), and a rich archeological record of Mode 1 (Oldowan) and Mode 2 (Acheulean) tool industries (Martini et al., 2004) dated to the late Early Pleistocene (Ghinassi et al., 2015).

This chapter is devoted to mammal paleoecology in the Buia-Dandiero Basin, with particular focus on the suid fossil record from the site. In the Pleistocene, suid species had a wider latitudinal and longitudinal distribution than at present and were adapted to diverse habitats and diets. Owing to their marked tolerance to cyclical paleoenvironmental changes and their rapid evolutionary changes, Pleistocene suids serve as important biochronological and paleoecological markers within mammalian ecosystems (Harris and White, 1979; White, 1995).

The present contribution presents a detailed study using "bed-by-bed" facies analyses and sequence stratigraphy of the Buia-Dandiero Basin Alat Formation (Ghinassi et al., 2009) and a recent, integrated, comparative review of the sedimentological, magnetostratigraphic, pedological, paleontological, and paleoanthropological record from the sedimentary succession exposed in the Mount Aalat area, in the northern part of the basin (Ghinassi et al., 2015).

Geology

The Dandiero Basin is characterized by *ca.* 1000-m thick sedimentary succession of late Early to early Middle Pleistocene age (Figure 16.2). This succession consists of six formations (Abbate et al., 2004), from bottom up: Bukra Formation (fluvial), Aalat Formation (fluvio-lacustrine), Wara Formation (fluvial), Goreya Formation (lacustrine), Aro Formation (fluvio-deltaic), and Addai Formation (alluvial fan). In the Mount Aalat area, the exposed basin-fill succession is about 300 m thick, as most of the basal fluvial Bukra Formation does not crop out. The Aalat section records repeated shifts from fluvial to lacustrine depositional settings, which occurred due to interactions between local tectonics and Pleistocene climate changes (Ghinassi et al., 2009, 2015). Accumulation was associated with axial sedimentation in a north–south-trending trough that was fed from the south. Lacustrine and deltaic deposits are dominant in the Aalat and Goreya Formations. Those also represent the most fossiliferous intervals of the whole basin-fill succession. Specifically, the Aalat Formation contains most of the vertebrate and archeological remains; those were concentrated in shallow-water fluvio-deltaic deposits. Sedimentological, pedological, and paleontological (Martínez-Navarro et al., 2004, Martínez-Navarro et al., 2010; Rook et al., 2010; Medin et al., 2015) records, including

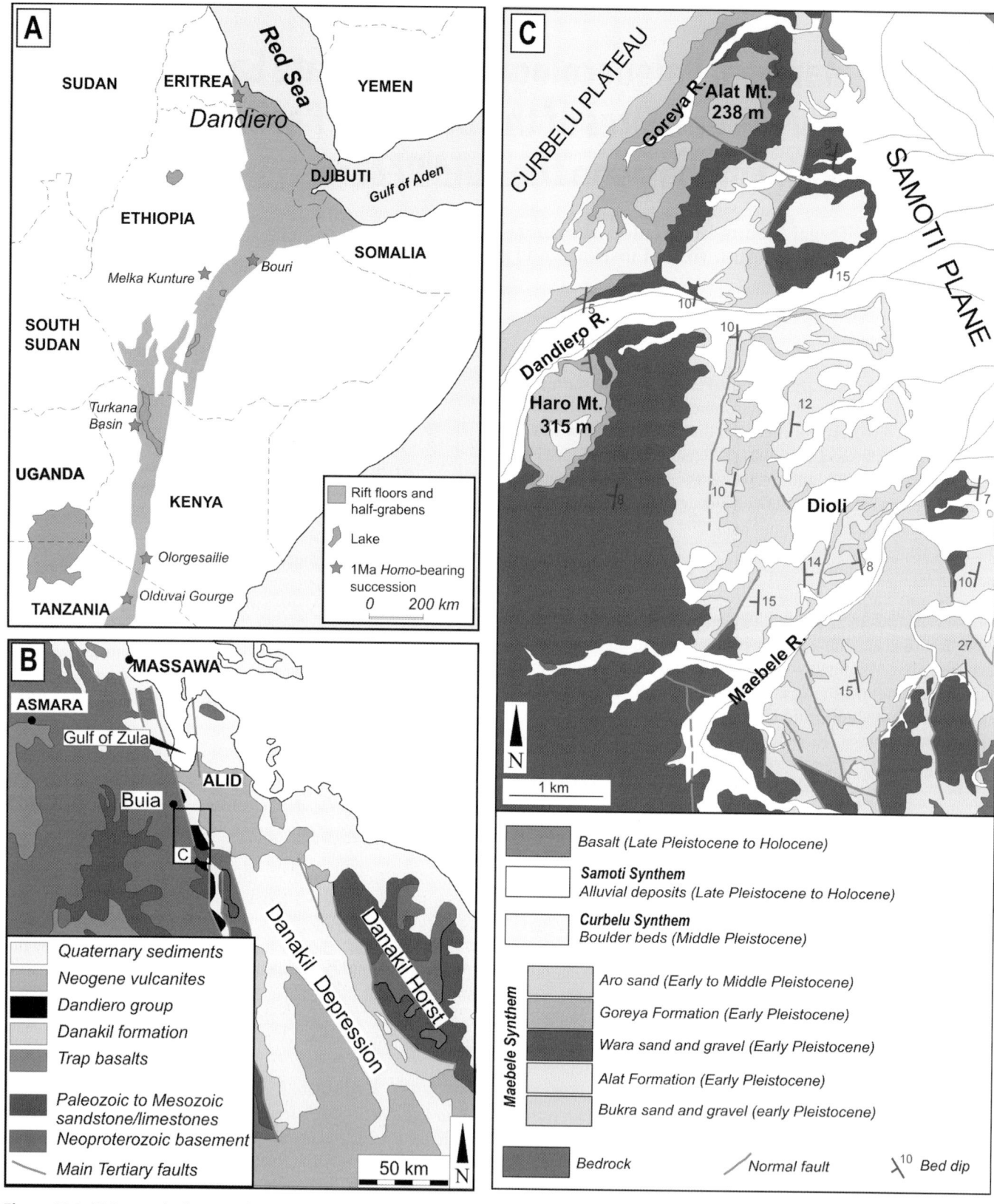

Figure 16.1 (A) Geographic location of the Dandiero Basin in the East Africa Rift System. Position of the well-known 1 Ma *Homo*-bearing sedimentary succession is also shown. (B) Position of the Dandiero Basin in the Danakil depression. (C) Geological map of the Dandiero Basin. After Ghinassi et al. (2015). (A black and white version of this figure will appear in some formats. For the color version, please refer to the plate section.)

ichthyofauna (Rook et al., 2013), show that the palaeoenvironment at this time was characterized by sources of water in close proximity to grassland and savanna-dominated habitats adjacent to coastal plains and floodplains (Ghinassi et al., 2009, 2015). The Aalat section displays three polarity chrons (Figure 16.2): a 70 m lower normal one (N1), a 165 m reverse one (R), and a 50 m upper normal one (N2). The quality of paleomagnetic data (Albianelli and Napoleone, 2004; Ghinassi et al., 2015), and their cross-correlation with absolute dating from a tephra layer (Bigazzi et al., 2004) and vertebrate paleontology, provide a robust chronology for the recorded magnetostratigraphy and indicate that N1 is C1 r.1 n (Jaramillo), R is C1 r.1 r, and N2 is C1 n (Brunhes). The earliest date for these deposits is ~ 1.07 Ma and the latest date represented is about 0.67 Ma (Albianelli and Napoleone, 2004).

Isotope Record

The stable isotope data from Dandiero Basin derive from authigenic carbonates and gastropod shells (*Melanoides tuberculata*) of the Goreya and Aalat Formations (Abbate et al., 2004). Specifically, samples from the Aalat Fm. show $\delta^{18}O$ ranging from −9.2‰ to 4.8‰ for the calcareous beds and from −10.6‰ to 1.6‰ for *Melanopsis tuberculata* shells. These values are very low for rift lowlands and can be accounted for by a very limited evapotranspiration and a substantial water-table recharge from plateau rainfall (Abbate et al., 2004). Moreover, the $\delta^{13}C$ record ranges from −4.8‰ to −2.1‰ for the calcareous beds and −5.4‰ to −3.2‰ for the gastropod shells. The absence of covariance of $\delta^{18}O$ and $\delta^{13}C$ is interpreted as representing an open-water lake, or ephemeral ponds with low residence times (Abbate et al., 2004).

Paleontology

Over 200 paleontological and archeological localities have been identified so far within the Dandiero Basin. Fossils from the Aalat Formation were mainly found at the base of the channel-fill deposits of a moderate- to high-sinuosity fluvial system unit (FL2b in Ghinassi et al., 2009, 2015), and secondarily in the fluvio-deltaic deposits (FL1–DL3 in Ghinassi et al., 2009, 2015).

The large mammal fossil record from Buia (see Tables 16.1 and 16.2) includes species such as geladas (*Theropithecus* cf. *T. oswaldi*), spotted hyenas (cf. *Crocuta crocuta*), extinct Reck's elephant (*Elephas recki*), white rhino (*Ceratotherium simum*), Grevy's zebra (*Equus grevyi*), species of hippo (cf. *Hippopotamus* sp., which is small-to-medium size; *Hippopotamus gorgops*), three species of extinct suids (*Kolpochoerus olduvaiensis, K. majus, Metridiochoerus modestus*), giraffe (*Giraffa* cf. *G. jumae*), and several species of bovids (*Bos buiaensis, Hippotragus gigas, Kobus ellipsiprymnus, Gazella* sp., *Tragelaphus* cf. *T. spekei*, and Caprini indet; Martínez-Navarro et al., 2004; Martínez-Navarro et al., 2010; Rook et al., 2010; Medin et al., 2015). The smaller vertebrate fauna include a large species of rodent (cf. *Thryonomys* sp.), some bird species (Rallidae indet., *Anhinga* sp., *Burhinus* sp.), and fish (*Clarias* sp.; Delfino et al., 2004; Rook et al., 2013). Finally, the faunal record also comprises a relatively well-represented herpetofauna: *Pelusios* cf. *P. sinuatus, Varanus niloticus, Python* gr. *P. sebae,* and *Crocodylus niloticus* (Delfino et al., 2004; Rook et al., 2013).

The Buia mammalian fauna is largely dominated by water-dependent species that typically inhabit grassland and savanna-dominated environments (Ghinassi et al., 2009, 2015). Several species, for example Kolpochoerus, Crocuta crocuta, *Hippopotamus gorgops*, and Theropithecus oswaldi, have been reported from the Early–Middle Pleistocene deposits of the Levantine corridor (Turner, 1984; Geraads et al., 1986; Tchernov

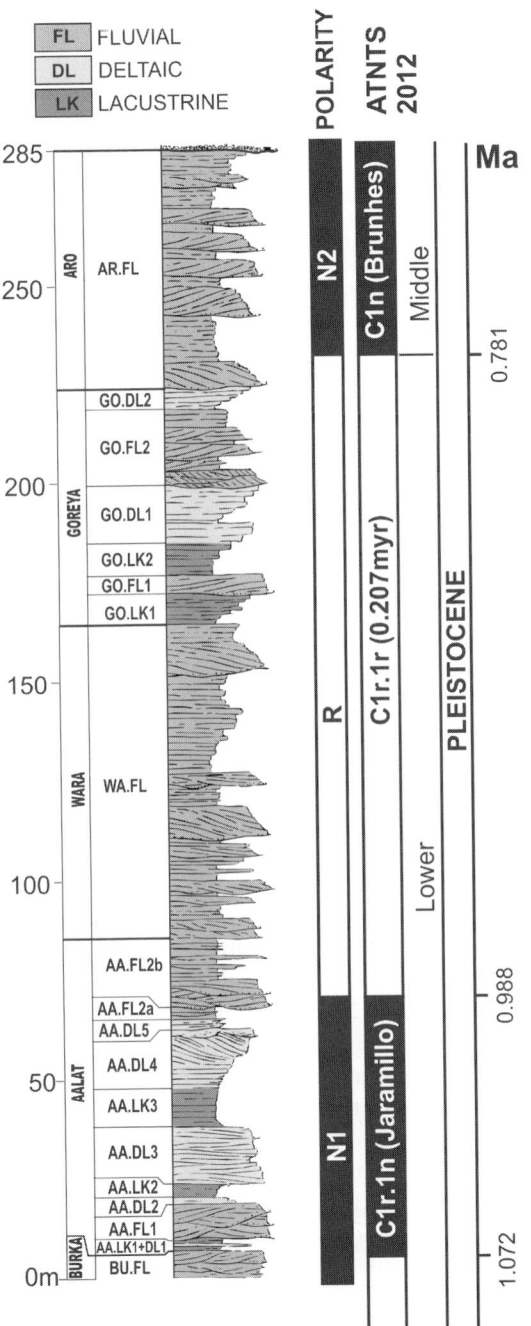

Figure 16.2 Sedimentary succession and magnetostratigraphy of the Dandiero Basin deposits. After Ghinassi et al. (2015). (A black and white version of this figure will appear in some formats. For the color version, please refer to the plate section.)

Table 16.1 Relationship between morphology and microwear results for the three suid species from Buia.

Species	Dental morphology	Diet based on microwear	Chronology of Buia suids	Extant descendants
K. olduvaiensis	Elongation of lower third molar and upper third molars Developed protocones Triangular median pillars with a butting base from the junction of the talonid and trigonid in lower third molars	Mixed-feeder	~1.0 Ma	–
K. majus	Upper third molars are short and low-crowned and upper molars are larger compared to K. olduvaiensis	Grazer-dominated	~1.0 Ma	Hylochoerus
	Teeth have thick cementum and show strongly crenulated enamel	Mixed-feeder		
M. modestus	Moderate to extremely hypsodont M3s with prismatic lateral pillars, numerous toll-shaped enamel islands and thick cementum	Grazer-dominated	~1.0 Ma	Phacochoerus

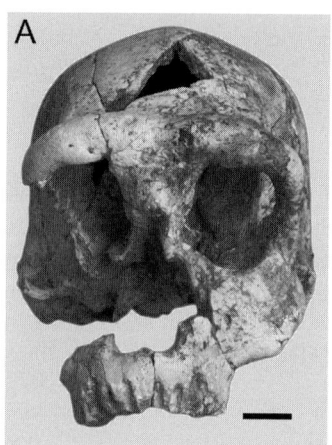 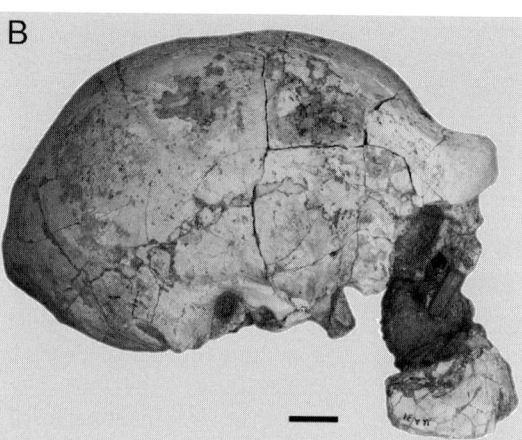

Figure 16.3 The human fossil cranium from the Homo site at Uadi Aalad (UA) in frontal (A) and lateral right (B) views. Scale bars equal 2 cm. After Ghinassi et al. (2015).

et al., 1994; Belmaker, 2006, 2010). They therefore show parallel dispersal events along hominins during the Early/Middle Pleistocene.

Hominin Record

Paleoanthropology

The Buia *Homo* remains (Macchiarelli et al., 2004b; Zanolli et al., 2014) come from the basal portion of the Aalat Formation of the Dandiero Group. The fossil human remains (Figure 16.3) are attributed to *Homo erectus/ergaster* and derive from two different sites. Uadi Aalad (also known as Buia *Homo*-site) was discovered in 1995 (Abbate et al., 1998; Ghinassi et al., 2009), while, more recently new hominin remains have been identified at the locality of Mulhuli-Amo (Coppa et al., 2012; Zanolli et al., 2014). Both the *Homo* sites of Uadi Aalad and Mulhuli-Amo (which is about 4.7 km southwest of Uadi Aalad) have been systematically surveyed and excavated since 2010. The fossil specimens from Uadi Aalad (UA) include two adult individuals, with a cranium (UA-31), two isolated permanent teeth (UA-222 and UA-369), and three pieces of pelves (UA-173, UA-405, UA-466; Abbate et al., 1998; Macchiarelli et al., 2002, 2004b, 2014; Bondioli et al., 2006; Zanolli et al., 2014).

The Buia *Homo* (UA-31) shows a blend of *H. erectus*-like and -derived morphoarchitectural features (Macchiarelli et al., 2007, 2014; Bruner et al., 2016). It has an absolutely long and proportionally high braincase with endocranial volume of 995 cm^3 (Macchiarelli et al., 2007, 2014; Bruner et al., 2011a). Viewed superiorly, it has an atypical dolium-shaped profile, which results from the combination of an anteroposteriorly and laterally projecting supraorbital torus, marked postorbital constriction, increasingly posterolateral enlargement of the parietal contour, and a smooth, rounded profile of the parietoccipital region, with no occipital torus (Ghinassi et al., 2015; Bruner et al., 2016). In coronal view, the braincase displays a low, intercristal positioning of the greatest breadth that is similar to all Early Pleistocene hominin crania. Moreover, it shows a modest lateral protrusion of the mastoid–supramastoid–auriculare complex, high positioning of the maximum parietal breadth, weak keeling along the midline, slight parasagittal flattening and, above all, from subvertical to slightly downwards converging parietal walls (Ghinassi et al., 2015; Bruner et al., 2016). It has a large zygomatic process filled with a voluminous maxillary sinus, and the height of the maxilla is larger than any known African Early Pleistocene hominin face (Macchiarelli et al., 2007; Ghinassi et al., 2015). The orbits are very tall, unlike any African or Asian Early to Middle Pleistocene specimens, and the sockets are very deep. Its primitive conditions and morphometric comparison show general phenotypic affinities to *Homo erectus*/*ergaster* rather than the younger *Homo* representatives (Bruner et al., 2011b; Ghinassi et al., 2015).

Two isolated permanent teeth, an upper left lateral incisor and a lower left central incisor with preserved crown and root (Macchiarelli et al., 2004b; Zanolli et al., 2014), belong to the cranium (UA-31) due to their original stratigraphic position (Ghinassi et al., 2015). Both crowns lack any expression of accessory features developed at the cingular region and exhibit relatively thin enamel (Zanolli et al., 2013, 2014). The breadth of the crown of the lower incisor falls within the range of variation of most Middle Pleistocene samples, but the upper incisor is relatively small compared to Early *Homo*; however, it is comparable to Indonesian *H. erectus* (Zanolli et al., 2013).

The shape and proportions of the three reconstructed partial hip bones show affinities with the early Middle Pleistocene OH 28 specimen from Olduvai Gorge, likely a female (Day, 1971). These specimens are related to UA-31 based on morphological, morphometric and techonomic criteria (Macchiarelli et al., 2004). However, the virtually intact left pubic symphysis provides the morphology of the subpubic ramus and shows a lack of anterior cresting and absence of a ventral arc; these indicate this specimen is from a male (Bondioli et al., 2006).

Furthermore, new specimens, consisting of a number of fragmentary human remains and a permanent crown molar, have been recovered from the site of Mulhuli-Amo. These specimens are not fully described yet (Coppa et al., 2012, 2014; Rook et al., 2014; Zanolli et al., 2014).

Archeology

The archeological record of Buia is similar to that of other eastern African sites like Olorgesailie, Bodo, and the Daka Member in the Middle Awash. The lithic assemblages from Buia region are mainly referred to Acheulean technology and are comparable to the Early Paleolithic complexes in eastern Africa (Martini et al., 2004). The Acheulean lithic assemblages in Africa span a wide chronological period; starting around 1.75 Ma (Lepre et al., 2011; Beyene et al., 2013), and Acheulean sites have been found in high concentration on several eastern African localities around 1.0 Ma.

The Acheulean assemblages are characterized by large bifacial tools, including choppers, handaxes, cleavers, and hammerstones (e.g., Kleindienst, 1962; Leakey, 1971; Beyene et al., 2013). In the Dandiero Basin the dominant raw materials are quartz, schist, basalt, and quartzite. The co-occurrence of Oldowan technology has been reported by Martini et al. (2004), but these are from surface collections with uncertain provenience.

Suid Microwear Record and the Diets Inferred for the Suids

Suid dentition was examined for microwear evidence that would indicate the likely diets of these species (Solounias and Semprebon, 2002). The microwear features (pits and scratches, etc.) observed on the molar enamel surface of the three suid species (Tables 16.1 and 16.2) revealed significant differences (Medin et al., 2015). The dental specimens of *Kolpochoerus olduvaiensis* show a significantly lower density of pits and scratches compared to *K. majus* and *Metridiochoerus modestus*. The analysis does not show any important difference in the average density of pits and scratches within *K. olduvaiensis* specimens; however, the record shows slight variation in *K. majus* and high variation in *M. modestus*. Fine scratches and small pits show identical densities in *K. olduvaiensis*. This is a comparable record of the average density of pits (70.3 pits/mm^2) to the density of scratches (70.3 scratches/mm^2). The scratches observed in *K. olduvaiensis* specimens are comparatively longer and deeper than scratches in *K. majus* and *M. modestus*. The majority of the specimens show fewer large pits than in *K. majus* and *M. modestus*. There is no evidence of gouges, while puncture pits are visible only on one specimen. Cross scratches and hyper-coarse scratches are abundant (i.e., high scratch width scores). In *K. majus*, we observe a similar quantity of pits (141.9 pits/mm^2) and scratches (120.6 scratches/mm^2). There is no significant difference between the densities of pits and scratches ($n = 5$, Mann–Whitney U-test; $U = 0$; $p = 0.0122$). However, *K. majus* specimens have more pits than *K. olduvaiensis* and fewer than *M. modestus*. Moreover, *K. majus* has a greater density of scratches than the other species. Large pits are also abundant. *Kolpochoerus majus* specimens have more large scratches than the other species; nevertheless, the fine scratches are still the most abundant and are denser and fainter than those observed in *K. olduvaiensis* and *M. modestus*. Small pits are dominant for *K. majus*, however; large pits are also recorded in low numbers on two specimens. Specimens show evidence of large pits, cross scratches, and low scratch width scores, but like *K. olduvaiensis*, puncture pits and gouges are almost absent. However, unlike *K. olduvaiensis* they have very few hyper-coarse scratches.

The very hypsodont specimens of *M. modestus* show the highest density of pits of all species (154.7 pits/mm^2) and an average density of scratches of 70.6 scratches/mm^2. However, *M. modestus* specimens have the same density of scratches as *K. olduvaiensis*, but lower than in *K. majus*. The average density of pits in *M. modestus* specimens is higher than the overall average density of scratches observed. The scratches in *M. modestus* specimens are quantitatively fewer, deeper, and discontinuous. The microwear features also include large pits and cross scratches. It has no record of hyper-coarse scratches or gouges.

Microwear data of extant suids species of *Hylochoerus meinertzhageni*, *Potamochoerus porcus* (red river hog), and *Sus scrofa* show close similarity considering most of the features (large pits, number of puncture pits, cross scratches, gouges); however, they have differences on values of their density of scratches and pits (Medin et al., 2015). These species show greater similarities in dietary habits than the extinct suid species and the peccary (*Tayassu pecari*). This shows that the counted value of the number of scratches and pits observed on the enamel surface of suids and peccaries has less impact in differentiating the dietary habits of omnivorous species compared to herbivorous animals. *Po. porcus* has very high numbers of pits and scratches relative to *H. meinertzhageni* (Medin et al., 2015). However, *H. meinertzhageni* has finely textured scratches, which are not seen in *Po. porcus*. The latter has a high percentage of coarse and mixed scratches (Solounias and Semprebon, 2002). The peccary falls within the grazing morphospace. *Po. porcus*, due to its rooting habits, scored a high average number of pits and an intermediate number of scratches in comparison to extant suids.

The present ecological habitat and dietary habits of the extant suid species have crucial resemblance to the paleoecological habitat of their fossil ancestors. However, variations in dental morphology among suid species cannot be solely related to a grazing C_4 diet. Our data show no relationship between dental hypsodonty and microwear dietary variations in suid and peccary species. This is most likely related to a decoupling between morphological changes over several generations (evolutionary process) and dietary changes recorded over the last days of life of an individual (microwear). Such discrepancies were observed in other ungulate species (Semprebon and Rivals, 2007, 2010; Mihlbachler et al., 2011).

Paleoecology of Buia: The Case of Suids

The Buia mammalian assemblage is mainly composed of strongly water-dependent taxa (hippos, waterbuck, sitatunga, *Kolpochoerus*) and other taxa typical of open environments (*Bos, Metridiochoerus, Giraffa, Hippotragus, Equus*; Martínez-Navarro et al., 2004). These mammalian fauna could have enjoyed an extended open grassland and adjacent lake habitat in this isolated basin of the northern-most end part of the rift valley. The paleoenvironmental setting of this basin (Dandiero Basin) shows that the suid species had access to a range of habitat types that permitted their varied dietary habits, much like the rest of the large mammalian fauna. The two suid genera (*Kolpochoerus* and *Metridiochoerus*) from the Buia site are recognized as evolved forms of *Kolpochoerus olduvaiensis, K. majus*, and one species of *Metridiochoerus* (*M.* aff. *modestus*; Martínez-Navarro et al., 2004; Medin et al., 2015). These suids are closely related to other conspecific populations of Early/Middle Pleistocene suid species from eastern Africa (Martínez-Navarro et al., 2004; Medin et al., 2015). Dental metric data of the two suid genera from Buia show close similarities to species from Daka and Olduvai Beds II/III/IV (Medin et al., 2015, and references therein).

African suids underwent dramatic adaptive radiations through time because of their successful and omnivorous diets and efficient mastication system. The transition to herbivory is basically characterized by the development of a complicated talon(id) in the third molars, with several pairs of cusp(id)s and an enamel that gets thinner over time (Harris and White, 1979; Cooke, 1978a). This evolutionary trend has been similarly documented on the suids from the Dandiero Basin. The development of an elongated talon(id) of the third molar for *K. olduvaiensis* and the very hypsodont *M. modestus* and moderately hypsodont *K. majus* crowns have permitted them to adapt feeding habits, that is, mixed-feeder, grazer-dominated mixed-feeder, and grazer-dominated, respectively (e.g., grasses, leaves, underground storage organs of plants –roots, tubers, corms, bulbs, rhizomes; Medin et al., 2015). The varied diets inferred for the three Buia suid species possibly reflect interspecific competition, as all three species were present at the same site (Medin et al., 2015). The microwear results are in agreement with the studies of sedimentary facies analysis (Ghinassi et al., 2009) and isotope record (Abbate et al., 2004), which support the existence of fluvio-deltaic and savanna environments (Ghinassi et al., 2009, 2015), with dominant monocot (C_4) plants in the Dandiero Basin and the existence of C_3 plants at the margins of the basin. Similarly, the Buia environment is also evidenced from the large terrestrial mammals that show strong water dependence and also the fossil birds that supports the presence of open water environment and dry areas nearby (Delfino et al., 2004; Martínez-Navarro et al., 2004; Rook et al., 2013; Medin et al., 2015). Moreover, the Buia ichthyofauna is dominated by catfish of the family Clariidae and is consistent with shallow-water fluvio-lacustrine paleobiotopes (Ghinassi et al., 2009, 2015).

The paleoecological habitat and dietary habits of the genus *Kolpochoerus* have been discussed from several Plio-Pleistocene African sites. Based on stable isotope data, the *Kolpochoerus* shows a negative record of $\delta^{18}O$ suggesting wet grass grazer feeding habits that perhaps related to a moister environment (Bobe et al., 2007a). In addition, Bishop (1999) reported a close habitat based on postcranial morphology and Harris and Cerling (2002) suggested a browser dietary habit based on dental morphology.

Based on microwear analysis, the species *K. olduvaiensis* from Buia shows a mixed feeding habit, inferred from the lower density of pits and scratches compared to *K. majus* and *M. modestus* and the absence of large and puncture pits and gouges (Table 16.1). This species might have fed upon soft vegetation and grasses found adjacent to the aquatic environments; that is, it had a mixed-feeder diet. Harris and Cerling (2002) reported stable isotope data for *K. olduvaiensis* (= advanced *K. limnetes*) from Koobi Fora, Kenya and suggested a grazer diet, although the species was dependent on water. According to Harris (1983b), earlier *Kolpochoerus* had similar dietary habits to the extant bushpig (*Potamochoerus*), but was recognized as a "browser." However, younger species of *Kolpochoerus* in the Pleistocene incorporated a grazing diet (Harris and Cerling, 2002; Bibi et al., 2013; Cerling et al., 2015a). As our microwear data suggest, occasionally differences within an ecosystem may be reflected in microwear and thus we may infer changes in dietary habits. Buia *K. olduvaiensis* had mixed dietary habits; although Buia fossil specimens are collected from the surface, they are found at the base of a channel/fill deposits and secondarily in the fluvio-deltaic deposits, along with other mammal and hominin fossil specimens (Ghinassi et al., 2015), in which the habitat could be interpreted as swamp areas adjacent to savanna rather than closed habitats (Ghinassi et al., 2015).

The moderate-sized *K. majus* was adapted to the open grasslands of the Dandiero Basin. Buia *K. majus* might have consumed dry leaves, grasses, wood bark, and, importantly, might have relied on a rooting diet. It had a mixed grass-dominated diet, implied by the high density of pits and scratches (Medin et al., 2015). Stable carbon isotope values (−0.5‰ to 0.9‰ for *K. majus* from Asbole) also show C_4-dominated dietary habits (Bedaso et al., 2010). Based on microwear data and morphology both *K. majus* and *M. modestus* might had similar dietary habits to their extant descendants *Hylochoerus* and *Phacochoerus*, respectively. The ecological habitat and dietary habits of the extant giant forest hog (*Hylochoerus meinertzhageni*: d'Huart, 1978) show crucial resemblance to the genus *Kolpochoerus*. *Hylochoerus meinertzhageni* is a specialized mixed-feeder herbivore inhabiting swamp areas and/or a variety of closed forested habitats of high humidity and low solar radiation (Meijaard et al., 2011). Moreover, Souron et al. (2015) reported modern *Hylochoerus* displayed more heterogeneous microwear surfaces than *Phacochoerus*, which indicates a mixed diet of various kinds of vegetation (grass, forbs, leaves, etc.). Isotope studies for *Hylochoerus* indicate a C_3 browsing diet; however, most of the specimens analyzed came from closed forests located at high altitude, where all the plants are C_3 (even the grasses; d'Huart, 1978; Viehl, 2003; Cerling and Viehl, 2004).

The extinct genus *Metridiochoerus* is at this time represented by several grass-eating species widespread through the whole African continent during the Plio-Pleistocene (Harris and White, 1979; Cerling et al., 2015a; Souron, 2017). *Phacochoerus africanus* and *Ph. aethiopicus* are the only extant *Metridiochoerus* descendants that display major morphological adaptations to diets dominated by tropical grass in open habitats (Souron, 2017). *Phacochoerus africanus* with a full set of incisors and not inflated zygoma have been reported from Eritrea (Yalden et al., 1996; d'Huart et al., 2016; Souron, 2017). The extinct and small-sized Buia *M. modestus* was a grazer mostly feeding on grasses, as was *K. majus* (Table 16.1). *M. modestus* has reduced premolars, thick cementum, and enamel surfaces dominated by pits (Medin et al., 2015), which were probably produced by grit and dust during rooting (Solounias and Semprebon, 2002). The dietary habits of the extant genus *Phacochoerus* resemble those of the extinct *Metridiochoerus* (*M. modestus*). *Ph. africanus* is mostly a grazer with reduced premolars and very hypsodont teeth and inhabits savanna grasslands and open bushlands (Cumming, 1975; Vercammen and Mason, 1993; Treydte et al., 2006).

Discussion

African Plio-Pleistocene suids show fairly rapid diversification that appears at odds with the paradigm of cyclical paleoenvironmental fluctuations proposed by various authors (Cooke, 1976, 1997; Geraads, 1993a, 2004b; Pickford, 1994b; Bishop, 1999, 2010; Harris and Cerling, 2002; Bishop et al., 2006a). In Africa, the period between *ca*. 2.0 and 1.0 Ma is characterized by intense and unstable arid conditions (Cerling et al., 1997; deMenocal, 2004). These climatic fluctuations promoted evolutionary changes in large mammalian fauna (for example, the elongation of the third molar in *Kolpochoerus olduvaiensis*), including *Homo* (technological innovations; enlargement of brain size, dietary shifts, etc.; Leakey, 1971; Grine, 1986; Aiello and Wheeler, 1995; Teaford and Ungar, 2000, among many others). According to Cerling et al. (2015a), in the last 2 Ma many of the C_4 grazing non-bovid herbivores became extinct, and some taxa that were previously C_4 grazers or C_3–C_4 mixed-feeders changed their diet to C_3 browsing.

The habitats of eastern Africa have shifted to cooler, drier, and more grassland-dominated environmental conditions, based on faunal evidence (Vrba, 1985b, 1988, 1995b; deMenocal, 2004). The earlier Pleistocene was characterized by low-amplitude 41-ka dominant climate cycles, but these were replaced progressively during the later Pleistocene by the high-amplitude 100-ka cycles (deMenocal, 2004; Head and Gibbard, 2005). These climate changes had profound effects on the African vegetation and thereby also on the fauna. The Dandiero Basin during the later Pleistocene was characterized by repeated shifts from fluvial to lacustrine depositional settings, indicating alternative wet and dry phases (Ghinassi et al., 2015). During these climatic shifts, the suid species from Buia were represented by *Kolpochoerus olduvaiensis*, *K. majus* and *Metridiochoerus* (*M.* aff. *modestus*).

These two suid genera, namely *Kolpochoerus* and *Metridiochoerus*, are known from several penecontemporaneous Plio-Pleistocene hominin sites in Africa (Cooke and Wilkinson, 1978; Harris and White, 1979; White, 1995; Suwa et al., 2003; Geraads et al., 2004c; Bobe et al., 2007a; Gilbert, 2008). Moreover, the genus *Kolpochoerus* has been reported from coeval sites from South Africa – e.g., the site of Elandsfontein Skurwerug and Cornelia (Hendey and Cooke, 1985, among many others) – and similarly from the North African sites of Ain Hanech Ain Boucherit, Mansourah (Sahnouni et al., 2002) and Thomas Quarry in Morocco (Geraads, 1993a). However, the suid genera from several other North African sites have been recently ascribed as *Metridiochoerus* (Souron, 2012). *Kolpochoerus* has also been found in the Levantine sites of Ubeidiya (*K. olduvaiensis*) and Evron Quarry (*K. evronensis*; Geraads et al., 1986). *Metridiochoerus modestus* has been reported from Koobi Fora (Harris and White, 1979), Olduvai Bed I (Cooke, 1982), Asbole (Geraads et al., 2004c), and other eastern African sites.

Changes in ecosystem structure and mammal diet have occurred in Africa in the past 4 million years (Cerling et al., 2015a), with C_4 plants becoming dominant in the warmer climates of tropical and subtropical regions through time (Edwards et al., 2010). The $\delta^{13}C$ values of C_3 plants range from −33‰ to −20‰, whereas those of C_4 plants range from −16‰ to −10‰, with isotopic differences of ~14‰ (Cerling et al., 1997). The $\delta^{13}C$ values from the Aalat Formation range from −4.8‰ to −2.1‰ for calcareous beds and −5.4‰ to −3.2‰ for gastropod shells. These stable isotope data show a tendency toward higher $\delta^{13}C$ values, suggesting C_4 plants dominate, but the data also show the presence of C_3 plants along the margins of the Dandiero Basin, and suggest fluvio-deltaic environments with a substantial water-table recharge from the plateau during the Middle/Early Pleistocene.

Although a comprehensive study of the isotope record from the Dandiero Basin will be forthcoming in the future, the presently available isotope values from Buia can be considered along with those from other sites. The Buia values fall within

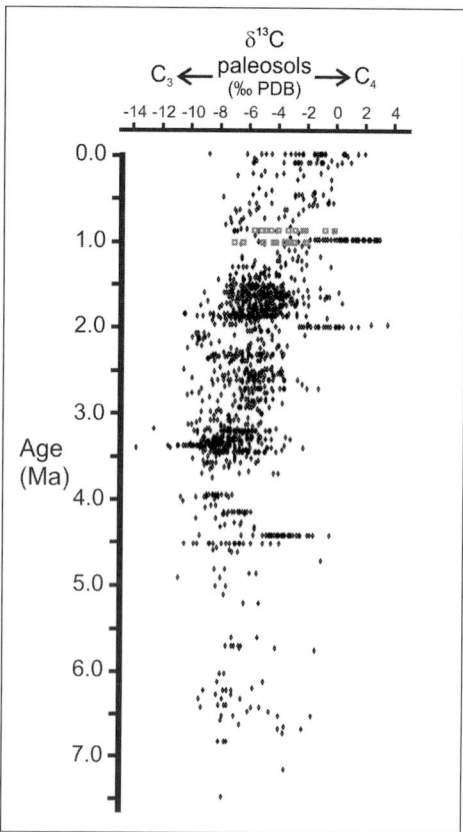

Figure 16.4 Graph showing paleosol records (δ¹³C) of Plio-Pleistocene eastern African sites and their geological age. Data in black for all eastern African sites from Levin (2013) and data in grey for Buia, Eritrea, from Abbate et al. (2004).

the range of known paleosol records from other eastern African Plio-Pleistocene sites (see Figure 16.4). Paleosol records from several eastern African sites, ranging from 7.0 Ma to the present, show a trend from predominately C_3 to C_4 plants starting in the late Pliocene or Early Pleistocene (Figure 16.4). Similarly, in the eastern Rift, C_3 plants dominated until the late Pliocene. Only at about 2.0 Ma are C_4 plants observed to become dominant (Lüdecke et al., 2016a). The paleoecological record from Buia indicates the dominance of monocot plants such as grasses and sedges, and the presence of dicots, which are mostly trees and sedges, on the margins of the Dandiero Basin during the interval analyzed here. These results differ from those of the contemporaneous site of Olorgesailie (Kenya), in which about 75–100 percent of the total biomass of the site consisted of C_4 plants (Sikes et al., 1999). The frequent shifts from fluvial to lacustrine environments in the Dandiero Basin (Ghinassi et al., 2009, 2013, 2015) likely led to a mosaic of environments that differed from similar-aged eastern African sites.

Studies focusing on the suid enamel stable isotope record (Cerling and Hay, 1986; Cerling et al., 1988, 2003a; Cerling, 1992; WoldeGabriel et al., 1994; Sikes et al., 1999; Bedaso et al., 2010; Lüdecke et al., 2016a, among others) help to reconstruct the paleoecology of several Plio-Pleistocene eastern and south-central African sites. For example, the δ¹³C values for Plio-Pleistocene African suids from the Chiwondo Beds (Malawi) show more positive values, with 7.7‰ (Lüdecke et al., 2016a); that is, an inferred major consumption of C_3 plants. This is interpreted as the environment possibly being much more closed compared to contemporary eastern African habitats (Lüdecke et al., 2016a); however, an alternative hypothesis is that the suids from Chiwondo Beds (Malawi) could have consumed a lot of C_3 grasses, perhaps because the environment was more humid (Antoine Soroun, pers. comm.). The *Kolpochoerus–Hylochoerus* lineage is generally adapted to more closed habitats and became C_3 browsers for the past 1.0 Ma, whereas the *Metridiochoerus–Phacochoerus* lineage continued as C_4 grazers (Cerling et al., 2015a). *Kolpochoerus* species from sites younger than 1.0 Ma years consume a high quantity of C_4 plants (Bedaso et al., 2010). According to Cerling et al. (2015a), from 4.0 to 1.0 Ma the genera *Kolpochoerus* and *Hylochoerus* were primarily C_4 grazers; however, at present their extant species are known as mixed-feeders. Similarly, suid enamel isotope data from the site of Asbole (0.8–0.64 Ma) shows an exclusive grazing diet for the two suid species of *K. majus* and *M. modestus* (Bedaso et al., 2010).

To date, stable isotope sampling has not been done for the Buia suids. However, microwear results together with stable isotopic data and faunal turnover records suggest a mixed diet for *K. olduvaiensis*, a graze-dominated/mixed-feeder diet for *K. majus*, and a graze diet for the hypsodont *M. modestus*. The microwear data and the turnover and taxonomy of the large mammalian community including hominins suggest a shift from forested/woodland habitats to more arid, open, and grassland-dominated habitats (Table 16.2). As in other eastern African sites the diverse taxonomic developments and dietary preferences of Buia suids have been greatly influenced by persistent climatic variability.

The large mammalian community from Buia was mainly represented by dominant grazing faunas. These include hippopotamids, equids, rhinoceros, and primates (*Theropithecus oswaldi*), and this supports the interpretation of open savanna and grassland vegetation. Studies focusing on understanding the abundance taxa of the basin is not yet initiated at the Buia Basin; for example, occurrence of the bovid tribes Alcelaphini are not yet known, in which their presence as indicators of dry and seasonal environments have been known from major eastern African sites (Greenacre and Vrba, 1984). In addition, the fluctuations of the isotopic range values were interpreted as demonstrating that a lake was present at specific time periods (Abbate et al., 2004). This interpretation is further supported by the herpetofauna from Buia, where abundant water taxa (crocodiles) and river–lake–swamp environment reptiles (rock pythons) are represented (Delfino et al., 2004; Rook et al., 2013).

The combined data from isotope analysis, paleontology, and sedimentology agree on the interpretations of fluvio-deltaic and savanna dominated environments at the Dandiero Basin (Abbate et al., 2004; Ghinassi et al., 2009, 2015). Therefore, the Basin's mosaic paleoenvironmental setting with associated diversity of food resources would have been attractive to the suids and other mammal species. The availability of water and grassland-dominated landscapes throughout the northern part of the rift valley would have presented an attractive habitat for mammals and hominins (Medin et al., 2015).

Table 16.2 Presence and absence of Plio/Pleistocene mammalian fauna and hominins from East Africa and the Levant. (1) Okote Member, (2) Nariokotome, (3) Olduvai Bed I, (4) Olduvai Bed II, (5) Olduvai Bed III, (6) Daka, (7) Buia, (8) Aïn Hanech, (9) Ternifine, (10) Ubeidiya, (11) Gesher Benot Ya'aqov. (X) Shows presence. Modified from Martínez-Navarro et al. (2004).

Fauna	1	2	3	4	5	6	7	8	9	10	11
Paranthropus	X		X	X							
Homo	X	X	X	X		X	X	X	X	X	X
Theropithecus	X	X	X	X		X	X	X	X		X
Kolpochoerus	X	X	X	X	X	X	X	X		X	
Metridiochoerus	X	X	X	X	X	X	X		X		
Sus										X	X
Megantereon	X								X		
Panthera	X		X	X		X					
Crocuta	X	X	X	X			X	X	X	X	
Canis			X							X	
Ursus									X		
Elephas	X	X		X		X	X				
Mammuthus											X
Bos						X					
Hippopotamus	X	X		X		X	X	X	X	X	X
Hexaprotodon		X					X				
Ceratotherium	X	X		X		X	X	X	X		
Equus	X	X		X		X	X	X	X	X	X
Giraffa	X			X		X	X	X	X		
Hippotragus			X	X	X	X		X			
Kobus	X	X	X	X	X	X	X		X		
Gazella	X		X	X		X	X	X	X	X	X
Tragelaphus	X	X	X	X	X	X	X		X		

Conclusions

Here we have used craniodental convergent morphology coupled with information from microwear and stable isotopic data to reconstruct the diets and habit preferences of the Buia suids. The specialized craniodental anatomy and efficient mastication process was a successful response to the dietary challenges that occurred during the trajectory of their evolution. These species had generally C_4-dominated diets and inhabited the mosaic environments of the Dandiero Basin. These advantages allowed the two genera, *Kolpochoerus* and *Metridiochoerus*, to evolve and adapt through appropriate and successful responses to the pressures of climate change, compared with other groups of mammals. Although further study is needed to better quantify the abundance of taxa in the Basin, it is inevitable that they show a better potential for presence in the fossil record together with hippopotamids, rhinoceros, and hominins than any other ungulates. Hominin presence is well documented in two different localities of the Basin accompanied by large accumulation of Acheulean lithic assemblages, showing parallel adaptation scenarios along the large mammalian fauna in general and the suid genera in particular. The suids were tolerant to the cyclical paleoenvironmental changes during Pleistocene times, had latitudinal and longitudinal dispersal scenarios (unlike carnivores and herbivores), and colonized vast territories. They served as important biochronological markers within the mammalian ecosystem of the Dandiero Basin and their presence alongside hominins in highest number and their diversity in the fossil record is a testimony to their adaptive strategies to mosaic environments.

Acknowledgments

The Buia Geo-Paleontological Research Project is an ongoing international project developed in agreement, and collaboration with, the Eritrean authorities. It is funded by the Italian

Ministry for Education and Research (PRIN2012 MY8AB2 to M.G.), the Italian Ministry for Foreign Affairs and International Cooperation (MAECI DGSP-VI to L.R.), and the University of Florence (Fondi di Ateneo 2012–2013 to L.R.). During the previous years, Buia geo-paleontological fieldwork has also benefited from support provided by the Leakey Foundation (2000–2005 to L.R.), the Wenner-Gren Foundation (7575/06 to L.R.), the National Geographic Society (7946/05 to L.R.), and the Spanish Ministry of Science and Education (CGL-2016-80975-P to B.M.N.), the Palarq Foundation (to B.M.N. and T.M.), and has been also supported by grants from the Atapuerca Foundation (to T.M.). For scientific collaboration during various phases of the field and laboratory work in the Buia Project, we are indebted to E. Abbate, E. Ghezzo, F. Landucci, M. Sagri, A. Urciuoli (Florence), M. Delfino, G. Carnevale, M. Pavia, A. Villa (Turin), A. Coppa, L. Bondioli, F. Candilio (Rome), C. Zanolli (Trieste; Pretoria), and R. Macchiarelli (Poitiers, Paris). We are also grateful for the comments and suggestions of A. Souron (Bordeaux), and analytical contribution of F. Rivals (IPHES, Tarragona). We dedicate this contribution to the late Piero Bruni (Florence), with whom we spent several enjoyable field seasons surveying the badlands of the Buia Dandiero Basin.

17 The 6-Million-Year Record of Ecological and Environmental Change at Gona, Afar Region, Ethiopia

Naomi E. Levin, Scott W. Simpson, Jay Quade, Melanie A. Everett, Stephen R. Frost, Michael J. Rogers, and Sileshi Semaw

Introduction

The rift setting of eastern Africa preserves exceptional records of mammalian (including hominin) fossils and archeology. The Afar region is host to multiple deposits with sediments ranging in age from >9 Ma to the present (Chorowicz, 2005; Katoh et al., 2016) and plays a major role in our understanding of human origins. The Gona project area contains fossiliferous deposits that span *ca.* 6.3 to <0.15 Ma (Quade et al., 2008); the duration of this record means that it can make a distinct contribution to understanding the environmental context for human evolution within the Afar and in eastern Africa (Figures 17.1 and 17.2). The primary units at Gona include the late Miocene Adu-Asa Formation, which contains fossils of *Ardipithecus kaddaba*; the early Pliocene Sagantole Formation with fossils of *Ardipithecus ramidus*; the mid- to late-Pliocene Hadar Formation; and the Busidima Formation (*ca.* 2.7 Ma to <0.15 Ma), which contains a record of some of the earliest Oldowan stone tools, fossils of *Homo erectus*, and Acheulean artifacts (Figure 17.2).

In this chapter, we review what is known about the environments preserved at Gona since the late Miocene. The majority of the paleoecological information from Gona is from geological, paleontological, and stable isotope information that is published in support of evidence of hominins and their behavior (e.g., Semaw et al., 2005, 2020; Simpson et al., 2008, 2015, 2020), although we also draw on studies that have focused on the geology and environmental change (e.g., Quade et al., 2004, 2008; Levin et al., 2004, 2008; Kleinsasser et al., 2008; López-Sáez & Domínguez-Rodrigo, 2009).

The content of this chapter reflects the data that are available from Gona, but not all units will be represented equally or in similar ways, given the extent of the studies done thus far. However, for all sections we review the basic geological setting, the depositional context for the mammalian fossils, and other relevant data (e.g., stable isotope results, faunal distributions) to the degree they are available. For some units, we present new data on faunal distributions that have not been published elsewhere (e.g., early Pliocene Sagantole Formation) or are only otherwise available in a dissertation (e.g., late Pleistocene Busidima Formation; Everett, 2010).

Methods and Overview of Work

The paleoenvironmental work at Gona has been conducted as part of efforts both to document the environmental context for specific fossil and archaeological finds and to build terrestrial records of regional climate and environmental change in eastern Africa. The data that we present and review in this chapter are based primarily on sedimentology, faunal analyses, and stable isotope geochemistry.

Sedimentological and Faunal Data

Sedimentological data and accompanying facies analyses provide the framework for all other environmental records at Gona. The sedimentological work has been conducted for units throughout the stratigraphic sequence at Gona and is summarized in Quade et al. (2008), although details on specific units also accompany papers that report fossil hominins and archeology (e.g., Semaw et al., 2005, 2020; Simpson et al., 2008, 2015, 2019). or that focus on the geology or paleoecology of units (Kleinsasser et al., 2008; Levin et al., 2008). For this chapter, we will briefly review the depositional information for all units at Gona, as it forms our primary understanding of the landscapes with which hominins interacted.

Faunal collection has been conducted throughout the stratigraphic sequence at Gona. The initial faunal surveys of the Gona Project study area were designed to document the presence of archeological and paleontological remains in service of better understanding hominin behavioral and anatomical evolution. Following initial survey of the study area, a more intensive survey and collection strategy was adopted. All fossils attributable to hominins, primates, carnivorans, and aves were collected. Diagnostic craniodental remains were collected for bovids, suids, hippopotamids, equids, rhinocerotids, and micromammals. Bovid, suid, and equid long bones that included an articular surface were collected, as were pedal bones. Complete or mostly complete proboscidean molars were recovered. Representative samples documenting the presence of fish, turtles, and crocodylians were collected. Collections were also made of taphonomically relevant specimens that demonstrate cut marks, carnivore damage, or weathering. At

---

Supplementary resources for this chapter are available on www.cambridge.org/africanpaleoecology

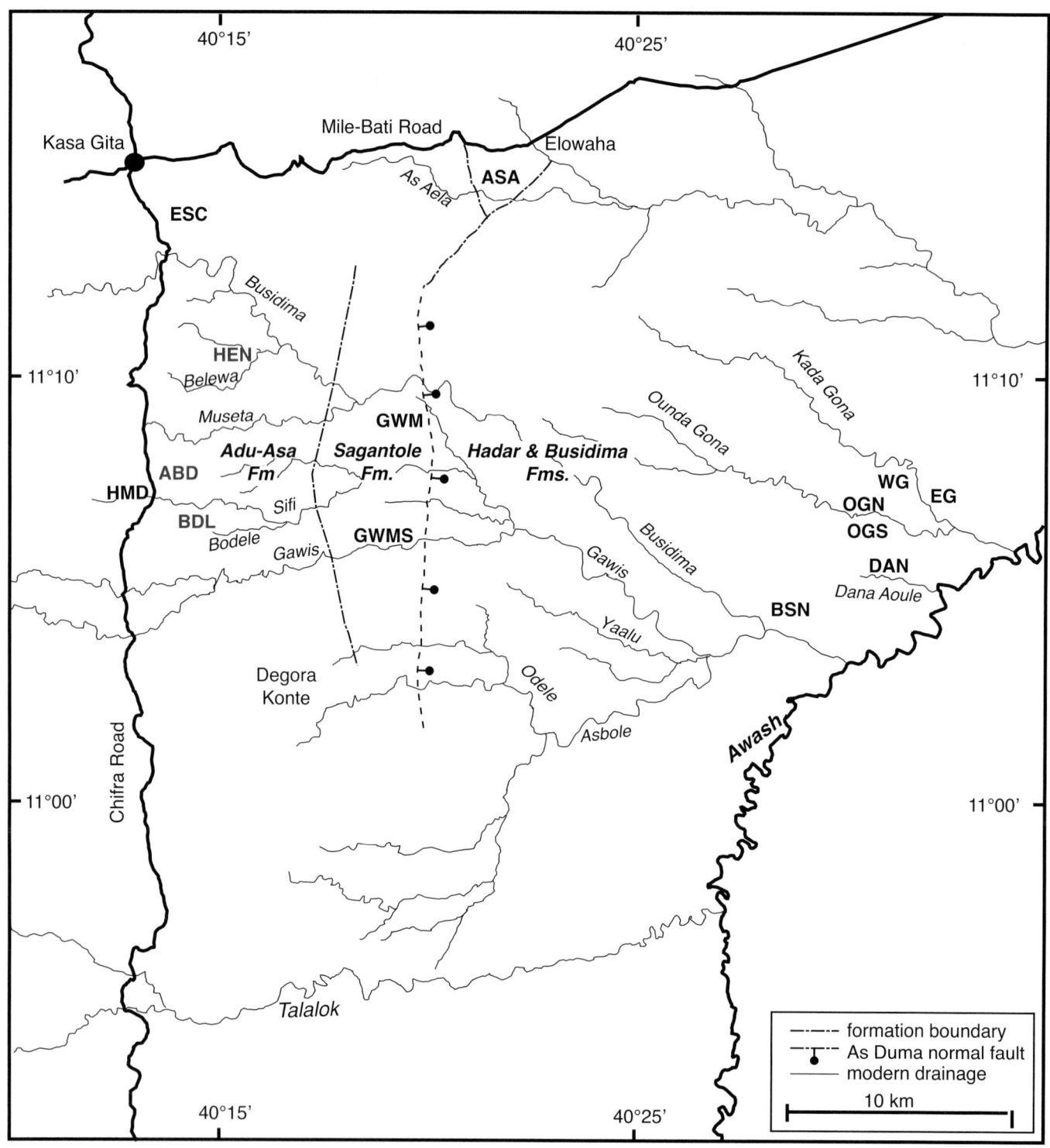

Figure 17.1 Location of the Gona Project study area with the locations of major drainages discussed, fossil collection areas (using three-letter abbreviations referenced in text), general formation boundaries, the As Duma normal fault, and nearby towns and roads from with the basic geology from Quade et al. (2008) and Kleinsasser et al. (2008).

hominin localities, crawling the area with a 100 percent recovery program was adopted. Because more time is spent at hominin localities, and every fossil in the vicinity of the hominin find spot is examined, there is the possibility that this strategy at hominin sites results in a biased composition of the fauna collected in both the taxonomic distribution and their frequency. Field notes describing all fossils at a locality were made, as were descriptions of the depositional context. Here, we review published faunal data that are available from all units and present new data from the Sagantole Formation and portions of the Busidima Formation, where available. Analysis of the faunal material from Gona is ongoing and the information presented here should be viewed as a preliminary status report on work in progress.

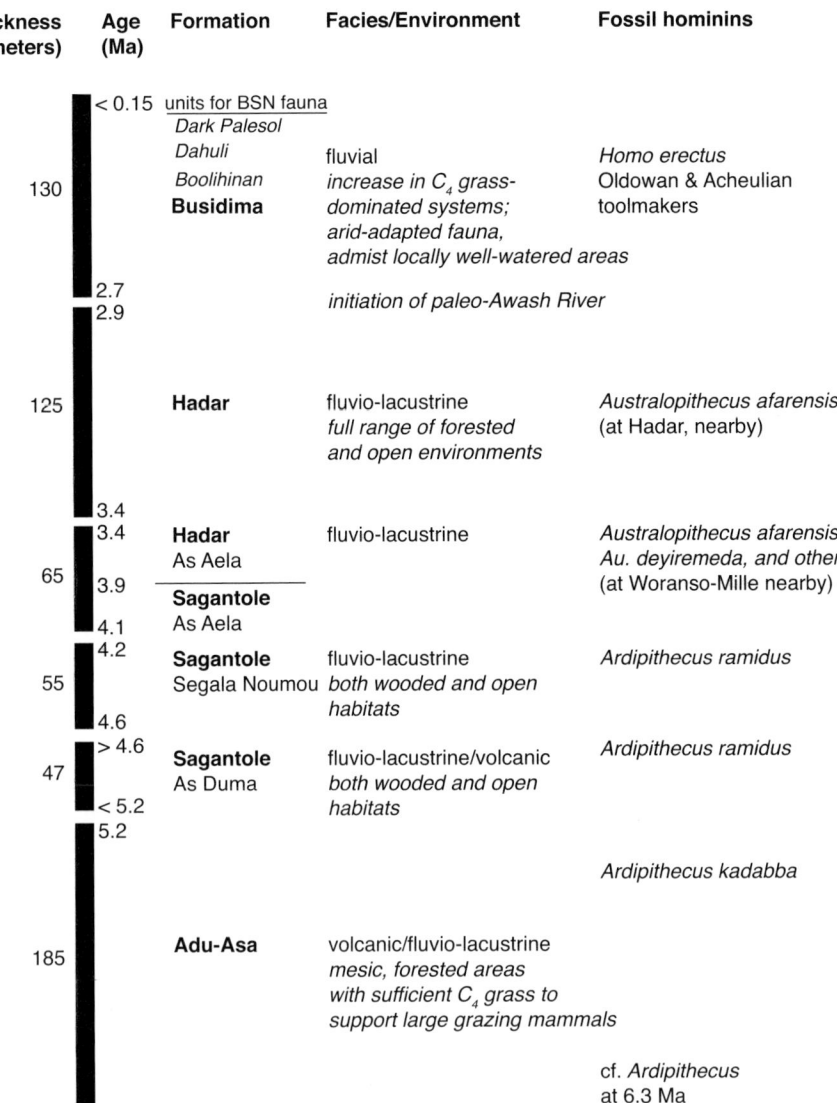

Figure 17.2 Composite stratigraphy of the Gona Project study area based on Figure 2 in Quade et al. (2008), with facies, environment, and relevant hominin activity marked. The three informal units used for describing the stratigraphy of fauna from Busidima North (BSN) in the Busidima Formation discussed in the text are also noted.

Isotopic Data Sets

Carbon and oxygen isotope records from soil carbonates and fossil teeth have played a significant role in our understanding of environmental change at Gona (Quade et al., 2004, 2008; Levin et al., 2004, 2008, 2011). The isotopic record has been developed for any part of the stratigraphic sequence where soil carbonates were present and could be sampled. The soil carbonate isotope records are discussed in the majority of publications from Gona, although they received particular focus in Quade et al. (2004) and Levin et al. (2004). The isotopic records from Gona have also played a major role in understanding temporal trends in vegetation and climate in the Afar and more broadly in eastern Africa since the early Pliocene (e.g., Cerling et al., 2011b; Levin et al., 2011). The most recent compilation of the soil carbonate stable isotope data from Gona was published by Levin (2013). We update this compilation for this chapter (Supplementary Table S17.1), with some new analyses (Supplementary Table S17.2), and include data from the pedogenic nodules first presented in Everett (2010). For consistency with the rest of the compiled data set of pedogenic carbonates from Gona, we only include data from soil carbonate nodules and exclude data from rhizoliths or vertic fill that Everett (2010) included in her analysis. Ages were assigned to soil carbonates as a function of their stratigraphic distance to the nearest marker bed and typical sedimentation rate for that part of the stratigraphic section; the ages listed in Supplementary Table S17.1 differ slightly from those in Levin (2013), as some of the ages for the marker units have been updated. Analytical methods for published data sets are in the corresponding publications.

Here we report new isotopic data from 16 paleosol units from the Busidima Formation (24 nodules total), where soil carbonate nodules were collected from distinct pedogenic carbonate horizons at least 40 cm below the top of the paleosol unit, which represents a minimum distance to the actual soil surface when nodules were forming, as the surfaces of most paleosols are not preserved. Micritic portions of carbonate nodules were powdered with a hand-held drill. Carbonate powders were then reacted in a bath of phosphoric acid (H_3PO_4) at 90°C on a custom-built device at Johns Hopkins University (see Passey et al., 2010 for description). The resultant CO_2 was cryogenically purified and its $^{13}C/^{12}C$ and $^{18}O/^{16}O$ ratios were measured on a Thermo 253 isotope ratio mass spectrometer. Isotope data are reported in standard δ-notation in per mil (‰) units, where $\delta^x = (^xR_{sample}/^xR_{standard} - 1) \times 1000$ and ^xR represents the ratio of the heavy to light isotope of the relevant isotope system (e.g., $^{13}C/^{12}C$). The $\delta^{13}C$ and $\delta^{18}O$ values are reported relative to the Vienna Pee Dee Belemnite (VPDB) standard and were measured in reference to in-house carbonate reference materials that have been calibrated to the isotopic composition of NBS-19. Within-run analytical precision of in-house standards was <0.3‰ for both $\delta^{13}C$ and $\delta^{18}O$ values during the specific analytical sessions in which these data were generated (1σ of multiple measurements). Where means of isotopic data are reported in the text below, the symbol ± is used to represent 1 standard deviation from the mean.

The carbon and oxygen isotope composition of soil carbonates has been widely used for reconstructing hominin environments at Gona and elsewhere in eastern Africa because it provides quantitative measures of the distribution of vegetation and water balance on a landscape, using materials (i.e., soil carbonates) that are abundant in rift basin sediments. Briefly, the $\delta^{13}C$ value of soil carbonate, when sampled at depth (>40 cm) from a pedogenic carbonate horizon in a paleosol, reflects the $\delta^{13}C$ value of vegetation that grew in that soil over the time interval of soil carbonate formation (10^3–10^4 years) and in turn the $\delta^{13}C$ value of vegetation reflects the photosynthetic pathway (C_3 or C_4) used by these plants, in addition to the $\delta^{13}C$ value of atmospheric CO_2 at the time the plants grew (e.g., Cerling et al., 1989). Carbon isotope analyses of soil carbonates are particularly useful in reconstructing paleovegetation in eastern Africa where the majority of grasses at lower elevations (<2000 m) use the C_4 photosynthetic pathway and have $\delta^{13}C$ values ca. −14‰ to −11‰, in contrast to trees and shrubs that use the C_3 pathway with $\delta^{13}C$ values that range from ca. −31‰ to −23‰ (Cerling et al., 2003a). As such, the $\delta^{13}C$ value of soil carbonates forming in a soil reflects the proportion of C_3 and C_4 plants growing in that soil and can be used as an indicator of woody cover (e.g., Cerling et al., 2011b). Likewise, the $\delta^{13}C$ values of fossil teeth reflect the carbon isotope composition of an animal's diet during the period of enamel mineralization; for herbivores at low elevations in eastern Africa, $\delta^{13}C_{teeth}$ values provide an indication of the proportion of grass (i.e., graze) relative to trees/shrubs (i.e., browse) in an animal's diet (e.g., Passey et al., 2005). The $\delta^{13}C$ values of both soil carbonates and fossil teeth provide detailed ecological and environmental information about specific locations (or species in the case of $\delta^{13}C_{teeth}$ values) and the broader ecosystem composition (e.g., Cerling et al., 2011b, 2015a; Wynn et al., 2013).

The oxygen isotopic composition of soil carbonates and fossil teeth provides information on both the water stress in an ecosystem and large-scale climate patterns, and has been the focus of studies of environmental change at Gona and other hominin sites in eastern Africa (e.g., Levin et al., 2004, 2011; Blumenthal et al., 2017). The interpretation of oxygen isotope records is complex and will not be a focus of this review. For a full treatment of the interpretation of carbon and oxygen isotope data from soil carbonates and fossil teeth, we refer the reader to the growing number of studies that provide in-depth presentation of these data from the Afar and elsewhere in eastern Africa (e.g., Levin et al., 2004, 2011, 2015; Cerling et al., 2011b; Levin, 2013, 2015; Sponheimer et al., 2013; Negash et al., 2015; Wynn et al., 2016; Blumenthal et al., 2017).

Review of Paleoenvironmental and Paleoecological Data from Fossil- and Artifact-Bearing Sediments at Gona

The fossil-bearing strata in the Gona Project study area include the Adu-Asa, Sagantole, Hadar, and Busidima Formations which sample the period between ca. 6.3 and <0.15 Ma (Quade et al., 2004, 2008; Kleinsasser et al., 2008; Figure 17.2). In the following sections, we provide an overview of environment and ecology for each of these time periods based on the data currently available.

Adu-Asa Formation (>6.4 to 5.2 Ma)

The late Miocene fossil-bearing deposits at Gona are exposed in the western-most portion of the Gona Project study area in small sedimentary packages intercalated with escarpment-forming basalts and assigned to the Adu-Asa Formation (Quade et al., 2008). These basalts are part of the Dahla Series fissure basalts that formed during the late stage of rifting associated with the southern Red Sea rift (Wolfenden et al., 2005); they set first-order controls on the landscapes and ecosystems of the Adu-Asa Formation. The hominin fossils recovered from these sediments are presented in Simpson et al. (2015), where the hominin paleoecology is also discussed. Here, we present an overview of the paleoecological information from these late Miocene sites. Our presentation of the faunal data draws on the overview presented in Simpson et al. (2015), but we also draw on the chronostratigraphic, sedimentological, and isotopic information presented in Kleinsasser et al. (2008), Quade et al. (2008), and Levin et al. (2008).

Adu-Asa Formation Fauna

The late Miocene fauna from the Adu-Asa Formation at Gona primarily come from two collection areas: (1) the ca. 6.3 Ma sediments along the Bodele and As Bole drainages and near an area known as Hamadi Das, and (2) the ca. 5.4 Ma sediments that are associated with the upper Busidima River that we labeled "Escarpment" (ESC) localities (Figure 17.1). The 6.3–5.4 Ma time interval is important in biotic evolution as a significant turnover in mammalian species occurs with the beginnings of a more grass-dominated landscape (e.g., Haile-Selassie et al., 2009a). This is also a critical period in human evolution, as current evidence suggests that the hominin and chimpanzee lineages separated about 7–5 Ma (Wilkinson et al., 2011). The available fossil hominin data indicate that two major changes in functional and behavioral anatomy – bipedal locomotion and reduction in size of the male canine teeth – were evident as early as 6 Ma (Senut et al., 2001). Over 900 fossils from both

Table 17.1 Fauna from the late Miocene (*ca.* 6.3 Ma and *ca.* 5.4 Ma) fossil localities, from Simpson et al. (2015).

- Mammalia
  - §Bovidae
    - *Zephyreduncinus oundagaisus*
    - Reduncini, gen. et sp. indet. (cf. *Kobus* sp.)
    - Reduncini, gen. et sp. indet. (cf. *Redunca* sp.)
    - Boselaphini, cf. *Tragoportax*
    - *Tragelaphus* sp.
    - Aepycerotini, gen. et sp. indet.
    - *Ugandax* sp.
  - §Suidae
    - *Nyanzachoerus* sp.
    - cf. *Nyanzachoerus kuseralensis*
  - §Hippopotamidae, gen. et sp. indet. A.
  - §Hippopotamidae, gen. et sp. indet. B.
  - §Giraffidae, gen. et sp. indet.
  - §Perissodactyla
    - *Eurygnathohippus* cf. *feibeli*
    - Dicerotini, *Diceros* sp.
  - §Proboscidea
    - *Anancus kenyensis*
    - Elephantidae gen. et sp. indet.
  - §Rodentia
    - cf. *Tachyoryctes*
    - cf. *Thryonomys*
    - Hystrichidae, gen. et sp. indet.
  - Primates
    - *Ardipithecus kadabba*
    - aff. *Ardipithecus* sp.
    - cf. *Kuseracolobus aramisi*
    - Colobinae, gen. et sp. indet.
    - Papionini, gen. et sp. indet.
    - cf. *Pliopapio alemui*
  - §Carnivora
    - *Machairodus* sp.
    - Mustelidae, gen. et sp. indet.
    - ?Viverridae
    - *Bonisicyon aakir*
- Reptilia
  - §Geochelonia
  - §*Varanus* sp.
  - §Crocodylia, gen. et sp. indet.
- Pisces
  - cf. Ciconiidae, gen. et sp. indet.

periods have been collected and are now curated at the National Museum of Ethiopia (Addis Ababa, Ethiopia). Most of these fossils represent terrestrial vertebrates, with a high percentage of bovids, carnivorans, suids, and cercopithecids, yet the assemblages also include crocodiles, turtles, fish, gastropods, and floral specimens (Table 17.1). The faunal collections have a high frequency of postcrania that precludes, in many cases, allocation to species or genus. In general, the fossils are well-preserved due in large measure to the low-energy environments in which they were deposited and the lack of weathering.

Ca. 6.3 Ma Fauna

The oldest fossils described from Gona come from the *ca.* 6.3 Ma sediments exposed along the Bodele and As Bole drainages and near an area known as Hamadi Das; they were primarily recovered from three collection areas, As Bole Dora (ABD), Bodele Dora (BDL), and Hamadi Das (HMD; Figure 17.1; Kleinsasser et al., 2008). The site from the Henali area (HEN1) to the north is likely of similar age to this oldest cluster of sites (Figure 17.1). Over 300 specimens were collected and catalogued from these areas (Simpson et al., 2015). A subset of 252 specimens that could be identified to order (Proboscidea, Carnivora) or better (Bovidae, Giraffidae, Suidae, Hippopotamidae, Rhinocerotidae, Equidae) are analyzed here. The majority of bovid remains from these localities are postcrania that are difficult to assign reliably beyond family. The three areas are nearly equally represented (ABD: numbers of individual specimens (NISP) = 77; BDL: NISP = 86; HMD: NISP = 89). At Hamadi Das, which has the thickest sedimentary exposures (>50 m), the two main collecting localities (HMD1 and HMD2), while separated by about 150 m, sample slightly different parts of the landscape, with HMD2 being more fluvial as evidenced by the higher frequency of water-associated fauna, e.g., hippopotamids and crocodiles. Both localities are dominated (≥50 percent) by bovids followed in frequency by carnivores (both large and small species) then suids and equids (each about 7 percent). Evidence of rodent gnawing on several fossils indicates that some of the bones were exposed on the surface prior to burial.

The stratigraphically equivalent ABD1 and ABD2 localities are similar in composition and species diversity. Both ABD localities have small sample sizes but the fauna are dominated by bovids, followed in frequency by hippopotamids and carnivores.

The BDL area appears to be sampling a more terrestrial (less aquatic) part of the paleolandscape with a lower frequency of bovids (49 percent), apparently mostly reduncines, fewer hippopotamids (*ca.* 6 percent vs 10–13 percent) and a much higher contribution by equids (23 percent vs 3–7 percent). While monkeys are rare at the *ca.* 6.3 Ma localities, colobines were recovered from ABD1 and ABD2 and a papionin from BDL2. Hominins are characteristically rare (*n* = 1, ABD1/P1; Simpson et al., 2015) such that it is difficult to draw conclusions about the landscape distribution and habitat preferences of this taxon.

A study of the bovid pedal remains (astragali, proximal and intermediate phalanges; *n* = 17) suggests the bovids were small in body size with an average mass of 50.4 kg (SD = 38.1; range: 23–139 kg) with the majority of specimens (14 of 17) having an estimated body mass between 23 and 48 kg (Fredieu et al., 2007). An ecomorphological analysis of these remains using criteria established by DeGusta and Vrba (2003, 2005) suggests that the majority of bovids preferred either a forest (*n* = 10) or heavy cover (*n* = 1), with the remaining specimens allocated to either light cover (*n* = 5) or open (*n* = 1) habitats. The smaller body size of the bovids and their anatomical adaptations are consistent with the overall faunal composition, isotopic, and geologic data indicating a habitat at the margins of a closed, riparian environment.

Ca. 5.4 Ma Localities

Eleven different localities in the *ca.* 5.4 Ma period are known and have yielded over 700 catalogued specimens. Localities ESC2 and ESC3 are especially fossiliferous. Localities ESC2, ESC3, and ESC8 have produced hominin remains that are assigned to *Ardipithecus kadabba* (Simpson et al., 2015). A sample of 554 larger mammal specimens identified to order or better were analyzed for faunal composition, with ESC2 being the richest locality (NISP = 352). The stratigraphically equivalent localities ESC4–ESC11 were combined together due to the small number of specimens recovered (NISP = 28).

Except for ESC1 (NISP = 43), the other localities are dominated (>50 percent) by bovids. ESC1 has a greater relative proportion of carnivores, monkeys, proboscideans, and suids than the other localities. While this is suggestive of a real difference in composition from ESC2 and ESC3, the small sample size may bias this comparison. The most common taxon is Bovidae followed by carnivores and suids. The bovids include tragelaphines and reduncines with antilopines a rare component. Monkeys and equids each represent about 6 percent of the total faunal composition with the other groups below 5 percent. The monkeys from the ESC localities include both colobines and cercopithecines. Among the colobines, a species similar in size to extant *Colobus* predominates, and a papionin similar in size to *Pliopapio alemui* is among the cercopithecines.

As above, analyses of the bovid pedal fossils (astragali; proximal, intermediate, and distal phalanges; *n* = 60) is informative about their biology. The estimated body size in this sample is much larger (mean = 193.5 kg; SD = 204.0; range = 32–1021 kg) than that from the 6.3 Ma localities at Gona; only 16 of the specimens provided an estimated body mass of less than 100 kg. Overall, the ecomorphological analysis indicates a preference for forest (*n* = 19) and heavy cover (*n* = 27); only 3 specimens were scored as light cover and 11 as open. It is important to note that while heavy cover allocations were made on all four pedal elements, assignment to light cover was made only on the astragali and assignment to open habitats was based on only the proximal and intermediate phalanges. Part of this discrepancy may be a function of using modern bovids as analogs for fossil collections, as this approach can be increasingly problematic in older deposits.

Comparing the *ca.* 6.3 Ma and the *ca.* 5.4 Ma faunal collections at Gona shows differences that may reflect their respective positions on the paleolandscape. Fluvial deposition at the *ca.* 5.4 Ma sites contrasts with fluvio-lacustrine deposition in the *ca.* 6.3 Ma sites. The younger deposits (ESC localities) have fewer hippopotamids, which suggests that fossil accumulation occurred along smaller or less-permanent sources of water (i.e., rivers versus lakes and rivers), although crocodiles were present at the ESC localities. Other differences include increased abundance of suids and carnivores with a reduction in the frequency of bovids and equids. Both areas share the presence of the small amphicyonid carnivore *Bonisicyon allicabo* (Werdelin and Simpson, 2009), a characteristically closed-habitat carnivore that may have been adaptively transitioning to more open habitats.

In addition to the faunal distributions and sedimentology, $\delta^{13}C$ values of 35 teeth from Adu-Asa Formation at Gona (Levin et al., 2008) add to our understanding of the environments of *Ar. kadabba*. The majority of teeth were sampled from the 5.4 Ma localities (ESC1, 2, 3, 6; *n* = 31) and yielded $\delta^{13}C$ values that indicate C_3 browsing diets of some herbivores (suids, bovids, giraffids) and C_4 grazing among other herbivores, including the proboscidean *Anancus* sp. and equid *Eurygnathohippus* cf. *feibeli*. The four Proboscidea and Equidae teeth from the older 6.3 Ma localities yield $\delta^{13}C$ values >−2.5‰, which suggests reliance on C_4 graze for these animals as well. This latter observation demonstrates that there were enough C_4 grasses and/or sedges on the landscapes where *Ar. kadabba* is found to support committed grazers (Levin et al., 2008; Simpson et al., 2015). It is also consistent with other carbon isotope records of teeth, such as those from Lothagam in the Turkana Basin that document proboscideans and equids in northern Kenya as committed grazers by 6.5 Ma (Uno et al., 2011).

Summary of Hominin Habitat in the Late Miocene at Gona

Overall, the late Miocene hominin environments from the Adu-Asa Formation at Gona were focused around lake and river systems in volcanic terrains and physically bounded by basalt flows. Hominins were associated with a combination of lakes and rivers in the older (*ca.* 6.3 Ma) units, whereas the younger sites (*ca.* 5.4 Ma) are associated mostly with rivers (Kleinsasser et al., 2008). The overall ecological reconstruction for *Ar. kadabba* at Gona included well-watered environments that were more wooded than in subsequent time intervals but where animals that ate solely C_4 grasses or sedges also thrived; this is reinforced by the sedimentology of the Adu-Asa deposits that indicates rapid deposition in lacustrine and fluvial settings. We also note that there is no evidence for soil carbonate development at, or near, hominin sites in the Adu-Asa Formation, which makes these sediments distinct from the younger hominin-bearing strata at Gona (Kleinsasser et al., 2008; Quade et al., 2008). The lack of soil carbonates may be a product of rapid deposition where soils did not have a long time to develop, a wetter climate (>1000 mm rainfall/year), or less seasonality. The dietary preferences of the herbivores, faunal composition, and absence of soil carbonates may reflect a different climate regime in the late Miocene at Gona that included more rainfall, less seasonality, higher depositional rates, and/or a higher elevation at the time than in the subsequent early Pliocene. These habitats of the Adu-Asa Formation at Gona Gona are consistent with habitat reconstructions for *Ar. kadabba* found in the Middle Awash, where stable isotope data from soil carbonates indicate the presence of woodland and grassy woodlands, whereas the fossil assemblages indicate wet and closed woodland or forest settings (WoldeGabriel et al., 2001). Both of these reconstructions are consistent with reconstructions of other late Miocene environments in eastern Africa that included woodland, wooded savannas, and wet and dry forests (as reviewed in Jacobs et al., 1999). They are also consistent with studies showing that the climate of northern Africa may have been wetter than it is today (Griffin, 1999). However, we need to be careful about making generalizations about large intervals of time and broad geographic regions that have not been sampled in detail, considering that (1) available records from marine cores indicate that the hydroclimate in northern and northeastern Africa was dynamic and variable in the late Miocene (e.g., van der Laan et al., 2012; Feakins, 2013; Colin et al., 2014), and (2) we do not yet have a full understanding for how the nascent stages of rifting at Gona and throughout eastern Africa in the late Miocene (Chorowicz, 2005) influenced landscapes, ecosystems, and even local climate at this time.

Sagantole Formation (<5.2 to 3.9 Ma)

Ardipithecus ramidus fossils from Gona were first reported by Semaw et al. (2005), with further description of the geology and ecological context of the sites in Quade et al. (2008) and Levin et al. (2008). Here, we review the contextual information of the *Ar. ramidus* fossils at Gona and provide preliminary analyses from the fossil mammalian, avian, and fish fauna that have not yet been reported.

The *Ar. ramidus* fossils at Gona come from two members of the Sagantole Formation, the older As Duma and younger Segala Noumou Members (Quade et al., 2008). Despite the abundance of volcanic materials in both units, the poor preservation of the tephra has made it difficult to determine the precise geochronological age of these fossils, or to correlate the deposits within the project area, or to strata in other areas. However, using the age information from ^{40}Ar/^{39}Ar geochronology that is available and the results from paleomagnetic sampling of the sediments (all samples are reversed), the fossil sites within the Segala Noumou Member must lie within the magnetozone of C3 n.1 r (4.493–4.300 Ma), whereas the As Duma Member sites likely lie within the older C3 n.2 r magnetozone (4.799–4.631 Ma; Quade et al., 2008; Simpson et al., 2019).

The As Duma and Segala Noumou Members represent distinct depositional environments in the Sagantole Formation at Gona. The As Duma Member sediments reflect primarily lacustrine deposition proximal to small volcanic centers, which is evident in volcanic deposits lateral to and below the fossil sites in section and the abundance of volcaniclastic material in the fossil-bearing sediments themselves (Quade et al., 2008). In contrast, the younger Segala Noumou Member is characterized by fluvial and lacustrine deposition. Although tephra are common in the Segala Noumou Member, including some containing coarse pumices indicating the area was close to volcanic activity, there are no basalts or thick units of volcaniclastic rocks. Despite the distinct depositional settings for *Ar. ramidus* in the As Duma and Segala Noumou Members, many of the *Ar. ramidus* fossils are associated with gastropod-rich carbonate horizons in both members, which indicate that these were relatively wet places on the landscape (Semaw et al., 2005; Simpson et al., 2019).

As of 2013, 105 paleontological localities have been recognized in the Sagantole Formation at Gona that contain fossil remains of terrestrial animals. The fossil preservation ranges from good to excellent and none of the fossils shows evidence of fluvial transport. A comparison of the fauna collected from the As Duma and Segala Noumou Members shows few differences in taxonomic composition and therefore will be grouped together for the analysis presented here. While more non-hominin localities have been documented (90 non-hominin versus 15 hominin), the total number of fossils collected is greater at the hominin localities (2181 hominin versus 862 non-hominin, at the end of the 2011 field season), and the collections at hominin localities yield markedly higher average numbers of fossils (mean = 145.6 fossils/locality; range: 27–507) compared to non-hominin localities (mean = 9.6 fossils/locality; range: 1–84). To test the possibility that sampling strategy may bias the composition of the collection, NISP of major components (i.e., bovids, suids, and monkeys) were compared for the hominin and non-hominin-bearing localities (Figure 17.3). Both collections are dominated by suids (>30 percent). Bovids are also common (>30 percent) with a preponderance of tragelaphines and aepycerotines, although the aepycerotines are slightly less common in the non-hominin localities. Monkeys are also common in both areas, with a slightly greater overall contribution, especially the papionines, in the hominin-bearing localities (Figure 17.3).

The presence of similarly aged *Ar. ramidus* localities at Aramis, *ca.* 70 km south of those at Gona, makes it possible to generate a broader view of *Ar. ramidus* habitat. The preliminary analyses of the fauna, taphonomy, and sedimentology of the *Ar. ramidus*-bearing localities from Aramis and its stratigraphic equivalents indicated a woodland habitat (WoldeGabriel et al., 1994), defined by a high proportion of primates, notably the colobine *Kuseracolobus aramisi*, and tragelaphine bovids – of which their modern relatives occupy closed habitats. Subsequent research reinforced the initial work and indicated that *Ar. ramidus* occupied closed woodland habitats, as two thirds of the taxonomically identifiable mammals (NISP = 1930) were either colobine monkeys or tragelaphine bovids. The more open-adapted alcelaphine and antilopine bovids (Louchart et al., 2009; White et al., 2009b) were rare components of the sample at Aramis. However, the only known equid, *Eurygnathohippus woldegabrieli*, was a "dedicated grazer with a coarse C_4 diet" (Bernor et al., 2013: 1472). Furthermore, ecomorphological analyses of the postcrania, study of enamel mesowear, and isotopic composition of the fauna were proposed as additional evidence of

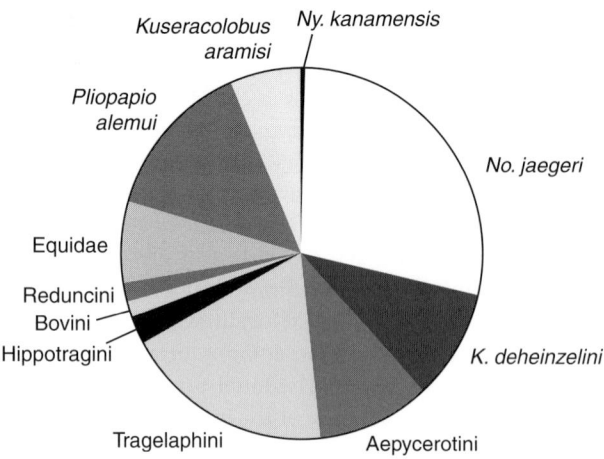

A. hominin-bearing localities
NISP = 566

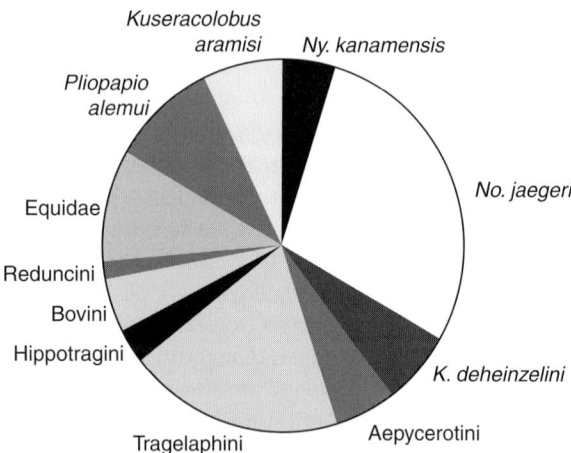

B. non-hominin-bearing localities
NISP = 320

Figure 17.3 Results of preliminary analyses in comparing faunal compositions at (A) fossil localities with hominins (*Ardipithecus ramidus*) (n = 15 localities) and (B) those without hominins (n = 90 localities) in the Sagantole Formation, Gona Project study area.

the closed woodland habitat reconstruction for *Ar. ramidus* at Aramis (White et al., 2009b). Comparisons of the Lower Aramis Member bovid composition with other paleontological localities [e.g., Hadar (see also Campisano et al., Chapter 18) and Shungura Member B in Ethiopia, Apak in Kenya, and Laetoli in Tanzania (Harrison et al., Chapter 34)] highlights the unusual nature of the Aramis sample by the high frequency of tragelaphine bovids to the very low frequency (<15 percent) of all other types of bovids (White et al., 2009a; Figure 17.4B). Equally unusual is the low diversity (two species) and high frequency of monkeys at Aramis. Clearly, this is a distinctive environment.

Given the data from Aramis, was *Ar. ramidus* restricted to this distinctive habitat as White and colleagues (2009b, 2010) propose? Or were they more broadly distributed across the ancient landscape? Independent interpretations of the Aramis isotopic data and comparisons with a broader diversity of contemporary isotope and phytolith data sets led Cerling and colleagues (2010, 2015b) to conclude that the Aramis pedogenic isotopic data were more consistent with a "tree- or bush-savanna" (2010: 1105-d) and a substantially more open habitat with less than 25 percent of woody canopy. This provides a very different context for the evolution of the early hominins than that offered by White and colleagues – a context that continues to evolve from that originally identified as a woodland (WoldeGabriel et al., 1994) to an environment that "ranged from forests to wooded grasslands ... [with] *Ar. ramidus* as a denizen of the closed habitats along this continuum" (White et al., 2009a: 87) to "woodland to grassy woodland" (White et al., 2010: 1105-e) to a "mosaic of available habitats that included forest patches and woodlands that graded into more open grasslands" (Suwa and Ambrose, 2014: 473).

The fossil data from Gona can be compared directly with those from Aramis (Figure 17.4). The faunal composition, while taxonomically similar, is markedly different in the relative abundances of those taxa. For example, the most common suid from Aramis is *Ny. kanamensis* followed in frequency by *K. deheinzelini* and *No. jaegeri*. Together, these suids make up 5.5 percent of the total NISP. At Gona, *Ny. kanamensis* is rare and *No. jaegeri* dominates the collection of suids followed in frequency by the suine *K. deheinzelini*. While both of the tetraconodont suids (i.e., *Notochoerus jaegeri*, *Nyanzachoerus kanamensis*) have $\delta^{13}C$ values suggesting a diet dedicated to grazing, the suine *K. deheinzelini* has enamel $\delta^{13}C$ values consistent with a diet composed of a mix of C_3 and C_4 plants; these results are comparable for fossils sampled at both Aramis and Gona (Levin et al., 2008; White et al., 2009a).

Similarly, the Aramis collections are dominated by the bovid *Tragelaphus* sp. (85 percent of the total bovid sample and 38.7 percent of the total large mammal NISP). Aepycerotin bovids represent less than 9 percent of the total bovids collected. The proportions at Gona are quite different. Bovids represent less than 32 percent of NISP, and while tragelaphines are the most common bovid, representing 55 percent of the bovid sample, aepycerotines account for 25 percent of the total number of bovids. Hippotragines, bovines, and reduncines account for the rest of the sample. The aepycerotine crowns are more hyposodont than the tragelaphines and have lower cuspal relief with rounded apices than the tragelaphines, indicating a more grazing diet (Figure 17.5). An ecomorphological analysis of the pedal remains (n = 41) shows an adaptive preference for more closed habitats (forest: n = 23; heavy cover: n = 2), although there is an increase in the frequency of specimens that are allocated to light cover (n = 12) areas than in the late Miocene samples. In addition, there is an increased frequency of smaller (<100 kg) bovids in the Gona Sagantole Formation sample (36/41) than in the *ca.* 5.4 Ma collection from the Adu-Asa Formation (16/60). Focusing just on the analysis of astragali, the relative allocation to light cover/open rises from less than 15 percent in the *ca.* 5.4 Ma collection to over 60 percent in the early Pliocene. This preliminary analysis of the bovid pedal remains from the Sagantole Formation at Gona suggests a near equal representation of forest/heavy cover and light cover adaptations, which is suggestive of habitat heterogeneity over small spatial scales (Fredieu et al., 2007).

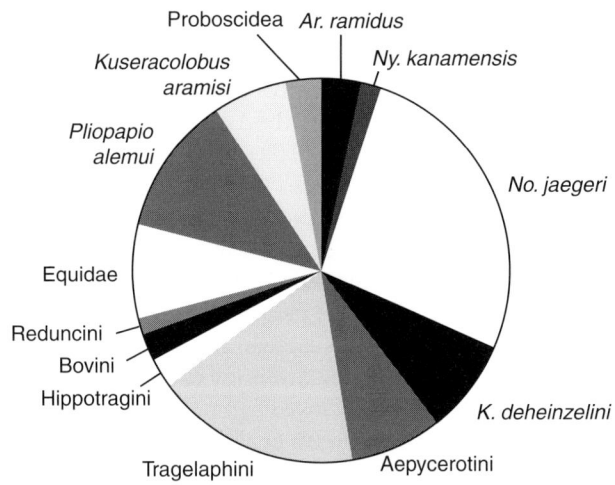

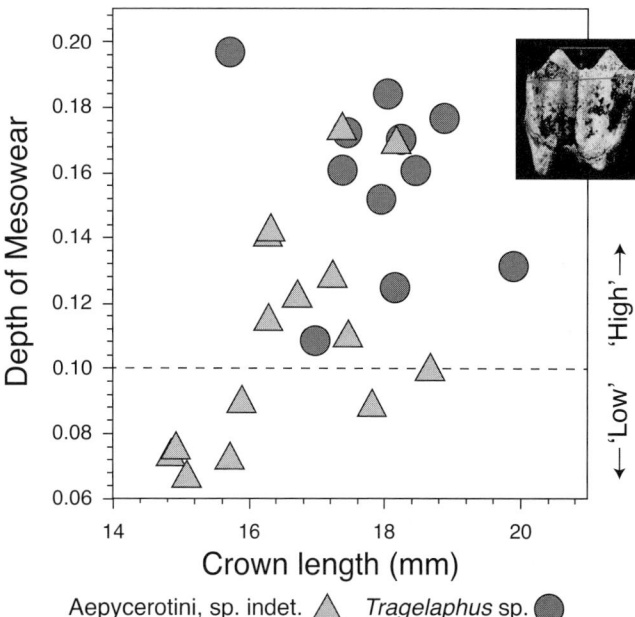

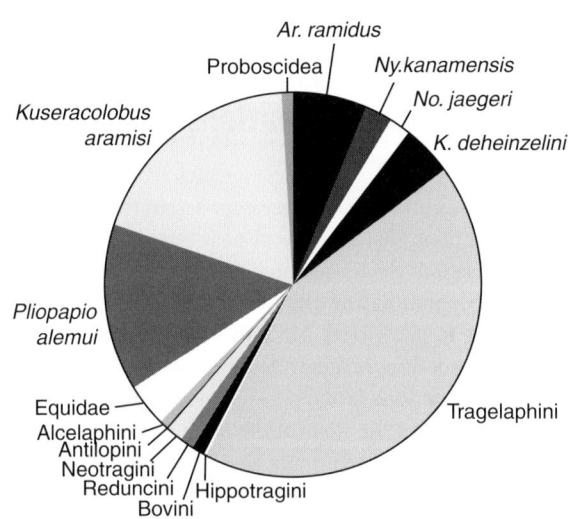

Figure 17.4 Results of preliminary analyses in comparing the frequency (NISP) of fauna in (A) the As Duma and Segala Noumou Members at Gona and (B) the Lower Aramis member. The Lower Aramis data are from White et al. (2009a, Supplementary Table S17.1).

Figure 17.5 Mesowear analysis of the aepycerotine and tragelaphine maxillary molars from the early Pliocene Sagantole Formation at Gona Project study area. Note that the aepycerotine molars have relatively lower crown apices when normalized by crown length. A relative value of 0.10 was suggested by Fortelius and Solounias (2000) to be a reasonable metric for distinguishing browsers from grazers.

Today, colobine monkeys are specialized arboreal folivores. This is reflected in numerous musculoskeletal, dental, and intestinal tract adaptations. The arboreal colobine *Kuseracolobus aramisi* is the most common primate at Aramis representing 58 percent of the total number of recovered monkey fossils, with the remaining 42 percent assigned to the somewhat more terrestrial papionine *Pliopapio alemui* (Frost, 2001; White et al., 2009a). Together, these monkeys comprise 29.1 percent of the total larger mammal assemblage NISP from Aramis. At Gona, cercopithecids make up a smaller portion of the fauna (18 percent) and *P. alemui* is nearly twice as common as *K. aramisi* (11.7 percent vs. 6.4 percent). The $\delta^{13}C$ values of enamel sampled from both Gona and Aramis indicates, not unexpectedly, that papionines consumed a greater fraction of C_4 resources than colobines at both sites, reflecting the more terrestrial behavior of the papionines (Levin et al., 2008; White et al., 2009a), which is consistent with sites from other time periods for which there are enamel $\delta^{13}C$ data for both papionines and colobines (Levin et al., 2015). Together, the relative frequency of the species and the isotopic composition of the enamel suggest that Aramis and Gona include habitats that differ in significant ways. Given that primate diversity in general increases with the prevalence of arboreal resources and cover (Chapman et al., 1999), both Aramis and Gona have an unusually low species diversity of primates "(one hominin and two monkeys at Aramis; one hominin and three monkeys at Gona)" compared to modern African forest ecosystems, suggesting a less densely wooded habitat than most primate habitats. While taphonomy may play a role in limiting primate species diversity at these localities, we think that this is unlikely at either Gona or Aramis due to the shared field research strategy of collecting all primate fossils, the intensive process of surveying for and collecting fossils in the hominin-bearing sediments, and the resulting large number of primate specimens collected.

While the identified avian fossils are few from the As Duma and Segala Noumou Members, they provide some additional information about the range of habitats that existed. These aves include two Phasianidae with different habitat preferences, with one (cf. *Francolinus s.l.*) that preferred more open habitats and *Pavo* sp. that was more forested. The recovery of a cormorant fossil, *Phalacrorax* sp., confirms the presence of a large lake.

The As Duma and Segala Noumou Member deposits are also rich in proboscideans with at least three different species, including *Deinotherium bozasi*, *Anancus* sp., and cf. *Loxodonta* sp. The $\delta^{13}C$ values from these taxa verify the widespread observation that *Deinotherium* was a dedicated browser and show that the other two species were reliant on C_4 grasses or sedges (Levin et al., 2008).

The amount of animal biomass (based on body mass and frequency) that is reliant on the significant intake of tropical grasses exceeds that of the browsers (grazers: *Anancus* sp., cf *Loxodonta*, *No. jaegeri*, *Ny. kanamensis*, *Ceratotherium*, *Eurygnathohippus*, Aepycerotini; mixed: *Kolpochoerus*, *Tragelaphus* sp.; browsers: *Deinotherium*, *Tragelaphus* sp., *Kuseracolobus*, *Pliopapio*). This indicates that abundant grass was available in, or very near, the habitats of *Ar. ramidus*. It is noteworthy that there was likely a juxtaposition of grass-dominated open habitats (*Eurygnathohippus*, *Loxodonta*, *No. jaegeri*, etc.), more closed, well-watered habitats (e.g., *Kuseracolobus*, *Pliopapio*, *Pavio* sp.), and riverine and open-water lacustrine habitats (Hippopotamidae, Crocodylia, and the cormorant *Phalocrorax*) on the early Pliocene landscape at Gona. This is consistent with the emergent stages of rift basin development where landscapes would have been patchy and fragmented (e.g., Gawthorpe and Leeder, 2000).

We note that the carbon isotopic composition of mammals from the As Duma and Segala Noumou deposits have similar distributions to similar taxa found at Aramis, which signals that although the relative distributions of these animals were different at Aramis and Gona during the Pliocene, their dietary behavior was fairly constant, regardless of where they lived (Levin et al., 2008; White et al., 2009a). The tragelaphine bovids provide a notable exception to this. At Aramis, tragelaphines had diets that were exclusively composed of C_3 vegetation, consistent with the traditional interpretation of them as browsers. However, in the Sagantole Formation at Gona the $\delta^{13}C$ values of tragelaphines indicate varying diets, with $\delta^{13}C$ values of teeth from some individuals reflecting diets dominated by C_3 vegetation, others with diets dominated by C_4 vegetation, and some that indicate mixed feeding. This range of $\delta^{13}C$ values for tragelaphine teeth at Gona is similar to that observed in the early Pliocene Lonyumun Member in Turkana (Cerling et al., 2015a). Cerling et al. (2015a) show that mixed feeding was typical for tragelaphine bovids through the Pliocene and Pleistocene. The aggregate of these carbon isotope data from tragelaphines from the early Pliocene indicate that in some settings, like the As Duma and Segala Noumou Members at Gona or the Lonyumun Member in Turkana, tragelaphines consumed a wide range of vegetation, whereas at other locations like Aramis their diets were restricted to more woody resources. This is a further indication that the environment that supported *Ar. ramidus* at Aramis was distinct from the environment that supported *Ar. ramidus* at Gona.

Fish remains were also recovered from the As Duma and Segala Noumou Members and represent five different genera from four families (Clariidae, Bagridae, Cyprinidae, and Cichlidae). The fish fauna of Gona indicates clear, oxygenated, inshore waters with at least some rocky areas. It could be either a river or lake environment, but likely was part of a larger water system connected by at least temporary streams. The small size of the fish and their diverse age range suggest that the bodies of water were permanent, albeit shallow.

Summary of Hominin Habitats in the Early Pliocene at Gona

The combination of evidence from the *Ar. ramidus*-bearing deposits at Gona indicates that these hominins had access to, and lived in, several distinct environments, both on the shores of small lakes in a volcanic terrain (i.e., the As Duma Member) and along the shores of both rivers and lakes that were in the vicinity of, but not adjacent to, volcanoes (i.e., the Segala Noumou Member). These different depositional settings supported similar taxonomic distributions of fauna. The combined data from the fauna at these sites (taxonomic distributions, mesowear, carbon isotopes, ecomorphology) indicate the presence of both arboreal and open resources available to *Ar. ramidus* at Gona. This is consistent with $\delta^{13}C$ values from soil carbonates at both Gona and Aramis that are indicative of a woodland or wooded grassland setting at the time (Levin et al., 2008; WoldeGabriel et al., 2009a; Cerling et al., 2011b). The similarity in faunal distributions in the As Duma and Segala Noumou Members at Gona is particularly notable because they are both distinct from the faunal distribution at Aramis, which is the only other known *Ar. ramidus* locality. This contrast in habitat between Aramis and Gona indicates that *Ar. ramidus* was able to negotiate landscapes of varying amounts of woody cover.

Sagantole and Hadar Formations at As Aela (4.1 to 3.3 Ma)

The As Aela fossil localities at Gona are exposed in the northern part of the project area, just southwest of the town of Eliwiha (Figure 17.1). The age of the 65-m thick sequence spans the top of the Sagantole Formation and the base of Hadar Formation, with tephra dating to 4.1 ± 0.07 Ma and 3.27 ± 0.1 Ma at the base and top of the section, respectively. Depositional environments in the lower portions of the As Aela deposits are similar to that of Segala Noumou Member of the Sagantole Formation, with fluvial and lacustrine sediments that are rich in volcaniclastic material. As in the Segala Noumou Member, fossils are associated with gastropod-rich carbonate zones, suggesting the presence of wet, paludal areas. $\delta^{13}C$ values from soil carbonates sampled from paleosols in the As Aela sequence range from −10.5 to −6.1‰ and average −7.9 ± 1.7‰ ($n = 5$), indicating environments that ranged from woodlands to wooded grasslands. Although no hominins have been found in the As Aela sequence at Gona, it is very close to deposits of similar age in the Woranso-Mille Project study area, just north of the Mile-Bati Road, where several hominin taxa have been recovered (e.g., Haile-Selassie et al., 2010b, 2012, 2015, 2019).

This small area is represented by only four fossiliferous localities but the few fossils recovered from the Asa Aela (ASA) sites are informative. Of these fossils comes the newly named suine *Kolpochoerus millensis* (Haile-Selassie and Simpson, 2013). This species is temporally intermediate and in all likelihood phylogenetically intermediate between the >4.3 Ma *K. deheinzelini* (Brunet and White, 2001) and the <3.4 Ma *K. afarensis* (Cooke, 1978b). *Kolpochoerus millensis* is distinguishable from the older taxon by having larger molar teeth (and probably body size too) and the enamel has slightly higher $\delta^{13}C$ values, suggesting that this lineage was increasing its dietary dependence on C_4 grasses. There are only two cercopithecid fossils from As Aela. The first is a well-preserved female mandible of a medium-sized papionin within the known size ranges for *Pliopapio alemui* and the smaller non-*Theropithecus* papionin material from Woranso-Mille (Frost, 2001; Frost et al., 2014), but smaller than *Parapapio* cf. *jonesi* from Hadar. The other specimen is an isolated molar of a larger papionin species, within the range of *Theropithecus oswaldi* cf. *darti* from Woranso-Mille and Hadar (Frost and Delson, 2002; Frost et al., 2014). Morphologically it is consistent with most non-*Theropithecus* papionins, but also with the very primitive morphology of some *T. o.* cf. *darti* specimens from Woranso-Mille.

Hadar Formation (3.8–2.9 Ma)

The Hadar Formation (*ca.* 3.8–2.9 Ma) is exposed at Gona primarily along the Kada Gona river in the badlands just west of the Awash River in the southeastern part of the project area, although it is also represented in the upper part of the section at As Aela, as discussed above. Although the Hadar Formation is represented by a thick sedimentary sequence (125 m) at Gona (Figure 17.2), it has not been a focus of study. The sediments of the Hadar Formation at Gona, like those in the neighboring Hadar and Dikika project areas, are dominantly lacustrine with intervals of fluvial–deltaic deposition (Quade et al., 2004). Soil carbonates from paleosols in the Hadar Formation at Gona (not including the As Aela paleosols) yield $\delta^{13}C$ values that range from −12.5 to −2.3‰ (−6.7 ± 1.7‰, *n* = 38; Supplementary Table 17.S1; Figure 17.6) and represent almost the full span of environments from forests to grasslands. This range of $\delta^{13}C$ values likely reflects both the diversity of vegetation at this time period (Campisano and Feibel, 2007; Reed, 2008) and that the soil carbonates from the Hadar Formation sample shorter time intervals, as the sedimentation rates in the Hadar Formation are high (20 cm/kyr in the Hadar Formation vs. 4–14 cm/kyr in the Busidima and Sagantole Formations; Quade et al. 2004, 2008). With the exception of fauna from As Aela, described above, studies of the faunal data from the Hadar Formation at Gona are limited and will not be discussed here, but see Campisano et al. (Chapter 18).

Busidima Formation (*ca.* 2.7 to <0.15 Ma)

The Busidima Formation is a 130-m thick sedimentary sequence that spans *ca.* 2.7 to <0.15 Ma in the Gona Project study area. Outcrops of the Busidima Formation are exposed in the badland topography formed by the Awash River today (Figures 17.1 and 17.2). The base of the Busidima Formation is defined by an erosional unconformity that represents a drop in base level and a shift to a fluvially dominated system between 2.9 and 2.7 Ma (Quade et al., 2004, 2008; Campisano, 2012). Fossils and artifacts are found in varying parts of fining-upward fluvial sedimentary packages, which represent an axial river system and its tributaries (Quade et al., 2004, 2008). For the purposes of this review we informally divide the Busidima Formation into lower and upper portions, which can be separated roughly by the presence

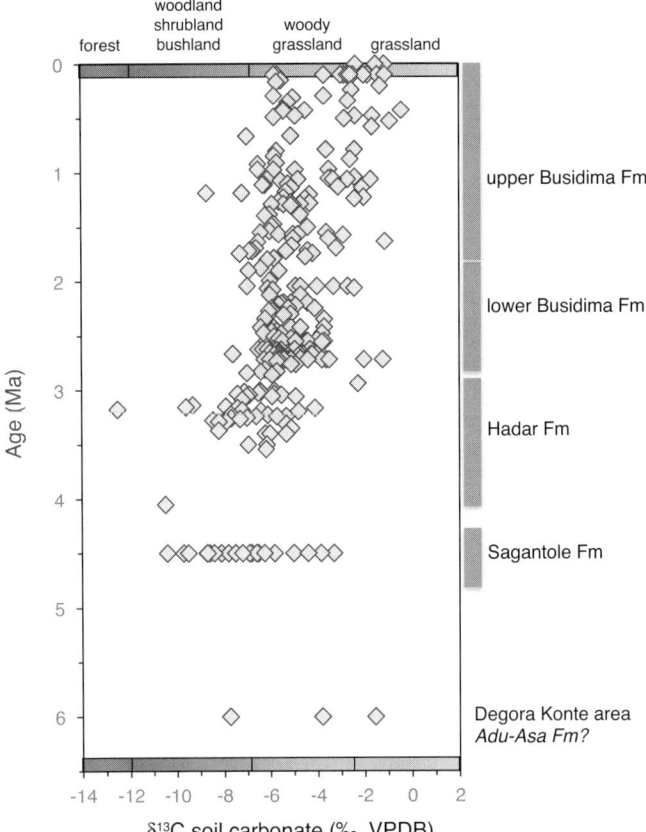

Figure 17.6 Summary of $\delta^{13}C$ values from soil carbonate in paleosols at Gona with interpretations of vegetation cover from Cerling et al. (2011b). Paleosols from the Adu-Asa Formation are generally non-calcareous, with the exception of three samples from the Degora Konte area which are not associated with fossil localities. Data are compiled in Supplementary Table 17.S1 and come from Levin et al. (2004), Quade et al. (2004), Semaw et al. (2005), Quade et al. (2008), Everett (2010), Cerling et al. (2011b), Levin (2013), and this study.

of the geomagnetic Olduvai Normal event. The lower portion of the Busidima Formation rests unconformably on the Hadar Formation, documents the period from about 2.7–1.8 Ma, and samples the main axial channel of the meandering paleo-Awash River (Quade et al., 2008). The younger portion of the Busidima Formation is marked by the prevalence of smaller channel systems that reflect secondary streams that drain into the paleo-Awash River and spans the period from about 1.8 Ma to <0.15 Ma (Quade et al., 2004, 2008; Levin et al., 2004; Simpson et al., 2008; Everett, 2010).

Lower Busidima Formation

The lower portions of the Busidima Formation are best exposed along the main Awash channel and within the Kada Gona, lower Ounda Gona, and Dana Aoule drainages (Figure 17.1). These deposits, composed of stacked fining-upward cycles, are exposed in deeply dissected cuts with steep banks. Fossils and artifacts (Oldowan and Acheulean) are found in the overbank and floodplain deposits of both the main axial river system (the paleo-Awash River) and of secondary streams (Semaw et al., 1997, 2003, 2009; Stout et al., 2005, 2010; Rogers and Semaw, 2009).

Most research in the lower Busidima Formation at Gona has focused on the rich archeological record (e.g., Semaw et al., 1997, 2003; Stout et al., 2005) with little focus on the fauna. However, we do have insights into the environments of these early tool makers from soil carbonate carbon isotope data and to a small degree from pollen data. The soil carbonate $\delta^{13}C$ values from the lower portions of the Busidima Formation range from −7.6 to −1.2‰ and average −5.2 ± 1.1‰ (n = 100; Supplementary Table 17.S1; Figure 17.6). Relative to the results from the Hadar Formation, this marks a distinct shift toward a more open, C_4-dominated landscape that likely reflects both a change in depositional mode at the beginning of the Busidima Formation and regional environmental changes (Levin et al., 2004, 2011; Quade et al., 2004). After 2.9 Ma, few soil carbonates yield $\delta^{13}C$ values <−8‰ at Gona, indicating that the vegetation growing on the floodplains of both the axial and tributary rivers at Gona was dominated by wooded grasslands and grasslands. Detailed sampling of soil carbonates lateral to river margins indicate that the proportion of C_4 grassy vegetation increases away from river channels and explains that the large (>8‰) range in $\delta^{13}C$ values observed at Gona during this time period reflects lateral gradients of vegetation on fluvial landscapes (Levin et al., 2004). Soil carbonate $\delta^{13}C$ values from Gona are higher on average than those from contemporaneous deposits in the Nachukui and Shungura Formations in the Omo-Turkana Basin, indicating that hominin riverine habitats at Gona were more open (grassy) than the habitats of their contemporaries in the Omo-Turkana Basin (Levin et al., 2011).

There is a limited amount of pollen data (three samples) from the lower Busidima Formation, collected at two 2.6 Ma archeological sites, OGS6 and OGS7. The pollen spectra are dominated by Afromontane and highland flora (ca. 40 percent) with smaller contributions from riparian trees (e.g., Moraceae; ca. 20 percent) and grasses (ca. 20 percent; López-Sáez and Dominguez-Rodrigo, 2009). More work is needed to reconcile the pollen spectra from these three samples with the sedimentology and isotopic data that indicate riparian habitats and large proportions of C_4 grasses on the landscape in the lower Busidima Formation.

Upper Busidima Formation

The upper portions of the Busidima Formation have laterally extensive and fossiliferous strata that are exposed by incision of the drainages that feed into the Awash River today (Figure 17.1). Strata exposed by the lower Busidima River, the Dana Aoule drainage, and the Kada and Ounda Gona drainages range from ca. 1.78 to 0.6 Ma. The Olduvai Normal event can be found at the base of most of these exposures and they all contain the Silbo Tuff (0.75 Ma), the Dahuli Tuff (ca. 0.8 Ma), the Ken-Di Tuff (ca. 0.5 Ma), and/or the Brunhes-Matuyama geomagnetic boundary (0.78 Ma) near their tops (Quade et al., 2008). Younger strata (ca. 0.6 to <0.15 Ma) that are rich in both fossils and artifacts predominate south of the Busidima River and are exposed along the Busidima, Gawis, and Ya'alu drainages (Figure 17.1). The Gawis Tuff (ca. 0.5 Ma) and the Waidedo Vitric Tuff (0.16 Ma) constrain the age of these sediments (Quade et al., 2008), but ongoing work indicates the presence of younger sediments >50-m thick stratigraphically above the Waidedo Vitric Tuff.

Much of the upper Busidima Formation is under active study and this review will highlight paleontological and geochemical research on the north side of the Busidima drainage (Busidima North) that was the focus of Melanie Everett's doctoral dissertation. Everett (2010) divided the fauna from the upper Busidima Formation in the Busidima North region into three informal stratigraphic units: the Boolihinan unit (ca. 1.3–1.1 Ma), the Dark Paleosol unit (ca. 1.1–0.9 Ma), and the Dahuli unit (ca. 0.9 to <0.64 Ma). Within this upper portion of the Busidima Formation in the Busidima North collecting area (BSN), a total of 43 paleontological localities were identified. While fossils are found throughout all of the facies, the densest accumulations of fossils are most commonly associated with the sandier facies of the units (Everett, 2010). Hominin fossils from the upper Busidima Formation in the Busidima North area have been attributed to *Homo erectus* (Semaw et al., 2001, 2020; Simpson et al., 2008). For comparison, there are also deposits of this age in the Dana Aoule and Ounda Gona drainages at Gona, where carbon isotope data from soil carbonates are available (Supplementary Table 17.S1; Figure 17.6).

The Boolihinan Tuff serves as a marker unit at the base of the upper Busidima Formation sequence in the Busidima North area (Quade et al., 2008; Simpson et al., 2008; Everett, 2010). The age of the Boolihinan Tuff (BHT) has been updated to 1.26 Ma (Semaw et al., 2020), based on correlation of its geochemistry to a tuff in Melka Kunture (MK27-05; Morgan et al., 2012), which is a better match than the initial correlation to a tuff in a deep-sea core dated to 1.6 Ma. As such, we revise the ages assigned to the Upper Busidima stratigraphic units defined by Everett (2010).

Boolihinan Unit (ca. 1.3–1.1 Ma)

Fossils associated with the Boolihinan unit come from sites associated with the Boolihinan Tuff (BHT), either within or just (<10 m) above the BHT, or in the package of silts or sands sandwiched between the BHT at the top and the widespread, prominent gravel, Gravel B3.0, that is 2–10 m below the BHT (Simpson et al., 2008; Semaw et al., 2020). Overall, these sediments represent a fining-upward sequence overlying a cobble conglomerate deposited by a meandering paleo-Awash River.

Within the Boolihinan unit, a large number of diverse taxa were preserved ranging from rodents (*Tatera, Taterillus, Gerbillus, Praomys, Golunda, Jaculus, Thryonomys, Hystrix*), birds (*Agapornis*, Anatidae, Phasianidae, Galliformes), to elephants (Table 17.2), including the hominin, *Homo erectus*. Bovids are the most common taxa in the Boolihinan unit and the two most common types are reduncines (36 percent of all bovids) and alcelaphines (29 percent). Both are grazers, although the reduncines are fresh-grass grazers and lack the marked hypsodonty of the more dry-grass grazers such as the alcelaphines. The frequency of alcelaphines and antilopines (38 percent) suggests, relying on Vrba's (1985a) "alcelaphine–antilopine" index, that the habitat was a mixed grassy-woodland. However, as Sponheimer and Lee-Thorp (2003) noted, ancient habitats may be difficult to infer based on the presence of antilopines as they had a more diverse diet, including browsing, in the past than they do currently. In addition, numerous lineages have changed their diet across time such that applying modern taxonomic composition in the reconstruction of ancient landscapes based on the diets of modern relatives may not provide the high resolution once hoped (Cerling et al., 2015a). Details of the index aside, the low frequency of bovids that in many studies are associated with more closed or shrubby environments (e.g., tragelaphines) would indicate a more open habitat. This is reinforced by the available carbon isotope data from bovid teeth from the upper Busidima Formation (Simpson et al., 2008; Everett, 2010). Of the 15 bovid teeth analyzed, the two tragelaphine teeth yielded $\delta^{13}C$ values of –7.2‰ and –2.4‰, while the rest of the teeth from the Alcelaphini, Hippotragini, Reduncini, and Bovini bovid tribes yield average $\delta^{13}C$ values of +2.2 ± 0.9‰, consistent with the grazing behavior of the majority of the bovids. (Simpson et al., 2008; Everett, 2010).

Table 17.2 Extended faunal list from the late Pleistocene fossil localities in the upper Busidima Formation, from Everett (2010).

	DAN5 level	BU	DPU	DU
Primates				
Hominidae				
Homo erectus	+	+	+	
Cercopithecidae				
cf. *Cercopithecoides* sp.	+	+		
Colobus sp.	+	+		+
Cholorcebus cf. *patas*		+	+	
Theropithecus oswaldi leakeyi		+		+
Papio sp.		+		
Carnivora				
Mustelidae cf. *Mellivora* sp.		+		
Canidae cf. *Vulpes* sp.		+		
Canidae cf. *Canis* sp.		+		
Vivveridae				
cf. *Mungos* sp.		+		
cf. Viverridae	+			
Hyaenidae				
Crocuta crocuta			+	+
Felidae				
Panthera leo (includes *P.* cf. *leo*)	+	+		
Panthera cf. *P. pardus*		+		+
Felis sp.		+		
Tubulidentata				
Orycteropus sp.		+		
Proboscidea				
Elephas recki		+	+	
Perissodactyla				
Rhinoceratidae				
Ceratotherium simum		+		
Equidae				
Equus sp.		+	+	
Eurygnathohippus sp.		+		

Table 17.2 (cont.)

	DAN5 level	BU	DPU	DU
Artiodactyla				
Hippopotamidae				
Hippopotamus sp.		+		
Suidae				
Kolpochoerus majus		+	+	
Metriodiochoerus compactus		+	+	
Metridiochoerus modestus		+	+	
Giraffidae				
Giraffa cf. *G. jumae*		+	+	
Sivatherium cf. *S. marusium*		+		
Giraffidae gen. et sp. indet.	+			
Bovidae				
Family indet., sp. nov.		+		
Bovini				
Pelorovis turkanensis		+		
Pelorovis cf. *P. oldowayensis*		+		
Syncerus sp. indet.		+		+
Tragelaphini				
Tragelaphus cf. *T. nakuae*		+		
Tragelaphus cf. *T. strepsiceros*		+		
Tragelaphus cf. *T. imberbis*			+	
Tragelaphus sp.	+	+	+	
Antilopini				
Antilopini gen. et sp. indet.		+	+	+
Gazella cf. *praethompsoni*		+		
Gazella sp.		+		
Gazella sp. nov.		+		
Alcelaphini				
Alcelaphini gen. et sp. indet.		+	+	+
Connochaetes taurinus		+		
Damaliscus niro		+		
Damaliscus sp. nov.		+		
Parmularius cf. *P. angusticornis*			+	
Parmularius sp.		+		
Rabaticeras sp.		+		
Alcelaphini gen. et sp. indet.	+			
Hippotragini				
Hippotragini gen. et sp. indet.		+	+	

Table 17.2 (cont.)

	DAN5 level	BU	DPU	DU
Hippotragus cf. *gigas*		+		
Reduncini				
Redunca sp.		+	+	+
Kobus cf. *K. sigmoidalis*		+	+	
Kobus cf. *K sigmoidalis/ellipsiprymnus*		+		
Kobus cf. *K. kob* (?*Menelikia* sp.)		+		
Kobus sp.		+	+	+
Reduncini gen. et sp. indet.	+	+	+	+
Neotragini				
cf. *Madoqua* sp.		+		
cf. *Raphiceras* sp.				
Rodentia				
Thryonomys cf. *swinderianus*	+	+	+	+
Taterillus sp.		+		
Tatera sp.	+	+		
Praomys sp.	+	+		
Gerbillus sp.		+		
Acomys sp.		+		
Jaculus sp.		+		
Golunda sp.		+		
Hystrix sp.		+		
cf. *Arvicanthis* sp.	+			
Lagomorpha				
Lepus sp.		+		
Aves				
Pternistis (s. l.) sp.		+		
Phasianidae, gen. et sp. indet.	+	+		
Columbidae, gen. et sp. indet.		+		
cf. Passeriformes		+		
Anatidae, gen. et sp. indet.		+		
Agapornis sp.		+		
Reptilia				
Varanus sp.	+	+		
Chelonia	+	+		
Crocodylia	+			
Pisces				
Siluriformes	+	+		
Bagridae, gen. et sp. indet.		+		
cf. *Chrysichthys* sp.		+		
Clarias sp.		+		

Further evidence of an open, grass-dominated landscape includes the presence of dedicated grazers such as the zebra (*Equus*), the white rhinoceros (*Ceratotherium*), the extinct gelada baboon *Theropithecus oswaldi leakeyi*, and the enigmatic large-bodied colobine primate *Cercopithecoides* – a genus that exhibits terrestrial locomotor adaptations and is often found at localities that are reconstructed as relatively open (Birchette, 1981; Frost and Delson, 2002; Jablonski et al., 2008; Frost et al., 2015). The metridiochoerine suids (*Metridiochoerus compactus* and *M. modestus*) have tall and elongate third molars and reduced premolars, both of which are adaptations to grazing and verified by $\delta^{13}C$ values of their enamel (Harris and Cerling, 2002). The presence of the jerboa rodent (*Jaculus*) provides evidence for proximity to an even more open, arid habitat, as the jerboa is now found in arid or semi-arid areas. While the environment had ample grass to support a diverse array of grazers, sediments from this interval were deposited on the margins of the ancestral Awash, consistent with the presence of hippopotamus (albeit rare), reduncine bovids, and the equid *Eurygnathohippus*. Browse must have been available from both bushes and trees as evidenced by the presence of giraffes, the suid *Kolpochoerus majus*, and the monkeys *Colobus*, *Papio*, and cf. *Chlorocebus* aff. *patas*.

The pedogenic carbonates from the Boolihinan unit yield $\delta^{13}C$ values that range from −8.7 to −2.1‰ with a mean of −5.3 ± 1.4‰ (n = 18), indicating a mix of grasses, shrubs, and trees on the landscape, equivalent to the "wooded grassland" category defined by Cerling et al. (2011b).

Dark Paleosol Unit (*ca.* 1.1 to 0.9 Ma)

The Dark Paleosol unit is recognized in Everett (2010) by its dark, carbonate-rich, mature vertisols immediately below the Dahuli Tuff. There are 14 paleontological localities identified in the Dark Paleosol unit. The fossils in this interval are eroding primarily from the sands associated with small ephemeral channels. While the unit is fossil-rich, it exhibits less taxonomic diversity than the underlying Boolihinan unit. The taxonomic distribution of the fauna from these sites indicates that it also was a grass-dominated, well-watered landscape. The only rodent species recovered from the Dark Paleosol unit is the cane rat (*Thryonomys*), a species that requires a permanent supply of water. Similarly, the high frequency of reduncine bovids, especially *Redunca* sp., also implies well-watered grasslands. The majority of the fauna suggests the absence of significant woody coverage, such as the presence of *Equus*, metridiochoere suids, alcelaphine, hippotragine, and bovine bovids, the unusual *Cercopithecoides*, the derived large-bodied theropith, *Theropithecus oswaldi leakeyi*, and the absence of *Colobus* as well as *Eurygnathohippus* equids. Overall, fossils from the Dark Paleosol unit sample a primarily grassy environment close to water. This is consistent with the carbon isotope data from soil carbonates in the Dark Paleosol unit that range in $\delta^{13}C$ values from −6.5 to −1.7‰ with a mean of −4.4 ± 1.6‰ (n = 14; Supplementary Table 17.S1), which suggests landscapes with a mix of grass and woody cover.

Dahuli Unit (*ca.* 0.9 to <0.65 Ma)

The Dahuli unit is the youngest fossiliferous unit in the Busidima North region, identified by Everett (2010), and contains fewer fossil localities (n = 7) than the underlying Dark Paleosol and Boolihinan units. Fossils are associated with gravels and sand at the base of fining-upward sequences and are heavily encrusted in carbonate. Taxonomic diversity is low in this unit, perhaps due to the few collecting localities. For example, no equids, rhinocerotids, giraffids, hippopotamids, or suids are known from this unit. However, primates are abundant and include the dedicated folivore *Colobus*, the large-bodied grazing *Theropithecus oswaldi leakeyi*, *Chlorocebus* cf. *aethiops*, and *Papio hamadryas*. The abundance of reduncine bovids (>50 percent) and the low frequency of alcelaphines (<5 percent) indicates a well-watered environment along a river margin with substantial grasslands and remnant woodlands. The $\delta^{13}C$ values of soil carbonates from the Dahuli unit range from −5.8 to −5.0‰ and average −5.4 ± 0.4‰ (n =4; Supplementary Table 17.S1), indicating a mix of grass and woody cover as in the other parts of the upper Busidima Formation. However, the restricted range of $\delta^{13}C$ values from soil carbonates in the Dahuli unit may reflect an environment with more woody cover than in the Boolihinan and Dark Paleosol units.

Summary of Hominin Habitats in the Upper Busidima Formation

The combination of mammalian fauna and carbon isotope data from the upper Busidima Formation indicates habitats focused along well-watered riparian corridors along the ancestral Awash, its tributaries, and adjacent floodplains that were covered by wooded grasslands and grasslands.

Summary of Paleoecological Change at Gona During the Last 6.3 Ma

The sedimentary sequence at Gona provides critical insights into ecological change during the last 6.3 million years in the Afar region. Starting in the late Miocene, when rift basin development was at an early stage, *Ar. kadabba* inhabited lake and river environments in volcanic terrains that were well-watered and more wooded than subsequent hominin habitats at Gona. Soil carbonates are missing from strata associated with these late Miocene hominins such that we cannot use them for direct comparisons with other sites or time intervals, but their absence does suggest one or a combination of the following, when compared with subsequent time intervals: more rainfall, less seasonality, faster landscape turnover, or higher elevation. As rifting continued into the early Pliocene, hominins at Gona still lived near volcanic centers, but their habitat was becoming more open and varied. *Ar. ramidus* lived alongside small lakes near volcanoes and also on landscapes that had both rivers and lakes. In these places, *Ar. ramidus* is found with other mammals that included browsers and grazers and those with both arboreal and terrestrial adaptations. The distribution of fauna associated with *Ar. ramidus* at Aramis, *ca.* 70 km south of Gona, is quite different and indicates a more wooded habitat, although soil carbonate $\delta^{13}C$ values near and between hominin sites at both Gona and Aramis are similar to one another and reflect woodland and wooded grasslands. The collective data on the habitat of *Ar. ramidus* from Gona and Aramis suggest that it inhabited a range of environments and was not restricted to a particular habitat. The presence of animals reliant on dietary inputs of C_4 grass in the ardipith habitats at Gona is consistent with the presence and abundance of C_4 grasses elsewhere in eastern African since the late Miocene (e.g., Uno et al., 2011).

A major subsidence event occurred around *ca.* 4 Ma, creating a basin to the east of the As Duma Fault in which the sediments of the Hadar and Busidima Formations would subsequently fill. The landscapes that span this transition and represent the beginnings of sedimentation in this larger rift basin are better represented in nearby project areas (e.g., Woranso-Mille and Hadar), but soil carbonate $\delta^{13}C$ values indicate the presence of wooded environments *ca.* 4.1 Ma at As Aela and then the full span of forested to grassland vegetation in the large lacustrine and deltaic systems of the Hadar Formation (3.8–2.9 Ma) that filled the basin as it continued to deepen.

The disconformity that defines the base of the Busidima Formation marks the end of the lacustrine- and delta-dominated environments of the Hadar Formation and the beginning of landscapes that were dominated by a meandering river system. Hominins from the Busidima Formation, which included the makers of the earliest known Oldowan stone tools and later *H. erectus*, occupied the banks and floodplains of this axial river system and its tributaries. This river system provided first-order controls on the distribution of water and vegetation on the landscape, with woodier and wetter environments closer to the river channel, as would be expected in a riparian ecosystem. The fauna and soil carbonate $\delta^{13}C$ values sampled from the Busidima Formation (*ca.* 2.7 to <0.15 Ma) indicate that the vegetation in this riparian system became more open through the Pleistocene, reflecting a trend toward more open environments that is also observed throughout eastern Africa throughout the Pliocene and Pleistocene (e.g., Bobe and Behrensmeyer, 2004; Frost, 2007; Jacobs et al., 2010; Cerling et al., 2011b; Levin et al., 2011).

The snapshots of information we have from Gona show that the ecology of hominin environments is strongly influenced by rift basin development; it placed a first-order control on the landscape and, in turn, the flora and fauna that inhabited it. Our comparisons of environments available to the hominins at Gona relative to those elsewhere (e.g., to Aramis in the early Pliocene and to parts of the Omo-Turkana Basin in later Pliocene) demonstrate the importance of sampling a wide and varied geographic area when assessing the biogeography and ecology of hominins. These intersite comparisons of hominin fossil localities are critical to developing more refined views of hominin ecology, and they are becoming more tractable with the increased number of comparable data sets from hominin fossil localities of similar ages as demonstrated in this volume.

Acknowledgments

The Gona Project would like to thank the Authority for Research and Conservation of Cultural Heritage (ARCCH) of the Ministry of Culture and Tourism and the National Museum of Ethiopia (NME) for research permit and support. We particularly appreciate the hospitality of the Afar Regional State administration at Semera and our Afar colleagues from Eliwiha. Fieldwork participants in the faunal surveys included but are not limited to Asahamed Humet, Yasin Ismail Mohamed, Wegenu Amerga, Mohamed Ahmedin, Kampiro Qairento, Bizuayehu Tegegne, T. Pickering, E. Smith, and S. Melillo. Major support for this research was provided by the L.S.B. Leakey Foundation (S.S., M.A.E.), and additional funding for field and laboratory research was provided by the U.S. National Science Foundation (NSF SBR-9818353 to S.S.; NSF HOMINID-RHOI BCS-0321893 to Tim White and F. Clark Howell; NSF SBR-9727519 to S.W.S.), predoctoral research grant to M.A.E.), the National Geographic Society (S.S.; J.Q.), Wenner-Gren Foundation (S.S.), NASA Astrobiology Initiative (M.A.E.), and grants from the European Union Marie Curie (S.S. FP7-303755), Spain's Ministry of Economy, Industry and Competitiveness (S.S. and Mahomed Sahnouni, HAR2013-41351-P), and the Connecticut State University system (M.J.R.). We thank Y. Haile-Selassie and L. Jellema of the Cleveland Museum of Natural History, Cleveland, Ohio, USA and the curators and staff at the Royal Museum for Central Africa in Tervuren, Belgium for allowing us to examine materials in their care. A number of researchers contributed to the faunal identifications: M. Asnake, F. Bibi, J.-R. Boisserie, R. Bernor, I. Giaourtsakis, Y. Haile-Selassie, A. Louchart, A. Murray, K. Stewart, H. Saegusa, L. Werdelin, H. Wesselman. Finally, we are grateful to the editors of this volume, Sally Reynolds and René Bobe, for their work organizing it, their invitation to contribute, and their patience in the submission process.

18 The Hadar Formation, Afar Regional State, Ethiopia: Geology, Fauna, and Paleoenvironmental Reconstructions

Christopher J. Campisano, John Rowan, and Kaye E. Reed

Introduction

Fossiliferous sediments of the Hadar Formation (Afar, Ethiopia) are preserved in the Hadar, Dikika, Gona, and Ledi-Geraru research areas, and have produced the most informative record of the mid-Pliocene hominin *Australopithecus afarensis*. Hundreds of specimens of *A. afarensis* have been recovered from the Hadar site, including a partial skeleton (A.L. 288–1), two nearly complete adult skulls (A.L. 444–2; A.L. 822–1), and a dense accumulation of hominin individuals of various ages (A.L. 333) (Johanson et al., 1978b; Kimbel et al., 1994; Kimbel and Delezene, 2009). Across the Awash River at Dikika, a juvenile hominin skeleton (DIK-1–1) was recovered and possible evidence of hominin carnivory ~3.4 Ma based on cut-marked bone was reported from Hadar Formation sediments (Alemseged et al., 2006; McPherron et al., 2010; Thompson et al., 2015). Thus, the outcrops of the Hadar Formation, particularly those at Hadar, have been tremendously important in interpreting Pliocene hominin evolution in eastern Africa.

The Plio-Pleistocene site of Hadar is located along the Awash River, approximately 300 km northeast of Addis Ababa in the Afar Regional State of Ethiopia (Figure 18.1). The site's name is derived from "Kada Hadar," the local Afar name for the large wadi (ephemeral streambed) that cuts through the central exposures in the area. The current Hadar Research Project (HRP) area is approximately 100 km², extending east–west between the Gona and Hurda wadis, and north–south between the Ledi wadi and the Awash River (Figure 18.1).

Hadar and neighboring paleoanthropological sites are situated within a unique geomorphological setting commonly referred to as the Afar Depression (also referred to as the Afar Triangle or Afar Triple Junction), a roughly 200,000 km² depression formed by extension of the Nubian, Arabian, and Somalian plates (McKenzie et al., 1970). This triple rift (RRR) junction marks the intersection of the spreading ridges forming the east-trending Gulf of Aden Rift, the northwest-trending Red Sea Rift, and the northeast-trending Ethiopian Rift. Sediments of the Hadar Formation (Taieb et al., 1976) are a component of an ill-defined sedimentary basin that lies parallel and adjacent to the Ethiopian Escarpment referred to as the West Central Afar Sedimentary Basin (Taieb et al., 1976) and the Hadar Formation is part of the Awash Group (Kalb et al., 1982c).

The first geological studies in the Afar region were conducted mainly by French, Italian, and German research groups and focused primarily on the structural, petrological, and geochemical aspects of the unique rift setting (e.g., Pilger and Rösler, 1976). The fossiliferous deposits of the Hadar region were first recognized as such by French geologist Maurice Taieb while conducting research on the evolution of the Awash River during the late 1960s and early 1970s (Taieb, 1974). Following a six-week survey of the central Afar in 1972 by Taieb, Donald Johanson, Yves Coppens, and Jon Kalb, the International Afar Research Expedition (IARE) was formed and launched its first major field campaign in 1973. The site of Hadar was targeted for paleontological survey due to its exceptionally rich and well-preserved fossil specimens, their Pliocene age, and the well-exposed, laterally continuous geological strata of the area (Johanson et al., 1982a). The first hominin remains were discovered during the initial IARE 1973 field season (Taieb et al., 1974), and Hadar was thrust into the paleoanthropological spotlight with the discovery of "Lucy" (A.L. 288–1), a 40 percent complete skeleton of *A. afarensis* in 1974, and the remains of the "First Family" (A.L. 333) in 1975, which now comprises the remains of some 17 individuals (Johanson, 1976; Johanson and Coppens, 1976; Behrensmeyer et al., 2003).

Fieldwork was suspended in 1977 to conduct extensive laboratory research on the hominin material. Before a new field campaign could begin, however, the project was placed on hold when the Ethiopian government declared an eight-year moratorium (1982–1989) on all prehistoric research in the country, during which time the Ethiopian Ministry of Culture established new rules and regulations (Lewin, 1983). Field research at Hadar was renewed in 1990 under the direction of the Institute of Human Origins (now at Arizona State University) as the Hadar Research Project and has continued, with intermittent breaks, until today. This most recent phase of research has proven as productive as the first explorations with important *A. afarensis* discoveries such as the skulls A.L. 444–2 and A.L. 822–1, as well as some of the earliest evidence of the genus *Homo* and Oldowan stone tools, e.g., A.L. 666–1 and the locality of A.L. 894 (Kimbel et al., 1994, 1996, 1997; Hovers, 2003), from the younger Busidima Formation. Currently, ~90 percent of all material attributed to the species *A. afarensis* has been recovered from Hadar (Lockwood et al., 2000).

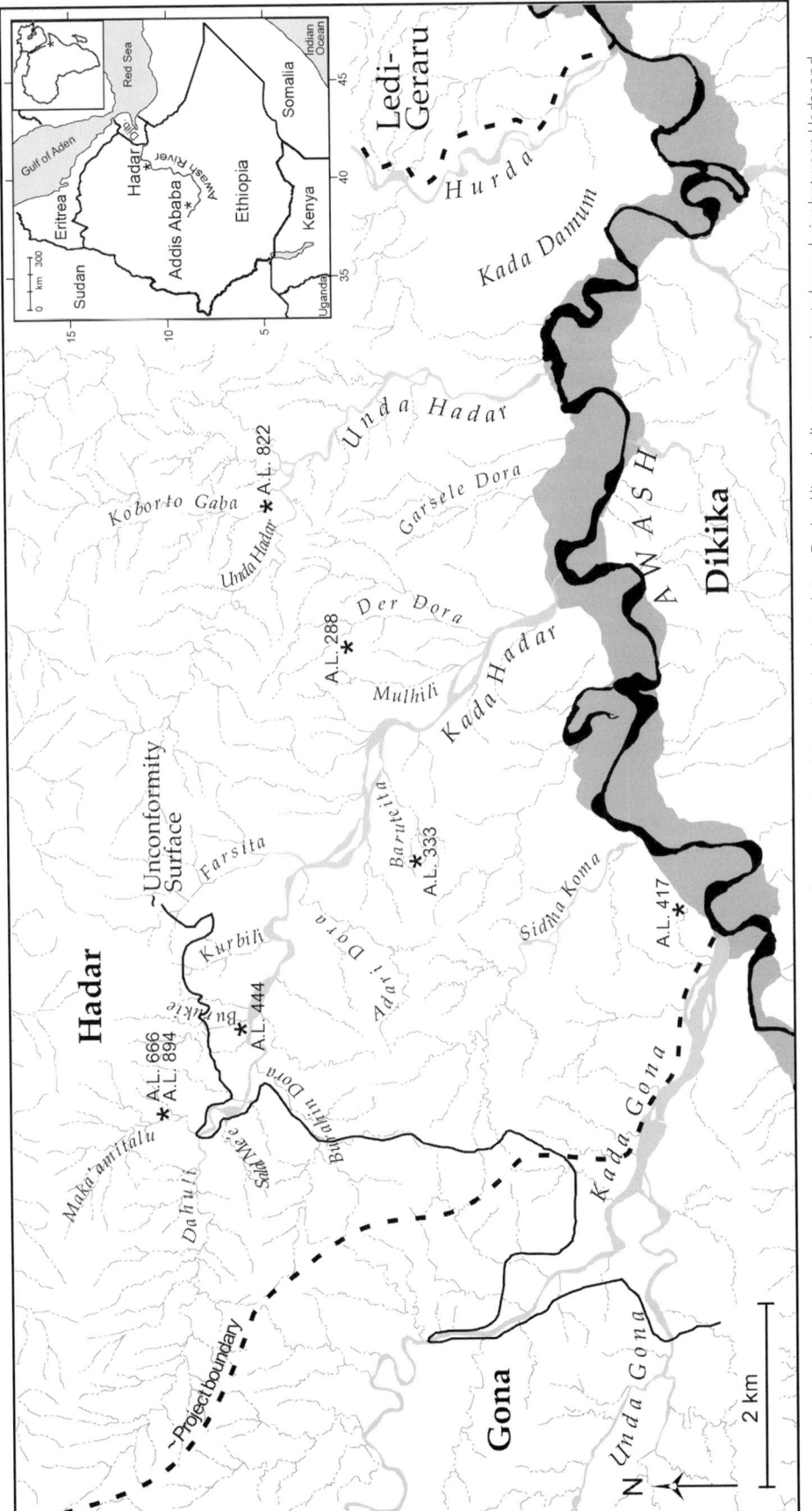

Figure 18.1 Location and drainage map of the Hadar paleoanthropological site with important hominin and archeological sites. Dashed lines indicate approximate boundaries between Hadar and adjacent research project areas. Location of unconformity surface in the Gona region adapted from Quade et al. (2004)

Stratigraphy and Geochronology

A system of several large wadis and their tributaries that ultimately drain into the Awash River are responsible for headland erosion into the badland topography and exposing the Plio-Pleistocene sediments in the region. The strata at Hadar are subhorizontal, with a general dip of only a few degrees, relatively uninterrupted by faulting, and are typically exposed on knolls and along ridges between 25 and 45 m in height.

As exposed in the Hadar project area, the Pliocene Hadar Formation is composed of close to 155 m of fluvio-lacustrine sediments (Figure 18.2) that preserve a high-resolution record of environmental conditions and change from ~3.45 to ~2.9 Ma (Campisano and Feibel, 2007, 2008). Sediments preserved south of the Awash River in the Dikika Research Project area extend the base of the formation to ~3.8 Ma (Wynn et al., 2008). A regional angular unconformity separates the Hadar Formation from the overlying Busidima Formation (Quade et al., 2004; Wynn et al., 2008). The Plio-Pleistocene Busidima Formation is poorly represented at Hadar (Campisano, 2012), but contains some of the earliest evidence of the genus *Homo* and Oldowan stone tools (Kimbel et al., 1996, 1997; Hovers, 2003).

The Hadar Formation was formally defined by Taieb et al. (1976) and their lithostratigraphic framework has essentially remained unchanged. Using laterally extensive dated tuff horizons, the Hadar Formation is divided into four members: the Basal Member (BM), the Sidi Hakoma Member (SH), the Denen Dora Member (DD), and the Kada Hadar Member (KH). These members have been further subdivided into submembers (e.g., DD-1, -2, -3) on the basis of other lithostratigraphic markers, primarily sand bodies, and some submembers have been divided into specific units (e.g., DD-3s, where the "s" represents a sand unit; Figure 18.2). Due to the lateral variation of the deposits, certain submembers or units are not consistently preserved and/or identifiable throughout the entire region. Although they do not always correspond to sedimentary cycles, and to an extent may even be time-transgressive, these submembers serve as the stratigraphic units to which paleontological specimens are assigned and the framework in which paleoenvironmental information has been analyzed (e.g., Johanson et al., 1978a; Gray, 1980; Campisano and Feibel, 2008; Reed, 2008).

As with most sites in eastern Africa, the chronological framework of Hadar is a combination of $^{40}Ar/^{39}Ar$ dating of feldspar-bearing tuffs and basalts, paleomagnetism, and tephra correlation (Figure 18.2). The Hadar site preserves five laterally extensive vitric/crystal–vitric and three crystal-bearing marker tephra, five of which have produced reliable $^{40}Ar/^{39}Ar$ ages: the Sidi Hakoma Tuff (SHT), Triple Tuff 4 (TT-4), the Kada Hadar Tuff (KHT), and the Bouroukie Tuff 2 Complex (BKT-2L, BKT-2U). The localized Kada Damum Basalt in the eastern area of Hadar has also been dated. The Hadar sequence was deposited during the Gauss Chron (C2An), and preserves both the Mammoth (C2An.2 r) and Kaena (C2An.1 r) Subchrons. Submember durations range from as little as 15–20 ka (DD-1, -2, and -3) to as much as 160 ka (KH-2). At 30 cm/ka, the rate of sediment deposition at Hadar is roughly twice that of comparably aged eastern African hominin localities, and is largely responsible for the rich paleontological record preserved (Figure 18.3; Campisano and Feibel, 2007).

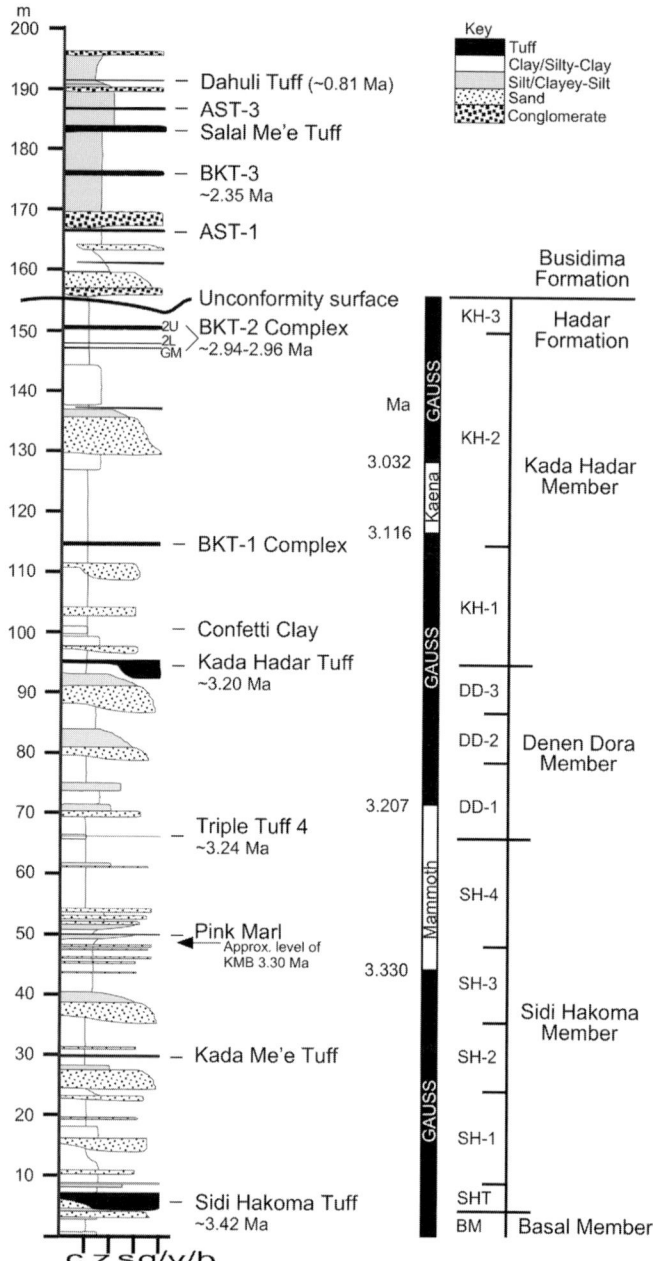

Figure 18.2 Composite stratigraphic section and member/submember divisions of the Hadar and Busidima Formations at Hadar. Tuffs and major marker beds are labeled alongside the section. $^{40}Ar/^{39}Ar$ dates and paleomagnetic transition are from Schmitt and Nairn (1984); Walter and Aronson (1993); Renne et al. (1993); Walter (1994); Kimbel et al. (1994, 1996, 2004); Campisano (2007); and DiMaggio et al. (2008). Previously published $^{40}Ar/^{39}Ar$ dates have been recalculated to reflect the age of the Fish Canyon sanidine standard (28.02 Ma, Renne et al., 1998) and the paleomagnetic timescale is ATNTS2012 (Hilgen et al., 2012).

Depositional Environments

Hadar Formation strata consist of floodplain paleosols (dominantly vertisols), fluvial and deltaic sands, and both pedogenically modified and unmodified lacustrine clays and silts.

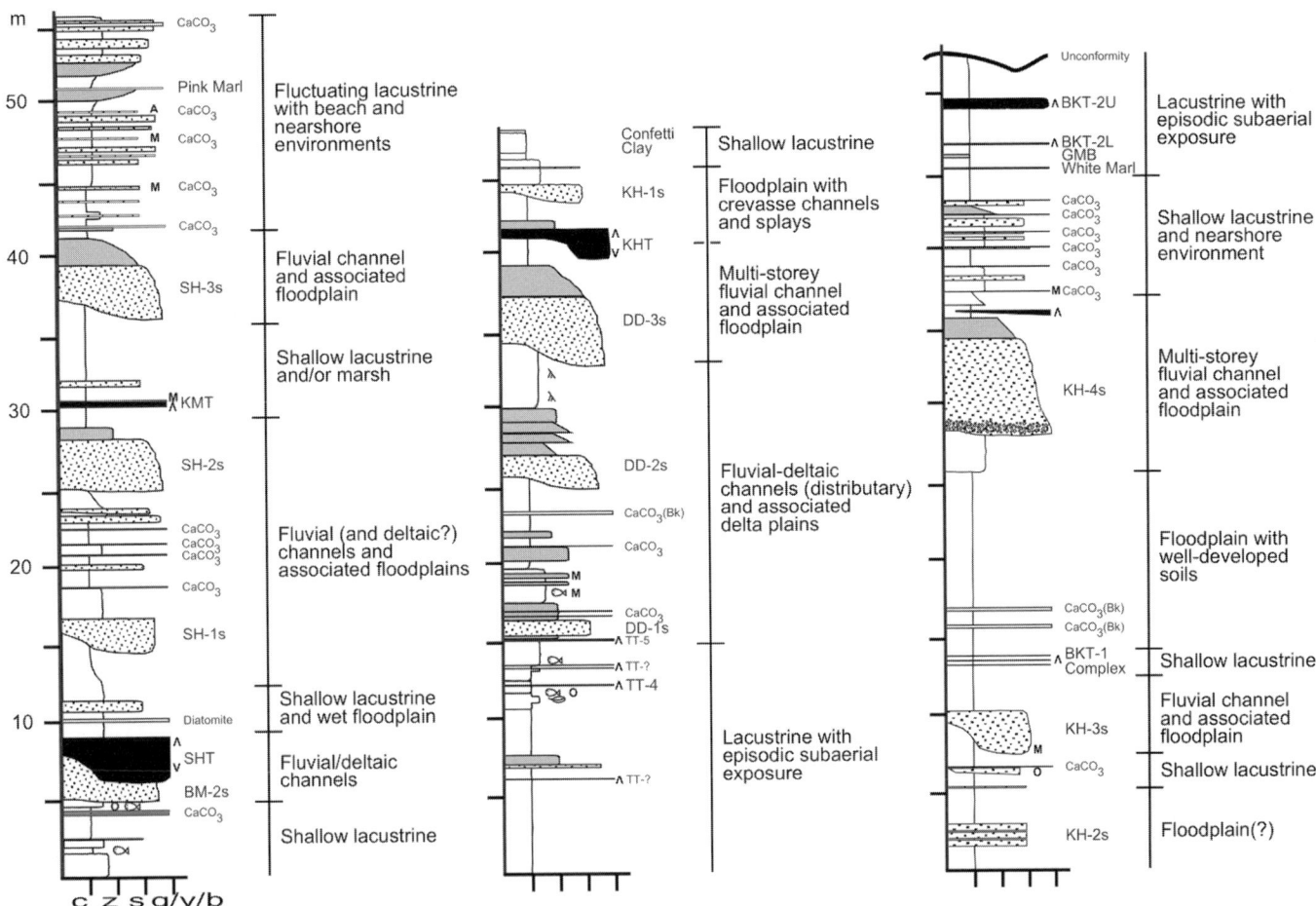

Figure 18.3 Summary of interpreted depositional environments for the Hadar Formation. Composite section constructed from stratigraphic sections located within the central region of the Hadar study area (Campisano and Feibel, 2008).

Sedimentological and petrographic analyses of many of the Hadar deposits were conducted by Yemane (1997). Clays and silts constitute the majority of the Hadar sediments while most sands can be attributed to channel and point bar deposits of a large-scale meandering river system or associated crevasse splay and distributary channel deposits (Campisano and Feibel, 2008).

Several conceptual models of depositional environments at Hadar have been proposed and modified over the decades (Taieb and Tiercelin, 1979, 1980; Aronson and Taieb, 1981), including some facies-based models (Tiercelin, 1986; Yemane, 1997). As currently understood, the strata of the Hadar Formation can be imagined as representing different components of a large-scale, but single fluvial–lacustrine system. The extensive sand bodies preserved at different stratigraphic levels within the Hadar sequence (e.g., SH-2s, DD-3s, and KH-4s) may be interpreted as representing meanders of a single fluvial system entering the Hadar region at different times. Hadar Formation conglomerate deposits are likely to have resulted from high-energy braided streams originating along the Ethiopian Escarpment either entering directly into the Hadar region or intersecting with the axial fluvial system nearby. Fluvio-deltaic deposition predominated at Hadar. The lacustrine depocenter was located east and northeast of Hadar, but lacustrine transgressions into the region were common. At least seven transgressive episodes are clearly recorded in the Hadar record with several more minor or ephemeral events possible (Campisano and Feibel, 2008). The most significant and persistent lacustrine episode at Hadar spans the upper Sidi Hakoma and lowermost Denen Dora Members, although the majority of the Basal Member preserved at Dikika is also lacustrine, likely related to the initial infilling of the Hadar Basin (Wynn et al., 2008). Evidence suggests that the paleolandscape at Hadar was topographically flat. During lacustrine-dominated intervals, lake water depths at Hadar were most likely relatively shallow and included repeated regression events across a low-gradient shoreline (Campisano and Feibel, 2008).

Non-Vertebrate Paleoenvironmental Proxies

Pedology

Most of the Hadar paleosols are Vertisols, which are typically found in flat terrains and characterized by strongly seasonal moisture regimes under semi-arid to subhumid climates (180–1520 mm/yr of precipitation) and can form in only a few hundred years (Retallack, 2001). Additionally, most of the Hadar mudstones are dominated by smectite (Yemane, 1997), which also develop under a warm climate with alternating humid and arid seasons (Paquet, 1970). Carbon isotopic analysis of pedogenic carbonates indicate a C_3-dominated environment during Hadar times, with an average of about 30 percent C_4 grasslands present and a range of 20–40 percent that shows no temporal trends ($\delta^{13}C$ average of −7.5±0.91‰, range −9.25 to −5.49‰; Hailemichael, 2000; Aronson et al., 2008). These values are comparable from Hadar Formation deposits at Dikika, immediately south of Hadar (Wynn et al., 2006), but slightly more depleted than Gona to the west (Levin et al., 2004), suggesting the woodland became subtly more abundant toward the lake (Aronson et al., 2008). A paleo-precipitation estimate based upon depth to Bk horizon at A.L. 333 (DD-2) yielded a mean annual precipitation (MAP) estimate of 900 mm/yr, which was at the low end of the range estimated by Bonnefille et al. (2004) using pollen. Oxygen isotopic analysis of paleosol carbonates average 6.35 ± 1.12‰ (Aronson et al., 2008). Compared with modern values, these oxygen isotopes argue for wetter conditions at Hadar during the Pliocene (consistent with Bk and pollen paleo-precipitation estimates), but interpretations differ on whether a stronger summer monsoon existed during the Pliocene (Aronson et al., 2008; Aronson and Hailemichael, 2010; Wynn and Bedaso, 2010).

Palynology

The Hadar fossil pollen record preserves a diversity of habitats including forest, woodland, and both wet and dry grassland. Palynological data indicate that Pliocene Hadar was cooler and wetter compared to the modern setting. Rainfall estimates range from 800 to 1200 mm/yr, with a mean temperature estimate of ~20.2°C, approximately 6.4°C cooler than present (Bonnefille et al., 2004). The Hadar pollen assemblage is dominated by subaquatic emergent reeds (*Typha*), sedges (Cyperaceae), and grasses (Poaceae) (Bonnefille et al., 2004), which is not surprising as most of the samples preserving pollen are derived from lacustrine or palustrine deposits that were likely fringed by herbaceous cover. With reference to modern biomes, steppe, tropical xerophytic woods/scrub, and temperate xerophytic woods/scrub have similar representation throughout the Hadar sequence with occasional incursions of warm mixed-forest biome elements (Bonnefille et al., 2004). Bonnefille et al. (2004) suggest that Hadar was located at the limit of the warm mixed-forest biome adjacent to xerophytic cold steppe along an escarpment slope. The lowermost Sidi Hakoma Member pollen assemblage is composed of taxa representing deciduous and evergreen forest or bushland, later replaced by high-elevation humid forest. The lacustrine-dominated upper Sidi Hakoma and lower Denen Dora Member assemblages indicate a succession from woodland to wet and dry grassland. The uppermost pollen sample close to BKT-2 near the top of the formation includes a peak in drier conifer forest, as well as the strongest seasonal contrast than any earlier or modern sample (Bonnefille et al., 2004).

Invertebrate Paleontology

Invertebrate material is associated with most lacustrine transgressions at Hadar, although in varying abundance. Diatomites are rather rare at Hadar, with only one unit well preserved above the SHT composed of *Aulacoseira granulata*, an indicator of turbid/well-mixed, but fresh waters (Tiercelin, 1986). A poorly preserved diatom flora composed of ?*Thalassiosira* sp. in the DD-1 submember suggests highly saline waters (Tiercelin, 1986). Thicker and more extensive diatomite deposits exist at the edge of, and outside, the Hadar project boundaries. For example, the Confetti Clay, in the KH-1 submember, becomes diatomaceous (*Aulacoseira* sp. and rare *Stephanodiscus* sp.) in the Hurda and into the Ledi-Geraru project area (Campisano and Feibel, 2008), and BKT-2 deposits in the Ledi-Geraru project area are encased in up to 8 m of laminated diatomite dominated by *A. granulata* (DiMaggio et al., 2008). A laminated diatomite sequence has also been noted from the Basal Member at Dikika (Campisano, pers. obs.).

Ostracods have been observed from multiple layers within the Hadar Formation, but only a single study by Peypouquet et al. (1983) exists for samples from the Basal and Sidi Hakoma Members. Virtually all of the Hadar ostracods belong to two varieties of *Cyprideis*. *Cyprideis* sp. SH1 dominates the ostracod assemblages except in the "ostracod fissile shale," located ~30–50 cm below TT-4, which is exclusively composed of *Cyprideis* sp. KH1 (Peypouquet et al., 1983). These ostracod assemblages indicate that Basal and Sidi Hakoma Member lakes had variable salinity, typically oligohaline, but ranging as high as mesohaline, and probably with seasonal variation (Peypouquet et al., 1983; Tiercelin, 1986). Additional features of the ostracod assemblage fit well with sedimentological evidence for fluctuating lacustrine and palustrine environments (Campisano and Feibel, 2008).

As with the ostracods, mollusk shells are recorded throughout the Hadar Formation, but only a few of the units have been studied in detail, and all from the Sidi Hakoma Member (Hailemichael, 2000; Hailemichael et al., 2002). With a focus on the main lacustrine phase of the upper Sidi Hakoma Member, isotopic analysis of the "Gastropod Beds" of the SH-3 submember represent the least evaporated condition of Lake Hadar (as represented by mollusk isotopes) with reconstructed lake water isotopic values much lower than modern lakes in Ethiopia and even lower than average modern Ethiopian Plateau rain (Hailemichael, et al., 2002). Combined with the paleosol carbonate data, this information has been used to suggest a strong summer monsoon during the Pliocene (Aronson et al., 2008). Mollusk oxygen isotope values from the lacustrine sequence in the SH-4 submember show more positive and more variable $\delta^{18}O$ values both within individual shells (6‰ range) and between shells (8‰ range), suggesting rapid expansions and contractions of Lake Hadar within the lifetimes of individual mollusks (Hailemichael et al., 2002). This is also in line with sedimentological evidence of lacustrine environments with episodic subaerial exposure (Campisano and Feibel, 2008).

Vertebrate Paleontology

The Hadar Formation has yielded one of the most taxonomically rich (Table 18.1) and abundant mid-Pliocene vertebrate faunas from eastern Africa. The Hadar mammalian fauna has been identified and subsequently re-evaluated by various researchers over the last four decades. Similarly, fossil collection protocol has varied over this time, with essentially three different protocols over the last 40 years. Researchers always collected craniodental material that could be identified to at least the family level; postcranial elements were always collected for primates and carnivorans, and often if postcranial elements were associated with craniodental remains. Since 2002, all identifiable postcrania were collected as to make the fauna comparable to other sites across Africa. More than 10,000 specimens have been collected and all are housed at the National Museum of Ethiopia (Addis Ababa).

Table 18.1 Fauna recovered from the Hadar Formation.

Mammalia
- Artiodactyla
  - Bovidae
    - Aepycerotini
      - *Aepyceros datoadeni*
      - *Aepyceros ?melampus*
    - Alcelaphini
      - *Damalborea elisabethae*
      - *Damalborea grayi*
      - *Damalborea* sp.
      - *Damalborea* sp. B
      - *Parmularius* cf. *P. pachyceras*
      - *Parmularius* sp. A
      - *Parmularius* sp. B
    - Antilopini
      - *Gazella* cf. *G. janenschi*
      - *Gazella* cf. *G. praethomsoni*
      - *Gazella harmonae*
      - *Gazella* sp.
    - Bovini
      - *Ugandax coryndonae*
      - *?Pelorovis* sp.
    - Caprini
      - *Budorcas churcheri*
    - Cephalophini
      - *Cephalophini* sp.
    - Hippotragini
      - *Oryx deturi*
    - "Neotragini"
      - *?Raphicerus* sp.
      - *Madoqua* sp.
    - Reduncini
      - *Kobus oricornus*
      - *Kobus* sp. B
      - *Kobus* sp. D
    - Tragelaphini
      - *Tragelaphus* aff. *T. gaudryi*
      - *Tragelaphus lockwoodi*
      - *Tragelaphus rastafari*
  - Giraffidae
    - *Giraffa jumae*
    - *Giraffa stillei*
    - *Sivatherium maurusium*
  - Hippopotamidae
    - aff. *Hippopotamus afarensis*
    - aff. *Hippopotamus coryndonae*
  - Suidae
    - *Kolpochoerus afarensis*
    - *Notochoerus euilus*
    - *Nyanzachoerus pattersoni*
- Carnivora
  - Canidae
    - *Canis* sp. A
    - *Canis* sp. B
    - *Nyctereutes lockwoodi*
  - Felidae
    - *Dinofelis aronoki*
    - *Dinofelis petteri*
    - *Leptailurus/Caracal*
    - *Felis* sp.
    - *Homotherium hadarensis*
    - *Panthera* sp.
  - Hyaenidae
    - *Chasmaporthetes* sp.
    - *Crocuta dietrichi*
    - *Crocuta* sp.

Table 18.1 (cont.)

			Hyaena sp.	Proboscidea	
			Ikelohyena abronia	Deinotheriidae	
			cf. Pliocrocuta perrieri		Deinotherium bozasi
	Herpestidae			Elephantidae	
			cf. Helogale sp.		Elephas ekorensis
			Herpestes sp.		Elephas recki
	Mustelidae				Loxodonta adaurora adaurora
			Large Mustelidae (Sivaonyx/Enhydriodon) sp. A		Loxodonta exoptata
			Large Mustelidae (Sivaonyx/Enhydriodon) sp. B		Mammuthus sp.
			Large Mustelidae (Sivaonyx/Enhydriodon) sp. C	Rodentia	
			cf. Poecilogale sp.	Hystricidae	
			Melivora benfieldi		Hystrix aff. H. cristata
			Mustelidae indet. sp.		Xenohystrix cf. X. crassidens
	Viverridae			Muridae	
			cf. Civettictis sp.	Gerbilinae	
			Viverridae indet.		Gerbiliscus sp.
Chiroptera				Murinae	
			Chiroptera indet.		Acomys coppensi
Lagomorpha					Golunda gurai
	Leporidae				Millardia taiebi
			Lepus sp.		Mus sp.
Perissodactyla					Oenomys tiercelini
	Equidae				Praomys sp.
			Eurygnathohippus afarense		Saidomys afarensis
			Eurygnathohippus hasumense	Spalacidae	
	Rhinocerotidae				Tachyoryctes pliocaenicus
			Ceratotherium mauritanicum	Sciuridae	
			Diceros praecox		Xerus sp.
Primates				Soricidae	
	Cercopithecidae				Soricidae indet.
		Papionini		Tubulidentata	
			Parapapio cf. P. jonesi	Orycteropodidae	
			Theropithecus darti		Orycteropodidae sp.
		Colobini		Aves	
			Cercopithecoides meaveae	Anseriformes	
			cf. Rhinocolobus turkanaensis	Anatidae	
	Hominidae				Anatinae sp.
			Australopithecus afarensis		Plectropterus sp.

Table 18.1 (cont.)

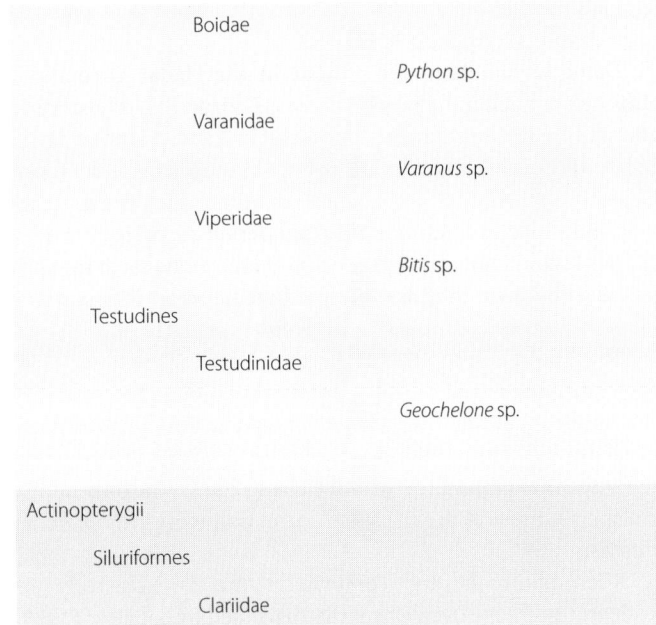

Taxonomy

The Bovidae from Hadar and surrounding regions were originally described by Gentry (1981), who included fossils collected from the International Afar Research Expedition. Subsequent papers have added to this initial list of fossil bovids (Gentry, 1996, 2006, 2010; Vrba, 1997; Reed and Bibi, 2010; Bibi, 2011a; Geraads et al., 2012a). The Hadar bovid fauna contains a great diversity of species representing most major tribes (Gentry, 1981; Geraads et al., 2012a), with notable taxa including the slender-horned *Aepyceros datoadeni*, the lyrate *Gazella harmonae*, and the greater kudu-like *Tragelaphus lockwoodi*, all three of which are known only from Hadar. Reduncini and Aepycerotini are the most common tribes overall, and changes in the relative abundance of bovid tribes through the Hadar Formation were previously discussed by Bobe et al. (2007b), Reed (2008), and Geraads et al. (2012a). New collections from fieldwork conducted from 2007 through 2012 have been added to the abundance data, and importantly both cranial and postcranial specimens have now been collected and used in estimating the overall number of taxa.

Among non-bovid artiodactyls, Giraffidae from Hadar were described by Geraads et al. (2013a), who recognized at least three species: *Giraffa jumae*, *G. stillei*, and *Sivatherium maurusium*. Boisserie (2005) provisionally recognized two hippopotamids, aff. *Hippopotamus afarensis* and the smaller aff. *H. coryndonae*. Weston and Boisserie (2010), however, noted that aff. *H. coryndonae* cannot be clearly distinguished from Omo-Turkana remains attributed to aff. *H.* cf. *protoamphibius* based on the diagnosis given by Gèze (1985). Boisserie (pers. comm.) is currently working on a revision of the Hadar hippopotamids. Suids have been described by Cooke (1978b, 1997, 2007), Harris and White (1979), Bishop (2010), Haile-Selassie and Simpson (2013), and Souron et al. (2013). Tetraconodontinae (*Nyanzachoerus* and *Notochoerus*) numerically dominate the suid fauna (63 percent), with *Notochoerus euilus* comprising the bulk of specimens (51 percent).

Carnivora are diverse and include at least three species of giant otter, referable to the genera *Sivaonyx* or *Enhydriodon* (Werdelin, pers. comm.) as well as several large felids (*Dinofelis*, *Homotherium*, *Megantereon*, *Panthera*) and hyaenids (*Chasmaporthetes*, *Crocuta*, *Hyaena*, *Ikelohyaena*). The canid *Nyctereutes lockwoodi* was described from Dikika (Geraads et al., 2011) and is also known from the Kada Hadar Member at Hadar (Werdelin and Lewis, 2014). Several smaller carnivoran taxa are also present, including members of the families Herpestidae and Viverridae. A full description of the Hadar Carnivora is forthcoming, although preliminary species lists can be found in Werdelin and Peigné (2010) and Werdelin and Lewis (2014).

Two species of the equid genus *Eurygnathohippus* have been identified from Hadar, the common *Eurygnathohippus hasumense* and the rarer *E. afarense*, which is known only from isolated teeth, a mandible, and a partial skull (Bernor et al., 2010). Bernor et al. (2005) recognized the species *E. hasumense* from the Sidi Hakoma and Denen Dora Members, and suggested that it derived from the earlier *E. feibeli*. *E. afarense* is known only from the Kada Hadar Member, where the type specimen was recovered. The status and phylogenetic relationships of *E. afarense* are uncertain, but Eisenmann (1976a) thought that *E. afarense* represented a central position in the evolution of Plio-Pleistocene Hipparionini, and was a possible ancestor to later species of the Pleistocene. Geraads (2005) revised the Hadar Formation Rhinocerotidae from both Hadar and Dikika, and recognized two species: *Ceratotherium mauritanicum* and *Diceros praecox*. He proposed that both of these species arose from within the genus *Ceratotherium*, specifically the taxon *C. neumayri*, with ecological divergence in the mid-Pliocene leading to the extant *C. simum* and *D. bicornis* from *C. mauritanicum* and *D. praecox*, respectively (Geraads, 2005).

Deinotherium bozasi is present in the Hadar Formation, although it is generally rare in the East African Plio-Pleistocene and was the last surviving deinotheriid in Africa (Sanders et al., 2010). Five different elephantids occur in the Hadar Formation: *Elephas ekorensis*, *E. recki*, *Loxodonta adaurora adaurora*, *L. exoptata*, and a species of *Mammuthus* (Sanders et al., 2010). White et al. (1984) could not classify the *Mammuthus* remains to the species level because they are intermediate between *Mammuthus subplanifrons* and *M. africanavus* (Sanders et al., 2010).

The Hadar cercopithecid fauna is diverse, with at least five taxa represented in the Hadar Formation. The colobines *Cercopithecoides meaveae*, *C. kimuei*, and cf. *Rhinocolobus turkanaensis*, and the papionins *Theropithecus darti* and *Parapapio* cf. *P. jonesi* are present (Frost and Delson, 2002). The only hominin species present in the Hadar Formation is *Australopithecus afarensis*.

Micromammals are comprised almost exclusively of Rodentia and have been primarily discussed by Sabatier (1978, 1982), Reed (2011b), and Reed and Geraads (2012). These include murines *Praomys*, *Acomys*, *Millardia*, *Golunda*, *Mus*, *Oenomys*, and *Saidomys*, and the gerbiline *Gerbiliscus*. The dominance of murines over gerbilines indicates the mesic nature of Hadar's paleoenvironments. The rhyzomyine spalacid *Tachyoryctes pliocaenicus* was named by Sabatier (1978) from the Kada Hadar Member. A sciurid, likely *Xerus*, is also known from this member. Hystricids occur throughout the Hadar Formation and are represented by *Xenohystrix* cf. *X. crassidens* and *Hystrix* aff. *H. cristata*. Indeterminate Chiroptera and Soricidae were reported by Sabatier (1982), but nothing else is known of these taxa. Reed (2008) reported leporids, herein referred to *Lepus*, from the Denen Dora and Kada Hadar Members.

Non-mammalian vertebrates are generally rare at Hadar. Archosaurs include *Crocodylus*, which is the most common among non-mammals, and the avians Anatinae sp., *Plectropterus*, *Balearica*, *Anhinga*, and *Struthio*. The former four taxa are highly dependent on permanent water bodies and, in the case of *Balearica*, wet grasslands and marshes. Likewise, the catfish *Clarias* is common. The prevalence of water birds and catfish is perhaps not surprising given the fluvio-lacustrine nature of the Hadar deposits. Squamate (*Bitis*, *Python*, *Varanus*) and testudine (*Geochelone*) genera present at Hadar are widespread in Africa today and do not provide much paleoenvironmental evidence.

Biogeography

The biogeographic relationships of the Hadar Formation mammalian fauna can be viewed as both limited and extensive, depending on the taxon of interest. For example, notable endemics include the bovids *Aepyceros datoadeni*, *Damalborea elisabethae*, *D. grayi*, *Budorcas churcheri*, *Tragelaphus lockwoodi*, *Gazella harmonae*, *Ugandax coryndonae*, the felid *Homotherium hadarensis*, the canid *Nyctereutes lockwoodi*, and the equid *Eurygnathohippus afarense*. The bovid *Oryx deturi* is shared exclusively with Laetoli, while *Parmularius* cf. *P. pachyceras* may be shared only with Koro Toro, Chad. On the other hand, other species, including the hominin *Australopithecus afarensis*, are comparatively widespread during the mid-Pliocene (*A. afarensis* occurs in the Middle Awash and Turkana Basin, as well as at Laetoli). Other regionally widespread species that are present at Hadar include the proboscidean *Deinotherium*, many of the hyaenid and felid taxa, and the giraffids *Sivatherium maurusium*, *Giraffa stillei*, and *G. jumae*. There are also some primate taxa shared with other localities, including the genera *Rhinocolobus* and *Cercopithecoides*. Interestingly, however, the dominant cercopithecid at Hadar is *Theropithecus darti*. This species is rare in the Turkana Basin where *T. brumpti* is common. *T. darti* and *Parapapio jonesi* are also present in South Africa. Thus, it seems that the regionally widespread species at Hadar tend to have larger body sizes, a carnivorous diet, or are cercopithecids.

Stable Isotope Ecology

Wynn et al. (2016) have recently provided an isotopic analysis (enamel $\delta^{13}C$ and $\delta^{18}O$) of the Hadar Formation mammalian fauna. The range of $\delta^{13}C$ values indicate the Hadar fauna span the entire spectrum from grazers (e.g., alcelaphins, reduncins, equids) to browsers (e.g., *Giraffa*) throughout the formation. The distribution of $\delta^{13}C$ values display is bimodal, with a minor mode at approximately −10‰ (browsers) and a major one at −1‰ (grazers). The majority of the Hadar taxa were mixed-feeders and show little change in consumption of C_3 or C_4 foods over time, although some browsing species, such as *Sivatherium*, switch to mixed feeding after ~3.0 Ma (Rowan et al., 2016). Oxygen isotope analysis of enamel suggests very little temporal variation of meteoric water $\delta^{18}O$ values over the Hadar Formation. Interestingly, *A. afarensis* displays a wide dietary range of both $\delta^{13}C$ and $\delta^{18}O$ values (Wynn et al., 2013), but in a unique combination that appears to fill a niche in isotopic space that does significantly overlap with other mammalian fauna (Wynn et al., 2016).

Mammalian Community Ecology (Methods)

Correspondence Analyses

A correspondence analysis (CA) is an exploratory multivariate technique that ordinates ecological information, such that each vector provides a range of variation among the data involved. To reconstruct paleo-habitats of the Hadar Formation, we first used the trophic and substrate traits of large mammal species from 203 modern African communities (national parks, game reserves, etc.) to collapse the data along several functional trait gradients (Figure 18.4). These functional traits also represent climatic features of various habitats, i.e., high representation of arboreal substrate use is indicative of forest, which in turn is associated with high mean annual precipitation (MAP). Although there were 18 categories of functional traits coded in the original data (see Reed, 2008), using only 6 in the CA (arboreal, aquatic, terrestrial, frugivory, fresh grass grazing, and grazing) produced the best results, with 76 percent of the variation represented on the first axis and 10 percent of the variation present on the

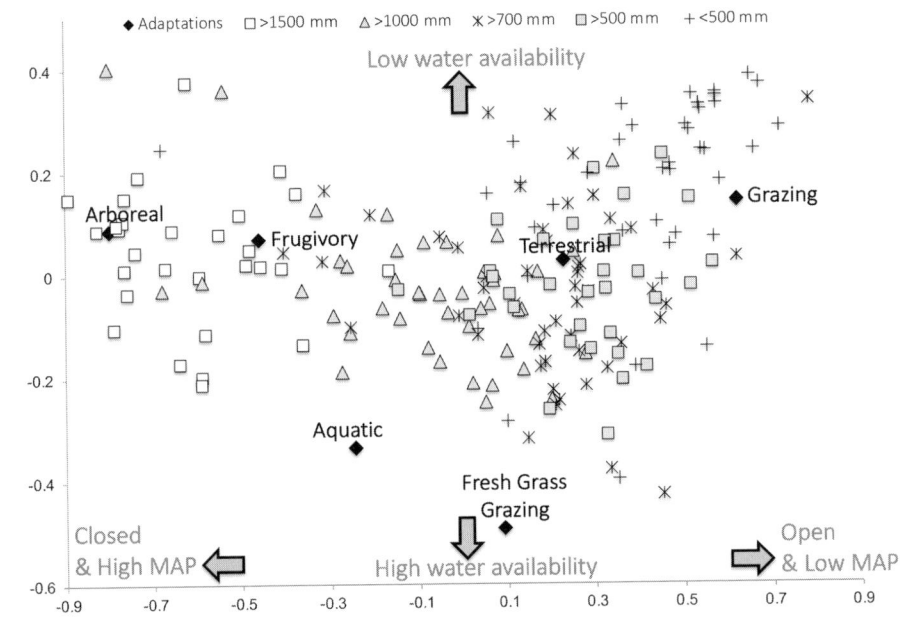

Figure 18.4 Correspondence analysis based on the functional traits of the mammals present in the 203 modern African communities. Each locality is coded by mean annual precipitation bins. See text for further information.

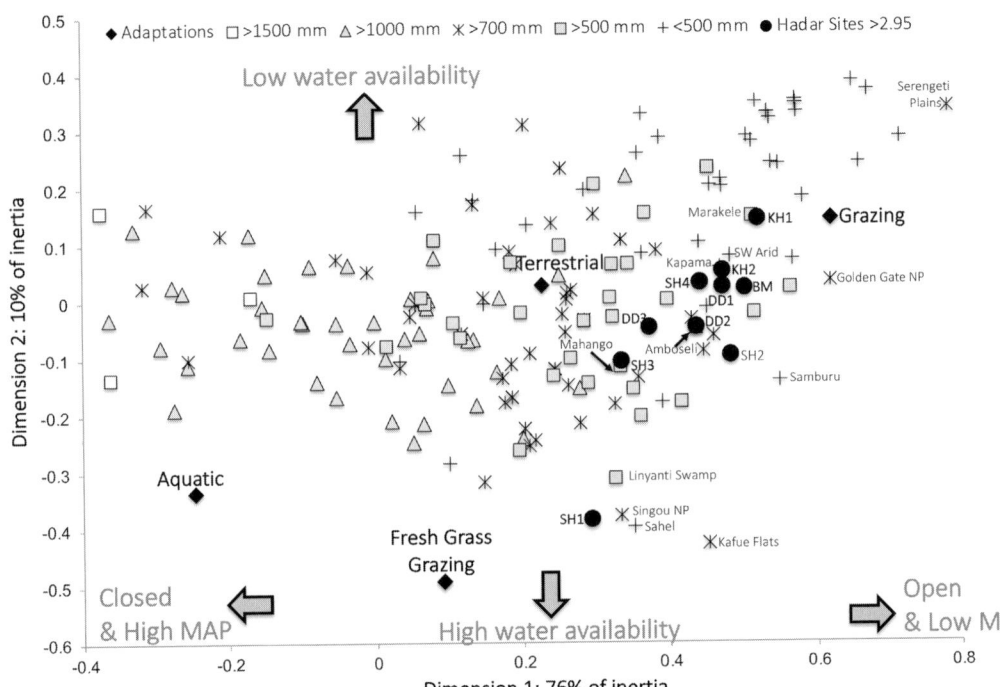

Figure 18.5 Correspondence analysis based on the functional traits of the mammals present in the 203 modern African communities and the same functional traits from the 10 Hadar assemblages added as supplementary points. A correspondence analysis that included the Hadar assemblages resulted in no discernible differences in placement. See text for further information.

second axis among the 203 modern sites. The first axis separates the localities based on high to low MAP, habitat physiognomy from closed to open, and also reflects soil types, such that sites on poorer soils, but with higher rainfall, have fewer trees than those with better soils. The functional traits that differentiate this axis include arboreality and frugivory (loading negatively), and grazing and terrestriality (loading positively). The second axis involves a separation of water availability, a phrase that we use to encompass the presence of ground water from rivers and lakes and flooding from higher elevations to low (e.g., Okavango Delta, Botswana). Thus, a site could have low MAP but high water availability. The traits associated with aquatic and fresh grass grazing pull sites with higher water availability toward the bottom/negative region of the graph.

Hadar Formation submembers were then superimposed onto this graph using an algorithm based on the modern data set to approximate what habitat physiognomy and MAP they might have when compared with these modern African localities (Figure 18.5). We also performed a CA using only the fossil submembers in order to understand how each member related to each other based on these same functional traits (Figure 18.6). Discussion of the placement of each of the Hadar submembers with modern analogs and their likely habitat physiognomy is presented in the following section.

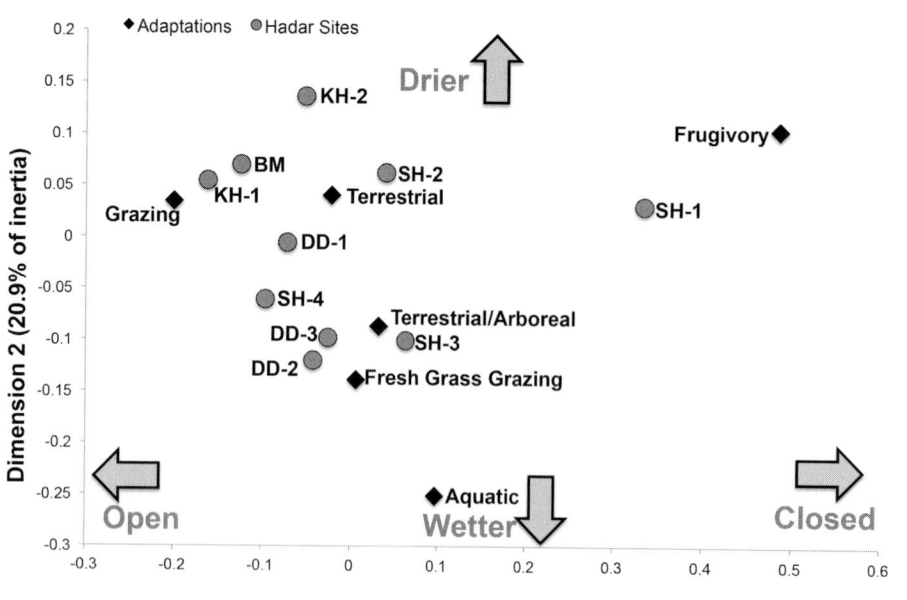

Figure 18.6 Correspondence analysis of Hadar Formation assemblage data. When the Hadar mammalian faunal data were analyzed separately, the ordination emphasizes the differences between the submembers. Because there are very few arboreal mammals recovered from Hadar, we used the functional trait "Terrestrial/Arboreal" rather than Arboreal in this analysis. The first two CA dimensions account for 75 percent of the variation among the submember assemblages, which was higher than any of the other combinations of functional traits in this analysis. It is clear that the SH-1 is different from the other submembers in having more animals with adaptations to frugivory. KH-2 appears more xeric than the other submembers, and KH-1 is suggested to have more open grasslands.

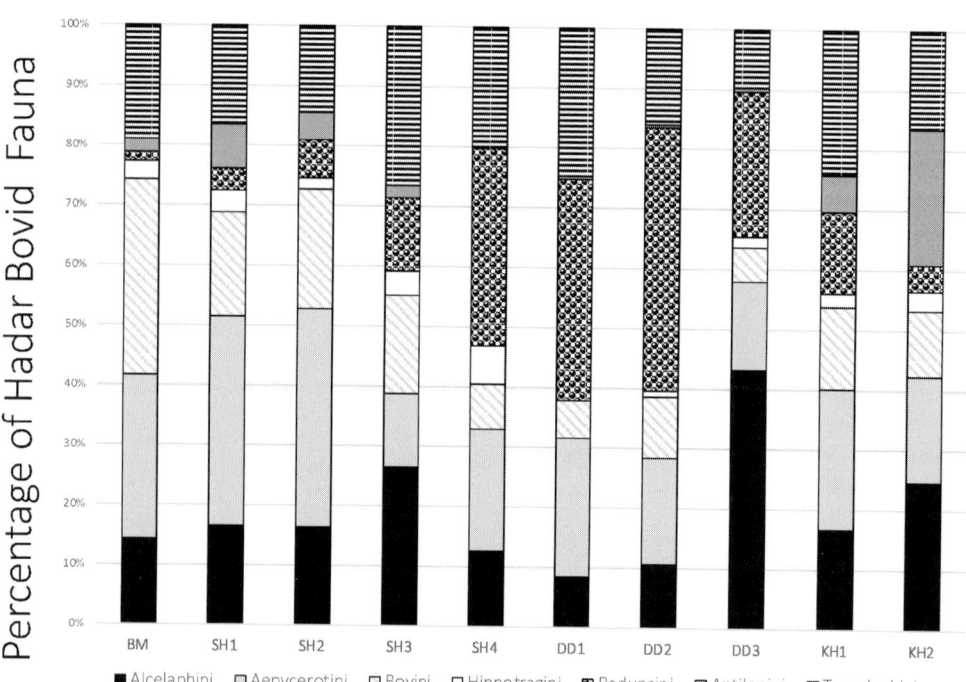

Figure 18.7 Relative abundance of bovid tribes through the Hadar Formation.

Temporal Trends in Taxon Abundances

Whereas correspondence analysis uses only species presence/absence data, we also used the numbers of individual specimens (NISP) of families and tribes to document changes in abundance through time. Bovid tribal percentages were calculated by dividing the total in each tribe by total identifiable bovids, thus excluding Bovidae indet. in these calculations (Figure 18.7). We compared bovid tribal abundances to abundance data from communities across Africa today (Figure 18.8A–C); to arrive at family percentages, we divided each by the total number of mammalian specimens in each submember (Figure 18.9). Again, results are discussed below with each of the individual submembers.

Hadar Paleoenvironmental Reconstructions

The Hadar Formation records approximately 900,000 years of time distributed across the Hadar, Dikika, and Ledi-Geraru Research Projects (Campisano and Feibel, 2008; DiMaggio et al., 2008; Wynn et al., 2008). Taxa recovered from each member/submember are frequently the same across these broad areas, although as Dikika alone preserves older components of the

Basal Member (Wynn et al., 2008), its faunal list includes a few taxa not found in the other project areas thus far, and are incorporated into Table 18.1. Analyses of the fauna have included habitat reconstruction using ecomorphology and community structure analysis (Reed, 2008; DiMaggio et al., 2015a), dental microwear of bovids (Scott, 2012), carbon and oxygen isotopes of enamel (Wynn et al., 2016), and taphonomic modification of bone, as well as new transect taphonomic data (Thompson et al., 2016). Other paleoenvironmental analyses have used paleosols (Hailemichael, 2000; Aronson et al., 2008), invertebrate paleontology (e.g., Tiercelin, 1986; Hailemichael, 2000; Hailemichael et al., 2002; Campisano and Feibel, 2008; DiMaggio et al., 2008) and pollen (Bonnefille et al., 1987, 2004). The results of these studies are synthesized below to provide a multiproxy depiction of environmental changes by submember for the entire Hadar Formation.

Basal Member (BM)

The large mammalian fauna suggest a woodland physiognomy with a riverine component (Figure 18.6), and is predicted to be similar to the Southern Savanna Grassland and Kapama Game Reserve areas of South Africa based on the CA analysis. The Basal Member has the greatest abundance of suids and bovins in the Hadar Formation, possibly indicating areas of woody grassland, as well as riverine forest (Figure 18.7). Aepycerotini are also abundant, and this tribe's preference for ecotonal habitats between grassland and woodland fits with the CA reconstruction. Complementary to the faunal evidence, paleosol data indicate only ~30 percent C_4 grass cover (Hailemichael, 2000; Aronson et al., 2008). Pollen also agrees with this overall habitat reconstruction, indicating high riverine forest pollen (Bonnefille et al, 2004). Finally, the lake during this time had variable salinity, ranging as high as mesohaline (Peypouquet et al., 1983). Overall, it is likely that the Basal Member encompassed woodlands, grasslands, and some riverine forest.

Sidi Hakoma Submember 1 (SH-1)

We include fauna associated with the SHT in this category, which, with SH-1, ranges in age from ~3.45 to 3.35 Ma. SH-1 functional traits of large mammalian fauna evince the most closed habitat of the Hadar Formation (Figures 18.5 and 18.6), and indicate riverine forests. Additionally, there were likely wetlands as the SH-1 aligns with the Singou Faunal Reserve, Burkina Faso, and the Sahel Savanna region around Lake Chad. Indicator taxa such as forest-dwelling Cephalophini sp., as well as five primate species recovered from this member, suggest, at the least, a large riverine forest with predominately woodland in the surrounding area. Aepyceros is by far the most abundant bovid, and SH-1 overall has the lowest proportion of grazing bovids of any submember at Hadar (Figures 18. 7 and 18.8). This closed woodland or forested habitat must have begun by the top of the BM, because the pollen assemblage recovered from directly beneath the SHT has the largest abundance of forest type taxa (Bonnefille et al., 1987, 2004). The vegetation of SH-1 might have resembled the Guinea or Sudanese savannas that interdigitate with the central African rainforest, creating a mosaic of grasslands, woodlands, and

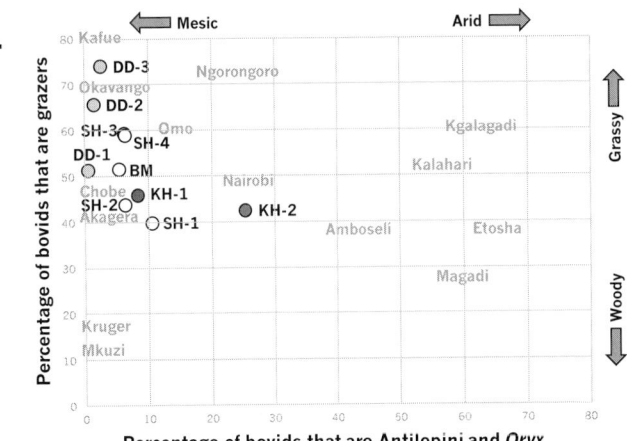
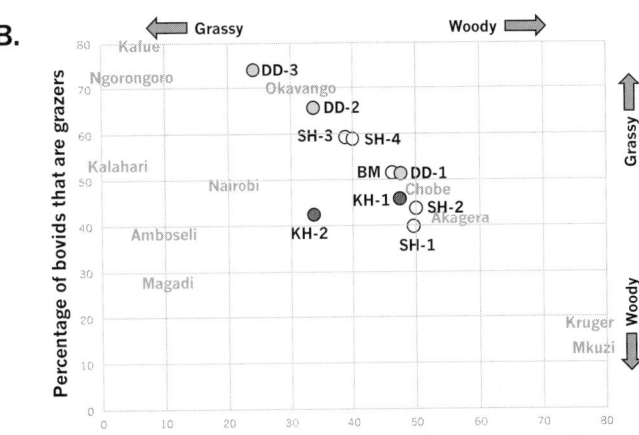
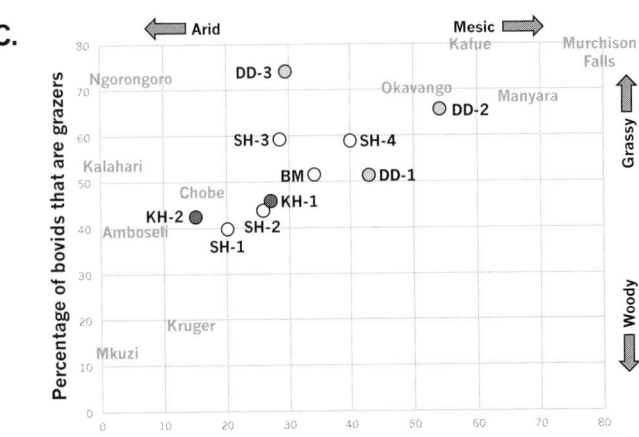

Figure 18.8 Biplots of bovid abundance data from Hadar compared to bovid census data from modern African communities. The y-axis shows the proportion of the bovid fauna comprised of grazers (Alcelaphini, Bovini, Hippotragini, and Reduncini) versus the percentage of bovids that are Antilopini and Oryx (A), the percentage of bovids that are Aepycerotini and Tragelaphini (B), and the proportion of bovids that are Reduncini and Bovini (C). Thus, the y-axis coarsely separates grassy cover from woody cover while the x-axes separate mesic from arid habitats (A), grassy open savanna from woody closed savanna (B), and arid grasslands/bushlands from wet edaphic grasslands (C).

some forest belts. Influence of the fluvial Basal Member sands and SHT are also reflected in the ostracod assemblage, which indicates relatively fresh (oligohaline) water input (Peypouquet

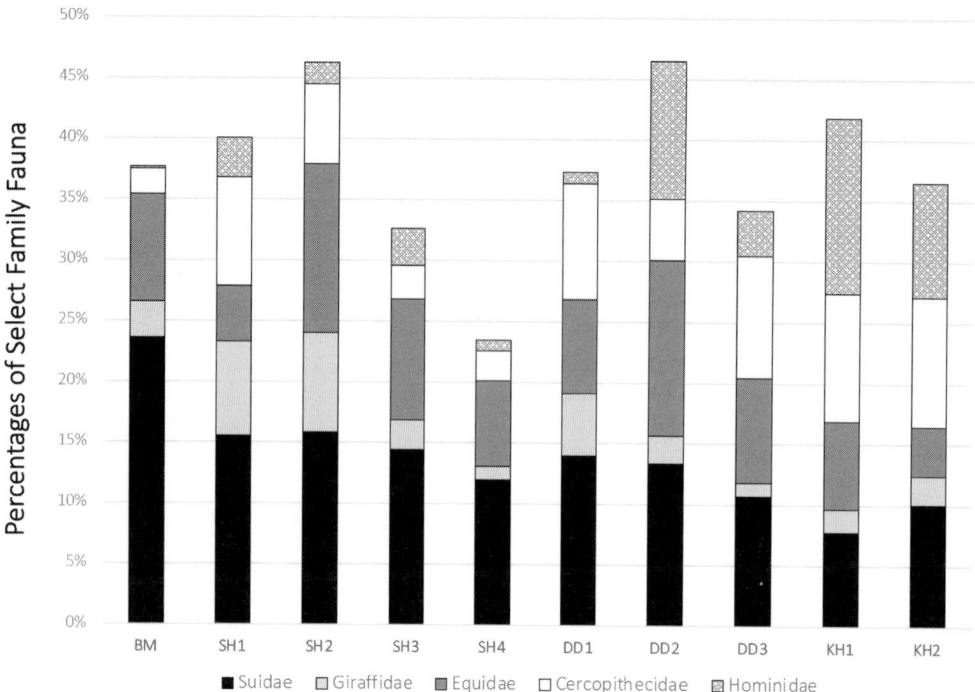

Figure 18.9 Relative abundance of five families through the Hadar Formation. Suid abundances decline about 15 percent throughout the sequence. Giraffids are most abundant in the SH-1 and SH-2, but maintain a similar percentage throughout the remaining submembers. Equids appear to be relatively constant except for lower percentages in the SH-1, which is more closed, and the KH-2, which is more arid. Cercopithecids increase in the KH-1 and KH-2, but these are almost exclusively *Theropithecus* specimens. There are hominins from every submember after the BM; hominin increases in DD-2 and KH-1 are due to the A.L. 333 hominins in DD-2 and to Lucy (A.L. 288) in KH-1.

et al., 1983). Finally, analysis of mollusk shells indicates only a three-month dry season for this member (Hailemichael, 2000), which is characteristic of the central African savanna–forest mosaics mentioned above. This factor is quite important, as no place in East Africa today has a single dry season; they are bimodal. The converse, that there is a nine-month rainy season, is not seen in East Africa today. This leads to the conclusion that the SH-1 was much more wooded with likely higher MAP than other submembers at Hadar.

Sidi Hakoma Submember 2 (SH-2)

Similar to SH-1, the SH-2 is reconstructed as woodland with some wet grassy plains based on the CA. This member is positioned near Réserve Intégrale du Lac Tonga and Réserve Intégrale du Lac Oubeïra, both in Algeria. These reserves encompass lakes that are surrounded by a variety of savanna-type habitats from woodland to open grassland and extensive wetlands, although geologic evidence suggests a fluvial-dominated system at Hadar. Aepycerotini have their highest abundance in this submember, likely reflecting the ecotone habitats between woodland and grassland near the river. The depositional environments indicate seasonal flooding through a meandering fluvial system. The pollen record indicates that this submember trended toward forest near the transition to SH-3, but also shows changing environments over approximately 20 ka (Bonnefille et al., 2004). Thus, all evidence points to woodlands and grasslands as the predominant habitat during SH-2 times.

Sidi Hakoma Submembers 3 and 4 (SH-3 and SH-4)

The CA for SH-3 suggests habitat of woodland with wet, grassy plains. This member is suggested to be similar to the Mahango Game Reserve, Namibia, which encompasses wetlands within a fairly dry environment. Wetland grasses are also indicated in the SH-3 by the slight increase in abundance of reduncins, although this submember has the highest abundance of tragelaphins across the Hadar Formation, which may indicate more closed habitats, or could also indicate wetlands if these tragelaphins are more sitatunga-like (*Tragelaphus spekii*). The largest micromammal assemblage from Hadar ($n = 1218$) comes from locality A.L. 327, which is in the SH-3 submember. This assemblage is dominated by extant murine genera (*Acomys*, *Golunda*, and *Oenomys*) and the extinct *Saidomys*. Only *Acomys* and *Oenomys* are present in Africa today, with species in the former genus preferring rocky habitats in savanna, whereas the latter prefers moist savanna–forest ecotones. These reconstructions are in concordance with mollusk shell analyses from just below the SH-3/SH-4 boundary that indicate the least evaporated condition of the lake (Hailemichael et al., 2002). Thus, the overall evidence suggests woodlands and grasslands with more lakeside habitats of wetlands than previously seen.

The CA for SH-4 indicates a habitat such Nkasa Rupara National Park, Namibia. Again, this includes wetlands in a possibly drier surrounding environment. However, there is a further increase in reduncin bovids and a decrease in alcelaphins, which likely indicates lake shore environments and surrounding wetlands, consistent with the reconstructed depositional environment. Bovid abundance data, when compared with abundances of grazers vs. tragelaphins and reduncins in modern bovid communities, suggests similar amounts of tree cover for SH-3 and SH-4, but that the former was slightly drier than the latter (Figure 18.8C). Pollen evidence for the SH-3 and SH-4 submembers indicates about 800–900 mm MAP and wetland grasses (Bonnefille et al., 2004). Ostracods and diatoms from the top of the SH-4 are consistent with a widespread lake, but much more saline (mesohaline) than earlier (Peypouquet et al., 1983; Tiercclin, 1986). The combined geological and paleontological evidence suggests habitats typical of those surrounding lakes in drier environments.

Denen Dora Submember 1 (DD-1)

Collections made from 2007 to present have greatly increased the number of specimens from the DD-1. In the CA, DD-1 is positioned near Kapama Game Reserve, South Africa and very close to SH-4 (Figure 18.5). Kapama is mostly rolling hills with grasslands interspersed with riverine forests. Reduncin bovids again increase in abundance in this submember (Figure 18.7), and there is also an increase in the abundances of cercopithecids and giraffids. Bovid abundance data indicate that DD-1 is slightly more mesic and wooded than SH-4 (Figure 18.8C).

The increase in reduncins is consistent with the fact that the upper Sidi Hakoma and the lower Denen Dora Members have the most persistent lake of the Hadar Formation (Campisano and Feibel, 2008). Pollen indicates a transition from woodland to wetlands and grasslands (Bonnefille et al., 2004). However, while there is a transition in physiognomy, the increase in cercopithecids and giraffids, as well as tragelphins and *Aepyceros* (Figure 18.7) suggests there were ecotone habitats of open wetlands and woodlands, which is our overall assessment of the DD-1 habitat considering all data.

Denen Dora Submember 2 (DD-2)

The DD-2 is the most fossiliferous submember of the Hadar site with 2596 identifiable fossils. The DD-2 is near Luiana National Park, Angola as well as Amboseli National Park, Kenya in the CA. Both of these modern localities indicate at least seasonal abundance of water within an open physiognomy and riverine forests. Bovid abundance data suggests DD-2 is most similar to Kafue Flats and the Okavango delta (Figure 18.8A–C), both of which are mesic and grassy but with patches of tree vegetation. This assessment also matches the reconstructed depositional environment of fluvial–deltaic distributary channels and delta plain (Campisano and Feibel, 2008). There is also an increase in equids and a decrease in cercopithecids and giraffids, suggesting a transition to more open vegetation, broadly speaking. Pollen also indicates wetlands (Bonnefille et al., 2004). MAP was estimated to be 900 mm/yr (Aronson et al., 2008), which agrees with the estimate based on pollen. The data for DD-2 indicate an overall habitat of large wetland areas perhaps interspersed with woodlands and riverine forests.

Denen Dora Submember 3 (DD-3)

In the CA, the DD-3 is positioned between the region of Kruger National Park that surrounds the Olifants River, and Amboseli National Park, Kenya. The Olifants River may be similar to the depositional environment of the DD-3, which has a meandering river system with overbank flood deposits (Campisano and Feibel, 2008). The number of reduncin bovids drops from a peak of ~45 percent in the DD-2 to 23 percent in the DD-3, while alcelaphin bovids peak at 42 percent of total bovids, indicating a transition from more mesic to drier habitats (Figure 18.8A–C). As there is no increase in antilopins in this submember, the indication is that there is an expansion of grasslands at the expense of some of the wetlands in the region without the bushes and shrubs on which antilopins thrive. There is also an increase in ceropithecids to greater than 10 percent, but most of those specimens are *Theropithecus*, which favored grasslands. Thus, our conclusion is that the DD-3 habitat was experiencing less flooding in the areas where we find fossils, and thus had more open woodlands and grasslands than DD-2.

Kada Hadar Submember 1 (KH-1)

The KH-1 is positioned on the top of Marakele National Park, South Africa in the CA, which is located between drier western and wetter eastern part of the country. Although there are small patches of seasonal grasses in this park, the dominant vegetation is low shrubs and bushes, with a patchy distribution of trees. There is an increase in tragelaphin and aepycerotin bovids, as well as in cercopithecids, and a decrease in alcelaphins, which suggests that the grassy and wetland-dominated habitats of the Denen Dora Member were receding and being replaced by woody vegetation. Antilopins also increase in abundance after being virtually non-existent from SH-4 to DD-3, which signals the presence of bushlands. The KH-1 includes several depositional environments, but most fossils are likely associated with fluvial systems. Overall, we consider the KH-1 to have habitats with shrub and bush vegetation, with scattered trees.

Kada Hadar Submember 2 (KH-2)

The CA positions KH-2 on top of the Kapama Game Reserve, South Africa, which, like the KH-1, has high numbers of species exhibiting grazing and mixed feeding – but not high abundances of those taxa. The KH-2 is dominated in abundances by antilopin species and *Oryx* (Figure 18.8A). Antilopins increase to 22 percent in the KH-2, with a previous high of 7 percent in the SH-1. Alcelaphins also increase to 24 percent from a large drop of 42 percent in the DD-3 to 16 percent in the KH-1. Equids are at their lowest abundance (4 percent) in the Hadar Formation, and suids, dominated by *Notochoerus*, increase to greater than 10 percent. Pollen data suggest, however, a return to more woodland-like conditions, although with evidence for the most seasonal environment in the Hadar sequence (Bonnefille et al., 2004). The spatial distribution of KH-2 fauna includes two distinct clusters ~5 km apart (Campisano, 2007; Campisano and Reed, 2007). The first is associated with a high-energy fluvial floodplain environment and includes predominantly terrestrial and open-adapted fauna (e.g., alcelaphins and antilopins). The second cluster is associated with a low-energy fluvial floodplain environment, is dominated by cercopithecids (including *Parapapio* and colobines), and includes more woodland fauna (e.g., tragelaphins) than the first cluster as well as the preservation of some smaller-bodied, semi-articulated specimens (e.g., snake vertebrae). This is suggested to represent two different habitats along the paleo-Awash River, the first being an open floodplain near the cutbank edge of the river with limited woodland or bushland habitats in the vicinity, and the second being a gallery forest/woodland located between the meanders of the fluvial system (Campisano, 2007; Campisano and Reed, 2007). Thus, the overall habitat reconstructed for KH-2 is much more xeric as indicated by pollen, antilopins, and *Oryx*, but the region still retained a riverine forest, similar to the Awash-Hadar landscape of today (although less arid).

Conclusions

Analysis of the Hadar faunal assemblage indicates that a range of habits were available to *Australopithecus afarensis* through time and space, including open and closed woodlands, gallery forests, edaphic grasslands, and shrublands. Some of the variation observed in these faunal communities can be explained by the spatial distribution of fauna across the landscape, as well as the depositional environments with which they are associated. Although there is no clear direction trend observed in habitats through time, reconstructions indicate slightly more xeric conditions beginning around 3.1/3.2 Ma.

The use of the presence and absence of species' functional traits in the correspondence analysis allows the assignment of habitats when compared with modern, known habitats. Most of the modern communities used in these analyses cover large areas and, as such, encompass more than one habitat type. The inclusion of species abundance data allows identification of perhaps the most important habitats within those areas. For example, we know that high numbers of reduncin bovids today indicate the presence of lakes, wetlands, and overbank flood deposits within other overall habitat types. Similarly, for our paleo-reconstructions, high numbers of reduncins do not mean wetlands were the only habitat present, but that they were important to the fauna that existed there. We note that, in general, there appears to be a slight trend toward more open and drier habitats through time in the Hadar Formation, but that "open" habitats are not necessarily synonymous with grasslands. In modern habitats that are fairly open vegetation can also be composed of shrubs and bushes, and modern shrublands, such as modern-day Hadar, are dominated by antilopin bovids and *Oryx*, similar to those found in KH-2.

Future paleoenvironmental analyses could focus on proxies for more refined paleoclimate reconstructions, such as seasonality, as we hypothesize that dry season months increased in duration in the younger submembers. For example, expanding the isotopic work on gastropods outside of the Sidi Hakoma Member would help in this endeavor. Additionally, increasing the sample size of paleosol carbonate and enamel isotopic analysis to specifically address (coupled) spatial distributions of habitats across the landscape could be critical to understanding the variability and relative proportion of habitats that *Australopithecus afarensis* is associated with, particularly as *A. afarensis* is one of only a handful of taxa that were able to persist throughout the entire Hadar sequence. Finally, phytoliths studies have yet to be attempted at Hadar, but can more readily resolve C_3 vs. C_4 grasses compared to pollen, as well as identifying C_4 grass subfamilies that have different temperature and precipitation requirements. For example, the abundance of the mesophytic Panicoideae has a positive relationship with precipitation, whereas the xerophytic Chloridoideae have an inverse relationship with precipitation (Taub, 2000; Cabido et al., 2008). Resolving the relative abundance of these grass types and others would greatly improve our understanding of the Pliocene environments of *A. afarensis*.

Acknowledgments

We thank all the researchers, from undergraduates to senior scientists, in both the field and laboratory that have contributed to our understanding of the Hadar Formation over the last four decades since Maurice Taieb recognized its importance for paleontology. This is a list far too long to include here, but is reflected in the diversity of names and dates in the references. For the most recent phases of fieldwork, we are indebted to the Institute of Human Origins and, in particular, the leadership provided by Bill Kimbel and Don Johanson. We would also like to thank the various organizations and foundations that have financially supported work at Hadar over the years, particularly the National Science Foundation. We would also like to thank the Authority for Research and Conservation of Cultural Heritage (ARCCH, and previous incarnations) and the Afar Regional State of Ethiopia for permission to conduct field and laboratory research. We thank Sally Reynolds, René Bobe, Terry Harrison, and an anonymous reviewer for constructive reviews of this manuscript. Last, but certainly not least, we thank our Addis-based camp staff and local Afar field crews, the unsung heroes, for their hospitality and generations of incredible contributions to the advancement of geology, archeology, paleontology, and human origins in the Hadar region.

19 Fossil Vertebrates and Paleoenvironments of the Pliocene Hadar Formation at Dikika, Ethiopia

René Bobe, Denis Geraads, Jonathan G. Wynn, Denné Reed, W. Andrew Barr, and Zeresenay Alemseged

Introduction to Dikika

The paleontological site of Dikika in the Afar Depression of Ethiopia (Figure 19.1) has been systematically studied since 1999, when a team led by one of us (ZA) launched the Dikika Research Project (DRP). This project set out to survey and document sedimentary exposures of the Hadar Formation south of the Awash River (Figures 19.2 and 19.3), and has produced important discoveries of fossil hominins and other mammals from the time between about 3.6 and 3.2 Ma. These discoveries include the earliest and most complete skeleton of an *Australopithecus afarensis* juvenile at locality DIK-1 (Alemseged et al., 2006); the earliest hominin from the Hadar Formation at locality DIK-2 (Alemseged et al., 2005); a new species of Canidae, *Nyctereutes lockwoodi* (Geraads et al., 2010b); a new species of gigantic otter, *Enhydriodon dikikae* (Geraads et al., 2011); and a new species similar to some modern otters, *Lutra hearsti* (Geraads et al., 2015b). Also, the earliest traces of stone-tool-modified bones were described from locality DIK-55 (McPherron et al., 2010). The study of these fossils and their paleoenvironmental context has offered new perspectives on the evolutionary forces that may have shaped early hominin adaptations (Wynn et al., 2006). The Dikika Research Project has therefore played a key role in deepening our understanding of *A. afarensis* paleobiology and its environmental context during the Pliocene.

The hominin species *A. afarensis* was named by Johanson and colleagues based on the specimen L.H. 4 from the Upper Laetolil Beds in Tanzania and multiple specimens including A.L. 288–1 ("Lucy") from the Hadar Formation (Johanson et al., 1978b). The most abundant record of this species is from the Hadar Formation. The Pliocene Hadar Formation, extensively exposed in a region bisected by the lower Awash River, was originally named by Maurice Taieb and colleagues to encompass the contiguous deposits of the Hadar Basin (Taieb et al., 1972, 1976). The Awash River is the main hydrological drainage in the Afar. It originates in the Ethiopian highlands to the southwest of Addis Ababa and drains into Lake Abhe

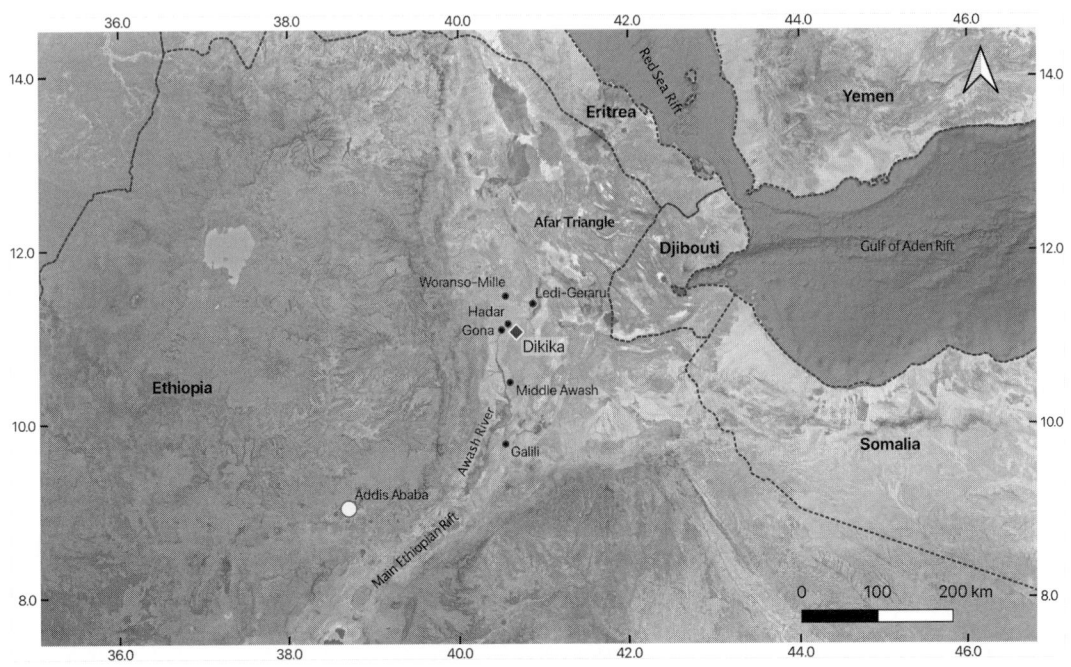

Figure 19.1 Satellite image of the Afar region. The site of Dikika is in the western margin of the Afar depression, a triple junction at the intersection of the Main Ethiopian Rift, the Gulf of Aden Rift, and the Red Sea Rift. The Dikika Research Project is located south of the Awash River, and the Hadar Research Project north of the river. (A black and white version of this figure will appear in some formats. For the color version, please refer to the plate section.)

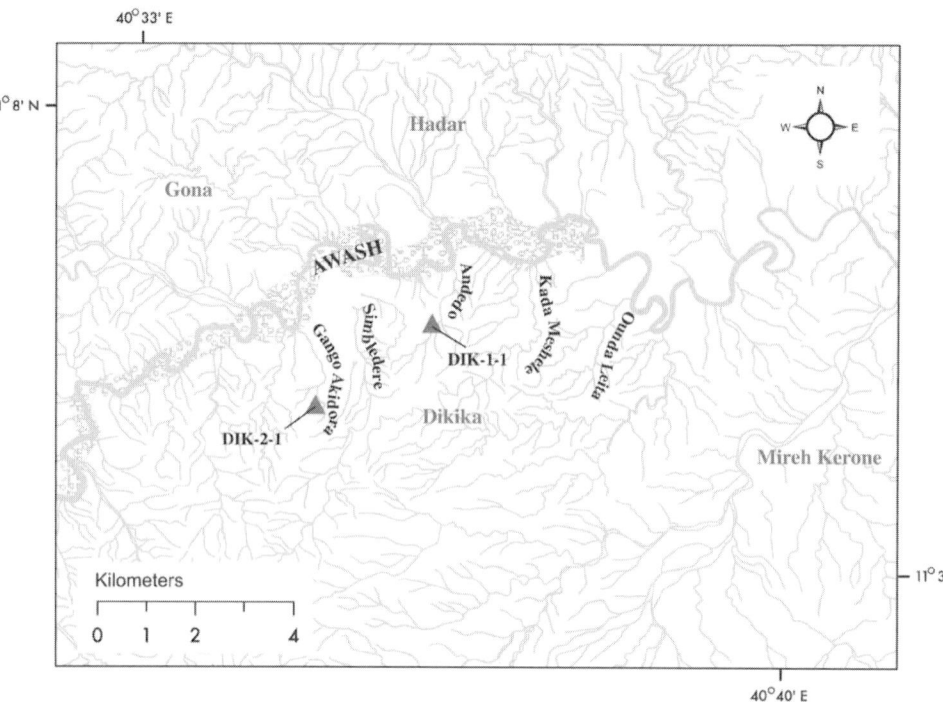

Figure 19.2 Drainage map of the Dikika Research Project and surrounding areas showing the location of two key sites: DIK-1 and DIK-2.

Figure 19.3 Photograph showing sediments of the Hadar Formation at Dikika in the foreground and of Hadar in the background separated by the Awash River and its riverine forest. The whitish–greenish layer is the Sidi Hakoma Tuff (SHT), dated to 3.42 Ma. In the foreground, sediments below the SHT belong to the Basal Member, and those above belong to the SH Member. Note the person sitting on top of the hill in the foreground for scale. (A black and white version of this figure will appear in some formats. For the color version, please refer to the plate section.)

near the Ethiopia–Djibouti border. Here we use the geographic term Dikika to refer to areas of the Hadar Basin south of the Awash River under the purview of the Dikika Research Project (DRP; positioned at approximately 11°5.5′N, 40°36.5′E), and we use the geographic term Hadar to refer to areas north of the river currently under the scope of the Hadar Research Project (HRP). Dikika is located about 300 km northeast of the Ethiopian capital, Addis Ababa (about 450 km by road).

The name Dikika derives from a distinctly pointed hill readily visible in the region (Figure 19.4). Since 1999, the DRP has documented 1381 fossil vertebrates from 116 paleontological localities of the Hadar Formation at Dikika. The project covers an area of approximately 500 km^2 of Hadar Formation exposures. Here we offer a review of Dikika's fossil record with a focus on the paleoenvironments and paleoecology of *A. afarensis*.

Figure 19.4 Photograph of Dikika Hill, a distinct pointed hill readily visible in the region, from which the name of the Dikika Research Project derives.

Geology and Paleoenvironments of the Hadar Formation at Dikika

The site of Dikika is close to the western margin of the Afar depression, a triple junction at the intersection of the Main Ethiopian Rift, the Gulf of Aden Rift, and the Red Sea Rift (Figure 19.1). Extensive geological and paleontological field work at Hadar in the 1970s led to a rich fossil record of hominins and other mammals from the time between 3.4 and 3 Ma (Johanson and Taieb, 1976; Gray, 1980; Johanson et al., 1982a, 1982b, 1982c; Kalb et al., 1982a; Kimbel et al., 1982, 1984; Eck, 1993; Kalb, 1993; Johanson, 2017). The deposits of the Hadar rift axial basin are exposed in parts of the adjacent Hadar, Dikika, Gona, and Ledi-Geraru research areas of the lower Awash Valley (Quade and Wynn, 2008), and conceivably as far as the Woranso-Mille research area (Deino et al., 2010) and the Middle Awash area (Renne et al., 1999). Deposits of the Hadar Formation contain several well-dated tuffs that provide a chronological framework for the Hadar Basin as well as tephrostratigraphic correlations over wider areas (Renne et al., 1993; Walter and Aronson, 1993; Walter, 1994; deMenocal and Brown, 1999; Campisano and Feibel, 2007; Roman et al., 2008).

Several faults transect the area and uplift the southern portions of the Hadar Basin. Although the base of the formation and its contact with the Sagantole Formation had been poorly known throughout the Awash Valley (Renne et al., 1999; Quade et al., 2008), research by the DRP established that deposits in the eastern Dikika area extend the defined lower boundary of the Hadar Formation to the contact with an erosional surface of basaltic basement (Wynn et al., 2006). This contact marks the onset to rapid deposition in the Hadar Basin (Wynn et al., 2008). The upper contact of the Hadar Formation is defined by the first of a sequence of unconformities marked by extensive conglomerates and an angular contact to the overlying Busidima Formation, deposited in a marginal basin along the western escarpment of the Ethiopian Rift (Quade et al., 2008; Wynn et al., 2008). Within the stratigraphic boundaries of its upper and lower contacts, the Hadar Formation is divided into four members: Basal, Sidi Hakoma, Denen Dora, and Kada Hadar Members (Figure 19.5), all of which are exposed in their entirety within the Dikika area. The Basal Member includes the initial deposits of the sedimentary basin (>3.8 Ma) up to one of the most prominent and widespread tuffs known throughout Pliocene sediments of eastern Africa, the Sidi Hakoma Tuff (SHT), dated to 3.42 Ma (WoldeGabriel et al., 2013). The remaining members of the formation are defined by prominent and widespread tuffs exposed throughout the region, including the SHT, as well as the Triple Tuff-4 (TT-4), dated to 3.24 Ma (Walter, 1994; Campisano and Feibel, 2007), and the Kada Hadar Tuff (KHT), dated to 3.20 Ma (Walter, 1994; Campisano and Feibel, 2007). Each member is defined as strata including the marker tephra up to the next marker tephra, finally ending with the upper boundary of the Kada Hadar Member at the Busidima Unconformity Surface. The Sidi Hakoma, Denen Dora, and Kada Hadar Members are further subdivided into sedimentary units. In the Sidi Hakoma Member there are four units above the SH Tuff (SH-1, SH-2, SH-3, SH-4); in the Denen Dora Member there are three units above the TT Tuff (DD-1, DD-2, DD-3); and in the Kada Hadar Member there are two units above the KH Tuff (KH-1, KH-2). The top of the Hadar Formation at the Busidima Unconformity Surface has an age range of 2.9–2.7 Ma (Wynn et al., 2006).

In the eastern Dikika area, the Hadar Formation is floored by the uppermost surface of a deeply weathered sequence of columnar basalts attributed to the Dahla Series (DSB; Wynn et al.,

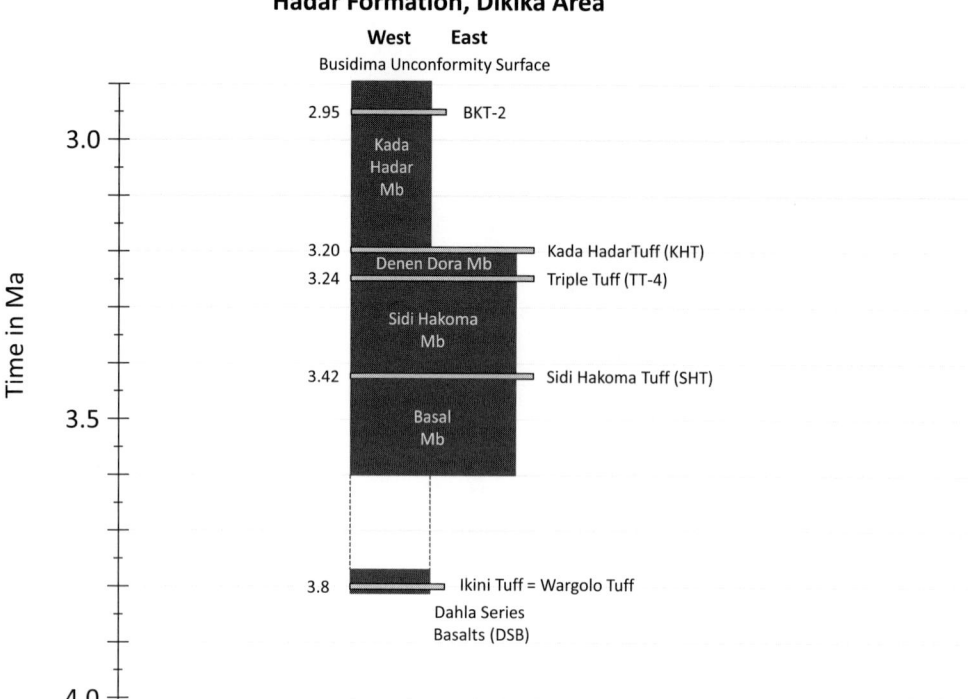

Figure 19.5 Schematic diagram of the Hadar Formation at Dikika illustrating strata exposed in western vs. eastern areas (approximately with respect to Dikika Hill). The Dahla Series Basalts unconformably underlie the sedimentary sequence in the eastern region. The basal contact of the formation is not exposed in the western region, although this area includes an uplifted area exposing the Ikini Tuff. The Busidima Unconformity Surface, which marks the uppermost contact, cuts across the Hadar Formation strata above the BKT-2 Tuff in the western region, but as deep as the Basal Member in the eastern region. The Hadar Formation is divided into the Basal Member, the Sidi Hakoma Member (including the SH Tuff), the Denen Dora Member (including the Triple Tuff), and the Kada Hadar Member (including the KH Tuff).

2006, 2008). Only the uppermost two flows of the Dahla Series are exposed in the area around the base of Andalee Ridge, and the uppermost surface is overlain by juvenile lithic sands deposited on the paleosol surface formed on relict topography of the initial basin floor. This weathering and erosional surface is overlain largely by laminated clays and diatomaceous mudstones of the Basal Member, indicating the onset of a period of extensive lacustrine deposition throughout the Hadar Basin with the formation of the Pliocene Lake Hadar. Locally, the Basal Member terminates in a brief lake regression below the deposits of the SHT, which marks the contact to the overlying Sidi Hakoma Member. Given the widespread nature of the exposure of SHT tephra deposits, which are in all cases reworked in sedimentary environments, this redeposited tephra can be used as a time horizon to map variations of depositional environments across a single landscape at the point of time of its deposition (3.42 Ma; Brown and Cerling, 1982; McDougall and Brown, 2008; WoldeGabriel et al., 2013). Within the Dikika area alone, the SHT is found in facies ranging from fluvial in the southwest, through deltaic facies, to entirely lacustrine facies in the northeastern part of the area around Andalee Ridge. However, despite this localized regression of Lake Hadar at ~3.42 Ma, there is evidence that continuous lacustrine deposition persisted during the entire interval from the Basal Member through lower Kada Hadar Member (~3.6 Ma to <3.2 Ma), evidenced by the section exposed at Andalee Ridge. Sections further southwest, however, document evidence of periodic expansion and contraction of Lake Hadar, with at least four periods of widespread lake transgression, and perhaps several other minor transgression events (Wynn et al., 2008). Hence, with a relatively complete picture of the exposures of the Hadar Formation in the greater Hadar–Dikika–Gona region, one could summarize the depositional environments of the Hadar Formation as continuously lacustrine deposition near the basin's depocenter to the northeast of Dikika, with periodic transgressions of the lake's shoreline across low-gradient topographic conditions toward the southwest.

Within the depositional framework described above, discrete exposures of fossiliferous strata of the Sidi Hakoma Member can be placed in the context of a lacustrine basin with a fluctuating shoreline. Locality DIK-55 locally exposes shallow lacustrine clays with some evidence of periodic subaerial exposure, and sheetflow sands deposited into the shallow lake waters (McPherron et al., 2010). The semi-adjacent localities of DIK-1 (Alemseged et al., 2006) and DIK-100 expose subaerial deltaic deposits of a braided fluvial system at the margin of Lake Hadar, whose shoreline was somewhere northeast of Dikika (Figure 19.6).

Our team has also analyzed $^{13}C/^{12}C$ ratios from pedogenic carbonates in the Basal, Sidi Hakoma, and Denen Dora Members at Dikika, from about 3.55 Ma to 3.2 Ma (Wynn et al., 2006). These analyses in the form of $\delta^{13}C$ values (with the standard Vienna Pee Dee Belemnite, $\delta^{13}C$VPDB) show spatial variability but overall a prevalence of woodlands and wooded grasslands

Pliocene Hadar Formation at Dikika, Ethiopia

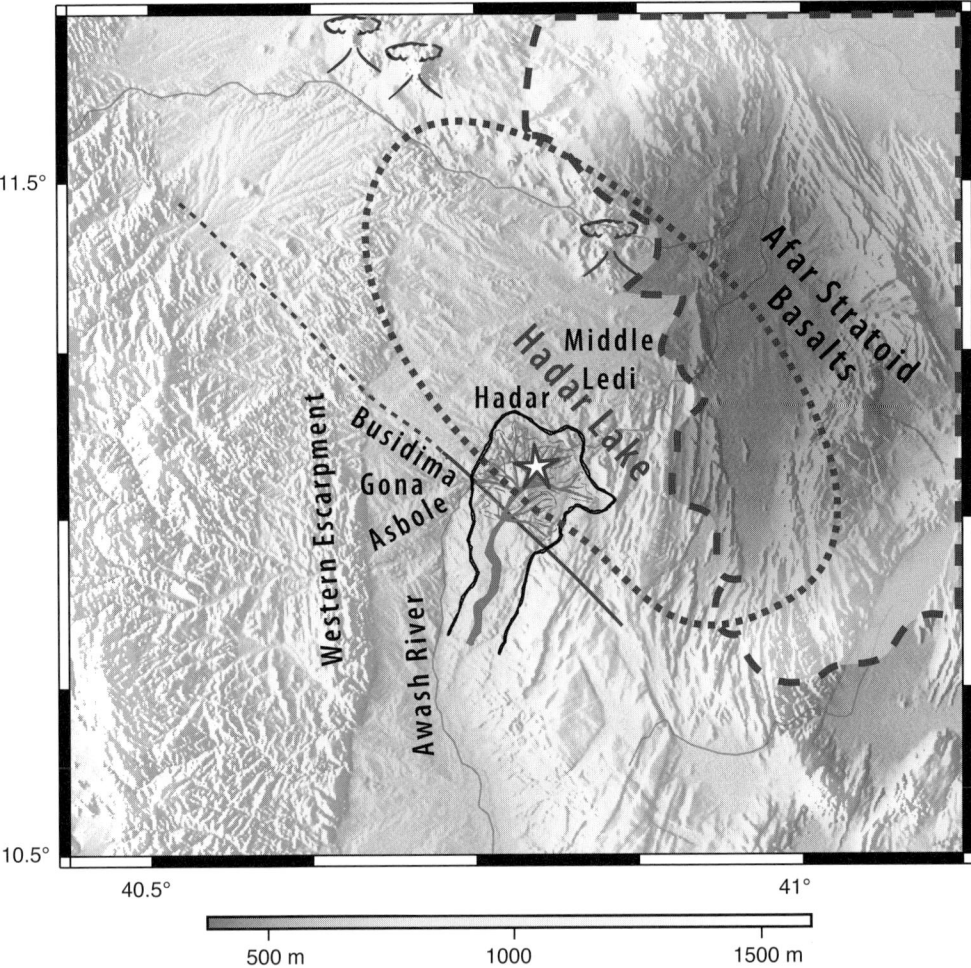

Figure 19.6 Paleogeography and paleoenvironments of the DIK-1 locality (red star) near the base of the Sidi Hakoma Member at 3.32 Ma, with a braided fluvial system (in blue) at the margin of Lake Hadar to the northeast (dashed blue line). Brown color indicates lower elevations in the modern regional landscape. The approximate locations of other areas are also indicated (Middle Ledi, Hadar, Gona, Busidima, Asbole, etc.). (A black and white version of this figure will appear in some formats. For the color version, please refer to the plate section.)

in the Dikika area during times of soil formation (Figure 19.7; Cerling et al., 2011). Stable carbon isotopes from mammalian dental enamel indicate that Dikika mammals relied on both C_3 and C_4 resources for their diet, with some taxa being primarily browsers (e.g., giraffids, deinotheriids), others primarily grazers (e.g., alcelaphin bovids, elephantids), and some mixed-feeders (e.g., *Kolpochoerus*; Bedaso et al., 2013). Mammals from Hadar were also sampled for stable isotopes (Wynn et al., 2016), and we integrate these results into our discussion of the Dikika fauna.

Vertebrate Paleontology

The Dikika Research Project has defined over 100 fossil vertebrate localities within the project area. Each locality is given the prefix DIK followed by a number, as in DIK-1. Fossil specimens in each locality are then numbered consecutively as in DIK-1-1, DIK-1-2, etc. Some localities may have a single fossil specimen, while the richest locality (DIK-41) has 163 identified specimens (NISP). Most localities occur in the SH Member, followed by the Basal Member. The DD and KH Members are not well exposed at Dikika, with only a few localities from these stratigraphic

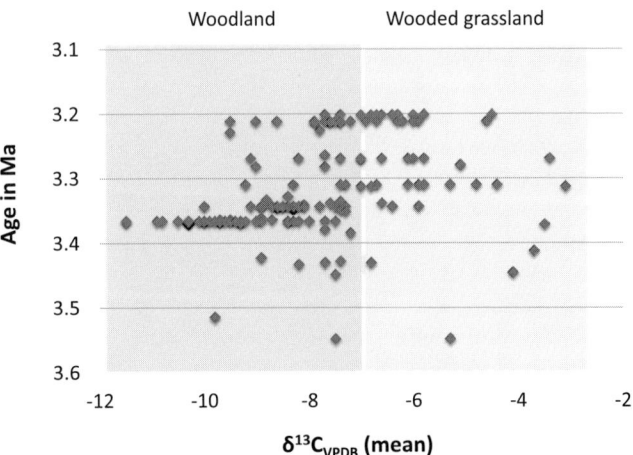

Figure 19.7 Pedogenic carbonate $\delta^{13}C$ values (with the standard Vienna Pee Dee Belemnite, $\delta^{13}C_{VPDB}$) showing $^{13}C/^{12}C$ ratios in the Basal, Sidi Hakoma, and Denen Dora members at Dikika, from about 3.55 Ma to 3.2 Ma, with data from Wynn et al., 2006 and Cerling et al., 2011b. The shaded areas indicate woodlands and wooded grasslands as in Cerling et al. (2011b). (A black and white version of this figure will appear in some formats. For the color version, please refer to the plate section.)

intervals. Thus, most of our discussions of Dikika fossil vertebrates refer to the Basal Member and Sidi Hakoma Member. In this regard, the Dikika paleontological record complements that of the Hadar Research Project, which has few samples from the Basal Member, and abundant fossils and localities from the DD and KH Members (Campisano and Feibel, 2007; Reed, 2008; Campisano et al., Chapter 18).

Collection Methods

Given the high abundance of fossils on the surface of the DRP area, it was clear from the first field surveys that not all specimens could be collected. Also, many parts of the Dikika exposures could only be reached on foot, and this made it logistically difficult to collect very large vertebrate elements, e.g., proboscideans, rhinocerotids, hippopotamids, and large turtles. These specimens were documented (e.g., taxon, skeletal element, stratigraphic level) and their GPS coordinates recorded, but were often left in the field. Thus, the DRP team established a set of criteria or collection protocols so that surface specimens could be collected in a systematic and consistent way from year to year. The criteria for the collection of surface fossils were the following (see also Reed et al., 2015; Thompson et al., 2015).

(1) All primate and carnivoran specimens, regardless of fragmentation or preservation.
(2) All mammalian cranial elements that could be identified at least to family. This category includes all bovid horn cores and giraffid ossicones. An exception was made for proboscideans and hippopotamids, which often proved to be logistically difficult to transport and curate. If uncollected, specimens were documented as to taxon, skeletal element, stratigraphic level, and GPS coordinates.
(3) All mammalian isolated teeth if at least half of the tooth was preserved.
(4) Complete crocodilian teeth were collected as bulk samples for each locality. In some localities they were very abundant.
(5) Relatively complete cranial elements of crocodiles, turtles, and fish.
(6) All mammalian astragali if at least half complete.
(7) All calcaneus, scapula, humerus, radius, ulna, femur, tibia, fibula, and metapodial fragments that were at least three fourths complete. Again, an exception was made for proboscideans and hippopotamids.
(8) All lizard and snake vertebrae.
(9) Mammalian long bones with at least one complete articular surface.
(10) Other specimens encountered in the field were not systematically collected but were always documented by taxon, skeletal element, stratigraphic level, and GPS coordinates.

Another collection methodology consisted of randomly choosing spots along a stratigraphic level for full surface collection and screening. We marked these spots with GPS coordinates and drew a circle with a radius of 3 m (Figure 19.8). All fossil specimens within the circle and to a depth of about 5 cm were collected. The purpose of these circle collections was to obtain a baseline of complete surface collections to assess paleoecological and taphonomic variables in relation to paleoenvironments and potential paleoecological interactions. These circle collections were analyzed by Thompson and colleagues (2015). Wet-sieving also took place in localities that were potentially rich in micromammals (see below). The DRP team has also pioneered the use of mobile devices and geospatial databases to systematically record collected specimens as well as those documented but left in the field (Reed et al., 2015).

Figure 19.8 Example of a circle collection (with 3 m radius) in the Andedo drainage locality DIK-41. The sample is 0.5 m below the Sidi Hakoma Tuff (the light color layer at the foot of the researchers) dated to 3.42 Ma. All surface specimens were collected as well as those retrieved from screening down to a depth of ~5 cm.

Overview of the Dikika Faunal Collections

Most of the fossil mammals in the Dikika Research Project faunal database derive from the Basal and Sidi Hakoma Members, with smaller samples from the Denen Dora and Kada Hadar Members (Table 19.1). Thus, the Basal and Sidi Hakoma Members form the basis of our discussions of the fauna. Table 19.1 provides the number of individual specimens in the Dikika database, and not necessarily the abundances of taxa in the exposures. These numbers reflect the different collection methods described above, and further taphonomic work is needed to establish relative abundances throughout the Hadar Formation exposures. Overall, there are six orders of mammals represented in the Dikika fossil sample. Artiodactyla is the most abundant order (817 specimens), followed by Proboscidea (138 specimens), Perissodactyla (89 specimens), Primates (67 specimens), Carnivora (33 specimens), and Rodentia (29 specimens). These orders include 18 families, with Bovidae the most abundant, followed by Hippopotamidae, Suidae, Equidae, Cercopithecidae, Giraffidae, Rhinocerotidae, and Elephantidae. These 8 families make up 95 percent of the fossils mammals. Figure 19.9 shows the abundance of fossil mammals identified to tribe or genus in the Sidi Hakoma Member. Here, the most abundant taxa are aff. *Hippopotamus*, *Aepyceros*, Bovini (mostly *Ugandax*), "*Hipparion*," *Kolpochoerus*, Alcelaphini, *Notochoerus*, *Nyanzachoerus*, *Giraffa*, *Tragelaphus*, and *Elephas*; these 11 taxa make up over 90 percent of the fossil mammals in the Sidi Hakoma Member (Figure 19.9). *Australopithecus* makes up about 1.2 percent of the mammals identified to tribe or genus. There are seven documented genera of megaherbivores (i.e., mammals weighing at least 1000 kg) in the collections: aff. *Hippopotamus*, *Giraffa*, *Sivatherium*, *Ceratotherium*, *Diceros*, *Elephas*, and *Deinotherium*. Below we provide further details of the Dikika fossil vertebrates.

Table 19.1 Mammal abundances, Dikika Research Project Hadar Formation. Includes documented but uncollected specimens.

	Hadar Formation Members					Hadar Formation Members			
	Basal	SH	DD	KH		Basal	SH	DD	KH
PRIMATES					*Crocuta dietrichi*	1	2	0	0
HOMINIDAE					*Crocuta* cf. *dietrichi*	0	2	0	0
Australopithecus afarensis	1	7	0	0	*Crocuta eturono*	0	0	0	1
CERCOPITHECIDAE					FELIDAE				
Cercopithecidae indet.	21	30	0	1	*Homotherium hadarensis*	0	1	0	0
Theropithecus darti	1	5	0	1	ARTIODACTYLA				
RODENTIA					BOVIDAE				
Rodentia indet.	4	5	0	0	Bovidae indet.	20	32	6	32
HYSTRICIDAE					*Tragelaphus* indet.	3	1	0	0
Hystix	0	3	0	0	*Tragelaphus* cf. *rastafari*	3	15	4	5
MURIDAE					Bovini indet.	3	8	0	1
Acomys coppensi	0	4	0	0	*Ugandax coryndonae*	5	55	1	0
Golunda gurai	2	7	0	0	*Aepyceros datoadeni*	14	64	1	2
Millardia taiebi	0	2	0	0	Reduncini indet.	4	2	0	0
aff. *Praomys* sp.	0	2	0	0	*Kobus* indet.	0	1	1	0
THRYONOMYIDAE					Hippotragini indet.	0	3	0	0
Thryonomys	2	0	0	0	*Oryx deturi*	0	2	0	0
CARNIVORA					Alcelaphini	5	42	1	2
Carnivora indet.	3	5	1	1	GIRAFFIDAE				
CANIDAE					Giraffidae indet.	5	8	0	0
Canidae indet.	0	2	0	0	*Giraffa jumae*	2	18	2	1
Nyctereutes lockwoodi	0	2	1	0	*Giraffa pygmaea*	0	1	0	0
MUSTELIDAE					*Sivatherium maurusium*	2	3	0	0
Enhydriodon dikikae	3	5	0	0	HIPPOPOTAMIDAE				
Lutra hearsti	0	1	0	0	aff. *Hippopotamus* sp. Hadar	53	180	5	8
HERPESTIDAE					SUIDAE				
cf. *Herpestes* sp.	0	1	0	0	Suidae indet.	14	28	1	0
HYAENIDAE					*Kolpochoerus afarensis*	14	45	0	2
Hyaenidae indet.	0	1	0	0	*Nyanzachoerus kanamensis*	11	20	0	1

Table 19.1 (cont.)

	Hadar Formation Members					Hadar Formation Members			
	Basal	SH	DD	KH		Basal	SH	DD	KH
Notochoerus euilus	16	31	3	5	Diceros praecox	0	1	0	0
PERISSODACTYLA					PROBOSCIDEA				
EQUIDAE					Proboscidea indet.	43	61	5	1
Equidae indet.	3	4	0	0	ELEPHANTIDAE				
"Eurygnathohippus" s.l. cf. hasumense	2	47	2	2	Elephantidae indet.	1	2	0	0
RHINOCEROTIDAE					Elephas recki	6	14	0	1
Rhinocerotidae indet.	2	21	1	1	DEINOTHERIIDAE				
Ceratotherium mauritanicum	0	3	0	0	Deinotherium bozasi	1	2	0	1

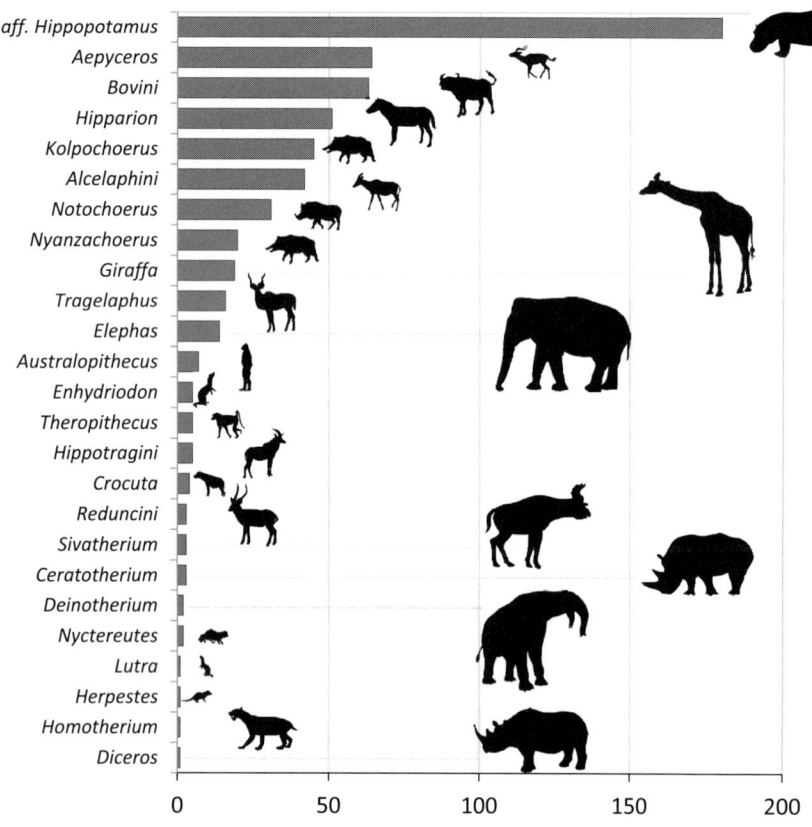

Figure 19.9 Abundance of fossil mammals identified to tribe or genus in the Sidi Hakoma Member. There are seven genera of megaherbivores, with *Hippopotamus* as most abundant. The relative abundance of *Australopithecus* is about 1.2 percent of the mammalian fauna. Silhouettes from phylopic.org.

Primates

There are eight hominin specimens from the Dikika Hadar Formation, all assigned to *Australopithecus afarensis*. The earliest of these specimens is the only known hominin from the Basal Member of the Hadar Formation, the mandible fragment DIK-2-1, with a date older than 3.42 Ma (Alemseged et al., 2005). The well-known Dikika juvenile, DIK-1-1 ("Selam"; Figure 19.10), derives from the lower SH Member and dates to about 3.32 Ma (Alemseged et al., 2006). This specimen provides key information about the ontogeny and adaptations of *A. afarensis*, and indicates that, although fully bipedal on the ground, the species also had arboreal adaptations (Green and Alemseged, 2012; DeSilva et al., 2018). The other Dikika hominins also derive from the SH Member. With a total of seven specimens in the SH Member, hominins make up about 1.2 percent of the fossil mammals in that member. Three hominin specimens have been sampled for stable carbon isotopes to infer dietary preferences, and these provide $\delta^{13}C$ values ranging from −10.6‰, indicating a C_3 diet, to −4.3‰, indicating a mixed C_3–C_4 diet (Wynn et al., 2013). These values fall within the range of variation of the hominin sample from Hadar (Wynn et al., 2016). Although other hominin species have been documented from this time elsewhere in eastern Africa, e.g. *Kenyanthropus platyops* in the Turkana Basin

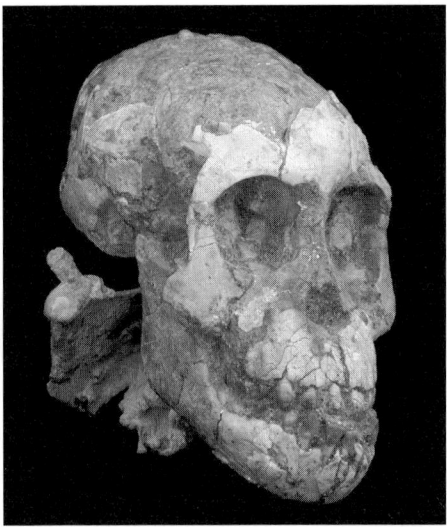

Figure 19.10 Specimen DIK-1–1 *Australopithecus afarensis* juvenile from the lower Sidi Hakoma Member, ~3.32 Ma.

(Leakey et al., 2001), *A. deyiremeda* in the Woranso-Mille area (Haile-Selassie et al., 2015), these have not been identified in the Hadar Formation.

There are 60 cercopithecid specimens from Dikika. Cercopithecids are the fifth most abundant mammalian family, but this important collection has yet to be described in detail and awaits further work. The species *Theropithecus darti* is represented by at least seven specimens. This species has been well described at Hadar (Eck, 1993), where it is the most abundant primate. At Hadar there are also specimens assigned to *Parapapio*, cf. *Rhinocolobus*, and *Cercopithecoides* (Frost and Delson, 2002). During equivalent periods in the Turkana Basin, *Theropithecus brumpti* is the most common primate in the Lokochot and lower Tulu Bor members of the Koobi Fora Formation (Jablonski and Leakey, 2008).

Rodentia

A small collection of micromammal specimens was recovered by dry-screening from three localities at Dikika: DIK-1 (12 specimens) and DIK-2 (2 specimens), and DIK-58 (12 specimens), and 5 larger rodent specimens were recovered from surface collections. Specimens were recovered by dry-screening at all localities down to 2-mm mesh, and wet-screening a subset of sediment from each locality down to 1 mm. Identifications are based on reference material from modern East African sites (Reed, 2007, 2011a), as well as published and newly collected Pliocene-age specimens from Hadar (Sabatier, 1982; Reed, 2011b; Reed and Geraads, 2012). The material comprises mostly well-preserved mandibles and isolated molars, but also includes a nearly complete skull of *Golunda gurai* from DIK-2.

The murid material comprises specimens assigned *Acomys coppensi*, *Golunda gurai*, *Millardia taiebi*, and aff. *Praomys* sp. These assignments are based on similarities to material from Hadar and using the taxonomic designations erected by Sabatier (1982), with the exception of *Acomys coppensi*, which is described by Sabatier as *Millardia coppensi*, but shows apomorphies attributable to *Acomys*, based on analysis of the latter by Denys, and is here referred to that genus (Denys, 1990a, 1990b). The validity of the other taxonomic attributions merits further comparison against a database of rodent character apomorphies from a broader geographic extent. In addition to the murid rodent remains, two larger rodent taxa are present: *Thryonomys* sp. and *Hystrix* sp. Cane rats (*Thryonomys*) are common to river margin grassland habitats in Africa and porcupines (*Hystrix*) are broadly distributed across the continent.

There do not appear to be significant differences in the taxonomic composition between localities. The two localities with the largest samples, DIK-1 and DIK-58, have largely overlapping taxonomic representation. The one exception is *Millardia taiebi*, which is known only from DIK-1. However, as there are only two specimens the difference may be due to chance.

The biogeographic and paleoecological significance of these taxa were previously described as indicating a relatively high level of species diversity for such a small sample, and also for indicating biotic exchange with Asia during the Pliocene because the genera *Golunda* and *Millardia* are today restricted to that continent (Sabatier, 1982; Reed and Geraads, 2012). The faunal composition indicates an intermediary, mesic bushland environment. The absence of arid-adapted taxa such as gerbillids is inconsistent with a dry grassland or semi-arid environment such as the Serengeti short grass plains (Reed, 2011a), and the absence of forest-adapted and arboreal taxa (e.g., *Thallomys*, *Oenomys*) argues against a dense or closed canopy, woodland/forest environment. However, the samples are very small, and span a roughly 200-kyr time interval from the Basal Member at *ca.* 3.5 Ma (locality DIK-58) up into the Sidi Hakoma Member at *ca.* 3.3 Ma (DIK-1).

Carnivora

This group has been studied in some detail at Dikika (Geraads et al., 2010b, 2011, 2015b), allowing precise identifications, and the naming of three new species. The canid *Nyctereutes lockwoodi* (Geraads et al., 2010b) belongs to a genus that is quite rare in Africa; it could be an immigrant from southern Asia. It was certainly an omnivorous form, as indicated by its dental morphology, perhaps feeding on plants, carrion, and small animals like its modern relative, *N. procyonoides*. There is no evidence in the Afar of a fox, jackal, or larger canid similar to the Simien wolf (*Canis simensis*). Among the Mustelidae, no form of small size has been discovered yet. The only mustelids are two new species of otters. *Enhydriodon dikikae* (Geraads et al., 2011) from the Basal Member of the Hadar Formation is a gigantic form, probably weighing around 200 kg (Figure 19.11). It is not closely related to modern otters, but instead to a group widespread in Africa and southern Asia in the Pliocene. It was probably less aquatic than living forms, although its diet may have consisted of mollusks, crabs, and perhaps catfishes that its powerful teeth were able to crush. *Lutra hearsti* (Geraads et al., 2015) is similar to modern Old World otters (*Lutra*, *Hydrictis*, and *Aonyx*) and could be close to the base of their phyletic tree. It likely had a similar ecology, feeding mostly on fishes. A mongoose, *Herpestes* sp., is represented by a single tooth, but it is likely that screening would increase the sample of Herpestidae. All specimens of Hyaenidae belong to the genus *Crocuta*, the most common

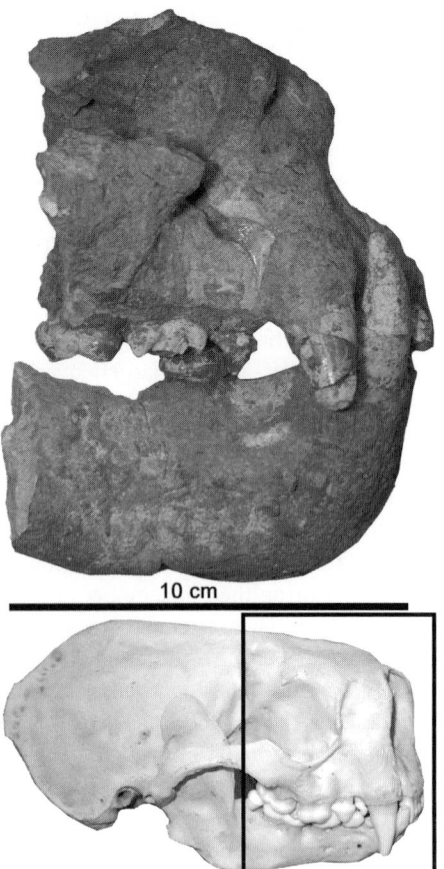

Figure 19.11 Specimen DIK-56–9 *Enhydriodon dikikae*, a giant otter from the lower Basal Member, ~3.8 Ma, compared to a modern sea otter, *Enhydra lutris*, at the same scale; the rectangle indicates the part preserved in the fossil. Modern otter photograph from https://commons.wikimedia.org/wiki/File:Enhydra_lutris_10zz.jpg.

large African carnivores today. All species are characterized by their robust crushing premolars, but differences in their size and proportions allow the distinction of two species, the primitive *C. dietrichi* that could be the stem group from which all later *Crocuta* arose, and the large *C. eturono*, which reached the size of the much younger cave and spotted hyenas. *Homotherium hadarensis* is the only Felidae recorded at Dikika, and it is also known from Hadar (Petter and Howell, 1988), but it is unlikely that this saber-tooth predator was the only one at the top of the food web. Further fieldwork at Dikika may yield a richer sample of felids.

Artiodactyla

Among Bovidae, Tragelaphini are relatively common in the Basal Member (about 16 percent of bovids identified to tribe) and the SH Member (about 8 percent of bovids identified to tribe), but few specimens are complete enough for species identification. The typical form of *T. nakuae*, best known from Omo, is certainly absent, and most large tragelaphins probably belong to its likely ancestor *T. rastafari* (Bibi, 2011a). Stable carbon isotopes from dental enamel indicate a mixed diet of C_3 and C_4 resources in Dikika Tragelaphini (Bedaso et al., 2013), similar to the diet derived from Hadar samples (Wynn et al., 2016). Bovini are identified to the species *Ugandax coryndonae* (Gentry, 2006). This early buffalo had short horns directed postero-dorso-laterally; thus, their orientation was rather different from those of other African bovins. The size range of the most common bone, the astragalus, encompasses that of the whole Hadar collection. This species is quite common at Dikika, as in the lower part of the sequence at Hadar. At locality DIK-41, for instance, where we carried out systematic paleontological sampling and screening, *Ugandax* makes up 16 percent of fossil vertebrates, which include abundant hippopotamids and crocodiles. This association with semi-aquatic and aquatic taxa might indicate *Ugandax*'s preference for environments close to water. *Ugandax* shows a mixed C_3/C_4 feeding strategy but with a preference for C_4 grasses (Bedaso et al., 2013; Wynn et al., 2016). The impala, *Aepyceros datoadeni* (Geraads et al., 2012a), is a common form (more than 33 percent of all bovids identified to tribe) at Dikika, as in the lower part of the sequence at Hadar. The range of variation of the horn-core measurements is large, one specimen even reaching the size of *Aepyceros afarensis* from Woranso-Mille (Geraads et al., 2009a), but some Hadar specimens are also quite large, and the Dikika form can be assigned to the Hadar species. *Aepyceros* diets as deduced from stable carbon isotopes ranged from C_4-dominated to C_3/C_4 mixed strategies (Bedaso et al., 2013; Wynn et al., 2016). Reduncini are rare from the base of the SH Member, as at Hadar, but a mandible might represent a species larger than the Hadar forms. In the abundant sample from the Denen Dora Member at Hadar, Reduncini make up about 30 percent of the bovid fauna and have a C_4-dominated diet (Wynn et al., 2016). Among Hippotragini, the species *Oryx deturi*, first recorded from Laetoli (Dietrich, 1950), differs from modern *Oryx* in that its horn cores are less transversally compressed and less inclined backwards. It may be relatively more common at Dikika than at Hadar (Geraads et al., 2012a). A few hippotragin teeth are probably of the same species. The tribe Alcelaphini is well represented by their robust dental remains, but horn cores do not preserve so well and only a few have been retrieved. Some belong to the first stage of the most common Hadar lineage, *Damalborea elisabethae* (Gentry, 2010), but two others belong to one or more of the rarest Hadar species, i.e., *Parmularius* cf. *pachyceras* and/or Alcelaphini gen. et sp. indet. A (Geraads et al., 2012a; please note that Table 19.1 provides only the total numbers of Alcelaphini in each member). The mean $\delta^{13}C$ of alcelaphin teeth is indicative of a grazing diet at Dikika (Bedaso et al., 2013) and at Hadar (Wynn et al., 2016). There is no evidence of *Gazella* or other Antilopini, but this tribe is rare at Hadar, especially in the lower part of the sequence, in contrast to the overlying Busidima Formation. A multivariate analysis of bovid tribal abundances from Dikika and other sites is shown below in the section entitled "Correspondence Analysis."

Among giraffids, *Giraffa* is more common than *Sivatherium* at Dikika, as at Hadar. Most of the specimens are of similar size, and can be identified as *Giraffa jumae*, a species that chiefly differs from the modern form in its less pneumatized skull (Geraads et al., 2013a). A radius and associated metacarpal from DIK-55 are of distinctly smaller size, and are in fact the only sound evidence for the presence of the rare *G. pygmaea* in the Hadar Formation. It confirms the suggestion by Geraads et al. (2013a) that its absence at Hadar itself was due to incomplete sampling. The large *Sivatherium maurusium* of buffalo-like proportions but of much larger size is much less common, especially as most giraffid bones unidentified to genus are probably of *Giraffa*.

Hippopotamids are the most common large mammals at Dikika, as in other eastern African sites. All specimens from Dikika fall within the usual morphological and metric ranges of a single species, and there is no evidence of a second one (Hadar hippos used to be considered two species: *Trilobophorus afarensis* and *Hexaprotodon coryndoni*; Gèze, 1985). The Dikika hippopotamids are probably the same taxon as those from Hadar, a hexaprotodont species with a wide symphysis and second incisors similar in size to the third incisors but distinctly smaller than the central ones. It is likely an early member of the *Hippopotamus protamphibius* lineage, first considered as a distinct species by Gèze (1985), but called aff. *Hippopotamus* cf. *protamphibius* by Weston and Boisserie (2010). More recently, Boisserie suggests the provisional label "aff. *Hippopotamus* sp. Hadar" until a comprehensive taxonomic revision can be published (Boisserie, 2020). This species would have been present from the Turkana Basin (at Kanapoi) to the Afar, from 4.2 Ma to 3 Ma. Dikika hippopotamids have $\delta^{13}C$ values indicative of a mixed C_3/C_4 diet (Bedaso et al., 2013).

Three species of Suidae are present at Dikika, as at Hadar. *Kolpochoerus* M3s/m3s from the SH Member are on the average intermediate in size between those of *K. millensis* from the earlier sites of Woranso-Mille (Haile-Selassie and Simpson, 2013) and those of *K. afarensis* from the overlying Denen Dora Member (Cooke, 1978b), but the smallest specimen is as small as *K. deheinzelini* from the lower Pliocene (Brunet and White, 2001), which indicates that isolated teeth should be used with caution in biostratigraphy. Teeth of *Nyanzachoerus kanamensis* are similar to those from Hadar, but one M3, uncollected because it was found at a time when its stratigraphic position was unknown, almost reaches the size of *Notochoerus jaegeri* from Kanapoi; we refrain from adding this name to the Dikika faunal list, however. Third molars of *Notochoerus euilus* do not increase in length, and may even undergo some shortening through the Hadar Formation, but there is no doubt that the last lower premolars from the Basal and Sidi Hakoma members are larger than those from the Denen Dora Member, thus clearly illustrating the transition from *Nyanzachoerus* to a typical *Notochoerus*. The three suid genera in the Hadar Formation have $\delta^{13}C$ values indicative of a mixed C_3/C_4 diet, but in some cases have a significant C_4 component (Bedaso et al., 2013; Wynn et al., 2016).

Perissodactyla

Equids appear to be represented by a single species at Dikika, "*Hipparion*" s.l. cf. *hasumense*. Identification of hipparion fossils on the basis of incomplete remains is risky, but the Dikika species does not seem to differ from the most common Hadar one. It is now usually assigned to *Eurygnathohippus* (Bernor et al., 2010), a genus said to include all Plio-Pleistocene African hipparions and defined by a single synapomorphy, the presence of an ectostylid. However, this structure is in fact lacking in some of them, and definite evidence that all Plio-Pleistocene African hipparions form a monophyletic group is still lacking (Eisenmann and Geraads, 2007). Most Dikika and Hadar equids have $\delta^{13}C$ values indicative of grazing, and serial samples from single teeth indicate that C_4 grasses were available year-round in the area (Bedaso et al., 2013; Wynn et al., 2016).

Among Rhinocerotidae, *Ceratotherium mauritanicum*, a primitive form of the white rhino, is probably the most common form (Geraads, 2005), although distinction of postcranial remains from those of *Diceros* on a size basis is impossible, as representatives of the latter genus were larger than modern ones. The site DIK-1 yielded a complete cranium (Geraads, 2005) of *Ceratotherium mauritanicum*. The species *Diceros praecox* used to be included in *Ceratotherium*, but the type specimen from Ekora is clearly a *Diceros*. A skull was found at the base of the SH Member but remains uncollected. Some of the Dikika rhinocerotids have $\delta^{13}C$ values that indicate a mixed C_3/C_4 diet, but two specimens identified to *Ceratotherium* from the Basal Member have a grazing signature (Bedaso et al., 2013). This would indicate that by 3.5 Ma *Ceratotherium* was already adapted to a grazing diet.

Proboscidea

Elephant remains are common, but collecting most of them proved logistically impossible. An uncollected cranium of *Elephas* from the base of the SH Member resembles *E. recki brumpti* more than *E. ekorensis*. However, isolated molars have various degrees of hypsodonty and plate numbers, regardless of their stratigraphic levels, and the more brachyodont ones are reminiscent of *E. ekorensis*, suggesting coexistence of these closely related species, whose evolution appears more complex than a single anagenetic lineage. *Loxodonta* may also be present, as its teeth at that stage are very similar. Dikika elephantids have $\delta^{13}C$ values that indicate a diet based primarily on C_4 grasses (Bedaso et al., 2013). *Deinotherium bozasi* is mostly represented by enamel fragments, but there are also some well-preserved teeth from the Kada Hadar Member. *Deinotherium* was a pure browser (Bedaso et al., 2013; Wynn et al., 2016), so that it is unlikely that its downwardly curved lower tusks were used for digging, but their function remains a matter of debate.

Other Vertebrates

Crocodile teeth are common in the Dikika exposures. Most of them belong to *Crocodylus*, although the piscivorous *Euthecodon* is also present. A snake vertebra from DIK-1 was identified as cf. *Naja* sp. A large terrestrial tortoise is moderately common, but its remains are not complete enough for species assignment, especially as the systematics of these forms is still debated, and we provisionally assign it to *Geochelone* s.l. Aquatic turtles are also common in the collections, with most specimens belonging to the family Pelomedusidae. In the circle collections (see "Collection Methods" above), fishes constitute about 35 percent of the fauna (Thompson et al., 2015).

Correspondence Analysis of Bovid Tribes

To place Dikika in the broader context of Africa, we conduct a CA of bovid tribes across several sites in the time range from 3.8 Ma to 3.0 Ma. CA is a multivariate ordination method to describe contingency tables with categorical data commonly used in ecology and paleoecology (Greenacre, 1993). Here we use Paleontological Statistics (PAST) software version 4.0 (Hammer et al., 2001, 2020). The time frame from 3.8 to 3.0 Ma encompasses the known time range of *A. afarensis*. From Dikika, we use only the Basal Member and the SH Member as analytical units, because the DD Member and KH Member have samples that are too small. From Hadar we use all four members of the Hadar Formation as separate analytical units with data from Campisano and Feibel (2007) and Reed (2008). Bovid tribal abundance data for other sites come from the following sources: Woranso-Mille localities Aralee Issie (ARI) and Mesgid Dora (MSD) (Haile-Selassie et al., 2010b; Curran and Haile-Selassie, 2016), Lower Laetolil Beds at Laetoli (LLB; Su, 2011), and Koro Toro locality KT13 in Chad (Geraads et al., 2001).

The correspondence analysis shows that the Dikika and Hadar members group close together in the upper right quadrant of the graph (Figure 19.12), indicating that Dikika and Hadar have comparable proportions of bovid tribes. Given the geographical proximity of these research areas, it is not surprising that they display similar bovid proportions during the same time intervals, although some minor local differences may occur (e.g., Dikika sampling habitats farther from the shores of Hadar Lake, as in Figure 19.6). In this regard, the Dikika and Hadar research areas sample different geographic regions of the same ecosystem. The Woranso-Mille localities of Aralee Issie (ARA) and Mesgid Dora (MSD) also plot close to the Hadar Formation Basal and Sidi Hakoma members. Again, this is not surprising given that Woranso-Mille is about 20 km north of Hadar, even if it samples a somewhat earlier time period. Along the first axis, it is Laetoli (Upper Laetolil Beds) that falls farthest from the Dikika and Hadar localities. Neotragini is the most abundant bovid tribe in the Upper Laetolil Beds, followed by Alcelaphini and Antilopini. These bovid proportions along with other lines of evidence indicate that Laetoli environments were probably drier, with greater proportions of grasslands and bushland than those in the Afar region (Su, 2011). Along the second axis, the Chad site of Koro Toro is farthest from the Dikika localities. At Koro Toro (KT13), the most abundant bovid tribe is Alcelaphini, followed by Reduncini and Antilopini. Aepycerotini and Tragelaphini are absent from Koro Toro (Geraads et al., 2001). Thus, the environments at Koro Toro were likely more open than those in the Afar during this time, with a greater proportion of grasslands.

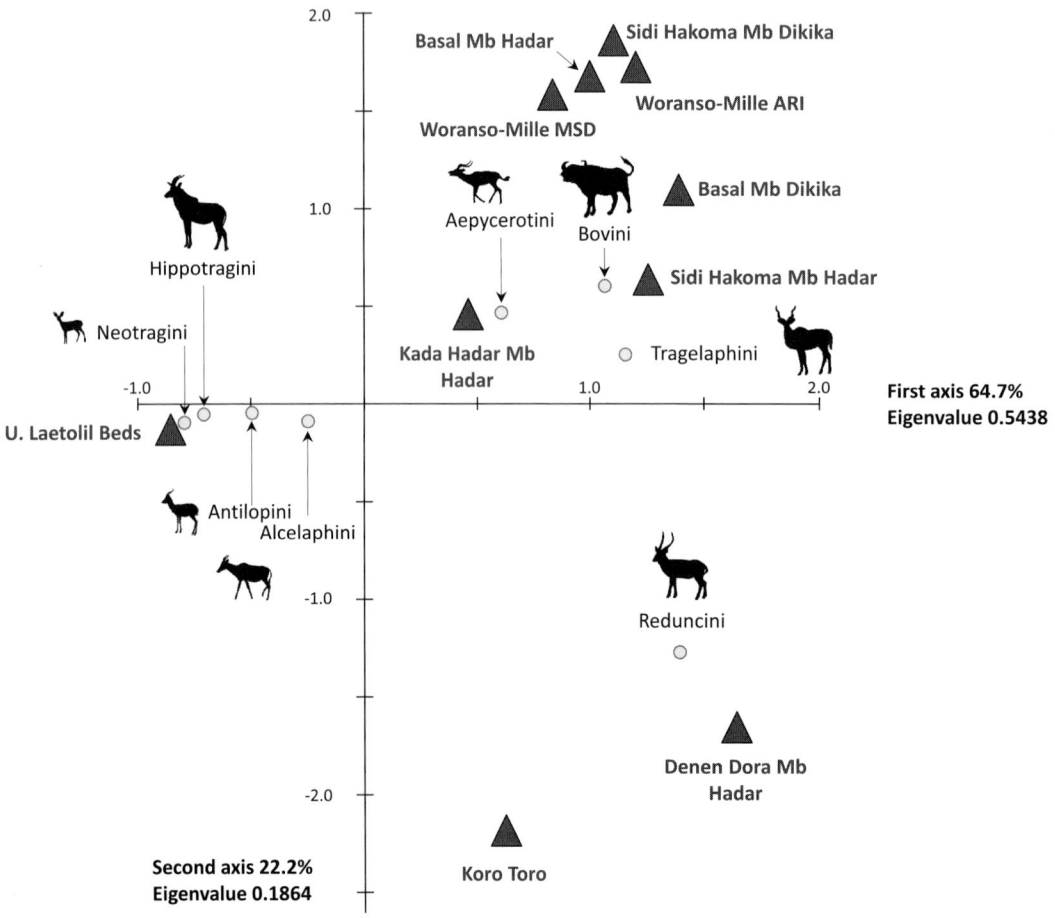

Figure 19.12 Correspondence analysis of bovid tribes (circles) from Dikika (Basal Member and Sidi Hakoma Member), Hadar (Basal, Sidi Hakoma, Denen Dora, and Kada Hadar Members), Woranso-Mille (localities ARI and MSD), Laetoli (Upper Laetolil Beds), and Koro Toro (KT13). Sites are represented by triangles. Bovid silhouettes from PhyloPic.org.

Australopithecus afarensis in Context

The genus *Australopithecus* has its earliest record at about 4.2 Ma in the Kanapoi Formation in the Turkana Basin of Kenya (Ward et al., 2020). The Kanapoi hominins are assigned to the species *A. anamensis* (Leakey et al., 1995, 1998), likely the direct ancestor of *A. afarensis* (Kimbel et al., 2006). By 4.1–3.9 Ma, there are records of *A. anamensis* at Asa Issie in the Afar region of Ethiopia (White et al., 2006), as well as elsewhere in the Turkana Basin (Allia Bay, Fejej; Fleagle et al., 1991; Ward et al., 1999a). Thus, by about 4 Ma *Australopithecus* was distributed from the Turkana Basin in the south to the Afar region in the north. At Kanapoi, *Australopithecus* thrived in complex and dynamic environments with a mix of woodlands, grasslands, and riverine forests in an ecosystem that had plenty of fresh water (Bobe et al., 2020a). It is noteworthy that there are other paleontological sedimentary sequences in eastern Africa from the interval 4.2 to 3.9 Ma (e.g., Mursi Formation, Lower Laetolil Beds, Wembere-Manonga Formation) that do not have evidence of *Australopithecus* or other hominins, even though other mammals were abundant (Drapeau et al., Chapter 23; Harrison, 1997a, 2011a, 2011b; Drapeau et al., 2014). It is likely that the high abundance of *A. anamensis* at Kanapoi, and to some extent at Asa Issie, may be explained by these sites having the right mix of woodland, grassland, and water resources that this species needed. It is interesting that even though C_4 dietary resources were clearly available at Kanapoi, *Australopithecus* at that time had an essentially C_3 diet.

In the transition between *A. anamensis* and its descendant *A. afarensis*, there was a dietary shift from a reliance on C_3 resources to a diet that included both C_3 and C_4 foods (Sponheimer et al., 2013; Wynn et al., 2013, 2016; Levin et al., 2015). It may be argued that this dietary shift led to an expansion in the geographic range of *A. afarensis*. By 3.6–3.3 Ma, *A. afarensis* had a wider geographic distribution, with records at Laetoli (Upper Laetolil Beds; Harrison, 2011b), Kantis (on the shoulders of the Kenya Rift; Mbua et al., 2016), Koobi Fora (Tulu Bor Member; Kimbel, 1988), Middle Awash (Maka; White et al., 1993; Lovejoy et al., 2002), Dikika (Alemseged et al., 2005, 2006), Hadar (Johanson et al., 1982b; Kimbel and Delezene, 2009), Woranso-Mille (Haile-Selassie et al., 2010a), and possibly as far west as Koro Toro in Chad, although the species there is often referred to *A. bahrelghazali* (Brunet et al., 1995).

Although *A. afarensis* had a wide geographic distribution in eastern Africa, in some places it was significantly more abundant than in others. In the Sidi Hakoma Member at Dikika, *A. afarensis* makes up about 1.2 percent of fossil mammals identified to genus or tribe (Figure 19.9), a relatively high proportion by hominin standards (Bobe and Leakey, 2009). This proportion may be slightly higher at Hadar (Campisano and Feibel, 2007; Reed, 2008). However, *A. afarensis* at Laetoli was a very rare species, making up about 0.2 percent of the identified large mammalian fauna (Su and Harrison, 2008). The higher proportion of *A. afarensis* in the Hadar Formation may be indicative of habitat preferences. The species *A. afarensis* seems to have preferred habitats similar to those of its putative direct ancestor, *A. anamensis*, with a mix of woodlands, grasslands, and riverine forests in ecosystems that had readily available fresh water. Dikika and Hadar seem to have provided the right balance of mixed habitats and resources for these hominins to thrive.

Conclusions

In the past two decades, the site of Dikika in the Afar region of Ethiopia has provided valuable new information about the adaptations and paleoenvironments of the species *Australopithecus afarensis*. The Dikika Research Project has documented about 1400 fossil vertebrates from the Pliocene Hadar Formation, especially from the Basal Member and the Sidi Hakoma Member. Of particular importance have been the discoveries of the *A. afarensis* juvenile skeleton DIK-1-1 and of three new species of carnivoran mammals. Dikika has also provided evidence of stone tool use in early hominins at 3.4 Ma at locality DIK-55. Analyses of Dikika's sedimentary environments, stable isotopes from paleosols and mammal teeth, and vertebrate communities indicate that *A. afarensis* occurred in dynamic environments with a mix of riverine forests, extensive woodlands, and wooded grasslands, in an ecosystem that had an abundant supply of fresh water. As a potential ancestor to both the *Homo* and *Paranthropus* lineages, *A. afarensis* played a pivotal role in hominin evolution. With the largest sample of *A. afarensis* in Africa, the Hadar Formation remains the key sequence for our understanding of this species.

20. Miocene to Pliocene Stratigraphy and Paleoecology of Galili, Ethiopia

Ottmar Kullmer, Oliver Sandrock, Thomas Bence Viola, Wolfgang Hujer, Zelalem Bedaso, Doris Nagel, Andrea Stadlmayr, Fritz Popp, Robert Scholger, Gerhard W. Weber, and Horst Seidler

History of Research

The first paleontological surveys of the Mullu basin in the Somali Region (Figure 20.1A,B) were conducted by Yohannes Haile-Selassie and colleagues in 1997. They collected several isolated hominin teeth, preliminarily attributed to *Australopithecus anamensis*, and a few other large mammal remains in the Galili area in the southern Afar depression of Ethiopia (Haile-Selassie and Asfaw, 2000). Subsequently, between 2000 and 2009, the International Paleoanthropological Research Team consisting of Ethiopian, Austrian, American, Italian, and German anthropologists, paleontologists, and geologists recovered and catalogued more than 2000 vertebrate fossils from Galili sites (Figure 20.1C) during annual field seasons. Besides a number of fish, reptile, bird, and small mammal remains, a great variety of large mammal species, including primates, carnivores, proboscideans, perissodactyls, and artiodactyls have been found (Kullmer et al., 2008). A right lower third molar (GLL 33) of a hominin was discovered on the surface near the foot of Galili hill by the local employee Mr. Abdellahi Ille during fieldwork in spring 2000. Macchiarelli and colleagues (2004a) attributed this specimen to the taxon *Australopithecus* cf. *afarensis*. Further hominin discoveries followed, including postcranial remains reported by Viola et al. (2008). Kullmer et al. (2008) described suid and proboscidean material, and interpreted their biostratigraphic correlations and the paleoecology in comparison to other Pliocene hominin sites in Kenya and Ethiopia. The first geological interpretations of the Galili Formation were published by Urbanek et al. (2005). A more detailed description of the lithostratigraphy and radiometric datings of the Galili Formation were provided in Hujer et al. (2015).

Geology, Radiometric Age, Paleomagnetism, and Lithostratigraphy

In a regional geological context, the volcano-sedimentary successions of the Galili Formation are located in the transition zone between the Northern Main Ethiopian Rift and the Southern Afar Rift. The sedimentary and volcanic deposits are ~230-m thick, constituting the Galili Formation which is subdivided in ascending stratigraphic order into the Lasdanan, Dhidinley, Godiray, Shabeley Laag, Dhagax, and Caashacado Members (Mbs; Figure 20.2). The individual members are defined by intercalated volcanic layers such as basalts, ignimbrites, and tuffs.

Radiometric and Paleomagnetic Data

Feldspar crystals separated from volcanic layers were dated by means of the $^{40}Ar/^{39}Ar$ method (Hujer et al., 2015). Paleomagnetic samples obtained from volcanic and mudstone intervals provided further age control, especially for intervals that have not been covered by radiometric dating. According to paleomagnetic investigations a total of 12 distinct paleomagnetic polarity intervals [N1–R6] could be identified in the Galili research area (Figure 20.2). The paleomagnetic study used primary magnetization vectors (PMVs) determined from magnetite, Ti–magnetite, hematite, and goethite out of volcanic and sedimentary layers from the Galili Formation. Thereby, in accordance with the radioisotopic data from tuff and ignimbrite layers intercalated in the sections (Hujer et al., 2015), these paleomagnetic polarity intervals were assigned to the Gilbert, upper Gauss and lower Matuyama polarity zones of the Global Polarity Time Scale (GPTS) from Cande and Kent (1995), thus providing a time frame of ~5.37 Ma to ~2.15 Ma for the deposition of the Galili Formation.

The lower four Members of the Galili Formation (Lasdanan, Dhidinley, Godiray, and Shabeley Laag Mbs.) containing fossil vertebrate remains cover nine magnetic polarity intervals (chrons C3r Gilbert [R6], C3 n.4 n Thvera [N6], C3n3 r Gilbert [R5], C3 n.3 n Sidufjall [N5], C3 n.2 r Gilbert [R4], C3 n.2 n Nunivak [N4], C3 n.1 r Gilbert [R3], C3 n.1 n Cochiti [N3], and C2Ar Gilbert [R2]) within a time span of 5.37–3.58 Ma for their deposition. The upper two members of the Galili Formation (Dhagax and Caashacado Mbs.) contain three polarity intervals (chrons C2An.1 n Gauss [N2], C2 r.2 r Matuyama [R1], and C2 r.1 n Reunion [N1]) ordered around a $^{40}Ar/^{39}Ar$ age of ~2.35 Ma for an ignimbrite layer, thereby providing the formation's upper age limit at ~2.15 Ma from magneto-stratigraphic aspects. In combination of the determined magnetic polarity data with this absolute age of 2.35 Ma, located in the middle of the upper Galili Formation sections, we must conclude that ~0.5 Ma and four polarity intervals are missing between the Galili Formation lower and upper members (Figure 20.2). We assign the resulting depositional gap to a crustal uplift process of the region due to intrusion of the Galili basalt magma in Upper Shabeley Laag Mb. times.

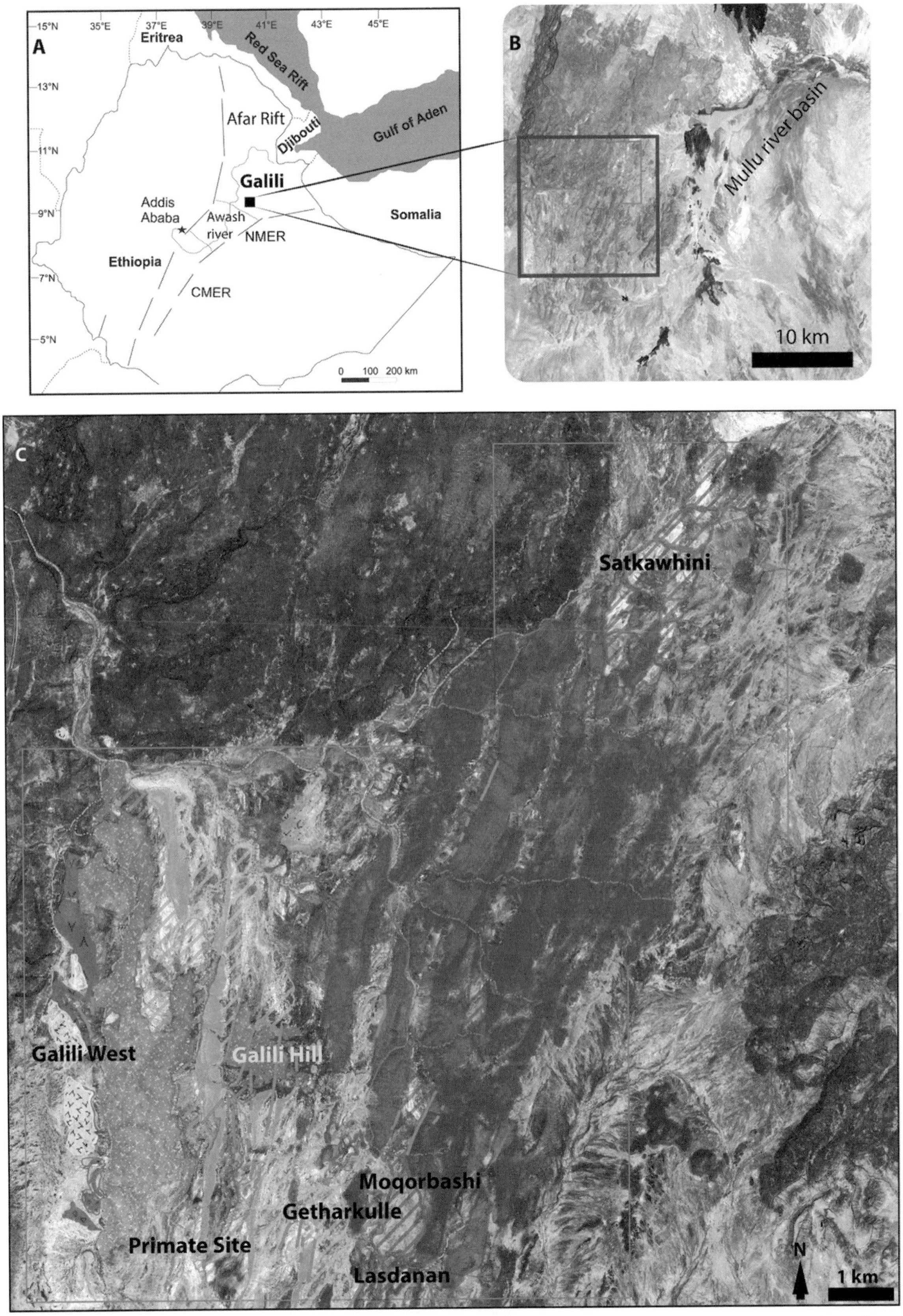

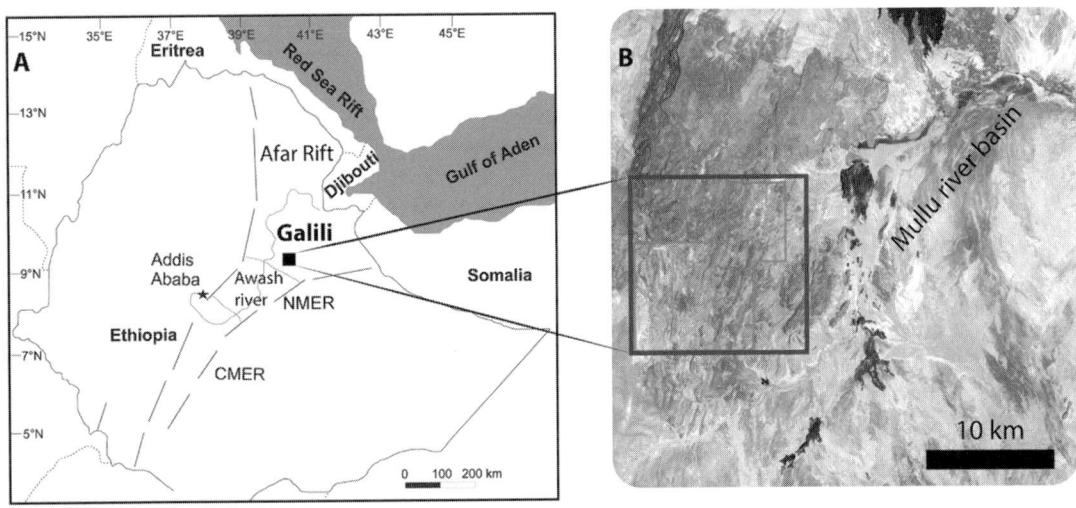

Figure 20.1 (A) The location map shows the Galili research area within the southwestern part of the Afar Rift, the Afar and the Northern Main Ethiopian Rift (NMER; modified from WoldeGabriel et al., 2013). (B) Satellite image showing the Galili research area (framed in black) west of the Mullu river basin. (C) Geological map of the research area based on IKONOS satellite image. Contoured areas represent volcanic layers whereas dashed lines refer to sediment and thin tuff exposures. Legend at the bottom refers to stratigraphic members: Lasdanan Mb., Dhidinley Mb., Godiray Mb., Shabeley Laag Mb., Dhagax Mb., Caashacado Mb., white lines: faults. Important fossil sites are named in white font (modified from Hujer et al., 2015). (A black and white version of this figure will appear in some formats. For the color version, please refer to the plate section.)

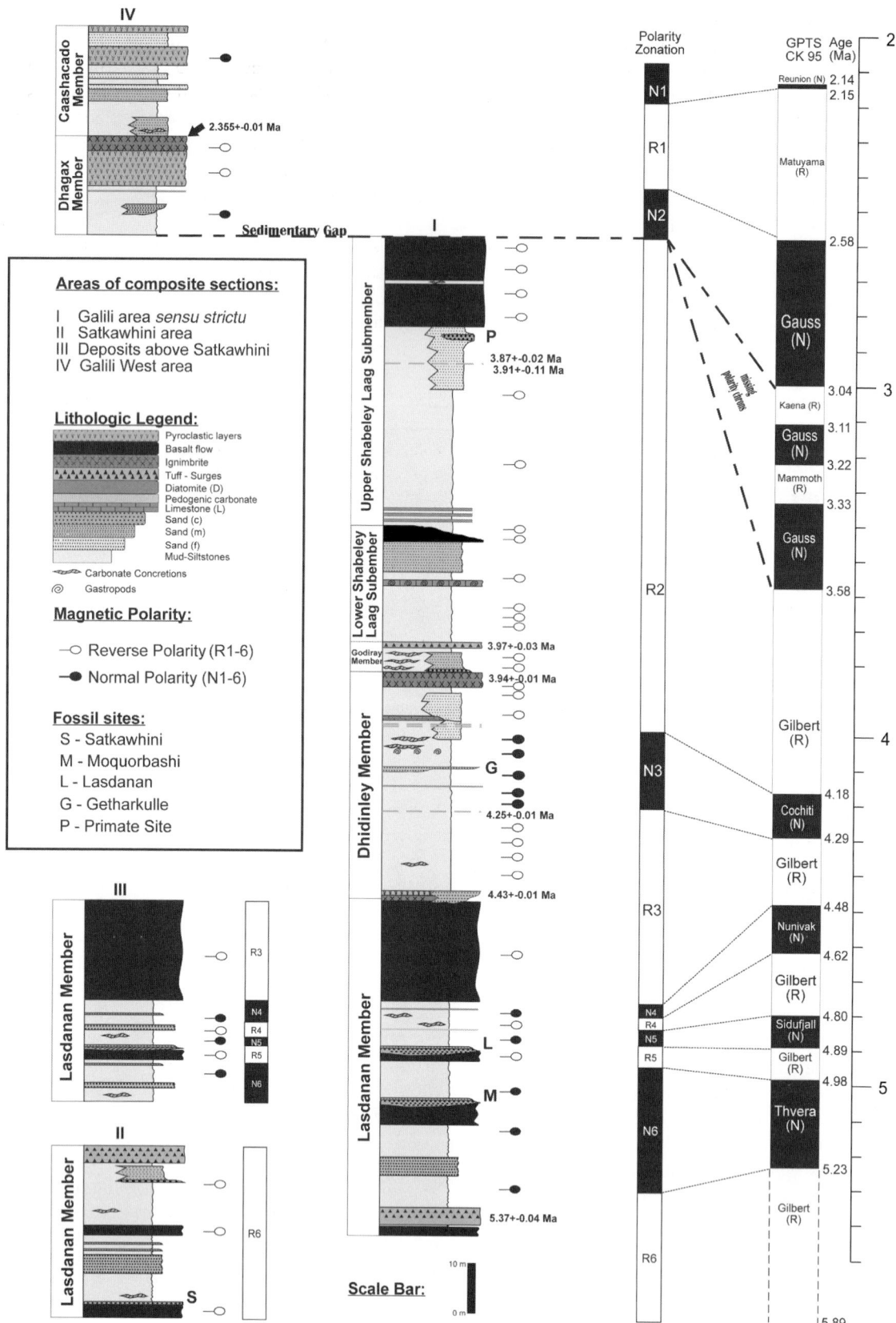

Figure 20.2 Composite lithostratigraphic chart of the Galili Formation with absolute age data, paleomagnetic polarity zonation, and correlation with the Global Polarity Time Scale (modified from Hujer et al., 2015). Column (I) gives the stratification of the Galili Formation, including the Lasdanan, Dhidinley, Godiray, Shabeley Laag Members. Column (II) is a generalized lithologic profile of the lower portion of the Lasdanan Member in the Satkawhini area. Column (III) indicates the portion of the Lasdanan Member above Satkawhini. Column (IV) shows the upper portion of the Galili Formation in the Galili West area with the Dhagax and Caashacado Mbs. above a sedimentary hiatus following the Shabeley Laag Mb. Capital letters in the columns indicate the stratigraphic position of important fossil sites.

Furthermore, the PMV data of volcanic layers indicate by their deviation from the expected paleodirection of the region at ~5 Ma (Besse and Cortillot, 2002) that the Galili research area was subjected thereafter (since the Pliocene) to rift-related tectonics involving crustal block rotation, tilting, and trans-tension relative to the stable African crust (Nubian plate).

In summary, we consider the Galili area being the place where stages of trans-tensional tectonics were active during the Pliocene/Pleistocene age, resulting in a lateral offset of magmatic segments marking the center of the Main Ethiopian Rift (Kidane et al., 2006). This trans-tensional movement is considered to belong to an arcuate accommodation zone in respect to the migration of the Afar triple junction since ~4 Ma (Wolfenden et al., 2005).

The sedimentary and volcanic successions of each member are briefly described below together with an interpretation of their depositional environments. A more detailed study on depositional settings is in preparation.

Lasdanan Member (<5.37–4.43 Ma)

The oldest Lasdanan Member describes the volcanic and sedimentary successions exposed below the fissure basalt flow capped by deposits of the basal Dhidinley Member. The Member varies in thickness between 60 and 80 m. At least five basalt horizons (1–5, Figure 20.2), most of them consisting of several flows, have been observed. The strong weathering and the lateral pinch out of intervening sedimentary successions complicate stratigraphic control of this member. Therefore, three composite columns (I–III) for the Lasdanan Member are represented in the composite stratigraphic chart (Figure 20.2). Column II (polarity zonation PZ R6) represents the stratigraphic successions of the Satkhawini area (Figure 20.1C). The sedimentary succession encased between basalt horizons 1 and 2 comprises basal pebbly–coarse-grained, cross-bedded sands to sandstones overlain by brownish mudstones containing root structures and carbonate concretions. These sandstones constitute the Satkawhini fossil site ("S," Figure 20.2). The muddy sequence is cut by a 3–5-m thick lenticular sandstone body followed by ~3 m interbedding of decimeter (dm)-thick siltstone and sandstone capped by a basalt horizon. The latter is overlain by 5–10 m of reddish–brownish to multicolored mudstones that are cut by ~4 m of pebbly sandstones to medium-grained sandstones. The top of the sedimentary succession exposed at Satkawhini is marked by an ~2-m thick whitish Lapilli tuff.

The sandstones are interpreted as fluvial channel to proximal overbank deposits whereas the mudstones represent vegetated floodplain to shallow lake sediments adjacent to the fluvial deposits.

The deposits described by stratigraphic column III are located ~6 km southwest of the Satkawhini region and describe the deposits overlying the Satkawhini succession. The ~40-m thick deposits are represented by polarity zonations N6–R3. The basal part of the deposits comprises multicolored mudstones containing carbonate concretions followed by brownish–grayish mudstones with intercalated fine- to medium-grained sand to sandstone layers. The latter exhibit parallel bedding and current ripples. The sedimentary succession is interrupted by deposition of a thin basalt layer (basalt horizon 4, ~1 m) that increases strongly (up to 10 m and more) laterally. The deposits between basalt horizons 4 and 5 consist of 1–2-m thick sandstone layers to lenticular-shaped sandstone bodies that exhibit cross-bedding. The sandstones are separated by brownish–grayish mud- to siltstones containing carbonate concretions.

The basal multicolored mudstones are interpreted as lake margin deposits affected by pedogenesis. The sequence above the lake margin deposits represents sedimentation by fluvial channels (lenticular sandstones), proximal overbank settings (fine-grained sandstone layers), and adjacent floodplains (mudstones). The latter shows evidence for pedogenesis. Deposition in the fluvial system has been halted by the eruption of basalt horizon 4.

The deposits of the Lasdanan Member exposed in the Galili area *sensu stricto* are described by the lower part of stratigraphic column (I). This sequence encompasses the Moquorbashi and Lasdanan fossil sites (Figure 20.1, "L" and M" in Figure 20.2) and is located ~3.2 km south of the exposures described by column III. The compiled thickness of the succession is ~65 m and has been deposited between chrons R6 and R3. Basalt horizon 2 constitutes the base of the succession. The basalts are overlain by a thin reddish mudstone followed by a ~3-m thick whitish tuff layer dated at 5.37 ± 0.04 Ma. The volcanic layer is overlain by multicolored mudstones and coarse-grained sandstones that are followed by brownish siltstones. The basal succession is overlain by basalt horizon 3. The basalts of this horizon are strongly eroded by bluish–grayish sandy conglomerates to sandstones that constitute the Moquorbashi fossil site ("M" in Figure 20.2). The fossiliferous deposits consists of several stacked fining-upward cycles starting from pebbly, cross-bedded sandstones to fine-grained, current rippled sands. The sandy deposits are overlain by brownish–grayish to slightly pinkish mudstones. The top of the muddy succession comprise a dark grayish mudstone that is overlain and partly baked by pillow basalt flow ("4" in Figure 20.2). This basalt flow is strongly eroded by pebbly to coarse-grained, orange-colored sandstones that constitute the Lasdanan fossil site. The sandy deposits pinch out laterally and are overlain by a 10-m thick succession of multicolored mudstones containing carbonate concretions and discontinuous carbonate layers. A thin limestone layer with gastropods is exposed at the top of the succession. The top of the sequence and the top of the Lasdanan Member comprise thick basalt horizons several tens of meters thick.

The sandy deposits, including those of the Moquorbashi and Lasdanan fossil sites, are interpreted as fluvial channel deposits. This interpretation is based on cross-bedding, fining-upward cycles and the overall coarse grain-size observed. The intervening muddy sequences represent deposition on floodplains and shallow lakes adjacent to the fluvial system. Pedogenesis is indicated by the presence of carbonate concretions in the muddy deposits.

The overall depositional setting of the Lasdanan Member is dominated by thick basalt flows with intervening fluvial sandstones, shallow lacustrine to floodplain mudstones, and locally acidic volcanic layers. The sedimentary successions pinch out laterally resulting in stratigraphic contact of encasing basalt flows. This outcrop situation indicates a landscape dominated by basalt ridges where deposition mainly took place in low areas between ridges and is stopped by eruption of additional basalt flows. Similar sedimentary settings are reported for the Adu-Asa Formation at Gona (Kleinsasser et al., 2008).

Dhidinley Member (4.43–3.94 Ma)

The Dhidinley Member is defined as the strata between the top of the uppermost Lasdanan basalt layer 5 and the top of the gray ignimbrite of the Dhidinley Member (Figure 20.2). The deposits of the Dhidinley Member encompass the upper part of the R3 chron, the complete N3 chron, and the lower part of the R2 chron. The Member is well exposed along the north–south striking ridges in the central and eastern parts of the research area and also north of Galili hill (Figure 20.1C). The thickness of this member varies between 18 and 70 m. The deposits of the Dhidinley Member exhibit a broad fivefold subdivision: basal muddy–sandy deposits; a basal tuff complex; multicolored mudstones with intercalated carbonate, diatomite, and sandstone layers; bluish–gray to greenish sandy deposits; and an ignimbrite layer.

The basal muddy deposits comprise thin, brownish, grayish to reddish colored mudstones characterized by root structures, prism cracks, and carbonate concretions. In the southern part of the research area, the basal muddy deposits are overlain by a ~2-m thick tuff complex that has been dated to 4.43 ± 0.01 Ma. The basal sandy deposits are mainly found in the eastern and northern part of the research area. They comprise 1–3-m thick bluish-gray to orange-colored, fine- to coarse-grained sands to sandstones that overlie or erode the basal muddy facies and rest partly on the uppermost Lasdanan basalt flow. Physical sedimentary structures identified in the sandy deposits comprise cross-lamination, current ripple structures, and trough cross-bedding. Fining-upward cycles are common. Abundant large mammal fossils have been recovered from exposures of these sands north of Galili Hill.

These basal sediments are overlain in almost all outcrops by multicolored mudstones that increase in thickness from 5 m in the south to more than 55 m in the east. The muddy deposits exhibit greenish, reddish, brownish, and gray to purple colors. Root structures and carbonate concretions are mainly present in the lower part of the sequence. Thin limestone and diatomite layers are intercalated within the mudstones. A prominent tuff layer dated at 4.25 ± 0.01 Ma is exposed in the eastern exposures of the multicolored mudstones where they reach their maximum thickness. The fine-grained deposits yield abundant fish, crocodile, and hippopotamid fossils. In the southern part of the research area, the muddy sequence is interrupted by a ~2–3-m thick succession of fine- to coarse-grained sandstones organized in a fining-upward cycle. These sandy deposits constitute the Getharkulle fossil site (Figure 20.1C, "G" in Figure 20.2). The upper part of the mudstone sequence again contains carbonate concretions and gastropods locally.

The upper half of the Dhidinley Member is generally more sandy and characterized by an up to 12-m thick sandy succession with minor intercalated brownish mud- to siltstones. The basal part of the sandy successions comprises ~2.5–9-m thick greenish–brownish, medium–coarse-grained sandstones that cut into the underlying muddy deposits. The sandstones exhibit cross-lamination to cross-bedding. Locally, the basal sandy deposits yield abundant mammal fossils, including equids and suids. This basal sandy succession is overlain by a thin whitish tuff layer followed by 2–3-m thick bluish–grayish, fine-grained tuffitic sandstones that are organized in decimeter-thick layers. The layers exhibit parallel lamination, ripples, and synsedimentary deformation structures. Lenticular 1-m thick medium–coarse-grained sand bodies cut into the fine-grained tuffitic sandstones. Sedimentary structures within these bodies comprise planar cross-bedding and lateral accretion surfaces.

The uppermost deposits of the Dhidinley Member comprise 3–5-m thick brownish siltstones to silty sandstones exhibiting root structures. The top of the Dhidinley Member is marked by a grayish ignimbrite. The thickness of the ignimbrite layer reaches its maximum with 4 m in the southern and central parts of the research area and thins to 0.5 m toward the northern parts.

The deposits of the Dhidinley Member are interpreted to reflect deposition in fluvial to lacustrine settings. Deposition of the basal sandy–muddy successions is still influenced by the topography of the basalt horizons of the underlying Lasdanan Member. Sandy deposits are interpreted as fluvial channel sediments that cut into floodplain mudstones affected by pedogenesis. This deposition is accompanied by acidic eruptions that sourced the basal tuff layer. The basal sandy–muddy deposition is followed by the development of a widespread lake system. Multicolored mudstones lacking evidence of pedogenesis are interpreted as lacustrine basin deposits. The sandy deposits of the Getharkulle fossil site represent a fluvial system that developed along the southern margins of the lake system. The lacustrine setting is followed by development of widespread fluvial deposition, probably triggered by increasing volcanic activity as indicated by bluish–grayish tuffitic sandstones. Sedimentary structures point to a system of meandering channels with adjacent sandy overbank to muddy floodplain deposits. Root structures and carbonate concretions point to development of vegetation on the floodplain. The deposition of the Dhidinley Member has been dramatically stopped by volcanic eruptions that sourced the grayish ignimbrite layer. Feldspars from this ignimbrite have been dated to 3.94 ± 0.01 Ma.

Godiray Member

The Godiray Member includes the ~5-m thick strata between the top of the gray ignimbrite and the top of the white Lapilli tuff. The latter yields a radiometric age of 3.97 ± 0.03 Ma. The sediments of the Godiray Member consists of sandy, muddy-silty and tuffitic deposits. The sandy deposits comprise coarse–medium- to fine-grained, cross-bedded greenish–gray sands that are in erosive contact with the grayish ignimbrite layer on top of the Dhidinley Member.

Lateral to the sandy deposits, gray, brownish to reddish mud- to siltstones are exposed. The fine-grained sediments are characterized by prism cracks, root structures, burrows, and nodular carbonate concretions and decimeter-thick, strongly cemented carbonate layers (calcrete). The top of the Godiray Member is marked by a 1-m thick whitish Lapilli tuff.

The sandy deposits are interpreted as fluvial channels with adjacent widespread floodplain areas as indicated by the mudstones. The floodplain areas of the Godiray Member have been affected by intense pedogenesis evidenced by precipitation of calcrete layers.

Shabeley Laag Member

The Shabeley Laag Member encompasses the sedimentary and volcanic strata between the top of the whitish Lapilli Tuff and the top of the uppermost basalt horizon capping this member.

The thickness of the Shabeley Laag Member varies between 35 and 70 m. This member is subdivided into a lower and an upper submember. The boundary between the two submembers is defined by the lower basalt flow.

The lower Shabeley Laag Submember starts with a 10-m thick interval of multicolored mudstones and siltstones with thin interbedded layers of fine- to medium-grained sandstone, limestone, and gastropod limestone. Carbonate concretions were found within the mud- and siltstones at several outcrops. Fossils recovered from the mudstones comprise hippopotamids, crocodiles, turtles, and abundant fish scales. A sandstone layer exposed below gastropod limestones yields several well-preserved mammal fossils.

The fine-grained deposits of the lower Shabeley Laag Submember are erosive and overlain by up to 5 m of coarse-medium-grained, bluish–gray friable sandstones organized in stacked sets that grade from cross-bedded into fine-grained, ripple-bedded sandstones. Several large mammal fossils, mainly elephants and the trunks of silicified wood, have been found within these deposits. Laterally, the bluish-gray sandy deposits grade into interbedded brownish siltstones and minor calcite-cemented sandstones. Carbonate concretions and layers occur frequently within the silty deposits. The bluish-gray sands are overlain and locally intercalated with whitish diatomites and gray mudstones. The top of the Lower Shabeley Laag Submember is marked by the lower basalt flow that is characterized by pillow structures.

The Upper Shabeley Laag Submember comprises the deposits between the top of the lower submember and the top of the upper basalt horizon. The submember starts with 10 m of multicolored mudstones intercalated with thin, whitish limestone layers. The muddy deposits are in followed by up to 11 m of fine-grained tuffitic sandstones locally showing abundant root and burrow structures. A thin tuff layer intercalated within the tuffitic sandstones has been dated to 3.87 ± 0.02 Ma, respectively, 3.91 ± 0.11 Ma. The tuffitic sandstones grade laterally into medium–coarse-grained, greenish–brownish sandstones. The latter exhibit stacked fining-upward cycles characterized by cross-bedding and ripple stratification. The fossil site called "primate-site" (Figure 20.1C, "P" in Figure 20.2) is formed by such a stacked fining-upward cycle. Locally, the sandy deposits grade upwards into 5 m of fine-grained, silty sands characterized by abundant root structures and carbonate concretions.

The top of the Shabeley Laag Submember is formed by stacked basalt flows with a total thickness ranging between ~2 and 30 m from south to north. At least four individual basalt flows have been observed. Locally, two reddish paleosol intervals are intercalated within the basalt flows.

The multicolored mudstones present in the basal parts of both the lower and upper Shabeley Laag Submembers are interpreted as lacustrine basin deposits. Lake margin areas are indicated by sandstone and gastropod limestone layers and the presence of pedogenic concretions. Whitish limestone and diatomite layers have been deposited during lake level highstands with low terrigenous influx. The lacustrine intervals of both submembers are followed by a fluvial system. The change to coarse-grained deposition is probably triggered by volcanic activity preceding the eruption of the basalt flows. The above-described stacked fining-upward sandstones characterized by cross-bedding are interpreted as channel deposits. Proximal overbank areas adjacent to channels are indicated by fine-grained sandstones containing root and burrow structures. The presence of vegetation is furthermore proven by silicified tree trunks. Brownish–grayish mudstones to silty sandstones have been deposited in more distal floodplain settings. The carbonate concretions within the floodplain deposits formed during pedogenic processes. The basalt flows on top of the upper Shabeley Laag Submember most likely almost covered the complete research area. The presence of reddish paleosol horizons between individual flows points to periods where eruption of basalts stopped, thus increasing the overall time span represented by the basalt horizons.

Dhagax Member

The Dhagax Member comprises the ~17-m thick volcano-sedimentary succession between the top of the uppermost basalt horizon capping the Shabeley Laag Member and the top of the reddish ignimbrite (Figure 20.2). The Dhagax and Caashacado Members constitute the deposits of the Galili West area (Figure 20.1, IV in Figure 20.2). The deposits of both members are restricted to this area.

The lower part of the member comprises 6 m of greenish, grayish to reddish mudstones with a thin intercalated limestone layer. The fine-grained deposits are laterally cut by bluish-gray, medium–coarse-grained, cross-bedded tuffitic sands that exhibit trough cross-bedding. The bluish-gray sands are overlain by 9-m thick, very fine-grained, bluish-gray pumice tuffs. The top of the Dhagax Member is built up by a 2-m thick reddish ignimbrite. Feldspars from this ignimbrite have been dated to 2.335 ± 0.01 Ma.

The muddy deposits are interpreted as deposits of a shallow lake, whereas the tuffitic sandstones represent channel-fills of a fluvial system adjacent to the lake. The thick acidic volcanic layers show a significant change from dominating basaltic volcanism of the Shabeley Laag Member. No fossil mammal remains have been recovered from the Dhagax Member.

Caashacado Member

The sedimentary–volcanic succession below the top of the uppermost pyroclastic layer is attributed to the Caashacado Member. The Caashacado Member is either overlying the reddish ignimbrite on top of the Dhagax Member or rests directly on the upper basalt horizon capping the Shabeley Laag Member. The thickness of the Caashacado Member is strongly variable and reaches a maximum of 25 m.

The basal part of the Caashacado Member comprise fine- to medium-grained, <1-m thick sand layers intercalated with brownish silty sands containing carbonate concretions. The sandy deposits are overlain by 5 m of light gray to brownish mudstones and 2 m of fine- to medium-grained, light gray to brownish sands to tuffitic sands and subordinately brownish siltstones. Observed sedimentary structures comprise horizontal and convolute lamination and abundant root structures. Bivalves have been found in the sandy deposits. The top of the member is characterized by a pyroclastic layer that is locally separated into two layers by a weathering horizon. No deposits overlying the uppermost Caashacado Member are exposed in the research area.

The deposits of the Caashacado Member are interpreted to reflect mainly deposition in shallow lakes with adjacent lake margin areas. Fluvial channel sandstones are present in the lower part of the member.

The recorded sedimentary hiatus between the Shabeley Laag Member and the Dhagax and Caashacado Members could be explained by the long time span recorded by the basalts and intervening paleosols on top of the Shabeley Laag Member. A stratigraphic correlation of the individual members of the Galili Formation with other fossiliferous formations of the southwest Afar Rift based on Ar/Ar dating and paleomagnetic results are shown in Figure 20.3.

Fauna

The Galili region east of Gedameyto is the first known locality in the Somali Region of Ethiopia to yield early hominin remains attributable to various taxa accompanied by a rich fossil vertebrate fauna (Kullmer et al., 2008). The Paleoanthropological Research Team recovered 10 isolated hominin molars (and molar fragments), the proximal half of an adult femur, a proximal fragment of a metatarsal V, and a distal humerus fragment of a juvenile hominin. The positions of major fossil localities are indicated in Figure 20.1 and in capitals in the composite stratigraphic columns in Figure 20.2.

A detailed description and analysis of the Galili hominin findings is in progress and not a central topic of this contribution. In brief, the dental remains from the Lasdanan Mb. are referred to cf. *Ardipithecus* sp. based on their small size, low

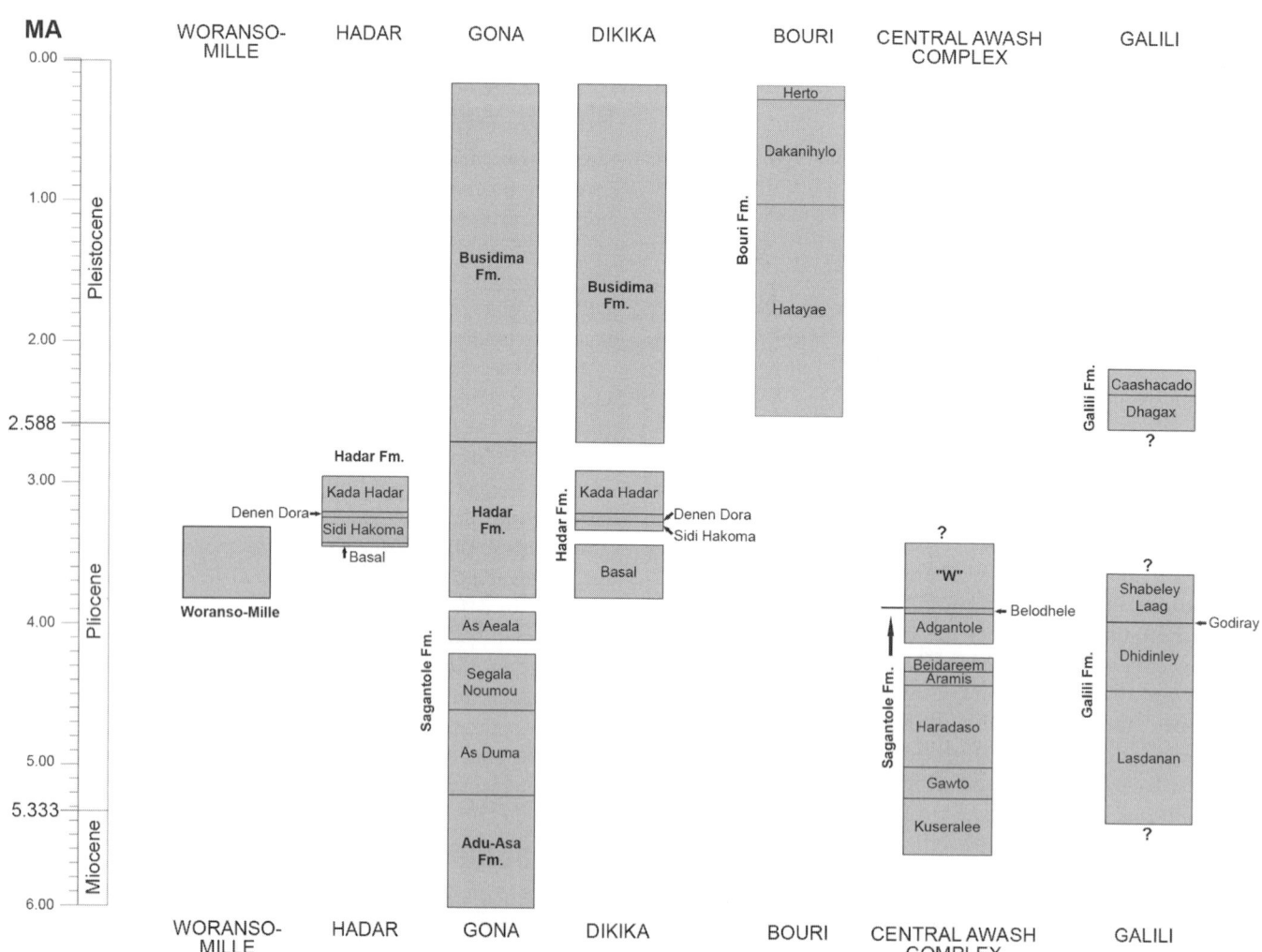

Figure 20.3 Age correlation of the Galili Formation with other Ethiopian hominin localities (from Hujer et al., 2015).

crown relief, and strong basal flare, while the dental material from the Dhidinley and Shabeley Laag Mbs. show clear affinities to *Australopithecus*. The Dhidinley and Shabeley Laag specimens are relatively large, making an attribution to the recently named *Australopithecus deyiremeda* (Haile-Selassie et al., 2015) unlikely. In general, some of the molars show a mixture of *A. anamensis*-like and *A. afarensis*-like features, supporting the idea of an anagenetic transition within a restricted area between these two taxa (Kimbel et al., 2006), also seen at the penecontemporaneous site of Woranso-Mille (Haile-Selassie, 2010).

The Galili Formation vertebrate fauna (see Table 20.1) is comparable to fossil assemblages from Woranso-Mille, Hadar, Gona, Dikika, the Central Awash Complex, and Omo in Ethiopia, as well as from the Turkana Basin in northern Kenya, such as Allia Bay, Lothagam, and Kanapoi (Kullmer et al., 2008).

Pisces and Reptilia teeth and bones are the most common elements in all three fossiliferous members, while Aves long bone fragment fossils are also present, but rare. Rodentia are collected only in Dhidinley and Lasdanan Mbs., and Lagomorpha and Hyracoidea only in Lasdanan Mb. In the three members, skull and jaw fragments, teeth, and longbones of artiodactyls (bovids and suids) and proboscideans dominate the large mammal assemblage, followed by perissodactyls (Table 20.1, Figure 20.4). The bovids are represented by at least eight taxa. Tragelaphins and alcelaphins constitute the majority. *Tragelaphus* sp., cf. *Ugandax* sp., *Gazella* sp., and Reduncini gen. et sp. indet. are common in the Shabeley Laag, Dhidinley, and Lasdanan Mbs.. *Hippotragus* sp., Alcelaphini gen. et sp. indet. and *Aepyceros* sp. occur in the Shabeley Laag and Dhidinley Mbs., while Neotragini gen. et sp. indet. was only found in the Shabeley Laag Mb. Giraffids are identified as *Giraffa* sp. and *Sivatherium* sp. Three suid genera (*Nyanzachoerus*, *Notochoerus*, *Kolpochoerus*) are present; *Nyanzachoerus pattersoni* dominates the suid assemblages of all three major fossiliferous Mbs., which also contain the taxon *Notochoerus jaegeri*, while *Notochoerus euilus* only occurs rarely in the Shabeley Laag Mb. Diverse Galili proboscidean remains consist of *Deinotherium bozasi*, *Anancus kenyensis* (advanced morph), *Loxodonta*, and *Elephas* with two species each, *Loxodonta* cf. *exoptata* and *L.* cf. *adaurora*, and *Elephas recki brumpti* and *E.* cf. *ekorensis*. Both *Elephas* taxa are only recovered from the Shabeley Laag Mb. All equid fossils are preliminarily attributed to the genus *Eurygnathohippus*.

The oldest Lasdanan Mb. contains a high percentage of cercopithecoid primates, with a relatively high proportion of colobines, accompanied by small-sized Papionini. Diversity increases in the upper members: in the Shabeley Laag Mb. five cercopithecoid taxa can be distinguished, including a large Papionini indet., aff. *Parapapio ado*, *Theropithecus* sp., and a large and a small Colobinae indet., as well as *Kuseracolobus aramisi* (Table 20.1). A large variety of carnivores, most abundant in the Lasdanan Member with *Chasmaporthetes* sp., Herpestidae gen. et sp. indet., and Lutrinae gen. et sp. indet., and *Dinofelis* sp. and Viverridae gen. et sp. indet. in the Dhidinley Mb., was discovered. *Homotherium* cf. *crenatidens* was identified only from the Shabeley Laag Mb.

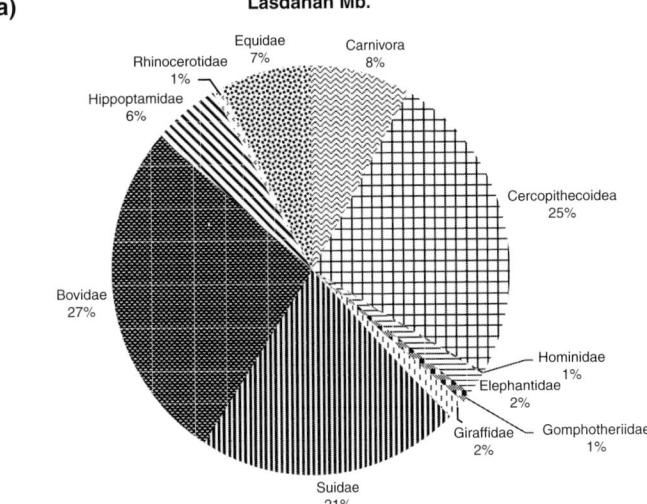

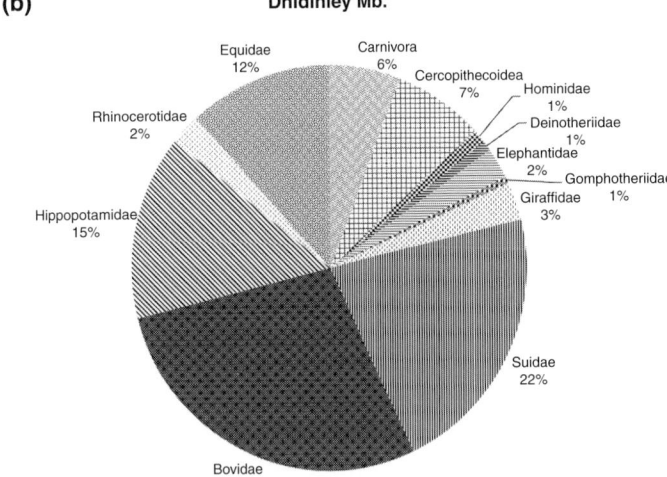

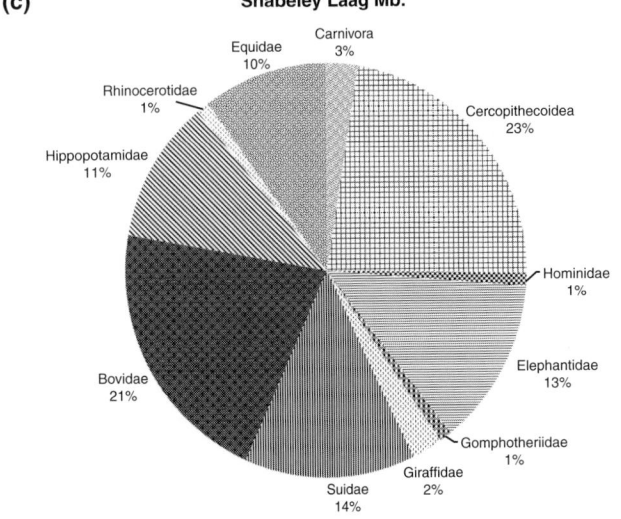

Figure 20.4 Pie charts showing the percentage of mammalian taxa from (A) Lasdanan Mb., (B) Dhidinley Mb., and (C) Shabeley Laag Mb.

Paleoenvironment

In terms of the abundance and distribution of fresh-grass grazers, faunal studies for paleoenvironmental reconstruction show

Table 20.1 Species list of Lasdanan, Dhidinley, and Shabeley Laag Members, which contain a rich mammal fauna, including biostratigraphically informative species of elephant and suids.

Fauna	Lasdanan Mb.	Dhidinley Mb.	Shabeley Laag Mb.
Pisces			
Barbus sp.	x	x	x
Clarias sp.	x	x	x
Reptilia			
Testudinata gen. et sp. indet.	x	x	x
Crocodylus cf. *niloticus*	x	x	x
Python gen. et sp. indet			x
Aves			
Gen. et sp. indet	x	x	x
Rodentia			
cf. *Atherurus* sp.	x	x	
cf. Muroidea indet.	x	x	
cf. *Thryonomys* sp.	x	x	
Lagomorpha			
Gen. et sp. indet.	x		
Hyracoidea			
Gen. et sp. indet.	x		
Carnivora			
Dinofelis sp.		x	
Homotherium cf. *crenatidens*			x
Chasmaporthetes sp.	x		
Viverridae gen. et sp. indet.		x	
Herpestidae gen. et sp. indet.	x		
Lutrinae gen. et sp. indet.	x		
Primates			
cf. *Ardipithecus* sp.	x		
Australopithecus cf. *anamensis/afarensis*		x	x
Colobinae indet. (large)	x		
Colobinae indet. (small)	x	x	x

Fauna	Lasdanan Mb.	Dhidinley Mb.	Shabeley Laag Mb.
Kuseracolobus aramisi			x
Papionini indet. (large)			x
aff. *Parapapio ado*	x	x	x
Theropithecus sp.		x	x
Proboscidea			
Deinotherium bozasi		x	x
Anancus kenyensis (advanced morph)	x	x	x
Loxodonta cf. *exoptata*		x	x
Loxodonta cf. *adaurora*		x	x
Elephas cf. *ekorensis*			x
Elephas recki brumpti		x	x
Perissodactyla			
Diceros bicornis	x	x	x
Eurygnathohippus sp.	x	x	x
Artiodactyla			
Hexaprotodon sp.	x		
Hippopotamus sp.		x	x
Nyanzachoerus kanamensis/pattersoni	x	x	x
Kolpochoerus deheinzelini		x	x
Notochoerus jaegeri	x	x	x
Notochoerus cf. *euilus*			x
Giraffa sp.		x	x
Sivatherium sp.	x		
Tragelaphus sp.	x	x	x
cf. *Ugandax* sp.	x	x	x
Hippotragus sp.		x	x
Reduncini gen. et sp. indet.	x	x	x
Alcelaphini gen. et sp. indet.		x	x
Aepyceros sp.		x	x
Gazella sp.	x	x	x
Neotragini gen. et sp. indet.			x

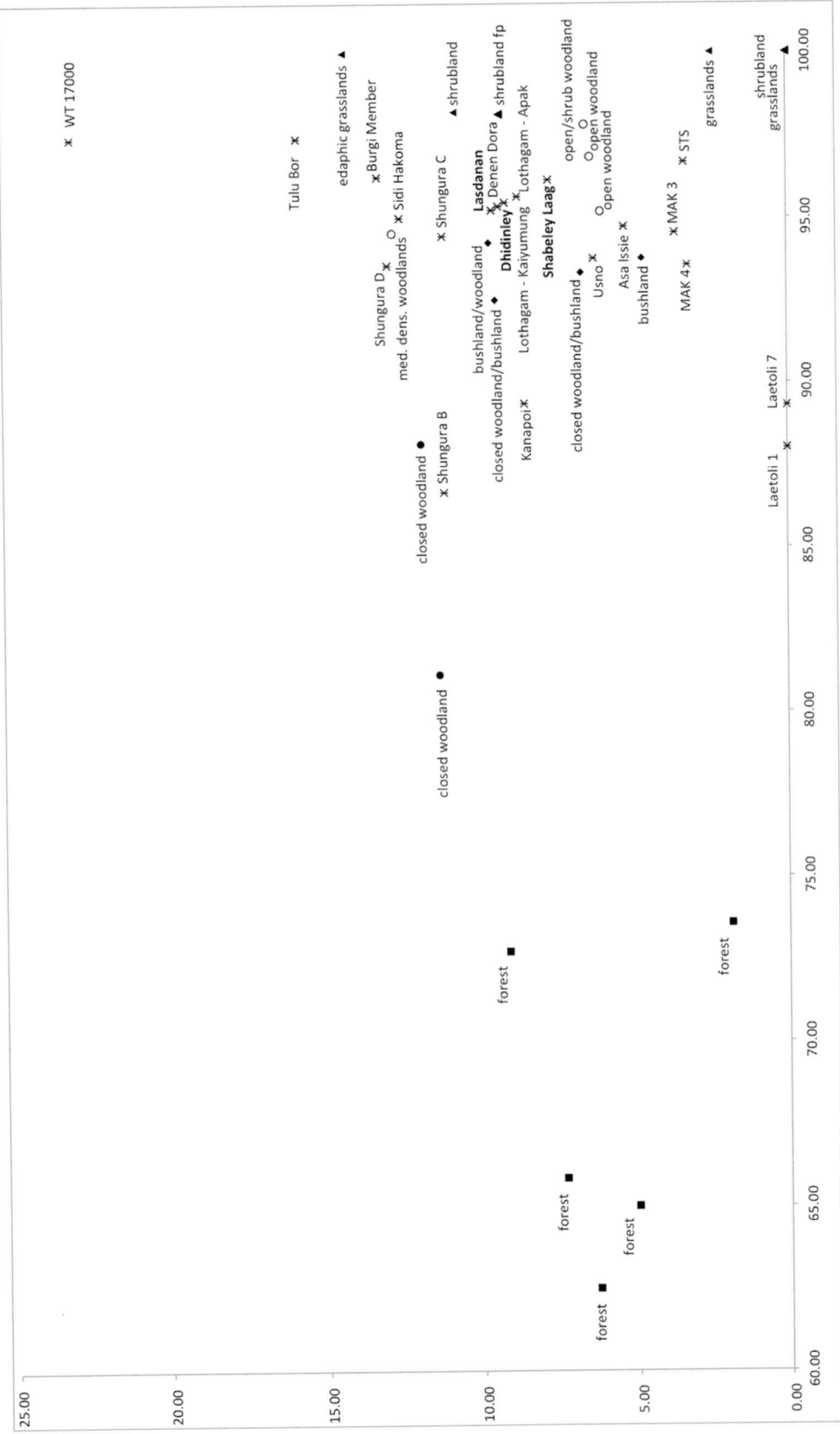

Figure 20.5 Bivariate plot of the percentages of total terrestrial mammals vs. fresh-grass grazers in vegetative habitats ranging from forests to grasslands. Comparison of data from Eastern and Southern African hominin localities and modern game park environments (data from Reed, 1997; Harris et al., 2003; Harris and Leakey, 2003a; White et al., 2006).

that communities of the Lasdanan and Dhidinley Mbs. plot close to bushland/woodland communities of modern analog game parks (Reed, 1997; Harris et al., 2003; Harris and Leakey, 2003a; White et al., 2006; Figure 20.5). A similar picture is given by the Denen Dora Member from Hadar as well as the Apak and Kaiyumung Members at Lothagam. The Shabeley Laag community points toward open/shrub woodland.

Regarding herbivore–frugivore non-hominin primate distribution, Shabeley Laag points to bushland/woodland and has affinities to Sterkfontein and the KNM-WT 17000 site in the Turkana basin (Figure 20.6). The Lasdanan fauna shows close affinities to Asa Issie and Lothagam Apak Member and points to open/shrub woodland. Dhidinley Mb. plots close to Lothagam Kaiyumung and Sidi Hakoma Mbs. and indicates open woodland.

Denen Dora Mb. is interpreted to represent woodland with forest regions near water sources and edaphic grasslands (Reed, 1997). Sidi Hakoma stands for medium to open density woodland communities rather than bushland, because of the lower percentage of fruit- and leaf-eaters (Reed, 1997). Sterkfontein Member 4 represents open woodland, with bushland and thicket areas and the KNM-WT 17000 locality is open woodland with bushland thickets, edaphic grasslands and wetlands, and a riparian woodland or forest (Reed, 1997). White et al. (2006) interpret the Asa Issie habitat as closed to grassy woodlands.

In general, communities from Lasdanan and Dhidinley at Galili are broadly comparable to the Denen Dora and Sidi Hakoma Members from Hadar and the Apak and Kaiyumung Members from Lothagam. Shabeley Laag represents the open woodland to bushland spectrum. These results correspond to the faunal analyses from Kullmer et al. (2008).

Stable carbon and oxygen isotopes in enamel were analyzed from 15 large mammalian taxa (Bedaso, 2011). Carbon isotope ratios in tooth enamel have been considered to faithfully record mammalian herbivore dietary preferences, which in turn reflect the standing C_3/C_4 vegetation (O'Leary, 1988). Carbon isotope analysis of the tooth enamel in the Galili Formation shows a range of dietary preferences including pure C_3 browsers, mixed C_3/C_4 feeders, and pure C_4 grazers (Figure 20.7). In the Galili Formation, dinotheres and giraffids show a C_3-dominated diet (exclusively browsers); Alcelaphini, equids, notochoere suids, elephantids, and gomphotheres (*Anancus*) show a mainly C_4-dominated diet with minor C_3 vegetation; while hippopotamids and Bovini point toward C_3/C_4 mixed-feeding strategies. However, other herbivore taxa such as Reduncini and Tragelaphini exhibit a wider range of feeding strategy and show changes in feeding habit in different members in the Galili Formation.

The oxygen isotopic composition of tooth enamel is related to the animal's body water, which reflects the oxygen isotopic composition of ingested water and closely track meteoric water (Bryant and Froelich, 1995; Kohn et al., 1996). However, this can be complicated by relative proportions of vegetation type and different parts of vegetation such as leaves and other parts consumed by the animal (Dongmann et al., 1974), physiology of the animal, and climatic conditions (Longinelli, 1984; Luz et al., 1984; Kohn et al., 1996).

In this respect the oxygen isotopic composition of tooth enamel in the Galili Formation shows a very wide range of variation. The $\delta^{18}O$ values range between −9.5‰ in hippopotamids in the Lasdanan member and +4.8‰ in Reduncini in the Dhidinley member. The $\delta^{18}O$ values also show a wide range of variation within a single taxon and sympatric taxa in each member and across time. In general, the range of $\delta^{18}O$ values are similar in different members throughout the Galili Formation. However, the taxa in the Lasdanan member exhibit ^{18}O-enriched values, whereas taxa in the Dhidinley and Shabeley Laag members show more ^{18}O-depleted values. This wide range of $\delta^{18}O$ values may represent a large degree of variation of water dependence and drinking habits. Using the average $\delta^{18}O$ values, the taxa can be categorized as water-dependent (evaporation-insensitive), where animals obtain their water from an open water source, and water-dependent, where animals obtain their water from the food they consume (Levin et al., 2006). At Galili, water-independent taxa include giraffids and tragelaphins, whereas hippopotamids, equids, and elephantids are water-dependent. The rest of the taxa, however, do not show a clear drinking habit. Although animal physiology may explain some of the oxygen isotopic variations, other factors such as spatial and temporal variation in the $\delta^{18}O$ of rainfall as well as different degrees of evaporation of the drinking water sources can control the distribution of oxygen isotopes in the Galili Formation.

The combined carbon and oxygen results from the Galili Formation indicate a range of variable environmental and climatic conditions from late Miocene through early Pleistocene (Figure 20.7). The Lasdanan Mb., between >5.37 and 4.43 Ma, at Galili was characterized by a wooded grassland paleoenvironmental condition with significant C_4 vegetation on the paleolandscape. But the lower part of Lasdanan (e.g., Satkawhini sites, see Figure 20.1) is dominated by grassland. In contemporaneous sites in the Awash Basin, Levin et al. (2008) at Gona indicated paleoenvironmental conditions with abundant C_4 vegetation, while at Aramis White et al. (2009a) suggest a wooded habitat including closed to open woodlands with patches of true forest. The middle Pliocene between 4.43 and 3.94 Ma at Galili (Dhidinley Mb.) was represented by wet wooded grassland to woodland environmental condition with significant C_3 vegetation on the landscape compared to the underlying member. The middle to late Pliocene part of the Galili Formation is characterized by relatively moist wooded grassland paleoenvironmental conditions where C_4 grasses dominated the landscape. The middle to late Pliocene environmental condition at Galili is in general agreement with paleoenvironmental reconstructions from contemporaneous deposits in Hadar and Dikika (Reed, 2008; Bedaso et al., 2013). Regarding the isotope data, the Galili Formation documents variable environmental and climatic conditions with abundant C_4 vegetation except for the time between 4.43 and 3.94 Ma, where C_3 vegetation was dominating.

The Galili faunal and paleoenvironmental data presented here match with contemporaneous fossil hominin localities in Eastern Africa, reflecting a patchwork of grassland and wooded habitats with lake and river settings, favorable for permanent residence of diverse large mammal communities including early hominins during most of the Pliocene.

Figure 20.6 Bivariate plot of the percentages of total terrestrial mammals vs. frugivores in vegetative habitats ranging from forests to grasslands. Comparison of data from Eastern and Southern African hominin localities and modern game park environments (data from Reed, 1997; Harris et al., 2003; Harris and Leakey, 2003a; White et al., 2006).

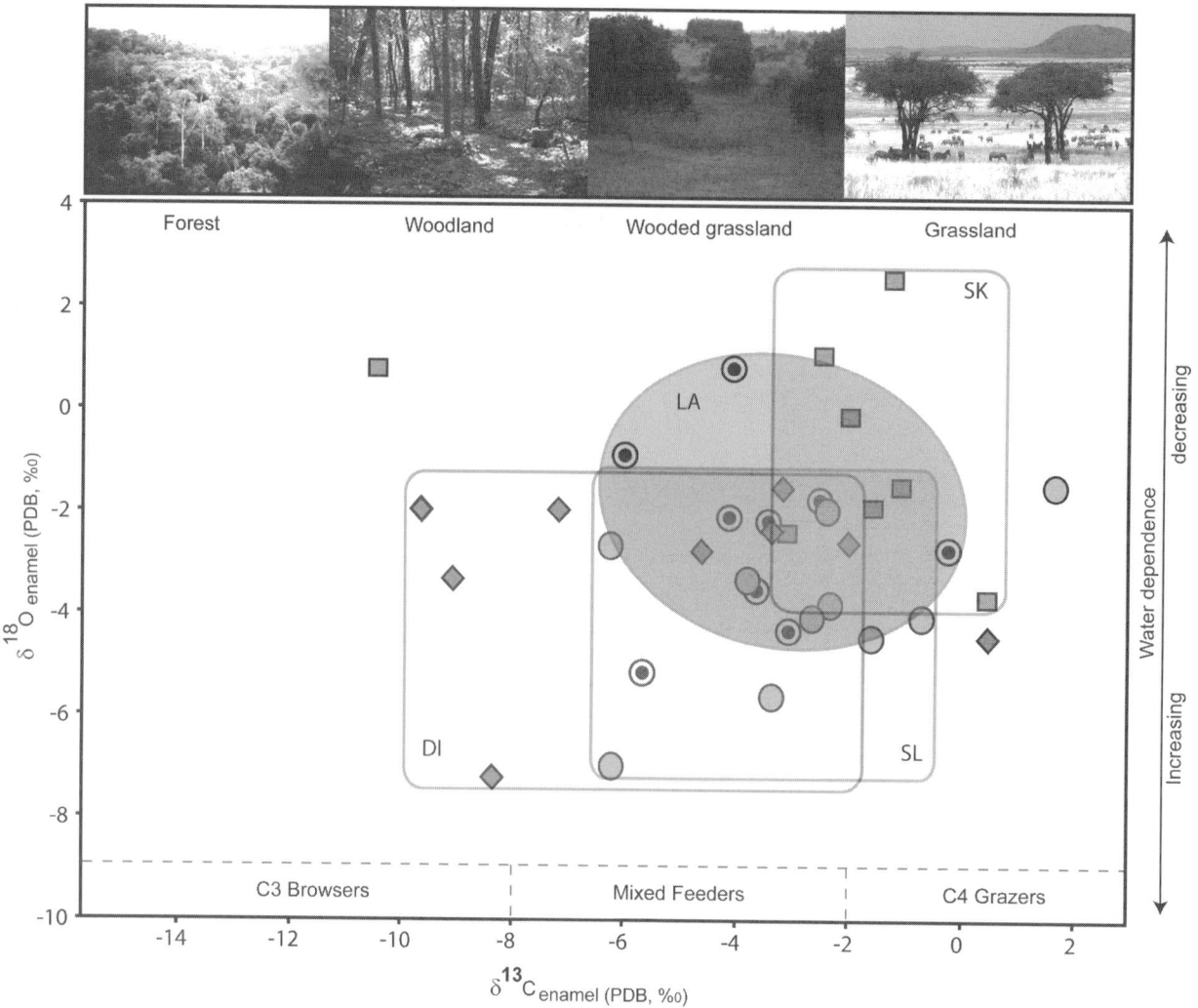

Figure 20.7 Combined δ¹³C and δ¹⁸O enamel isotope plots for the Galili Formation by member. Individual points represent average carbon and oxygen isotope value of taxa and the polygons define the majority of the isotope values in the respective members (LA, Lasdanan member – black circle; DI, Dhidinley member – grey diamond; SL, Shabeley Laag member – grey circle; and Sk, Satkawhini fossil site, which is the lower part of the LA – grey cube. The dotted lines indicate mammalian feeding preference. The upper panel shows representative modern environment/habitats: forest, woodland, wooded grassland, and grassland. The carbon isotope boundaries of canopy covers are based on Cerling et al. (2011b).

Conclusions

The Galili Fm. represents a Miocene to Pliocene fossiliferous 230-m thick sedimentary and volcanic sequence in the Southern Afar Rift. The exposures are situated about 35 km east of the Awash River in the vicinity of the town of Gadameyto. Lithostratigraphically, the Galili Fm. is subdivided by volcanics in the Lasdanan, Dhidinley, Godiray, Shabeley Laag, Dhagax, and Caashacado Mbs. with a radiometric age between >5.37 and <2.35 Ma. The first three members contain a rich mammal fauna, including a number of biostratigraphically relevant elephant and suid remains representing a minimum age boundary of 3.87 ± 0.02 Ma (Table 20.1). The deposits and the fauna of the Lasdanan, Dhidinley, and Godiray Mbs. are time-equivalent to the Sagantole Formation exposed at the Central Awash Complex and Gona. The Shabeley Laag Member has been formed during similar time as the "W" Formation of the Central Awash Complex, the basal Hadar Formation at Dikika and Gona, the Sidi Hakoma Member at Hadar, and deposits at Woranso-Mille. The fauna is comparable to large mammal assemblages also from other Eastern African sites outside the Afar Rift, such as the Apak and Kaiyumung Mbs. of Lothagam, Kanapoi, the Kataboi Mb. of the Nachukui Fm. at West Turkana, and the Moiti and Lokochot Mbs. at East Turkana representing diverse habitats from grassland to wooded grassland and woodland. Geological, paleontological, and isotopic results show that fluctuation in environmental conditions through time was present during sedimentary deposition favoring faunal communities with more or less water dependency. In lake, river, and floodplain deposits in these environments several hominin specimens were recovered by the international PAR Team between 2000 and 2009. At Moquorbashi and Lasdanan fossil sites in the Lasdanan Mb., several teeth dated to <5.37 to >4.43 Ma show similarities to specimens of the genus *Ardipithecus* from the Central

Awash Complex. At the locality of "Getharkulle" (Dhidinley Member), molar crowns and a proximal femur from the time period between <4.43 and 3.94 Ma may reflect the presence of *Au. anamensis*. Several hominin molars have been collected from sandy deposits of the so-called "primate-site" and other localities in the slightly younger Upper Shabeley Laag Submb. showing distinct affinities with *Au. afarensis* teeth. Therefore, Galili is one of the very few hominin sites covering the time range of the transition between *Ar. ramidus*, *Au. anamensis*, and *Au. afarensis*. Further fieldwork is necessary to exploit the paleoanthropological potential of the Galili area to enlighten this crucial time interval in human evolution.

Acknowledgments

We want to express our gratitude to A. Dessie and G. Assefa from the Authority for Research and Conservation of Cultural Heritage (ARCCH) in Addis Ababa, and Hasan Said from Addis Ababa University, Institute of Ethiopian Studies for their professional advice and help in the field. Also we thank the ARCCH and the Ethiopian Government for giving the permission to undertake fieldwork in the Somali Region in the Afar Depression. Fieldwork would not have been possible without the permission and support of the people of the local Issa community in Gadameyto and Galili. We are indebted to all members of the PAR Team including Kummelatshu and his staff for their hard work during the annual field seasons between 2000 and 2009.

21 Melka Kunture, Ethiopia: Early Pleistocene Faunas of the Ethiopian Highlands

Denis Geraads, Rosalia Gallotti, Jean-Paul Raynal, Raymonde Bonnefille, and Margherita Mussi

Introduction

The large complex of archeological and paleontological sites of Melka Kunture is located about 50 km SSW of Addis Ababa (base camp coordinates 8.708° N, 38.594° E), on the banks of the Upper Awash in the Ethiopian plateau at elevations of 2000–2200 m a.s.l. (Figure 21.1); it includes numerous archeological sites that yield tens of thousands of artifacts. It has no equivalent in East Africa in documenting the full evolutionary sequence of lithic industries, from the late Oldowan to historic times, on the Ethiopian Highlands. It is also unique in providing abundant faunal remains that help reconstruct the diet of early hominins and, together with rich floral spectra, their environment at high altitudes.

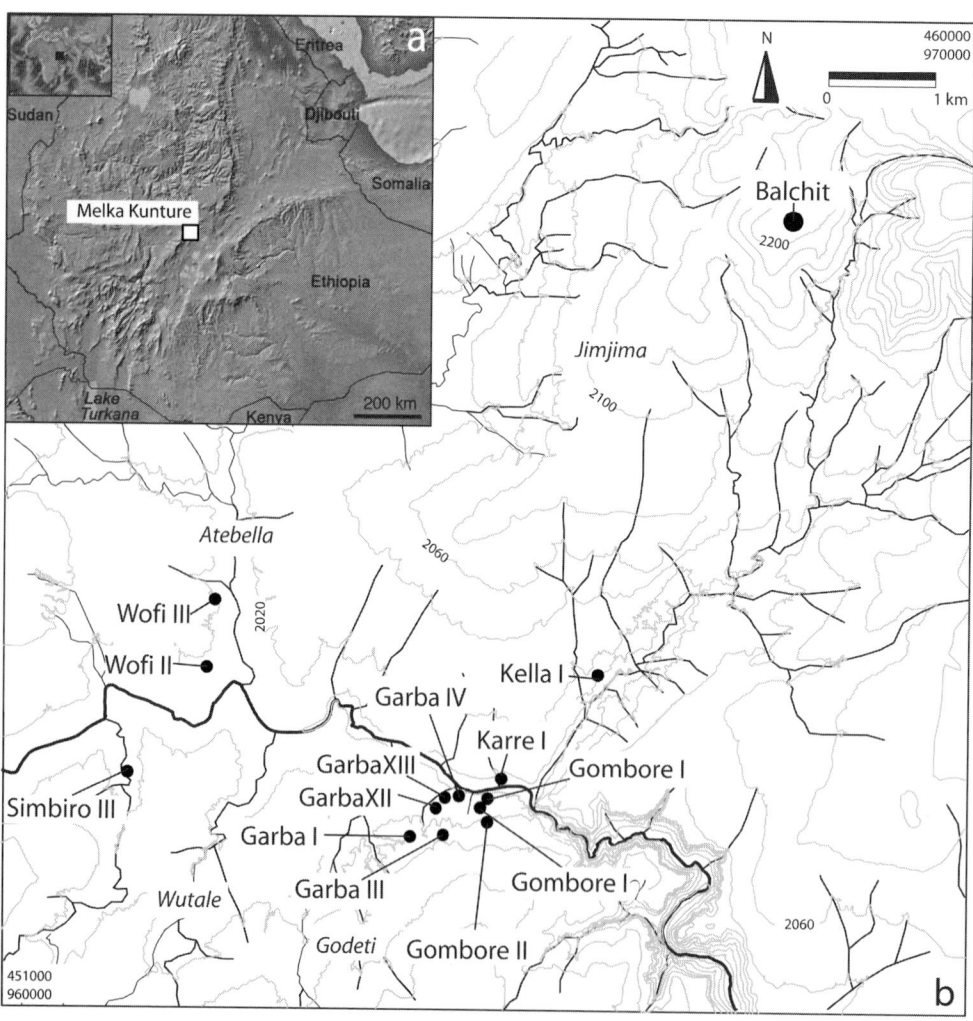

Figure 21.1 (a) Location of Melka Kunture on the shoulder of the Main Ethiopian Rift and map of Ethiopia with surrounding countries. (b) Map of the Melka Kunture area with the major excavations.

History of Research

Melka Kunture was first mentioned in print in 1931 by Father F.B. Azaïs when reporting a previous journey from Addis Ababa to Butajira (Azaïs and Chambard, 1931). In 1963, Gerard Dekker, a Dutch hydrologist and a friend of L.S.B. Leakey, discovered Acheulean artifacts at Kella (currently one of the sites of Melka Kunture) and informed the Ethiopian authorities in Addis Ababa (Chavaillon and Piperno, 2004a). In 1963–1964, Gérard Bailloud, a French archeologist, carried out the first systematic surveys, making collections at Kella, Gombore (currently Gombore II), Godeti, and Tcharri Aroussi (Figure 21.1; Tcharri Aroussi, about 1 km southeast of Gombore gully, is outside the map area). In 1965, he published his analysis of the lithic assemblages, placing them in chronological order from the Middle Acheulean to the Epipaleolithic (Bailloud, 1965).

Systematic research at Melka Kunture was conducted by Jean Chavaillon, director of the French Archaological Mission from 1965 to 1981, and again from 1993 to 1995. Chavaillon and his team described the sedimentary deposits of the Upper Awash Valley (Chavaillon and Taieb, 1968; Taieb, 1971, 1974; Chavaillon, 1979), and surveyed a region of approximately 100 km². Many sites were discovered, with lithic industries from the Oldowan to the Acheulean, and from the Middle Stone Age to the Late Stone Age. They were named after the gullies where they are exposed, i.e., after the seasonal tributaries of the Awash that drain the area. The nomenclature combines the name of a gully – e.g., the Garba gully – with the consecutive number of the site discovered in the area and the successive archeological units identified by letters, from top to bottom. Several archeological layers were excavated: Karre I, Gombore IE to IC, and Garba IVG to IVE (from 1.8 to 1.7 Ma); Garba IVD and Gombore IB (1.6 Ma); Gombore Iγ (1.3 Ma); Garba XII and Simbiro III (more than 1.0 Ma); Gombore II (from 0.85 to 0.7 Ma); Garba I (*ca.* 0.5 Ma); Garba III (*ca.* 0.2 Ma); Wofi II–III, Kella I (Late Stone Age); Balchit (Late Stone Age to historic) (Chavaillon and Chavaillon, 1971; Chavaillon, 1973, 1980, 1982; Hivernel-Guerre, 1976; Hours, 1976; Chavaillon et al., 1979; Gallotti and Piperno, 2003; Chavaillon and Berthelet, 2004; Chavaillon and Piperno, 2004a, 2004b; Piperno et al., 2009; Gallotti et al., 2010; Gallotti, 2013; Mussi et al., 2014, Gallotti and Mussi, 2015, 2018; Altamura et al., 2019, 2020). In 1999, the Italian Archeological Mission at Melka Kunture and Balchit, directed by M. Piperno (1999–2010), resumed systematic research. Another Acheulean site was also discovered and excavated, i.e., Garba XIII, of late early Pleistocene age (Gallotti et al., 2014). The volcanic tuffs, which are the main chronological markers, were resampled and dated by $^{40}Ar/^{39}Ar$ analysis (Morgan et al., 2012). Since 2011, the Italian Archeological Mission at Melka Kunture and Balchit is directed by one of us (M.M.), who leads investigations aimed at completing the general chronostratigraphy and at reassessing the archeological, geological, and paleoanthropological record, which is the outcome of 50 years of research. In 2019 the Italo-Spanish Archaeological Mission at Melka Kunture and Balchit became active. The new discoveries include Gombore Iδ, a new Acheulean site (1.4 Ma), and ichnosurfaces in the Gombore gully where animals and hominins printed tracks (0.9 to 0.7 Ma) (Altamura et al., 2019, 2020; Perini et al., 2021).

Geological Background

Melka Kunture is located in a half-graben depression that belongs to the Upper Awash basin, on the Ethiopian Plateau along the western border of the Main Ethiopian Rift. The basin surface is of *ca.* 3000 km² and is delimited by Pliocene volcanic centers. The main centers are Wochacha and Furi to the north, Boti and Agoiabi to the south. The eastern limit is marked by the main graben of the Ethiopian Rift, which is part of the East African Rift System (Mohr, 1999). The area of Melka Kunture is made up of valleys whose inner terraces resisted erosion. The visible thickness of these deposits is around 30 m, but the cumulative thickness of the various levels is estimated at about 100 m (Kieffer et al., 2002, 2004; Bardin et al., 2004; Raynal and Kieffer, 2004).

The phases of human occupation so far identified post-date large regional eruptions, which erased prior archeological evidence (if any existed), modified the environment, and increased the river bed load. The Awash regularly reestablished its course toward a new basal level of erosion. The sedimentation that preserved the archeological localities was controlled by reactivation episodes of the border faults and the subsidence of the half-graben and consequently by the level of the Awash sill at the exit of the basin. Upstream of gorges deeply incised in the western rift border, the sill remained high for a long period of time, reducing until recently the likelihood of regressive erosion.

The alluviums of the right bank tributaries document an evolution that is related to the successive geodynamic phases of the Melka Kunture fault and associated volcanism. Those of the left bank record different stages of dismantling the superficial formations of parts of the basin between Melka Kunture and the northern volcanic centers. The piling of alluviums, volcano-derived sediments and direct tephric inputs built the Melka Kunture Formation (MKF; Raynal et al., 2004). This geological formation documents the human occupation of this part of the Upper Awash Valley between the Olduvai Polarity Subzone and the Brunhes-Matuyama Reversal, if not later (Schmitt et al., 1977; Cressier, 1980; Morgan et al., 2012; Tamrat et al., 2014). Four Oldowan sites (Karre I, Gombore I, Gombore Iγ, and Garba IVG-E) and four Acheulean sites (Garba IVD, Garba XII, Garba XIII, and Gombore II, which includes several sublocalities) have been recorded and extensively excavated in this formation; Gombore II-2, which is one of the subsites of Gombore II, as well as Garba I, are of early Middle Pleistocene age. (Figures 21.1 and 21.2). Recent work, based upon radiometric dating, paleomagnetism, and lithic industries, has greatly improved the understanding of their succession. A major point concerns the extensively excavated archeological layer of Gombore IB that was thought to document the earliest industries of Melka Kunture, but in fact is broadly contemporaneous with the other major level of Garba IVD, which rests upon the "Grazia tuff."

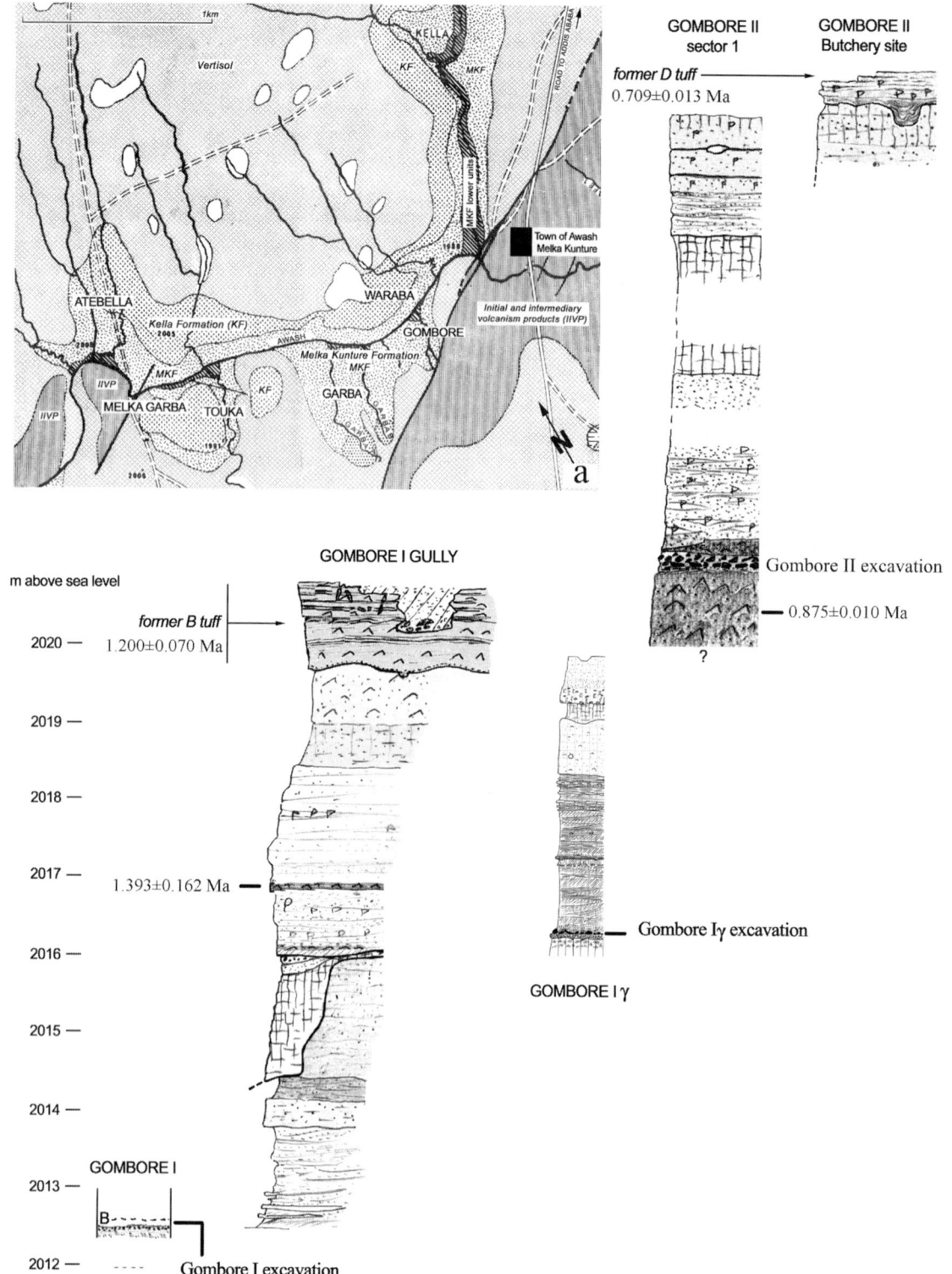

Figure 21.2 Geological sketch map of the Melka Kunture area (after Taieb, 1974, revised) and sections of the Melka Kunture Formation at Gombore (after Raynal et al., 2004, revised; 40Ar/39A dates from Morgan et al., 2012).

Sedimentation and Site Formation

Lithostratigraphic analyses of sedimentary sections at Kella, Gombore, Garba, and Simbiro have clarified the dynamics of the depositional processes of the Melka Kunture Formation during the Lower Pleistocene. Downstream transport and accumulation dominated. Channel-lag petrographic suites reflect the basin's structural geology and point to a period of global dismantling of ancient volcanic reliefs, as well as to important lateral contributions to alluvial accumulation by the tributaries of both banks. Volcanic activity was the main source of fine-grained sediments. Pumice derived from pyroclastics of penecontemporaneous plinian eruptions were the main contribution to channel lags and to major accretion events (Sl, Sp, St facies; Miall, 1996). Reworked coarse tuffs formed massive beds (Sm facies), while cinereous tephras were mainly responsible for silt deposition (Fsm, Fm facies). Resistant and opaque minerals make up the matrix of bed lags and are the principal components of the sandy bases of current structures.

Six superposed and partly embedded channels were identified in Gombore gully. At Garba IV, i.e., within Garba gully, three channels are superimposed and partly embedded one within the other. Each exhibits a logical facies succession, ultimately leading to complete infilling and abandonment while the main stream migrated farther southeast. Archeological layers are associated with the bedform, local erosional surfaces, or abandoned channels. The input of volcanic products overloaded the streambeds and forced new channel routes. Facies and sedimentary structures are fluvial. The "major cut-and-fill" events may partly represent major erosional phases but mostly local evolutionary channel developments within an active half-graben. The different identified facies indicate a shallow, seasonal, low-sinuosity braided river environment, indicative of a well contrasted dry-wet seasonal climate.

Archeology

The long stratigraphic sequence of Melka Kunture allows the technological trends to be followed from the Oldowan to the Later Stone Age and the impact of high mountain ecological condition on cultural productions to be evaluated, while hominins usually evolved in East Africa as lowlanders.

Lithic industries at Melka Kunture were performed on volcanic raw materials (Piperno et al., 2009; Gallotti et al., 2010, 2014; Gallotti, 2013 Gallotti et al., 2014; Mussi et al., 2014).

The Oldowan is dated to >1.8 Ma at Garba IVE. A single *chaîne opératoire* was aimed at the production of small to medium-sized flakes through unprepared débitage methods and retouch produced small pointed tools (Piperno et al., 2009; Gallotti and Mussi, 2015, 2018). Obsidian is the most frequently exploited raw material. Except for a few Middle Pleistocene Acheulean sites, elsewhere in East Africa obsidian was typically utilized later, i.e., from the Middle Stone Age onwards (Merrick et al., 1994).

Early Acheulean technology appears in the record approximately at 1.6 Ma at Garba IVD and Gombore IB. Stone working includes now two *chaînes opératoires*, i.e., small débitage and Large Cutting Tool (LCT) productions. Both *chaînes opératoires* document a strict differential use of raw materials, whereas the procurement system – from secondary sources close to the site – is the same as the one of the Oldowan. Prepared methods appear both to produce large flakes as potential blanks for LCTs and small–medium-sized flakes. Shaping (*sensu* Inizan et al., 1999) is absent and when any retouch occurred both in large and small–medium flakes, it was a scraper-like retouch (Gallotti, 2013).

During the late early Pleistocene, a set of innovations emerges, as well documented at Garba XIIIB (~1.0 Ma) and Gombore II (~0.85 Ma): (1) a new procurement system, right at the primary sources for large flake débitage; (2) temporal and spatial fragmentation of the LCT *chaînes opératoires*; (3) systematic use of the Kombewa method for LCT flake blank extraction; (4) bifacial and bilateral management of large flake blanks for biface manufacture; (5) intensive production of cleavers; and (6) exclusive use of the discoid technology for small *débitage* (Gallotti et al., 2014). Additionally, knappers at Gombore II enlarged the provisioning area in searching for high-quality basalts for bifaces and cleaver manufacture, reaching a distance of *ca.* 15–20 km. A unique aspect of the bifacial process is the production of obsidian twisted bifaces (Gallotti et al., 2010). The Early Middle Stone Age is documented at Garba III, of late Middle Pleistocene age (Mussi et al. 2014).

Later, in the Middle Pleistocene, at Melka Kunture as elsewhere in East Africa, biface and cleaver manufacture became the main objective of technical activities. Garba I (~0.5 Ma) is a good example, with large amounts of bifaces and cleavers intensely shaped and refined, achieving a high degree of morphological and metrical standardization (Chavaillon and Berthelet, 2004).

Human Remains

Human fossil remains were discovered at four sites during the excavation of archeological levels. Accordingly, there is each time co-occurrence between hominins, lithic productions, fauna, and other environmental indicators.

The earliest fossils attributed to *Homo erectus sensu lato* were found in the basal part of the MKF: the immature mandible of Garba IVE (~1.8 Ma) (Zilberman et al., 2004; Le Cabec et al., 2019) and the humerus of Gombore IB (Chavaillon et al., 1977; Di Vincenzo et al., 2015). Later remains (0.85 Ma) are the cranial fragments of Gombore II-1, recovered with a middle Acheulean assemblage including twisted bifaces and recently attributed to an ancestor of *Homo heidelbergensis* (Chavaillon et al., 1974; Chavaillon and Coppens, 1975, 1986; Profico et al., 2016).

Cranial fragments of archaic *Homo sapiens* are also part of the archeological assemblage of Garba III, belonging to the Early Middle Stone Age (final Middle Pleistocene; Chavaillon et al., 1987; Mussi et al., 2014).

Flora

At present, the Melka Kunture region belongs to a single vegetation type that includes all the plant ecosystems existing between 1800 and 3000 m, called "Dry evergreen Afromontane forest and grassland complex: DAF" (Friis et al., 2011), ranging from forest to grassland and bushland, according to variations in the density of trees, although the plant species remain the same.

Samples collected in various levels from 1.8 to 0.12 Ma yielded 22 pollen assemblages. Altogether, they include over 10,000 grains distributed among a total of 114 distinct fossil plant taxa. Many of them (70, i.e., 61 percent) are not found in the modern pollen assemblage extracted from mud of the Awash River, which is not surprising, considering the highly impoverished natural vegetation around the site because of cultivation and grazing. A great number of pollen taxa ($n = 69$) belongs to trees and shrubs that are listed as components of the present-day "DAF"; thus, the mountain character of the vegetation started from the bottom of the sequence at *ca.* 1.8 Ma until the present day. The evolution of the floral spectrum is detailed below.

Five distinct pollen assemblages, at Kella, Gombore, and Garba, document the past vegetation at the time of the emergence of the Acheulean (Table 21.1; Figure 21.3). At Kella, a

Table 21.1 Composition of pollen samples from Melka Kunture.

		Garba IV	Gombore I	Kella	Gombore II	Garba I
Approx. age (Ma)		1.6	1.6	1.6	0.7	0.5
Arboreal pollen						
Pistacia	Anacardiaceae			3		
Rhus	Anacardiaceae				1	
Heteromorpha	Apiaceae		2			
Carissa edulis	Apocynaceae		1			
Polyscias ferruginea	Araliaceae		1			
Piliostigma thionningii	Caesalpiniaceae			1	3	
	other Caesalpiniaceae				1	
	Combretaceae			1		1
Juniperus procera	Cupressaceae			100	2	
Encephalartos	Cycadaceae			32		
Euclea + Maba	Ebenaceae			2	4	
Hymenocardia acida	Euphorbiaceae					2
Cadia	Fabaceae			4	1	
Calpurnia subdecandra	Fabaceae			1		
Hypericum	Hypericaceae		2			
	Loganiaceae			1		
Acacia	Mimosaceae				5	10
Trilepisium	Moraceae				5	
Myrica salicifolia	Myricaceae			1	2	
Myrsine africana	Myrsinaceae	1		1		
Syzygium guineeense	Myrtaceae			8	2	
Olea	Oleaceae		2	6	7	1
	Palmae			16		
Podocarpus	Podocarpaceae	1	11	11	10	29
Clematis	Ranunculaceae		1	1		
	Rhamnaceae				1	
Hagenia abyssinica	Rosaceae			1	4	
Pygeum africanum	Rosaceae				1	
Psychotria	Rubiaceae			5		
Fagaropsis angolensis	Rutaceae				1	
Dodonaea viscosa	Sapindaceae		1	4	44	17
Sapium ellipticum	Sapotaceae				3	
Brucea antidysenterica	Simarubaceae				1	2
Tamarix	Tamaricaceae			2		
Celtis	Ulmaceae				1	5
Lianas						
Cissus quadranguaris	Vitaceae			1		

| | | Garba IV | Gombore I | Kella | Gombore II | Garba I |

Table 21.1 (cont.)

		Garba IV	Gombore I	Kella	Gombore II	Garba I
Non-Arboreal pollen						
Barleria	Acanthaceae					1
Dyschoriste	Acanthaceae			3		
Achyranthes aspera	Amaranthaceae			1		
Arabis + other Apiaceae	Apiaceae		3	5	2	
	Aster. Cichoriae					6
	Aster. Tubuliflorae	10	2	7	5	8
Artemisia	Asteraceae					1
Carduus	Asteraceae		1			
	Caryophyllaceae				1	
	Chenopodiaceae		4	8	2	5
	Cyperaceae		11	5	2	10
Euphorbia	Euphorbiaceae			1	1	
Rhynchosia	Fabaceae		1			
Plectranthus	Labiateae		1			
Plantago africana	Plantaginaceae	2	6	17	6	5
	Poaceae	96	290	169	442	555
Rumex	Polygonaceae		1	2	2	4
Anthospermum	Rubiaceae		3			
Osyris	Santalaceae				1	
Typha	Typhaceae			1		
	Pteridophyta	1	9	2	1	6
TOTAL		110	446	321	561	662

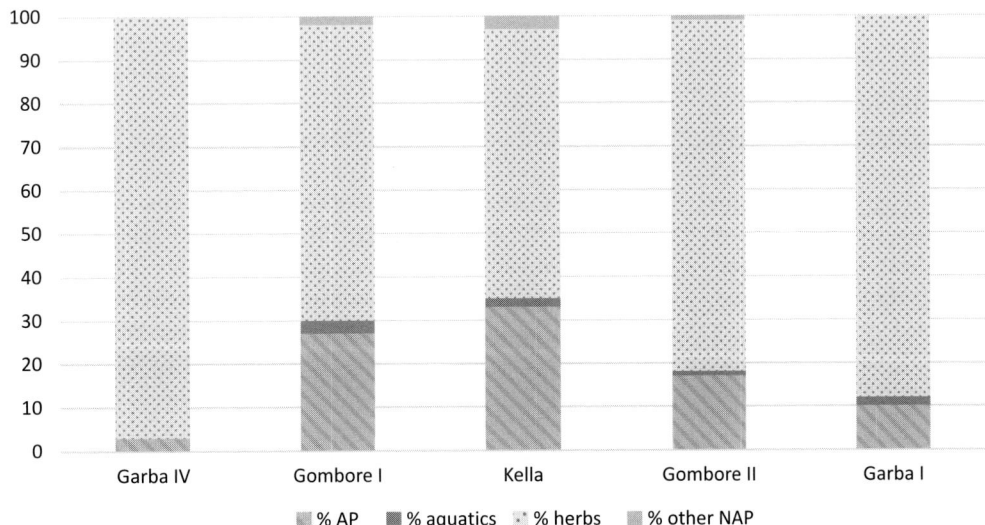

Figure 21.3 Percentages of the main pollen categories in the five samples of Table 21.1.

pollen sample was extracted from a layer located just below that containing the first biface ever found there, but above a volcanic ash that has been dated 1.65 Ma at this spot (but 1.85 Ma a few hundred meters downstream). Although not accurately placed in the stratigraphy, this pollen sample yielded a high diversity of tree taxa of the DAF, with a few still occurring in riparian wooded vegetation (Bonnefille, 1968), although the high percentage of grasses and the occurrence of herbs document large extents of mountain grassland. There is also a palm tree, *Encephalartos*, probably *E. tegulaneus*, absent from Ethiopia today but present in the evergreen forest of Kenya at 2000 m, where it needs a moist, well-drained, frost-free location.

The most common trees of the mountain forests of the northern plateau are present at Gombore IB (Bonnefille, 1971): *Podocarpus*, *Olea*, *Polyscias*, *Hypericum*, and *Myrica*; they are associated with many *Juniperus*, known to disperse its pollen not far from the tree, showing that the earliest known inhabitants of Melka Kunture lived close to a DAF forest dominated by junipers, which extending far beyond the nearby Wochacha volcano. Mountain grasslands were present as well and expanded during Gombore IC occupation (Bonnefille, 1972; Bonnefille et al., 2018).

At Garba IV, pollen assemblages bracketing the Grazia tuff strongly differ from those obtained at Gombore IB. They are dominated by grasses that, together with *Plantago* and Asteraceae, are indicative of an extensive mountain, cool grassland, confirmed by the shrub *Myrsine africana*, a good marker of the DAF. A few pollen grains from *Podocarpus*, a gymnosperm tree whose pollen is widely dispersed, associated with *Dodonea viscosa*, a fire-resistant shrub, point to existing spots of forest, rather limited, or located far away from the site. In the most recent sample of this group, the small highland tree *Myrica salicifolia* is present, while *Celtis* and *Trema* document riparian trees.

A similar vegetation, with grasslands and a dry mountain woodland, persists for some time higher in the sequence, but a significant change occurs at *ca.* 1.3 Ma, documented on the Kella outcrops. The abundance of herbaceous plants, such as Asteraceae, Resedaceae, and Fabaceae, together with the occurrence of *Acacia* trees, resembles the vegetation occupying wadis on the slopes of the Sahara Tibesti mountain, suggesting some affinities with the dry summer conditions of the Mediterranean/Saharan mountains, but trees like Rhamnaceae and *Trilepisium* were present along the Awash.

Before the Bruhnes/Matuyama reversal, the vegetation was an Afroalpine grassland, with abundant grasses and the small shrub *Artemisia*, under climatic conditions much cooler than today, with riparian vegetation (*Myrica salicifolia*, *Salix*). Slightly later, shrubs increase in abundance and diversity (*Dodonaea viscosa*, *Rumex*, *Jasminum*, *Rhus*, and *Myrsine africana*), indicating a dense evergreen bushland, with a dry mountain forest in the far background, while *Typha* (cattail) and *Phragmites* occupied locally humid flat land or freshwater ponds. Just before the archeological levels discovered at Gombore II, a diversified mountain forest including *Juniperus* and *Maesa* was associated with dry evergreen bushland (*Pterolobium*, *Carissa edulis*, *Croton*, *Heteromorpha*, Asteraceae, and Ebenaceae), becoming more humid just after 0.8 Ma.

Younger samples, but still older than Garba I, show an increase in the total of arboreal pollen, many of them from trees that do not disperse their pollen far, indicating that a mountain seasonal forest had reached areas closer to the site. Later, the forest remains highly diversified, including the beautiful tree *Hagenia abyssinica*, associated with *Anthospermum* and Asteraceae, attesting to an Afroalpine vegetation nowadays occupying cold areas above the forest belt. Freshwater swamps including *Typha* and sedges were locally present. A pollen assemblage at Garba I (Bonnefille, 1969) shows a reduced proportion of forest pollen replaced by mountain evergreen bushland (*Brucea*, *Shrebera*, *Dodonaea viscosa*, and *Podocarpus*), with riparian trees of the genus *Celtis*.

Pollen assemblages likely immediately posterior to the archeological assemblage of Garba III are remarkable by the great proportion of tree taxa of the high-elevation diversified *Podocarpus* forest, accompanied by several types of Acanthaceae (*Justicia*, *Mimulopsis*, and *Hypoestes*) known in their understory today, and many taxa of the mountain grassland (Friis et al., 2011). The occurrence of *Hypericum* and *Hagenia abyssinica* trees together with *Alchemilla* and Ericaceae (heath) shrubs, now located above the upper limit of the forest zone, indicates a climate slightly cooler than today.

In summary, there is no evidence of the warmer and drier vegetation encountered in the Rift valley today, and the pollen flora always belongs to the "Dry evergreen afromontane forest and grassland complex," with more or less wooded mountain grasslands. It implies mountain ecological conditions, experiencing cool nights and warmer days. These conditions persisted throughout the whole sequence from 1.7 Ma onwards.

Regarding reconstruction of paleolandscape (Figure 21.4), the pollen data register the occurrence of three different vegetation types. Mountain grassland and evergreen bushland was probably the regional vegetation in the basin whereas mountain forests were present along the escarpment, although their proximity to the site and their composition varied a great deal through time. The floodplain was occupied by local grasslands, and subaquatic vegetation surrounded rivers and ponds. Isolated riparian trees occurred but never constitute a dense forest. Only soon after *ca.* 0.2 Ma, a closed-canopy forest is documented at the Kella site. The two periods during which forest was considerably reduced and during which mountain grasslands were the most extensive correspond with the Garba IV and Garba I archeological occupations, so there is no general trend toward aridity through the whole sequence.

A notable point is the difference between the grasslands documented at Garba IV and the more densely wooded vegetation, close to a juniper forest, of Gombore IB. This might seem surprising if the two sites are chronologically close, but one must remember that wet–dry climate variability on the timescales of 20-ky precessional monsoon cycles might be sufficient to cause such a major shift in the vegetation cover. We may consider that this vegetation change had some bearing on the emergence of the early Acheulean. Unfortunately, the chronology is not accurate enough to address this question at Melka Kunture.

Later, when hominins were making the evolved Acheulean stone tools of Gombore II or Garba XII, many plant resources were available to them from at least three distinct vegetation types: the subaquatic and riparian vegetation near the river, the

Figure 21.4 Past environments at Melka Kunture must have been similar to these grasslands, with montane forests in the background, in the Chyulu Hills in Southern Kenya. Photo: R. Bonnefille, 2010.

Figure 21.5 Detail of the archaeological floor of Gombore II, at the open air museum.

local mountain grasslands, and different types of forests, located at walking distances. The forests occurred in the basin, but were sometimes restricted, sometimes located farther away, or reaching closer to the site. Their composition was always changing and offered a great variety of food resources and shelter.

Fauna

All faunal remains from Melka Kunture were found associated with lithic artifacts in occupation floors frequented by hominins (Figure 21.5), and we can assume that, whatever their origin, these faunal remains do not faithfully reflect the biocenosis. In early publications, Chavaillon posited that they were leftovers of butchering and consumption activities of hominins. More recently, Fiore and Tagliacozzo (2004) conducted a taphonomic analysis of the site of Garba IVD, by far the richest in number of specimens. They observed that only 10 percent of the faunal remains preserve their surface intact or are only moderately abraded, and that the representation of the anatomical elements is far lower than what would be expected in calm depositional settings, suggesting transport before deposition. Also, the distribution of the various anatomical elements across the categories distinguished by Badgley (1986) compares best with her Group I, again indicating transport. Fiore and Tagliacozzo (2004) concluded that in this site the faunal assemblage was subjected to hydraulic sorting, lacking elements that floated farther downstream, but probably also including elements redeposited from upstream. Although no detailed taphonomic analysis has been undertaken yet in the other localities, it is clear that in all main localities, the relative proportions of the main anatomical element are also biased (Table 21.2). Garba IVD has many bovid horn-cores, whereas Gombore II has few horn-cores but many postcranial elements, and Gombore IB appears intermediate in this respect. At Gombore II, large distal humeri and astragali are remarkably common, especially as there is no horn-core of corresponding size (Bovini); hydraulic sorting is certainly responsible for this overrepresentation of these compact, robust bones, as already surmised by Geraads (1985). We suspect that the overrepresentation of horn-cores at Garba IVD could be attributed to a similar process. Although only horn-cores can be easily identified to genus, it is likely that the various bovid taxa were differentially affected by these preservation biases, *Connochaetes* horn-cores being overrepresented in respect to those of *Damaliscus*, whose teeth and perhaps limb bones are more common. Of course, this seriously hinders any interpretation of hominin behavior, and also, although perhaps less seriously, the paleoecological conclusions.

Table 21.2 Number of the main anatomical elements in the richest levels of Melka Kunture

	Garba IVD	Gombore IB	Gombore II
Bovidae HC* (total)	108	38	21
Bovidae teeth (total)	140	61	114
Bovidae postcrania	96	90	172
Alcelaphini HC	60	20	11
Alcelaphini teeth	70	25	83
Antilopini HC	14	0	3
Antilopini teeth	3	0	1
Bovini HC	5	0	0
Bovini teeth	22	0	17
Reduncini HC	0	0	2
Reduncini teeth	0	0	3

*HC, horn-cores.

The following account on the taxonomy is based upon the detailed studies by Geraads (1979, 1985), Geraads et al. (2004a), and Gallotti et al. (2010), with some updates. The faunal list is as follows (see also Table 21.3).

Table 21.3 Distribution of the vertebrate taxa in the various sites of Melka Kunture.

	GAR IVEF	GAR IVCD	GOM IBC	GOM Iγ	SIM III	GAR XIII	GAR XII	GOM II	GAR I	GAR III
Pseudocivetta ingens	+									
cf. *Hyaena* sp.								+		
Megantereon sp.			+							
Lupulella sp.				+				+		
Theropithecus oswaldi		+					+			
Elephas recki recki		cf.	cf.				cf.		+	
Stylohipparion sp.		+	+	+				+		
Equus cf. *capensis*	cf.	+								
Equus cf. *stenonis*	cf.	+	+							
Equus cf. *mauritanicum*								+		
Equus sp.	cf.	+	+	+	+	+	+		+	+
Diceros sp.								+		
Hippopotamus cf. *amphibius*	+	+	+	+	+	+	+	+	+	+
Hippopotamus cf. *aethiopicus*			+							
Kolpochoerus majus	+	+								
Kolpochoerus cf. *olduvaiensis*	+		+							
Metridiochoerus cf. *andrewsi*	+	+		sp.	+			sp.		
Metridiochoerus modestus		cf.						+		
Phacochoerus sp.										+
Suidae indet.				+					+	

	GAR IVEF	GAR IVCD	GOM IBC	GOM Iγ	SIM III	GAR XIII	GAR XII	GOM II	GAR I	GAR III
Giraffa cf. *camelopardalis*		+			cf.			+		+
Sivatherium maurusium		+		+						
Pelorovis oldowayensis								sp.		
P. turkanensis brachyceras	?	+	sp.		+					
Bovini indet.						+	+	+	+	+
Hippotragini indet.				+	?		?			
Kobus sp. (small)	+	+		+	?			+	+	+
Kobus cf. *ellipsiprymnus*								?		
Connochaetes gentryi leptoceras	cf.	+	cf.	?	cf.					
Connochaetes taurinus						sp.		+	+	+
Damaliscus strepsiceras	cf.	+	+		sp.					
Damaliscus cf. *korrigum*		+		+	+		+	+	+	+
Parmularius cf. *angusticornis*		+		+						
Gazella cf. *rufifrons*	sp.	+	sp.	+				sp.		sp.
Antidorcas cf. *recki*		+								
Antilopini indet.									+	
Stenocephalomys sp.									+	
Oenomys kunturensis									+	
Arvicanthis sp.		+								
Muridae indet.					+					
Otomys cf. *typus*										+
Tachyoryctes konjitae		+		+	+			+		+
Hystrix cf. *cristata*									+	
Hystrix sp.		+								
Tadorna sp.								+		
Cygnus sp.		+								
Crocodylus sp.		+	+					+		
Chelonia indet.		+								

The Carnivora are extremely rare compared to ungulates. A lower carnassial tooth from Garba IVE was assigned to *Enhydriodon* by Petter (in Geraads et al., 2004a) but belongs in fact to the viverrid *Pseudocivetta ingens*, also known from Omo Member G until Olduvai Bed II. A distal humerus from Gombore II resembles more *Hyaena* than *Crocuta*. A distal humerus and proximal left ulna from Gombore IB, probably of the same individual, must be referred to *Megantereon*, a widespread dirk-toothed felid whose systematics is not fully agreed upon (Werdelin and Peigné, 2010, and references therein). Two axis vertebrae belong to jackals (*Lupulella* sp.), perhaps of two distinct species.

Besides hominins, there is only one species of primate, *Theropithecus* cf. *oswaldi*, a relative of the gelada baboon, which is quite rare, in contrast with its high frequency in many other African Pleistocene sites. There is a molar fragment from Garba IVD, and a maxilla from Garba XIIJ. These remains are too incomplete to infer any useful biochronological conclusion.

Elephants are extremely rare, as there are only pelvis and tooth fragments. Piperno and Bulgarelli-Piperno (1975, figure 21.17.5) also figured a dp3 from Garba IVD, which looks similar to those of *Elephas recki recki* from the upper Omo Shungura members (Beden, 1979, figure 21.89C).

The Equidae are represented by the monodactyl *Equus* and the tridactyl "*Hipparion*" (s.l.); taxonomic identifications are difficult, but several species are present. At Garba IVD and E (Geraads et al., 2004a), there were probably three species of *Equus*, one with large and plicated teeth and probably long protocones, which was very tentatively referred to the South

African *E.* cf. *capensis*; one of medium size referred to a smallish and robust form close to the European *E.* cf. *stenonis*; and a smaller form *Equus* sp. It is surprising that the forms most similar (or less different) are not East African, but either European or South African.

A mandibular symphysis, some teeth and incomplete limb bones from Garba IVD, Gombore IB, and Gombore Iγ are among the few remains of hipparions of this age, while a few teeth from Gombore II are among the latest known representatives of this group. The only definite comparison is that the symphysis of Garba IVD cannot belong to the same hipparion as the symphysis of Olduvai Bed II referred (Eisenmann, 1998) to *Hipparion* cf. *cornelianum* (often called *Eurygnathohippus*). All this material can be identified as *Stylohipparion* sp.

The single remain of Rhinocerotidae from Melka Kunture is a maxilla from Gombore II, outside archeological excavations. It can unambiguously be referred to *Diceros* rather than to the much more common grazer *Ceratotherium*.

The hippo is the most common large mammal of Melka Kunture, and the dominant one in terms of biomass, but its remains consist mostly of bone and teeth fragments. Almost all of them belong to a large-sized species, similar to, or slightly larger than, the modern common hippo, *Hippopotamus amphibius* L., and there is no positive evidence that it differed from it at the species level. However, the earliest populations, from Gombore IB and Garba IVD, are distinctly more brachyodont than those from Gombore II and later sites, which can more confidently be assigned to the modern species. The large hippo from the earliest localities of Melka Kunture is clearly distinct from the large Olduvai hippo known as *H. gorgops*. This confirms the diversity of Plio-Pleistocene African hippos, probably linked to the isolation of local hydrographic systems. A single tooth from Gombore IB belongs to a dwarf hippo; it resembles a P4 of *Hippopotamus aethiopicus* from Omo (Coryndon and Coppens, 1973), a species that lasts until Shungura Member L.

The Suidae are quite rare compared to either the hippos or bovids. *Kolpochoerus* cf. *majus* is represented by a few incomplete tooth remains from Garba IVD. The M3 is well distinct from that of the contemporaneous *K. olduvaiensis* (= evolved morph of *K. limnetes*) in its short, simple talon, but is more reminiscent of *K. majus*, a species that ranges from ca. 1.9 to 0.3 Ma (Souron, 2012). A few more or less complete teeth seem to belong to another species of *Kolpochoerus*, probably *K. olduvaiensis*; a molar fragment lacks the pillar isolation of *K. majus*. Still, the occurrence of two species of *Kolpochoerus* in the earliest levels of Melka Kunture rests upon very scant evidence.

Several third molar fragments from the early localities belong to at least one species of *Metridiochoerus* but none is diagnostic to species. They are rather small, but an M2 from Gombore Iγ is very large. Some of them should probably be referred to *M. andrewsi*, being too small for *M. compactus*, too complex for *Phacochoerus*, and lacking the pillar isolation of *M. hopwoodi*. In addition, an incomplete m3 from Garba IVD matches better *M. modestus*, and this species is definitely present at Garba XIIJ. *Phacochoerus* sp., the modern warthog, appears only at Garba III.

A proximal metatarsal from Garba IVD is definitely of *Giraffa* rather than of *Sivatherium*; it is the size of a large modern giraffe, *G. camelopardalis*, but a few East African fossil specimens are larger still. In addition, a lower premolar from Gombore Iγ and some tooth fragments from Garba IVD demonstrate the occurrence of *Sivatherium maurusium*, a shorter-limbed giraffid.

Together with hippos, the Bovidae make up the bulk of the large mammal fauna of Melka Kunture, being far more common than equids, suids, and giraffids. Most of them belong to the tribe Alcelaphini, and only a few specimens belong to buffaloes (tribe Bovini), kobs (tribe Reduncini), and gazelles (tribe Antilopini).

A partial cranium with complete left horn-core from Simbiro III is most similar to a skull from Olduvai Bed II that Gentry (1967) thought to be a female of *Pelorovis oldowayensis*, a large, long-horned species, best known from Olduvai but also present in Kenya (Harris, 1991) and Israel (Geraads, 1986). There is also a short-horned species of the same genus, *Pelorovis turkanensis*, best known from Koobi Fora (Harris, 1991a), but in contrast to the Kenyan ones, all horn-cores from Garba IVD and Simbiro III are short and taper toward the tips, demanding taxonomic distinction as *P. t. brachyceras*. Fragments from Gombore IB and Karre I probably attest to the presence of the species in these sites as well.

The only definite record of the Hippotragini at Melka Kunture is a lower molar from Gombore Iγ; very few other specimens could be of the same tribe.

Reduncins are rare in all localities, but size indicates that two different species are present. The smallest one is not larger than a large *Redunca*, but a horn-core piece fits better with *Kobus*, while a second species, perhaps the waterbuck, is represented by teeth from Gombore II.

The Alcelaphini are by far the most common bovid tribe. Dental remains can seldom be identified to genus, but horn-cores are also relatively common, allowing identification of several taxa.

Connochaetes gentryi was previously known from the Late Pliocene and Early Pleistocene of Kenya and Tanzania. Gentry and Gentry (1978a, 1978b), Harris et al. (1988a), and Harris (1991a) believed that the form present at Koobi Fora and Olduvai could be ancestral to the living *C. taurinus*, the blue wildebeest, but the subspecies present in the earliest localities of Melka Kunture, characterized by horn-cores with a very long, slender distal part, which are remarkably frequent at Garba IVD, is certainly a distinct lineage and was called *C. g. leptoceras* by Geraads et al. (2004a). The wildebeest from later Acheulean localities has stout horn-cores and is certainly much closer to the modern form, *C. taurinus*, but the Gombore II form at least is more primitive, as at Olduvai and Tighenif.

Damaliscus strepsiceras is also an Oldowan/early Acheulean form, reminiscent of *D. agelaius* from Olduvai (Gentry and Gentry, 1978a, 1978b), but with a shorter tooth-series, longer premolars, and more spiraled horns; they are longer at Gombore IB than at Garba IVD. A single incomplete horn-core from Garba IVD, as well as poorly preserved horn-cores from later localities, can be tentatively identified as the modern East African form, *Damaliscus korrigum*, probably being too small to belong to the common *Damaliscus* of the Pleistocene of Africa, *D. niro*.

Parmularius is a common and widespread genus in the Plio-Pleistocene of Africa, but it is quite rare at Melka Kunture. A few horn-cores from Garba IVD and Gombore Iγ can be referred to it, but identification as *P. angusticornis* is tentative.

Antilopini are much less common, probably in part because of their fragile remains. Gazelle horn-cores from Garba IVD-E and Gombore Iγ are probably of the modern species *Gazella rufifrons*, but do not differ from the North African Pleistocene *G. pomeli*. A few dental remains from Garba IVD and horn-cores from surface collection best match *Antidorcas recki*, the Plio-Pleistocene springbok of East Africa.

In addition to the large mammals, a number of rodent teeth have been collected by screening, but mostly from localities lacking large mammals. Sabatier (1979) recognized several species, two of which are new: *Oenomys kunturensis* from Garba III, which is closer to *O. olduvaiensis* than to the modern *O. hypoxanthus*, and *Tachyoryctes konjitae* that could be ancestral to the modern *T. splendens* and is by far the most common rodent in all localities, although it may be that hydraulic sorting increased its relative abundance.

Biochronology

The lists of the large mammals from the various archeological localities are given in Table 21.3. It is interesting to evaluate how this distribution and the evolutionary stages of some species fit into the stratigraphic succession. In all localities, sampling of the biocenosis was certainly far from complete, so that conclusions are hard to draw from absences, but bovids, which are abundant, provide some reliable information. The best-documented level is Garba IVD; it clearly belongs to the same faunal unit as Gombore IB, as they share the most characteristic taxa: *Connochaetes gentryi leptoceras* and *Damaliscus strepsiceras*. However, the latter is represented by a slightly distinct variety, which is certainly a different evolutionary stage of the same lineage; thus, the only chronological relationship that can be discarded is exact contemporaneity. In the belief that Gombore IB was the earlier site, a shortening of the horn-cores had to be assumed (Geraads et al., 2004a), but this is perhaps a less likely evolutionary trend than the lengthening that should be posited if the succession is the reverse. The fauna of Gombore Iγ does not significantly differ from those of these sites, but is too poor for definite conclusions. Simbiro III has *Pelorovis turkanensis brachyceras* and *Connochaetes gentryi*, so that on faunal grounds it is not very remote from these early localities.

Paleoecology

The ecological implications of the faunal assemblage are clear. The complete lack of tragelaphins, the rare occurrence of reduncins, the presence of the probably grazing *Pelorovis*, the striking dominance of alcelaphins among identified bovids (Table 21.4), and the high frequency of equids strongly suggest that, during the whole sequence of Melka Kunture, the environments documented by the large mammal fauna were open grasslands, with rare bushes and thickets, in agreement with the abundance of the rodent *Tachyoryctes*. The virtual lack of monkeys speaks against the presence of a significant riverine forest along the paleo-Awash, although it may be that their small size acted against their preservation, given the taphonomic conditions.

In the early localities, equid morphology provides some further details. At Garba IVD, a hipparion mandibular symphysis is of a grazer, and a terminal phalanx from Gombore Iγ probably reflects hard ground; however, the robustness of the *Equus* metapodials and the extreme plication of their teeth point to an environment that was not very dry (Geraads et al., 2004a). The giraffe implies the presence of some trees.

The large hippo displays interesting changes in its tooth morphology. In early sites, its molars are distinctly more brachyodont than those of the modern *H. amphibius* or of the fossil *H. sirensis* and *H. gorgops*, their lateral sides converging toward the apex of the tooth. From Gombore II onwards, they become more hypsodont, with more nearly parallel borders. One might expect that this increase in hypsodonty was correlated to a change in diet, but the isotopic analysis (Bocherens et al., 1996) found no evidence of it, the $\delta^{13}C$ being even less negative than in modern hippos, showing that it fed mainly on C4 grasses; perhaps these grasses were softer than those consumed by other large Pleistocene and recent hippos.

Table 21.4 Number of identified specimens in the main sites of Melka Kunture.

	Total Bovidae	Alcela.	Antilopini	Bovini	Redun.	Hippotr.	Bovidae indet.	Equidae	Hippo.	Suidae	TOTAL
GAR III	36	12	2	1	2	0	19	6	15	1	58
GAR I	21	10	2	1	1	0	7	6	23	1	51
GOM II	312	100	5	63	5	0	139	59	325	1	697
GAR XIII	3	0	0	1	0	0	2	1	7	0	11
SIM III	30	11	0	4	1	1	13	8	18	1	57
GAR XII	25	10	0	2	0	1	12	8	32	4	69
GOM Iγ	15	3	4	0	1	1	6	22	24	1	62
KARRE	5	1	0	3	0	0	1	0	7	0	12
GAR IV C-D	350	130	10	15	0	0	195	113	362	15	840
GOM IB	205	45	1	4	0	0	155	66	293	13	577
GAR IV E-F	59	29	4	3	4	0	19	15	70	7	151

Conclusion

Despite its fragmentary nature, which often precludes precise identification, the fauna from Melka Kunture is quite interesting because many mammals are distinct at specific or subspecific levels from contemporaneous forms in the Turkana Basin or at Olduvai. This is true for the alcelaphins, the large hippo, and probably for most of the equids. Because the time range of the best-documented part of the Melka Kunture sequence certainly falls within that of these sites located at lower latitudes and altitudes, those distinctions are clearly of geographical or ecological origin. They point toward an isolation of some part of present-day Ethiopia. Whether this part includes only a small area, such as central Shoa, or most of the Ethiopian highlands is not known, because no other fauna has been described from these highlands, but it is clear that this geographic isolation must be taken into account when dealing with hominin biological and cultural evolution. At present, Melka Kunture is the only archeological site with a long stratigraphic sequence allowing understanding of how hominins first developed the capacity of living at high altitude. The ecological conditions did not impact on the lithic industries, whose technical structure is shared by other Oldowan and Acheulean techno-complexes in East Africa. This means that similar lithic productions were successfully adopted in various contemporary environments.

The faunal and floral data agree to reconstruct the environment of most Melka Kunture sites as dominated by open grasslands, with aquatic vegetation and some trees near the river. This kind of landscape is particularly well documented at Garba IV. However, there is no evidence in the fauna of the forest that is definitely attested by pollen in most levels of Melka Kunture. Several factors may account for this absence of inhabitants of thick bushland, woodlands, or forests. We cannot rule out a preservation or collecting bias in the absence of some faunal elements, such as the small primates, but this does not hold for, e.g., tragelaphin horncores that are robust. More likely explanations are that the pollen sampled a broader geographic area than the faunal remains, because if most of the fossils were water-transported, bones from forest animals were not included, or that, if the faunal remains are really leftovers of hominin food processing, these hominins only occupied the sites during the driest phases. Unfortunately, Melka Kunture still lacks a natural, well-preserved fossil accumulation that would allow controlling for these factors.

Acknowledgments

We thank the Authority for Research and Conservation of Cultural Heritage of the Ministry of Culture & Tourism, the National Museum of Addis Ababa, and the Oromia Culture and Tourism Bureau for permits for fieldwork and access to the collections. Véra Eisenmann provided much help with the Equidae. The Archeological Mission at Melka Kunture and Balchit is directed by M.M., with J. Panera and E. Mendez-Quintas as co-Directors. This chapter reflects geology (J.-P.R.), Oldowan archeology (R.G.), Acheulean archeology (M.M.), human paleontology (M.M.), vertebrate paleontology (D.G.), and flora (R.B.).

22 Early Pleistocene Fauna and Paleoenvironments at Konso, Ethiopia

Gen Suwa, Berhane Asfaw, Hideo Nakaya, Shigehiro Katoh, and Yonas Beyene

Background

The Konso Formation (Fm) is exposed in the southernmost part of the Main Ethiopian Rift, >400 km SSE of Addis Ababa, approximately 160–240 km northeast of the fossiliferous exposures of the northern Turkana Basin (Figure 22.1). It occurs at the southwestern part of the Ganjuli graben, ~25–40 km south of Lake Chamo, at an altitude mostly between 1150 and 1400 m. To the north, the Konso Fm basin is separated from the lower (in altitude) Lake Chamo by a ~1200–1300 m drainage divide. Currently, the Konso Fm basin drains southeast into the Segen River that then courses due west to the northern end of the Chew Bahir rift. The Konso area is separated from the southern lowlands (Weyto/Chew Bahir basin) by a mountainous terrain of 1700–2000 m. Some degree of geographic discontinuity and altitudinal difference between the Konso and the Turkana basins probably existed in the Early Pleistocene as well, judging from the differences observed in the mammalian fauna (Suwa et al., 2003). Tentatively, we interpret the Early Pleistocene Konso Fm to represent a rift-induced small depositional basin that was distinct from the Lake Chamo depression (Nagaoka et al., 2005; Katoh et al., 2014). Most likely, the Konso basin had subsided before rifting had advanced in the Lake Chamo area to recent downthrown levels. The occurrence of the high-altitude ranging rodent *Tachyoryctes* at the ~1.4 Ma levels of localities KGA7 and KGA12 (currently 1400 and 1340 m altitude, respectively) suggests that Early Pleistocene deposition may have occurred at a similarly high altitude. Maximum lake expansion in the Early Pleistocene Konso Fm basin is estimated to be ~8 km (NE–SW) at <1.3–1.4 Ma (Suwa et al., 2003; Nagaoka et al., 2005).

A recently updated chronostratigraphy of the Konso Fm is presented in Beyene et al. (2013, 2015) and Katoh et al. (2014). Early Pleistocene sediments and fossils range from ~1.95 Ma, close to the Olduvai event lower boundary, upwards mostly to ~1.2 Ma. At the southern basin margins, the uppermost Konso Fm sediments, younger than 1.0 Ma, unconformably overlie the main Konso Fm sequence. Twenty-seven tephra units are recognized, 11 or 13 of which are considered correlative to those described in the Omo-Turkana basin (Katoh et al., 2014). Depositional gaps occur at ~1.8 Ma, ~1.7 Ma, ~1.5 Ma, ~1.4 Ma, and ~1.2–<1.0 Ma, enabling partitioning of the Konso Fm faunal assemblages into six non-overlapping chronostratigraphic intervals (Intervals 1 to 6, hereafter INT-1 to INT-6; Figure 22.2). A comprehensive schematic summary of the chronological positions of the faunal collection localities and levels were initially presented in Suwa et al. (2003), with minor revisions added in Katoh et al. (2014; see their figure 3.2).

The Konso fossils were systematically collected mostly by surface survey at 21 collection localities, each about ~1 to several km diameters (see figures 2.1 and 2.2 of Suwa et al., 2014a). The details of the localities and collection methods are outlined in Suwa et al. (2014a). In 1993, a systematic collection strategy was explicitly set and thereafter rigorously followed. This resulted in what we consider a highly reliable relative abundance record of the fossils that we encountered and collected. Although the fossiliferous exposures occur within the Konso people's traditional farmland areas, when we started our work in the early 1990s, only few farms had encroached the fossil localities (e.g., at KGA4 and KGA7). At this time, the villagers appeared not to have engaged in any noticeable degrees of fossil picking. The surface scatter looked quite fresh and minimally disturbed. We

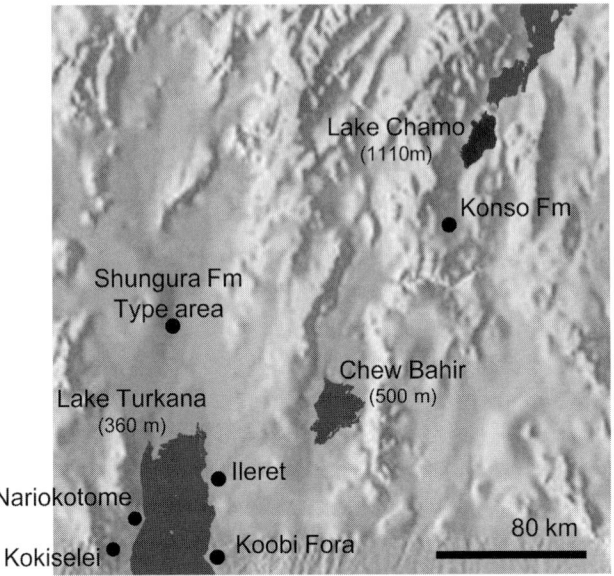

Figure 22.1 Digital elevation map showing locations of the Omo-Turkana and Konso Formation basins. Topographic imagery from National Geophysical Data Center, with superimposed lake contours taken from Landsat 8 image available from U.S. Geological Survey. Present-day lake level altitudes are shown in parentheses.

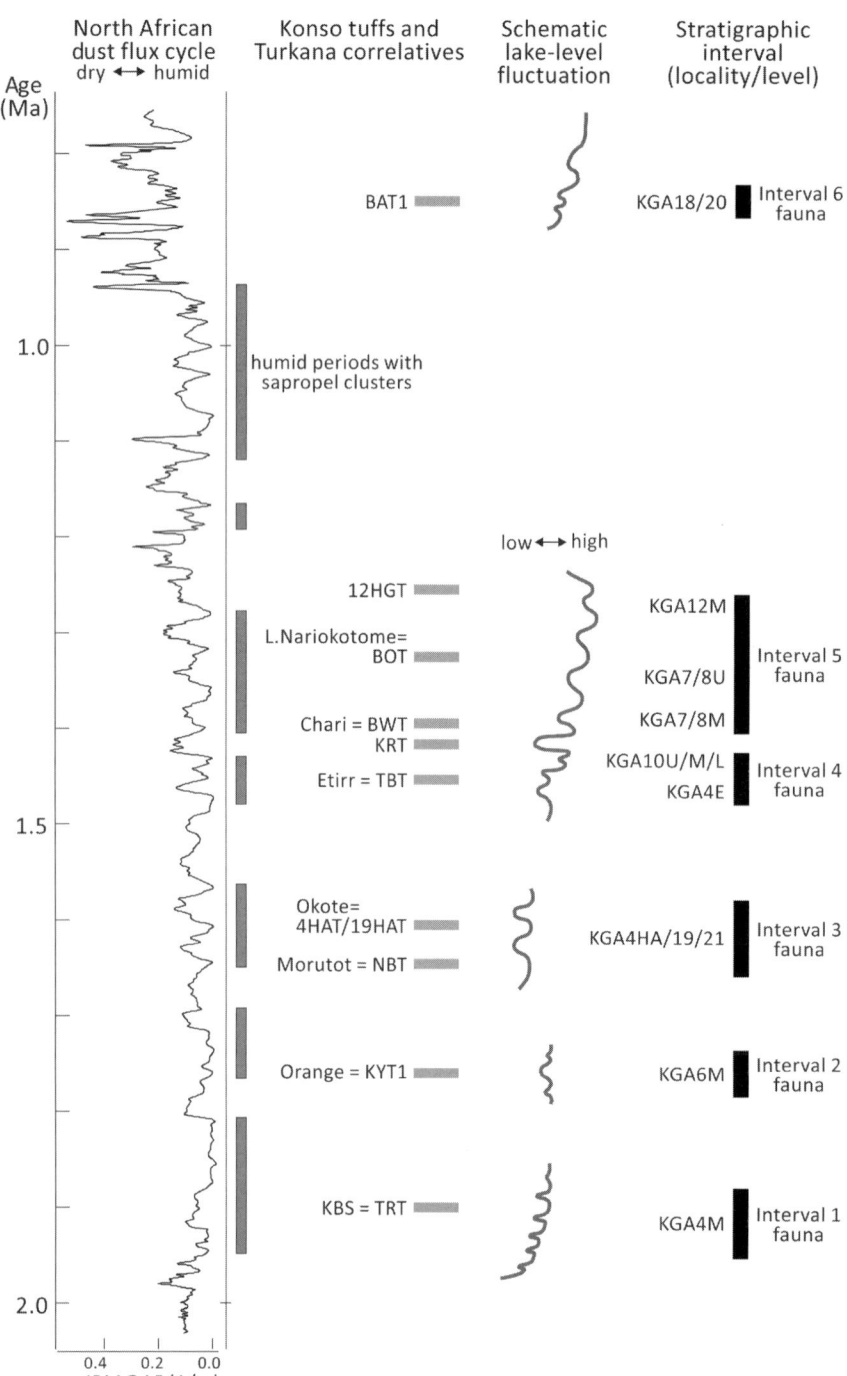

Figure 22.2 Simplified schematic relationship of Konso Formation chronostratigraphy and cyclic changes in regional/continental environments. From left to right columns: North African dust flux cycles and sapropel cluster periods, modified from Larrasoana et al. (2003) and Trauth et al. (2009). Konso tuffs and Turkana basin correlatives, simplified from Beyene et al. (2013) and Katoh et al. (2014). Note that the Okote tuff of the Koobi Fora Formation is similar in elemental compositions to four closely spaced tuffs at Konso, the 4HAT, 19HAT, BRT, and DBT (Beyene et al., 2013). Schematic depiction of presumed lake level fluctuations inferred from the Konso Formation, after Suwa et al. (2003), Nagaoka et al. (2005), and unpublished data. Chronological distributions of the Konso Formation fossiliferous stratigraphic intervals after Katoh et al. (2014).

conducted the bulk of the systematic collecting in the central localities between 1993 and 1997, and in the peripheral localities through 2000. During this period of annual systematic paleontological survey, we were fortunate to have had the full support of the Konso administration and agricultural associations so that the scientific collecting of the fossils was not disturbed.

Our collection strategy and methods were similar to that described in detail by Eck (2007) for the American Omo collection, but with several important differences. From the very start of the work, we aimed to exhaustively sample the fossils in an unbiased way as possible, so we systematically collected both craniodental and postcranial materials. The exception was that for the large proboscidean fossils, only craniodental fossils were systematically collected. Another notable exception regarded the ubiquitous hippopotamus fossils, which as a rule we did not collect. These exceptions stemmed from laboratory and storage limitations in the 1990s, and the expectation that much of such large fossils would remain available for collection in the future. In 2010, we collected a small representative sample of hippopotamus fossils from two major localities (KGA4 and KGA10), as well as including hippopotamids in systematic collecting at a newly recognized small fossiliferous patch (the KGA4 EE exposure). The latter was done so as to obtain information regarding relative abundance of hippopotamids in a sandy unit that is otherwise dominated by terrestrial mammalian fossils. Such sandy units comprise the majority of fossiliferous units intercalated throughout the Konso Fm.

Although we consider much of our surface collection to be relatively well-constrained in stratigraphic levels of derivation, and hence chronologically well-controlled for general paleontological evaluations, this is not the case if one's interest is in the unit-specific relative abundances or other characteristics. For the purpose of catalog documentation and collection analyses, fossils were logged as deriving from one of several "collection levels" at each locality, such as the KGA10 "main level" or KGA10 "upper level." Typically, these "levels" would include one to several fossiliferous sandy units that intercalate the predominantly silt to clay sequences. These units represent floodplain or fluvial lake margin facies associated with successive periods of lake regression (see Nagaoka et al., 2005, for an interpretation of cyclic sedimentation in INT-4 and INT-5 of the Konso Fm). Therefore, faunal assemblages allocated to collection levels represent varying degrees of chronological and depositional mixtures. These collection levels may comprise sedimentary units spanning up to several precession cycles. Alternatively, some collection levels (such as those at KGA10) appear to be confined to subprecession timescale cycles of sedimentation. The collection level designations of each locality and their vertical extents are shown in the stratigraphic columns published in Katoh et al. (2014, their figures 3.5–3.10).

A schematic depiction of the chronostratigraphic context of lake level regression–transgression cycles and how they relate to the Konso Fm stratigraphic intervals and locality collection levels are shown in Figure 22.2. Typically, the predominantly silt/clay Konso Fm sediments intercalating thinner sandy fossiliferous units represent extended periods of relatively high lake levels in the Konso basin. Conversely, the conspicuous depositional hiatuses between stratigraphic intervals represent extended periods of low lake levels. Importantly, the Konso Fm sedimentary pattern corresponds well with several time scales of humid and arid periodicities (~40 kyr, 100 kyr, and 400 kyr) documented for northern Africa as represented by the dust flux data and sapropel clusters of the eastern Mediterranean (Larrasoana et al., 2003). Sedimentation of the fossiliferous units at Konso appears associated with regression events interspersed within extended periods of high lake levels. The latter was most probably driven by humid conditions that recurrently characterized large areas of the Sahara and surrounding regions via cycles of particularly strong northern penetration of the African summer monsoon (Larrasoana et al., 2003). Larrasoana et al. (2003) and Trauth et al. (2009) attributed such long-term (100 or 400 kyr) Saharan environmental periodicity to the effects of precession amplified by eccentricity.

The Konso Faunal Assemblages

Over 8000 vertebrate fossils from the Konso Fm were collected from systematic paleontological survey, mostly between 1993 and 2010. A total of 8176 fossil specimens are currently entered in the Konso vertebrate paleontology catalog (January 2014 version) as independent cases (i.e., specimens assumed to belong to different individuals; Suwa et al., 2014a). These fossils include 8102 mammalian fossils identified to family and/or order, 26 specimens not yet allocated to mammalian order, 36 bird fossils, and 12 fossils identified as reptilian. Crocodilian and chelonian fossils were common at some of the localities (e.g., KGA 4, a locality dominated by lacustrine clay/silts), but were generally fragmentary and not collected. Fish fossils, when present, were fragmentary and identifiable elements were rare.

All bird fossils noticed in the field were collected ($n = 36$). These were described by Louchart (2014), who reports 12 distinct taxa, including swimming and diving piscivores (grebe, cormorant, and darter), shore predators (ibis, heron, and stork), probably a swan, the terrestrial francolin and guinea fowl, and raptors. These bird fossils come from the fossil-rich stratigraphic intervals, INT-1, INT-4, and INT-5. The fossil assemblages from INT-2, INT-3, and INT-6 are much smaller (see below), and do not contain birds. Terrestrial bird fossils are fewer in number. They are as frequent as aquatic taxa only at KGA10, a locality considered to have been dominated by dry grassland-adapted mammals (Suwa et al., 2003; and below). Louchart (2014) considers the Konso avian fossils to indicate presence of freshwater courses and water bodies.

Of the 8102 mammalian fossils identified to taxa, the vast majority have been attributed to stratigraphic level. A limited number of specimens from KGA4 and KGA11 have indeterminate chronostratigraphic provenience. At KGA4, the INT-1, INT-3, and INT-4 sedimentary units are lithologically similar, and at some places juxtaposed in fault contact. While we were able to allocate most fossiliferous units to fault blocks, this was not possible for some of the surface scatters. Likewise, at the western end of KGA11, the INT-4 sediments lie unconformably on the INT-1 sediments, making judgments as to stratigraphic provenience of fossils problematic in some instances. A few other specimens collected from KGA2, KGA3, and KGA9 were also not allocated to stratigraphic levels. The stratigraphic provenience levels of the remaining 7877 fossils were estimated in relation to the more than 20 marker tuffs spanning the ~1.95–0.85 Ma time period (Katoh et al., 2014). Our analyses of relative abundances are based on this sample of 7877 specimens. Sample sizes (number of collected fossils) are small for the INT-2 ($n = 57$) and INT-6 ($n = 125$) faunal assemblages, so that much of the analyses and discussion that follow focus on the INT-1, INT-3, INT-4, and INT-5 fossils. Sample sizes for these intervals are: INT-1, $n = 1887$; INT-3, $n = 491$; INT-4, $n = 3308$; and INT-5, $n = 2009$. The richest locality, KGA10 ($n = 2697$, all from INT-4), contributes 82 percent of the INT-4 fauna. Another particularly rich locality, KGA4 ($n = 2410$), contributes 98 percent of the INT-1 fauna, 42 percent of the INT-3 fauna, and 11 percent of the INT-4 fauna. The large majority of the INT-5 fauna (95 percent) is represented by fossils from KGA7/8 ($n = 813$) and KGA12 ($n = 1046$).

The mammalian taxa identified to genus and species were listed in Suwa et al. (2003). This fauna list needs only minor modifications. The INT-1 notochoere n. sp. has since then been named *Notochoerus clarki* (White and Suwa, 2004). Suwa et al.

(2014b) furthermore provided a comprehensive descriptive analysis of the Konso suids, and noted several minor changes from the Suwa et al. (2003) listing: one change is to conservatively call the Konso *Kolpochoerus majus* lineage fossils *K.* cf. *majus*, because of its primitive intermediate condition between the 2.5 Ma *K. phillipi* (Souron et al., 2015) and the ~1 Ma and later *K. majus*; a second minor change involves allocation of the *Kolpochoerus limnetes/olduvaiensis* lineage materials; while the INT-2, INT-3, and lower INT-4 materials are attributed to *K. limnetes/olduvaiensis*, the other INT-4 and INT-5 materials are now allocated to *K. olduvaiensis*. A third taxonomic change stemmed from reevaluation of fragmentary metridiochoere dental elements, leading to the conclusion that Konso *Metridiochoerus andrewsi* is represented only in INT-1 and INT-2, and not in INT-3 (as listed in Suwa et al., 2003). The cercopithecids have also been comprehensively described and analyzed (Frost, 2014), necessitating the following remarks. *Theropithecus oswaldi* from INT-4 and INT-5 are allocated to the advanced subspecies *T. oswaldi leakeyi*, although they are not quite as advanced as the ~1 Ma and later examples of the derived subspecies. At Konso, Colobinae is very rare, but now recorded in both INT-4 and INT-5.

In analyzing relative abundances, we first compare body part representation among fossils of the Konso stratigraphic intervals (Table 22.1), and between Konso and the Omo-Turkana basin fossil assemblages (Figure 22.3). Overall, close to 60 percent of the Konso fossils are isolated teeth, 30 percent are postcrania, and 10 percent are partial crania and jaws (including small fragments). The KGA4-dominated INT-1 fauna is characterized by a greater proportion of cranial (~20 percent) and postcranial (~40 percent) fossils with only 40 percent isolated teeth, whereas the INT-4/5 fauna, largely represented by KGA10 and KGA7/8/12, consists of around 65 percent isolated teeth. This difference may stem in part from the tendency for more solidified matrix at KGA4 that might have prevented postexposure fragmentation of jaws better than at the other localities. However, the greater postcranial frequency at KGA4 cannot be explained by such a factor, and may relate to a more lacustrine habitat sampled at KGA4 (e.g., abundance of hippopotamids and crocodiles). Compared with the Omo Shungura Formation fossils (Alemseged et al., 2007; Eck, 2007), relative body part representation at Konso is closest to that of the French Omo collection (Figure 22.3). Eck (2007) detailed that, while the French team collected postcrania across taxa, the American team collected only limited postcranial elements. The published database entries of the Koobi Fora Formation collection (Bobe, 2011) appear to be biased in favor of crania and jaws. This most probably stems from a difference of collection strategies. The Konso Fm is characterized by an overall smaller exposed area. Much of the outcrops are hidden by Middle Pleistocene and later deposits as well as by modern vegetation and farmlands. Hence, in most localities and outcrops, systematic survey would generally follow the ribbon-like zone of exposed fossiliferous units along the main ridge margins and flanks. This somewhat simplified the systematic collecting, and enabled strict imposition of a comprehensive collection strategy.

The order/family breakdown of the 7877 Konso fossil specimens and results of the comparisons with the Omo Shungura Fm assemblages are shown in Table 22.2 and Figure 22.4. Here, we focused on comparisons using the French Omo collection, which seems more comparable in body part representation with the Konso fossils than the American Omo collection. Overall, bovids dominate the Konso mammalian assemblage, close to 70 percent of all catalogued mammals, which is a high

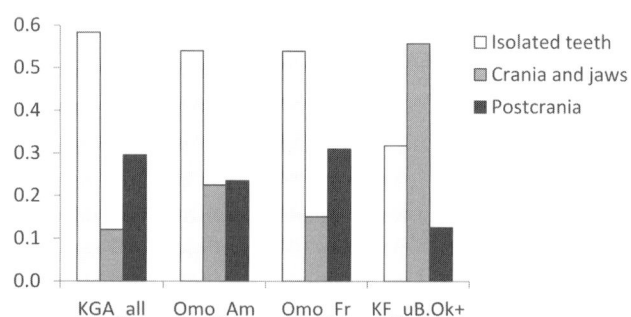

Figure 22.3 Relative abundance of body parts of the Konso Formation mammalian fossils and comparisons with the Omo-Turkana Basin. KGA all: combined total of 7877 specimens allocated to stratigraphic intervals 1 through 6 (Table 22.1). Omo Am and Omo Fr are the Omo Shungura Formation American and French collections, respectively (combining Members A through L; after Alemseged et al., 2007). KF uB-Ok+ shows the combined frequencies of the Koobi Fora Formation upper Burgi, KBS, and Okote Members, data from the Turkana Basin Published database (Bobe, 2011) omitting specimens that lack stratigraphic provenience and not counting suffix entries that represent the same individual.

Table 22.1 Body part representation of the Konso Formation mammalian fossil assemblages

Body part	Stratigraphic intervals													
	All		Interval 1		Interval 2		Interval 3		Interval 4		Interval 5		Interval 6	
	No.	%	No.	%	No.	%	No.	%	No.	%	No.	%	No.	%
Isolated teeth	4597	58.4	754	40.0	37	64.9	302	61.5	2075	62.7	1330	66.2	99	79.2
Mandible (and frags)	302	3.8	109	5.8	5	8.8	15	3.1	125	3.8	43	2.1	5	4.0
Maxilla (and frags)	80	1.0	35	1.9	1	1.8	6	1.2	27	0.8	9	0.4	2	1.6
Crania (includes horn cores)	567	7.2	224	11.9	4	7.0	21	4.3	251	7.6	63	3.1	4	3.2
Postcrania	2331	29.6	765	40.5	10	17.5	147	29.9	830	25.1	564	28.1	15	12.0
Total	7877		1887		57		491		3308		2009		125	

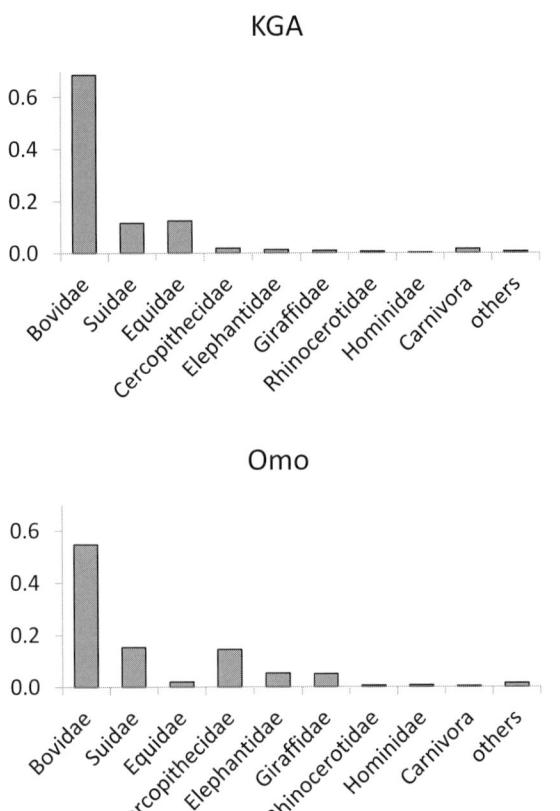

Figure 22.4 Relative taxonomic abundances of the Konso Formation mammalian fossils and comparison with the Omo Shungura Formation. Because hippopotamids were not systematically collected at Konso, the diagrams are depicted with the hippopotamids omitted. Data are from Table 22.2 combining Konso stratigraphic intervals 1 through 6. Rare taxa are combined in the category labelled as "others."

fossiliferous units were thin sandy inclusions within lacustrine clays and exhibited an extreme dominance of hippopotamids (e.g., KGA10U), while other units appeared to be rare in hippopotamid fossils.

Among the four most common medium to large body-sized mammalian families, bovids, suids, equids and cercopithecids, some differences were observed between Konso and Omo, and among Konso stratigraphic intervals (Table 22.3). Possible meaningful interpretations of these patterns are: (1) a bovid dominance that intensifies after ~2.0 Ma (Bobe and Behrensmeyer, 2004), (2) a greater abundance of cercopithecids at Omo prior to ~2 Ma (Bobe and Behrensmeyer, 2004; Eck, 2007), (3) a consistently low (~1–3 percent) frequency of cercopithecids at Konso, and (4) a greater abundance of equids throughout the Konso sequence, subequal to suids and apparently increasing after ~1.45 Ma.

The largest body-sized families, the elephants, giraffes, and rhinos, are rare at Konso (~1 percent); the former two are somewhat more common at Omo (~5 percent, not including hippopotamids in the counts). Carnivores are more common at Konso than at Omo, perhaps several times the relative abundance. Whereas felids considerably outnumber hyaenids at Omo (Alemseged et al., 2007), this is not the case at Konso. Hyaenids are dominant at most, but not all, Konso localities, and the pattern suggests locality differences in habitat sampling (hyaenids representing more open habitats). At Konso, KGA10 (INT-4) and KGA7/8 (INT-5) show strong dominance of hyaenids. Other Konso localities/levels exhibit either coequal occurrences of hyaenids and felids (KGA4 INT-1 levels), felid dominance (KGA4 INT-4 levels), or felid/viverrid dominance (KGA12 INT-5 levels). The rodents of Table 22.2 are mostly porcupine (*Hystrix*), documented in all Konso stratigraphic intervals except INT-2 and INT-6. At KGA12, the cane rat (*Thryonomys*) is also common. Two specimens of a mole-rat (*Tachyoryctes*) indicative of high altitude were found during paleontological survey despite their small sizes. So far, no patches of high micromammal concentration have been discovered. However, wet-sieving at an archeological excavation site (KGA4-A3) yielded several murid species (*Thallomys*, *Arvicanthis*?, and cf. *Saidomys*), indicating the presence of a wider range of micromammals than known from the systematic paleontological surface collecting.

Paleoenvironments

The paleoenvironmental implications of the Konso fauna are derived using the numerical abundances of bovid fossils assigned to tribes. It is well-established that Alcelaphini and Antilopini are good indicators of predominantly open and dry grassland environments, both in the present and in the past. While Reduncini indicates wet grasslands, Bovini are considered to be associated with wet grasslands and/or woodlands. Tragelaphini and Aepycerotini represent woodland or woodland/forest edge habitats. The relative abundance of Alcelaphini and Antilopini (proportion of AA to all bovids identified to tribe; or AAH including Hippotragini) has been extensively used as an indicator of arid and/or open habitats in the African Pliocene and Pleistocene (e.g., Vrba, 1975; Bobe et al., 2007b; Bibi and

degree of bovid dominance stronger than seen in the Shungura Fm. This is the case even when we take into account that hippopotamids (as a rule) were not collected at Konso (Figure 22.4, Table 22.2).

As briefly mentioned in the introductory passages, in 2010, we included hippopotamids in the systematic collecting of a newly recognized small exposure KGA4 EE (see figure 2.3 of Beyene et al., 2015). As is the case with many other Konso localities, fossils and artifacts were found eroding out of a thin sandy unit intercalated in dark colored silts/clays. Although this was a small collection of 70 mammalian specimens, it exhibited a relative abundance pattern typical of many Konso localities and levels; bovids were by far the most abundant (47 percent), followed by roughly equal frequencies of suids and equids (13 percent and 14 percent, respectively). Elephantids and rhinocerotids were represented by one specimen (1.4 percent) each. In this collection, hippopotamids (23 percent) were the second most common after bovids, similar to the Shungura Fm French collection in relative abundances (Table 22.2). Although we did not collect quantitative data regarding hippopotamids at the other Konso localities, the general impression was that KGA4 EE probably falls within a relatively common condition at Konso. However, clearly, each fossiliferous unit would differ in abundance of hippopotamids. Some

Table 22.2 Taxonomic (order and family) representation of the Konso Formation mammalian fossil assemblages

Taxon	Konso Fm stratigraphic intervals													Omo Shungura Fm		
	All		Interval 1		Interval 2		Interval 3		Interval 4		Interval 5		Interval 6		Mbs A–L Fr collection		
	No.	%	No.	%	No.	%	No.	%	No.	%	No.	%	No.	%	No.	%	% (– hippo)
Bovidae	5356	68.0	1415	75.0	37	64.9	385	78.4	2266	68.5	1170	58.2	83	66.4	11,007	43.0	54.7
Suidae	912	11.6	243	12.9	5	8.8	47	9.6	380	11.5	225	11.2	12	9.6	3087	12.1	15.3
Equidae	978	12.4	96	5.1	7	12.3	39	7.9	411	12.4	401	20.0	24	19.2	397	1.6	2.0
Cercopithecidae	147	1.9	36	1.9			5	1.0	51	1.5	55	2.7			2917	11.4	14.5
Elephantidae	101	1.3	16	0.8	7	12.3	2	0.4	34	1.0	38	1.9	4	3.2	1062	4.2	5.3
Giraffidae	72	0.9	23	1.2			2	0.4	23	0.7	23	1.1	1	0.8	1007	3.9	5.0
Rhinocerotidae	48	0.6	1	0.1			1	0.2	21	0.6	24	1.2	1	0.8	109	0.4	0.5
Hippopotamidae	65	0.8	10	0.5			1	0.2	41	1.2	13	0.6			5472	21.4	0.0
Hominidae	19	0.2							16	0.5	3	0.1			135	0.5	0.7
Chalicotheriidae	16	0.2	1	0.1					1	0.0	14	0.7			4	0.0	0.0
Deinotheriidae	2	0.0	2	0.1											196	0.8	1.0
Orycteropodidae	1	0.0	1	0.1													
Carnivora	127	1.6	37	2.0	1	1.8	6	1.2	58	1.8	25	1.2			79	0.4	0.4
Rodentia	32	0.4	6	0.3			3	0.6	6	0.2	17	0.8			93	0.5	0.5
Lagomorpha	1	0.0									1	0.0			3	0.0	0.0
Others															16	0.1	0.1
Total	7877		1887		57		491		3308		2009		125		25,584		

Omo collection data from Eck (2007).
% (– hippo) is relative frequency calculated by omitting the hippopotamids.
Konso hippopotamids include INT-4 specimens systematically collected at KGA4 EE (*n* = 16), others were selectively collected.

Table 22.3 Relative abundance of four major families: bovids, suids, equids and cercopithecids

Taxon	Konso stratigraphic intervals					Omo Fr collection	
	All	Int-1	Int-3	Int-4	Int-5	A-lowG	upG-J
Bovidae (%)	72.4	79.1	80.9	72.9	63.2	63.1	80.0
Suidae (%)	12.3	13.6	9.9	12.2	12.2	17.1	14.5
Equidae (%)	13.2	5.4	8.2	13.2	21.7	2.0	3.7
Cercopithecidae (%)	2.0	2.0	1.1	1.6	3.0	17.9	1.8
Total	7393	1790	476	3108	1851	11,966	1674

Omo collection data from Eck (2007).
Total is total number of specimens of the four families.
Intervals 2 and 6 not tabulated due to small sample sizes.

Kiessling, 2015). The analyses of these authors showed that relatively high AA (or AAH) values that exceed 0.2–0.4 commonly occurred in northern Tanzania, the Afar, and West Turkana as early as 4–3 Ma. In contrast, probably because of the more stable water source of the Omo-Turkana Basin, AA values remained low in the lower Omo Valley and East Turkana throughout the Pliocene (mostly 0.1 or lower), and it was only after 2.0 Ma that AA values of ~0.2–0.3 are observed. The implication is that the large water bodies of the Omo-Turkana basin enabled retention of more mesic and denser environments and habitats compared to the other regions and areas (Bobe et al., 2007b). It is also interesting to note that, compared to the impoverished Konso cercopithecid representation, the Omo-Turkana basin cercopithecids exhibit considerable taxonomic diversity and numerical abundance extending into post-2 Ma times (Jablonski and Leakey, 2008). This may also be underlain by such aspects of the Omo-Turkana basin environmental setting.

Against this background, we examined the bovid tribe frequencies of the Konso fossil assemblages. Suwa et al. (2003) presented Konso bovid tribe specimen counts, segregated by locality and collection levels. This was done by means of a strict method of relative abundance counts, restricted to molars and controlling for degree of breakage. We termed this the "standardized molar NISP" and also applied it to equids and suids (Suwa et al., 2003). In Table 22.4 we summarize the Suwa et al. (2003) bovid tribe dataset by stratigraphic intervals, and also present an alternative version based on raw NISP counts of all collected specimens. The results of the two methods are very similar (Table 22.4). The Konso bovid tribe frequencies suggest greater dominance of open dry grasslands in INT-1, INT-3, and INT-4 (AA values range from ~0.4 to ~0.7), but not in INT-5 (AA value of <0.2; Figure 22.5A). However, a more detailed look at the relatively densely sampled and well-calibrated INT-4 and INT-5 fossils indicates that abundance of bovid tribes actually fluctuates radically (Figure 22.5B). The AA values of the individual collection levels of KGA10 and KGA7/8 vary from as high as 0.86 (KGA10M) to as low as 0.08 (KGA7/8U). We also tallied the abundance of *Equus* relative to total bovid tribe counts. In the Shungura Fm, even after 2 Ma, equids (and *Equus*) are rare (Bobe and Behrensmeyer, 2004; Eck, 2007), whereas at Konso, equids occur in subequal numbers with suids (Table 22.3). A peculiar pattern of equid frequency was observed at Konso as follows. Contrary to Alcelaphini, *Equus* becomes increasingly abundant through INT-4/5, and particularly so at the main and upper collection levels of KGA7/8 (Figure 22.5A,B). This suggests a broad association of *Equus*, not with dry grasslands, but rather with mosaics of wet grasslands and woodlands, and that the genus became more abundant and/or may have undergone conspicuous range expansion between ~1.9 and ~1.25 Ma.

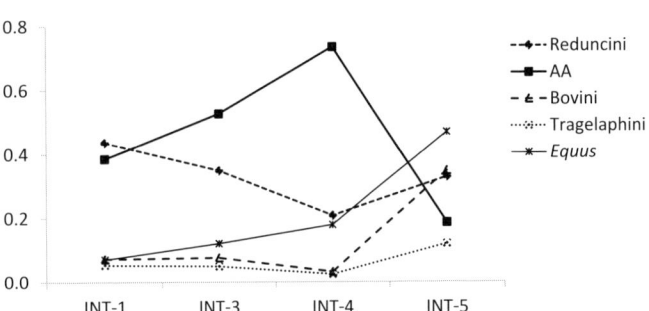

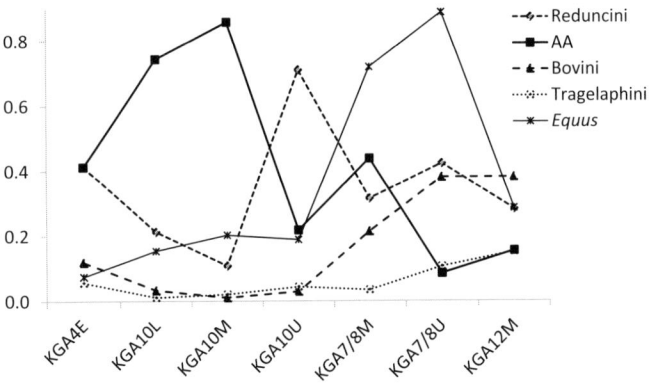

Figure 22.5 Relative abundance of bovid tribes and *Equus* in the Konso Formation. The number of specimens attributed to each bovid tribe divided by NISP (number of identified specimens). Data are from Table 22.4, only craniodental specimens have so far been identified to tribe. AA is combined total of Alcelaphini and Antilopini. *Equus* (counting only craniodental specimens) NISP is also shown relative to bovid tribe total NISP. (a) Comparison of stratigraphic intervals 1–5 (intervals 2 and 6 are not shown due to small sample sizes). (b) Detailed pattern within stratigraphic intervals 4/5. Only localities/levels with relatively large samples are shown. Localities KGA7 and KGA8 are geographically adjacent and were combined.

Table 22.4 Relative abundances of the Konso Formation bovid tribes

Taxon	Konso Fm stratigraphic intervals											
	All		Interval 1		Interval 2		Interval 3		Interval 4		Interval 5		Interval 6	
	dNISPstd	%	dNISPstd	%	dNISPstd	%	dNISPstd	%	dNISPstd	%	dNISPstd	%	
Alcelaphini	1068	53.0	157	39.5	5	31.3	84	50.9	751	74.4	71	16.6	
Antilopini	55.8	2.8	13.8	3.5	1	6.3	6	3.6	31	3.1	4	0.9	
Reduncini	561	27.9	158	39.8	10	62.5	55	33.3	192	19.0	146	34.2	
Bovini	224	11.1	36	9.1			15	9.1	25	2.5	148	34.7	
Tragepahini	83	4.1	20	5.0			5	3.0	8	0.8	50	11.7	
Aepycerotini	12.2	0.6	12.2	3.1									
Hippotragini	10	0.5							2	0.2	8	1.9	
Total	2014		397		16		165		1009		427		

Taxon	rawNISP	%	rawNISP	%	rawNISP	%	rawNISP	%	rawNISP	%	rawNISP	%	rawNISP	%
Alcelaphini	1490	48.4	220	32.2	8	32.0	111	49.6	1028	70.3	108	17.4	15	23.1
Antilopini	105.5	3.4	42.5	6.2	1	4.0	7	3.1	46	3.1	7	1.1	2	3.1
Reduncini	932	30.3	297	43.5	15	60.0	78	34.8	303	20.7	203	32.8	36	55.4
Bovini	339	11.0	49	7.2	0	0.0	17	7.6	46	3.1	215	34.7	12	18.5
Tragepahini	157	5.1	36	5.3	1	4.0	11	4.9	35	2.4	74	12.0		
Aepycerotini	35.5	1.2	35.5	5.2										
Hippotragini	17	0.6	2	0.3					3	0.2	12	1.9		
Neotragini	2	0.1	1	0.1					1	0.1				
Total	3078		683		25		224		1462		619		65	

dNISPstd is standardized molar NISP (standardized number of identifed specimens, see Suwa et al., 2003);
rawNISP is NISP of all collected specimens. So far, only cranial and dental specimens are allocated to tribe Antilopini and Aepycerotini dentitions were sometimes difficult to distinguish, in which case allocations followed cranial (horn core) frequencies (see Suwa et al, 2003).

Antilopini and Aepycerotini dentitions were sometimes difficult to distinguish, in which case allocations followed cranial (horn-core) frequencies (see Suwa et al., 2003).

The KGA10 and KGA7/8 fossiliferous units are particularly enlightening, because these localities occur adjacent to each other and can be inferred to have occupied a similar lake margin setting at the time of deposition. KGA7/8 occurs just 1–2 km south of KGA10. The three KGA10 collection levels are temporally closely spaced, all probably lying within a single precession cycle, possibly between 1.45 and 1.42 Ma. These collection levels combine one to several sandy silt to gravelly sand fossiliferous depositional units. They represent either small-scale lake margin fluvial systems, or, in the case of the KGA10M level, a small alluvial fan. These fossiliferous units at KGA10 were probably associated with millennium or shorter-scaled fluctuations of humid–dry cycles, superimposed on a period of overall lake transgression at the precession (or longer) timescale (Figure 22.2).

At Konso, a prolonged period of generally high lake levels continued from ~1.45 through <1.3 Ma, with an overall trend for an increase of lake levels through time. The bovid tribe frequency data strongly suggest that, during the early part of this period, extensive stretches of open dry grasslands occurred close to the lake margins at and before ~1.43 Ma (KGA10L and M, AA values of 0.74 and 0.86, respectively). The Reduncini- and hippopotamus-rich KGA10U level comprises (a) thin sandy layer(s) within thicker lacustrine clays, and probably samples fauna of a marshy lakeshore setting. Then there appears to have been a period of greater lake level decrease, expressed by reduced sedimentation at around the time of deposition of the Karat Tuff (KRT, ~1.42 Ma). Following this regression, an extensive diatomite unit just below the Bright White Tuff (BWT, equivalent of the Omo-Turkana basin Chari tuff) indicates a period of stable high lake levels just at or before ~1.40 Ma. Thereafter, further cyclic increase of lake level continued until ~1.3–1.25 Ma. These are schematically shown in Figure 22.2. The chronology of the fossiliferous units above BWT are not resolved well enough to form a hypothesis of possible associations with precession or longer-scaled cycles. However, contrary to the apparent predominance of dry grasslands prior to ~1.43 Ma, bovid tribe abundances after ~1.4 Ma suggest transition from a mix of dry and wet grasslands and woodlands (KGA7/8M), to wet grassland and woodland dominance (KGA7/8U), followed by a greater contribution of woodlands (KGA12M; Figure 22.5b). The latter may in part represent location (habitat sampling) differences (3–4 km distance).

In summary, the INT-4 and INT-5 faunal assemblages of the Konso Fm document paleoenvironments of the Konso basin from >1.45 to <1.3 Ma with some considerable resolution. This is the time period thought to have been characterized by recurrent humid environments extending north of the central Saharan watershed (Larrasoana et al., 2003; Trauth et al., 2009). It seems possible that the Konso INT-4 and INT-5 sediments and faunas were formed and preserved via the modally high lake levels associated with the hypothesized periods of strong northern excursions of the African monsoon. Previous workers have suggested that one such period would have been centered at ~1.4 Ma corresponding to the 400-kyr cyclicity of extreme modulation of precession by eccentricity (Larrasoana et al., 2003; Trauth et al., 2009). In the Konso basin, the earlier part (~1.45–1.4 Ma) of this period appears to have been drier than after 1.4 Ma. Sediments and fossils immediately prior to this, at and before ~1.5 Ma, are not sampled at Konso, presumably because there was little deposition at this time due to it being overall an even drier period.

We reported previously on the distinct taxonomic differences between the Konso faunas of INT-1/2, INT-3, and INT-4/5. The latter is characterized by a suite of immigrant dry grassland-adapted bovids with Olduvai Bed II taxonomic affinities (Suwa et al., 2003). These taxa may have been going through a phase of range expansion (or shifts) at or around the 1.55–1.5 Ma period of Saharan relative aridity. Alternatively, such range expansions might have occurred earlier at >1.6 Ma. The current small samples of the Konso INT-3 fossils preclude a definitive conclusion. It is of interest to note that, at Konso, judging from the continuous record of Acheulean assemblages, the *Homo erectus* lineage appears little affected by the rather large fluctuations of Saharan and regional environments spanning 1.65 to 1.25 Ma. We have recently evaluated the tempo and mode of Acheulean technological development through this time period (Beyene et al., 2013, 2015). Significant technological changes within the early Acheulean seem gradual and accretionary rather than abrupt. However, there are flaking technology enhancements that start to appear at early INT-4 levels at ~1.45 Ma, and such appear to intensify through the INT-5 levels. It is possible that, with establishment of the (largely) immigrant dry grassland-adapted mammalian (especially bovid) community, subsistence strategies of the resident *H. erectus* populations changed somewhat. This may have included experimentation in new tool techniques that led to the technological and functional enhancements of the handaxe tool category documented at Konso (Beyene et al., 2013, 2015).

Acknowledgments

The fossil specimens described here are predominantly based on results of field research undertaken by the Konso-Gardula Paleoanthropological Research Project (KGA Project), co-directed by Yonas Beyene and Gen Suwa, by the permission of the government of Ethiopia. We thank the Authority for Research and Conservation of Cultural Heritage of the Ministry of Culture and Tourism of Ethiopia for the continued support to this project over the years. All fossils and artifacts are currently stored in the laboratory facilities of the ARCCH, Addis Ababa. We thank the Southern Nations, Nationalities, and People's Regional State (SNNPRS), the Culture and Tourism Bureau of the SNNPRS, and the Konso administrative district for their support and facilitation to the research. Aside from the coauthors of this paper, many individuals participated in the KGA field and laboratory research and are gratefully acknowledged. We are particularly grateful to the local field assistance provided by Dinote Kusia, Kampiro Kayrante, and Kusia Shekaido, although many more individuals kindly assisted us. The KGA field and laboratory research has been supported by the Mitsubishi Foundation in 1993 and by the Japan Society for the Promotion of Science (JSPS) from 1994 and thereafter. The ongoing KGA project curatorial and research work is funded primarily by JSPS grant number 24000015.

23 Paleontology and Geology of the Mursi Formation

Michelle S.M. Drapeau, Jonathan G. Wynn, Denis Geraads, Laurence Dumouchel, Christopher J. Campisano, and René Bobe

Introduction to the Mursi Formation

The importance of the Turkana Basin (northern Kenya) and lower Omo Valley (southern Ethiopia) in our understanding of the environments in which early hominins lived, and on how climate changes may have influenced the emergence and disappearance of species, is undeniable (e.g., Bobe and Leakey, 2009; Levin et al., 2011). The majority of the Plio-Pleistocene sediments belong to the Omo Group, which consists of the Shungura, Usno, Nkalabong, and Mursi formations in Ethiopia and of the Nachukui and Koobi Fora formations in Kenya (e.g., Brown and McDougall, 2011). The Shungura, Nachukui, and Koobi Fora formations are well-studied (e.g., Howell and Coppens, 1976; de Heinzelin, 1983a, 1983b; Harris et al., 1988a, 1988b; Koobi Fora Research Project Volumes). The Mursi Formation of the lower Omo Valley, with a date of more than 4 million years, is among the oldest formations of the Omo Group in Ethiopia. However, it has been poorly documented despite its importance in informing us on the mid-Pliocene, a period in which the genus *Australopithecus* arose, but that is presently inadequately known. This chapter will present the formation with the history of the research in the area, including renewed fieldwork. It will be followed by a description of the geology and taphonomy and, finally, a preliminary analysis of the fauna found to date.

Importance of the Formation

The genus *Australopithecus* has its first appearance date at about 4.2 Ma at Kanapoi (Leakey et al., 1995), and a member of the genus is the most likely ancestor to the genus *Homo*. Understanding how and why australopithecines evolved, with their novel adaptive niche, which included habitual bipedalism (Leakey et al., 1995; White et al., 2006) and a diet of tough foods (White et al., 2006), will help us define the processes that led eventually to the rise of the genus *Homo*. Although the appearance of the genus *Australopithecus* is characterized by clear morphological traits, the environmental context in which this morphological transition occurred is poorly understood and subtler morphological and behavioral adaptations need to be identified. The first *Australopithecus* species, *A. anamensis*, is documented in only a handful of localities: Allia Bay, Kanapoi, and Fejej in the Turkana Basin and Asa Issie, Aramis, and possibly Woranso-Mille in the Afar Triangle (Leakey et al., 1995; White et al., 2006; Haile-Selassie, 2010; Ward, 2014). Given that the period between 4.5 and 4 Ma is poorly documented, any localities from that time period will provide significant information on the environment in East Africa at that important time period. Further investigation of the Mursi Formation, in which no hominins have been found to date, is important to document different areas and environment that were available but that may not have been favorable to hominins.

History of Research

The lower Omo Valley was first identified as a fossiliferous area by Emil Brumpt, the naturalist of the Bourg de Bozas expedition (de Heinzelin et al., 1976; Guillemot, 1997). They encountered what is now known as the Shungura Formation in 1902, and fossils were collected and sent to the Muséum National d'Histoire Naturelle in Paris (de Heinzelin et al., 1976; Guillemot, 1997). The fossils were studied for the next couple of decades by various researchers, among them Camille Arambourg, who organized a new expedition to these sediments in 1932–33 (Arambourg, 1948). The sediments were revisited occasionally, but it was not until 1966 that geologist Frank Brown confirmed that the sediments were Plio-Pleistocene in age (Brown, 1969; Guillemot, 1997). Systematic paleontological work in the lower Omo Valley was initiated in 1967 by the International Omo Research Expedition (IORE; Howell and Coppens, 1983). The IORE consisted of American, French, and Kenyan teams led by Francis Clark Howell, Camille Arambourg, and Richard Leakey, respectively. Each team surveyed different areas and Richard Leakey was assigned to the eastern bank of the Omo River, at the southern limit of the Nkalabong Range, to survey the relatively younger Kibish sediments and the Yellow Sands locality. These had been recognized during an aerial reconnaissance by Howell, Leakey, Arambourg, and Yves Coppens in early June 1967 (de Heinzelin et al., 1976). During his first year of work, Leakey discovered, in the Kibish Formation, the Omo skulls that are among the earliest specimens of *Homo sapiens*. He also surveyed the much older Yellow Sands sediments, the type area for the Mursi Formation (Butzer and Thurber, 1969), and collected 30 fossils there. After 1967, Leakey concentrated his efforts on Koobi Fora further south, which he had discovered while flying to the Omo from Nairobi, and never returned to the Yellow Sands.

The French and American teams worked in the lower Omo Valley for seven more seasons. The Yellow Sands locality, because it was on the eastern bank of the Omo River, was difficult to access from the Shungura Formation because it involved crossing the Omo River either by boat or by helicopter. In part for that reason, the teams only returned to the Yellow Sands three times to collect fauna. The French crossed via helicopter in 1968 and collected 31 fossils. In 1969, a French and American contingent crossed via helicopter, and collected about 130 fossils. Their work was interrupted because the helicopter crashed in the afternoon and they needed to concentrate their efforts on building a landing strip so that they could be flown out by plane (which occurred the next day with a plane from Nairobi). Finally, in 1973, the Americans crossed the river by boat and collected fossils for a day, returning with 28 fossils. Forty years later, in 2002 and 2003, a team led by John Fleagle surveying the overlying Kibish sediments collected about 30 fossils from the Mursi Formation, including a beautifully preserved skull of a new species of fox, *Vulpes mathisoni* (Geraads et al., 2015a).

When visiting the Yellow Sands for the first time in 1969, the American contingent identified 10 different localities (Butzer, 1976). When they returned in 1973, the focused solely on Locality 4, which was the locality that yielded the most fossils in 1969. Unfortunately, the French and Kenyan contingent did not map their finds, and it is unknown where within the Yellow Sands area of the formation they were collected, although, given the relative abundance of Locality 4, they may have collected there as well. All specimens collected in 2002 and 2003 by John Fleagle, except for one, were from Locality 4 area (Figure 23.1).

Karl Butzer, assisted by Claudia Carr, studied and mapped the Yellow Sands in 1968 (Butzer and Thurber, 1969), which was divided into three sedimentary members topped by an olivine basalt dated to about 4 million years (Brown, 1969). In August 1973, Jean de Heinzelin, Paul Haesaerts, and Frank Brown also studied the stratigraphy (de Heinzelin et al., 1976; Haesaerts, pers. comm., Dec. 31, 2013), broadly concurring with Butzer's work (de Heinzelin and Haesaerts, 1983c). In 1972–73, an Ethiopian–Canadian team of geologists produced an extensive map of the lower Omo basin (Davidson, 1983) and documented that the Mursi sedimentary sequence extended to the north of the Yellow Sands area along the western slope of the Nkalabong Range for about 35 km (Davidson et al., 1973; Davidson, 1983). In 2009 and 2012, exploration by the Mursi Paleontology Project, led by Michelle Drapeau at the Université de Montréal, focused on the northern exposures of the sediments, gaining access from the Mursi Basalt plain that extends west and northwest of the Nkalabong Range. Difficulty with access limited the number of hours surveying, but a new fossiliferous locality was discovered in 2009 and was briefly revisited in 2012. This new locality, which we named Cholo (derived from the name given to the area by the local Mursi people), is located approximately

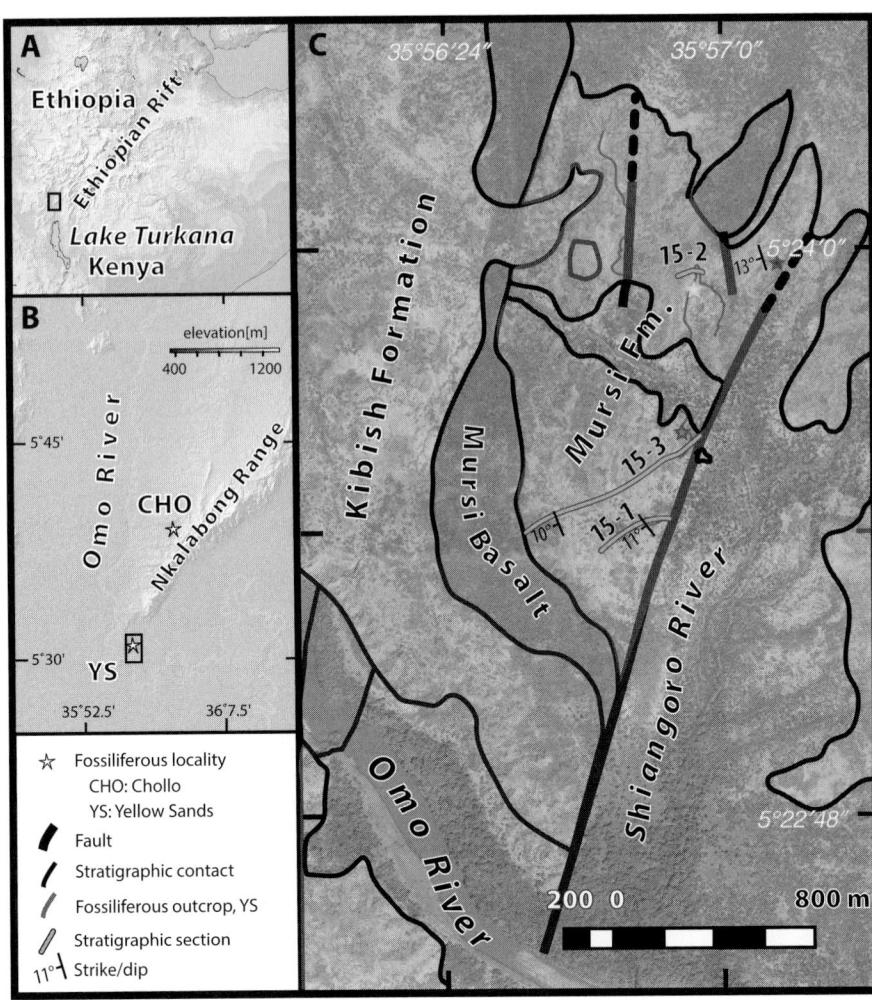

Figure 23.1 Outcrop map of the Mursi Formation exposed at Yellow Sands. (A) Location map of Mursi Formation in eastern Africa; outlined box shows area mapped in (B). (B) Location map of fossiliferous localities: Yellow Sands and Cholo. (C) Outcrop map of the Yellow Sands with the localities identified in 1969 by the IORE (red star, locality 4; yellow star, localities 1–3 and 7–10; green star, locality 6). (A) and (B) are overlain on Shuttle Radar Tomography Mission (SRTM) digital elevation model (DEM) data. (C) is overlain on Landsat Imagery from Google Earth. (A black and white version of this figure will appear in some formats. For the color version, please refer to the plate section.)

28 km to the northeast of the Yellow Sands (Figure 23.1). This discovery of the new locality at the northern extent of the formation suggests that the formation is fossiliferous throughout (Drapeau et al., 2014).

Cholo

In 2009, we found a thick tuff with fossils nearby. However, as the team only held an exploration permit at the time, fossils were documented, but could not be collected. North of the exposed tuff, on a steep slope in an area we named Cholo 1, we observed turtle, fish, crocodile, and hippo remains. Southwest of the exposed tuff, in an area we named Cholo 2, we observed fossilized remains in moderate density of bovids, hippos, suids, elephants and elephant-sized postcrania, crocodiles, fish, and wood. Other fossils were found scattered around in lower densities.

We attempted to return to Cholo in 2012, but because of increased rains in the region and thick grass overgrowth, access, exposure visibility, and fossil relocation proved challenging. At Cholo 1, we found crocodiles and *Euthecodon* teeth, one bovid tooth, gastropod casts, and a few other unidentifiable fragments. The predominance of aquatic taxa is in line with what we had observed in 2009. At Cholo 2, where we had identified elephants, suids, and bovid remains in 2009, we found two elephant tooth fragments and a giraffid femur fragment. In contrast to the predominantly aquatic taxa identified at Cholo 1, the taxa from Cholo 2 are predominantly terrestrial. All finds are currently housed at the National Museum of Ethiopia in Addis Ababa. One of us (J.G.W.) was able to draw a contiguous section through Cholo 1 and identify the most fossiliferous layers (Drapeau et al., 2014).

Return to the Yellow Sands

In February 2015, the Mursi Paleontology Project team returned to the Yellow Sands. More than 30 years after the IORE expeditions, access was still easiest coming from the western bank of the Omo River and crossing the Omo by boat. That year, it was possible to relocate the localities identified by the American team in 1969 and to reinitiate sampling of the fossil fauna. Although the 2015 expedition surveyed for only 9 days, we collected 645 fossil specimens, tripling the existing fossil sample for the formation. Our work confirmed that Locality 4 has the highest density of fossils. Fossils were found in two other areas, one was identified as Locality 6 by the American contingent of the IORE, while the other included Localities 1, 2, 3, 7, 8, 9, and 10 (Figure 23.1). Except for localities 1 and 9, which are on the western slope of the valley-like exposures, we observed no significant reason for giving different locality numbers to pre-existing Localities 2, 3, 7, 8, and 10, all located on the eastern slope of the valley-like area. Of the 645 specimens collected in 2015, 68 percent were collected at Locality 4, 11 percent at Locality 6, and 19 percent at the other cluster of localities (1, 2, 3, 7, 8, 9, 10). A few specimens (2 percent) were collected in a previously undocumented locality with very low fossil density. Although the 2015 season yielded a much greater number of specimens from Locality 6 than previous expeditions (11 percent of the collection versus 0.6 percent), the proportions of specimens collected at Locality 4 versus the proportion collected at the other cluster is identical (78 percent and 22 percent, respectively) to the previous expeditions. The proportion of time spent at each locality is unknown for the previous teams, but given the similarity in numbers, it may have been proportionally similar to the amount of time spent by the 2015 expedition (ratio ~4:1).

Geology: Stratigraphy and Paleoenvironments

Although the Mursi Formation outcrops in a 40-km band along the western slope of the Nkalabong range (Davidson, 1983), only two regions of outcrops, the Yellow Sands and Cholo, have been described in any detail (e.g., Butzer, 1976; de Heinzelin and Haesaerts, 1983c; Drapeau et al., 2014). To this previous work, we have added new geological observations at the Yellow Sands locality as a context for the renewed paleontological work at this locality.

The Shiangoro River, near its intersection with the Omo River, exposes ~120 m of sediments including the Yellow Sands, a ~10 m package of distinctly colored (10YR 5/6 yellowish brown) cross-bedded sandstones near the base of the sequence locally exposed (Figure 23.2). The western side of the Shiangoro Valley is an uplifted fault block that is capped by the Mursi Basalt, which locally holds up badland exposures of the Mursi Formation below (Figure 23.1). The outcrops are bounded on the eastern side by a normal fault, which follows the western banks of the river and marks a knickpoint in the Omo River. The outcrops are bounded on the west, north, and south sides by a crescent-shaped ridge forming in the plateau surfaces held up by the resistant Mursi Basalt; the latter is overlain unconformably by the Kibish Formation capping the plateau. The Mursi Formation is not exposed on the eastern side of this fault, constraining the fault's activity to between deposition of the Mursi and Kibish Formation. Two other faults cut through the Mursi Formation exposures in the northern area of outcrop, and repeat the section such that the Yellow Sands are exposed on at least two of the fault-bounded blocks. Other minor slump-block faults mapped by Butzer (1976) have offsets <5 m and are not shown in Figure 23.1.

In this area of limited outcrop, a continuous section from the Shiangoro River up to the Mursi Basalt has thus far provided a type section for the formation (Butzer and Thurber, 1969; de Heinzelin and Haesaerts, 1983c). However, the ~120 m exposed here is a minimum thickness of the formation because the lower contact is not exposed in the immediate vicinity of the Yellow Sands, although the sediments are known to unconformably overlie Paleogene–Neogene volcanics throughout outcrops further north, as in the vicinity of Cholo (Davidson, 1983; Drapeau et al., 2014). The sedimentary sequence at Shiangoro ends at the contact to the Mursi Basalt and the "Shiangoro Alteration Zone", as defined by Butzer and Thurber (1969). Although Butzer's stratigraphy indicates that the Mursi Basalt is to be included in the Mursi Formation, we propose to use the mapping unit definitions of Davidson (1983), which maps this as a separate stratigraphic unit; thus, a more complete definition

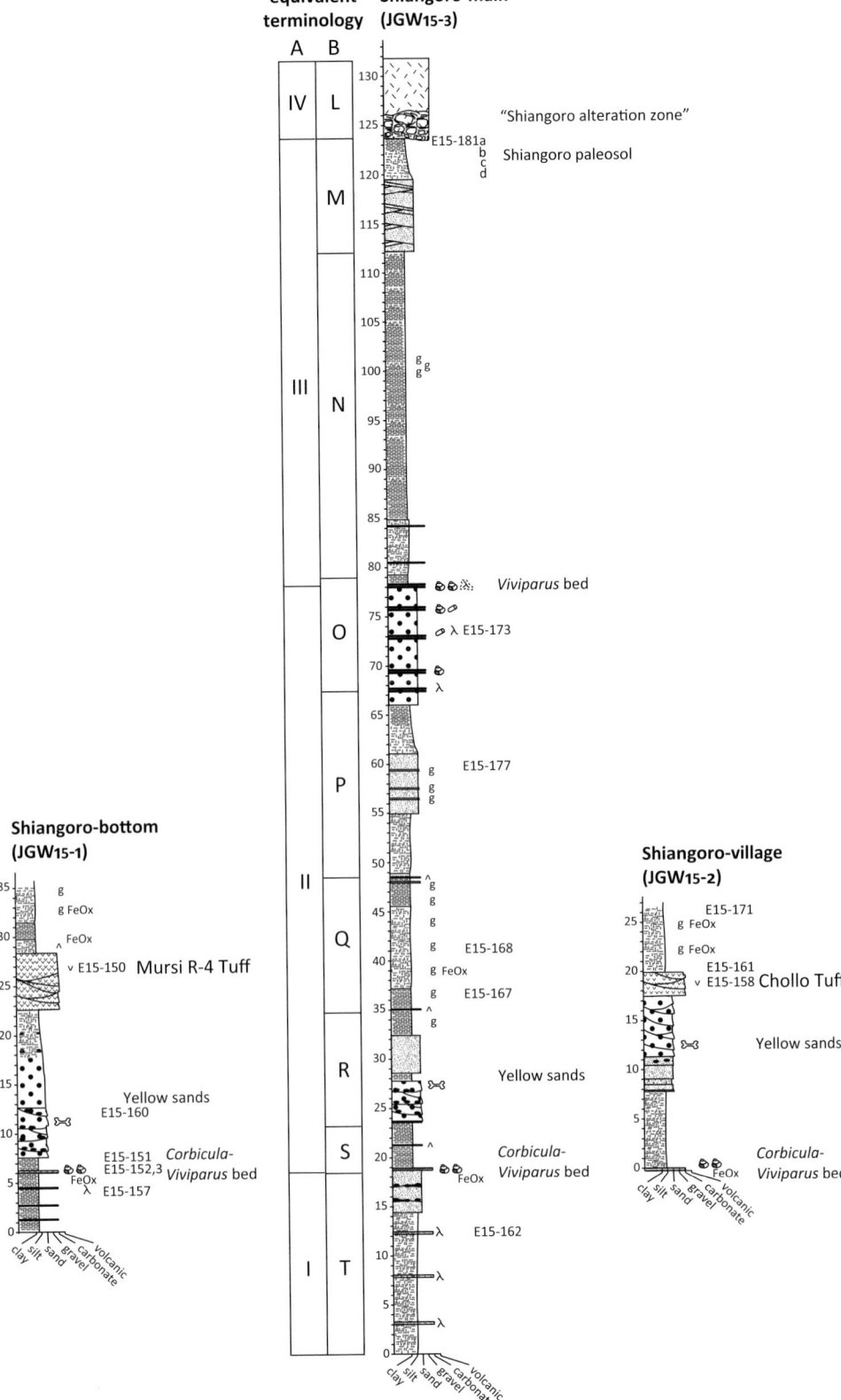

Figure 23.2 Stratigraphic sections measured through the Yellow Sands in the Shiangoro area (see Figure 23.1 for the location of each section). Approximate equivalent stratigraphic terminology of (A) Butzer and Thurber (1969) and (B) de Heinzelin and Haesaerts (1983c) are shown next to the main section.

of the Mursi Formation extends from the contact with the Paleogene–Neogene volcanics to the base of the Mursi Basalt. A complete section of this sequence has not yet been measured in any locality, although we provide evidence here of a composite section of the entirety of the Mursi Formation totaling ~150 m (Figure 23.2).

The age of the sedimentary sequence is poorly constrained by the uppermost of the Paleogene volcanic sequence and the age of the Mursi Basalt (*ca.* 4.0 Ma; Brown, 1969; McDougall, 1985; Ebinger et al., 2000). To date, there has been no material identified within the sedimentary sequence to provide a more reliable age. Previous chemical analyses of glass shards of the Cholo Tuff at Cholo (Drapeau et al., 2014) found this tuff is not an equivalent to the Mursi R-4 Tuff described by de Heinzelin and Haesaerts (1983c) and analyzed by Brown and Fuller (2008; sample Kib99-44). Hence, the only prior correlation between the Cholo and Shiangoro areas was the overlying Mursi Basalt, which rests unconformably on the sedimentary strata, with an unconstrained gap between. However, our new work in the Shiangoro area has identified two chemically distinct tephras in approximately the same stratigraphic position, one of which (not the original R-4 Tuff) now establishes a new correlation between the Cholo and Shiangoro fossil localities. First, we note that our stratigraphic section differs slightly from both previous groups' descriptions, in that vitric glass shards of the Mursi R-4 tephra do not occur in the only measurable contiguous stratigraphic section (section JGW15-3: "Shiangoro-main" in Figure 23.2). Rather, it is exposed in a lenticular, reworked channel deposit approximately 150 m to the south (section JGW15-1, "Shiangoro-bottom" in Figure 23.2), although the section here is not contiguous with the overlying strata through the Mursi Basalt. Chemical analysis of glass shards from this tuff (sample E15-150; Table 23.1) confirms its identity as that measured by Brown and Fuller (2008). A second outcrop of tuff occurs ~700 m to the north in a section between two fault blocks and not contiguous with the Mursi Basalt (section JGW15-2, "Shiangoro-village" in Figure 23.2). This tuff (sample E15-158) correlates geochemically to the Cholo Tuff at Cholo (Table 23.1; Drapeau et al., 2014). Both the Mursi R-4 and the Cholo Tuff at Shiangoro lie just above the distinctive Yellow Sands, and are thus rough lateral equivalents, but ironically, not derived from the same eruption, nor likely the same volcanic source. Given this lateral equivalence, a composite thickness may be estimated from the 63 m of sediments below the Cholo Tuff at Cholo and the 90 m of sediments above the Yellow Sands at Shiangoro. This is somewhat longer than the 143 m measured by Butzer and Thurber (1969), especially given the fact that we observed a much shorter exposure than the stated 43 m of Member I below the gastropod bed (*Corbicula–Viviparus* bed).

Overall our sedimentological observations and paleoenvironmental interpretations follow those of Butzer (1976), who suggested an environment characterized by piedmont alluvial deposits interfingering with shoreline deposits of paleo-Lake Turkana. Largely we refer the reader to the interpretations of this previous work, although we note a few additional features. The abundance of medium-sand-sized muscovite grains, as well as abundant subangular quartz and feldspars, in many of the sand beds is consistent with high-energy deposits of alluvium, derived from crystalline basement rocks of the Hamer Range to the east (Davidson, 1983). The fine-grained mudstones with beds and occasional dispersed and bedded *Viviparus* fossils are evidence of low-energy shallow water with abundant decomposing vegetation. Gypsum, as well as iron oxides, and or hydroxides, particularly surrounding lacustrine fossils of plant detritus, fish, and often decalcified mollusc shells, are very distinctive in the low-energy mudstones. This association is entirely consistent with reducing conditions resulting in reduction of sulfate to sulfide, using the energy gained by bacterial sulfate reduction with an energy source provided by abundant organic matter in shallow-burial diagenesis typical of delta systems, such as the lower Omo River Valley. The illuvial nature of the Shiangoro paleosol profile (see also Haesaerts et al., 1983) is consistent with the wooded conditions indicated by carbon isotopic composition of the Shiangoro paleosols (Drapeau et al., 2016) and it suggests a relatively lush wooded landscape compared to later paleosols of the Pliocene Shungura Formation (Haesaerts et al., 1983) and other localities of the Omo Group deposits (Levin et al., 2011).

Taphonomy

For a better understanding of the local environment around the time of accumulation of the bones of the Mursi Formation, we compared the taphonomy of a sample from that collection (*n* =

Table 23.1 Electron microprobe analyses of vitric tephra from the Mursi Formations[a].

Tuff	Sample	n	SiO_2	TiO_2	Al_2O_3	Fe_2O_3	MnO	MgO	CaO	Na_2O	K_2O	Total
Cholo[b]	E12-106	20	72.01 ± 1.27	0.36 ± 0.07	10.90 ± 0.12	1.55 ± 0.05	0.09 ± 0.02	0.06 ± 0.01	0.15 ± 0.01	3.69 ± 0.27	3.80 ± 0.12	92.61 ± 1.36
Cholo[b]	E12-107	16	72.57 ± 0.99	0.37 ± 0.05	10.92 ± 0.13	1.54 ± 0.05	0.09 ± 0.02	0.06 ± 0.01	0.14 ± 0.01	3.47 ± 0.88	3.81 ± 0.43	92.97 ± 1.22
Cholo[c]	E15-158	18	75.60 ± 0.44	0.26 ± 0.02	11.37 ± 0.09	1.56 ± 0.03	0.08 ± 0.02	0.08 ± 0.01	0.16 ± 0.01	3.74 ± 0.36	2.58 ± 0.47	95.42 ± 1.11
Mursi R[d]	KIB99-44	13	72.13	0.15	10.73	4.22	0.1	0.06	0.23	1.33	2.5	92.2
Mursi R	E15-150	20	72.31 ± 0.39	0.24 ± 0.01	10.83 ± 0.11	4.12 ± 0.07	0.14 ± 0.02	0.05 ± 0.01	0.21 ± 0.02	2.49 ± 0.40	2.41 ± 0.22	92.81 ± 0.70

[a] All values reported as wt% with ± equal to 1σ. EMP settings: 15 keV, 25 nA, 10 μm.
[b] From Drapeau et al. (2014).
[c] Slightly higher Al_2O_3 values and lower TiO_2 values reported here compared to Drapeau et al. (2014) are due to instrument variation and are also reflected in analysis of internal standards.
[d] From Brown and Fuller (2008).

24) to samples from other collections of similar ages from the Omo-Turkana Basin: Kanapoi ($n = 45$) and Allia Bay ($n = 161$). Specimens of fossilized mammal bones larger than 5 cm were scored for traces left by seven taphonomic agents (Table 23.2). The taphonomic agents (e.g., carnivore tooth marks, water abrasion) were evaluated by observing the surface of each specimen with a hand-held magnifying lens and by recording the type and intensity of the traces on each bone (Blumenschine et al., 1996).

The intensity of traces on each specimen was scored following previously established documentation protocols (Behrensmeyer, 1978b; Binford, 1981; Brain, 1981; Fiorillo, 1988; Andrews, 1990; Lyman, 2010). The Mursi collection was compared to the two sites using Monte Carlo analyses. Results indicate that overall, the Mursi assemblage is taphonomically similar to that of both Allia Bay and Kanapoi (Table 23.2). Only a handful of taphonomic differences have been identified between the sites.

Table 23.2 Taphonomic agents for faunal collection of Mursi, Kanapoi, and Allia Bay and comparison with the Mursi

	Kanapoi ($n = 45$)	Comparison Kanapoi–Mursi	Mursi ($n = 24$)	Comparison Allia Bay–Mursi	Allia Bay ($n = 161$)
Trampling[a]					
Absent	40 (89%)	NS	19 (79%)	NS	125 (78%)
Present	5 (11%)		5 (21%)		36 (22%)
Carnivore[b]					
Absent	38 (84.5%)	NS	18 (75%)	NS (0.053)	144 (89.5%)
Present	7 (15.5%)		6 (25%)		17 (10.5%)
Insect					
Absent	32 (71%)	0.003	24 (100%)	NS	157 (97.5%)
Present	13 (29%)		0		4 (2.5%)
Polishing[c]					
Absent	17 (38%)		11 (46%)		66 (41%)
Light	19 (42%)	NS	7 (29%)	NS	54 (33.5%)
Moderate	9 (20%)		5 (21%)		30 (18.5%)
High	0		1 (4%)		11 (7%)
Weathering[d]					
Absent	8 (18%)		5 (21%)		112 (69.5%)
Very light	28 (62%)		11 (46%)		15 (9%)
Light	6 (13%)	NS	7 (29%)	0.008	20 (12.5%)
Moderate	3 (7%)		0		13 (8%)
High	0		1 (4%)		1 (1%)
Extreme	0		0		0
Digestion[e]					
Absent	45 (100%)		23 (96%)		154 (96%)
Very light	0		0		7 (4%)
Light	0	NS	1 (4%)	NS	0
Moderate	0		0		0
High	0		0		0
Extreme	0		0		0
Root etching					
Absent	40 (89%)	NS	18 (75%)	NS	92 (57%)
Present	5 (11%)		6 (25%)		69 (43%)

[a] Domínguez-Rodrigo et al. (2009a).
[b] Binford (1981).
[c] Fiorillo (1988).
[d] Behrensmeyer (1978b).
[e] Andrews (1990).

Differences in carnivore tooth mark traces between Mursi and Allia Bay fossils approach statistical significance, but neither collection, nor Kanapoi, can be characterized as being specifically carnivore-accumulated. The weathering profile is significantly different between the localities of Mursi and Allia Bay, with the Mursi fossils presenting more weathering than the Allia Bay specimens. Weathering is predominantly present (79 percent) in the Mursi collection, while it is much less present on the Allia Bay fossils (30.5 percent). Thus, the Mursi specimens were generally exposed longer at the surface before burial than the Allia Bay specimens, which appeared to have generally been buried rapidly. This could be the result of slightly drier local conditions at Mursi than at Allia Bay. However, the most common weathering stage recorded within both the Mursi and Kanapoi assemblages is a light weathering. Although statistically significant, the differences between the Mursi and Allia Bay remain minor and these results indicate that the predepositional processes would have been broadly similar within the Omo-Turkana Basin at the time possibly due to similar paleoenvironments. The surface modifications on the Mursi fossils differ significantly from those of Kanapoi only in terms of traces left by termites and other insects. No insect traces were recorded on the Mursi postcranial remains, whereas about a third of the bones from the Kanapoi collection preserve such traces. The ecological meaning of the presence of insect traces in the Plio-Pleistocene fossil record is still relatively poorly understood. However, actualistic studies have shown that termites and other insects destroy bones, which can significantly impact site formation processes, as well as the taxonomic representation of small elements at sites (Backwell et al., 2012; Pirrone et al., 2014). Given that only one third of fossils from Kanapoi present traces of insects, it remains unlikely that the impact of insects resulted in significant faunal proportion differences between the two localities.

Overall, despite some statistically significant differences between Mursi and the other two localities, the taphonomic processes appear to have been broadly similar throughout the Omo-Turkana Basin around 4 million years ago. The analysis of the complete collections from each site is needed in order to confirm the patterns observed in this preliminary study, but we can state at this point that the differences observed between the Mursi Formation collection and the other penecontemporaneous localities of the Turkana Lake Basin are not due to widely differing taphonomic processes.

Fauna

The Mursi faunal assemblage collected in the 1960s and 1970s is characterized by a high proportion of suids, particularly when compared to bovids. Nearly 44 percent of all identifiable mammals are suids, while less than 14 percent are bovids, with a suid-to-bovid ratio of 3.3:1. Unsurprising for sediments of that age, hippos and elephantids are also fairly abundant (14 percent and 13 percent, respectively). The formation is notable for its high proportion of deinotheres, consisting of 7 percent of the identifiable mammals. Other, rarer mammalian taxa include giraffids, rhinocerotids, equids, a gomphothere, and carnivores. Notably, the older collection did not include any primates. The faunal assemblage collected in 2015 is similar in numerous points to the older collection (Table 23.3). It has a similar proportion of suids to bovids with a nearly identical ratio of 3:1. The proportion of deinotheres is also 7 percent of the identifiable mammals. However, the new collection has significantly more hippos than the old collection (25.5 percent and 14.3 percent, respectively) and significantly more elephantids (23.5 percent and 13.3 percent, respectively). We believe that these differences between the two samples reflect differences in collecting strategies. Because all collected specimens by the IORE at the Yellow Sands are identified and do not include any small tooth fragments, it can be reasonably assumed that they collected only identifiable specimens that presented reasonably complete anatomical units (mainly teeth and horn-cores). In 2015, however, all specimens that were suspected to be mammalian were collected, including numerous small teeth fragments of hippos and elephants that were likely ignored 40 years ago. As a consequence, the number of teeth flakes identified to hippos and elephantids is important in the 2015 collection and explains the higher proportions of these taxa compared to the 40-year-old collection. Similarly, the 2015 collection presents a larger number of crocodiles and euthecodons. These taxa were very common in the sediments and only a sample of the exposed remains was collected; as a consequence, crocodilian numbers in the 2015 collection underestimate their numbers in the sediments. We suspect that the IORE collected an even smaller proportion of the crocodilian remains that were exposed, so differences in the two collections likely reflect, again, differences in sampling strategy. As a result of the differences in collecting strategy, the proportion of suids and bovids appear proportionally lower (31 percent and 10 percent of identifiable mammals, respectively) in the 2015 collection, but given that the ratio of one to the other is nearly identical in both collections, we feel confident that the large proportion of suids and low proportion of bovids reflect accurately the relative frequency of these fossils in the sediments. In 2015, we also found a primate (see below), the first reported from the collection.

Taxon-Specific Descriptions

Hippopotamidae

Teeth and limb bones can all be assigned to a single species of hippo, tentatively assigned to "*Hippopotamus*" *protamphibius*, but Pliocene and Pleistocene African hippos are still in need of revision before a definite species identification can be made. The large size of this species in the Mursi Formation is noticeable for its geological age: two astragali are close in size to the largest specimens of "*Hippopotamus*" *protamphibius* from the younger Shungura Formation (Gèze, 1980), paralleling the large size of the crocodylians (see below).

Suidae

The most abundant family of the Mursi fauna, about 200 fossil specimens have been collected thus far. By far the most common taxon is *Nyanzachoerus kanamensis* (of which *N. pattersoni* is a junior synonym); the most informative teeth are the

Table 23.3 Fauna from Yellow Sands of the Mursi Formation.

Family or Group		1960 and 1970 Collection[a]		2015 Collection	
		Total	% of mammalian taxa	Total	% of identified mammalian taxa
Pisces		8		108	
Crocodylidae		14		107	
	Euthecodon cf. *brumpti*	9		26	
	Crocodylus cf. *cataphractus*	4		11	
	Crocodylidae indet.	1		70	
Chelonia		3		9	
Reptilia indet.				4	
Suidae		89	48.8	119	32.6
	Notochoerus jaegeri	4		1	
	cf. *Notochoerus* sp.			1	
	Nyanzachoerus kanamensis	59		29	
	Nyanzachoerus sp.			17	
	Suidae indet.	26		71	
Hippopotamidae		29	14.3	89	24.4
	"*Hippopotamus*" cf. *protamphibius*	12		1	
	Hippopotamidae indet.	17		88	
Giraffidae		1	0.49	2	0.55
	Giraffa cf. *stillei*	1			
	Sivatherium sp.			2	
Bovidae		28	13.8	40	11.0
	Aepyceros sp.	13		17	
	Reduncini indet.	1			
	Tragelaphus cf. *saraitu*	9			
	Tragelaphini			8	
	Bovidae indet.	5		15	
Tragulidae ?				1	0.27
Rhinocerotidae		7	3.4	2	0.55
	Ceratotherium sp.	2			
	Diceros sp.	5			
	Rhinocerotidae indet.			2	
Equidae		2	0.99		0
Gomphotheriidae		1	0.49		0
Elephantidae		27	13.3	83	22.7
	Loxodonta adaurora	15			
	Elephantidae indet.	12		83	
Deinotheriidae		14	6.9	26	7.1

Table 23.3 (cont.)

		1960 and 1970 Collection[a]		2015 Collection	
	Deinotherium bozasi	14		26	
Proboscidea indet.		2	0.99	1	0.27
Carnivora		3	1.5	1	0.27
	Vulpes mathisoni	1			
	cf. Hyaenidae			1	
	Carnivora indet.	2			
Primates			0		0.27
	aff. Cercopithecoides			1	
Mammalia indet.				29	
Indet.				71	
Total		228		685	

[a] Includes a few specimens collected in 2003 by John Fleagle.

upper third molars, intermediate in size between the slightly smaller *Nyanzachoerus* specimens from Kanam and the upper Nawata Formation at Lothagam, and the slightly larger ones from Kanapoi and the Hadar Formation. Further analysis may show whether size and chronology are correlated. Given its postcranial and dental morphology, it can reasonably be assumed that *Nyanzachoerus* was an inhabitant of woodland (e.g., Bishop, 2011) and carbon isotope values indicate that it consumed a mixed diet of leaves/grass more ^{13}C-depleted than in Aramis, Gona, or Kanapoi (Drapeau et al., 2014). Four specimens only can be assigned to *Notochoerus jaegeri* (formerly called *Nyanzachoerus jaegeri*, but Harris et al., 2003 corrected this generic assignment); this species is also present at Kanapoi (Geraads et al., 2013c; Geraads and Bobe, 2020a). No specimens can be unambiguously assigned to *Kolpochoerus*, a genus that is also absent at Kanapoi.

Tragulidae(?)

Specimen Mursi-742 is the posterior part of a heavily worn lower third molar of a ruminant. It resembles the Tragulidae (of which the water chevrotain, *Hyemoschus aquaticus*, is the only modern African representative) in that the entoconid is unconnected to the third lobe and to the distolingual arm of the hypoconid. This is in contrast to most Bovidae, although this identification cannot be definitely ruled out. *Dorcatherium* is common in the Miocene of Kenya (see review in Geraads, 2010c), but has not been reported from Ethiopia to date. However, a late *Dorcatherium*, or early *Hyemoschus*, was described by Pickford et al. (2004) from the early Pliocene Mabaget Formation of Kenya, indicating that the family was present in eastern Africa at that time. It is likely that the rarity of tragulids in the African fossil record owes much to their forested environment and, if confirmed by more complete material, their occurrence in the Mursi Formation would point to the presence of some dense wood cover.

Giraffidae

There are only three specimens from this family, but they document two species, a medium-sized giraffe probably close to *Giraffa stillei*, and a large *Sivatherium*, which was a browser at that time (Cerling et al., 2015a).

Bovidae

The new collections confirm the poor taxonomic richness of this family. There are only four taxa: the impala *Aepyceros*, a relative of the kudu, *Tragelaphus*, a reduncin (a single tooth identified by A.W. Gentry, not seen by us), and a member of the bovini, represented only by a calcaneum. Only one of the *Aepyceros* horn-cores is virtually complete, so species identification remains tentative, but it resembles *Ae. datoadeni* from Hadar (Geraads et al., 2012a). It differs from those of *Ae. afarensis* from the somewhat younger sites of Woranso-Mille (Geraads et al., 2009a), and perhaps from Kanapoi (Geraads et al., 2013c; Geraads and Bobe, 2020b) in its small size and lack of outward curvature in front view. The *Tragelaphus* is also hard to identify with certainty, but is close in size and development of the keels on the horn-cores to *T. saraitu* from Woranso-Mille (Geraads et al., 2009a). Some horn-cores not seen by us were identified as *T.* aff. *gaudryi* by Gentry (1985), but we assume that they belong to the same species. Delimitations and relationships between these early *Tragelaphus* species are still unclear, but the four lower third molars have mid-height lengths ranging from 23.3 to 25.2 mm, compatible with a single species. These three tribes of bovids (Aepycerotini, Tragelaphini, and Reduncini) are the most abundant bovids in the subsequent strata (*ca.* 3.5–1.2 Ma) of the nearby Shungura Formation (Bobe and Eck, 2001). In terms of paleoenvironment, the rarity of reduncins (wetlands) and the absence of grassland-inhabiting alcelaphins is notable, especially when compared with the relative abundance of the former tribe in the early part of the Omo sequence (Bobe and Eck, 2001; Bobe and Behrensmeyer, 2004) or of the latter tribe at Kanapoi (Geraads and Bobe, 2020b). Carbon isotope values (Drapeau et al., 2014) show that the enamel of both *Tragelaphus* and *Aepyceros* was more ^{13}C-depleted than in other sites, indicating a greater emphasis on browsing at Mursi. On the whole, the Mursi bovids point to some kind of bushland or closed woodland. Another interesting aspect of the bovid assemblage is its low diversity, which the limited sample size alone fails to explain, even though it is likely that further collecting would increase the number of species (*S*). For instance, Shannon's index $H'' = -\Sigma(N_i/N * \ln N_i/N) - (S-1)/N$ equals 0.742 (N; N_i being the number of identified specimens in each species: 30, 14, 1, 1), a value lower than that of all other Plio-Pleistocene African sites but the Moiti Member at Koobi Fora (Geraads, 1994b), including those with low sample size. Such a low value might indicate that either the Mursi collection sampled only a very homogeneous habitat, or that the environment was ill-suited for bovids; by comparison, the roughly contemporaneous sites of Kanapoi and Laetoli have a greater diversity of bovids (Gentry, 2011; Geraads et al., 2013c; Geraads and Bobe, 2020b).

Rhinocerotidae

Both the grazer *Ceratotherium* and the mixed-feeder *Diceros* are represented among the rhinos. The latter genus may have been more common, but sample sizes are very low.

Equidae

There are only two specimens of *Hipparion senso lato* in the old collections, a lower second premolar and a distal metacarpal; recent collecting has yielded no new specimens. Precise taxonomic assignment is impossible, but the family is remarkably rare by comparison with other Pliocene and Plio-Pleistocene East African sites, probably reflecting the rarity of grass in the vicinity because, although some Pliocene Equidae were partly browsers, it is hard to imagine a grassland or savanna with so few equids.

Proboscidea

In terms of number of specimens, *Deinotherium* is among the most common large mammal; even though most of them consist of tooth fragments, which are easily identifiable, this very large browsing animal must have represented a significant proportion of the biomass, pointing to preponderance of closed woodland or forested environments. A single tooth fragment belongs to *Anancus* (Beden, 1976). Most of the elephantid material belongs to *Loxodonta adaurora*, a primitive cousin of the present-day African elephant. Again, most specimens are tooth fragments, but this mixed-feeder (Drapeau et al., 2014) was certainly among the dominant large mammals.

Carnivora

Only two carnivore specimens have been collected, a Hyenidae distal humerus and a skull of a new species of small fox, *Vulpes mathisoni* (Geraads et al., 2015a). Most fox species are open-country forms, but being represented by a single specimen, ecological conclusions are hard to draw.

Primates

The only primate specimen is an edentulous right mandibular corpus in two pieces in which only the roots or alveoli of the incisors, canine, and p4 can be unambiguously identified. Although the two pieces do not articulate, their proximity at discovery, their similar size, weathering, and color strongly suggest that they are fragments of the same hemi-mandible. The break is at the posterior part of the alveolar row, and presents some alveolar resorption, making the remaining roots difficult to identify to specific molars. The reconstructed minimal length of the specimen with the identifiable roots is consistent with the possibility of it having had four molars. The specimen has a very long, thick, but shallow corpus, giving it a robust appearance. The body has a clear lateral prominence that makes an inferior bulge in profile. The symphysis is quite sloping and marked by a single median mental foramen under the p3/4 contact. There are no mental ridges. The superior torus reaches back to the mesial root of the p3, and the inferior torus back to the p4/m1. The incisor roots are fairly small and mediolaterally compressed and the whole incisor area is quite crowded. The canine root is small and is more consistent with a female. It is similar in size to *Cercopithecoides meaveae* from Leadu and Hadar but distinct from it, and also from the Kanapoi mandible (KP 29255) assigned to cf. *Cercopithecoides* by Harris et al. (2003) or to cf. *Kuseracolobus* by Frost et al. (2020) by having a more sloping symphysis and a median mental foramen. Unlike the Kanapoi mandible, its body does not deepen posteriorly and it is smaller and much shallower than *Kuseracolobus aramisi*. Compared to mandibles of *Parapapio* cf. *ado* from Kanapoi and *Pliopapio alemui* from Aramis, the Mursi specimen has weaker mental ridges and is shallower, but with a thicker corpus. Although different from all known taxa, we do not assign it to a new species given the pathological resorption of the alveolar area.

Reptilia

Crocodiles are represented by numerous cranial and dental remains of the piscivorous *Euthecodon* and of a large *Crocodylus* (Drapeau et al., 2014), obviously implying the presence of rivers or large bodies of water. A few specimens of turtle were also recovered.

Overall, the fossil fauna recovered in 2015 is broadly similar to the collection from the 1960s and 1970s. As stated above, the suid-to-bovid ratio is nearly identical and the broad categories of taxa are similar. The 2015 collection does include taxa that were not represented in the older collection: a large *Sivatherium*, perhaps a Tragulidae, a Hyaenidae, and a primate. Although each is represented by only one or two specimens, it broadens moderately the particularly low species diversity of the Mursi Formation.

Paleolandscape

The Mursi deposits, with evidence of abundant organic vegetation in shallow-burial diagenesis, is typical of delta systems, as observed currently in the lower Omo delta. The proximity of a large body of water is also evidenced by the abundance of aquatic taxa such as hippos, crocodiles, and fishes. The low-diversity bovid assemblage, although relatively small, is dominated by *Aepyceros* (63 percent of the identified bovids) and, to a lesser degree, Tragelaphini (35 percent) with only one reduncini (2 percent). The combination of the large number of specimens from aquatic taxa but few reduncini is intriguing, particularly because the sedimentology suggests low-energy alluvial and littoral conditions with abundant aquatic vegetation. The C_3-enriched stable carbone isotope values for the Tragelaphini and *Aepyceros*, as well as those of hippos, when compared to other penecontemporaneous localities (Drapeau et al., 2014; Dumouchel, 2017), suggest relatively more closed conditions in the Mursi.

The small sample of diagnostic fossil wood suggests riverine forest and some grasslands. In addition, one *Anancus* specimen and one *Hipparion* specimen indicate that there were grasses in the vicinity, but their low frequency suggests that it was not an extensive part of the landscape. The relatively numerous *Loxodonta adaurora* specimens could also indicate the presence of grass, although given the mixed diet of these specimens from the Mursi (Drapeau et al., 2014) and the likely large range of the species, it is also possible that the C_4 component of their diet was acquired at another location. The high frequency of deinotheres (that are pure C_3 plant consumers), the highest frequency of any locality in East Africa, combined with more depleted enamel carbon isotopic values than these other deinotheres (Drapeau et al., 2014), support the interpretation of habitats in the Mursi that are more closed than what is inferred from other localities.

The absence of *Kolpochoerus* and the abundance of *Nyanzachoerus* in the Mursi fauna could suggest that the landscape was more dominated by bushland and thickets than forested conditions; however, the stable carbone isotopes values (Drapeau et al., 2014) indicate that the *Nyanzachoerus* and *Notochoerus* from the Mursi were characterized by a C_3-enriched diet relative to those from other penecontemporaneous localities (e.g., Kanapoi), but comparable to the diet of *Kolpochoerus* at Gona (Levin et al., 2008) or Aramis (White et al., 2009a). This underscores the dietary flexibility of the *Nyanzachoerus* genus (e.g., Zazzo et al., 2000) and of suids in general (Levin et al., 2008), and it indicates, again, relatively closed conditions in the Mursi. The presence of other taxa, such as a primate, and particularly a possible tragulidae, suggest the presence of closed wooded conditions nearby.

Overall, the sedimentology, the faunal proportion, and inferred diet of the fauna (and the lack of obvious taphonomic bias) suggest that the Mursi paleolandscape had some wooded condition with some grasses but to a lesser extent than what is inferred from other penecontemporaneous localities of East Africa. The paleosol stable carbon isotopes indicate closed wooded conditions (Drapeau et al., 2016), suggesting that the Mursi Formation might sample a forest edge. The relative rarity of primates may indicate that they inhabited the forested part of the available habitats, a type of environment that might not favor their preservation. This forest habitat combined with fewer grasses does not appear to have been favored by hominins because they are not found in the Mursi. It suggests to us that more open grassy settings might have been an essential aspect of the early hominin adaptive complex and its absence (or relative rarity) in the Mursi landscape may have hindered their occupation of that area.

Conclusions

The Mursi Formation covers a time period that is important paleoanthropologically because it is only poorly documented in eastern Africa. Our renewed work in the formation has identified a new fossiliferous locality further north, Cholo. A new faunal collection from the Yellow Sands has confirmed the general reconstructions drawn from the old collection, while adding modestly to the diversity of taxa. There are two tephra in the Mursi Formation that are uncorrelated with others from East Africa. However, one tephra from Cholo is also found in the Yellow Sands, allowing for sedimentary correlation of the two localities. Interpretation of the sedimentology of the Yellow Sands concurs with Butzer (1976), who suggested an environment characterized by piedmont alluvial deposits interfingering with shoreline deposits of paleo-Lake Turkana. In addition, we propose that the fine-grained gypsum-bearing deposits indicate depositional conditions of shallow freshwater with abundant decomposing vegetation. Taphonomic comparison with Kanapoi and Allia Bay do not suggest significant differences in depositional environment among these localities; all other lines of evidence suggest a relatively closed landscape at the Yellow Sands when compared to other penecontemporaneous hominin localities from the East African Rift. This rather lush, wooded environment in the Mursi may sample a habitat that was not well-suited for hominins during the Pliocene.

24 Mammalian Diversity Patterns and Paleoecology in the Lower Omo Valley, Ethiopia

Enquye W. Negash, René Bobe, Zeresenay Alemseged, and Jonathan Wynn

Introduction

The Omo-Turkana Basin of southern Ethiopia and northern Kenya preserves a rich record of late Cenozoic fossil vertebrates and plays a central role in our understanding of early hominin evolution. In this chapter we focus on the northern area of the basin, the lower Omo Valley of Ethiopia. We provide a brief history of research in the area, present a review of previous studies focused on the paleoenvironment of the Shungura Formation (Figure 24.1), and offer a fresh perspective for the paleoecological context of hominin evolution in the lower Omo Valley with analyses of mammalian diversity patterns from ~3.6 to 1 Ma.

History of Research in the Lower Omo Valley

The first expedition to document fossil vertebrates in the lower Omo Valley was the French expedition of Bourg de Bozas in 1902–1903, which subsequently led Camille Arambourg to establish the Mission Scientifique de l'Omo in 1932–1933, with further documentation of the geology and paleontology of the Omo beds (Arambourg, 1947; Harris et al., 2006). Between 1967 and 1976, the International Omo Research Expedition (IORE) conducted yearly campaigns composed of two primary teams: the American contingent of the expedition led by F. Clark Howell and the French contingent led by Yves Coppens (Howell, 1968, 1969, 1978a; Coppens, 1975). The American team worked primarily in the northern sectors of the Plio-Pleistocene Shungura Formation, as well as in the Usno and Mursi Formations, while the French team focused its efforts in the southern sectors of the Shungura Formation. In 1967, a Kenyan contingent of the IORE worked briefly in sediments of the late Pleistocene Kibish Formation (Leakey, 1969), but subsequently turned its attention to the Koobi Fora deposits in Kenya (Leakey, 1970). By the end of the 1976 field season, the American contingent of the IORE had documented nearly 23,000 fossil vertebrates, while the French contingent had amassed more than 27,000 specimens. Most of these specimens are housed at the National Museum of Ethiopia in Addis Ababa, and the data are accessible through the Omo American database (Bobe, 1997; Eck, 2007) and the Omo French database (Alemseged, 1998; Alemseged et al., 2007). Ongoing paleontological work in the lower Omo Valley continues to be productive (Boisserie et al., 2008; Drapeau et al., 2014; Drapeau et al., Chapter 23).

Geology and Stratigraphy of the Lower Omo Valley

The Omo Group deposits encompass Pliocene and Pleistocene sediments in the lower Omo Valley (Ethiopia) and in the Lake Turkana Basin (Kenya). The Omo Group includes the Mursi, Usno, Shungura, Koobi Fora, Nachukui, and Kanapoi Formations, with deposition beginning about 4.3 Ma (Feibel et al., 1989; Brown and McDougall, 2011). Tectonic activity associated with the Main Ethiopian Rift led to the onset of sedimentation of the Omo Group deposits in the Pliocene lower Omo Valley (Brown and de Heinzelin, 1983; McDougall and Brown, 2008; Feibel, 2011). Active volcanism in the region resulted in the deposition of tuffaceous material that intercalates with fluvio-lacustrine sediments, and allows for excellent geochronological control, both within basins as well as across basins in the region (Brown et al., 1978; Brown, 1982; Brown and Cerling, 1982; Brown and McDougall, 2011). In this contribution we focus on the Shungura Formation (Figure 24.1).

The Shungura Formation

The Shungura Formation consists of sedimentary deposits that are exposed on the west side of the Omo River. These deposits have a composite thickness of greater than 760 m and are divided into 12 members: Basal, A, B, C, D, E, F, G, H, J, K, and L (there is no member I in the sequence; Figure 24.1B; de Heinzelin, 1983). Except for the Basal Member, each member commences with a volcanic ash layer that is labeled with the same letter as the member: Tuff A underlies Member A; Tuff B underlies Member B, etc. These members are further subdivided into units or submembers ranging in thickness from 2 to 20 m with an average thickness of 7 m (de Heinzelin and Haesaerts, 1983a). Submembers or sedimentary units are labeled starting with number 1 at the bottom of the member. Thus, for example, in Member F there are five units above Tuff F, and these are labeled F-1, F-2, F-3, F-4, and F-5, with F-1 at the bottom and F-5 at the top of the member. The sediments consist of fluvial, lacustrine, and deltaic sediments that were deposited by the Pliocene and Pleistocene Omo River, with some intermittent lake phases in the basin characterized by relatively slow sedimentation rates. K/Ar, Ar/Ar, and magnetostratigraphic dating of the Shungura

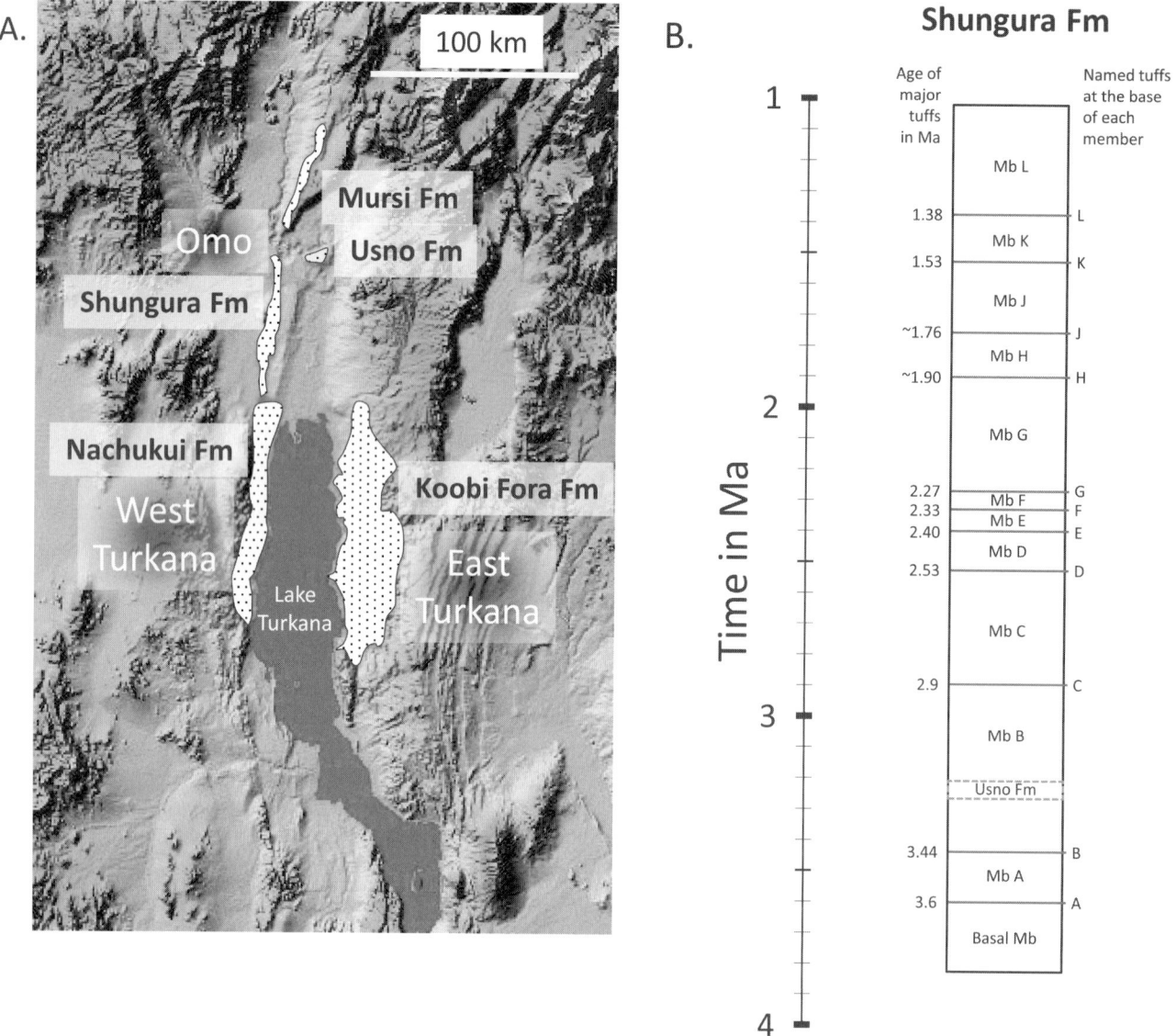

Figure 24.1 (A) Location of the Shungura Formation in southwestern Ethiopia. (B) Chronstratigraphic sequence of the Shungura Formation, redrawn after Blondel et al. (2018). (A black and white version of this figure will appear in some formats. For the color version, please refer to the plate section.)

Formation provides a chronological framework that ranges from >3.6 Ma to ~1 Ma (Brown and McDougall, 2011; Kidane et al., 2014). The Shungura Formation is exposed in two major areas; the "Type locality" is found in the northern part near Shungura village and exposes the Basal Member up to Member J, and the "Kalam locality" which is found in the south contains exposures of Member C to Member L (de Heinzelin et al., 1976).

The Hominin Fossil Record in the Lower Omo Valley

The lower Omo Valley preserves a rich record of fossil hominins. Although most specimens are isolated teeth, there is also a large sample of cranial, mandibular, and postcranial elements (Howell, 1969; Howell and Coppens, 1973, 1974; Coppens, 1977; Suwa et al., 1996). The hominin taxa currently recognized in the Shungura Formation include *Australopithecus* (Suwa et al., 1996), *Paranthropus aethiopicus* (Arambourg and Coppens, 1968), *Paranthropus boisei* (Alemseged et al., 2002), *Homo* cf. *habilis*, and *Homo erectus* (Wood and Leakey, 2011). The record from the lower Omo Valley spans the time period between 2.0 and 3.0 Ma that encompasses the earliest records of *Homo* and *Paranthropus*, for which there is a limited hominin fossil record in eastern Africa (Wood and Constantino, 2007; Villmoare et al., 2015). In addition, archeological occurrences with evidence of hominin tool use have been reported dating to ~2.3 Ma (Chavaillon, 1976; de la Torre et al., 2004; Delagnes et al., 2011).

A Synthesis of Paleoenvironmental and Paleoecological Studies of the Lower Omo Valley

Depositional Environments and Paleosols

Sedimentological studies have been used to investigate depositional environments, climate, and structural changes in the Shungura Formation. These studies document three main phases of deposition: fluvial, deltaic, and lacustrine (de Heinzelin and Haesaerts, 1983a). A lacustrine phase occurs in the first unit of the Basal Member, which is followed by a long fluvial sequence up to the middle of Member G, with units G-11 to G-13 showing a transition to deltaic conditions (Haesaerts et al., 1983). Upper Member G (units G-14 to G-27) consists of lacustrine deposits, and presents a shift in taphonomic conditions relative to the older part of the Shungura Formation (Bobe and Eck, 2001). Units G-28 to H-7 are again deltaic, and fluvial channel sedimentation resumes from the uppermost units of Member H to the middle of Member L. Lacustrine deposits characterize the very top of the Shungura Formation, units L-7 to L-9.

Well-developed paleosols are documented in Shungura Members A and B that reflect high precipitation and warm climate in the absence of a pronounced dry season. However, in the later members there is progressive change toward more sporadic precipitation and a generally drier climate (de Heinzelin et al., 1976; Haesaerts et al., 1983).

Stable isotopic study of paleosol carbonates has provided detailed information about the proportions of C_3 and C_4 vegetation in the lower Omo Valley from about 3.4 Ma to nearly 1.0 Ma (Levin et al., 2011). Pedogenic carbonates indicate more woodland/bushland relative to grassland compared to contemporaneous sediments in the Nachukui and Koobi Fora Formations (Levin et al., 2011). In other words, the Omo had more wooded environments than other parts of the basin. Woodlands dominated the lower Omo Valley from 3.4 Ma to about 2 Ma while wooded grasslands became the dominant vegetation structure from 2 Ma to 1 Ma.

Paleobotanical Remains

Fossil wood, fruit, and pollen have been recovered and analyzed from the Shungura and Usno Formations. Although this record is discontinuous through the sequence, it provides important information about the kinds of trees and grasses that were present in the Omo. Member A preserves fossil fruit of the genus *Antrocaryon*, a genus that today occurs primarily in the dense and humid tropical forests of West and Central Africa (Bonnefille and Letouzey, 1976). Member D has a sample of fossil wood that includes the genera *Platysepalum* and *Psorospermum* (Bonnefille and Dechamps, 1983). *Platysepalum* is indicative of closed riverine forest while *Prosospermum* indicates more open savanna conditions. Fossil wood from Members F and G indicates a persistent riverine forest, but surrounded by more arid conditions than in earlier members (Bonnefille and Dechamps, 1983). Members J, K, and L preserve fossil wood of *Steganotaenioxylon*, a genus characteristic of arid habitats (Dechamps and Maes, 1985). Fossil pollen derives only from Members B, C, E, and G, and shows the highest proportion of arboreal vegetation in Member B, and the lowest in Members E and G (Bonnefille and Dechamps, 1983).

Faunal Analysis

Analyses of first appearance data (FADs) and last appearance data (LADs), presence/absence, and relative abundance of environmentally informative taxa, as well as origination and extinction rates have been used to infer paleoecological information from the Omo faunal collections. Vrba argued that there was a pulse of faunal turnover in the Omo between 2.8 and 2.5 Ma characterized by a replacement of woodland-adapted taxa by more open-adapted taxa (Vrba, 1985a, 1985b, 1995b; Hernandez Fernández and Vrba, 2006). However, Behrensmeyer and colleagues used Omo-Turkana Basin-wide data set and concluded that there was no turnover pulse, but instead a prolonged period of gradual faunal turnover (Behrensmeyer et al., 1997). Using faunal abundance data from the American collections, Bobe and colleagues found that there was indeed an episode of rapid faunal change in the Omo at about 2.8 Ma, followed by further faunal changes between 2.5 and 2.3 Ma (Bobe, 1997; Bobe and Eck, 2001; Bobe et al., 2002). Based on his work on the French collections, Alemseged concluded that the most important faunal changes in the Omo occurred closer to 2.3 Ma (Alemseged, 2003).

Micromammal assemblages in the Omo are rare, but there are important samples from five different levels: Shungura B-10, C-8, Tuff F, F-1, and G-3. These samples derive from excavated localities and have been thoroughly analyzed by Wesselman (1984, 1995), who identified 47 species in the sequence. The Omo micromammals indicate mesic and forested conditions in Member B, with slightly more open conditions in Member C. Samples from Members F and G indicate a shift to more open, xeric conditions in the lower Omo Valley.

Ecomorphological Analysis

The fossil record of the lower Omo Valley is characterized by a high proportion of isolated teeth, which reflects the dominance of high-energy fluvial depositional environments. Collection methods in the Omo targeted complete mammalian teeth as well as other cranial and mandibular elements (Bobe, 1997; Eck, 2007). Among postcranial elements, the IORE targeted astragali for collection. Systematic collection of these skeletal elements facilitates comparisons across members. Thus the Omo fossil record has a relatively high abundance of astragali, which have been the subject of ecomorphological analyses (Barr, 2015; Plummer et al., 2015). Plummer and colleagues used discriminant functional morphology analyses linking particular astragalar shapes in bovids to discrete vegetation categories: open habitat, light cover, heavy cover, forest, and wetlands. They found that Shungura bovids exhibit the full range of ecomorphological categories, which indicates that a wide range of environments were present in the lower Omo Valley. However, this evidence indicates that wetland, forest, and heavy cover dominated the axis of the basin from Member B to Member G (Plummer et al., 2015). Using the same astragalus specimens but analyzed at the submember level while controlling for body size and phylogenetic signals, Barr found that a shift to more open habitats occurred in submembers C-8, C-9, and in Tuff F (Barr, 2015).

Stable Isotopes from Dental Enamel

Studies of stable carbon isotopes from tooth enamel in the bovid genus *Tragelaphus* and the suid genus *Kolpochoerus* indicate a dietary shift toward higher consumption of C_4 resources in these mammals at about 2.8 Ma (Bibi et al., 2013), a result in accordance with previous work in the Omo indicating a major shift in ecological conditions between Members B and C (Bobe and Eck, 2001). Also, stable isotope analysis of the dietary adaptations of four bovid tribes (i.e., Reduncini, Tragelaphini, Aepycerotini, and Alcelaphini) across Shungura members revealed an overall increase in C_4 vegetation after 2.3 Ma (Negash et al., 2015). Detailed analysis of bulk enamel samples of the large mammal faunal assemblage at a higher temporal resolution is also currently in progress by the same authors.

Dental Microwear Studies

Another approach to studying the diet of herbivores is to assess dental microwear (i.e., microscopic wear or scars on the surface of the tooth), which provides information on the mechanical properties of foods, i.e., toughness, hardness, and abrasiveness (Scott et al., 2006; Calandra and Merceron, 2016). Martin et al. (2018) adopted this approach to study the diet of cercopithecines in the Shungura Formation and results from their study show a change in the dental microwear of the primate genus *Theropithecus* at 2.92 Ma (between Members B and C) and at 2.32 Ma (between Members E and F), indicating higher intake of herbaceous monocots. Similarly, Blondel et al. (2018) performed dental microwear texture analysis on *Tragelaphus* and showed that a browsing diet characterized the three species of *Tragelaphus* encountered across the Shungura sequence. However, a multiproxy approach used in their study, which combined microwear, mesowear, and stable isotopic studies, shows a dietary shift at ~2.8 Ma, which might reflect environmental changes in the Shungura sequence at that time.

Diversity Patterns

Species diversity is influenced by many ecological factors, and it is often measured in terms of species richness (number of species) and evenness (abundance and dominance; Magurran, 1988; Rosenzweig, 1995). Thus, establishing patterns of diversity in the fossil record provides an informative way of exploring potential changes in paleoecological conditions. Apart from previous studies that looked at diversity patterns in specific taxa (e.g., Bobe and Eck, 2001; Bobe, 2011) and a more recent study by Du and Alemseged (2018) that focused on diversity patterns across formations in the Omo-Turkana region, detailed analysis of species richness and diversity patterns of mammalian communities in the Shungura Formation is currently lacking. In this contribution we assess the mammalian fauna from the Shungura Formation (to the exclusion of the patchily distributed micromammals) to establish the main patterns of abundance and diversity from 3.6 Ma to 1 Ma. We examine the diversity patterns at both the genus and species levels, compare how these diversity patterns are related to faunal composition and similarity between stratigraphic units, and evaluate how this information ties to the paleoenvironmental patterns inferred from different proxies.

Methods

Here we explore patterns of mammal taxonomic diversity in the lower Omo Valley Shungura Formation during a time interval that spans from 3.6 Ma to 1 Ma. Data from both the French and American collections are combined in order to have a robust and representative data set that covers a wide spatial and temporal frame. Diversity patterns were observed in two sets of time bins. The first time bin used is the member level. This analysis has the disadvantage that each member comprises different time spans. The second approach uses time bins of 200 kyr. Although this approach has the advantage of comparing time intervals of equal duration and allowing us to examine finer temporal differences, it has the limitation of combining members/stratigraphic units that represent different depositional conditions. Diversity patterns were assessed at both the species and genus level. Tables 24.1 and 24.2 show the stratigraphic units representing each time bin used in the analysis along with the time interval represented at the species and genus levels, respectively. When analyzing diversity patterns, only dental and cranial

Table 24.1 Member level and 200-kyr bin classification with information on time interval represented and the sample size used for analysis in each time interval at the species level in the Shungura Formation. Age ranges of submembers were determined by regression of stratigraphic heights of de Heinzelin (1983) to chronostratigraphic units reported in Kidane et al. (2014).

Member	Time in Ma	Sample size	Stratigraphic units in 200-kyr time bins	Time in Ma	Sample size
Member A	3.60–3.44	153	A1	3.7–3.5	53
Member B	3.44–2.91	1022	A2–B0	3.5–3.3	117
Member C	2.91–2.53	1260	B1–B2	3.3–3.1	403
Member D	2.53–2.40	401	B3–B11	3.1–2.9	531
Member E	2.40–2.32	937	B12–C3	2.9–2.7	94
Member F	2.32–2.27	1527	C4–D1	2.7–2.5	1313
Member G	2.27–1.90	5486	D2–F1	2.5–2.3	2597
Member H	1.90–1.76	86	F2–G11	2.3–2.1	4355
Member J	1.76–1.53	26	G12–G29	2.1–1.9	1323

Table 24.1 (cont.)

Member	Time in Ma	Sample size	Stratigraphic units in 200-kyr time bins	Time in Ma	Sample size
Member K	1.53–1.38	103	H1–J1	1.9–1.7	86
Member L	1.38–1.05	164	J2–K0	1.7–1.5	59
			K1–L2	1.5–1.3	101
			L3–L9	1.3–1.1	133

Table 24.2 Member level and 200-kyr bin classification with information on time interval represented and sample size used for analysis in each time interval at the genus level in the Shungura Formation. Age ranges of submembers were determined by regression of stratigraphic heights of de Heinzelin (1983) to chronostratigraphic units reported in Kidane et al. (2014).

Member	Time in Ma	Sample size	Stratigraphic units in 200-kyr time bins	Time in Ma	Sample size
Member A	3.60–3.44	188	A1	3.7–3.5	65
Member B	3.44–2.91	2139	A2–B0	3.5–3.3	145
Member C	2.91–2.53	2429	B1–B2	3.3–3.1	1071
Member D	2.53–2.40	611	B3–B11	3.1–2.9	935
Member E	2.40–2.32	1319	B12–C3	2.9–2.7	163
Member F	2.32–2.27	2316	C4–D1	2.7–2.5	2486
Member G	2.27–1.90	7053	D2–F1	2.5–2.3	3870
Member H	1.90–1.76	210	F2–G11	2.3–2.1	5628
Member J	1.76–1.53	68	G12–G29	2.1–1.9	1693
Member K	1.53–1.38	163	H1–J1	1.9–1.7	211
Member L	1.38–1.05	289	J2–K0	1.7–1.5	116
			K1–L2	1.5–1.3	168
			L3–L9	1.3–1.1	234

elements were used because isolated postcranial elements are usually not identified to the species or genus level.

It is well known that different taphonomic processes and depositional settings might introduce biases in diversity analyses (Behrensmeyer and Kidwell, 1985). Even though only cranial elements are used in this analysis, making our comparisons across time more robust, differences in size and durability of cranial and dental remains among taxa and differences in collection strategies might introduce additional biases. However, previous studies in the Shungura Formation (e.g., Bobe et al., 2002; Alemseged, 2003) that examined and compared the effect of taphonomy on taxonomic and biological signals have indicated isotaphonomic conditions (i.e., assemblages that indicate similar preservation or taphonomic settings) in parts of the Shungura sequence. We consider these taphonomic issues in our discussions of our results.

Several measures and indices have been used in the past to calculate taxonomic diversity. While some of the most commonly used indices mainly focus on calculating taxonomic richness, other indices take relative abundance of each species into account. Here, we evaluate diversity patterns using Hill numbers (effective number of species), which have been shown to overcome the shortcomings of other diversity indices. Thus, while most diversity indices provide information about the entropy (uncertainty) that are difficult to interpret and compare across communities, the effective number of species (Hill numbers) reduces this problem by providing the number of equally common species (Hill, 1973; Jost, 2006, 2007; Ellison, 2010).

The Hill number is calculated as:

$$^qD = \left(\sum_{i=1}^{S} P_i^q\right)^{1/(1-q)}$$

where S is the number of species in the assemblage, p_i is the relative abundance of the ith species, and q is the order of diversity that determines the sensitivity to relative frequencies. As such, when $q = 0$, the number represents species richness where abundance does not contribute to the calculation of diversity. When $q = 1$ the equation is undefined but its limit as q tends to 1 is the exponential of the Shannon diversity index, given as:

$$^1D = exp\left(-\sum_{i=1}^{S} P_i \log P_i\right)$$

In this case the equation weighs all species by their relative abundance without favoring either common or rare species (Jost, 2006; Chao et al., 2014). When $q = 2$, the equation provides

Simpson diversity, which favors abundant species and discounts rare species.

Traditional methods of comparing diversity across communities mainly relied on standardizing samples using rarefaction (downsampling larger samples to the smallest sample; Sanders, 1968; Tipper, 1979). However, this approach is not optimal as it can undersample and artificially compress species richness in diverse assemblages (Close et al., 2018). More recently, a new approach of standardizing samples by coverage, which refers to comparing samples of equal completeness instead of equal size, has shown to be more effective in estimating diversity (Chao and Jost, 2012; Chao et al., 2014; Close et al., 2018; Du and Alemseged, 2018). Coverage is defined as the proportion of the total number of individuals in a community that belong to the species represented in the sample, and it is calculated as:

$$\hat{C}n = 1 - \frac{f1}{n} \frac{(n-1)f1}{(n-1)f1 + 2f2}$$

where n is the total number of individuals in a sample, and $f1$ and $f2$ are the numbers of singletons (taxa represented by one individual) and doubletons (taxa represented by two individuals), respectively (Chao and Jost, 2012).

Analysis of diversity was performed using iNEXT R package (version 2.0.19). This package allows an integrated rarefaction and extrapolation methodology using a coverage-based approach to calculate diversity (Hsieh et al., 2016). The package also allows estimation of 95 percent confidence interval by a bootstrapping method of 200 replications. Here the coverage-based approach is used to examine diversity patterns in the Shungura Formation through time. In this analysis, diversity estimates are computed for minimum sample coverages at the species ($C = 0.888$ for member level and $C = 0.895$ for 200-kyr time bin) and genus level ($C = 0.927$ for member level and $C = 0.940$ for 200-kyr time bin).

To analyze faunal dissimilarity between consecutive members at the genus and species levels, chord distance, a distance measure for abundance data is used. The chord distance between two assemblages, j and k, is calculated as:

$$D_{chord}(jk) = \sqrt{2\left(1 - \sum^{S}(X_{ij} * X_{ik}) \Big/ \sqrt{\sum^{S} X_{ij}^2 \sum^{S} X_{ik}^2}\right)}$$

Here, X_{ij} represents the abundance of the ith species (taxon) in the jth assemblage, X_{ik} represents the abundance of the ith species (taxon) in the kth assemblage, and S is the total number of species (taxa) in the two assemblages. Chord distance can have values ranging from 0 for assemblages with identical taxonomic composition to $\sqrt{2}$ for assemblages with no taxa in common (Legendre and Gallagher, 2001; Bobe et al., 2002; Faith and O'Connell, 2011; Legendre and DeCáceres, 2013). The chord distance for successive time units (i.e., members or 200-kyr time bin) was calculated for both taxonomic (i.e., species and genus) levels using Vegan R package (Version 2.5–6).

Results and Discussion

Diversity Patterns Across Geological Members

Both species and genus diversity patterns across members of the Shungura Formation are presented in Figure 24.2. In terms of species richness, relatively higher species richness is observed in Members B, E, F, G, H, and K (despite the wide confidence interval in H), while slightly lower values are observed for Members A, C, D, J, and L. Although overlapping confidence intervals do not indicate the lack of significant differences, the fact that the confidence intervals between Members A and B, B and C, and F and G do not overlap indicates significant differences in species richness between these members. When looking at Shannon diversity patterns that take abundance into account without favoring either common or rare species, diversity is low in Member A and increases to stable values in Members B through F, with some increase in Member E. Diversity increases in Members G and H, drops in Member J, increases again in Member K, and decreases in Member L. Simpson diversity, which favors abundant species, shows a slightly lower diversity in Member A followed by a relatively stable diversity patterns from Members B to E, with a slight drop in Member F. Diversity increases in Member G, remains relatively stable until Member K, and then slightly decreases in Member L. Overall, when looking at species richness, there are notable peaks and valleys. However, when taking abundance into account (i.e., Shannon or Simpson diversity), diversity appears to be less variable in the lower members (B–E) compared to the upper members (H–K). This difference does not appear to be a result of differences in depositional environments because fluvial conditions predominate in Members B–E as in Members H–K. However, samples are larger in the lower than in the upper members.

Looking at diversity at the genus level, taxonomic richness is relatively low in Member A, increases in Member B, decreases in Member C, and increases up to Member G. Richness decreases in Members H and J, increases in Member K, and drops in Member L. Both Shannon and Simpson diversities show similar patterns, with slightly higher diversity in Members A and B, a small drop in Member C, an increase in diversity in Members D and E, and a slight decrease in Member F. Diversity increases in Member G, decreases in Members H and J, increases again in Member K, and drops in Member L. Compared to what is observed at the species level, diversity patterns (i.e., Shannon or Simpson diversity) at the genus level appear to be more variable. These differences in the diversity patterns between the genus and species level analysis could be a result of a combination of a generally smaller number of genera compared to the number of species in an assemblage (i.e., several species might belong to the same genus), and also the differences in sample size between the two analysis (i.e., there are more samples for the genus level analysis as fossil specimens can sometimes be attributed to the genus level but not to the species level).

Diversity Patterns at 200-kyr Time Intervals

When assessing diversity patterns at 200-kyr time intervals at the species level, richness appears to increase from ~3.6 to 2.9

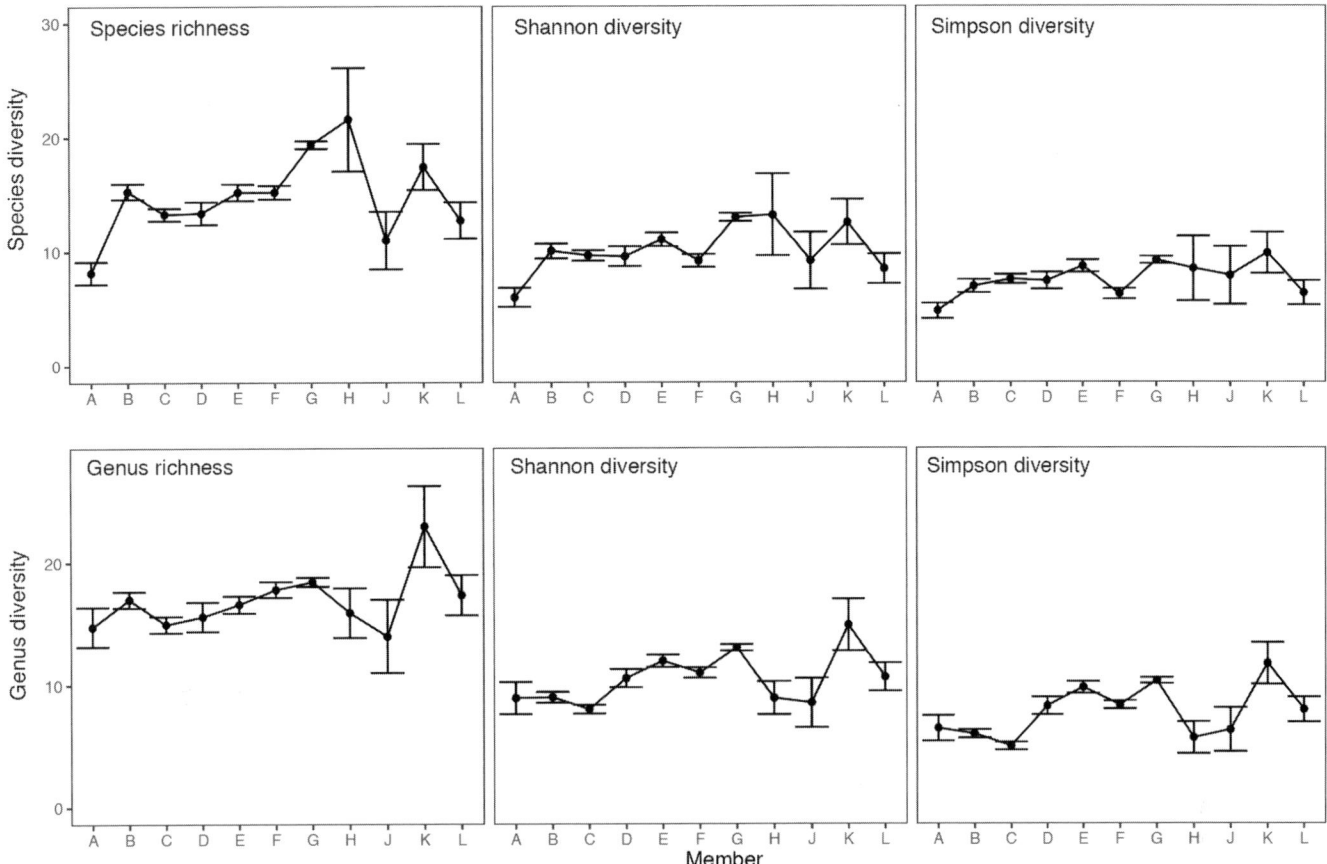

Figure 24.2 Species and genus richness and diversity patterns through time at the member level in the Shungura Formation. Error bars indicate 95% confidence intervals.

Ma; it decreases between 2.9 and 2.7 Ma; it increases from 2.7 to 1.7 Ma, and decreases afterwards (Figure 24.3). The analysis at the 200-kyr time bins shows some similar patterns to the member level analysis but highlights the time periods where diversity peaks occur. For instance, it indicates that the peak observed in Member B is a result of an increase in species richness that reaches its maximum at ~2.9 Ma, while the peak in Member G and H corresponds to an increased species richness between 2.1 and 1.7 Ma. When taking abundance into account, both Shannon and Simpson diversities show similar patterns, where diversity increases from 3.6 to 2.9 Ma, 2.7 to 2.1 Ma, 1.9 to 1.7 Ma, and decreases between 2.9 and 2.7, 2.1 and 1.9 Ma, and after 1.7 Ma.

At the genus level, richness shows an increase from 3.6 to 2.7 Ma, a decrease between 2.7 and 2.5 Ma, and remains stable between 2.5 and 1.9 Ma. Richness decreases between 1.9 and 1.7 Ma, increases between 1.7 and 1.3 Ma, and decreases afterwards. The sharp increase in species richness between 2.1 and 1.9 Ma at the species level is not reflected at the genus level. Both Shannon's and Simpson's diversities show similar patterns where diversity appears to increase between 3.5 and 3.3 Ma, 3.1 and 2.7 Ma, 2.5 and 2.1 Ma and between 1.7 and 1.3 Ma. Diversity is relatively lower prior to 3.5 Ma, from 3.3 to 3.1 Ma, 2.7 to 2.5 Ma, 2.1 to 1.7 Ma, and after 1.3 Ma.

Faunal Dissimilarity

To examine the faunal compositional similarity, chord distance was computed between consecutive members and at 200-kyr time intervals at the species and genus levels (Figure 24.4). As noted above, the chord distance has values ranging between 0 and √2, with values close to 0 indicating assemblages with very similar taxonomic composition and values close to √2 implying assemblages with no taxa in common. At both taxonomic levels, the faunal communities between Members A and B and between Members B and C show higher faunal dissimilarity compared to the fauna from Members C to G, which are more similar in species and genus composition to each other. The transition from Member G to Member H is signified by a higher dissimilarity, and the adjacent Members H through L also show the same pattern of higher dissimilarity. The slightly lower species and genus richness observed in Members A and C compared to the relatively higher richness in Member B might relate to this causing adjacent Members A–B and B–C to have higher faunal dissimilarity. Similarly, the higher faunal dissimilarity after Member G might relate to the differences in species and genus richness between these members. Assessing faunal compositional similarity at 200-kyr time bins at the species level reveals a similar pattern where higher faunal dissimilarities are observed at 3.5

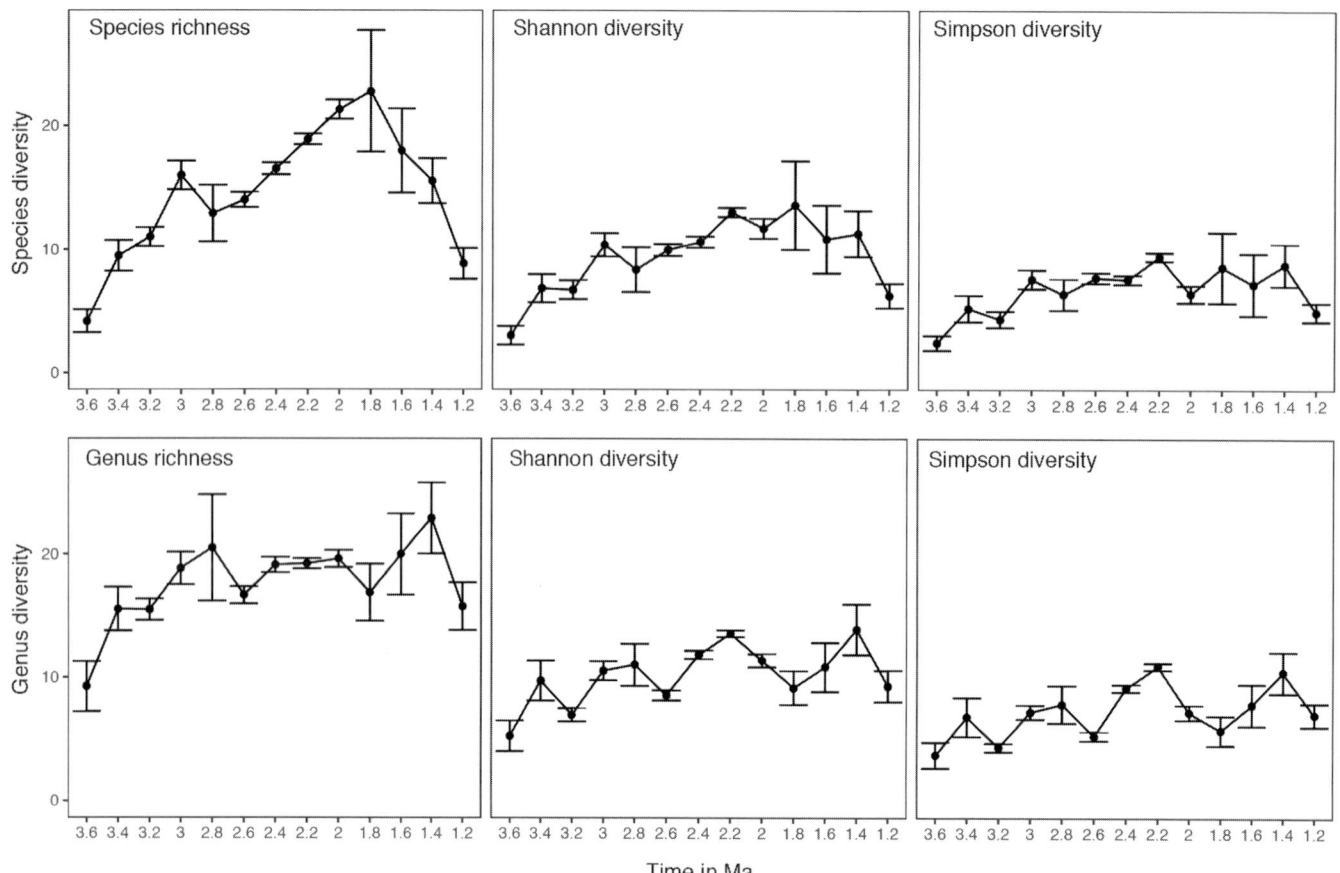

Figure 24.3 Species and genus richness and diversity patterns through time at 200-kyr intervals in the Shungura Formation. Points are plotted using the 200-kyr interval midpoints. Error bars indicate 95% confidence intervals.

Ma, between 3.1 and 2.9 Ma, and after 1.9 Ma. Faunal assemblages between 2.7 and 2.1 Ma appear to be similar to each other. At the genus level, while higher dissimilarity is observed at 3.5 Ma and 1.9 Ma, the assemblage between 3.1 and 2.1 Ma appear to be similar.

Comparison with Previous Studies

As presented earlier, several lines of paleoecological evidence have indicated changes in the paleoenvironmental conditions in the Shungura Formation. Bobe and colleagues (2002) explored changes in mammalian proportions (i.e., relative abundance of mammalian families) in the Omo sequence and reported differences in proportions that show a succession of the dominant mammalian families across time. Their study reported the dominance of suids prior to 3.4 Ma, succeeded by dominant cercopithecids and bovids between 3.4 and 2.5 Ma, and then a dominance of bovids over other mammalian families after 2.5 Ma. The faunal dissimilarity patterns presented this study might attest to these faunal successions at the genus and species levels.

A large body of evidence (paleosol carbonates, stable isotopes from dental enamel, large mammal abundances, micromammals, dental morphology, microwear, and paleobotanical remains) from the Shungura Formation coincides with the idea of a significant change in environmental conditions in the transition between Members B and C, approximately 2.8 Ma (Bonnefille and Dechamps, 1983; Wesselman, 1995; Bobe and Eck, 2001; Cooke, 2007, Martin et al., 2018). This shift in fauna and environments occurs in the absence of changes in taphonomic conditions and depositional environments (Bobe et al., 2002). The peak in species richness observed in this study in Member B (or more specifically between 2.9 and 3.1 Ma), which is followed by a slight drop in richness in Member C (around 2.9–2.7 Ma), and the differences in faunal compositional similarity observed between these time periods might reflect a response of the fauna to these changing environmental conditions. Similarly, data from paleosol carbonates and ecomorphological studies indicated the presence of wooded settings prior to 2 Ma, which were later replaced by more open and wooded grassland settings (Levin et al., 2011; Plummer et al., 2015). A study by Bobe et al. (2007) that assessed the proportion of bovids in the Shungura Formation through time has also indicated a low proportion of arid adapted taxa prior to 2 Ma that increased afterwards, indicating that the Omo was wetter and more wooded than other parts of the Omo-Turkana Basin. In this study we observe a peak in species richness ~2 Ma that is followed by a decline afterwards. This time period also coincides with a time of higher faunal dissimilarity compared to preceding time periods. Overall, peaks in the faunal diversity and dissimilarity patterns observed in this study appear to coincide in time with previously reported changes in the paleoenvironment

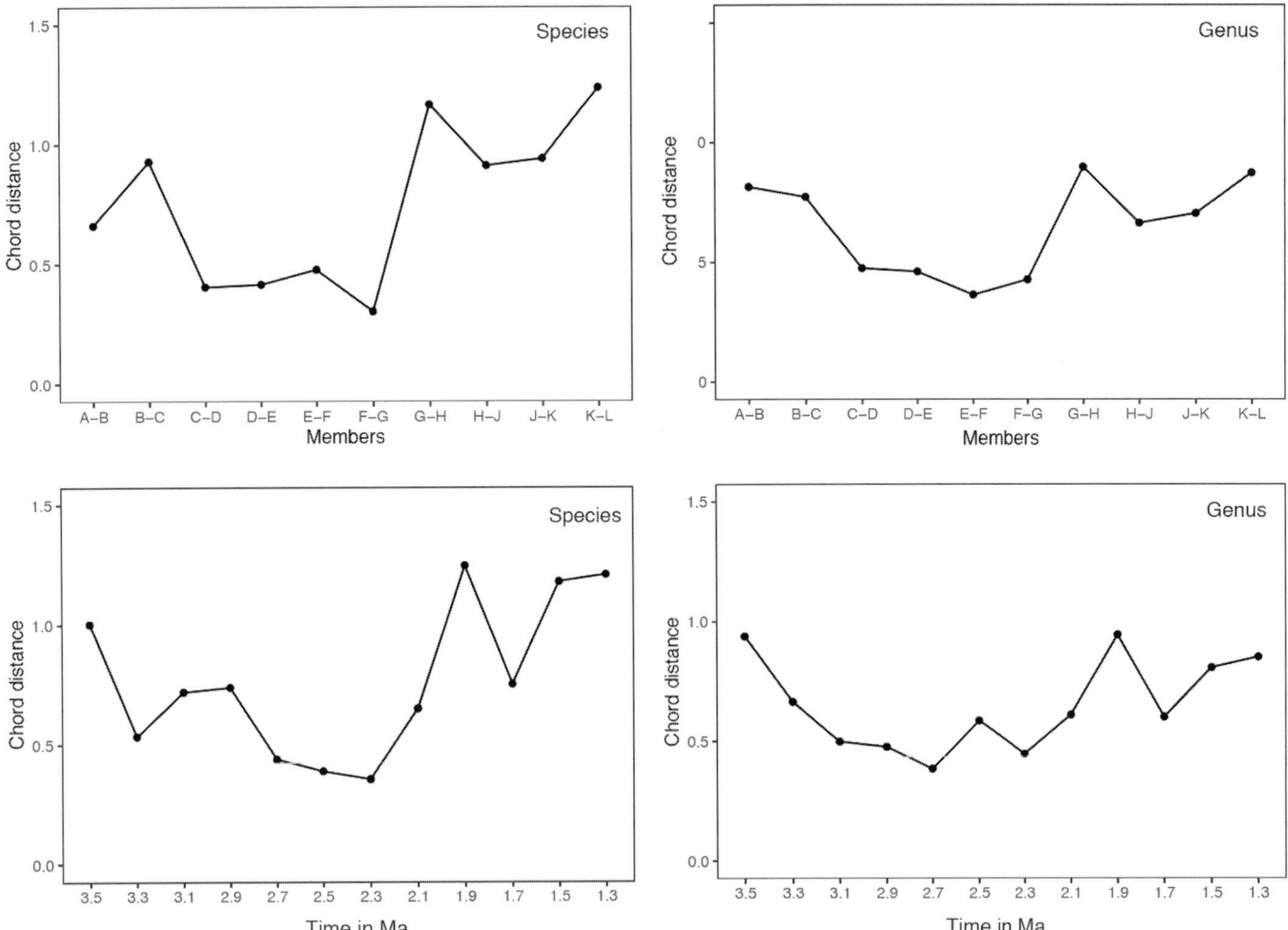

Figure 24.4 Faunal dissimilarity at the species and genus level through time at the member level (top) and at 200-kyr intervals (bottom) in the Shungura Formation. Faunal dissimilarity was measured using chord distance.

of the Shungura Formation. This indicates that these major paleoenvironmental changes might have affected the species abundance, composition, and overall community structure.

Concluding Remarks

The Shungura Formation provides one of the most continuous records of fossiliferous sediments that have contributed to our understanding of human evolution in Africa from about 3.6 Ma to 1 Ma. Here we have reviewed studies that focus on the paleoenvironments of the Shungura Formation, and provide analyses of diversity patterns at the species and genus levels at different time bins. We analyzed taxonomic diversity using a coverage-based approach across stratigraphic members and 200-kyr time bins. Notable peaks and drops in diversity show significant differences between stratigraphic levels. We also conducted analyses of faunal dissimilarity across stratigraphic members and 200-kyr time intervals, and highlight differences in faunal composition at the species and genus level across time. Several lines of paleoenvironmental evidence presented here indicate that changes in paleoenvironmental conditions occurred at about 2.8 Ma and after 2.0 Ma. Taxonomic diversity and faunal dissimilarity patterns show peaks that coincide with previously suggested environmental changes. This might imply that environmental changes likely caused a change in the vegetation structure and distribution as well as the faunal community structure and composition.

25. Paleoecology and Paleoenvironments of Early Quaternary Faunal Assemblages from the Nachukui Formation in Kenya: Insights from the West Turkana Archeological Project

Jean-Philip Brugal and Hélène Roche

Introduction

The Omo-Turkana Basin is a hotspot in Africa for paleontological, paleoanthropological, and paleoclimate studies. It contains several sedimentary formations spanning the Miocene, Pliocene, and Pleistocene distributed around Lake Turkana in Kenya and Ethiopia, yielding very rich and diverse records of vertebrate faunas and hominin species, as well as very early, and early, archeological sites (Bobe, 2011; Feibel, 2011; Harmand et al., 2015). During the last decades, researchers from various scientific disciplines have clarified the fine chronostratigraphic scale and the sedimentological and paleo-eco-ethological context of this area (including isotopes; for example, Negash et al., 2020). Taken together, these data comprise one of the best frameworks for the paleoenvironment and paleoecology of early hominins.

The Nachukui Formation, on the west side of Lake Turkana in the northern Kenya Rift, is comprised of a thick sequence (ca. 730 m of fluvio-lacustrine sediments) divided into eight members and dated from >4 to 0.7 Ma. Intensive fieldwork has been conducted particularly from the end of the 1980s by the National Museum of Kenya (NMK; Harris et al., 1988b with the WTRP) followed by a French–Kenyan project, the West Turkana archeological Project (WTAP, joint-project NMK/French Mission *Préhistorique au Kenya*). These projects have highlighted the importance of this formation, by providing evidence of the succession of hominin occupation sites (Oldowan, Acheulean) within the time interval of 2.4–0.7 Ma (Roche, 2011) as well as the oldest stone tools dated at 3.3 Ma (Harmand et al., 2015: Lomekwian industry). The fieldwork and surveys led to the discovery of some 40 archeological sites of which the most important were excavated.

Here we present a first overview of the faunal associations and paleocommunities during the period of 2.35 and 1.65 Ma where cultural transitions occurred (from early Oldowan, to Oldowan, to early and recent Acheulean). This period coincides with the earliest appearance of the genus *Homo* in the Kenyan region (although present earlier in Afar, Ethiopia at 2.8 Ma; Villmoare et al, 2015), and also with the appearance of the *H. erectus* clade and the presence of the genus *Paranthropus*. It is a time interval where hominin diversity was the highest in Africa. This period coincides with the onset of the Northern Hemisphere glacial cycles with a 41-kyr periodicity, around 2.7–2.5 Ma (deMenocal, 2004, 2011). Paleovegetation proxies (as well as isotopic values) record abrupt and marked shifts toward cooler and drier climate with an increase of C_4 grassland and shrubs (Bonnefille, 2010; Cerling et al., 2013a). The terrestrial fauna, especially the bovids, record turnover events (high levels of speciation and extinction) around 2.8 and 1.8 Ma, which are characterized by the appearance of greater numbers of grazing species (i.e., those possessing hypsodont teeth and molarized premolars; Vrba, 1995b; Bobe and Behrensmeyer, 2004).

This interval is characterized by a general aridification trend, although this appears not to have been uniform both in space and time. Moreover, at a regional scale and when dealing with hominin (*Homo* and/or *Australopithecus*) occupational sites (i.e., those with stone tools), we would expect local faunal associations with differing ecological signatures. The knowledge of habitat diversity and faunal variability through space and time constitutes one of the main scientific goals of previous decades of research from the Omo-Turkana basin. In this paper, we focus on faunal lists from 14 archeological sites in the Nachukui Formation to provide new insights on taxonomic diversity and paleoenvironmental contexts for early hominins and to make some preliminary comparative analyses with other Basin faunal assemblages.

Faunal Collections: Sampling and Counting Procedures

The questions of temporal and spatial scales combined with analytical resolution from taxonomy, taphonomy, and sedimentological settings are critical methodological steps into the study of faunal collections to infer paleo-context *sensu lato* (Behrensmeyer et al., 2007a). We provide a brief account of how the studied Nachukui collections were collected.

The first faunal collection was the result of systematic fieldwork surveys and geological and paleontological investigations made between 1980 and 1990 (West Turkana Research Project, WTRP), and the results were published in an important and seminal monograph (Harris et al., 1988b) that documented the discovery of numerous (n = 47) paleontological localities or areas distributed across the entire stratigraphical sequence. Generally these paleontological localities were relatively large (sometimes several km² in spatial extent). Such spatially extensive collection areas probably represent great sedimentary thicknesses and longer time intervals (see Note 1). The recovered vertebrate fossils come mostly from Plio-Pleistocene exposures, collected from the surface and rarely *in situ*, but the 'majority of surface specimens were not far removed from their original site (or level) of preservation'' Harris et al., 1988b: 22), with no systematic sieving except at hominin localities or to specifically recover fossil micromammal specimens.

Primate and carnivore specimens were comprehensively collected. The collection protocol for herbivores and large mammals focused on specimens that could be identified, i.e., well-preserved, often complete, and identifiable specimens, which means essentially cranial specimens and mandibles, horn-cores, and isolated teeth for herbivores and large mammals; postcranial material was not usually collected unless associated with cranial or dental remains. Almost 1000 specimens from more than 90 mammal species have been identified with preliminary descriptions in the monograph, providing an important basis for further work.

Surveys and surface collections continued until 1999 throughout the Lake Turkana basin by staff of the NMK supervised by M.G. and L.N. Leakey, R. Bobe, and others that are documented in the fossil inventory database described and used by Bobe (2011; www.mnh.si.edu/ete/ETE_Datasets_Turkana.html). So far, 1572 mammal specimens are recorded from the Nachukui Formation with 87.8 percent of cranial and dental material for all Orders and Families. For comparison, cranial and dental material represents 79.2 percent of the 8851 specimens collected from the Koobi Fora Formation.

Following observations of lithic materials by the WTRP participants, one of us (H.R.) was invited to visit West Turkana by R. Leakey, then director of NMK. This led to the creation of a joint project – the West Turkana Archeology Project (WTAP), which has surveyed archeological sites and conducted excavations since 1996. Almost 40 archeological sites have been located in different members of the Nachukui Formation. After locating stone tools, with or without bones, within a surface concentration, the following procedure was followed.

- *Surface/subsurface collection*: documentation of the entire surface of the exposure and presence of stone tools within meter squares (in very few cases we used a larger zone, 5 × 5 m^2). All items (bones, teeth, and artifacts) are collected and often the loose soil was removed and the sediments sieved and any retrieved material was sorted.
- *Excavation areas*: several square meters were selected according to the topography and exposure in order to be excavated to document the archeological level *in situ*. The classic excavation procedure was used: taking 3D coordinates of visible items, plotting them within the meter squares, and photographing them. The enclosing matrix was dry-sieved (some was tested with wet-sieving) and all sorted material was assigned to the meter square of origin. During this process, many supplementary observations were made on sediment type, geological sections were documented, special features were sampled (carbonates, pumices, termite nests, roots, etc.). It is noteworthy that all organic material whatever its size or state of preservation was retrieved, including small splinters or tooth fragments and microfragments.
- *Extension zone*: for a few sites in which faunal material was abundant and more spatially scattered, systematic surveys were made in which all fossils were documented (including carnivores, primates, and bones marked by biological agents) and all identifiable remains (cranial, teeth, postcranial, marked bones) were collected. This surface collection rarely exceeds ~100 m in extent around the excavation areas, and notes were kept on from which part of the site the specimens were retrieved and located.

The two collecting/sampling procedures mentioned lead to major differences that may impose limitations on our interpretations. These include the following.

1. *Temporal resolution*: the WTAP focused on archeological sites that were chronologically limited (i.e., of shorter duration), but that was not always the case for the WTRP collections. Each "fossil unit" ranges from a relatively restricted climatic event/phase for single excavations to several climatic phases/cycles for larger-scale collecting; that is to say, concerning the "short-term" versus "longer-term" *sensu* Behrensmeyer and colleagues (2007a). However, even short-term is often a time-averaged accumulation for which the duration is unknown and which may range from decades, centuries, to millennia.

2. *Taxonomy*: all specimens, and even small fragments or bone splinters, were collected by the WTAP, which increased the probability for sampling a wider taxonomical representation coupled with a relatively higher rate of taxon identification (notably for smaller species). However, most of the fossil materials from archeological excavations were fragmented, whereas only relatively complete specimens were collected during the paleontological surveys, resulting in a significant gap between numbers of specimens collected. This point is especially relevant for tooth fragments because even a very small piece (in mm^2) could be attributed to a family level (bovid, suid, hippopotamid, etc.), and if larger to a genus or tribe level (such as Alcelaphini, Antilopini). For remains of bovids, and also with respect to postcranial material, size classes are used to categorize these fossils (Brugal, 2017). Excavation procedures that yield mainly bone and tooth fragments, more or less identifiable, will strongly influence the counting process (i.e., higher count of fragments, and therefore higher numbers of specimens). Bone splinters are not considered here, even though a category of large mammal (such as a pachyderm) can be readily distinguished from other bone fragments.

3. *Taphonomy*: the scale of temporal resolution and the ease of identification of fossil material will influence the accuracy of interpretations of depositional environment and site formation processes. The degree of completeness of the fossil material and the use of size classes, the time/duration of accumulations and their spatial distribution will in turn influence the accuracy of the taxonomic representation and the taphonomic interpretations.

Sites and Materials

The Nachukui Formation is divided into eight members, bounded by volcanic tuffs that are correlated by mineralogy and geochemical signatures with the radiometrically well-dated tuff sequence of the Shungura Formation, near the Omo River, in Ethiopia (Harris et al., 1988b). We focus on sites from two main members: the Kalochoro Member (2.34–1.88 Ma) represented by four sites and the Kaitio Member (1.88–1.62 Ma) with nine sites, and one site is added from the Upper Lokalalei Member (2.52–2.34 Ma). This last is Nasura 2 (NAS2), which is located just below the Kalochoro tuff (= tuff F of the Shungura Formation dated at 2.34 ± 0.05 Ma; see Harris et al., 1988b) that formed the boundary between the Lokalalei Member and the Kalochoro Member. The KBS tuff (= H-2 of Shungura dated at 1.88 ± 0.02 Ma) is the boundary between the Kalochoro and Kaitio Members, and the upper boundary of the Kaitio Member is formed by the Lower Koobi Fora tuff dated at 1.62 ± 0.02 Ma (= tuff J6-2 of Omo; Bobe et al., 2007b).

According to the tuff correlations, the Kalochoro Member corresponds to Members F, G, and the basal part of H of the Shungura Formation and the Upper Burgi Member of the Koobi Fora Formation. The Kaitio Member corresponds to H and the basal part of J of the Shungura Formation and the KBS and lowest part of the Okote Members of the Koobi Fora Formation (see figure in Harris et al., 1988b: p. 12). The Kalochoro Member has a total thickness estimated at 78 m with a time span of 450 ka, whereas the Kaitio Member has a thickness of 169 m for a temporal span of 250 ka. From these data, we infer a higher sedimentation rate for the second member and increased levels of hydrological activity (at least in terms of sedimentation). For these two members, laminated claystone and siltstone, as well as fine sandstone, dominated the section (see Harris et al., 1988 for further detail).

WTAP Sites

One site is located at the top of the Lokalalei Member. Nasura 2 (NAS2) is placed just below the Kalochoro Tuff, and tentatively dated to 2.4 Ma. This site has yielded very poor fossil material, essentially deriving from surface collections. Four sites derive from the Kalochoro Member From oldest to youngest these are: Nasura 1 (NAS1), Lokalalei 1 (LA1), Lokalalei 2 (LA2), and Lokalalei 3 (LA3) – all bracketed between ~2.4 and 2.2 Ma (see details in Tiercelin et al., 2010). Material from LA1 and LA2 derives from excavation, surface collections and an extension zone (corresponding to *ca*. 2000 m^2 and *ca*. 1000 m^2). LA3 is a more limited collection coming only from surface–subsurface of *ca*. 300 m^2 (for comparison, one European football field is equal to 10,800 m^2 and a tennis court for doubles is 261 m^2).

In the Kaitio Member, there are two main complexes of sites dated to between 1.8 and 1.7 Ma: one along the Kokiselei river (with three sites – KS1, KS5, and KS6 – that are the richest sites in this area, and three others that yielded few fossil remains: KS2, KS3, KS4) and the other adjacent to the Naiyena Engol river (with six sites NY1, NY2, NY6, NY10, NY11, and NY12). The KS sequence seems older than the NY sequence, and we tentatively organized them chronologically (from oldest to youngest) as follows: KS5 = KS6 → KS1 and NY12 → NY1 → NY6 → NY10 → NY11 → NY2. The KS faunal collections come mainly from excavations and limited collection from the site surface (see Table 25.1). This is also the case for NY2, NY6, NY10, and NY12. The NY1 and NY11 faunal collections come from excavations, surface site, and extension zones which represent a prospection area of between 1500 and 2000 m^2 in extent.

Several published papers document the work over the period considered here, including Kibunjia (1994), Roche and Kibunjia (1996), Roche et al. (1999, 2003), Brugal et al. (2003), Prat et al. (2003, 2005), Delagnes and Roche (2005), Roche (2005, 2011); Texier et al. (2006), Harmand, (2009), Tiercelin et al. (2010), and Quinn et al. (2013, 2020).

WTRP Sites

There are six paleontological localities within the Kalochoro Member (one of which yielded only two fossil remains – KG2 – and is therefore excluded) and seven within the Kaitio Member (originally this was nine localities, but two of these – NY1 and

Table 25.1 West Turkana sites – Nachukui Formation, Kalochoro and Kaitio Members (n = specimen included large mammal category) – area: km^2 for WTRP, m^2 for WTAP

			Kalochoro				
Ma	WTRP[a]		Area	n Specimens	WTAP	Area	n Specimens
1.87	KL4	= KL4	0.053	19			
2.0–1.8	KK	= KK	0.508	70			
2.0–1.8	KG1	= KG I	0.156	35			
2.4–1.8	KI3*	= KI III	0.186	6			
ca. 2.2					LA3	500	61
ca. 2.3					LA2	1000	175
2.34	LA1	= LA I	0.25	62	LA1	2000	758
ca. 2.4					NAS1	150	45

[a] KGII(2) excluded *Kalochoro?

Table 25.1 (cont.)

Ma	WTRP[b]		Area	n Specimens	WTAP	Area	n Specimens
				Kaitio			
1.9–1.6	KL3	= KL III	0.146	36			
1.9–1.6	KL6	= KL VI	0.103	58			
1.9–1.6	LK4	= LK IV	1.13	13			
1.9–1.6	NY2	= NY II	0.245	55			
1.9–1.6	NY3	= NY III	0.396	42			
1.9–1.6	NY4	= NY IV	0.18	48			
1.8–1.75					KS5	70	186
1.8–1.75					KS6	85	202
1.8–1.75	KS1	= KS I	0.135	20	KS1	875	610
1.8–1.7					NY12	70	65
1.8–1.7					NY1	2500	856
1.8–1.7					NY6	64	106
1.8–1.7					NY10	130	42
1.8–1.7					NY11	2000	229
1.8–1.7					NY2	340	247

[b] KSII(2) and NYI(1) excluded (one remains, respectively).

KS2 – yielded very few remains and are therefore excluded; see Harris et al., 1988b). In Table 25.1 we provide the estimated surface areas of these localities, as well as indications of WTAP sites for comparison. In some cases the same acronym was given with number in both expeditions, and it appears that some same places were investigated by the both teams. To avoid confusion, we decided to follow the previous numbering system of Harris et al. (1988b: 21) with a roman numeral associated with an acronym: for example, Lokalalei 1 (LA1) would be LA I, or Naiyena Engol 3 (NY3) would be NY III, etc. for WTRP sites. The same sites refer to LA I similar to LA1 and KS I to KS1 (see Table 25.1 for the correspondence of sites between WTAP and WTRP). Overall a total of 20 sites are available for the time period and area considered, with 8 sites from the Kalochoro Member (1261 specimens) and 12 from the Kaitio Member (3189 specimens).

Methods and Preliminary Results

We compare here the data from the WTAP to the WTRP, and to other paleontological assemblages (Shungura and Koobi Fora from for the Omo-Turkana Basin). We use the extant African mammalian communities as modern faunal proxies to interpret different climatic biomes, environments and habitat categories (e.g., Greenacre and Vrba, 1984; Shipman and Harris, 1988; Hernandez Fernandez and Vrba, 2006; Alemseged, 2003).

We provide an initial overview of faunal assemblages from WTAP, essentially at a family level but also at the tribal level for Bovidae. African bovids display a wide species spectrum intensively used in ecology, paleoecology as well as in zooarcheology (e.g., Jarman, 1974; Vrba, 1980; Cerling et al., 2003a; Gordon and Prins, 2008) with numerous paleoenvironmental and paleoanthropological implications (e.g., Vrba, 1995b; Kappelman et al., 1997; Reed, 1997). At this stage only general comparisons are possible; however, one of the main uncertainties about locality/site level is their chronological succession within a member, which often constrains consideration of them as a "package," allowing only a relatively crude assumptions to be made. This is especially the case in the Kaitio Member, within and particularly between the two site complexes Kokiselei and Naiyena Engol, and constitutes a real limitation for a dynamic, high-resolution, comparative paleoenvironmental reconstruction (see Behrensmeyer et al., 2007a). Moreover, the taphonomic and geological contexts remain poorly understood.

WTAP Sites

Table 25.2 gives a comprehensive overview of the faunal associations found from, and in the near vicinity of, archeological sites presented at different taxonomic levels (family, genus/tribe) including mammal size classes. It is important to note here that we do not include in our calculations all the smallest fraction of material coming from sieving, corresponding to small mammal, reptile, or fish bone splinters. These results give the first indications of ecosystems present around the sites and in each member. However, data on bovid size-classes need to be improved in order to accurately reflect their tribe status. Bovid size-classes often represent a high percentage of remains, partly due to a high degree of fragmentation (Table 25.2).

The sites can be divided in three categories following the number of remains (i.e., NISP and size-classes) as well as the

Table 25.2 Vertebrate distribution (NISP/size classes) per WTAP sites (tot = total for sites including excavations + surface site + extension zone, see text)

		Member	Lokalalei	Kalochoro				Kaitio									
		Sites	NAS2	NAS1	LA1 tot	LA2 tot	LA3	KS5	KS6	KS1	NY12	NY1 tot	NY6	NY10	NY11 tot	NY2
		Surface excavation (m²)	2C=20	126	60	2C=17	2	65	78	38	45	55	15	70	22	32
		Surface collection	?	ca. 140	cuvett	ca. 100	ca. 500	ca. 70	ca. 85	875	70	ca. 2500	64	130	ca. 2000	ca. 340
		Thick level (cm)	ca. 40	Max.50	ca. 35	ca. 50	?	ca. 30	ca. 25	ca. 40	ca. 50	ca. 40	ca. 50	ca. 80	ca. 40	40–73
		Lithic *in situ*	85	920	380	2122	10	1779	5584	526	433	ca. 2640	259	ca. 1300	153	320
		Lithic surface	?		ca. 320		98	?	?	1727	?	ca. 940	?	?	473	300
Bovids		Small (1 + 2)	6		124	7		43	11	60	6	141	7	2	40	13
		Small–medium (2–3)						30	25	36	6	42			3	2
		Medium (3)	2	1	85	7	2	5	2	63	4	90	7	2	20	4
		Large (4)			5				6	2		21	2		3	
		Indet.	1		17	10				87	5	74	6		5	23
		Neotragini	1		6					6		1				
		Antlopini			81	3	1	15	1	2	1	12	4	2	13	13
		Aepycerotini			14				3	7	1	31	1?		1	
		Alcelaphini			117	4	1	16	3	42		10	1	2	7	2
		Reduncini	1		16	4	3	6		37		23	5		18	15
		Tragelaphini	1		5	2				77		19	1	1		9
		Hippotragini			3	1						1				
		Bovini			12		1		3	8		10			2	7
Equids		Indet.			12	4		6	6	10		18	1		3	3
		Hipparionin	1		11	5		1	1	3	3	27	3	1	32	
		Zebrine			3	1	1	2	2	5		16	1	1	2	
Suids		Indet.	1	9	5	4	1			27	7	23	3	1	13	2
		Metridiochoerus			1					23		7	2		11	9
		Kolpochoerus			4	2				9	2	9	5	2	6	7
		Notochoerus			7	2	1					2				2

Taxon	Sub-taxon														
Giraffid															2
Hippopotamids		11	11	3		8	12	44	17	5	3				
Rhinocerotids	*Ceratotherium*	1		3	10		4	11	7		5	3	10	3	12
Proboscids	*Elephas/Loxodonta*	21		2	1		2					1	2		11
	Deinotherium		3					4	1						
Large mammals	Indet.	31	11	42	9		34	34	5	28	6	10	2		2
Primates	Non-hominid			13				2		6	1				2
	Hominin	1		1			10			1					
Carnivores	Hyenid			3	1						1		1		
	Felid						5	5	5				1		
	Canid						2		2						
	Mustelid														
	Viverrid			1		5				1	1				
	Indet.			1		1?	1		3				1		
Rodents	Small					11	7		6						2
	Hystrix			1			3								
Hyracoid							1								
Leporid				3		7									1
Aves	*Struthio* (egg)	2		4	18		1	1	1		1		26		
	Other			2		13	1		2						
Reptiles	Crocodile	5	1	34	8	4	7	13	8	35	18	2	5		7
	Chelonid	9	1	88	27	1	5	2	2	43	4	1	4		1
	Indet.			4	47										
Pisces		14	8	18	5	28	80	9	5	91	10	11	2		88
Total		100	45	758	175	61	186	202	610	65	856	106	42	229	247

Data compiled at April 2015 (JPB).

Table 25.3 Some descriptors of WTAP sites: percentages of cephalic (horn-core, cranial, and teeth), aquatic, and small vertebrate stock

	Lokalalei	Kalochoro			Kaitio									
	NAS2	NAS1	LA1 tot	LA2 tot	LA3	KS1	KS5	KS6	NY1 tot	NY2	NY6	NY10	NY11 total	NY12
% Cephalic*	77.3	–	53.5	86.2	87.5	51.5	38.6	55.8	45.0	68.9	48.8	78.3	58.1	54.3
% Small vertebrate	43.5	29.4	21.4	60.6	73.1	6.4	34.4	54.8	21.5	40.1	29.4	43.8	16.4	25.0
Main small vertebrate	Fish	Fish	Chelonid	Reptile	Fish	Crocodile	Fish/rodent	Fish	Fish	Fish	Crocodile	Fish	Struthio	Crocodile
% Aquatic	30.4	58.8	8.8	9.1	71.2	3.8	17.2	56.5	20.5	42.5	45.0	56.3	4.4	41.7
Main aquatic	Fish	Hippo	Crocodile	(Crocodile)	Fish	Crocodile	Fish	Fish	Hippo	Fish	Crocodile/hippo	Fish	Crocodile	Hippo

*Calculation on identifiable material of bovid, equid, suid, carnivoran, primate, rhino, hippo, giraffid, proboscid, and crocodylian.

Table 25.4 General description of faunal associations of WTAP sites: main families (bovid size classes were not considered in the ranking); in parentheses: (aquatic component dominant: >50%) and underlined: small vertebrate remains dominant

1st rank		2nd rank			
	Bovids	Equids	Suids	Hippopotamids	Large mammals
Bovids	KS5	LA2, NY1, NY11	KS1, (NY2)	(NY6), (NY12)	LA1, (KS6)
Suids					(NAS1)
Large mammals	NAS2, (LA3), (NY10)				

biodiversity (i.e., number of taxa), from the richest site (n = 600–850: LA1, KS1, and NY1), intermediate (n = 100–300: NAS2, LA2, KS5, KS6, NY2, NY6, NY11) to the more impoverished sites (n < 100: NAS1, LA3, NY10, NY12; Table 25.1). Two other broad descriptive categories could be estimated for each assemblage: one about the prevalence of aquatic species (hippopotamids, crocodile, and fish) and another on the frequency of large versus small vertebrate species (this last category includes rodents, birds, reptiles/chelonids, and fish). Lastly, we rank and organize sites according to the dominance of the two most important large mammal families in the faunal associations. All these data – together with proportion of dental and cranial remains, especially composed of dental material (see above) – are given in Table 25.3 then summarized in Table 25.4, which provides an overview of the variability in the fossil assemblages.

The aquatic component (mostly fish) is minimal in the site of LA1 and LA2, and even less at KS1 and NY11. The small vertebrate component is especially high for LA2 and LA3, but low at KS1 and NY11. We also note a relatively high proportion of ostrich eggshell occurring at NY11. Moreover, a relatively high proportion of terrestrial tortoises is present at LA1, which has been interpreted as possible hominin exploitation with cutmarks present on a few shell fragments (Brugal et al., 2003) as has been observed for later periods (Braun et al., 2010). It appears that the sites of KS1 and NY11 are suggestive of complex taphonomic histories (a mixture of naturally occurring faunas with intervention by potential predators, whether hominins or not) and are related to a depositional environment marked by more or less proximity to water sources, such as lakes, rivers, or marshes. Information on sediments and other geological features needs to be combined with these first observations before determining the range of habitats used by hominin groups; however, at this point, they indicate that hominins were using a wide range of paleoenvironments.

Unsurprisingly, fossil bovids dominate in all localities (except NAS1) and size-classes (especially small size-classes). Bovid material fluctuates through the sites from 38.9 percent to 94.3 percent without any obvious explanation for such variation (Figure 25.1). However, bovids are more frequent in the Kokiselei complex and seem to decrease during the period of the Naiyena Engol complex; a general trend toward fewer bovids could occur during the temporal period represented by the Kaitio Member. If we consider analyses at the tribe level (assemblages with more than 10 remains: 9 sites), Alcelaphini and Antilopini are frequent in Kalochoro sites with a slight increase of Reduncini from LA1 to LA3; in the latter site, Bovini are frequent. KS5 shows the same picture, but KS1 is peculiar in possessing abundant Tragelaphini and Alcelaphini. The NY sites display a relative abundance of Reduncini associated with Aepycerotini or Antilopini.

African bovids possess various locomotory and dietary adaptations which facilitate classification into broad habitat types defined primarily by their proportions of grass and wood cover (i.e., closed versus open) with climatic features (i.e., arid/dry versus wet). Dietary categories from grazer, mixed-feeder to browser are reflected in modern record of behavior for the different tribes (Jarman, 1974; Vrba, 1980; Gordon and Prins, 2008; and see Cerling et al., 2003a). In order to facilitate their comparisons we will follow the groups outlined by Shipman and

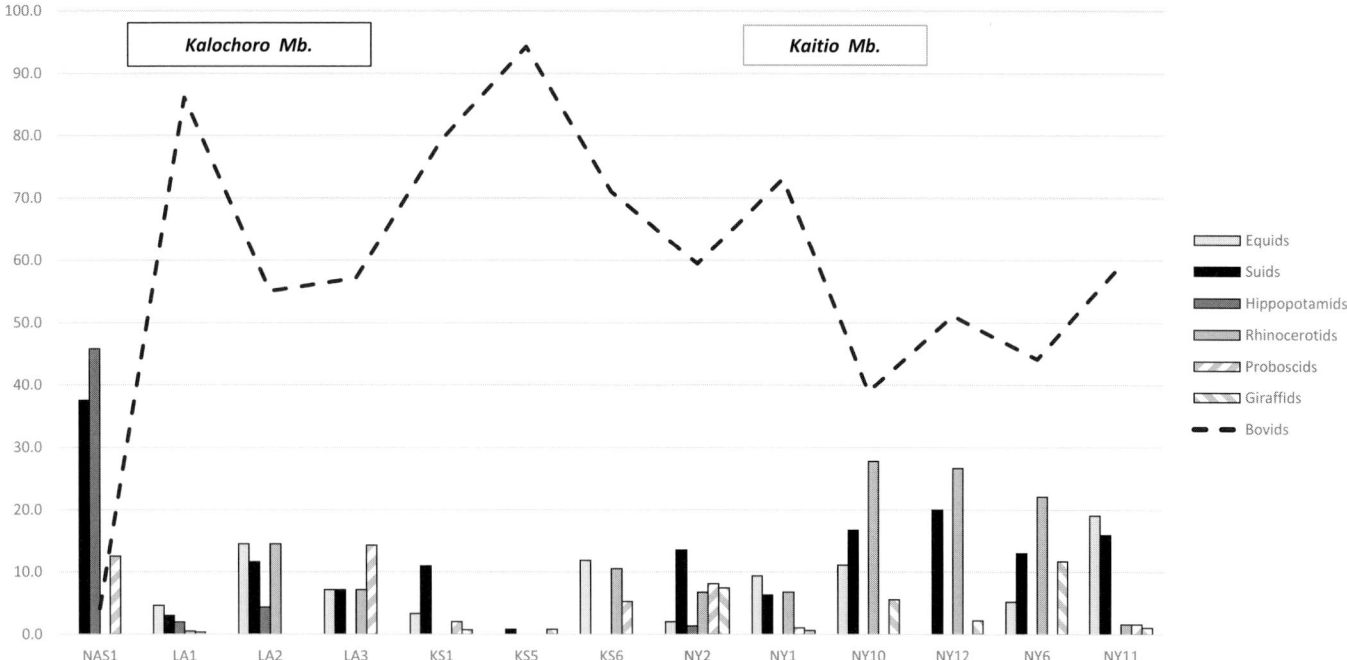

Figure 25.1 Distribution of main mammal families in the WTAP sites.

Harris (1988) and Bobe et al. (2007b) expressed and modified as follows: (i) a group composed of Alcelaphini + Antilopini + Hippotragini (AAH group), which represents open and seasonally arid grasslands; (ii) a group with Aepycerotini + Tragelaphini (AT), which represents woodland or forest as well as ecotonal zone with grasslands or bushlands; and (iii) a last group with Reduncini + Bovini (RB) associated with moist grasslands near wooded habitats. Cephalophini, Neotragini, and Caprini are not taken into account in this approach. The place of Bovini could be questioned and could be combined with Tragelaphini although they indicate a wetter setting. As noted by Bobe et al. (2007b: 145) "The cluster formed by the 'moist-grass grazers' (Reduncini) plus Bovini, Aepycerotini, and Tragelaphini likely represents vegetation types that depend on moister climatic or groundwater conditions with less severe dry seasons, while the cluster formed by Alcelaphini, Antilopini, and Hippotragini represents open or bushy vegetation that characterizes environments with marked dry seasons." According to the ternary diagram taking into account the sites with sufficient material ($n > 15$), following Shipman and Harris' (1988) method, and excluding the relatively rare Neotragini (Figure 25.2) we can distinguish three groups of sites based on percentage frequency (NISP):

1. Dominance of AAH group, represented by Kalochoro sites (LA1 and LA2 in a lesser degree, and KS5).
2. Faunal associations with subequal proportion of AAH and RB groups, represented by NY6, NY11 and NY2.
3. A relative higher proportion of AT group, represented by NY1 and KS1 sites.

As seen here, the bovid taxonomic abundance varies according to the sites, which could be related to different biomes and requires further information about depositional contexts. It is important to remember that taxa representation in one site includes species living close to the site (representing a single habitat type) as well as species deriving from a wider catchment area around the site (covering several different habitat types). For Naiyena Engol sites, we observed abundant aquatic components (especially hippo at NY1, NY6, and NY12) with a good representation of Reduncini indicating closer habitats near a lake. The Kokiselei sites seem located in a relatively more terrestrial (drier) context within a more open environment (Brugal et al., 2003). The Kalochoro sites (Lokalalei) also seem to be located in a relatively more open and drier context with a seasonal contrast, although evidence of the woodland/bushland/shrubland areas structural category is present associated with wooded grassland (Quinn et al., 2013; see below).

Second to bovids in abundance of species/families are mainly equids (LA1, LA2 with rhino, KS6, NY1, NY11) or suids (KS1, NY2 with proboscideans), then rhinocerotids (NY6, NY10, NY12). Large mammals are overall relatively important (NAS1, NAS2) and regularly present except at LA1, KS1, and KS5, where there might have been less vegetation cover, specifically trees. Giraffids, primates (including hominins), and carnivores are never abundant.

WTRP versus WTAP

We have followed the same analytical procedure at the bovid tribal level in order to compare sites from the two members from the two collections (WTRP versus WTAP; see top of Figure 25.2). We notice a discrepancy between the two sets of data in terms of bovid group frequency. It is less obvious when comparing LA1 ($n = 248$) to LA I ($n = 25$), but is quite noticeable when comparing KS1 ($n = 173$) and KS I ($n = 16$). If the former shows more evidence of the AT representatives (especially Tragelaphini), the latter is more situated toward the RB cluster.

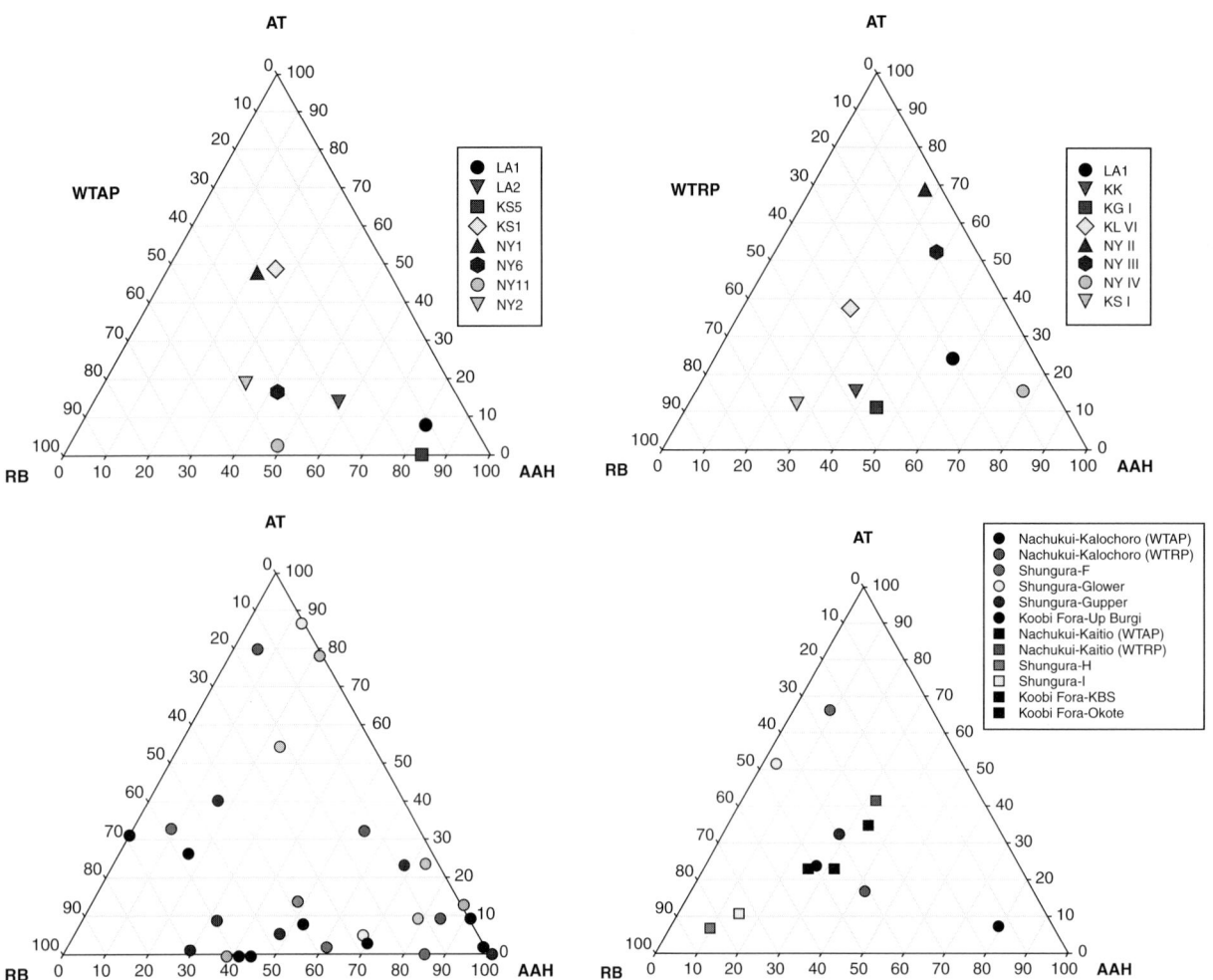

Figure 25.2 Ternary plots of bovid tribe representation (see text for explanation of grouping) for WTAP sites (top, left) versus WTRP sites (top, right): square = Kalochoro Member, triangle = Kaitio Member; ternary plots of modern bovid tribe representation from 29 game parks (Shipman and Harris, 1988; Alemseged, 2003: table 25.3) (bottom, left) and for different members of Nachukui, Shungura, and Koobi Fora Formations between *ca*. 2.3 and 1.6 Ma: circle = Kalochoro Member and equivalent, square = Kaitio Member and equivalent. (A black and white version of this figure will appear in some formats. For the color version, please refer to the plate section.)

Further inference is not possible, but we do note the large size sample differences between the two collections.

Globally speaking, sites belonging to the Kalochoro Member are located between AAH and RB poles with less dispersion (Figure 25.2). The sites from the Kaitio Member show a higher distribution occurring between the AT and RB poles, except for two sites (KS5 and NY IV) which essentially yield taxa from the AAH group. As a first indication, the Kaitio interval would indicate less open and arid components than Kalochoro, with a higher diversity in habitats and biomes associated with more wooded and bushy environments. This point could be linked with a higher sedimentation rate and wetter conditions during the deposition of the Kaitio Member, as highlighted above.

Member Comparisons

In this section we compare compiled non-bovid data from each site and collections of the Nachukui and Shungura formations at the family level (Figure 25.3). The proportion of mammals other than bovids is especially high in the WTAP collections (71.6–79.4 percent), whereas they are lower in the two other faunal data sets (WTRP: 45.3–50.5 percent; Shungura: 52.4–53.5 percent). This seems related to the degree of tooth fragmentation (more abundant in the archeological site which tends to inflate the most frequent taxa, i.e., bovids) and the different sampling procedures. The WTAP and WTRP assemblages display relatively similar patterns, but the Shungura representations are very different for the two time periods considered.

The comparison between the two members of the Nachukui Formation shows significant differences in taxonomic abundance marked by more suids and hippopotamids during the Kaitio Member, whereas equids and to a lesser degree primates seem more frequent in the Kalochoro Member. This is also the case in both members of Shungura, with a high frequency of suids and above all hippopotamids associated for levels H + J with more primate remains.

A first picture can be seen for the bovids (Figure 25.4) between Kalochoro and Kaitio members from WTAP sets based on seven main tribes (Antilopini, Aepycerotini, Alcelaphini, Reduncini, Tragelaphini, Bovini, Hippotragini). Such representation is compared with a global picture of African bovids taken at a continental scale (from 29 game parks: Alemseged, 2003).

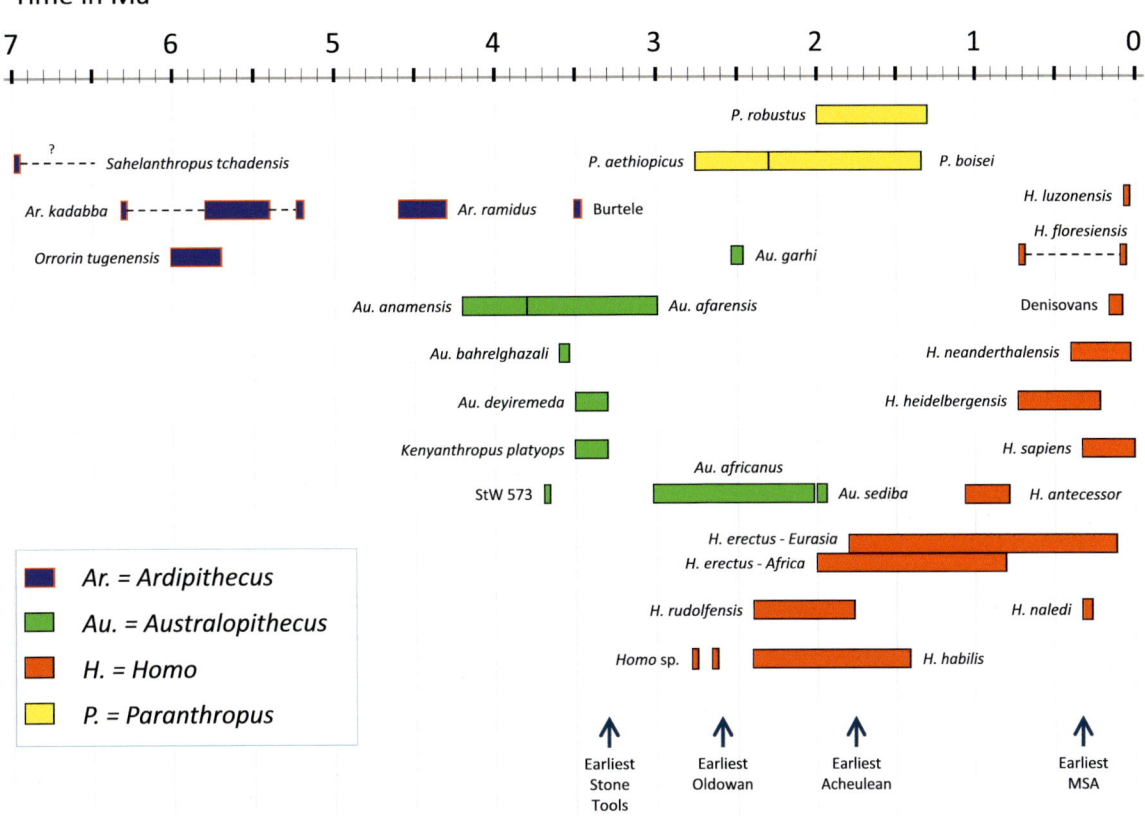

Figure 1.5 Chronology of hominin species. There are alternative interpretations to the hominin taxa depicted here. (A black and white version of this figure will appear in some formats.)

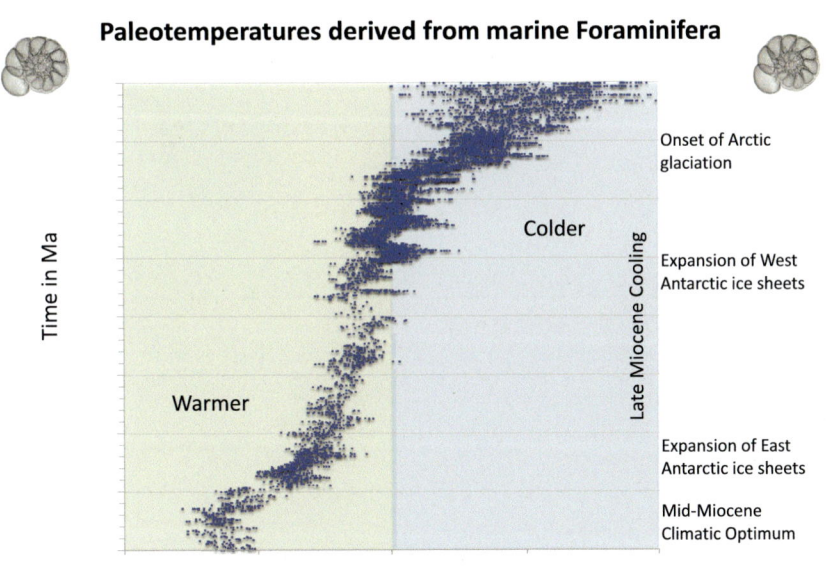

Figure 1.6 Paleotemperatures derived from benthic Foraminifera with $\delta^{18}O$ values in ‰ on the horizontal axis and time in Ma (million years) on the vertical axis. Graph drawn with data from the Deep Sea Drilling Project and the Ocean Drilling Project summarized in Zachos et al. (2001). This graph provides a view of global temperatures during the past 16 million years as a general background to understanding evolution in Africa. (A black and white version of this figure will appear in some formats.)

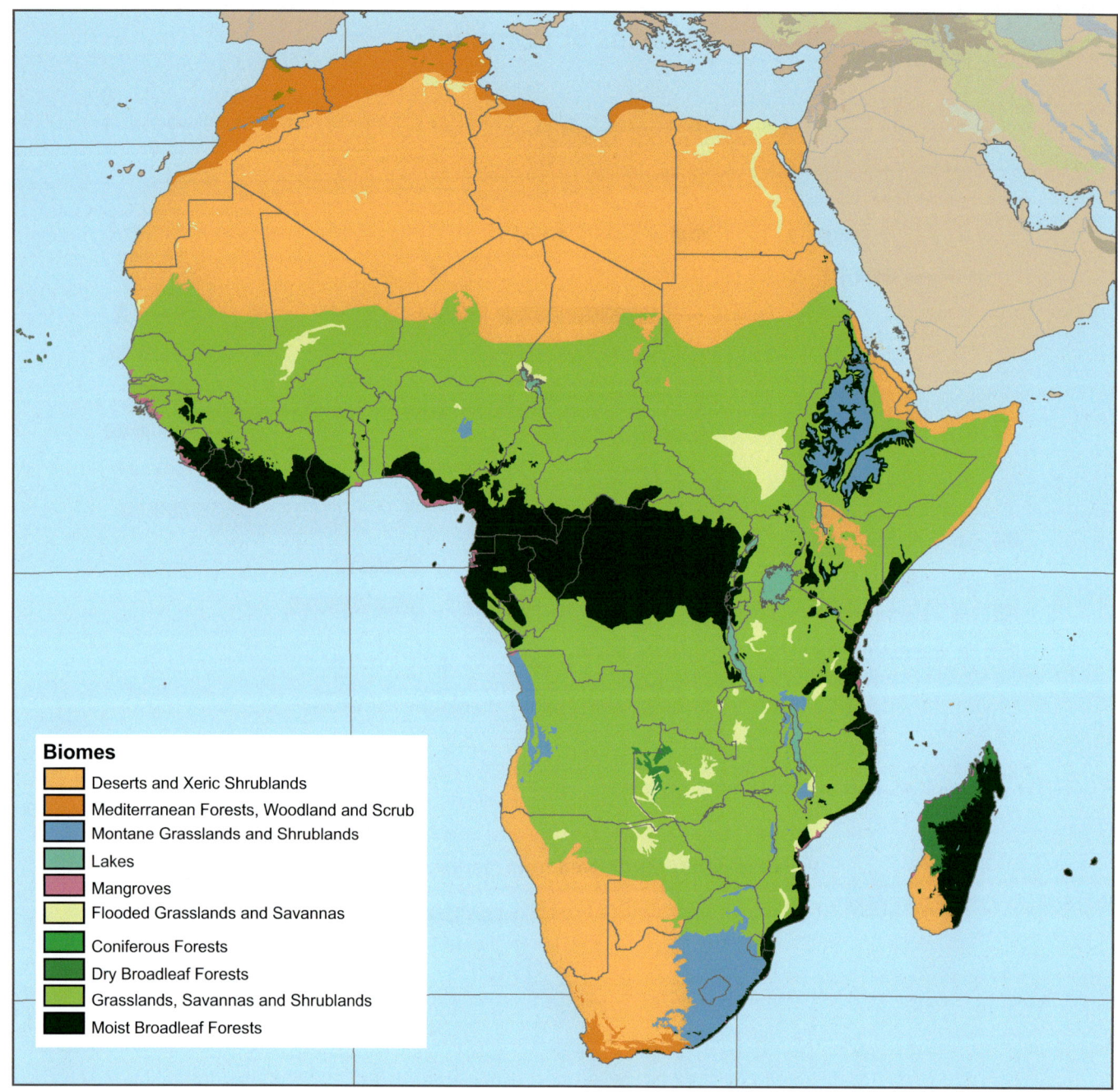

Figure 2.1 Simplified biome map of Africa, with emphasis on the major biomes of interest in the fossil record, namely forest, savanna, grassland, and desert. (*Source*: Modified from https://sedac.ciesin.columbia.edu/data/set/nagdc-population-landscape-climate-estimates-v3/maps based on WWF (2006) World Biomes Data set, www.worldwildlife.org/biome-categories/terrestrial-ecoregions). (A black and white version of this figure will appear in some formats.)

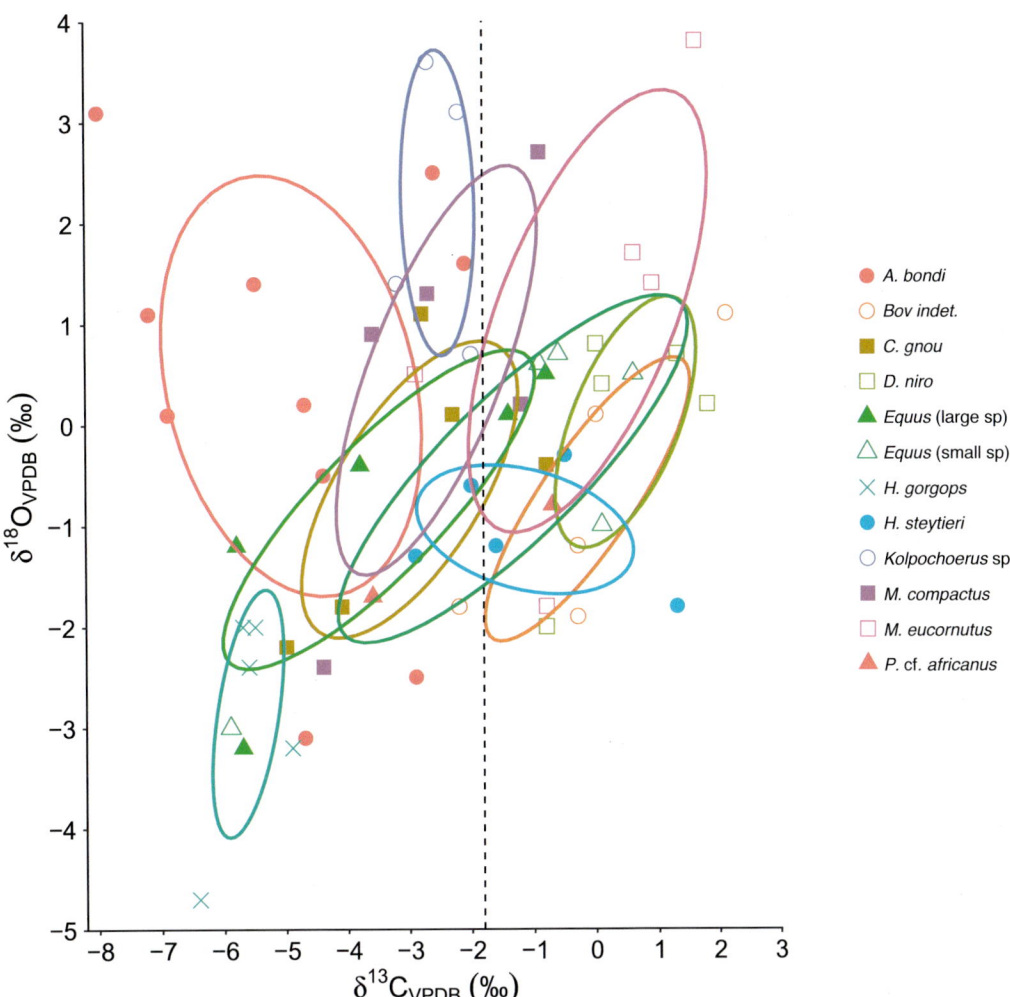

Figure 12.8 Stable carbon and oxygen isotope compositions of Cornelian grazer fauna. Ellipses for each taxon are standard ellipse areas (SEAc) used to depict isotopic niche breadths. The vertical dashed line represents a threshold for interpreting herbivore diets: to the right of the vertical, i.e., higher $\delta^{13}C$ values, individuals' diets are expected to be entirely C_4-derived, whereas lower values depict diets comprising a mixture of C_3/C_4 foods (see Discussion text for details). Note that a similar vertical delineating pure C_3 diets would be positioned at approximately –12.3‰ along the $\delta^{13}C$ axis. Data are from Codron et al. (2008). (A black and white version of this figure will appear in some formats.)

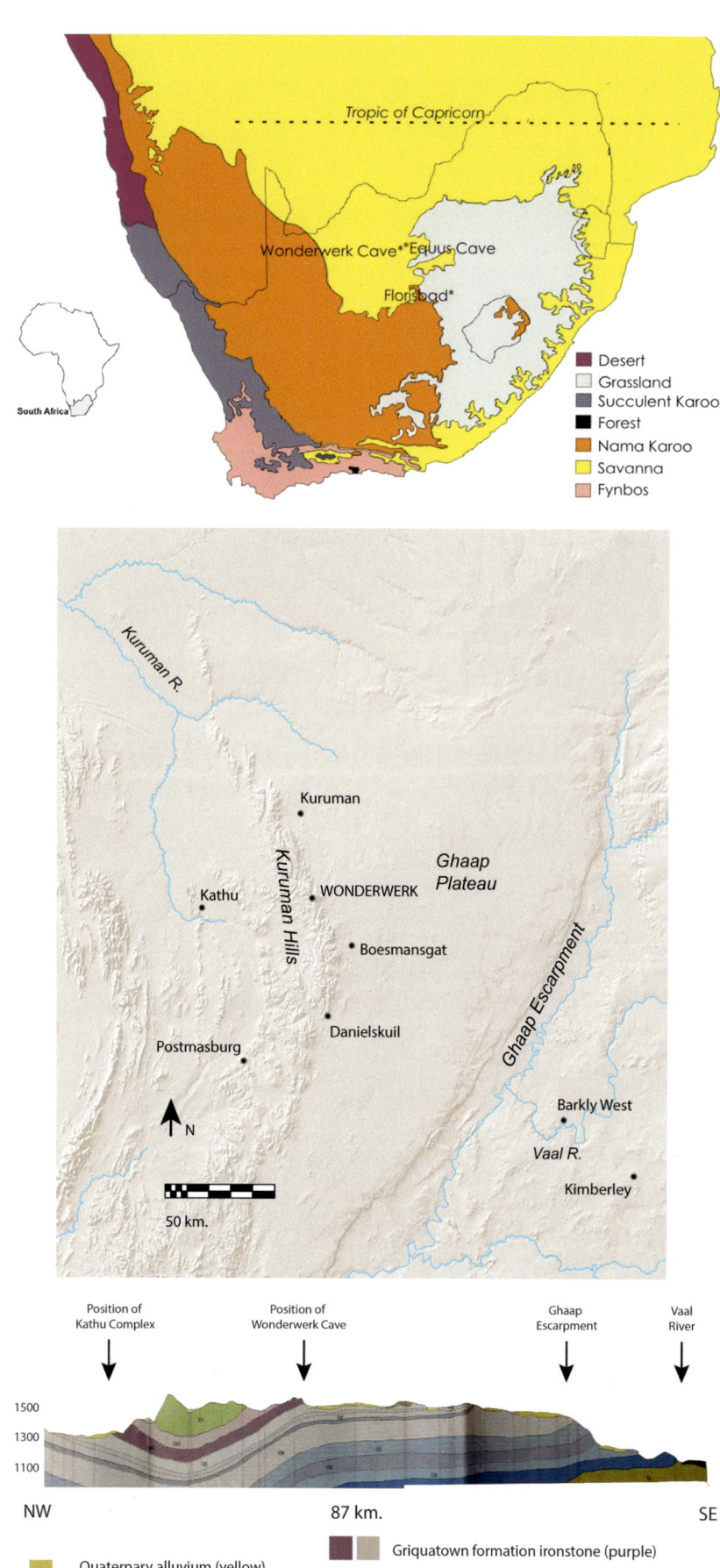

Figure 14.1 (a) Map showing location of Wonderwerk Cave and vegetation biomes of South Africa. (b) Detailed map showing site location and landscape features. (A black and white version of this figure will appear in some formats.)

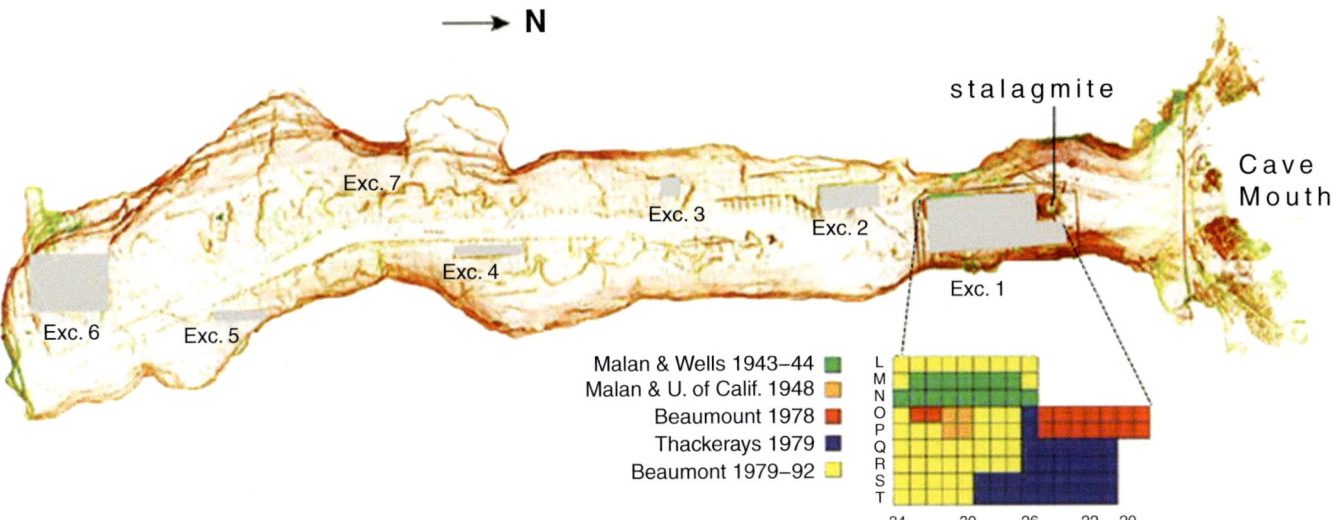

Figure 14.3 Plan of the interior of cave showing the location of the different areas excavated by P.B. Beaumont (figure generated from a 3D scan of the cave – see Rüther et al., 2009). Enlarged view of excavation grid from Beaumont and Vogel (2006). Grid scale is in yards (1 yard = 91.44 cm). (A black and white version of this figure will appear in some formats.)

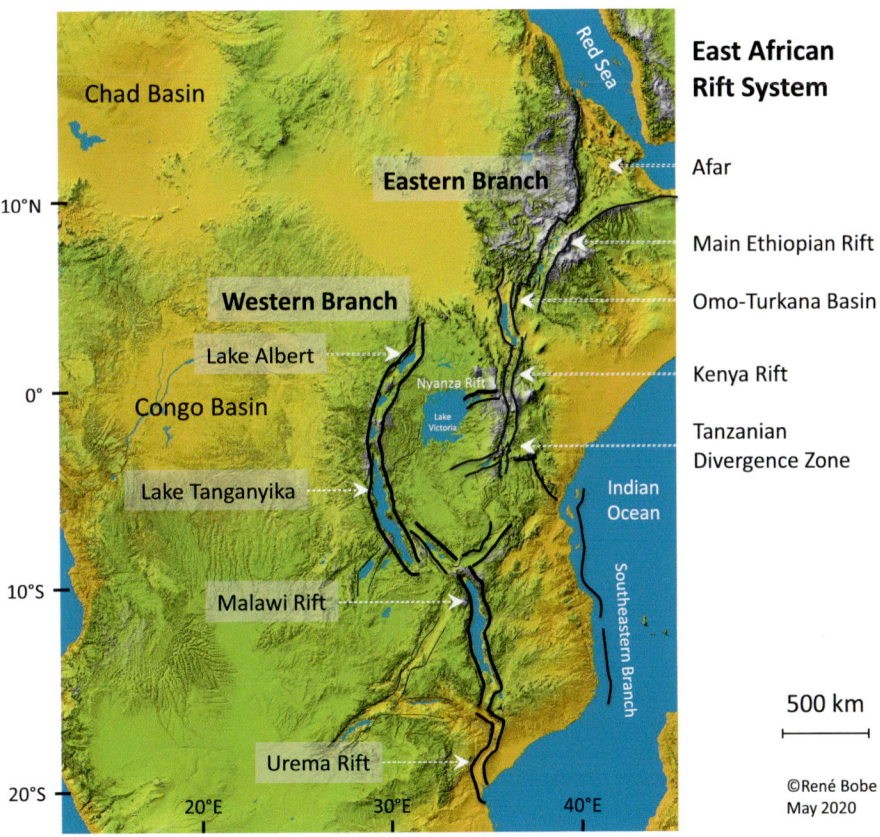

Figure 15.3 The East African Rift System with the Eastern Branch, the Western Branch, and some of the major basins and rifts. The development of the East African Rift System since the Miocene has played a major role in shaping the physical environments and modifying the conditions under which which plants and animals have been evolving in eastern Africa. Base map from NASA Shuttle Radar Topography Mission (www2.jpl.nasa.gov/srtm/). (A black and white version of this figure will appear in some formats.)

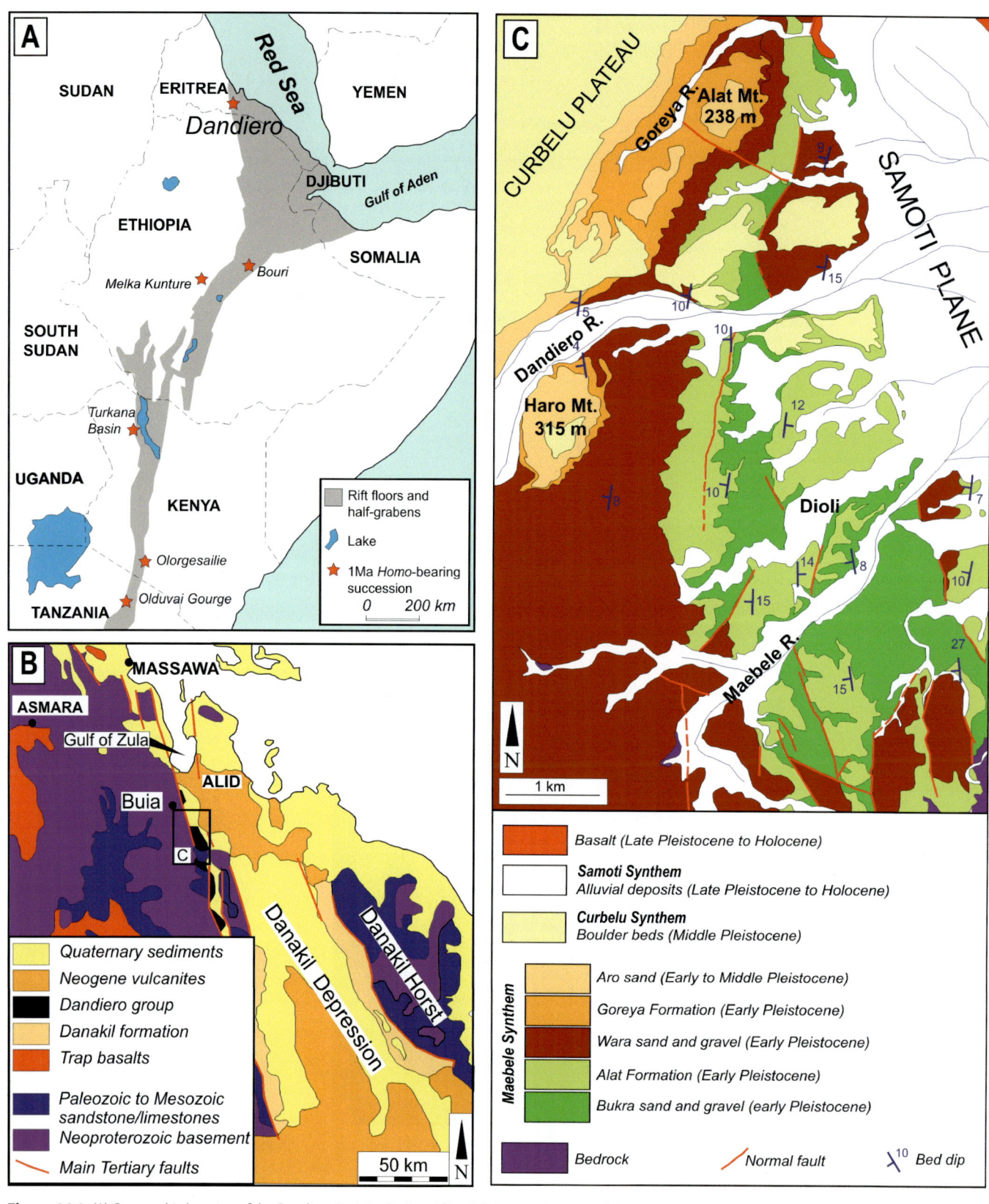

Figure 16.1 (A) Geographic location of the Dandiero Basin in the East Africa Rift System. Position of the well-known 1 Ma *Homo*-bearing sedimentary succession is also shown. (B) Position of the Dandiero Basin in the Danakil depression. (C) Geological map of the Dandiero Basin. After Ghinassi et al. (2015). (A black and white version of this figure will appear in some formats.)

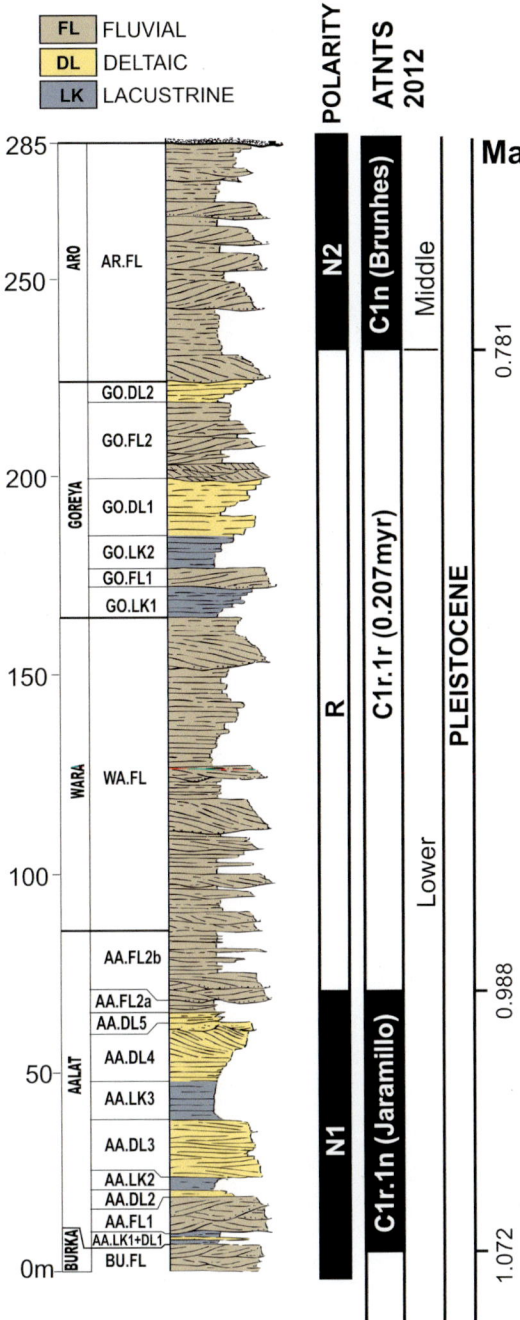

Figure 16.2 Sedimentary succession and magnetostratigraphy of the Dandiero Basin deposits. After Ghinassi et al. (2015). (A black and white version of this figure will appear in some formats.)

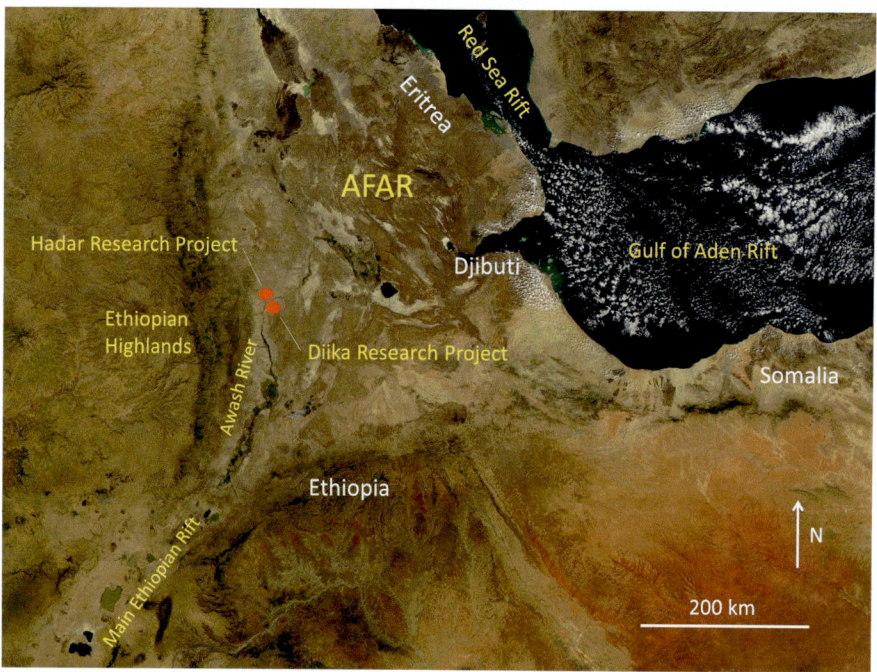

Figure 19.1 Satellite image of the Afar region. The site of Dikika is in the western margin of the Afar depression, a triple junction at the intersection of the Main Ethiopian Rift, the Gulf of Aden Rift, and the Red Sea Rift. The Dikika Research Project is located south of the Awash River, and the Hadar Research Project north of the river. (A black and white version of this figure will appear in some formats.)

Figure 19.3 Photograph showing sediments of the Hadar Formation at Dikika in the foreground and of Hadar in the background separated by the Awash River and its riverine forest. The whitish–greenish layer is the Sidi Hakoma Tuff (SHT), dated to 3.42 Ma. In the foreground, sediments below the SHT belong to the Basal Member, and those above belong to the SH Member. Note the person sitting on top of the hill in the foreground for scale. (A black and white version of this figure will appear in some formats.)

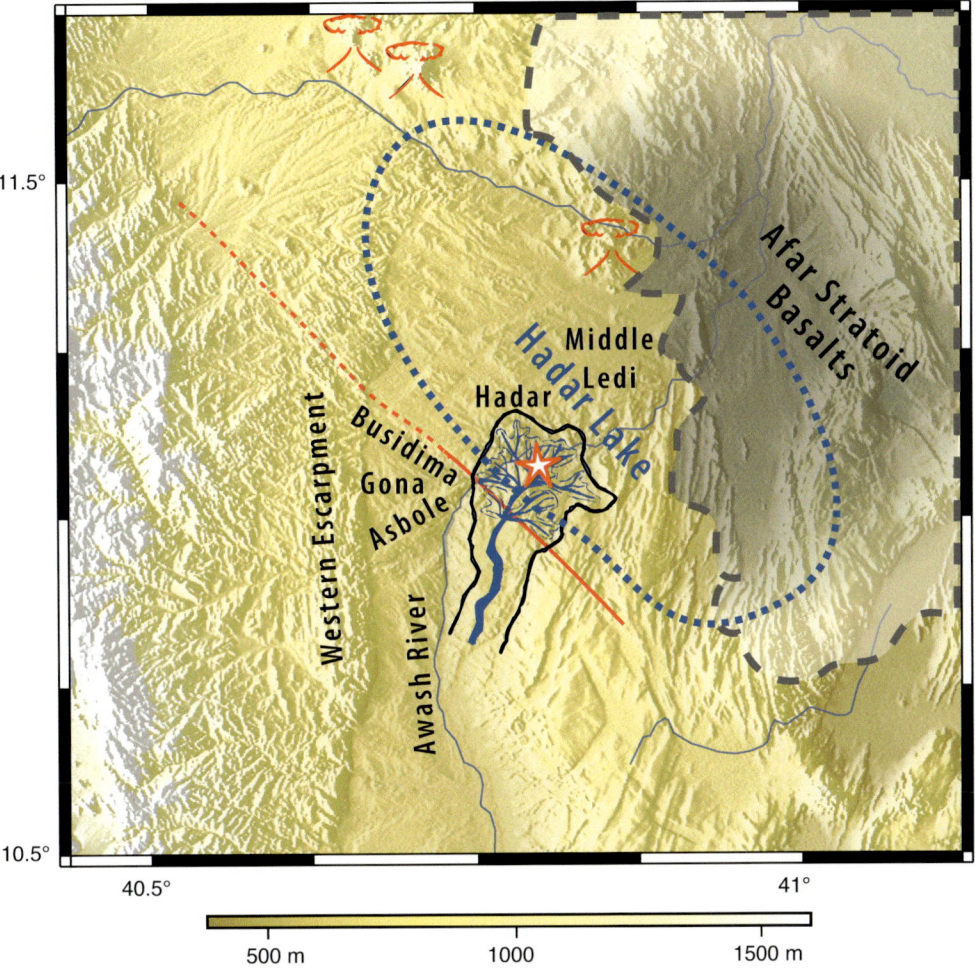

Figure 19.6 Paleogeography and paleoenvironments of the DIK-1 locality (red star) near the base of the Sidi Hakoma Member at 3.32 Ma, with a braided fluvial system (in blue) at the margin of Lake Hadar to the northeast (dashed blue line). Brown color indicates lower elevations in the modern regional landscape. The approximate locations of other areas are also indicated (Middle Ledi, Hadar, Gona, Busidima, Asbole, etc.). (A black and white version of this figure will appear in some formats.)

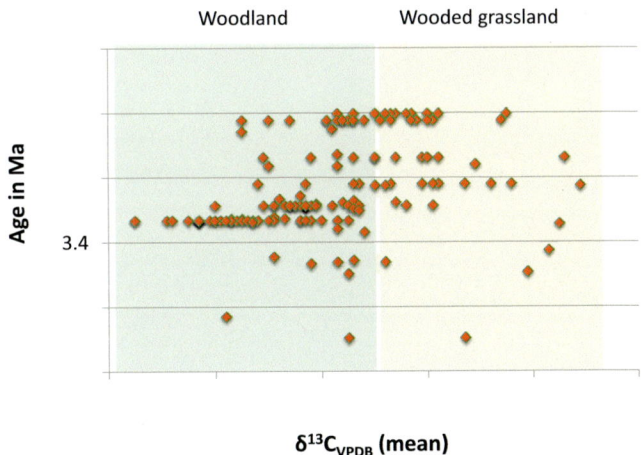

Figure 19.7 Pedogenic carbonate $\delta^{13}C$ values (with the standard Vienna Pee Dee Belemnite, $\delta^{13}C_{VPDB}$) showing $^{13}C/^{12}C$ ratios in the Basal, Sidi Hakoma, and Denen Dora members at Dikika, from about 3.55 Ma to 3.2 Ma, with data from Wynn et al., 2006 and Cerling et al., 2011b. The shaded areas indicate woodlands and wooded grasslands as in Cerling et al. (2011b). (A black and white version of this figure will appear in some formats.)

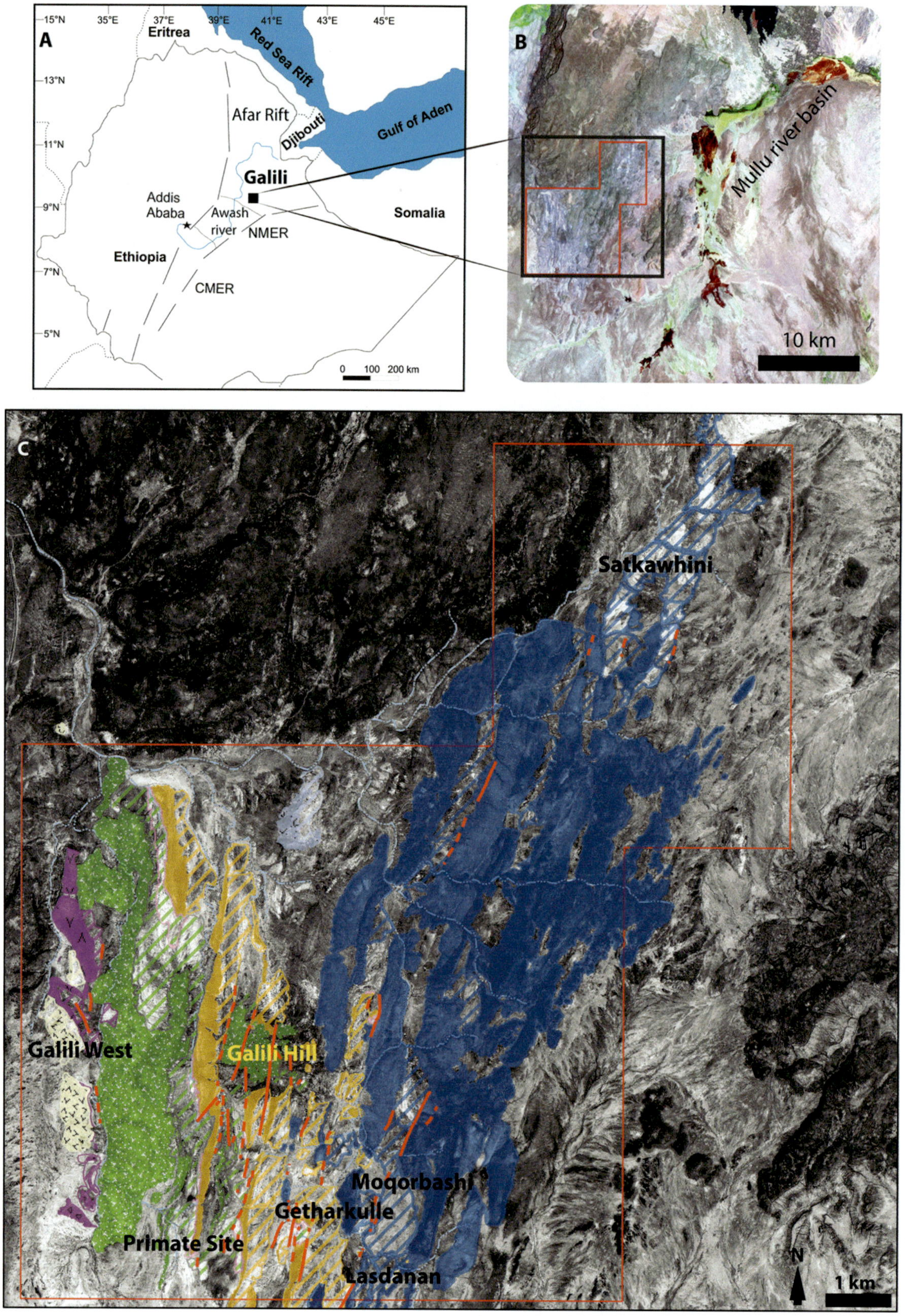

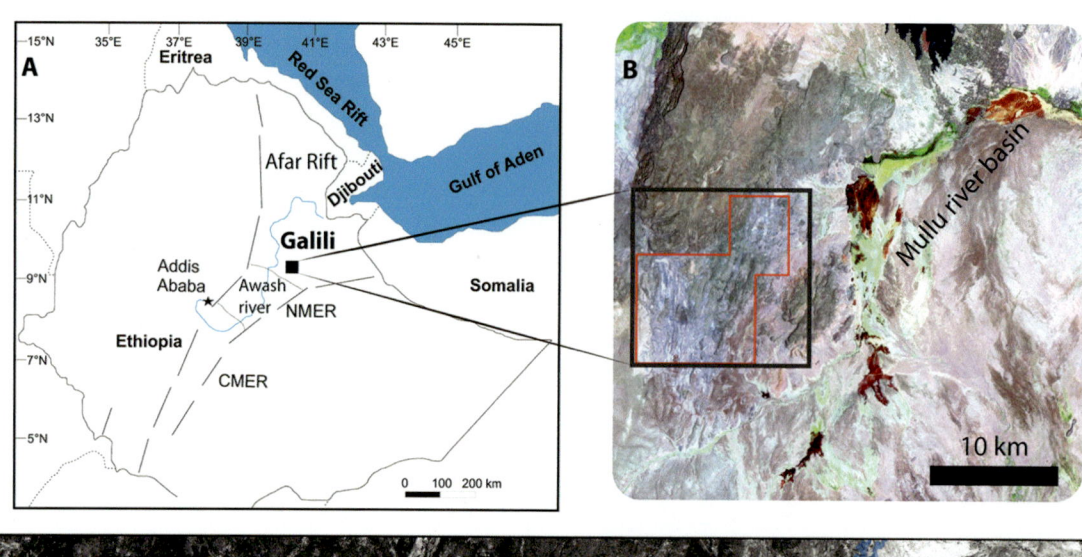

Figure 20.1 (A) The location map shows the Galili research area within the southwestern part of the Afar Rift, the Afar and the Northern Main Ethiopian Rift (NMER; modified from WoldeGabriel et al., 2013). (B) Satellite image showing the Galili research area (framed in black) west of the Mullu river basin. (C) Geological map of the research area based on IKONOS satellite image. Contoured areas represent volcanic layers whereas dashed lines refer to sediment and thin tuff exposures. Legend at the bottom refers to stratigraphic members: Lasdanan Mb., Dhidinley Mb., Godiray Mb., Shabeley Laag Mb., Dhagax Mb., Caashacado Mb., white lines: faults. Important fossil sites are named in white font (modified from Hujer et al., 2015). (A black and white version of this figure will appear in some formats.)

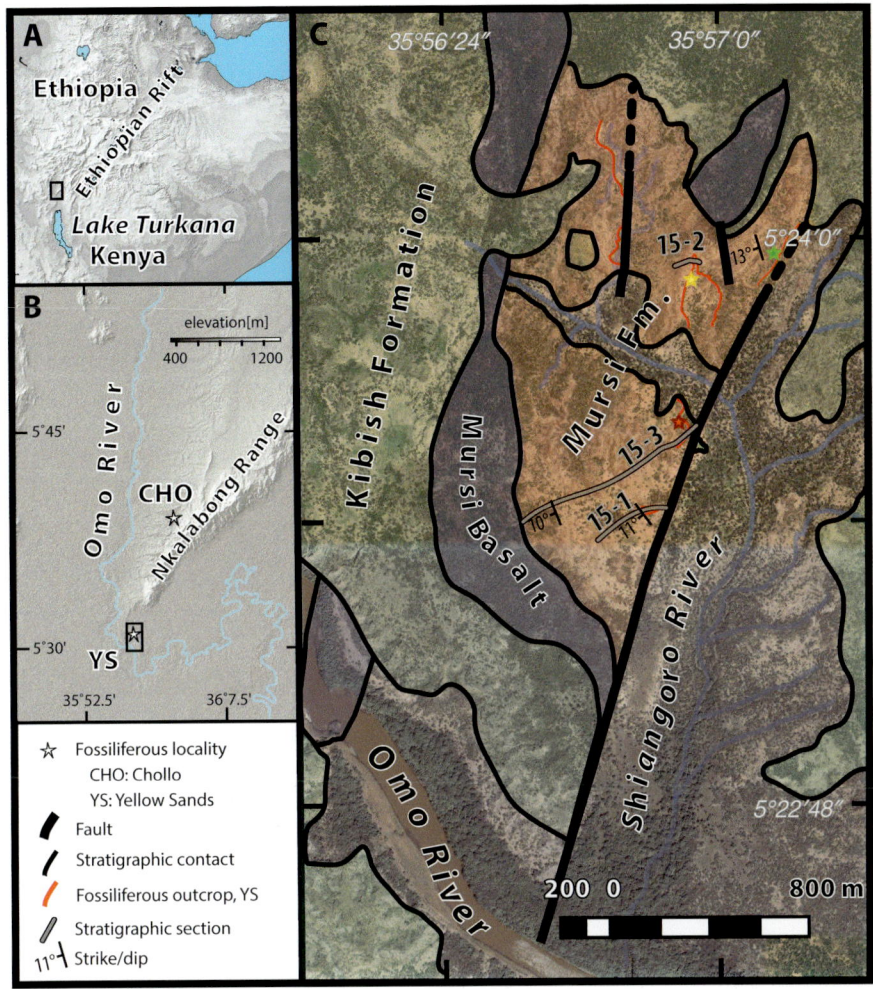

Figure 23.1 Outcrop map of the Mursi Formation exposed at Yellow Sands. (A) Location map of Mursi Formation in eastern Africa; outlined box shows area mapped in (B). (B) Location map of fossiliferous localities: Yellow Sands and Chollo. (C) Outcrop map of the Yellow Sands with the localities identified in 1969 by the IORE (red star, locality 4; yellow star, localities 1–3 and 7–10; green star, locality 6). (A) and (B) are overlain on Shuttle Radar Tomography Mission (SRTM) digital elevation model (DEM) data. (C) is overlain on Landsat Imagery from Google Earth. (A black and white version of this figure will appear in some formats.)

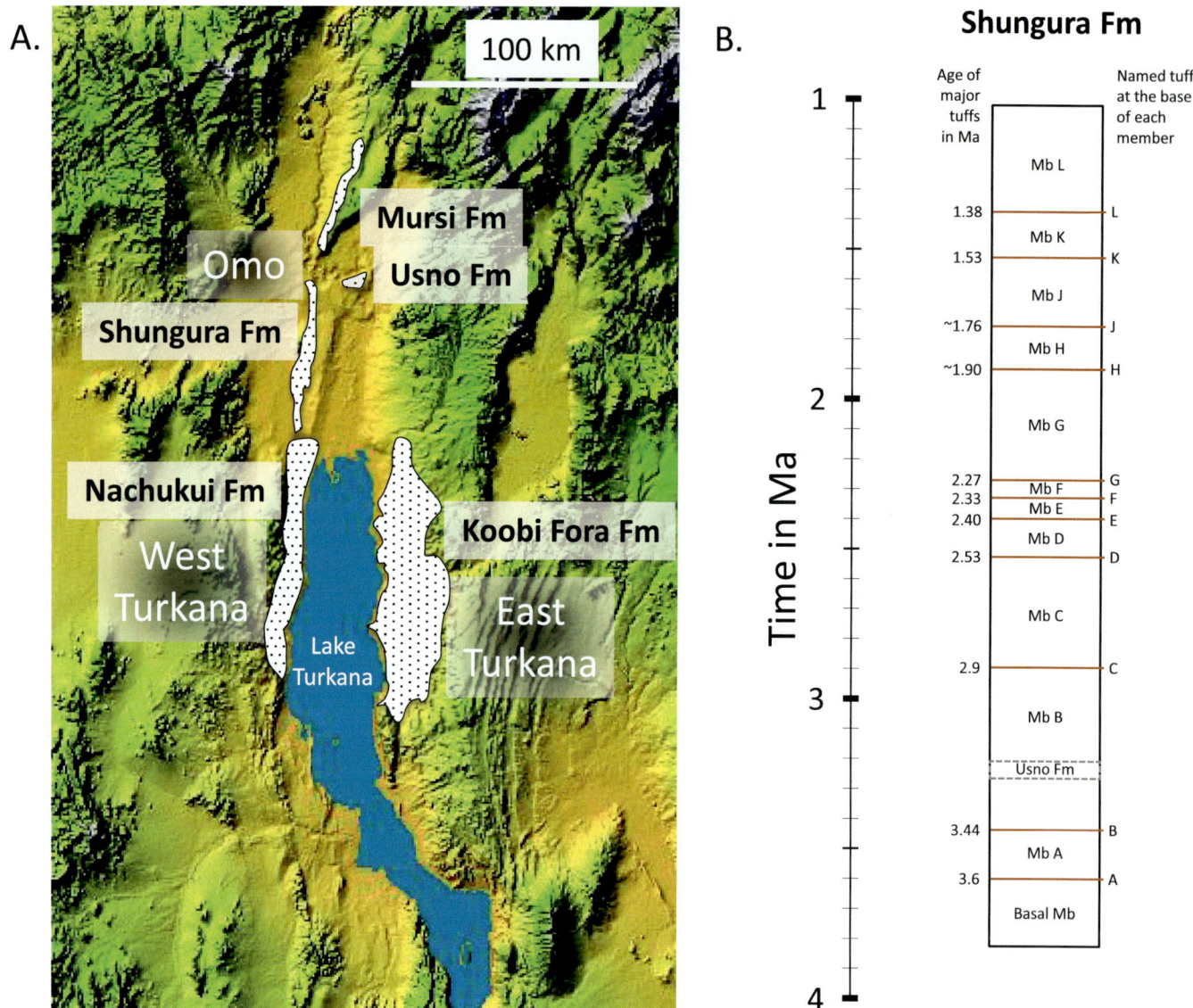

Figure 24.1 (A) Location of the Shungura Formation in southwestern Ethiopia. (B) Chronstratigraphic sequence of the Shungura Formation, redrawn after Blondel et al. (2018). (A black and white version of this figure will appear in some formats.)

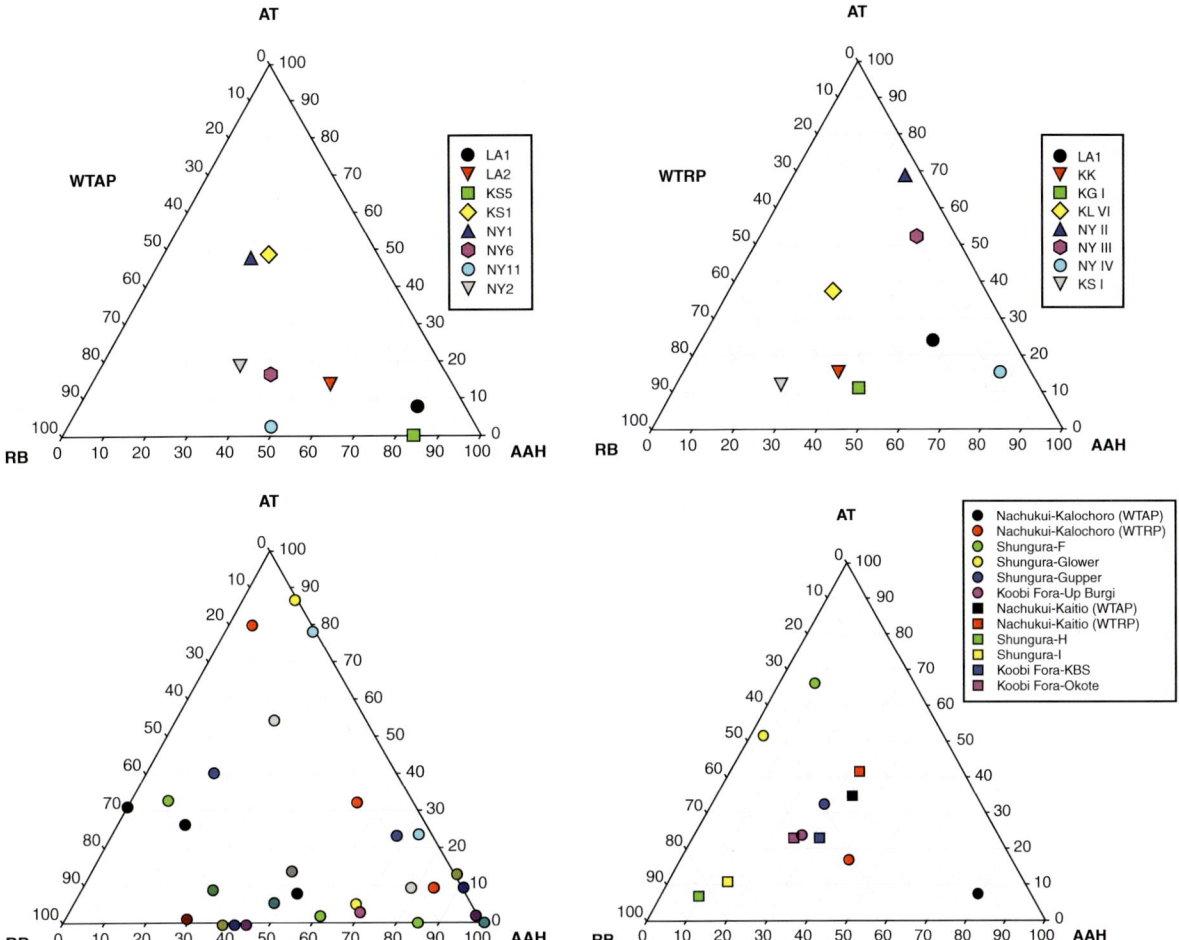

Figure 25.2 Ternary plots of bovid tribe representation (see text for explanation of grouping) for WTAP sites (top, left) versus WTRP sites (top, right): square = Kalochoro Member, triangle = Kaitio Member; ternary plots of modern bovid tribe representation from 29 game parks (Shipman and Harris, 1988; Alemseged, 2003: table 25.3) (bottom, left) and for different members of Nachukui, Shungura, and Koobi Fora Formations between *ca*. 2.3 and 1.6 Ma: circle = Kalochoro Member and equivalent, square = Kaitio Member and equivalent. (A black and white version of this figure will appear in some formats.)

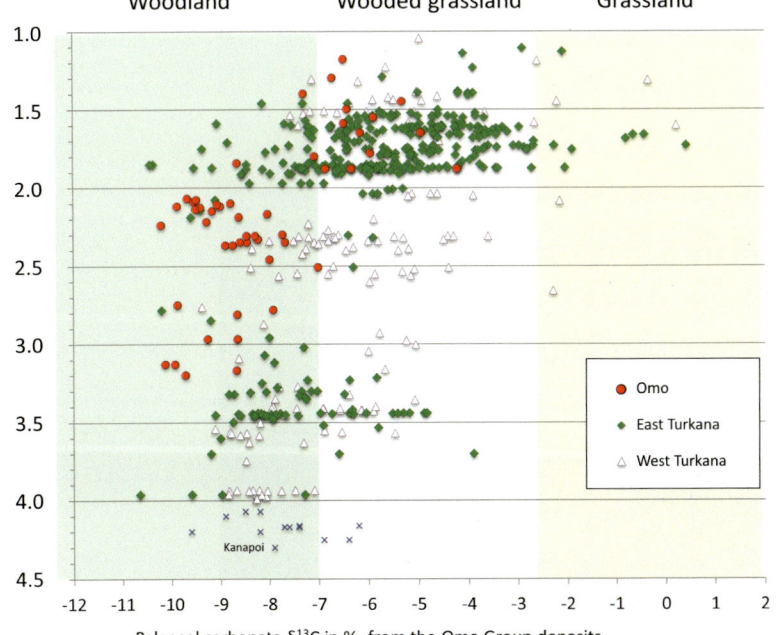

Figure 26.6 Paleosol carbonate $\delta^{13}C$ in ‰ from the Omo Group deposits reflecting C_3 and C_4 vegetation in the Omo-Turkana Basin from 4.3 Ma to 1.0 Ma. Data from Quinn et al. (2007) and Levin et al. (2011). (A black and white version of this figure will appear in some formats.)

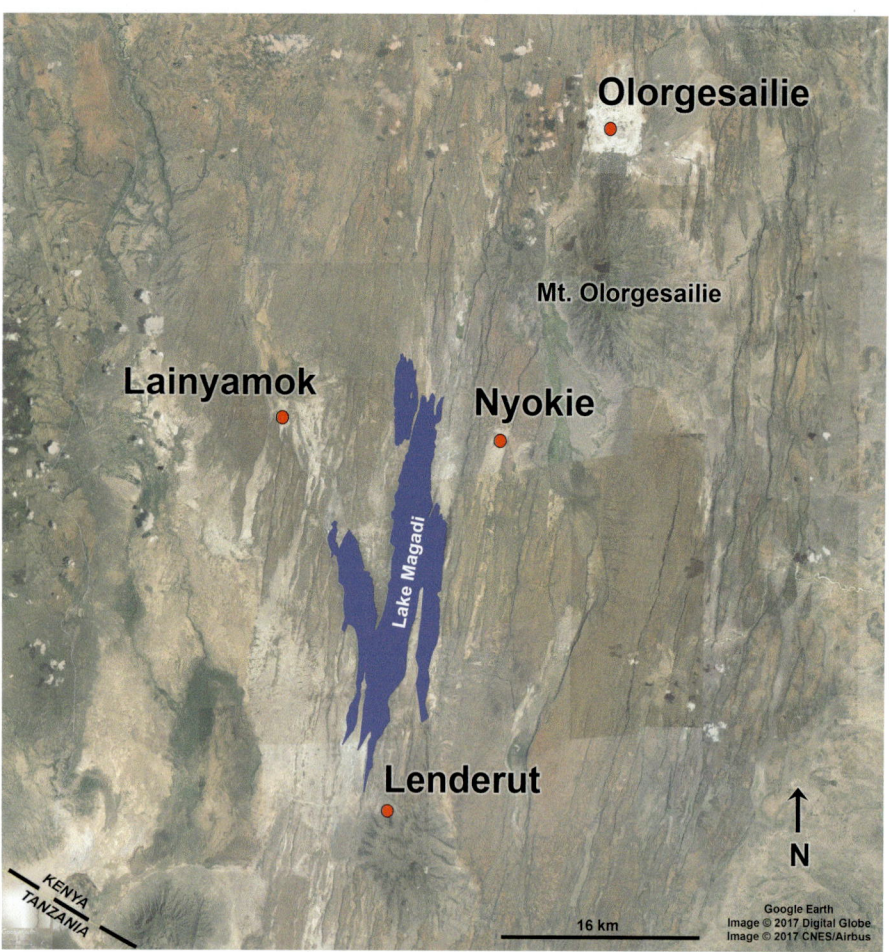

Figure 30.1 Map of the southern Kenya rift showing the location of fossil sites discussed in the text. (A black and white version of this figure will appear in some formats.)

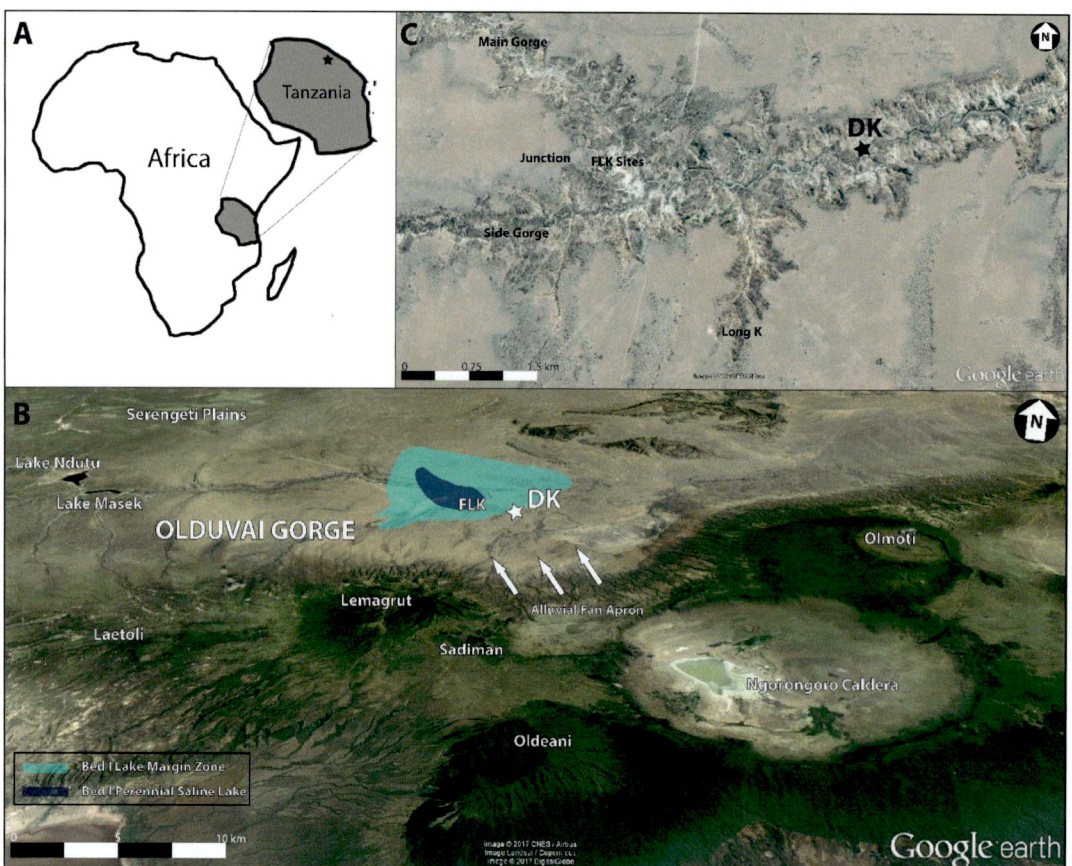

Figure 32.1 (A) Location of Olduvai Gorge in northern Tanzania. (B) Google Earth image of the Ngorongoro volcanic highlands showing Olduvai Gorge with the minimum and maximum levels of Paleolake Olduvai. Arrows indicate direction of mudflow influence from Ngorongoro. (C) Location of DK site relative to other Bed I sites. (A black and white version of this figure will appear in some formats.)

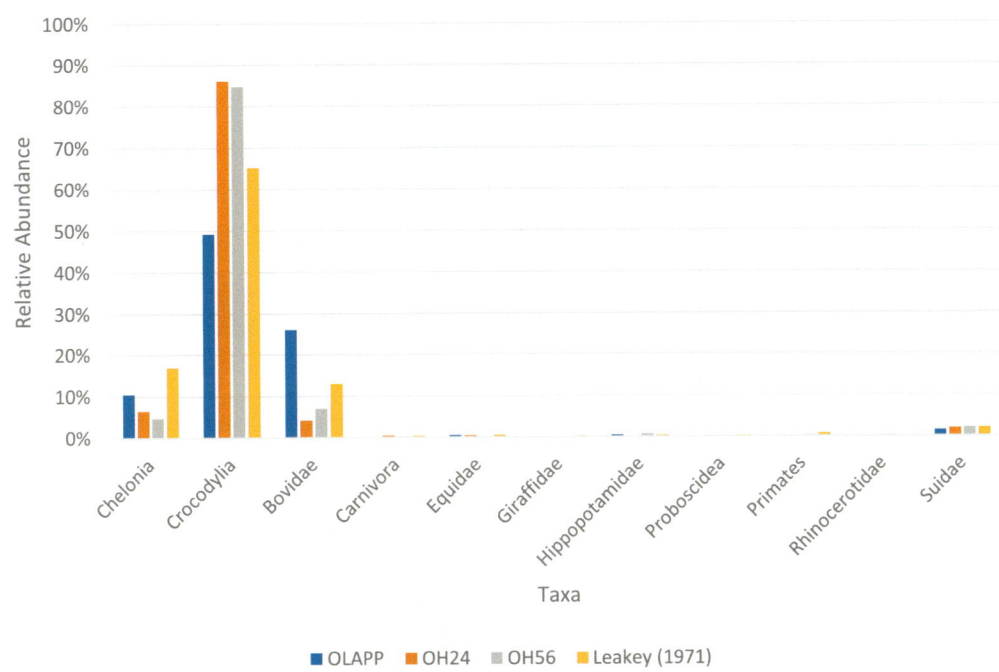

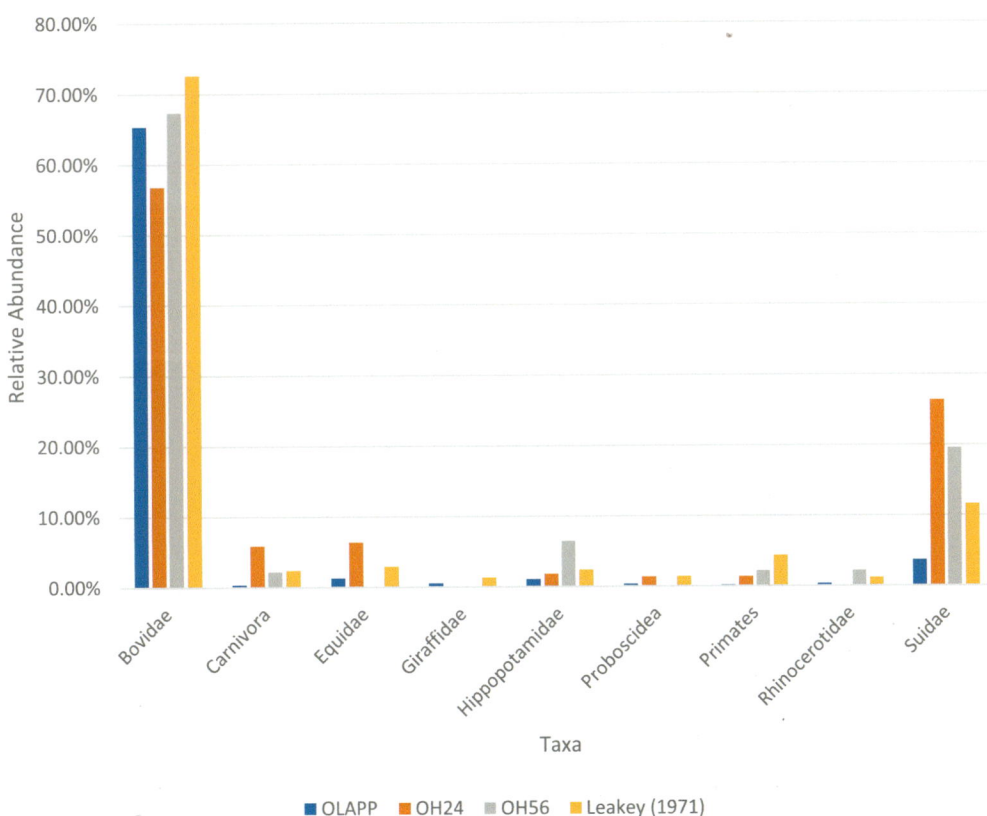

Figure 32.5 Frequencies of large vertebrate bones, teeth, scutes, and carapace fragments from DK site. (A) All large vertebrates. (B) Large mammals only. Analysis of the OLAPP, OH 24 and OH 56 assemblages include over 500, 2200, and 300 isolated crocodile teeth, respectively. M.D. Leakey's (1971) assemblage includes over 4500 crocodile teeth. (A black and white version of this figure will appear in some formats.)

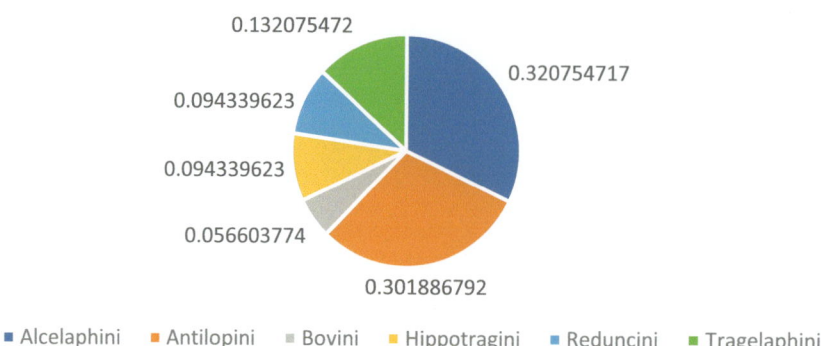

Figure 32.11 Proportions of bovid tribes in the OLAPP DK fossil assemblage. These numbers include specimens from OLAPP and Potts (1988). (A black and white version of this figure will appear in some formats.)

Figure 37.1 The site of Ahl al Oughlam in the early 1990s (A) and in 2007 (B). (A black and white version of this figure will appear in some formats.)

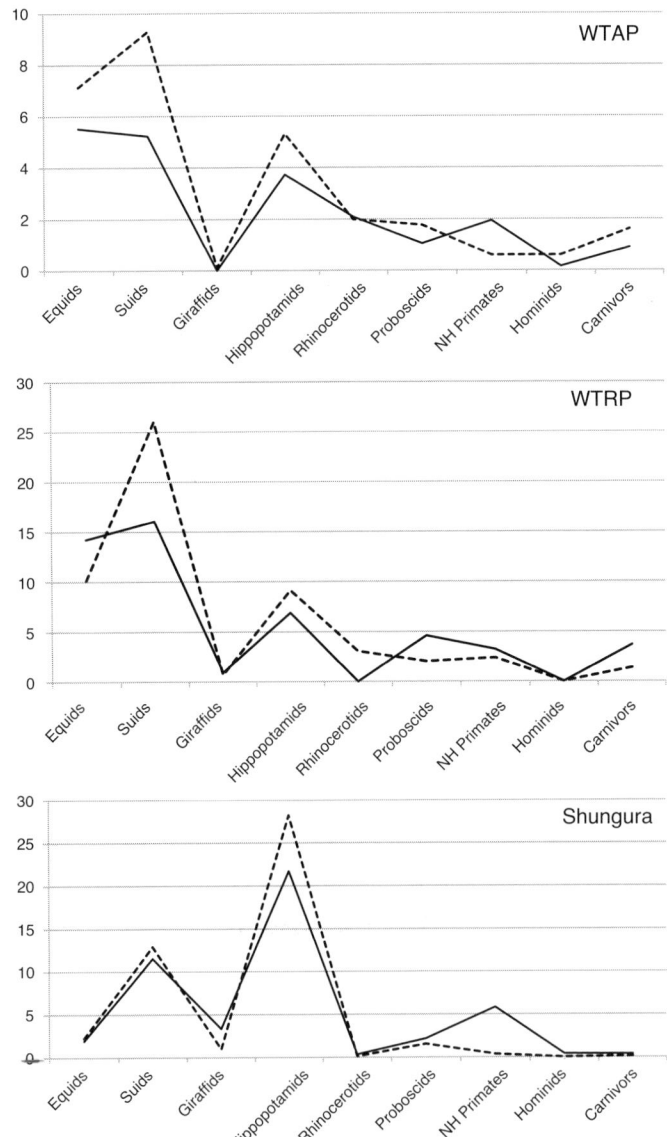

Figure 25.3 Distribution of mammals (%NR, except bovid) of different Omo-Turkana formations. Plain line = Kalochoro and Shungura F + G; dotted line = Kaitio and Shungura H + J. *Note:* Bovid abundance is higher in WTAP as seen in the *y*-axis. Shungura data from Alemseged (2003).

Alcelaphini represent the most abundant tribe in the extant African record followed by Antilopini and Aepycerotini (total of around 76 percent), with the two last in a subequal proportion. It is roughly the same pattern observed in the Kalochoro, with dominance of Alcelaphini and Antilopini (around 75 percent), but these are less abundant during Kaitio (roughly 33 percent, and 43 percent with Aepycerotini). In this last interval, Reduncini and Tragelaphini are better represented (around 48 percent) and Alcelaphini and Antilopini formed only 33 percent. This is a crude approximation, which nonetheless distinguishes the differences between the two members.

A second approach uses the grouping method (see above) to compare bovid representations between Nachukui (WTAP and WTRP), Shungura and Koobi Fora (data in Bobe et al., 2007b) within ternary plots (created with the SigmaPlot package, Figure 25.2). At first glance, the relatively high dispersion of data within each member from these various sedimentary formations is clear. Nonetheless, many faunal associations are positioned in the center of the diagram, giving a mixed picture, both in terms of climate and habitats. Faunal compositions are different within the Omo-Turkana Basin, implying distinct paleoenvironments around the lake. However, the three Koobi Fora sets are closely grouped, with a slight dominance of Reduncini. The results between WTAP and WTRP from Nachukui are similar for the Kaitio Member, but not for the Kalochoro Member. Some are outliers from this central position, e.g., LA1 and Shungura F and Shungura H and J.

During the time interval dated at 2.34–1.88 Ma (Kalochoro for Nachukui), we note a clear difference between the data from WTAP and WTRP, with the first record occurring close to the AAH pole; it is noteworthy that WTAP results come mainly from site LA1 situated at the base of the Kalochoro Member, around 2.4–2.2 Ma. The analysis of pedogenic carbonates from LA sites demonstrates dominant vegetation from woodland/bushland to wooded grassland (Quinn et al., 2013). The archeological site of LA1 was interpreted as a floodplain or ecotonal zone, close to riparian woodlands near a large perennial river system. The paleobiodiversity is high at LA1, implying a developed habitat with various vegetation types, and grazer species are abundant with Alcelaphini and Antilopini accompanied by equids, which suggests open settings. However, the equids are mainly represented by hipparionins, while the Alcelaphini remains (almost all teeth) indicate small–medium-sized taxa which do not necessarily point to open habitats. The tribe Alcelaphini had an important evolutionary radiation during the Plio-Pleistocene with a wide range in body size (from small to very large, as *Megalotragus*) and some small forms (Thomson's gazelle size). These smaller-sized alcelaphines could have been more adapted to closed habitats (as in Aepycerotini) even if these taxa possess hypsodont teeth. Full adaptation of all the Alcelaphini representatives for open habitats was established later (by the early Pleistocene). Moreover, to end with the LA1 example, other species represented include the smallest bovids (Neotragini), primates (*Cercopithecoides* and other Colobinae – *Rhinocolobus*?, *Parapapio* – and the presence of *Galago* sp.), or Aves (Kori bustard *Ardeotis* sp. living in open grassy areas), or reptiles (large *Varanus* sp.), among other taxa which clearly indicate wooded to grassland vegetation zones.

In the Shungura sequence, Member F yields the higher proportion of AT, especially Aepycerotini (41 percent), with a trend in the upper members (lower G and upper G) toward a reduction of this group coupled with more Reduncini taxa. This change continues in the other upper members (H and J) that are clearly located near the RB pole. These members are especially rich in Reduncini (72–82 percent). It seems that the habitats in Shungura were regularly dominated by a diverse vegetation cover, from wooded area to bushland with the development of wet weather, especially around *ca.* 1.9–1.8 Ma. This general trend toward humid conditions through time in Shungura evidences the differential response to global climate change in relation to more localized site-specific habitat (geo-topography) conditions.

The central position of most of the fossil faunal collections in the ternary diagram is noticeable, and AT and RB are the dominant bovid groups, suggesting landscapes with more wooded

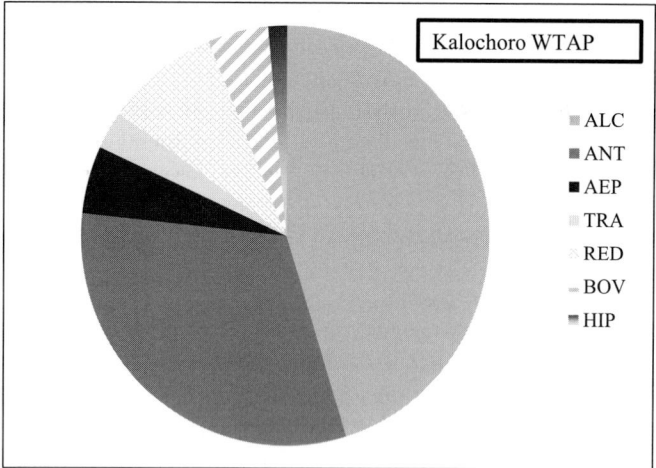
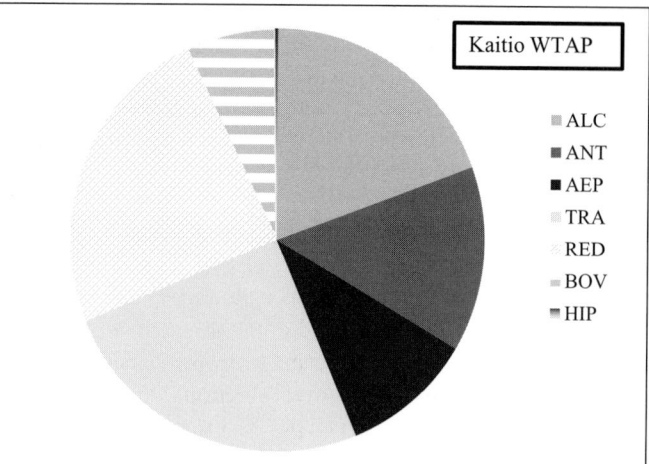
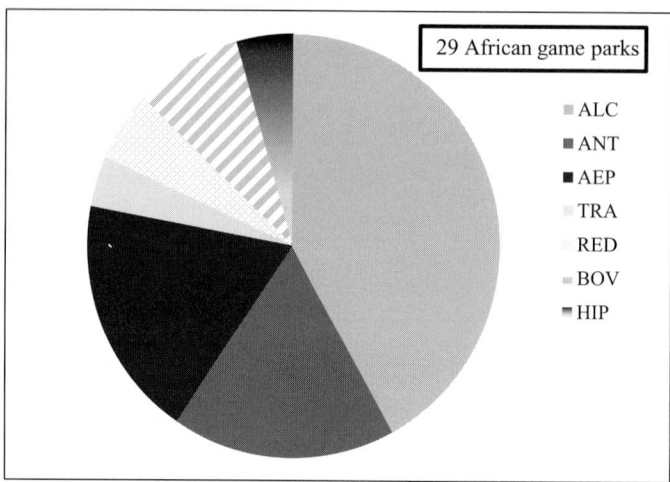

Figure 25.4 Abundance of bovid tribes in Nachukui Formation (WTAP data) and global African modern faunas. Legend key: ALC, Alcelaphini; ANT, Antilopini; AEP, Aepycerotini; TRA, Tragelaphini; RED, Reduncini; BOV, Bovini; HIP, Hippotragini.

and forested zones, and with more or less humidity. Overall, the AAH group is least represented, except for the site LA1 (see above). Koobi Fora does not show variation between its members, during the period considered, whereas in the Nachukui the representatives of AT + RB increase, which could indicate a trend for more humid and denser habitats for Kaitio compared to drier conditions during the Kalochoro interval. However, the fossil faunal associations indicate a relatively balanced bovid tribe composition with all tribes represented, which overall could indicate the existence of mosaic landscape sustaining a high diversity of species from grazers to mixed-feeders to browsers. Such ecological characteristics may be typical of Plio-Pleistocene environments (e.g., Reynolds et al., 2015), but imply a large range of biomes without present-day analog environments (see below).

Modern versus Fossil Comparisons

The modern African bovid distribution from 29 game parks and reserves (e.g., Shipman and Harris, 1988; Alemseged, 2003) is used following the same combined methods. Figure 25.2 (bottom left) displays all these localities with different groupings according to three clusters. This representation was also illustrated by Shipman and Harris (1988), who recognized the oversimplification but defined the limits of clusters by statistical procedure. We modify this scheme by adding Hippotragini, but this tribe is never abundant, especially in the fossil record. Within the ternary diagram, the largest area concerns the RB cluster, when AAH and AT areas are more reduced. In the RB area, two subassociations are distinguishable: one with a second main component of AAH, and the other with relatively more AT elements. According to the distribution, most of the modern associations correspond to closed/wet cluster (RB, *ca.* 45 percent), followed by an open/arid cluster (AAH, *ca.* 38 percent) when closed/dry clusters are few (AT, *ca.* 1.3 percent), even if such representation is likely to be an oversimplification.

When compared with the fossil associations, one striking observation concerns the relative lack of comparability between the two sets of data, modern versus fossil (see bottom of Figure 25.2). The latter are often located in empty areas, even if they fall closer toward the RB cluster. This suggests that there are likely no modern analogs to what is observed in the fossil record and the areas within the ternary plot of extant species are empty where fossil associations are found. While the modern record does not sample all possible types of environments present, it does seem to be the case that the fossil fauna was peculiar in possessing a more mixed taxa composition. However, this comparison points to the relative predominance of a closed and rather humid environment from the fossil data, which also could be linked with the depositional context, near water – river, lake, or marshes (see percentage of aquatic species). Naturally, not only bovids but all vertebrate species need to be further evaluated and considered in such meta-analyses.

All these preliminary results indicate what has been suggested by ourselves and other researchers about the mixed and diverse nature of paleocommunities with a higher paleobiodiversity (many extinct species), and probably a different picture of ecosystem relationships (in terms of trophic level and ecological niches, biomass and resource partitioning, competition, and reproductive strategies). Such patterns may also explain the observed higher diversity in hominins, both anatomically and culturally.

Conclusions

The time interval between *ca.* 2.4 and 1.7 Ma constitutes an important chronological window because of several climatic and paleoenvironmental changes that would have affected hominin diversity (*Australopithecus*, *Homo*). Following the onset of glacial conditions in the Northern Hemisphere, marked with high climatic variability, different studies indicate general aridification and opening up of grasslands often associated with the term "savanna" (see Dominguez-Rodrigo, 2014). The Nachukui Formation yields a diverse fossil record and provides a first overview of the vertebrate paleocommunities, compared with faunal associations from other Omo-Turkana Basin formations (Shungura, Koobi Fora) at a supra-taxonomical level. The West Turkana Archeological Project (WTAP) has investigated four archeological sites from the Kalochoro Member (*ca.* 2.4–2.2 Ma) and nine from the Kaitio Member (1.9–1.7 Ma) that complemented data from previous work by the West Turkana Research Project (WTRP; Harris et al., 1988b). One of the goals of this paper was to provide a preliminary analysis of vertebrate assemblages based on different criteria (faunal lists, proportion of aquatic species, small vertebrate components, supra-taxonomical analysis of large mammals and bovids). However, the collections focused essentially on two specific time intervals (with a gap in between of 300 kyr) and the interplay between different sets of data still needs to be better controlled and revised (such as for the bovid size-classes in the WTAP collections) with better taphonomic considerations (degree of fragmentation of material, skeletal representation, age structure) and placement within a precise depositional context (for better spatiotemporal resolution). At this point we can merely comment on the faunal succession following the member comparisons at the Nachukui Formation.

The Kalochoro Member shows more species adapted to arid and seasonal environments, as evidenced by the presence of Antilopini, Alcelaphini, and equids. Nonetheless, other faunal elements and isotopic analyses demonstrate more wooded cover (roughly 40 percent in Quinn et al., 2013, 2020), especially at archeological site LA1. This calls into question the importance of Alcelaphini, and possibly also small equids, as indicators of fully open habitats. The Kaitio Member seems more diverse in terms of taxonomical representation, particularly with more species (Reduncini, Bovini, Tragelaphini, suids) that are associated with a range of wetter environments and closed vegetation, ranging from wooded areas or bushland to wet grassland. This confirmed the first interpretation proposed for the Kaitio Member (Brugal et al., 2003). This time interval preserves evidence of a wider range of habitats and geological reconstruction indicates pronounced hydrological activity in conjunction with less seasonality, leading to higher precipitation, as well as dense lake and river networks. This agrees with what has been previously noted from the different faunal associations of the Nachukui Formation with less mesic habitats prior to 1.9 Ma and expansion of wet grassland in the Kalochoro Member followed by predominance of woodland in the Kaitio Member (Harris et al., 1988b). These observations underline the importance of depositional contexts in the fossil vertebrate assemblages, as well as the significant hydrological and geo-topographical factors affecting the basin through time that are partly connected with local tectonic activity.

From 2.15 to 2.13 Ma we have clear evidence of the development of paleo-lake Lorenyang in the basin, expanding asynchronously in the rift, reaching its highest level between 2.2 and 2.0 Ma essentially due to an eruptive phase that blocked the southeast outlet (Lepre, 2014). This coincides with the time interval studied in this chapter, and between Kalochoro and Kaitio deposits we have a major hydrological change in the Omo-Turkana Basin. The paleogeographic reconstruction (Rogers et al., 1994) shifts from a dominantly fluviatile system (paleo-Omo) to a lacustrine one at about 1.89 Ma with climatic fluctuations implying unstable lake levels. From 1.7 to 1.5 Ma the paleogeographic setting is complex, oscillating between a major fluvial channel and a more meandering system. Such landscape transformations are controlled to a lesser extent by climate, which interplays with geological factors (volcanism, tectonism) to fragment and diversify the environments. Other studies, such as those on the terrestrial biomarkers from the Olduvai sequence (2.0–1.8 Ma), demonstrate repeated short-term (*ca.* 100–1000 years) ecosystem variations passing abruptly from C_4 grasslands to closed C_3 forests (Magill et al., 2013a; Tipple, 2013). The transition from wooded to grassland habitats could oscillate with changing climatic cycles rather than reflecting a gradual process (Brugal, 2014) and might be considered a dynamic seasonal mosaic environment.

The importance of paleobiogeography is obvious from the data coming from the different sedimentary formations in the basin, controlled both by tectonic activities and climate with some asynchronicity (Lepre, 2014). These factors, in combination, influenced high environmental variability and probably some localized differential instability in habitats, which would imply differential and selective responses and adaptations for hominins (see Potts, 2013). Each area in the Omo-Turkana Basin shows some peculiarities in terms of faunal associations, with Koobi Fora remaining relatively stable while Shungura, and to a lesser extent Nachukui, trend toward wetter conditions through the interval under consideration. Such habitat changes and diversity have important implications for global biome structure and composition, offering new habitats at regular intervals as well as higher and diverse resource availability, that would favor speciation and changes of adaptive strategies (morphology, and behavior including technology). Such changes also shape hominin diversity especially for this time period with many short-term wet–dry cycles before a period of relatively stable climatic conditions (longer cycles?) when the African climate became gradually more arid after 1.7 ± 0.1 Ma and 1.0 ± 0.2 Ma (deMenocal, 2004, 2011) associated with lower hominin diversity (the disappearance of *Paranthropus* and the first *Homo erectus*) and probably a first "out of Africa" event.

Although our spatiotemporal resolution is still quite limited (diachrony and synchrony), we suggest that the earliest hominins were probably not associated with dense or closed forest habitats, but rather lived within a large range of habitats that periodically changed through short-term climatic phases. Such mosaic, patchy environments with their diversity, discontinuity, and variability of habitats may help us understand the ecomorphological changes, cultural emergence, and variability observed in hominins.

Note

1. To illustrate the relationships between sedimentary thicknesses and longer time intervals, there is 11.20 m between LA1 and LA2C, meaning a time interval of *ca.* 74 ka based on an assumed sediment accumulation rate of 152 mm/ka for the Kalochoro Member (Tiercelin et al., 2010), to be compared with a value of 174 mm/ka for the Lomekwi Member (Harmand et al., 2015).

Acknowledgments

We want to thank the office of the President of Kenya, the Ministry of Education, Science and Technology, the National Council for Science and Technology of the Republic of Kenya, the French Ministry of Foreign Affairs, and ANR-12-CULT-006-02, for all their support, as well as the Turkana people. We greatly thank the editors who invited us to participate to this volume. We thank R. Bobe, S. Reynolds, and J.M. Harris for their comments and editing work.

26 Early Hominins and Paleoecology of the Koobi Fora Formation, Lake Turkana Basin, Kenya

René Bobe, João d'Oliveira Coelho, Susana Carvalho, and Meave Leakey

Introduction

The Koobi Fora Fm (Formation) east of Lake Turkana in northern Kenya is one of the most important paleoanthropological rock units in the world (Figure 26.1). Nearly 250 hominin specimens are documented from East Turkana, representing the species *Australopithecus anamensis*, *A. afarensis*, *Paranthropus boisei*, *Homo rudolfensis*, *H. habilis*, and *H. erectus* (or *ergaster*) (M.G. Leakey, 1970; R.E. Leakey, 1973, 1976; Day et al., 1976; M.G. Leakey and R.E. Leakey, 1978; Kimbel, 1988; Wood, 1991; M.G. Leakey et al., 1995, 2012; Spoor et al., 2007; Wood and Leakey, 2011). Spanning from about 4.3 Ma (million years ago) to about 0.7 Ma, the abundant paleontological and sedimentological records of the Koobi Fora Fm offers a rich picture of hominin evolution and paleoenvironments during the Pliocene and early Pleistocene. In this contribution we present a synthesis of previous paleoecological work at East Turkana and add new paleontological analyses relevant to understanding the ecology of early hominins.

The Lake Turkana Basin today is a hot and dry place, with mean annual temperature of 29.2°C (Passey et al., 2010) and mean annual precipitation of 180 mm/year (Cerling et al., 2003a). Turkana is a closed hydrological basin at low elevation. With the lake at ~400 m above sea level, Lake Turkana has the lowest elevation of the major rift valley lakes. Most of the water flowing into the lake (~80 percent) comes from the Omo River (Avery and Tebbs, 2018), originating in the Ethiopian highlands, with further contributions from the Turkwel River, originating on Mount Elgon, and the Kerio River flowing from high areas of western Kenya (Feibel et al., 1991). The predominant vegetation today east of Lake Turkana is composed of *Acacia–Commiphora–Salvadora* trees and bushes, with grasslands near the lake margins (Bamford, 2017).

Historically, the first reports of fossils found in the Turkana region are attributed to the French expedition led by Bourg de Bozas in 1902 and 1903, who discovered vertebrate fossils in the lower Omo Valley (Harris et al., 2006). These discoveries led to the subsequent expeditions by Camille Arambourg with the Mission Scientifique de l'Omo in 1932 and 1933 (Arambourg, 1947). In 1964, Bryan Patterson initiated systematic geological and paleontological surveys (continued from 1965 to 1972) between the Kerio and Turkwel rivers southwest of Lake

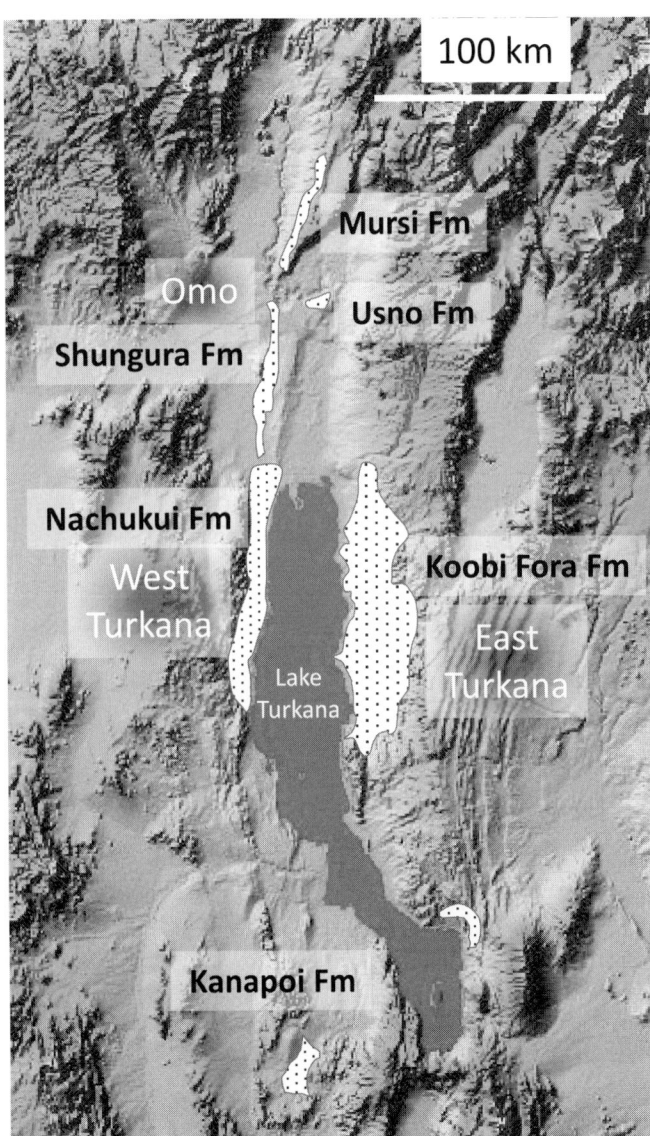

Figure 26.1 Map of the Omo-Turkana Basin including the lower Omo Valley of Ethiopia and the Lake Turkana Basin of Kenya. The Pliocene and Pleistocene Omo Group deposits include the Mursi, Nkalabong, Usno, and Shungura formations in Ethiopia, and the Koobi Fora, Nachukui, and Kanapoi formations in Kenya. The Nkalabong Formation is not known to be fossiliferous and is not shown on this map.

Supplementary resources for this chapter are available on www.cambridge.org/africanpaleoecology

Turkana, leading to the earliest reports of fossils from Kanapoi and Lothagam (Patterson, 1966; Patterson et al., 1970). In 1967, the International Omo Research Expedition (IORE) launched a long-term geological and paleontological project that conducted annual field seasons until 1976 (Howell, 1968, 1978a; Coppens et al., 1976; de Heinzelin, 1983b).

The East Turkana (then called East Rudolf) exposures came to the attention of Richard Leakey as he flew on his way to the Omo from Nairobi in 1967. The following year, Leakey began to explore the fossiliferous deposits east of Lake Turkana, accompanied by Bernard Wood, John Harris, Kamoya Kimeu, Bob Campbell, Paul Abell, and Margaret Leakey. Only a limited number of fossil specimens were collected in 1968, but the paleoanthropological potential of the region became clear. In 1969, Anna K. Behrensmeyer and Meave Leakey joined the team, and in 1970 Glynn Isaac agreed to lead archeological research at Koobi Fora (M.D. Leakey, 1978). Thus, Leakey established the East Rudolf Research Project (from 1969 to 1975) followed by the Koobi Fora Research Project (from 1975 to the present; Harris et al., 2006). In 1975 the government of Kenya changed the name of the lake from Lake Rudolf to Lake Turkana. Several researchers joined the team in the early 1970s, including geologists Carl Vondra, Bruce Bowen, Ian Findlater, and Thure Cerling; paleontologists Vince Maglio, Shirley Savage, Basil Cooke, Craig Black, Tim White, and Peter Williamson; paleoanthropologists Michael Day and Alan Walker; and archeologists Jack Harris and John Barthelme, among many others (M.D. Leakey, 1978). In 1979, Frank Brown, who had been working in the Omo since 1966, was invited to study the tuffs from the Koobi Fora region. Today, extensive research continues at East Turkana under the auspices of the National Museums of Kenya in collaboration with interdisciplinary teams from several institutions.

The Koobi Fora Formation

The Koobi Fora Fm, within the Turkana Depression, or the Omo-Turkana Basin, is part of the eastern branch of the East African Rift System (Brown and McDougall, 2011). Exposures of the Koobi Fora Fm occur from the Kenya/Ethiopia border in the north to the Loiyangalani area in the south. On the west side of the lake, West Turkana includes the sedimentary sequences of the Nachukui and Kanapoi Fms, while the lower Omo Valley on the Ethiopian side north of the lake encompasses the Shungura, Usno, Mursi, and Nkalabong Fms (Figure 26.1). These sedimentary sequences constitute the Omo Group (Figure 26.2), fossiliferous deposits associated with the ancient Omo river as well as its main tributaries (de Heinzelin, 1983b; Brown and McDougall, 2011; Feibel, 2011). In various parts of the Turkana Basin, Plio-Pleistocene deposits are covered by sediments of the younger Galana Boi Fm, which dates from the latest Pleistocene to the Holocene (Bowen and Vondra, 1973; Owen and Renaut, 1986; Beck et al., 2019).

The tectonic, sedimentary, and chronological framework of the Omo Group deposits, including the Koobi Fora Fm (Figure 26.3 and Table 26.1), has been well established after decades of research in the region, and it is concisely summarized by Brown and McDougall (2011) and Feibel (2011). The Koobi Fora Fm was formally defined by Brown and Feibel (1986: 299) as "sedimentary strata of the Koobi Fora region of Pliocene and Pleistocene age that lie disconformably or unconformably on, or are in fault contact with, Miocene and Pliocene volcanic rocks and/or associated sediments, and are disconformably overlain by the late Pleistocene and Holocene Galana Boi Beds of Bowen and Vondra (1973)." The formation, with a composite thickness of 565 m, is divided into eight members. The oldest is the Lonyumun Mb (Member), followed by the Moiti Mb, Lokochot Mb, Tulu Bor Mb, Burgi Mb, KBS Mb, Okote Mb, and Chari Mb. Each member, except for the Lonyumun, is defined by a volcanic ash layer at its base with the same name as the member (Figure 26.2): the Moiti Tuff defines the base of the Moiti Mb, the Lokochot Tuff defines the base of the Lokochot Mb, the Tulu Bor Tuff defines the base of the Tulu Bor Mb, etc. There is a major unconformity in the Burgi Mb, which is usually divided into a lower and upper Burgi Mb. The Koobi Fora Fm spans from about 4.3 Ma to 0.7 Ma.

The Koobi Fora Fm deposits represent fluvial, lacustrine, and deltaic paleoenvironments. The fossiliferous portions of the Koobi Fora Fm are primarily lake margin and fluvial, the latter laid down by the paleo-Omo river during times when a lake was either absent or restricted to portions of the rift basin. During times when the lake was absent, the river meandered through the basin and exited to the southeast via the Turkana River (inferred to have existed at times during the Pliocene and Pleistocene) through the Lamu embayment (Feibel, 1988, 1994). The paleo-Omo river originated in the Ethiopian highlands and is assumed to have been perennial, as it is today. Other rivers flowed into the basin from the south (paleo-Kerio River), west (paleo-Turkwel River), and the northeast. The fluvial sequences were interrupted episodically by lakes of varying size and duration. At various times during the Pliocene and Pleistocene the basin had hydrological connections to the Nile River drainage (Feibel, 2011). Thus, the rich geological, paleobotanical, and paleontological record of the Koobi Fora Fm includes elements from areas proximate to the depositional environments, e.g., the surrounding floodplains and lake shores, as well as elements transported downstream from more distant regions or reworked from previous deposits. The Appendix (Supplementary material) provides details of the Koobi Fora Formation exposures across Paleontological Collection Areas.

The PaleoTurkana Database

Most fossil vertebrates collected from the Koobi Fora Fm and housed at the National Museums of Kenya (NMK) in Nairobi were incorporated into a database created by the first author in collaboration with A.K. Behrensmeyer (Smithsonian Institution), Meave Leakey (then at NMK, now at the Turkana Basin Institute), and Emma Mbua (NMK). Since 2004, a public version of the database has been available to the scientific community through the NMK, the Smithsonian Institution (Bobe, 2011), and the Turkana Basin Institute (Fortelius et al., 2016). In this chapter we use a current version of the database, the PaleoTurkana Database, maintained by the first author (Bobe

The Omo Group deposits in Ethiopia and Kenya

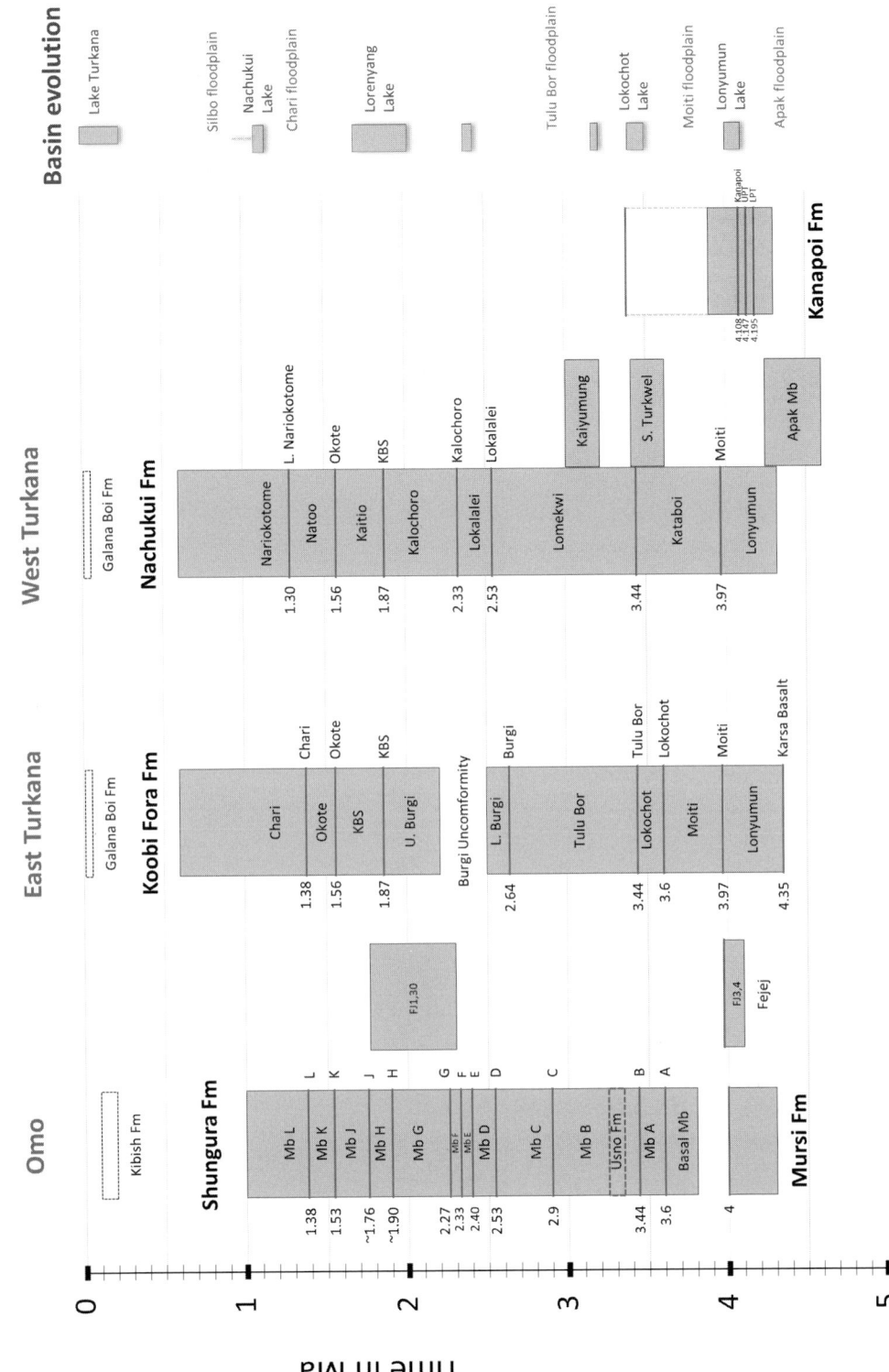

Figure 26.2 Schematic sequence of the Omo Group deposits including the Mursi, Usno, Shungura, Koobi Fora, Nachukui, and Kanapoi formations. Major tephra and basalts are indicated with horizontal lines, with their names on the right side of the column. Dates in Ma are indicated on the left of the column. The Kibish and Galana Boi formations constitute the Turkana Group deposits, and are depicted here in dashed rectangles. Major intervals in the evolution of the Omo-Turkana Basin are depicted on the right side of the figure.

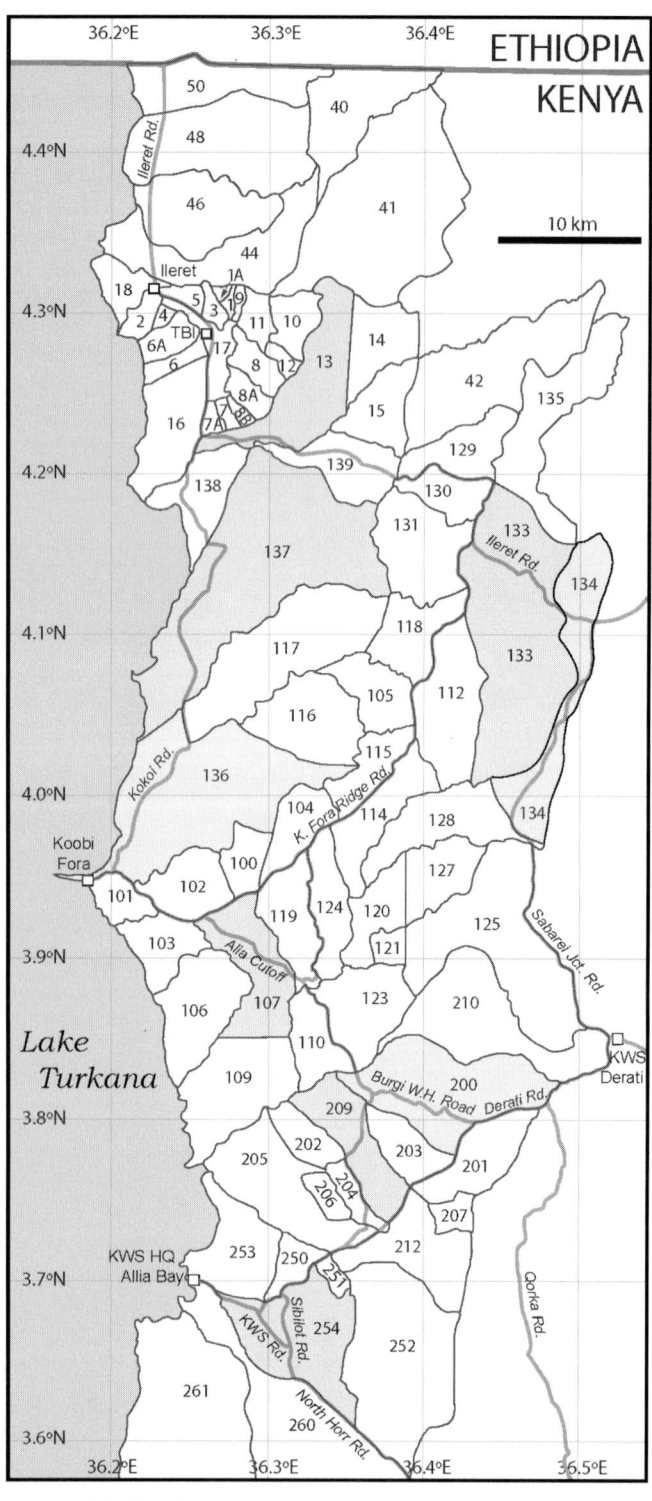

Figure 26.3 Map of paleontological collecting areas of the Koobi Fora Formation revised and modified by Frank Brown.

Table 26.1 Paleontological collection areas of the Koobi Fora Formation.

Area#	Area in km²	Area#	Area in km²
1	1.29	114	28.10
1A	0.93	115	17.80
2	5.88	116	37.90
3	3.63	117	69.88
4	1.53	118	25.60
5	3.65	119	24.70
6	5.62	120	19.40
6A	8.90	121	5.68
7	2.22	123	32.00
7A	2.49	124	22.10
8	9.24	125	82.70
8A	6.68	127	22.90
8B	1.68	128	37.40
9	1.43	129	35.30
10	12.50	130	15.60
11	7.52	131	39.20
12	3.12	133	115.00
13	47.40	134	46.70
14	23.30	135	37.80
15	21.80	136	103.00
16	34.40	137	140.00
17	11.30	138	25.90
18	11.90	139	27.20
40	41.70	200	65.70
41	116.00	201	26.50
42	58.00	202	13.00
44	49.20	203	17.50
46	42.40	204	7.84
48	69.00	205	47.90
50	33.80	206	6.28
100	12.20	207	6.63
101	11.40	209	31.70
102	22.30	210	60.20
103	19.30	212	36.50
104	18.80	250	9.45
105	20.90	251	3.74
106	37.10	252	85.80
107	38.30	253	32.80
109	46.60	254	54.00
110	18.50	260	67.20
112	42.40	261	86.20

and Carvalho, 2019). This database currently has about 12,000 records of fossil vertebrates from the Koobi Fora Fm. Table 26.2 provides a list of taxa known from the formation across geological members.

To determine taxonomic abundances, we use mNISP, a modified form of NISP (Number of Identified Specimens), whereby all specimens known to represent a single individual animal are counted as one, even if they have multiple records in

Table 26.2 Fossil mammals from the Koobi Fora Formation across members, with numbers representing modified numbers of identified specimens (mNISP) in the PaleoTurkana Database. P refers to specimens present but without abundance data. See main text for details.

	Lonyumun-Moiti	Lokochot	Tulu Bor	Upper Burgi	KBS	Okote	Chari
PRIMATES							
HOMINIDAE							
Hominini indet.	1	4	3	4	6	7	0
Australopithecus anamensis	46	0	0	0	0	0	0
Australopithecus afarensis	0	0	1	0	0	0	0
Paranthropus boisei	0	0	0	5	43	21	0
Homo indet.	0	0	1	26	29	10	0
Homo habilis	0	0	0	1	1	2	0
Homo rudolfensis	0	0	0	4	1	0	0
Homo erectus	0	0	0	4	9	11	0
CERCOPITHECIDAE							
Cercopithecidae indet.	2	0	0	0	0	1	3
Cercopithecinae indet.	70	24	6	27	24	18	0
Cercopithecus sp. indet. A	0	0	0	0	2	1	0
Cercopithecus sp. indet. B	0	0	1	0	0	0	0
cf. Papionini	3	0	0	1	0	1	0
Papionini indet.	16	11	1	1	7	11	0
Cercocebus indet.	0	0	0	0	0	1	0
cf. *Lophocebus*	0	0	0	0	0	6	0
Lophocebus cf. *albigena*	0	0	0	0	4	42	0
cf. *Parapapio*	40	0	0	1	1	2	0
Parapapio indet.	55	1	0	2	1	6	0
Parapapio cf. *ado*	52	1	1	0	0	0	0
Parapapio indet. A	0	0	0	3	1	2	0
Parapapio indet. B	7	3	0	0	1	0	0
Parapapio indet. C	0	1	0	0	0	1	0
cf. *Theropithecus* sp.	9	2	9	25	17	20	0
Theropithecus indet.	3	2	7	3	11	3	0
Theropithecus darti	0	1	0	0	0	0	0
Theropithecus brumpti	0	24	30	0	0	0	0
Theropithecus cf. *brumpti*	0	2	0	0	1	0	0
Theropithecus oswaldi	0	0	1	110	125	103	0
Theropithecus cf. *oswaldi*	0	0	0	10	9	4	1
cf. Colobinae	37	4	0	1	3	3	0
Colobinae indet.	19	6	0	8	17	15	0
cf. *Cercopithecoides*	40	4	2	0	0	0	0
Cercopithecoides williamsi	0	0	1	6	2	0	0
Cercopithecoides kimeui	0	0	2	6	6	0	0
Colobus indet.	0	0	0	0	0	2	0
Colobus freedmani	0	0	0	0	2	12	0
Paracolobus mutiwa	0	0	0	2	0	0	0
Rhinocolobus turkanaensis	0	2	0	10	14	0	0
cf. *Rhinocolobus*	0	4	0	1	8	2	0

Table 26.2 (cont.)

	Lonyumun-Moiti	Lokochot	Tulu Bor	Upper Burgi	KBS	Okote	Chari
RODENTIA							
THRYONOMYIDAE							
Thryonomis indet.	0	0	0	0	0	3	0
MURIDAE							
Aethomys indet.	0	0	0	0	0	6	0
Arvicanthis indet.	0	0	0	0	7	0	0
Mus indet.	0	0	0	0	5	0	0
Praomys cf. *minor*	0	0	0	0	24	0	0
Thallomys quadrilobatus	0	0	0	0	10	0	0
HYSTRICIDAE							
Hystrix indet.	1	1	0	0	0	1	0
DIPODIDAE							
Jaculus orientalis	0	0	0	0	0	3	0
SCIURIDAE							
Sciuridae indet.	1	0	0	0	0	0	0
CARNIVORA							
Carnivora indet.	0	0	2	8	1	1	0
CANIDAE							
cf. Canidae	0	0	0	0	1	0	0
Lupulella sp.	0	0	0	6	2	0	0
Vulpes sp.	0	0	0	0	1	0	0
MUSTELIDAE							
Mustelidae indet.	0	1	0	2	2	1	1
Enhydriodon afman	0	1	0	0	0	0	0
Enhydriodon cf. *afman*	1	0	2	1	0	0	0
cf. *Torolutra* sp.	0	0	0	9	1	1	0
Torolutra cf. *ougandensis*	0	0	0	2	1	0	0
cf. *Hydrictis*	0	0	0	1	1	0	0
Hydrictis gudho	0	0	0	1	0	0	0
cf. *Aonyx*	0	0	0	0	1	0	0
Lutrinae gen. sp. nov.	0	0	0	1	0	0	0
Lutrinae indet.	0	0	0	1	0	0	0
Mellivora indet.	0	0	0	1	0	1	0
aff. *Plesiogulo*	0	0	1	0	0	0	0
aff. *Ictonyx*	0	0	1	0	0	0	0
URSIDAE							
cf. *Agriotherium* sp.	1?	0	2	0	0	0	0
VIVERRIDAE							
cf. *Civettictis*	0	0	0	4	0	0	1
cf. *Pseudocivetta* sp.	0	0	0	1	2	0	0
Pseudocivetta ingens	0	0	0	1	3	0	0
aff. *Genetta*	0	0	0	1	0	0	0
Genetta genetta/maculata	0	0	0	2	0	2	0
Genetta nyakitongwer	0	0	0	0	1	0	0
Viverridae indet. sp. A	0	0	0	1	0	0	0

Table 26.2 (cont.)

	Lonyumun-Moiti	Lokochot	Tulu Bor	Upper Burgi	KBS	Okote	Chari
Viverridae indet. sp. B	0	0	1	0	1	0	0
Viverridae indet.	1	1	0	0	1	1	0
HYAENIDAE							
Hyaenidae indet.	0	1	1	1	1	0	0
Hyaenidae indet. sp. A	0	0	0	0	0	1	0
Crocuta indet.	0	1	0	2	1	2	0
Crocuta eturono	0	0	1	0	0	0	0
Crocuta dietrichi	0	0	0	2	0	0	0
Crocuta cf. *dietrichi*	0	1	0	4	0	0	0
Crocuta ultra	0	0	0	2	8	9	0
Crocuta cf. *ultra*	0	0	0	1	6	3	0
Hyaena sp.	0	1	0	0	0	4	0
Hyaena cf. *makapani*	0	0	0	3	1	0	0
Hyaena cf. *hyaena*	1?	0	1	0	1	0	0
cf. *Parahyaena*	0	0	0	0	0	1	0
FELIDAE							
Felidae indet.	0	0	1	3	1	0	0
Homotherium sp.	3	1	4	10	7	1	0
cf. *Megantereon* sp.	0	0	0	0	2	1	0
Megantereon whitei	0	0	0	0	1	2	0
Dinofelis indet.	0	0	0	0	2	0	0
Dinofelis petteri	1	0	1	5	1	0	0
Dinofelis aronoki	0	0	0	1	1	0	0
Dinofelis piveteaui	0	0	0	0	0	9	0
Machairodontinae indet.	0	0	0	1	0	0	0
Panthera pardus	0	0	0	3	1	0	0
Panthera leo	0	0	0	5	1	11	0
Acinonyx sp.	0	0	0	2	0	0	0
Acinonyx sp. nov.	0	0	0	0	2	1	0
Caracal or *Leptailurus*	0	0	4	0	0	0	0
ARTIODACTYLA							
BOVIDAE							
Bovidae indet.	353	0	3	0	13	15	1
Tragelaphini sp.	P	6	12	12	35	14	0
Tragelaphus kyaloi	P	1	0	0	0	0	0
Tragelaphus nakuae	0	0	0	16	7	0	0
Tragelaphus rastafari	0	20	27	1	0	0	0
Tragelaphus strepsiceros	0	0	0	37	79	19	0
Bovini sp.	0	0	0	4	2	0	0
Simatherium cf. *khollarseni*	0	4	25	0	0	0	0
Pelorovis oldowayensis	0	0	0	2	12	7	0
Pelorovis turkanensis	0	0	0	6	52	8	1
Aepyceros sp.	P	0	0	3	7	1	0
Aepyceros shungurae	0	16	4	0	0	0	0
Aepyceros melampus	0	0	0	33	71	5	0

Table 26.2 (cont.)

	Lonyumun-Moiti	Lokochot	Tulu Bor	Upper Burgi	KBS	Okote	Chari
Reduncini sp.	P	1	25	55	66	15	0
Kobus sp.	0	0	0	1	1	2	0
Kobus ancystrocera	0	0	9	6	43	0	0
Kobus ellipsiprymnus	0	0	0	0	5	0	0
Kobus aff. *kob*	P	1	4	0	0	0	0
Kobus kob	0	0	0	2	28	48	0
Kobus aff. *leche*	0	0	0	3	15	1	0
Kobus oricornus	P	6	30	0	0	0	0
Kobus sigmoidalis	P	2	13	104	82	3	0
Menelikia leakeyi	P	0	13	0	0	0	0
Menelikia lyrocera	P	0	2	23	78	2	0
Hippotragus gigas	0	0	0	3	2	0	0
Oryx sp.	0	0	0	2	12	0	0
Alcelaphini sp.	P	0	0	8	39	7	1
Beatragus antiquus	0	0	0	2	8	2	0
Beatragus cf. *hunteri*	0	0	0	0	0	0	1
Connochaetes aff. *gentryi*	0	7	3	0	0	0	0
Connochaetes gentryi	0	0	0	12	16	6	0
Damaliscus indet.	0	1	0	0	0	3	0
Damaliscus cf. *eppsi*	0	0	4	0	0	0	0
Damaliscus eppsi	0	0	0	3	66	7	0
Damaliscus cf. *niro*	0	0	0	0	3	0	0
Damaliscus sp. nov.	0	0	0	0	0	1	0
Megalotragus sp.	0	1	6	0	0	0	0
Megalotragus isaaci	0	0	0	34	38	9	0
Parmularius sp.	0	0	0	0	1	0	0
cf. *Parmularius angusticornis*	0	1	1	0	0	0	0
cf. *Parmularius altidens*	0	0	0	0	1	0	0
Caprini indet.	0	0	0	0	1	0	0
Antilopini indet.	P	0	0	0	0	0	0
Antidorcas recki	0	0	3	14	49	3	0
Gazella sp.	P	1	0	12	15	1	0
Gazella aff. *granti*	0	0	0	0	1	1	0
Gazella cf. *janenschi*	0	0	0	3	5	0	0
Gazella praethomsoni	0	4	4	18	11	2	1
Raphicerus	0	0	0	1	5	0	0
Madoqua	0	0	0	0	2	0	0
GIRAFFIDAE							
Giraffa indet.	33	5	10	8	39	8	0
Giraffa jumae	4	1	2	1	6	2	0
Giraffa pygmaea	1	4	1	9	19	3	0
Giraffa stillei	9	3	1	8	16	0	0
Sivatherium maurusium	3	2	3	8	32	0	0
HIPPOPOTAMIDAE							
Hippopotamidae indet.	118	0	0	0	0	0	0

Table 26.2 (cont.)

	Lonyumun-Moiti	Lokochot	Tulu Bor	Upper Burgi	KBS	Okote	Chari
aff. *Hippopotamus* cf. sp. Hadar	5	0	0	0	0	0	0
aff. *Hippopotamus protamphibius*	0	8	18	0	0	0	0
aff. *Hippopotamus aethiopicus*	0	0	0	3	25	13	0
aff. *Hippopotamus karumensis*	0	0	0	37	50	13	0
Hippopotamus gorgops	0	0	0	6	17	6	1
SUIDAE							
Nyanzachoerus kanamensis	105	1	10	0	0	0	0
Notochoerus jaegeri	8	0	0	0	0	0	0
Notochoerus euilus	25	1	58	0	0	0	0
Notochoerus scotti	0	0	4	104	6	0	0
Kolpochoerus limnetes	0	1	7	152	138	19	0
Metridiochoerus andrewsi	0	0	0	66	217	1	0
Metidiochoerus compactus	0	0	0	0	10	65	0
Metridiochoerus modestus	0	0	0	1	4	1	0
Metridiochoerus hopwoodi	0	0	0	2	27	6	0
CAMELIDAE							
Camelus	0	0	4	0	0	0	0
PERISSODACTYLA							
EQUIDAE							
Equidae indet.	45	0	3	3	1	2	0
Eurygnathohippus sp.	0	0	1	3	10	0	0
Eurygnathohippus cornelianum	0	0	0	1	0	0	0
Eurygnathohippus cf. *ethiopicum*	0	0	1	22	24	4	0
Eurygnathohippus hasumense	1	1	18	1	0	0	0
Equus sp.	0	0	0	15	80	7	0
Equus koobiforensis	0	0	0	36	23	1	0
Equus cf. *tabeti*	0	0	0	0	2	4	0
Equus cf. *grevyi*	0	0	0	0	0	8	0
Equus cf. *burchelli*	0	0	0	0	0	1	0
RHINOCEROTIDAE							
Rhinocerotidae indet.	11	0	0	0	0	0	0
Ceratotherium praecox	2	0	3	0	0	0	0
Ceratotherium simum	0	0	0	8	21	1	0
Diceros bicornis	0	0	0	1	9	0	0
PROBOSCIDEA							
DEINOTHERIIDAE							
Deinotherium bozasi	13	1	16	12	12	0	0
ELEPHANTIDAE							
Elephas recki	23	0	0	0	2	0	0
Elephas recki atavus	0	0	0	9	18	0	0
Elephas recki brumpti	0	0	26	0	0	0	0
Elephas recki ileretensis	0	0	0	0	17	0	0
Elephas recki recki	0	0	0	0	0	10	0
Elephas recki shungurensis	0	0	7	33	0	0	0
Loxodonta adaurora adaurora	8	0	0	0	0	0	0

Table 26.2 (cont.)

	Lonyumun-Moiti	Lokochot	Tulu Bor	Upper Burgi	KBS	Okote	Chari
Loxodonta adaurora kararae	0	0	0	6	0	0	0
Loxodonta exeptata	0	0	12	0	0	0	0
TUBULIDENTATA							
ORYCTEROPODIDAE							
Orycteropus indet.	0	1	0	1	3	1	0

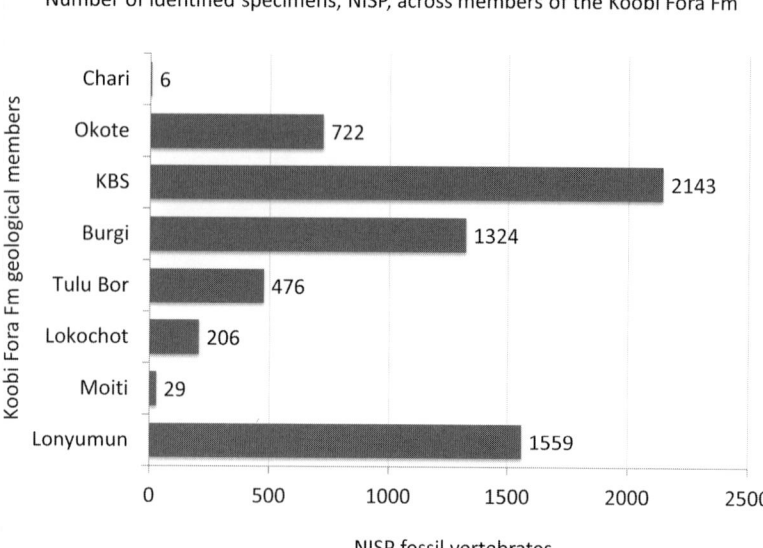

Figure 26.4 Abundance of fossil mammals (NISP) per geological member of the Koobi Fora Formation.

the database. For example, the newly described partial skeleton KNM-ER 47000 is represented by nine records in the database (partial scapula, humeral fragments, ulna, etc.; Richmond et al., 2020), but as all specimens belong to a single individual animal, it is counted as one in Table 26.2. Faunal abundances in Table 26.2 indicate the number of fossils in the database, but not necessarily relative abundances of these taxa in the exposures. Some taxa (e.g., Primates) have been more thoroughly collected, studied, identified, and published than others (e.g., Hippopotamidae) and their abundances in Table 26.2 will be inflated relative to other taxa. The numbers provided here are not adjusted for collection efforts and taphonomic factors that undoubtedly play an important role affecting the abundance data. Even considering these caveats, however, it still is clear that fossil vertebrates are unevenly distributed across members of the Koobi Fora Fm (Figure 26.4). Some of the lower members, i.e., Moiti, Lokochot, and Tulu Bor, have lower sample sizes than the upper members (Table 26.2). Many specimens from these lower members have yet to be fully studied and published, but ongoing work on these fossils will significantly improve our understanding of the interval between about 4 Ma and 3 Ma (Villaseñor, 2017; Dumouchel, 2018). Thus, for the lower part of the Koobi Fora sequence we focus on those taxa that have been well published: hominins (Leakey and Leakey, 1978; Wood, 1991; Leakey et al., 1995; Ward et al., 2001), cercopithecids (Jablonski and Leakey, 2008), and carnivores (Werdelin and Lewis, 2013b).

Paleoenvironments and Fossil Mammals

The hydrology of the Omo-Turkana Basin and its evolution during the late Cenozoic has played a central role in shaping the water balance and vegetation of the region. A brief outline of key intervals in the history of the basin is sketched in Figure 26.2, derived from the work of Craig Feibel and Frank Brown (Brown and Feibel, 1991; Feibel et al., 1991; Feibel, 1999a). Alongside changes in basin evolution, the region has been affected by frequent volcanism in the form of volcanic ashes (Feibel, 1999b) and lava flows (Haileab et al., 2004). Some tephra in the Koobi Fora Fm were the result of massive eruptions that likely blanketed large areas of eastern Africa (e.g., Moiti Tuff, Tulu Bor Tuff, Chari Tuff), while others corresponded to smaller, and sometimes frequent and complex episodes of deposition by fluvial systems (e.g., Okote Tuff Complex). Figure 26.5 presents the number of separate tephra per unit of time in the Omo-Turkana Basin from 4.2 Ma to 1.0 Ma (after an illustration by Feibel, 1999b) with data published by McDougall and colleagues (McDougall, 1985; McDougall

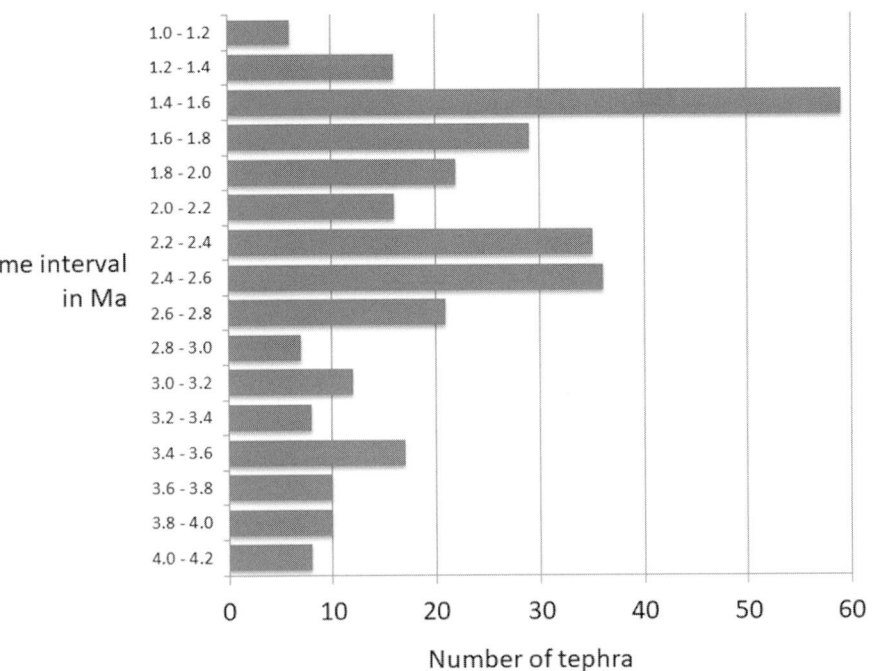

Figure 26.5 Number of tephra in the Omo-Turkana Basin between 4.2 to 1.0 Ma. Data compiled and redrawn from McDougall et al. (2012) and Feibel (1999b). Some of these tephra are airfall deposits from massive volcanic eruptions that likely produced major disruptions of regional ecosystems

et al., 1985; Brown et al., 2006; Brown and McDougall, 2011; McDougall and Brown, 2006, 2008; McDougall et al., 2012). There were three increasingly higher peaks of tephra deposition in the basin with intervals of about 1 million years: first at about 3.5 Ma, then at about 2.5 Ma, and finally at about 1.5 Ma. Whether these peaks relate to broader-scale tectonic cycles remains to be determined. The magnitude and frequency of volcanism in the region provided some degree of environmental disruption and heterogeneity that influenced the vegetation and fauna at various times (Bobe and Carvalho, 2019).

Temperatures in the Turkana Basin appear to have been relatively stable over the past 4 Myr, with surface temperatures during soil formation typically above 30°C (Passey et al., 2010). Along with consistently high temperatures, water deficit in the basin (a measure of aridity) shows no discernible trends over the past 4.4 Myr (Blumenthal et al., 2017). Nevertheless, stable carbon isotopes from paleosols are indicative of an overall shift toward increasingly C_4 environments in the region between 4.2 and 1 Ma (Wynn, 2004; Levin et al., 2011). Thus, there seems to be a decoupling between long-term changes in aridity, which were minimal, and the documented increase in C_4 vegetation in the region. The vegetation history of the basin can be well summarized by stable carbon isotopes from pedogenic carbonates as published by several colleagues (Wynn, 2000; Cerling et al., 2003b, 2011b; Quinn et al., 2007; Levin et al., 2011; Quinn and Lepre, 2020). The pedogenic carbonate isotope data from the basin between about 4.3 Ma and 1 Ma is synthesized in Figure 26.6. Stable carbon isotopes have also been obtained from dental enamel from a range of fossil mammals in the Turkana Basin (Cerling et al., 2003a, 2011a, 2013a, 2013b, 2015; Patterson et al., 2017a, 2017b, 2019). Here we illustrate previously published data from hominins (Figure 26.7) and from the cercopithecid genus *Theropithecus* (Figure 26.8).

In our discussions we use the term megaherbivore to refer to herbivorous mammals estimated to weigh 1000 kg or more (Owen-Smith, 1988). Today there are six species of megaherbivores in Africa: elephants – *Loxodonta africana* and *Loxodonta cyclotis*; rhinocerotids – *Ceratotherium simum* and *Diceros bicornis*; giraffe – *Giraffa camelopardalis*; and hippos – *Hippopotamus amphibius*. However, in the past African megaherbivores were significantly more abundant and diverse (Faith et al., 2018).

Below we summarize the geology and reconstructed paleoenvironments for each of the Koobi Fora Fm members, based on sedimentological, faunal, and stable isotopic evidence. By presenting the data on a member by member basis, we are dealing with samples that are time-averaged and derive from different depositional environments. Thus, these samples do not necessarily represent paleocommunities except in a very broad sense. We suggest that further taphonomic work is needed to evaluate the ideas, paleoenvironmental reconstructions, and faunal associations tentatively presented here (Behrensmeyer, 1985).

Lonyumun Member: 4.3–3.97 Ma

The Lonyumun Mb is composed of sediments deposited over Miocene and early Pliocene volcanic rocks, and capped by the base of the Moiti Tuff, dated to 3.97 Ma (McDougall et al., 2012).

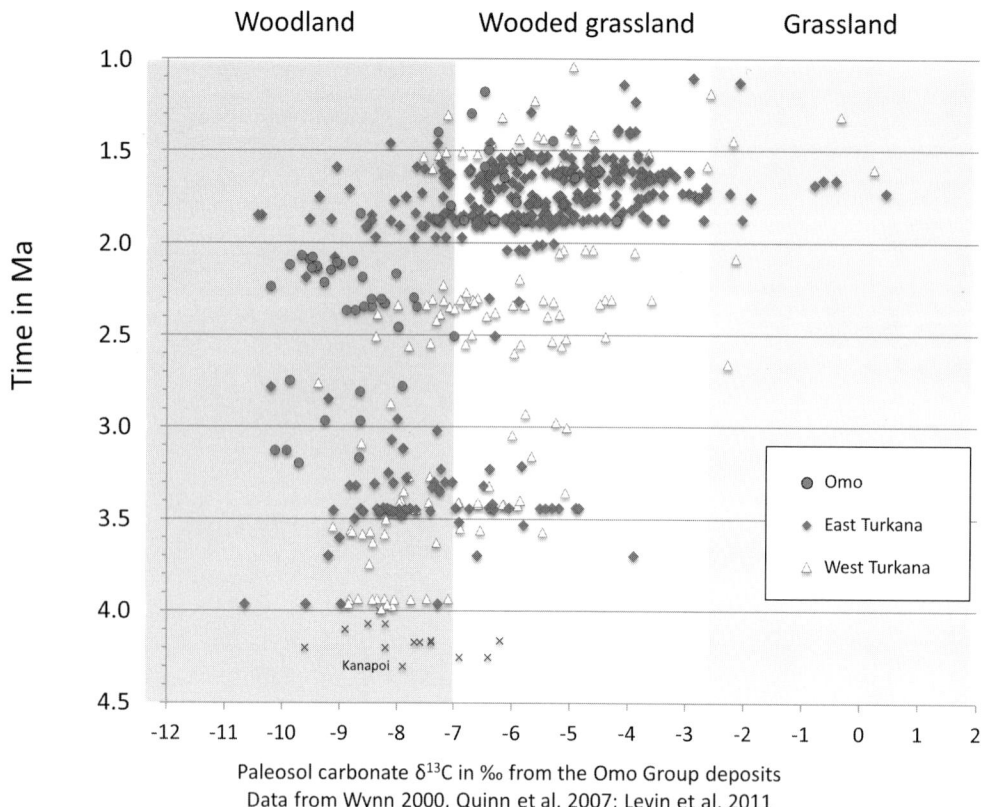

Figure 26.6 Paleosol carbonate δ¹³C in ‰ from the Omo Group deposits reflecting C₃ and C₄ vegetation in the Omo-Turkana Basin from 4.3 Ma to 1.0 Ma. Data from Quinn et al. (2007) and Levin et al. (2011). (A black and white version of this figure will appear in some formats. For the color version, please refer to the plate section.)

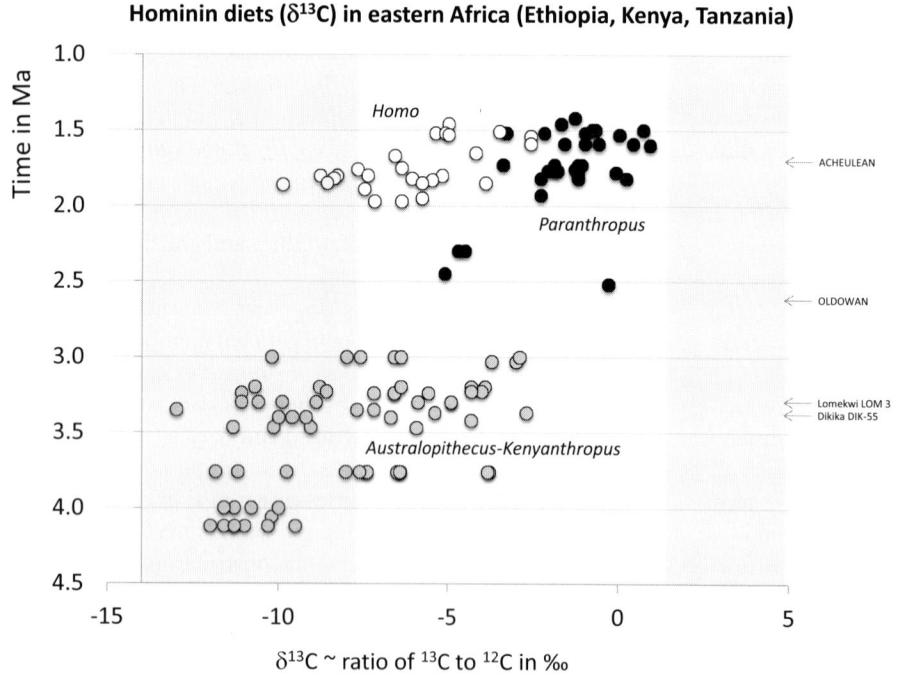

Figure 26.7 Stable carbon isotopes, δ¹³C in ‰, in hominin dental enamel in East African sites (Ethiopia, Kenya, Tanzania) from 4.2 Ma (*Australopithecus anamensis*) to 1.5 Ma (*Homo* and *Paranthropus*).

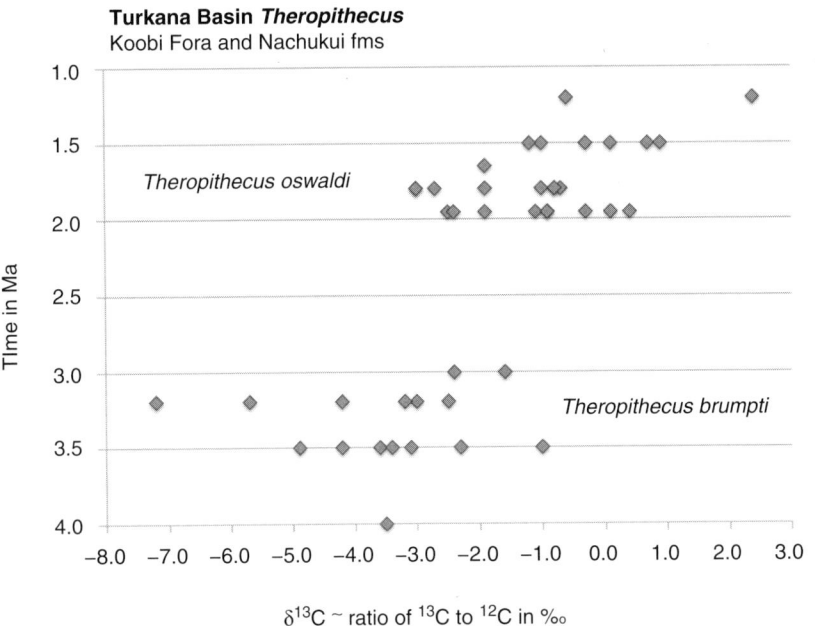

Figure 26.8 Stable carbon isotopes, $\delta^{13}C$ in ‰, in *Theropithecus* dental enamel in the Turkana Basin (Koobi Fora and Nachukui formations) from 4 Ma to 1.2 Ma.

The type section is defined in Area 260, where it is 36.8-m thick (Brown and Feibel, 1986). This member is exposed in areas 13–15, 40–41, 117, 129, 133, 136–139, 200, 212, 251–252, 254, 260–261, and in the Loiyangalani region. Fossiliferous sediments of this age range are also well represented in the Apak Mb of the Nachukui Fm at Lothagam, in the Kanapoi Fm, and in the Omo Mursi Fm. In the lower part of the Lonyumun Mb about 4.3 Ma fluvial deposits of the Apak floodplain record the onset of sediment accumulation associated with the integrated Omo Group, but by 4.1 Ma a major freshwater lake formed and covered most of the basin: the Lonyumun Lake lasted for about 100 ky (Feibel et al., 1991; Feibel, 2011). By about 4 Ma, the extensive flood basalts of the Gombe Group intruded into the Lonyumun Mb landscape (Haileab et al., 2004), and the lake was replaced by a depositional system dominated by a large river (Figure 26.2; Feibel et al., 1991). Pedogenic carbonates from paleosols in the Allia Bay region indicate that woodland was the dominant type of vegetation during this time (Levin et al., 2011; Figure 26.6), but stable isotopes from mammalian dental enamel indicate that grasses were also widely available (Cerling et al., 2015).

The richest faunal sample from the Lonyumun Mb comes from the very top of the sequence, just below (or within) the Moiti Tuff at Locality 261–1 (in Area 261), the site of *Australopithecus anamensis* at Allia Bay (Leakey et al., 1995). Specimens in the 261–1 excavation derive from a densely packed bone bed, about 20 cm thick, with abundant but abraded and fragmentary bones and teeth (Coffing et al., 1994; Hagemann, 2010). This means that many of the specimens from the bone bed have only been identified to order or family rather than to genus or species. There are about 2000 specimens of fossil fish, with the lungfish *Protopterus* being particularly abundant and indicating floodplain, swampy habitats. Other fishes including *Gymnarchus*, *Hydrocynus*, *Sindacharax* are indicative of fluvial settings (Coffing et al., 1994). The reptiles, Trionichidae (soft-shelled turtles), *Crocodylus*, and *Euthecodon* are all indicative of aquatic conditions. The horned crocodile *Crocodylus thorbjarnarsoni* is documented at the nearby site of Kanapoi and in later intervals at Koobi Fora (Brochu, 2020), and it is also likely that it was one of the top predators at Allia Bay. The primate and carnivoran faunas from Allia Bay are well studied and published (Jablonski and Leakey, 2008; Werdelin and Lewis, 2013b), while other taxa including bovids and suids are currently under review (Dumouchel, 2018). All hominins are attributed to the species *Australopithecus anamensis*, which, with a total of 46 specimens (Table 26.2), is relatively abundant at 261–1. This hominin is also present in the older deposits of the nearby site of Kanapoi (Ward et al., 2001). Comparisons between 261–1 and Kanapoi are difficult because the two sites are taphonomically very different: Allia Bay 261–1 hominins derive from a fluvial channel bone bed (Coffing et al., 1994), whereas Kanapoi hominins come primarily from paleosols (Wynn, 2000).

Among Allia Bay monkeys, cercopithecines are about 2.5 times more abundant than colobines, with *Parapapio* as the dominant primate. This is the only member of the Koobi Fora Fm in which *Parapapio* is more abundant than *Theropithecus*. Sometime after 3.9 Ma, *Theropithecus* became the dominant cercopithecid genus in the basin. Both *Australopithecus* and *Theropithecus* co-occurred at Allia Bay, as they did at Kanapoi. Among carnivores, *Homotherium* was a ubiquitous predator in the Turkana Basin during this time, both at Kanapoi and Allia Bay (Werdelin and Lewis, 2013b). Bovids are currently under review, so here we report taxonomic presence or absence. As at Kanapoi, Tragelaphini was the most abundant bovid tribe at Allia Bay 261–1, followed by Alcelaphini. Most of the suids belong to the species *Nyanzachoerus kanamensis*, with a few specimens of *Notochoerus jaegeri* and *Not. euilus*. Hipparionin equids were common. The diversity of megaherbivores in the

Allia Bay deposits appears lower than at Kanapoi, where there were 10 species of mammals weighing over 1000 kg. However, the lower diversity at Allia Bay could result from the fragmentary nature of the fossils, which limits identification to species. Overall, the paleoenvironments of *A. anamensis* at East Turkana appear to have been similar to those of the well-studied site of Kanapoi, with a mix of woodlands and grasslands and abundant freshwater in rivers and/or lakes (Bobe et al., 2020a).

Moiti Member: 3.97–3.6 Ma

The Moiti Tuff, well-dated to 3.97 Ma, defines the base of the Moiti Mb, and the base of the Lokochot Tuff, dated to 3.6 Ma, caps the member. The type section of the Moiti Mb is defined at Jarigole in Area 261, where it measures 59.9 m in thickness (Brown and Feibel, 1986). Outcrops of the Moiti Mb occur in areas 13, 40–41, 129, 133–134, 200, 205, 212, 250–252, 254, and 260–261. The Moiti Tuff is the earliest of the major volcanic eruptions to blanket the Turkana Basin, measuring up to 17 m in parts of the Allia Bay Region (Brown and Feibel, 1991). This ash layer is also found in the Gulf of Aden about 1600 km to the northeast, indicating that it was the product of a massive volcanic eruption (Sarna-Wojcicki et al., 1985). Paleogeographically, this interval was dominated by a large meandering river flowing across the Moiti Floodplain from about 4 Ma to 3.6 Ma, with no evidence of lacustrine sediments (Figure 26.2; Feibel et al., 1991; Feibel, 2011). The fossil record of the Moiti Mb is relatively sparse, except for the very base of this member at Locality 261-1, where a dense concentration of bones occurs below or within the base of the Moiti Tuff, as discussed in the section above. Paleosols from this level indicate a mixture of woodlands and wooded grasslands (Figure 26.6; Levin et al., 2011). Fossil samples other than those from Locality 261-1 show a dominance of Reduncini among the bovids.

Lokochot Member: 3.6–3.44 Ma

The Lokochot Mb ranges from the base of the Lokochot Tuff, dated to 3.6 Ma, to the base of the Tulu Bor Tuff, dated to 3.44 Ma (McDougall and Brown, 2008). Its type section as defined in Area 261 measures 34.4 m (Brown and Feibel, 1986). This member is also exposed in areas 13, 40–41, 117, 129, 133–134, 136–139, 204–206, 210, 212, and 250–253. A major lake, Lake Lokochot, was the dominant paleogeographic feature during this interval. This was a relatively shallow lake with fluctuating margins that persisted for about 60 ky (Feibel, 2011; Figure 26.2). Although the published paleontological record of the Lokochot Mb is relatively sparse (Figure 26.4), significant fieldwork in recent years has added important new faunal samples to the collections, including hominins, but these fossils are still under study (Villaseñor, 2017) so they are not discussed here. So far only four hominins have been published from the Lokochot Mb, and these are considered Hominini indet. The holotype of the hominin *Kenyanthropus platyops*, KNM-WT 40000, derives from sediments of Lokochot age west of Lake Turkana (Leakey et al., 2001). At Koobi Fora, *Theropithecus brumpti* became the most abundant primate during this time. Stable carbon isotopes from dental enamel indicate that *Theropithecus* was a mixed feeder of C_3 and C_4 vegetation during this time (Figure 26.8; Cerling et al., 2013c). As with the Moiti Mb, the Lokochot pedogenic carbonates indicate a mixture of woodlands and wooded grasslands in the region (Figure 26.6). The Lokochot Mb correlates with Mb A of the Shungura Fm, where suids were the most abundant family of mammals (Bobe and Behrensmeyer, 2004). The higher abundance of suids in the Shungura Fm and monkeys in the Koobi Fora Fm may relate to differences in depositional environments between the Omo and East Turkana. Taphonomic factors remain to be fully analyzed.

Tulu Bor Member: 3.44–2.63 Ma

The Tulu Bor Mb spans from the base of the Tulu Bor Tuff to the base of the Burgi Tuff. At the type section in Areas 202 and 204, it measures 86.2 m in thickness (Brown and Feibel, 1986). This member is exposed in areas 13, 40, 116–117, 129–130, 133, 136–139, 202, 204–209, 212, 250, 260–261, and in the Loiyangalani Region. The Tulu Bor Tuff is a major marker bed for dating and correlations. It occurs from the Gulf of Aden in the north to the Lake Baringo basin in the south, and it is found in sedimentary sequences in the Afar (where it is called the Siki Hakoma Tuff), the lower Omo Valley (where it is called Tuff B), and the Turkana Basin (Figure 26.9; Brown, 1982; WoldeGabriel et al., 2013). This tuff provides an unparalleled opportunity for extensive faunal and sequence correlations across eastern Africa (Bobe et al., 2007b; Villaseñor, 2017).

By 3.4 Ma, the Lokochot Lake no longer existed, and the region was dominated by a large river that exited the basin through a southeast outlet toward the Indian Ocean (Bruhn et al., 2011). The Tulu Bor Floodplain characterized the paleogeography of the basin for about one million years (Feibel, 2011). Pedogenic carbonates indicate woodlands and wooded grasslands in the region (Levin et al., 2011), while dental enamel isotopes provide evidence of both woodland and grassland dietary resources for mammals (Cerling et al., 2013a). Important new paleontological collections from this time are currently under study by A. Villaseñor and colleagues, and these include new hominins as well as abundant fossil mammals. On the west side of the lake, the paratype of *Kenyanthropus platyops*, KNM-WT 38350, derives from strata equivalent to the lower Tulu Bor Mb (Leakey et al., 2001), and in temporal association with the earliest known archeological site at Lomekwi 3 (Harmand et al., 2015). Although rare, *Australopithecus afarensis* (KNM-ER 2602) has been identified in the Tulu Bor Mb (Kimbel, 1988). The most abundant species in the lower Tulu Bor Mb are *Notochoerus euilus*, *Theropithecus brumpti*, *Kobus oricornus*, *Tragelaphus rastafari*, and *Elephas recki*, in that order (Harris, 1983, 1991; Jablonski and Leakey, 2008). The upper part of the Tulu Bor Mb has a sparse fossil record, but it may hold one of the earliest specimens of the genus *Homo*, KNM-ER 5431 (Wood, 1991). The earliest record of *Paranthropus* also dates to this time, about 2.7 Ma, in Mb C of the Shungura Fm in the Omo (Suwa et al., 1996; Bobe and Carvalho, 2019).

Figure 26.9 The Tulu Bor Tuff, dated to 3.44 Ma, caps this sequence with Lokochot Member sediments below, in Area 117 of the Koobi Fora exposures. The Tulu Bor Tuff is a widespread volcanic ash layer, found from the Gulf of Aden in the north to the Tugen Hills in the south. It is a major marker in the correlation of sedimentary sequences in the Afar region, the lower Omo Valley, the Turkana Basin, and the Tugen Hills. In this view, it forms the white, erosion-resistant layer capping the ridge.

Burgi Member: 2.63–1.87 Ma

The Burgi Mb is defined by sediments from the base of the Burgi Tuff, dated at 2.6 Ma, to the base of the KBS Tuff, dated at 1.87 Ma (Brown and Feibel, 1986; McDougall and Brown, 2008). Burgi sediments occur in areas 10, 12–13, 40–41, 44, 48, 50, 100, 102, 104–105, 110, 114–118, 123, 125, 127, 129–131, 134, 136, 139, 200, 202–203, 207, 210, and in the Loiyangalani Region. A major unconformity – the Burgi Unconformity – separates the lower Burgi Mb (Feibel, 2011), with a sparse fossil record, from the upper Burgi Mb, which has a rich fossil record in its uppermost sediments. The type section of the lower Burgi in Area 207 measures 26.9 m in thickness, whereas the upper Burgi type section in Area 102 measures 120.1 m (Brown and Feibel, 1986). The longest lived of the late Cenozoic Turkana Basin lakes, the Lorenyang Lake, developed in the later stages of the Burgi Mb, and remained in place in varying configurations until about 1.5 Ma. The gigantic crocodile *Crocodylus thorbyarnarsoni* was abundant in the rivers and lake of this period: measuring over 6 m in length (larger than any living crocodile) it would have been a formidable predator of water-dependent hominins and other vertebrates (Brochu and Storrs, 2012). During much of this time, the basin continued to have a hydrological outlet to the Indian Ocean through the Turkana River, as attested by the presence of stingrays in the upper Burgi, KBS, and Okote Mbs (Feibel, 1994). Pedogenic stable isotopes (Quinn et al., 2007; Levin et al., 2011) and fossil wood (Braun et al., 2010; Bamford, 2011) indicate that during the upper Burgi times the vegetation in the region continued to be a mix of woodlands and wooded grasslands with an ample supply of fresh water.

By 2.3 Ma, species of *Homo* and *Paranthropus* appear to have been well-established in the Omo-Turkana Basin, with three or four hominin species co-occurring by 2 Ma (Bobe and Carvalho, 2019; Grine et al., 2019). Key hominin fossils from the upper Burgi Mb include the lectotype of *Homo rudolfensis*, KNM-ER 1470 (Figure 26.10A) and the KNM-ER 1813 cranium usually referred to *Homo habilis* (Figure 26.10B). The earliest records of *H. erectus* are from the upper Burgi with specimens KNM-ER 1481, 1812, 2598, and 3228. In the upper Burgi Mb, specimens of *Homo* are more abundant than those of *Paranthropus* (Table 26.2). The earliest well-documented archeological site at East Turkana is in the upper Burgi Mb and dates to 1.95 Ma (Braun et al., 2010), although there are earlier Oldowan sites both in the Omo Shungura Fm (Howell, 1987) and west of the lake in the Nachukui Fm (Roche et al., 1999). These sites prior to 2 Ma have low densities of artifacts and appear restricted to specific points in the landscape with an intersection of key ecological resources (Rogers et al., 1994).

Upper Burgi cercopithecids are represented by *Parapapio*, *Theropithecus*, *Rhinocolobus*, *Cercopithecoides*, and *Paracolobus*, with *Theropithecus* as the most abundant primate. Koobi Fora carnivorans reach a peak of species richness in the upper Burgi Mb, with at least 18 documented species (Table 26.2; Werdelin and Lewis, 2013b). Reduncini are the most abundant bovids, followed by Tragelaphini, Alcelaphini, Antilopini, and Aepycerotini, in order of diminishing abundance. Among suids, the genus *Kolpochoerus* is most abundant, followed by *Notochoerus* and *Metridiochoerus*. The earliest record of *Equus* in Africa is in Shungura Mb G, at about 2.3 Ma (Eisenmann, 1976b), and by upper Burgi times, around 2 Ma, *Equus* is about twice as abundant as *Eurygnathohippus*. The megaherbivore fauna is dominated by *Elephas recki* and hippopotamids.

KBS Member: 1.87–1.56 Ma

KBS Mb sediments span from the base of the KBS Tuff, dated to 1.87 Ma, to the base of the Okote Tuff, dated to 1.56 Ma. This member outcrops in areas 1–1A, 6, 8–8A, 9–13, 16, 41, 44, 48,

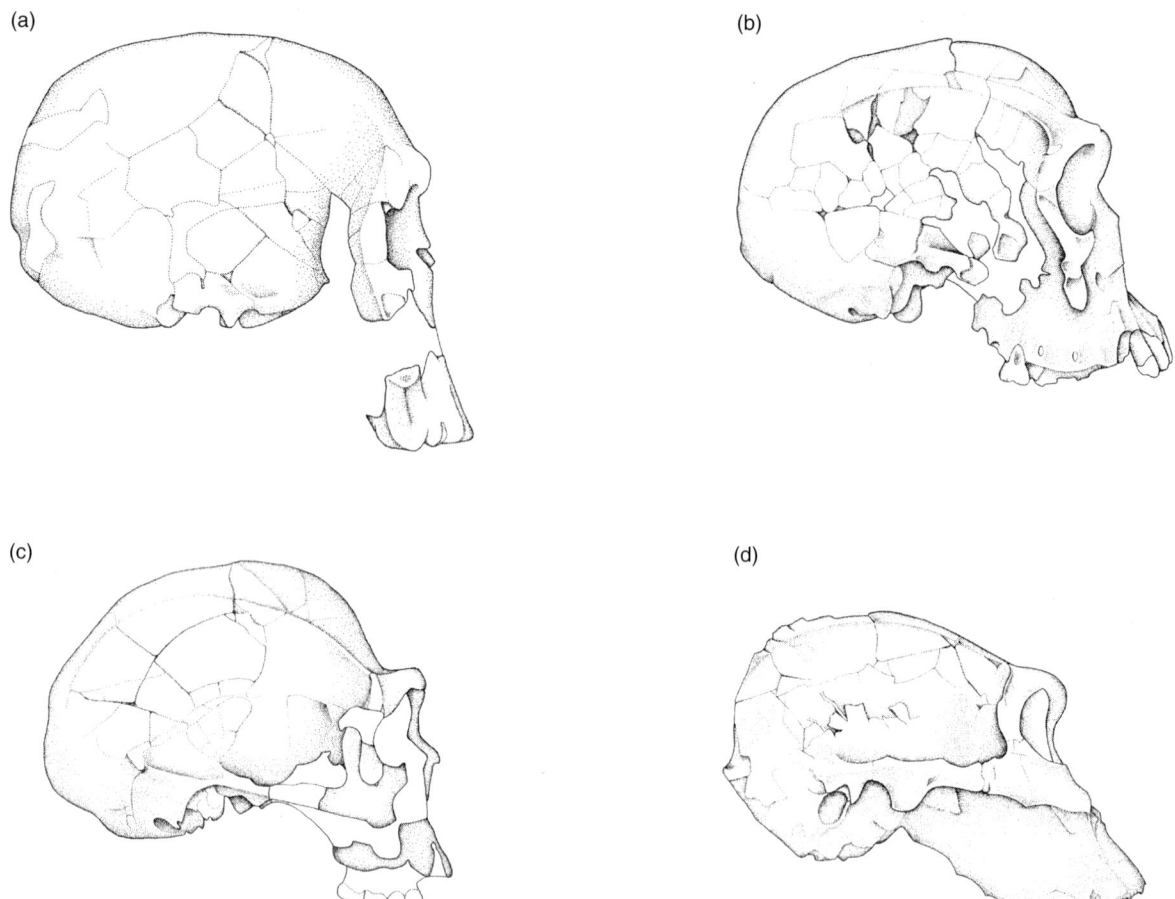

Figure 26.10 Illustration of hominin species co-occurring in the upper Burgi and KBS members of the Koobi Fora Formation. Lateral views of (A) *Homo rudolfensis* specimen KNM-ER 1470, (B) *Homo habilis* specimen KNM-ER 1813, (C) *Homo erectus* specimen KNM-ER 3733, (D) *Paranthropus boisei* specimen KNM-ER 406. Artwork by Vanessa Cannon.

50, 101–112, 114–115, 117–134, 200, and in the Loiyangalani Region. During this time the Lorenyang Lake dominated the basin. Stable carbon isotopes from pedogenic carbonates in the KBS Mb are more enriched than in the upper Burgi Mb, indicating a modest but significant shift toward greater expansion of C_4 vegetation in the region (Patterson et al., 2019). Nevertheless, throughout the interval encompassed by the upper Burgi, KBS, and Okote Mbs there was environmental heterogeneity in the East Turkana region (Behrensmeyer, 1985; Quinn et al., 2007; Patterson et al., 2017a). KBS is the only member in the Koobi Fora Fm with a substantial sample of micromammals, and these indicate relatively arid environments with some riverine forests and arid scrub (Black and Krishtalka, 1986). The basin retained a mix of woodlands, wooded grasslands, and extensive mesic grasslands, as attested by the isotopic signatures and the overall composition of the fauna. The KBS Mb has the highest abundance of fossil vertebrates in the Koobi Fora Fm (Figure 26.4). The well-known hominin specimens KNM-ER 3733 (*Homo erectus*) and KNM-ER 406 (*Paranthropus boisei*) derive from this member (Figure 26.10C,D). The last appearance record of *H. rudolfensis* is in the KBS. Unlike in the upper Burgi Mb, in the KBS Mb specimens of *Paranthropus* are more abundant than specimens of *Homo* (Table 26.2). Within the genus *Homo*, there is a shift in isotopic signature indicating significantly greater consumption of C_4 resources beginning about 1.65 Ma, in the upper part of the KBS Mb (Patterson et al., 2019). Archeological sites at Koobi Fora become more common than in previous members (Figure 26.11; Bunn, 1997; Braun and Harris, 2009), and the earliest record of Acheulean technology is documented on the west side of the lake at Kokiselei locality KS4, dated to 1.76 Ma (Lepre et al., 2011). Monkeys are represented by *Cercopithecus*, *Lophocebus*, *Parapapio*, *Theropithecus*, *Colobus*, *Rhinocolobus*, and *Cercopithecoides*, with *Theropithecus* far outnumbering other primate genera. Among carnivorans, species richness is lower than in the upper Burgi Mb both in absolute terms (16 vs. 18 species) and relative to sample size (Werdelin and Lewis, 2013b). The most abundant bovid tribes are Reduncini, Alcelaphini, Tragelaphini, Antilopini, and Aepycerotini, in that order. Among suids, *Metridiochoerus* became more abundant than *Kolpochoerus*, and *Notochoerus* became rare (Patterson et al., 2017b). The most common suid species was *Metridiochoerus andrewsi*. Among equids, specimens of *Equus* are three times more abundant than those of *Eurygnathohippus*. The megaherbivore fauna was dominated by hippopotamids, *Elephas*, *Giraffa*, *Sivatherium*, and *Ceratotherium*.

Okote Member: 1.56–1.38 Ma

The Okote Mb is defined as those sediments from the base of the Okote Tuff to the base of the Chari Tuff, dating from 1.56 Ma to 1.38 Ma (Brown and Feibel, 1986). The type section in Area 131

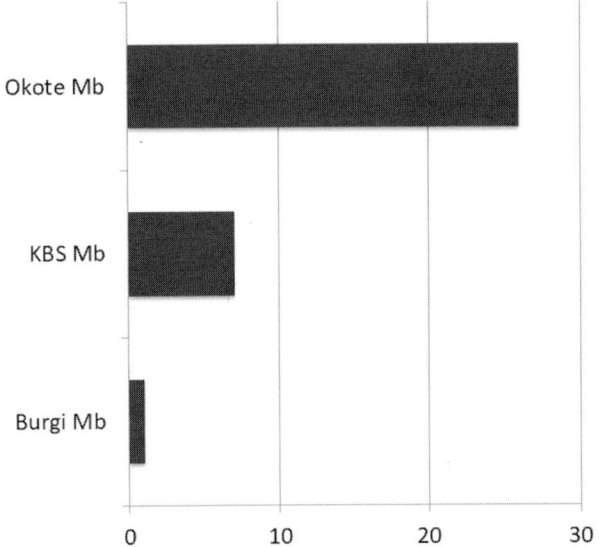

Figure 26.11 Number of archeological sites per member of the Koobi Fora Formation. Data from Isaac (1997) and Braun et al. (2009).

measures 21.6 m, and Okote exposures occur in areas 1–4, 6–6A, 7A, 8–11, 16, 44, 46, 101, 103–105, 112, 118–119, 128–134, and 200. The Okote sediments include very complex fluvial deposits, with brief lacustrine intervals constrained to only parts of the basin (Behrensmeyer and Isaac, 1997). The time interval around the Okote Mb has the highest number of tephra in the Omo-Turkana Basin from 4 Ma to 1 Ma (Figure 26.5). It is likely that frequent volcanism added to the environmental heterogeneity of the basin during this time (Feibel, 1999b; Bobe and Carvalho, 2019). Stable carbon isotopes indicate heterogeneous vegetation dominated by wooded grasslands (Figure 26.6). The paleobotanical record of the Okote Mb includes over 100 specimens of silicified wood from the site FwJj14 in Area 1A. This site is of particular importance because of the well-preserved hominin trackways attributed to *Homo erectus* (Bennett et al., 2009), as well as a newly described upper limb skeleton attributed to *Paranthropus boisei* (Lague et al., 2019b; Richmond et al., 2020). The vessel structure and configuration of the fossil wood specimens from this site indicate large to medium trees from mesic, megathermal environments with no water stress (Bamford, 2017). The most common genus identified from the fossil wood is *Drypetes*, indicative of dense, semideciduous forests. Other taxa indicate gallery forest, Miombo and wooded grasslands, and mangroves. Several of the wood specimens identified derive from genera that are not found in Kenya today but occur in Central and West Africa (Bamford, 2017).

In the Okote Mb, specimens of *Homo* are slightly more abundant than those of *Paranthropus*. The last appearance of *Homo habilis* is documented in the Okote Mb (Spoor et al., 2007), as *Homo erectus* becomes the increasingly dominant species within the genus. At the site FxJj 14E in Area 1A there is a series of hominin trackways produced by at least 20 individuals tentatively attributed to *Homo erectus* (Bennett et al., 2009; Hatala et al., 2016, 2017). These hominin tracks are comparable in morphology, and similar in age, to those found in the 1970s at the site GaJi 10 in Area 103 (Behrensmeyer and Laporte, 1981), about 45 km to the south of FxJj 14E. The site FxJj 14E also produced the newly described partial upper limb skeleton of *Paranthropus boisei*, KNM-ER 47000 (Richmond et al., 2020), which indicates that this species spent at least some time in the trees (Green et al., 2016; Lague et al., 2019a, 2019b).

The abundance of archeological sites is significantly greater than in any of the earlier members (Figure 26.11). Archeological sites are also more widely distributed in relation to paleogeographic and environmental settings (Rogers et al., 1994), with most sites having abundant lithic materials and a few including fossil bones (Harris and Isaac, 1976; Isaac, 1978a; Isaac and Harris, 1978; Harris and Isaac, 1997; Stern et al., 2002; Braun et al., 2008; Merritt, 2017; Presnyakova et al., 2018). It is noteworthy that the fauna from archeological sites has a higher proportion of Alcelaphini than in the general landscape, suggesting that hominins may have had a preference for hunting or scavenging bovid remains in relatively open environments (Patterson et al., 2017b). Okote sediments also contain the earliest evidence of possible hominin control of fire at the FxJj 20 site complex in the Karari Ridge (Hlubik et al., 2017, 2019).

The sample of Okote cercopithecids includes the genera *Cercopithecus*, *Cercocebus*, *Lophocebus*, *Parapapio*, *Theropithecus*, and *Colobus*. The dominant primate was *Theropithecus oswaldi*, a C_4 grazer (Figure 26.8; Cerling et al., 2013b), but other common monkeys, e.g., *Lophocebus* cf. *albigena* and *Colobus freedmani*, are consistent with the arboreal vegetation inferred from the fossil wood specimens (Bamford, 2017). *Parapapio* was still present during Okote times but in very small numbers. It is noteworthy that the large colobines that were present in earlier members (*Rhinocolobus*, *Paracolobus*, *Cercopithecoides*) all appear to have gone extinct by the time of the Okote Mb. Carnivoran species richness is lower in the Okote Mb than in the Burgi or KBS Mbs, both in absolute terms and relative to sample size (Werdelin and Lewis, 2013b). The broad decline in the functional and taxonomic diversity of African carnivorans was well underway by the time of the Okote Mb, e.g., the last occurrence of *Homotherium* (Werdelin and Lewis, 2013a), but the abundance of *Crocuta* increased relative to earlier members. The bovid fauna is dominated in abundance by Reduncini, followed by Alcelaphini, Tragelaphini, and Bovini, in that order. Among suids, the most abundant species is *Metridiochoerus compactus*, followed by *Kolpochoerus limnetes*. Among equids, the genus *Equus* is five times more abundant than *Eurygnathohippus*. Thus, from the upper Burgi to the Okote Mb, *Equus* became increasingly more abundant in relation to *Eurygnathohippus*. The megaherbivore fauna is dominated by *Hippopotamus*, *Elephas*, and *Giraffa*. The megaherbivore fauna is less diverse in the Okote than in earlier members.

Chari Member: 1.38–0.7 Ma

The base of the Chari Mb is defined by the base of the Chari Tuff, dated to 1.38 Ma, and the top is estimated to be 0.7 Ma. The

Chari Mb is 42.7 m thick at the type section (Brown and Feibel, 1986). Exposures of this member occur in areas 1, 2–7, 7A, 16, 44, 46, 112, 128, 130–131, 133–134, and 138. Most of the deposition of the Koobi Fora Fm during this time took place in the northern areas. The Chari Tuff was deposited in a fluvial context that marked the onset of Chari Floodplain, dominated by a large meandering river and episodic lacustrine intervals (Feibel et al., 1991). The Chari Tuff is the result of a massive volcanic event, as it is found throughout the Turkana Basin (= Tuff L in the Shungura Fm) and as far north as the Gulf of Aden. Other major markers within the Chari Mb include the Gele Tuff (1.25 Ma), the Silbo Tuff (0.75 Ma), and the Matuyama/Bruhnes Chron boundary (0.78 Ma). The lower part of the Chari Mb correlates with Mb L of the Shungura Fm, and with the upper Natoo/lower Nariokotome Mbs of the Nachukui Fm. Sedimentation of the Koobi Fora Fm, and the Omo Group, ended by about 0.7 Ma (Feibel et al., 1989, 1991). Although fossil mammals are sparse in the Chari Mb, there are sand sequences that contain abundant fossil fish, ostracods, and bivalves. In the Omo, the Shungura Mb L mammalian fauna is dominated by hippopotamids, Reduncini, and to a lesser extent by Alcelaphini, indicating extensive grasslands in the vicinity of a major river in the Chari Floodplain. It is most likely that *Paranthropus* went extinct during the time of the Chari Mb, but better samples are needed to establish the timing of this extinction event.

Patterns of Faunal Associations

The best sampled and most continuous part of the Koobi Fora Fm is from the upper Burgi Mb to the Okote Mb, i.e., from about 2 Ma to 1.4 Ma. The fossil record of the upper Burgi, KBS, and Okote Mbs has been more thoroughly studied and published, and here we present new analyses of faunal associations based on these upper members. Ever since the first coefficient of association between species was devised by pioneer ecologist Stephen Alfred Forbes (Forbes, 1907), numerous quantitative metrics have been defined, aiming at clarifying how species combine themselves into larger communities (Dice, 1945). We use a version of Table 26.2 that includes only genera across the upper Burgi, KBS, and Okote Mbs to detect patterns of association in relation to taxonomic abundance data. All extremely rare genera ($N \leq 10$) were excluded from the following analysis. To reveal faunal patterns, we employed APRIORI (Agrawal et al., 1993), an *if A then B* algorithm for mining association rules, typically used to analyze transaction data for retail markets and online e-commerce stores (Hahsler, 2017; Hahsler and Karpienko, 2017). Instead of looking at transactions per se, we transformed our count data (a proxy for the abundance of taxa) of genera across geological members into "association" data. The data transformation involved three steps: first the data set was double-standardized per *max* value of each column (member) and per the *sum* of each row (genus; Legendre and Gallagher, 2001); second, a Euclidean distance matrix D_{mn} was calculated; and third, a matrix X_{ij}, where each value ij is a binarized logical solution for $D_{mn} < \overline{D}_n$. This Boolean matrix X_{ij} can then be fed into the APRIORI algorithm to understand associations *if i then j* between any paleotaxa *i* and *j*. Then, the associations calculated were analyzed, scored and ranked by the following thresholds:

$$\text{Support} = \frac{\text{\# of Associations between A and B}}{\text{Total \# of Associations}} = P(A \cap B)$$

(eq. 1)

$$\text{Confidence} = \frac{\text{\# of Associations between A and B}}{\text{Total \# of Associations with A}} = \frac{P(A \cap B)}{P(A)}$$

(eq. 2)

$$\text{Lift} = \frac{\text{Confidence}}{\text{Expected Confidence}} = \frac{P(A \cap B)}{P(A) \times P(B)}$$

(eq. 3)

Here we introduce FARUBO, a flexible web application for rule-based learning and visualization of paleofaunal associations, available through the "osteomics" web platform. FARUBO (http://osteomics.com/FARUBO) was fully developed in R using shiny, arules and arulesViz packages (Hahsler et al., 2005, 2011; Hahsler, 2017; R Core Team, 2019). FARUBO is designed with a side panel for interactive functionalities and a main panel with three menu tabs: "Data Exploration," "Paleofaunal Network," and "Clustered Rules." The side panel allows users to control interactively all parameters as minimum thresholds (eqs. 1–3). The fourth parameter of the side panel, "Rules length," allows one to define the number of taxa in the left-hand side (LHS) of the if–then rule, while the last parameters are all related to filtering taxa for the analyses. Regarding the main panel, the first tab "Data Exploration" is the landpage; it summarizes all rules being generated in real-time by the web application and it allows users to download them anytime as a .csv table. In the "Paleofaunal Network" tab, interactive networks of associations can be visualized; in the default display, circle size increases with support and circle shading saturates (to red) with confidence, while the rules' number decreases with lift. If hundreds or thousands of rules are being generated the graph visualization gets too convoluted, and therefore users can alternatively use the "Clustered Rules" tab to see a summarized visualization of the rules. The current version of the webapp loads with the hominins as required RHS (right-hand side) taxa, but this is also an option that can be manipulated in the side panel. *Homo* associations tend to rank higher than *Paranthropus* in terms of Support and Confidence, but lower in terms of Lift. This is due to *Paranthropus* being comparatively underrepresented in the upper Burgi Mb, which leads to lower expected confidence.

For the results presented here, we defined the same minimum thresholds of support = 0.4, confidence = 0.6, and lift = 1, as in the web application defaults, resulting in 23 association rules. The top 10 identified rules (Figure 26.12) show the major importance and representativeness of *Theropithecus* (9/10 rules) overall for hominin assemblages, with *Metridiochoerus* following closely (but more relevant toward *Paranthropus*). Indeed, the best rule in terms of lift (1.938) was (*Metridiochoerus, Theropithecus*) ⇒ (*Paranthropus*)

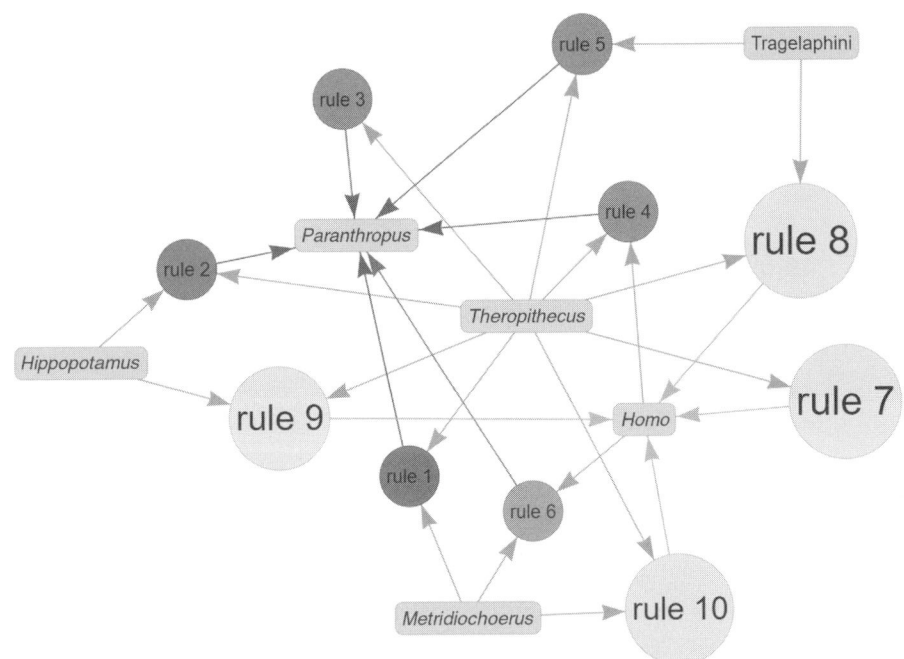

Figure 26.12 Faunal associations in the Koobi Fora Formation upper Burgi, KBS, and Okote members with abundance data at the genus level. Extended Hominin graph model showing the top 10 rules (by lift). Parameters: minimum support = 0.4; minimum confidence = 0.6; minimum lift = 1; maximum length = 3; RHS = c("*Paranthropus*," "*Homo*"); maximum rules displayed = 10.

with 81.3 percent confidence, while the top five rules for *Homo* all contained *Theropithecus* in the LHS. From this, their combined potential as paleontological predictors for hominins in the region can be inferred. Both *Theropithecus* and *Metridiochoerus* are more abundant than hominins, and thus are easier to detect during paleontological surveys.

The fossil record indicates that *Theropithecus* was a successful primate lineage, comparable to some early hominins in terms of geographic range and terrestriality (Elton, 2006). At the site of Olorgesailie in Kenya, there is direct evidence of coexistence and interactions between *Theropithecus* and Pleistocene hominins from cut-marked bones of *T. oswaldi* (Shipman et al., 1981). Additionally, *Theropithecus* has been central as a comparative model for hominin locomotor evolution (Jolly, 1970; Wrangham, 1980; Kingdon, 2003) and behavioral adaptations (e.g., diet) to changing habitats and climate (Dunbar, 1983; Foley, 1993). As for *Metridiochoerus* and its stronger association to *Paranthropus*, we tentatively attribute this to overlapping habitat preferences, and to possibly similar strategies of resource exploitation. It is known that in eastern Africa grasses were an important component of both of their diets, and *Metridiochoerus* species (advanced forms of the genus) have been interpreted as indicators among suids of seasonal grassland habitats (Bobe and Behrensmeyer, 2004). However, taphonomic factors likely play a role: *Paranthropus* and *Metridiochoerus* teeth are both abundant in the fluvial deposits of the KBS Mb, where their durable teeth may survive better during fluvial transport.

Also important are the hominin associations to *Hippopotamus* and *Tragelaphus* most likely demonstrating the importance of close sources of fresh water and trees in the life history of hominins. Furthermore, if we look at the lower-ranking rules, we see that *Crocuta* is also associated with *Homo* in multiple rules (but with lower support values), and other bovid tribes such as Reduncini and to a lesser extent Bovini also show some degree of association to the hominins (not depicted), which further illustrates the complexities of the environmental context.

It is also possible to look exclusively at paired associations, that is, associations that do not need combined taxa to be detected. As an example, if one is only interested in pair relationships related to hominins, the maximum value of the "Rules length" parameter should be kept at 2 in FARUBO, and "*Homo*" and "*Paranthropus*" have to be selected in "Require taxa in RHS." Considering only pair relationships, the association of *Crocuta* with *Homo* becomes more evident (lift = 1.192; Figure 26.13), and this might indicate commonalities in the way both taxa exploited resources, as the *Homo* lineage is thought to have increasingly adopted meat and marrow into its diet by opportunistic scavenging and eventually by hunting (Moleón et al., 2014). Further relaxing the minimum support value in FARUBO will allow users to detect a few more interesting pair associations with *Homo* that might also indicate some ecological overlaps, notably *Dinofelis* and *Parapapio* at 29 percent support and *Panthera* (25.8 percent).

The evolutionary and ecological significance of these associations needs further work to assess the role of collection biases and taphonomic factors such as the durability of teeth and mandibles in different depositional contexts (Behrensmeyer, 1975, 1978b, 1985). Thus, these associations are best considered as tentative hypotheses to be tested with further taphonomic analyses.

Summary and Conclusions

In this chapter we have focused on the fauna and paleoenvironments of the Koobi Fora Fm (Formation) from about 4.3 Ma to about 1 Ma. It is important to keep in mind that Koobi Fora

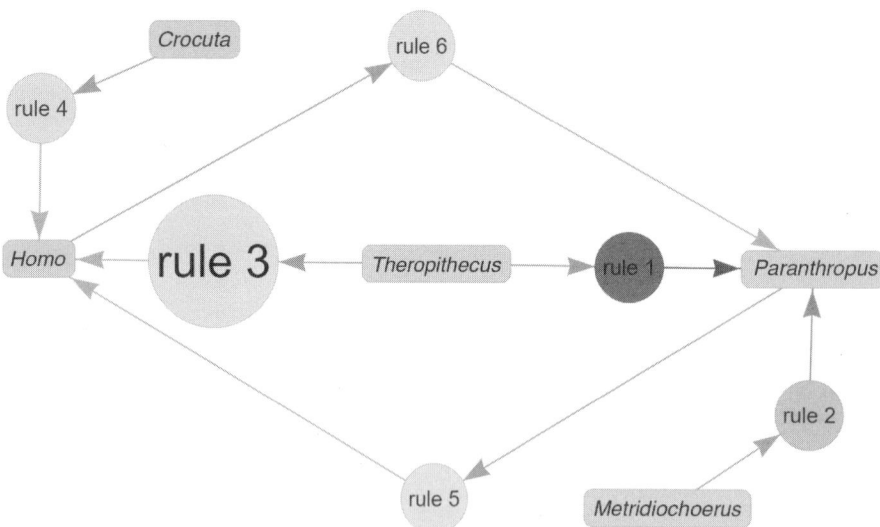

Figure 26.13 Faunal associations in the Koobi Fora Formation upper Burgi, KBS, and Okote members with abundance data at the genus level. Main taxa associated with *Homo* and *Paranthropus*, with a central role of *Theropithecus*, and with *Crocuta* and *Metridiochoerus* as the respective satellite associations in this reduced graph model. Parameters: minimum support = 0.4; minimum confidence = 0.5; minimum lift = 1; maximum length = 2; RHS = c("Paranthropus," "Homo").

was part of the larger ecosystem of the Omo-Turkana Basin (Figure 26.1), and that an ecosystem perspective is the best way to understand the evolution of hominins and their landscapes as documented in the Omo Group deposits (Figure 26.2) (Feibel, 1999a). The East Turkana region is central to our understanding of hominin evolution during the Pliocene and early Pleistocene, and here we provide a new map drafted by Frank Brown of the Koobi Fora Fm Paleontological Collection Areas (Figure 26.3). During the time documented by the Koobi Fora Fm hominins underwent profound changes in anatomy, behavior, and diversity. The vegetation and paleogeography of the region also changed significantly during this time (Feibel et al., 1991), as did ecological relationships among species.

The earliest intervals of the Koobi Fora Fm, between 4.3 and 3.6 Ma, have small samples of fossils, except for Locality 261-1 in Allia Bay (Figure 26.4). However, fossils from the Kanapoi and Nachukui Fms provide a rich picture of hominins and their environments during the early Pliocene of the Omo-Turkana Basin. The earliest record of *Australopithecus anamensis* is from Kanapoi at 4.2 Ma (Ward et al., 2020), and important collections of this species also derive from Allia Bay Locality 261-1 dated to 3.97 Ma (Leakey et al., 1995). The species *A. anamensis* is also found at the site of Asa Issie in the Afar region of Ethiopia (White et al., 2006), indicating that the geographic range of this species extended at least from the southern Turkana Basin to the middle Awash River in the Afar. It is noteworthy that the earliest records of both *Australopithecus* and *Theropithecus* occur at the same time and in the same place, Kanapoi at 4.2 Ma (Frost et al., 2020; Ward et al., 2020), establishing a long-lasting association between hominins and *Theropithecus* what would persist for millions of years. Both genera were also present at Allia Bay preserved within basal deposits of a massive volcanic eruption, the Moiti Tuff (Figure 26.5). It was only in these early intervals that *Parapapio* was more abundant than *Theropithecus* among the primates. In later periods, *Theropithecus* far outnumbered *Parapapio* and other primates. At Kanapoi, *Australopithecus* inhabited an ecosystem dominated by megaherbivores, with 10 species of mammals weighing 1000 kg or more (Bobe et al., 2020a). These megaherbivores included five species of proboscideans (Sanders, 2020), which undoubtedly had a profound impact on the local ecology, e.g., clearing paths for terrestrial animals, dispersing seeds, providing food for hunting and scavenging carnivores. These were proboscidean-dominated landscapes. The basin at this time was dominated by woodlands, although grasslands were an important element of the ecosystem (Figure 26.6). Hominins were feeding mostly on C_3 resources (Figure 26.7) even though C_4 resources were clearly available in the landscape. Fresh water in rivers, streams, and lakes was a persistent feature of the ecosystem.

By 3.4 Ma, hominins had diversified into at least two species, with evidence of *Australopithecus afarensis* and *Kenyanthropus platyops* in the basin (Kimbel and Delezene, 2009; Spoor et al., 2010). The vegetation in the basin remained a mosaic of woodlands and grasslands but with a greater proportion of grasslands than before (Figure 26.6). By this time hominins had shifted from a largely C_3 diet to a mixed diet of C_3 and C_4 resources (Cerling et al., 2013a; Figure 26.7). The reasons for this shift in hominin diets remain to be fully explored, because C_4 resources were clearly present and available to early *Australopithecus* at Kanapoi and Allia Bay, but apparently not exploited. The earliest archeological site, with lithic artifacts that emphasize percussive activities, dates to 3.3 Ma (Harmand et al., 2015), and signals the deep roots of hominin use of technology.

After 3 Ma there is evidence of further hominin diversification, with the earliest records of *Homo* and *Paranthropus*. Earliest *Homo* derives from the Afar site of Ledi-Geraru (~2.8 Ma) and from the upper Tulu Bor Mb at East Turkana (~2.7 Ma; Villmoare et al., 2015), while the earliest record of *Paranthropus* is from Shungura Mb C (~2.7 Ma; Bobe and Carvalho, 2019). In the Shungura Fm there is evidence of important faunal changes at about 2.9–2.8 Ma (Bobe and Eck, 2001; Bobe et al., 2007b; Bibi et al., 2013), but the overall composition of the vegetation in the basin seems to have remained relatively stable (Figure 26.6). *Homo* and *Paranthropus* coexisted in the Omo-Turkana Basin for about 1.5 million years (Bobe and Carvalho, 2019). Further faunal changes are documented in the Omo during the interval from 2.5 to 2.3 Ma, with an increase in the abundance and diversity of grazing bovids (Bobe and Eck, 2001) and frequent deposition of volcanic ash (Figure 26.5).

The richest and most continuous record of fossil vertebrates in the Koobi Fora Fm comes from the upper Burgi, KBS, and Okote Mbs, from about 2 Ma to 1.4 Ma (Figure 26.4). Beginning at about 2 Ma there were major paleogeographic and environmental changes in the basin, with more extensive wooded grasslands, although gallery forests likely played a key ecological role as relatively stable habitats associated with river corridors (Figure 26.6). The center of the basin was dominated by the Lorenyang Lake, the longest-lived of the paleo-lakes documented in the Omo Group deposits (Figure 26.2; Feibel, 2011). Relative to earlier hominins, *Homo* and especially *Paranthropus* consumed greater proportions of C_4 resources after 2 Ma (Figure 26.7). *Theropithecus* shifted from a mixed diet to a C_4-dominated diet during this time (Figure 26.8). After 2 Ma, hominins had diversified into three or four species (depending on taxonomic attributions): *Homo habilis*, *H. rudolfensis*, *H. erectus*, and *Paranthropus boisei* (Figure 26.10). Thus, there may have been four hominin species coexisting in the highly variable and dynamic environments of the Omo-Turkana Basin (Bobe and Carvalho, 2019).

The abundance and distribution of archeological sites changed dramatically from a few Oldowan sites before 1.9 Ma (Braun et al., 2010) to a large number of sites with thousands of artifacts and bones across multiple landscapes by 1.5 Ma (Figure 26.11; Isaac and Harris, 1978; Rogers et al., 1994; Presnyakova et al., 2018). The earliest Acheulean technologies appeared by 1.76 Ma at Kokoselei 4 on the west side of Lake Turkana (Lepre et al., 2011), and possibly the earliest indications of hominins using fire appear at 1.5 Ma at the FxJj 20 site complex (Hlubik et al., 2017, 2019). Analyses of the fauna from archeological sites indicate that hominins accessed alcelaphin bovids in higher proportion than their overall representation in the paleo-communities (Patterson et al., 2017b). This happened as *Homo* underwent a significant shift toward greater reliance on C_4 resources (Patterson et al., 2019) and *H. erectus* was becoming the dominant species of the genus. It is likely that hominins accessed animal resources in grassland habitats at this time.

In our analyses of Koobi Fora faunal associations between 2 Ma and 1.4 Ma, some significant patterns emerged. We found *Theropithecus* to be a key taxon in predicting the occurrence of both *Homo* and *Paranthropus* (Figure 26.12 and Figure 26.13). The combined association of *Theropithecus* and the suid *Metridiochoerus* proved to be a particularly strong predictor of *Paranthropus*, while *Tragelaphus* and *Crocuta* also associated with *Homo*. It is noteworthy that some of these associations were also found for earlier periods in the Omo Shugura Fm. At around 2.3 Ma (a time "missing" from the Koobi Fora Fm because of the Burgi Unconformity), *Theropithecus* was significantly associated with *Paranthropus*, while *Parapapio* and *Tragelaphus* were significantly associated with *Homo* (Bobe and Behrensmeyer, 2004). These associations provide an indication of the ecological communities in which these hominins lived during the early Pleistocene, with monkeys like *Theropithecus* and *Parapapio* likely sharing the hominin landscapes. We can speculate that the association of *Homo* with *Crocuta* may indicate a shared interest in animal carcasses, but further work is needed to test these ideas.

In sum, the Koobi Fora Fm preserves a record of hominin evolution spanning nearly 3 million years, from the earliest species of *Australopithecus* prior to 4 Ma to a time of high hominin diversity between 2 Ma and 1.4 Ma with *Homo habilis*, *Homo rudolfensis*, *Homo erectus*, and *Paranthropus boisei* occupying the Omo-Turkana ecosystem. This time also saw the rise of *Theropithecus* from a rare taxon around 4 Ma to the most common primate in the landscape by 1.5 Ma, as well as a decline in the diversity of carnivorans and megaherbivores. During the time span from *Australopithecus anamensis* to *Homo erectus* the environments in the Omo-Turkana Basin shifted from extensive woodlands and wooded grasslands to diverse and dynamic habitats that included a greater proportion of grasslands. The archeological record underwent a dramatic transformation from a few Oldowan sites before 1.9 Ma to numerous Developed Oldowan and Acheulean sites at about 1.5 Ma, a transformation associated with the increasingly prevalent species *Homo erectus*.

Acknowledgments

This work is dedicated to the memory of Frank Brown (1943–2017), a generous colleague who spent his lifetime dedicated to studying the geology, paleontology, vegetation, and cultures of northern Kenya and southern Ethiopia. Frank drafted the map presented here as Figure 26.3, and wrote the notes accompanying the map of paleontological collection areas (Appendix). Richard Leakey passed away as this chapter went to press. We are immensely grateful for his enormous contribution to the development of vertebrate paleontology and paleoanthropology in the Lake Turkana region, and for the support and encouragement that he provided to so many colleagues and students of human evolution in Africa. We are very thankful to David Patterson, Sally Reynolds, and Anna K. Behrensmeyer for thoughtful comments and corrections that greatly improved this chapter.

27. Early Pliocene Faunal Assemblages from the Tugen Hills, Kenya: A Comparison of Field Collection Methods and Some Implications for Paleoenvironmental Reconstruction

Katie M. Binetti, Andrew Hill†, and Joseph V. Ferraro

Geological Context of the Tugen Hills Fossil Sites

The Tugen Hills range in Central Kenya is a 75 km north–south-oriented horst block tilted to the west (Chapman, 1971; Chapman et al., 1978; Hill et al., 1986; Williams and Chapman, 1986). The range is situated to the west of Lake Baringo and forms the eastern margin of the Kerio Valley (Figure 27.1).

The Tugen Hills (previously known as the Kamasia Range) were first recognized as volcaniclastic in origin during Gregory's (1921) investigations of the Kenya Rift Valley. The sedimentary and volcanic rocks of the Tugen Hills are characterized by *en echelon* fault scarps stepped eastward into the Lake Baringo catchment (Chapman et al., 1978). The eastern foothills of the range expose approximately 3000 m of lava and sediment that comprise the six major formations of the Tugen Hills succession (Bishop et al., 1971; Hill, 1999). The complex rift–fault history of the succession has resulted in geological units that are progressively younger from the top of the Tugen Hills range down toward Lake Baringo. From oldest to youngest the main geological units are the: Muruyur Formation (16–13 Ma), Ngorora Formation (13–8.5 Ma), Mpesida Beds (7–6.2 Ma), Lukeino Formation (6.2–5.6 Ma), Chemeron Formation (5.6–1.6 Ma), and Kapthurin Formation (700 to <200 ka; Chapman and Brook, 1978; Hill, 2002). The succession is fossiliferous throughout with a number of fossil-bearing localities known in each time interval (Hill, 1999, 2002). Fossils of paleoanthropological significance occur in each major formation and include a number of primate taxa, several of which are type specimens or unique fossil occurrences, including the types of *Equatorius africanus*, *Paracolobus chemeroni*, *Theropithecus baringensis*, *Simiolus minutus*, and the only known fossil occurrence of *Pan troglodytes* (Hill and Ward, 1988; Hill, 1999; McBrearty and Jablonski, 2005; Gilbert et al., 2010; Rossie and Hill, 2018). The particular focus of this chapter are two early Pliocene fossil-bearing sites from the basal Chemeron Formation, Tabarin and Sagatia, which are associated with the early hominin species *Ardipithecus ramidus*.

The Chemeron Formation (5.6–1.6 Ma) is conformably underlain by the Kaparaina Basalts, which serve as an important stratigraphic marker within the greater Tugen Hills sequence (Martyn, 1967; Chapman et al., 1978). The sites of Tabarin and Sagatia were first discovered and investigated by the Baringo Paleontological Research Project (BPRP) in 1984 (Hill, 1985; Hill et al., 1986). They are part of the northern extension sediments of the lower Chemeron, which are characterized by lake-margin to fully lacustrine facies moving westward away from the main Tugen Hills scarp (Pickford et al., 1983; Hill, 1985; Hill et al., 1985, 1986). Pickford et al. (1983) suggest that the sedimentology of the northern extension indicates the persistence of a lake throughout the early Pliocene. Lithologically, the BPRP northern extension sites comprise sandstones and mudstones intercalated with low-energy conglomerates and tuffs (Hill, 1985; Deino et al., 2002). This lithology is generally consistent with the gradual transgression Pickford et al. (1983) posit for the early Pliocene Tugen Hills.

The chronostratigraphy at Tabarin was refined in 2002 (Deino et al., 2002) and the *Ar. ramidus* mandible has an $^{40}Ar/^{39}Ar$ date of 4.42 Ma. While Sagatia has not been dated radiometrically, it is considered contemporaneous with Tabarin on the basis of its biostratigraphically constrained early Pliocene fauna (Hill, 1985). Preliminary paleomagnetic polarity studies of Sagatia are also consistent with this interpretation (D. Peppe, in preparation) and radiometric dates are pending. Following Hill (1985) the faunal assemblage from Sagatia is considered coeval with that from Tabarin and is regarded as a stratigraphic equivalent with respect to paleoenvironmental interpretation(s) (Binetti, 2011).

Tabarin

Tabarin (BPRP site #77) is located approximately 20 km northwest of Lake Baringo (Figure 27.1). The exposures at Tabarin are situated in a series of fossiliferous gullies that together comprise approximately 100 m of largely conformable fine- to medium-grained sediments periodically interspersed with dateable tuffaceous layers (Deino et al., 2002). The BPRP initiated research at Tabarin in 1984 and shortly thereafter a fragmentary hominin left mandibular corpus preserving the M_1 and M_2 was recovered (Hill, 1985). The Tabarin mandible (KNM-TH 13150) was found in association with abundant faunal remains.

The Tabarin mandible was immediately recognized as hominin; however, its species attribution was uncertain (Hill, 1985). With the 1993 discovery of *Ar. ramidus* at Aramis, Ethiopia paleoanthropological interest in the Tabarin mandible was revived. Specifically, KNM-TH 13150 and *Ar. ramidus* share small, thin-enameled, narrow molars garnering the Tabarin

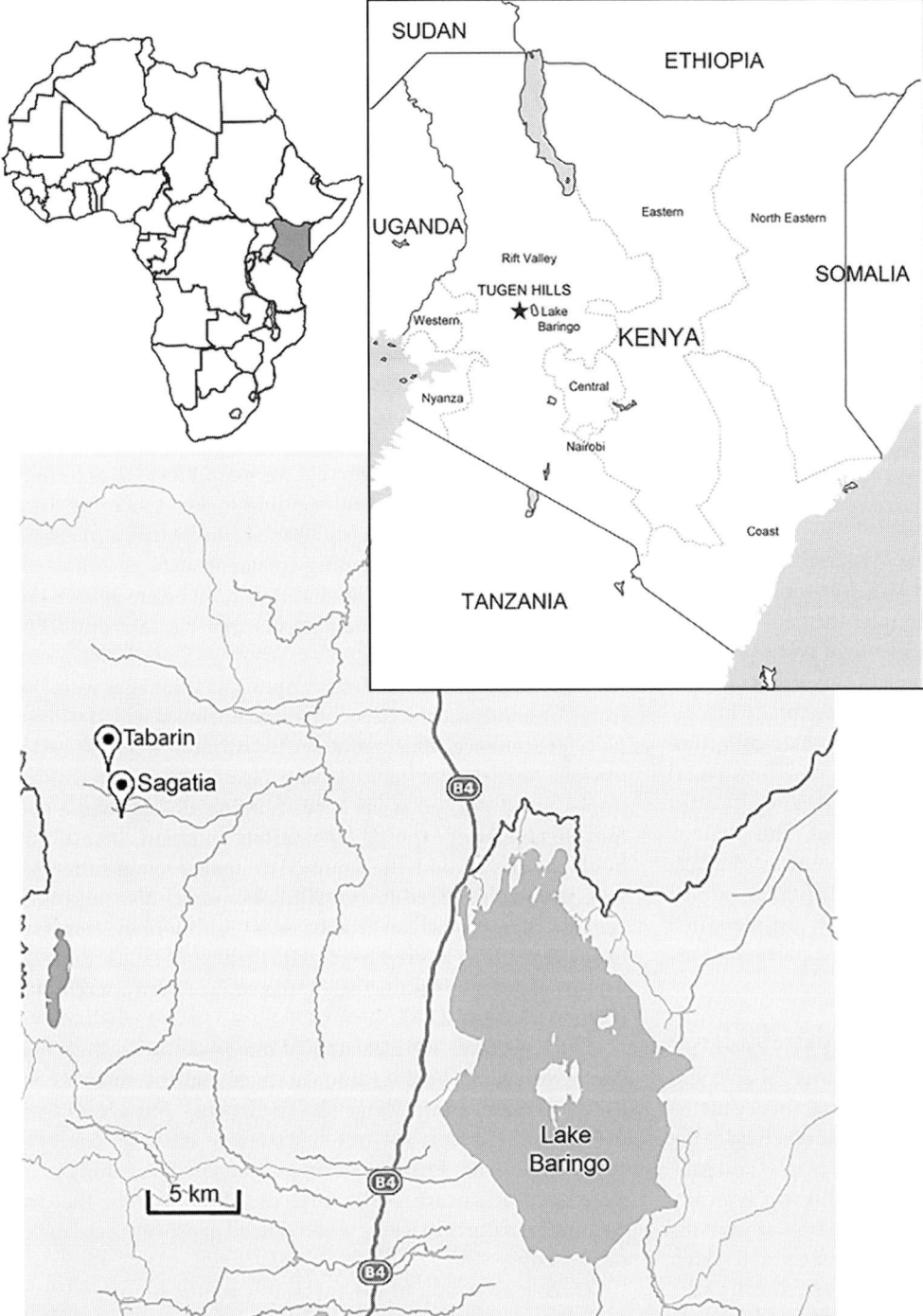

Figure 27.1 Location of the Tugen Hills fossil sites.

specimen general acceptance as a southern representative of the otherwise Ethiopian species (Hill, 1995, 1999; Deino et al., 2002; MacLatchy et al., 2010).

Sagatia

Sagatia (BPRP site #75) is situated approximately 2.5 km southeast of Tabarin (Figure 27.1). The locality is also part of the northern extension sediments of the Chemeron Formation (Loc. 2/232 in Pickford et al., 1983). It was first investigated by the BPRP in 1984 during the same field season that produced the hominin mandible at Tabarin. While the locality did not produce hominin specimens, abundant and speciose mammalian fossils were recovered, including several carnivoran taxa (e.g., hyenids, felids, and mustelids; Hill, 1985).

Relative to Tabarin the geology at Sagatia is not well-understood. Although there are a number of tuffaceous units in all three of the primary drainages, none have yet yielded radiometric dates (new dating is currently in progress). Lithologically, the

Sagatia drainages are similar to Tabarin and are characterized by lacustrine and fluvial deposition as silts, sands, and conglomeritic layers, some of which represent fairly high-energy depositional episodes (D. Peppe, pers. comm.). Fossils are not limited to a single horizon, but are scattered throughout the site and within the larger stratigraphic sequence. There is also evidence at Sagatia of moderate paleosol development in a floodplain setting (D. Peppe, pers. comm.) that has produced some important fossil specimens, including a relatively complete cranium of a female primate, *Parapapio* sp. nov. (C. Gilbert, pers. comm.). Considering the dynamic nature of the deposition at Sagatia, the abundant fossils are remarkably well-preserved, with many recovered *in situ*. Preservation quality of *in situ* specimens is especially good, suggesting that many of the more poorly preserved surface-collected specimens were damaged after erosion due to modern weathering rather than prior to deposition.

Materials and Methods

The BPRP has regularly monitored the fossiliferous exposures at Tabarin and Sagatia since the early 1980s. More focused work at Tabarin and Sagatia began in 2003 under the field direction of K.M. Binetti. This period of intensive field work provided more than just an opportunity to augment the fossil assemblages from the two sites with additional paleoenviromentally indicative taxa; it also offered a chance to test an alternate collection strategy (as advocated by White, 2004 and others). Thus, a total collection regimen was developed and employed at Tabarin and Sagatia during the 2003–2006 field seasons. This strategy also afforded an opportunity to compare and contrast the taxa yielded via each collection method (earlier traditional survey and later total collection) and to determine how any identified collection bias might influence faunally based paleoenvironmental interpretations.

Traditional Survey Field Methods (1980s–2002)

In the early years of the BPRP's investigations at Tabarin and Sagatia, fossil recovery proceeded via traditional survey methods. The main goal was to document taxonomic diversity at the sites by creating faunal lists useful for biostratigraphy and general paleoenvironmental characterizations. This was typically accomplished by walking the exposures in search of identifiable surface specimens. Several constraints determined which specimens were collected and which were not; specifically, specimen quality and transport capabilities in the form of vehicle packing space were primary factors. Generally, a rule of collecting only "better bones" defined by W.W. Bishop as specimens "preserving recognizable facets and form" (Bishop and Whyte, 1962: 1286; Bishop, 1968) and not duplicating previously collected taxa and/or skeletal parts from each site was set. Exceptions to this rule were made when partial skeletons or taxa otherwise undocumented in the National Museums of Kenya's (NMK) paleontology collections were encountered. Another exception to the "better bones" rule was when the research question or field collection method dictated that all encountered specimens be recovered, such as occurs during systematic excavation of *in situ* specimens. An example of the latter was the several square meter area at Tabarin where the hominin mandible was found, which was excavated thoroughly with all fossils encountered on the surface and *in situ* collected and transported to Nairobi.

Total Collection Field Methods (2003–2006)

While Bishop instigated the idea of collecting only the "better bones" in the Tugen Hills, he also strongly cautioned that critical information may be lost when doing so (Bishop, 1971). Thus, another departure from the collection of only "better bones" in the Tugen Hills came during the reinvestigation of these sites that commenced in 2003. During the period associated with this project, fossil recovery and collection at Tabarin and Sagatia proceeded according to the following total collection protocol.

Initial reconnaissance surveys were conducted to determine whether sediments were still yielding fossils. Once the localities were determined to be sufficiently productive, a rough site sketch was drawn documenting erosional surfaces and drainages. All erosional slopes and drainage gullies were given either alphabetic (for erosional slopes) or numeric (for drainages) designations.

Visible surface fossils from slopes and drainages were collected by hand and placed in sample bags labeled with drainage/gully provenance information. After surfaces were cleared of obvious fossils, large boulders were cleared from the erosional slopes and deposited at the base of drainages. This had a twofold effect: first, it exposed fossiliferous sediments beneath the boulders, and second, the dammed drainages retain runoff soil from the newly cleared erosional hillocks, which also minimizes the loss of any newly exposed fossils. Additionally, low-lying bushy vegetation was removed to further expose the sediments. Trees that did not obscure the ground surface were not removed (Figures 27.2 and 27.3).

Once surfaces were cleared of major obstacles they were swept with hand brushes into dustpans and the soil was collected in metal *karais* (large shallow basins). Surface soil was then sieved through 1/4″ mesh screens to ensure recovery of small specimens. Prior to sieving, designated screening areas were swept to ensure sterile surfaces. All fossil bone that was encountered during sieving was collected in provenance labeled sample bags.

During sweeping of the exposures *in situ* specimens were often encountered and GPS points were taken to mark their location. They were then excavated and plastered in jackets for transport to the NMK in Nairobi, where they were cleaned in the preparation laboratory to facilitate identification and analysis.

After sieving, collected fossils were given preliminary field identifications so that any particularly rare, important, or previously unknown specimens or species could be further investigated. For instance, when primate teeth were encountered in the sieves, the area yielding the specimen was swept a second or third time to make sure nothing had been missed. The outlined procedures were followed for all fossiliferous sediments in the targeted drainages at Tabarin and Sagatia.

Figure 27.2 Sagatia "B" before sweeping and sieving. Photo credit: K.M. Binetti.

Figure 27.3 Sagatia "B" after sweeping and sieving. Photo credit: K.M. Binetti.

Results

Tabarin Results

Table 27.1 lists all mammal taxa currently known from Tabarin and includes specimens recovered during all collection periods from 1984 through 2006. There are 21 different species known from Tabarin, including the hominin mandible. Figure 27.4 depicts the number of taxa exclusively recovered during each collection interval at Tabarin. The 1984–2003 collection period (field work was concentrated in the beginning of this period, but continued sporadically throughout it) clearly yielded many more new taxa.

Rarefaction curves also document this pattern (Figure 27.5). Rarefaction is a statistical sampling method that facilitates comparison of species richness between samples of different sizes (Sanders, 1968; Hurlbert, 1971; Simberloff, 1972). This method can be used to approximate whether maximal species richness has been achieved at a given sample size, and to generally

Table 27.1 Mammal taxa currently identified from Tabarin fossil locality. This includes specimens recovered during all collection periods from 1984 to 2006.

Family	Species
Bovidae	*Aepyceros* sp.
Bovidae	Antilopini sp.
Bovidae	Bovini sp.
Bovidae	Reduncini sp.
Bovidae	Tragelaphini sp. (large)
Bovidae	*Tragelaphus* sp.
Cercopithecidae	Colobini sp.
Cercopithecidae	Papionini sp.
Deinotheriidae	*Deinotherium bozasi*
Elephantidae	
Equidae	cf. *Eurygnathohippus*
Felidae	cf. *Homotherium*
Giraffidae	
Gomphotheriidae	*Anancus kenyensis*
Hippopotamidae	*Hexaprotodon* sp.
Hominidae	cf. *Ardipithecus ramidus*
Hyaenidae	
Rhinocerotidae	*Ceratotherium* sp.
Rhinocerotidae	*Diceros* cf. *bicornis*
Suidae	*Nyanzachoerus* cf. *kanamensis*
Suidae	*Notochoerus* cf. *jaegeri*

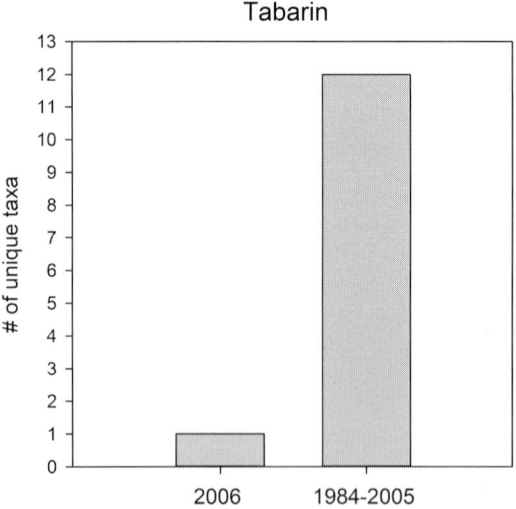

Figure 27.4 Number of new taxa identified during the two collection intervals at Tabarin. The 2006 interval represents the total collection strategy.

estimate the overall taxonomic completeness of a given sample (Hammer and Harper, 2006; Smith et al., 2018). Rarefaction was performed using PAST statistical software (Hammer et al., 2001) and the resulting curves for each collection interval, as well as for the complete Tabarin assemblage, are presented in Figure 27.5.

All three collection intervals from Tabarin have rarefaction curves that are not yet flattened (Figure 27.5). However, the curve representing the complete assemblage is nearly so, suggesting that most of the taxonomic diversity of the site has been realized. In comparison to the early and late collection intervals, the combined Tabarin fossil assemblage also demonstrates that the 2006 fieldwork served to augment the overall assemblage, even though a comparably small number of specimens were recovered during this second collection interval. Many of the specimens collected in 2006 were taxonomic duplications from the earlier collection period, causing the combined Tabarin rarefaction curve to begin flattening. Overall, the rarefaction curves suggest that the larger Tabarin assemblage is probably a fairly accurate representation of the fossil fauna preserved at the site, making any paleoenvironmental interpretations based on the fauna more robust. Conversely, as the curve has not completely flattened, additional fieldwork at Tabarin might still prove fruitful.

Sagatia Results

Fossil collection at Sagatia for this project also followed the protocols outlined above. Reconnaissance survey and total collection were completed for the Sagatia "A" drainage in 2003. At the very end of the 2003 field season, surveys were also conducted at Sagatia "B," which resulted in the recovery of several primate teeth. This provided the impetus for the 2004 field season that focused on total collection at Sagatia "B," which yielded several additional primate teeth and revealed a number of *in situ* specimens that were excavated, plastered, and transported to Nairobi for laboratory preparation. Survey at Sagatia "C" also took place during the 2004 field season, resulting in the discovery of several *in situ* specimens in the drainage. Follow-up total collection at Sagatia "C" in 2005 produced a number of additional fossils, including the mostly complete primate cranium referenced previously. Although no hominin specimens were recovered, the field seasons spent at Sagatia greatly augmented the earlier faunal assemblage for the site.

Table 27.2 lists all taxa recorded at Sagatia. Included are specimens recovered during the later bout of fieldwork, as well as those known from earlier BPRP field expeditions. There are 24 distinct taxa known from Sagatia, some of which are also known from Tabarin. Figure 27.6 depicts the number of distinct species collected solely during the early expeditions (1984–2003) and those only associated with the later field seasons (2003–2005). The later total fossil collection episodes at Sagatia yielded four new taxa. Three of these are small-bodied species, including Antilopini sp., *Theropithecus* sp., and *Parapapio* sp. nov., indicating that the total collection effort recovered taxa that had not been recorded previously at Sagatia through other collection methods.

Rarefaction curves for Sagatia reflect a similar pattern to those from Tabarin (Figure 27.7). Considering that Sagatia had been surveyed previously, the rarefaction curves predictably demonstrate that new taxa are more abundant in the earlier collection interval than in the later collection period. However, the total collection method used from 2003 to 2006 was more intensive than the surface survey used in the earlier years at Sagatia, which may explain the addition of three relatively small-bodied

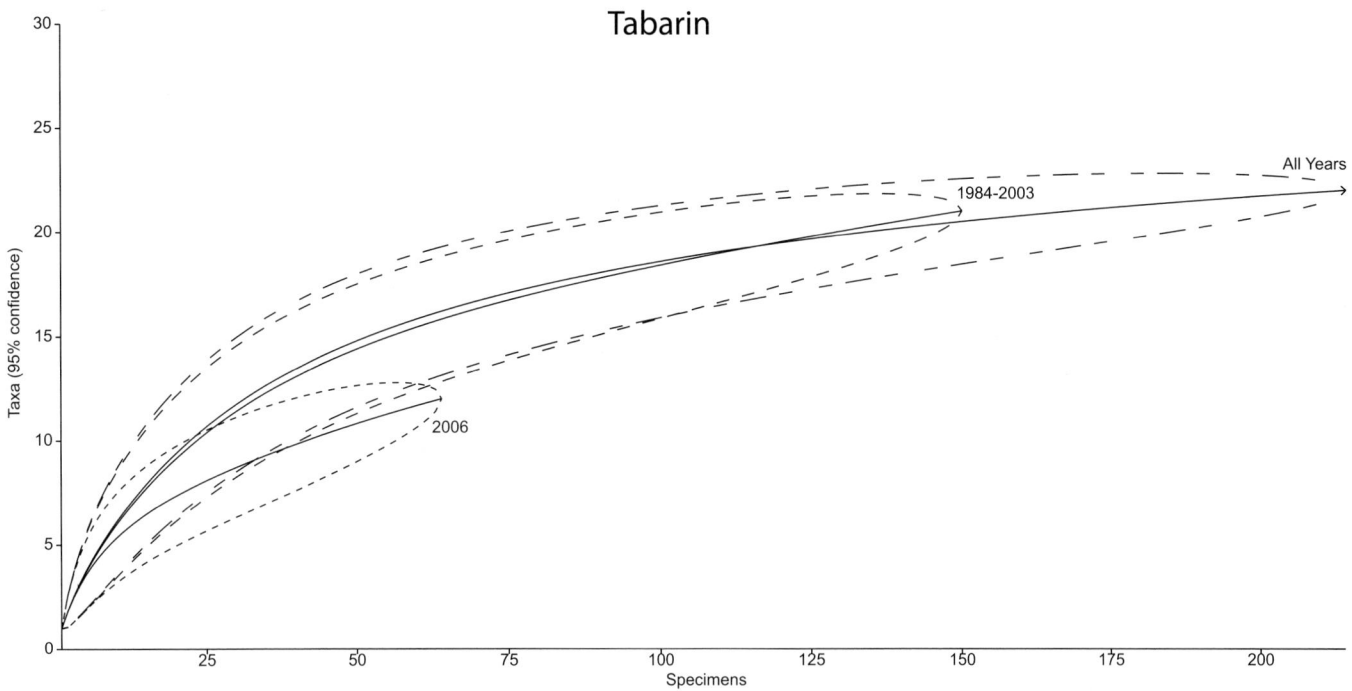

Figure 27.5 Rarefaction curves for the two collection intervals. Because the complete assemblage (all years) is beginning to asymptote it likely represents most of the faunal taxa present at Tabarin.

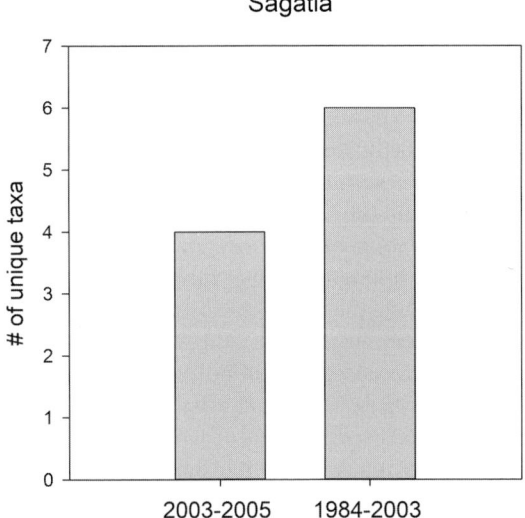

Figure 27.6 Number of new taxa identified during the two collection intervals at Sagatia. The 2003–2005 interval represents the total collection strategy.

Table 27.2 All mammalian taxa recorded at Sagatia fossil locality. This includes specimens recovered during the later fieldwork seasons, as well as those known from earlier BPRP field expeditions.

Family	Species
Mustelidae	Enhydriodon sp.
Bovidae	Aepyceros sp.
Bovidae	Antilopini sp.
Bovidae	Simatherium cf. kohllarseni
Bovidae	Traglephus sp.
Cercopithecidae	
Cercopithecidae	Parapapio sp. nov.
Cercopithecidae	Theropithecus sp.
Deinotheriidae	Deinotherium bozasi
Elephantidae	
Equidae	cf. Eurygnathohippus
Felidae	cf. Homotherium
Giraffidae	cf. Sivatherium sp.
Gomphotheriidae	Anancus kenyensis
Hemicyonidae	Agriotherium sp.
Hippopotamidae	Hexaprotodon sp.
Hyaenidae	cf. Parahyaena
Hystricidae	Hystrix sp.
Mustelidae	Lutrinae sp.
Rhinocerotidae	Ceratotherium sp.
Rhinocerotidae	Diceros cf. bicornis
Suidae	cf. Kolpochoerus deheinzelini
Suidae	Notochoerus cf. jaegeri
Suidae	Nyanzachoerus cf. kanamensis

species to the assemblage during the second collection interval. The fourth taxon added to the assemblage is a large-bodied bovid, *Simatherium* cf. *kohllarseni*. The primary specimen representing this species is a partial cranium that was discovered *in situ* after the area had been cleared of surface detritus and swept for sieving. These four taxonomic additions to the Sagatia assemblage suggest that the total collection strategy was useful in recovering additional taxa that might not otherwise have been recorded. The rarefaction curve for all collection years also reflects this pattern (Figure 27.7). It is beginning to reach an asymptote, suggesting that most of the taxa present at the site have likely been identified. However, as with Tabarin, the

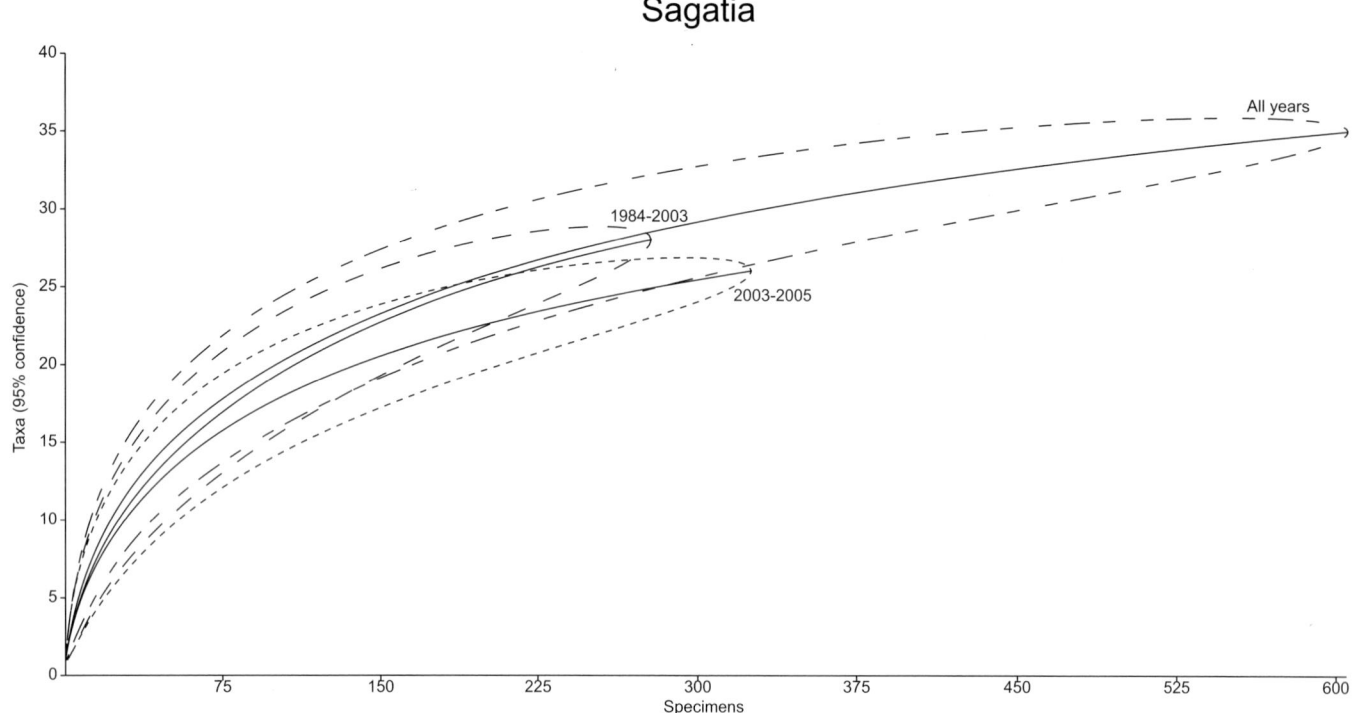

Figure 27.7 Rarefaction curves for the two collection intervals. Because the complete assemblage (all years) curve is just starting to asymptote it likely represents most of the faunal taxa preserved at Sagatia.

curve has not completely flattened, indicating that additional fieldwork may be productive. Ultimately, though, the Sagatia assemblage is probably a fairly accurate representation of the mammalian taxa preserved there.

Discussion

In comparing the two different collection strategies used in the Tugen Hills over the last 30+ years, some clear benefits emerge from implementing the total collection strategy. In the collections derived from the traditional survey field method, the most commonly missing components of the fossil assemblages were the small-bodied taxa. In contrast, more small species were recovered during the later collection periods when total collection was used. Additionally, many of the fossils recovered through total collection exhibited better preservation characteristics (personal observation), irrespective of body size, because they were found either *in situ* or early enough in the erosional process that modern weathering had not affected their identifiability. This was likely the result of the more intensive searching in general that is inherently part of the total collection protocol. The recovery of more readily identifiable fossil specimens, from a broader range of taxa, has important implications for faunal-based paleoecological reconstructions at these sites and others like them.

General Taphonomic Effects on Faunal Assemblages

Taphonomic processes responsible for the transition of biological remains from the living world to the lithic one include decomposition, disarticulation, weathering, geochemical and biological alteration, and, for a select few remains, fossilization (Weigelt, 1927, 1989; Hill, 1975, 1979a, 1979b, 1980, 1989; Behrensmeyer, 1978b; Hill and Behrensmeyer, 1984; Hedges, 2002; Trueman and Martill, 2002). Unfortunately, while taphonomic processes create the fossil record, these same processes are also well known for introducing biases into the record (Efremov, 1940).

Differential preservation of remains can result in biases at the level of missing skeletal elements, inaccurate counts of individual animals, and/or the complete absence of once-present taxa from fossil assemblages (Lyman, 1994 and references therein). Thus, careful consideration of potential taphonomic biases should be undertaken as early as possible in paleontological studies. Below, we discuss a series of general taphonomic processes that have potentially biased the Tabarin and Sagatia faunal collections, and outline possible theoretical, practical, and analytical steps that may mitigate their effects.

Taphonomy and Animal Body Size

Because of a long-recognized taphonomic bias against small animals, we suggest that faunally based paleoenvironmental analyses should be limited to mammals with a species mean body weights of 15 kg or greater (Voorhies, 1969; Dodson, 1973; Behrensmeyer et al., 1979; Behrensmeyer and Dechant Boaz, 1980; Soligo and Andrews, 2005; Andrews, 2006; Western and Behrensmeyer, 2009; but see, Miller et al., 2014). This is a departure from many faunal-based paleoecological analyses, where body-size thresholds are either fairly small (e.g., 500 g or 4 kg) or non-existent (e.g., all species present are included in analyses; Reed, 1996, 1997, 1998, 2008; Harris et al., 2003; Reed and Fish, 2005; Su, 2005; Reed and Rector, 2006; Campisano, 2007;

Su et al., 2009; Teague, 2009). Due to this potential taphonomic bias, the paleocommunity analyses performed for Tabarin and Sagatia included only species with mean body weight estimates greater than 15 kg (Binetti, 2011). The rationale for this decision is detailed over the next few sections, where we review the literature on the topic and further discuss the implications of our field collection study on paleoecological analyses and paleoenvironmental interpretations.

Known Taphonomic Biases Involving Small(er) Mammals

Taphonomic processes begin with the death of an organism, often followed by varied amounts of disarticulation, decomposition, consumption, and/or skeletonization of the carcass (Weigelt, 1927, 1989; Toots, 1965; Hill, 1975, 1979a, 1979b, 1980; Hill and Behrensmeyer, 1984). With regard to destructive processes, Hill (1980) suggests that larger skeletal elements and taxa may be more likely to survive than smaller ones. For example, some carnivores, hyenas in particular, will completely consume small and medium-sized animal carcasses within hours of death, thereby negating opportunities for fossilization (Kruuk, 1972; Crader, 1974; Blumenschine, 1986, 1987; Hill, 1989). In addition to biotic agents, abiotic factors can also contribute to the preferential obliteration of small(er) skeletons. Behrensmeyer (1978b) clearly demonstrates that the skeletons of small-bodied species (as well as the juveniles of larger taxa) are destroyed faster than their larger counterparts when subjected to subaerial weathering. Small skeletons are also highly susceptible to fluvial transport, which may result in differential movement of smaller animals either into or out of faunal assemblages (Voorhies, 1969; Dodson, 1973).

In contrast, *if* small mammal skeletons are available for deposition, they are more likely than larger mammal skeletons to be buried intact (Coe, 1980; Behrensmeyer, 1991). While burial is a necessary step, interment alone does not ensure fossilization. Buried bones are subject to the chemical and microbial action of the surrounding soil, which can either facilitate or arrest bone preservation and subsequent mineralization (Gordon and Buikstra, 1981; White and Hannus, 1983). With regard to small interred bones, Von Endt and Ortner (1984) suggest that subterranean chemical weathering progresses more rapidly than in larger bones, resulting in fewer small bones, and smaller-sized species, in fossil assemblages. Finally, the weight of overlying sediment can cause buried skeletal elements to further fragment (Klein and Cruz-Uribe, 1984; Villa and Mahieu, 1991), which Lyman and O'Brien (1987) suggest leads to the "analytical absence" of very small bones due to the loss of potentially identifying features on the remaining absolutely tiny bone surfaces.

Reduced Taphonomic Biases Against Larger Mammals?

In contrast to the problems associated with the preservation of small mammal skeletons, pioneering neotaphonomic work on modern bone accumulations in Amboseli National Park, Kenya, has demonstrated relative fidelity between skeletal remains and living populations of mammals larger than 15 kg (Behrensmeyer et al., 1979; Behrensmeyer and Dechant Boaz, 1980; Western and Behrensmeyer, 2009). In fact, the skeletal population at Amboseli reflected 95 percent of herbivore species and 100 percent of carnivore species greater than 15 kg in the living population, while species between 1 and 15 kg were only represented at 60 percent (herbivores) and 21 percent (carnivores) in the skeletal sample (Behrensmeyer and Dechant Boaz, 1980). The same study also found a bias against small species with respect to researchers' ability to locate the skeletal remains of animals smaller than 15 kg visually (Behrensmeyer et al., 1979; Behrensmeyer and Dechant Boaz, 1980; Western and Behrensmeyer, 2009). The survey methods employed in the neotaphonomic research at Amboseli are similar to, if not more systematic than, the survey techniques commonly employed in fossil collection (Eck, 2007). A major implication of this study is that small species are "missed" with greater frequency than larger taxa; this is a finding with important consequences when considering the taxonomic composition of fossil assemblages in comparison with modern faunal communities (Coe, 1980; Western, 1980). Our paleontological study accords with modern bone and ecological surveys, in that mostly small-bodied species were added to the Tabarin and Sagatia faunal lists during our later collection efforts.

Issues of Recovery Techniques and Collection Strategies

A complementary body of actualistic research has considered the effects of sieving or screen-washing sediments in terms of taxonomic and skeletal part recovery. Sieving experiments were devised to simulate both paleontological (Wolff, 1975) and archeological (Payne, 1972, 1975; Shaffer, 1992; Shaffer and Sanchez, 1994) scenarios. In all cases, researchers demonstrated improved recovery using sieves, with better results associated with smaller mesh sizes. Specifically, taxa with body weights greater than ~5 kg had an almost 100 percent recovery rate with 1/4″ screens (Shaffer, 1992), while 1/8″ mesh allowed for reliable recovery of fauna greater than just 42 g (Shaffer and Sanchez, 1994). The results of these experiments imply that taxa smaller than 5 kg cannot be reliably recovered in the absence of at least some screen-washing, and these taxa should probably not be utilized in subsequent paleoecological analyses where small-bodied species are important paleoenvironmental indicators (e.g., Andrews et al., 1979).

Given the well-documented actualistic evidence for significant sampling bias against small animals, a number of paleontological field projects have begun to examine and quantify the differences in fossil yields at localities where collections were achieved via differing collection strategies (Sheehan et al., 1991; Suwa et al., 2003; White, 2004; Behrensmeyer and Barry, 2005; Eck, 2007). This research has demonstrated that more systematic and thorough fossil survey produces greater numbers of identifiable skeletal elements and a greater number of recognizable taxa in paleontological assemblages (Sheehan et al., 1991; Suwa et al., 2003; White, 2004; Behrensmeyer and Barry, 2005; Eck, 2007).

Unfortunately, many fossil assemblages were not, and are still not, collected this way (White, 1988; Eck, 2007). This is problematic, because small and large taxa are not equally likely to be recorded, making analytical techniques based on the presence/absence of species (such as those used in many faunally based paleoecological analyses) of questionable utility. In particular, when the collection methodologies are either unknown, or were more opportunistic than systematic, it is arguably best to exclude small taxa from ensuing analyses. Doing so ensures that only reliably recoverable taxa are analyzed. Ultimately, this conservative approach was the tactic adopted for paleocommunity analyses of Tabarin and Sagatia because the assemblages are the result of two different field collection strategies (Binetti, 2011). A cautious approach requires applying the lowest common denominator, which in this case means limiting analysis to taxa that can be reliably recovered via traditional survey-based collection. As suggested by the survey-collected modern bone assemblages from Amboseli (Behrensmeyer et al., 1979; Behrensmeyer and Dechant Boaz, 1980; Western and Behrensmeyer, 2009), that threshold was set at a species mean body weight of 15 kg or greater for the analyses applied to the Tabarin and Sagatia assemblages.

Taphonomic Effects on Data Analysis

From an anthropological perspective, one unfortunate consequence of imposing a 15 kg threshold is that the vast majority of primate species are not included in any subsequent analyses. Binetti's (2011) paleoenvironmental analyses of the Tabarin and Sagatia faunal assemblages only include those species that are baboon-sized and larger. Not only does this mean excluding many primates, but also a number of other common mammals must be omitted due to small body size, including hyraxes, some larger rodent species, and several small bovids. With specific regard to bovids, the excluded species are primarily forest dwellers, which, coupled with the loss of all the arboreal primates, posed a potential problem for distinguishing between forest and non-forest environments on the basis of faunal community composition. Fortunately, this was not the case and larger mammals proved adequate for differentiating forest from non-forest habitats (Binetti, 2011 and in preparation).

Although excluding small species certainly removed some variation from the faunal data sets, there were associated beneficial effects on the analyses. There is a well-known bias in anthropologically relevant fossil collections *in favor* of primates with many field projects preferentially collecting primate specimens for a variety of perfectly valid reasons (White, 1988, 2004; Suwa et al., 2003; Alemseged et al., 2007; Eck, 2007). It is possible, however, that this bias results in an overrepresentation of primate taxa in fossil assemblages relative to fauna generally of less "anthropological" interest (at least when fossil collection expeditions are being run by anthropologists). It may also result in an overrepresentation of fossil primate taxa relative to those reported in living communities. At least in part, this is because many modern primate species, as well as small taxa in general, are nocturnal and are less frequently documented in published faunal censuses (Graham and Bell, 1969; Pennycuick and Western, 1972). Furthermore, even diurnal small arboreal primate species commonly go unrecognized in modern communities. For example, the Udzungwa Mountains of Tanzania recently yielded a previously unidentified species of mangabey (*Rungwecebus kipunji*) that would not have appeared in faunal censuses taken prior to 2005 (Jones et al., 2005; Davenport et al., 2006). This is potentially problematic, as the goal of many paleoecological studies is to use modern mammal communities as models for paleocommunities. Thus, if paleontological data sets overrepresent one group (e.g., primates), then the results of comparisons between modern and fossil communities are of questionable utility. By limiting fossil faunal data sets to taxa greater than 15 kg, primate species are largely excluded from analyses mitigating possible primate-centric biases in the fossil data and subsequent paleoenvironmental interpretations (Alemseged et al., 2007).

To demonstrate the effect of including primates (and other small-bodied taxa) in some types of paleocommunity analyses, we use faunal data from Sagatia and apply a well-known and accepted modern African community model to predict habitat type (Reed, 1996, 1997). Reed (1996, 1997) demonstrated a predictive relationship between the proportion of arboreal mammal species in African faunal communities and broad habitat types; generally, the more arboreal taxa present in a community, the more vegetative cover the landscape supports (from forests with the most cover, to grasslands and deserts with the least). This can then be applied to paleocommunities that contain mammals of similar locomotor repertoires as their modern counterparts. As discussed previously, African arboreal mammals are very frequently small-bodied and/or primates, both of which may have positively and/or negatively biased representation in modern and fossil communities.

At Sagatia, the percentage of small arboreal taxa in the fossil assemblage has changed as a function of collection strategy. In a system such as Reed's (1996, 1997), the Sagatia paleoenvironmental interpretation changes in relation to this shift in abundance of arboreal taxa. In the early assemblage (traditional survey), the proportion of arboreal mammals that made up the total number of species was approximately 3 percent. In the second collection interval (total collection), arboreal mammals made up 12.5 percent of taxa in the assemblage. When the two intervals (and collection strategies) are combined, the arboreal mammal species make up approximately 7 percent of the entire faunal assemblage. The effect on Sagatia's paleoenvironmental interpretation is shown in Figure 27.8. Dependent upon which collection interval is used, Sagatia can be reasonably interpreted as closed woodland (7.5–15 percent arboreal mammals), bushland/woodland (5.5–6.5 percent arboreal mammals), or open woodland (2.9–5 percent arboreal mammals) under this system. An argument can be made that the combined assemblage provides the "true" proportion of arboreal taxa from Sagatia, and certainly other paleoecological indicators should be used to corroborate any final interpretations; however, the fact remains that collection strategy seemingly biased these assemblages and subsequent analytical outcomes. We suggest, therefore, that paleoecological analyses be applied with caution to assemblages collected by less-systematic, or unknown, means as they may

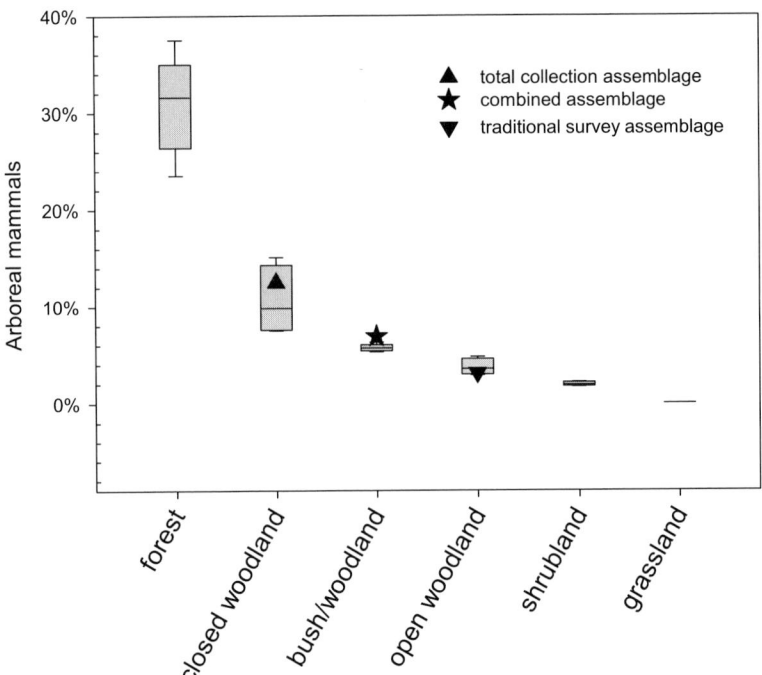

Figure 27.8 The paleoenvironmental interpretation of Sagatia based on the proportion of arboreal mammals (after Reed, 1996, 1997).

be biased representations of the once-present paleocommunity, which can influence paleoenvironmental interpretation(s) (Figure 27.8). As previously indicated, this may often mean excluding small-bodied taxa from analysis.

Finally, there may be one additional benefit to using only larger mammals in data analysis. As previously noted, small, rare, and cryptic species are often missed in modern censuses as well as in fossil collection (Graham and Bell, 1969; Pennycuick and Western, 1972; White, 1988, 2004; Suwa et al., 2003; Eck, 2007). However, there are times, both in modern ecological work as well in paleontology, when very thorough survey can yield virtually complete faunal lists (see Yalden et al., 1996 and Miller et al., 2014 for modern examples; White et al., 2009a, 2009b for a paleontological example). This creates a situation of analytical equivalence between common taxa and those that are less common, or even rare, when considering species lists. By removing the smaller mammals from the fossil data sets, we have also likely removed some of the rarer species (Hutchinson and MacArthur, 1959; Peters and Raelson, 1984). This mitigates the potential problem of allowing rare species to unduly influence data analysis and subsequent paleoenvironmental interpretations by ensuring that only relatively common (and environmentally indicative) taxa are considered.

Conclusion

As Bill Bishop argued long ago, there is a great deal of "information that can be obtained from the total investigation of natural associations of bone and tooth" (Bishop, 1971: 499), especially with respect to paleoenvironmental reconstruction. In more recent years, others have echoed this sentiment and begun to institute field collection protocols aimed at "total" or "complete" fossil collection for a variety of very good scientific reasons (White, 2004; Behrensmeyer and Barry, 2005; White et al., 2009a, 2009b). Based on our comparative study, we contend that a total collection approach is almost always preferable when and where logistically possible. Our data indicate that a total collection approach more reliably yields small-bodied taxa and that fossils recovered through this method may be better preserved, and therefore more readily identifiable to both skeletal part and taxon.

Increasing the number of identifiable fossils is of universal interest to paleontologists, but it is of particular importance in some types of faunal analyses used for paleoenvironmental reconstruction. Specifically, our data suggest that faunal assemblages resulting from traditional survey techniques, or those collected by unknown methods, may be of limited analytical utility in paleoecological analyses where small-bodied taxa are key environmental indicators (Andrews et al., 1979; Avery, 1982a). Incomplete fossil assemblages can also be problematic for analyses that rely on the mere presence (and by extension, absence) of specific indicator taxa to predict environmental affinity (Vrba, 1980), particularly if those species are also among the rarer components of the faunal paleocommunity (e.g., many carnivorans; Belmaker, 2018) as non-abundant taxa are also more likely to be missed during traditional survey.

Unfortunately, due to a variety of logistical constraints, a total collection approach may not always be feasible. One reason total collection was possible at Tabarin and Sagatia was that the fossil-bearing exposures of the Northern Chemeron tend to be relatively small and discrete areas. For example, the three Sagatia drainages range in total area from 2000 to 8000 m², and although Tabarin has more drainages, they are each similar in size to those at Sagatia. This made completing the total collection task easier and more straightforward than it might be at other fossil localities. At sites where fossils are widely dispersed, or where the fossils themselves are concentrated but the fossiliferous sediments are more extensive, total collection may be more difficult to accomplish. This is especially challenging if time and/or personnel are also limited, both of which may be a function of adequate expedition funding.

Another logistical issue surrounding total collection relates to space constraints. The transport of fossils, which are often large and/or fragile, from remote field locations to modern laboratory and collections facilities may be hindered by the availability of vehicle space. If specimens can be transported from the field, then the designated archival facility must also be willing to accept and curate the additional fossil material generated through total collection. These space issues are becoming increasingly problematic for a number of museums that are at, or close to, capacity and often without means for significant expansion. Field projects are addressing limited curation space in a variety of ways, but this issue could deter some projects from using a total collection protocol as described here. We urge current and future field expeditions to consider a total collection approach, though, especially when the project goals include recovering fossils from groups such as primates, rodents, carnivores, and other small-bodied or non-abundant taxa. If a total collection strategy remains untenable, then analytical adjustments such as those outlined above should be made to include only species of body sizes that are reliably recoverable using less-intensive field collection methods.

Acknowledgments

Funding for this project was provided to K.M.B. from the L.S.B. Leakey Foundation, the Wenner-Gren Foundation, the Fulbright-Hays DDRA Program, the Geological Society of America, and the Bill Bishop Memorial Trust. We gratefully acknowledge the assistance of Bonface Kimeu in the field, and of the curatorial and administrative staff in the Paleontology Department at the National Museums of Kenya in Nairobi. We also thank René Bobe and Sally Reynolds for their patience and perseverance in organizing this volume and for their helpful comments on the manuscript. Kris Kovarovic also provided helpful suggestions that greatly improved this chapter. Nothing presented here would have been possible without A.H.'s initial and sustained work in the Tugen Hills spanning the better part of 40 years. His impact on the field of African paleoecology is immeasurable and will be greatly missed, but the greatest loss is of his guidance as mentor and friend. Thank you for everything, Andrew.

28. The Southern Chemeron Formation, Tugen Hills, Kenya: A Review and a Paleoecological Analysis of the Bovid Fauna

Emily Goble Early

History of Exploration in the Baringo Basin

The Baringo Basin first came to the attention of European explorers during a geological survey by Joseph Thomson in 1884. The Cambridge Expedition to the East African Lakes discovered fossils in 1930 and 1931, but descriptions were delayed until a report by Vivian E. Fuchs (1950). During the 1950s, Robert M. Shackleton worked in the Baringo Basin and was followed by geologists from the Kenya Geological Survey, who also contributed to the basic geological mapping and framework, particularly in the southern portion of the Tugen Hills that is the focus of this chapter (McCall et al., 1967; Walsh, 1969).

Research was later taken over by the East African Geological Research Unit (EAGRU). EAGRU's geological mapping included extensive surveying that resulted in the discovery of fossils. A member of the team, John Kimengich, working with John Martyn, discovered one of the first fossil hominins (KNM-BC 1) from Kenya in 1965. KNM-BC 1 is the Chemeron temporal bone (Martyn, 1967 and Tobias, 1967b), and possibly one of the earliest members of our own genus *Homo* (Hill et al., 1992; Hill, 1999). From 1968 onwards Andrew Hill, working with Bill Bishop, was attached to this team to explore the increasing number of fossil sites then being discovered (Bishop et al., 1971). He, and later Martin Pickford – working with the same group – considerably added to the fossil collections. In 1980 the Baringo Basin Paleontological Project (BPRP) was established by David Pilbeam, then at Yale University, subsequently at Harvard, with Andrew Hill as field director. This resulted in the discovery of a hominin at 4.4 Ma that remained plausibly the oldest known hominin for a period of 10 years (Hill, 1985). The project was turned over to Andrew Hill in 1985. Since then, the project has been affiliated with Yale University, working consistently in the region in association with the National Museums of Kenya (for more detailed history, see Hill, 2002). After 1985 a few other hominin fragments have been discovered from the sites analyzed in Goble Early's thesis (Goble, 2011), including either a late-occurring *Australopithecus afarensis* or an early *Paranthropus*.

One of the major contributions of the EAGRU in the 1960s and 1970s was to establish a stratigraphic framework (see Hill, 2002). The most simplified version consists of, from bottom to top, the Muruyur Beds (16–13 Ma), the Ngorora Formation (13–8.5 Ma), the Mpesida Beds (7–6.2 Ma), the Lukeino Formation (6.2–5.6 Ma), the Chemeron Formation (5.3–1.6 Ma), and the Kapthurin Formation (700 to <200 ka). The sedimentary units are frequently separated by volcanic flows and within each unit are a number of paleontological sites.

Stratigraphy and Geochronology

The Tugen Hills are located west of Lake Baringo in the Kenya Rift Valley and extend 150 km in a north to south direction. They are formed by a tilted horst block and expose over 3000 m of rocks covering 16 million years. The Chemeron Formation, Tugen Hills, Kenya is a fossiliferous unit covering the time period from 5.3 to 1.6 Ma. Martyn examined the Chemeron and Kapthurin Beds in 1965. He made a lithological distinction between the Upper Tuffs (*ca.* 6–30.48 m), the Upper Fish Beds (up to 76.2 m), the Lower Tuffs (roughly 2.7–4.87 m), the Lower Fish Beds (up to 97.5 m) and the Basal Beds (0–45.7 m or more). The Basal Beds are derived from a breakdown of the underlying basalts. They run approximately 5 miles in a north to south depression. Although water was involved in their accumulation it appears there was no permanent lake in the depression. The Fish Beds dominate the Chemeron and are divided by a tuff into Upper and Lower. They are almost entirely lacustrine and fluviatile, as indicated by their name. Martyn was, unfortunately, incorrect in his naming of members, and as such BPRP has since dropped any such system in favor of simply using formations and individual sites within them. Within the Chemeron Formation are the Barsemoi, Ndau, and Kapthurin Rivers and their tributaries. These drainages expose the majority of sites relevant to this chapter. They are comprised of successions of gravels and sands on top of a fluviatile plain along with lacustrine silts. The lacustrine silts are most often associated with the paleontological remains and contain the majority of the sites (Martyn, 1967). As with all formations in the Tugen Hills, the Chemeron sediments display a high degree of faulting. Tracing horizons more than a few hundred meters is difficult due to extreme variability in lateral facies. In spite of these difficulties, recent work undertaken by BPRP has managed to refine our knowledge of the stratigraphy. The sites included in this chapter are predominantly located in the southern portion of the eastern foothills, between the Tugen Hills and Lake Baringo. The vast majority of sites lie within the Kapthurin, Barsemoi, and Ndau River drainages or their tributaries.

History of Faunal Research in the Chemeron Formation

In 1965 John Kimengich discovered a hominin temporal bone weathered out on the surface of the Upper Fish Beds at BPRP #2, then referred to as JM 85 (JM for John Martyn). The site is almost a bedding plane slope (Martyn, 1967). The temporal bone was initially identified as hominin by Jonathan Leakey and later described by P.V. Tobias (1967b). Closer scrutiny of the temporal bone came much later, once other hominin comparative material became generally available and the chronostratigraphy of the succession became better understood (Hill et al., 1992; see Hill, 1999 for an account of the discovery and subsequent opinion).

Past work on the fauna from the formation includes intensive study of BPRP #2 where the hominin temporal was found (Hill et al., 1992; Deino and Hill, 2002), and for the formation as a whole, a brief overview of monkey specimens (Gundling and Hill, 2000), and in-depth taxonomy and ecology of suids (Bishop, 1994; Bishop et al., 1999).

As part of her dissertation, Bishop (1994) examined and refuted the Turnover Pulse Hypothesis (Vrba, 1985b) using FADs and LADs of hominins and suids. She found evidence that East African hominin species went extinct either before or after the 2.6–2.4 Ma interval, with the exception of *Paranthropus aethiopicus*. This is not the case for the suids, with 13 extinct and one modern species having a record in the Pliocene and Pleistocene. The four suid species extant at 2.6 Ma survive through Vrba's critical 2.5 Ma date, with no speciation until 2.2 Ma and no extinction until 2.1 Ma. Additional work on Chemeron fauna from northern sites at and near the location of a hominin discovery has been undertaken by Katie Binetti (2011).

BPRP Precession Group

An intensive three-year survey of the Chemeron Formation undertaken by the BPRP Precession Group focused work in the Barsemoi, Kapthurin, and Ndau main river beds and tributaries. Over the course of three years, 105 faunal sites were revisited, or discovered, and surveyed. The Precession Group uses C and O isotopic analysis of mammalian dental enamel, diatomite taxonomy, examination of microflora remains, C/N/O/Si analysis of diatom inorganics and biosilica, and a more traditional faunal approach to examine the paleoenvironment. While all of these avenues of paleoenvironmental research are of interest to reconstructing the past environment, the most necessary aim of the survey for integrating paleoecological research has been creating a detailed chronostratigraphic framework. The area was initially selected due to a sequence of diatomites best exposed within the Barsemoi river section that has been correlated with high insolation packages linked to Milankovitch cycles (Deino et al., 2006a; Kingston et al., 2007).

Milankovitch cycles involve movements of the Earth's axis or orbit that individually and collectively affect climate on a global scale. There are three cycles and they are described here from longest cycle to shortest. Orbital eccentricity refers to the variously elliptical or circular path of the Earth around the sun and occurs on an average 100-kyr cycle. This cycle changes the distance of the Earth from the sun and affects seasonality by lengthening or shortening the duration of the season. Obliquity, or axial tilt, refers to variations in the tilt of the Earth's axis. Tilt angle ranges from 22.1° to 24.5° on a 41-kyr cycle. Variations in obliquity affect the amount of sunlight striking the Earth in different places at different times. Precession occurs on a 24–26-kyr cycle. It is a gyroscopic motion of the axis of rotation that is frequently likened to the motion of a spinning top. Differences in the alignment of the axis alter the level of seasonal extremities. Within the Chemeron Formation there is evidence from diatomites of a fluctuating lake system aligned with precessional cycles modulated by eccentricity. This is the first undisputed terrestrial evidence linking astronomical forcing to changes in paleoenvironment.

The interface between an organism and its environment is where natural selection occurs and as such paleoenvironments must be examined to study changes in lineages. Between 5 and 3 Ma global climate shifted from warm and stable to a prolonged cooling period, resulting in the Northern Hemisphere Glaciation (NHG). As a result of the southward migration of the Intertropical Convergence Zone with the NHG after 2.7 Ma there is evidence for an intensification of climatic variability in the tropics and subtropics (deMenocal, 1995; Trauth et al., 2005; Broccoli et al., 2006). According to Trauth and colleagues (2005), three major humid periods coincident with global climate shifts interrupt the trend toward aridification in East Africa. The first humid period between 2.7 and 2.5 Ma is believed to have occurred in response to the glaciation that created a drop in sea level and subsequently changed deep-water circulation patterns that increased atmospheric moisture (Haug and Tiedemann, 1998). At the same time, evidence from the Chemeron Formation, Tugen Hills suggests the Rift Valley was dominated by large freshwater lake systems resulting from intensified monsoonal circulation over the African continent (Kingston et al., 2007). High-resolution (millennial-scale) analysis of paleoclimatic and mammalian fossil records is made possible in the Tugen Hills due to the frequency of diatomites and volcanics interwoven with fossiliferous sediments and allows local trends to be linked to global-scale events (Deino et al., 2006a; Kingston et al., 2007). Diatomite packages such as these indicate large fluctuations in water availability that likely altered the paleolandscape. As orbitally forced climate changes should have global impact, then patterns of change, once identified, should be found across Africa. The common element across hominin localities tends to be large mammalian fauna; therefore, any change identified within faunal lineages or mammalian communities is potentially the most useful for locality comparison. Once recognized, those faunal patterns may be linked directly or indirectly with astronomically forced climate change.

A sequence of diatomites occurs in the southern portion of the Chemeron between 2.7 and 2.55 Ma (Kingston et al., 2007). The combined use of traditional geological methods and manipulation of remotely sensed images has suggested that following the precession cycle of 23,000 years there were alternating cycles of very large lakes and dry lake basins (Kingston et al., 2007). Goble Early and colleagues (Goble et al., 2008) used remotely sensed images as a heuristic tool to ask and answer paleogeographical questions. Kingston and colleagues (2007) suggest large-scale faunal turnovers, such as those described by Vrba (1995b), Dynesius and Jansson (2000), and deMenocal (2004), cannot be linked to orbital forcing in the Tugen Hills. However, this is not to suggest orbitally forced climate change would have no effect on the mammalian community. Rather, precession modulated cycling of precipitation patterns would likely have resulted in changes in the size and location of species' geographic distribution (Bennett, 1997; Kingston et al., 2007). Continuous fragmentation and recombination of faunal communities in response to a rapidly changing environment that includes large swings in water availability and extent would result in microevolutionary changes in isolated populations. This sort of genetic mixing over time could have a significant effect on speciation (Barnosky, 2005; Kingston et al., 2007).

One of the aims is to determine what, if any, effect these environmental changes had on the animal community. The idea that changing environments constitute a main ingredient in evolution and can be examined by studying faunal material is not new and has been attempted at a variety of African localities. Large mammalian fauna is a common denominator at sites and consequently is often the focus of paleoenvironmental reconstruction. Diatomites, volcanics, invertebrates, and eggshell may not be available to provide paleoecological data at most sites. Unlike many other localities, the Baringo Basin provides a unique opportunity to link paleoenvironmental reconstruction using the mammalian fauna to already known, well-dated environmental fluctuations caused by Milankovitch cycles. If megafauna can be linked to environmental shifts in the Baringo Basin, where it can be compared and contrasted to other proxies, then reconstruction at other localities based solely on mammalian fauna is supported. At a later stage this work will be integrated with that of other members in the BPRP Precession Group to achieve our larger paleoecological goals.

Collection and Recording of Fossils

When fossils are retrieved in the field they are individually wrapped and placed in bags on which is recorded the site and horizon and date of collection. Back in camp a number is written on the fossil in permanent ink which records the year of collection followed by a sequential number (e.g., 08–125). This number is recorded in the field catalog and faunal database along with a field taxonomic identification, an identification of body part, the site number, and any additional notes (e.g., if we believe it is part one of two). They are then rewrapped in labeled bags that correspond to sites.

The field catalogs remain in Nairobi. We hold onto Xeroxes of them for security. When the specimens are accessioned, this information is transferred to the accessions register. It is also incorporated in our flexible computer database of all specimens. A copy of this is stored on the KNM Paleontology Division computer.

Prospecting for New Sites and Fossils

Protocols for prospecting for new sites and fossils were led by Andrew Hill, in collaboration with other senior team members, and built on past collection methods of groups who had worked in the area before BPRP. The vast majority of fossils found in the Tugen Hills are fragmentary surface finds. As such they have already been excavated by erosion from their immediate stratigraphic context. For this reason any person in our team may collect these specimens, taking note of position, without risk of damage. Teams in other areas may leave even surface finds until a more senior member of the team may examine them. However, the Tugen Hills have three extenuating circumstances to not follow that practice. First, the Tugen Hills are a relatively populous area, at least compared to Koobi Fora or West Turkana, and it would be irresponsible to leave fossils in the field for any length of time. Even if locals did not see us locate them, and we were to hide them, they often note a site of disturbance and naturally explore. The second reason is frequent, violent rain. Fossils are often exposed in river beds or gulleys and would be easily washed away if left in the field. The third reason, as previously mentioned, is that most of the fossil material we collect is already fragmentary. There is no known instance in Baringo where the collection of a surface fossil has resulted in damage to a specimen or confusion about provenance that would have been avoided by leaving it in the ground.

In cases where a specimen is still embedded in the rock it is only retrieved after consultation, and only by an experienced excavator. We follow conventional excavation procedures. Specimens are reinforced with Butvar or a similar plastic fluid. Separate parts are glued together. If necessary the specimen is wrapped in plaster bandages. We take photographs of some specimens during excavation, to assist with subsequent preparation.

When prospecting we are most often in groups and individuals are rarely far from one another. Upon discovery of a new collection area many or all of the group visit it to record and more intensely collect. If a person becomes isolated, and some distance away from a rendezvous point, he or she might collect fossils and bring them back without others having seen the situation. This could happen with a new or previously known site. Such fossils would only be surface finds. In these cases the group visits the area as soon as possible, typically on the same day but if extenuating circumstances arise then it is revisited no later than within 2 days of the initial collection.

Site Analysis

Chemeron Formation collections primarily come from the Barsemoi, Ndau, and Kapthurin River drainages and their tributaries, as well as a few other scattered localities, ranging from 5.14 to 2 Ma. Fossil vertebrates, accessioned and unaccessioned, are housed in the National Museum of Kenya in Nairobi (NMK) and were studied there. Study included identification to the lowest taxonomic level possible, comparison with other material, taking appropriate measurements and photography. Tugen Hills sites were originally recorded by EAGRU in various and distinctive ways. For example, JM 511 is the site of Kibingor, discovered by John Martyn. To conform to EAGRU mapping this method was systematized by Andrew Hill by adding a prefix to the site number that would indicate its location based on the geologist who studied the area. JM 511 is 1/511. With the formation of BPRP a database was created to catalog old sites and incorporate them into a uniquely BPRP numbering scheme, as well as newly discovered ones. In this way 1/511 became BPRP #1. BPRP numbers are given wherever possible for the sites, but a few of the older localities have not yet been incorporated in the BPRP catalog. When this is the case the EAGRU format numbers are provided, as they are the only numbers on the specimen cards. A specimen from what is now referred to as BPRP #1 may have a location on the museum card of JM 511, 1/511, Kibingor or BPRP #1 due to the changes in naming schemes. In some cases the specimen card was unclear on provenience. Fossils without well-recorded provenience were not included in this study.

Faunal lists were created for each site with one specimen number listed as an example of each identified taxon. Descriptions of a few of these are included in this chapter as examples. While many methodologies argue the importance of relative abundances (Vrba, 1974; Andrews and Evans, 1979; Andrews, 1989; Reed, 1997; Su and Harrison, 2007), Behrensmeyer (1991) and Behrensmeyer and Western (2009) demonstrated that taphonomy has little impact on the assemblage in terms of broad-scale paleoenvironment reconstructions. The paleoecological reconstructions of the southern Chemeron Formation are the result of a conventional analysis of individual faunal assemblages from relevant sites. The paleoecological reconstruction of each site is based on the presence or absence of taxa. Other methods are presently precluded due to limited sample sizes. Larger-scale reconstructions rely on geologic dates to pool sites and produce larger sample sizes. Paleoecological information on the fossil species and bovid tribes used modern analogs and isotopic and paleoecomorphologic work that had been carried out directly on the relevant fossil taxon to reconstruct that animal's environment. Only when no work had been done on the paleospecies, or tribe, was a modern analog used. Although much paleoecomorphological work has been done on bovids, much of it remains relatively taxon-free, as the postcrania are infrequently associated with crania or horn-cores used to identify to species. Therefore, inferences about bovid paleoenvironments are at the tribal rather than species level.

A small note is needed here in reference to the term mosaic as it refers to environment. There has been much discussion about mosaicism in the paleoecological community. My own personal classification of a mosaic is that it requires three or more different habitats in the reconstruction. Therefore, an environment with animals indicating open areas and wooded ones would be categorized as an open woodland rather than a mosaic.

Relative abundances of families are calculated by number of specimens. Skeletal element abundances are calculated the same way and for complete or partial skeletons they are counted as postcrania as given in Bobe and Behrensemeyer (2004). Bovid tribe abundances are calculated using minimum number of individuals (MNI), which is the most accurate method but gives low sample sizes even for large sites. For sites with 30 or more specimens, or ones of particular interest due to the presence of primates, I have included data on relative abundances of families, skeletal element abundances, and bovid tribe abundances. These data are available for all sites, but as many have very small sample sizes those data are not statistically significant without packaging by geologic date. BPRP does not separate formations into members. In an effort to be conservative, BPRP has named discrete sites where there are occurrences of bones in the same local area but separated by gullies, in case they prove not to be from the same horizon. This is in part due to past mistakes in geology at other localities in East Africa, and the complicated stratigraphy of the Tugen Hills, as well as the possibility of obtaining fine-resolution dates for each of our sites. Unless otherwise noted, all site ages are known from personal communication with John Kingston and Al Deino.

I have examined 105 sites within the southern part of the Chemeron Formation as part of my dissertation work. Due to this large number of sites, many of which have very few fossils that are not identifiable to anything more than the family level, only a small number of them will be discussed in detail. These sites were chosen either for having among the largest collection of faunal material, or for having a moderate collection with a specimen of particular interest, such as a hominin.

Paleoenvironments were reconstructed using a combination of paleoecomorphological studies, isotopic studies, and information on modern indicator taxa. Isotopic work on extinct proboscideans from work done by Cerling and colleagues (1999) was used to indicate preferences of a variety of those taxa. Preferences for the genus *Homo* were reconstructed by consulting MacLatchy et al. (2010) and Ungar et al. (2006). Coombs and Cote (2010) was consulted for information on chalicothere paleoenvironments. Kingston and Harrison's (2007) isotopic study was used to identify equid dietary preferences. Geraads' (2010c) chapter was used to reconstruct tragulid paleoenvironments. Bovid family preferences were reconstructed using work by Brooks (1961), Cerling et al. (2003c), Estes (2012), Gagnon and Chew (2000), Kingdon (2015), Maddock (1979), Smithers (1983), and Sponheimer and Lee-Thorpe (2003). Research by Cerling et al. (2005), Harris (1991d), Kingston and Harrison (2007), and Solounias et al. (2000) were used to reconstruct the favored paleoenvironment of giraffids. Suid environments were reconstructed referencing Bishop (1994, 2010), Bishop et al. (1999a), Cooke and Wilkinson (1978), Harris (1983b), Harris and Cerling (2002), and Plummer and colleagues (1999). References used in reconstructing hippopotamid environments were Bocherens et al. (1996), Boisserie and coauthors (2005a), Cerling et al. (2003b), Franz-Odendaal et al. (2002), Kingston (1999), Morgan et al. (1994), Schoeninger et al. (2003), and Zazzo et al. (2000).

BPRP #1 Reconstruction

Kibingor, alternatively referred to as JM 511 and BPRP Site #1, is radiometrically dated to 5.14 Ma (Deino, pers. comm.). It was discovered to be fossiliferous in 1965 or 1966, and due to its reasonably high annual yield of fossils and convenient location near the road it has been visited on a regular basis. Specimens from Kibingor have been collected by a variety of researchers and field teams including EAGRU, the Leakeys, and BPRP. It is a well-sampled site that includes a number of rare taxa, such as *Ancylotherium hennigi*, yet there are no hominins and few primates in general.

Four hundred forty six mammalian specimens were found and studied, with 433 identifiable to family (Figure 28.1). There are 58 deinothere teeth and fragments, presumably all belonging to the only recognized species, *Deinotherium bozasi*. Forty gomphotheres are present and all are presumably *Anancus ultimus* (Sanders, 2011). Of the 34 elephantids only 7 specimens are complete enough for species designation. The remainder of the proboscidean material is not identifiable to family. One papionin is present on the basis of a molar. Two of the three hyaenid specimens are identifiable to genus as *Ikelohyena*. One felid specimen is classified on the basis of a tooth root. One of the three chalicothere specimens is complete enough to attribute to *Ancylotherium hennigi*. Of the 36 rhinocerotid specimens, 9 can be attributed to genus. There are only two equids, both incisors, only distinguishable to family. Two tragulid specimens, including a mandible fragment with dentition, were recently collected. Fifty four specimens are bovids with 30 of them identifiable to tribe. Five are giraffids with two specimens attributed to species. Seventy two are suids with 54 identifiable to genus. One hundred twenty two are isolated hippopotamid teeth or postcrania and, therefore, given current reclassifications (Boisserie, 2005), only recognizable to family.

Much of the fauna indicates a wooded environment. Deinotheres were dedicated browsers found in woodland environments. *Anancus* is an exception to the woodland reconstruction as it was a grazer. Schizotheriinae, the subfamily of chalicotheres which *Ancylotherium* belongs to, is typically found in sites reconstructed as being relatively moist with a forest component. The only two equid specimens are incisors not attributable to genus but likely of the "hipparion" group, of which the vast majority of species are mixed feeders. Modern species of tragulids are always found near a water source in dense cover. *Giraffa jumae* is present, albeit in small numbers, and indicates a need for drinking water and a specialization in mid-slope *Acacia–Commiphora* woodland. Modern tragelaphines prefer woodland environments, and are water-dependent browsers. Extant bovines are grazers with a penchant for areas with a modicum of tree cover to provide shade. Living antilopines are browsers or mixed feeders and prefer a grassland habitat. Modern reduncines are water-dependent grazers. Living alcelaphines are also grazers, but their water dependency varies by species. Neotragini and Hippotragini are the only bovid tribes missing from BPRP #1. Tragelaphini, Bovini, and Antilopini are equally distributed, but this is actually closely followed by Reduncini and Alcelaphini, given that the sample sizes are very small. *Nyanzachoerus devauxi* had a diet of browse or a mixed diet that incorporated grass. Study of the postcrania of *N. devauxi* indicates it lived in a woodland or bushland environment. Isotopic work on the dentition of *N. syrticus* from the Tugen Hills and Laetoli identifies diets that range from mixed feeding to complete browsing. The same carbon isotope studies demonstrate *N. kanamensis* also had a diet ranging from mixed feeding to browsing. Paleoecomorphological studies conducted on *N. kanamensis* skeletons indicate a preference for woodland or bushland habitats. The presence of *Notochoerus jaegeri* at one of the earlier sites for the species indicates, similar to its

BPRP #1 Family Distribution

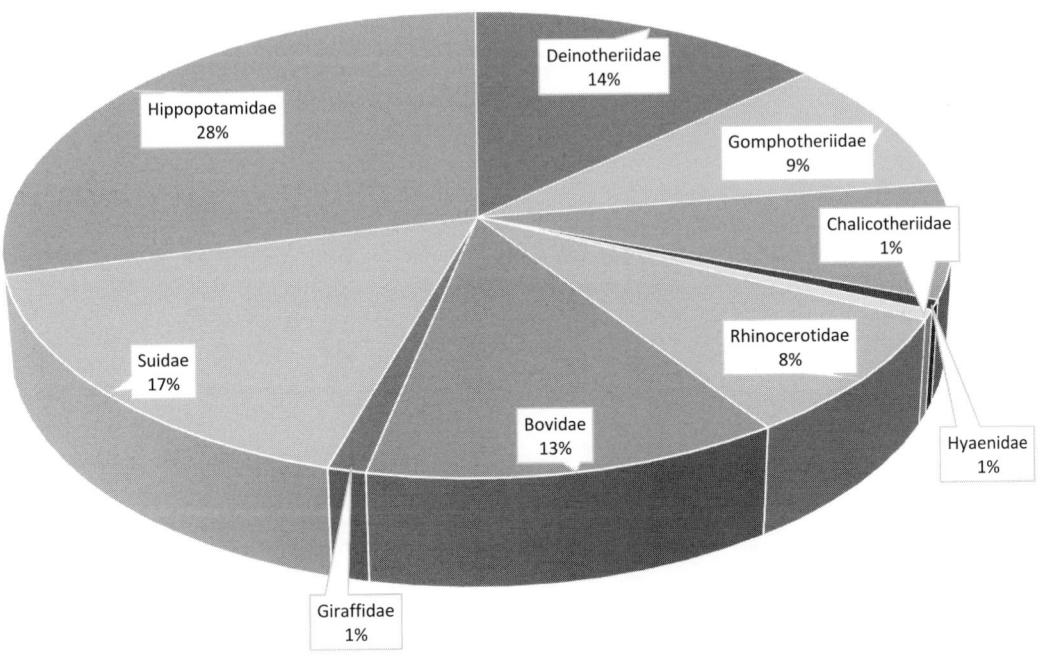

Figure 28.1 Pie chart of BPRP #1 Mammalian Family Distribution. The four most abundant families represented at Site 1 are Hippopotamidae, Suidae, Bovidae, and Deinotheriidae.

conspecifics in other portions of the Tugen Hills, a diet that included grass and browse. *Kolpochoerus heseloni* at Kibingor are likely most similar to other earlier members of that species in having morphology more suited to a wooded environment while their diet was that of a grazer. The presence of hippopotamids indicates a body of water and grazing area, likely comprised of C_4 grasses.

Hippopotamids and suids make up the majority of the specimens, with bovids and deinotheres following. The presence of large numbers of deinotheres, representing 13 percent of the specimens, is unusual for Neogene Africa. While deinotheres are ubiquitous at sites, they typically represent an uncommon element in terms of abundance and their presence is frequently known only through enamel fragments. BPRP #1 has a number of complete isolated teeth and their abundance may indicate a more wooded environment than that found at other East African sites of a similar age.

As with most sites in the Chemeron Formation, and particularly the larger sites, BPRP #1 is dominated by isolated teeth, making it comparable to the Turkana material.

BPRP #2 Reconstruction

BPRP #2 (EAGRU site JM 85) is located in a tributary drainage of the Kapthurin River and the hominin temporal bone found there is dated to 2.43 ± 0.02 Ma (Hill et al., 1992). More radiometric dates were obtained from the lapilli tuffs bookending the BC-1 fossiliferous unit with ages of 2.456 ± 0.006 Ma and 2.939 ± 0.013 Ma. In the Kapthurin River the base of the Chemeron Formation is dated at 3.19 ± 0.03 Ma and the top at 1.60 ± 0.05 Ma. The sediments were deposited at an average rate of 11 cm/ka (Deino and Hill, 2002).

Mammalian family distribution is dominated by bovids, as shown in Figure 28.2. One proboscidean tooth fragment has been recovered from this site. A temporal bone, plausibly one of the earliest representatives of *Homo*, is also the only evidence of the genus in the formation. The only indication of Rhinocerotidae is an ilium fragment. The majority of the fauna are specimens belonging to Bovidae. One tragelaphine, a neotragine identified as *Madoqua*, and an antilopine identified as *Antidorcas* have been recovered, along with 20 alcelaphine fragments. Two pigs, *Notochoerus euilus* and *Kolpochoerus heseloni*, are present at the site. Only one hippopotamid tooth has been found.

Using modern analogs, the tragelaphine specimen indicates the area had some woodland component and a source of water. The living *Madoqua* is an arid-adapted bovid that prefers low thicket areas with succulents. Extant antilopines vary in dietary preferences from mixed feeders to browsers. The majority of bovids are alcelaphines. Modern species of this family are grazers. Both species of extinct pigs are, through stable carbon isotope analysis, known to have been mixed feeders. The single hippopotamid specimen indicates a body of water in the area. This produces an overall environmental picture of a predominantly grassland area with some bushland and a permanent water source.

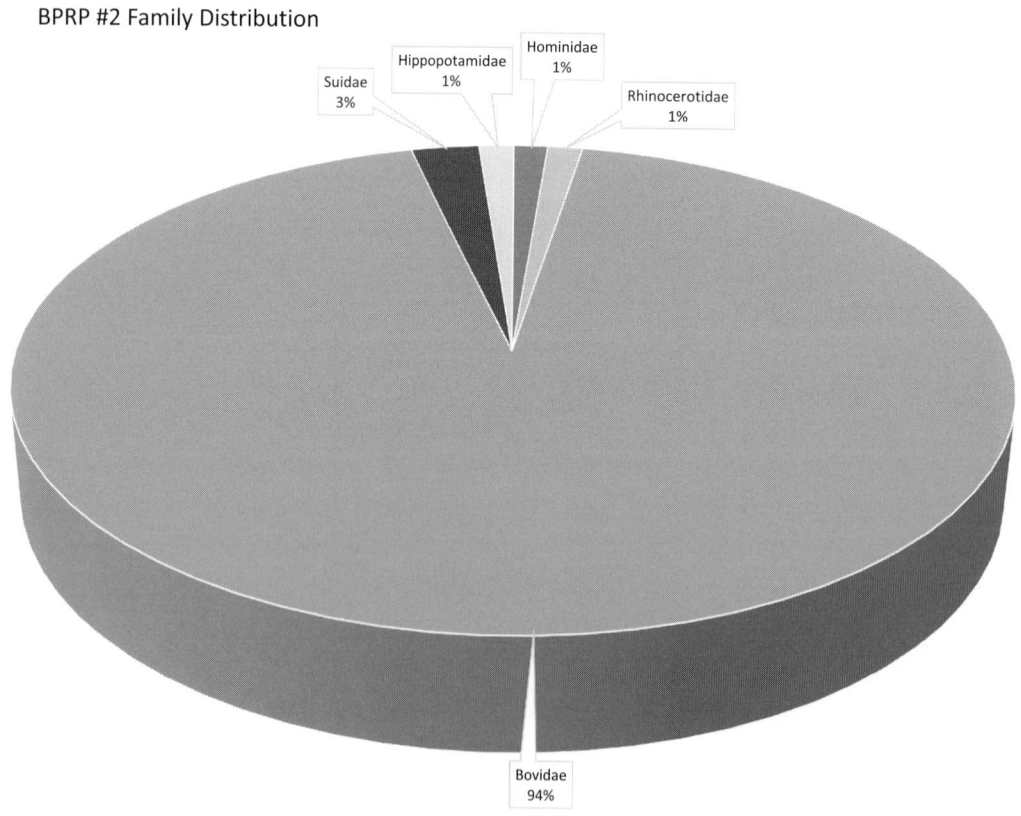

Figure 28.2 Pie chart of BPRP #2 Mammalian Family Distribution. Bovidae overwhelmingly make up the majority of the fossils found at Site 2.

BPRP #15 Reconstruction

Also located in the original Ndau tributary, this site is approximately 5 Ma. The majority of specimens are isolated teeth (Figure 28.3). Thirty three specimens are *Deinotherium bozasi* teeth or fragments of teeth. Eight *Anancus* teeth are from site 15. Five are available for identification and are assigned to *Anancus ultimus*. Five elephantids are present, two identified to *Loxodonta adaurora*. One other proboscidean tooth fragment cannot be identified to family. A hyaenid ulna fragment, larger than *Ikelohyena* at Langebaanweg, is the only carnivore. There is one chalicothere molar, presumably *Ancylotherium hennigi*. Of the 12 rhinocerotid fragments, 2 are missing from the NMK, 6 are *Ceratotherium* sp. and one is *Brachypotherium lewisi*. A tragulid mandible fragment with dentition is part of the assemblage. Twelve bovid specimens are present. The majority are reduncines, with the other specimens equally distributed between tragelaphine, antilopine, hippotragine, and alcelaphine tribes. There is one giraffid, *Giraffa* sp. indet. Only three suids are part of the collection, one identifiable to *Nyanzachoerus kanamensis*. There are 27 hippopotamid specimens, including a recently discovered cranium as yet undescribed.

Deinotheres were browsers. *Anancus* species and elephantids were and are habitual grazers. Chalicotheres were adapted for browsing. The living tragulid, *Hyemoschus aquaticus*, is a browser preferring dense cover near a water source. Living reduncines, hippotragines, and alcelaphines are all grazers, but reduncines require water. Extant tragelaphines are also water-dependent but are browsers like antilopines. *Giraffa* species are browsers today and were in the past. *Nyanzachoerus kanamensis* was a mixed feeder. Hippopotamids require permanent water. The most abundant species, simply by specimen count, are browsers, but many of the deinothere specimens are fragments and the minimum number of individuals is three. There seems to be an even split between browsers and grazers, possibly indicating a truly mosaic habitat. Regardless, there must have been a wooded component with grass and permanent water.

Methods and Results for Skeletal Element Abundance

Fossils have been collected from the Tugen Hills since 1930 with systematic collection and description beginning with the work of the EAGRU in the 1960s and continuing through work undertaken by the Leakeys and the BPRP. As with most paleontological collections, there is a bias toward identifiable material, particularly if that material can be classified to a level more specific than family. Typically, postcranial elements, which frequently cannot be identified beyond family, are collected. Exceptions occur if the specimen is too large to be carried, too worn to be useful, or would likely be rejected for accessioning due to lack of storage space. These caveats notwithstanding, my familiarity with the collection and field sites, plus knowledge of past collection practices, suggests that the sample presented here is a good representation of Chemeron fossils (Figure 28.4). It should also be noted that many isolated teeth or fragments thereof are not collected as they would be difficult to identify, sometimes to even the family level, and therefore would be rejected for storage and not particularly useful in paleoecological reconstruction or taxonomic studies. The majority of specimens found and collected are isolated teeth (Figure 28.5). This is surprising, as the Chemeron deposits are lacustrine. Typically this pattern would be indicative

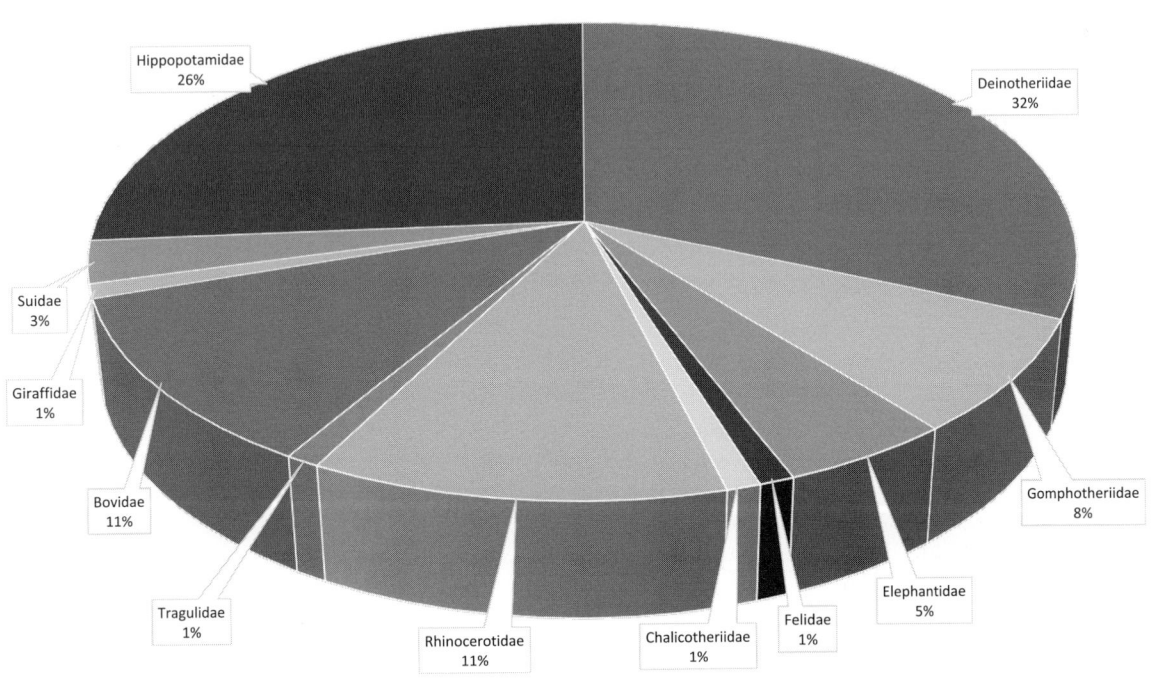

Figure 28.3 Pie chart of BPRP #15 Mammalian Family Distribution. Deinotheriidae, Hippopotamidae, Rhinocerotidae, and Bovidae are the four most represented faunas at Site 15.

of a fluviatile environment as demonstrated in taphonomic studies and found at Omo Shungura (Behrensmeyer, 1988; Bobe et al., 2002). It is of interest that the proportion of isolated teeth in the Chemeron as a whole, 74 percent, closely corresponds to the lowest percentage accumulated in the lacustrine sediment of upper Member G in Omo Shungura (70 percent; Bobe et al, 2002). At the scale of 100-ka intervals isolated teeth in the Chemeron still tend to dominate the assemblages (with the two exceptions of tying with the category "other skull parts" for most abundant) and those abundances range anywhere from 33 percent in the 3.2 Ma interval to almost 90 percent at the 4.1 Ma interval (Figure 28.6). When compared to the same time intervals found in the Omo Shungura (Bobe and Behrensmeyer, 2004; Table 28.1), the proportions are almost identical.

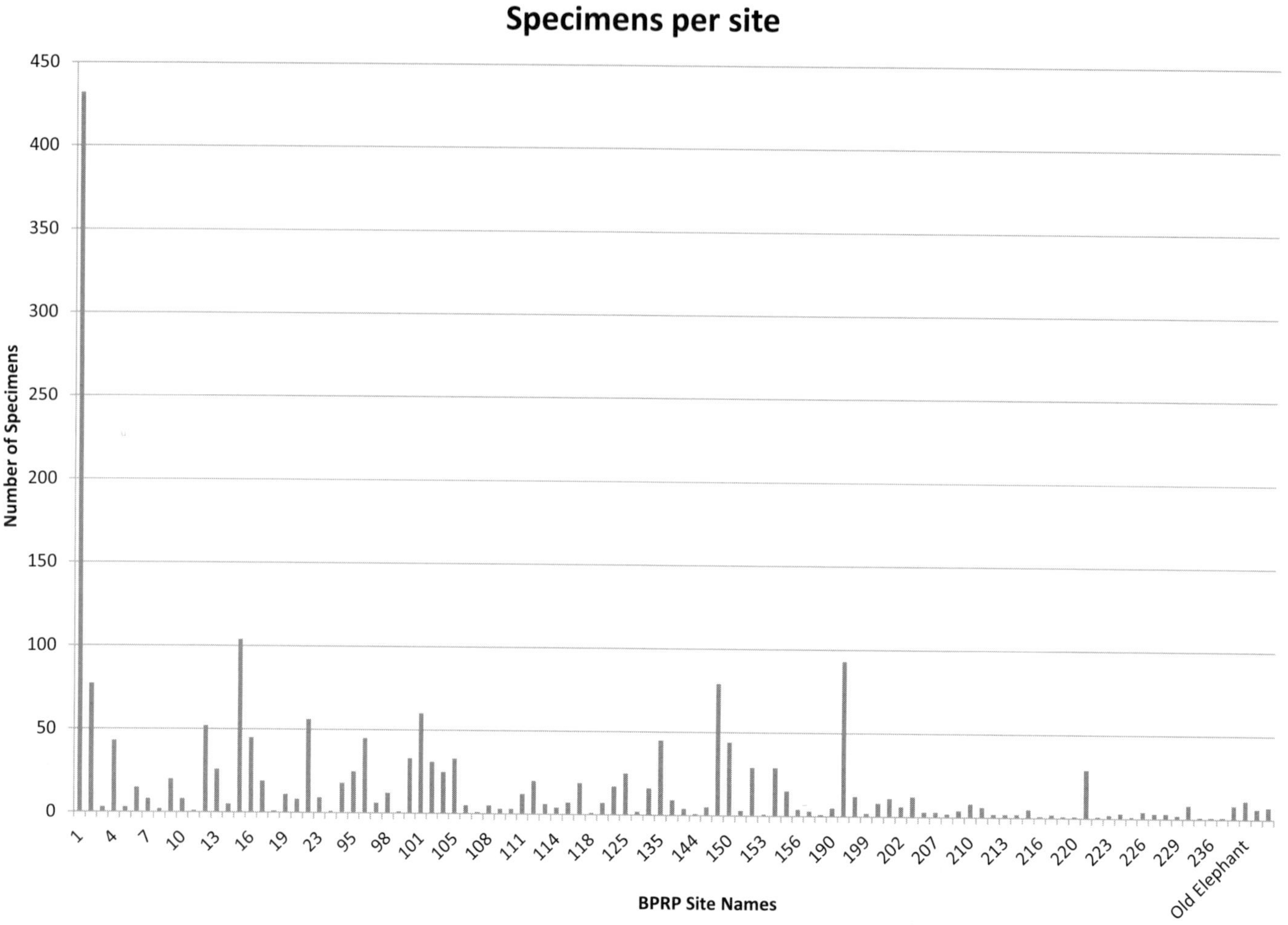

Figure 28.4 Specimens per site by count in the Chemeron Formation, Tugen Hills, Kenya. BPRP #1 has the most extensive collection.

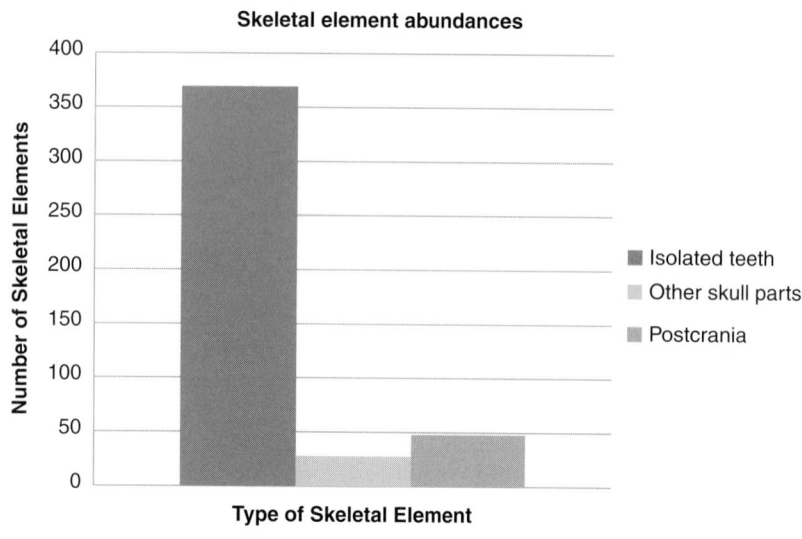

Figure 28.5 Numbers of skeletal element abundances at Chemeron sites. Isolated teeth are far more abundant than other skull parts or postcrania.

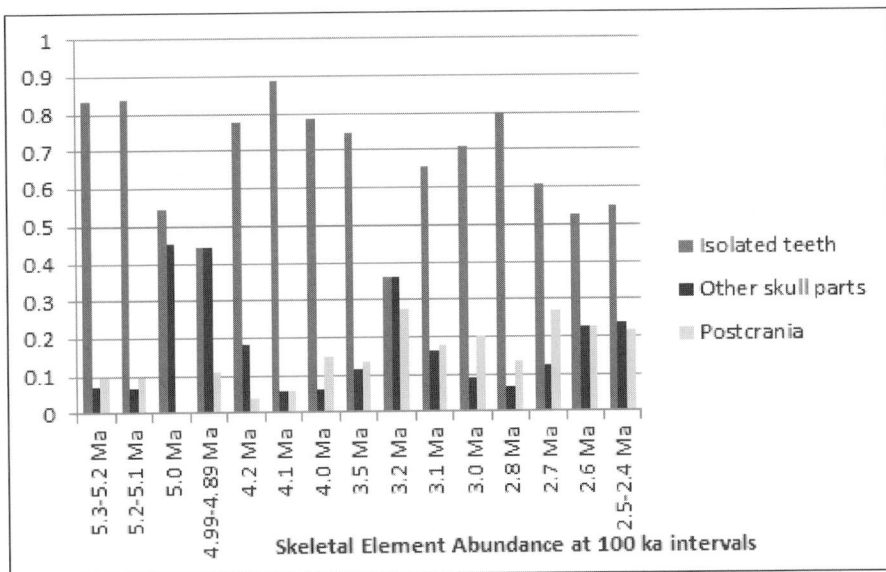

Figure 28.6 Skeletal element abundance found at Chemeron sites grouped by date in 100-ka intervals.

Bovid Tribe Abundance

Bovids are the most abundant specimens in the Chemeron Formation, followed closely by hippopotamids (Figure 28.7). Relative proportions of bovids to all other mammal specimens in each 100-ka time interval were calculated using specimen counts (Figure 28.8). Specimen counts were used rather than MNIs due to the high numbers of isolated hippopotamid teeth that cannot be identified to serial position in many cases. This relative abundance varies widely throughout the sequence but seems largely unrelated to sample size as the biggest site samples also vary in bovid abundance from roughly 12 percent to 92 percent. Some of the earlier-collected bovid specimens were initially identified by Alan Gentry, John Barry, or Andrew Hill, and I reconfirmed or changed the identifications as needed. MNIs were used to calculate bovid tribe abundances at each site, which were then used to calculate percentages of each tribe throughout the entirety of the formation and at various time intervals (Tables 28.1–28.3; Figure 28.9). This choice was made, in part, for taphonomic reasons, as sites within the Tugen Hills are small in extent and contain either isolated teeth or partial skeletons. It is unclear if many of the isolated teeth at a site came from one individual originally but, given the low numbers of overlapping elements of each taxa at a site, it is the most conservative approach. Geologic dates for each site (John Kingston and Al Deino, pers. comm.) were then used to create different categories of time intervals, 100 ka, 200 ka and 400 ka, where possible. MNIs of bovids from sites of similar ages were pooled in each of those cases and percentages of abundance for each tribe at those intervals were calculated. Because of our collection and geologic methods, i.e., not using members and instead using time intervals, there is no need to test if sample size is correlated to time represented (as done in Bobe and Eck, 2001). Unfortunately, we do not have information on the geographic area represented by each site and I am unable to determine if that influences sample size. Chi-square statistics were performed on each interval group to test the null hypothesis that taxonomic abundance is uniform across time intervals. Chi-square (or Cochran's) test of linear trend is preferable for small sample sizes as it reduces the amount of Type I and II errors (Cannon, 2001), and as such this statistic was also used on the bovid tribe sample. Cochran's test of linear trend tests the same null hypothesis as the chi-square statistic, that a taxon is uniform across time intervals.

Use of the chi-square statistic resulted in failure to reject the null hypothesis. Low sample sizes and the number of cells with zeroes as values were considered as potential complicating factors. Elimination of the minor component of Neotragini, the tribe contributing several zero count cells, did nothing to alter significance. Bovid tribe abundances do not appear to change significantly throughout time in the Tugen Hills according to the chi-square statistic. This is interesting, as we know from independent evidence that there were climatic fluctuations during this period. However, as my results from chi-square tests may be due to small sample sizes, Cochran's test for linear trend (Cannon, 2001) was used to better examine potential trends for each bovid tribe at every time interval used in this study. When this test was performed for each tribe significant results were obtained only for alcelaphines. Alcelaphines were the sole tribe to show any significant trend and demonstrate that there is not an even distribution through time. Rather, alcelaphines increase through time (i.e., as sediment packages get younger there are more alcelaphines). Overall abundances for the entirety of the formation show that tragelaphines are the most abundant with 46 percent of the specimens. Alcelaphines and antilopines tie for second with 17 percent each. This is interesting, because while tragelaphines suggest a closed environment and the other two tribes suggest open, all three indicate dry environments. This is the opposite of what is seen in the Omo Shungura Formation (Bobe and Eck, 2001) and may suggest that Chemeron sites with high percentages of bovids were deposited in drier intervals. Tragelaphine abundance declines throughout the sequence, although not significantly. This may suggest some shift from more closed wet environments to more open areas.

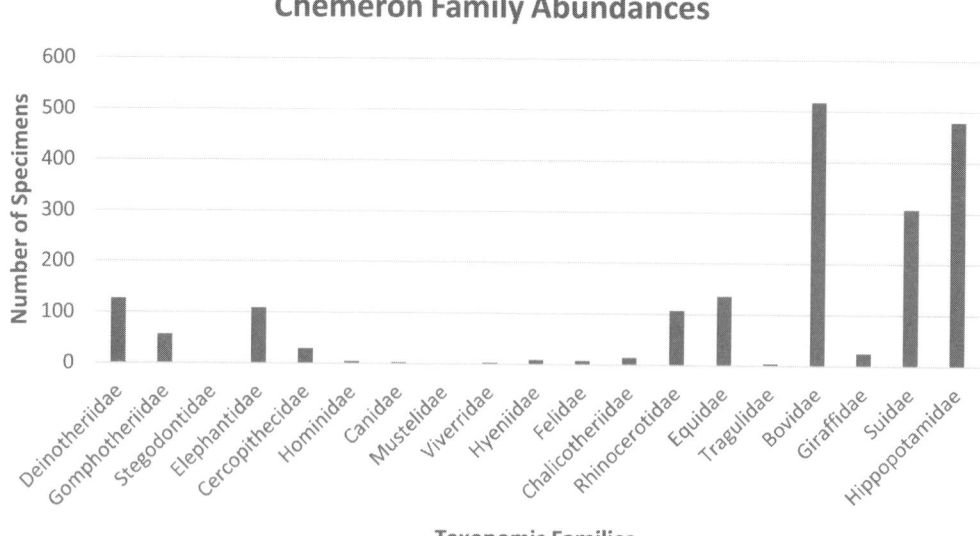

Figure 28.7 Chemeron Formation taxonomic abundances by family. Bovidae are the most abundant, followed closely by Hippopotamidae.

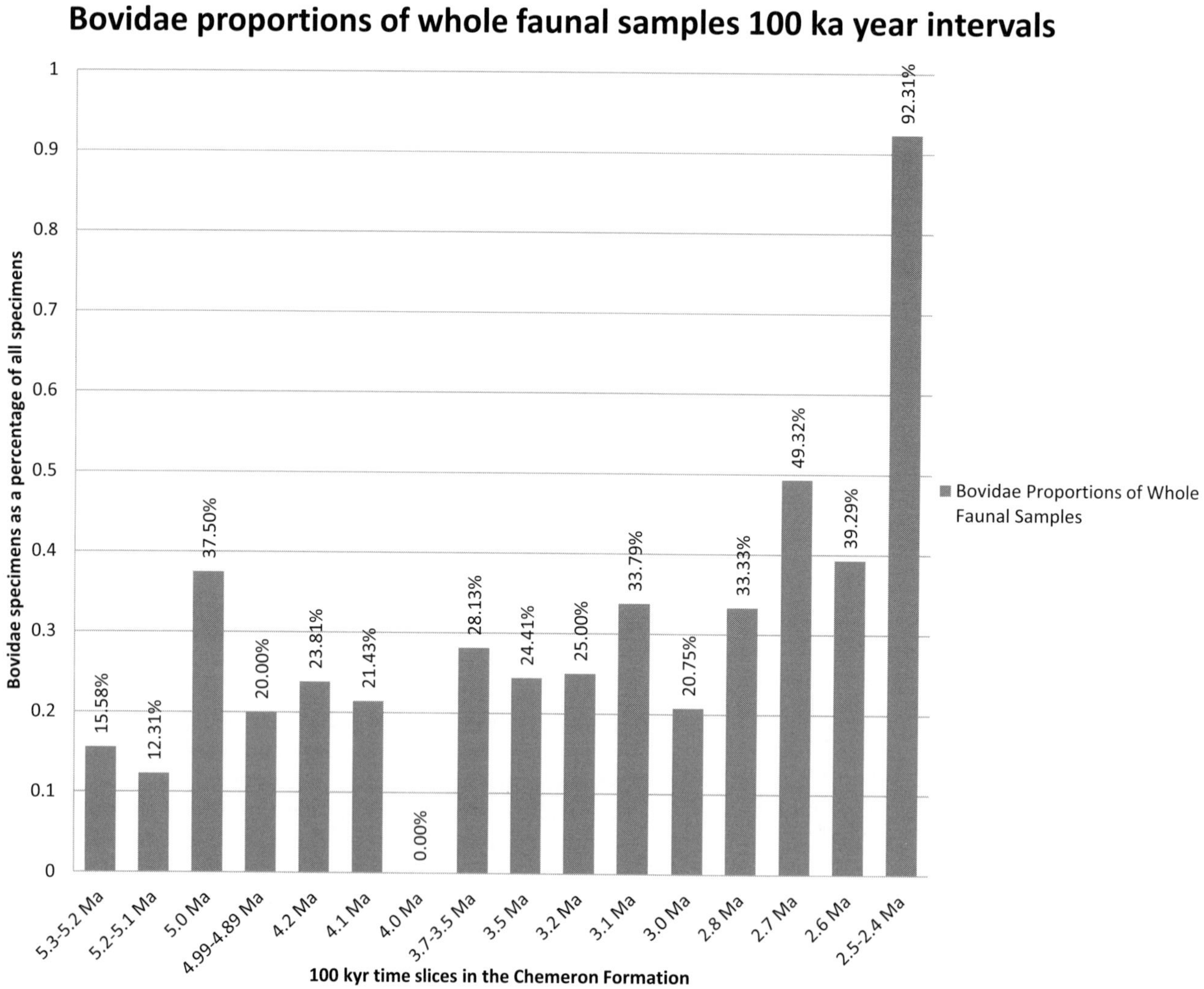

Figure 28.8 Bovidae percentages as proportions of whole faunal samples at Chemeron sites grouped by date in 100-ka intervals.

Many individual sites within the southern Chemeron Formation are reconstructed as a mosaic environment. Relative proportions of bovid tribes as shown in Figure 28.10 show roughly the same results, with the added component that alcelaphines begin to increase as the sediments get younger, indicating the environment was becoming more open or perhaps seasonally drier.

Given that bovids may only have been sampled from sites deposited in drier intervals between the megalakes, their abundances were plotted against hippos. At certain intervals there appears to be a strong inverse relationship between the two. This may be due to lake size waxing or waning during a particular interval and is perhaps supported by the higher proportions of bovid tribes preferring drier environments. When we look for faunal trends during the high insolation period we certainly do not see the same signature in each. Further work will focus on including the site location relative to the location of the diatomites in order to determine if some of the differences are due to proximity to the paleo-lake.

Table 28.1 Bovid tribe abundances at 400-ka intervals in the Chemeron Formation

	5.3–4.9	3.2–2.8	2.7–2.3	Totals
Tragelaphini	7	4	6	17
Bovini	4	1	5	10
Neotragini	0	0	2	2
Antilopini	5	9	6	20
Reduncini	3	1	4	8
Hippotragini	2	3	2	7
Alcelaphini	5	8	14	27
Totals	26	26	39	91
%Tr	26.92	15.38	15.38	
%Bov	15.38	3.85	12.82	
%Neo	0.00	0.00	5.13	
%Ant	19.23	34.62	15.38	
%Red	11.54	3.85	10.26	
%Hipp	7.69	11.54	5.130	
%Alc	19.23	30.77	35.90	

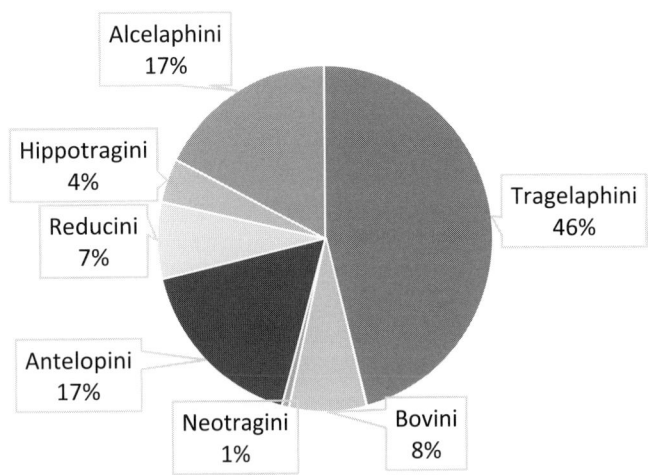

Figure 28.9 Pie chart showing percentages of Bovidae tribes for the Chemeron Formation. Tragelaphini are the most common.

Table 28.2. Bovid tribe abundances at 200-ka intervals in the Chemeron Formation

	5.3–5.1	5.1–4.9	4.2–4.0	3.7–3.5	3.2–3.0	2.8–2.6	2.5–2.3	Totals
Tragelaphini	4	3	4	7	4	5	1	28
Bovini	4	0	2	6	1	4	1	18
Neotragini	0	0	0	0	0	1	1	2
Antilopini	4	1	3	4	9	4	2	27
Reduncini	3	0	1	1	1	4	0	10
Hippotragini	2	0	1	1	2	3	0	9
Alcelaphini	4	1	2	8	6	9	7	37
Totals	21	5	13	27	23	30	12	131
%Tr	19.05	60.00	30.77	25.93	17.39	16.67	8.33	
%Bov	19.05	0.00	15.38	22.22	4.35	13.33	8.33	
%Neo	0.00	0.00	0.00	0.00	0.00	3.33	8.33	
%Ant	19.05	20.00	23.08	14.81	39.13	13.33	16.67	
%Red	14.29%	0.00	7.69	3.70	4.35	13.33	0.00	
%Hipp	9.52	0.00	7.69	3.70	8.70	10.00	0.00	
%Alc	19.05	20.00	15.38	29.63	26.09	30.00	58.33	

Table 28.3 Bovid tribe abundances at 100-ka intervals in the Chemeron Formation

	5.3–5.2 Ma	5.2–5.1 Ma	5 Ma	4.99–4.89 Ma	4.2 Ma	4.1 Ma	4 Ma	3.5 Ma	3.2 Ma	3.1 Ma	3 Ma	2.8 Ma	2.7 Ma	2.6 Ma	2.5–2.4 Ma	Totals
Tragelaphini	1	3	2	1	2	1	1	3	0	2	2	0	2	3	1	24
Bovini	2	2	0	0	2	0	0	4	0	1	0	0	2	2	0	15
Neotragini	0	0	0	0	0	0	0	0	0	0	0	0	0	1	1	2
Antilopini	1	3	0	1	1	2	0	1	1	5	2	0	4	0	1	22
Reduncini	0	3	0	0	0	0	1	1	0	1	0	0	3	1	0	10
Hippotragini	1	1	0	0	0	0	1	0	0	1	1	1	2	0	0	8
Alcelaphini	2	2	1	0	0	0	2	5	0	3	2	2	5	2	5	31
Totals	7	14	3	2	5	3	5	14	1	13	7	3	18	9	8	112
%Tr	14.29	21.43	66.67	50.00	40.00	33.33	20.00	21.43	0.00	15.38	28.57	0.00	11.11	33.33	12.50	
%Bov	28.57	14.29	0.00	0.00	40.00	0.00	0.00	28.57	0.00	7.69	0.00	0.00	11.11	22.22	0.00	
%Neo	0.00	0.00	0.00	0.00	0.00	0.00	0.00	0.00	0.00	0.00	0.00	0.00	0.00	11.11	12.50	
%Ant	14.29	21.43	0.00	50.00	20.00	66.67	0.00	7.14	100.00	38.46	28.57	0.00	22.22	0.00	12.50	
%Red	0.00	21.43	0.00	0.00	0.00	0.00	20.00	7.14	0.00	7.69	0.00	0.00	16.67	11.11	0.00	
%Hipp	14.29	7.14	0.00	0.00	0.00	0.00	20.00	0.00	0.00	7.69	14.29	33.33	11.11	0.00	0.00	
%Alc	28.57	14.29	33.33	0.00	0.00	0.00	40.00	35.71	0.00	23.08	28.57	66.67	27.78	22.22	62.50	

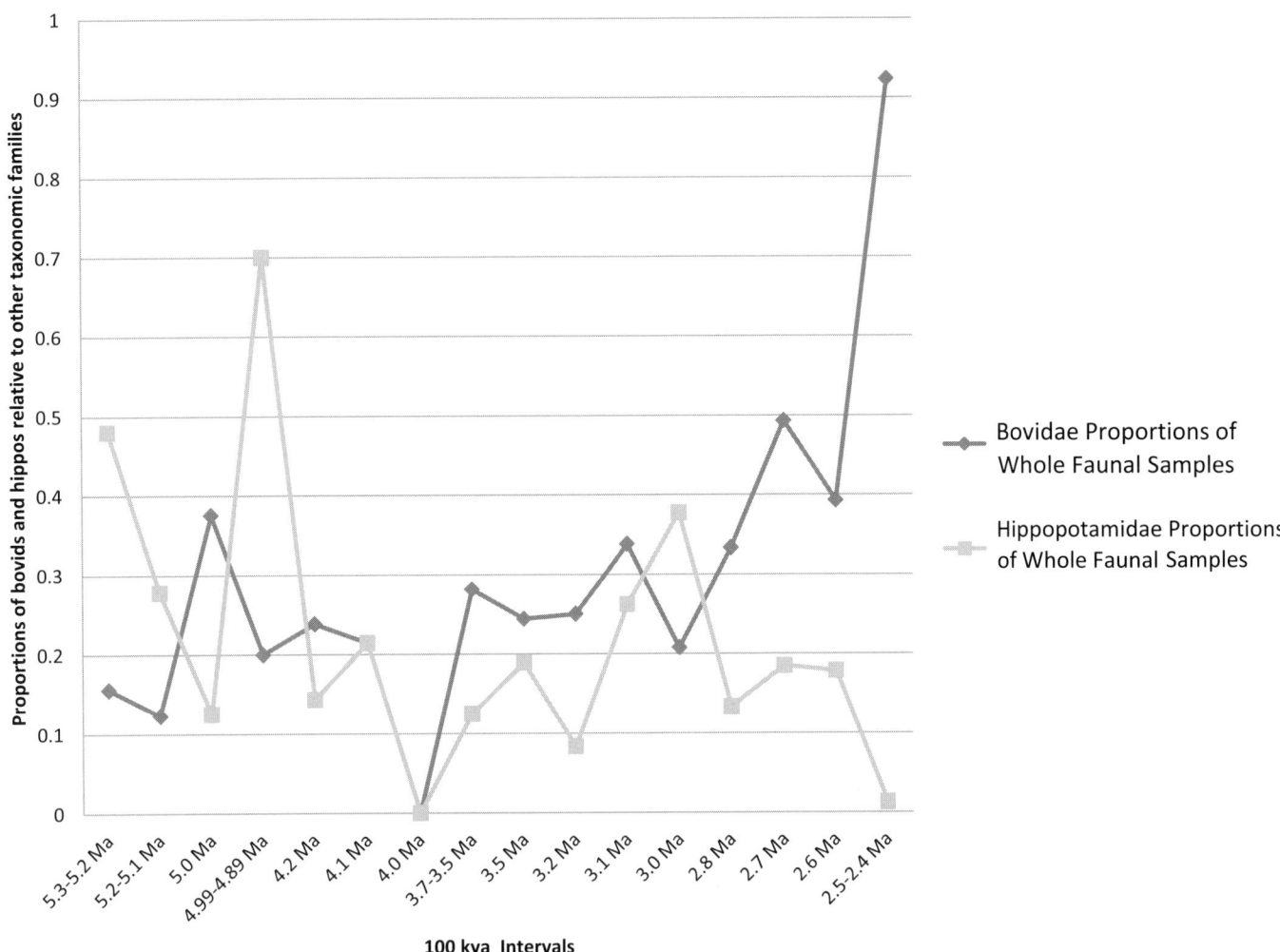

Figure 28.10 Comparison of proportions of Bovidae and Hippopotamidae specimens at Chemeron sites grouped by date in 100-ka intervals.

At sites just older than 5 Ma, with relatively few bovids, we have unusual fauna for East Africa. Two sites in particular, BPRP #1 and #15, have an abundance of deinotheres, several chalicotheres and two tragulids. It may be that the constant fracturing of the paleoenvironment by the fluctuating lake system created sanctuaries or isolated areas for these rare groups as the megalakes created a larger woodland or bushland area or pocket of such than would be typically be found in this region. We have evidence of high insolation and paleo-lake systems at 5.8–5.7 Ma, 4.9–4.8 Ma, 3.8–3.7 Ma, and 2.7–2.5 Ma. When we look for faunal trends in those time periods we certainly do not see the same signature during each insolation period. Further work will focus on including the site location relative to the location of the diatomites in order to determine if some of the differences are due to proximity to the paleo-lake.

Stepping back from examining particular taxa and looking at faunal reconstructions as a whole provides a slightly different viewpoint. Paleoecological reconstruction of each site is based on presence or absence of taxa due to small sample sizes. Many individual sites within the southern Chemeron Formation are reconstructed as a mosaic environment and many of the time slices at both the 500-ka interval grouping and the 200-ka interval grouping support the idea that if you sample at such large hundred thousand year intervals the paleolandscape will look like a mosaic. The relative proportions of bovid tribes show the same results and also support grasslands increasing between 2.4 and 2 Ma, indicating the environment was becoming more open or perhaps seasonally drier. The insolation periods seem to have some of the highest variation in environment type.

Paleoenvironmental Reconstruction in Regard to Time

Most paleontological projects use the standard geological framework of dividing up stratigraphic units into formations and then further subdividing those into members. As referenced earlier in the text, BPRP does not subdivide Tugen Hills' Formations into members. This affords the opportunity to examine paleoenvironmental reconstruction in a variety of packages that are not constrained by a geologic subdivision as each site, no matter the wealth or dearth of specimens, is individually dated. I used the same 500–ka (Figure 28.11), 200–ka (Figure 28.12), and 100-ka (Figure 28.13) intervals as in the bovid analyses to determine what effect, if any, rearrangement of time slices had on paleoenvironmental reconstruction.

At 500-ka intervals the Tugen Hills are dominated by grasslands toward the beginning and end of the formation, from 5.5 to 5.9 Ma and from 2.0 to 2.4 Ma. It should be noted that from 2.0 to 2.4 Ma there is a small bush/grass component and that sample sizes in both of those time intervals are very small. From 5.0 to 5.4 Ma there is a mixture of closed environments as well as sites that are comprised solely of aquatic animals. No grassland element is present during this time and there are a number of sites such as BPRP #1 and BPRP #15, described earlier, that include unusual fauna such as chalicotheres. It is hypothesized that perhaps the Tugen Hills were more densely wooded than other areas during that time and served as a refuge for those animals. From 4.5 to 4.9 Ma we see a strong water component, the return of grassland and also a bushland environment. When that 500-ka time frame is compared to our precession peaks, we see that at around 4.9 Ma we have a high-insolation package and an abundance of hippopotamids at sites and that quickly drops off by 4.2 Ma, when bovids outnumber hippos. Specimen counts of both families are relatively low and there is not as great a disparity between the two by 4.2 Ma as in other times. However, this is a good indication that 500-ka packages are not of fine enough resolution to tease apart what is linking the orbitally forced waxing and waning of the lake system. At a 500-ka interval that paleoenvironment may be reconstructed as a mosaic as there are sites indicating both grassland and bushland when it may simply be artificially imposed time-averaging. From 4.0 to 4.4 Ma there is clear evidence of a true mosaic paleoenvironment as well as a range of closed environments from bush with a grass component to fully wooded. The environment may well have been more fragmented after a period of high lake levels followed by drying. The time interval of 3.5–3.9 Ma has the highest occurrence of sites reconstructed as mosaic. Additionally, the remainder of the sites covers a much larger spectrum of environments than other 500-ka time slices including everything except bush/grass. The time interval of 3.0–3.4 Ma also sees a wider range of environments from grassland to completely wooded, but has fewer sites that fall into my strict mosaic category than the earlier interval and a greater number of sites reconstructed as grassland. The interval from 2.5 to 2.9 Ma continues the trend in increasing numbers of grassland paleoenvironments as well as the reappearance of sites reconstructed as bush/grass. Numbers of sites reconstructed as

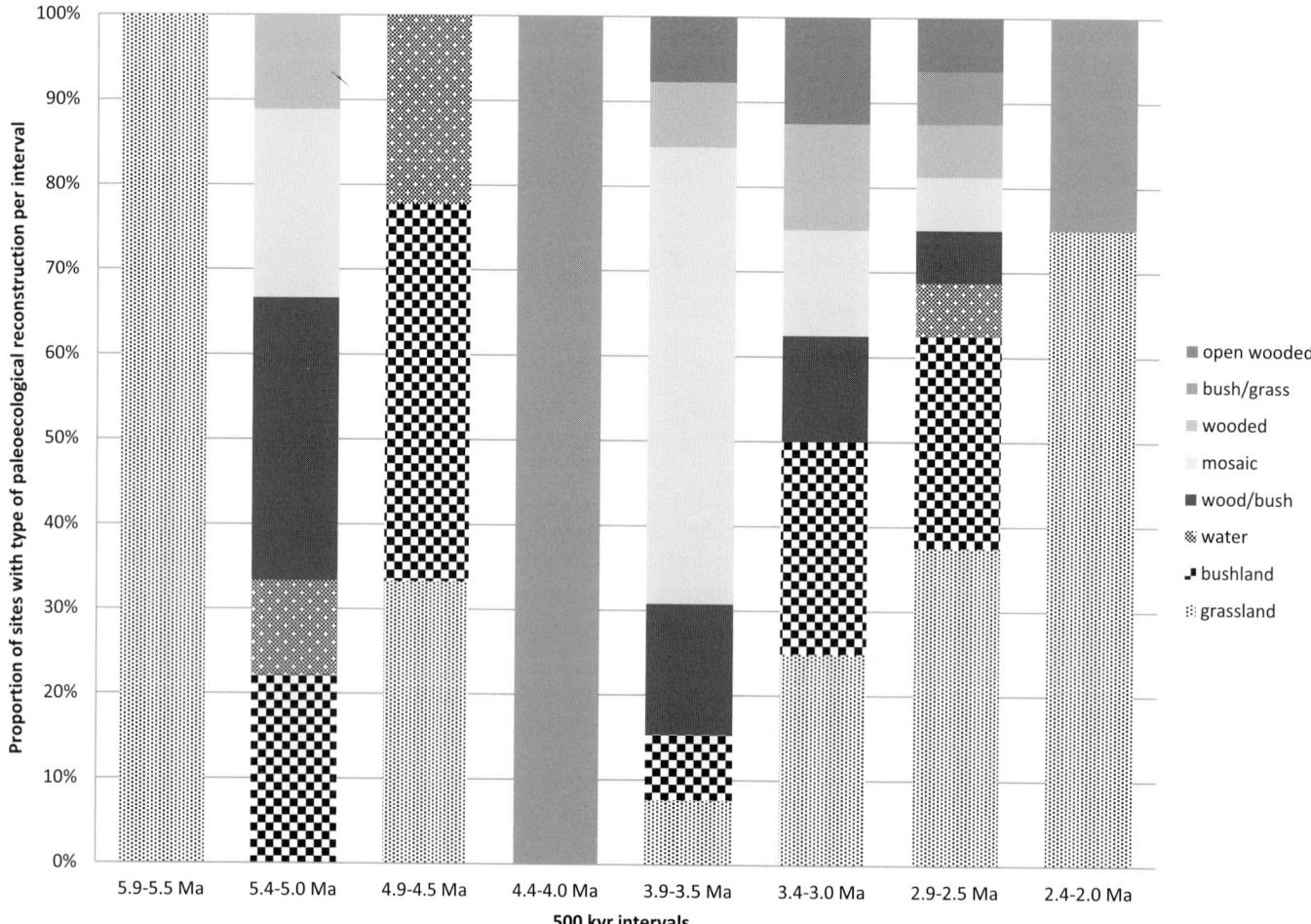

Figure 28.11 Proportions of Chemeron sites with type of paleoecological reconstructions grouped in 500-ka intervals.

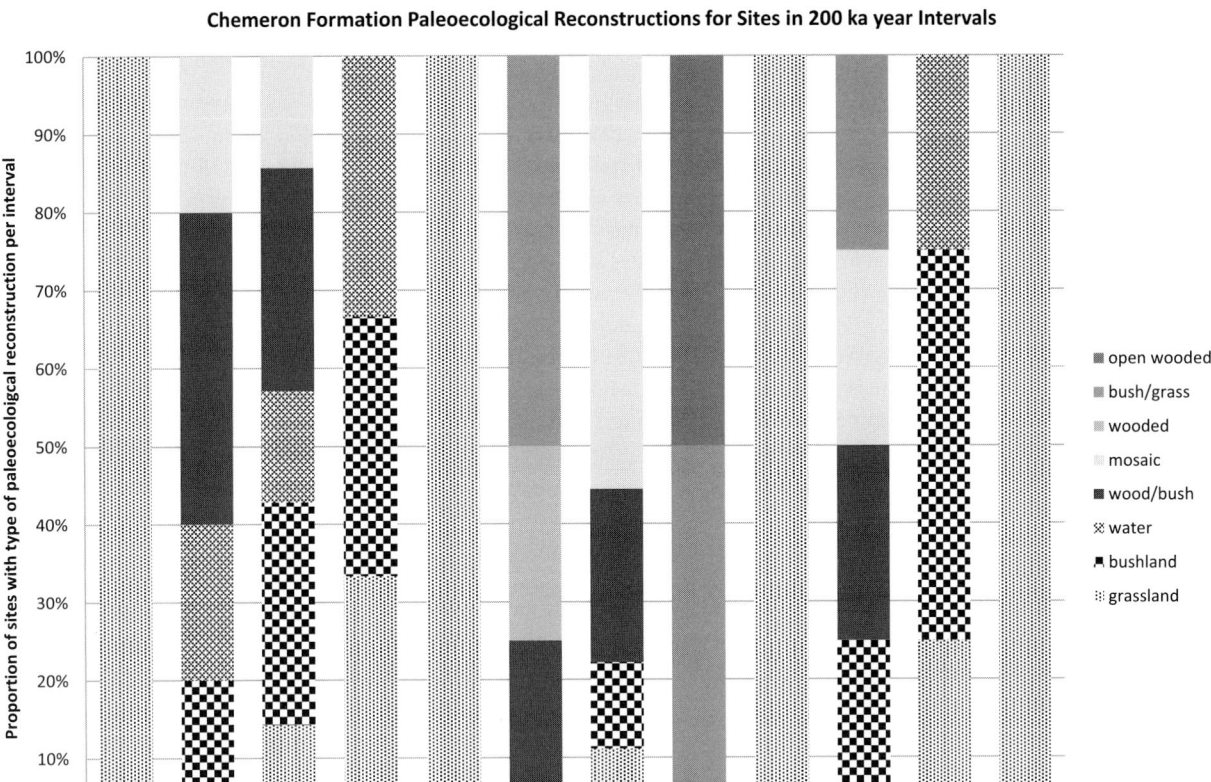

Figure 28.12 Proportions of Chemeron sites with type of paleoecological reconstructions grouped in 200-ka intervals.

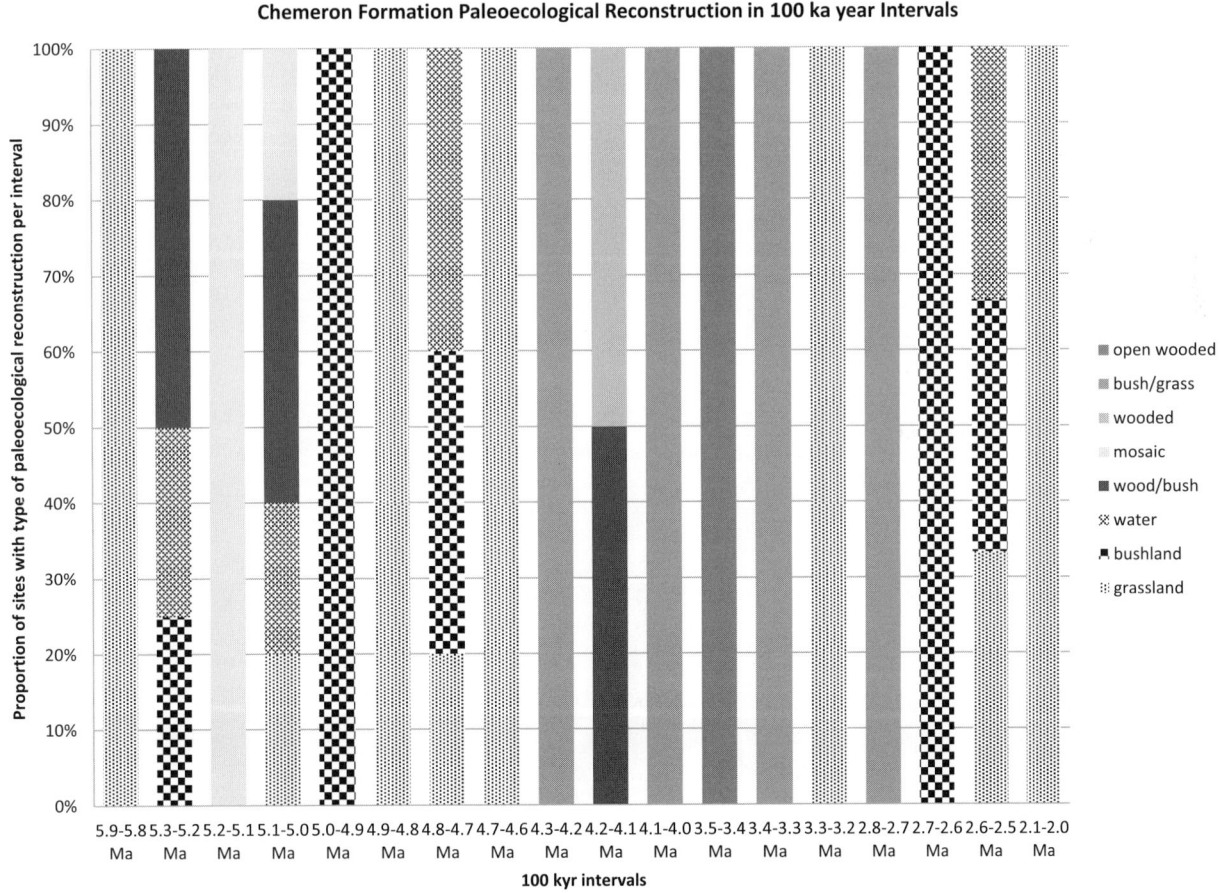

Figure 28.13 Proportions of Chemeron sites with type of paleoecological reconstructions grouped in 100-ka intervals.

more closed environments decrease from the last time interval to this one as well and that trend continues to the extreme with the 2.0–2.4 interval that is predominantly grassland with some bush/grass paleoenvironments. In examining paleoecological reconstructions at 200-ka intervals the picture changes a bit. There are four, rather misleading, intervals that are 100 percent grassland. The oldest interval has only one site at 5.8 Ma reconstructed as a grassland. Two of the other pure grassland reconstructions, 4.7–4.5 Ma and 2.1–1.9 Ma, are also based on single sites and the 3.3–3.1 Ma interval reconstruction is only based on two sites. The highest percentages of wood/bush environments are at 5.3–5.1 Ma and 5.1–4.9 Ma, which still supports the idea that the Tugen Hills may have been a more closed environment refuge for certain rarer animal groups. Reconstructions at this level do not support a gradual spread of grasslands leading up to 2.1–1.9 Ma and instead suggest that the data may be skewed due to smaller sample sizes.

When we examine at the 100-ka interval scale the first glaring issue is the lack of sites in particular time periods, especially from 3.7 to 3.5 Ma where we previously had data. Currently that range is the best we have for the dating of those sites; therefore, they cannot be separated into smaller units of time and were left out of this interval analysis. Several sites in the 2.9–2.7 Ma category were also eliminated for the same reason. There are also several intervals with only one site, giving the reconstruction of that site 100 percent of the reconstruction for the interval. It is also worth noting that at 100-ka intervals there are some intervals such as 5.3–5.2 Ma that, if not considering individual sites in those time slices, may have been reconstructed as simply mosaic, regardless of the geographic distribution, as there is more than one environment represented. This highlights the need to be cautious when categorizing a locality as mosaic, as time-averaging and geographic extent of the locality must be taken into careful consideration.

The presence or absence of water in intervals of time has also been compared (Figures 28.14 and 28.15). Water in the paleoecological reconstructions was a category signifying the definitive presence of water within the environment. Reconstructions of bush/grass or open wood may have included a collection with a crocodile tooth or some hippo bones but the water was not included as a separate category and its inclusion did not qualify a reconstruction as mosaic. The vast majority of Chemeron sites have fauna indicative of a reasonably large water source, likely paleo-lake Baringo. Again, when examining the data it is important to remember that there is only one site included in the 5.9–5.5 Ma interval and one at the 2.4–2.0 Ma interval. This

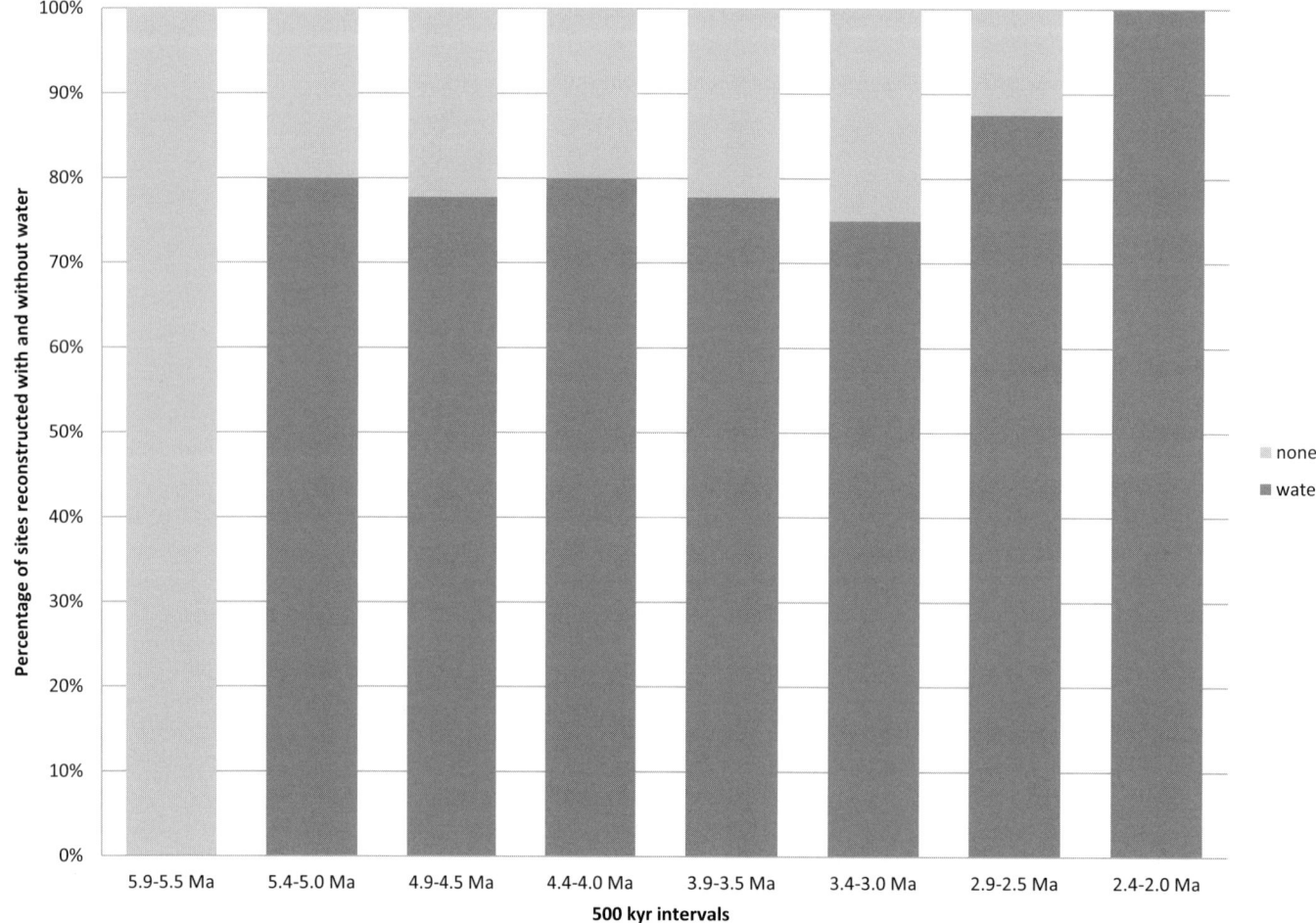

Figure 28.14 Proportions of Chemeron sites reconstructed with and without water grouped in 500-ka intervals.

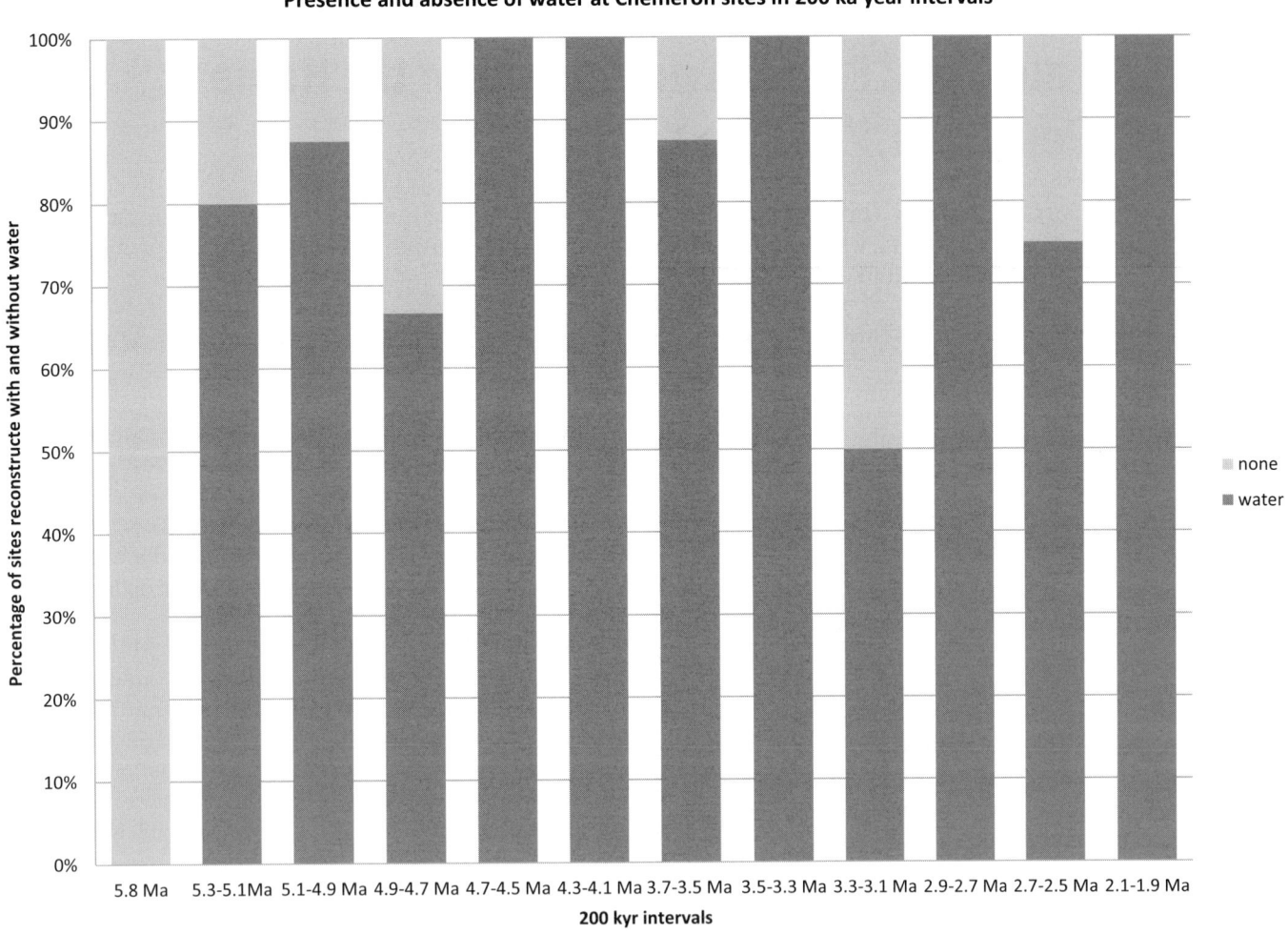

Figure 28.15 Proportions of Chemeron sites reconstructed with and without water grouped in 200-ka intervals.

means it is unlikely that there was absolutely no water in the earlier interval and further exploration is needed for sites in that time period. The picture looks slightly more complex at 200-ka intervals, but it is important to keep in mind that some intervals represent only a single site or a cluster of sites that are geographically close. These graphs may not be capturing the peaks and valleys of insolation or waxing or waning of the paleo-lake, but they do indicate that future research needs to be in the direction of tracking the extent of the paleo-lake throughout time.

Summary

Analysis of the fauna from the Chemeron Formation does not answer all of the broad questions posed by paleoecologists. It does, however, caution against cavalier use of the term mosaic and affords an opportunity to examine the scope of our studies. If we were working in the art world it would be akin to questioning how to examine an Impressionist painting – do you study the brush strokes or step back and take in the whole? The answer is to do both, but with the understanding that different questions must be asked and, hopefully, answered at each level.

The abundance of rare fauna at individual sites in the Chemeron Formation is fascinating and certainly tells us something unique was occurring in that place at that time. Does the presence of deinotheres at BPRP #15 tell us more than that, though? For that we must step back. Are there deinotheres at other sites around that time in the Tugen Hills? Yes. Are there any elsewhere in Kenya at that time? No. Which indicates the Tugen Hills must have had a unique ecology for that time [although there are similarities to the Mursi Formation in the Omo Valley at a later time of slightly older than 4 Ma (Drapeau et al., 2014) which may be further explored upon completion of isotope studies in the Chemeron]. Are we able to pull further back and make statements about the paleoenvironment for all of the Tugen Hills during that time or to include 100 ka before or after? Not without some major caveats. Sample size is an ongoing problem in the Tugen Hills, but the area certainly does not lack in opportunities related to chronostratigraphy. Future fieldwork targeting areas of interest and the reconstruction of the paleo-lake through time, combined with the wealth of information yet to be mined from core samples and concerted efforts, like this edited volume, to share our resources will continue to further our ability to view that larger picture.

29 Fauna and Paleoenvironments of the Homa Peninsula, Western Kenya

Laura C. Bishop, Thomas W. Plummer, David R. Braun, Peter W. Ditchfield, Emily Goble Early, Fritz Hertel, Cristina Lemorini, James S. Oliver, Richard Potts, Thomas Vincent, Elizabeth Whitfield, and Rahab N. Kinyanjui

Background

The Homa Peninsula has been known to science since 1911, and fossil specimens from the area comprise many type specimens for common African mammalian paleospecies. Here we discuss the fauna and the paleoenvironmental information from the Homa Peninsula. The Homa Peninsula is a 200 km² area in Homa Bay County, situated on the southern margin of the Winam Gulf of Lake Victoria in Kenya (Figure 29.1). Lake Victoria is estimated to be the third largest lake in the world, with a surface area of 68,900 km² and a maximum length of approximately 616 km. Although its catchment is extensive, it is relatively shallow compared to any other lake of similar size, with a maximum depth of 84 m. Lake Victoria is located in a depression formed by the western and eastern branches of the East African Rift System (EARS), and is at an average elevation of 1135 m a.s.l. (Database for Hydrological Time Series of Inland Waters, 2017).

The easternmost extension of Lake Victoria is the Winam (formerly Kavirondo) Gulf, into which the peninsula juts. The Gulf is approximately 25 km wide and extends for 64 km from Rusinga Island in the west to Kisumu and Sondu in the east. The Winam Gulf is formed in the western half of the Nyanza Rift, a depression extending from the Kenya Dome, on which the eastern branch of EARS, the Gregory Rift, is also centered. There are extensive Neogene deposits in this valley, with Miocene sediments cropping out around their source volcanoes and more recent sediments accumulating on the floor of the valley. Numerous sources of evidence point to a relatively recent origin for the modern Lake Victoria [approximately 200 Kya (Meyer

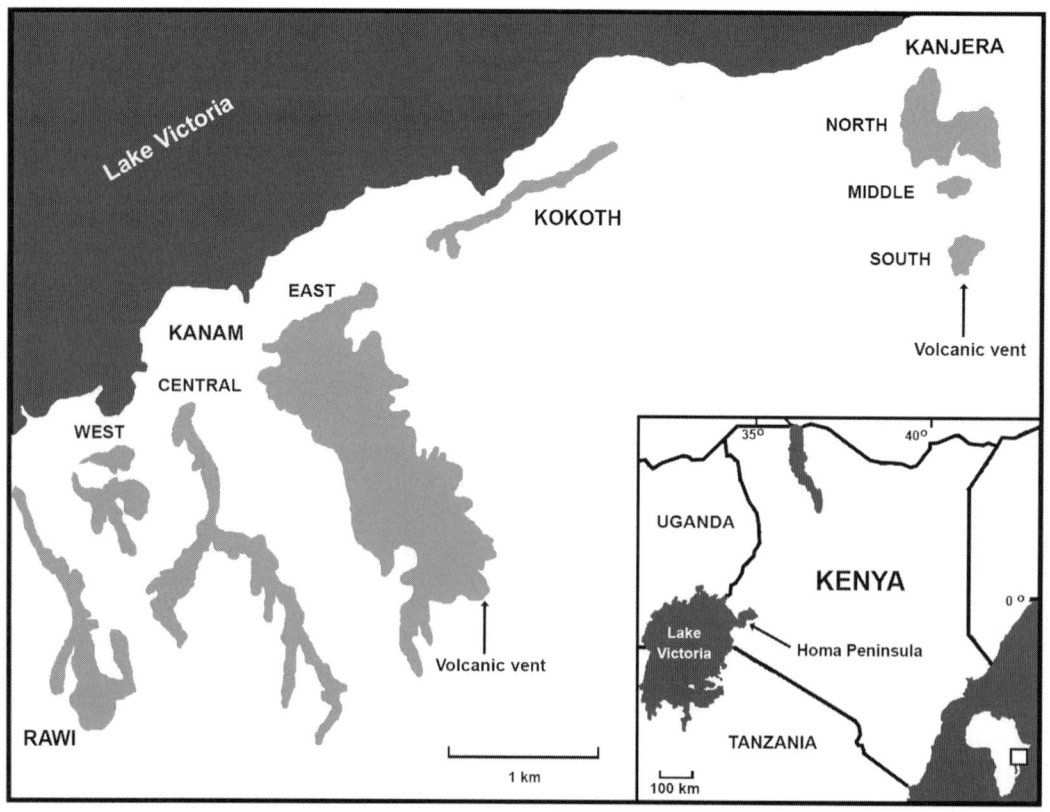

Figure 29.1 Map showing the Homa Peninsula localities discussed in the text (after Pickford, 1984).

et al., 1990), although there is evidence for more recent drying events (e.g., Verheyen et al., 2003)]. Many of the fossiliferous sediments of the Homa Peninsula have more ancient origins, with lacustrine deposits up to 225 m above current lake level (Plummer, 1992).

The landscape of the peninsula is dominated by Homa Mountain (latitude 0.38°S, longitude 34.5°E, elevation 1751 m), a carbonatite volcano complex that was active from the Late Miocene to the Pleistocene (Le Bas, 1977). Volcanic activity in the region began approximately 13 Ma, with doming of the mountain commencing approximately 11–10 million years ago (Ma) and continuing until 5 Ma (Le Bas, 1977). Later volcanic activity persisted, centering on peripheral vents, and continues today at active geothermal hot springs at Kanjera and Kanam. The peninsula has a varied topography, and the exposures to the north of Homa Mountain vary in relief from several meters to cliffs of 20 m and higher. The published fossiliferous exposures occur in a series of gullies radiating toward the lake from Homa Mountain in the south, shaped by modern river activity. These are Rawi, Kanam West, Kanam Central, Kanam East, and Kanjera, named from west to east. The Kokoth exposures are oriented as an east–west cliff of sediments located between the Kanam East and Kanjera gully systems. Homa Peninsula sedimentary stratigraphy from the Late Miocene to the Pleistocene preserves a range of depositional environments formed under varied fluvial–lacustrine and subaerial regimes, with many sediments and clasts sourced from the eruption products of Homa Mountain and underlying basement rock. Recent exploration of the western and southwestern flanks of Homa Mountain has discovered new fossil- and artifact-bearing deposits that are currently under investigation, and beyond the scope of this chapter.

Geology of the Homa Peninsula

Sedimentary strata preserved in the region north of Homa Mountain have been defined as the Kanam, Homa, Rawi, Abundu, Kasibos, and Kanjera Formations (Ditchfield et al., 1999). The Apoko Formation (Fm) was defined by Pickford (1984) as a series of paleosols and fluviatile sediments sitting unconformably above the other deposits. The Apoko Fm is time-transgressive, incorporating sediments that vary in age from the late Middle Pleistocene to the Late Pleistocene or even Holocene. The fossiliferous Kanam Fm (Kent, 1942; refined by Pickford, 1984, 1987) forms the base of the sequence with outcrops best exposed in the Kanam West, Kanam Central, and Kanam East gullies. The Kanam Fm is comprised of six beds of alternating clay/silt and tuffaceous deposits, as summarized by Pickford (1984, 1987), and named (from oldest to youngest) beds K1 to K6. The Homa Fm lies unconformably on the Kanam Fm, with this relationship observable in the Kanam West gully system; geological trenches on the eastern side of the Kanam East gully (~20 m south of the main road that cuts across the gully) also show the unconformable superposition of Homa on Kanam Fm. The Homa Fm is best exposed and most fossiliferous in the Kanam West inland gullies, where the relationships among the sedimentary beds are complicated due to ancient infilling of complex paleoerosion surfaces, probable falls and displacements of former sedimentary cliffs, and also deformed by faulting and subsidence related to the later eruptive stages of the Homa Mountain volcanic complex. Pickford (1984, 1987) defined the Homa Agglomerate (now considered to be part of the Homa Fm), which unconformably overlies the Kanam Fm and is exposed in all three of the Kanam gullies.

The Kanam and Homa Formations are unconformably overlain by the Rawi Fm, which is equivalent to Kent's (1942) Rawe Beds and Pickford's (1984, 1987) Rawi Member. Outcrops of the Rawi Fm are exposed in the Rawi Gulley, where its lower member has a relatively planar, weakly erosive contact overlying the Homa Fm, and in Kanam Central gully, where the formations are separated by a pronounced angular unconformity (Ditchfield et al., 1999). The sediments of the lower member of the Rawi Fm, show a fining upwards sequence from pebble- to granule-grade matrix-supported conglomerates to a fine- to medium-grained micaceous sandstone, suggesting that it was formed by a fluvial system, which might have been intermittently active with only seasonal flow (for detailed sedimentological descriptions, see Ditchfield et al., 1999). The upper member of the Rawi Fm, which is exposed in the "Fish Cliffs" in the Rawi Gully and Kanam Central (Kent, 1942), consists of very fine sand and silt that occur in centimeter-thick couplets with laterally continuous horizontal laminations 1–2 mm thick. These couplets are interbedded with thin, tabular, fine- to medium-grade sandstones that, along with the commonly preserved fish remains and evaporate crystal pseudomorphs, suggest a rapidly forming, shallow lake environment that periodically dried, causing mass mortality of fish and evaporate formation (Ditchfield et al., 1999).

The Abundu Fm crops out in the Kanam East and Kanam Central Gullies. It has two members that directly overly the Homa Fm and interdigitate with coarse-grained biotite-rich debris from a small volcanic vent in the southern part of the Kanam East gully. The lower member is characterized by a 3–7 m thick moderately well-sorted and well-cemented medium–coarse-grained yellow to orange sandstone, in planar beds of between 10 and 60 cm thickness, with occasional outsized clasts (Ditchfield et al., 1999). Their depositional environment is uncertain because they are poorly exposed and, where visible, lack sufficient internal structure for this to be determined. The upper member of the Abundu Fm is up to 25 m thick and consists of interbedded poorly sorted conglomerates that vary in clast size from pebble to boulder. The pebbly conglomerates are clast-supported and the conglomerates with larger clast sizes are matrix-supported. The regional geology makes it difficult to determine the precise stratigraphic position of the Abundu Fm, and it is possible that its lower member is a lateral equivalent of the lower Rawi Fm.

The Kasibos Fm is only exposed in the Kanam East gully, where it unconformably overlies the Abundu Fm and oversteps the more ancient Kanam Fm (Ditchfield et al., 1999). Its thickness of up to 7 m is comprised of fine-grained poorly consolidated red clays and siltstones, interbedded with 10–20 cm thick pebble-grade conglomerate horizons, which are occasionally cemented with coarse-grained carbonate cement. Few sedimentary structures have been observed in the Kasibos Fm, but one location in Kanam East, Felid Hill, preserves large-scale cross-bedding defined by thin pebble layers in an otherwise clay-dominated sequence. This may represent lateral accretion surfaces on point-bars within a moderately sized fluvial system. Elsewhere in Kanam East gully (Equid Tooth Site) the red clay facies dominates, and may represent floodplain or overbank deposits of the fluvial system. The volcanic vent that interfingers with the Abundu Fm and exhibits dips of up to 25° is overlain by Kasibos Fm strata having horizontal bedding, suggesting this as the temporal limit to the activity of this volcanic vent and its effect on the local topography.

The Kanjera Fm is exposed at Kanjera, in the Southern, Northern, and Middle Exposures (Behrensmeyer et al., 1995; Ditchfield et al., 1999, 2019; Plummer et al., 1999). The oldest units, Beds KS-1 to KS-5, make up the Kanjera South Member and are exposed at the Kanjera South locality (Figure 29.1). They have been the subject of extensive archeological enquiry (Plummer et al., 1999, 2009a, 2009b; Plummer, 2004; Braun et al., 2008, 2009; Ferraro et al., 2013; Lemorini et al., 2014, 2019; Plummer and Bishop, 2016; Oliver et al., 2019). These beds are gently dipping to the north and are affected to a minor extent by normal faults down-stepping to the north, and associated minor folding. The Kanjera South Member is overlain unconformably by the beds of the Kanjera North Member (Beds KN-1–KN-5), which also dip northwards but are more intensively deformed by faulting associated with the Winam Gulf graben. These members were previously informally referred to as Kanjera Fm (S) and Kanjera Fm (N) (Plummer et al., 1999; Ditchfield et al., 2019). Both Kanjera South and Kanjera North Members are unconformably overlain by the Kanjera Middle Exposure Member (KME-1 to KME-3), which seems to represent a west–east-directed alluvial fan sequence, which is erosive into both underlying members.

The Kanjera South Member in the southern exposures of the Kanjera gully system is subdivided into five beds, KS-1 through KS-5. All beds yield fossils, although the densest concentrations of fossils and artifacts are found in Beds KS-1 to KS-3. Sandy silts and fine sands characterize KS-1. KS-2 has two facies, one a pebbly fine to medium sand and the other a discontinuous patchy conglomerate. Further sandy silts and patchy conglomerates characterize the KS-3 deposits. The lower sequence suggests deposition in a floodplain environment by low aspect channels with diffuse flow. Recent analysis indicates that the bulk of these deposits were formed by intermittent hyperconcentrated-to-mudflow events that buried an *in situ* accumulation of artefacts and fossils (Ditchfield et al., 2018). These are overlain by KS-4 clays deposited in a low-energy lacustrine or swamp environment, which is in turn overlain by KS-5, which includes both gravel facies and clay facies with paleosol carbonates indicative of the formation of stable land surfaces. The sequence ends with a clay grading upwards into gravelly clay and capped with an irregular, massive limestone containing plant casts. This terminal unit had been designated KS-6 in Behrensmeyer et al. (1995), but is considered the top of KS-5 here. This suggests a range of depositional phases, including low-energy and fluvial deposits, and ultimately consolidation of sediments cemented by calcium-saturated water from a spring.

The Kanjera North Member is exposed in the Middle and Northern Exposures of the Kanjera Gully. North of the locality, a shallow saline lake or playa, unrelated to modern Lake Victoria, was present during Kanjera North Member deposition (Behrensmeyer et al., 1995). Five beds have been identified, that were deposited by alternating delta, lake, and mudflat systems. The basal beds are KN-1 and KN-2, which have alluvial fan deposits (KN-1a and KN-2a) that interfinger with lacustrine silts and clays (KN-1b and KN-2b). The lacustrine layers preserve mudcracks and evaporitic layers, which suggest that the lake was saline and occasionally dried up. KN-3 silts and clay alternate with sands, suggesting quiet water alternating with fluvial deposition. The sandy silts of KN-4 were deposited under more subaerial conditions, most likely in a mudflat environment. The thick, homogenous KN-5 clays unconformably overlie KN-4, and suggest swamp or lacustrine deposition at the base of the unit, returning to subaerial mudflat deposition toward its top.

Age of Homa Peninsula Formations

It has been difficult to use radiometric methods to determine absolute ages of the Homa Peninsula strata and for the fauna and archeological occurrences recovered from these contexts. Primarily this has been because of a lack of igneous rocks suitable for these methods. Most known tuffs are altered, and other igneous occurrences and layers derived from the Homa Mountain carbonatite complex have chemical compositions that are not amenable to radiometric methods. Therefore, field observations covering conformable and unconformable contacts between formations exposed in the Homa Peninsula gullies inform the interpretation of the overall lithostratigraphic sequence in the region. These observations are further informed by biostratigraphy and magnetostratigraphy. A composite stratigraphy based on field observations, bio-, and magnetostratigraphy is shown in Figure 29.2.

Vertebrate Paleontology

The Kanam Formation and Homa Formation

The Kanam and Homa Formations are currently recognized as the oldest sedimentary units along the northern rim of the Homa Peninsula and are mainly exposed in the Kanam West, Kanam Central, and Kanam East gullies. During field research in the Kanam gullies over the past century, mammalian fossils have been surface-collected, recovered on steeply eroded slopes of superposed sedimentary units that are potentially as old as 6 million years. The early expeditions organized by Louis Leakey had poor control over spatial locations and left no field documentation. An expedition by David Pilbeam in 1974 and later research visits by Martin Pickford provided sedimentary descriptions and sketch maps that assist in provenancing some of their surface finds (Pilbeam, 1974; Pickford, 1984). In general, though, the lack of precise coordinates makes it difficult to make definitive associations between fossils collected during the past expeditions and specific geological units. Until the 1990s, provenances of surface-collected fossils were rarely tested by excavation or geochemical methods (see Plummer et al., 1994, for an example of the latter research at Kanjera).

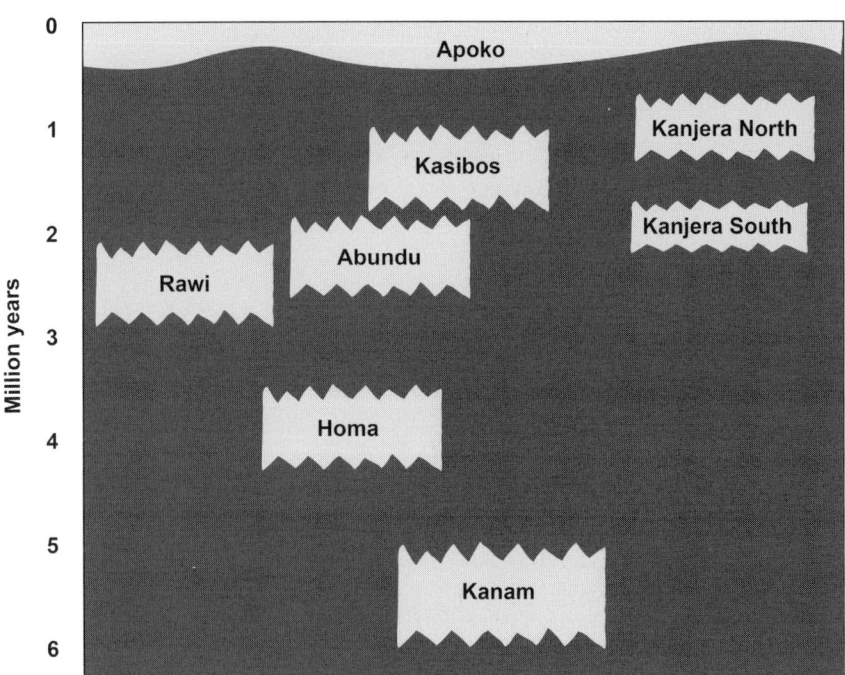

Figure 29.2 Schematic composite stratigraphy of sedimentary formations discussed in the text. The numerical scale on the right shows the approximate age of units in millions of years (before present).

Excavations carried out by the Smithsonian–National Museums of Kenya (SI-NMK) research group since 1985 demonstrate that *in situ* fossils of the Kanam and Homa Fms are typically fragmentary and found in isolation rather than in bone concentrations. As a means of recovering fossil samples, therefore, *in situ* recovery is less effective than collecting surface fossils following seasonal rains.

Unpublished age estimates have been reported to the authors as ~6.12 Ma for Kanam Fm Bed K2 and 6.06 Ma for K6 (Alan Deino, Robert Drake, pers. comm.); however, the chronological analyses are not definitive and are considered preliminary estimates until refined analyses are published. Fossils in this formation have been recovered mainly from Kanam West, which encompasses northern lakeside exposures and a southern inland gully system. Proboscidean taxa from Kanam West include *Paleaoloxodon* (*Elephas*) *recki* and *Stegotetrabelodon* sp., both from bed K5, which have biostratigraphic ranges of ~5.0–0.5 Ma and 7.4–4.2 Ma, respectively. In Kanam East, fauna associated with sediments mapped by Pickford as Kanam Fm include *Kolpochoerus heseloni*, which has a biostratigraphic range of 3.26–0.7 Ma, and *Phacochoerus* sp., which is likely derived from eroded remnants of the Middle/Late Pleistocene Apoko Fm. Kanam Central does not include specimens from the Kanam Fm that are identifiable to a useful level for biostratigraphic or chronological purposes.

As defined in the Kanam West gullies, the odd-numbered beds of the Kanam Fm are fossil-bearing (K5, K3, and K1, in decreasing abundance). The even-numbered beds are typically tuffaceous and less fossiliferous except in pedogenic units intercalated with tuff horizons. Sedimentary facies are consistently fluvial channel and floodplain with reworked airfall tuffs. The six beds of the Kanam Fm are visible in limited exposures in the southeastern branch of Kanam Central, where recent erosion has begun to expose strata potentially lower than K1, and in limited exposures on the eastern side of the Kanam East gully.

The richest fossil-bearing strata of the Homa Fm occur in the southeastern portion of the Kanam West inland gullies, ~50–10 m north of the southern erosional lip of the gully. In this location a prominent, fossil-bearing, orange pebbly conglomerate (PC) bed overlies a fossil-rich dark concretionary clay (DCC) unit. An orange-banded sand/silt (OBS) bed appears on the surface to underlie DCC; however, test trenching shows that OBS is either a very steep channel that cuts into the lower part of DCC or the two beds are in contact at a fault. Geological observations in test trenches further illustrate the complications in attributing some surface-eroded fossils to particular geological beds: near the southern lip of this area, the DCC unit of the Homa Fm lies on top of bed K4 of the Kanam Fm, whereas 30 m northeast, bed K4 is overlain by a draping of dark concretionary gritty clay that is only slightly distinct from the Homa DCC bed, but is likely Middle/Late Pleistocene Apoko Fm. In some instances, it is possible to mistake the Homa OBS bed to be laterally equivalent to the banded Homa Agglomerate (HA), which is prominent in the mid- to westernmost exposures of the Kanam West inland gullies and appears to represent the oldest bed of the Homa Fm, stratigraphically beneath the OBS, DCC, and PC beds. The HA preserves fragmented fossil mammals and plants.

For the reasons noted here, taxa claimed historically to derive from the Kanam and Homa Formations must be treated with utmost caution as to their actual provenance. Type specimens attributed to these formations include the suids *Nyanzachoerus kanamensis* (Kanam West) and *Metridiochoerus andrewsi* (locality unrecorded), and the gomphotherid *Anancus kenyensis* (Kanam East). Table 29.1 provides a provisional faunal list

Table 29.1 Mammalian fauna currently assigned to the Kanam and Homa Formations based on fossils collected from the Kanam gullies, Homa Peninsula. X: taxon present. Body size class 2: 23–113 kg; class 3: 113–340 kg.

	Taxon	Kanam Fm	Homa Fm
Cercopithecidae			
	Parapapio ado		X
	Theropithecus darti		X
	Cercopithecidae indet.		X
Carnivora			
	Canis sp.		X
	Hyaenidae indet.		X
Suidae			
	Nyanzachoerus cf. *N. syrticus*	X	
	Nyanzachoerus kanamensis		X
	Notochoerus jaegeri		X
	Notochoerus cf. *N. scotti*		X
	Kolpochoerus heseloni		X
	Metridiochoerus cf. *M. andrewsi*		X
Hippopotamidae			
	Hexaprotodon sp. (*H. imagunculus*)	X	X
	Hippopotamus sp.		X
Giraffidae			
	Sivatherium sp.		X
Bovidae			
	Tragelaphus cf. *T. kyaloae*		X
	Tragelaphini (size class 2)	X	X
	Tragelaphini (size class 3)	X	
	?Hippotragini sp.	X	
	Reduncini indet.	X	X
	Alcelaphini indet.	X	X
	Aepyceros sp.		X
	Antilopini indet.		X
	Neotragini indet.	X	
	Cephalophini indet.	X	
Rhinocerotidae			
	Ceratotherium sp.	X	
	Diceros bicornis		X
Equidae			
	cf. *Eurygnathohippus* sp.	X	
Proboscidea			
	Palaeoloxodon (*Elephas*) sp.	X	X
	Loxodonta adaurora		X
	Stegotetrabelodon orbis	X	
	Deinotherium bozasi	X	X
	Anancus kenyensis	X	

by formation (Potts et al., 1997) based on Pickford (1984) supplemented by SI-NMK field research in 1994 and 1996. Fossil identifications from field geological studies at Kanam West and careful surface-collecting of the Homa Fm in 2012 and 2014 are in progress.

In Kanam West the Homa OBS bed yielded *Tragelaphus* cf. *kyaloi*, which has an age range of ~6.5–3.4 Ma. From the Homa DCC/PC beds, a single specimen of *Parapapio ado* was collected *in situ*, which has a range of ~4.1–3.5 Ma. The Homa Fm surface collection includes another example of *P. ado*, as well as *Kolpochoerus* cf. *K. heseloni*, currently known from ~3.3 to 0.7 Ma and *Ancancus* cf. *A. progressus* at ~5.0–3.5 Ma. It is likely, therefore, that the Homa Fm surface collection represents material from approximately 3.5 Ma. Mammalian taxa associated with the Homa OBS bed in the Kanam Central gully overlap in age from ~4.2 to 1.6 Ma. At Kanam East a fossil of *Aepyceros* cf. *A. melampus* was associated with the mapped HA bed, yet its biostratigraphic range of ~2 Ma to present suggests a spurious spatial association with a geological unit that is at least 3.3–3.5 Ma. All biostratigraphic ranges are from Werdelin and Sanders (2010), augmented by field and laboratory research by E.G.E. as part of the Baringo Paleontological Research Project study of the Chemeron Fm, Tugen Hills, Kenya.

The Rawi Formation

The Rawi Fm is highly fossiliferous in patches, and as such was one of the earliest areas in the peninsula to receive concentrated and systematic attention from scientific researchers. In the 1930s Louis Leakey's expeditions extensively trenched the Rawi Fm in the area of the Fish Cliffs in the Rawi Gully. A diverse fauna was recovered then, including the holotype skeleton of *Giraffa jumae*, a skeleton of the rhinoceros *Ceratotherium simum*, a cranium and mandible of *Metridiochoerus andrewsi*, remains of *Hippopotamus gorgops*, and a pygmy hippopotamus mandible (cf. *Hexaprotodon imagunculus*), all of which are currently housed in the Natural History Museum, London. These specimens are exceptionally well-preserved and complete, preserving the platy sand matrix from which our expedition also surface-collected fossils near the Fish Cliffs. In 1994 we were aided in relocating two of Leakey's trenches by a local informant who was at Leakey's excavations as a child. Subsequently, the SI-NMK team has recovered additional taxa from one of the trench sites, including *Notochoerus*, and some hippo and bovid remains, as well as a partial cranium of *Cercopithecoides kimeui* from the base of the main Fish Cliffs sequence. The primate specimen conjoins with a mandibular fragment collected in the 1970s by Pilbeam (1974) and is likely from the same individual as mandibular fragments in the NHM's Rawi collection found by Leakey's expedition (Frost et al., 2003).

Numerous taxa recovered from Rawi have biostratigraphic relevance (Table 29.2). *Cercopithecoides kimeui* has a documented age range between 2.6 and 1.5 Ma in eastern Africa (Frost et al., 2003; Jablonski and Frost, 2010). The Suidae are also relevant, with *M. andrewsi* known in East Africa from at least 2.95 Ma until 1.7 Ma, and *Notochoerus* known from the Pliocene until 1.8 Ma, although it is both rare and derived after 2 Ma (Bishop, 1994, 2010; Ditchfield et al., 1999; White, 1995). The height, length, and complexity of the *M. andrewsi* and *Notochoerus* teeth are suggestive of an age older than 2 Ma (Bishop, pers. obs.), making the most likely biostratigraphic interval from 2.6 to 2 Ma. Magnetostratigraphy of the Rawi Fm sampled in two localities showed a completely normal sequence, excepting one short antipodal reversed site (Ditchfield et al., 1999). The bio- and magnetostratigraphy are concordant with several possible dates: the Rawi Fm was deposited either during the Olduvai Subchron (1.922–1.775 Ma) or during the C2An1 n Subchron (3.05–2.59 Ma) of the Gauss Chron. The latter, Gauss Chron date is more concordant with the biostratigraphic data.

The Abundu Formation

The Abundu Fm was described as a separate geological sequence in 1999; earlier reports considered it to be part of the Rawi Fm (Kent, 1942; Pickford, 1984; Ditchfield et al., 1999). Its age is not well-constrained and currently few taxa can be attributed to it. Those that have been recovered are not very informative as to the biostratigraphic age of the Abundu Fm (Table 29.2). Hyenidae, Hippopotamidae, Rhinocerotidae, *Paleoloxodon* (*Elephas*) *recki*, and the Bovidae Tragelaphini, *Kobus* sp., and Alcelaphini sp. have been attributed to the Abundu Fm since its recognition and definition. However, these taxa are not particularly informative because they mostly lack species-level taxonomic attribution, and those that are identifiable have long known time ranges (e.g., *P. recki* 4.1–0.3 Ma: Todd, 2006). No *in situ* artifacts have been recovered from the Abundu Fm. Attempts to attain a meaningful magnetostratigraphic result have not been successful to date (Ditchfield et al., 1999). Therefore, the stratigraphic succession is our best guide to the age of this formation, which may be equivalent to the Rawi Fm and is in turn overlain by the Kasibos Fm.

The Kasibos Formation

The only known outcrops of the Kasibos Fm are found in the Kanam East gullies, unconformably overlying the Abundu Fm. In this setting the Kasibos exposures show up to 7 m of thickness that consist of fine-grained, poorly consolidated red clays and siltstones with occasional pink paleosol nodules, in beds from 40 to 150 cm thick. These are interbedded with thin, pebble-grade conglomerate horizons that comprise angular to subangular clasts of carbonatite lavas with very occasional rounded clasts of basement schists in occasionally cemented horizons approximately 20 cm thick.

Despite its rare exposure, the Kasibos Fm can be very fossiliferous where it is exposed. Several sites have been identified, with Felid Hill and the *Equus* Tooth Site the most important. Geochronology is established by studies of paleomagnetism in conjunction with the biostratigraphic estimates for this site. Kasibos Fm sediments demonstrate normal polarity but, along with the magnetostratigraphy, the fauna recovered suggest that the age of these deposits best corresponds with the Jaramillo Subchron (1.070–0.990 Ma), with a maximum age of approximately 1.8 Ma circumscribed by the first appearance datum (FAD) of *Kolpochoerus majus* (Table 29.2; Ditchfield et al., 1999).

Table 29.2 Identified mammalian taxa collected from the Rawi, Abundu, Kasibos, and Apoko formations.

	Taxon	Rawi	Abundu	Kasibos	Apoko
Hyracoidea					
	Heterohyrax sp.			X	
Cercopithecidae					
	Cercopithecoides kimeui	X			
	Cercopithecidae indet.	X		X	
Carnivora					
	Felidae	X		X	
	Dinofelis piveteaui			X	
	Hyaenidae		X		
Suidae					
	Notochoerus sp.	X			
	Metridiochoerus sp.	X			
	M. andrewsi	X			
	M. cf. *modestus*			X	
	Kolpochoerus sp.				X
	K. majus			X	
	Phacochoerus sp.				X
	Hylochoerus meinertzhageni				X
Hippopotamidae					
	Hippopotamidae (cf. *H. imagunculus*)	X			
	Hippopotamidae, large	X	X	X	X
	Hippopotamus cf. *gorgops*	X			
Giraffidae					
	Giraffa jumae	X			
Bovidae					
	Tragelaphini	X	X	X	X
	Bovini			X	X
	Syncerus sp.				X
	Pelorovis sp.				X
	Reduncini	X		X	
	Kobus sp.		X		
	K. kob	X			
	Neotragini			X	
	Alcelaphini		X	X	X
	Antilopini			X	
	Hippotragini				
Equidae					
	Equidae	X		X	X
	Equus sp.			X	X
Rhinocerotidae					
	Rhinocerotidae	X	X		
	Ceratotherium simum	X			
Proboscoidea					
	Elephantidae	X		X	
	Palaeoloxodon (*Elephas*) *recki*		X		

Another consideration is the skeleton of *Dinofelis piveteaui* recovered from the Kasibos Fm site at Felid Hill over successive expeditions, most notably in the conjoinable ulna fragments of this specimen recovered in 1974 and 1994 (KNM-KE 21; Ditchfield et al., 1999). The Kasibos specimen shows more derived morphology than material from the Okote Member, suggesting a later date for the former specimen (Werdelin, pers. comm.). Another major consideration supporting a Jaramillo Subchon age for the Kasibos Fm deposits is the known temporal distribution of *D. piveteaui*, which does not extend into the Middle Pleistocene (Turner, 1990; Werdelin, pers. comm.). A Jaramillo Subchron age for the Kasibos *D. piveteaui* would make it the most recent known specimen of this taxon from Africa (Ditchfield et al., 1999).

Felid Hill has yielded a wide range of faunal specimens, which along with representatives of the taxa above include Cercopithecidae, Canidae, Felidae, *Equus*, specimens from six bovid tribes, *K. heseloni*, *Metridiochoerus* cf. *modestus*, hippopotamus, elephantid, lizard, and bird fossils. Considering the limited distribution of Kasibos Fm sediments, the fauna recovered has been quite diverse (Table 29.2). As is true for the Abundu Fm, no *in situ* artifacts have been recovered from the Kasibos Fm; however, surface artifacts including Acheulean bifaces reported by Pickford (1987) and Ditchfield et al. (1999) from the Kanam East gully may ultimately be found *in situ* in the Kasibos Formation.

The Kanjera Localities

Kanjera has been the focus of the most recent scientific investigations on the Homa Peninsula. Sediments crop out in three exposures over a distance of approximately 0.5 km. The Northern and Southern Exposures are separated by the Middle Exposures, which are lower in height and less well-exposed. Between them, the sediments of the localities of Kanjera South and Kanjera North preserve archeology and fauna intermittently sampling the past two million years. Kanjera South is older, with sediments estimated to cover the period from approximately 2 million to older than 1.775 Ma, because the preserved sediments cap out before reaching the top of the Olduvai Subchron (Ditchfield et al., 2019). Sedimentation in Kanjera North is more recent, with excavations recovering material dating from just over 1 Ma to the Middle Pleistocene. There are more recent, undated occurrences in the latest part of the sequence, the Apoko Fm, and black cotton soils of the Kanjera North Member.

Kanjera South Member

Although the Kanjera localities have been known to science since 1911, it was relatively recently that the temporal differences between the Southern and Northern Exposures (and the related geological formations) have come to light (Ditchfield et al., 1999; Plummer et al., 1999). Repeated attempts to date overlying volcanics at Kanjera South using Ar–Ar methods have been unsuccessful. However, a combination of paleomagnetic and biostratigraphic studies using the abundant mammalian fauna allows us to delimit the age of the archeological deposits. The proboscidean *Deinotherium* sp., the suids *M. modestus* and *M. andrewsi*, and the extant genus of equid *Equus* have all been recovered. The earliest African appearance of *Equus* dates to 2.3 Ma as does the FAD for *M. modestus* (Cooke, 2007). *Metridiochoerus andrewsi* is known from 3.36 Ma to 1.7 Ma elsewhere in Africa and *Deinotherium* sp. is known from deposits older than 1.5 Ma. These taxa indicate that archeological materials were deposited between 2.3 and 1.7 Ma. Moreover, the Olduvai Subchron (1.922–1.775 Ma; Singer, 2014) has been detected in the sediments of Beds KS-4 and KS-5 (Ditchfield et al., 1999, 2019). The underlying archeological occurrences in Beds KS-1 to KS-3 must therefore predate the base of the Olduvai Subchron at 1.92 Ma, yielding a date of between 2.3 and 1.92 Ma for hominin activity. Given the apparent rapidity of deposition, it seems likely that the archeological occurrences are closer to the younger end of this time interval, with an approximate age of ~2 Ma. Table 29.3 shows the fauna recovered from the Kanjera South and Kanjera North Members.

Kanjera North Member

A combination of paleomagnetic determinations and biostratigraphy suggests that the Kanjera North Member deposition spans a relatively long interval. At the base of the sequence, the polarity is reversed (Behrensmeyer et al., 1995). KN-1 is not fossiliferous and has a reversed polarity, which almost certainly post-dates the Olduvai Subchron based on the prevalence of the derived suid *M. compactus* in Beds KN-2 to KN-4. Beds KN-3 and KN-4 are reversed at their bases and normal at their tops. The upper normals in these units were originally attributed to the Jaramillo Subchron (0.99–1.07 Ma) for KN-3 and the Brunhes/Matuyama boundary (0.780 Ma) for KN-4 (Behrensmeyer et al., 1995). However, it now appears that KN-3 and KN-4 are laterally equivalent, and that normal samples in each likely correspond to the Jaramillo (Ditchfield, pers. obs.). Thus, the KN-1 to KN-4 sequence largely predates the Jaramillo, and the fauna and artifacts from these beds largely predate *ca.* 1.1 Ma. The contact between KN-5 and the underlying units is downfaulted and so cannot be seen, but the abundant fauna from this bed is similar to Bed IV Olduvai (Plummer, 1992). Its magnetostratigraphy is consistently normal, indicating a Middle Pleistocene (Brunhes Chron) age for its deposition (Plummer, 1992; Leakey and Roe, 1994; Behrensmeyer et al., 1995; Ditchfield et al., 1999).

The Apoko Formation

The ~4 m of clay and gravel channel facies of the Apoko Fm unconformably overlies the other formations found on the Homa Peninsula (Pickford, 1984; Ditchfield et al., 1999). Because of its unconformable nature, normal polarity, and a fauna that is dominated by modern or recently extinct taxa, it is likely that nowhere is the Apoko Fm older than the late Middle Pleistocene (Pickford, 1984; Behrensmeyer et al., 1995; Ditchfield et al., 1999). The Apoko Fm has been best explored at Kanjera, particularly in the Northern Exposures, where it is very fossiliferous (see Table 29.2 for faunal taxa recovered from the Apoko Fm). The Apoko Fm has yielded remains of an anatomically modern human in addition to a wide range of mammalian taxa, all of which were well fossilized (Ditchfield et al., 1999).

Eastern and Central Africa

Table 29.3 Fauna from the Kanjera South and Kanjera North formations.

	Taxon	Kanjera South	Kanjera North
Cercopithecidae			
	Cercopithicinae indet.	X	
	Cercopithecus sp.		X
	Theropithecus indet.	X	
	Theropithecus oswaldi		X
Carnivora			
	Carnivora, size 2	X	
	Canidae indet.	X	
	Felidae indet.		X
	Felidae, size 3	X	
	Hyaenidae indet.		X
	Crocuta sp.	X	
	cf. *Civetta viverina*	X	
Suidae			
	Metridiochoerus andrewsi	X	
	M. modestus	X	
	M. compactus		X
	M. hopwoodi		X
	Kolpochoerus heseloni		X
	Kolpochoerus sp.	X	
	Phacochoerus sp.		X
Giraffidae			
	Giraffidae indet.	X	
Hippopotamidae			
	Hippopotamidae, size 3		X
	Hippopotamus, size 6	X	X
	Hippopotamus cf. *gorgops*		X
Bovidae			
	Tragelaphini		X
	Tragelaphini, size 3	X	
	Tragelaphus, size 2	X	
	Bovini	X	
	Pelorovis		X
	Pelorovis cf. *oldowayensis*		X
	Syncerus acoelotus		X
	Reduncini, sizes 1–3	X	X
	Kobus sp.	X	X
	Cephalophini indet.		X
	Alcelaphini, sizes 2 and 3	X	
	Parmalarius altidens	X	
	Parmularius agusticornis		X
	Connochaetes sp.	X	
	Megalotragus sp.		X

Table 29.3 (cont.)

	Taxon	Kanjera South	Kanjera North
	Antilopini, sizes 1 and 2	X	X
	Antidorcas recki	X	
	Gazella sp.		X
	Hippotragini indet.		X
Equidae			
	Equus sp.	X	X
	Eurygnathohippus sp.	X	X
Rhinocerotidae			
	Rhinocerotidae indet.	X	
	Diceros bicornis		X
	Ceratotherium simum		X
Proboscoidea			
	Elephantidae indet.	X	
	Loxodonta africana		X
	Paleoloxodon recki		X
	Deinotherium sp.	X	
Lagomorpha			
	cf. *Lepus*	X	
Manidae			
	Phataginus giganteus		X
Rodentia			
	Thryonomyidae	X	
Aves			
	Accipitridae *Gyps*	X	
	Phalacrocoracidae		
	Phasianidae		
	Struthionidae		
Gastropoda		X	X

The Apoko *Homo sapiens* may predate the other remains of modern *Homo* from Kanjera North (Plummer and Potts, 1995), or it could represent a more recent burial into an Apoko outcrop.

Hominin Behavior and Ecology on the Homa Peninsula

Although stone artifacts are found on the surface of deposits all over the Homa Peninsula, their relationship to the underlying *in situ* sediments has not always been straightforward. Kanjera South and Kanjera North have extensive, dense surface accumulations of artifacts and fossil fauna. Excavations at these sites provide the best evidence of hominin behavior and ecology on the Peninsula. As noted above, extensive investigations at the Kanjera locality have shown that the north and south are temporally distinct, and thus reveal the details of hominin occupation of the region over hundreds of thousands of years. Analysis of well-preserved *in situ* and surface-collected finds has allowed reconstruction of hominin behavior in detail, and several lines of evidence have put this behavior into a well-evidenced environmental setting (Plummer et al., 1999, 2009a, 2009b; Ferraro et al., 2013; Lemorini et al., 2014, 2019; Ditchfield et al., 2019; Oliver et al., 2019).

Kanjera South

Kanjera South is older than many known Oldowan sites from which large assemblages of artifacts and well-preserved faunal remains have been recovered. Our interdisciplinary team of paleontologists, archeologists, and geologists has been excavating at Kanjera South since 1995, when it was recognized that these sediments predated those at Kanjera North, where previous research was concentrated (Behrensmeyer et al., 1995). The largest excavation is a 169 m^2 area (Excavation 1) from which approximately 3700 fossils and 2900 artifacts have been recovered and individually piece plotted using a laser transit system, making it one of the largest collections of Oldowan archeological material from a single site. Artifacts and bones are found successively in three beds (from oldest to youngest, KS-1 through KS-3) that occur over a 3 m depth of sediment. Analyses confirm that the primary agent of accumulation of the archeological material at Kanjera South was hominin activity (Plummer et al., 1999; Bishop et al., 2006b; Ferraro et al., 2013; Ditchfield et al., 2019).

Oldowan Hominin Habitats

At Kanjera, isotopic and faunal data document an Oldowan site complex formed in an open habitat within a grass-dominated ecosystem (Plummer et al., 2009a, 2009b). Repeated deposition of artifacts and bones from butchered macromammals provide the first clear evidence of recurrent hominin activities in such an open setting. Whereas the hominin fossil record suggests that some evolutionary innovations in the human genus *Homo* reflect an increased reliance on relatively open, arid savanna environments, direct evidence of grass-dominated settings and of early *Homo* within these open settings during the Plio-Pleistocene (2.5–1.5 Ma) had been lacking until Kanjera South paleoenvironments were reconstructed (Plummer et al., 2009a). Activities in this open habitat and their comparison to activities undertaken in more closed habitats, e.g., the woodlands of FLK-Zinj, have implications for understanding early *Homo* behavioral ecology (Oliver et al., 2019).

The KS-2 fauna from Excavation 1, for example, is composed of a variety of taxa, indicating a range of inferred habitat preferences and diets (Table 29.3). One indication that the secondary grassland component of the floral community was significant is the relative proportion of taxa preferring open grasslands versus other habitat types. Bovids make up 82.6 percent of the 886 KS-2 fossils attributable to macromammalian families (Ferraro et al., 2013). Ninety-two percent of the KS-2 bovid specimens attributable to tribe ($n = 143$) fall into the Alcelaphini and Antilopini, which in modern settings are good indicators of open grassland ecosystems (Vrba, 1980; Bobe and Behrensmeyer, 2004). Moreover, the high frequency of equids in KS-2 (11.6 percent) is similar to the relative abundance of zebras in modern, grassland-dominated ecosystems such as the Serengeti, Tanzania (Potts, 1988; Plummer et al., 1999).

In modern ecosystems, trees, shrubs, herbs and high-elevation grasses preferring cool, wet growing seasons use the C_3 photosynthetic pathway, which strongly discriminates against ^{13}C (Ehleringer et al., 1997; Plummer et al., 2009a, 2009b). Grasses and sedges in warm, arid, open environments, such as those commonly found in sub-Saharan Africa, predominantly use the C_4 photosynthetic pathway. Terrestrial plants using these photosynthetic pathways can thus be identified by the relative abundance of ^{12}C and ^{13}C in their tissues. The isotopic composition of pedogenic carbonates reflects the relative proportion of surface vegetation using each photosynthetic pathway. Thus, the isotopic signature of pedogenic carbonates found associated with large concentrations of archeological debris can be used to reconstruct the habitat structure at points on the landscape recurrently visited by hominins (Sikes, 1994; Levin et al., 2004; Quinn et al., 2007). This is one of the few available ways to make linkages between hominin activities and specific habitat types. Stable carbon isotope studies of pedogenic carbonates from Beds KS-1 and KS-2 at Kanjera indicate that site formation occurred in an open (wooded grassland to open grassland) setting (Plummer et al., 1999, 2009a, 2009b; Ditchfield et al., 2019).

Paleoenvironmental context is also assessed using taxon-free faunal analyses including ecomorphic analysis of long bones and tarsals (Plummer and Bishop, 1994; Kappelman et al., 1997), and isotopic analyses of tooth enamel (Plummer et al., 2009a, 2009b). The limb element ecomorphic analyses (Plummer et al., 2006) indicate that the bovid postcranial sample is dominated by individuals with open- and light-cover habitat preferences.

Assessment of the carbon isotopic ratios in the teeth from the Kanjera excavations allows us to assess the diets of specific taxa, as well as the relative proportion of browsing versus grazing strategies (Morgan et al., 1994; Cerling et al., 2003c; Kingston and Harrison, 2007). By sampling a wide range of herbivores, general dietary preferences of the fauna can be used to infer microhabitats and vegetation present in the region. Stable carbon isotopic analysis of herbivore tooth enamel shows that all taxa except some surface-collected tooth fragments of the proboscidean *Deinotherium* subsisted largely or entirely on grass (Table 29.4; Ditchfield et al., 2006; Kingston et al., 2006; Plummer et al., 2009a, 2009b). This finding is striking, as taxa such as the tragelaphine bovids and the Cercopithecinae indet. (Table 29.3) were assumed to have consumed predominantly C_3 plant products based on comparison with living relatives. There is a strong C_4 dietary signal across the spectrum of animals found at Kanjera South, including non-migratory taxa such as the monkeys, rhinos, tragelaphine antelopes, and pigs. This makes it unlikely that the grassland dietary signal results from a prevalence of mobile grazing herbivores at the lake edge overwhelming the signal from the resident mammalian community, because these latter also show a preference for C_4 diets.

Oldowan Hominin Faunal Acquisition

Generally, debate on the mode of carcass acquisition has been based on data from Bed I Olduvai, particularly FLK-Zinj, and focused on whether Oldowan hominins were primarily scavenging or hunting prey, and if they were scavenging whether it was active or passive (Plummer, 2004). Because medium-sized mammals are the most common within the Bed I faunas, discussion of carcass acquisition strategies has focused on this size class (e.g., Bunn and Kroll, 1986; Oliver, 1994; Blumenschine, 1995; Dominguez-Rodrigo et al., 2007; Bunn and Pickering, 2010; although see Fernandez-Jalvo et al., 1998). A dichotomy of scavenging versus hunting oversimplifies and artificially partitions what is likely to have been a complex, flexible foraging strategy. Moreover, it presupposes that scavenging and hunting would be equally visible in the archaeological record. This seems unlikely, given the taphonomic biases acting on the animals most likely to have been hunted (i.e., small mammals) versus those most likely to have been scavenged (i.e., medium and large mammals) and potential differences in transport behavior based on carcass size (Lyman, 1994; Plummer and Stanford, 2000; Ferraro et al., 2013).

Although there is evidence of both hominin and carnivore involvement with excavated faunal remains from Excavation 1 (NISP = 3600+, macromammal MNI = 80+ for the KS-1 to KS-3 sequence), analyses of site sedimentology and bone taphonomy clearly indicate that hominins were the primary agent of assemblage formation (Ferraro et al., 2013; Ditchfield et al.,

Table 29.4 Carbon and oxygen stable carbon isotope values for mammalian enamel samples from Kanjera South, Kenya. After Plummer et al. (2009b).

Field Number	Taxon	δ¹³C VPDB	δ¹⁸O VPDB	Field Number	Taxon	δ¹³C VPDB	δ¹⁸O VPDB
2218	Cercopithecidae	0.763	−1.215	14416	Antilopini, size 1	0.537	0.514
10501	*Cercopithecus* sp.	−1.384	0.468	14452	Antilopini, size 1	1.009	−0.799
859	*Theropithecus*	0.572	−0.817	14655	Antilopini, size 1	0.881	0.327
2066	Hyaenidae–*Crocuta*-sized	0.801	−1.621	15580	Antilopini, size 1	1.946	0.704
63	Suidae	1.105	−2.012	20515	Antilopini, size 1	1.033	1.435
3775	Suidae	−0.885	−0.596	21420	Antilopini, size 1	−0.419	0.417
5386	Suidae	−0.932	−1.016	732	Antilopini, size 1	0.834	−0.392
4718	Suidae	−1.72	−2.677	6512	Antilopini, size 2	−1.148	−0.378
14363	Suidae, cf. *Metridiochoerus* sizes 2/3a	−0.007	−0.745	12522	Antilopini, size 2	0.59	0.046
5888	*Metridiochoerus* sp.	1.246	−0.452	17737	Antilopini, size 2	2.369	−0.08
KJ95-17	*M. andrewsi*	1.741	−1.385	18386	Antilopini, size 2	1.953	−0.066
5162	*M. modestus*, size 2	0.549	−0.997	21053	Antilopini, size 2	1.934	0.272
2	*Hippopotamus* sp.	−3.351	−2.984	203	Bovidae, size 3	−8.238	−2.054
8	*Hippopotamus* sp.	0.092	−2.153	14525	Bovidae, size 3b	2.808	0.251
25	*Hippopotamus* sp.	−1.001	−2.112	16443/c	Bovidae, size 3x	2.071	1.306
49	*Hippopotamus* sp.	0.851	−0.459	299	Bovini size 5	1.948	−0.621
365	*Hippopotamus* sp.	0.666	−1.935	3654	Bovini, size 5	1.76	−0.743
792	*Hippopotamus* sp.	2.051	−1.626	286	Reduncini, size 2	1.979	−2.936
2039	*Hippopotamus* sp.	−1.219	−2.216	6296	Reduncini, size 2	1.318	−1.122
5004	*Hippopotamus* sp.	0.12	−1.174	12043	Reduncini, size 2	−0.256	−1.034
7211	*Hippopotamus* sp.	2.041	0.238	13837	Reduncini, size 2	1.794	1.622
7900	*Hippopotamus* sp.	−0.328	−1.708	9	Reduncini, size 3a	2.578	−0.794
8898	*Hippopotamus* sp.	1.683	−0.317	438	Reduncini, size 3a	1.806	0.037
10188	*Hippopotamus* sp.	0.386	−2.829	2168	Reduncini, size 3a	0.328	0.881
17990	*Hippopotamus* sp.	2.661	−1.178	12045	Reduncini, size 3a	2.424	−0.562
586	Alcelaphini, sizes 2/3a	2.544	−0.781	23316	Reduncini, size 3a	0.677	−3.399
632	Alcelaphini, sizes 2/3a	1.967	−0.527	408	Reduncini, size 3x	2.251	−0.85
755	Alcelaphini, sizes 2/3a	2.063	−0.485	3333	Tragelaphini, size 3a	−1.655	0.057
922	Alcelaphini, sizes 2/3a	2.134	−0.09	13490	Tragelaphini, size 3a	−2.473	−0.374
4280	Alcelaphini, sizes 2/3a	2.275	0.83	21035	Equidae, size 3b	1.376	−0.776
4549	Alcelaphini, sizes 2/3a	1.141	−1.549	68	Equidae, size 3x	1.556	−0.981
6428	Alcelaphini, sizes 2/3a	2.718	0.818	76	Equidae, size 3x	1.201	1.252
4564	Alcelaphini, size 3a	1.914	0.475	408	Equidae, size 3x	1.332	−1.297
4714	Alcelaphini, size 3a	1.987	0.324	638	Equidae, size 3x	1.455	−0.018
4807	Alcelaphini, size 3a	1.592	0.999	1352	Equidae, size 3x	1.351	0.366
5233	Alcelaphini, size 3a	2.505	−0.582	1764	Equidae, size 3x	2.05	−0.985
5475	Alcelaphini, size 3a	2.947	−0.959	2840	Equidae, size 3x	1.528	0.414
6318	Alcelaphini, size 3a	0.212	0.855	3673	Equidae, size 3x	1.258	−0.128
6351	Alcelaphini, size 3a	2.675	−0.532	4942	Equidae, size 3x	0.721	0.574
6436	Alcelaphini, size 3a	4.565	1.954	5117	Equidae, size 3x	1.553	−1.024
6510	Alcelaphini, size 3a	2.037	0.059	5256	Equidae, size 3x	1.621	0.869
6511	Alcelaphini, size 3a	2.338	0.316	6104	Equidae, size 3x	1.76	−1.483
7309	Alcelaphini, size 3a	2.385	−0.213	6891	Equidae, size 3x	1.552	−1.08
8191	Alcelaphini, size 3a	2.091	−1.003	7463	Equidae, size 3x	1.765	0.525
15868	Alcelaphini, size 3a	2.019	−0.205	10746	Equidae, size 3x	1.135	−0.05

Table 29.4 (cont.)

Field Number	Taxon	δ¹³C VPDB	δ¹⁸O VPDB	Field Number	Taxon	δ¹³C VPDB	δ¹⁸O VPDB
22830	Alcelaphini, size 3a	2.417	−1.126	15507	Equidae, size 3x	1.405	−0.171
4003	Alcelaphini, size 3b	2.441	0.825	160	*Equus*, size 3x	1.67	0.812
4300	Alcelaphini, size 3b	2.899	−0.607	700	*Equus*, size 3x	1.617	0.615
4511	Alcelaphini, size 3b	2.971	−0.313	720	*Equus*, size 3x	1.368	−1.612
4801	Alcelaphini, size 3b	2.521	1.112	3388	*Equus*, size 3x	1.283	−1.521
5991	Alcelaphini, size 3b	2.541	−0.507	3934	*Equus*, size 3x	1.602	−0.678
6541	Alcelaphini, size 3b	1.829	1.016	66	*Eurygnathohippus*, size 3x	1.344	−0.635
9770	Alcelaphini, size 3b	2.104	−1.159	102	*Eurygnathohippus*, size 3x	1.185	0.62
10941	Alcelaphini, size 3b	2.433	0.229	865	*Eurygnathohippus*, size 3x	1.997	−1.364
10949	Alcelaphini, size 3b	2.448	−0.046	2871	*Eurygnathohippus*, size 3x	1.476	−1.855
17469	Alcelaphini, size 3b	3.318	−1.283	3664	*Eurygnathohippus*, size 3x	1.171	−0.942
166	Antilopini, size 1	1.231	1.595	3905	*Eurygnathohippus*, size 3x	0.908	−0.66
4172	Antilopini, size 1	0.916	−0.335	5762	*Eurygnathohippus*, size 3x	1.236	−1.936
4313	Antilopini, size 1	2.773	−1.114	19677	*Eurygnathohippus*, size 3x	1.295	−2.312
4320	Antilopini, size 1	1.248	1.635	6369a	*Eurygnathohippus*, size 3x	−0.019	−2.657
5165	Antilopini, size 1	1.567	1.406	6369b	*Eurygnathohippus*, size 3x	1.555	−2.762
5579	Antilopini, size 1	1.176	−0.756	6291	Rhinocerotidae, cf *Ceratotherium*	2.224	−0.58
5631	Antilopini, size 1	1.644	−0.018	5873	Elephantidae	1.611	−2.485
6360	Antilopini, size 1	0.668	0.917	8512	Elephantidae	1.973	−2.481
6417	Antilopini, size 1	1.358	0.459	KJ-95	*Deinotherium* sp	−10.616	−2.37
6432	Antilopini, size 1	0.256	1.137	KNM KJ 189	*Deinotherium* sp.	−7.556	−2.292
11317	Antilopini, size 1	1.26	1.29				

2019). Furthermore, research indicates that hominins had early access, likely through hunting, to many small (sizes 1–2) bovids (Ferraro et al., 2013; Parkinson, 2013; Oliver et al., 2019). At the five Bed I Oldowan levels studied by Potts (1988), sizes 1 and 2 mammals make up an average of only 20 percent of the assemblage total, compared to 36 percent from Excavation 1. The proportion of juvenile individuals within the KS-1 and KS-2 small size class is also high relative to the only other large Oldowan assemblage, FLK-Zinj (50 percent, versus an average of 14 percent for FLK-Zinj; Bunn and Pickering, 2010; Oliver et al., 2019). The overall sense of the Excavation 1 faunal samples is that they contain a higher proportion of small, frequently immature mammals than do the Bed I Olduvai assemblages. The mortality profile and anti-predator defensive strategies of small antelopes combined with the grassland setting suggest that Kanjera South hominins acquired small bovids via short chases (Oliver et al., 2019). Two other Early Pleistocene Oldowan samples, Lokalalei and FwJj20, from west and east of Lake Turkana in Kenya, also have a high proportion of sizes 1 and 2 mammals (Kibunjia, 1994; Braun et al., 2010), suggesting that as sampling extends beyond Olduvai, a better sense of variation in Oldowan faunal acquisition strategies will be obtained.

Analyses of skeletal part frequencies suggest that these size 1 and 2 animals were frequently transported whole to the site (Ferraro et al., 2013). Cut and percussion mark frequencies, although low (4 percent and 7 percent, respectively; Parkinson, 2013), are similar to those of other Oldowan assemblages (Ferraro et al., 2013), and show patterns consistent with carcass exploitation for meat, organ, and marrow resources. In contrast, hominins were at least at times passively scavenging large bovid and equid carcasses (sizes 3–4; wildebeest/buffalo size), which are best represented by skulls and distal limb bones. With respect to carnivore involvement, the fauna generally reflects low to moderate levels of carnivore activity (9.8 percent; Ferraro et al., 2013: table S2) to 13.8 percent; Parkinson, 2013: table 3.4). Most carnivore bone modifications are plausibly related to gaining access to the marrow. Notably, the intensity of carnivore activity differs dramatically from that modeled in the modern Serengeti (Blumenschine, 1987). Taken together, the record suggests marked variability in the carnivorous foraging behaviors of hominins making Oldowan tools (Ferraro et al., 2013; Oliver et al., 2019). It also suggests that by ca. 2.0 Ma some hominins had at least occasional access to substantial amounts of meat and within-bone resources (marrow, brains, etc.), resources which, some have argued, fueled dramatic anatomical and social adaptations in the genus *Homo* (Isaac, 1978a; Plummer, 2004). The Kanjera data further demonstrate that Oldowan hominins possessed the cognitive, behavioral, and technological abilities to forage in a diversity of habitats.

Early Pleistocene Hominin Technology and Behavioral Ecology

Combining the intensive studies of past environments with analyses of hominin technology has enabled us to examine how these factors interact. In particular, our studies of hominin raw material sourcing, manufacture, and curation have enabled us to examine how hominins have used their capabilities to ensure efficient use of hard-won commodities (Braun et al., 2008). Furthermore, by looking at use wear on Oldowan stone tools, we can understand what materials were processed by tool-using hominins.

Studies of Oldowan behavior have suggested that transport of resources was a major factor in hominin technological organization (Schick, 1987; Potts, 1991). The diversity of raw materials used by Oldowan hominins on the Homa Peninsula greatly exceeds that documented for other Oldowan localities, and many of the artifacts recovered during excavations were made from materials not available locally (Braun, 2006; Braun et al., 2008). Extensive raw material surveys sampled over 300 potential primary and secondary sources for tool stones on the Homa Peninsula and in the surrounding region. Samples at each primary source and some secondary sources were analyzed using geochemical and material sciences techniques. Raw material samples from primary and secondary sources were analyzed both destructively and non-destructively, and specific sets of elements were identified to distinguish the different raw material types. We used EDXRF (energy-dispersive x-ray fluorescence; Latham et al., 1992) to accurately and non-destructively determine the elemental composition of a large sample of Kanjera artifacts. Local raw materials associated with the Homa Mountain carbonatite complex (e.g., carbonatite, fenetized rocks) were used in the manufacture of approximately 70 percent of the artifacts, but a substantial proportion of artifacts (25–30 percent) were made of materials sourced off the peninsula. These "non-local" raw materials were transported a minimum of 10 km, a level of raw material transport not previously documented for the Oldowan (Plummer, 2004; Braun, 2006; Braun et al., 2008).

Material sciences analyses suggest that this relatively high degree of transport occurred because the "non-local" raw materials were of much higher quality for artifact manufacture and use than the "local" ones. Tests assessed fracture predictability (the consistency with which a particular type of stone fractures) and edge durability (the ability of an edge to resist degradation by a static or dynamic force; Braun et al., 2009). Analyses of the raw materials at Kanjera demonstrate that the stones used to make artifacts display a great deal of variation in raw material "quality." Specifically, raw materials originating off the peninsula are harder and tend to fracture more consistently than those deriving from the carbonatite complex.

Edge durability is another critical aspect of raw material quality, particularly when tasks increase raw material consumption (Brantingham, 2003). Studies show that the capacity of tool edges in the Kanjera raw material assemblage to resist wear ranges from some of the lowest possible (carbonatite) to the highest possible values (quartzite). As with fracture predictability, the "non-local" raw materials were more suited for artifact manufacture as they generally hold an edge longer than the "local" raw materials (Braun et al., 2009). Technological analysis is consistent with the idea of preferential transport of non-local raw materials. The non-local raw materials are more extensively and carefully flaked than the local ones (e.g., flakes were thinner, providing more perimeter per unit mass) and they were more frequently retouched. This study suggests that very early in stone tool use hominins had a keen understanding of raw material source distributions and raw material quality, and incorporated an economy of resources into their behavioral repertoire (Braun, 2006; Braun et al., 2008).

Analyses of the Kanjera South Oldowan assemblage initially identified traces of use-wear (Lemorini et al., 2014, 2019). A series of controlled experiments with replicated artifacts made from raw materials used at Kanjera was undertaken to help interpret these. Experiments involved butchery (skinning, defleshing), woodworking (hard and soft wood), cutting of grass, and peeling and sectioning of tubers and roots including wild African tubers by Hadza women foraging in Tanzania. Analysis of the experimental assemblage allowed creation of a use-wear framework linking the processing of specific materials and tool motions to their resultant use-wear patterns. Sixty-three of 87 archeological artifacts sampled from Kanjera South showed use-wear that was attributable to the processing of specific materials. On 10 of these (12 percent), use–wear corresponded to animal tissue processing, providing additional evidence to corroborate zooarcheological studies demonstrating that butchery took place at the site. The processing of plant tissues, including wood, grit-covered plant tissues (underground storage organs or USOs), and stems of grass or sedges accounted for the use-wear on 33 tools (40 percent). The rest of the tools showed use-wear attributable to generic soft or medium material processing.

Use-wear analysis demonstrates that hominins used artifacts to process materials that otherwise would be invisible to standard archeological methods, such as the cutting and scraping of wood, which may represent the production and/or maintenance of wooden tools. Evidence that USOs were processed shows that hominins acquired and processed this resource 1.5 Ma earlier than previously known (Lemorini et al., 2014, 2019). It is unclear the extent to which use-wear indicating the cutting of grasses, sedges, or reeds is subsistence (e.g., grass seed harvesting, cutting out papyrus culm for consumption) or non-subsistence (e.g., production of "twine," simple carrying devices, or bedding) related. To date, the Kanjera South artifacts are the earliest known tools on which this type of analysis has been successfully carried out. Use-wear highlights the adaptive significance that using lithic technology had for Kanjera South Oldowan hominins (Lemorini et al., 2014, 2019).

Although several analyses are still underway, our studies demonstrate that hominins were transporting artifactual raw materials that were superior to those available locally to Kanjera South over relatively long distances. Once brought to the locality, hominins were carefully curating the resources so as to maximize their utility. Use-wear analysis, which has so far concentrated on the tools made from transported raw materials, shows that these artifacts were used on a range of animal and plant substances. The overall picture is one which shows that hominins exercised considerable cognitive awareness and behavioral flexibility (Lemorini et al., 2014, 2019). The reasons for the recurrent use of the Kanjera South locality, for what was likely hundreds of years, is poorly understood. The use-wear and zooarcheological evidence indicate that that hominins were butchering whole young gazelles and processing tubers through the 3 m KS-1 to KS-3 sequence. This suggests that both of these resources were available nearby, and perhaps it was foraging for these resources and the local availability of potable water that repeatedly drew the hominins back to this locale.

Kanjera North

As discussed above, the Kanjera North sediments postdate those in the south (Ditchfield et al., 1999; Plummer et al., 1999). The evidence from Kanjera North also preserves bones and artifacts in spatial association, but none of the excavated or surface occurrences found so far has similar density or persistence as the Kanjera South Excavation 1 assemblage. The Kanjera North site formation took place under a slightly different sedimentary regime than did the deposits in the south, with alternating deltaic, lake, and mudflat systems (Plummer, 1992; Behrensmeyer et al., 1995).

Evidence from carbon stable isotope analyses of soil carbonates suggests that the local environment at Kanjera North exhibited a greater degree of habitat heterogeneity than found at Kanjera South, with elements of both grassland and C_3 plants in more equal balance (Ditchfield, unpublished data). Results are suggestive of mixed vegetational habitats with considerable variability across the landscape (Nicholson, 2003). Many of the δ^3C values fall within the range usually associated with grassy woodland (Cerling, 1992; Plummer et al., 1999). This is consonant with the mixed depositional environments which are suggested by the sedimentary regimes that prevailed during Kanjera North deposition.

Although fossil fauna are common at Kanjera North, the extensive collection of *Theropithecus oswaldi* is notable. These fossils derive from the KN-2A "Island," a small, circumscribed outcrop that produces a unique chemical signature high in uranium, rubidium, radon, zirconium, and yttrium in fossils preserved there (Plummer et al., 1994). Eighty-five skeletal elements representing 13 individuals are housed in the collections of the National Museums of Kenya and The Natural History Museum, London (Plummer, 1992). Kanjera is the type locality for this species, first described in 1916, which is now known to be widespread and characterized by both geographic and temporal variation (e.g., Jablonski, 2002).

Hominin occupation of the Homa Peninsula during the Kanjera North deposition is evidenced by the artifacts recovered from each site where there are major accumulations of fossils (Plummer, 1992). Kanjera North artifacts can be described as Developed Oldowan or Acheulean (Leakey, 1972). Hominins used relatively poor local raw materials, such as vesicular lavas, carbonatites, and welded tuff to make a significant proportion of artifacts. They also used other raw materials that may have been sourced from local streams or transported from farther afield, as has been demonstrated for Kanjera South (Braun et al., 2008). The use of cobbles, which are otherwise absent in the Kanjera North sediments, as artifactual material is suggestive of transport of lithic raw materials by hominins, as these are not locally available (Plummer, 1992).

One excavation at the AC Site in Bed KN-4 yielded a nearly complete subadult hippopotamus skeleton (KNM-KJ 20653) in close spatial association with several cores, all of which were probably deposited in an ephemeral channel (Plummer and Potts, 1989; Plummer, 1992). The bones are tightly clustered together and are relatively unweathered and unbroken, suggesting that they were not transported and were buried soon after death (Plummer and Potts 1989; Plummer, 1992). Although there are numerous linear marks, pits, and abrasions on the bones, the most likely indication of interaction between hominins and the hippo carcass comes from probable cutmarks on the ilium; these are found in an area of muscle attachment that was unlikely to have been affected by trampling or sedimentary abrasion (Plummer and Potts, 1989; Plummer, 1992). Other indications of hominin faunal processing include a size 2 bovid distal humerus with cutmarks excavated from KN-3, and a medium mammal long bone shaft fragment with chop marks surface collected from KN-4. Other excavations from Kanjera North (e.g., GP site in KN-5) did not produce firm evidence of hominin/faunal interactions, although fossils and artifacts were spatially associated (Plummer and Potts, 1989; Plummer, 1992).

Discussion and Conclusions

The Homa Peninsula records evidence of hominin presence, both intermittent and more continuous, over nearly 6 million years of human evolution. The Homa Peninsula's location between the two branches of the Great Rift Valley makes it significant for studies of the evolution of East African landscapes because this area is otherwise poorly sampled. The region has significance in any examination of the evolution of hominin behavior and hominin dispersals given that it supplies information about both in a unique ecological and geographical context.

Our record of the evolution of hominins and their behavior is serendipitously preserved, and the archive presented by the sediments of the peninsula is no less compelling for its episodic nature. By the time hominins are making observable alterations in their environment with the advent of stone tool manufacture, the evidence of hominin occupation is less sporadic. Why were hominins either resident or frequent visitors to this region? The main attractor must have been the existence of both ephemeral and more permanent bodies of water and the diversity of habitats surrounding Homa Mountain. The sedimentation in many paleontological and archeological sites is associated with fluvial and lacustrine sources. However, the Kanjera sedimentological evidence points to the near-constant presence of fresh, likely potable water in the vicinity of Homa Mountain. The combination of wooded slopes on the mountain as well as open expanses of grassland nearby would have provided hominins with an attractive setting and a diversity of resources.

At Kanjera South, where repeated hominin activities are evidenced, many of our analyses show that nearby fresh water may have been a local attraction. For example, use-wear on stone tools demonstrates that wood, tubers, and herbaceous plants such as sedges were processed. These plants are likely to be found near permanent or seasonal water sources. The presence of fresh water, particularly following seasonal rains, is also strongly indicated by the mortality profiles of antelopes, particularly the dominance of the juvenile small antelope, *Antidorcas recki* (Plummer et al., 2018). Modern springboks (*A. marsupialis*) are seasonal breeders most likely to give birth during the rainy season, when ephemeral sources of water are more plentiful and permanent ones refreshed (Furstenburg, 2002). The low frequency of carnivore damage at Kanjera may suggest reduced risks of predation and fewer competitive interactions that also may have promoted recurrent occupation of the area.

The presence of water and of the concomitant food resources on the slopes and lowlands surrounding Homa Mountain would have made the region attractive to hominins. Moreover, tool use seems to have been adaptively significant, as hominins preferentially transported and used stones that were hard and, because of this, produced flakes that held a sharp edge for a long time. Hominins consumed foods including animal carcasses and USOs that would have required stone tool use to acquire and/or process, that were of high nutritional value, and in the case of whole gazelle carcasses and dense patches of tubers came in packets large enough to be shared. The fact that evidence of these activities is found through 3 m of sediment indicates that these were not ephemeral behaviors but were sustained activities by multiple generations of hominins in the vicinity of Kanjera South (Ditchfield et al., 1999, 2019; Ferraro et al., 2013). The behaviors evidenced at Kanjera, just prior to the first appearance of *H. erectus*, may be the archeological expression of this shift toward the tool-dependent foraging of high-quality foods within a cooperative group context that provided the evolutionary milieu for the evolution of this taxon.

Acknowledgments

The authors would like to thank the editors for their invitation to contribute to this volume and for their patience in awaiting the final result. We also appreciate the positive suggestions of the anonymous reviewers, which improved this chapter immeasurably. Permission to conduct this research was granted by various agencies of the Government of Kenya, under the joint cooperation agreement between the National Museums of Kenya and the Smithsonian Institution. We thank the National Museums of Kenya and M. Kibunjia, F.K. Manthi, J. Kibii, and E. Ndiema for support. J.M. Nume and B. Onyango have managed the Kenya field teams. We acknowledge Kenya Government permission granted by the Ministry of Sports, Culture and the Arts, and by NACOSTI permit P/14/7709/701. T.P. acknowledges grants from the L.S.B. Leakey Foundation, the National Geographic Society, the National Science Foundation, the Wenner-Gren Foundation, and the Professional Staff Congress–City University of New York Research Award. L.C.B. would like to thank the Leverhulme Trust for the funding that supported her research. R.P. gratefully acknowledges support received from the Peter Buck Fund for Human Origins Research (Smithsonian Institution), and E.G.E. thanks the Peter Buck Postdoctoral Fellowship. Many thanks to Jennifer Clark for redesigning and redrawing Figures 29.1 and 29.2. Finally, we wish to acknowledge the contributions of the late Professor Andrew Hill to this research and to the field he influenced both through his own innovative research and through his enthusiastic and insightful mentorship of students and colleagues.

30 Mammalian Fauna of the Olorgesailie Basin and Southern Kenya Rift

Richard Potts and J. Tyler Faith

Geological Framework

The eastern branch of the East African Rift System developed over the past 20 million years (Ma), with uplift and large-scale faulting manifested since the early Miocene south of the Afar Triangle (Ethiopia) and predominantly during the late Miocene farther south (Partridge, 2010). Tectonic faulting and volcanism in the southern Kenya rift is younger – predominantly Pliocene and Pleistocene – with the formation of sedimentary basins mainly during the early and middle Pleistocene. The oldest of these basins in which intensive geological, paleontological, and paleoanthropological study has been conducted is Olorgesailie (Figure 30.1; e.g., Isaac, 1977, 1978b; Shackleton, 1978; Potts, 1989, 1994, 2007; Deino and Potts, 1990; Behrensmeyer et al. 2002; Potts et al., 2018). The mammalian fauna of the Olorgesailie Basin is the focus of this chapter. Several other depocenters to the south and west of Olorgesailie, including west of Lake Magadi, have produced less-extensive middle Pleistocene mammalian fossil discoveries (e.g., Lainyamok, Oldonyo Nyokie, Lenderut); the faunas from these sites will also be discussed briefly here.

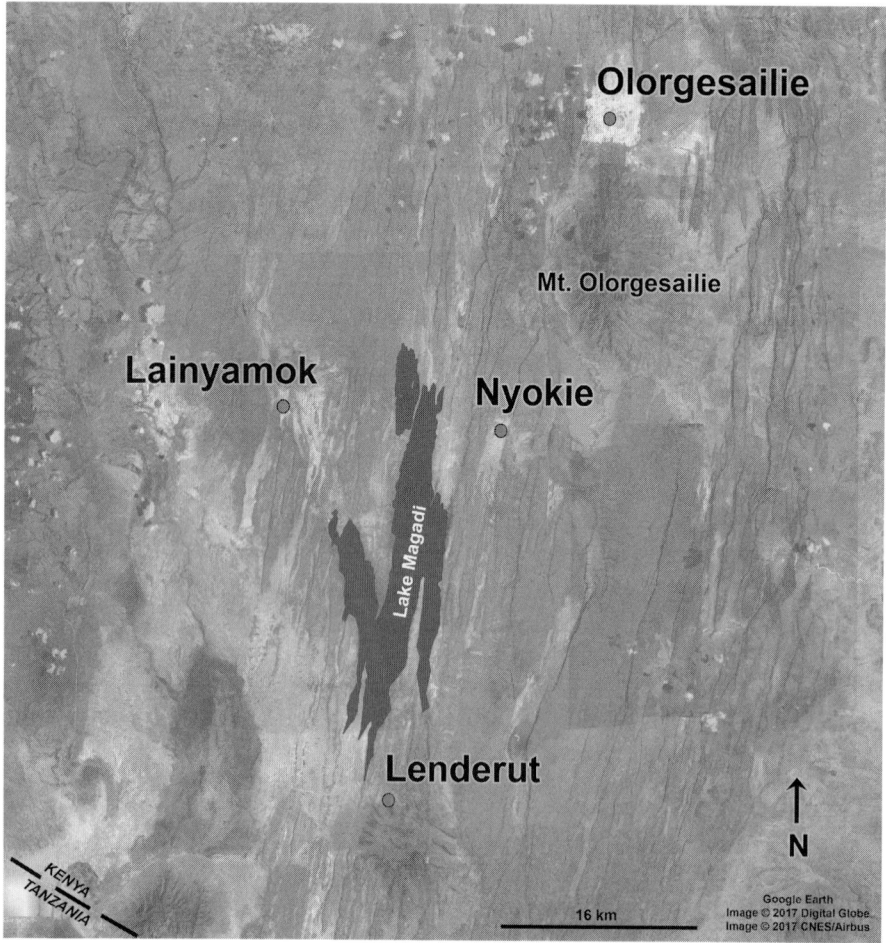

Figure 30.1 Map of the southern Kenya rift showing the location of fossil sites discussed in the text. (A black and white version of this figure will appear in some formats. For the color version, please refer to the plate section.)

The lacustrine, fluvial, floodplain, volcaniclastic sedimentary sequence of the Olorgesailie Basin is divided into two formations. The Olorgesailie Formation is divided into stratigraphic units named Members 1 through 14, dated 1.2 Ma to 499 ka, and largely characterized by aggradational and stable (pedogenic) sedimentary environments with minor erosional phases (Deino and Potts, 1990; Behrensmeyer et al., 2002). Acheulean archeological sites are preserved throughout most of the 700-kyr deposition of the Olorgesailie Fm (Isaac, 1977; Potts, 2013). Tectonic displacement initiated erosion of the Olorgesailie Fm that lasted for ~180 kyr. Deposition of the Oltulelei Formation, dated ~320–36 ka, ensued and is represented by episodes of channel filling and valley erosion controlled by tectonics and climate dynamics (Behrensmeyer et al., 2018; Deino et al., 2018; Potts et al., 2018). The Oltulelei Fm preserves a sequence of Middle Stone Age (MSA) archeological sites (Brooks et al., 2018).

Mammalian faunal preservation in the basin is stratigraphically discontinuous and falls into four principal time units (Table 30.1). Because it has undergone extensive study (e.g., Potts et al., 1999, 2018; Owen et al., 2008; Behrensmeyer et al., 2018), the Olorgesailie stratigraphic sequence presents the opportunity to examine how mammalian taxonomic persistence and turnover relate to the tempo and amplitude of environmental dynamics.

Taphonomic and Environmental Contexts

Member 1 Fauna, Olorgesailie Fm, ~1 Ma

The lowest stratigraphic unit in the Olorgesailie Basin ranges from ~1.2 to 1.0 Ma (Deino and Potts, 1990; Behrensmeyer et al., 2002). Fossil remains are concentrated in the upper Member 1 paleosol, or UM1p (Potts et al., 1999), while dispersed fauna has been uncovered immediately below the upper Jaramillo boundary, ~1.0 Ma (Isaac, 1977; Tauxe et al., 1992). More than 100 excavated areas have sampled >4 km of linear outcrop of UM1p, and have uncovered dispersed and clustered mammalian fossil assemblages; faunal and Acheulean stone artifact concentrations roughly coincide across this paleo-landscape. The largest faunal sample in M1 thus largely reflects remains that were accumulated during a period of stability and pedogenesis following lake regression, along with minor floodplain channeling, footprint trails, and burrows that were also traps for silt, sand, and fauna (Potts et al., 1999).

Member 1 paleoenvironments are reflected by a series of fluctuations between shallow and deep lakes (Owen et al., 2008), intermittent, short-duration pedogenesis, and the most mature soil of UM1p, probably representing ~500–1000 years based on sediment weathering, rootmarking, soil cutans development, and $^{40}Ar/^{39}Ar$ ages and sediment deposition rates above and below the paleosol (Potts et al., 1999). Carbonate isotopic data show that the UM1p fauna accumulated in a grassland that approached 100 percent C_4 plants (Sikes et al., 1999).

Member 7 Fauna, Olorgesailie Fm, ~900 ka

The next youngest faunal unit is derived from lower M7, primarily from a sedimentary unit called M6/7s. The fauna is preserved in (1) fine-to-coarse sands deposited in shallow channels (up to 50 cm deep) in which *Theropithecus oswaldi* remains are concentrated; (2) overbank coarse sands (originally misidentified as a Member 6 of the Olorgesailie Fm), which were accumulated as thin floodplain deposits adjacent to the channels of lower M7; and (3) diatomaceous silts that represent the uppermost sediments and overtopping phases of the lower M7 channels fills. The paleo-landscapes of lower M7 consisted of a network of braided streams and floodplains. Fauna and Acheulean stone artifacts are strongly associated and highly concentrated with very few remains preserved away from the main channel fills. Although animal bone concentrations preserved in lower M7 were subject to moving water, the shallowness of the channels and nature of the sand–gravel lenses deposited within them suggest that water flow was not sufficiently energetic to be the primary agent responsible for accumulating the bones; instead, water flow appears to have caused relatively minor redistribution of the remains of animals that had died in spatially delimited locations within the channels. On the basis of renewed, ongoing studies, hominin and other animals may have been attracted to dry-season waterholes in the channels without much direct interaction (Potts et al., 1999).

Although fragmentary diatoms indicative of freshwater lakes are rare in the channel fills and floodplain sands of lower

Table 30.1 Stratigraphic and temporal units of faunal preservation in the Olorgesailie Basin.

Age range	Formation	Member	Principal lithologies	Sedimentary environments	Key references
320–298 ka	Olutelei	Olkesiteti	Sands, silts, paleosols	Repeated cycles of fluvial cut-and-fill and floodplain development	Behrensmeyer et al. (2018); Potts et al. (2018)
671–609 ka	Olorgesailie	M10–M11	Pumicious gravels, sands, diatomites, paleosols, reddened diatomaceous melt zones	Fluctuating land–lake conditions: includes channel fills, sheetwash, shallow lakes, soils, and burning of concentrated wetland plant matter indicative of wet–arid fluctuation	Behrensmeyer et al. (2002); Melson and Potts (2002); Isaac (1977)
~900 ka	Olorgesailie	M7	Gravelly sands, diatomaceous silts, paleosols	Filling of a shallow channel system, broad overbank flooding, development of wetlands and long-duration soils	Potts et al. (1999); Isaac (1977)
~1.0 Ma	Olorgesailie	Upper M1	Paleosols developed on diatomaceous silts and sands	Short-duration (1–2 kyr) grassland with ephemeral wetlands within a lengthy interval of strong lake-land oscillation	Potts et al. (1999); Sikes et al. (1999)

M7, paleo-channel directions trend toward wetland facies of limited exposure toward the Mt. Olorgesailie foothills. One or more cycles of lake transgression–regression deposited sediments immediately above the channels, followed by long-term pedogenesis recorded at the top of M7.

Members 10–11 Fauna, Olorgesailie Fm, ~671–609 ka

Faunal remains uncovered and collected from Members 10 and lower 11 (M11′) are preserved in reworked volcaniclastic sands and gravels. Concentrations of animal bones were recovered in M10 by L.S.B. Leakey in the 1940s and G.Ll. Isaac in the 1960s (Isaac, 1977) and by Potts' team (Haradon, 2010) from volcaniclastic sediments that rapidly filled channels and depressions. M10 pumices are dated ~671 ka (Deino and Potts, 1990; Deino et al., 2018). Faunal concentrations in these pumice gravels appear to represent rapid-death assemblages in sediment-choked shallow rivers and streams, with the remains disarticulated and winnowed prior to final burial. The fossils in M10 tend to be fragile and surface features are poorly preserved.

M10 deposition ended as the basin stabilized, followed by the return in M11′ of several cycles of wetland/lake deposition and pedogenesis. The paleosols contain spatially discontinuous, reddened diatomaceous lenses that consist of burned plant material from wetland habitats; these reddened beds reflect intense moist–dry fluctuations because marked lowering of the water table was necessary to initiate burning of plant matter (Melson and Potts, 2002). The upper strata of M11′ consist of a series of gravelly sands that were distributed on top of a lactustrine/fluvial floodplain. The sands, which were deposited roughly contemporaneous with intrabasinal faulting, preserve faunal concentrations in some locations closely associated with Acheulean stone artifacts and evidence of tree roots and freshwater ponds.

Mammalian faunal remains are scarce in Members 12, 13, and 14 of the Olorgesailie Fm, typically consisting of isolated fragments. One exception is a site excavated in M13 in the lower foothills of Mt. Olorgesailie, which preserved one main skeleton of *Palaeoloxodon* (*Elephas*) *recki* and fragments of another conspecific individual. The elephant from this previously unreported excavation represents the last known reliable appearance of this species in the southern Kenya rift, ~550 ka.

Olkesiteti Member Fauna, Oltulelei Fm, ~320–295 ka

Fauna of the Olkesiteti Member (OK Mbr) is ~300–230 kyr younger than the youngest faunal-preserving units of the Olorgesailie Fm (Potts et al., 2018). The fossil sample was obtained in association with a series of excavated MSA sites situated in a complex of paleo-channel fills in a relatively small area of ~3400 m^2 (Brooks et al., 2018). These strata represent a duration of ~7–22 kyr, and thus represent a relatively short time interval. The fauna throughout the OK Mbr shows no obvious changes in taxonomic composition. Although the fossilized bones were originally deposited in abandoned channels along with the MSA artifacts, both the faunal and lithic assemblages contain abundant small fragments indicative of burial at the site with minimal disturbance by water flow.

The combination of sedimentary lithologies, $\delta^{13}C$ values of soil carbonates, phytolith assemblages, and mammalian taxa indicates that the habitats of the channel filling phases (the preservation environment) included arid, sparsely wooded grasslands, grassy wetlands, and spring deposits, while channel erosional phases may have resulted as higher amounts of seasonal precipitation led to downcutting in the area (Potts et al., 2018; Behrensmeyer et al., 2018).

Early and Middle Pleistocene Faunas of the Olorgesailie Basin

Tables 30.2 and 30.3 list the mammalian fauna currently identified from the Olorgesailie and Oltulelei Fms. Recovery of fauna from Olorgesailie is ongoing, and new taxonomic identifications will very likely be added over the next decade, probably increasing the currently known taxonomic diversity. The Olorgesailie Fm fauna (1.2 Ma to 500 ka) is unusual in its low relative representation of bovids. Previous description of this fauna in Potts (2007) also inferred a relay over time of relative abundance among the non-bovid large mammals, with equids prominent in M1 (~1 Ma), *Theropithecus* abundant in M7 (~900 ka), and suids and hippopotamids dominant in M10–M11 (671–609 ka). (See Deino et al., 2018, for this revised chronology of Olorgesailie Fm members.) This apparent shift in the mammalian paleocommunity is hypothesized to be related to environmental dynamics, particularly climatic and resource variability that affected lake level, lake presence/absence, and access to fresh water, graze, and browse (Potts, 1998, 2007).

Building on the observations in Potts (2007), a contingency table analysis of taxonomic abundances (NISP) reinforces the broad family-level changes in faunal composition through the Olorgesailie and Oltulelei Fms (Table 30.4; taxa aggregated at the family level). Chi-square tests indicate highly significant differences across adjacent stratigraphic intervals (Mbr 1 vs. Mbr 7: $\chi^2 = 1555.4$, $p < 0.001$; Mbr 7 vs. Mbrs 10–11: $\chi^2 = 985.7$, $p < 0.001$). Adjusted residuals (ARs), which can be interpreted as standard normal deviates (absolute values greater than 1.96 are significant at $\alpha = 0.05$), indicate those taxa whose abundance changes significantly, with the sign of the AR indicating the direction of change relative to the underlying assemblage (+ = increase; − = decrease; Table 30.4). The transition from M1 (dominated by equids and to a lesser degree, bovids) to M7 is characterized by a massive increase in cercopithecids (*T. oswaldi*) and significant declines in all other families (barring the poorly sampled giraffids); equids and hippopotamids are the dominant ungulates, with bovids representing a smaller portion of the large mammal fauna in the M7 sample. Between M7 and M10–M11, *Theropithecus* declines while suids, hippopotamids, and bovids increase; suids and hippopotamids dominate the ungulate fauna from M10 to 11. Drawing from biogeographical and ecological theory (e.g., Belyea and Lancaster, 1999; Hubbell, 2001), it appears likely that a combination of dispersal

Table 30.2 Mammalian fauna of Members 1, 7, and 10/11 of the Olorgesailie Formation, Olorgesailie, Kenya; unique taxa only with adult body size >2 kg. Where present, taxa are represented as number of individual specimens and, in parentheses, minimum number of individuals. Faunal samples are in stratigraphic order from left (oldest) to right (youngest).

Acheulean-associated Taxa (1.0 Ma–609 ka)	Mbr 1	Mbr 7	Mbrs 10–11	Diet	Body mass – modern range (kg)	Body mass – ~average (kg)	Body size category
Theropithecus oswaldi	3	1931 + (49+)	0	G+		200	3
Homo cf. H. erectus	1	1 (1)	1	O		70	2
Genetta sp.	0	2 (1)	0	C(O)	1.5–3.0	2	1b
Panthera leo	1	0	0	C	120–260	200	3
Crocuta crocuta	0	0	1	C	40–90	65	2
Crocuta sp. nov.	600+ (5)	0	0	C		60	2
Canis cf. C. mesomelas	4	0	0	C	7–14	10	1c
Palaeoloxodon (Elephas) recki	200+ (4)	12 (2)	4	G+		8000	6
Equus oldowayensis	156	112 (5)	0	G+		450	4
Equus cf. E. grevyi	64	3 (2)	6	G	350–450	400	4
Equus cf. E. quagga	10	0	0	G	175–325	250	3b
Eurygnathohippus sp.	5	1 (1)	0	G		200	3a
Ceratotherium simum	32	38 (4)	0	G	1400–3600	2500	5
Diceros bicornis	0	0	2	B	800–2900	2000	5
Kolpochoerus majus	0	0	29	G/M		120	3a
Metridiochoerus compactus	16	5 (2)	2	G		150	3a
Metridiochoerus hopwoodi	9	0	0	G+		250	3b
Phacochoerus sp.	11	0	0	G	45–150	100	2
Hippopotamus cf. H. gorgops	69	112 (10)	32	G+		3000	6
Giraffa sp.	0	2 (1)	0	B	450–1950	1500	5
Tragelaphus scriptus	1	2 (1)	1	M	24–80	50	2
Taurotragus sp.	3	2 (1)	1	B	300–940	600	4
Syncerus (Pelorovis) cf. S. antiquus	16	2 (2)	0	G		900	5
Redunca sp.	6	5 (2)	3	G		50	2
Connochaetes sp.	49	9 (3)	3	G		250	3b
Megalotragus sp.	12	4 (1)	2	G		400	4
Alcelaphus sp.	16	0	0	G	116–218	175	3a
Aepyceros sp.	0	4 (1)	1	M		60	2
Gazella sp.	21	15 (5)	1	G		40	2

Diet: B, browser; C, carnivore (mostly animal tissue); G, grazer; G+, hyper-grazing adaptations; M, mixed grazer/browser; O, omnivore (including vertebrate tissue).
Body size: 0: indet 1: <23 kg (1a: <1 kg; 1b: 1–10 kg; 1c: 10–23 kg); 2: 23–113 kg; 3: 113–340 kg (3a: topi size; 3b: wildebeest/zebra size); 4: 340–900 kg; 5: 900–2700 kg; 6: >2700 kg.

Table 30.3 Mammalian fauna of the Olkesiteti Member of the Oltulelei Formation, Olorgesailie, Kenya; unique Middle Stone Age-associated taxa only with adult body size >2 kg (Potts et al., 2018). Where present, taxa are represented as number of individual specimens and, in parentheses, minimum number of individuals. Faunal samples are in stratigraphic order from left (oldest) to right (youngest).

Middle Stone Age-associated taxa (~320–298 ka)	BOK-1East	BOK-3	BOK-2	BOK-4	Diet	Body mass – modern range	Body mass – ~average	Body size category
Madoqua sp.			3 (1)		B	4–7	6	1b
Antidorcas marsupialis			19 (3)		M	20–59	40	2
Gazella thomsoni		1 (1)	1 (1)		G	15–35	25	2
Damaliscus hypsodon	3 (2)		3 (1)		G+		70	2
Oryx gazella – Hippotragin oryx size	1 (1)		3 (2)		G (M)		200	3a
Hippotragin – roan size			1 (1)		G		280	3b
Taurotragus oryx	2 (1)		17 (4)	1 (1)	B	300–940	600	4
Tragelaphus strepsiceros			4 (2)		B (M)	120–315	250	3b
Tragelaphus cf. *T. imberbis*			1 (1)		B	56–108	80	3a
Phacochoerus sp.			1 (1)		B	45–150	100	2
Suidae sizes 2/3a	2 (2)				?		125	3a
Hippopotamus cf. *H. amphibius*			3 (1)	2 (1)	G	600–3000	1500	5
Equus aff. *E. capensis*	6 (2)		26 (4)	4 (1)	G		600	4
Equus cf. *E. quagga*	24 (2)		60 (3)	5 (2)	G	175–325	250	3b
Diceros bicornis			1 (1)		G	700–1400	1100	5
Bovidae/Equidae body sizes 3b/4		2 (1)						
Elephantidae cf. *Loxodonta africana*	2 (1)		1 (1)	1 (1)	M	2200–6300	4500	6
Felis sp. indet.			1 (1)		C		10	1c
cf. Hyenidae			1 (1)		C		65	2
Otocyon megalotis			8 (2)		C		4	1b
Canidae size 1b1c			4 (1)		C		10	1b/1c
Hystrix cristata	1 (1)				M (O)	12–27	15	1c
Pedetes sp.			25 (3)	1 (1)	G		3	1b
Lepus sp.			1 (1)		G		2	1b
Totals	41 (12)	3 (2)	184 (36)	14 (7)				

Diet: B, browse; M, mixed feeder; G, grazer.

Table 30.4 Taxonomic abundances (NISP) and adjusted residuals (ARs) derived from a contingency table analysis of the Olorgesailie faunas. The sign of the ARs (+ = increase; − = decrease) indicates to the change in abundance relative to the underlying stratum. Significant ARs in bold. Counts include only taxa identified to genus or lower.

	Mbr 1	Mbr 7		Mbrs 10–11	
	NISP	NISP	AR	NISP	AR
Cercopithecid	3	1931	37.79	0	−20.41
Equid	235	116	−25.38	6	0.83
Rhino	32	38	−6.05	2	0.49
Suid	36	5	−11.65	31	26.93
Hippopotamid	69	112	−7.20	32	12.47
Giraffid	0	2	0.67	0	−0.27
Bovid	124	43	−19.39	12	7.39

constraints (mobility, landscape connectivity between regions, random geographic factors), taxonomic environmental preferences, and internal community dynamics (e.g., competition, mutualism) in the context of shifting climate variability helped shape changes in species assembly and community composition between 1.0 Ma and 500 ka in the southern Kenya rift (Potts, 2007; Potts and Faith, 2015).

Although faunal change recorded in this interval was associated with fluctuating climatic variability, it took place in a relatively stable, consistently aggrading lake–basin system with few and relatively minor periods of erosion. A far more abrupt shift in the mammalian community took place between 500 and 320 ka, which is evident by comparing the faunas of the Olorgesailie Fm (Table 30.2) with the overlying Olkesiteti Member of the Oltulelei Fm (Table 30.3). On the basis of taxa currently identified, the degree of turnover is estimated at 85 percent during this period (i.e., only 15 percent of taxa are shared; Potts et al., 2018). Large-scale downfaulting in the Olorgesailie region led to a first period of extensive erosion and valley formation starting 500 ka and lasting ~180 kyr. The lake basin was replaced by a fluvial cut-and-fill system, with limited periods of wetlands and lacustrine facies. This Oltulelei Fm was further characterized by two subsequent periods of dramatic basin erosion and filling (Behrensmeyer et al., 2018). Extensive faulting of the southern Kenya rift after 500 ka was essential to this dramatic alteration in the depositional system. A prolonged phase of highly variable climate, predicted to have been concurrent with the Oltulelei Fm record (Potts and Faith, 2015), would have led to alternating intervals of strong aridity and rainfall necessary to build up and subsequently erode and displace large volumes of sediment over most of the past 320 kyr (Behrensmeyer et al., 2018).

While the Olorgesailie Fm fauna is characterized by large-bodied herbivores (e.g., *T. oswaldi*, *P. (Elephas) recki*) that possessed hyper-grazer craniodental adaptations, the mammalian community of the interval between 320 and 295 ka is dominated by grazers that appear to have evolved and migrated into the southern Kenya rift in response to heightened aridity (Faith et al., 2012; Potts et al., 2018). The current first appearance of the high-crowned bovid *Damaliscus hypsodon* (Faith et al., 2012) in this region is indicative of a bovid-dominated fauna adapted to aridity, presumably with a reliable supply of grass but also potentially affected by strong grazing competition during times of scarcity. The southern African springbok *Antidorcas marsupialis* is present in the Olkesiteti Mbr fauna, reflecting an instance of long-distance range extension into southern Kenya around 320–295 ka (Potts et al., 2018). The presence of brown hyena *Parahyaena brunnea* in the middle Pleistocene Oloronga beds southwest of Olorgesailie (Werdelin and Barthelme, 1997) further suggests a connection with southern Africa; the Oloronga beds are most likely equivalent to the <400 ka fossil-rich sediments exposed at Lainyamok (see below). Another unusual aspect of the Olkesiteti Mbr fauna is a very large *Equus* species (*Equus* aff. *E. capensis*) currently unidentified in other middle Pleistocene African faunal assemblages (Potts et al., 2018); whether this zebra is endemic to the southern Kenya rift is currently under investigation.

Lainyamok, Lenderut, and Oldonyo Nyokie Mammalian Faunas

Mammalian faunal remains have been recovered from several other distinct catchments in the southern Kenya rift (Figure 30.1), and these are discussed briefly here.

Lainyamok

The Lainyamok fauna described in Potts and Deino (1995) is the largest of these fossil assemblages, consisting of at least 42 mammalian taxa. It is one of the rare middle Pleistocene fossil localities in Africa with precise age calibration. This fauna is undergoing further study by the authors and therefore the species list is likely to be revised. The most important revision published so far is the transfer of the dominant bovid species initially referred to *Damaliscus* cf. *D. dorcas* (blesbok) to the recently described species *D. hypsodon* (Faith et al., 2012). The type specimen and most complete skeletal remains of *D. hypsodon* are from Lainyamok. This species is characterized by simple molar morphology, the lack of upper and lower P2, very high-crowned teeth relative to molar heights of other African bovids, along with a distinctive horn-core morphology and insertions, among other features (Faith et al., 2012).

The sedimentary sequence at Lainyamok, ~9 m thick, is exposed over an area of ~1.5 km^2 within a small north–south trending half-graben. Fossil bone concentrations and stone artifacts are preserved in poorly sorted, khaki-colored mudflows, particularly within the massive silts of the Khaki 2 bed (Potts et al., 1988). While abundant stone flakes, broken cores, and other artifact debris have been collected from the eroded surface, lithic artifacts are rare and dispersed within the Khaki beds, evidently having been transported as part of the sediment load of the mudflows. By contrast, faunal remains were densely packed in elongated concentrations, most likely representing hyena den accumulations dug into the Khaki 2 layer after settling of the mudflow. The stone artifacts are thus associated with tephra within Khaki 2 dated 397 ± 8 ka, while the fauna is bracketed from 397 ± 8 ka to the superjacent Khaki 1 bed dated 334 ± 12 ka (Deino et al., 2018); these dates are a revision of $^{40}Ar/^{39}Ar$ ages of 392 ± 4 to 330 ± 6 ka reported in Potts and Deino (1995).

On the basis of surface finds, the Lainyamok fauna and artifacts were once hypothesized to reflect a series of single carcass butchery sites (Shipman et al., 1983); however, detailed excavation, laboratory analyses, and taphonomic tests indicate that the tools and bones are disassociated, and the bone concentrations were the result of carnivore activity (Potts et al., 1988). Of 851 mammalian remains (NISPs) identified to family level, bovids represent ~70 percent, equids ~13 percent, carnivorans >7 percent, and hominins <0.5 percent of the fauna. Taxonomic composition is consistent with an open, grass-dominated environment, although the presence of impala (*Aepyceros melampus*), eland (*Taurotragus oryx*), and giraffes (*Giraffa camelopardalis*) signal bushy and woody vegetation. This taxonomic combination is consistent with strong topographic relief that developed in the southern Kenya rift, where woody vegetation has often covered the ridges on the upthrust sides of faults while the grabens have been susceptible to aridity, grassland development, denuded landscapes, and also episodic lakes.

The fauna is similar to that of the Olkesiteti Member in the Olorgesailie Basin. It lacks the large-bodied specialized grazing elephants, baboons, suids, and hippos that typify the Olorgesailie Basin fauna up to 600–500 ka (Potts and Deino, 1995; Potts et al., 2018), and it includes *D. hypsodon* and other taxa (e.g., *Gazella thomsoni, Oryx*) which typify the fauna ≤320 ka at Olorgesailie, ~42 km to the northeast.

As implied by the mudflow sediments in which stone artifacts occur at Lainyamok, as well as in debris flow units more widely distributed around Lake Magadi and assigned to the Oloronga Beds (Baker, 1958; Eugster, 1981; Potts et al., 1988), hominins post-500 ka lived in the southern Kenya rift during a time of heightened tectonic activity. Faulting apparently resulted in destabilization of the landscape and the massive transfer of silt-to-cobble-sized debris into lower-elevation grabens. Handaxes are rare among archeological materials, and the Lainyamok assemblage cannot be easily assigned to either the Acheulean or Middle Stone Age. The fact that the lithics are associated with mudflow deposits suggests that the assemblage is likely to have low analytical integrity.

Lenderut

Located on the northwest side of the Lenderut volcano, this site preserves Acheulean artifacts and a small faunal assemblage. As described by Barthelme (1991), the Lenderut sequence consists of 7 m of lacustrine silts, fluvial deposits, and carbonate layers consistent with lake, lake margin, and riverine environments. The stone artifacts and fauna are largely derived from cut-and-fill deposits. Excavations by Barthelme recovered the remains of *T. oswaldi, Equus* spp., a suid, and dental and horn-core fragments representing alcelaphin, hippotragin, antilopin, and tragelaphin bovids (Barthelme, 1991). No radiometric dates have been reported; the presence of Acheulean remains and *T. oswaldi* leads one to suspect an age between 900 and 500 ka based on the well-calibrated fauna of the Olorgesailie Fm.

Nyokie Fossil Site

The Nyokie site is located SSW of Olorgesailie, directly west of the Oldonyo Nyokie volcanic complex. Fossil recovery primarily by excavation and geological research began at this site in 2015 by R.P., and studies of the taphonomic complexity of the site, along with paleoecological and biogeographical implications, are in their initial phases. Animal remains and stone tools occur within silts and injectite deposits situated within volcanic sediments deposited 1 million years ago following the eruption of a 30-m thick deposit of ash from the nearby Oldonyo Nyokie. Fluids injected upward through the main tephra unit either tracked existing weaknesses in the consolidated tephra unit or helped to create zones susceptible to fissuring in response to tectonic events. The majority of fossils formed as animals fell into and were buried by sediment in fissures that developed in the volcanic plain as earthquakes shook the region. Stone tools and isolated bones of animals were also washed into these openings probably due to sheetwash.

Well-preserved mammalian fossils provide evidence of a taxonomic combination and a faunal community previously undocumented in the southern Kenya rift. Two unusual aspects of the excavated fossil sample include: (1) evidence of a very large lion – see Manthi et al. (2018) for a similar example from ~196 ka deposits in northwest Kenya – along with a large species of African wild dog with distinctive similarities to Pleistocene finds of *Lycaon magnus* and *L. sekowei* discovered previously in northwestern and southern Africa, respectively (Geraads, 2011; Hartstone-Rose et al., 2010); and (2) evidence of the bovid *Rabaticeras* cf. *R. arambourgi*, a species found throughout the continent and typically thought to be the immediate predecessor of the hartebeest *Alcelaphus buselaphus* (Vrba, 1997). The rich bovid fauna is dominated by *Oryx* cf. *O. beisa*, indicative of arid environments, and a variety of other dry grassland species also occur in the fauna, such as the leopard tortoise *Stigmochelys pardalis* and the extinct antelope *Damaliscus hypsodon*.

Efforts to obtain radiometric ages are in progress at the time of writing. Stone tools in the excavations demonstrate that early human toolmakers were present in the vicinity of the Nyokie Fossil Site at the time of this faunal community. The presence of small, refined handaxes, the absence of archaic species that typify the Olorgesailie Fm (e.g., *Theropithecus, Palaeoloxodon, Eurygnathohippus*), and the overall combination of mammal taxa suggest that the fossils and archeological remains fall in the interval between 500 and 397 ka (the younger date based on the lower age constraint on the Lainyamok fauna), a period poorly represented in the fossil record of East Africa. If this estimate is correct, the Nyokie Fossil Site represents the youngest occurrence of *Rabaticeras* in East Africa, though the species may have persisted up to ~500 ka in north-western Africa (Geraads, 2011). Such a young record of *Rabaticeras* in East Africa would call to question proposed relationships with hartebeest, which is present at Bodo in Ethiopia ~600 ka (Vrba, 1997), or imply that hartebeest emerged from *Rabaticeras* via cladogenetic rather than anagenetic speciation.

Conclusion

What is often considered paleoecological analysis based on the faunas associated with paleoanthropological sites has tended to focus on habitat or overall paleoenvironmental reconstructions. With the exception of researchers engaged in dietary analysis (e.g., stable isotopic studies) or the documentation of bone damage indicative of species interactions, direct investigation of ecological relationships, food webs, and processes of species assembly has been somewhat limited. Study of such topics demands in-depth evaluation of taphonomic processes, strong time–space controls, and minimal time-averaging in order to address past species associations on ecological timescales. These criteria are rarely met in the study of surface-collected assemblages that integrate many thousands of years and potentially numerous environmental shifts.

Faunas of the southern Kenya rift have mainly been recovered by precise excavation techniques within narrow, well-defined strata with excellent age control relative to what could be determined several decades ago. Faunas of the Olorgesailie Basin, coupled with fossil assemblages from Lainyamok and potentially the Nyokie Fossil Site, illustrate the potential to identify dramatic faunal shifts directly and precisely linked in time and space with major evolutionary change in hominin behavior, such as the replacement of the Acheulean by MSA technology and other behavioral innovations (Brooks et al., 2018; Potts et al., 2018). The relay of taxonomic dominance in the Olorgesailie Fm from 1 Ma to 600 ka, taxonomic and ecological reorganization of the faunal community between 500 and 320 ka, and evidence of biogeographic influx of taxa to the southern Kenya rift during this interval are all indicative of important shifts in the ecological setting associated with hominins in this region.

Only a single fossil hominin has been described so far from the Olorgesailie stratigraphic sequence; this fossil appears to represent the last definite appearance of *Homo erectus* in eastern Africa, at ~900 ka (Potts et al., 2004). With a recalculated argon-constrained age of <540 ± 61 ka for Acheulean tools associated with the non-*erectus* cranium from Bodo, Ethiopia (Deino et al., 2018), it is possible that the Acheulean of eastern Africa, including the archeological sequence at Olorgesailie, was produced by more than one hominin species between 1 Ma and 500 ka. Nonetheless, the Olorgesailie Acheulean represents a lithic industry that was produced nearly continuously in lacustrine and low-energy fluvial floodplains and paleosols reflecting a structurally stable basin and relatively stable aggrading sedimentary regime. Along with the entire mammalian community, hominin populations experienced a range of moist–arid oscillations. The Olorgesailie Acheulean thus reflects a resilient adaptive repertoire that could be accommodated to shifting environments over hundreds of thousands of years. The large mammal community comprised mainly grazing taxa, the relative proportions of which changed substantially over time (Tables 30.2 and 30.3).

The Acheulean of the southern Kenya rift came to an end following major structural change of the Olorgesailie Basin and tectonic reshaping of the southern Kenya rift that began ~500 ka. Approximately 100–180 kyr later, mammalian communities had undergone large-scale taxonomic and ecological revision. During this time of tectonic, climatic, landscape, and biotic change, hominins who made MSA tools, transported obsidian over wide distances, and modified and used pigments had emerged and occupied this region. Shifts in the mammalian community and in hominin behavior were concentrated near the onset of a prolonged period of high insolation, typically associated with pronounced wet–dry climate variability. The success of a novel system of hominin adaptation based on wider mobility, social networks, and innovations in lithic technology significantly revised the ways in which early hominins near the origin of *Homo sapiens* adjusted to increasingly unpredictable resource landscapes and the expansion of arid grasslands in southern Kenya.

Acknowledgments

We acknowledge the long-term collaboration of the National Museums of Kenya, and thank M. Kibunjia, I.O. Farah, F.K. Manthi, E.N. Mbua, and M. Muungu for their support, and J.M Nume, C.M. Kilonzi, S.M. Musyoka, J.N. Mativo, and A.M. Kioko for their skillful participation in the field and laboratory efforts of the Olorgesailie, Lainyamok, and Oldonyo Nyokie projects. We further acknowledge Kenya Government permission granted by the Ministry of Sports, Culture and the Arts, and by NACOSTI permit P/14/7709/683. A.K. Behrensmeyer, A.L. Deino, A.S. Brooks, J.E. Yellen, among other colleagues, played vital roles in understanding the geology, geochronology, and archeological finds of the southern Kenya rift. J.B. Clark handled logistics and field operations, and produced Figure 30.1. The Olorgesailie project has been supported by the Peter Buck Fund for Human Origins Research, Smithsonian (R.P.), the Human Origins Program (R.P.), and NSF HOMINID Program grant BCS-0218511 (R.P.). J.T.F.'s analysis of some of the faunas discussed here was supported by an Australian Research Council DECRA Fellowship.

31 Context and Environments of the Lower Pleistocene Hominins of Peninj, Tanzania

Denis Geraads, Ignacio de la Torre, and Christiane Denys

History of Research

In the 1880s, Gustav Fischer was the first European to see the Oldoinyo Lengai volcano (Dawson, 2008) and, with Joseph Thomson, to visit Lake Natron (Gregory, 1921). The first systematic geological studies in the area were carried out by Carl Uhlig, who in 1904 surveyed the Manyara–Natron fault and noted the asymmetry of this sector of the rift (Dawson, 2008). Guest (1953) mapped and studied the volcanics of Lake Natron, and Baker (1963) compared the lacustrine beds of lakes Magadi and Natron. However, it was only in 1959 when Mary Leakey (1984: 124) drove across the area and realized the paleoanthropological potential of the area.

The Leakeys confirmed by aerial reconnaissance in 1963 the interest of West Natron, and in 1964 a field expedition in the area was led by Glynn Isaac and Richard Leakey (Isaac, 1965). The only hominin remain so far discovered in the area belongs to this very first expedition in 1964, when a mandible of *Paranthropus boisei* was discovered in Plio-Pleistocene sediments of the Peninj river (Leakey and Leakey, 1964). Isaac (1965) mapped systematically the West Natron sediments, and documented the existence in Pleistocene deposits of vertebrate remains and Acheulean sites. Preliminary reports on the geology and archeology of Peninj (Isaac, 1965, 1967) were followed by the first radiometric dating of the sequence (Isaac and Curtis, 1974), which situated the Peninj assemblages among the earliest Acheulean sites worldwide.

Fieldwork at Peninj resumed in September 1982, when G. Isaac, A. Mturi and M. Taieb co-directed a new field project, with archeological, geological, and paleontological components (Figure 31.1). The untimely death of G. Isaac in 1985 prevented publication of his results, but a detailed study of the sedimentology, geochemistry, and other aspects of the Lake Natron basin were published by Taieb and Fritz (1987). The paleontological field work was conducted by E. Chacha, D. Geraads, and B. Hanson, who collected a number of large mammals and other vertebrates; B. Hanson also coordinated systematic bulk sampling at some selected localities in various levels of the Humbu Formation. Systematic collecting was also undertaken at Kipalagu, an archeological site in the upper part of the Humbu Formation. Geraads (1987a) published an

Figure 31.1 G.Ll. Isaac and E. Chacha at the site of the *Paranthropus boisei* mandible in 1982.

account on the large vertebrates collected in 1963, 1964, and 1982, except the primates and suids, which were supposed to be studied at Berkeley and Dar-es-Salaam, respectively. No report on these latter groups has been published so far, so our account here for Primates and suids is based upon very sketchy notes and photos.

Geological survey and fieldwork organized by M. Taieb, N. Thouveny and P. Manega were conducted in 1984 in the Kipalagu area. During this survey, the Moinik and Humbu Formation sections were sampled for paleomagnetism (Thouveny and Taieb, 1986, 1987). In addition, washing and screening of about 450 kg of sediment from the Basal Sandy Clays below the Main Humbu Tuff and the Gabbia limestone were performed (Denys, 1987b).

A new phase of archeological research was initiated in the mid-1990s (Dominguez-Rodrigo et al., 2009b), which is still ongoing (Dominguez-Rodrigo et al., 2014b).

Geographic Setting

The Peninj area is located in the Lake Natron basin, Tanzania. Lake Natron lies on an elongated depression that runs North-South (approximately S2°05 to S2°35 and E35°–36°) as a southern continuation of the Magadi Basin in Kenya (Figure 31.2). The present lake is around 20 km wide and 50 km long, with an approximate surface area of 1039 km^2 and an average altitude of 608 m above sea level (Vincens and Casanova, 1987), and is very shallow (3–4 m depth) and saline, with a high evaporation rate (Dawson, 2008).

Lake Natron is surrounded by five volcanoes (clockwise from the north: Shombole, Gelai, Lengai, Embagai, and Sambu), one of which (Oldoinyo Lengai) is still active. Four permanent rivers flow into the lake. In the north, the Engare Nyiro feeds Lake Natron from Kenya; the Engare Sero enters into the lake from the southwest; the Peninj and the Moinik rivers flow into the lake from the west, and cut through Plio-Pleistocene sediments.

Plio-Pleistocene deposits have been reported on the western part of Lake Natron only, across the Peninj and Moinik river courses. Deposits extend from the Precambrian hills to the west to the area close to the lake shoreline. Fossiliferous sediments are particularly relevant in three areas across the Peninj river: Maritanane-Type Section, closest to Lake Natron; MHS (also known as Bayasi-South Escarpment), in the middle course of the Peninj river; and RHS (Mugulud-North Escarpment), upper in the fluvial course of the Peninj river (Figure 31.2).

Geological Context

Structurally, Lake Natron is located in the northern Tanzania section of the Gregory Rift Valley. Like other basins of the northern Tanzania Rift Valley, Lake Natron is not enclosed within opposed faults, but is a half-graben rift basin with a maximum depth of 3.3 km (Dawson, 2008) that lies between the Archaean Tanzanian craton and the reworked craton margin (Neukirchen et al., 2010). Two major episodes of faulting took place in the area of Lake Natron (Macintyre et al., 1974); the first produced the accommodation space for the deposition of the Peninj

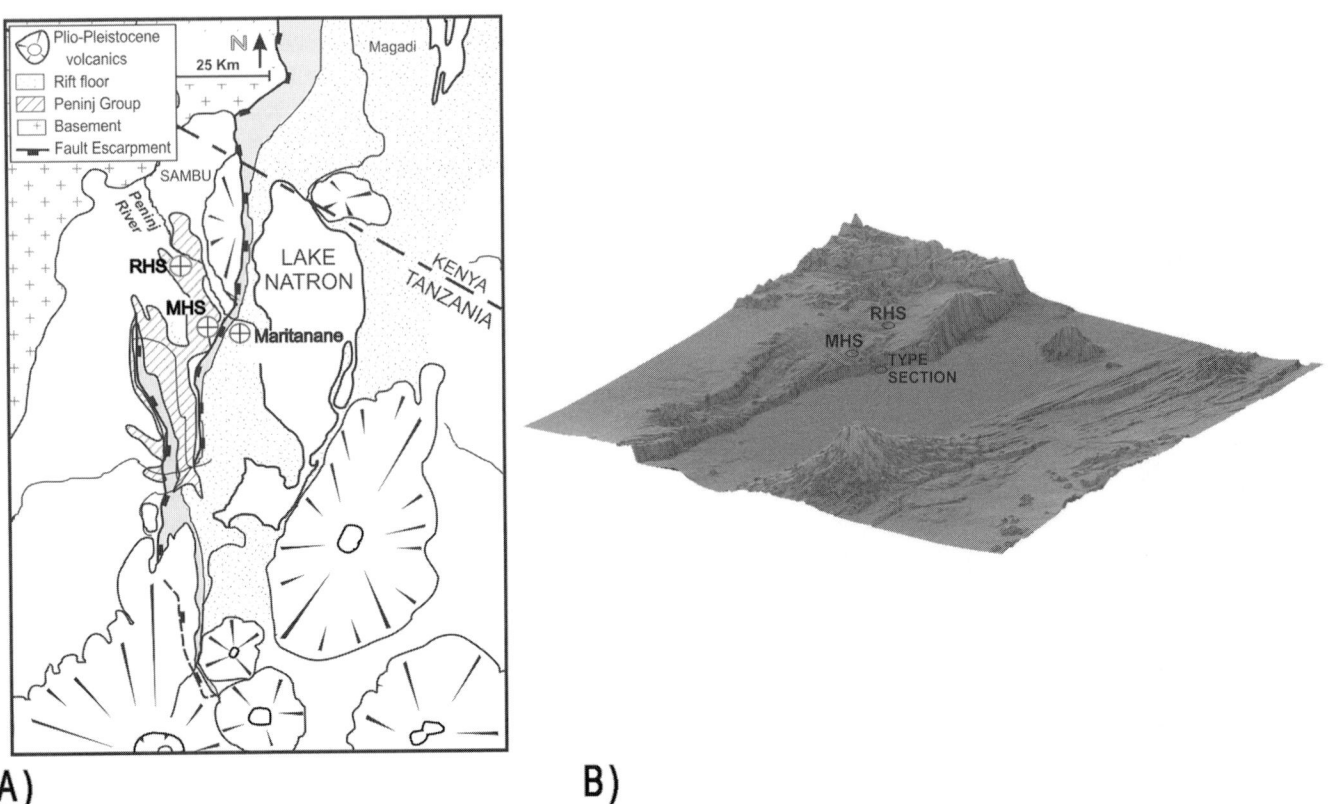

Figure 31.2 (A) Map of Lake Natron and Lake Magadi basin (adapted from Luque, in Mora et al., 2003). (B) Digital elevation model of Lake Natron, with the fossiliferous areas mentioned in the text.

Group into a shallow fault-bounded basin. The second and main faulting episode occurred between 1.2 and 1.15 million years ago, and created the escarpment of the Manjara–Natron Fault (Macintyre et al., 1974), which caused the termination of the Peninj Group sedimentation (Isaac and Curtis, 1974).

The Precambrian basement (quartzites, gneisses, and quartz micaschists) is exposed in the Sonjo fault, and is separated from Plio-Pleistocene basalts and nephelinites derived from the Sambu and Mosonik volcanoes (Isaac, 1967). These lavas were deposited in a fault-generated shallow depression and fill up most of the basin. The Sambu lavas are more than 250 m thick and are overlain by the Hajaro Beds, which contain sediments and lavas (Isaac, 1967). Between the Precambrian hills eastwards to Lake Natron, extensive clastic deposits with interbedded tuffs and lavas lie on top of the Sambu and Hajaro Beds, forming the Peninj Beds (Isaac, 1965) or Peninj Group (Isaac, 1967), which are the main fossiliferous deposits in Lake Natron.

The Peninj Group (Figure 31.3), as defined by Isaac (1967), corresponds to *ca*. 100-m thick fluvial and lacustrine sediments deposited in a wide and shallow basin, previous to the major faulting that created the escarpment of the Manjara–Natron Fault. Isaac (1967) distinguished two major units within the Peninj Group, namely the Humbu Formation and the Moinik Formation. The Humbu Formation consists of clays and sands, which vary laterally and contain basaltic tuffs and flows, and is largely deltaic. The Moinik Formation sits conformably on top of the Humbu Formation. It consists of sands, clays, and trachytic tuffs and lavas, and is largely lacustrine, although there is considerable lateral variation, with lacustrine deposits dominating in the east and south, and alluvial and deltaic facies in the northwest (Isaac, 1967).

Within the Peninj Group, it is the Humbu Formation that yields most of the archeological and paleontological evidence. Isaac (1967) subdivided the *ca*. 40-m thick Humbu Formation into three members (see also Icole et al., 1987; Luque et al., 2009). At the bottom, the Basal Sandy Clays (BSC) Member contains basaltic tephra and coarse-grained alluvial sands. This is overlaid by the Main Humbu Tuff (MHT, 1.6 m thick), which contains numerous fish and gastropod remains, and which to the south includes a lava flow (Wa-Mbugu basalt) with normal polarity. It is overlain by the Middle Zone (MZ) that contains numerous root casts, followed by the Upper Sandy Clays Member (USC; 20–30 m thick), which lies on top of the Main Humbu Tuff and caps the Humbu Formation. It contains a variety of facies, including channels, fluvial and deltaic environments, and lacustrine conditions. This upper member of the Humbu Formation is the richest in archeological terms within the Peninj Group.

Geochronology

Radiometric dating of the Peninj beds has proven difficult, and disparate – and often contradictory – results exist. The first K/Ar dates of the Peninj sequence were obtained by Isaac and Curtis (1974), who privileged an interpretation of the Moinik Formation basalt at 1.35 My, the Sambu lavas at 3.5 ± 0.46 My, and the Wa-Mbugu basalt at 1.91 My. Manega (1993) dated by $^{40}Ar/^{39}Ar$ the bottom of the Humbu Formation (1.72 My), and the base (1.33 My) and the top (1.06 My) of the Moinik Formation. More recently, Deino et al. (2006b) used $^{40}Ar/^{39}Ar$ to place the Wa-Mbugu basalt at 1.19 ± 0.03 My, and the tuff at the top of the Moinik Formation at 1.01 ± 0.03 My. Given that the Moinik Formation was deposited before the Manjara–Natron Fault offset the deposits (Isaac, 1967), and that such episode of major faulting is dated at 1.2–1.15 My (Macintyre et al., 1974), an interpretation of the whole of the Humbu Formation as older than 1.33 My (Isaac and Curtis, 1974; Manega, 1993) is probably more consistent than placing the post Wa-Mbugu units at <1.19 My (Deino et al., 2006b).

Paleomagnetism (Thouveny and Taieb, 1986, 1987) has not settled radiometric discrepancies, especially concerning the Wa-Mbugu, whose correlation with the Olduvai positive event is unlikely (see below). Tephra correlations between Olduvai Gorge and Peninj are also uncertain, as basaltic tuffs from the Humbu Formation are not comparable with those from Olduvai, and the Moinik trachytic tephras could only be correlated with Olduvai Bed IV (McHenry et al., 2011).

Archeology

The archeological record of the Peninj Group was first reported by Isaac (1965, 1967), and has been the subject of a number of monographic volumes in recent years (de la Torre and Mora,

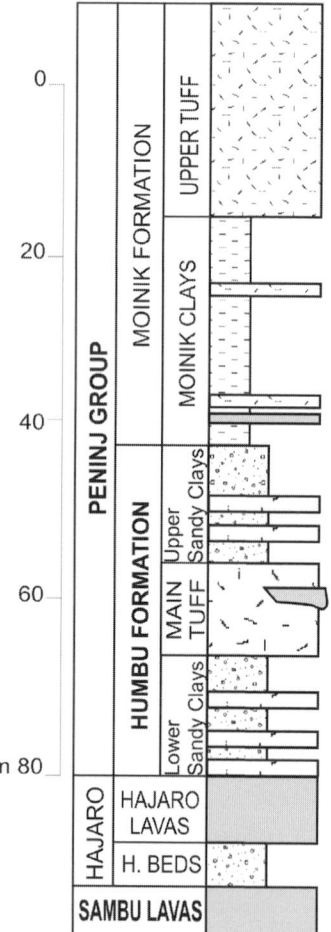

Figure 31.3 General stratigraphic column of the Peninj Group (adapted from Luque, in Mora et al., 2003).

2004; de la Torre, 2006; Dominguez-Rodrigo et al., 2009b, 2014b). Isaac (1965, 1967, 1981–1982) documented fossils and artifacts in three geographic areas across the Peninj river; in the northernmost outcrops (by the Sambu foothills), Isaac (1965, 1967) found the Acheulean site of MHS – later renamed as Mugulud (Isaac, 1981–1982) – which is stratigraphically located at the top of the Humbu Formation/bottom of the Moinik Formation (de la Torre, 2006; Dominguez-Rodrigo et al., 2009b). Further south, Isaac (1965, 1967) excavated another Acheulean site (MHS, later renamed as Bayasi), located in the USC Member of the Humbu Formation. Closer to the shoreline of Lake Natron and on the hanging wall of the Sambu Fault that offsets the Peninj Group, Isaac (1967) located the Type Section or Maritanane (Isaac, 1981–1982). Here, fossils are found in the BSC Member – e.g., the *Paranthropus boisei* mandible (Leakey and Leakey, 1964) – the Main Humbu Tuff and the USC Member of the Humbu Formation (Denys, 1987b; Geraads, 1987a; Dominguez-Rodrigo et al., 2009b). Stone tools are reported in the USC Member of the Humbu Formation and in the Moinik Formation (de la Torre and Mora, 2004; de la Torre, 2006; Dominguez-Rodrigo et al., 2009b).

In the Type Section/Maritanane, archeological occurrences are found throughout the whole of the USC Member of the Humbu Formation, albeit most is surface material (de la Torre, 2006, 2009). Fossils and artifacts are particularly clustered in the denominated ST Site Complex (Dominguez-Rodrigo et al., 2002, 2009b; Mora et al., 2003; de la Torre and Mora, 2004), where some mammal bones are cut-marked (Dominguez-Rodrigo et al., 2002, 2009b) and cores and flakes predominate (de la Torre and Mora, 2004). Although handaxes are yet to be found, hand axe flakes may exist in the ST Site Complex (de la Torre, 2006, 2009), and handaxes are found elsewhere in the Type Section. Therefore, despite the predominance of cores and flakes, it is plausible to attribute the whole of the archeological sequence of the USC Member to the Acheulean technology (de la Torre, 2009), rather than to the Oldowan (de la Torre et al., 2003).

While in the deltaic environments of the Type Section/Maritanane fossils are relatively abundant, bone preservation in the MHS and RHS areas is poorer. This contrasts with the lithic assemblages, which are much denser in the middle course of the Peninj River, and contain large concentrations of handaxes (Isaac, 1967; de la Torre, 2009). The MHS and RHS assemblages show attributes typical of the early Acheulean, i.e., the manufacture of handaxes that are often flaked unifacially and that show limited shaping and asymmetrical platforms (de la Torre et al., 2008). Albeit attributed to the same Acheulean techno-complex as the Type Section/Maritanane assemblages, the considerably higher density of artifacts and abundance of handaxes in the MHS and RHS areas when compared to the deltaic settings may be a reflection of distinct technological and subsistence activities by Lower Pleistocene humans across the varied landscapes of the Peninj river (de la Torre, 2009).

Fauna

Based on our own field notes, on bovid identifications by Gentry (in Isaac, 1967) and Gentry and Gentry (1978a, 1978b) of specimens that we have not seen, and on unpublished field notes by B. Hanson, we were able to combine a catalog of 380 identified large vertebrates, of which 353 are mammals, and within which 344 were identified by D.G. to family level or below. In addition, there are many fragments collected by bulk sampling procedures, but they have not been entered in the catalog. The micromammals were obtained after sieving the sediment with a 0.2-mm mesh in the field and in the laboratory, and sorted under the microscope. Rodents, primates, and lagomorphs were identified by C.D., while Soricomorpha and Chiroptera were identified by P.M. Butler. In total, 276 microvertebrate skeletal elements were found among which rodents and shrews predominate (NR = 255). A short account of the faunal taxonomic composition, updated from Denys (1987b) and Geraads (1987a), is given below.

Mammalia

Primates – Cercopithecidae: Cf. *Cercopithecoides kimeui*. Besides the well-known mandible of *Paranthropus boisei* (Leakey and Leakey 1964), there is no evidence of more than three primate species. An unidentified colobine, represented by a mandibular fragment with two teeth, is the same size as those present at Olduvai.

Theropithecus oswaldi. An unpublished skull, associated mandible and some limb bones, found by B. Hanson in 1982, as well as some isolated teeth, probably represent this species.

Galago sp. A single upper right canine was recovered by screening (Denys, 1987b) and may have affinities with *G. senegalensis*, also found at Olduvai Bed I and Omo Member G.

Carnivora – Viverridae: an unidentified viverrid milk tooth was identified by P.M. Butler (pers. comm.).

Hyaenidae: *Crocuta crocuta* cf. *ultra*. This is a close relative of the modern spotted hyena, relatively common in the African Plio-Pleistocene; a mandible is more primitive than the modern form in the presence of metaconid on the lower carnassial tooth.

Felidae: *Panthera pardus*. A leopard skull is one of the most valuable Peninj fossils, and probably the most complete *Panthera* specimen from the Plio-Pleistocene of East Africa.

Canidae: *Lupulella* cf. *adustus*. A single maxilla is more similar to this species than to *L. mesomelas* in its large M2, but species identification is tentative.

Rodentia – Muridae: This is by far the most abundant family. *Thallomys quadrilobatus* is the most abundant rodent. Besides isolated molars, a half anterior skull and a lower mandible show typical characters of this species found at Olduvai Bed I, Bed II, Omo F and G.

Arvicanthis primaevus is represented by isolated molars whose characters match those of specimens described from Olduvai Bed I, but differ from modern representatives.

Aethomys cf. *lavocati* is represented by a single juvenile molar very similar to the Olduvai Bed I specimens.

Mus sp. is smaller than *M. petteri* from Olduvai Bed I and Bed II and larger than the very small modern *M. minutoides*.

Nesomyidae: *Saccostomus* cf. *mearnsi* is represented by a single broken upper M1, which was further identified following taxonomic revision of the modern species as well as the Olduvai Bed I fossils (Denys, 1992).

Dendromus sp. is very small when compared to specimens of Olduvai Beds I, II and modern East African representatives. It could be very close to modern *D. mystacalis*, but the genus is in need of taxonomic revision.

Myoxidae: *Graphiurus* sp. is the oldest representative of the genus in East Africa, but based upon a single upper molar species identification remains tentative.

Soricomorpha – cf. *Suncus infinitesimus* were represented by 12 isolated teeth which agree closely in size with modern *S. infinitesimus* and with *S. leakeyi* from Olduvai. It differs from *S. leakeyi* in the absence of postentoconid ledge on lower m1–m2, but has a smaller lingual cingulum of M1. Another Soricomorph indet. was also found, but remains unidentifiable (P.M. Butler, pers. comm.).

Chiroptera – cf. Rhinolophidae: a single molar obtained from the BSC by screening may be attributed to this family of bats (P.M. Butler, pers. comm.).

Lagomorpha –*Lepus* sp. is represented by a broken lower mandible with p3–m1, an isolated M3, and upper molars obtained by screening of the sediment. They differ somewhat in size from modern *L. capensis* and Omo E, F, and G specimens attributed to this species.

Proboscidea – Elephantidae: *Elephas recki* cf. *recki*. Several more or less complete teeth are clearly identifiable as a much derived form of this common African species. They are definitely more hypsodont than those of *E. recki atavus* from Olduvai Bed I and lower Bed II, and even than those of *E. recki ileretensis* from upper Bed II (Beden, 1979).

Perissodactyla – Rhinocerotidae: *Ceratotherium simum*. A virtually complete skull, found in 1982, is more similar to the modern "white" rhino than to the East African Pliocene *C. mauritanicum* (Geraads, 1987a, 2005). There is no evidence of *Diceros*.

Equidae: "*Hipparion*" (s.l.) cf. *cornelianum*. Three-toed African equids are usually assigned to *Eurygnathohippus* (Bernor et al., 2010), but this is debatable (Eisenmann and Geraads, 2007).

Equus sp. Monodactyl equids are more common, but their remains are too fragmentary for species assignment.

Cetartiodactyla – Hippopotamidae: *Hippopotamus* cf. *gorgops*. This is the most common species in terms of number of specimens, and probably also in terms of biomass, but most fossils come from the archeological site of Kipalagu.

Suidae: *Kolpochoerus olduvaiensis*. An unpublished female complete skull is of a derived stage of this lineage (Harris and White, 1979), and a few other specimens are probably of the same species.

Metridiochoerus cf. *andrewsi*. Most suid remains probably belong to a species of *Metridiochoerus* that is intermediate in size between *M. andrewsi* and *M. compactus* (see, e.g., Cooke, 2007, figures 7–8), thus similar to *M. hopwoodi*. However, an M3 lacks the pillar isolation of this species, and precise identification must await study of the material.

Giraffidae: *Sivatherium maurusium*. A few remains, including a well-preserved snout and a horn piece, can be assigned to this large, buffalo-like giraffid.

Giraffa cf. *camelopardalis*. A few teeth and some limb-bones are of a large *Giraffa* that is more robust than the late Pliocene *G. jumae* (see Geraads et al., 2013a), and which could be an ancestor of the modern form.

Giraffidae indet. A single tarsal bone attests to the occurrence of another smaller giraffid.

Bovidae: *Tragelaphus strepsiceros grandis*. This is a large relative of the greater kudu, known from Middle Bed II to Bed IV at Olduvai.

Taurotragus sp. The eland is represented by a single molar.

Pelorovis sp. Fragmentary remains of a large buffalo cannot be identified to species.

Kobus cf. *kob*. A close relative of the common kob is present throughout the sequence.

Hippotragus gigas is represented by a single horn-core.

The alcelaphins are the most common and diverse bovids. In addition to many dental remains unidentifiable beyond tribe level, a number of more or less complete horn-cores and cranial remains can be assigned to four species: *Parmularius angusticornis*, *Megalotragus kattwinkeli*, *Connochaetes taurinus prognu*, and *Damaliscus niro*.

Aepyceros cf. *melampus*. Several impala horn-cores and dental remains cannot be separated from the living form.

Among the Antilopini, *Antidorcas* (the springbok), is the most common genus; it resembles the Olduvai form, but could be more derived toward the modern *A. marsupialis*, and can be identified as *A.* cf. *recki*.

A few *Gazella* horn-cores are similar to those of an unidentified Olduvai species.

Ndessokia (1987) also reported *Sylvicapra*, but none of the fossils that we have seen can be assigned to this genus.

Reptilia

Crocodylidae: *Crocodylus* cf. *anthropophagus*. It is likely that the two species tentatively distinguished by Geraads (1987a) are in fact one and the same. The most noticeable skull feature is the upturned postero-lateral squamosal angle, one of the characters defining *C. anthropophagus* from Olduvai (Brochu et al., 2010). Given the close chronological and geographic proximity of Olduvai and Peninj, this attribution is likely, but only a full study of the Peninj material could confirm it. The virtually parasagittal orientation of the lateral borders of the cranial table distinguishes it from *C. thorbjanarsoni* Brochu and Storrs, 2012 in the Turkana basin.

Chelonia indet. A number of tortoise shell fragments have been collected, especially from bulk sampling, but are yet to be identified; there is no evidence of a giant form.

Serpentes – Colubridae indet. Three different types were recorded (J.-C. Rage, pers. comm.), as well as other isolated vertebrae of Serpentes indet., all from the BSC sieved material.

Amphibia – Anura indet. were also represented by long bones (J.-C. Rage, pers. comm.) found in the screened material from BSC.

Pisces – Pisces indet.: a few small fish teeth were found in the BSC sieved material.

Biochronology

All of the Peninj large mammals (Table 31.1) are also present at Olduvai, and it is with this nearby site that comparisons should be made. Gentry and Gentry (1978a, 1978b) correlated the Middle Zone with Middle or Upper Bed II, and further research

Table 31.1 Distribution of the Peninj large mammals across the sequence.

	BSC	MZ	USC	Unknown
cf. *Cercopithecoides kimeui*				+
Theropithecus oswaldi		+		
Galago sp.	+			
Viverridae indet.	+			
Crocuta crocuta cf. *ultra*	+			
Panthera pardus	+			
Lupulella cf. *adustus*		+		
Elephas recki cf. *recki*	+	+	+	
Ceratotherium simum		+		
"*Hipparion*" (s.l.) cf. *cornelianum*			+	
Equus sp.	+	+	+	
Hippopotamus cf. *gorgops*	+	+	+	
Kolpochoerus olduvaiensis		+	+	
Metridiochoerus cf. *andrewsi*	+	+		
Sivatherium maurusium		+		
Giraffa cf. *camelopardalis*		+	+	
Giraffidae indet.		+		
Tragelaphus strepsiceros grandis	+	cf.	+	
Taurotragus sp.	+			
Pelorovis sp.		+	+	
Kobus cf. *kob*	+		+	
Hippotragus gigas				+
Parmularius angusticornis		+		
Megalotragus kattwinkeli		+	+	
Connochaetes taurinus prognu	+	+	cf.	
Damaliscus niro		+	+	
Aepyceros cf. *melampus*	+		+	
Antidorcas cf. *recki*	+	cf.	+	
Gazella sp.	+			

supports this proposal. The Peninj *Elephas* is decidedly more hypsodont than that of Olduvai Bed I and Lower Bed II, as the hypsodonty index of a molar fragment from the BSC reaches 202; even though the validity of the subspecies recognized by Beden (1979) is questionable (Ferretti et al., 2003a), there is no doubt that elephants point toward an age younger than Bed I. *Ceratotherium* is similar to *C. simum* and more derived than *C. mauritanicum*, which precedes *C. simum* in East Africa in its strongly oblique molar lophs (Geraads, 2005). The suids have not been studied, but if the *Metridiochoerus* is effectively intermediate between *M. andrewsi* and *M. compactus*, it could be positioned close to Olduvai Middle to Upper Bed II. Among the bovids, *Tragelaphus* is larger than that from Bed I, *Megalotragus kattwinkeli* is present in Bed II but is not known from Bed I, and the Peninj *Parmularius* is definitely *P. angusticornis*, rather than the Olduvai Bed I *P. altidens*. Thus, the conclusion that the Peninj large mammals biochronologically correlate with Middle or Upper bed II is supported. The only argument against this correlation would be the identification of *Theropithecus* as *T. oswaldi oswaldi* by Frost and Delson (2002); according to them, this subspecies, also present at Olduvai Beds I and Lower Bed II, is more primitive than *T. oswaldi leakeyi* from Upper Bed II; only a full study of this material could confirm this taxonomic assignment, which is debatable, given the very large size of the Peninj *Theropithecus* fossil.

Some rodent species like *T. quadrilobatus* and *A. primaevus* are found both in Peninj and Olduvai Bed I and Lower Bed II, as well as at Omo Shungura Mb F and G, while *A. lavocati* is also found at Olduvai Bed I; we can thus compare the evolutionary stages of these taxa. Figure 31.4 plots the M1 and m1 of various fossil and modern *Arvicanthis*; we observe that the Peninj lower m1s are among the smallest ones, close to modern *A. somalicus* and Olduvai Bed I and East Turkana *A. primaevus*. They differ from the *A. primaevus* from Lower Bed II that are larger and from modern and fossil *A. niloticus* from Upper Bed II. *A. primaevus* could represent the ancestral species leading to the divergence between *A. somalicus* and *A. niloticus*. Morphological characters indicate that the early modern *A. somalicus* appears at Olduvai Bed IV (ca. 0.8 Ma) and that *A. niloticus* appears at Olduvai Upper Bed II; this suggests that the cladogenesis dates at least to 1.4 Ma and that Peninj is older than this level but younger than Upper Bed I (1.79 Ma). In preserving ancestral *A. primaevus* characters, the Peninj molars suggest an age between Upper Bed I and lower Middle Bed II for the BSC (Denys, 1987b). The Peninj *Thallomys* and *Aethomys* also bear similar characters and the same size as the fossil *T. quadrilobatus* and *A. lavocati* recovered at Olduvai Bed I and Lower Bed II. The fact that the Peninj *Mus* sp. differs from *Mus petteri* present at the base of Bed II and the absence of some Muridae like *M. minor*, *Oenomys olduvaiensis*, and *Zelotomys leakeyi* at Peninj also suggests an intermediate age of BSC between the base and the top of Bed II sites (HWK and FCW localities; Table 31.2).

As a whole, and as was already apparent in earlier papers (Denys, 1987b; Geraads, 1987a), some discrepancies remain concerning the biostratigraphic ages provided by the Peninj large and small mammals. While large mammals suggest a correlation with Middle or Upper Bed II of Olduvai, small mammals may indicate an earlier age. Incomplete sampling and/or evolutionary stasis probably played a role; in any case, the Peninj mandible remains among the last known *Paranthropus*, although it is probably not younger than the Olduvai BK II fossils.

Table 31.2 Distribution of small mammals across the Peninj and Olduvai sequences (after Butler and Greenwood, 1976; Jaeger, 1976, 1979).

Species	BSC	Olduvai Upper Bed I	Olduvai Lower Bed II	Olduvai Upper Bed II
Thallomys quadrilobatus	+	+	+	
Arvicanthis primaevus	+	+	+	A. niloticus
Aethomys cf. lavocati	+	+	+	
Mus sp.	+	M. petteri	M. petteri	
Graphiurus sp.	+			
Dendromus sp.	+	+	+	
Saccostomus cf. mearnsi	+	+		
Cf. Rhinolophus sp.	+			
S. infinitesimus	+	S. leakeyi		

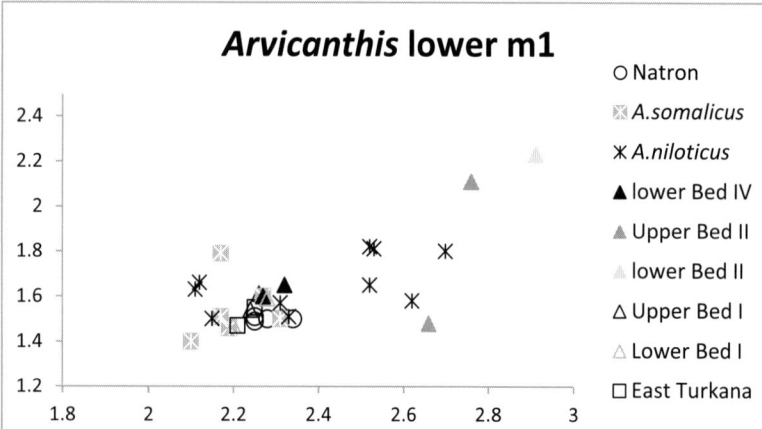

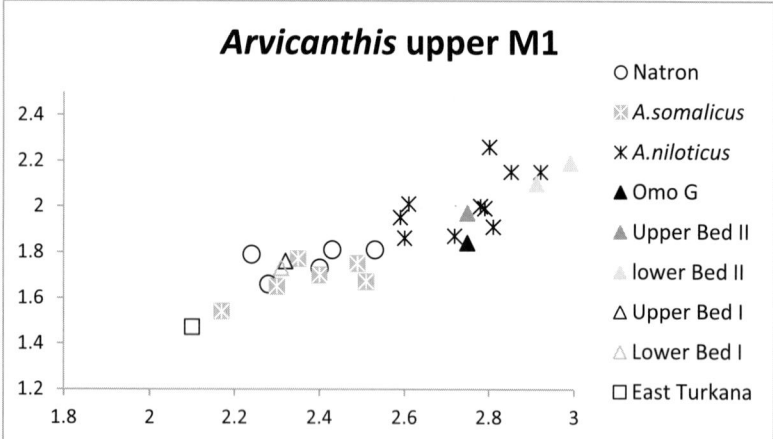

Figure 31.4 Scatterplots of the length × width proportions of fossil and modern *Arvicanthis* spp. (A) Lower m1; (B) upper M1. Measurements in mm.

Taphonomy

Systematic collecting at selected localities from various levels in 1982 recovered a total of 595 specimens. Table 31.3 provides percentages of the various anatomical elements per sample plot (numbered 82A through 82I). There are important differences in the proportions of elements, but there is no obvious trend through the sequence. The heavy fragmentation of most specimens is noticeable, in accordance with the deltaic conditions that prevailed during most of the time of deposition, implying significant water transport of most specimens. However, there is also evidence of deposition in lower-energy settings; for instance, the *Panthera* skull at the base of the BSC could not have been transported for a long distance, and the same is true of other relatively complete skulls, such as those

Table 31.3 Number of collected fossils and percentages of anatomical elements in the 1982 sample plots, arranged by stratigraphic order.

	Level	Sample total	Horn-cores	Dental elements	Vertebras	Epiphyses	Limb bone shaft fragments	All others (mostly bone fragments)
Sample plot 82B	USC	42	0	69	0	2	0	29
Sample plot 82C	USC	27	0	3	0	4	4	89
Sample plot 82D	USC	46	2	2	0	24	11	61
Sample plot 82E	MZ	75	0	11	1	5	12	71
Sample plot 82F	MZ	84	1	5	7	12	0	75
Sample plot 82A	MZ	78	13	1	4	5	13	64
Sample plot 82G	BSC	42	5	38	0	0	7	50
Sample plot 82H	BSC	24	0	8	0	0	0	92
Sample plot 82I	BSC	177	0	14	9	28	16	33
Total		595	2	15	4	14	9	56

Table 31.4 Taphonomic and paleoecological parameters of the BSC small mammals fauna in comparison with selected predation assemblages. Average PR is calculated from Dodson and Wexlar (1979) as the mean bone representation for all skeletal elements (original data on skeletal representation were taken from Denys, 1987b). The Gerbillinae/Murinae ratio is adapted from Fernandez-Jalvo et al. (1998). Data for *B. lacteus* and *B. africanus* are from Andrews (1990) and Denys (1997), those for *G. genetta* are from Denys et al. (1999 and unpublished).

	BSC	B. africanus	B. lacteus	G. genetta
% digested incisors	65.1	57	25	35
Average PR	23.4	28.8	58.6	40.7
Gerbillinae/Murinae ratio	0	0–0.4	1–3	0.5
N rodent species	7	4–9	1–4	5

of *Ceratotherium* and *Kolpochoerus*. Ndessokia (1987) also observed that few bones seem to have been transported over long distances. Significant parts of suid and hippo limbs were also recovered from Kipalagu.

Because all small vertebrates obtained by screening were recovered from a small surface (10 m²) of the BSC, we infer that they all were subjected to the same taphonomic history. Usually microvertebrate concentrations result from predation. Here, the potential prey species are small, from about 10 g (*Mus*, *Suncus*) to 2–3 kg (*Lepus*). We observe a wide spectrum of prey including snakes, shrews, amphibians, Lagomorpha, Rodentia, small primates; such a wide spectrum is generally observed for large birds of prey like *Bubo*, *Asio* spp., some eagles, as well as some mammalian Carnivora such as *Genetta* or medium-size Canidae (Andrews, 1990; Denys et al., 1996; Denys et al., 1999). Most of the prey are nocturnal or semidiurnal, which suggests a nocturnal predator. Denys (1987b) found a 23.4 percent average bone representation percentage (PR), which is lower than what is known for *Bubo lacteus* and *Genetta*, but is similar to *Bubo africanus* (Table 31.4). The fragmentation is very high, but may also been accentuated by the sieving process. However, there is a good representation of skull fragments, vertebrae, and phalanxes. There is a lack of some long bones (tibia, mandible) and very low proportions of femora, humeri, radii, ulnae, pelvis, and scapulae, which suggest slight hydrodynamic sorting (Denys, 1987b). New re-examination of the material shows clear evidence of the characteristic polishing and epiphyses alterations resulting from digestion (according to Andrews, 1990) both on long bones and teeth (Table 31.4). The percentage of digested elements was analyzed only upon incisors, and 65.1 percent showed evidence of digestion; digestion was light for 48.9 percent of them, against 24.4 percent for which it is moderate, 24.4 percent strong, and only a single incisor showing extreme digestion (2.4 per cent). All epiphyses also show evidence of light to moderate digestion. These values may correspond to accumulation by the spotted eagle owl (*Bubo africanus*) and are higher than for *Genetta*. Other taphonomic alterations include, e.g., low weathering and polishing, potential burning, and carbonate coating in some large bones.

Paleoenvironment

We have computed the proportions of the large mammals in the Humbu Formation, either considered as a whole (344 identified mammals, of which 109 have no precise stratigraphic provenance), or divided for convenience into a lower part (BSC + MHT + MZ), and an upper part with the USC only, with comparable numbers of identified specimens (respectively, 121 and 114). The main difference is that the upper part of the sequence contains more hippos, but they are mostly from Kipalagu, and their abundance might have a local significance only. By contrast, the scarcity of hippos in the lower part may be an artifact of field collection strategies, as often occurs in East Africa. We have not included them in the graph of Figure 31.5A.

As a whole, relative abundances of the diverse families do not differ from the usual ones in other late Pliocene or early Pleistocene East African sites. Bovids make up more than half of the total, with Suidae, Elephantidae, and Equidae also being common. Tooth preservation in this latter family is favored by their robustness, but their abundance is the first indication of an open landscape. The number of specimens in non-bovid families is low, and therefore inferences must be drawn with caution. We should note the absence of any brachyodont form apart from *Giraffa*, well-known to feed upon *Acacia* trees in open savannas.

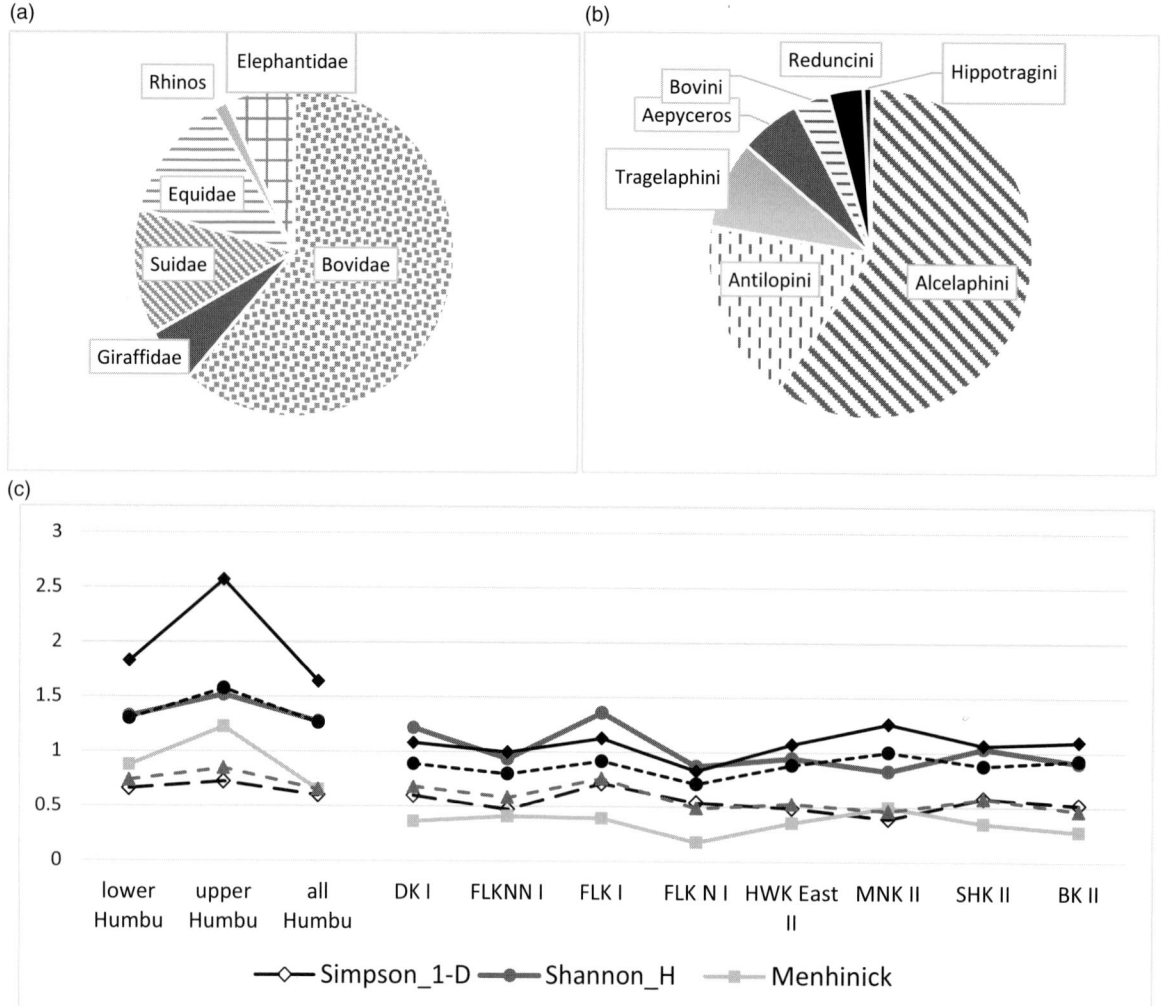

Figure 31.5 (A) Proportions of large mammals in the Humbu Formation. (B) Proportions of bovid tribes in the Humbu Formation. (C) Values of some bovid diversity indices at Peninj and in some Olduvai sites (Olduvai data from Gentry and Gentry, 1978a, 1978b).

This absence is not too significant, as in fact such brachyodont forms are virtually unknown in the East African Pleistocene, with the exception of the small Cercopithecidae. The latter are the best indicators of forest, and their virtual absence here attests to a minimal wood cover.

The proportions of bovid tribes (Figure 31.5B) support such inferences. As documented by Vrba (1980), Alcelaphini and Antilopini are indicators of open, dry environments. At Peninj, they amount to about 75 percent of the total number of bovids, so that the overall picture was certainly that of an open savanna. On the other hand, other bovids indicating somewhat distinct environments are not uncommon. Tragelaphini favor more closed settings, *Aepyceros* prefers the savanna/woodland ecotone, and the Reduncini suggest presence of wetlands; these bovids show that the landscape was probably not a uniform savanna. The overall similarity with Olduvai is obvious because of the taxonomic similarity and general dominance of the same two tribes; for instance, HWK II East (Lower and Middle Bed II), is very similar in terms of bovid proportions. However, proportions are far from uniform at Olduvai, with some sites, especially in Bed I, having many reduncins, or alternatively virtually yielding only alcelaphins and antilopins (Gentry and Gentry, 1978a, 1978b). On the whole, however, the dominance of alcelaphins and antilopins at Peninj is less sharp than at Olduvai. This is reflected in the Peninj diversity indices, several of which have higher values than in Olduvai (Figure 31.5C). Some assumptions should be made prior to interpreting these results. First, we must keep in mind that sample size is low, although the presence of several specimens of impala, an antelope virtually unknown at Olduvai, demonstrates a real difference. We also assume that the fossil abundances roughly reflect those of the biocenosis, i.e., that they are not biased by hominid selection and/or taphonomic processes. Absence of hominid selection (outside of archeological sites) is supported by the lack of systematic association between faunal remains and artifacts in the assemblages collected in the 1960s–1980s; taphonomic processes certainly altered the proportions (e.g., preserving preferentially alcelaphin teeth because of their robustness), but we may surmise that the same factors acted at Olduvai. Thus, even though conclusions remain tentative, and although the meaning of these diversity indices is far from fully understood, it is not unreasonable to assume that they reflect a more diverse

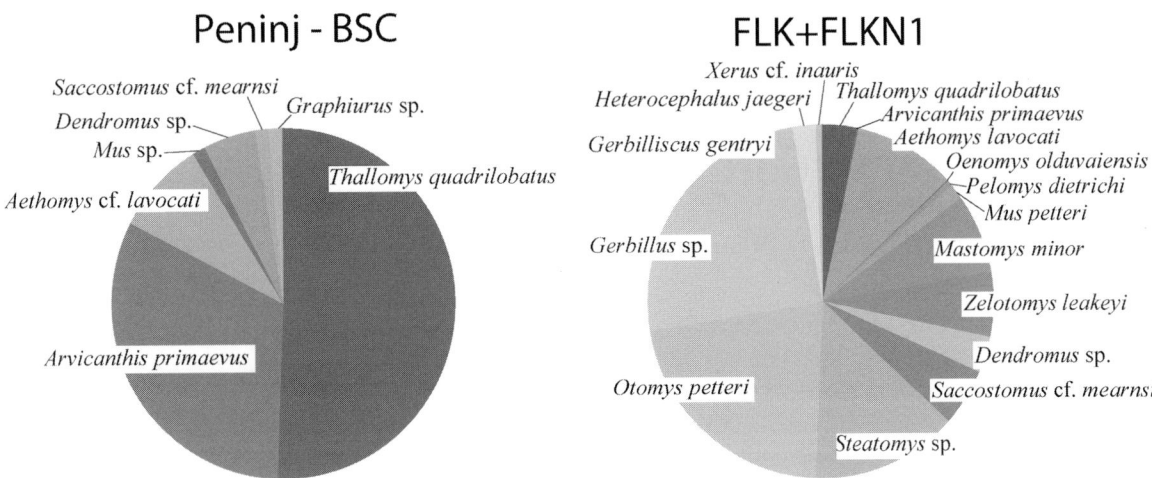

Figure 31.6 Proportions of BSC rodent species based upon the mandible and molar frequencies, compared to Olduvai Upper Bed I (FLK + FLKN sites, after Jaeger, 1976, 1979).

ecological setting than at Olduvai. The two sites are geographically quite close, but Olduvai is presently located at a significantly higher elevation (*ca.* 1500 m instead of *ca.* 700 m at Peninj).

Differences observed between the lower and upper parts of the Humbu Formation are few and of doubtful significance, given the low numbers of specimens. The upper part has fewer suids and more elephants and equids, but the proportions of the bovid tribes are similar.

On the whole, the faunal indications agree with those provided by the pollen and phytolith assemblages, which point to a savanna grassland with xeric grasses, where trees and shrubs of *Acacia*, *Commiphora*, and *Salvadora persica* were scarce, similar to the present-day vegetation (Barboni, 2014). Herbivores must have been dominated by C_4 eaters (including *Paranthropus* – van der Merwe, 2013), but these arboreal plants must have been able to also sustain giraffes, and probably tragelaphins at least.

Micromammal communities from the BSC have been compared with modern ones. Most of the rodents and shrews indicate the presence of savanna during the deposition of the Humbu Formation. Three taxa are arboreal or semi-arboreal (*Thallomys*, *Graphiurus*, *Galago*) and *Thallomys* is associated with *Acacia*. *Aethomys* is considered as a bush rodent. *Suncus*, amphibians, and *Dendromus* are indicators of water proximity. *Saccostomus* is found in woodland savanna and floodplains. *Arvicanthis* and *Lepus* are grazers, which indicates grassland areas and a relatively open savanna environment, in agreement with paleoecological inferences provided by Bovidae and other large mammals. The absence of Gerbillinae (*Gerbillus* and *Gerbilliscus*) and of some Murinae like *Mastomys* and *Otomys*, which are very abundant at Olduvai Bed I (Figure 31.6), may be explained either by differences in predators/prey specificity and/or by the altitude. A complete absence of Gerbillidae has been recorded only in lowland rainforest and montane forests of Africa (Denys, 1999), but it is not in agreement with the presence of numerous savanna species in Peninj. Due to the absence of true lowland forest Murinae species in BSC, the Gerbillinae/Murinae ratio is here probably biased by predators' dietary habits. It has been shown that *Bubo lacteus* favors Gerbillinae in its diet (Andrews, 1990; Denys, 1997) and was supposed to be one of the accumulators of Olduvai Bed I small mammals (Fernandez-Jalvo et al., 1998), whereas *B. africanus*, which we consider here as the most probable accumulator for BSC, avoids Gerbillinae in its diet. Both *Bubo* spp. predators catch fewer Murinae prey than *Tyto* spp. (barn owls; Denys, 1997). This may explain differences between the Olduvai Bed I and Peninj assemblages better than a difference in the type of vegetation. The absence of *Otomys* at Peninj compared to its abundance at Olduvai Bed I (Figure 31.6) may be explained by the altitudinal differences between the two sites. Today *Otomys* is a savanna genus and most of the recognized East African species live in highlands. Denys (1999) found that the Peninj rodent community has its highest affinities with modern Somali–Masai savanna (eight common genera) but also with Zambezian (seven), southwest arid (seven) and Highveld (six) savannas of South Africa. The same result was obtained for Olduvai Middle and Upper Bed I, and Lower and Upper Bed II, which confirms continuity through time of the savanna environment of Northern Tanzania.

Conclusion

While dating problems are still unsolved, the early Acheulean sequence and the main fossiliferous sequence in the Humbu Formation are most likely 1.3 million years or older. The vertebrate fauna from Peninj testifies to an environment similar to, but not identical with, those of Olduvai, and provide important insights into the dynamics of the paleoecology of the early Pleistocene in northern Tanzania. Despite the need for further paleoecological, archeological, and radiometric investigations, Peninj remains a key place for understanding the late survival and final demise of *Paranthropus*, and early *Homo* adaptations associated to the emergence of the Acheulean in East Africa.

Paleoecology and Vertebrate Taphonomy of DK Site (Bed I), Olduvai Gorge, Tanzania

Paul Farrugia and Jackson K. Njau

Introduction and Background

History of Research at Olduvai Gorge

Louis and Mary Leakey drew worldwide attention to Olduvai Gorge with their discoveries of the Olduvai Hominin (OH) 5 and OH 7 fossil remains. OH 5, a cranium representing the holotype of *Paranthropus boisei*, was found at the Frida Leakey Korongo (FLK) site in 1959 and assigned the genus name of *Zinjanthropus*, which is still used informally today (LS.B. Leakey, 1959). In 1960, OH 7, the holotype for *Homo habilis*, was found at the FLK North North (NN) site and consists of a mandible, two parietals and other cranial fragments, and hand bones (Leakey et al., 1964).

The Leakey's site-based excavations revolutionized the field of archeology as this method allowed exposures of penecontemporaneous paleo-land surfaces (up to 100 m²), and permitted detailed analysis of lithology and bone assemblages, some containing dense concentrations of stone artifacts, bone fragments of large mammals, and many early hominin fossils representing about five dozen hominin individuals (OH 2 to OH 60; e.g., L.S.B. Leakey, 1959, 1960; Leakey and Leakey, 1963; M.D. Leakey, 1971; Day, 1986; for complete database see https://olduvai-paleo.org/). Some of the fossil bones show both butchery marks and traces of animal ravaging. Where these butchered fossils occur in conjunction with stone tools, the sites were interpreted as "living sites" or "occupation floors" (L.S.B Leakey, 1959; M.D. Leakey, 1971), and later reclassified as "home bases" by Isaac (1971, 1978a).

Leakey's five decades of work at Olduvai (1931–1983) was followed by the Institute of Human Origins (IHO) team, led by Donald Johanson, Tim White, and Fidelis Masao, whose continued exploration at the site focused on the expansion of the hominin and vertebrate fossil record. IHO's most notable discovery was the OH 62 postcranial skeletal remains of *H. habilis* found near the FLK "*Zinjanthropus*" site (Johanson et al., 1987).

Since 1989, the Olduvai Landscape Paleoanthropology Project (OLAPP), co-led by Robert Blumenschine (Rutgers University, USA), Fidelis Masao (University of Dar Es Salaam, Tanzania), and Jackson Njau (Indiana University, USA), has been conducting fieldwork research at Olduvai (Blumenschine and Masao, 1991; Blumenschine et al., 2003, 2012a; Njau, 2006; Njau and Blumenschine, 2012). Expanding on Leakey's work, their goal is to understand the ecological basis for variation in the fossil record for hominin land-use behavior in Bed I and Lower Bed II at increasingly finer scales of temporal and spatial resolution using a landscape approach. One of the notable hominins recovered by OLAPP is OH 65, a complete maxilla with complete dentition of *H. habilis* (Blumenschine et al., 2003). This larger-brained early *Homo* is the first Pleistocene hominin recovered from the western side of the ancient lake margin, and its cranial size is considerably larger than the OH 24 skull that was found at the DK site (M.D. Leakey et al., 1971).

On the one hand, the sites were favorable locations on the landscape that hominins periodically exploited for food, water, and arboreal refuge, while traversing the paleo-lake basin, before returning to the safety of the volcanic highlands (Peters and Blumenschine, 1995; Blumenschine and Peters, 1998; Potts et al., 2004). On the other hand, the locations also presented high predation risks for our earliest, stone-tool using ancestors as evidenced by the abundance of tooth-marked bones indicating that these locations were also attractive to carnivores (M.D. Leakey, 1971; Binford, 1981, 1986; Bunn and Kroll, 1986, 1988; Blumenschine, 1987, 1995; Binford et al., 1988b; Oliver, 1994; Peters and Blumenschine, 1995; Blumenschine and Peters, 1998; Selvaggio, 1998; Capaldo, 1997; Njau, 2006; Njau and Blumenschine, 2006, 2012; Domínguez-Rodrigo et al., 2007; Blumenschine et al., 2012b; Pante et al., 2012, 2015). At the FLK "*Zinjanthropus*" and FLK NN sites, tooth-marked hominin bones suggest that hominins were killed or scavenged by crocodiles and large mammalian carnivores (e.g., M.D. Leakey, 1971; Davidson and Solomon, 1990; Njau and Blumenschine, 2006, 2012).

Since 2006, The Olduvai Paleoanthropology and Paleoecology Project (TOPPP), which is co-led by Manuel Domínguez-Rodrigo (Complutense University of Madrid, Spain) and Audax Mabulla (National Museum of Tanzania), has also been conducting research at Olduvai (Domínguez-Rodrigo et al., 2007, 2012), followed by the Olduvai Geochronology and Archaeology Project (OGAP) in 2007. This project, which is co-directed by Ignacio de la Torre (University College London, UK), Lindsay McHenry (University of Wisconsin-Milwaukee, USA), and Jackson Njau (Indiana University, USA), seeks to understand the timing and nature of the extinction of *H. habilis* along with its Oldowan industry, and the emergence of *H. erectus* along with its Acheulean industry in Middle Bed II (McHenry et al. 2016; de la Torre et al., 2018).

Geological Setting

Olduvai Gorge is located on the western flank of the East African Rift System (a great "seam" in the Earth's crust where eastern Africa is diverging from the African continent) in the eastern Serengeti Plains. It is split into the Main Gorge and Side Gorge and has been carved out over the past 200,000 years by streams originating from Lakes Masek and Ndutu, and from the slopes of the Lemagrut volcano (Figure 32.1). The gorge exposes Pleistocene beds that were deposited over the last 2.0 Ma in a broad, lake basin on the foothills of the western Ngorongoro Volcanic Highlands. The recent drilling project by the Olduvai Gorge Coring Project (OGCP), co-directed by Jackson Njau, Nicholas Toth and Kathy Schick (Indiana University and Stone Age Institute, USA), and Ian Stanistreet (University of Liverpool, UK), extends the sedimentary sequence considerably, indicating that the Olduvai record is much longer than previously recognized (Njau et al., 2015; Colcord et al., 2018).

Hay's (1976) seminal work at Olduvai established a stratigraphic framework, measured from the exposed outcrops across the gorge, laying the foundation for all further interpretations of biological, cultural, climatic, and paleoenvironmental change through time. Initially the stratigraphy was subdivided into five mappable horizontal beds known collectively as the "Beds" by the pioneering volcanologist, Hans Reck (1914), and were named from oldest (lowermost) to youngest (topmost) rock units (Beds I, II, III, IV, and V). Hay (1976) improved and refined the Olduvai sequence by reassigning Bed V into three distinct geological units, Masek, Ndutu, and Naisiusiu Beds (Figure 32.2).

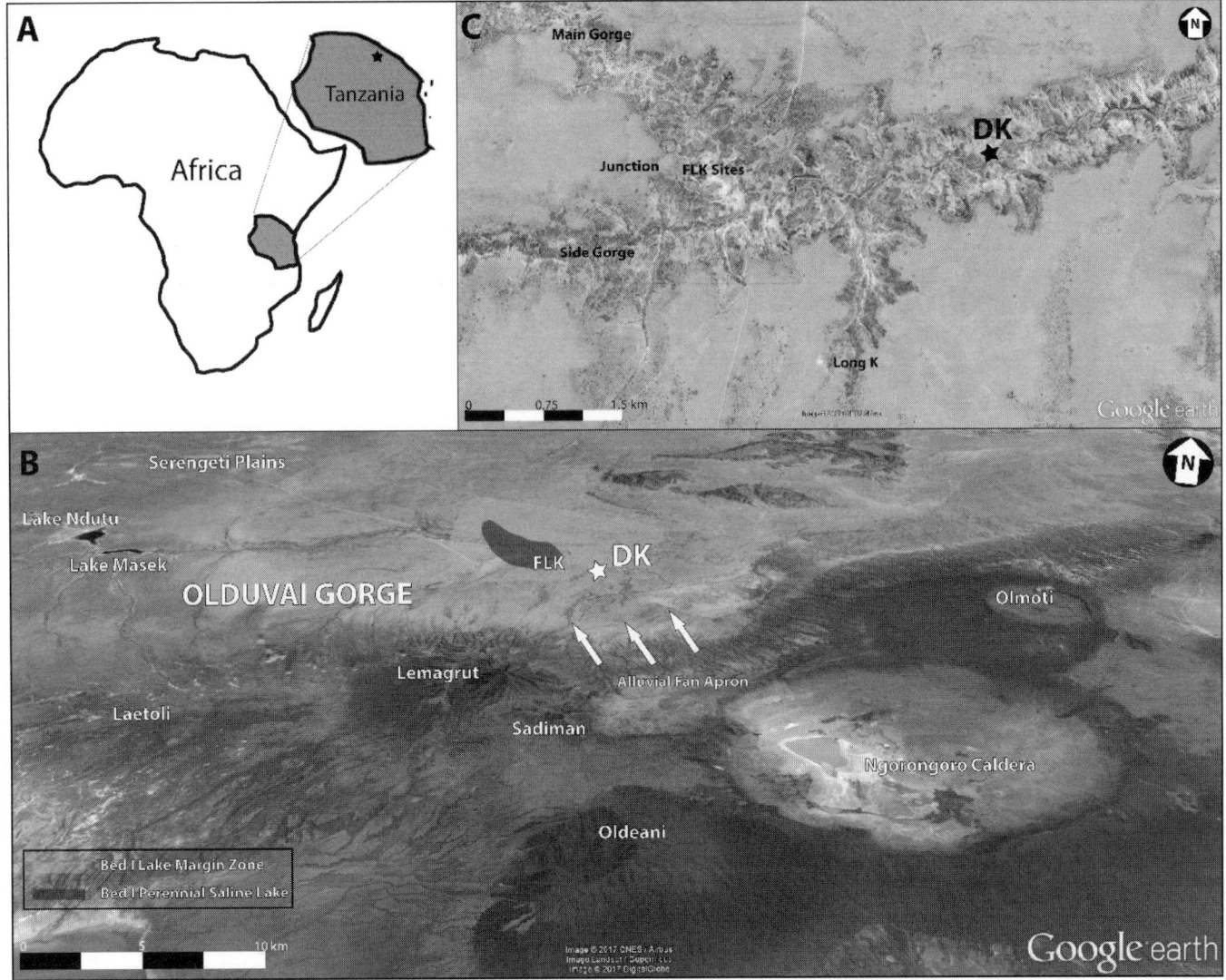

Figure 32.1 (A) Location of Olduvai Gorge in northern Tanzania. (B) Google Earth image of the Ngorongoro volcanic highlands showing Olduvai Gorge with the minimum and maximum levels of Paleolake Olduvai. Arrows indicate direction of mudflow influence from Ngorongoro. (C) Location of DK site relative to other Bed I sites. (A black and white version of this figure will appear in some formats. For the color version, please refer to the plate section.)

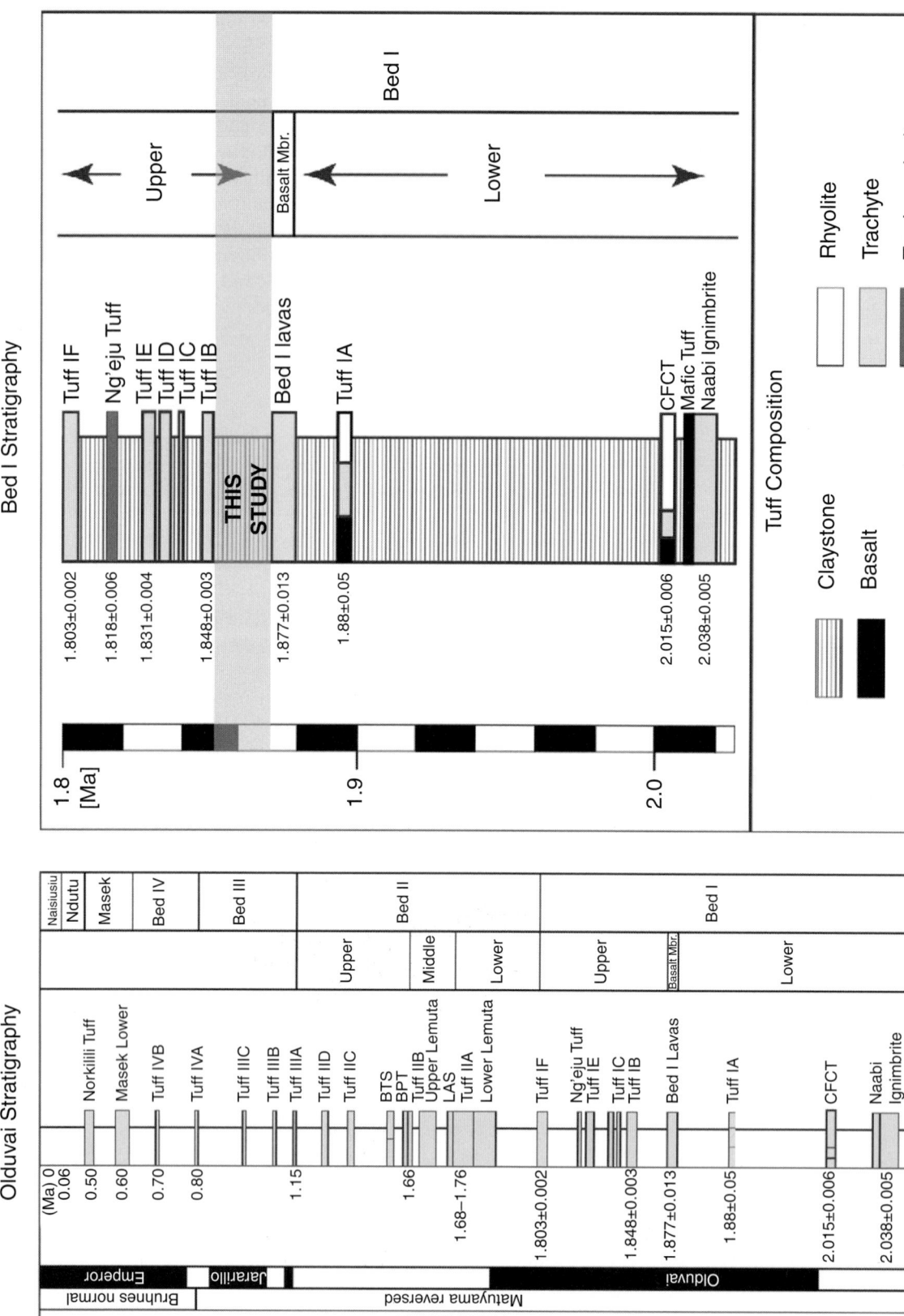

Figure 32.2 Olduvai stratigraphy showing (A) complete sequence after Hay (1976) and (B) detail of Bed I with new dates adopted from Stanistreet et al. (2018) after Hay (1976).

The base of Bed I dates to approximately 2.03 Ma, and comprises a series of lavas, originating from the Ngorongoro volcano (McHenry et al., 2008; McHenry, 2012; Mollel and Swisher, 2012), which is overlain by approximately 40–60 m of sedimentary and volcanic deposits. Tephostratigraphy (Hay, 1976; McHenry, 2012), magnetostratigraphy (Hay, 1976; Tamrat et al., 1995; Hay and Kyser, 2001), whole-rock and single-grain geochemistry (McHenry, 2005; McHenry et al., 2013), and $^{40}Ar/^{39}Ar$ dating (Walter et al., 1991; Deino, 2012) have been used to date the prominent marker tuffs within Bed I (e.g., ignimbrite, Tuff IA, Tuff IB, Tuff IC, Tuff ID, Tuff IE, Ng'eju Tuff, and Tuff IF). The ignimbrite (2.03 Ma) and Tuff IA (1.88 Ma), which are restricted to the western basin, are the lowermost and oldest units of the sequence. Tuff IF (~1.80 Ma), the most widespread tuff throughout the basin, marks the boundary between Bed I and Bed II.

Paleoenvironmental and paleogeographical reconstructions of the local environments developed by Hay (1976, 1990) showed that the center of the basin was occupied by a small, shallow, saline, and alkaline lake during Bed I times. The perennial portion of the lake measured approximately 10 km long and 5 km wide and intermittently flooded across the low terrain surrounding it in response to rainfall input and freshwater streams draining from the volcanic highlands. Due to the lack of drainage outlets, the lake underwent cycles of expansion and contractions (parasequences) between the Tuff IA and Tuff IF interval that flooded and exposed marginal areas (Hay, 1976). The episodic flooding caused interfingering of lake deposits with tuffs and the alluvial fan deposits that formed on the eastern margin of the basin, and with lavas from the eastern highland volcanoes (Figure 32.1). These cycles had a frequency of approximately 4000–5000 years (Stanistreet, 2012) and were affected by a combination of tectonism, orbital forcing, and climate change (Hay, 1976; Potts, 1988, 1998a, 1998b; Trauth et al., 2005, 2007). Each lake parasequence is associated with a phase of basin-wide erosion, which resulted in shifts in terrestrial habitats and generated undulating land surfaces upon which Leakey's "occupation floors" are deposited.

During times of high lake stands the lake was freshest, particularly on the eastern side and near the mouths of the streams that drained the eastern and southeastern volcanic highlands. This condition is supported by the presence of *Typha* (cattail) or reed marshes as evidenced by apparent root casts, *Typha* pollen, and fossil rhizomes of papyrus found in the sediments (M.D. Leakey, 1971; Hay, 1976, 1990; Bonnefille, 1984a; Masao et al., 2013; Albert et al., 2015; Peters et al., Chapter 33).

During the deposition of Bed I, the lake was at its maximum extent prior to the deposition of Tuff IB and at intermediate levels during the deposition of Tuff IB and Tuff ID. The presence of urocyclid slugs (Verdcourt, 1963; Hay, 1976) and closed-habitat rodents (Jaeger, 1976; Fernández-Jalvo et al., 1998) in the lowermost deposits of Upper Bed I indicate that densely vegetated and humid habitats were common (Kappelman, 1986). Bovid remains suggest that more closed and mixed habitats were common below Tuff ID (Gentry and Gentry, 1978a, 1978b; Kappelman, 1984; Potts, 1988; Shipman and Harris, 1988; Plummer and Bishop, 1994; Kappelman et al., 1997).

Between the deposition of Tuffs ID and IF, the climate became more arid, and pollen evidence indicates that annual rainfall dropped to about 350 mm (Bonnefille, 1984) causing lake levels to decrease. At this time open-habitat bovids and rodents became widespread (Plummer and Bishop, 1994; Fernández-Jalvo et al., 1998). Just prior to the deposition of Tuff IF, the lake expanded and contracted intermittently, and the eastern lake margin became flooded (Hay, 1976; Plummer and Bishop, 1994; Bamford et al., 2008). Hay and Kyser (2001) infer that between the deposition of Tuff IB and Tuff IF the eastern lake margin was probably flooded due to downward tilting. Evidence of this is provided by the high values of $\delta^{18}O$ isotope in the uppermost Bed I clays, which were caused by brine from the central basin flooding into the eastern lake margin (Hay and Kyser, 2001).

The DK Site

The site was discovered by Mary Leakey in the 1960s. It is located about 3 km east of the FLK "*Zinjanthropus*" site, at the edge of the paleo-lake margin and the alluvial fan, in the eastern part of the Olduvai Basin (Figure 32.1; M.D. Leakey, 1971; Hay, 1976). Stratigraphically, the site is constrained by Bed I lavas (1.877 ± 0.013) and Tuff IB (1.848 ± 0.003 Ma), making it the oldest paleontological and archeological site in the eastern basin. Bed I lavas form the base of the sedimentary rock sequence, observed from the outcrops in this eastern part of the basin.

M.D. Leakey (1971) divided the site into four distinct levels, DK 1–4, based on differences in the lithology, mainly color and texture, of the sediments (Figure 32.3). Fine grain sediments dominate the stratigraphy, although pebbles and gravel are interspersed throughout (M.D. Leakey, 1971; Hay, 1976), due to the actions of sheet-wash (Hay, 1976; Potts, 1988) and/or mudflows (Stanistreet et al., 2018). The "occupation floor" is situated at the base of Level 3, on top of "tuff" (Leakey's terminology). Recent higher-resolution studies of DK stratigraphy recognized that lake-parasequences created additional surfaces within Leakey's four levels and that the "tuff" is volcaniclastic sandstone that was deposited during a regression phase of the paleo-lake (Figure 32.3; Stanistreet et al., 2018).

Remains recovered from the site, previously, include not only hominin remains, faunal remains, Oldowan stone tools, and associated butchered bones, but also a circle of loosely piled stones at the base of Level 3 (Figure 32.4). This ring of stones was speculated to have been a supporting structure for tree branches or poles erected to serve as a windbreak or shelter. Later arguments propose that the circle could have been formed naturally by the radial distribution of tree roots that penetrated and broke up the underlying basalt (Potts, 1984; Stanistreet et al., 2018).

The stone tools found at DK were typical of the Oldowan Industry (M.D. Leakey, 1971). A total of 106 cores were recovered, of which 97 were produced on basalt and 8 on quartzite (M.D. Leakey, 1971). Quartzite cores were of better craftsmanship and showed more reduction than those produced on basalt (M.D. Leakey, 1971; Reti, 2016). Imported basalt manuports were difficult to distinguish from broken up lava, although some were identified (M.D. Leakey, 1971). Broken lava was common

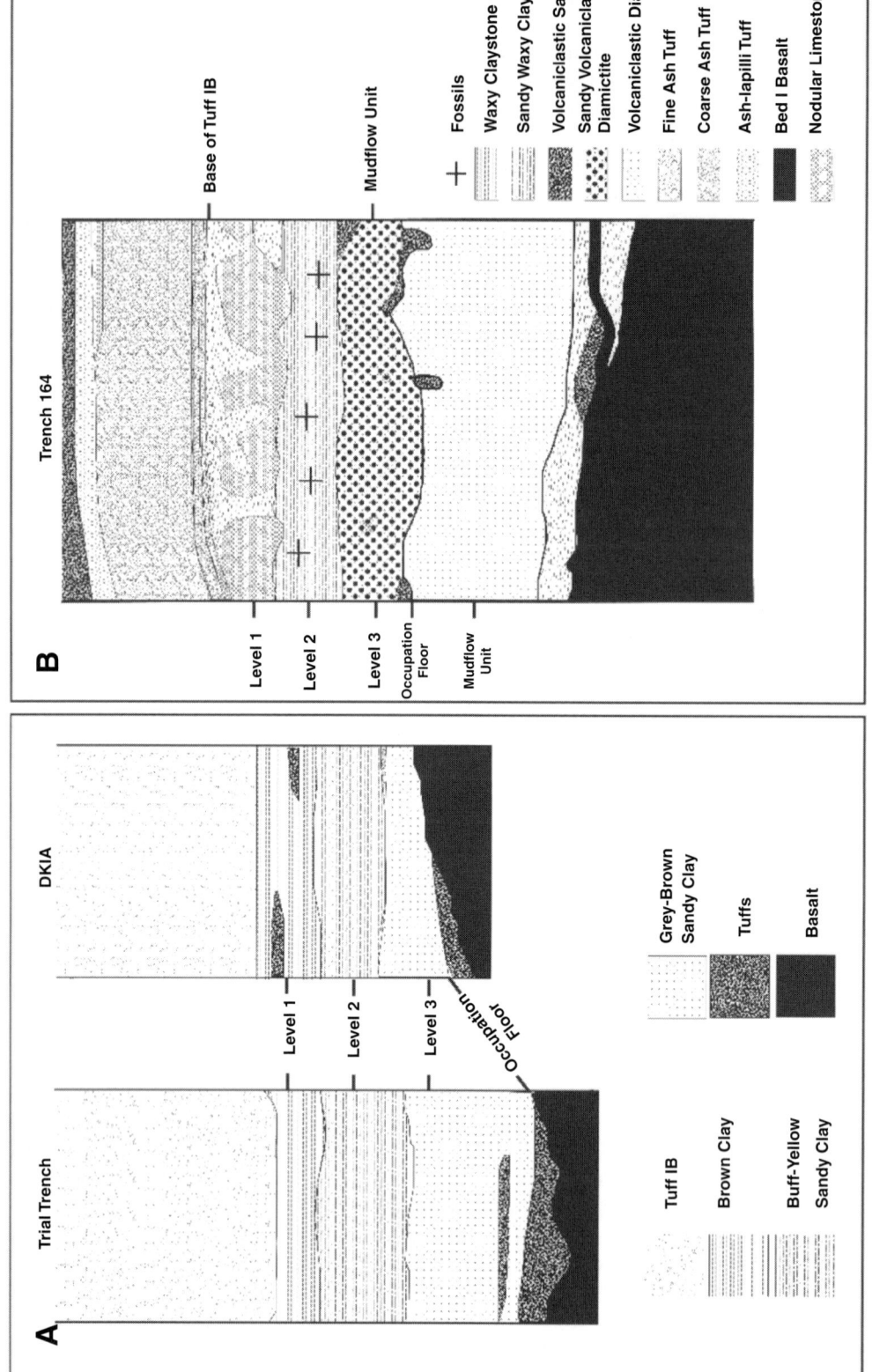

Figure 32.3 Correlation of the lithostratigraphy of DK Bed I interval site showing the location of archeological levels including the "occupation floor" sitting on an uneven surface of the basal Bed I lavas exposed on the eastern side. (A) M.D. Leakey (1971) sections and (B) archeological bearing levels exposed by OLAPP excavation showing additional surfaces created during lake parasequences. Leakey's "tuff" is volcaniclastic sandstone deposited during a lake regression. The correlated "occupation floor" sits on top of a previous mudflow. Modified after Stanistreet et al. (2018).

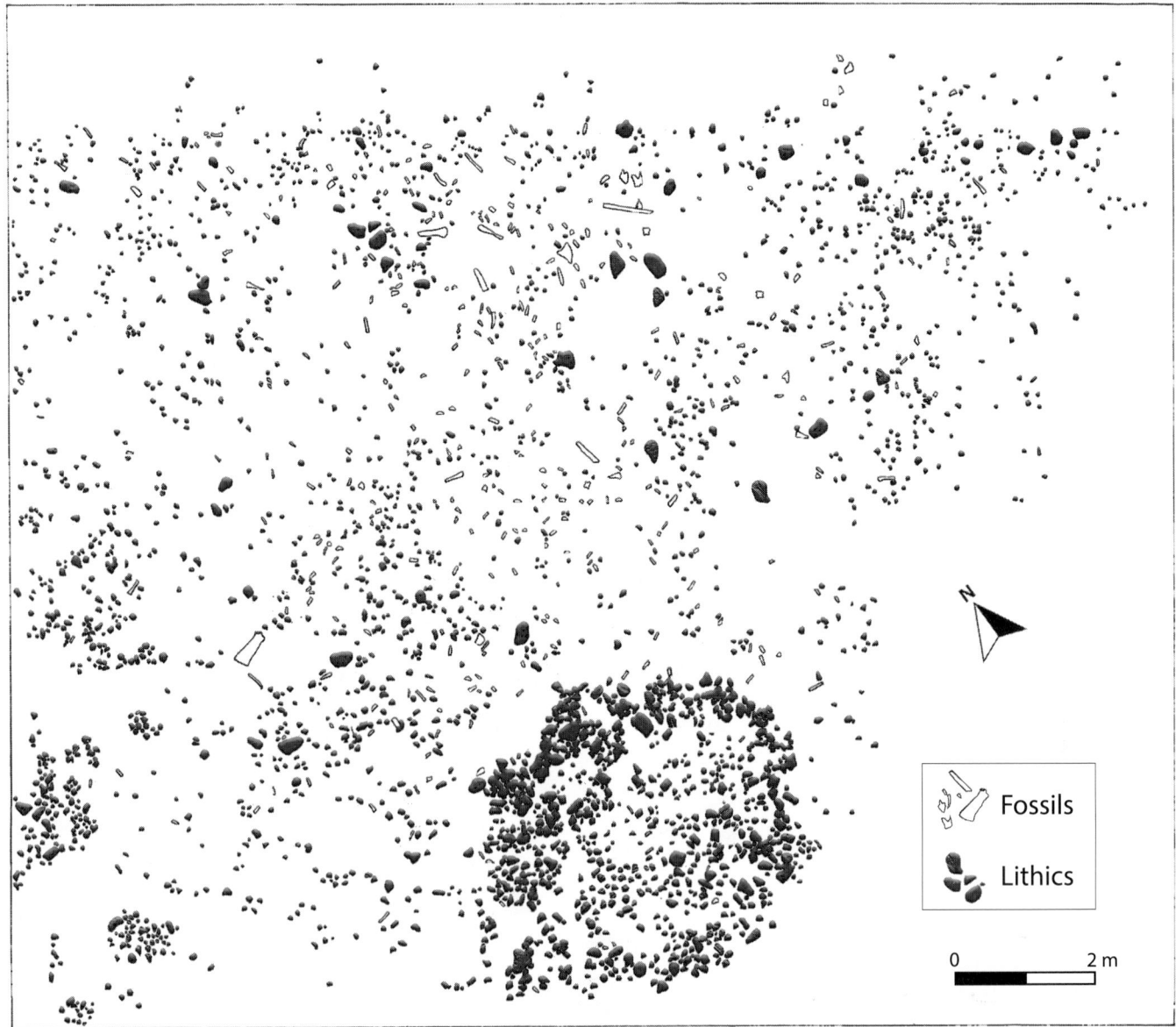

Figure 32.4 DK site plan showing stone tools, faunal remains, and stone circle from M.D. Leakey (1971; Figure 32.5A,B).

due to the stratigraphic position of the site on top of an uneven topographic surface of Bed I lavas.

Since Leakey's publication in 1971, competing theories as to how the site was formed have been proposed. For example: (1) Potts (1988) provided a holistic study of hominin behavior at Olduvai using a variety of methods including taphonomic analysis of Leakey's faunal and lithic material from DK and other Bed I sites. He concluded that DK was a location to which hominins were transporting carcasses to and that the Stone Circle was produced by the radial distribution of tree roots that broke up bedrock. He also suggested that water may have carried some artifacts into the site. (2) Njau's (2006, 2012a) taphonomic study concluded that the abundance of manuports could be due to hominins deploying them as probing stones or defense tools against crocodiles in wetland settings. (3) A zooarcheological study of Leakey's assemblage by Egeland (2007) suggested that the site was a palimpsest formed largely by the actions of large carnivores, mainly felids, with some minor input by hominins. (4) Masao et al. (2013) reported on the finds from excavations, including the discovery of remains from two hominins (OH 71 and OH 72). They concluded that DK was a location on the landscape that provided hominins with temporary refuge from predators and favorable resources, i.e., carcasses for scavenging, plant food, and fresh water. (5) GIS analysis of Leakey's (1971) site plan maps of DK and other Bed I sites (FLK North 1–6, FLK NN 3, and FLK "*Zinjanthropus*") by Benito-Calvo and de la Torre (2011) and de la Torre and Benito-Calvo (2013) showed that the DK assemblage showed preferential orientation either northeast–southwest or north–south, indicating that the site was disturbed, probably by sheet-wash and wave action, although a definitive process could not be ascertained (but see Stanistreet et al., 2018). (6) Using actualistic methods on the effects that moving water has on bone orientation, data from Egeland (2007) and M.D. Leakey's (1971) maps, Domínguez-Rodrigo et al. (2012, 2014a) determined that the DK assemblage was of an autochthonous origin. (7) Albert et al. (2015) reported on plant

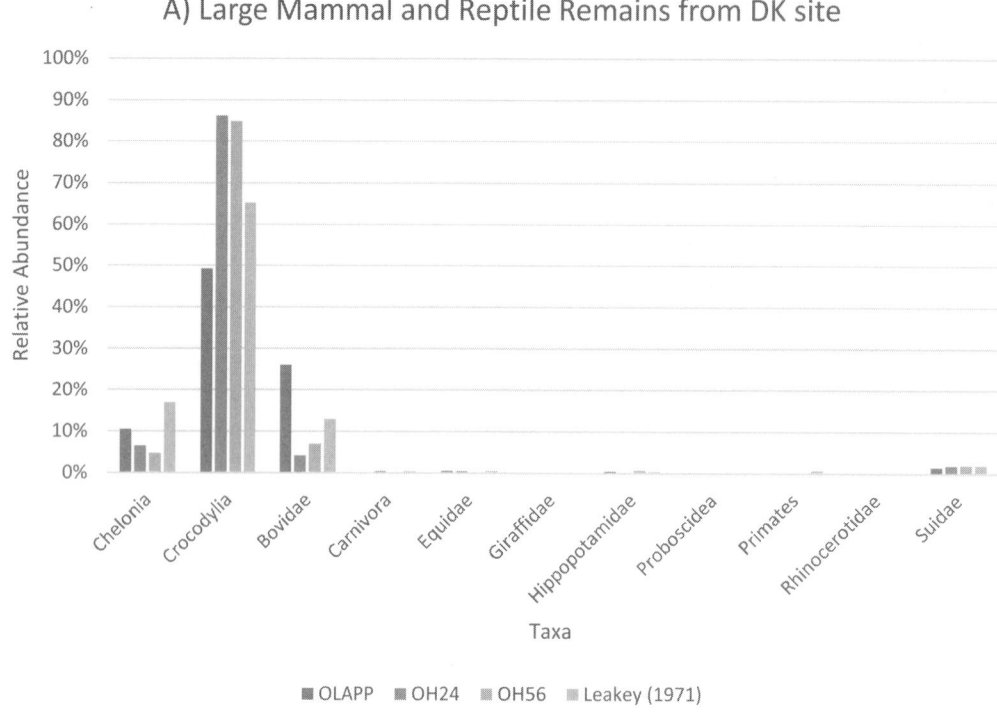
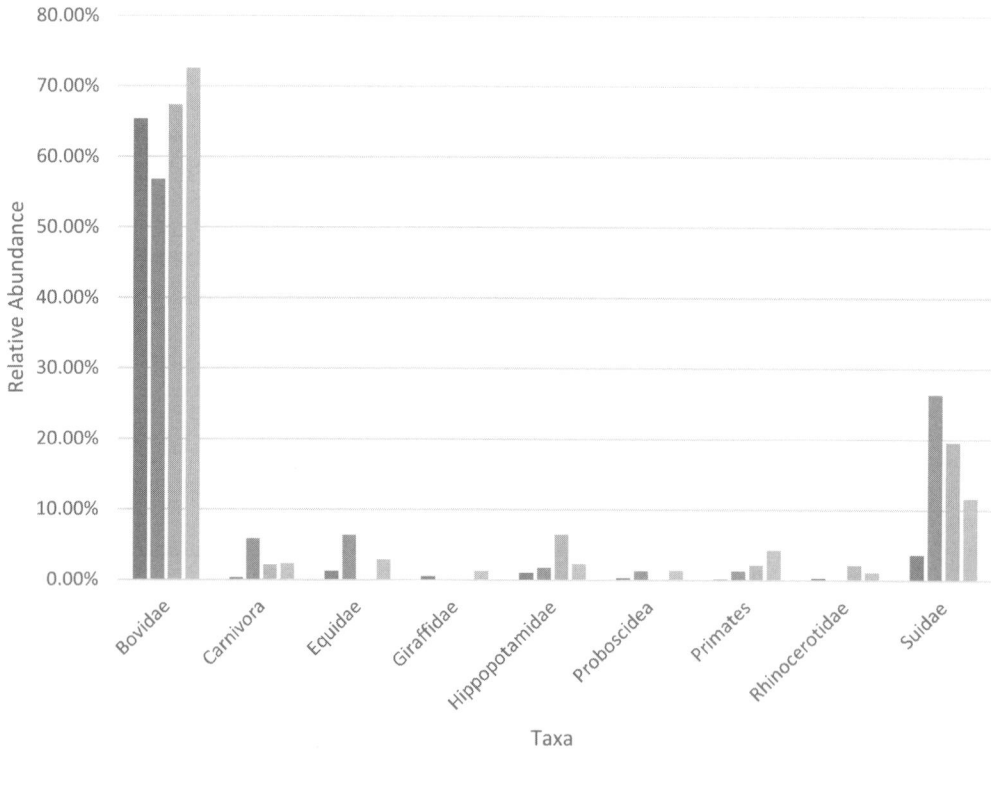

Figure 32.5 Frequencies of large vertebrate bones, teeth, scutes, and carapace fragments from DK site. (A) All large vertebrates. (B) Large mammals only. Analysis of the OLAPP, OH 24 and OH 56 assemblages include over 500, 2200, and 300 isolated crocodile teeth, respectively. M.D. Leakey's (1971) assemblage includes over 4500 crocodile teeth. (A black and white version of this figure will appear in some formats. For the color version, please refer to the plate section.)

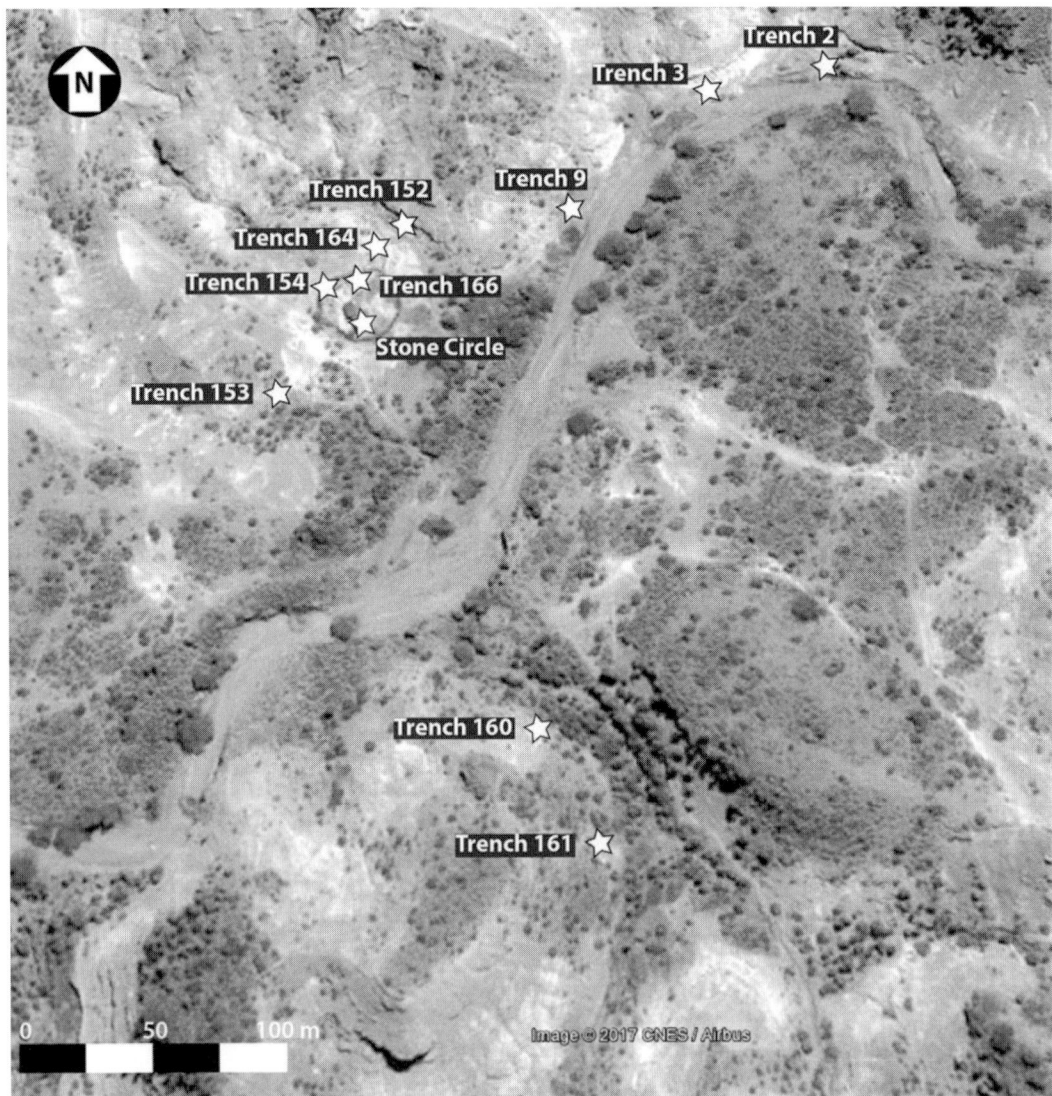

Figure 32.6 Location of the 10 trenches excavated by OLAPP. The Stone Circle is in the structure.

remains and the associated sediments to reconstruct the DK paleoenvironment, and in the process identified the presence of lush vegetation and a freshwater pool that would have drawn hominins and other animals to the site. (8) Ashley et al. (2016) interpreted the limestone bodies in the stratigraphy as spring seeps that provided hominins with a freshwater source during the dry season, although these limestones may have been deposited thousands of years after the "occupation floor" (Stanistreet et al.,2018). (9) Actualistic studies by Reti (2016) compared the stone tools recovered by Leakey to an experimental assemblage to show statistically that, based on the number and quality of flakes and cores, hominins were transporting both basalt and quartzite tools to the site. (10) Recent sequence stratigraphy combined with *in situ* archeological remains recovered from new excavations (Stanistreet et al., 2018) suggest that DK was a location to which hominins visited for safety while exploiting resources from a nearby freshwater pool. More importantly, during the eruptions of Ngorongoro the site was disturbed as smaller fragments were removed, objects were reoriented (e.g., Benito-Calvo and de la Torre, 2011), and buried by laharic mudflow (Stanistreet et al., 2018).

Fauna Composition

Fauna provided the basis for habitat reconstruction of Olduvai, e.g., savanna, forest, woodland, mosaic, etc. Evidence from small mammal remains indicates that the overall Bed I environment was more wooded with denser and wetter woodlands (Andrews, 1983). In Upper Bed I, rodent remains show that there is a shift from rich, closed woodland environments, in the middle of Upper Bed I, to more open seasonal woodlands and grasslands in the uppermost levels (Fernández-Jalvo et al., 1998). This environmental shift is also observed in larger mammals. Plummer and Bishop (1994) used antelope metapodial morphology to show that during the lower to middle of Upper Bed I times there was a higher proportion of intermediate and closed habitats in the lake margin, than had previously been proposed, with a shift to more open woodland and grasslands throughout top of Upper Bed I times.

Evidence of diverse faunal communities has been recovered throughout the gorge, documented (e.g., Reck, 1914; L.S.B. Leakey, 1951, 1959, 1960, 1961a, 1961b; M.D. Leakey, 1969; Leakey and Leakey, 1964; L.S.B. Leakey et al., 1973) and broadly summarized by L.S.B. Leakey (1965) and M.D. Leakey (1971). Subsequent analyses have provided revisions to the original taxonomic identifications, and the addition or deletion of species (e.g., Werdelin and Sanders, 2010 and references therein). Many different species of animals are represented, including bovids, which make up most mammals (Figure 32.5).

Material and Methods
Faunal Analysis
The large vertebrate faunal remains reported here were recovered from excavations of 10 trenches, in the DK locality (Figure 32.6), conducted by OLAPP under the direction of the one of the authors (J.N.) from 2010 to 2014 and from those published in M.D. Leakey (1971). Analysis of the OLAPP faunal material was conducted over three field seasons (2013–2016) at the Mary Leakey Camp, Olduvai Gorge Research Station. All specimens were cleaned with water, labeled, and bagged. Analysis was conducted with a 16× hand lens under a 75-watt light source. Measurements were taken with a Vernier caliper. Comparative material housed in the lab was used for taxonomic and skeletal part portion and identification. Taxonomic identifications were made to family level except for bovid teeth, which were identified to tribe. Taphonomic data recorded included condition of cortical surface and degree of weathering based on Behrensmeyer (1978b). Minimum number of elements (MNE) and minimum number of individuals (MNI) in the assemblage were calculated using animal body size (Bunn, 1982; Bunn and Kroll, 1986), skeletal element, skeletal portion, and body side (right or left).

Additionally, faunal remains from the OH 24 and OH 56 sites were found in medium-sized wooden boxes in the old Leakey Laboratory at Olduvai Gorge Research Station and were curated, inventoried, and studied by the authors (Farrugia and Njau, unpubl. data). This material is included in this analysis for taxonomic identification. The OH 24 skull was found about 300 m from the Stone Circle, at the DK East site in 1968, and briefly summarized in M.D. Leakey et al. (1971). The OH 56 fossils were found at the DK site in 1977 (Day, 1986). Small mammals and birds are present in the assemblages excavated by both Leakey and OLAPP; however, an analysis of the material has yet to be conducted.

Bovid Diversity
Bovid diversity was calculated using Simpson's Diversity Index (Simpson, 1949) and compared to other Bed I sites using data

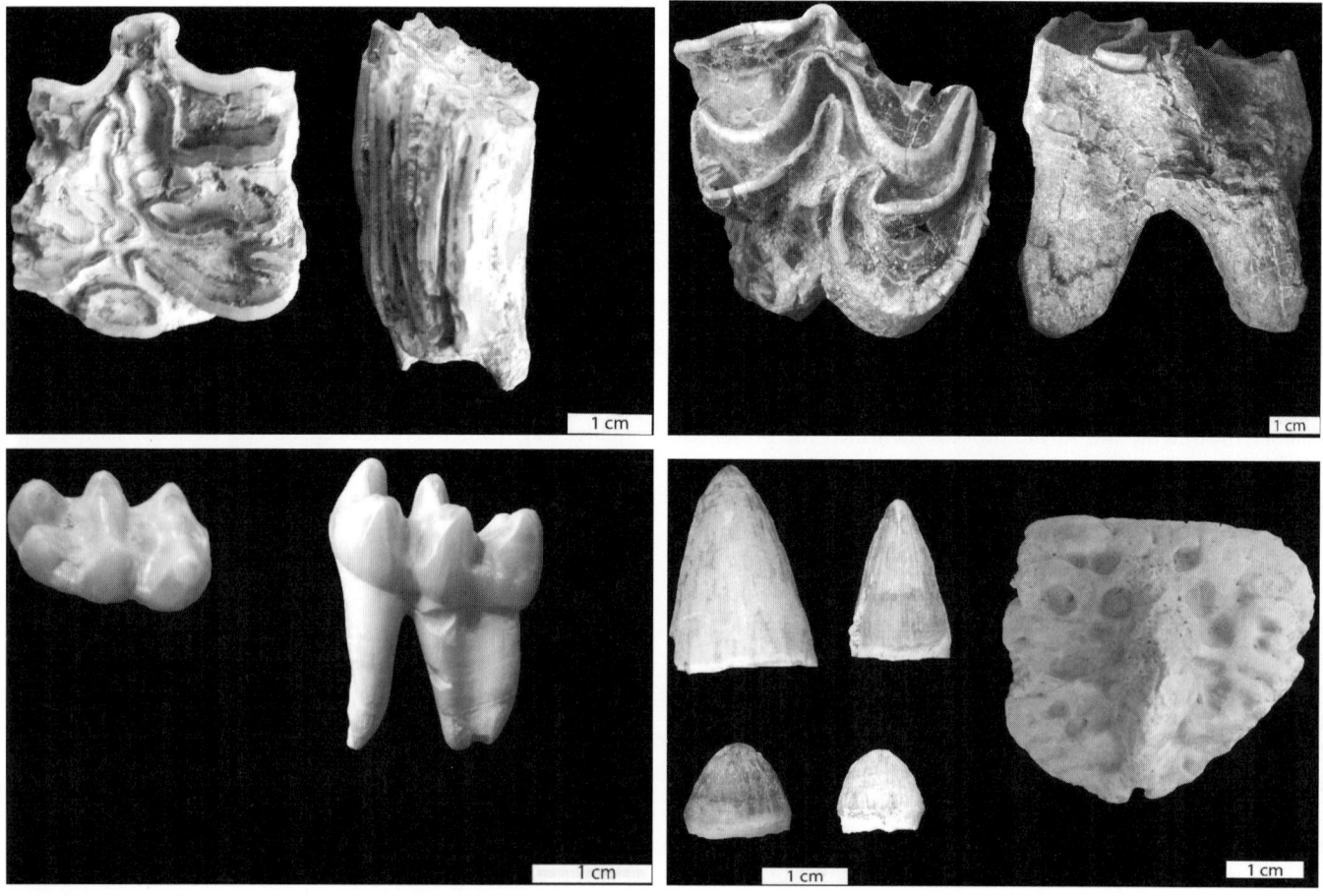

Figure 32.7 Examples of fossils from DK. (A) Partial *Eurygnathohippus cornelianus* s.s molar. (B) Partial right upper *Sivatherium* molar. (C) M_3 from *Theropithecus* cf. *oswaldi*. (D) Fossilized crocodile scute and teeth found in the OH 24 collection.

from: (1) FLK "*Zinjanthropus*" from Bunn (1982) and Bunn and Kroll (1986); (2) FLK N from Domínguez-Rodrigo et al. (2007) and Potts (1988); (3) FLK NN from Potts (1988) and Domínguez-Rodrigo et al. (2007); (4) Long K from Potts (1988).

Precipitation Estimates

Degree of hypsodonty in herbivorous species can be used to estimate annual precipitation values in living and fossil communities (Eronen et al., 2010a, 2010b). Using a non-linear regression of the relationship between tooth crown height and precipitation levels (Eronen et al., 2010a, 2010b), we estimated annual precipitation and precipitation of the wettest and driest quarters for Olduvai during the formation of the DK site. Herbivores were classified as having hypsodont (high-crowned), mesodont (medium-crowned), or brachydont (low-crowned) teeth based on assessments from the NOW Database (www.helsinki.fi/science/now/) and published literature. Elephants were excluded from the analysis as per Eronen et al. (2010a). The values of 3, 2, and 1 were assigned to each category, respectively (as described in Fortelius et al., 2002; Table 32.1). These categories are found to be conservative values as the ratio of the molar crown height of a hypsodont to that of a brachydont is generally greater than 3:1. A regression tree, created by Eronen et al. (2010b) by calculating the correlation between tooth crown height and precipitation, was used to predict precipitation values based on living and fossil communities. To utilize the regression tree, the number of species for a given site (in this case DK) was adjusted based on the species count in Eronen et al. (2010b; Table 32.2). The regression tree was calculated using a data set containing 584,341 species occurrences and 53,054 grid cells, yielding an average of 11.014 species per locality (Eronen et al., 2010a). The fossil data set includes 7594 species occurrences and 1266 localities, yielding an average of 5.998 species per locality (Eronen et al., 2010b). The correction factor, or ratio between extant and fossil species, was therefore 11.014/5.998, or 1.832.

The DK faunal list includes 21 herbivorous species. Because we are using only one locality, there is no average, so a new correction factor was calculated by combining DK data with the

Table 32.2 Adjusted number of species for the DK site.

Tooth height	No. species	Adjusted No. species	Percentage
Brachydont	7	12.82	0.33
Mesodont	1	1.83	0.04
Hypsodont	13	23.81	0.62

Table 32.1 DK herbivores and associated hypsodonty values (H-value). Elephants were excluded from the analysis following Eronen et al. (2010a).

Genus	Species	Subspecies	Crown height	H-value
Megalotragus	?*kattwinkeli*		Hypsodont	3
Parmularius	*altidens*		Hypsodont	3
Antidorcas	*recki*		Brachydont	1
Syncerus	sp.		Hypsodont	3
Hippotragus	*gigas*		Hypsodont	3
Kobus	*sigmoidalis*		Hypsodont	3
Redunca	*redunca*		Hypsodont	3
Tragelaphus	*strepsiceros*	*maryanus*	Brachydont	1
Giraffa	*stillei*		Brachydont	1
Sivatherium	*maurusium*		Brachydont	1
Hippopotamus	*gorgops*		Mesodont	2
Kolpochoerus	*heseloni*		Hypsodont	3
Metridiochoerus	*andrewsi*		Hypsodont	3
Metridiochoerus	*compactus*		Hypsodont	3
Metridiochoerus	*modestus*		Hypsodont	3
Equus	*oldowayensis*		Hypsodont	3
Eurygnathohippus	*cornelianus* s.s.		Hypsodont	3
Ceratotherium	*simum*		Hypsodont	3
Theropithecus	*oswaldi*		Brachydont	1
Gorgopithecus	*major*		Brachydont	1
Galago	sp.		Brachydont	1

fossil data from Eronen et al. (2010b), producing 7617 species occurrences from 1267 localities, with an average of 6.01 fossil species per locality. This gave a correction factor of 1.83 (11.014/6.01). The DK species counts per crown height were multiplied by the correction factor to calculate precipitation estimates based on the regression tree in Eronen et al. (2010a).

Results and Discussion

A total of 7202 bone fragments and teeth were recovered from all levels within the 10 OLAPP trenches, of which approximately 19 percent were identifiable. Crocodile fossils dominate the assemblage (49 percent of the identified material). Tortoise shell fragments are also found in large quantities (Figure 32.5). Teeth make up about 58 percent of the identified specimens (Table 32.3). The assemblage is taxonomically diverse. Bovids make up about 65 percent of the mammals followed by suids, then equids and hippopotamuses (Table 32.4). All six bovids tribes are represented, with alcelaphines and antilopines being the most common. Bones are highly fragmented, represented primarily by long-bone fragments (Table 32.5). All six animal size groups are represented with elephants only by a few tooth fragments. Size 2 animals are the most common, followed by size 3 and size 1.

The revised list consists of 34 species from DK including one hominin species. Each taxon that has been identified, either through our analysis or previously published reports, will be described briefly below.

Bovidae

Within the bovids, six tribes were identified: Tragelaphini, Bovini, Reduncini, Hippotragini, Alcelaphini, and Antilopini.

Tragelaphini: *Tragelaphus strepsiceros maryanus* was a large local variant of the extant greater kudu.

Bovini: Remains of *Syncerus* were recovered at DK and possibly belong to *S. acoelotus*, although the fossils are too fragmentary to assign to a definite species. This extinct bovid was an ancestor to the modern African buffalo (Gentry and Gentry, 1978a, 1978b).

Reduncini: *Kobus* is the most common reduncine found at DK. *Kobus sigmoidalis* is the ancestor of the extant waterbuck, *K. ellipsiprymnus*, and the central African lechwe, *K. leche* (Gentry and Gentry, 1978a, 1978b). In addition, a lower right molar that is similar to the living Bohor reedbuck, *Redunca redunca*, was recovered and assigned to *Redunca* sp. (Gentry and Gentry, 1978a, 1978b).

Hippotragini: *Hippotragus gigas* was a large relative of the modern hippotragines. It is the only species found at Olduvai but is relatively uncommon in Beds I–III when compared to other bovid tribes (Gentry and Gentry, 1978a, 1978b).

Alcelaphini: *Parmularius altidens* was the most common alcelaphine at Olduvai. *Parmularius* may have derived from the same ancestry as *Damaliscus* and *Alcelaphus* but had more specialized features. The holotype skull is about the same size as the modern blesbok, *D. dorcas*, and the body size of the modern hartebeest, *A. buselaphus* (Gentry and Gentry, 1978a, 1978b).

Megalotragus ?*kattwinkeli* was one of two species of extinct giant alcelaphines (the second being *M. priscus* of South Africa).

Several unidentifiable remains were assigned to Alcelaphini sp.

Antilopini: *Antidorcas recki* was the most common antilopine in Bed I. *A. recki* was smaller than the modern South African springbok, *A. marsupialis* (Gentry and Gentry, 1978a, 1978b). Several indeterminate remains were assigned to Antilopini sp.

Hippopotamidae

Hippopotamus gorgops remains are found in all levels at DK. This extinct hippo was larger than the modern African hippo, *H. amphibius*, and had more elevated orbits and higher-crowned molars (Coryndon, 1970; Harris, 1991b; Weston and Boisserie, 2010).

Suidae

Suids are the second most abundant mammal family found at the site. Originally, five separate species of suid were identified in DK material (M.D. Leakey, 1971) including: *Potamochoerus*

Table 32.3 Taxonomic composition based on teeth count only (NISP).

Family	NISP
Bovidae	178
Carnivora	2
Cercopithecidae	4
Crocodylidae	573
Elephantidae	2
Equidae	5
Giraffidae	2
Hippopotamidae	5
Rhinocerotidae	2
Suidae	17
Total	790

Table 32.4 Minimum number of individuals (MNI) based on bones and teeth.

Family	Tribe	MNI
Bovidae	Alcelaphini	7
	Antilopini	8
	Bovini	1
	Hippotragini	1
	Reduncini	3
	Tragelaphini	2
Carnivora		2
Cercopithecidae		1
Elephantidae		2
Equidae		4
Giraffidae		2
Hippopotamidae		4
Rhinocerotidae		2
Suidae		6
Total		45

Table 32.5 Skeletal part profiles for the OLAPP DK sample. Body size groups follow Bunn (1982).

	Size 1		Size 2		Size 3		Size 4		Size 5		Size 6		Total	
	MNE	NISP	MNE	NISP	MNE	NISP	MNE	NISP	MNE	NISP	MNE	NISP	MNE	NISP
Cranial fragment	0	0	1	0	1	0	0	0	0	0	0	0	2	0
Frontal	0	0	0	0	0	0	0	0	0	0	0	0	0	0
Horn-core	0	0	1	1	1	1	0	0	0	0	0	0	2	2
Hyoid	0	0	0	0	0	0	0	0	0	0	0	0	0	0
Maxilla	0	0	0	0	1	1	0	0	0	0	0	0	1	0
Mandible	0	0	2	2	1	1	0	0	0	0	0	0	3	3
Nasal	0	0	0	0	0	0	0	0	0	0	0	0	0	0
Occipital	0	0	0	0	0	0	0	0	0	0	0	0	0	0
Premaxilla	0	0	0	0	0	0	0	0	0	0	0	0	0	0
Sphenoid	0	0	0	0	1	1	0	0	0	0	0	0	1	0
Temporal	0	0	0	0	0	0	0	0	0	0	0	0	0	0
Zygomatic	0	0	0	0	0	0	0	0	0	0	0	0	0	0
Cranial total	0	0	4	3	5	4	0	0	0	0	0	0	9	5
Atlas	0	0	0	0	0	0	0	0	0	0	0	0	0	0
Axis	0	0	0	0	0	0	0	0	0	0	0	0	0	0
Caudal vertebra	0	0	0	0	0	0	0	0	0	0	0	0	0	0
Cervical vertebra	0	0	2	2	0	0	0	0	0	0	0	0	2	2
Clavicle	0	0	0	0	0	0	0	0	0	0	0	0	0	0
Lumbar vertebra	0	0	1	1	0	0	0	0	0	0	0	0	1	1
Rib	0	0	10	8	30	12	0	0	0	0	0	0	40	20
Rib 1	0	0	0	0	0	0	0	0	0	0	0	0	0	0
Sacrum	0	0	0	0	0	0	0	0	0	0	0	0	0	0
Sternum	0	0	0	0	0	0	0	0	0	0	0	0	0	0
Thoracic vertebra	0	0	0	0	0	0	0	0	0	0	0	0	0	0
Vertebra fragment	0	0	0	0	2	0	0	0	0	0	0	0	2	0
Axial total	0	0	13	11	32	12	0	0	0	0	0	0	45	23
Femur	0	0	2	2	0	0	0	0	0	0	0	0	2	2
Fibula	0	0	1	1	0	0	0	0	0	0	0	0	1	1
Humerus	2	2	6	5	4	3	1	1	0	0	0	0	13	11
Long-bone fragment	19	19	101		23		2		0		0		145	
Metacarpal	0	0	2	2	0	0	0	0	0	0	0	0	2	2

Element												
Metapodial	1		9	1	0	0	0	0	0	0		
Metatarsal	1	1	3	2	0	0	0	0	0	0	11	3
Radius	3	1	5	4	0	0	0	0	0	0	4	5
Tibia	0	0	9	6	2	0	0	0	0	0	8	8
Ulna	1	1	3	3	0	0	0	0	0	0	4	4
Appendicular total	27	5	141	25	30	5	3	1	0	0	201	36
Astragalus	1	1	1	1	0	0	0	0	0	0	2	2
Calcaneus	0	0	1	1	1	0	0	0	0	0	2	2
Carpal or tarsal	0	1	1	0	0	0	0	0	0	0	2	
Cuneiform	0	0	0	0	0	0	0	0	0	0	0	0
External cuneiform	0	0	0	0	0	0	0	0	0	0	0	0
Fibula	0	0	1	1	0	0	0	0	0	0	1	1
External–lateral cuneiform	0	0	0	0	0	0	0	0	0	0	0	0
Lunate	0	0	0	0	0	0	0	0	0	0	0	0
Magnum	0	0	0	0	0	0	0	0	0	0	0	0
Navicular-cuboid	0	0	0	0	0	0	0	0	0	0	0	0
Patella	0	0	0	0	0	0	0	0	0	0	0	0
Phalange proximal	0	0	1	0	0	0	0	0	0	0	1	1
Phalange intermediate	0	0	1	1	0	0	0	0	0	0	1	1
Phalange distal	2	2	0	0	1	0	0	0	0	0	3	3
Phalange fragment	0	0	1	0	1	0	0	0	0	0	2	
Pisiform	0	0	0	0	0	0	0	0	0	0	0	0
Sesamoid	0	0	0	0	0	0	0	0	0	0	0	0
Scaphoid	0	0	0	0	0	0	0	0	0	0	0	0
Trapezoid	0	0	0	0	0	0	0	0	0	0	0	0
Unciform	0	0	0	0	0	1	0	0	0	0	1	1
Compact total	3	3	7	5	4	2	0	1	1	0	15	11
Innominate	0	0	2	1	1	0	0	0	0	0	3	0
Scapula	0	0	2	1	1	0	0	0	0	0	3	3
Pelvis/scapula total	0	0	4	3	2	0	0	0	0	0	6	5
Total identified	30	8	169	47	73	25	3	1	1	0	276	80
Indeterminate mammal fragments											53	
Grand total	30	8	169	47	73	25	3	1	1	0	329	80

intermedius, *Promesochoerus mukiri*, *Ectopotamochoerus dubius*, *Pronotochoerus* cf. *jacksoni*, and *Notochoerus* sp. However, subsequent analyses have reduced the number to four. Harris and White (1979) re-examined the material and reclassified three of the species, *Pot. intermedius*, *Pr. mukiri*, and *E. dubius* to *Mesochoerus limnetes*, which is now known as *Kolpochoerus heseloni* (Cooke, 1997; Bishop, 2010). *Pronotochoerus* cf. *jacksoni* was reassigned to *Metridiochoerus andrewsi*, and *Notochoerus* sp. to *Metridiochoerus modestus* (Harris and White, 1979). A third molar of a fourth species, *Metridiochoerus compactus*, was also identified (Bishop, 2010).

Equidae

Many equid limb bones and tooth fragments were recovered. *Equus oldowayensis* was the most common equid species in Tanzania during the Lower Pleistocene (Hooijer and Churcher, 1985). Most are assigned to *E.* c.f. *oldowayensis*. A fragmentary upper molar of a "hipparion" was recovered from the OH 24 level at DK East (Figure 32.8) and probably belongs to *Eurygnathohippus cornelianus* s.s., as this was the most common species of hipparion during Bed I times (Armour-Chelu et al., 2006).

Giraffidae

Two species of giraffe were identified in the DK deposits.

Giraffa stillei: Originally identified as *Okapi* sp. by M.D. Leakey (1971) and later reclassified as *G. stillei* by Harris (1976a).

Sivatherium cf. *maurusium*: Remains of this large giraffid were originally assigned to *Libytherium olduvaiensis*. A partial upper right molar was recovered by OLAPP in recent excavations (Figure 32.8). This robust giraffid was probably the largest ruminant mammal during this time period (see Basu et al., 2016).

Giraffa sp.: Remains from an indeterminate giraffe species were found by M.D. Leakey (1971) and a molar fragment was recovered in recent excavations.

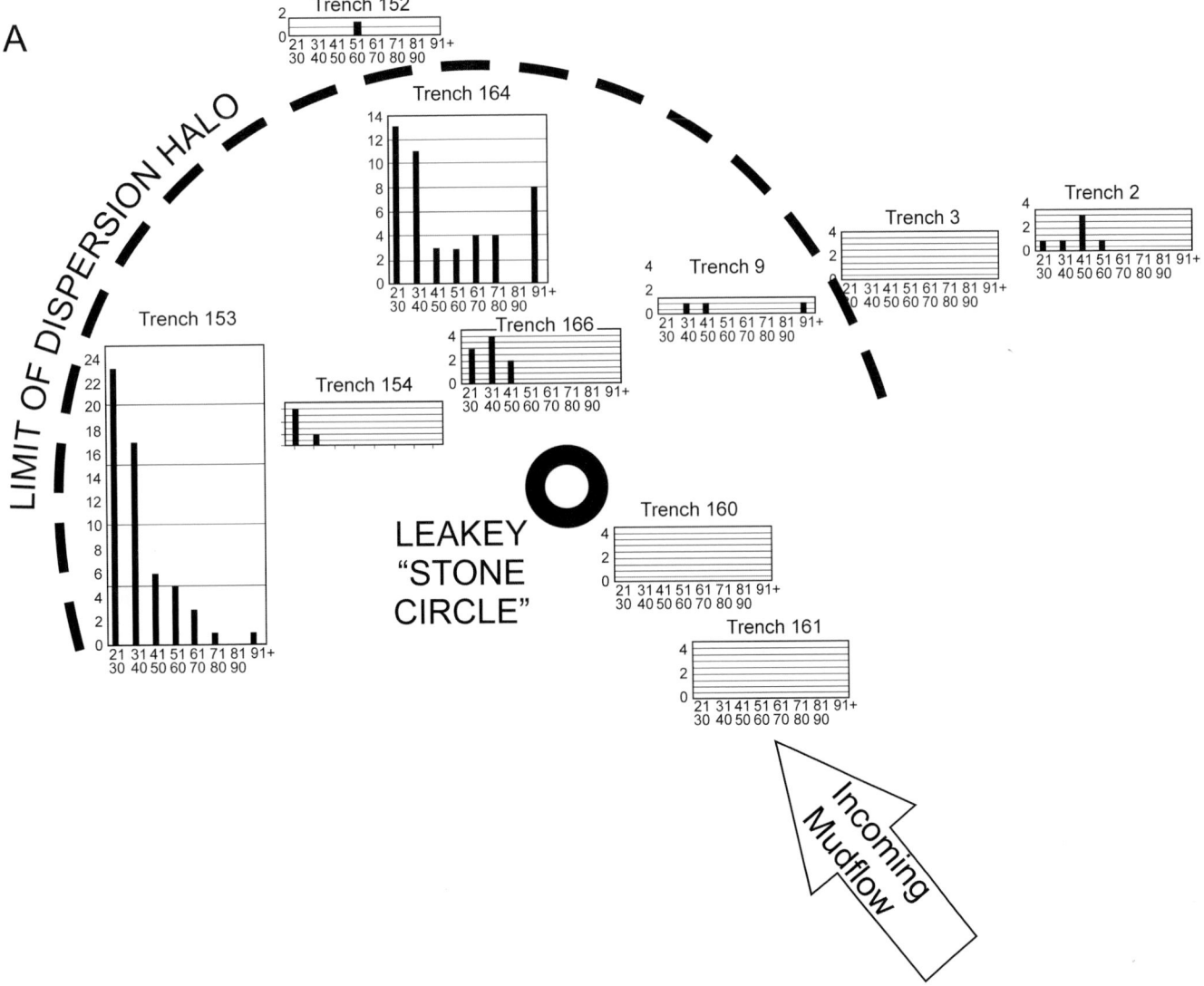

Figure 32.8 Analysis of dispersion "halo" of assemblage using (A) long-bone midshaft fragments and (B) Voorhies Groups in the levels corresponding to Leakey's occupation floor (after Stanistreet et al., 2018).

Eastern and Central Africa

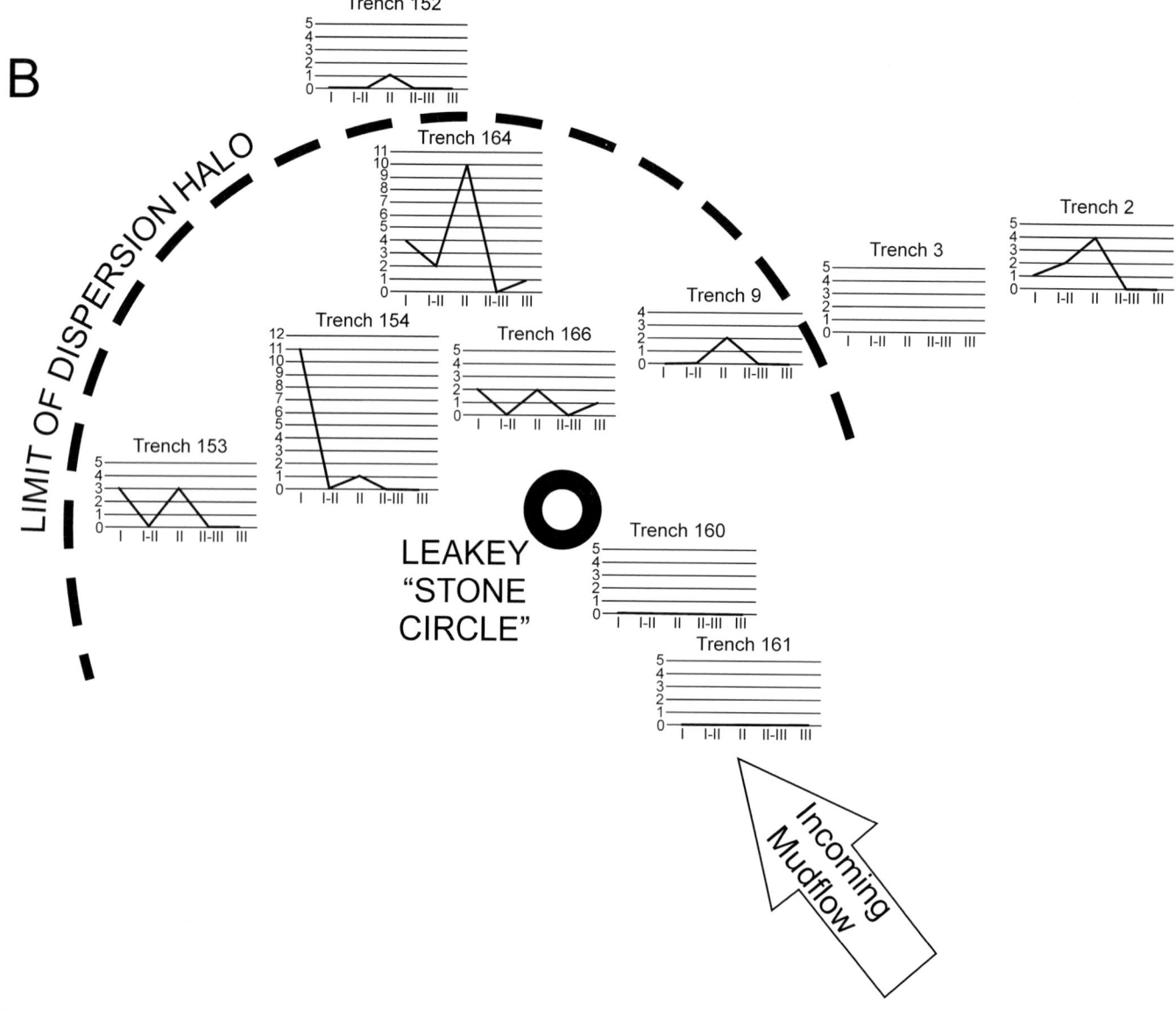

Figure 32.8 (Continued)

Proboscidea
Two species of proboscidean, *Deinotherium bozasi* and *Elephas recki atavus*, were recovered. Deinotheres are extinct relatives of modern-day elephants (Sanders et al., 2010) and are distinguished from other proboscideans by the presence of large, recurved tusks in the lower jaw and the absence of upper tusks (Harris, 1976b). *D. bozasi* is the species found at DK and other Bed I and Bed IIA (Bibi et al., 2018) sites. *E. recki* was a large relative of the extant Asian elephant (*E. maximus*). Standing at nearly 14 feet tall, it was the most common elephant in East Africa from the late Pliocene to the middle Pleistocene, when it became extinct due to the expansion of grasslands and increased competition from *Loxodonta* (Sanders et al., 2010). The subspecies *E. recki atavus* was common during Bed I times.

Rhinocerotidae
The white rhino, *Ceratotherium simum*, is the only rhino found at DK and other Bed I sites (Geraads, 2010d).

Hyaenidae
Crocuta ultra, a relative of the extant spotted hyena, and an indeterminate specimen, *Crocuta* sp., are present in the assemblages.

Canidae
The black-backed jackal, *Canis mesomelas*, is present.

Felidae
Machairodontinae indet.: Remains of a machairodont were recovered, but could not be assigned to any particular species. *Homotherium* is the most likely candidate as it was one of the most common carnivores found in East African Plio-Pleistocene sites, while *Dinofelis* is the most common fossil felid found in the African Neogene (Werdelin and Peigné, 2010).

Herpestidae
Specimens of mongoose were found but could not be identified to species.

Viverridae

Remains of the extinct large civet *Pseudocivettictis ingens* were recovered (Petter, 1973).

Cercopithecidae

Theropithecus oswaldi oswaldi: This is a common gelada found at DK. A lower third molar was found among the OH 24 site fossils (Figure 32.7).

Remains of an unknown species of medium-sized baboon were found and assigned to *Papio* sp. (Leakey and Leakey, 1976). However, recent analysis by Gilbert et al. (2016) has identified it as *Gorgopithecus major*, a species that was previously only known from South Africa.

Galagidae

Galago sp.: M.D. Leakey (1971) reports that remains of an unknown species of bushbaby were recovered, but no further information is given. The species could be related to the extant *G. senegalensis*, which is also found at the FLK "*Zinjanthropus*" site in middle Bed I and described in detail by Simpson (1965).

Hominidae

Remains of five hominins have been recovered. OH 24 "Twiggy" is a severely crushed and distorted *Homo habilis* skull. It is the oldest known fossil skull from Olduvai. OH 52 is an incomplete left temporal bone which may have been from *H. habilis* (Day, 1986). OH 56 is represented by a few cranial fragments that also probably belong to *H. habilis*. An upper incisor fragment belonging to an indeterminate hominin was assigned to OH 71, and a cranial fragment identified as *Homo* sp. to OH 72 (Masao et al., 2013).

Crocodylia

Crocodile remains include numerous skeletal fragments and teeth (Figure 32.7). DK is unique among the Olduvai sites in that it yielded the highest concentration of crocodile teeth among all Olduvai sites. In total, nearly 8000 isolated crocodile teeth were recovered from all excavations. Identification of the teeth to any particular species is not possible at present. *Crocodylus anthropophagus* is the only crocodylian to be found at Olduvai and is the most likely candidate (Brochu et al., 2010). *C. thorbjarnarsoni* is a close relative of *C. anthropophagus* but has only been found in the Turkana Basin (Brochu and Storrs, 2012; Brochu, 2020).

Chelonia

Fragments of tortoise carapaces and plastrons make up the majority of chelonian remains. Three species (two of which are extant) have been identified by Auffenberg (1981). Most of the chelonian remains (98 percent) found at Olduvai belong to *Pelusios sinuatus*, the extant serrated hinged terrapin. It was found in DK Levels 1 and 2. The extant leopard tortoise, *Geochelone pardalis*, now referred to as *Stigmochelys pardalis*, was also found in Level 1 (Gerlach, 2001). In Level 2, *Latisternon microsulcae*, an extinct turtle, was identified.

Remains of other reptiles were also found during Leakey's excavations, including pythons, puff adders, and monitor lizards.

Flora

Phytoliths represent a variety of plant groups and components, including grasses and other monocots, which dominate the plant matter, and wood/bark of dicots (Albert et al., 2015, their table 2 and their figure 5). Diatoms were also extracted from the deposits and studied (Albert et al., 2015, their table 3). M.D. Leakey (1971) recovered fossil rhizomes that were similar to papyrus, but these could not be found by Albert et al. (2015), but see Peters et al. (Chapter 33).

Taphonomy

In the mudflow levels, the size distribution of long bone midshaft fragments shows an abundance of smaller pieces, <40 mm in maximum dimensions (Figure 32.8). Leakey's original assemblage was lacking in this size group (Egeland, 2007). Flume experiments show that bones within this size group are more likely to be transported by fluvial processes than larger fragments (Pante and Blumenschine, 2010). Additionally, Voorhies' (1969) grouping of skeletal elements places most of the bones into groups (I, I–II, and II) that are capable of being transported (Figure 32.8). The condition of the bones varied from moderate to highly weathered (stages 2–4), according to Behrensmeyer's (1978b) criteria, and approximately 45 percent of the assemblage show signs of transport (rounding).

Hominid-modified bone is relatively low compared to carnivore-ravaged bone in the OLAPP assemblages from all levels (Figure 32.9). This pattern is like the analysis of the Leakey assemblage (Egeland, 2007). Considering that crocodiles were

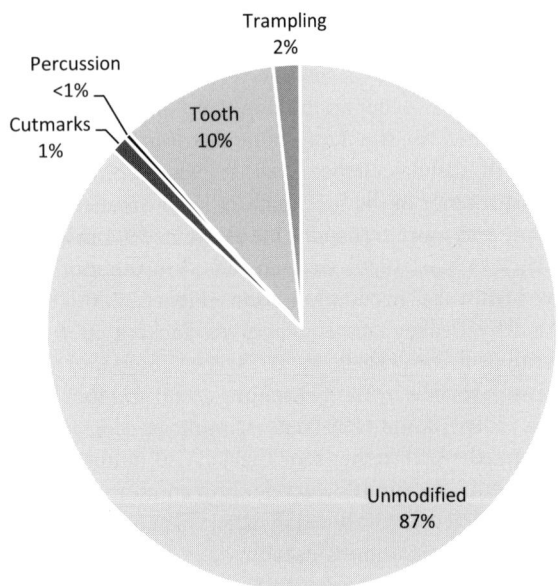

Figure 32.9 Percentages of modified bones from all levels of the OLAPP excavations.

present, because DK produced more crocodile teeth than any other Bed I site, further evaluation may reduce these numbers due to new evidence that crocodile tooth marks can be indistinguishable from cut marks (Njau, 2012b; Sahle et al., 2017). Approximately 10 percent of the bones show tooth markings from carnivores. Previous studies indicate that DK contains a higher frequency of animal bones bearing crocodile tooth marks than other Bed I and Lower Bed II lakeshore assemblages (Njau, 2006, 2012a).

Paleoenvironment

Sedimentary structures and processes and paleontological remains provide a basis for interpreting the environmental conditions of the DK locality. Taphonomic, taxonomic, and ecometric analyses were conducted on faunal remains recovered from recent excavations and those published in existing literature. This includes analysis of long-bone size distribution and Voorhies grouping of skeletal elements, bovid diversity, and relationships between tooth crown height and precipitation, respectively.

The depositional history of DK is unique among the Bed I sites in that it is not buried by volcanic ash (Hay, 1976). The overall environment is indicative of lower-energy processes, i.e., fine-grained sediments; however, the presence of pebbles and gravel intermixed with the fine sediment overlaying the site suggests some periodic pulses of higher-energy input (Hay, 1976; Potts, 1988). Recent refinement of the stratigraphy by Albert et al. (2015) and Stanistreet et al. (2018) has identified these pebbles and gravel as sandy diamictites and volcaniclastic sandstone, which are indicators of mudflow. Using the evidence from sediments and bones, Stanistreet et al. (2018) concluded that following the eruption of the Ngorongoro volcano, laharic mudflows slightly modified, buried, and preserved the DK site prior to the deposition of Tuff IB.

Stanistreet et al. (2018) discovered that within the mudflow levels of the OLAPP trenches (trenches 9, 153, 154, 164, and 166) remains were dispersed and spread in a "halo"-like pattern surrounding the Stone Circle (Figures 32.4 and 32.8A,B). These levels overlay the "occupation floor" level and formed as mudflows inundated the site. Long-bone distribution and Voorhies grouping of skeletal elements all indicate some postdepositional disturbance of the "occupation floor." Smaller fragments (<40 mm) and more transportable elements (Voorhies Groups I and II; Voorhies, 1969) were entrained in the mudflow and removed from the "occupation floor" (Figure 32.8). This could explain why Leakey's assemblage was lacking in fragments smaller than 40 mm (Egeland, 2007) when compared to experimental assemblages by Blumenschine (1995) and Pickering and Egeland (2006). Potts (1984) also commented on the lack of bone fragments within the Stone Circle. Also, almost 45 percent of the bones in the mudflow levels show rounding, as opposed to all the other levels combined in which 35 percent are rounded (Farrugia and Njau, unpubl. data).

Furthermore, M.D. Leakey (1971) noticed that the remains on the "occupation floor" appear to be more plentiful to the north and northwest of the Stone Circle, which would have been the downflow direction of the mudflows (Stanistreet et al., 2018). Remains from the OLAPP trenches were more concentrated in trenches in this same general direction and diminished laterally, as seen in trench 3. No remains were recovered from mudflow levels in trenches 160 and 161, indicating that remains were not carried into the site (Stanistreet et al., 2018). Regarding trench 2, Stanistreet et al. (2018) suggest that these remains could belong to a separate hominin accumulation, but the modern Olduvai River has removed most of the area, preventing further investigation.

Paleontological evidence indicates that the site was in a freshwater wetland. Fish, hippopotamuses, turtles and tortoises, and crocodile remains all confirm this interpretation. The large amount of isolated crocodile teeth (>8000 teeth from OLAPP, OH 24 and 56, and Leakey's excavations combined) are evidence that crocodiles occupied this wetland because as polyphyodonts, crocodiles continuously shed teeth throughout most of their lives (Poole, 1961). Furthermore, Njau (2006) observed that crocodile remains are found in greater numbers in crocodile-inhabited pools when compared to adjacent riverbanks, overbanks or distal floodplains. Additionally, at the base of Level 3, steep-sided channels were found that strongly resemble game trails formed by hippos at lake-margin wetlands along the modern Lake Magadi (Makat) in the Ngorongoro crater (M.D. Leakey, 1971; Deocampo, 2002). The freshwater source was most likely a crocodile pool like those seen on the modern Grumeti River during the dry season (Gereta and Wolanski, 1998; Njau, 2006; Albert et al., 2015; Stanistreet et al., 2018).

Plant remains support the sedimentary and faunal evidence. M.D. Leakey (1971) recovered fossilized rhizomes resembling papyrus, which are only found near fresh water, and Albert et al. (2015) identified plant phytoliths from diverse vegetation, including grasses, trees and shrubs, diatoms and sandy diatomite,s which also grow in the presence of permanent freshwater pools.

Bovids are good indicators of environmental conditions, and their diversity at DK was like other Bed I sites (Figure 32.10). As originally pointed out by Potts (1988), many bovid tribes are represented by only a few individuals. Alcelaphini and Antilopini make up 60 percent of the total amount of bovids (Figure 32.11). These tribes prefer more open and drier habitats (Gentry and Gentry, 1978a, 1978b; Vrba, 1980). The presence of Tragelaphini and Hippotragini suggests that the landscape was more mixed, rather than open, because these tribes prefer more closed and mixed habitats, respectively (Gentry and Gentry, 1978a, 1978b). Reduncini are associated with near-water habitats (Gentry and Gentry, 1978a, 1978b; Vrba, 1980), thus supporting the sedimentary and plant evidence that there was a nearby freshwater source.

Using the criteria established in Eronen et al. (2010a, 2010b) annual precipitation was estimated to be approximately 882 mm, which agrees with previous studies using paleosol carbonates (Cerling and Hay, 1986) and fossil pollen (Bonnefille and Riollet, 1980) both of which estimated that rainfall was greater than 800 mm annually. Average precipitation during the wettest quarter was estimated to be 542.6 mm and during the driest quarter 14.98 mm. During the time interval below Tuff

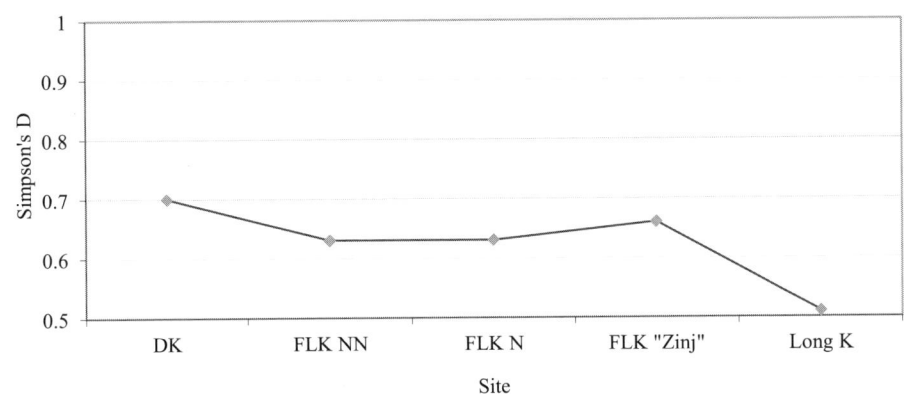

Figure 32.10 Bovid diversity (Simpson's Diversity Index) in the DK faunal assemblage. Data for other Bed I sites were compiled from the following sources: (1) FLK "Zinjanthropus" from Bunn (1982) and Bunn and Kroll (1986); (2) FLK N from Domínguez-Rodrigo et al. (2007) and Potts (1988); (3) FLK NN from Potts (1988) and Domínguez-Rodrigo et al. (2007); (4) Long K from Potts (1988).

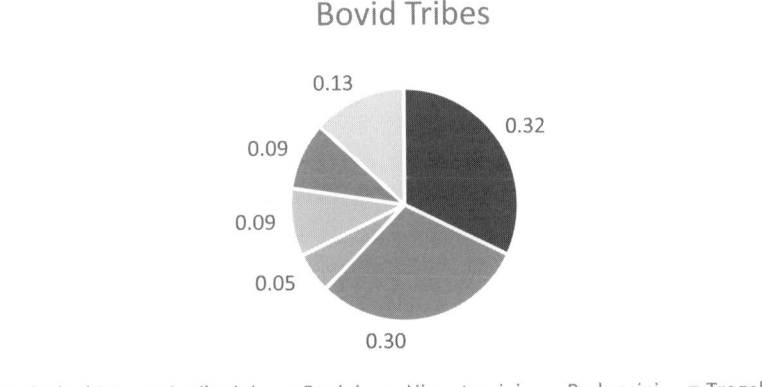

Figure 32.11 Proportions of bovid tribes in the OLAPP DK fossil assemblage. These numbers include specimens from OLAPP and Potts (1988). (A black and white version of this figure will appear in some formats. For the color version, please refer to the plate section.)

IB (~1.85 Ma) Olduvai was wetter than the region today (Table 32.6). These values are more in line with precipitation in the modern-day Serengeti National Park (Norton-Griffiths, et al. 1975; Sinclair et al., 2000; Ritchie, 2008).

Conclusion

DK site is the oldest archeological site at Olduvai Gorge and the first known to have been disturbed, buried, and preserved by laharic mudflows. Uncovered in the 1960s, the DK site gained worldwide recognition because it contained evidence of possibly the oldest known shelter. Referred to, archeologically, as a "living site" or "occupation floor" by Mary Leakey, the site also contained Oldowan stone tools and modified bones in association with *H. habilis* remains (OH 24, OH 56).

The depositional environment and fossil evidence indicate that the site was situated within a large wetland habitat near a freshwater pool, like the crocodile and hippo pools found along the Grumeti River in the Serengeti (Njau, 2006, 2012a). The abundant vegetation, tree cover, and fresh water would have attracted an assortment of animals, including hominins, to the area. Bovids from diverse habitats were plentiful. The presence of reduncines confirms that a freshwater source was nearby and would accommodate both grazers (e.g., alcelaphines, antilopines) and browsers (e.g., hippotragines, tragelaphines, *Giraffa*). Predation risks would have been high because of the presence of crocodiles and other carnivores. Hominins would have made temporary visits to acquire water, plant food, and to scavenge crocodile and felid kills.

The Stone Circle was probably the location of a tree that was used by hominins for refuge. From this tree they would have used manuports to probe the water for crocodiles and perhaps scare them off. During the eruption of the Ngorongoro

Table 32.6. Precipitation estimates for DK time frame compared to the modern Olduvai Basin (after Hay, 1976; Cerling and Hay, 1986) and the Serengeti (after Norton-Griffiths et al., 1975; Sinclair et al., 2000; Ritchie 2008). Numbers in parentheses are the range.

	Annual precipitation (mm)	Precipitation of wettest quarter (mm)	Precipitation of driest quarter (mm)
DK	882 (493.82–1270)	542.6 (317–715)	14.98 (0–82)
Modern Olduvai Basin	566	332	38
Modern Serengeti	800	266	74

volcano the tree was uprooted by mudflows. The mudflows would have displaced some of the accumulated material on the "occupation floor" below the tree, then buried and preserved the site.

Olduvai Gorge has yielded a wealth of information not only for paleoanthropology, but also for paleontology and paleoecology. The exposed two million years of sediments in a layer-cake stratigraphic sequence allows for the tracing of evolutionary events through time. Paleoenvironmental reconstructions using paleosol carbonate isotopes have shown that both Beds I and II were cooler and wetter than today while Beds III and IV were warmer and drier (Cerling and Hay, 1986). The DK study supports the Bed I interpretation. Correlations between herbivore tooth crown height and annual precipitation confirms that during Bed I times the Olduvai Basin was wetter than it is today. Future studies will apply these methods to Beds II, III, IV, Masek, and Ndutu. During these times, the increasing aridity (Cerling and Hay, 1986) eventually led to more open habitats and the emergence of *Homo erectus* and eventually early *Homo sapiens* in the region.

33 Lower Bed II Olduvai Basin, Tanzania: Wetland Sedge Taphonomy, Seasonal Pasture, and Implications for Hominin Scavenging

Charles R. Peters, Marion K. Bamford, and John P. Shields

Introduction

This chapter examines plant macrofossils from Lower Bed II, Olduvai Gorge (Tanzania). During field surveys in 1998, pieces of fossilized sedge culm were identified eroding from the earthy clay exposures of Lower Bed II. The gaps in plant taphonomic literature relating to sedges and marshlands led us to initiate a long-term actualistic field study in a modern seasonal wetland, specifically the living seasonal wetland plant community at Seekoeivlei (South Africa). The results of this study, as applied to the fossil evidence from Olduvai, are invaluable in interpreting the nature of the marshland of Lower Bed II.

This contribution consists of five parts: (1) overview of Olduvai Gorge and previous interpretations of Lower Bed II; (2) field observations of the extant seasonal wetland, in which the litter of one wetland species, the sedge *Cyperus fastigiatus*, is seen to be relatively destruction-resistant; (3) we then examine the pre-burial micro-scale taphonomy of culm disintegration in *C. fastigiatus*, before (4) the analysis and interpretation of the micro-scale taphonomy of Olduvai Gorge fossil sedge culm "species X," using *C. fastigiatus* as guide. Within a volume on paleoenvironments based largely on vertebrate paleontology, we showcase the vital contribution that plant macrofossils make in reconstructing specific aspects of the landscape and vegetation which indicates the past significance to hominins and other fauna utilizing the Olduvai area at that time. The fifth part of this contribution is the implications for clarifying the context of land use, potential scavenging, and predation risk to Olduvai hominins.

Olduvai Gorge Study Site

Olduvai Gorge boasts sediments in Lower Bed II with key archeological evidence within the context of varying paleoenvironments on the margin of a paleo-lake during the interval 1.715–1.735 Ma (M.D. Leakey, 1971; Hay, 1976; Stanistreet, 2012). This record has been used to generate models of landscape archaeology and of hominin land use (Blumenschine and Masao, 1991; Peters and Blumenschine, 1995). This chapter focuses on the Lower Bed II earthy clay sediment that Hay (1976, 1996) interpreted as a marshland facies. During field surveys in 1998, the first author recognized that among the nondescript siliceous fragments eroding from the earthy clay exposures there were pieces of fossilized sedge culm like that of the larger sedges found today in African seasonal wetlands (e.g., Haines and Lye, 1983; pers. obs.).[1] The presence of sedge macrofossils corroborated Hay's prior interpretation and prompted additional research into the extant seasonal wetland plant taphonomy to understand the Olduvai paleorecord. Examination of a living seasonal system with its death assemblages, litter formation and its subsequent destruction reveals taphonomic patterns comparable to those preserved at Olduvai, which indicate the seasonality of the paleo-marsh. We use modern studies of a seasonal wetland to interpret the Olduvai plant material taphonomy and its ecological significance to hominins and other fauna.

Olduvai Gorge is in the eastern Serengeti Plain of northern Tanzania (Peters et al., 2008). The Gorge, which began to erode *ca.* 500 ka, has a southern branch and a northern main branch that join to drain east into a contemporary rift valley abutting the western foot of the nearby volcanic highlands. Sediments exposed in different parts of the Gorge record the paleogeography of a shallow, closed basin evolving over the past two million years, chiefly in response to rift-related earth movements and ashfalls from the volcanos to the east (Hay, 1976). A saline–alkaline lake was present from *ca.* 1.9 to 1.2 Ma. In the junction of the Gorge and to the east, paleo-lake margin and alluvial fan deposits are exposed. Figure 33.1 shows a partial reconstruction of the paleo-lake area for Lower Bed II times, superimposed on the present-day gorge outline.

The ecogeological dynamics of the eastern portion of the basin were driven by lake level fluctuations and nearby volcanics. The volcano Mt. Olmoti lies to the east and was active at that time. A broad piedmont (bajada-like) volcaniclastic alluvial plain (a coalescence of alluvial fans) is suggested by the less-dense pattern of stippling in Figure 33.1. The synsedimentary microfaulting common at this time (not indicated in Figure 33.1) probably resulted in local micro-relief of less than one meter (Stollhofen and Stanistreet, 2012).

Supplementary resources for this chapter are available on www.cambridge.org/africanpaleoecology

1 The largest triangular-culmed sedges of perennial wetlands are more robust than the Olduvai macrofossils. Across tropical and subtropical Africa, *Cyperus papyrus* is the dominant sedge in perennial, shallow, freshwater wetlands, especially marshes, lake margins, and along slow-moving river courses (Peters, 1999). In eastern Africa these culms reach up to 5 m in height and 40 mm thick (Haines and Lye, 1983).

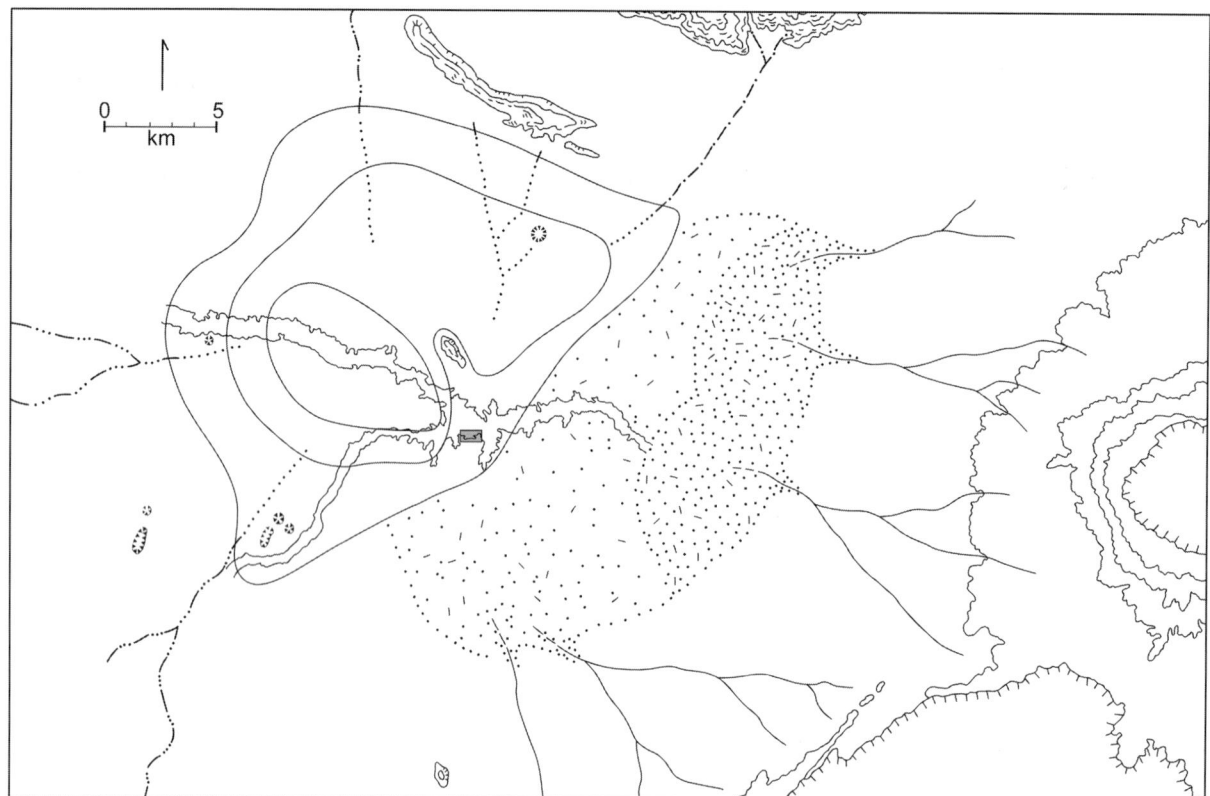

Figure 33.1 Paleogeography of the Lake Olduvai area for Lower Bed II times. Adapted from Peters and Blumenschine (1995), based on Hay (1976, 1996, plus pers. comms.), and 1:50,000 scale topographic maps. The outline of present-day Olduvai Gorge follows Hay (1976). There are three paleo-lake zones: (1) an inner perennial zone of saline–alkaline lake water; (2) an intermittently dry lake margin zone; and (3) an outer zone of intermittently flooded lake margin. To the north of the lake are ancient hills of metamorphic rock, which outcrop locally as inselbergs or kopjes. To the east and southeast is the western edge of the volcanic highlands with their piedmont paleo-alluvial fan system (stippled area). The shaded rectangle indicates the approximately 1 km area of exposures of paleo-marshland sediments along the south side of the Gorge just east of the junction of its two branches.

Hay (1996) distinguishes two main types of sediments for Lower Bed II in what was the eastern lake margin zone: (1) a *waxy clay* which is widespread and indicative of saline–alkaline lake waters; and (2) the more limited *earthy clay* interpreted as marshland and relatively freshwater conditions (Hay 1976, 1996). The earthy clays are discontinuously exposed in gullies for *ca.* 1 km along the south side of the gorge just east of the junction indicated by the shaded rectangle in Figure 33.1 (Hay, 1976, 1996).

Most of the earthy clay beds are *ca.* 30 cm to 1 m in thickness, have an erosional basal contact on lake-margin waxy clay, and grade upwards into waxy clay (Hay, 1996). The accommodation space for the deposition of these deposits was created by synsedimentary micro-faulting (Stollhofen and Stanistreet, 2012), and the basal earthy clay sediments were deposited on an erosional (valley bottom) land surface (Stanistreet, 2012). Considering the erosional disconformities in Lower Bed II, and Hay's estimates of average sedimentation rates, the earthy clays may represent a time period of several hundred to a few thousand years duration (also see Stanistreet, 2012).

The sedge fossils discussed here derive from the earthy clays in Lower Bed II. Hay (1976, 1996) describes these sediments as fine-grained deposits with a chalk-like luster, composed of variable proportions of biogenic silica, fine grained calcite, sand, volcanic glass, and smectite clay. Earlier, Hay (1976) referred to these sediments as siliceous earthy clays. These earthy clays contrast with the greenish waxy clays, which are lacustrine clays with a waxy luster. The beds of both clays are for the most part massive in structure, representing muds that were churned by bioturbation. Hay (1976, 1996) mentions common fossils of the earthy clays, including phytoliths, and lacustrine diatoms and chrysophyte algal spore cases, as well as small fragments of silicified plant material. Faunal remains include hippopotamus and crocodile teeth, and the bones of small fish in the sand fractions of the deposits. We now know the phytoliths include those of sedges, grasses, woody dicots, and palms (Albert and Bamford, 2012).

Freshwater streams from the volcanic highlands probably entered the southeastern margin of the lake. Sandy deposits in some of the earthy clays (Hay, 1996) indicate the presence of such a stream system in association with the marshland (suggested in Figure 33.1). The freshwater marshland was intermittently flooded by the saline–alkaline lake (Hay, 1976, 1996). During relatively short periods of flooding, freshwater stream flow apparently diluted the lake water, and the marshland was subject to brackish conditions. During longer episodes of high lake levels, parts or all of the marsh died off and the geoecological succession returned to lakeshore mudflats, to be succeeded again by marshland during lower lake levels (e.g., Hay, 1996, HWK localities).

Fossil Plant Collection

Plant macro-fossils were recovered from surface exposures and excavations into the earthy clays in the 1998 field season of the Olduvai Landscape Paleoanthropology Project. The systematic collection from the 1998–2000 field seasons forms the focus of this report. The collection in its entirety includes fossil sedge fragments from virtually all areas of exposed earthy clays in Lower Bed II; in particular, in M.D. Leakey's (1971) Korongo site-location nomenclature, from West HWK to MCK. Most of the fossil sample derives from the relatively extensive exposures of earthy clays in the HWK gullies (occurring along about half a kilometer of the gorge). They are also well-preserved and representative of the whole collection. In addition to sedge culm (including numerous tiny fragments), the macro-fossil plant collection includes some cylindrical hollow monocot stem fragments (likely grass culm), small irregularly shaped stems that may be roots, and a few pieces of small branches from trees or large bushes (Bamford, 2012). The fossil sedge (species X) reported here is the dominant culm recovered from the earthy clay of Lower Bed II.

Questions regarding what plant taphonomic features might be expected in a seasonal wetland and whether they could be recognizable in the fossil fragments required observations in a living ecosystem, in this case the Seekoeivlei Nature Reserve. These observations are a partial guide for interpreting the Olduvai material in terms of macro-ecological processes with signatures at the level of micro-scale taphonomy, informed by culm anatomy.

Seekoeivlei Nature Reserve, Eco-Botanical and Neotaphonomic Methods

The first two authors selected the Seekoeivlei Nature Reserve as a suitable location for field studies of plant decomposition, and observations were made annually 2000–2010. The reserve is in the northeastern-most Free State. The sandstone river valley along the upper Klip River has extensive floodplains and numerous oxbow ponds (Figure 33.2). A nickpoint further downstream, where a dolerite intrusion is resistant to erosion, maintains this floodplain and its sediments (McCarthy and Hancox, 2000; Tooth et al., 2002).

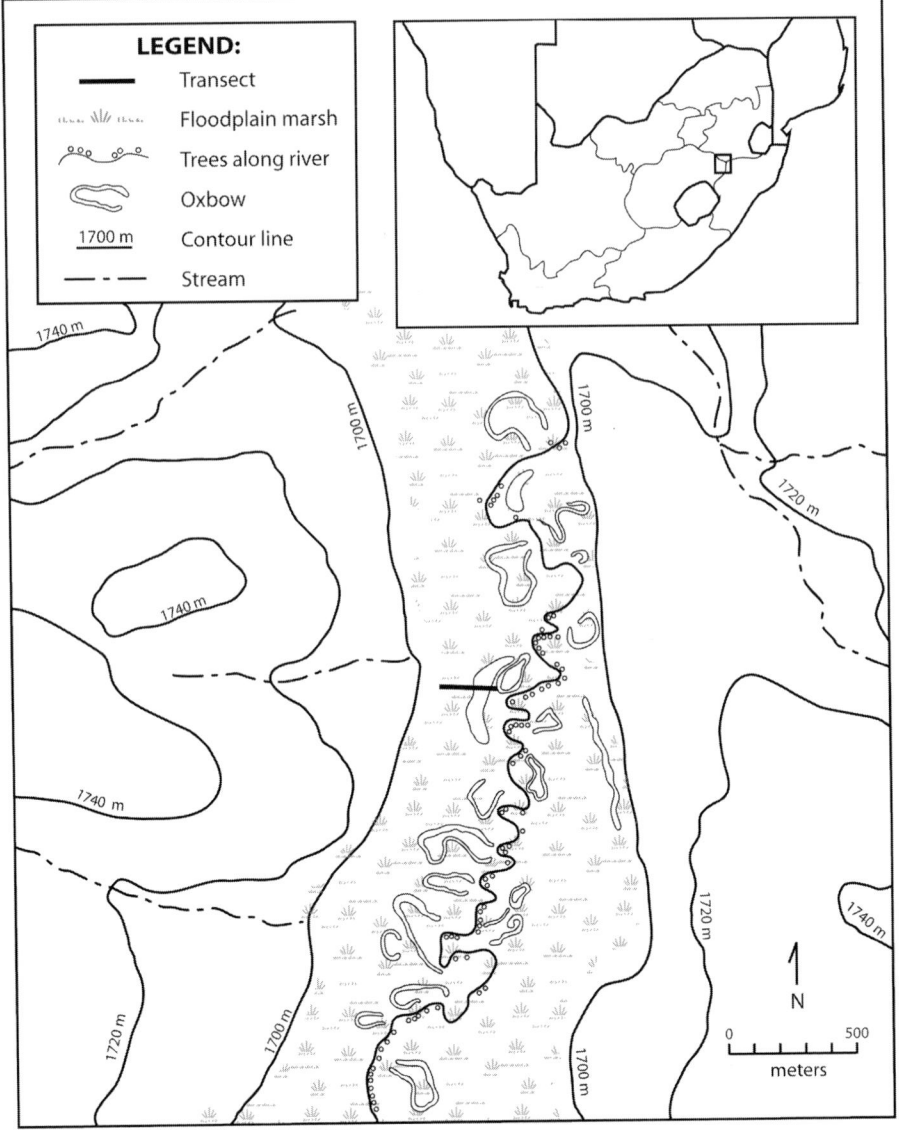

Figure 33.2 Study site in the southern part of the Seekoeivlei Nature Reserve, South Africa. The Reserve encompasses most of the seasonal wetland along a 20 km stretch of the Klip River in the Free State province, which is marked with a square in the regional map insert. Klip River landscape features and valley topography based on 1:50,000 scale South Africa map 2729 DA Memel (2nd ed., 1987), supplemented with 1:30,000 air photo 341–17435 (1954). The study site transect is indicated as a black line.

Historically, large herds of wild ungulates grazed the region, but it has since been cultivated and has supported livestock since 1890 (Bulpin, 1980). Recently, wetland rehabilitation was begun, and in the northern part of the Reserve hippos were reintroduced in 1999, along with African buffalo (*Syncerus caffer*) and several other common wild ungulates, such as zebra (*Equus quagga*), and various alcelphins, such as black wildebeest (*Connochaetes gnou*) and red hartebeest (*Alcelaphus buselaphus caama*), among others.

The study site is in the southern part of the Reserve where the floodplain is grazed by horses, zebras, and occasionally the common reedbuck (*Redunca arundinum*). Large numbers of migratory waterfowl visit these wetlands during the summer rainy season.

The rainy season is from October to April (summer), with an average annual rainfall of *ca*. 700 mm (Tooth et al., 2002), and seasonal inundation of the floodplain occurring during the midsummer months, with maximum flood levels occurring December through March (G. Wandrag, pers. comm.) with progressive recession thereafter followed by surficial desiccation through the winter. Interannual variation, as well as monthly variation, in rainfall is also significant. During the years of our research the annual rainfall ranged from 528 to 1019 mm (Supplementary Information). Summer temperatures are hot to moderate during the day and cool at night. Winter days are cold, and night temperatures from −5°C to −10°C are common.

The study site and location of the belt transect for the floodplain vegetation survey (Figure 33.2) were chosen after reconnaissance of the area. The belt transect was about 10 m wide and included several meters of floodplain, a shallow crescent-shaped flood basin, and the western channel of a pear-shaped oxbow pond. Plant taxonomic identifications were made by specialists at the National Herbarium in Pretoria and our vouchers are deposited there (Bamford and Peters numbers 1–73, 105–123, 150–154).

Individual species distributions were recorded and estimates of dominance made based upon observations of relative density. Species with a C_4 photosynthetic pathway were identified by the late John C. Vogel at the CSIR facility in Pretoria.

Observations on dead plant material and types of degradation were made with the goals of understanding the etiology of damage (agents and processes of destruction), and the possibility of identifying macro-remains to plant part and taxon. Subaerial versus subaqueous weathering signatures and mechanical damage were distinguished. The *in situ* potential longevity of the standing litter was restricted to a few years because the floodplain has been burned every two or three years since 1995 (G. Wandrag, pers. comm.).

Limited excavations (shovel and cores) at multiple locations exposed the living root system and soil to a maximum depth of *ca*. 40 cm, with recordings made of root growth forms and possibilities for burial. Some additional observations and plant collections were made at a seasonal wetland, the Nylsvley Nature Reserve, close to the Makapan valley (Limpopo Province, South Africa), and in a perennial papyrus marsh in the Okavango Delta, Botswana. These confirmed our observations at Seekoeivlei that ungulate trampling creates a taphonomic signature in the destruction-resistant sedge litter of seasonal wetlands, and that relatively rapid progressive decomposition of plant tissues by rotting is the taphonomic process characteristic of continuous subaqueous aerobic conditions.

Microscopy Methods and Techniques

The collections were studied at both the Center for Ultrastructural Research (now Georgia Electron Microscopy) at the University of Georgia and at the Evolutionary Studies Institute at the University of the Witwatersrand, where they are currently housed. Specimens selected for further study were examined by a 10× hand lens, supplemented with 16× (monocular) and 40× (binocular) light microscopy. At the University of Georgia, light microscopy observations and photography were made by the first author using a Leica binocular microscope outfitted with a Spot digital camera (Leica Microsystems Inc., Buffalo Grove, IL, and Spot Imaging Solutions, Sterling Heights, MI). For scanning electron microscopy (SEM), specimens were imaged with a Zeiss 1450EP variable pressure SEM (Carl Zeiss Microscopy, Thornwood, NY).

For SEM, the extant specimens (*Cyperus fastigiatus*) were sputter-coated with gold (*ca*. 15 nm thick) to be conducting and avoid charging artifacts. They were imaged with either a backscatter electron detector or a secondary electron detector, at 20 Kev and a high vacuum. For observations of tissue anatomy, specimens were cryo-fractured to obtain good cross-sectional views. The resulting anatomical descriptions, by the first author, follow the terminology in Esau (1960) and Metcalfe (1971). In contrast, the fossil specimens (Olduvai Gorge culm-species X) were not coated for SEM. They were imaged with a backscatter electron detector at 20 Kev and a vacuum of 20 pascals. The SEM work was conducted jointly by the first and third authors.

Results

This section is in three parts: (1) field observations of the living seasonal wetland plant community at Seekoeivlei, where the sedge *C. fastigiatus* is seen to be relatively destruction-resistant in the litter of this wetland; (2) the pre-burial micro-scale taphonomy of culm disintegration in *C. fastigiatus*; and (3) the analysis and interpretation of the micro-scale taphonomy of Olduvai Gorge fossil sedge culm-species X.

1. Field Observations in the Seasonal Wetland at Seekoeivlei

Wetland Transect: The Terrain

The transect begins at the western edge of the floodplain (see Figure 33.2) and that point is demarcated as zero in Figure 33.3. This is the beginning of the wetland vegetation, and the edge of the maximum seasonal floodwater. Topography, as reflected in maximum floodwater depth observed by us in March, changes by several centimeters along the 250-m transect shown in Figure 33.3A. Moving west to east out into the floodplain, in the first 110 m the maximum floodwater depth is *ca*. 40–50 cm at *ca*. 40 m out. From this moderate depth it becomes shallower eastwards, so that across the area between *ca*. 100 m and 140 m out into the floodplain there is relatively high ground, resulting in a maximum floodwater depth of *ca.* 15–25 cm. From 140 m to 230 m out, the transect crosses a crescent-shaped small flood basin (see Figure 33.2) where the maximum floodwater depth is *ca.* 80 cm (Figure 33.3A). Between this flood basin and the pear-shaped oxbow to the east (see Figure 33.2), there is a bank about 30 cm high (Figure 33.3A) which separates the two features. Just beyond this bank, the oxbow pond at the end of the transect is *ca.* 1.3 m deep. During the maximum floods of our tenure this bank was covered by *ca.* 40–50 cm of water. At these observed flood stages water enters the oxbow pond from the adjacent north-flowing Klip River through a shallow breach (an otter trail) in its higher south bank and exits as overflow back into the river through another (shallower) bank breach in its northeast corner.

Wetland Transect: The Vegetation

Most of the plant species in this seasonal wetland are also found in eastern Africa or have close relatives there. The plants of the seasonal wetland are patchy in their distributions (Figure 33.3B), related in large part to maximum floodwater depth (Figure 33.2A). None occur in the deeper water of the oxbow pond. Here aquatic species dominate; specifically, the pondweed, *Potamogeton* spp. and the oxygen weed *Lagarosiphon muscoides*. The moderately deep to shallow portion of the seasonal wetland (the western end of this transect) has the greatest diversity of plant species, while only sedges are present in the deeper water of the flood basin (*ca.* 160–200 m on the transect).

The only common forb is the dicot *Persicaria attenuata* (Figure 33.3B), subspecies *africana*, with conspicuous pink-noded stems (and pink inflorescences), emergent above or floating partially submerged in moderately deep water. Otherwise, the plants are dominated by three families of monocots: cattails (Typhaceae), grasses (Gramineae), and sedges (Cyperaceae) (Figure 33.3B). Most of these plants reach standing foliage heights of 1 m or less, or float partially emergent above the low floodwaters, apart from *Typha* (*ca.* 1.5–2.0 m in height) and *Cyperus fastigiatus*, which reaches heights of 1.5–2.0 m next to deeper water. A filamentous blue–green alga, *Oscillatoria* (Cyanophyta), also occurs across the wetland, but not in the oxbow pond.

In the floodplain the sedges usually occur as small patches or scattered tufts mixed with grasses in a dense mosaic. However, in the deeper water of the small flood basin the sedges *Eleocharis dregeana* and *E. limosa* provide a dense uniform cover.[2]

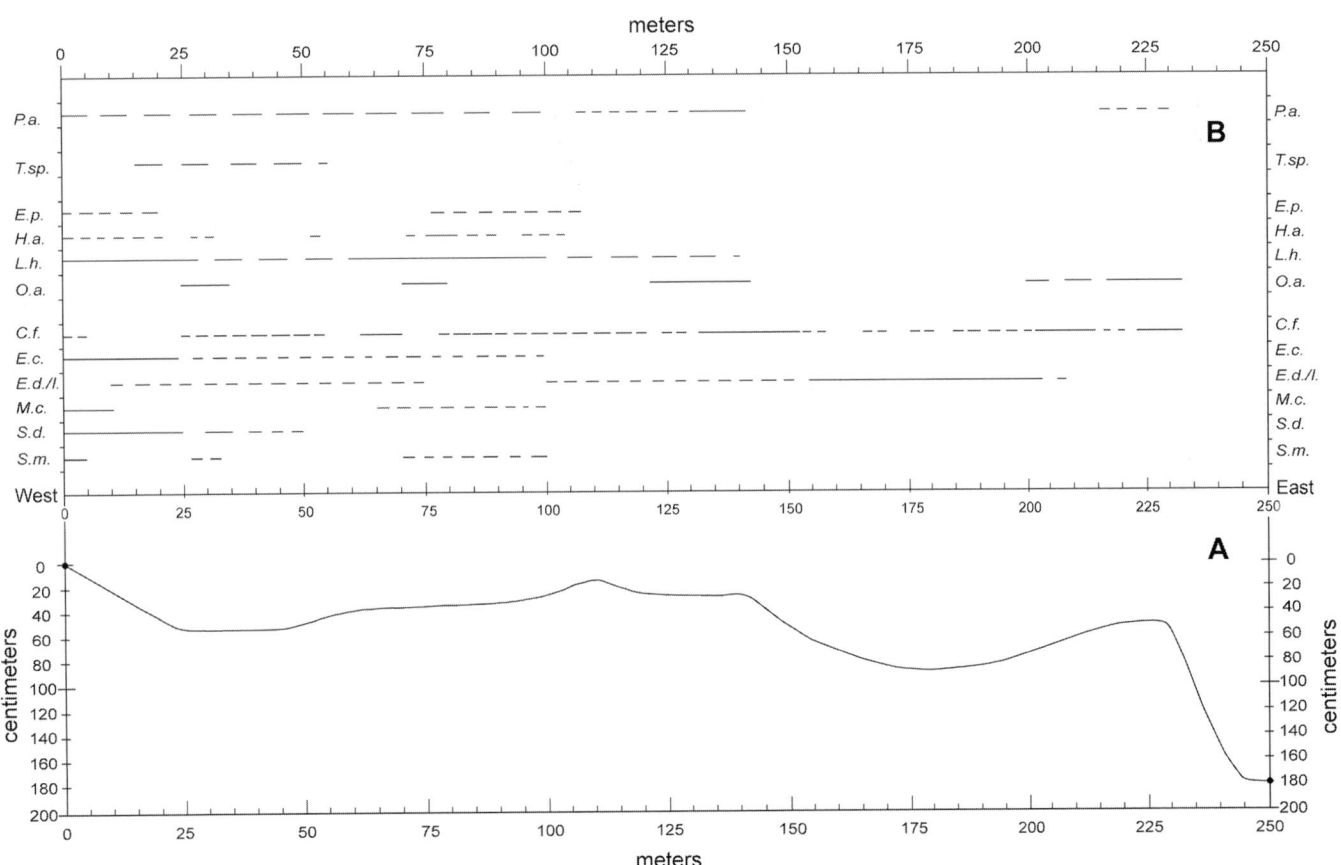

Figure 33.3 Terrain relief (A) and the common plants (B) of the study site transect indicated in Figure 33.2. (A) Seasonal floodwater depth varies with terrain: with the edge of the floodplain at zero depth at the west end of the transect, the oxbow pond (former river channel) is at 180 cm floodwater depth at the east end of the transect. (B) Plant species. Dicotyledonae. *P.a.* = *Persicaria attenuata* (wetland forb). Monocotyledonae. *T. sp.* = *Typha* sp. (cattail, reedmace). Grasses: *E.p.* = *Eragrostis planiculmis**; *H.a.* = *Hemarthria altissima**; *L.h.* = *Leersia hexandra*; *O.a.* = *Odontelytrum abyssinicum**. Sedges: *C.f.* = *Cyperus fastigiatus**; *E.c.* = *Eleocharis caduca*; *E.d./l.* = *Eleocharis dregeana* and *E. limosa*; *M.c.* = *Mariscus congestus**; *S.d.* = *Schoenoplectus decipiens*; *S.m.* = *Schoenoplectus muriculatus*. Asterisks indicate species with a C_4 photosynthetic pathway.

---

2 Both *Eleocharis* species occur in this wetland but were indistinguishable in the field.

Cyperus fastigiatus also occurs as dense stands, in shallow water at the edge of the floodplain and along the edges of the deeper water of the flood basin and oxbow. *Leersia hexandra* is the most widespread floodplain grass. It is absent only from the deeper water of the small flood basin and the edge of the oxbow pond. *Odontelytrum abyssinicum* is the dominant grass near the western edge of the floodbasin and the only grass at the edge of the oxbow pond.[3] Except for *C. fastigiatus*, all the sedges and grasses are sometimes grazed. Only the grasses *L. hexandra* and *Odontelytrum abyssinicum* are commonly grazed and comprise the main wet-season pastures across the shallowly flooded areas sampled by the central and east portions of the transect.

Observations of Seasonal Wetland Litter and its Disintegration

Systematic field observations on the seasonal wetland litter, its disintegration, and the role of the perennial root system were begun in the summer of 2003. The lack of burning in 2002 and a poor rainy season facilitated observations of the mostly dry floodplain and flood basin by March–April 2003 fieldwork. Representative observations are presented below for *Persicaria*, *Typha*, the grasses, and the sedges. Observations during seasonal flooding in other years showed that prolonged wet conditions amplified ongoing litter decomposition.

As expected in a seasonal marshland, complete dieback of above ground stems and foliage occurs at the beginning of the dry season, with regrowth from perennial rootstock in the subsequent rainy season. In 2003, the resulting year-old litter had been subjected to the conditions of one dry season, followed by the shallow temporary standing water of a rainy season without the usual accompanying flood. Commonly, a pattern of disintegrating leaf remains, rotten stem bases, and very fragile remaining stems (disintegrating under slight pressure into longitudinal fragments) were observed. *Cyperus fastigiatus* was the notable exception; the mid to upper portions of its culms were destruction-resistant compared with the other wetland species.

In the *Persicaria* variant of this one-year-old litter pattern the leaves had completely disintegrated. The stems had lost their pith, were detached from their rhizomes, and broken between their nodes. These remnant hollow pieces of stem were very fragile.

For *Typha* the culm bases were rotten, and the plants bent over *ca.* 8–14 cm from the base, lying prostrate on the litter-covered ground. Above their rotten bases the pith of the culms was for the most part lost, and slight pressure easily broke the culms longitudinally. Upper portions of the culms were still firm to the touch where the pith remained intact, but lengthways, cracks were beginning to develop. Leaf blades still attached to the culms were split longitudinally, exposing the interior cell boxwork. On the ground, pieces of leaf-blade formed a very fragile litter covered with a skin of dried mud and algae. Fine *Typha* rootlets were growing upward into this leaf litter.

The grass litter was mainly *Leersia* and *Odontelytrum*. For the one-year-old litter the culms were fragile, broken into various lengths, some still round, but most were shrivelled (ridged longitudinally), crimped, flattened, or split open. Some were still attached to their roots but easily torn away at the base. Leaf fragments (some still attached to the culms) were very fragile, and disintegrated upon touch with very little pressure.

The disintegrating condition of the one-year-old *Eleocharis* litter in the flood basin was representative, for the most part, of the wetland sedges. The litter formed a layer a few millimeters thick of shriveled (ridged longitudinally) and flattened culms that had broken away from their bases. This material was very fragile, disintegrating completely upon the slightest pressure. Fine *Eleocharis* rootlets penetrated the litter layer from the root mat below. Dead culm bases, still rooted, were chartaceous (paper-like), flattened, shriveled, and fibrous; very fragile, they were easily torn away by hand. Adhering basal leaf sheaths disintegrated upon touch.

The *C. fastigiatus* litter was composed almost entirely of culm fragments. Leaf blade fragments were rare. Leaf sheaths adhering to pieces of basal culm disintegrated upon touch. Culm bases still attached to the root mat were rotted (shriveled or decomposed lengthways into fiber bundles). What was notably different were the culm fragments that made up the litter, which although broken into pieces were still largely intact in cross-section and firm to the touch. They were destruction-resistant, and their distinctive triangular cross-section was clearly identifiable.

Usually, the litter-forming process starts when the floodwaters recede. The standing green culms begin to dry out and are dead by June, along with the other wetland species. The resulting dry-season floodplain litter consists predominantly of *C. fastigiatus* culms and a fragile surficial mat of the culms and leaf fragments of the other sedge species and the grasses. Equid trampling (incidental to their movements across the floodplain) snap-breaks the dead culms into short, segment-like pieces, and further reduces the fragile litter layer of the other wetland species to indistinguishable fibrous plant material. However, the *C. fastigiatus* culm fragments persist as the only common identifiable litter on the floodplain, with hundreds to thousands of pieces in a hectare. More detailed observations as a partial analog for Olduvai Gorge fossil sedge culm-species X are presented below in the microscopy section of the results.

The Seasonal Wetland Root Mat as a Barrier and a Net

Outside of the oxbow ponds the root mat is virtually continuous across the floodplain. It acts as a barrier to litter burial, even where trampling hooves drive plant fragments down several centimeters into the mud. In effect they are buried in the root mat and subsequently subject to rootlet invasion and accelerated decomposition during the wet season (see Supplementary Information). A similar result occurs when the mud cracks during the dry season. The litter that falls into the cracks becomes incorporated into the root mat when the cracks close during the early rains.

---

3 Beyond our transect, the largest grass of the wetland is *Phragmites australis*. It reaches *ca.* 2.0–2.5 m in height and occurs in dense patches at seepages at the edge of the floodplain.

2. Micro-Scale Taphonomy of the Culm of *Cyperus fastigiatus*

Culm Tissue Anatomy

The culm of *C. fastigiatus* at Seekoeivlei reaches between one and two meters tall, with a maximum width at the base of 5–10 (13) mm, and an uppermost width (just below the inflorescence) of 2–4 (5) mm. The sheath leaves are relatively thin and basal, contributing little, if anything, to the protection of the culm. The basic architecture of the culm is that of a transversely subcircular (at the base) to acutely triangular (at the top) upright stem composed mostly of pith a few millimeters wide surrounded by cortex a few micrometers thick. The data in Appendix A present an introduction to the previously undescribed culm tissue anatomy of *C. fastigiatus*. None of the tissue types are unique to this species. See Metcalfe (1971) for their diverse expressions in other species and genera. The standing, somewhat flexible, rigidity of the culm results from numerous long fiber strands and vascular bundles that run lengthwise up the stem, which influences the response of the culm to mechanical damage. The cortex of the culm is layered, outward in, with an epidermis, immediately subepidermal fiber strands, and an inner cortex of chlorenchyma (cellular tissue with chlorophyll) cells. This laminar cortical structure deteriorates progressively in response to weathering in the changing seasonal environments of the wetland.

Pre-Burial Taphonomy

The destruction-resistant *C. fastigiatus* preserves taphonomic damage sustained over approximately 2–3 years in this modern wetland ecosystem, limited by periodic controlled burning. In the first year after controlled burning, the litter assemblage of the sedge begins to show the accumulating mixture of characteristic taphonomic signs. Some processes occur widely over the floodplain, while others are restricted to micro-environments. Use of the wetland by large ungulates leads to repeated trampling, specifically green bends in live culms, and breakage of the brittle, dead culms into short pieces. Other animals, insects and birds cause minor forms of damage. Standing dead culms experience subaerial laminar weathering of the cortex, while the pith remains relatively intact except for rotting due to flooding. As litter, snap-broken pieces of culm undergo dry season subaerial weathering, followed by incipient rotting of waterlogged pith in the subsequent wet season. Complete disintegration of these pieces begins in the second wet season after death. Based on experiments and observation, the process of culm rot and disintegration appears to occur within 3–5 years. The biomechanical damage is largely due to ungulate trampling, which is evident in close-up observations of the dry culms in the hoof-printed pastures and trackways of the Seekoeivlei floodplain. The most obvious and reliably judged forms are transverse snap-breaks, and crimping of the culms (both common) and pressure-molding (less common). The common processes of pre-burial taphonomic damage observed in *C. fastigiatus* are described in Table 33.1, and illustrated below.

Snap-Broken Segment-Like Pieces

For the dead sedge culm, trampling causes breakage into shorter segments. Early-stage necrotic processes cause the dead culm to become brittle and exhibit snap-breaks of various forms. Most snap-breaks are planar, transverse, or somewhat angled

Table 33.1 Pre-burial neotaphonomic processes modifying destruction-resistant sedge culm in a modern seasonal wetland: the features, their inferred causal agents/processes, and their micro-environmental space–time correlates. (Based on *Cyperus fastigiatus* actualistics, 2000–2010, at Seekoeivlei Nature Reserve, South Africa.)

Taphonomic features	Inferred causal agents/processes	Spatial and temporal correlates
Snap-broken segment-like pieces of culm in-the-round, a few centimeters long	Incidental trampling of the dead dry sedge culms by large ungulates: usually the culm does not break by splitting; rather, it breaks cross-wise into segments intact in-the-round	Trackways across the floodplain between pastures and open water, trails along banks, hoof-printed fields from recurrent grazing; dominantly occurs after the rains begin and during the early dry season; can occur even under floodwaters when the dead culms remain brittle
Crimping: transverse creases or folds in the green culm	Trampling of the green culm; less frequently the least brittle lower portions of the newly dead culm, and the basal-most (sheath-leaf protected) portion of year-old standing dead	Trampling spatial correlates similar to that of snap-broken segment-like pieces: the firm substrates of moist mud and herbaceous vegetation facilitate crimping by trampling during the wet season
Molding: a concave or U-shaped depression across one side of the culm	Trampling whereby one culm is pressed down crossways on and into another culm, both prostrate on a firm substrate	Trampling spatial correlates similar to that of snap-broken segment-like pieces: occurs when the culm is firm and green, and with the less brittle portions of the newly dead
Micro-ridging of the epidermis (= the first stage of subaerial weathering in this species): especially well-developed on the upper portion of the dying culm where the epidermis begins to drape the thread-like longitudinal subepidermal fiber strands	Rapid drying (desiccation) of the exposed portions of the senescing culm by sun and wind: the inter-fiber strand epidermal cells collapse, forming surficial micro-grooves	Spatially ubiquitous, the end of the wet season into the dry season, then the second and third stages of subaerial weathering begin
Rhreadbare surficial micro-ridges (= the second stage of subaerial weathering in this species): the formerly subepidermal fiber strands are now partially to wholly exposed, and appear threadbare	Deterioration of the epidermis of the dead culm in subaerial conditions	Open canopy of the standing-dead, and the prostrate-dead on bare ground: develops on the upper culm during the first annual dry season following death at the end of the rainy season; observed the next wet season on the *least* exposed side of the culm (the south facing side, or the inner side of a bowed culm, or the underside of a prostrate culm)

Table 33.1 (cont.)

Taphonomic features	Inferred causal agents/processes	Spatial and temporal correlates
Disintegration of the outer cortex (= the third stage of subaerial weathering in this species): the uncovered fiber strands break up and exfoliate; the resulting surface consists of collapsed chlorenchyma	Greater exposure of the most unprotected side of the dead culm in subaerial conditions: particularly, prolonged direct exposure to the sun	Open canopy of the standing-dead, and the prostrate-dead on bare ground: cortical disintegration develops during the first annual dry season after death, occurring on the side of the upper culm facing the sun (the north-facing side, or the outer side of the bowed standing-dead, or the upper side of the prostrate culm)
Disintegration of the inner cortex (= the fourth stage of subaerial weathering in this species): the chlorenchyma disintegrates and the vascular bundles at the chlorenchyma–pith interface are exposed; the resulting surface is dominated by the destruction-resistant sclerenchyma remnants of these vascular bundles	Continued exposure of the most unprotected side of the upper mid-culm to direct sunlight (the deteriorated uppermost culm, which includes the base of the inflorescence, has already broken away in the wind)	Open canopy of the standing-dead: disintegration of the inner cortex and the newly exposed peripheral vascular bundles develop during the second annual dry season after death, occurring on the side of the upper mid-culm facing the sun; the less-exposed sides of the culm are in the second and third stages of subaerial weathering
Contraction of the ends of snap-broken pieces of culm	With successive aquatic and dry subaerial conditions a portion of the exposed pith deteriorates and the resulting rim of cortex subsequently enfolds over the lost pith when the ends dry quickly	Occurs when there is seasonal standing water in an area of trampled culms, especially at the edges of the flood basin and oxbow pond, where snap-broken pieces are caught in the dense floating stems of aquatic grass
Cortical sheet-peeling	Subaqueous followed by subaerial conditions	Well-developed in prostrate culms lying over onto patches of bare ground immediately adjacent of well-vegetated sedge clumps along the western bank of the flood basin
Micro-wrinkling of the cortex on a lower section of the standing culm	Alternating water line wet–dry or persistent subaqueous conditions followed by repeated desiccation: present on both the newly dead green culm at the end of the wet season, and older dead culms with deteriorated pith	Wet season in standing water followed by dry exposure; well-developed on the standing dead of the shallow flood basin, and elsewhere across the floodplain in high flood years
Shriveled, convoluted, and collapsed basal culm: loss of pith parenchyma, a shell of inner cortex and vascular bundles remains	Persistent (shallow) subaqueous conditions in the lowermost culm of the standing dead; the pith parenchyma rot away in the basal section of the culm below the floodwater line; the softened and weakened culm is easily torn away at the base; subsequent drying gives remnants their shriveled convoluted appearance	Develops in the rainy season after the first dry season of death; well-developed in the flood basin, and elsewhere across the flood plain in high flood years
Aquatic rootlet invasion of snap-broken pieces of culm	Snap-broken pieces of the previous growing season's trampled culms float into adjacent grass (with the help of ungulate movement) where they are trapped by floating grass stems; rootlets from the floating grass roots grow into breaks in these pieces of dead sedge culm	Aquatic floating-grass pasture fringed by the sedge; growth of floating grass roots occurs during the floodwater stages of the wet season

end-breaks (Figure 33.4Aa and 33.4Ab). Judging by the weathering of the specimen, two generations of snap-breaks can be seen (e.g., Figure 33.4Ab and 33.4Ac). The snap-broken culm pieces range from *ca.* 1 to 30 cm in length, with shorter lengths indicating repeated trampling.

Contraction of the Ends of Snap-Broken Pieces
Contraction of the ends of snap-broken pieces of destruction-resistant sedge culm occurs under a successive combination of floodwater and dry subaerial conditions. From field observations and experiments, we infer that the process begins when previous snap-broken pieces experience a few weeks of aquatic conditions. The exposed waterlogged pith at the ends of the pieces deteriorates and when floodwaters recede the culm pieces are exposed to full subaerial conditions. The fast-drying ends cause the small rims of cortex to enfold over the micro-space left by the lost pith (Figure 33.4Aa and 4Ac).

Crimping
Defined as transverse creasing or folding of the culm, this is commonly seen in green culm trampling (e.g., Figure 33.4B). Green bends occur when ungulates walk over a sedge clump, or insect holes in the green culm sometimes result in the culm bending over at that point. Rarely, green culms are bent by take-off and landing by large water birds. Whenever the culm dries out, the crimps are especially vulnerable to breaking.

Moulding
This is less common than other forms of trampling damage. It is most likely to occur where culm density is high. Under pressure, green or newly dead culms are trampled (molded) one onto another. The result is deformation and a concave depression in the culm (Figure 33.4C). If the trampling occurs when the culm is partially dry, the resulting concave depression in the culm is visibly cracked and vulnerable to further drying and breaking.

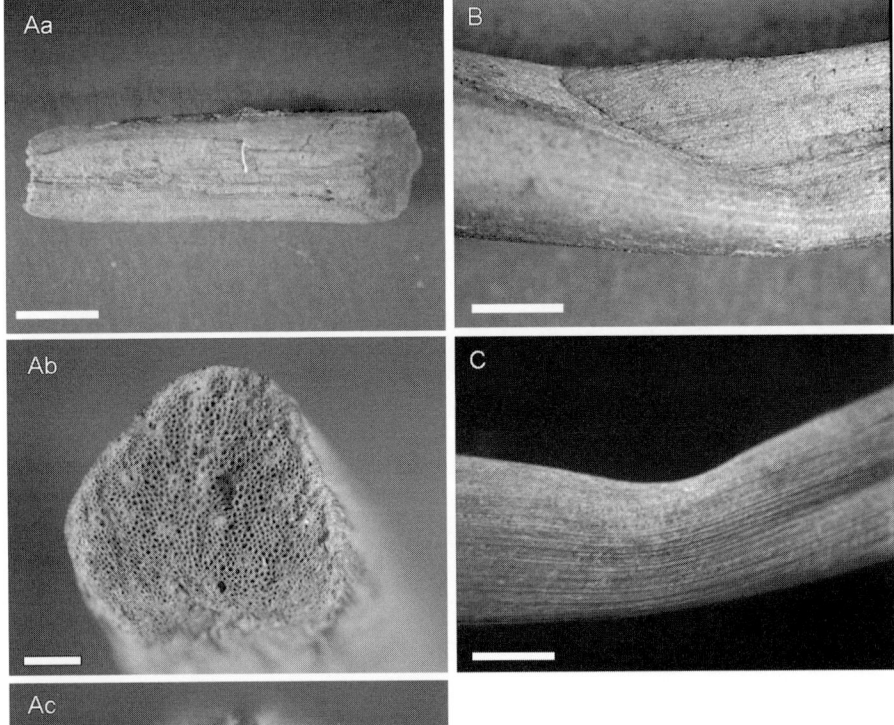

Figure 33.4 Optical micrographs of extant sedge *Cyperus fastigiatus* culm damaged by ungulate trampling.
Aa Extant snap-broken ends from trampling: side view of a culm specimen with evidence of two episodes of trampling. The right end (the thicker end) shows a recent break (also see Figure 33.4Ab) and the left end shows an earlier snap-break, with the partial collapse of its cortex over deteriorated peripheral pith (also see Figure 33.4Ac). The specimen was floating in a net of aquatic grass *Odontelytrum abyssinicum* and has been partially invaded by its roots (one visible as white near mid-center of image, also see Figure 33.7). Scale bar 4 mm.
Ab End view of the right snap-break in Figure 33.4Aa. This is a relatively fresh break, with comparatively clean exposed pith. Scale bar 1 mm.
Ac End view of the left snap-break in Figure 33.4Aa. This is an older break, with a collapsed rim of cortex over deteriorated peripheral pith. Scale bar 1 mm.
B Extant crimp (transverse fold) caused by trampling. Scale bar 4 mm.
C Extant mold (concave depression and deformation) formed by a culm trampled onto this one. Scale bar 4 mm.

Micro-ridging

This is the first stage of subaerial weathering in this species. The senescing or newly dead standing culm is sun/wind air-dried and is turning from green to tan in color. In contrast to the smooth appearance of the live green culm, the surface of the drying culm is finely ridged and shallowly micro-grooved lengthways (Figure 33.5A), with a relief of *ca.* (5) 10–20 (30) µm. The second stage of subaerial weathering shows threadbare surficial micro-ridges. The portion (side or triangular edge) of the culm in this stage is light brown, to gray, in color. The surface has lost its luster and appears "threadbare" (Figure 33.5Ba). The epidermal cells have collapsed. Amorphous remnants of epidermis are draped over the fiber strands, revealing in outline the underlying individual fiber cells (Figure 33.5Bb). In advanced stage two weathering, open cracks develop (some as wide as *ca.* 20 µm) in the troughs between the exposed fiber strands.

Disintegration of the Outer and Inner Cortex

In the third stage of subaerial weathering the culm is dull gray in color. The outer cortex, namely the epidermis and the outer chlorenchyma between the fiber strands, has decomposed into an amorphous surface layer *ca.* 1–2 µm thick. The exposed fiber strands break, the broken ends disintegrate while the strands exfoliate in long strips individually, or as plates a few fiber strands in width, up to *ca.* 8 mm long (Figure 33.5C).

The fourth weathering stage is seen only in the open canopy of the standing dead, in untrampled clumps of sedge. The chlorenchyma has for the most part decomposed, and the peripheral vascular bundles at the chlorenchyma–pith interface are exposed. Rare chlorenchyma remnants composed of collapsed cells in isolated layers no more than *ca.* 20 µm thick are resting on (partially collapsed) pith. The surface appearance is now that of a dense field of partially broken up sclerenchyma (rigid, supporting tissue) strands *ca.* 25–100 µm in width, *ca.* 75–100 µm apart, with skins of amorphous collapsed chlorenchyma or well-defined pith cells in between (Figure 33.5D). Their constituent sclerenchyma cells are sometimes seen to be loosely tangled and bent, resembling the unbound wires of a broken multistrand cable.

We did not see a fifth stage of subaerial weathering. Pieces of weathered dead culm consisting primarily of exposed pith were not observed. By the second rainy season after death, and the fourth stage of subaerial weathering, the mid to upper sections of the destruction-resistant sedge culm are very brittle: few remain standing and most now form part of the waterlogged litter, disintegrating to the touch.

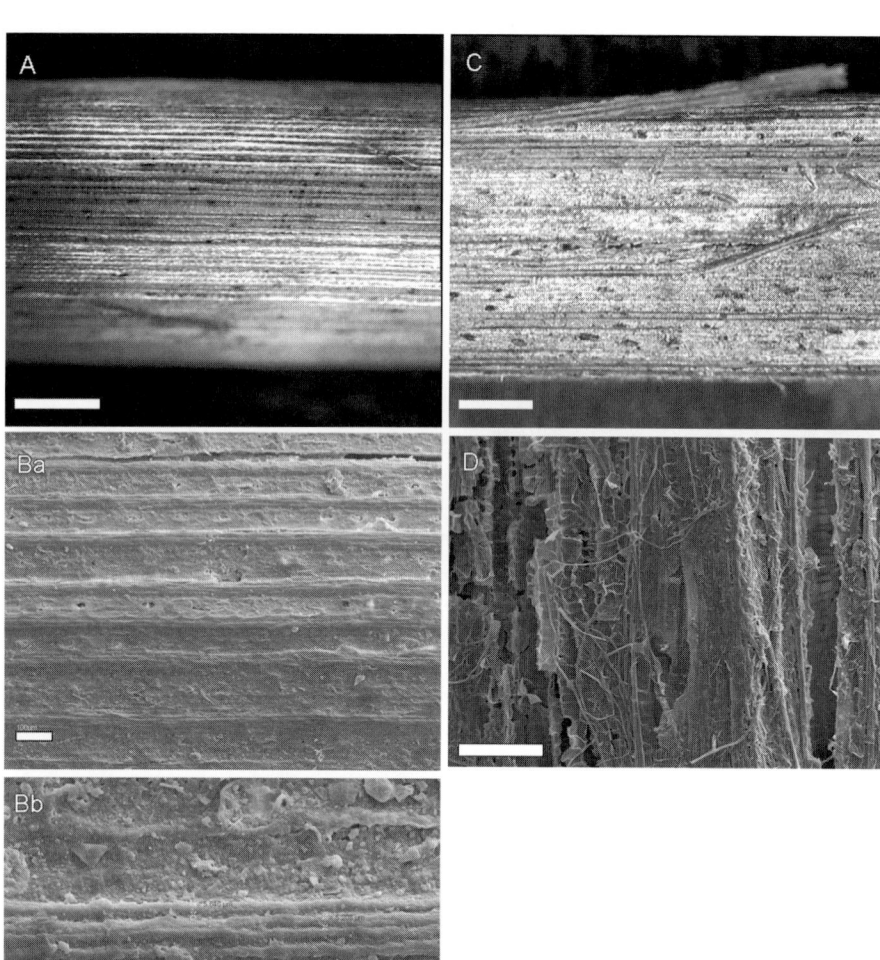

Figure 33.5 Extant sedge *Cyperus fastigiatus* culm damage from subaerial weathering.
A Extant micro-ridging of the culm epidermis. The first stage of subaerial weathering in this species. Optical micrograph. Scale bar 2 mm.
Ba Extant threadbare surficial micro-ridges. The second stage of subaerial weathering in this species. Due to subaerial weathering of the culm epidermis, the formerly subepidermal fiber strands are now exposed at the culm surface. These fiber strands are *ca*. 30–40 μm wide. Scanning electron micrograph. Scale bar 100 μm in length.
Bb Detail of one threadbare fiber strand with some of its individual fiber cells visible. The individual long cells are *ca*. 5.2–5.6 μm wide. Scanning electron micrograph. Scale bar 20 μm in length.
C Extant disintegration of the outer cortex of the culm in subaerial conditions. The third stage of subaerial weathering in this species. The exposed fiber strands break up and exfoliate individually and as plates. The formerly underlying chlorenchyma is now exposed as a weathered amorphous surface. Optical micrograph. Scale bar 2 mm.
D Extant disintegration of the inner cortex of the culm in subaerial conditions. The fourth stage of subaerial weathering in this species. The inner cortex of chlorenchyma and the vascular bundles at the cortex–pith interface have decomposed. The destruction-resistant vascular-bundle sclerenchyma sheaths can be seen as cable-like strands and wire-like individual sclerenchyma cells, which are resting on amorphous collapsed chlorenchyma and outer pith. Image in vertical orientation, side view. Scanning electron micrograph. Scale bar 200 μm in length.

Other forms of weathering occur under a combination of subaerial and subaqueous conditions, as described previously (snap-broken ends) and below.

Cortical Sheet-Peeling

In some cases, a skin of cortex exhibits longitudinal blisters, or has peeled away from the underlying pith as a sheet, leaving the culm surface with exposed pith, ridged by vascular bundles. Prostrate culms lying on bare ground, subject to floodwater, alternating with dry unprotected conditions, sometimes exhibit well-developed sheet-peeling (Figure 33.6A). In some instances, the cortex alone has peeled away, along the chlorenchyma–pith interface, or the cortex plus *ca*. 200–400 μm of the outer pith has peeled away as one skin-like unit, along an outer ring of large vascular bundles or between the two most peripheral rings of vascular bundles in the outer pith.

Surface Micro-Wrinkling

The incipient signature of damage to the lower portion of the culm is caused by standing in water during the rainy season, experiencing alternating subaqueous and subaerial conditions around the water line (Figure 33.6B). This micro-wrinkling was only discernible using a hand lens (10×) after experience finding it with binocular microscopy (40×).

Shriveled, Convoluted, and Collapsed Basal Culm

Culms standing dead in water during most of the rainy season rot at the base below the water line. The waterlogged shell and remnant central vascular bundles are fragile, and the standing culm is easily torn away at the base: undisturbed, the clump of living and dead culms helps support the more rotten cohort.

The exterior surface of the lower culm experiences alternating subaqueous and subaerial weathering as the water line moves up and down, while the interior of the base (the pith) remains waterlogged for the most part. As a result, the parenchyma (cellular tissue) of the pith disintegrates and the interior of the culm becomes hollow except for loose remains of the ground-mass vascular bundles. The lowermost culm is now primarily a shell of inner cortex, held together by the chlorenchyma, collenchyma (supporting cells) bundles, and the chlorenchyma–pith interface vascular bundles. The chlorenchyma–pith interface vascular bundles form the interior surface of the cortical shell. Our field observations suggest that when the torn away culm dries, the flaccid basal shell shrivels

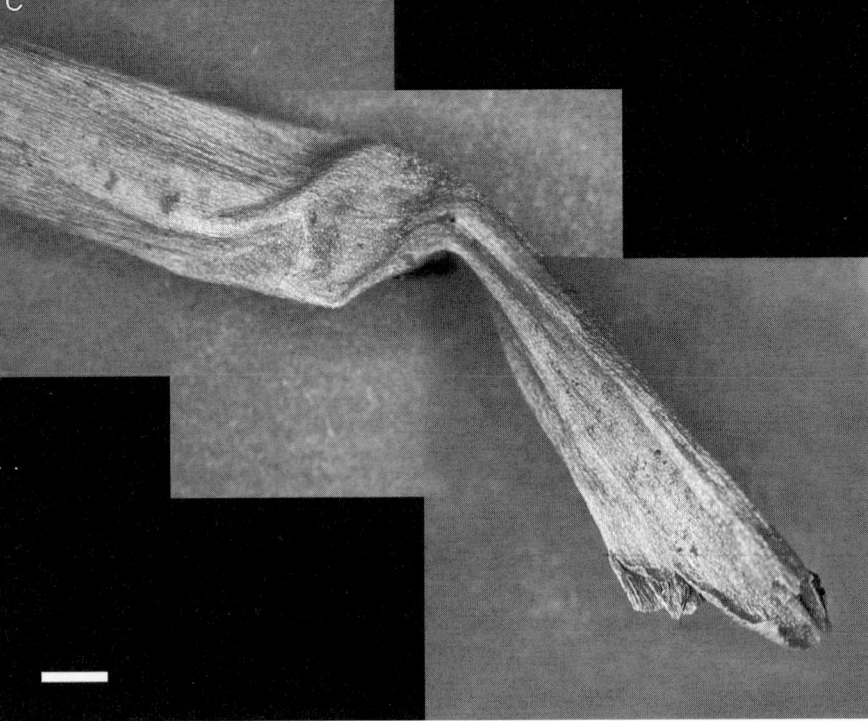

Figure 33.6 Extant sedge *Cyperus fastigiatus* culm damage from alternating subaqueous and subaerial conditions.
A Extant cortical sheet-peeling in a prostrate culm (partly trampled) lying on bare ground subject to alternating floodwater and dry conditions. Optical micrograph. Scale bar 4 mm.
B Extant micro-wrinkling of the cortex at the alternating wet–dry water line on a standing culm in flood season. Optical micrograph. Scale bar 1 mm.
C Extant shriveled, convoluted, and collapsed basal culm torn away and dried out, after standing dead with pith rotted away in shallow floodwater. Composite optical micrograph. Scale bar 2 mm.

and creases along its axis, resembling a twisted ribbon at the torn end (Figure 33.6C). This process occurs in the flood basin even in relatively dry years where there is long-standing rainwater: in drought years there is an absence of standing water. In wet years with high floods, it also occurs along the edge of the oxbow channel, and on the higher ground of the floodplain.

Aquatic Rootlet Invasion

Subaqueous invasion of aquatic rootlets into pieces of *C. fastigiatus* culm (Figure 33.7, also see Figure 33.4Aa) occurs in flooded *Odontelytrum* pasture. The aquatic grass *Odontelytrum* has long, soft (spongy), stolon-like stems that float in the seasonal floodwaters and produce masses of fleece-like floating rootlets from their nodes. These rootlets invade the destruction-resistant broken pieces of dead sedge culm that become trapped in the grass.

Uncommon Forms of Microdamage

These were round to oval borings; torn-open sections of culm; and cone-shaped micro-excavation. These probably reflect invertebrate and bird activity (Supplementary Information).

Figure 33.7 Extant aquatic rootlet invasion of a snap-broken segment of *Cyperus fastigiatus* culm. The adhering floating roots are of *Odontelytrum abyssinicum*. Broken sedge culm segments float into (and are trapped by) the floating stems of the aquatic grass whose rootlets then invade the litter. Optical micrograph. Scale bar 1 mm.

Table 33.2 Inferred pre-burial taphonomy of Olduvai Gorge fossil sedge culm-species X: taphonomic features, interpretations of causal agents/processes, and supporting notes. (The interpretations are based for the most part on the neotaphonomy summarized in Table 33.1.)

Taphonomic features	Interpretation of causal agents/processes	Supporting notes
Segment-like broken pieces of culm in-the-round a few centimeters long with transverse end-breaks	*Snap-broken* dead dry culms: breakage due to trampling	The comparatively short lengths of the pieces suggest multiple trampling
Transverse creases and abrupt bends in the culm specimens	*Crimping* of the green culm, or the least brittle (lower) portion of the recently dead culm, by trampling	Recognized from broken halves, which is consistent with neotaphonomic observations that modern pieces are very fragile after they dry, easily broken at the crimp
Transverse concave and U-shaped depressions a few millimeters wide in the culm specimens	*Molding* from trampling of one green culm onto and into another	Commonly seen in fossils of medium width, suggesting it occurred to green culms well into the wet season
Shallow, broad, longitudinal furrows across the surface of the culm: imperfectly correlated with the air cavities of the innermost cortex	*Micro-fluting* of the outer cortex due to drying out of the senescing culm: the first stage of subaerial weathering in this species	Also seen to be present under partially broken away sheath leaf, but not always, or at least not well-developed under some of them
The chlorenchyma can be seen over the majority of the surface on one or more sides of the culm specimen: the outer cortex of the culm (the epidermis/hypodermis) has been lost	*Disintegration of the outer cortex* from continued exposure of the dead culm to subaerial conditions: the second stage of subaerial weathering in this species	Remnant small lumps of cemented Lower Bed II earthy clay sediment covering parts of the chlorenchyma indicate this weathering occurred prior to paleo-burial in mud
The air cavities of the innermost cortex are exposed at the surface of the culm: the chlorenchyma has been lost	*Disintegration of the inner cortex* from extended (more than one dry season?) exposure of the dead culm to subaerial conditions: the third stage of subaerial weathering in this species	Lower Bed II earthy clay sediment infill of the cortical air cavities indicates this weathering occurred prior to paleo-burial in mud
In some specimens with a node, the culm surfaces below the node show more deterioration of the cortex than the culm surfaces above the node	*Greater subaerial weathering below the node vs. above it*, due to the (temporary) presence of the base of the sheath leaf above the node, and an absence of sheath leaf immediately below the node	In extant sedge species the sheath leaf grows upwards from its base around the node; the upper part of the leaf is subsequently lost in weathering before the base of the leaf breaks away from the node
One end of the culm specimen is collapsed, folded, and twisted in shape	*Shriveled, convoluted, and collapsed section of culm* wherein the parenchyma of the pith rotted away and a shell of cortex remained: due to rotting below the waterline in the standing dead, followed by tearing away of the culm and convolution of the flaccid end	In the modern analog the curlicued torn ends of the culm distinguish this form of subaqueous pith-rot from the rot of prostrate pieces in shallow water

3. Micro-Scale Taphonomy of Olduvai Gorge Fossil Culm-Species X

Fossil Sedge Culm Tissue Anatomy

The largest pieces of culm-species X in the Olduvai Gorge sample are broken segments *ca.* 31 mm long. Preserved in the round, intact widths that range from *ca.* 3 to 9 mm (like *C. fastigiatus* at Seekoeivlei). Unlike that extant species, the sheath leaves of the fossil species are thick, providing some protection from weathering. The basic architecture of culm-species X is that of an obtusely to triangular-shaped stem, mostly composed of pith a few millimeters wide surrounded by a cortex a few micrometers thick. None of its tissue types are unique (cf. Metcalfe, 1971), but together they form a distinctive morphotype (Appendix B). It is the common sedge morphotype represented in the macro-fossil botanical material from the Lower Bed II earthy clay deposits at Olduvai Gorge.

Pre-Burial Taphonomy

We infer the pre-burial taphonomy of Olduvai Gorge fossil sedge culm-species X, based on the neotaphonomy of the extant sedge *C. fastigiatus* in the Seekoeivlei Nature Reserve (Table 33.2). The three main signs of trampling prior to burial (snap-breaking, crimping, and pressure molding of the culm) are present in the Olduvai fossil species X. This trampling suggests the importance of this seasonal wetland as a pasture. Taken together with the evidence of cortical weathering and pith rot, we see taphonomic features probably from the end of the wet season near the time of herbaceous plant dieback, the first dry season after annual dieback, and the first wet season with standing water after that. These are cumulative stages of seasonal cohort death history, one or more of which are seen in individual specimens, and illustrated in the following sections. Additional destruction stages are not identified, presumably because tissue integrity was lost with further pre-burial disintegration.

Snap-Broken Culm Pieces

These specimens have the three sides present for the most part, confirming the original breaks were end-breaks. The maximum length is *ca.* 3 cm. In some cases, the original transverse snap-breaks are preserved, but often, recent damage has caused jagged ends. Smoothly curved end-breaks are also seen in the Olduvai fossil sedge material, and some of these may be post-fossilization pressure breaks (see Supplementary Information). The comparatively short lengths of the specimens may be due to a combination of multiple trampling, which in living systems can be common in the dry season, and post-fossilization breakage. Figure 33.8Aa and 8Ab illustrate a relatively well-preserved fossilized snap-break on a segment-like piece of culm, which compares well with trampling damage observed on extant sedge *C. fastigiatus* (Figure 33.4Aa and 4Ab).

Crimping

No full crimping was preserved intact: only a portion of the "left" or "right" half of the fossilized crimp is seen in broken ends, sometimes including sheath leaf (e.g., Figure 33.8B, compared with Figure 33.4B). This agrees with Seekoeivlei observations that the transverse folds resulting from trampling of green culms are vulnerable to breakage after drying. For the fossils, portions of the preserved abrupt bends at broken ends were recognized at low magnifications and confirmed with SEM. Overall, transverse creases and the broken remnants of crimping are well represented in the fossils. Shallow, longitudinal creases and folds are also seen in the fossils, related to partial collapse of underlying air cavities, also consistent with pre-burial trampling.

Molding

Transverse concave and U-shaped depressions with preserved green-bends are seen in the fossil specimens. Recently broken specimens show fossilized bent subsurface tissue consistent with trampling of these culms, when they were green, crosswise on one another. Figure 33.8C shows a fossil specimen with multiple recent breaks and only remnants of epidermis, but with a well-preserved molded profile, and the breakage reveals the bent cortical air-cavity vascular-bundle walls underlying the depression. In the extant sedge, the concave bend of the underlying tissue can be seen surficially after the culm dries out and the weathered epidermis drapes the immediately subepidermal fiber strands (Figure 33.4C). While the fossil and the extant sedge tissues differ somewhat, the green bending process appears similar.

Micro-Fluting of the Outer Cortex

This was the first stage of subaerial weathering of the culm in this species. Fossilized micro-fluting is seen across the epidermal surfaces and across the surfaces of broadly exposed chlorenchyma in initial stage two subaerial weathering (e.g., Figure 33.8Aa). It is generally correlated with the spacing of the air cavities of the innermost cortex, and the fluting is amplified with partial accordion-like deformation of these underlying air cavities (Figure 33.8Ab).

Disintegration of the Outer and Inner Cortex

This was the second stage of subaerial weathering in this species. The chlorenchyma is exposed as the surface on one or more sides of the fossil culm specimens. This inferred weathering stage is judged to have occurred prior to paleo-burial based on cemented remnants of paleo-mud covering parts of the exposed chlorenchyma (e.g., Figure 33.9Aa and 9Ab). Typically, the loss of the epidermis means the hypodermis is gone also; thus, broad areas of hypodermis are not exposed. If hypodermis is exposed, it is generally at the edge of remaining epidermis, or as a remnant narrow band next to a node, suggesting that both layers were lost as one tissue. This probably occurred in the dry season after the culm's death, and continued after trampling of the culm, especially on the most exposed (upward-facing) sides.

The third stage of subaerial weathering is the disintegration of the inner cortex, where previously exposed inner cortex of chlorenchyma is lost, exposing the underlying air cavities (e.g., the left side of Figure 33.9Ba). This stage is judged to have occurred prior to burial, inferred from the paleo-mud infill of the cortical air cavities (Figure 33.9Bb). The loss of the chlorenchyma layer happened progressively. This can be seen on

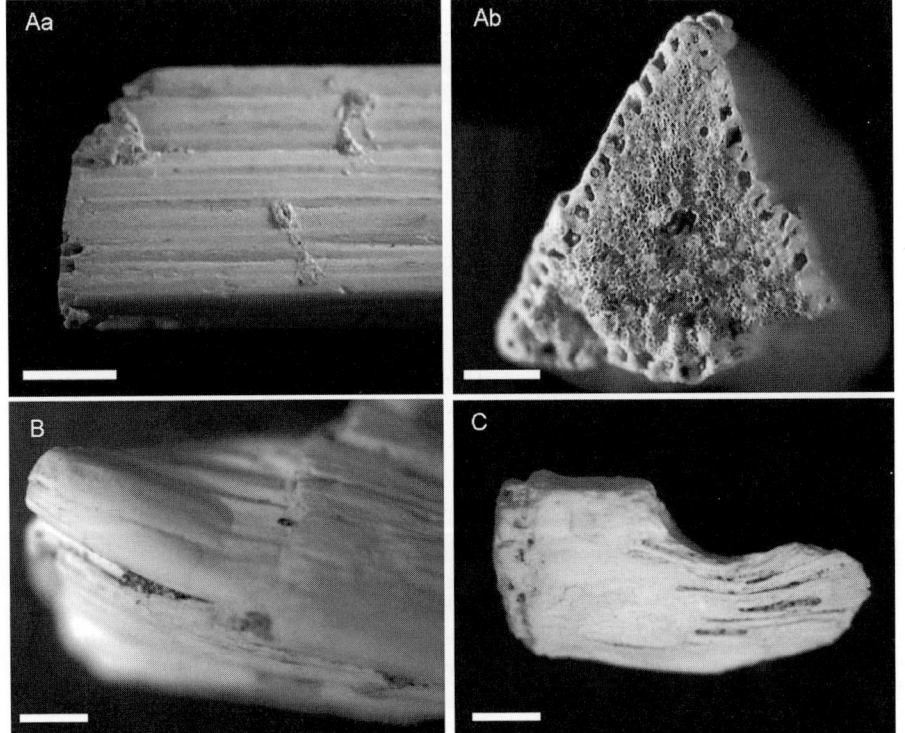

Figure 33.8 Optical micrographs of fossil sedge, Olduvai Gorge culm-species X damage interpreted as pre-fossilization trampling.
Aa Fossilized snap-break: side view of culm specimen. Note micro-flutes along the culm surface. Scale bar 4 mm.
Ab Fossilized snap-break: end view of culm specimen seen in Figure 33.8Aa. Scale bar 2 mm.
B Broken fossilized crimp, with an associated crease in the culm preserved under (now broken away) sheath leaf. Scale bar 1 mm.
C Fossilized U-shaped mold in a culm specimen, with recent breakage exposing the underlying fossilized bent cortical air cavity walls along one side of the culm. Scale bar 2 mm.

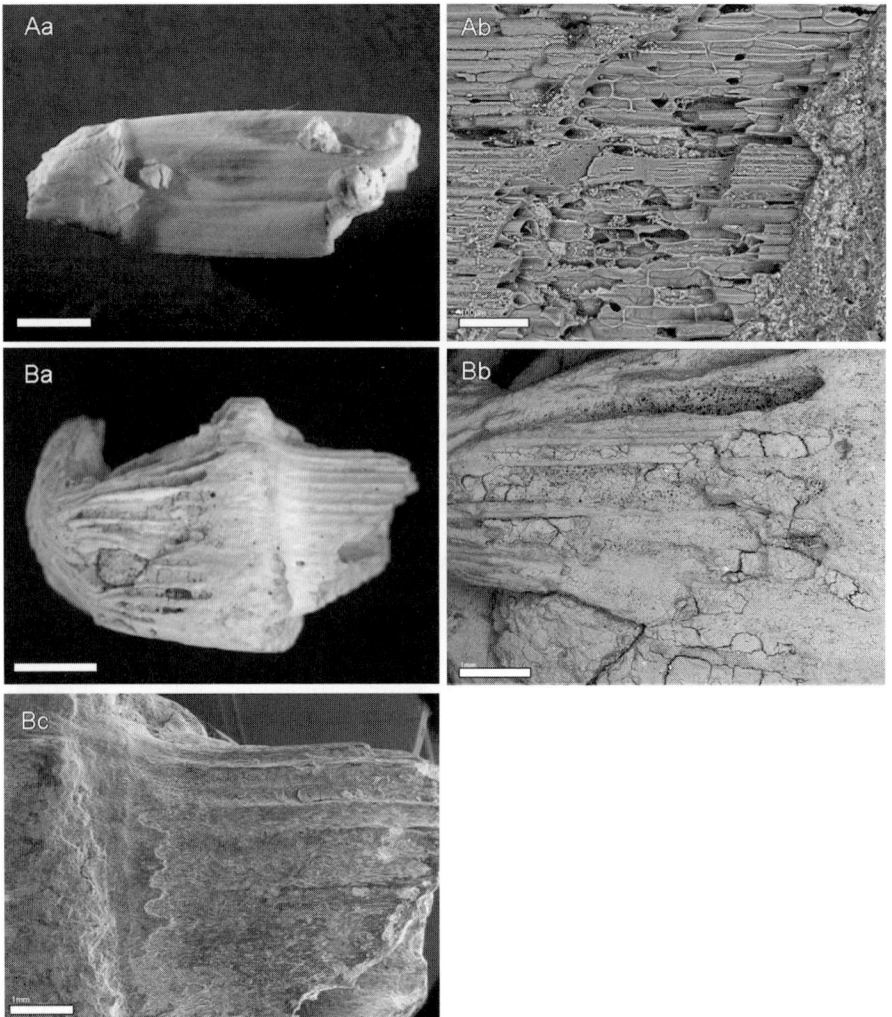

Figure 33.9 Fossil sedge, Olduvai Gorge culm-species X damage interpreted as pre-fossilization subaerial weathering.
Aa Fossil culm specimen with small mounds of paleo-mud adhering to its weathered surface of exposed inner cortex (chlorenchyma). Part of the mound of paleo-mud in the upper right of the image was removed to confirm that the immediately underlying tissue was chlorenchyma and not outer cortex (see Figure 33.9Ab). Optical micrograph. Scale bar 3 mm.
Ab Fossilized inner cortex of chlorenchyma originally exposed by disintegration of the outer cortex in subaerial weathering before burial in mud. Laboratory removal of a piece of the adhering paleo-mud confirmed, as seen here, that the fossilized culm surface was mud-covered chlorenchyma. The experimentally broken edge of the paleo-mud can be seen at the right of the image. Scanning electron micrograph. Scale bar 100 μm in length.
Ba Fossilized culm specimen with a node. Below node portion is to the left, with a curled end. Above node portion, smaller in width, with a recently broken end, is to the right. On the left side of the image (i.e., below the node) the air cavities of the innermost cortex were originally exposed by disintegration of the overlying chlorenchyma in subaerial weathering before burial in mud and fossilization. Some of the paleo-mud infill was removed in the laboratory to expose the air cavity walls. Optical micrograph. Scale bar 4 mm in length.
Bb Detail of the below-the-node surface of the fossil culm specimen seen in Figure 33.9Ba (left side of that image). The air cavity walls and paleo-mud infill are highlighted. Scanning electron micrograph. Scale bar 1 mm.
Bc Enlargement of the above-the-node portion of the fossil culm specimen seen in Figure 33.9Ba (right side of image). The surface has a scallop-shaped remnant of outer cortex preserved near the shelf of the node to the left. To the right is chlorenchyma, more deeply weathered progressing to the right, away from the node. There are also patches of paleo-mud covering parts of this chlorenchyma. Scanning electron micrograph in secondary electron mode. Scale bar 1 mm.

different specimens with inner, versus outer, chlorenchyma exposed, and on single specimens where adjacent parts of the same surface show inner, versus outer, chlorenchyma (e.g., Figure 33.9Bc). The inner chlorenchyma is distinguished by fiber strands (ridges in Figure 33.9Bc), and shorter cells.

Chlorenchyma deterioration is sometimes more advanced on one side of the fossil culm, suggesting that it was leaning over, or that some of the weathering occurred on snap-broken pieces resting one side up on the ground. Once the inner chlorenchyma disintegrated, the underlying cortical air cavities were exposed.

These large air cavities may have then persisted for some time (exposed to weathering), because of the destruction-resistant side walls that lie between them.

Lack of Further Subaerial Weathering

No fossil specimen with all cortex lost (pith only) was observed, which probably reflects the vulnerability of pith parenchyma to rot under prolonged aerobic waterlogging (as discussed in the neotaphonomy section). In a few fossil specimens the walls of the cortical air cavities are lost on a portion (usually one side) of the specimen. This damage may reflect recent erosional exposure at Olduvai Gorge, because none of these surfaces show sediment covering.

Weathering Below Nodes

Some fossil specimens with a node show greater subaerial weathering below the node compared to above it, with chlorenchyma lost and cortical air cavities exposed below the node only (e.g., Figure 33.9Ba and 9Bc). This is seen in specimens with Lower Bed II earthy clay sediment infill, which show adhering patches of cemented earthy clay sediment. The interpretation is therefore that, prior to burial, the culm immediately above the node was protected for some time by the base of its sheath leaf, which was subsequently lost. Consistent with this are specimens showing a progression above the node from more intact cortex nearest the node to less intact cortex away from the node (e.g., Figure 33.9Bc). This pattern may have been the result of a fine-scale subaerial weathering front proceeding down the culm toward the node, in relation to deterioration and loss of the sheath leaf.

Partly Shriveled and Collapsed Specimens

Signs of waterlogged pith rot at one end of specimen are seen in the Olduvai fossils (e.g., Figure 33.10). At Seekoeivlei, this type of damage occurs when a lower portion of an upright dead culm rots in standing seasonal water and the upper portion of the culm is subsequently torn away, with part of the rotten end. Large grazers likely visited the Olduvai paleo-wetlands and tore up the vegetation while grazing.

Figure 33.10 Fossilized shriveled and convoluted fossil culm where the pith had rotted away, leaving cortex shell. Optical micrograph. Fossil sedge, Olduvai Gorge culm-species X. Scale bar 2 mm.

Inferred Seasonality of the Paleo-Marshland

Neotaphonomic observations indicate that in modern seasonal wetlands, a diversity of taphonomic processes mark the annual-death cohort of the destruction-resistant sedge. The process of ubiquitous rotting that occurs in continuously waterlogged conditions is repeatedly suspended in the seasonal wetland, and trampling, progressive subaerial weathering, and partial pith rot create an accumulating mixture of characteristic taphonomic signs. Similar signs are evident in the Olduvai fossil sedge culms, indicating that the paleo-marshland was a seasonal wetland, without perennial standing water.

Pre-Burial Neotaphonomic Type Features Not Observed in the Fossil Sample

Not all the features associated with waterlogging and pith-rot seen in the extant species at Seekoeivlei are observed in the Olduvai fossils. The lack of culm micro-wrinkling, cortical sheet-peeling, and contraction of snap-broken ends may reflect a combination of differences in tissue anatomy, lack of preservation, and sampling of different parts of the wetland. Possible aqueous rootlet invasion in the Olduvai specimens prior to their burial is problematic. It is confounded by what was apparently rootlet invasion after shallow burial in mud (see below). This also complicates judgments about the presence of possible insect holes in the surfaces of the culms because they may have been invaded by those rootlets. Fossilized hollowed-out sections of pith are seen, however, like that of extant insect damage. Signs of bird damage from extracting insects from inside extant culms are lacking in the fossil assemblage. Other forms of possible invertebrate damage to the culm cortex are not seen in the fossils. Recent breakage and disintegration of the surfaces of the fossil specimens may have destroyed evidence for this type of damage, but a larger sample may clarify this in future.

Rootlets in the Culm Pieces

Fossilized rootlet remains are commonly present in culm specimens and in patches of adhering (cemented) earthy clay sediment and are *ca*. 85 μm to 1.5 mm in diameter. They are seen primarily in the form of cell walls of root cortex, in side views of the rootlet cylinder (Figure 33.11Aa and 11Ab). Oval to round holes through the culm cortex, and sometimes completely through the pith, also show traces of these rootlets (Figure 33.11Ba and 11 Bb). Sometimes the culm tissues near the edges of the holes are deformed, curved as in a green bend (Figure 33.11Bb). Fracture lines do not emanate from the holes in the fossil plant tissues nor in adhering indurated paleo-sediment, suggesting that the rootlets invaded the specimens prior to fossilization. These rootlets may have invaded the culm litter in seasonal shallow water (as seen at Seekoeivlei), and/or after shallow burial in mud. Modern bank edges of oxbow ponds or abandoned channels offer a microenvironment with abundant rootlets, and potential shallow burial in mud. The fossil rootlets were present in weathered, but not rotten, culm tissue. This indicates that aerobic waterlogged conditions in shallow mud did not persist long enough for the culm pieces to rot and that potentially deeper burial and fossilization proceeded quickly.

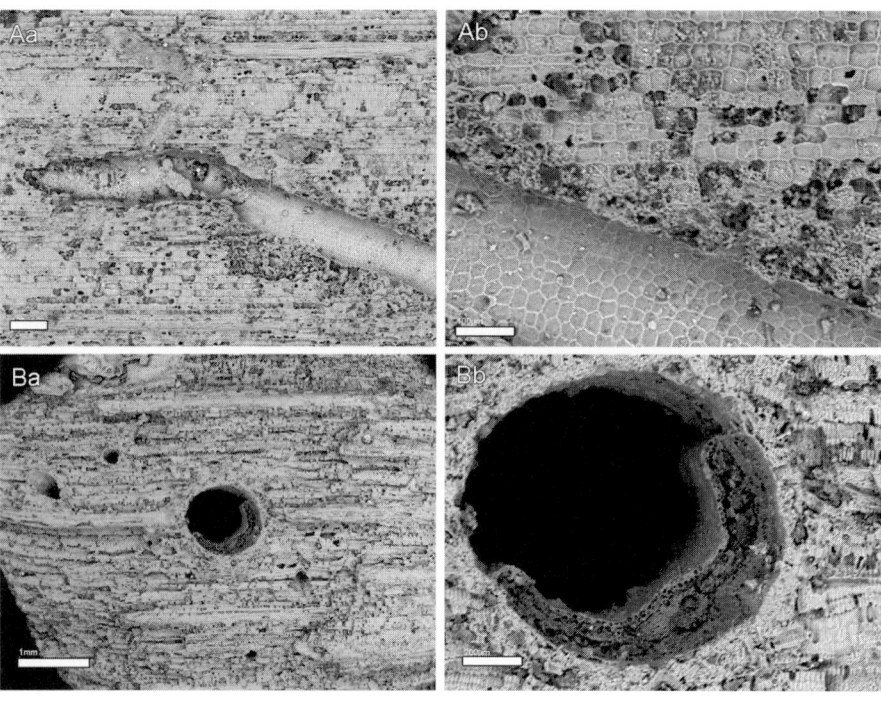

Figure 33.11 Fossilized invasive rootlets in fossil sedge, Olduvai Gorge culm-species X, the invasions interpreted as occurring prior to, or during, early burial of the culm.
Aa Fossilized invasive rootlet into culm inner chlorenchyma. Scanning electron micrograph. Scale bar 200 μm in length.
Ab Detail of the right side of Figure 33.11Aa showing the fossilized cell walls of the rootlet cortex (lower) and the culm chlorenchyma (upper). Scale bar 100 μm in length.
Ba Fossilized rootlet hole 1.145 mm wide (center of image) in culm pith. Scanning electron micrograph. Scale bar 1 mm.
Bb Detail of fossilized collapsed rootlet in the hole in Figure 33.11Ba. Also note fossilized deformation (splaying) of the immediately adjacent cellular tissue (pith) can be seen on the right. Scale bar 200 μm in length.

Post-Fossilization Damage

Post-fossilization *in situ* damage, and recent damage with modern erosional exposure, are also seen on the specimens of culm-species X (see Supplementary Information).

Discussion

Implications of the Paleo-Marsh Seasonal Wetland for Hominin Scavenging Strategies

The seasonal aspect for the paleo-marshland is crucial for understanding its significance to the grazer/predator community, and for landscape models of hominin foraging. Seasonal marshes differ from perennial marshes in that they do not offer refuge for grazers in drought years (Western, 1997; Peters et al., 2008), and they do not offer an abundance of edible C_4 rootstocks, such as *C. papyrus* (Peters and Vogel, 2005).

Here we recast the previous interpretations of the Olduvai Basin landscape ecology and hominin foraging patterns during Lower Bed II times (Hay, 1976, 1996; Peters and Blumenschine, 1995, 1996; Supplementary Information). Some suggested revisions to those models, for future model building, are presented below, including the seasonal earthy clay marshland at Olduvai, and possible tests of contrasting theoretical views of hominin scavenging capabilities/strategies more broadly in the landscape context of seasonal marshland. As recognized in earlier models, the local climate in the paleo-Olduvai basin was mainly influenced by the rain shadow caused by the volcanic highlands capturing most of the monsoon rain coming from the east. Directly east of the lake in Lower Bed II times, the poorly developed and apparently sparsely vegetated volcaniclastic alluvial fan soils noted by Hay (1976) are consistent with this rain shadow effect.

During the rainy season, mountain top cloud capture and resulting precipitation on the uppermost west-facing slopes of Mt. Olmoti (the volcano east of the lake) would have created stream flow down the western side of this highland, as it does today (Figure 33.1). The strongest storms could have generated flash flooding in the streams crossing the alluvial fans, inundating the earthy clay marshland where the fan topographic gradient was at its lowest. Small stream courses would have likely entered the east side of saline–alkaline Lake Olduvai.

The western side of the lake would have been even drier, likely with bush or scrubland. The Serengeti ecosystem did not exist at that time (Peters et al., 2008). Hominins would have inhabited the eastern basin during times when it was habitable.[4] There the hominins would have encountered two pasture lands and opportunities for scavenging. The remainder of our discussion will be limited to activities of scavenging hominins, defined in more detail below, while recognizing that they were probably also fruit- and root-eating foragers.

The lacustrine shoreline would have provided pasture. By analogy with modern saline–alkaline lakes in east Africa, the lower part of the beach and seasonally exposed mud flats would have been unvegetated, with a relatively narrow strip of pasture, a few to several meters wide, parallel to the shoreline along the upper beach. Usually only one, sometimes two, halophytic (salt-tolerant) grass species make up this pasture in extant ecosystems.

---

4 From a metapopulation point-of-view the Olduvai Basin was probably a demographic sink, the demographic source population, or subregional heartland, lying on the eastern, ecologically richer, monsoonal side of the Crater Highlands (Peters and Blumenschine, 1995, 1996; also see Peters, 2007).

Sporobolus spicatus is the most common (e.g., Capaldo and Peters, 1995). These grasses are low-growing, forming a ground surface mat, and able to withstand intensive grazing.

From a hominin standpoint, this shoreline pasture would have offered good visibility. Carnivores entering the pasture nearby from the bush or woodland above the upper beach would be visible, and the hominins could avoid them due to limitations in weaponry and defensive/offensive behavior (Blumenschine and Peters, 1998). Blumenschine and Pobiner (2007) describe this as "passive scavenging." Earlier, Binford (1983), in the context of Bed I Olduvai, used the phrase "marginal scavenger." In the Blumenschine and Peters models, these hominins were scavenging carcasses from which the bulk of readily accessible flesh and bone marrow were previously consumed.

This scenario contrasts with Bunn's (2007) concept of the "power scavenging" hominin. Theoretically, this scavenging hominin would be able to confront large carnivores at kill sites along the lakeshore and regularly carry away more of the fleshy, bone marrow-rich limbs of prey. This scenario suggests that hominins likely possessed carrying devices with an ample supply of stones for use as missiles in these confrontations. Perhaps the power scavenger would consume some of the kill at the site, abandoning some stone tools or flaking debris, but would still require transport of carcass parts to nearby trees due to safety considerations and potentially to share the kill with the rest of the social group.

What can the identification of the earthy clay marshland contribute to the conceptual and predictive implications of these contrasting hypotheses about hominin scavenging? Located a short distance inland from the lakeshore, the earthy clay marsh was a separate, second pastureland, based on circumstantial evidence of the sedge taphonomy, and on the importance of marshy seasonal wetlands for a diversity of wild grazers and domestic stock in modern Africa ecosystems (e.g., Hughes and Hughes, 1992). The earthy clay paleo-marsh was probably heterogeneous, and due to annual variation in the shallow, temporary, stream–floodwater regime and minor variations in topography (e.g., buffalo wallows) would have supported high sedge and grass diversity. In the wet season one could expect to see both sward-forming and tufted species, as well as semiprostrate species with floating foliage or stolons. Adding to this heterogeneity would be clumps or patches of the taller sedges and grasses, plus *Typha* (cattail/reedmace). Compared to the lakeshore grassland, this seasonal marsh would have offered a diversity of productive pasture, and possibly drawn a denser, greater variety of grazers in a seasonal grazing succession. These are possibilities for future model building.

Other critical considerations for the hominin scavenger models are limited (vegetation-interrupted) visibility and impeded bipedal locomotion that we experience in these marshlands, and the presence of a variety of predators. This type of marsh would offer concealment and ambush hunting opportunities to early Pleistocene large felids, as has been observed for lion prides in the marshy areas of Masai Mara (Jackman and Scott, 1983). The early Pleistocene and Olduvai basin would have hosted lions and other carnivorans, including crocodiles (Peters et al., 2008). True and false saber-toothed cats were also present in east Africa at that time, and it is likely they were capable of hunting in marshland.

Carefully considered, there is nothing in the marginal scavenger model that would unequivocally consign those hominins to this part of the landscape, not even for wetland rootstock or seed foraging. It may be that any archeological evidence for hominin use of the earthy clay marsh would, on the face of it, favor the power scavenger model. Hominins would also benefit from plausibly associated plant-food foraging (Peters, 2007), which would increase the hominin C_3 dietary signature with plant foods common in seasonal wetlands (cf. Peters et al., 1992, with Peters and Vogel, 2005, e.g., *Typha*, wild rice, water lilies).[5]

Based on current evidence, hominins probably seasonally abandoned the basin, given its small size, its location in a rain shadow, the local aridity created by Mt. Olmoti (Peters and Blumenshine, 1995), and the compounded dry season problems of deteriorating surface freshwater quality and scarcity (e.g., Peters and Blumenschine, 1996). The stratigraphic sequence in the clay deposits of Lower Bed II indicate an alternating geosuccession of earthy and waxy clays recorded by Hay (1996), implying that during extended periods of high lake levels both types of primary pasturelands at Olduvai were destroyed. Consequently, hominins may have been repeatedly forced to abandon the basin for several years at a time.

Conclusion

This research, as part of the Olduvai Landscape Paleoanthropology Project, was to redirect inquiry from a largely discovery-driven and inductive mode toward a science that builds models with testable implications that can be challenged by the paleo-record, starting with lowermost Bed II (Blumenschine and Masao, 1991). The project developed a three-stage conceptual view of inquiry. The first stage is that of building models of the landscape ecology of the paleo-lake basin, highlighting the foraging opportunities and hazards likely encountered by hominins based partly on modern analogs (Peters and Blumenschine, 1995, 1996). The models will naturally be revised considering new paleontological observations (recognition of the sedge fossils) and inferences based on modern African ecosystems (sedge size and taphonomy indicates seasonal wetland). The modern ecosystem is not assumed to be an exact analog of the Olduvai paleo-environment. Rather, it reveals the taphonomic character of the system (in this case the seasonal signs that mark sedge remains), which aids interpretation of the fossil sedges. Our results suggest that both the models of landscape ecology and hominin foraging (particularly scavenging) previously developed for Lower Bed II will need revision.

---

5   To clarify comments made in Peters (2007), cattails (*Typha*) and reeds (*Phragmites*), both seasonal wetland C_3 plants with edible rootstocks, are also found at the edges of perennial marsh, where they are not partially submerged in water year-round.

The second stage of inquiry is that of building predictive models of the paleo-landscape distribution and relative density of stone-tool and butchery-marked bone residues from hominin scavenging of carcasses (Blumenschine and Peters, 1998). The methodology is an integration of refined first-stage models of landscape eco-structure, functional interpretations of stone-tool technology, neotaphonomic studies of carcass availability and bone modification, plus postulates about hominin capabilities. The scavenging hominin assumed in the previously developed predictive models is an australopithecine-like *Homo habilis*. This aids in setting theoretically conservative limits on the scavenger's capabilities in comparison with a presumably more physically powerful and behaviorally capable *H. erectus*. In hindsight, this view of *H. habilis* may have been inappropriate (cf. Blumenschine et al., 2003), and at this stage, it is probably unnecessary to link the archeological models to a single hominin species. Methodologically, the model-building process may be better served by considering theoretically contrasting formulations of hominin scavenging capabilities, in the context of renewed paleo-environmental reconstructions.

These two stages of model building move the conceptualization of research from a pre-theoretic to an intuitive-theoretic level of development (*sensu* Pickett et al., 1994). One of the benefits of this is that model building helps make explicit the assumptions underlying our ecological understandings of the past, which is vital in a discipline where ideas and interpretations carry a good deal of uncertainty (Willig and Scheiner, 2011).

The third stage of inquiry for Lower Bed II is testing the models of scavenging against the archeological record, and this work lies in the future. Blumenschine and Peters (1998) point out that it will probably entail multiple cycles of ecological research, model building, and hypothesis testing. As a part of this process, our findings and their implications show the importance of carrying out new ecological and theoretical work independently of that anticipated archeological work intended to test previously formulated models.

In conclusion, this work has employed microscopic analysis to identify and reconstruct the elements of the taphonomy of a seasonal marshland pasture preserved in the Olduvai Lower Bed II. The research on the modern analog environment that was developed in the floodplain marsh of the seasonal wetland at Seekoeivlei Nature Reserve (South Africa) enabled us to identify taphonomic processes including trampling by ungulates, as well as a seasonal mixture of subaerial and subaqueous weathering. The results aid our understanding of the role of the Olduvai paleo-pasture, which we suggest would have provided hunting/scavenging opportunities during the seasonal grazing succession, and wetland plant foods at the end of the rains, before seasonal abandonment of the basin by the hominins.

Acknowledgments

We would like to thank Georg and Erla Wandrag (Seekoeivlei Nature Reserve) for their invaluable assistance. We are indebted to Clare Archer, Lynn Fish and Rene Glen at the national herbarium (PRE) in the South African National Botanical Institute in Pretoria, for plant identifications and to Stuart Sym (University of the Witwatersrand) for algae identifications. Spike McCarthy of the School of Geosciences, University of the Witwatersrand provided geological information and loaned the sediment corers we used at Seekoeivlei and in the Okavango Delta. James W. Morgenthaler assisted with the optical micrograph composite of the *C. fastigiatus* culm. Financial assistance was provided by the Anthropology Department of the University of Georgia to C.R.P. (as Professor Emeritus), and by the South African Palaeontology Scientific Trust (PAST), the National Research Foundation-Department of Science and Technology, and the University of the Witwatersrand to M.K.B. The Olduvai Gorge research was conducted as part of the Olduvai Landscape Paleoanthropology Project under Robert J. Blumenschine and Fidelis T. Masao. C.R.P. would like to acknowledge all the field botanists, ecologists, and anthropologists that facilitated his landscape reconnaissance program in Africa over 30 years.

Appendix A: Extant Sedge *Cyperus fastigiatus* Culm Tissue Anatomy

Outline (transverse view): culm subcircular at the base, becoming obtusely triangular upwards along the lower culm, progressing to acutely triangular at the mid to upper culm below the inflorescence. Sheath leaves from a single node at the base of the culm.

Maximum width (transverse to the long axis of the culm): 4–6 mm for the culm pieces (obtusely triangular to subcircular) utilized for the optical and scanning electron microscopy relied upon in this analysis. A transverse section through a culm is shown in Figure 33.A.1A and A.1B.

Surface of air-dried fresh culm shallowly micro-grooved lengthways: individual micro-grooves *ca.* (50) 75–100 (125) μm wide, with micro-ridges on each side and a ridge–groove relief of *ca.* (5) 10–20 (30) μm. The micro-ridges are imperfectly correlated with subepidermal fiber strands. Stomata, *ca.* 50 μm long, occur in a single (sometimes staggered) row in the furrows between the ridges. Laterally adjacent epidermal cells are united at the surface by toothed articulations of their outer (top) horizontal (periclinal) walls.

Cortex *ca.* (75) 100–175 (215) μm thick, composed of the epidermis, subepidermal fiber strands, and chlorenchyma with collenchyma bundles.

Epidermis: one to two cells thick: one cell thick over fiber strands, two cells thick otherwise. All the epidermal cells are *ca.* 10–15 μm wide. These cells are smaller over the fiber strands: here they are *ca.* 7–10 μm thick. Where two cells thick, the outer epidermal cells are long cells, *ca.* (40) 70–130 (max. 200?) μm long and *ca.* 10–20 μm thick. The inner epidermal cells are relatively short, about one half the length of the overlying cells.

Subepidermal fiber strands: *ca.* 25–50 μm wide and *ca.* 20–30 μm thick. They are located immediately below the epidermis and form a single ring, individual strands *ca.* (50) 115–145 μm apart. They are composed of long fiber cells *ca.* 5–7 μm in diameter, thick-walled with tapered ends.

Chlorenchyma: thin-walled polygonal cells *ca.* (10) 20–40 μm wide and *ca.* 30–60 μm long. They form a zone about 6–8 (10?) cells thick between the epidermis and the pith. Within

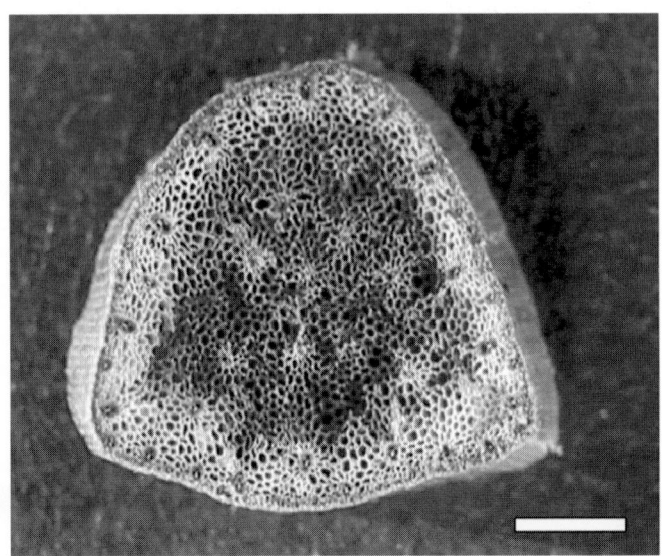

Figure 33.A.1A Transverse section of a culm showing the pith (honeycombed in appearance), and the culm perimeter of cortex. Optical micrograph. Extant sedge, *Cyperus fastigiatus*. Scale bar 2 mm in length.

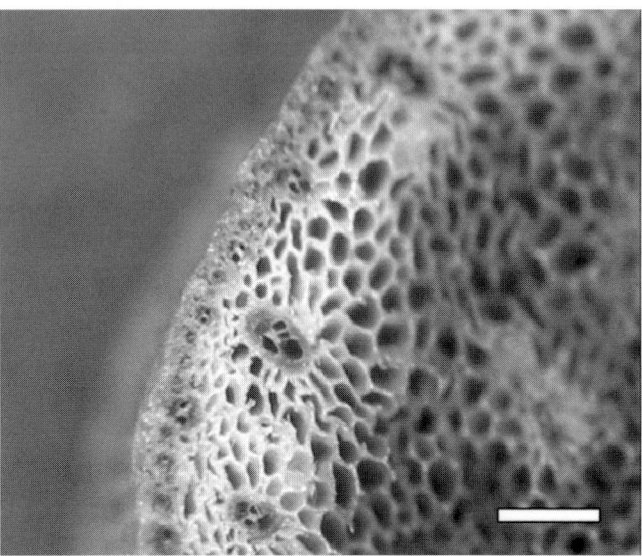

Figure 33.A.1B Outer portion of the culm in transverse section, showing large vascular bundles at the periphery of the pith, and smaller vascular bundles at the narrow cortex–pith interface. Optical micrograph. Extant sedge, *Cyperus fastigiatus*. Scale bar 0.5 mm in length.

this zone there are collenchyma bundles, each *ca.* 20–25 μm in diameter, spaced *ca.* 125–200 μm apart in a ring, each bundle surrounded by chlorenchyma.

Vascular bundles: thinly surrounded to well-capped (longitudinally braced) with fiber cells. Relatively small vascular bundles of two sizes, *ca.* 50 and 100 μm in width, are located *ca.* 100–200 (300) μm apart, alternating in a ring at the cortex (chlorenchyma)–pith interface. They are partially correlated with the spacing of the subepidermal fiber strands, from which they are separated by 3–4 chlorenchyma cells. Larger vascular bundles are found in the pith.

Pith: central ground tissue, parenchyma of the aerenchyma type, with (usually) polygonal intercellular air spaces forming longitudinal air cavities *ca.* (50) 75–100 (150) μm in diameter. Large vascular bundles, *ca.* (110) 125–150 by 200–250 μm in cross-section and *ca.* (300) 400–800 μm apart, form a peripheral ring in the pith. Other large vascular bundles are scattered throughout this central ground tissue.

Appendix B: Fossil Sedge Culm-Species X, Interpretation of Culm Tissue Anatomy

Outline (transverse view): culm cavities. Sheath-leaf is thick, with large air cavities. Culm with nodes at and above the base: obtusely to acutely triangular, with large cortical air growth points for a series of sheath-leaves up the length of the culm (inferred). An approximately transverse section of broken culm, with sheath-leaf intact, is shown in Figure 33.B.1.

Maximum width of the culm (transverse, across one face of the triangle): 3–8 mm for the specimens relied upon in this diagnosis.

Surface of the culm shallowly micro-fluted: individual flutes $ca.$ 400 μm wide. The shallow furrows imperfectly correlate with the underlying cortical air cavities of the culm.

Cortex $ca.$ 270–530 μm thick: composed, outwards in, of epidermis, a hypodermis, chlorenchyma with fiber strands, and an innermost cortex of peripheral vascular bundles separating large cortical air cavities that encircle the pith of the culm.

Epidermis: one cell thick, elongated cells $ca.$ 3 μm wide with sinuous vertical (anticlinal) walls. Silica bodies present, conical in shape, without satellites, 6–10 per cell, in one row. The midline along the top surface of the epidermal cell has a row of small dark depressions that correspond to the apices of the underlying cones. The top of the epidermal cell breaks off intact revealing the cones inside, filling most of the otherwise now empty cell, their bases resting on the inner periclinal wall. At the base of a node the shape of the epidermal cells is irregularly angular, the cells forming a swirled pavement, the silica bodies per cell sometimes few in number or partially arranged in two rows. The epidermis together with the hypodermis constitutes the outer cortex.

Hypodermis: fibrous, $ca.$ 20–50 μm thick. Consisting of thick-walled (to near solid) rounded to cylindrical cells $ca.$ 100–300 μm long of two sizes: outer ones $ca.$ 5 μm in diameter, inner cells $ca.$ 10 μm in diameter. These sclerenchyma cells are immediately subjacent to the epidermis and appear to form a continuous fiber plate around the perimeter of the culm between the epidermis and the chlorenchyma. In SEM backscatter mode the naturally broken transverse sections of culm usually show the fossilized plate as more or less solid matter; only rarely are individual fiber cells discernible, and the secondary electron detector only reveals a few fiber cell ghost-like features. The damaged longitudinal surfaces of culm locally preserve the fiber cells of the plate as remnant islands overlying chlorenchyma. Here the internal cellular structure of the plate can sometimes be seen, and less-damaged specimens reveal the upper (i.e., outer) surface of the plate as a fiber cell sheet.

Chlorenchyma with fiber strands: zone $ca.$ 100–200 μm thick of thin-walled polygonal cells (presumed to be chlorenchyma) overlying a ring of cortical air cavities and their associated

Figure 33.B.1 Approximate transverse section of a broken culm with surrounding sheath-leaf mostly intact. The sheath-leaf ($ca.$ 1.3 mm thick) is relatively well-preserved along the outside of the lower left and bottom portions of the culm triangle. As can be seen there, large rectangular air cavities constitute most of its volume. The sheath-leaf is broken away (apparently recent, fresh breakage) at the top and along the right side of the culm, highlighting the obtusely triangular shape of the culm with its top and bottom right corners well defined. Inside the culm itself, part of its perimeter of cortical air cavities is faintly seen as a row of several dark depressions across the bottom of the triangle. The air cavities of the leaf and the cortex of the culm are, at a glance, the most conspicuous anatomical features of this fossil sedge. Optical micrograph. Fossil dedge, Olduvai Gorge culm-species X. Scale bar 2 mm in length.

vascular bundles. These thin-walled cells are *ca.* 13–30 μm thick, *ca.* 20–200 μm long, and *ca.* 20–50 μm wide. An outer and inner chlorenchyma can be distinguished. Each is only a few cells thick. Together they constitute the inner cortex. The cells of the outer chlorenchyma are long and narrow. Those of the inner chlorenchyma are short and wide. Fiber strands *ca.* 45–100 μm wide (variously shaped in transverse view) occur in the inner chlorenchyma, correlated in position with the subjacent vascular bundles that separate the cortical air cavities. The strands are composed of fiber cells (sclerenchyma) *ca.* 5 μm and 10 μm in diameter, and do not appear to be directly connected to the overlying fiber plate or the underlying sclerenchyma around the peripheral vascular bundles, although their separation from the latter can be as little as two chlorenchyma cells.

Cortical air cavities: conspicuous (as much as 300 μm across in transverse view), numerous (between 30 and 40 not uncommon), irregular to subrectangular or box-shaped in cross-section, peripheral (encircling the pith), they are formed by the disintegration of cellular tissue between large vascular bundles. The vascular bundles lie just below the fiber strands of the inner chlorenchyma. Each vascular bundle, ensheathed by its own sclerenchyma, constitutes a wall *ca.* 175–230 μm wide between adjacent air cavities. This ring of longitudinal cortical air cavities and their associated vascular bundles form an innermost cortex, and a structural transition between the chlorenchyma (inner cortex) and the central ground tissue (pith). The floors of the air cavities are pith.

Pith: parenchyma of the aerenchyma type, with polygonal (sometimes rounded) intercellular air spaces forming longitudinal air cavities *ca.* 50–100 μm in diameter. Vascular bundles (*ca.* 180–290 μm in diameter) are scattered throughout this central ground tissue.

34 Paleoecology of Laetoli, Tanzania

Terry Harrison, Amandus Kwekason, and Denise F. Su

Introduction

Laetoli in northern Tanzania is one of the most important paleontological and paleoanthropological sites in eastern Africa. Fossils were first discovered in the area in the 1930s, but its significance for hominin evolution was only appreciated after Mary Leakey's research began in the 1970s (Leakey and Harris, 1987). The site has yielded fossil hominins from the Upper Laetolil Beds (referred to as ULB; dated to 3.6–3.85 Ma), Upper Ndolanya Beds (referred to as UNB; dated to 2.66 Ma), and Upper Ngaloba Beds (>200 ka). The sample of hominins from the ULB is relatively small (just over 30 specimens), but is one of the largest and geologically oldest samples of *Australopithecus afarensis* (Harrison, 2011a). Moreover, the material includes the holotype of *Praeanthropus* (Garusi I) and the lectotype of *A. afarensis* (L.H. 4) (Hennig, 1948; Weinert, 1950; Şenyürek, 1955; Johanson et al., 1978b; Harrison, 2011a). Laetoli is also important for preserving trails of hominin footprints (Hay and Leakey, 1982; Leakey and Harris, 1987), which were presumably made by *A. afarensis*. The footprint trails corroborate inferences based on the postcranial anatomy that bipedalism was an important component of the terrestrial locomotor behavior of Pliocene hominins (Leakey and Hay, 1979; Day and Wickens, 1980; White, 1980a; Charteris et al., 1981, 1982; M.D. Leakey, 1978, 1979, 1981, 1987a; Hay and Leakey, 1982; Stern and Susman, 1983; Susman et al., 1984, 1985; Tuttle, 1987, 2008; Latimer et al., 1987; White and Suwa, 1987; Tuttle et al., 1990, 1991, 1992; Latimer, 1991; Susman and Stern, 1991; McHenry, 1986, 1991, 1994; Feibel et al., 1996; Agnew and Demas, 1998; Stern, 2000; Ward, 2002; Meldrum, 2004; Schmid, 2004; Harcourt-Smith and Aiello, 2004; Sellers et al., 2005; Berge et al., 2006; Raichlen et al., 2008, 2010; Crompton et al., 2012; Harcourt-Smith, 2015).

Upper Ndolanya Beds (UNB) hominins include the first specimen of *Paranthropus aethiopicus* recovered from outside the Turkana Basin, and one of the oldest securely dated specimens attributable to this taxon (Harrison, 2002, 2011a). Localities to the south and southwest of Laetoli have yielded small fossil assemblages from the Lower Laetolil Beds (LLB; 3.85 Ma to older than 4.36 Ma), but without hominins. Finally, a partial cranium of an archaic *Homo sapiens* has been recovered from the Late Pleistocene Upper Ngaloba Beds in association with Middle Stone Age artifacts (Day et al., 1980; Magori and Day, 1983; Ndessokia, 1990).

The ULB and UNB sediments offer insights into the faunal and floral diversity of the African Pliocene and provide a well-dated reference for Plio-Pleistocene faunal comparisons. The inferred paleoecological setting at Laetoli is unusual for hominin-bearing sites in East Africa in the absence of evidence for rivers or lakes and in being less-densely wooded (Harris, 1985; Leakey and Harris, 1987; Andrews, 1989, 2006; Cerling, 1992; Andrews and Humphrey, 1999; Musiba, 1999; Kovarovic et al., 2002; Kovarovic, 2004; Harrison, 2005, 2011b, 2017; Su, 2005, 2011; Kingston and Harrison, 2007; Kovarovic and Andrews, 2007, 2011; Musiba et al., 2007; Su and Harrison, 2007, 2008, 2015; Andrews and Bamford, 2008; Peters et al., 2008; Bishop et al., 2011; Kaiser, 2011; Kingston, 2011; Rossouw and Scott, 2011; Barboni, 2014; Louys et al., 2015).

Recent investigations at Laetoli have critically re-examined the paleoecology using a broader range of taxonomic evidence (i.e., plants, invertebrates, reptiles, birds and mammals), modern-day ecosystems (i.e., soils, vegetation, invertebrates, and vertebrates), and paleoenvironmental proxies (i.e., sedimentology, geomorphology, palynology, phytoliths, coprolites, stable isotopes, mesowear, ecomorphology, and gastropod and mammal community structure; Kovarovic et al., 2002; Harrison, 2005, 2011b, 2011c, 2017;Harrison and Msuya, 2005; Su, 2005, 2011; Kingston and Harrison, 2007; Su and Harrison, 2007, 2008, 2015; Andrews and Bamford, 2008; Andrews et al., 2011; Bamford, 2011a, 2011b; Bishop et al., 2011; Denys, 2011; Ditchfield and Harrison, 2011; Hernesniemi et al., 2011; Kaiser, 2011; Kingston, 2011; Kovarovic, 2004; Kovarovic and Andrews, 2007, 2011; Peters et al., 2008; Reed, 2011; Reed and Denys, 2011; Rossouw and Scott, 2011; Tattersfield, 2011). The paleoecology of this region offers insights into early hominin ecology and paleobiology, which have implications for debates about the mode and tempo of speciation and extinction among Pliocene African hominins (Bobe and Behrensmeyer, 2004; deMenocal, 2004, 2011; Bobe and Leakey, 2009; Maslin and Trauth, 2009; Reed and Russack, 2009; Trauth et al., 2010; Harrison, 2011a; Potts, 2013; Shultz and Maslin, 2013; Macho, 2014; Maslin et al., 2014, 2015).

ULB paleoecology has been reconstructed as an open woodland, shrubland, and grassland mosaic, with closed woodland and gallery forest bordering seasonal watercourses and more mesic and more densely wooded than the modern-day Laetoli ecosystem (Andrews and Bamford, 2008; Andrews et al., 2011; see Su and Harrison, 2015). Turnover in the Laetoli large mammal fauna during the one-million-year gap in the fossil record between the ULB and UNB (3.6–2.66 Ma) points toward somewhat drier habitats with a greater proportion of grasslands in the UNB. However, alternative lines of evidence suggest relatively mesic conditions, dominated by open and closed woodlands in the UNB (Harrison, 2017).

History of Research

The 1930s witnessed the earliest research in the Laetoli (= Garusi) area, when Louis and Mary Leakey visited in 1935, collecting fossil vertebrates from Laetoli, Naibadad, Ngai, and Endolele. These included a hominin lower canine, the first early hominin to be recovered from East Africa, although not identified as such until decades later (White, 1980b, 1981). Ludwig and Margrethe Kohl-Larsen made extensive collections in the area in 1938–1939 (Dietrich, 1941, 1942a, 1942b, 1945, 1950, 1951; Kohl-Larsen, 1943; Petter, 1963). These collections included a hominin maxilla, an isolated M^3, and a lower incisor (Hennig, 1948; Remane, 1950, 1954; Weinert, 1950; Robinson, 1953a, 1955; White 1980b; Ullrich, 2001; Harrison, 2011a). Hennig (1948) described the hominins as belonging to a new genus, *Praeanthropus*, but failed to provide a species name, making it a *nomen nudum*. Weinert (1950) referred the Garusi hominins to a new species, *Meganthropus africanus*, and Senyürek (1955) later transferred the species to *Praeanthropus*, making Hennig's genus name available. Louis and Mary Leakey revisited Laetoli briefly in 1959 and 1964 (M.D. Leakey, 1987b), and Hay (1976) reported fossils from the Laetolil Beds at Silal Artum and the Olduvai Side Gorge.

The first comprehensive investigation of the Laetoli area was directed by Mary Leakey in 1974–1982 (Hay, 1976, 1978, 1981, 1986, 1987; Leakey et al., 1976; Hay and Reeder, 1978; M.D. Leakey, 1981; Hay and Leakey, 1982; Leakey and Harris, 1987). Leakey's team recovered a large collection of fossils from the ULB, including 25 hominins (Leakey et al., 1976; White, 1977, 1980b, 1981, 1985; M.D. Leakey, 1987c). A partial mandible, L.H. 4, was designated as the holotype of *A. afarensis* (Johanson et al., 1978a), and all other fossil hominins recovered from the ULB were attributed to the same taxon. A mandibular fragment (L.H. 29), initially attributed to *Homo* cf. *H. erectus* (M.D. Leakey, 1978), was later reassigned to *A. afarensis* (Harrison, 2011a). In addition to *A. afarensis*, a partial cranium (L.H. 18) assigned to *H. sapiens* was recovered from the Late Pleistocene Upper Ngaloba Beds (>200 ka; Day et al., 1980; Magori and Day, 1983; Manega, 1993). With the discovery of fossilized footprints of hominins at Laetoli in 1978, the main focus of Leakey's investigations shifted to the study of these trails and their significance for early hominin locomotor behavior, before being reburied in 1979 to conserve them (M.D. Leakey, 1978, 1979, 1981, 1987a; Leakey and Hay, 1979; Day and Wickens, 1980; White, 1980a; Charteris et al., 1981, 1982; Hay and Leakey, 1982; Tuttle, 1985, 1987, 1990, 1994, 2008; Robbins, 1987; White and Suwa, 1987; Tuttle et al., 1990, 1991, 1992).

The Institute of Human Origins (IHO; Arizona State University, USA) carried out paleoanthropological research in northern Tanzania from 1985 to 1988 and recovered a small collection of fossils from Laetoli, including an isolated upper molar of *A. afarensis* (Kyauka and Ndessokia, 1990). Ndessokia (1990) made a detailed study of the fauna and archeology of the Ndolanya and Olpiro Beds, and Manega (1993) carried out investigations of the geochronology and geochemistry. In 1993–1994 the joint American–German Hominid Corridor Research Project (HCRP led by Friedemann Schrenk and Timothy Bromage) surveyed localities in the Laetoli area and collected additional fossils (Kaiser et al., 1995; Kaiser, 2000).

The hominin footprint trails were re-excavated in 1994–1997 by the Getty Conservation Institute and the Government of Tanzania to study and conserve the footprints (Agnew et al., 1996; Feibel et al., 1996; Agnew and Demas, 1998), after which the trails were reburied. During the 1990s, Charles Musiba worked on the ecomorphology, taphonomy, and paleoecology of Laetoli (Musiba, 1999), and continued research at the site, principally on the paleoecology and animal trackways (Musiba et al., 2007, 2008; Meldrum et al., 2011).

Presently, full-scale paleontological and geological investigations at localities on the Eyasi Plateau, including Laetoli, have been led by two of the authors (T.H. and A.K.) since 1998 (Harrison, 2011b, 2011c, 2011d, 2011e). This has resulted in the discovery of new localities, the recovery of over 20,000 fossils, and a more detailed understanding of the geology and geochronology. The collections include additional finds of *A. afarensis* from the ULB and the first discovery of *Paranthropus aethiopicus* from the UNB (Harrison, 2002, 2011a).

Geology and Dating

The geology and geochronology of the Laetoli region are well-documented (Kent, 1941; Pickering, 1969; Hay, 1976, 1978, 1987; Hay and Reeder, 1978; Hay and Leakey, 1982; Drake and Curtis, 1987; Ndessokia, 1990; Manega, 1993; Mollel, 2007; Deino, 2011; Ditchfield and Harrison, 2011; Harrison and Kweka, 2011; McHenry, 2011; Mollel et al., 2011), but the nature of the depositional environment, the source of the volcanic sediments, and correlation of the Laetoli and Olduvai stratigraphic sequences require better resolution (Barker and Milliken, 2008; Ditchfield and Harrison, 2011; Zaitsev et al., 2011, 2012, 2015).

The Eyasi Plateau is an uplifted fault block, with a general elevation of 1700–1800 m, bordering the northwest margin of Lake Eyasi (Figure 34.1). The rugged escarpment of the rift is almost 2000 m high at Eseketeti, but the plateau slopes away to the north and west to grade into the southern Serengeti Plains. To the east is the Ngorongoro Volcanic Highland Complex (NVHC), comprising a series of Pliocene and Pleistocene volcanoes, most notably Lemagurut, Satiman, Ngorongoro, Olmoti, and Oldeani. Satiman, the oldest of the volcanic centers in the NVHC, located 20 km to the east of Laetoli, has been identified as the most likely source of the Laetolil Beds (older than 4.36 Ma to 3.6 Ma) and Ndolanya Beds (2.66 Ma; Hay, 1978, 1986, 1987). However, its known age of activity (4.8–4.0 Ma) overlaps only with deposition of the oldest of the Laetolil Beds (Mollel et al., 2011), and the geochemistry and mineralogy of the Laetolil tuffs are not consistent with having been derived from Satiman

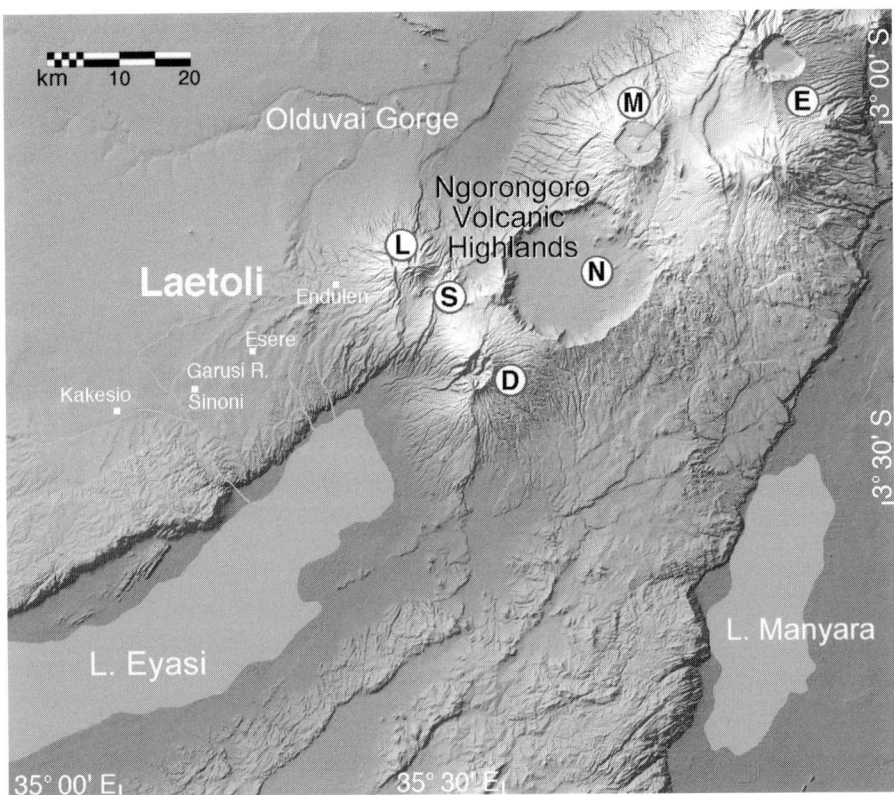

Figure 34.1 Satellite image of the Eyasi Plateau and the Ngorongoro Volcanic Highlands area of northern Tanzania, showing the location of Laetoli and the Garusi River Valley (adapted from NASA Earth Observatory, 2004). Volcanoes = large circles: D, Oldeani; E, Embagai; L, Lemagurut; M, Olmoti; N, Ngorongoro; S, Satiman. Villages = small white squares.

(McHenry, 2011; Zaitsev et al., 2011, 2015). Lavas dating from 4.0 Ma to 2.5 Ma have not been recorded in the NVHC, so no direct correlation exists currently between Satiman and the Laetolil and Ndolanya Beds (Mollel, 2007; Mollel et al., 2008, 2011). It is conceivable that the volcano that produced the Laetoli tephra was buried by the subsequent activity of Ngorongoro (2.4–2.2 Ma) and Lemagurut (2.3–2.0 Ma; Mollel et al., 2011). Given the nature and distribution of the Laetoli tuffaceous sediments, it seems unlikely that a more distant center, such as Mosonik (3.5–3.2 Ma), represents the source of the Laetolil Beds (Zaitsev et al., 2015).

During the Pliocene, volcanic ashes were blown from the NVHC toward the southwest, which is the direction of the prevailing wind today. The tephra settled on a gently undulating peneplain with little topographic relief and sloping at a low gradient away from the NVHC. The Laetolil Beds can be traced more than 50 km from Laetoli, with those closer to the NVHC being substantially thicker than distal beds (Hay, 1987; Ditchfield and Harrison, 2011). Lake sediments in the Manonga Valley, 170 km to the southwest of Laetoli, apparently derived from the same volcanic source (Mutakyahwa, 1997). The age of the Ibole fauna in the Manonga Valley (~5.0–5.5 Ma; Harrison and Baker, 1997) is estimated to be older than the oldest radiometrically dated sediments at Laetoli (4.36 Ma; Deino, 2011). It would appear, therefore, that deposition of the Laetolil Beds began regionally as early as 5.5 Ma, but discernible accumulation of sediments in the Laetoli area occurred later (Ditchfield and Harrison, 2011).

A composite stratigraphic section of the sediments on the Eyasi Plateau shows the Laetolil Beds at the base are about 300 m thick (Figure 34.2; Hay, 1987; Ditchfield and Harrison, 2011). They are subdivided into two lithological units, the Lower Unit of the Laetolil Beds and the Upper Unit of the Laetolil Beds, which are conventionally referred to as the Lower Laetolil Beds (LLB) and the Upper Laetolil Beds (ULB). The LLB are widely exposed to the south and west of Laetoli (Figure 34.3). Radiometric dating of the LLB indicates an age of 3.85 Ma to older than 4.36 Ma (Drake and Curtis, 1987; Deino, 2011). The sediments consist mainly of subaerially deposited eolian tuffs, interbedded with air-fall and water-worked tuffs. The eolian tuffs are massive, crudely bedded, with moderate levels of bioturbation by termites and other invertebrates. At Kakesio, about 30 km to the west of Laetoli, the base of the LLB consists of 3 m of regolith, conglomerates, and sandstones, deposited in a low-energy fluvial or paludal environment, unconformably overlying the Precambrian basement. South of Laetoli, at Noiti and Esere, the LLB is dominated by fluvial, deltaic, and lacustrine deposit in a 30 m section of tuffaceous clays, sandstones and conglomerates, interbedded with air-fall tuffs. In the upper part of the LLB at Noiti and Esere, paleochannels were filled by lahars, presumably from the NVHC, and which contain abundant fossil wood (Bamford, 2011a).

Fossil vertebrates from the LLB are far less common and more fragmentary than in the overlying ULB. Despite extensive and lacustrine sediments in the LLB, aquatic vertebrates are extremely rare (a crocodile and an otter are known from

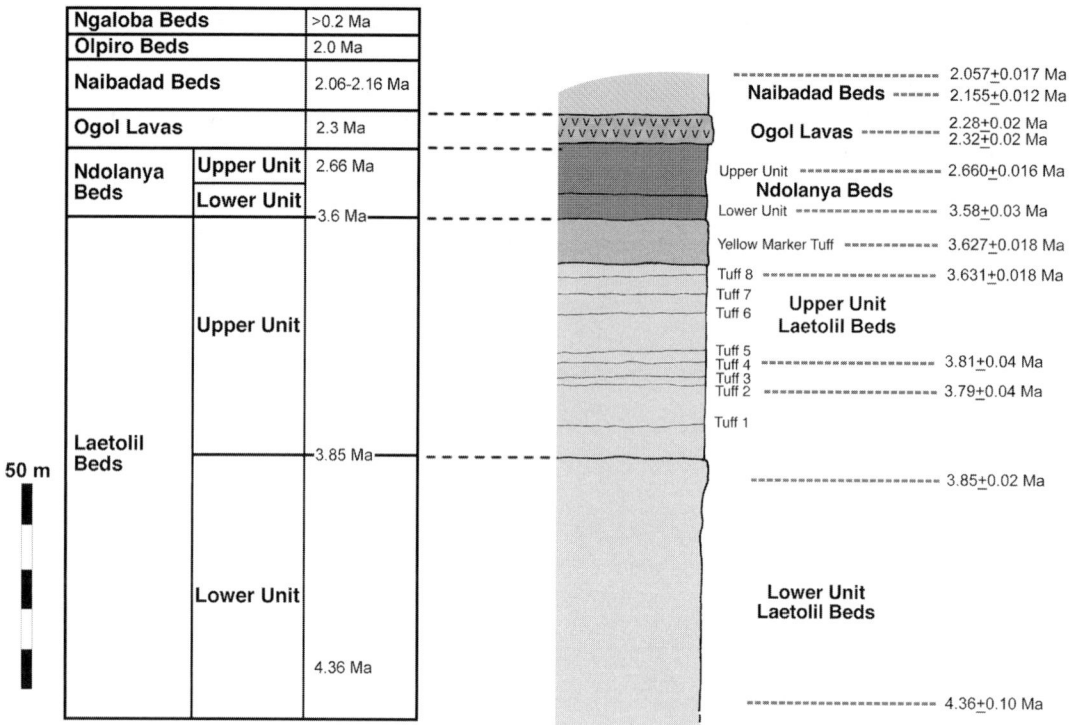

Figure 34.2 Simplified stratigraphic scheme and geochronology of the main lithological units at Laetoli (after Harrison, 2011b).

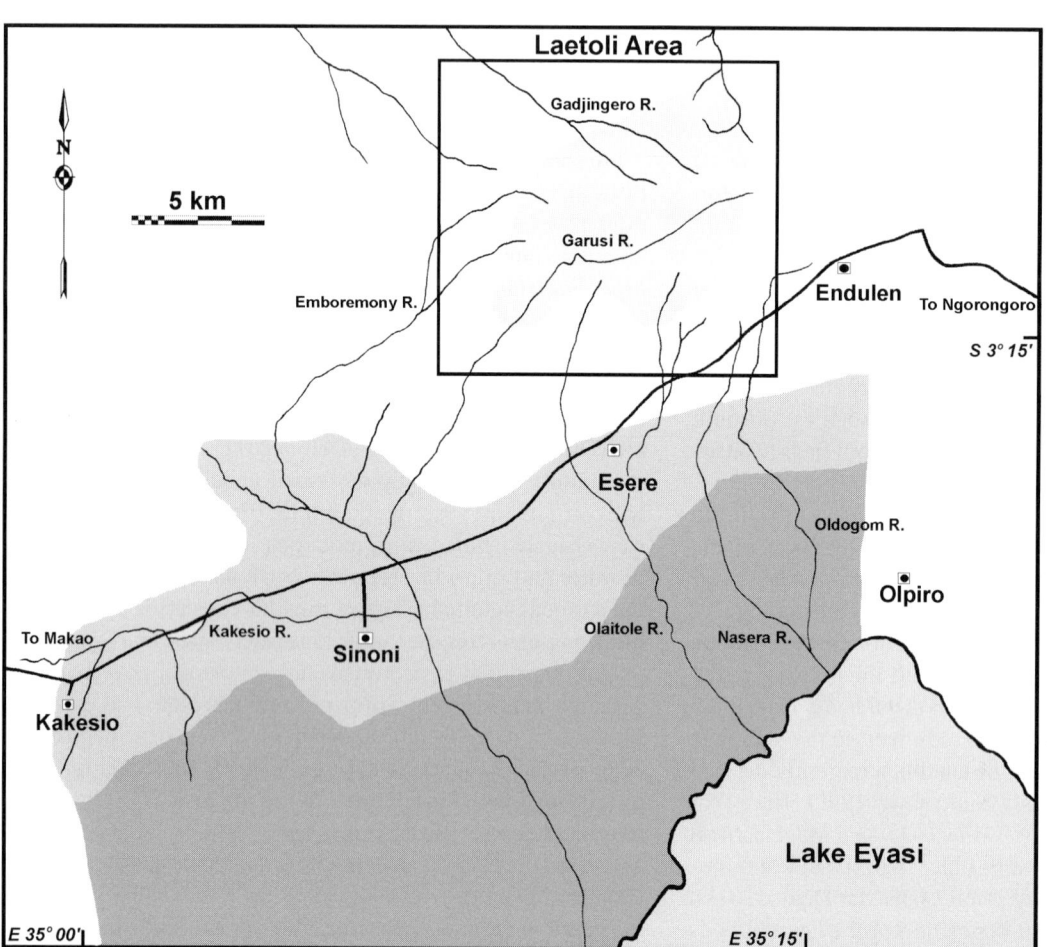

Figure 34.3 Map of the Eyasi Plateau, including the Laetoli area showing the main exposures of Upper Laetolil Beds and Upper Ndolanya Beds (light gray), Lower Laetolil Beds (medium gray) and Precambrian basement (dark gray). Motor track from Ngorongoro to Makao, passing through Endulen and Kakesio, is shown as a dark solid line. Rivers are indicated as fine lines, and villages are indicated as black dots inside open squares.

Kakesio, but no hippopotamids, turtles, fishes [*contra* Harris, 1987] or freshwater invertebrates), suggesting that the hydrology was impermanent and labile, with no communication to other regional rivers and lakes (Ditchfield and Harrison, 2011). Fossil hominins have not yet been recovered from the LLB, but this may be due to sampling issues. Given that the time period spans the last occurrence of *Ardipithecus*/first appearance of *Australopithecus*, any LLB fossil hominins could be of immense interest.

The ULB consists of a series of eolian, air-fall, and water-worked tuffs (Hay, 1978, 1987; Ditchfield and Harrison, 2011). The eolian tuffs are often heavily bioturbated, primarily by termites and other insects. The water-worked sediments are associated with small ephemeral ponds and minor channel fills produced by seasonally active streams. The direction of flow of these channels is principally toward the south and southwest, toward the present-day Eyasi basin (Hay, 1987; Ditchfield and Harrison, 2011). The channels indicate a relatively extensive fluvial system that was larger than the modern-day Garusi River system (Ditchfield and Harrison, 2011), implying that abundant water was available during and shortly after the rainy season. However, there is no evidence, geological or paleontological, for permanent water sources such as rivers or lakes. Today, subsurface run-off from the NVHC emerges at the interface between the basement and the Laetolil Beds as perennial springs which drain into Lake Eyasi. Given similar geomorphological and hydrological conditions during the Pliocene, it appears that perennial springs were dotted along the margin of the Eyasi Plateau and a reliable water source.

Radiometric dating provides an age of 3.6–3.85 Ma for the ULB (Deino, 2011). The Yellow Marker Tuff delimits the top of the ULB, which lacks fossils. Other distinctive air-fall tuffs throughout the ULB are designated as marker tuffs (Tuffs 1–8), which range in thickness from a few centimeters to substantial layers of calcrete (Hay 1978, 1987). Tuff 7, the thickest of the marker tuffs (30–40 cm thick), consists of an upper coarser part, the Augite Biotite Tuff, and a lower fine-grained and laminated Footprint Tuff, which preserves the hominin and other animal trails (Leakey and Hay, 1979; Hay and Leakey, 1982; Hay, 1987; Leakey, 1987a, 1987d; Robbins, 1987; Tuttle, 1987). The ULB are highly fossiliferous, with over 20,000 mammal specimens recovered since 1974, and large collections of birds, reptiles, invertebrates, and plants. Most of the Laetoli fossil hominins, all attributed to *A. afarensis*, are from the ULB.

Disconformably overlying the Laetolil Beds are a series of eolian tuffs and calcretes comprising the Ndolanya Beds (Hay and Reeder, 1978; Hay, 1987; Ditchfield and Harrison, 2011). These are subdivided into upper and lower units separated by a disconformity. The Lower Ndolanya Beds (LNB) consist of reworked tuffs and poorly cemented tuffaceous clays, with limestone nodules and concretions (Hay, 1987). The LNB are separated from the Yellow Marker Tuff of the ULB by a thin tuffaceous limestone and from the UNB by a massive pedogenic calcrete. Apart from traces of bioturbation and root markings, the LNB are not fossiliferous. The UNB, dated to 2.66 Ma (Ndessokia, 1990; Manega, 1993; Deino, 2011), contain a rich assemblage of fossil vertebrates, including hominins. The ~1 myr depositional hiatus between the Laetolil and Ndolanya Beds is the critical time period when *A. afarensis* disappears and *Paranthropus* first appears.

The UNB are overlain by a series of lavas, the Ogol Lavas, which date to 2.3 Ma (Drake and Curtis, 1987; Deino, 2011; Mollel et al., 2011) and are presumed to be part of the same eruptive complex as Lemagurut (2.4–2.2 Ma). The lavas originate from a range of volcanic cones flanking both sides of the Olaitole Valley (Hay, 1987). The overlying Naibadad Beds consist of eolian and air-fall tuffs, 20–30 m thick (Hay, 1987; Manega, 1993). Radiometric dates give an age of 2.3–2.1 Ma (Ndessokia, 1990; Manega, 1993), with Ngorongoro (2.3–2.0 Ma) being the most likely source of the tephra (Hay, 1976, 1987; Mollel et al., 2008). Few fossils have been recovered from the Naibadad Beds.

The Olpiro Beds, 3–5 m thick, are mainly comprised of tuffaceous claystones, sandstones, and conglomerates. The age (2.00–2.06 Ma) and lithological composition of the Olpiro Beds suggests that the tuffs are probably derived from Olmoti (2.0–1.8 Ma), and likely correlate with Olduvai Lower Bed I (Ndessokia, 1990; Manega, 1993; McHenry et al., 2008; Mollel et al., 2009; Deino, 2011). The sparse fauna is consistent with an Early Pleistocene age (Ndessokia, 1990; Harrison, unpubl. data). Excavations in the Olpiro Beds have produced Oldowan artifacts in association with large mammals (Ndessokia, 1990).

The overlying Ngaloba Beds are subdivided into upper and lower units. The Lower Ngaloba Beds consist of conglomerates, sandstones, and clays, while the Upper Beds are composed of tuffaceous clays and sandstone. The Ngaloba Beds have been dated to older than 200 ka and they possibly correlate with the Ndutu Beds at Olduvai (220–450 ka; Hay, 1987; Manega, 1993). Both units are fossiliferous, but the Upper Beds are the most productive. The fauna from the Upper Ngaloba Beds includes a partial cranium of an archaic *H. sapiens* (L.H. 18; Day et al., 1980; Magori and Day, 1983). Acheulian and Middle Stone Age artifacts have been recovered from the Lower and Upper Ngaloba Beds, respectively (Harris and Harris, 1981; Hay, 1987; Leakey, 1987b; Manega, 1993; Adelsberger et al., 2011).

Hominins

The sample of 32 ULB fossil hominins are all attributed to *A. afarensis* (Table 34.1; Harrison, 2011a). The sample includes eight jaw fragments, four associated dentitions, 19 isolated teeth, and a partial skeleton of an infant with associated cranial and postcranial elements (Leakey et al., 1976; White, 1977, 1980b, 1981; Leakey, 1987c; Kyauka and Ndessokia, 1990; Kyauka, 1994; Ullrich, 2001; Harrison, 2011a). Additional cranio-dental specimens recovered in 2012 and 2014 await description. In addition, the ULB preserves trails of hominin footprints (Leakey and Hay, 1979; White, 1980a; Hay and Leakey, 1982; Leakey 1987a; White and Suwa, 1987).

Although the Laetoli *A. afarensis* sample is far smaller than the Hadar sample, it is still a significant collection (Kimbel and Delezene, 2009; Harrison, 2011a). The Garusi maxilla is the holotype of *Praeanthropus* and L.H. 4 is the lectotype of *A. afarensis* (Hennig, 1948; Weinert, 1950; Johanson et al., 1978a; Harrison, 2011a). Moreover, the *A. afarensis* material from Laetoli is older (3.83–3.63 Ma) than the sample from Hadar

Table 34.1 Coordinates of paleontological localities at Laetoli and at other localities on the Eyasi Plateau

Locality	WGS84 coordinates		UTM (Zone 36)	
	South	East	Easting	Northing
Laetoli				
Loc 1	3° 11′ 18.6″	35° 13′ 30.7″	747290	9647304
Loc 1NW	3° 10′ 49.4″	35° 13′ 01.9″	746402	9648203
Loc 2	3° 13′ 05.4″	35° 11′ 38.3″	743811	9644042
Loc 3	3° 12′ 23.7″	35° 12′ 41.2″	745757	9645307
Loc 4	3° 12′ 32.4″	35° 13′ 19.0″	746923	9645037
Loc 5	3° 12′ 45.1″	35° 12′ 25.0″	745255	9644651
Loc 6	3° 12′ 56.1″	35° 12′ 07.7″	744720	9644314
Loc 7	3° 13′ 09.7″	35° 12′ 10.6″	744809	9643896
Loc 8	3° 13′ 31.1″	35° 11′ 21.4″	743287	9643241
Loc 9	3° 12′ 19.8″	35° 10′ 09.2″	741063	9645437
Loc 9S	3° 13′ 01.4″	35° 10′ 05.7″	740952	9644159
Loc 10	3° 13′ 46.3″	35° 09′ 49.9″	740461	9642781
Loc 10E	3° 14′ 01.0″	35° 10′ 13.0″	741173	9642327
Loc 10W	3° 14′ 04.4″	35° 09′ 28.4″	739796	9642226
Loc 10NE	3° 13′ 35.0″	35° 10′ 31.0″	741731	9643125
Loc 11	3° 13′ 10.0″	35° 12′ 50.0″	746026	9643884
Loc 12	3° 13′ 37.6″	35° 13′ 09.7″	746632	9643034
Loc 12E	3° 13′ 33.7″	35° 13′ 31.8″	747315	9643153
Loc 13	3° 12′ 32.4″	35° 11′ 11.5″	742986	9645046
Loc 14	3° 12′ 14.6″	35° 11′ 28.8″	743521	9645592
Loc 15	3° 13′ 21.0″	35° 08′ 38.0″	738242	9643653
Loc 16	3° 12′ 11.6″	35° 12′ 56.7″	746236	9645678
Loc 17	3° 12′ 09.0″	35° 13′ 31.0″	747296	9645755
Loc 18	3° 12′ 03.5″	35° 11′ 55.6″	744349	9645931
Loc 19	3° 13′ 51.6″	35° 12′ 42.3″	745785	9642606
Loc 20	3° 13′ 58.6″	35° 12′ 42.4″	745788	9642391
Loc 21	3° 14′ 16.1″	35° 12′ 33.2″	745502	9641854
Loc 22	3° 14′ 30.3″	35° 11′ 10.0″	742932	9641423
Loc 22E	3° 14′ 43.6″	35° 11′ 32.2″	743617	9641013
Loc 22S	3° 15′ 01.4″	35° 11′ 09.3″	742908	9640468
Loc 23	3° 11′ 23.4″	35° 12′ 37.7″	745653	9647160
Loc 24	3° 13′ 19.0″	35° 10′ 38.0″	741948	9643616
Other localities				
Aldarapoi	3° 14′ 36.2″	35° 15′ 37.2″	751184	9641224
Emboremony 1	3° 17′ 50.2″	35° 02′ 08.0″	726182	9635317
Emboremony 2	3° 17′ 22.0″	35° 04′ 30.0″	730568	9636174
Emboremony 3	3° 19′ 52.3″	35° 04′ 05.7″	729808	9631558
Engeju-Enacho	3° 15′ 36.7″	35° 10′ 01.6″	740815	9639388
Engesha	3° 17′ 13.0″	35° 12′ 52.0″	746071	9636417
Esere 1	3° 18′ 48.7″	35° 11′ 04.0″	742729	9633484
Esere 2	3° 20′ 05.0″	35° 11′ 06.0″	742786	9631139
Esere 3	3° 21′ 48.0″	35° 10′ 44.0″	742099	9627976
Kakesio 1	3° 21′ 03.0″	34° 59′ 20.0″	720982	9629404
Kakesio 2	3° 21′ 03.0″	34° 59′ 50.0″	721908	9629402
Kakesio 3	3° 21′ 00.0″	35° 00′ 08.0″	722464	9629493
Kakesio 4	3° 20′ 50.0″	35° 00′ 16.0″	722712	9629800
Kakesio 5	3° 20′ 49.0″	35° 00′ 35.0″	723299	9629829
Kakesio 6	3° 20′ 37.0″	35° 00′ 47.0″	723670	9630197
Kakesio 7	3° 21′ 51.0″	35° 01′ 45.0″	725456	9627920
Kakesio 8	3° 22′ 16.8″	35° 01′ 08.3″	724321	9627130
Kakesio 9	3° 22′ 58.1″	35° 01′ 31.1″	725022	9625859
Kakesio 10	3° 23′ 03.1″	35° 00′ 23.5″	722935	9625710
Kakesio South	3° 23′ 22.0″	34° 59′ 00.0″	720356	9625135
Lobeleita	3° 23′ 57.0″	35° 05′ 50.0″	733012	9624033
Olaltanaudo	3° 20′ 16.1″	35° 04′ 14.4″	730075	9630826
Oleisusu	3° 14′ 12.6″	35° 15′ 35.1″	751120	9641949
Ndoroto	3° 11′ 04.4″	35° 16′ 57.0″	753663	9647727
Noiti 1	3° 18′ 30.5″	35° 12′ 50.0″	746004	9634036
Noiti 2	3° 18′ 30.4″	35° 12′ 31.6″	745436	9634040
Noiti 3	3° 18′ 24.8″	35° 13′ 43.8″	747666	9634207
Silal Artum	3° 10′ 06.4″	35° 12′ 37.1″	745639	9649526

(3.4–2.9 Ma), as well as those from Dikika, Maka, and Koobi Fora (slightly older than 3.4–3.3 Ma), and comparable in age to those from Belohdelie (3.8 Ma) and Woranso-Mille (3.8–3.6 Ma; Alemseged et al., 2005; Kimbel and Delezene, 2009; Deino et al., 2010). Comparisons of the sample from Laetoli with the later and more derived material from Hadar have proved critical in debates about intraspecific variation and evolutionary trends in the species (Lockwood et al., 2000; Ward et al., 2001, 2010; Kimbel et al., 2004, 2006; Haile-Selassie et al., 2010b; Harrison, 2011a).

Few Laetoli hominins have been recovered *in situ*, but information concerning their discovery locations and the occurrence of fossiliferous horizons in the ULB (Harrison and Kweka, 2011) allows most of the hominins to be placed into stratigraphic context (Figure 34.4). *Australopithecus afarensis* occurs throughout the ULB, with dates ranging from 3.63 Ma to 3.83 Ma. Most of the ULB hominins derive from above Tuff 5, but this largely reflects the greater paleontological productivity of the upper ULB.

Two hominin specimens have been recovered from the UNB. A proximal tibia (EP 1000/98) is similar to *Australopithecus* and *Paranthropus*. In the absence of a direct association with craniodental material, its taxonomic identity is unclear (Harrison, 2011a). The other UNB specimen, an edentulous maxilla fragment (EP 1500/01), is more informative with a unique combination of features resembling *P. aethiopicus*. This is the only *P. aethiopicus* specimen recorded from outside the Turkana Basin, and is one of the oldest securely dated specimens definitively attributable to this taxon (Feibel et al., 1989; Suwa et al., 1996; Harrison, 2002, 2011a; Wood and Constantino, 2007; Bobe and Leakey, 2009). The proximal tibia from UNB may belong to the same species, but the possibility of a second hominin taxon in the UNB cannot be discounted.

Figure 34.4 Stratigraphic distribution and chronology of *Australopithecus afarensis* specimens in the Upper Laetolil Beds (adapted from Harrison, 2011a).

Yellow Marker Tuff	3.63 Ma
L.H. 15, EP 2400/00	
Tuff 8	3.63 Ma
L.H. 1, 2, 3/6, 8, 22, EP 162/00	
Tuff 7	3.66 Ma
L.H. 4, 5, 13, 21, 23, 24, 25, 26, 27, 28	
Tuff 6	3.70 Ma
L.H. 7, 14, 16, 19	
Tuff 5	3.79 Ma
Tuff 4	3.79 Ma
L.H. 12	
Tuff 3	3.80 Ma
Tuff 2	3.81 Ma
L.H. 10, 11	
Tuff 1	3.83 Ma
LOWER LAETOLIL BEDS	3.85–4.36 Ma

Collection Methods

Paleontological localities on the Eyasi Plateau occur in three main geographical areas: Laetoli, Kakesio, and Esere-Noiti (Figure 34.5). Sixty paleontological localities and sublocalities have been designated (Table 34.1), extending over an area of ~400 km². However, most of the fossils have been recovered from localities in the Laetoli area, where exposures of the ULB and UNB occur in the Garusi, Nompopong, Olaitole, and Gadjingero River valleys (Figure 34.6). This is where researchers have concentrated their efforts, and where all the fossil hominins and footprint sites have been discovered (Leakey, 1987a, 1987b, 1987c; Harrison, 2011a, 2011b; Harrison and Kweka, 2011). The Kakesio and Esere-Noiti areas have extensive exposures of the LLB, but fossils are much rarer than in the Laetoli area, and with no hominins recovered as yet.

Since 1998, the following collection methods have been employed: fossils are primarily recovered from the surface of outcrops after they have eroded out of the sediments. Partially exposed fossils *in situ* are excavated, but full-scale excavations to recover unexposed fossils have not been fruitful (Leakey, 1987b; Ndessokia, 1990). No systematic screening for microvertebrates and invertebrates was undertaken, although dry screening was used to recover associated remains and

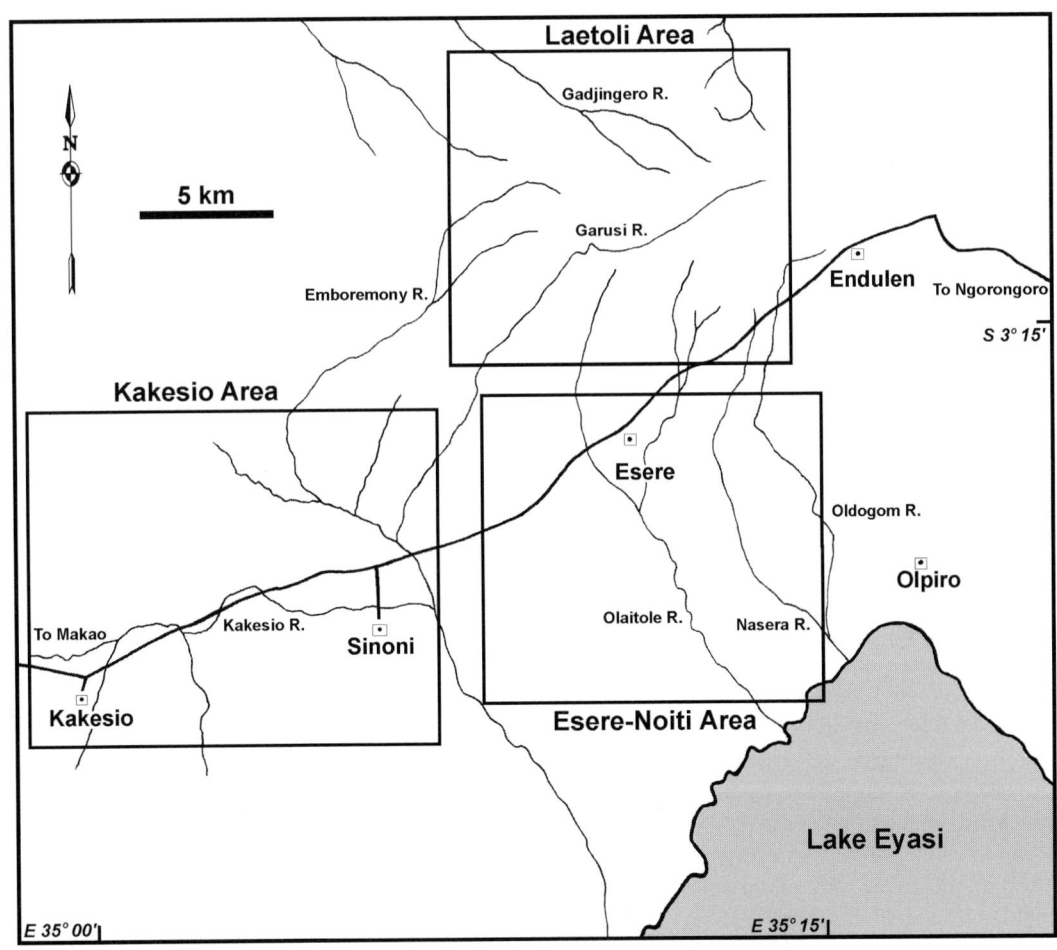

Figure 34.5 Sketch map of the Eyasi Plateau showing the three main paleontological collecting areas: Laetoli, Esere-Noiti, and Kakesio (from Harrison and Kweka, 2011). See Figure 34.6 for details of the Laetoli collecting area.

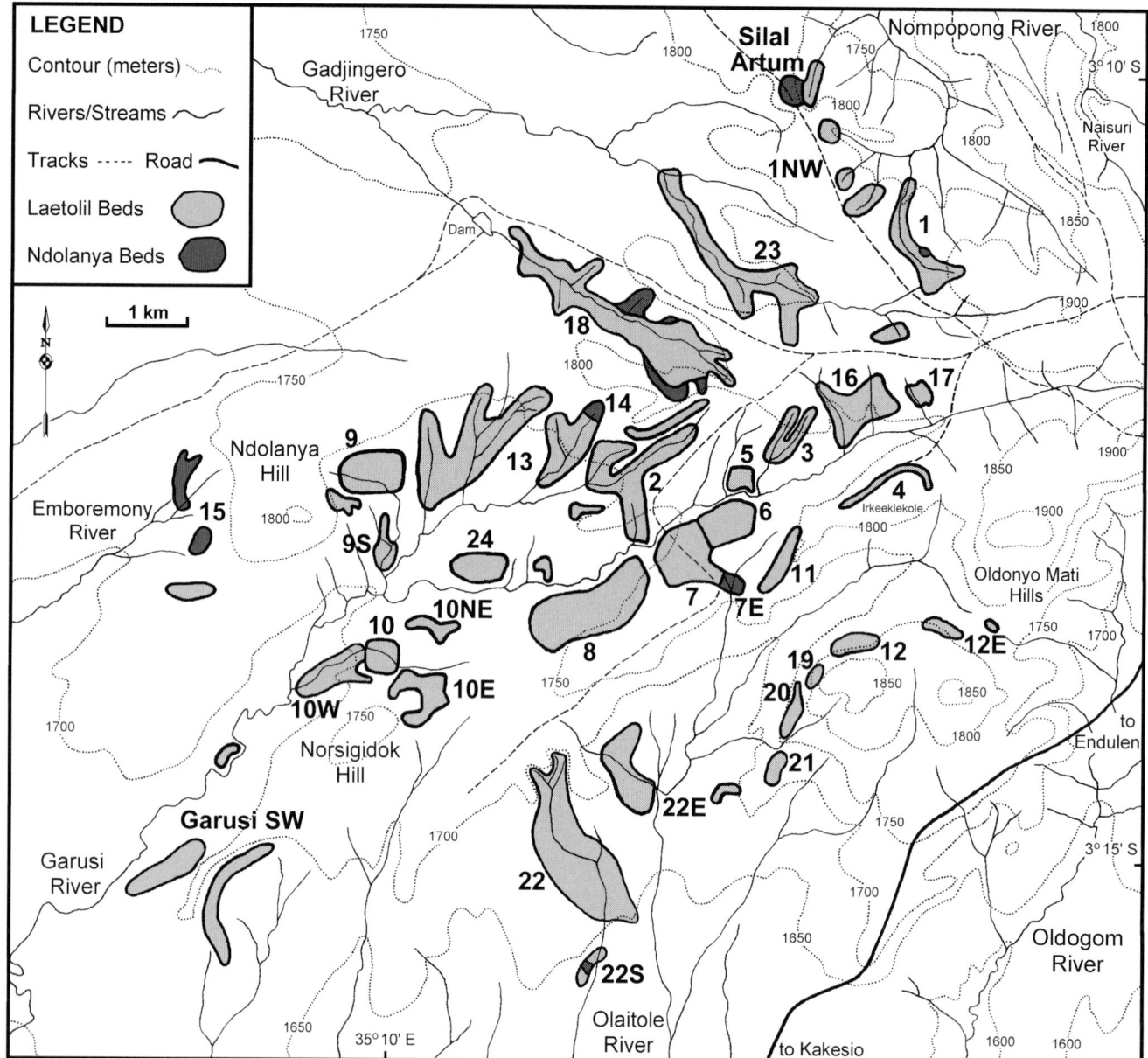

Figure 34.6 Map of the Laetoli area showing the main outcrops of Upper Laetolil Beds and Upper Ndolanya Beds, and the paleontological collecting localities (adapted from Harrison and Kweka, 2011).

at hominin localities. All anatomically identifiable bones (except rib fragments and limb bone shaft fragments lacking a portion of at least one articular surface) of all fossil vertebrates are recovered. Isolated fragments of tortoise shells and ostrich eggshell, gastropods, insect traces, and undiagnostic macrobotanical remains are not collected systematically, but representative specimens from each locality are obtained as reference samples. This collection strategy is designed to ensure a comprehensive representation of the entire fauna and flora, as well as to gather the kinds of data that are essential for analyzing the taphonomy, ecomorphology, community structure, and paleobiology of the fauna. All material collected is catalogued in the field, with a field number, locality, stratigraphic provenance, anatomical element, and provisional taxonomic identification.

Taphonomy

Vertebrate remains are primarily isolated elements, although partial skeletons of small- and medium-sized mammals (less than 5 kg) are quite common (Su and Harrison, 2008). The sedimentary setting and the preservation of bones at Laetoli indicate that the skeletal remains of vertebrates were scattered on successive land surfaces before burial by subaerially deposited volcanic ashes (Hay, 1987; Su, 2005; Su and Harrison, 2008). The remains included carcasses and individual bones in various stages of decomposition, disarticulation, and weathering. Prefossilization damage to the bones (i.e., breakage, weathering, root etching, insect damage, rodent gnawing, carnivore bite marks and chewing) is common and demonstrates that specimens often lay exposed on the surface for some time (Su and

Harrison, 2008). The high taxonomic diversity of carnivores (28 species of carnivores in the ULB compared with 25 species in the modern-day Serengeti fauna), the common occurrence of bite marks on bones (over 6 percent of large mammal bones), and the abundance of carnivore coprolites all confirm the taphonomic impact of carnivores on carcasses and individual bones (Su, 2005; Su and Harrison, 2008). Fossils are exclusively preserved in subaerially deposited sediments, with little to no evidence for fluvial transport.

Paleontological Collections

A small sample of fossil vertebrates collected by Louis and Mary Leakey in the 1930s from Laetoli and other localities on the Eyasi Plateau are housed in the Natural History Museum (London). Major collections made by Kohl-Larsen in 1938–1939 are housed at the Museum für Naturkunde (Berlin), the Institut für Ur- und Frühgeschichte und Archäologie des Mittelalters, and the Institut und Museum für Geologie und Paläontologie at Eberhard Karls Universität, both in Tübingen. Unfortunately, these collections lack provenance and stratigraphic information. Mary Leakey's collections from the 1970s, totaling over 10,000 specimens and originally stored at the Leakey camp at Olduvai Gorge and at the National Museum of Kenya in Nairobi, have recently been reassembled and curated at the National Museum of Tanzania in Dar es Salaam. More than 30,000 fossils have been collected at Laetoli since 1998 (Table 34.2). These consist of fossil mammals (almost 19,000 specimens), birds, reptiles, amphibians, invertebrates, and plants. Most of the fossil mammals are from the ULB (82.3 percent), with smaller samples from the LLB (1.9 percent) and UNB (15.7 percent). Representative fossil vertebrates have also recovered from the Pleistocene deposits of the Olpiro and Ngaloba Beds and are all curated in the National Museum of Tanzania.

Eighty-five species of mammals are recorded from the ULB (Table 34.3). The large mammal fauna is dominated by bovids (33.8 percent of all mammal specimens), with *Madoqua avifluminis* (an extinct species of dik-dik) being the most common species (representing 18.1 percent of all bovids; Table 34.4). Rodents and lagomorphs are well represented (45.4 percent), with the leporid *Serengetilagus praecapensis* being the most common mammal (38.1 percent of all mammal specimens). Rodents and other micromammals (with body mass under 200 g) are likely underrepresented due to taphonomic and collecting biases (see Soligo and Andrews, 2005). Giraffids (6.4 percent), rhinocerotids (3.7 percent), and carnivorans (3.6 percent) are relatively common. Equids and suids, which typically represent a significant component of other eastern Africa Pliocene faunas, are relatively rare at Laetoli. Primates (i.e., hominins, cercopithecids, and galagids) are also rare, and comprise less than 1 percent of mammalian specimens (Harrison, 2011a, 2011f, 2011g; Table 34.4). Among the large mammals, hominins occur about as frequently as aardvarks, chalicotheres, and large felids, which may offer clues to the specialized nature of their ecological or dietary niche (Su and Harrison, 2008, 2015).

Other common vertebrates in the ULB include galliform birds (and their eggs), ostriches (represented by eggshell fragments only), tortoises, and snakes (Harrison, 2005, 2011h; Harrison and Msuya, 2005; Louchart, 2011; Rage and Bailon, 2011). Terrestrial gastropods are ubiquitous (Peters et al., 2008; Tattersfield, 2011; Harrison, 2017). Trace fossils and natural casts of insects are common, especially termitaries, hymenopteran cocoons and brood cells, and dung beetle brood balls (Sands, 1987; Darlington, 2005, 2011; Kitching and Sadler, 2011; Krell and Schawaller, 2011). Macrobotanical remains are represented by seeds, root casts, twigs, wood fragments, and *in situ* tree stumps (Bamford, 2011a; Barboni, 2014). Fossil leaf impressions are rare but are occasionally preserved in primary ash falls (Bamford, 2011b).

A small assemblage from the LLB includes 27 species of mammals and the mammal fauna is dominated by bovids (31.1 percent, in terms of specimen counts), equids (19.2 percent), and proboscideans (12.5 percent; Table 34.4). Small mammals are uncommon, with a strong taphonomic bias favoring the preservation of large mammals. Most of the mammalian species (78 percent) in the LLB also occur in the ULB, despite the age difference, implying a strong biogeographic provinciality and ecological continuity through time (Table 34.4). Nevertheless, a few mammalian taxa occur in the LLB that are not present in the ULB (Harrison, 2011b). The presence of *Petromus*, *Proteles*, and an aonyxin otter in the LLB probably relates to ecological differences, while the occurrence of *Anancus kenyensis*, *Loxodonta cookei*, and *Heterocephalus manthii*, which are replaced in the ULB by more advanced congeners, presumably reflects a biochronological distinction (Denys, 2011; Sanders, 2011; Werdelin and Dehghani, 2011). Fossil tortoises, ostrich eggshell fragments, termitaries, and terrestrial gastropods are

Table 34.2 Number of fossils collected at Laetoli and other localities on the Eyasi Plateau (1998–2014)[1]

Taxon	LLB[2]	ULB	UNB	Total	% of total
Mammals[3]	367	15,594	2976	18,937	57.1
Birds[4]	4	238	13	255	0.8
Struthio[5]	787	431	453	1671	5.0
Reptiles and amphibians[6]	136	408	36	580	1.7
Molluscs[7]	508	5639	400	6547	19.7
Insects[8]	773	2312	1250	4335	13.1
Plants[9]	279	571	5	855	2.6
Total	2854	25,193	5133	33,180	100.0

[1] Specimen counts do not include fossils from the Olpiro Beds or Ngaloba Beds.
[2] Abbreviations: LLB, Lower Laetolil Beds; ULB, Upper Laetolil Beds; UNB, Upper Ndolanya Beds
[3] For more detailed information on fossil mammals see Table 34.4.
[4] Includes bones and eggs, except for those assigned to *Struthio*.
[5] Eggshell fragments of *Struthio* spp.
[6] Mostly the remains of tortoises, but the count includes snakes, lizards, and anurans.
[7] Terrestrial gastropods.
[8] Mostly cocoons and brood cells of solitary bees and wasps, but also includes casts of insects, termitaries, and brood balls of dung beetles.
[9] Includes wood, twigs, seeds, and leaf impressions.

Table 34.3 List of the fauna from Laetoli (LLB, Lower Laetolil Beds; ULB, Upper Laetolil Beds; UNB, Upper Ndolanya Beds). After Harrison (2011b).

Class	Order	Family	Genus and species	LLB	ULB	UNB
Insecta	Hymenoptera	Indeterminate		X	X	X
	Coleoptera	Tenebrionidae	Tentyriini sp. A (*?Tentyria*)		X	
			Tentyriini sp. B		X	
			?Tentyriini sp. C		X	
			Molurini sp. A (*?Arturium*)		X	
		Scarabaeidae	*Calcitoryctes magnificus*		X	
			Melolonthinae: Schizonychini, sp. A		X	
			Coprinisphaera ndolanyanus			X
			Coprinisphaera laetoliensis			X
			Lazaichnus amplus			X
	Diptera	Indeterminate			X	
	Lepidoptera	Saturniidae	Bunaeini indet.		X	
	Isoptera	Termitidae	*Macrotermes* spp.		X	
			Apicotermitinae indet.		X	
		Indeterminate		X		
Gastropoda	Pulmonata	Succineidae	"*Succinea*" sp. A	X		
		Cerastidae	*Gittenedouardia laetoliensis*	X	X	
			Cerastus sp. A	X		
		Subulinidae	*Subulona pseudinvoluta*		X	
			Pseudoglessula (*Kempioconcha*) aff. *gibbonsi*		X	
			Kenyaella leakeyi	?	X	
			Kenyaella harrisoni			X
			Subuliniscus sp. A			X
		Vertiginidae	*Pupoides coenopictus*	X		
		Streptaxidae	*Streptostele* (*Raffraya*) aff. *horei*		X	X
			Streptostele sp. A		X	
			Gulella sp. A		X	
		Achatinidae	*Burtoa nilotica*	X	X	
			Limicolaria martensiana	X	X	
			Achatina (*Lissachatina*) indet.	X	X	
		Urocyclidae	*Trochonanina* sp. B	X	X	X
			Urocyclinae sp. A		X	X
			Urocyclinae sp. B		X	X
			Urocyclinae sp. C		X	X
			Urocyclinae sp. D		X	X
			Urocyclinae sp. E		X	X
			Urocyclinae sp. F		X	X
		Bradybaenidae	*Halolimnohelix rowsoni*		X	
Amphibia	Anura	Indeterminate			X	
Reptila	Chelonii	Testudinidae	*Stigmochelys brachygularis*	X	X	X
			"*Geochelone*" *laetoliensis*	X	X	
	Crocodilia	Crocodylidae	*Crocodylus* sp.	X		
	Squamata	Acrodonta indet.			X	
		Scincomorpha indet.				X
		Boidae	*Python sebae* or *P. natalensis*		X	

Table 34.3 (cont.)

Class	Order	Family	Genus and species	LLB	ULB	UNB
		Colubridae	cf. *Thelotornis* sp.		X	
			cf. *Rhamphiophis* sp.		X	
			Indeterminate sp. A		X	
			Inderterminate sp. B		X	
		Elapidae	*Naja robusta*		X	
			?indeterminate sp.		X	
		Viperidae	*Bitis* sp. nov. or *Bitis olduvaiensis*	X	X	X
Aves	Struthioniformes	Struthionidae	*Struthio kakesiensis*	X	X	
			Struthio camelus		X	X
	Galliformes	Phasianidae	*Francolinus* sp. A aff. *F. (Peliperdix) sephaena*		X	X
			Francolinus (Pternistis) sp. B		X	X
			cf. *Francolinus* sp. indet.		X	
		Numididae	cf. *Agelastes* sp.		X	
			Numida/Guttera sp.	X	X	X
			Acryllium vulturinum		X	
	Ciconiiformes	Ardeidae	cf. *Ardea* sp.			X
			Aegypius sp.		X	
	Charadriiformes	Scolopacidae	Calidrinae indet.		X	
	Accipitriformes	Accipitridae	cf. *Buteo* sp.		X	
			Aquilini indet. sp. A		X	
			cf. Aquilini indet sp. B		X	
	Falconiformes	Falconidae	*Falco* cf. *eleonorae*			X
			Falconiformes indet.		X	
	Columbiformes	Columbidae	*Columba* sp. (sp. A)		X	
			Streptopelia sp. (sp. B)		X	X
			Columbidae indet. (sp. C)			X
	Strigiformes	Tytonidae	*Tyto* sp.		X	
		Strigidae	*Bubo* cf. *lacteus* (sp. A)		X	
			Asio sp. (sp. B)		X	
			cf. Strigidae (sp. C)		X	
	Coliiformes	Collidae	*Colius* sp.		X	
	Passeriformes	Indeterminate	cf. Passerida indet.		X	
Mammalia	Macroscelidea	Macroscelididae	*Rhynchocyon pliocaenicus*		X	
	Tubulidentata	Orycteropodidae	*Orycteropus* sp.		X	
	Proboscidea	Deinotheriidae	*Deinotherium bozasi*		X	?
		Gomphotheriidae	*Anancus kenyensis*	X		
			Anancus ultimus	X	X	
		Stegodontidae	*Stegodon* sp. cf. *Stegodon kaisensis*		X	
		Elephantidae	*Loxodonta* sp. cf. *Loxodonta cookei*	X		
			Loxodonta exoptata	X	X	X
	Primates	Galagidae	*Laetolia sadimanensis*		X	
		Cercopithecidae	*Parapapio ado*		X	X
			Papionini indet.		X	
			cf. *Rhinocolobus* sp.		X	X
			Cercopithecoides sp.		X	
		Hominidae	*Australopithecus afarensis*		X	

Table 34.3 (cont.)

Class	Order	Family	Genus and species	LLB	ULB	UNB
			Paranthropus aethiopicus			X
	Rodentia	Sciuridae	*Paraxerus meini*		X	X
			Xerus sp.		X	
			Xerus janenschi		X	X
		Cricetidae	*Gerbilliscus satimani*		X	
			Gerbilliscus winkleri			X
			Gerbilliscus cf. *inclusus*		X	
			Dendromus sp.		X	
			Steatomys sp.		X	
			Saccostomus major	cf.	X	cf.
			Saccostomus sp.			X
		Muridae	*Aethomys* sp.		X	
			Thallomys laetolilensis		X	X
			Mastomys cinereus		X	
			Mus sp.		X	
		Thryonomyidae	*Thryonomys wesselmani*			X
		Petromuridae	*Petromus* sp.	X		
		Bathyergidae	*Heterocephalus quenstedti*		X	
			Heterocephalus manthii	X		
		Hystricidae	*Hystrix leakeyi*		X	
			Hystrix makapanensis		X	X
			Xenohystrix crassidens		X	
		Pedetidae	*Propedetes laetoliensis*		X	
			Propedetes sp.			X
	Lagomorpha	Leporidae	*Serengetilagus praecapensis*	X	X	X
	Soricimorpha	Soricidae	?*Crocidura* sp.			X
	Carnivora	Canidae	?*Nyctereutes barryi*		X	
			cf. *Canis* sp. A		X	
			cf. *Canis* sp. B		X	
			aff. *Otocyon* sp.		X	
		Mustelidae	*Propoecilogale bolti*		X	X
			Mellivora sp.		X	
			Aonyxini gen. et sp. nov.	X		
			Mustelidae indet.		X	
		Viverridae	*Viverra leakeyi*		X	
			Genetta sp.		X	
			aff. Viverridae		X	
		Herpestidae	*Herpestes palaeoserengetensis*		X	
			Herpestes ichneumon		X	
			Galerella sp.		X	
			Helogale palaeogracilis	X	X	X
			Mungos dietrichi		X	X
			Mungos sp. nov.		X	
		Hyaenidae	*Crocuta dietrichi*		X	X
			Parahyaena howelli	X	X	
			Ikelohyaena cf. *I. abronia*		X	?

Table 34.3 (cont.)

Class	Order	Family	Genus and species	LLB	ULB	UNB
			Lycyaenops cf. *L. silberbergi*		X	
			?*Pachycrocuta* sp.		X	
			aff. *Proteles* sp.	X		
		Felidae	*Dinofelis petteri*		X	X
			Homotherium sp.		X	X
			Panthera sp. aff. *P. leo*		X	
			Panthera sp. cf. *P. pardus*		X	X
			Acinonyx sp.		X	
			Caracal sp. or *Leptailurus* sp.		X	X
			Felis sp.		X	X
	Perissodactyla	Equidae	*Eurygnathohippus* aff. *hasumense*	X	X	
			Eurgnathohippus aff. *cornelianus*			X
		Chalicotheriidae	*Ancylotherium hennigi*		X	
		Rhinocerotidae	*Ceratotherium efficax*	X	X	X
			Ceratotherium cf. *simum*			X
			Ceratotherium sp.			X
			Diceros sp.		X	
	Artiodactyla	Suidae	*Notochoerus euilus*	X	X	
			Notochoerus jaegeri	X	X	
			Nyanzachoerus kanamensis		X	
			Potamochoerus afarensis		X	
			Kolpochoerus heseloni		X	X
			Metridiochoerus andrewsi			X
		Giraffidae	*Giraffa stillei*	aff.	X	aff.
			Giraffa jumae		aff.	
			Giraffa pygmaea			aff.
			Sivatherium maurusium	X	X	aff.
		Camelidae	*Camelus* sp.			X
		Bovidae	*Tragelaphus* sp.		X	
			Tragelaphus sp. cf. *T. buxtoni*			X
			Simatherium kohllarseni		X	
			Brabovus nanincisus		X	
			Bovini sp. indet.	X	X	X
			Cephalophini sp.		X	?
			Hippotragus sp.	X	X	
			Hippotragus sp. aff. *cookei*?			X
			Oryx deturi		X	
			Oryx sp.			X
			Parmularius pandatus	X	X	
			Parmularius ?*altidens*			X
			Parmularius parvicornis			X
			Alcelaphini, larger sp. indet.	X	X	
			Alcelaphini, small sp.		?	
			Megalotragus kattwinkeli or *M. isaaci*			X
			?*Connochaetes* sp.			X
			Reduncini sp. indet.		X	X

Table 34.3 (cont.)

Class	Order	Family	Genus and species	LLB	ULB	UNB
			Madoqua avifluminis	X	X	X
			?*Raphicerus* sp.	X	X	X
			Aepyceros dietrichi	X	X	
			Aepyceros sp.			X
			"*Gazella*" *kohllarseni*		X	
			Gazella janenschi	X	X	X
			Gazella sp.			X
			Nanger granti	X	?	?
			Antidorcas recki			X

Table 34.4 Number of specimens and the frequency of fossil mammals collected at Laetoli and other localities on the Eyasi Plateau (1998–2014).

Taxon	Lower Laetolil Beds		Upper Ndolanya Beds		Upper Ndolanya Beds	
	N	%	N	%	N	%
Macroscelididae	0	0	7	0.05	0	0
Galagidae	0	0	3	0.02	0	0
Cercopithecidae	1	0.27	141	0.91	1	0.03
Hominidae	0	0	6	0.04	2	0.07
Rodentia	15	4.16	1123	7.28	138	4.78
Leporidae	24	6.66	5873	38.09	497	17.23
Carnivora	17	4.72	553	3.59	65	2.25
Proboscidea	45	12.50	181	1.17	28	0.97
Orycteropodidae	1	0.27	26	0.17	2	0.07
Equidae	69	19.17	410	2.66	129	4.47
Rhinocerotidae	43	11.94	577	3.74	30	1.04
Chalicotheriidae	0	0	8	0.05	0	0
Suidae	16	4.44	287	1.86	30	1.04
Camelidae	0	0	27	0.18	6	0.21
Giraffidae	17	4.72	984	6.38	89	3.08
Bovidae	112	31.11	5214	33.81	1868	64.75
Total	360	99.96	15,420	100.0	2885	99.99

common in the LLB (Harrison and Msuya, 2005; Darlington, 2011; Harrison, 2011h; Tattersfield, 2011). Fossil wood from Noiti has aided the LLB paleoenvironmental reconstruction (Bamford, 2011a).

Fossil mammals are abundant in the UNB with 49 species identified (Table 34.3). There is a significant taxonomic turnover of the fauna during the gap in deposition between the ULB and UNB (between 3.6 Ma and 2.66 Ma), with only 69 percent of the UNB species shared with the ULB. *Eurygnathohippus* aff. *cornelianus* replaces *E.* aff. *hasumense*, *Gerbilliscus winkleri* replaces *G. satimani*, and *Paranthropus aethiopicus* replaces *A. afarensis*. Other taxa making their first appearance include *Thryonomys wesselmani*, *Ceratotherium simum*, *Metridiochoerus andrewsi*, *Giraffa pygmaea*, *Parmularius altidens*, *Parmularius parvicornis*, *Megalotragus* sp., *Tragelaphus* sp. cf. *T. buxtoni*, and *Antidorcas recki* (Armour-Chelu and Bernor, 2011; Bishop, 2011; Denys, 2011; Gentry, 2011; Harrison, 2011b; Hernesniemi et al., 2011; Robinson, 2011).

The UNB mammalian fauna is dominated by bovids (64.8 percent of all specimens), especially medium- and large-sized alcelaphins, probably due to ecology and taphonomic factors (Table 34.4). *Madoqua avifluminis* and *Serengetilagus praecapensis* are still common in the UNB, but they occur much less frequently than in the ULB (Table 34.4). Other common mammals in the UNB include rodents (4.8 percent of all specimens), equids (4.5 percent), giraffids (3.1 percent), and carnivorans (2.3 percent; Table 34.4). As in the ULB, ostrich eggshell fragments, gastropods, and traces of hymenoptera are well represented in the UNB.

Paleoecology

Previous inferences about Laetoli suggested that the ULB was predominantly semi-arid grassland with scattered bush and tree cover and patches of acacia woodland, similar to the modern-day ecosystem in the southern Serengeti (Harris, 1985, 1987; Bonnefille and Riollet, 1987; Denys, 1987a; Gentry, 1987; Hay, 1987). The UNB fauna was generally interpreted as indicating more arid habitats with open woodland and grassland (Gentry, 1987; Harris, 1987; Hay, 1987). However, other evidence from fossil mammals and gastropods pointed to somewhat wetter conditions in the UNB with a more extensive representation of woody vegetation (Denys, 1987a; Gentry, 1987; Harris, 1987; Verdcourt, 1987). The LLB was viewed as ecologically similar to the ULB, except that sedimentological evidence and the presence of aquatic vertebrates indicate shallow lakes and marshes (Harris, 1987). Recent studies, however, have revised these previous paleoecological scenarios.

The Pliocene geomorphological evidence indicates that Laetoli had relatively low topography, with a gently undulating terrain. Unlike most Pliocene sites in eastern Africa, there is no evidence of permanent bodies of water in the ULB, and this is consistent with the absence of aquatic and hydrophilic vertebrates (i.e., hippopotamids, crocodiles, turtles and fishes; Harrison, 2011b). The ULB sediments provide evidence of small rivers and streams, probably with a greater extent and capacity than the present-day hydrological system. However, these flowed only during the rainy season and were otherwise dry for most of the year (Ditchfield and Harrison, 2011). Ephemeral wet-season ponds account for the rare finds of anurans (Ditchfield and Harrison, 2011; Rage and Bailon, 2011). The intricate network of small watercourses would have supported a complex vegetational mosaic, including dense stands of riverine woodland and bushland (Ditchfield and Harrison, 2011). Wading birds (Scolopacidae) and sedge and bulrush pollen grains suggest nearby wetlands, which were rare in the lower part of the ULB (Louchart, 2011).

The evidence suggests that the Eyasi Plateau would have been dry for much of the year with no standing water. However, run-off from the volcanic highlands probably occurred year-round, just as it does today, with water flowing subsurface during the dry months. Today, springs and seepages, dotted along the margin of the Eyasi escarpment, provide a perennial source of water. These springs were very likely present during the Pliocene and would have offered an important source of water for animals during the long dry season in what would otherwise have been a dry landscape.

This absence of standing water explains the uniqueness of the Laetoli fauna. Two of the most common mammals in the ULB, the leporid *Serengetilagus praecapensis* and the extinct dik dik *Madoqua avifluminis*, are closely related to modern arid-adapted taxa (Maloiy et al., 1988; Kingswood and Kumamoto, 1997; Kingdon, 2015). Additionally, the sample of *Loxodonta exoptata*, the most common proboscidean in the ULB, is remarkable in being heavily skewed numerically toward calves and juveniles, with two thirds of the cranio-dental specimens represented by deciduous teeth (Sanders, 2011). Modern African elephants (*L. africana*) experience high levels of mortality among the youngest age classes during severe drought (Corfield, 1973). During the Pliocene at Laetoli, when the rains failed and even the springs dried up, younger elephants would have been less able to move to other water sources and so been prone to greater mortality (Sanders, 2011). In addition, the occurrence in the ULB of fossorial rodents, traces of termitaries, extensive termite bioturbation, burrows and nests of solitary hymenoptera, and achatinid gastropods estivating underground during diapause all indicate that soils were dry and well-drained for much of the year.

Inundations of volcanic ashes periodically covered the terrain, and occasionally a sufficient volume of ash fell that seriously disrupted the local and regional ecosystem. Heavy inundations would have buried ground vegetation, stripped trees of their leaves and branches, and contaminated standing water (Peters et al., 2008). Over time, thick deposits of ashes formed impervious calcretes and hardpans that were unsuitable for trees, leading to a landscape that was dominated by grasslands and scattered woodlands. These periods of disruption were probably relatively rare and short-lived (in the order of decades).

Initial pollen studies from the ULB indicated similar vegetation to present-day Laetoli, including herbaceous plant families common in the area today, with a high proportion of grass pollen (Bonnefille and Riollet, 1987; Andrews and Bamford, 2008, Andrews et al., 2011). Arboreal pollen was mostly derived from afromontane forest trees, including *Juniperus* and *Podocarpus*, which presumably originated in the NVHC. Pollen of *Acacia* is also common. While Bonnefille and Riollet (1987) concluded that the ULB vegetation was principally grassland and open woodland, recent renewed sampling of the ULB sediments failed to recover any palynomorphs, suggesting that pollen preservation is extremely poor or that the initial results were contaminated by modern pollen (Rossouw and Scott, 2011). Study of the phytoliths indicates that grasses were common in the ULB, but that woodland and shrubland dominated (Rossouw and Scott, 2011).

Plant macrofossils from the ULB consist of wood, root casts, leaf impressions, fruits, and seeds. The wood and root casts are generally not well enough preserved for taxonomic identification, although a number of fossil twigs with small thorns are likely to belong to *Acacia*. The fruits and seeds have proved difficult to identify, but some are provisionally recognized as from woodland taxa, such as *Ximena*, *Celtis*, *Boscia*, and *Cryptocarya* (Bamford, 2011a). Small seeds found in bovid coprolites are probably derived from *Acacia* pods (Harrison, 2011i). Leaf impressions of Euphorbiaceae, *Dombeya*, and *Acacia* have also been identified (M.D. Leakey, 1979; Hay, 1987; Bamford, 2011b; Harrison, unpublished). The abundance of microphylls among the fossil leaves indicates a deciduous woodland with a seasonal climate (Bamford, 2011b). The plant fossils mostly belong to taxa that occur today in the open and closed woodland communities on the Oldonyo Mati Hills to the south of Laetoli (Andrews et al., 2011).

Studies of the stable isotopes, mesowear, bovid postcranial ecomorphology, small and large mammal community structure, and avifauna largely agree with paleobotanical evidence (Andrews, 1989; Andrews and Humphrey, 1999; Kovarovic, 2004; Harrison, 2005, 2011b; Su, 2005, 2011; Kingston and Harrison, 2007; Kovarovic and Andrews, 2007, 2011; Su and Harrison, 2007, 2015; Bishop, 2011; Bishop et al., 2011; Denys, 2011; Hernesniemi et al., 2011; Kaiser, 2011; Kingston, 2011; Louchart, 2011). Overall, the evidence suggests that the paleoecology of the ULB was a heavily vegetated woodland, bushland and grassland mosaic, with dense stands of riverine woodland and gallery forest fringing the seasonal watercourses. A recent study of the mammalian community in relation to arboreal heterogeneity reconstructs the ULB paleoecology as predominantly light woodland and grassland, with ~10 percent heavy tree cover (Louys et al., 2015). However, there is substantial evidence for densely wooded conditions during the ULB, and one can conclude that the model does not provide an accurate predictor of tree cover, at least to the ULB.

The ungulates are dominated by browsing taxa (50 percent of ungulate species) and mixed feeders (45 percent of ungulate species; Kingston and Harrison, 2007; Kaiser, 2011; Kingston, 2011). The diverse guild of large browsers (i.e., three species of giraffids, Cephalophini, *Brabovus*, *Tragelaphus*, "*Gazella*" *kohlarseni*, *Gazella janenschi*, *Aepyceros*, *Nyanzachoerus*, *Potamochoerus*, *Ancylotherium*, *Ceratotherium*, *Deinotherium*, *Anancus*, and *Stegodon*) has no modern analog outside tropical forest communities, underlining the importance of dense woodland and shrubland habitats. The only obligate grazer in the ULB fauna was *Eurygnathohippus* aff. *hasumense* (Kaiser, 2011; Kingston, 2011), although alcelaphins appear to have occupied the grazing end of the dietary spectrum of intermediate feeders. Ecomorphological analyses of the bovid postcranials also suggest ULB was woodland-dominated (Kovarovic and Andrews, 2007, 2011; Bishop et al., 2011).

The primate fauna provides further support for the inference that the ULB paleoecology consisted of extensive tree cover. The postcranial morphology of the three most common monkeys shows that they were either arboreal (cf. *Rhinocolobus* sp. and *Cercopithecoides* sp.) or semiterrestrial (*Parapapio ado*; Harrison, 2011f; Harrison and Rein, 2016). Only the very rare large papionin was terrestrial. Moreover, the co-occurrence of a hominoid (*A. afarensis*) with four species of cercopithecids is found today in East Africa only in evergreen and semi-evergreen forests (Su and Harrison, 2008). The unique locomotor and dietary profiles of the primates and other large mammals indicate that there is no modern ecological counterpart in Africa for the ULB woodland–shrubland.

The ULB rodent fauna compares well with modern-day faunas in the dry savannas (i.e., wooded grasslands) and woodlands of the northern Serengeti region. The relatively high proportion of arboreal rodents (i.e., *Paraxerus*, *Dendromus*, and *Thallomys*) supports the presence of woodlands (Reed and Denys, 2011). The terrestrial gastropods suggest relatively mesic and heavily vegetated conditions during ULB times (Peters et al., 2008; Tattersfield, 2011; Table 34.5).

Overall, the evidence suggests that the ULB paleoecology was a mix of closed woodland, open woodland, shrubland, and grassland habitats. It was more mesic and more densely wooded than the modern-day Garusi valley ecosystem, which is dominated by grassland and scattered acacia woodland–bushland (Andrews et al., 2011). However, the modern vegetation has been negatively impacted by recent anthropogenic activities (Andrews et al., 2011), with a greater proportion of woody plant cover in the historic past. The closed and open woodlands (a mix of broad-leaved species and acacias, with a diverse herbaceous understory) on the Oldonyo Mati Hills along the southern margin of the Garusi River valley probably provide a suitable analog (Andrews et al., 2011). Dense stands of riverine woodland and gallery forest would have bordered the ephemeral watercourses. Water was probably more abundant during the rainy season, judging from the size and frequency of watercourses and small-scale fluvial deposits, but the region would have been arid for much of the year, except for perennial springs along the edge of the Eyasi Plateau.

Based on the large mammal fauna and stable isotopes, the paleoecology of the LLB appears to have been broadly like that of the ULB (Harrison, 2011b; Kingston, 2011). Aquatic vertebrates are extremely rare in the Lower Laetolil Beds, but the fossils of an otter and a crocodile do indicate the presence of water bodies. Harris (1987) reported the presence of fish from the LLB, but this has not been substantiated, and their record has been removed from the faunal list (Table 34.3). The sedimentological evidence confirms that marshes, shallow pools, and small lakes dotted the landscape with dense woodland–bushland around larger water bodies.

The paleobotanical evidence for the LLB, specifically fossil wood from Noiti, indicates that dense woodlands and forest covered the lower slopes of the volcanic highlands to the east, and a mix of woodland, bushland, and wooded grasslands occurred nearer to Laetoli (Bamford, 2011a). A fossil sedge from Oleisusu indicates the presence of a perennial water source. Phytoliths from the LLB are indicative of a relatively mesic habitat dominated by C_3 grasses (Rossouw and Scott, 2011). Volcanic ash falls in the LLB were more substantial and more frequent than in the ULB and would have caused disruptions to the local ecosystem. However, the greater degree of fluvial reworking of the tuffs and heavy bioturbation by invertebrates, especially termites, indicates that the sediments soon formed weakly developed paleosols that would have supported a rapid re-establishment of the climax vegetation.

The mammal fauna from the LLB shares most of its species (78.6 percent) with the ULB and there appears to be a strong ecological and zoogeographic continuity between the two faunas. Nevertheless, novel taxa in the LLB do indicate ecological

Table 34.5 Stratigraphic distribution and habitat preferences of most common fossil terrestrial gastropods from Laetoli (excluding urocyclid slugs).

Stratigraphic unit	Horizon	#1 ranked taxon	#2 ranked taxon	#3 ranked taxon	Paleoecological inference
Upper Ndolanya Beds		*Kenyaella* (72%)	*Subuliniscus* (16%)	*Streptostele* (4%)	Closed woodland and forest Rainfall: 760–1500 mm
Upper Laetolil Beds	Above Tuff 7	*Gittenedouardia* (45%)	*Trochonanina* (30%)	*Subulona* (10%)	Open and closed woodland; forest patches Rainfall: 500–1270 mm
	Between Tuffs 5 and 7	*Subulona* (50%)	*Achatina* (23%)	*Trochonanina* and *Burtoa* (both 6%)	Woodland and forest Rainfall: 760–1500 mm
	Between Tuffs 3 and 5	*Subulona* (44%)	*Kenyaella* (41%)	*Achatina* (10%)	Closed woodland and forest Rainfall: 760–1500 mm
	Below Tuff 3	*Kenyaella* (77%)	*Achatina* (6%)	*Pseudoglessula* (6%)	Woodland and forest Rainfall: 760–1200 mm
Lower Laetolil Beds		*Limicolaria* (52%)	*Achatina* (28%)	*Burtoa* (11%)	Dry open woodland Rainfall: 760–1020 mm

Data on Laetoli gastropods from Tattersfield (2011), Harrison (2017), Harrison (unpubl. data).
Data on habitat preferences and rainfall from Verdcourt (1963, 1987), van Bruggen (1978), Pickford (1995, 2004, 2009), and Tattersfield (2011).

differences, mostly related to the presence of semipermanent sources of water. For example, a clawless otter is known from the LLB, and *Anancus kenyensis* occurs at several LLB localities associated with lakeside or paludal settings. The occurrence of *Proteles* in the LLB is probably related to the abundance of small termite nests found throughout the LLB, termites being the major food source of the extant aardwolf (Kingdon, 2015). The large herbivore community is dominated by browsers and intermediate feeders, which suggest a woodland–shrubland ecosystem (Kaiser, 2011; Kingston, 2011). Micromammals from the LLB are not particularly informative from a paleoecological perspective, although *Heterocephalus* indicates relatively dry woodland habitats, while *Petromus* suggests the presence of rocky outcrops (Reed and Denys, 2011; Kingdon, 2015).

Unlike the mammal fauna, the terrestrial gastropod community from the LLB is strikingly different from that of the ULB (Table 34.5). It is dominated by large achatinids belonging to *Limicolaria*, *Achatina*, and *Burtoa*. These taxa have broad ecological tolerances and can be found in habitats ranging from grassy woodland to tropical forests. *Limicolaria* and *Achatina* occur today at Laetoli, where they are associated with grasslands and open woodlands. The occurrence of *Burtoa nilotica* suggests an annual precipitation of between 760 and 1020 mm (Pickford, 1995). *Limicolaria martensiana* (which comprises more than 50 percent of the land snails from the LLB) is an adaptable species that occurs commonly in shady plantations, agricultural plots, and other disturbed habitats (Owen, 1965; Pickford, 1995), and it is likely that its dominance in the LLB is associated with the ecological disruptions that accompanied the periodic volcanic eruptions. As Pickford (1995) has noted, many of the *Limicolaria* specimens from the LLB exhibit ovoviviparity (with young individuals preserved inside the shells of estivating adults), which represents a reproductive strategy in extant populations living in marginal environments. *Pupoides*, which is known from Kakesio (Pickford, 1995), is found today in semi-desert and dry woodland habitats (van Bruggen, 1978; Pickford, 1995). The composition of the gastropod fauna, along with the absence of urocyclid slugs, suggests that the LLB was a dry open woodland habitat (Table 34.5).

Overall, the LLB appears to have been a relatively dry open woodland–shrubland, with extensive areas of closed woodland surrounding larger bodies of water. Water was evidently more abundant year-round than in the ULB, with semipermanent marshes and lakes. Just to the east of Laetoli, relatively dense woodland and forests blanketed the lower slopes of the volcanic highlands.

The paleoecology of the UNB has proved more difficult to reconstruct because of conflicting lines of evidence. Analyses of stable isotopes, mesowear, ecomorphology, phytoliths, and the mammalian community structure all indicate that there was a shift from a woodland–bushland–grassland mosaic in the ULB to drier habitats with a greater proportion of grasslands in the UNB (Kovarovic et al., 2002; Kovarovic, 2004; Kingston and Harrison, 2007; Kovarovic and Andrews, 2007, 2011; Gentry, 2011; Harrison, 2011b; Hernesniemi et al., 2011; Kaiser, 2011; Kingston, 2011; Rossouw and Scott, 2011; Su, 2011; Barboni, 2014). The timing coincides with global climate changes at ~2.8–2.5 Ma, associated with increased intensification of northern hemisphere glaciation and greater aridity in East Africa (Bobe and Behrensmeyer, 2004; deMenocal, 2004, 2011; Feakins et al., 2005; Sepulchre et al., 2006; Bonnefille, 2010; Feakins and deMenocal, 2010). However, stable isotope data from ostrich eggshells and the habitat preferences of the rodents and terrestrial snails indicate that the UNB resembled the ULB in being a relatively mesic habitat dominated by woodlands (Kingston and Harrison, 2007; Peters et al., 2008; Kingston, 2011; Denys, 2011; Reed and Denys, 2011; Tattersfield, 2011). This latter interpretation accords well with evidence for increased moisture availability in East Africa at 2.6 Ma, associated with 400-kyr eccentricity maxima and elevated lake levels (Deino et al., 2006b; Trauth et al., 2005, 2007, 2009, 2010; Kingston et al., 2007; Maslin and Trauth, 2009; Maslin et al., 2015).

The most compelling evidence for an ecological shift in the UNB toward drier habitats comes from the composition and paleobiology of the large mammal fauna, which shows that most large mammal herbivores that make their first appearance in the UNB (nine species) are mixed-feeders or grazers, whereas the relative proportion of large browsing mammal taxa declines (Bishop, 2011; Harrison, 2011b, 2017; Kaiser, 2011; Kingston, 2011). The UNB also has a higher proportion of alcelaphin and antilopin bovids (77.4 percent of bovid specimens) compared with the ULB (50.1 percent), and these taxa are predominantly mixed-feeders. These changes indicate a notable shift in the UNB large herbivore dietary guild to one with a greater emphasis on taxa that included a significant proportion of grasses in their diets (59 percent of ungulate species are grazers or mixed feeders in the UNB, compared with 41 percent in the ULB). Stable carbon isotope and mesowear analyses confirm a greater emphasis on C_4 diets among equids and alcelaphin bovids in the UNB (Kingston and Harrison, 2007; Kaiser, 2011; Kingston, 2011).

Based on the ecological diversity of the mammal fauna, Kovarovic et al. (2002) and Andrews (2006) inferred that the UNB was predominantly a bushland-grassland that was drier and more open than the ULB. Ecomorphological studies of UNB bovid postcrania indicate that the majority preferred open or lightly vegetated habitats (65.4 percent in the UNB versus 23.3 percent in the ULB; Kovarovic and Andrews, 2007; Bishop et al., 2011). Phytolith evidence indicates that there was a relatively higher frequency of C_4 grasses in the UNB compared with the ULB (Rossouw and Scott, 2011), which is further supported by stable carbon isotope analyses of carbonates in paleosols that indicate a shift to open woodland or bushland dominated by C_4 grasses in the UNB (Cerling, 1992).

Overall, this evidence indicates that the UNB and ULB were both woodland–bushland–grassland mosaics, in which the ULB appears the more mesic and more densely wooded, while the UNB is viewed as being more arid with extensive grasslands. Basically, only the relative proportions of each vegetation type changed in the Laetoli area (Kovarovic and Andrews, 2007). This gradational ecological transition between the ULB and UNB is reflected in comparisons of large mammal faunas, in which 62.5 percent of UNB species also occur in the ULB. Closer scrutiny of the large mammal fauna shows that the evidence for a profound ecological change in the UNB is largely based on taxonomic and paleobiological changes in the bovids and equids. For example, the UNB sees the arrival of several new species of antilopin and alcelaphin, as well as a replacement species of hipparionine, all of which were apparently more specialized than their ULB predecessors for grazing and increased cursoriality in open country environments. However, the actual changes in the composition of the large mammal fauna were primarily limited to just a few taxonomic groups, and it is these that influence the outcome of analyses that favor interpretations of a major paleoecology distinction between the ULB and UNB.

As noted above, however, other lines of evidence run counter to the interpretation that the UNB was characterized by drier grassland and open woodland habitats compared with the ULB. Apart from the alcelaphin bovids and equids, none of the other UNB mammals demonstrate a significant difference in carbon isotopic signatures or mesowear from those from the ULB (Kingston and Harrison, 2007; Kaiser, 2011; Kingston, 2011). In contrast, carbon and oxygen isotopes of ostrich eggshell indicate that the UNB climate was cooler and more humid than the ULB (Kingston, 2011).

Based on modern-day habitat preferences, the rodents from the UNB indicate the presence of open woodlands and sparsely wooded grasslands that were more mesic than those in the ULB (Campbell et al., 2011; Denys, 2011; Reed, 2011; Reed and Denys, 2011; Granjon and Dempster, 2013; Kingdon, 2015). The terrestrial gastropod community in the UNB is restricted today to forest and closed woodland habitats (Verdcourt, 1963, 1987; Pickford, 1995, 2004, 2009; Tattersfield, 2011; Harrison, 2017; Table 34.5), and they simply cannot be found today in the type of dry open woodland–grassland habitats that have been inferred from the large mammal fauna. The same gastropods occur at all UNB localities, suggesting that woodland–forest habitats were widespread, not patchily distributed.

A plausible argument is that ostrich eggshells, terrestrial snails, and micromammals provide a better reflection of fine-grained ecological differences over relatively small spatial scales and thus represent more accurate indicators of local environmental conditions, in which case, the UNB was dominated by woodland–shrubland, and not profoundly different from the ULB, at least in the general composition of its vegetation. Nevertheless, the UNB and ULB faunas do provide evidence for an ecological difference, but this may have been more subtle than has been previously deduced using the large mammal fauna (Harrison, 2017). It is likely that a woodland–shrubland–grassland mosaic persisted at Laetoli throughout the Pliocene, but that the UNB experienced greater aridity with an increased proportion of grassland compared with the ULB. Of the changes in the fauna that took place in the UNB, it is the appearance of a new species of *Eurygnathohippus* and of several new alcelaphins and antilopins that had the greatest impact on the results of stable isotope, mesowear, and ecomorphological analyses. These taxa were apparently more specialized for exploiting open woodland and grassland environments compared to their ULB counterparts and were able to take advantage of grasslands that already existed within the Laetoli mosaic. The most plausible interpretation of the evidence suggests that the overall ecology remained broadly similar in the ULB and UNB, but that the composition of the large mammal fauna changed with the arrival in the UNB of more advanced and specialized herbivores that were better adapted for exploiting this grassland component (Harrison, 2017).

Conclusions

Fossil mammals, including hominins, were first discovered at Laetoli in the 1930s, but the significance of the site was only realized when Mary Leakey initiated research in the 1970s. Laetoli is best known for the skeletal remains of *Australopithecus afarensis* and trails of footprints from the ULB (3.6–3.85 Ma). Fossil hominins from the UNB (2.66 Ma) include the first specimen of *Paranthropus aethiopicus* from outside the Turkana Basin, and one of the oldest securely dated specimens of this taxon. A small collection of fossils, but no hominins, has been recovered from the LLB (3.85 Ma to older than 4.36 Ma).

Laetoli is unusual for early hominin sites in the absence of permanent bodies of water, and in having less densely wooded habitats. The evidence indicates that the ULB was a mosaic of woodland, shrubland, and grassland, with closed woodland and gallery forest fringing seasonal watercourses. The LLB is similar, but with marshes and shallow lakes. These bodies of water were probably associated with dense stands of fringing woodland–shrubland, but that generally, the LLB was probably open woodland dominated. The hiatus between the deposition of the ULB and UNB coincides with climatic changes that impacted on the regional and local environments, including the Laetoli faunal composition. Evidence from the large mammals suggests that the UNB samples drier habitats with a greater proportion of grasslands compared with the earlier ULB. However, other evidence indicates that UNB habitats resembled the ULB in being relatively mesic with a predominance of closed woodlands. The UNB may have been slightly drier with more grassland than the ULB, but woodland and shrubland still dominated the ecosystem.

Acknowledgments

We thank Sally Reynolds and René Bobe for the invitation to contribute to this volume, and for their patience in waiting for the final product. We also acknowledge the following colleagues whose work and discussions have contributed much to our understanding of the paleoecology at Laetoli: Peter Andrews, Marion Bamford, Laura Bishop, Jo Darlington, Peter Ditchfield, Christiane Denys, Mikael Fortelius, Alan Gentry, John Kingston, Thomas Kaiser, Kris Kovarovic, Charles Peters, Denné Reed, Kaye Reed, Lloyd Rossouw, William Sanders, and Louis Scott. The Tanzania Commission for Science and Technology, the Department of Antiquities, and the National Museum of Tanzania granted research permission. Peter Andrews, Sally Reynolds, and René Bobe provided helpful feedback on an initial version of this chapter. We are grateful to the following institutions and their staff for access to the fossil and skeletal collections in their care: National Museum of Tanzania, National Museum of Kenya, American Museum of Natural History, and The Natural History Museum, London. The National Geographic Society, the Leakey Foundation, and NSF (Grants BCS-0309513, BCS-0216683 and BSC 1350023) provided funding.

35 The Paleoenvironment of the Plio-Pleistocene Chiwondo Beds of Northern Malawi

Ottmar Kullmer, Oliver Sandrock, Harrison Simfukwe, Timothy G. Bromage, and Friedemann Schrenk

History of Research

The Plio-Pleistocene sedimentary deposits in Northern Malawi were first described as Chiwondo and Chitimwe Beds by Dixey (1927). In the 1920s and 1930s Dixey collected vertebrate remains mostly from localities close to "Uraha Hill" and attributed the deposits based on the interpretation of the fossils to the Pliocene and Pleistocene. Further studies have been undertaken by Clark and colleagues (1966, 1970), Coryndon (1966), Clark and Haynes (1970), Mawby (1970), Kaufulu and colleagues (1981), and by the Hominid Corridor Research Project (HCRP) since 1983 (e.g., Bromage et al., 1985, 1995). More than 1200 vertebrate fossils were collected by the HCRP from around 150 localities between Karonga in the north and Uraha in the south (Figure 35.1). The significance of the assemblage lies in its geographic position between the classical eastern and southern African hominid sites (Bromage et al., 1995; Kullmer et al., 1999a; Sandrock et al., 2007; Kullmer, 2008). The first evidence of a fossil hominin in Malawi, a fragmentary *Homo rudolfensis* mandible (HCRP-UR 501) from the Chiwondo Beds, was recovered from the southern locality U18 at Uraha in 1991 (Schrenk et al., 1993). The second hominin, a maxillary fragment of a *Paranthropus boisei* (HCRP-RC 911), was excavated at the northern locality RC 11 in Malema (Kullmer et al., 1999b); and the third hominin specimen, a *Homo rudolfensis* lower molar fragment (HCRP-MR 1106), was found at locality MR 10 in Mwenirondo just north of Malema in 2009 (Kullmer et al., 2011).

Geology and Biostratigraphy

The Chiwondo and overlaying Chitimwe Beds can be separated into five sedimentary units (Figure 35.2). From bottom to top, Units 1 to 4 refer to the Chiwondo and unit 5 refers to the Chitimwe Beds. The lithostratigraphic succession was described by Ring and Betzler (1995) and Betzler and Ring (1995), and consists of lake beds and fluviatile layers, as well as alluvial fan deposits. The accumulation of sediment in the northern Malawi Rift ("Karonga Basin") is attributed to subsidence processes and shoulder uplifts in a north–south direction along the youngest section of the East African Rift System. It is part of its western branch and rifting commenced around 8.6 Ma in the Late Miocene south of the Rungwe volcanic province (Ebinger et al., 1989, 1993). The sedimentary bodies in the Karonga Basin were formed during transgression and regression cycles of Paleo-Lake Malawi. Adjacent to the recent northwestern Lake Malawi shore a strip of 70-km sediments of a halfgraben structure is exposed between the towns of Karonga in the north and Chilumba in the south.

Unit 1 overlies Mesozoic deposits and consists of braided river sediments including reworked cretaceous Dinosaur

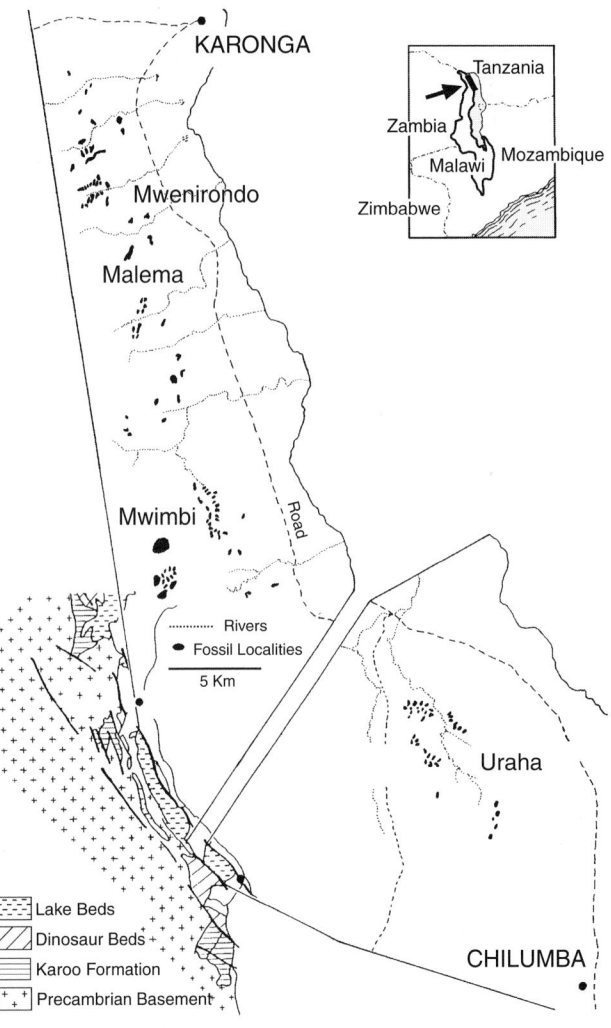

Figure 35.1 Topographic map and geological setting of the Chiwondo Beds, Northern Malawi.

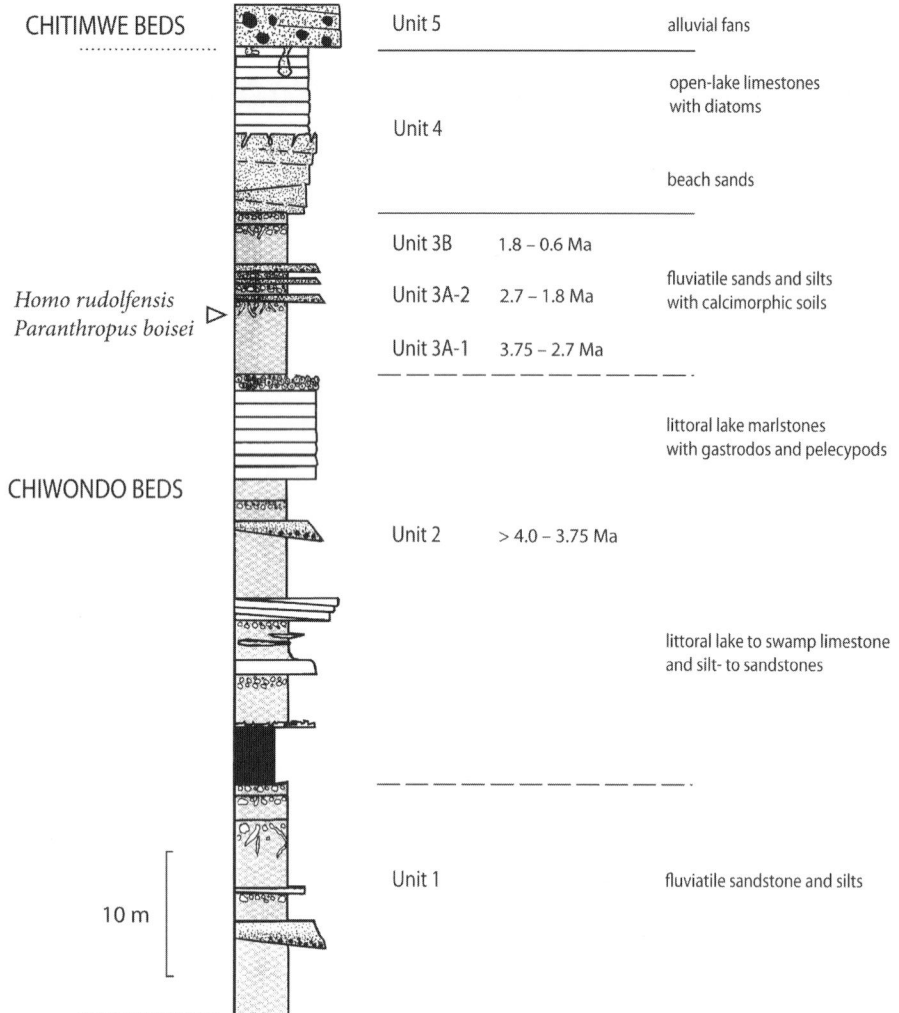

Figure 35.2 Generalized stratigraphic profile of Chiwondo and Chitimwe Beds Units 1–5 including their age ranges. Solid lines mark major unconformities; dashed lines mark minor unconformities.

Beds (Betzler and Ring, 1995). Unit 2 is dominated by fine- to medium-grained lake beds. Unit 3 comprises two subunits; unit 3A refers to meandering rivers and small lagoons and Unit 3B, only occurring in the south, is composed of paleosols. Unit 4, only occurring in the south, represents limestones with abundant diatoms due to a lake level high stand. During lake regression, gravels of Unit 5 were deposited.

No datable volcanic ashes or lava were found in the Chiwondo lithostratigraphic sequence.

Thus, an age determination of sedimentary units of the Chiwondo Beds relies on biostratigraphic correlation of proboscidean and suid remains with fossils from radiometrically dated localities in the East African Rift (Bromage et al., 1995; Kullmer, 1999, 2008; Kullmer et al., 1999a).

No age determination can be given for Unit 1, because no fossils have yet been found at Unit 1 localities. A few fragmentary proboscidean molars identified as *Anancus* aff. *kenyensis*, early *Loxodonta* sp., and *Mammuthus subplanifrons* (Bromage et al., 1995) were collected from Unit 2 sediments at northern (Mwimbi) and southern (Uraha) localities (Table 35.1). *Anancus* aff. *kenyensis* specimens are comparable with remains recovered in the Adu-Asa Formation (WoldeGabriel et al., 2001; Haile-Selassie et al., 2004b), the Kuseralee Member of the lower Sagantole Formation (Kalb et al., 1982b; Kalb and Mebrate, 1993; Renne et al., 1999), and in the Mursi Formation (Beden, 1976) at an age of >4 to <4.15 Ma (Brown and Nash, 1976; Brown et al., 1985; Feibel et al., 1989). In addition, early *Loxodonta* (*L. adaurora*) is known from the Mursi and Hadar Formations (Kalb et al., 1982b; Beden, 1987; Kalb, 1995). *M. subplanifrons* was identified at Aramis (<4.1–3.75 Ma; Kalb et al., 1982b; White et al., 1993) and Langebaanweg (*ca*. 5 Ma; Sanders, 2007). Suid dental remains from Unit 2 are invariably attributed to the species *Notochoerus jaegeri*, known from East African localities, such as the type site Hamada Damous, the Middle Awash, the Mursi Formation, Lothagam Apak Member and Kaiyumung Member, Kanapoi, Ekora, Atetir and Chemeron Formation, supporting an age older than 3.75 Ma (Kullmer, 2008). Morphometric studies of Plio-Pleistocene suid third molars (Kullmer, 1999) have led to a refinement of the biostratigraphy of the Chiwondo Beds Unit 3A, separating the pig sample into two time-consecutive biozones (Figure 35.2). Unit 3A-1 contains early *Not. euilus* specimens, reflecting an evolutionary stage of the species also

Table 35.1 List and abundance of identified mammal taxa at fossiliferous areas of the Chiwondo Beds (modified after Bromage et al., 1995 and Kullmer et al., 2011). X marks the presence of a taxon, those in parentheses refer to Kaufulu et al. (1981).

Stratigraphic Unit 2	Uraha	Mwimbi	Malema	Mwenirondo	Mwamberu	Sadala
Notochoerus jaegeri	4	3				
Notochoerus sp.	8					
Anancus aff. *kenyensis*	2					
Early *Loxodonta* sp.		3				
Mammuthus subplanifrons	1					
Stratigraphic Unit 3A						
Damaliscus sp.	6	10	2	2		
Connochaetes sp.	1	1				
Megalotragus sp.	9	2	31	2		
Gazella sp.	1	2	1			
Gazella sp. aff. *vanhoepeni*						(X)
Antilopini gen. indet.	14	7	5	1		
Tragelaphus cf. *angasi*	1			(X)		
Tragelaphus sp.	1		1			
Tragelaphini gen. indet.	4	3	2			
Kobus aff. *patulicornis*		(X)		1	(X)	
Kobus sp.	1	2	1			
Oryx aff. *gazella*	2					
Hippotragus sp.	3	2	19	1		
Hippotragini gen. indet.	3	2	2	1		
Syncerus sp.	1	1	13	2		
Ugandax sp.				(X)		
Aepyceros sp.	12	1	5	1	(X)	
Neotragini gen. indet.	1		3			
Bovidae gen. indet.	20	26	56	9		
Giraffa aff. *pygmaea*	1		4			
Giraffa gen. indet. small	2	5	14	1		
Giraffa gen. indet. large			7			
Sivatherium sp.			3			
Hippopotamus sp.	12	18	12	13		
cf. *Potamachoerus porcus*		1				
Metridiochoerus andrewsi	6	3				
Metridiochoerus sp.	1	1				
Notochoerus euilus	3	9		2		
Notochoerus scotti	1	1	6	1		
Notochoerus capensis		3		(X)		
Notochoerus sp.		3	7			
Suidae gen. indet.	3	5	3	2		
Diceros bicornis	1					
Ceratotherium simum	1		1	1		
Rhinocerotidae gen. indet.		2	1	1		
Eurygnathohippus sp.	24	30	42	4		
Elephas recki ssp.	3		11			
Elephantidae gen. indet.	4	4	27	1		
Deinotherium sp.	1		5			

Table 35.1 (cont.)

Stratigraphic Unit 2	Uraha	Mwimbi	Malema	Mwenirondo	Mwamberu	Sadala
Parapapio sp.	1		6	4		
Theropithecus sp.			1	1		
Papionini gen. indet.	1			2		
Cercopithecidae gen. indet.	1	1				
Homo rudolfensis	1			1		
Paranthropus boisei			1			
Camelidae gen. indet.	1			1		
Stratigraphic Unit 3B						
Metridiochoerus compactus	2					

represented in Member B (Harris and White, 1979) of the Shungura Formation (3.36–2.85 Ma) and in the Kataboi, lower Lomekwi, and middle Lomekwi members on the western shore of Lake Turkana (Harris et al., 1988a, 1988b). In East Turkana, *Not. euilus* is identified as an abundant faunal element in the Lokochot and the Tulu Bor Members (Harris, 1983b), confirming a time interval from 3.75 to 2.7 Ma. Unit 3A-2 covers a time span from 2.7 to 1.8 Ma determined through *Not. scotti*, which occurs up to the lower part of Member G of the Shungura Formation (Harris and White, 1979), but primitive members are noted as early as Member C (Cooke, 1976). *Not. scotti* is abundant also in the Middle and Upper Lomekwi Members in the West Turkana assemblage (Harris et al., 1988a, 1988b). The last occurrence of *Not. scotti* in the West Turkana succession is known in the Kaitio Member, equivalent to the KBS Member at Koobi Fora. In Koobi Fora, *Not. scotti* is the dominant suid in the Upper Burgi Member, but it also occurs with advanced forms in the lower KBS Member (Kullmer, 2008). Unit 3A also contains the Suidae species *Metridiochoerus andrewsi* stages I and II, and proboscidean remains attributable to former *Elephas recki shungurensis* species (today *Paleoloxodon recki*; Todd, 2010), both confirming a younger age than Unit 2 fauna.

The uppermost fossiliferous Unit 3B is estimated to an age of ca. 1.8–0.6 Ma yielding *Met. andrewsi* III and *Met. compactus* third molar remains known from just below the Okote Tuff in Koobi Fora and in Olduvai Bed IV (Harris and White, 1979; Kullmer, 2008).

Vertebrate Fauna and Paleoecology

The first comprehensive interpretation of the vertebrate fauna from the Chiwondo Beds was published by Bromage et al. (1995). Large mammals, represented by isolated molars, mandible fragments, or high-density limb bones, attributed to Primates, Proboscidea, Equidae, Rhinocerotidae, Suidae, Bovidae, Giraffidae, and Hippopotamidae were described, and their occurrence at northern Karonga localities and southern Uraha localities was determined. Sandrock et al. (2007) further subdivided the northern localities into Mwenirondo, Malema, and Mwimbi areas (Figure 35.1). The fauna at all areas is dominated by bovids, followed by equids, suids, hippopotamids, giraffids, and primates (Schrenk et al., 1995; Sandrock et al., 2007; Kullmer et al., 2011; Table 35.1). Equids, all identified as belonging to the genus *Eurygnathohippus* sp., have about the same relative abundance in the north and south. Slight differences are recognized in the occurrence of suids between Malema, where only early *Not. scotti* specimens are recorded, and Uraha with remains of *Not. jaegeri*, *Not. euilus*, *Not. scotti*, *Met. andrewsi*, and *Met. compactus*, reflecting the occurrence of all fossiliferous Units and sub-Units in the area. All suid species, except *Met. compactus*, also occur in Mwimbi. Besides *Giraffa pygmaea*, two size groups of giraffes can be distinguished in the Chiwondo Beds. The large giraffe and *Sivatherium* only occur in Malema locality RC 11. Among bovids, Bovini are identified as *Syncerus* sp. and *Ugandax* sp., the latter only occurring in the north. Alcelaphini are identified as *Damaliscus* sp., *Connochaetes* sp., and *Megalotragus* sp., which, like Antilopini and Aepycerotini (*Aepyceros* sp.), occur in the south and north. Hippotragini occur as *Oryx* sp. at Uraha and *Hippotragus* sp. in both regions (Sandrock et al., 2007). The *Ugandax* sp. specimens from Malema share morphological affinities with specimens of the Mwenirondo region that are curated at the University of California Museum of Paleontology (UCMP; Kaufulu et al., 1981). Tragelaphini and Reduncini occur in the north and south. As very rare elements, specimens of the cercopithecid primates, such as *Parapapio* sp., were identified at northern and southern localities (Bromage and Schrenk, 1987; Frost and Kullmer, 2008), while *Theropithecus* sp. was only found in the Malema and Mwenirondo area (Kullmer et al., 2011).

Just based on bovid abundances at Malema and Uraha, the Chiwondo Beds resemble the Somalia–Masai arid grassland pattern. Today, the region belongs to the Zambezian phytochorion (Sandrock et al., 2007). Combing comparative data from modern African habitats and fossil communities, the percentages of large terrestrial mammals versus frugivorous or fresh grass grazing mammals in the Chiwondo Beds areas reveal a different paleoecological picture (Figures 35.3 and 35.4). The Mwimbi area with almost no arboreal animals is similar to the Tulu Bor Member in Koobi Fora, and can be interpreted as scrubland plus adjacent wetlands. At Mwenirondo most of the frugivores (>15 percent) and fresh grass grazers (>10 percent) are found. It is similar to the Shungura Formation Member C, and can be characterized as bushland to woodland with edaphic

Figure 35.3 Bivariate plot of the percentages of total terrestrial mammals vs. frugivores in vegetative habitats ranging from forests to grasslands. Comparison of data from Eastern and Southern African hominin localities and modern game park environments including Mwenirondo, Malema, Mwimbi, and Uraha from the Chiwondo Beds.

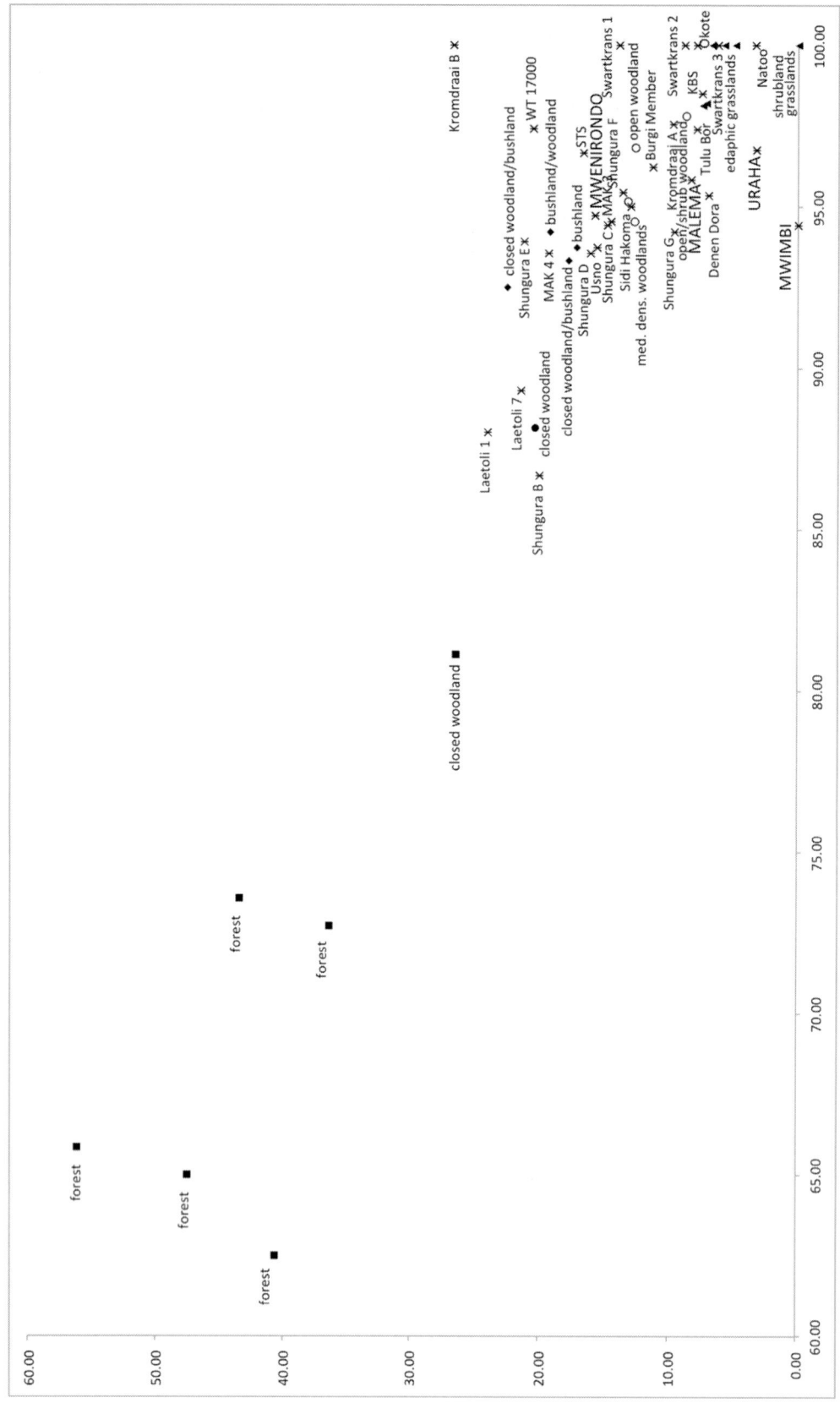

Figure 35.4 Bivariate plot of the percentages of total terrestrial mammals vs. fresh grass grazers in vegetative habitats ranging from forests to grasslands. Comparison of data from Eastern and Southern African hominin localities and modern game park environments including Mwenirondo, Malema, Mwimbi, and Uraha from the Chiwondo Beds.

grasslands. Malema is similar to Denen Dora, Hadar, and is seen as open scrubland to woodland. At Uraha in the South only a few arboreals/frugivores (3.2 percent) are found. It has the lowest proportion of fresh grass grazing mammals in the Chiwondo Beds and is interpreted as open woodland to shrubland. These paleoenvironmental reconstructions are supported by recently analyzed isotope data from pedogenic carbonates and suid enamel that indicate persistent C_3 vegetation during early hominin occupation in the Northern Malawi rift in the Late Pliocene to Early Pleistocene (Lüdecke et al., 2016a). Continuative isotope results including supplementary $\delta^{18}O$ analyses on faunal remains incorporating bovid, equid, hippopotamid, elephantid, and additional suid faunal samples support previous interpretations, adding detailed information that only *Connochaetes* sp. samples contain a typical grazer signal, while *Megalotragus* sp., *Eurygnathohippus* sp., *Hippopotamus* sp., and elephantid remains carry mixed-feeder signals (Lüdecke et al., 2016b). The results underline that grasslands did not play a major role during Plio-Pleistocene time in the southern part of the Karonga Basin. Many large mammals representing typical grazing $\delta^{13}C$ at eastern African localities between *ca.* 4 and 0.6 Ma provide evidence for their flexibility coping with more generalized C_3/C_4 diets in the Malawi rift (Lüdecke et al., 2016b). $\delta^{18}O$ results reveal a water signature in the range of present-day drinking water in the Karonga basin reflecting seasonality, elevation, and evaporation (Lüdecke et al., 2016b). Relatively low and fluctuating $\delta^{18}O$ values particularly in some equid and bovid samples suggest a higher seasonal humidity than at most eastern African localities. The Plio-Pleistocene in the Karonga basin was characterized by high ecosystem diversity throughout the time period (Lüdecke et al., 2016b), offering versatile foraging grounds for mammals and early hominins in the vicinity and along the northern shoreline of paleo-lake Malawi.

Conclusions

The fauna of the Chiwondo Beds is similar to those in localities from the Turkana Basin. The majority of the fauna has an age between 2 and 3 Ma, although some sites may be older than 4 Ma. Localities closer to the lake are dominated by large grazing herbivores, while isotope results show that even most large mammal taxa known as typical grazers in eastern African localities exhibit a much more versatile feeding behavior in the northern Malawi rift. C_3 vegetation in the Karonga basin persisted into the Early Pleistocene and likely formed hideaway conditions. A higher seasonal humidity in the northern Malawi Rift contrasted the increasing C_4 vegetation that became prevailing in large parts of Eastern Africa. These favorable conditions most likely triggered extended hominin dwell times in this part of the East African Rift valley along the northern margins of the Zambesian phytochorion.

Part IV Northern Africa

36 The Northern African Sites: Paleoenvironmental Syntheses

Denis Geraads

Introduction

The history of paleontological research in northern Africa goes back to the first half of the nineteenth century, when French zoologists discovered the first fossil mammals in Algerian caves. In 1851, Duvernoy described the long-horned buffalo *"Bubalus" antiquus*, the first fossil mammal ever named from Africa. Further discoveries and descriptions of fossil mammals were made in Algeria by French paleontologists (Gervais, Gaudry) in the mid-nineteenth century. Philippe Thomas (1884) named several species, including the first fossil monkey reported from Africa, *"Cynocephalus" atlanticus*, and he established the co-occurrence of *Hipparion* and *Equus* at Aïn Jourdel. However, it is only with the first excavations made at Palikao (Tighennif) near Oran that extinct mammals were found definitely associated with a Paleolithic industry (Pomel, 1886). Between 1893 and 1897 Pomel published a series of monographs on Algerian fossil mammals: even though most of the finds that he described are of late Pleistocene age, with the notable exception of those from Tighennif, his work, which includes a number of new species, remains a benchmark in African paleomammalogy, at a time when virtually nothing was known south of the Sahara. Research on early hominin sites in the twentieth century is associated with the name of Camille Arambourg, who spent most of his childhood in Algeria, and excavated a number of fossil sites of various ages there (Hadjouis, 2010). His early research focused on upper Pleistocene caves along the Algerian shoreline, but as early as 1931 he started excavating several sites known since the nineteenth century near El Eulma. He discovered the Pliocene sites of Lake Ichkeul and Aïn Brimba in Tunisia and the lower Pleistocene sites of Aïn Boucherit and Aïn Hanech in Algeria (Arambourg, 1970, 1979). The latter site yielded the earliest known man-made artifacts of North Africa; it has been under renewed research by Sahnouni and colleagues for more than 20 years (Sahnouni et al., 2018, and references therein), making it one of the most important North African sites. Later, Arambourg conducted large-scale excavations at Tighennif, but published only the hominin fossils from this site, erecting for them the binomen *Atlanthropus mauritanicus*, probably a synonym of *Homo heidelbergensis* or *H. rhodesiensis*; they remain the earliest North African fossil hominins. The last important site excavated by Arambourg in Algeria is that of Bou Hanifia (also known as Oued el Hammam), of late Miocene age (Arambourg, 1959).

The French Protectorate in the early twentieth century allowed French geologists to work in Morocco, and they soon focused on the chronology of uplifted beaches, intertidal and continental deposits of the Atlantic coast, trying to correlate them with the European Quaternary chronology. Development of the Casablanca harbor requested huge volumes of sandstones that were readily available there, and a number of quarries were opened in these Plio-Quaternary sequences, leading to the discovery of a number of caves and fossils, unfortunately rarely collected in secure stratigraphic context (Rabat: Marçais, 1934; Sidi Abderrahmane: Arambourg and Biberson, 1955). Stratigraphy remained a matter of discussion for many decades, involving correlations between marine and continental deposits, pluvials and interpluvials, and long-distance correlations with Mediterranean stages. Biberson (1961a, 1961b) published his elaborated conception on this topic, synthetizing data on the malacofauna, mammalian faunas, human fossils (especially those that he discovered at Sidi Abderrahmane), industries, and paleoclimatic interpretations. More recently, a Moroccan–French project initiated in 1978 has been aiming at deciphering the complex stratigraphy by trying to correlate the succession of transgressive/regressive phases to isotopic stages, and at putting hominin remains and lithic industries in paleoenvironmental context (Raynal et al., 2010 and references therein). The discovery of Ahl al Oughlam, close to the Plio-Pleistocene boundary, and of rich faunas, hominin fossils, and early Acheulean industries in the Thomas-Oulad Hamida quarries are the most significant recent improvements to Moroccan hominin history (see relevant chapters in this volume).

In the North-Eastern part of the continent, the earliest significant Neogene discoveries were those of Fourtau (1918, but this work is known through its 1920 more widely distributed second edition) at Moghra, and of Stromer (1902) at Wadi Natrun, both in Egypt. The former site has been subject to recent in-depth investigation by E. Miller and colleagues (see below), but the latter remains understudied. In Libya, at that time an Italian colony, Italian geologists made the first reports of fossil mammals in Jebel Zelten (Desio, 1935) and Sahabi (historical account in Rook, 2008); renewed research has been conducted on both sites since then.

Still, compared to some other regions of Africa, the North African record remains very patchy, so that human history in this province can only be reconstructed very tentatively. In contrast to East and South Africa, early hominin fossils are rare. Most are isolated teeth or bones, and more or less complete mandibles. The only published significant cranial remain before the late Pleistocene is the partial skull of Salé, whose stratigraphic context is unclear, and which might be pathological (Hublin, 2001).

Environmental Context

This incompleteness of the hominin fossil record in North Africa is certainly one of the main reasons why environmental studies have been far less extensive there; isotopic studies, for instance, are virtually non-existent, and there is relatively little environmental information deriving directly from primate-bearing sites. Because of its position, between the Mediterranean Basin and tropical Africa, North Africa can be expected to have been influenced, climatically and biogeographically, by both provinces, and most studies have been conducted in this context.

In the early to middle Miocene, as elsewhere, the climate was warmer than today. Faunas of this period document warm, humid environments with swamps in Libya and Egypt, and there is paleobotanical evidence of forests in Egypt (El Saadawi et al., 2014). It is likely that this environment was widely distributed in coastal lowlands, but grasslands were already present in Arabia, and might have been widespread farther inland. Mountain ranges (Atlas) were covered by forests, including conifers (Ben Moktar and Mannaï-Tayech, 2015). This distinction between coastal areas, hinterland, and mountain ranges remains valid in later periods. An *Avicennia* mangrove was still present on the coasts in the upper Miocene, while temperatures decreased and grasslands expanded inland (Bachiri-Taoufiq et al., 2008).

Various lines of evidence show that the late Miocene climate in the Sahara was far from desertic. Fossil localities within its present-day extant are few, but an abundant, diverse fauna was thriving in Chad, and Egypt was humid enough to house forest-dwelling primates. Large rivers were flowing northward into the Mediterranean, especially along the Eonile. They deposited thick sapropel layers that help to reconstruct the climate in this area. Some of this fluvial input probably originated from East Africa, but there were also rivers flowing into the Gulf of Syrt, originating from present-day central Sahara (e.g., Köhler et al., 2010); large lakes there (Larrasoaña et al., 2013) and south of the Atlas range (Boulton et al., 2019) unambiguously demonstrate that the environment was generally far from desertic, as the intertropical convergence zone was located north of its present position. A humid climate (Zeit wet phase) is documented in northeast Africa. Aeolian dunes were deposited in Chad as early as 7 Ma (Schuster et al., 2006), and computer models (Pound et al., 2011; Zhang et al., 2014) suggest dry or desert areas over the Sahara at that time, but other evidence shows that they were certainly of limited extant. It is tempting to relate the origin of the Sahara to tectonic events, such as the shrinkage of the Tethys (which would have reduced the African summer monsoon), or the uprising of the Atlas, or to the Mediterranean Salinity Crisis, but, paradoxically, the impact of the latter was probably less local than global (Fauquette, 2006; Ivanovic et al., 2014; Flecker et al., 2015).

At the end of the Messinian, drier conditions were progressively installed. Temperatures were still warmer than today at the beginning of the Pliocene, but the amount of precipitations differed with areas. The reorganization of the atmospheric circulation reduced them, and temperatures lowered (Colin et al., 2008, 2014). The last mangroves with *Avicennia* disappeared (Suc et al., 2018), steppes expanded over most of the area at the end of the Pliocene, with herbaceous plants (*Artemisia*) and shrubs (*Ephedra*), including some desert elements, while forests colonized the highlands (Dupont and Leroy, 1995; Feddi et al., 2011). However, arid periods were less marked than they became in the late Pleistocene (Leroy and Dupont, 1997). For instance, a (middle?) Pliocene flora from north Tunisia still possesses the boreal taxa *Fagus* (beech) and *Ulmus* (elm), attesting to a mild climate, with cool winters, and low seasonality (Arènes and Depape, 1953). The north–south thermal gradient increased toward its present-day high values, with cooler winters and drier summers in North Africa (Suc et al., 2018), a contrast especially marked during glacial periods. In the Pleistocene, climate cycles prompted fluctuations of the relative abundances of Mediterranean taxa (e.g., *Quercus*, *Pinus*, *Cedrus*, *Olea*) and steppes dominated by *Artemisia* and Amaranthaceae–Poaceae.

A major advance of recent research is the recognition of numerous fluctuations of vegetation cover in the Sahara, driven by both precessional (eccentricity) and obliquity forcing (e.g., Marzocchi et al., 2015). Green Sahara Periods (GSP) were relatively well-known for the late Pleistocene, but recent combination of the study of sapropel deposits in the Eastern Mediterranean, which record river run-off into the Mediterranean, and dust records from the same area have led to the recognition of no less than 30 GSPs, each of them of short duration, over the whole Plio-Pleistocene (Grant et al., 2017). It is now clear that the scale of climatic change in the Pleistocene is in ky, not My.

Mammal-Bearing Sites

Additional information on the environment can be drawn from mammalian assemblages, but they always reflect local environments, and we should be cautious not to extrapolate the indications that they provide to wider areas, as a marshy delta, a riverine gallery forest, a sandy seashore, a cave, etc., can all be surrounded by, e.g., open grasslands. Depositional and taphonomic biases should especially be kept in mind in the Pleistocene; cave sites are unknown in the first half of this period, while open-air sites are rare after that, and are therefore hardly comparable. The following account includes only the main Neogene and Quaternary sites that yielded large mammals, arranged by decreasing age and these localities are shown in Figure 36.1.

Wadi Moghra

Wadi Moghra (= Moghara), in northern Egypt, has been known since the nineteenth century, but the first description of mammals from the site was published by Fourtau (1920). Moghra is the earliest Neogene locality in North Africa, and preserves several stacked deltaic and fluvial deposits dating from about 21 to 17 Ma, with most of the fossils coming from layers dated to 18–19.5 Ma, but time-averaging is certainly present in museum collections (Morlo et al., 2019). The rich fauna (Sanders and

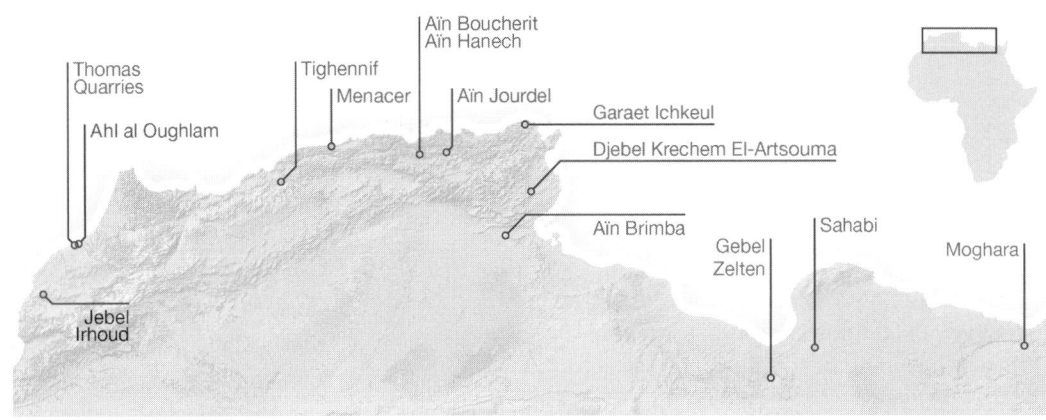

Figure 36.1 Fossil localities reviewed in this chapter, and in the following chapters.

Miller, 2002; Morlo et al., 2007, 2019; Miller et al., 2009, 2014; Pickford et al., 2010) documents a humid, forested environment with abundant evidence of water-dwelling vertebrates, such as turtles (*Podocnemis*, *Trionyx*), crocodiles, including a fish-eating relative of the gavial (*Tomistoma*), dolphins, several suoids, a hippo-like rhinoceros (*Brachypotherium*), as many as six species of anthracotheres (an extinct family of artiodactyls possibly related to hippos), and a small chevrotain-like animal. In addition, there are several proboscideans, a small giraffoid with palmate cranial appendages (*Prolibytherium*), and various predators, including both small and large true carnivores, as well as members of Creodonta, including the gigantic hyena-like *Megistotherium*. Primates are represented by early members of the cercopithecoid radiation (*Prohylobates tandyi* and another species), but no hominoids have been described from the site. The Moghra fauna includes some taxa that originate from Eurasia (e.g., suids, giraffoids, rhinocerotids), but also many that are intra-African (e.g., cercopithecoids, proboscideans). Several taxa are shared with East African sites, probably testifying to north–south exchanges along the Eonile Valley.

Jebel Zelten

The site was discovered by an Italian team led by A. Desio in 1935, but only fishes were reported at that time. The first mammalian fossils were found by A. Magnier during petroleum explorations in 1960. Camille Arambourg accompanied him the same year, and collected some fossils, including the first material of the strange giraffoid *Prolibytherium* (Arambourg, 1961), but the main collecting field seasons were led by R.J.G. Savage in 1964–1968. More mammals, especially rodents, were collected by R. Daams and colleagues in 1997.

The fauna from Jebel Zelten (or Zaltan), like that of Moghra, documents fluviatile deposits close to the shore, in a partially forested environment. It is, on the whole, somewhat younger than Moghra, although the assemblage is also heterochronous, as first clearly recognized by Wessels et al. (2003). Fishes and crocodiles are plentiful, anthracotheres and suoids are diverse (although less so than at Moghra), and there are also several proboscideans and sirenians, and a hyracoid. The carnivore assemblage is also less diverse that at Moghra, but includes a barbourofelid (*Afrosmilus*), a group that parallels machairodont felids. Significant additions, relative to the Moghra fauna, are a hyracoid (a group that was quite diverse in the Paleogene of Africa), another giraffoid, *Canthumeryx*, and true bovids. Cercopithecoid primates are related to those of Moghra; there is no hominoid (Hamilton, 1973a, 1973b; Savage and Hamilton, 1973; Pickford, 2006; Miller et al., 2009; Morales et al., 2010; Morlo et al., 2019). Among rodents (Wessels et al., 2003), some taxa are shared with south Asia, but also with younger sites in East Africa (Fort Ternan) and Morocco (Beni Mellal; see below).

On the whole, similarities with Moghra are not unexpected given the geographic and chronologic proximity of the sites, but the noticeable similarities with East Africa point to easy faunal exchanges with southern latitudes.

Beni Mellal

Beni Mellal in central Morocco is not a rich site, but is important in documenting the only large mammal fauna of North Africa between *ca*. 15 and 11 Ma (Lavocat, 1952). It is certainly of middle Miocene age, and not immediately anterior to the late Miocene. There are numerous birds and squamates, but large ungulates are rare (Rémy, 1976; Ginsburg, 1977a, 1977b; Guérin, 1976); the most abundant is the giraffid *Palaeotragus* (Heintz, 1976), and there is a single bovid (*Benicerus*; Heintz, 1973), which is the earliest African representative of the northern tribe Caprini. Carnivores are diverse (Ginsburg, 1977c) and include early members of the Mustelidae, and the earliest Hyaenidae of Africa (*Protictitherium* and *Hyaenictis*). No Primate has been reported. The rich micromammal fauna (Jaeger, 1977b) includes bats of northern origin (*Megaderma*). Most of the rodents have a wide geographic range (Pedetidae, *Paraphiomys*, *Atlantoxerus*); the Cricetidae and Ctenodactylidae are Asian immigrants, while the Gliridae came from the north. Thus, on the whole, there is a strong northern component on the faunal assemblage. The large mammal fauna is too poor to draw conclusions from absences, but that of anthracotheres is significant, as they are so abundant in earlier and later localities of Tunisia and eastern Algeria.

Several other late middle Miocene to late Miocene sites in Morocco and Algeria allow the establishment of a biochronological scale based on rodents, but they yield virtually no large mammals (Zouhri et al., 2017, and references therein).

Beglia Formation

The Beglia Formation at Bled Douarah in central Tunisia was first reported by Robinson et al. (1969). It yielded a large number of fossils, part of which only has been studied or revised recently (Robinson and Black, 1974; Kurtén, 1976; Crusafont-Pairó, 1979; Pickford, 1990, 2000, 2008; Werdelin and Peigné, 2010). The locality was said to be and is commonly regarded as straddling the middle–upper Miocene boundary, based upon the absence of *Hipparion* s.l. in the lower part of the sequence, and its presence in the upper part. However, in addition to fishes, crocodiles, and birds, the mammalian fauna is poor in taxa, with only nine ungulates, and it remains to be further substantiated that the absence of this equid in the lower part is not due to incomplete sampling or slight ecological difference, as this taxon is quite rare in the upper part (Forstén, 1972; Geraads, 1989). The most remarkable elements of the fauna are the abundant antracotheres (but, in contrast to earlier sites, a single species is present), an early representative of the suid *Nyanzachoerus*, very hypsodont antelopes, and a barbourofelid (*Vampyrictis*). No primate has been reported. The assemblage suggests a riverine environment with extensive open habitats.

Bou Hanifia

Also known as Oued el Hammam, this site near Oran in Algeria yielded a large mammal fauna that is rich in number of specimens but consists of a few taxa only. Arambourg (1959) regarded this assemblage as reminiscent of the classic Pikermian fauna of Eurasia, but it is in fact contemporaneous with the Vallesian, as shown by the rodents (Ameur et al., 1976). The dominant taxa are a giraffe ("*Palaeotragus*"), a hipparion, and a rhinoceros close to the common ancestry of the modern "white" and "black" rhinos; the virtual absence of bovids and suids can be explained by a strong taphonomic (or collecting!) bias toward large taxa, but again, the absence of anthracotheres is noticeable. No hominid has been reported. The abundance of hipparion and of a long-limbed giraffid suggests an open landscape.

Bahariya-Farafra

This now arid region of Egypt enjoyed a humid climate during the first part of the late Miocene. Over a large area, limestones are deeply hollowed by karsts attesting to important water circulation. This is confirmed by the presence of a humid forest fauna, including the small primate *Galago*, whose modern representatives need trees and significant rainfall (Pickford et al., 2006).

Skoura

The upper Miocene deposits of Skoura near Ouarzazate in Morocco belong to the Aït Kandoula Formation that yielded important rodent faunas farther north. Vertebrate fossils were first reported by Zouhri et al. (2012). Further survey, complemented by fossils collected by fossil hunters, increased the sample, which remains small but includes at least two species of hipparions, two rhinos (Geraads and Zouhri, 2021), a caprine bovid (*Skouraia*) that might be related to *Benicerus*, and the early elephant *Tetralophodon* (Geraads et al., 2012b, 2019). The site is probably contemporaneous with the European Vallesian.

Menacer

The scrappy fauna of this site (formerly called Marceau) near Oran in Algeria was first published by Arambourg (1959), who regarded it as of early late Miocene age, comparable to that of Oued el Hammam. Thomas and Petter (1986) revised the fauna and concluded that it is in fact significantly younger. However, the carnivores *Dinocrocuta* and *Indarctos* do support a rather ancient age, earlier than the latest Miocene. Two cercopithecids coexist, one of which is the only definite occurrence of a true colobine in North Africa, but the fauna is too poor for paleoecological conclusions.

Sahabi

This Libyan site was first reported by Petrocchi (1934; but see Rook, 2008). The now desertic area was surveyed by a number of Italian geologists, who also collected and studied some fossils, but it was made famous through the work of N.T. Boaz and colleagues (1987), who described one of the richest faunas of the African Neogene. Following the geologists' (who thought that the deposits were post-Messinian) conclusions, most paleontologists regarded the fauna as Pliocene (Boaz et al., 1987), to the notable exception of Howell (1987), who pointed out the Miocene character of the Carnivora. Geraads (1989) confirmed that the bulk of the fauna, which he regarded as heterochronous, is of Miocene age. It took some years (Boaz et al., 2008b) for this age to be accepted, and for the time-averaged nature of the assemblage to be fully acknowledged (although El-Shawaidhi et al., 2016 still provide only a composite list). Most of the fauna comes from sediments of Messinian age (but anterior to the salinity crisis), corresponding to the European Turolian mammal age.

Taken as a whole, the mammalian fauna (see Boaz et al., 2008b, for an update) includes terrestrial forms whose habitats range from subdesert or at least very dry steppes (the gerbil *Abudhabia*) to savanna (various antelopes, including grazing ones; rhinos) and woodlands (the cercopithecids *Libypithecus* and *Macaca*) that were probably close to water (as shown by the last African anthracotheres, the earliest hippos – along with the Chadian and Lothagam ones – and perhaps amebelodont proboscideans), in addition to fully aquatic forms (whale, dolphin, seal, crocodiles, and fishes). Fossil woods confirm the importance of swampy environments, but also of very dry areas nearby.

The Sahabi fauna consists of a mixture of taxa with northern, eastern, and southern affinities, but most of its ungulates are already of fully African type, foreshadowing later faunas. This is especially true of the bovids, with the establishment of the Afro-Indian alcelaphin–hippotragin–reduncin cohort that will later dominate African savanna–grassland faunas. By contrast, the affinities of the rodents already lie with the east (the gerbil *Abudhabia*) and north (the murid *Progonomys*), as in later faunas. The carnivores also incorporate European immigrants (*Adcrocuta* and the hunting hyena *Chasmaporthetes*). No hominid is known from Sahabi.

Lissasfa

Lissasfa is a fissure filling near Casablanca, slightly earlier than the Miocene–Pliocene boundary. It yielded a rich rodent fauna that attests to exchanges with Spain (Geraads, 1998; Raynal et al., 1999), but only a few large mammals, including a canid that is among the earliest of its family in Africa.

Wadi Natrun

This interesting site in northern Egypt was first published by Stromer (1902), and it is unfortunate that its fauna has not been revised recently. Its most significant components are *Libypithecus*, endemic to northeast Africa, which is perhaps a basal colobine, and a camel that is among the earliest ones of Africa. Otters (*Enhydriodon* and *Lutra*), hippos, a seal, and *Euthecodon* reflect an estuarine environment. The murine rodent *Saidomys* attests to exchanges with both eastern Africa, along the Eonile Valley, and southern Asia (Brandy et al., 1980).

Lake Ichkeul

This site in northern Tunisia was excavated by Arambourg in 1947–1949 and the large mammals published by him (Arambourg, 1970, 1979), while Jaeger (1971) published a short description of the rodents. The age of the site is not well constrained, but the rodents show that it is certainly earlier than the late Pliocene. The antelopes are mostly of African type, but the flora (Arènes and Depape, 1953), which includes beech and elm, indicates a temperate, mild climate with low seasonality.

Aïn Brimba

The large mammals of this site, perhaps roughly contemporaneous with Ichkeul, were also described by Arambourg (1970, 1979); the rodents (Jaeger, 1975) suggest an open, if not arid environment, with gerbillids and *Jaculus*. The only primate is *Macaca*.

Ahl al Oughlam

Geraads et al. (Chapter 37) provide a more detailed account of this important site. In brief, Ahl al Oughlam is an abandoned quarry at the eastern fringe of Casablanca, first mentioned by Biberson (1961a, 1961b) who reported the occurrence in a "Messaoudian" marine layer of broken pebbles that he regarded as man-made artifacts. Raynal and Texier (1989) demonstrated that they are in fact of natural origin, and discovered the first fossil mammals in karstic and fissure fillings. The site, which is no longer accessible, has yielded more than 100 species of vertebrates (Geraads, 2006, 2010a; Zouhri et al., 2017, and references therein), as discussed in more detail by Geraads and colleagues (Chapter 37). Biochronology indicates an age close to the Plio-Pleistocene boundary, at *ca.* 2.5 Ma, but, as in many other North African sites, there is no radiometric control. With the notable exception of carnivores, each of the various faunal groups lacks diversity, partly because of the absence of time-averaging, but also because the relatively open environment was rather cold, with little arboreal cover. Rodents are largely endemic, or of Mediterranean type, but the large mammals have clear African affinities, testifying to intensive latitudinal exchanges. Thus, it is probably this harsh environment that explains the absence of any hominin.

Aïn Boucherit

Arambourg first excavated this site in 1931 and published (posthumously) in 1970 and 1979 a large mammal fauna whose most significant elements are the mastodont *Anancus*, a primitive wildebeest *Connochaetes tournoueri*, the endemic antilopin *Parantidorcas*, a bovin perhaps akin to the East African *Pelorovis*, and both *Equus* and *Hipparion* s.l. Sahnouni and colleagues conducted new multidisciplinary researches on the site recently, and reported (Sahnouni et al., 2018) a lithic industry and traces of butchering activity, contemporaneous with this fauna, which they estimate to be 2.44 Ma old. This would be the earliest evidence of human presence in North Africa. Independent points of view on various aspects of their results would be welcome, but no details have been provided on the very small lithic assemblage or purported butchery marks, and it remains to be explained how an ESR date of <1.92 Ma can form the basis of a paleomagnetic date of 2.44 Ma. In any case, the site is younger than Ahl al Oughlam, which lacks *Equus*. Still, there is no doubt that Aïn Boucherit is a major site in North Africa, and further publication of results is eagerly awaited.

Aïn Hanech

Aïn Hanech is very close to, but stratigraphically above, Aïn Boucherit. Its large mammal fauna, also studied by Arambourg (1970, 1979), is ecologically similar, with alcelaphins and gazelles indicating open landscapes, but it differs in its taxonomic composition, especially in the likely absence of *Anancus* and the disappearance of hipparions. Arambourg (1949, 1979) published unquestionable polyhedric artefacts, and the site yielded to Sahnouni and colleagues (Sahnouni et al., 2013, 2018) a large sample of stone artifacts, in association with the vertebrate fauna. The main levels belong to the base of member T, which mostly consists of silts and clays deposited in floodplains, in a calm environment and showing no disturbance. The environmental context is interpreted as sampling a riparian habitat becoming drier through time; the abundance of *Equus*, alcelaphins, and gazelles is significant in this regard. The lithic industry is made on limestone and flint, making it hard to compare with East African industries prepared on volcanic material, but it is clearly an Oldowan industry, in which no hand axe has been reported. Microwear analysis on stone tools and cutting-marks on bones provide a rare glimpse into the behavior of the earliest human immigrants in northwestern Africa. Thus, the site is central in documenting the context of early hominins in this region, but its dating remains conjectural. It has repeatedly been said to be *ca.* 1.78 Ma by Sahnouni and colleagues (2013, 2018 and references therein), but the interpretation of paleomagnetic results is not unambiguous, so that this issue, raised by Geraads et al. (2004b), remains open. A strong argument in favor of an early age would be the mastodont *Anancus*, a tooth of which has been reported, but unfortunately not described or illustrated by Sahnouni et al. (2013). As almost everywhere else in northwestern Africa, and in sharp contrast with eastern Africa, the lack of volcanic tephra suitable for radiometric dating is seriously felt here.

Mansoura

Located near the city of Constantine in Algeria, this site is known since the mid-nineteenth century. It consists of a thick fluvio-lacustrine sequence. The basal travertines yielded quartzite polyhedrons and choppers, but no bifacial tools (Laplace, 1956), and some remains of large mammals, among the first to be described from Africa (Gervais, 1869). The most significant are *Tragelaphus* and *Kolpochoerus*, suggesting an age similar to Aïn Hanech (Chaid-Saoudi et al., 2006), but only renewed study of the site could confirm its antiquity. Interestingly, and keeping in mind the small size of the sample, the bovid fauna consists mostly of tragelaphins and reduncins, attesting to an environment that is definitely more wet and/or wooded than in other North African sites, including Aïn Hanech which is geographically and chronologically close.

Tighennif

Formerly known as Palikao or Ternifine, the site is known since the late nineteenth century, and provided part of the material upon which Pomel based his classic monographs (1893–97). Later excavations, especially by Arambourg in 1954–1956, yielded a large faunal collection, an abundant early Acheulean industry, and several hominin fossils that remain the earliest ones in North Africa to date. He called them *Atlanthropus mauritanicus*, but they are now taken as representing members of the *H. heidelbergensis/rhodesiensis* group.

Unfortunately, the original depositional conditions have been seriously disturbed by artesian upwelling, and Arambourg (1963b) did not provide any indication regarding the stratigraphic origin of his material. The large mammal fauna suggests a very open landscape surrounding a lake inhabited by hippos. Alcelaphins, gazelles, zebras, white rhino, and the hypsodont suid *Metridiochoerus andrewsi/compactus* form the bulk of the assemblage, and the rodents, among which the gerbils dominate, confirm this. Taken as a whole, the large mammal fauna is reminiscent of late early Pleistocene East African sites, such as Olduvai upper beds, and is probably around 1 Ma (see Chapter 38 for further details and faunal lists).

Aïn Maarouf

The fauna of this site near El Hajeb in central Morocco bears definite similarities with that of Tighennif, so that a femoral diaphysis is certainly the earliest human fossil from this country (Geraads et al., 1992; Hublin, 1992; Geraads and Amani 1997). It probably also belongs to the *H. heidelbergensis/rhodesiensis* group.

Thomas Quarries

These quarries (see Chapter 39), now incorporated within the limits of the ever-expanding city, were among those that provided building material for the development of the Casablanca harbor. Intertwining of marine and continental levels builds up a complex stratigraphy, first studied by Biberson (1961a, 1961b).

Following the discovery of a human mandible (Ennouchi, 1969; Sausse, 1975) and the first descriptions of mammalian fossils and artifacts (Geraads, 1980a; Geraads et al., 1980), a new research program was established in the 1980s, allowing the deciphering of the stratigraphy and depositional conditions, as well as the discovery of more human fossils (now assigned to *H. rhodesiensis/heidelbergensis*), of large fossil assemblages, and of lithic industries that document several successive stages of the local Acheulean, from the early Pleistocene to the early Middle Pleistocene.

Sidi Abderrahmane

Sidi Abderrahmane is a huge quarry located close to Thomas Quarries, also studied by Biberson (1961a, 1961b). It also yielded artifacts and faunas, but unfortunately without reliable stratigraphic control, and the site, which has been largely destroyed, has not been worked recently. Hominid remains (Arambourg and Biberson, 1955) and rodent faunas are certainly younger than those of Thomas Quarries.

Salé

A quarry in Salé near Rabat yielded a partial cranium probably assignable to a primitive *Homo sapiens*, but it might be pathological (Hublin, 2001). The associated large mammal fauna is quite poor, but rodents collected from a red breccia above the human skull (Jaeger, 1975, 1981) indicate an age younger than Thomas Quarries, and perhaps also than Sidi Abderrahmane.

Jebel Irhoud

Jebel Irhoud is a hill of Cambrian schists in central Morocco, hollowed by numerous caves of various ages, which yield several important rodent faunas (Jaeger, 1975). One of them is remarkably rich in hominin remains. A first cranium was unearthed (by very productive excavation methods!) in 1961, followed by several other human remains, most of them out of stratigraphic context. Ennouchi (1962, 1968) assigned them to Neandertals, but they belong instead to primitive representatives of *Homo sapiens*. Most of the hominid cave was destroyed by quarry works, but Tixier conducted small-scale excavations on remaining sediments (Hublin et al., 1987). Recent excavations allowed the discovery of new human remains in the very limited remaining volume of sediment, showing that the whole cave must have been extraordinary rich in human remains. Most importantly, they also allowed their dating that, at *ca.* 315 ka, makes them the earliest representatives of our own species (Hublin et al., 2017; Richter et al., 2017). The mammalian fauna (Thomas, 1981a; Amani and Geraads, 1993; Geraads et al., 2013b; Richter et al., 2017), where gazelles dominate among ungulates, and murids among rodents, indicates an environment that is less dry and open than in other Middle Pleistocene Moroccan sites, but the precise origin of the museum collections is unknown, and the faunal sample might be biased by hunting preferences.

Biogeographic Issues

Because of its wide connections with the rest of Africa, and potential connections with Europe and Asia, North Africa has a complex biogeographic history, which is blurred to the modern zoologist by the erection of the Sahara barrier, by relatively recent immigrations from the north, and by human catastrophic impact on wildlife (remember that elephants were living in Casablanca in Roman times!). These changes have largely obscured its original Ethiopian affinities, so that it is now part of the Palearctic realm.

Miocene North African fishes (best sampled at Bled Douarah; Stewart, 2001), for instance, are pan-African, unambiguously testifying to braided fluviatile networks throughout the continent. As mentioned above, there is also abundant evidence from large and small mammals of exchanges with East Africa, even South Asia, and the poorly known western Africa (e.g., Pickford et al., 2009). However, water-dwelling anthracotheres, widespread elsewhere, never colonized the lowland areas of Morocco and eastern Algeria, showing that the Atlas range acted as an effective barrier. Later, the numerous GSPs allowed latitudinal exchanges throughout the Plio-Pleistocene, at least for grazing large mammals, but it may be that arboreal cover was insufficient for those mammals relying on leaves or fruits, such as browsing antelopes, monkeys, and early hominins.

Direct trans-Mediterranean exchanges are poorly documented (e.g., *Stegotetrabelodon* in Sicily; Ferretti et al., 2001) because relevant fossil sites are rare, but several north–south crossings in the westernmost Mediterranean occurred at various periods. At the time of the final closure of the Mediterranean, before the Messinian salinity crisis, rodents crossed the Gibraltar straits in both directions (see review in Garcia-Alix et al., 2016), together with hippos (definitely in a south–north direction) and perhaps camels (long thought to have followed the same direction, but their recent discovery in the upper Miocene of Italy shows how such scenarios are fragile). However, Neogene exchanges were probably not restricted by land bridges, and may have involved swimming and natural rafts.

As hominins settled in the whole Maghreb, sometime between 2 and 1 Ma, the Gibraltar issue arises again, but it is often hard to exclude dispersal from Asia along both shores of the Mediterranean. Among the very few definite dispersal events from Africa to Europe across the western Mediterranean, that of the gelada baboon *Theropithecus* in the early Pleistocene is the most firmly supported, as it is wholly unknown in Europe outside southern Spain. Humans arrived in Spain earlier (see Gibert et al., 2016, for a review), even though general agreement on dates has yet to be reached. Because it is unlikely that a 10-km wide channel could have acted as a barrier for a long time, the duration of the time gap between Aïn Hanech and the expansion of *Homo* in Europe has bearing on his ability to colonize new environments. This gap might be as long as 0.5 million years or much shorter, depending on the dates: further documenting the early Pleistocene record, which remains undersampled, and providing reliable dates for major sites should be the aim of future research in northwestern Africa. We may hope that raising concern about the remote past will help protect previously known and newly discovered sites, so that northwestern Africa could occupy the place it deserves in early human history.

37 Ahl al Oughlam, Morocco: The Richest Fossil Site in North Africa at the Pliocene/Pleistocene Boundary

Denis Geraads, David Lefèvre, and Jean-Paul Raynal

Introduction

The quarry in which the paleontological site of Ahl al Oughlam (33°34′11″ N, 7°30′44″ W) is located was previously known as "carrière Déprez" and was investigated in 1953 by Biberson (1961a, 1961b). It was one of the numerous quarries that were worked at that time to provide building materials for the developing Casablanca city. A marine level assigned to the Messaoudian yielded to this author a rich fauna of mollusks of "Senegalian" type, thus contributing to the precise regional stratigraphic frame and paleoclimatic conditions at the time. However, its main interest was the discovery, at the base of this level (Biberson, 1961b, plate 11), of broken pebbles that Biberson considered as a man-made lithic industry referable to an archaic stage of the pebble culture.

In 1985, in the frame of the general revision of the stratigraphy and prehistory of Casablanca, Jean-Paul Raynal and Jean-Pierre Texier discovered mammalian fossils in a complex of karst and fissure fillings within the consolidated dune (calcarenite) that overlies this marine level. Suspecting their antiquity, they showed them to D.G. who confirmed it, leading to a revision of the age of the Messaoudian marine stage (Raynal et al., 1990). D.G. undertook excavations from 1989 onwards, in the frame of the "Programme Casablanca," led at the time by Jean-Paul Raynal, Fatima-Zohra Sbihi-Alaoui, and Abderrahim Mohib. The material is stored at the Institut National des Sciences de l'Archéologie et du Patrimoine (INSAP), Rabat (Raynal et al., 1990; Geraads et al., 1998, 2010a; Geraads, 2006, 2010a, 2010b).

Stratigraphy and Age

The Casablanca hinterland is characterized by a succession of longitudinal dune ridges parallel to the modern shoreline composed of littoral–marine and eolian calcarenites, associated with stepped erosional platforms developed into the Paleozoic substratum.

Up to 80 m a.s.l., we recognize several morphostratigraphic units (MSU) from the oldest to the most recent (Lefèvre and Raynal, 2002):

- The Marchich/Bouskoura MSU, associated with several platforms between 150 and 170 m a.s.l. The fillings of a karstic cave at the top of one the most recent formations of this MSU at Lissasfa (Raynal et al., 1999) yielded a micromammal association dated to close to the Miocene–Pliocene boundary at ca. 5.5 Ma (Geraads, 1998), thus pushing the earlier formations of this MSU back into the late Miocene Messinian Stage.
- The Dehar Mouak MSU is associated with a platform developed at about 130 m a.s.l., formerly included in the Fouaratien–Late Pliocene (Stearns, 1978), and it belongs to the Pliocene.
- The Oulad Malik MSU is associated with a platform developed about 110/115 m a.s.l.
- The Ahl al Oughlam MSU associated with a platform developed about 100 m a.s.l., formerly included in the Messaoudian (first stage of Quaternary of the Moroccan Quaternary chronostratigraphy: Biberson, 1961a, 1961b; Stearns, 1978) belongs to the upper Pliocene.
- The Sidi Messaoud MSU, probably associated with two platforms developed between 80 and 90 m a.s.l. and formerly included in the Messaoudian (Biberson, 1961a, 1961b), belongs to the Lower Pleistocene.

The stratigraphic succession at Ahl al Oughlam, first established by Biberson (1961a, 1961b) was revised by Raynal et al. (1990) and more recently by Raynal, Lefèvre, and El Graoui (unpublished); it reads as follows, from bottom to top:

- Cambrian quartzites at 100.7 m a.s.l..
- Unit 1 (G and F of Biberson, 1961; M1 of Raynal et al., 1990): on the erosional surface, intertidal deposits preserved in the eastern part of the quarry are made of a calcirudite with quartzite pebbles and boulders, then of a coarse biocalcarenite, laid in decimetric layers dipping 8–10° NNW.
- Unit 2 is subdivided into Unit 2a and Unit 2b. On an erosional disconformity dipping 10–15° NNW at 102.6 m a.s.l., intertidal deposits of Unit 2a (E and D according to Biberson, 1961; M2 of Raynal et al., 1990) are made of a calcirudite (E of Biberson) with quartzite and sandstone pebbles embedded in a matrix of shell sands, irregularly preserved in depressions, and by a coarse biocalcarenite with numerous *Trochatella trochiformis* Gmelin and *Purpura plessisi* Lecointre (Biberson, 1961a); upwards, it shifts to a stratified biocalcarenite, dipping 5–7° N to NNW; large blocks of an older calcarenite point to the nearby presence of a cliff shore. A planar disconformity separates Unit 2a and Unit 2b. Unit 2b (C of Biberson,

1961a; D2 of Raynal et al., 2002) consists of a succession of four distinct eolianites separated by planar disconformities. The whole Unit 2 today reaches 118.69 m a.s.l., and records a succession of intertidal, supratidal, and eolian facies correlative of a highstand sea level.

- Unit 3: at the northern end of the quarry, upon a planar surface at 108 m a.s.l., a chaos of plurimetric calcarenite blocks is associated with a paleoshoreline cut into the Unit 2 calcarenites. A sandy fossiliferous filling (C1) fills the gaps between these blocks.

Biberson (1961b) had distinguished two assemblages among the broken pebbles found in the marine conglomerates of Unit 2. One, more weathered, he considered as representing reworked artifacts of the "archaic pebble culture," the other, fresh and thus contemporaneous with the deposits he called "ancient pebble culture." However, there is no conclusive evidence that these objects are really man-made, and it has been demonstrated that they present all characteristics of "geofacts" that are still produced today by the waves striking boulders on each other in intertidal and infratidal environments (Raynal and Texier, 1989). We found no hint at all of human or hominin presence in any of the Ahl al Oughlam deposits.

The fillings (C1) are not stratified, and as the populations of the various rodent species from the different interconnected fissures do not significantly differ in tooth measurements, they can be considered as instantaneous at the geological scale. No absolute dating or paleomagnetic analysis is possible, so that the age of the fossiliferous fillings rests upon the identification and evolutionary stages of several taxa (Geraads, 2002, 2010b; Geraads et al., 2010a). The abundance of *Hipparion* and absence of *Equus* imply an age greater than 2.3 Ma. Postcranial dimensions of the giraffid *Sivatherium* best fit into the Pliocene/Pleistocene boundary. At species level, few bovids are identical with well-dated East African forms, one exception being *Beatragus whitei* (formerly called *Beatragus antiquus remotus* by Geraads and Amani, 1998) also known at Matabaietu 3-5, dated to *ca.* 2.5 Ma (Vrba, 1997). The cheetah *Acinonyx aicha* much resembles the European *A. pardinensis*, best known from Les Etouaires and Saint-Vallier, close to the Pliocene/Pleistocene boundary. A tooth of *Viverra leakeyi* best matches a specimen from Omo E3, *ca.* 2.4 Ma. Other taxa are similar to East African ones, but differences at species level make precise correlations problematic.

However, it is difficult to establish a maximum age for Ahl al Oughlam. The dental morphology of "*Kolpochoerus*" *phacochoeroides* is distinctly more derived than that of *K. afarensis* from Hadar, but this biochronological argument falls if these species belong to different lineages (see below). Among carnivores, *Crocuta dbaa* is certainly close to the Laetoli form, and the presence of a hyena still bearing an m2 is also indicative of an early age. On the other hand, the "*Parmularius*" *atlanticus* is distinctly more derived than the Hadar and Laetoli *Damalborea*. Thus, on the whole, the best fit of Ahl al Oughlam is about 2.5 Ma, but the full possible range is perhaps 2.4–2.8 Ma. In any case, it demonstrates than the lower units (1 and 2) of the AaO morphostratigraphic unit are in fact of Pliocene age and its unit 3 is close to the Pliocene/Pleistocene boundary.

The excavations involved mostly D.G., INSAP paleontologist Fethi Amani, and the local workers Abdeslam Nader and Abdelali Khaddouma. The fissure system was accessible through several points in the quarry cliff, but most of the excavations were conducted in an exceptionally rich small cave, about 1 m high after removal of the sediment and only accessible by crawling, from which about 3–4 m^3 of sediment were excavated and screened. The highly calcareous fossiliferous sediments C1 fill the fissures between the broken up and partly karstified blocks of consolidated calcarenite from Unit 2. They consist of loose clays with very friable bones and teeth, and concrete-hard calcified breccias, from which bones and teeth were extracted by acid cleaning. The concentration of fossils varies, but is always high, and the volume of fossils sometimes exceeds that of the sediment itself.

Unfortunately, despite frequent requests for its effective protection, and although it is officially classified as a protected site, the quarry has been transformed over the years into a rubbish dump, and is no longer accessible for excavation purposes (Figure 37.1). Extension of the excavations would still be possible by moderate blasting of the quarry, but is unlikely to happen.

Taphonomy

Obviously, several factors contributed to the faunal assemblage, but the destruction of part of the site by quarry works and the difficulties of excavations in narrow fissures prevent a reconstruction of the full topography of the fossiliferous deposits and their contents, which might have improved our understanding of the site formation. Furthermore, because the excavations, conducted in difficult conditions, were primarily aimed at collecting an identifiable faunal sample, and because of storage problems, not all bone fragments were collected and some information was certainly lost, but it is clear that some sorting occurred prior to fossilization. No detailed taphonomic analysis of bone breakage has been undertaken yet, but it seems that most of it occurred on green bone, probably as a result of the animals falling into pits; they probably attracted carnivores, whose remains are quite numerous, but there is little evidence of chewing. Some micromammals are associated with macromammals, but most of them are concentrated in special areas, and probably come from regurgitation pellets; the proportions of the various rodent taxa differ in the various loci, likely reflecting different predators, such as owls and small canids.

The topography of the main cave, where many bones of large mammals were found below a vertical chimney, strongly suggests that many bones fell through a pit, contributing to breakage and crushing of many of them. Still, there is no doubt that the main contributors to the taphocenosis were carnivores. They are far more abundant than in any biocenosis, both in number of species and in number of specimens: the ratio (NISP of carnivores) / (NISP of other mammals) is higher than 1/5 (Table 37.1). This implies that the carnivores preferentially used the fissures as dens or shelters. Although there are few conspicuous carnivore tooth marks, and although a detailed analysis of bone surfaces has yet to be undertaken, we may surmise that most killed or scavenged animals were brought into the fissures,

Figure 37.1 The site of Ahl al Oughlam in the early 1990s (A) and in 2007 (B). (A black and white version of this figure will appear in some formats. For the color version, please refer to the plate section.)

attracting other carnivores that were later killed or trapped as well. This would explain heavy breakage of most bones. By contrast, we believe that porcupines (*Hystrix*) did not significantly contribute to the assemblage, as not only are porcupine gnawing marks rare, but their fossil remains are also uncommon.

The relative proportions of anatomical elements in the various species strongly differ from those of the living animals (Geraads, 2006). Some of these differences are hard to explain, such as the very high numbers of bovid distal humeri, especially those of size class III, compared to the astragali, whereas *Hipparion*, whose bones are of similar size and robustness, displays the opposite pattern. Suid postcranials are remarkably rare, as elsewhere in Africa, but it may be that it is in fact their teeth that are overrepresented because of their robustness. Besides this, most of the apparent discrepancies in anatomical representations can probably be attributed to carnivore action. Limb bones of small- to medium-sized ungulates are underrepresented, but the most obvious distortion is that all very large animals, the giraffid *Sivatherium*, the rhino *Ceratotherium*, and both species of proboscideans are better represented by milk teeth than by third molars, and this proportion of juvenile individuals increases with size: there is not even a fragment of proboscidean permanent tooth. By contrast, the sample of medium-sized animals includes significant, and sometimes

Table 37.1 Faunal list of Ahl al Oughlam. In brackets, number of identified large mammals, and number of rodent lower m1s.

Mammalia

Primates:

Theropithecus atlanticus (Thomas, 1884) (90)

Carnivora (652):

Herpestidae (29):

Herpestes abdelalii Geraads, 1997

Ichneumia nims Geraads, 1997

Viverridae (2):

Viverra leakeyi Petter, 1963

Genetta sp.

Hyaenidae (194):

Crocuta dbaa Geraads, 1997

Pliocrocuta perrieri latidens Geraads, 1997

"*Ikelohyaena*" sp.

Chasmaporthetes nitidula darelbeidae Geraads, 1997

Felidae (100):

Acinonyx aicha Geraads, 1997

Panthera pardus (L.)

?*Lynx* sp.

Felis cf. *silvestris* Schreber, 1777

Dinofelis sp.

Homotherium sp.

Canidae (124):

Nyctereutes abdeslami Geraads, 1997

Lupulella paralius Geraads, 2011

Vulpes hassani Geraads, 2011

Mustelidae (31):

Prepoecilogale cf. *bolti* (Cooke, 1985)

Ictonyx libyca minor (Geraads, 1997)

Mellivora cf. *capensis* (Schreber, 1776)

Lutra fatimazohrae Geraads, 1997

Ursidae (9):

Ursus cf. *etruscus* Cuvier, 1823

Odobenidae (21):

Ontocetus emmonsi Leidy, 1859

Rodentia

Paraethomys chikeri Jaeger, 1975 (868)

Praomys skouri oughlamensis Geraads, 1995 (58)

Mus haouzi Jaeger, 1975 (975)

Gerbillus bibersoni Geraads, 1995 (454)

Irhoudia aff. *bohlini* Jaeger, 1971 (0)

Hystrix sp. (0)

Lagomorpha (*ca.* 100):

Lepus sp.

?*Trischizolagus* sp.

Prolagus n.sp.

Insectivora:

Suncus barbarus Geraads, 1995

Asoriculus maghrebiensis (Rzebik-Kowalska, 1988)

Erinaceus (*Atelerix*) sp.

Chiroptera:

Myotis darelbeidensis Gunnell et al., 2011

Miniopterus horaceki Gunnell et al., 2011

Emballonuridae indet.

Rhinolophus maghrebensis Gunnell et al., 2011

Proboscidea (65):

Elephas recki Dietrich, 1915?

Anancus cf. *osiris* Arambourg, 1945

Perissodactyla:

Ceratotherium sp. (108)

Hipparion pomeli Eisenmann & Geraads, 2007 (477)

Artiodactyla:

Delphinus sp. or *Stenella* sp. (11)

Kogia sp. (1)

?*Kolpochoerus phacochoeroides* (Thomas, 1884) (581)

Camelus sp. (5)

Sivatherium maurusium (Pomel, 1893) (223)

Bovidae (1582):

Tragelaphini (10)

Tragelaphus sp.

Bovini indet. (325)

Reduncini (81):

Kobus barbarus Geraads & Amani, 1998

Alcelaphini (110)

Beatragus whitei Vrba, 1997

?*Damalops atlanticus* (Geraads & Amani, 1998)

Antilopini (475)

Gazella (*Deprezia*) *psolea* Geraads & Amani, 1998

Gazella thomasi (Pomel, 1895)

Amphibia:

Bufo viridis Laurenti, 1768

Bufo sp.

Hyla cf. *meridionalis* Boettger, 1874

Reptilia:

Testudo oughlamensis Gmira et al., 2013

?*Centrochelys marocana* Gmira et al., 2013

Mauremys cf. *leprosa* (Schweigger, 1812)

Crocodylus sp.

Trogonophis darelbeidae Bailón, 2000

Blanus sp.

Gekkonidae indet.

Eumeces algeriensis Peters, 1864

Table 37.1 (cont.)

Chalcides sp.	*Mergus* sp.
cf. *Acanthodactylus* sp.	*Plioperdix africana* Mourer-Chauviré & Geraads, 2010
Ophisaurus koellikeri Günther, 1873	Rallidae size of *Porzana pusilla* (Pallas, 1776)
Coluber hippocrepis Linnaeus, 1758	*Otis* sp. size of *Otis tarda* Linnaeus, 1758
Malpolon sp.	*Chlamydotis* cf. *mesetaria* Sanchez-Marco, 1990
cf. *Macroprotodon* sp.	cf. *Lophotis* sp.
Macrovipera sp.	cf. *Pluvialis* sp.
Bitis sp.	cf. *Charadrius* Linnaeus, 1758
Aves:	*Catharacta* cf. *skua* Brünnich, 1764
Struthio asiaticus Milne-Edwards, 1871	*Alca ausonia* (Portis, 1889)
Phoebastria anglica (Lydekker, 1891)	*Columba* cf. *pisana* (Portis, 1889)
Phoebastria cf. *albatrus* (Pallas, 1769)	*Columba* sp. size of *C. palumbus* Linnaeus, 1758
Phoebastria cf. *nigripes* (Audubon, 1849) *Calonectris* cf. *diomedea* (Scopoli, 1769)	*Agapornis atlanticus* Mourer-Chauviré & Geraads, 2010
Pelagornis mauretanicus Mourer-Chauviré & Geraads, 2008	*Tyto alba* (Scopoli, 1769)
Morus peninsularis Brodkorb, 1955	*Tyto balearica* Mourer-Chauviré et al., 1980
Geronticus olsoni Mourer-Chauviré & Geraads, 2010	*Surnia robusta* Janossy, 1977
Anserinae indet.	Alaudidae indet.
Alopochen cf. *aegyptiacus* (Linnaeus, 1766)	**Pisces**
Tadorna tadorna (Linnaeus, 1758)	Sparidae indet.
Tadorna sp.	Squaliform indet.

very high, numbers of permanent teeth. However, this under-representation of adult individuals of the largest species does not hold for the distal parts of the limbs, as carpals and metapodials of the above-mentioned taxa are quite numerous. We may hypothesize that the carnivores ate many of the small- to medium-sized bones, or broke them into unidentifiable or discarded fragments. By contrast, they were unable to carry into the caves heavy elements such as heads of the largest adult ungulates, or large elements of their limbs, as explained by Klein et al. (1999) in the context of the Duinefontein 2 site in South Africa.

In spite of its age, contemporaneous with several famous eastern African sites, the locality has not attracted much paleoecological interest, probably because it lacks hominins. It is unlikely, anyway, that recently developed analyses, on microwear, mesowear, or isotopes, would seriously alter the pattern provided by the mere observation of the mammalian faunal list and abundances. In particular, because of the geographic location of the site north of the Atlas Range in the Mediterranean domain, it probably lacked C_4 grasses, and carbon isotope analyses (in progress) would be unable to tell apart grazers from browsers, although the ^{18}O might tell us more about the abundance of permanent fresh water in the surroundings.

Faunal Composition

The faunal collection consists of more than 4000 identified remains of large mammals, plus thousands of rodents, insectivores, and bats, to which should be added a remarkable collection of birds, plus reptiles, amphibians, and fishes. The faunal list (Table 37.1) includes more than 100 species of vertebrates, of which 56 are mammals. It is based upon the studies of the following taxa: Cercopithecidae (Alemseged and Geraads, 1998), Carnivora (Geraads, 1997, 2004a, 2008, 2011), Rodentia and Insectivora (Geraads, 1995), Chiroptera (Gunnell et al., 2011), Proboscidea (Geraads and Metz-Muller, 1999), Equidae (Eisenmann and Geraads, 2007), Suidae (Geraads, 1993b, 2004b), Giraffidae (Geraads, 1996), Bovidae (Geraads and Amani, 1998), Amphibia and Reptilia (Bailón, 2000; Gmira et al., 2013), Aves (Mourer-Chauviré and Geraads, 2008, 2010), and on preliminary identifications for the few taxa not studied yet.

Ahl al Oughlam is by far the richest site of the late Neogene of North Africa, only matched by Fayum in Egypt for the whole Cainozoic, and the only one that stands comparison with the most famous East and South African sites.

Some of the early identifications have been questioned. Frost and Delson (2002) considered *Theropithecus atlanticus* a synonym of *T. oswaldi darti*; both taxa are indeed at the same evolutionary grade, but we believe, pending discovery of more complete remains, that some of the dental features of the North African form prevent assignment to the southern one. The primitive hyenid first tentatively referred to *Hyaenictitherium* could in fact be a primitive *Hyaena*; it was called *Ikelohyaena* cf. *abronia* by Werdelin and Peigné (2010), but definitions and limits of these taxa are blurry. *Crocuta dbaa* was synonymized with *Crocuta dietrichi* by Werdelin and Peigné (2010), but we disagree; this issue still has to be worked on. It may be that the differences between *Acinonyx aicha* and the European *A. pardinensis*, although real, do not warrant specific distinction (Geraads, 2014). Souron (2012) concluded that *Kolpochoerus phacochoeroides* should be transferred to *Metridiochoerus*, a close relative of *Phacochoerus*; as shown by its name, the similarities of this species with the warthog have long been recognized, but the generic assignment remains debatable. Gentry (2010) suspected that *Parmularius atlanticus* Geraads and Amani, 1998 is in fact close to *Damalops*, and we are now inclined to follow him, but both generic names could be synonyms.

As most of the sediment was carefully screened (at 0.8 mm), and the number of identified fossils is quite high, we may assume that Table 37.1 includes virtually all vertebrates that were actually present at Ahl al Oughlam. In spite of this, there are a number of noticeable absences. The mention of *Macaca* in previous lists (Geraads, 2006) was based upon erroneous identifications of *Theropithecus* deciduous teeth, so that the latter genus, a large ground-dwelling form, is the only Primate present. The most surprising absence is that of hominins. None of the smaller cercopithecid monkeys commonly found in East Africa is present; because they are among the best indicators of wood cover, their absence argues against the presence of significant wood cover in the landscape. Among ungulates, the absence of the browsing *Diceros*, of the so-called "Neotragini" (dik-diks and allies), of the Cephalophini, and of the impala *Aepyceros* may have a biogeographic origin, as none of these forms has been reported from the Plio-Pleistocene of northwestern Africa, but it must be observed that these species need some wood cover, and it may be that none of the environments there was suitable for them. By contrast, the Tragelaphini did reach northwestern Africa, so that their scarcity at Ahl al Oughlam, which sharply contrasts with their abundance in some East African sites, strongly favors the hypothesis of an open environment. The otters attest to the presence of streams, as modern *Lutra* and "*Hydrictis*" need freshwater, but the complete absence of hippos and large freshwater fishes, and the scarcity of crocodiles, may reflect that of large permanent rivers or ponds, although the nature of the site certainly acted against the preservation of these taxa. This relatively xeric habitat is confirmed by the avifauna that differs from most other African ones in the virtual absence of aquatic forms living on the shores of lakes or rivers (Mourer-Chauviré and Geraads, 2010).

Among the taxa that are present at Ahl al Oughlam, Carnivora are not good ecological indicators, and their proportions are certainly biased by the nature of the site. At least the cheetah *Acinonyx* and the hunting hyena *Chasmaporthetes* were certainly open-country forms; but the leopard is not normally found in open landscapes, and the same was probably true of the bear. The latter documents the earliest dispersal of *Ursus* into North Africa, where it survived until historic times, but apparently never made it south of the present-day Sahara. It is seemingly absent from east Africa, suggesting that it crossed the Gibraltar Straits. *Nyctereutes* is also probably of Eurasian origin, with only a sparse record elsewhere in Africa.

Among Perissodactyla, the abundance of equids and presence of *Ceratotherium* are indicative of abundant grasses, although the dental adaptations of *C. mauritanicum* for grazing are less advanced than those of the modern *C. simum*. The suid, whatever its genus, has rather long, complex, and hypsodont third molars, and could have occupied a feeding niche intermediate between those of *Notochoerus* and *Kolpochoerus limnetes*. The diet of the giraffid *Sivatherium maurusium* has been disputed and may have changed through time (Harris et al., 2010b; Geraads et al., 2013a, and references therein), but regarding this large and abundant large mammal as a browser would be so sharply at variance with the rest of the faunal evidence that we can reject this hypothesis.

The number of bovid specimens of the various tribes may not, for taphonomic reasons, faithfully reflect their living abundances, but it is clear that open-country forms (Alcelaphini, Antilopini, and probably Bovini) largely predominate over the browsing Tragelaphini.

Among rodents, the gerbillids are today clear indicators of arid environments, and it is commonly assumed that the gerbillid/murid ratio roughly reflects the openness of the landscape. This ratio is low at Ahl al Oughlam, even if *Mus*, whose abundance in Upper Pleistocene sites demonstrates adaptability, is excluded from the count. Thus, this ratio does not fully agree with the conclusions drawn from large mammals, but it may be that this is because the most common murid, the extinct *Paraethomys*, was adapted to the Mediterranean steppes. In any case, the proportions of the rodent taxa in the various fissures differ, showing that they are also influenced by taphonomic factors, such as predator choice.

A taxon-free estimate of the forest cover is the height/width proportions of bovid tali (DeGusta and Vrba, 2003). Here, all bovid tali are low relative to their width: the ratio minimum height vs. median width (LI/WI of DeGusta and Vrba, 2003) never exceeds 1.4 (Figure 37.2), while it often exceeds this value in forest dwellers, confirming the absence of heavy wood cover.

Another taxon-free approach is the use of the so-called cenograms that display species by decreasing body weight; it has been assumed that the general shape of the graph, if not the slopes of the regression lines drawn through the points corresponding to the "large" or "small" species, provide indications about wood cover or temperature (e.g., Legendre, 1989, and references therein). We provide the updated cenogram here (Figure 37.3), but the validity of this method has been seriously questioned by Rodríguez (1999), who found that only the number of species between 0.5 and 8 kg and, to a lesser extent, between 0.5 and 25 kg can provide some indication on the vegetation physiognomy. These numbers at AaO (respectively, 5 and 7) are compatible with any environment except forest and desert, but best fit shrubland.

Not many of the species present at Ahl al Oughlam provide indications about the temperature or seasonality. None of the bird species definitely indicates cold weather, but the occurrence of more species with Eurasian than African affinities suggests a milder climate than further south. Several African antelopes are able to cope with rather low temperatures, and this was certainly also true of most carnivores; the walrus *Ontocetus* certainly preferred cold waters, as Ahl al Oughlam is its southernmost record in the Western Atlantic. So, even if it is generally agreed that the global climate at that time was warmer than today, the Ahl al Oughlam fauna provides no evidence for such difference in Morocco at that time.

One of the most remarkable features of the Ahl al Oughlam mammalian assemblage, contrasting with the high number of carnivore species, is the low diversity in all other groups, especially by comparison with most East or South African sites of

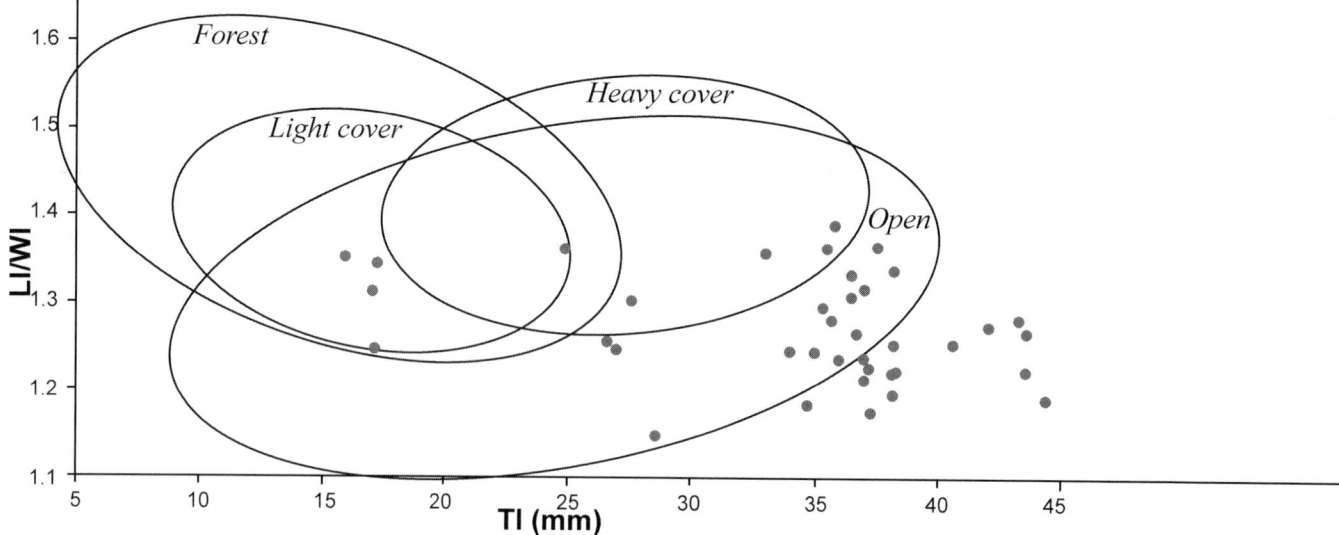

Figure 37.2 Plot of the ratio minimum length (LI)/width at mid-length (WI) vs. thickness at mid-length (TI) of bovid astragali from Ahl al Oughlam (dots), compared to the 90% probability ellipses for antelopes of various habitats (from DeGusta and Vrba, 2003).

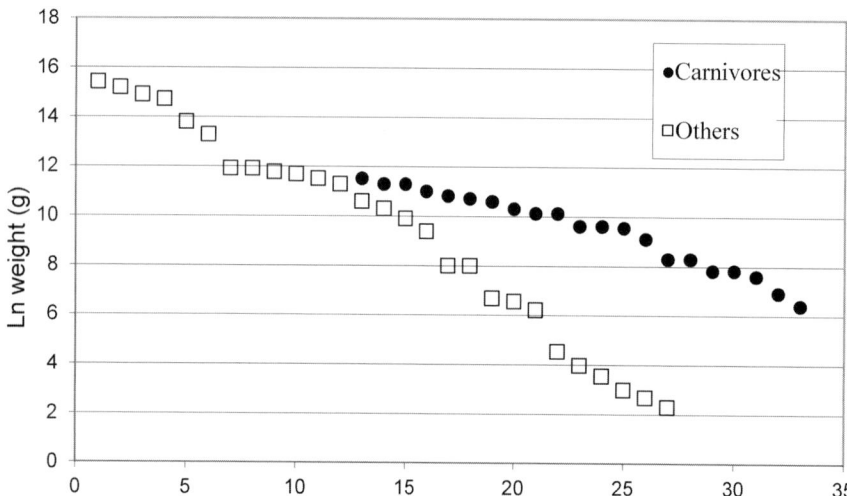

Figure 37.3 Cenogram of Ahl al Oughlam. Species arranged by decreasing weight from left to right.

similar age. There is only one species of Primate, whereas several are usually found elsewhere in Africa; the number of micromammal species is quite low, although collecting of thousands of teeth ensured that sampling of the living assemblage was virtually exhaustive; Rhinocerotidae, Equidae, Suidae, and Giraffidae are each represented by a single species, whereas two or three are usually recorded in East Africa; there are 7 species of bovids, but even this number is rather low when compared with well-sampled more southern sites, which often yield 10 species or more. One of the reasons for this low richness is probably that the assemblage of Ahl al Oughlam samples only α-diversity, whereas open-air sites may combine faunal remains from several habitats (β-diversity). Still, its fauna is poorer in species than those of the South African cave sites with similar taphonomic context, implying that, although species richness is not easily interpreted in terms of ecology, Ahl al Oughlam is not a sample from a very favorable environment. Perhaps high seasonality could explain some of the apparent inconsistencies in faunal indicators (especially those of birds) and the stress on the mammalian fauna.

Conclusion

On the whole, the vertebrate association unambiguously points to an open landscape, with no evidence of significant wood cover nearby, and no large permanent river or lake. More tentatively, we can hypothesize a marked seasonality with a cold winter temperature and imagine that these conditions could have been unsuitable for hominins of that time. Of course, whatever the quality of sampling, the absence of hominins is merely absence of evidence, and one can always hope that future work will bring one to light.

Acknowledgments

Excavations at Ahl al Oughlam were conducted in the frame of the Franco-Moroccan Préhistoire de Casablanca program and supported by the Institut National des Sciences de l'Archéologie et du Patrimoine (INSAP) of the Ministère de la Culture, de la Jeunesse et des Sports of the Kingdom of Morocco, the Ministère de l'Europe et des Affaires Étrangères of France, and the Collège de France.

38 Tighennif (Ternifine), Algeria: Environments of the Earliest Human Fossils of North Africa in the late Early Pleistocene

Denis Geraads

Introduction

The site of Tighennif (also known as Ternifine, from the old name Tighenifine, and as Palikao) is located about 20 km east of Mascara in northern Algeria, about 60 km from the Mediterranean sea, at a present-day altitude of around 500 m a.s.l. It was discovered in 1872, soon after the creation by French settlers of the village of Palikao. The sand quarry, west of the village (N 35°24′55″, E 0°19′17″), was worked from 1872 onwards; Pomel (1879) gave the first report on fossil finds and undertook a small excavation in 1882 with Tommasini. Numerous fossils were discovered during the last part of the nineteenth century, and many of them were described in Pomel's classical monographs, published from 1893 to 1897. However, sand extraction had to be stopped when the excavations reached a famous cemetery. Man-made artifacts were first identified by Tommasini (1886), but doubts were still frequently expressed as to the antiquity of the site, and it is only with the discovery by Pallary in 1928 of a canine of the saber-tooth cat *Homotherium* that its antiquity was confirmed (Pallary's material is held at the Institut de Paléontologie Humaine, Paris). Arambourg led new excavations in 1931, but was soon stopped by upwelling of artesian water from the bottom of the deposits; nevertheless, he was the first to reach a clayey level at the base of the deposits. The largest excavations, conducted by Camille Arambourg and Robert Hoffstetter, took place in 1954, 1955, and 1956 on a large scale, employing up to 80 workers. They resulted in the collection of thousands of fossils, numerous artifacts, and several hominin remains that Arambourg (1963a) assigned to *Atlanthropus mauritanicus* Arambourg, 1954, and that are still the earliest hominin fossils found in North Africa, even though they are now usually assigned to *Homo rhodesiensis* Woodward, 1921. This material is now deposited at the Muséum National d'Histoire Naturelle, Paris (MNHN). However, upwelling waters necessitated continuous pumping and hindered the study of the stratigraphy and the excavations themselves. Partly for this reason the digging stopped in 1956. Afterwards, thanks to a considerable lowering of the water table that had dried almost all of the fossiliferous levels, small-scale excavations were undertaken by a Franco-Algerian team led by Jean-Jacques Hublin in 1982–1983 (Figure 38.1; Geraads et al., 1986).

Figure 38.1 Excavations at Tighennif in 1982.

Geological Setting

The large-scale excavations undertaken by Arambourg and Hoffstetter allowed them to establish the basic stratigraphy of the site (Arambourg and Hoffstetter, 1963). Geraads and colleagues (1986) reconstruct its history as follows, on the basis of the sedimentological analyses:

First, a layer of virtually sterile varicolored clay allowed the formation of a shallow lake, fed by artesian springs, into which a gray clay layer, from 0.20 to 1.5 m thick, was deposited. It functioned in a closed system, as shown by the presence of montmorillonite, and periodically dried out, as shown by carbonate nodules. This layer is not easily accessible, which explains why it has provided relatively few fossils, despite its apparent richness.

Second, at a later stage the artesian springs brought up the underlying marine Miocene sands, filling the basin, while subsidence in its central part increased the dip of the basal layers toward the center, creating microfaults and disturbing their horizontal arrangement. These sands yielded most of the material, but the great number of fossils is misleading, being due to the loose nature of the sands that allow easy and fast excavations; in fact the density of fossils is low and some parts of the quarry are sterile.

As elsewhere in North Africa, no absolute age determination is possible, and the dating of the site mostly rests on mammalian biochronology. Unfortunately, well-dated faunas are quite rare in North Africa, and there are very few sites of comparable age. Aïn Hanech, also in Algeria, whatever its real age (Sahnouni et al., 2002; Geraads et al., 2004b), is significantly older than Tighennif. Most levels of the Thomas quarries in Morocco (Geraads et al., Chapter 39) are younger, but as they are certainly older than the 400 ka assigned to them by Geraads et al. in 1986, their age becomes more relevant to that of Tighennif. If not due to different ecological conditions or to biogeographic factors, the absence in the Moroccan sites of several taxa present in the Algerian site (*Homotherium*, *Metridiochoerus andrewsi/compactus*, cf. *Macedonitherium*, *Parmularius ambiguus*, *Mascaramys*), together with the greater evolutionary stage reached by most rodent genera (Jaeger, 1975; Tong, 1986, 1989; Geraads, 2002, 2010b), imply a significant age difference, but that is hard to quantify exactly. On the whole, even though comparisons are difficult because of the great distance, the evolutionary stage of the Tighennif fauna, especially that of the suids and alcelaphin bovids, is that of the upper Olduvai beds, therefore in the region of 1 Ma.

Paleomagnetic analyses attempted by Sevket Sen were reported by Geraads et al. (1986). No signal could be recognized in the sands, but the nodular gray clay has a normal polarity that is probably original, indicating either the Brunhes epoch or the Jaramillo event. In contrast to the suggestion made by these authors of an age close to 700 ka within the Brunhes epoch, it looks more likely now that if the normal polarity is indeed meaningful, an age closer to 1 Ma in the Jaramillo event is more likely.

The fauna and hominin remains were associated with many artifacts of early Acheulean type. They were studied by Djemmali (1985), who concluded that two different industries were present, one containing many large tools, including cleavers and handaxes, mostly made on quartzite, and one lacking these tools and mostly made on flint. However, it is unlikely that Arambourg and Hoffstetter would have missed this distinction if it was linked to the stratigraphy, and the technological differences probably result merely from the raw materials used. The most conspicuous hominin activity on bone is a zebra distal metacarpal exhibiting spiral fracture and retouches, and is one of the most convincing pieces of evidence so far for bone tool use during the lower Paleolithic (Denys et al., 1984; Geraads et al., 1986). Unfortunately, this find remains isolated, and cannot be placed in a broader taphonomic context at present (see below).

Arambourg and Hoffstetter (1963) did not provide any information on the stratigraphic origin of their fossils and artifacts, although they extracted fossils from both the gray nodular clay and the overlying sands, as definitely documented by the nature of the matrix still adhering to many fossils. Hublin and co-workers did record this provenance, but their collection is too small for any difference between layers to be considered as significant. Several species are known only from the 1982–83 excavations in the lower nodular clay, but this is probably only because of the different sedimentological context, or of a bias against the small forms in the 1954–56 excavations. I believe that no difference between layers is biostratigraphically meaningful, and no conclusive evidence refutes their contemporaneity at the geological scale.

Taphonomy

No taphonomic analysis of the whole fauna has ever been undertaken, in part because we know nothing of the collecting procedures of Arambourg and Hoffstetter, but we may suspect that they did not follow what is now considered as standard procedures. For instance, the collections of the MNHN include few bovid postcranials compared to the cranial and dental remains (respectively 134 vs. 378 fossils), whereas the small collection made by Hublin and co-workers who collected all fossils shows that these postcranial remains were not rare.

The Institut de Paléontologie Humaine (IPH), Paris collection includes an associated set of anterior rhino limb bones, but all bones found in 1982–1983 are isolated; the same is true of those of the Arambourg and Hoffstetter collection, although it may well be that associated bones were not recorded as such. It is likely that fossilization was usually not fast enough to prevent skeletons deposited in the lake bottom from being disturbed by living animals or artesian springs; this is true also of the artifacts, as Djemmali (1985) was unable to refit any flakes. Some animals certainly also died in the surroundings, as Denys et al. (1984) observed that some bones remained exposed for some time before burial.

Pending a detailed taphonomic analysis of the collection, hypotheses on the origin of the faunal assemblage must be put forward cautiously. As noted above, conclusions are hard to draw for large mammals; overall condition of the fossils is good, with little weathering and preservation of delicate specimens (such as *Homotherium* canines), suggesting little transport; most of the bone breakage clearly occurred during the excavations. The abundance of carnivores would perhaps designate them as responsible for the bone accumulation, but no carnivore marks have been reported, and truly hunting forms are few compared to scavengers, which probably came where food was available. Denys et al. (1984) surmised that hominins were the main agent of the bone accumulation, but reported traces of their activities are scarce. The overall evidence suggests that most large mammals died naturally in the lake or nearby. Denys et al. (1984, 1987) observed few discrepancies between the relative abundance of anatomical elements with those of living rodents, and concluded that they have not undergone much transport, and therefore reliably document the environment.

Vertebrate Fauna

The fauna of Tighennif remains largely unpublished, and the only descriptions and illustrations of some taxa are still those of Pomel (1893–1897). Arambourg never described the fauna, and mentioned only some taxa in passing. Only the equids (Eisenmann, 1979a, 1979b, 1980, 1981), the suids (Pickford, 2020), the camels (Martini and Geraads, 2018), the ruminants (Geraads, 1981), the rodents (Jaeger, 1975; Tong, 1986, 1989), the Cercopithecidae (Delson and Hoffstetter, 1993; Delson et al., 1993), and the carnivores (Geraads, 2011, 2016) have been studied in some detail. Maglio (1973) illustrated some elephants, and Harris et al. (2010) illustrated some *Camelus*. The faunal list provided in Table 38.1 has been compiled from these publications, and complemented by the faunal lists of Geraads et al. (1986) and Denys et al. (1987).

The number of specimens of the various taxa in Table 38.1 is based upon these publications and my personal observations, but the number of elephants, rhinos, hippos, and suids are based upon the catalogs only, as most of the Tighennif collection of very large mammals stored in the MNHN is presently unavailable. Thus, identifications were not checked but it is unlikely that the true numbers much differ from those of Table 38.1. The collection made by Arambourg and Hoffstetter is much larger than that made by Hublin and co-workers, especially for equids. It may be that the abundance of the latter is overestimated, as almost 3/5 of their sample consists of isolated teeth, perhaps as a consequence of breakage during the excavations. Still, there certainly remains a sampling difference for this group, which cannot be explained at present.

Table 38.1 Updated faunal list of Tighennif vertebrates (see text for the origin of identifications). The numbers of rodents in the various layers were provided by Tong (1986); those given here are the totals for all levels. "X" indicates presence.

Faunal list	Hublin	Arambourg & Hoffstetter
Ungulates – number of specimens		
Loxodonta atlantica	4	90
Ceratotherium mauritanicum	5	105
Equus mauritanicus	15	1548
Hippopotamus sirensis	49	454
Metridiochoerus andrewsi/compactus	3	98
Camelus thomasi	1	46
cf. *Macedonitherium* sp.		10
Bovidae (total)	14	530
Bovidae – number of m3s		
(x = present but no m3)		
Tragelaphus algericus		x
"*Bos*" cf. *bubaloides*	x	x
Oryx gazella	x	3
Hippotragus cf. *gigas*		6
Kobus sp.		1
Connochaetes taurinus prognu	2	48
Parmularius ambiguus	1	62
Gazella dracula	x	28
Gazella cf. *atlantica*		2
Gazella sp. B		2
Caprini indet.		1
Carnivora and Primates – number of dental remains (MNI)		
Hyaena hyaena		6 (4)
Crocuta crocuta	2	36 (15)
Homotherium sp.		7 (2)

Table 38.1 (cont.)

Faunal list	Hublin	Arambourg & Hoffstetter
Felis silvestris		4 (2)
Lynx sp.		18 (6)
Panthera aff. *leo*		9 (4)
Vulpes cf. *rueppelli*		9 (4)
Lupulella mohibi	2	47 (10)
Lycaon magnus		6 (2)
Mellivora capensis		9 (4)
Poecilictis cf. *libyca*		1 (1)
Enhydrictis hoffstetteri		1 (1)
Ursus aff. *bibersoni*		6 (2)
Theropithecus oswaldi		52 (7)
Homo cf. *rhodesiensis*		13 (5)
Erinaceidae indet	x	
Crocidura sp.	x	
Lepus sp.	x	
Rodentia – number of molars		
Ellobius africanus	62	
Paraethomys tighennifae	44	
Arvicanthis arambourgi	115	
Praomys (Berberomys) eghrisae	28	
Meriones maximus	135	
Meriones maghrebianus	5	
Gerbillus cingulatus	157	
Gerbillus major	887	
Mascaramys medius	83	
Amphibia:		
Discoglossus sp.	x	
Pelobates sp.	x	
Bufo cf. *bufo*	x	
Ranidae indet.	x	
Reptilia:		
Amphisbaenia indet.	x	
Erycinae indet.	x	
Matrix sp.	x	
Colubridae indet.	x	
Vipera sp.	x	
Lacertilia indet.	x	
Emys cf. *orbicularis*	x	

It is hard to be sure that Arambourg and Hoffstetter fully sampled the taphocoenosis. The list looks biased against small- to medium-sized mammals, such as herpestids, small felids, mustelids, and perhaps small bovids, which were probably not searched for with great care. Still, I believe that the absence of small cercopithecids is real, as they are usually common when present. In view of the frequency of carnivores, the absence of leopard (*Panthera pardus*) is probably not a sampling bias either. The lack of crocodiles, particularly given the abundance of hippos, is also remarkable.

The ecological preferences of the large ungulates provide detail regarding the nature of the environment. Obviously, the abundance of hippos, certainly the dominant mammals in terms of biomass, is linked to the nature of the deposits, but large extents of grassy areas must have been available nearby. If the Tighennif lake was really part of an endorheic system, as suggested by the clays, this system must have been large enough to enable the survival of a large hippo population. The white rhinoceros (*Ceratotherium*) is an exclusive grazer; *Equus*, also a grazer, is very abundant; the only suid, *Metridiochoerus andrewsi/compactus*, is a large-size cousin of the warthog with very hypsodont teeth; by contrast, no brachyodont suid is present, and the browsing giraffid is extremely rare (Figure 38.2A). Among the Bovidae, the Alcelaphini and Antilopini, together with *Oryx*, make up 95 percent of the total bovid assemblage, an extremely high proportion. These antelopes are well-known (e.g., Vrba, 1980) to indicate dry, open country, as opposed to the Tragelaphini, Reduncini, and Aepycerotini that prefer more wet and/or more forested areas. The absence of the leopard, a predator not normally found in open spaces, confirms this. Thus, the whole large mammal assemblage demonstrates that the environment surrounding the Tighennif lake was extremely open (Figure 38.2B). These indicators of open, dry environments are found in several other Pleistocene North African sites, such as Ain Hanech in Algeria (Arambourg, 1970, 1979), Thomas Quarries and Ain Maarouf in Morocco (Geraads et al., Chapter 39; Geraads and Amani, 1997), and we may surmise that it was widespread in the region, although there is also some evidence of more humid and wooded habitats, with tragelaphins and reduncins (Mansoura: Chaid-Saoudi et al., 2006).

The rodents tell a similar story. It is usually admitted that the relative proportions of gerbils vs. murins provide a rough estimate of the openness of the landscape; here, with 84 percent of the total rodent assemblage, contrasting with a mere 12 percent for the murins, the gerbils clearly point to a similar type of environment as that which is suggested by the large mammal assemblage, i.e., a "relatively dry climate and a steppe environment" (Tong, 1986: 214). Tong (1986) observed some variations in the percentage of Gerbillinae across the Tighennif layers, but it never goes below 66 percent of the rodents, showing that all Tighennif layers document the same type of environments (Figure 38.2C).

Although the evidence for grassland habitats is very clear, there are a few discordant indications. For instance, Eisenmann (1984, 1985) tentatively assumed from its relatively stout metapodials and broad third phalanges that *Equus mauritanicus* indicated relatively wet conditions and a relatively soft soil. No other ecomorphological analysis has been undertaken, mostly because postcranials are too rare to draw significant conclusions, and because there is no complete bovid cranium, but on balance, I regard this single evidence as less conclusive than the conclusions drawn from the taxonomy. The burrowing *Ellobius* also

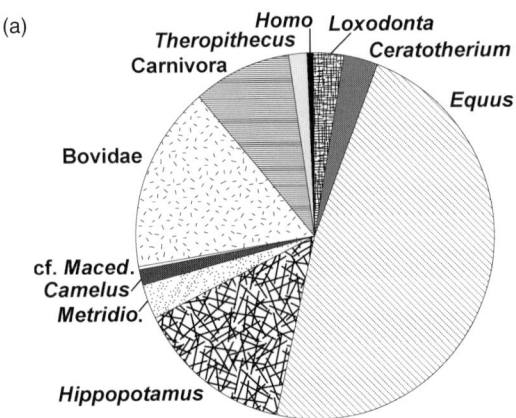
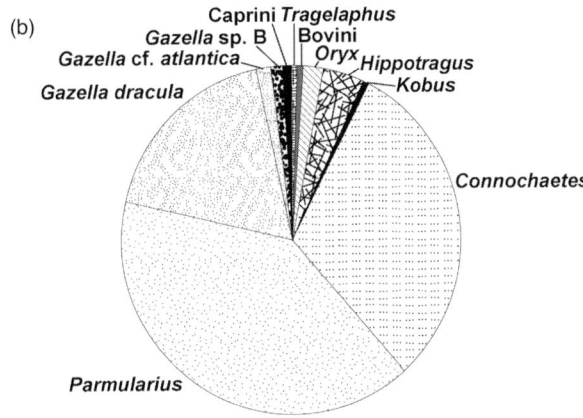
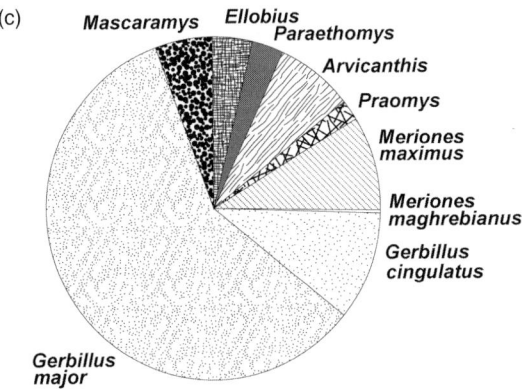

Figure 38.2A–C Proportions of the various mammals at Tighennif. (A) Pie diagram of the number of large mammals (NISP) in the MNHN collection. (B) Number of bovid m3s in the MNHN collection (taxa present but not represented by m3s counted as 1); dotted sectors represent open-country forms. (C) Number of rodent molars collected in 1982; dotted sectors represent open-country forms.

needed a soft soil, but this does not exclude a savanna or steppe habitat. The absence of the cheetah, a fast-running felid of open landscapes, is surprising, but it may be that it avoided competition at the lake margins, where other large predators abounded.

Like that of the much earlier site of Ahl al Oughlam, the mammalian assemblage of Tighennif is noticeable by its low species richness. Proboscideans, Rhinocerotidae, Equidae, Suidae, Giraffidae, and Cercopithecidae are each represented by one species only, and some African groups are wholly absent (aardvarks, hyraxes, tragulids). Even the Bovidae, with their 11 species, are not very diverse given the abundance of specimens, and are dominated by a few very common forms. By contrast, there are 13 species of carnivores, but several of them preyed upon lower vertebrates, or were partly omnivorous. This low diversity suggests that the fossil assemblage samples only the α-diversity of the site and immediate surroundings, and not the mosaic habitat of the Eghris plain, so that it represents only the fauna closely associated with *Homo*, in agreement with the absence of water transport. Still, even for a single mammalian community, this low diversity points to an environment that was not very favorable. This probably means colder than in more southern sites, although no taxon is indicative of a cold climate, except perhaps the bear, which is similar to the present-day brown bear (*Ursus arctos*), not found at low latitudes. Geraads et al. (1986) also observed that the Tighennif rodent assemblage differs from that of the earlier site of Sidi Abdallah in Morocco in the appearance of the cool-adapted *Ellobius*, and extinction of the thermophilous Ctenodactylidae.

No systematic analysis of tooth wear or isotopes has been undertaken, and the isotopic composition of only four taxa from Tighennif was analyzed by Bocherens et al. (1996): *Hippopotamus*, *Connochaetes*, *Ceratotherium*, and *Equus*. All of them have strongly negative $\delta^{13}C$ values, much lower than those found in modern African representatives of these genera and similar to those of browsers, but this only means that C_4 grasses were not present in the area, like today. Still, none of these taxa displays the extremely negative values that would have been expected in a wooded environment, thus underlining the open nature of the surrounding landscapes.

Unfortunately, other climatic proxies are almost completely lacking. Geraads et al. (1986) found eolian sands mixed with the Miocene ones in the deposits, confirming the presence of open, if not subdesertic areas in the vicinity, but no plant remains (including pollens) have been found at the site, so that the physiognomy of the landscape remains vague. However, palynological data from the Alboran sea (Feddi et al., 2011) have shown that the western Mediterranean Pleistocene saw a relative decrease of forest cover and an expansion of steppes and grasslands, with average temperatures not much higher than today, meaning it was quite cold in winter, especially at the altitude of Tighennif.

Changes across the Tighennif succession are poorly documented. As mentioned above, no stratigraphic provenance was recorded by Arambourg and Hoffstetter, and the collection of large mammals made by Hublin and co-workers is too small to be significant. By contrast, the proportions of the various rodent taxa vary significantly between levels. Geraads et al. (1986) attributed these changes to climatic fluctuations, a conclusion rejected by Dauphin et al. (1994) on the basis of taphonomic and chemical analyses. These changes are likely to reflect localized habitats.

Conclusion

There are probably few sites where the available paleoenvironmental indicators agree as closely as at Tighennif, and it is unlikely that, should more proxies become available, they would change the overall picture of an open, dry landscape that was probably valid for the whole, short stratigraphic succession. The absence of local floral indicators prevents any reliable reconstruction of the Tighennif "diorama," especially as the most likely modern equivalents, the Saharan steppe and Sahelian acacia savanna, have been deeply impacted by humans, but Tighennif shows that around 1 Ma *Homo* was able to thrive in an environment that was suitable to a small number of large mammal species only.

Acknowledgments

I am grateful to S. Reynolds and R. Bobe for inviting me to contribute this chapter, and for their editorial comments. Many thanks also to Camille Daujeard for her comments, and to the reviewer M. Belmaker for her constructive criticism.

39 Early *Homo* on the Atlantic Shore: The Thomas I and Oulad Hamida 1 Quarries, Morocco

Denis Geraads, Camille Daujeard, David Lefèvre, Rosalia Gallotti, Abderrahim Mohib, and Jean-Paul Raynal

Introduction

The sites discussed here were first reported by Biberson (1961a) under the name of "carrières Thomas" derived from the name of the worker of these quarries. There were three of them, called Thomas I, II, and III from the NE to the SW, at 33.568° N, 7.698° W, in what are now the suburbs of Casablanca. Biberson did not use them much in his major synthesis (1961a) and proposed simplistic correlations based on mollusk faunas between Sidi Abderrahmane and Thomas Quarries successions, but this did not help to clarify the complex stratigraphy of the beginning of the Moroccan coastal Middle Pleistocene, where continental and marine deposits interdigitate; finally, Biberson reported some fossils of unknown whereabouts. In 1969, while the quarries were being worked for their calcarenite, a young student, Philippe Beriro, found a human mandible in a cave opened by quarry works at Thomas I. The mandible was first reported by Ennouchi (1969, 1970) and studied in more detail by Sausse (1975). Soon after, hominin remains were discovered in a cave in Thomas Quarry III (Ennouchi, 1972, 1975, 1976), but the site was rapidly destroyed by quarry works. All hominin fossils from Thomas quarries were at the time referred by Ennouchi (1970) to *Atlanthropus mauritanicus*. Later, Thomas Quarries I and II were merged into Thomas I, and the name of Thomas Quarry III changed first to "Ben Sina" and later to "Oulad Hamida 1," which is the local toponym. Fossils associated with the human remains, as well as other fossils and Acheulean artifacts, were briefly studied by Geraads (1980a) and Geraads et al. (1980). At that time, one of us (J.-P.R.), together with Jean-Pierre Texier, was starting a revision of the Moroccan coastal Quaternary, for which the Thomas Quarries were key localities; he was joined by D.L. in 1989. Archeological excavations in several levels of Thomas Quarry I have been undertaken from 1988 onwards by J.-P.R. and colleagues, to be complemented in 1991 by the excavation in Oulad Hamida 1 Quarry of a large cave called "Grotte des Rhinocéros (GDR)," which is in geometric continuity with what Geraads (1980a) had called "fissures dans le Tensiftien de Thomas III."

These controlled excavations in the several *loci* of the Thomas–Oulad Hamida Quarries (Th-OH) resulted in the discovery of several thousand artifacts and fossils, of several more hominin remains in the "Grotte à Hominidés" of Thomas Quarry I (ThI-GH), and in the renewal of the stratigraphic scheme, within which all finds can be precisely positioned. All excavations were conducted with modern methodology, and all lithic and large faunal material was recorded stratigraphically and three-dimensionally. In the richest squares, sediment was treated with formic acid to remove the calcareous matrix and wet-screened at 0.8 mm, yielding thousands of rodent teeth.

Stratigraphic Context

The Casablanca hinterland shows a vast system of longitudinal dune ridges parallel to modern coast. These morpho-sedimentary units are composed of marine and aeolian calcarenites that have left a record of an exceptional succession of paleo-shorelines since the end of the Miocene (Biberson, 1961a; Stearns, 1978; Raynal et al., 1995, 1999; Lefèvre, 2000; Lefèvre and Raynal, 2002).

In the new Casablanca stratigraphic scale, four formations, associated with four platforms and including several members, have been defined, from the late Lower Pleistocene to the Upper Pleistocene: the Oulad Hamida Formation (late Lower Pleistocene–early Middle Pleistocene), the Anfa Formation, the Kef Haroun Formation (Middle Pleistocene), and the Dar Bou Azza Formation (Upper Pleistocene) (Figure 39.1). Their age estimates have been established by lithostratigraphy, biostratigraphy, absolute dating (OSL, ESR, U/Th), aminochronology, and paleomagnetism (Lefèvre et al., 1994; Texier et al., 1994, 2002; Lefèvre, 2000; Lefèvre and Raynal, 2002; Occhietti et al., 2002; Rhodes et al., 2006). The Th-OH sites belong to the Oulad Hamida Formation (Raynal et al., 1995, 2001, 2002, 2010, 2011).

The Oulad Hamida Formation (OHF) is based on a major unconformity formed at an altitude of around 28 m asl (general levelling of Morocco) at the expense of the Cretaceous or Palaeozoic substratum. The OHF includes five members, OH1 to OH5, from base to top (Lefèvre et al., 2016). A member is defined by a unit sequence, characterized by a succession of intertidal, supratidal and dunal or continental deposits bounded at its base and top by unconformities or erosional surface. It records highstand sea levels associated with the formation of a shoreline marked by a cliff. The unconformities or sequence boundaries that separate them sign the regression of the ocean and the continentalisation of the coast. The OHF Members are thus correlative of cyclic sea level fluctuations in relation to global glacio-eustatic changes and the extent of glaciation at high

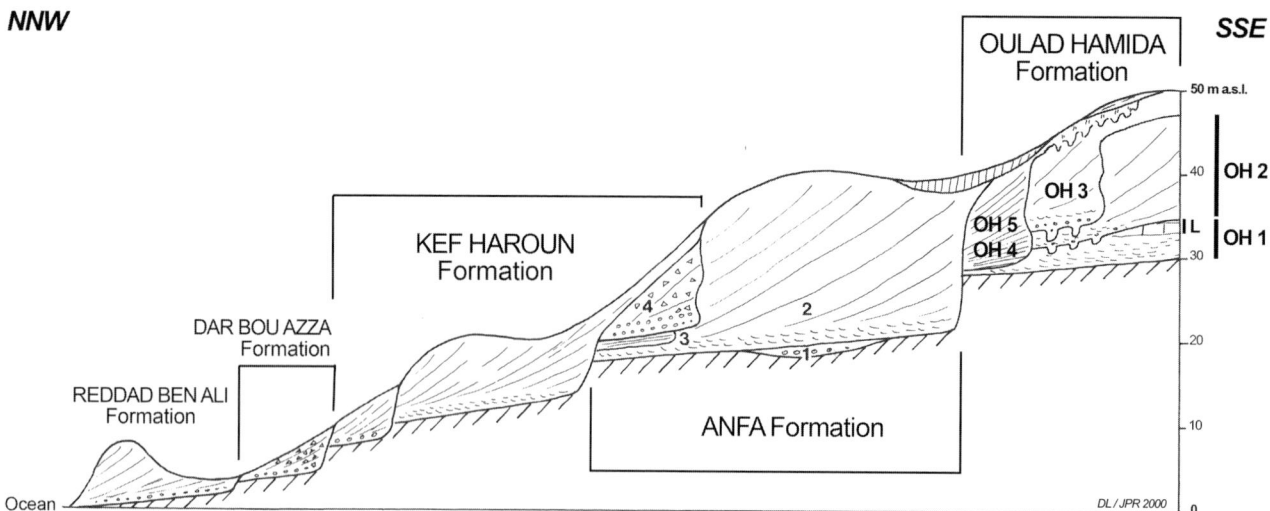

Figure 39.1 Stratigraphic succession of the Casablanca coastal formations, from the late Lower Pleistocene to Recent.

latitudes, preserved thanks to regional tectonic uplift (Lefèvre, 2000; Lefèvre et Raynal, 2002). Their lithostratigraphy is as follows, from base to top:

OH1 Member: Bed 1 is composed of coarse calcirudite at the base and coarse, stratified biocalcarenite; intertidal depositional environments.

Bed 2 is a 2–3 m succession of yellow lenticular limestone banks (Unit L) with cross-bedding structures, composed of microsequences of mudstones, intraclast sands separated by emergent surfaces formed in a continental fluviolacustrine hydrosystem with shifting channels and a temporary water table, followed by pedogenized aeolian sands. First tests using OSL dating provide an age of between 0.8 and 1.2 Ma for the unit L limestone deposits (Rhodes et al., 2006) which should thus belong to the Matuyama chronozone. This has to be confirmed, but an age of c. 1 Ma is for now the best estimate for Bed 2, either before or immediately after the Jaramillo subchronozone.

OH2 Member: Overlying an erosional surface above the OH1 Member deposits, there are coarse biocalcarenites with curved cross-bedding followed by finer inclined planar-bedding biocalcarenites formed within intertidal depositional environments; vertically there follow massive banks of aeolianites about 10 m thick, their upper part affected by fersialsol pedogenesis. The OH2 intertidal deposits register a highstand sea level followed by the regression of the ocean, which is conveyed by the formation of aeolianite.

OH3 Member: This is composed of coarse and/or coquinoid biocalcarenites (with inclined planar bedding), overlying an abrasion platform with associated calcarenite and lacustrine limestone blocks and pebbles that truncate the deposits of OH1 and OH2 Members and cut a cliff into the OH2 Member deposits, the base of which sits at an altitude of 37 m a.s.l. The OH3 deposits register a highstand sea level associated with the formation of a palaeoshoreline followed by the regression of the ocean. Several formations–OH4 and OH5 Members - are associated with a complex of palaeoshorelines cut into the earlier OH1, OH2 and OH3 Members.

OH4 Member: Composed of fine, gray, planar bedded calcarenites with, at the bottom inside the cavities, calcirudite mixed with blocks from earlier formations; these intertidal facies, which can be seen at an altitude of up to 34 m a.s.l., are associated with the formation of a paleo-shoreline with deep cavities.

OH5 Member: Composed of bedded, fine, gray sands (with millimetric to centimetric planar bedding) that pass down vertically to an aeolianite made up of layers of weakly cemented gray sands, with pronounced cross-bedding. These deposits are associated with a paleo-shoreline cliff, which partly follows the same path as the one associated with OH4 Member. The way they could interfinger with the upper half of the Hominid Cave continental filling (see *infra*) remains unclear. The Hominid Cave of Thomas Quarry I (ThI-GH) and Rhinos Cave of Oulad Hamida Quarry (GDR) belong to this complex of palaeoshorelines.

The Hominid Cave ("Grotte à Hominidés," ThI-GH)

This is a large cavity on the north side of Thomas Quarry I (Figure 39.2); it has a complex sedimentary infilling (Raynal et al., 2010, 2011). The upper set is of Upper Pleistocene age, and is separated from the underlying deposits by speleothems.

The lower set belongs to OH4 Member and to its associated paleo-shoreline. From bottom to top it is composed of:

1. A calcirudite with a coarse coquinoid matrix, which is associated with a well-defined notch shaped at the expense of the OH1 and OH3 Members at an altitude of about 34 m a.s.l. and also associated with plurimetric collapsed blocks of biocalcarenites with smoothed surfaces, originating mainly from OH3 Member which constitutes the cavity ceiling.

Figure 39.2 The northeastern flank of Thomas Quarry I with the main stratigraphic units; excavations of ThI-Hom are located below the shelter. To the right are the excavations in Unit L. RS, rubefied sands.

2. Laterally and vertically between and above the block fields is set a fine, planar-bedding biocalcarenite, becoming massive upwards. Some of the hominin fossils were discovered at its very top.
3. Without any apparent disconformity, a continental complex of bioclastic and quartzose sands containing lithic objects, macrofauna, microfauna, and hominin fossils were deposited, hence the cavity's name (Raynal et al., 2010, 2011). This unit was probably edified in several episodes. The well-graded sorting as well as the mineralogical and petrographical constitution of the sediment indicate that it originates mainly from reworked loose littoral deposits. Clays associated with these well-sorted sands could be due to an *in situ* weathering of the sediments and/or were brought into the cavity with the rest of the sediment, together with rare soil aggregates coming from the ground surface by mud-flows.

The ages calculated by OSL for the deposits of the continental complex that yielded most of the hominin fossils range from 370 to 440 ka (Rhodes et al., 2006). A hominin tooth was also dated to around 500 ka using ICP-MS laser ablation, but with a 20 percent error margin (Raynal et al., 2010, 2011). However, given both the stratigraphic position of the Oulad Hamida Formation in the Casablanca sequence, which predates MIS 13/15, and the biostratigraphic data (see below), an even earlier date within the Middle Pleistocene, closer to 0.6/0.7 Ma, could be proposed for the formation of this coastline and the oldest associated deposits containing at their top some of the hominin remains.

The Rhinos Cave ("Grotte des Rhinocéros," GDR)

The Rhinos Cave is a cavity formed in the biocalcarenite of the OH2 Member (Figure 39.3). What the quarry works removed was probably the bottom of this deposit. The GDR cavity developed within a palaeoshoreline whose associated deposits are not known. Its walls show traces of shaping and polishing in places, which can be linked to coastal marine weathering in the context of a palaeoshoreline cliff. The 7m thick infilling of the cavity, whose base has not been clearly identified, consists of a superposition of yellowish and reddish calcarenitic deposits (Raynal et al., 2016). They contain Acheulean lithic artefacts and faunal remains.

The infilling is divided into two lithostratigraphic sets separated by gradual transition. In both sets, the stratification is flat with a regular dip towards the north and the bottom of the cave.

The lower set (units 5 and 6) is characterized by a succession of clayey brown-red sands (unit 6) that fill the gaps between the calcarenitic megablocks from the collapse of the ceiling, followed by carbonate-bearing sands (unit 5). The sedimentary material originates mainly from reworked sandy dune mixed with aggregates resulting from the erosion of red soils, as well as from the dismantling of calcareous duricrust.

The upper set (units 1 to 4) shows a more regular stratification dominated by yellowish stratified sands. Architecture of the deposits, sedimentary structures and microfacies suggest that sedimentary material results of flow and/or wind-reworked coastal deposits from a backshore very close to the entrance of the cavity, or even deposits directly blown into an open cavity.

Within the stratigraphic pattern of the Oulad Hamida Formation as a whole, the cavity can be linked to the complex of compound shorelines of stratigraphic members OH4/OH5. The microfacies of the coarse sands of stratigraphic unit 4 seem to rule out a correlation with the OH5 Member deposits. Therefore, the cavity most likely belongs to the deep cavity shoreline of the OH4 Member of the Oulad Hamida Formation.

Four teeth of the rhinoceros *Ceratotherium mauritanicum* were used for ESR dating (Rhodes et al., 1994). Their average ESR age was 279 ± 49 ka according to the early uranium uptake model, and 476 ± 75 ka according to the linear uptake model. These ages were later recalculated (Rhodes et al., 2006), giving 435 ± 85 for early uptake and 737 ± 129 ka for linear uptake.

Figure 39.3 Excavations at the Rhinos Cave (GDR).

However, given both the stratigraphic position and the biostratigraphic data, an even earlier age within the Middle Pleistocene, closer to 0.6/0.7 Ma, could be proposed for the bottom deposits of the cave while some uncertainty remains about the real age of the cavity formation.

Hominin Remains

In addition to the mandible found by P. Beriro (Ennouchi, 1969, 1970; Sausse, 1975), from 1996 to 2009 ThI-GH yielded several isolated teeth (Raynal et al., 2010), plus craniofacial fragments, mandibular remains, and a femoral diaphysis (Daujeard et al., 2016; Raynal et al., 2017). To these must be added the cranial fragment and teeth from the cave at Thomas III (Ennouchi, 1972, 1975, 1976) and an isolated tooth at GDR. All teeth are remarkably large and these fossils can be ascribed to the Middle Pleistocene form *Homo heidelbergensis/rhodesiensis*. There is little doubt that they are close to the ancestry of *H. sapiens*, but they may even pre-date the divergence of this lineage from that of *H. neanderthalensis* (Hublin, 2001; Stringer, 2012).

Archeology

The archeological sites of Thomas-Oulad Hamida Quarries have yielded rich lithic assemblages that represent the only North Africa Acheulean recorded in an undisputable stratigraphic context (Raynal and Texier, 1989; Raynal et al., 2001). In Unit L of Bed 2 of OH1 Member at Thomas I lithic activities related to the early Acheulean have been documented for the subunits L1 and L5. The industry of L1 is mainly focused to trihedral and bifacial tool production, made of large cobbles and boulders of quartzite collected near the site. It also contains spheroids and subspheroids, a large variety of polyhedrons, centripetal and true discoid cores, and hammer-stones of quartzite, as well as small flint pebbles flaked using bipolar reduction techniques (Gallotti et al., 2020). In contrast, L5 yielded a large number of flaked medium-sized pieces, detached following flaking methods already performed in L1 (Raynal et al., 2002), rare biface-like cores, and no cleavers. This early Acheulean has a techno-economic structure distinct from what is claimed to be the preceding regional Oldowan culture in Algeria (Sahnouni, 2006) and from the East African early Acheulean (Lepre et al., 2011; Beyene et al., 2013). We consider it as the "First Regional Acheulean" (Raynal et al., 2017).

The Middle Pleistocene lithic assemblage recovered at Th1-GH unit 4, largely on quartzite cobbles, was mainly oriented toward medium-sized flake production performed through a large variability of flaking modalities. Some cores were turned into choppers by shaping a long cutting edge. Flint pebbles were also flaked by direct and bipolar techniques. A bifacial *chaîne opératoire* on quartzite was processed out of the cave to obtain large cutting tools and heavy pointed tools, successively imported into the site (Raynal et al., 2009, 2010, 2011).

The Rhino Cave at Oulad Hamida 1 Quarry yielded a large assemblage that is rich both in large cutting tools (bifaces and few cleavers), in many sorts of cores, and in flakes of various sizes. The bifaces are highly variable in shape and size, but there is a consistent effort to produce pieces with convex and/or concave edges and a pointed extremity. We can also observe an increase in the number of discoid cores, resulting in the production of medium-sized flakes. The edges of these flakes were rarely modified (Raynal et al., 2002). Like the lower occupations of the nearby Hominid Cave, GDR assemblage represents a facies of the "Second Regional Acheulean" (Raynal et al., 2017). ThI-GH and GDR assemblages are broadly similar with other Acheulean lithic series present in Atlantic Morocco and southern Europe at the same time (Raynal et al., 2010). Notches and denticulates predominate in tools on flakes, but various other types of scrapers and some multiple tools are represented.

Fauna

The earliest mammalian assemblage comes from unit L, deposited in a lacustrine or marshy environment (Geraads, 2010b; Geraads et al., 2010a); its most significant components are the suid *Kolpochoerus* and some rodents that differ from those of later levels in the Th-OH Quarries. These scarce faunal remains are in agreement with the age of ca. 1 Ma suggested by the stratigraphy, OSL dating, and paleomagnetism. The richest samples of large mammals, first studied by Geraads (1980a) and Bernoussi (1997), come from GDR and from the carefully excavated cave deposits, here called ThI-Hom, which yield hominin fossils in the OH4 Member at ThI-GH. The whole fauna from GDR has recently been published in detail (Geraads, 2016b,c; Geraads and Alemseged, 2016; Geraads and Amani, 2016; Geraads and Bernoussi, 2016a,b,c,d). On the basis of rodents, as detailed below, it seems that ThI-Hom is somewhat older than GDR.

Mammalia

Rodentia – The very large collection from GDR forms the basis of comparisons with the smaller sample from ThI-Hom. As noted by Geraads (2002, 2016a), it is likely that the rodent sample from Thomas I studied by Jaeger (1975) does not come from ThI-Hom proper, but from a connected filling that was called ThI-ABCE (Geraads, 2002), and is probably slightly younger than ThI-Hom, although there is no obvious stratigraphic discontinuity between them

Muridae: *Mus hamidae*, defined at GDR, slightly differs from the modern *Mus musculus* and *M. spretus* in the shape of its first lower molar (m1) (Geraads, 1994a). It is also present at ThI-ABCE, but the species from ThI-Hom is significantly larger.

According to Jaeger (1975), the evolution of *Praomys* (*Berberomys*) in North-Western Africa is anagenetic; however, *Praomys darelbeidae* from GDR is smaller than those of Tighennif and ThI-ABCE, so that it is likely that its evolution is more complex than previously suggested.

Paraethomys tighenifae. Apart from two teeth from ThI-L that have a different morphology, the populations of this extinct genus are very similar at all sites, and also similar to those of Tighennif.

Gerbillus grandis. Two isolated molars from ThI-L have peculiar morphologies and are perhaps of different species; besides this, there are two species of *Gerbillus* s.l. that can be separated on the basis of m1 length. Subtle size differences can be documented between the various populations of *Gerbillus grandis* and of *Dipodillus* cf. *campestris*, a smaller species formerly included in *Gerbillus* (Tong, 1986, 1989; Geraads, 2002, 2010a, 2010b).

There are two species of jird; *Meriones maximus* is already present at ThI-L, and virtually unchanged in later sites, while the modern *Meriones shawi* (including *M. grandis*), which includes the fossil form formerly called *M. maghrebianus*, appears only at ThI-Hom.

Arvicolidae: The mole vole *Ellobius* immigrated from Western Asia in the latest Lower Pleistocene; a tooth from ThI-Hom is reminiscent of those from Tighennif, but the *E. atlanticus* populations from GDR and ThI-ABCE are similar to each other.

Gliridae: *Eliomys* sp., the garden dormouse, from ThI-Hom is much smaller than *E. darelbeidae* from GDR and ThI-ABCE.

Hystricidae: The porcupine *Hystrix* cf. *cristata* is rare at all sites, and few gnawing marks have been documented.

Lagomorpha – *Trischizolagus raynali* is a survivor of the extinct group *Trischizolagus–Serengetilagus* that is best known from the Pliocene of the Mediterranean and Laetoli. *Lepus* cf. *capensis*, a true hare, is also present but less common.

Primates – Cercopithecidae: A few teeth, plus a mandible from fissures near GDR, are similar to *Theropithecus oswaldi* from Tighennif (Delson and Hoffstetter, 1993; Geraads and Alemseged, 2016), but contrary to what was assumed by these authors, the Moroccan populations did not undergo size reduction; the canines and lower third premolars (p3s) are quite small but the lower fourth premolars (p4) are rather large, as at Tighennif.

Insectivora – Shrews are extremely numerous at GDR, where two species could be identified (Geraads, 1993a, 2016c); it is likely that the same forms are also present at ThI-Hom and ThI-ABCE. *Crocidura darelbeidae* is the most common and larger one, it might be identical with *C. maghrebiana* Hutterer, 1991. A second species is close to the modern *C. tarfayaensis*, but it may be that its divergence from *C. darelbeidae* is not very old.

There are also some bats, as yet unidentified to genus or species.

Carnivora – As in most cave fillings, carnivores are common both at GDR and ThI-Hom, which they probably used as dens or shelters (Daujeard et al., 2012, 2016; Geraads and Bernoussi, 2016a). They include at least 11 species: 2 species of hyenas, a panther, a wild cat, a lynx, a bear, a honey-badger, an otter, a fox, a wild dog, and a peculiar canid.

Hyaenidae: Both species of hyenas are present in the main sites, and likely contributed to the fossil assemblage. As at Tighennif, *Hyaena hyaena* is less common than *Crocuta crocuta*, the modern spotted hyena, which appears at Aïn Hanech.

Felidae: Two lower carnassials, from GDR and ThI-Hom, are intermediate in size between *P. pardus* and *P. leo*, and are thus similar to the European *P. gombaszoegensis* that could be a jaguar, but such identification would be too speculative.

Several specimens, including a skull, represent a wildcat, *Felis* cf. *silvestris*, a group that is already present in the Pliocene of Laetoli (Werdelin and Dehghani, 2011).

The lynx *Lynx thomasi*, known by a single mandible from fissures probably contemporaneous with GDR, is most interesting in documenting a likely crossing of the Gibraltar Straits (Geraads, 1980b, 2010b). Another lynx is present as well.

There are four species of Canidae. As at Tighennif, the endemic canid *Lupulella mohibi* is the most common carnivore in all sites. Most specimens consist of isolated teeth, but a complete cranium from GDR allowed elucidating its affinities (Geraads, 2011): it has very omnivorous dental adaptations, but otherwise resembles the African jackals. A species similar to the modern Saharan fox, *Vulpes rueppelli*, is present but rare, while the presence of the red fox *V. vulpes* is doubtful. The Th-OH sites also document two of the few known occurrences of the hunting dog *Lycaon magnus* in Africa.

Mustelidae: The honey-badger *Mellivora capensis* which already had a pan-African distribution in the Pliocene, is not rare at the main sites. An otter m1 described by Bernoussi (1997) may indicate an extinct species of *Lutra*.

Ursidae: Bears are probably descended from the Tighennif species, but they are more common than in this site. They differ from contemporaneous European forms in their narrow teeth and long m2s; there is no compelling evidence that they are closely related to them; thus, they are best assigned to the endemic species *Ursus bibersoni*.

Rhinocerotidae: The "Grotte des Rhinocéros" owes its name to the abundance of *Ceratotherium mauritanicum*, represented by 12 more or less complete skulls (Geraads and Bernoussi, 2016b; see "Taphonomy" below), in addition to other remains, although only a small part of the cave has been excavated yet. The species, which is larger and more cursorial than the modern *C. simum*, although its teeth are less adapted for grazing (Geraads, 2005), survives here later than in East Africa, where the modern form appears in the Lower Pleistocene.

Equidae: The Th-OH Quarries are among the few sites where the *Equus* displays definite similarities with the Tighennif zebra, *Equus mauritanicus*, in contrast to many localities where the species has been cited on mere geographic grounds. However, there are some metric differences that forbid formal identification (Geraads and Bernoussi, 2016c).

Hippopotamidae, Suidae, Camelidae (Geraads and Bernoussi, 2016d): A single carpal bone from GDR belongs to a hippo, probably the *Hippopotamus sirensis* defined at Tighennif. There is no evidence of the *Metridiochoerus compactus* that was present at Tighennif; it is replaced here by the smaller, but probably ecologically similar warthog, *Phacochoerus* cf. *africanus*. An M3 from ThI-L and an incomplete tooth from ThI-Hom are probably close to the Eastern African *K. majus*. A few remains do not differ from *Camelus thomasi*, defined at Tighennif but not definitely known elsewhere.

Bovidae (Geraads and Amani, 2016): A large buffalo is present, but the absence of horn-core prevents formal identification as *Syncerus antiquus*. A braincase of *Oryx* sp. shows that, as at Olduvai (Gentry and Gentry, 1978a), the horn-cores were probably more upright than in modern forms. Alcelaphins are the most abundant bovids, but the most common species is represented by fragmentary remains only; it resembles the "?*Damaliscus* sp. nov." from the Okote Member of Koobi Fora, Kenya (Harris, 1991a) in its maxilla abruptly narrowing in front of the molars, and in its short, straight horn-cores that quickly taper above the base. Some of them resemble *Rabaticeras arambourgi* in their slight homonymous torsion, but the single specimen that we refer to this latter taxon is from the now-destroyed cave of Thomas III (Geraads, 1980a). Still another alcelaphin, *Connochaetes taurinus prognu*, a primitive subspecies of the blue wildebeest known in East Africa as *C. taurinus olduvaiensis*, is present, but rare, at the main sites. It may be that two species of gazelles are present, but horn-cores best match the North African species *Gazella atlantica*.

The birds were studied by Mourer-Chauviré (2016). There are some marine birds: albatrosses, gannet, ducks, scaup, but most of them are terrestrial: ostrich, partridge, quail, sandgrouse, pigeon, owl, swift, and jackdaw. Reptiles were studied by Bailón (2016). There is a lizard, and two colubrid snakes.

Biochronology

The vertebrate faunas from the Thomas and Oulad Hamida Quarries, the composition of which is provided in Table 39.1, are among the richest of the North African Pleistocene, and the only site with which they can be fruitfully compared is Tighennif in Algeria, which probably dates from the late Lower Pleistocene (Geraads et al., Chapter 38). Their relative ages can be estimated by the number of mammal species that are probably extinct. In the whole sample from the Thomas Quarries, it amounts to 24, versus 14 that are still living, in contrast to 28 versus 7 at Tighennif: this strongly suggest that Tighennif is earlier, and this conclusion is confirmed by detailed analysis of the fauna.

The cercopithecid *Theropithecus oswaldi* is represented at Tighennif by a form very similar to that of Th-OH; its LAD in East Africa is Kapthurin, Kenya, a site about 0.5 Ma (Deino and McBrearty 2002), but there are too few well-dated later sites to be sure about its extinction date. It is still present in North Africa at Aïn Bahya, a site that is probably younger than Kapthurin (Geraads, 2012).

As at Tighennif, the carnivore fauna lacks a number of the Pliocene forms that were present at Ahl al Oughlam, and it further lacks the saber-toothed genus *Homotherium* that is present at Tighennif; besides this, the whole carnivore fauna is virtually identical, the most significant common forms being the African wild dog *Lycaon* (also found at Elandsfontein ca. 0.5 Ma), perhaps a large *Panthera* different from modern lion (*P. leo*), and the rare extinct jackal *Lupulella mohibi*.

The rhino *Ceratotherium mauritanicum* differs from the modern form, but it certainly went extinct in North Africa later than further south. The zebra *Equus* cf. *mauritanicus* differs slightly from the Tighennif form, but not necessarily for chronological reasons.

Among suids, the presence of *Kolpochoerus* in the lower levels is indicative of an older age, but the *Metridiochoerus compactus* of Tighennif is here replaced by the modern *Phacochoerus*.

The Bovidae, instead, differ markedly from the Tighennif bovids. It is likely that this could be partly explained by ecological factors linked to the geographic location of the sites; we may note, for instance, that the alcelaphin *Parmularius ambiguus* is present in the hinterland sites of Tighennif and Aïn Maarouf in Morocco (Geraads and Amani, 1998), but not in the coastal sites of Thomas Quarries. However, these ecological factors were probably not of prime importance, because the environments appear to have been generally similar (see below), and the differences therefore are likely to reflect different ages of deposits. None of the taxa from Th-OH is definitely more advanced than the Tighennif ones; indeed, the alcelaphin that is reminiscent of the Okote Mb ?*Damaliscus* sp. nov. of Harris (1991a) suggests an even earlier age for the Moroccan sites.

The hare *Trischizolagus raynali* is definitely indicative of an older age, because both this genus and *Serengetilagus*, to which this species was first assigned (Geraads, 1994a), are unknown elsewhere after the late Pliocene (Ahl al Oughlam).

The evolution of several rodent lineages was studied by Jaeger (1975, 1988), Tong (1986, 1989), and Geraads (1994a, 2002). It may be that, in these sites at least, the evolution of some

Table 39.1 Faunal lists for the various localities of the Th-OH Quarries. The largest assemblage is that from GDR, complemented by the contemporaneous fossils from ThIII-fissures. The collection from ThI-Hom is less rich, but still substantial. The assemblage from ThIII-cave is known only by old collections. That of ThI-L is small and poorly preserved. ThI-ABCE yielded almost only micromammals.

	ThI-L	ThI-Hom	GDR	ThIII-cave	ThIII-fissures	ThI-ABCE
Mus hamidae		+	+			+
Praomys darelbeidae	+	+	+			+
Paraethomys tighenifae	+	+	+		+	+
Gerbillus grandis minor	+	+	+		+	+
Dipodillus cf. *campestris*	+	+	+		+	+
Meriones shawii		+	+		+	
Meriones maximus	+	+	+			+
Ellobius atlanticus		cf.	+		+	+
Eliomys darelbeidae		cf.	+			+
Hystrix aff. *cristata*		+	+	+	+	+
Trischizolagus raynali			+			
Lepus cf. *capensis*	?	?	+			
Crocidura darelbeidae	cf.	?	+		+	
Crocidura cf. *tarfayaensis*			+			
Theropithecus oswaldi		+	+	+	+	
Herpestes sp.		+				
Hyaena hyaena		+	+			
Crocuta crocuta		+	+		?	
Panthera aff. *leo*			+			
Panthera pardus		+				
Felis cf. *silvestris*		cf.	+		+	
Lynx thomasi					+	
Vulpes cf. *rueppelli*		+			+	
Vulpes vulpes		+				
Lupulella mohibi		+	+	+		
Lycaon cf. *magnus*		+	+			
Mellivora capensis		+	+			
Lutra sp.		+				
Ursus bibersoni		+	+	+		
Monachus sp.		+				
Elephantidae indet.	+				+	
Ceratotherium mauritanicum		+	+	+	+	
Equus cf. *mauritanicus*	sp.	+	+			
Camelus cf. *thomasi*			+			
Hippopotamus cf. *sirensis*	+		+			
Kolpochoerus cf. *maroccanus*	+	+				
Phacochoerus cf. *africanus*		+	+	+	+	
cf. *Syncerus antiquus*		+	+		+	
Redunca sp.		+	+			
Oryx sp.		cf.	+		+	
cf. ?*Damaliscus* sp. nov. Harris, 1991a		+	+	+	+	
Rabaticeras arambourgi				+		
Connochaetes taurinus prognu		+	+		+	
Gazella cf. *atlantica*	?	+	+	+	+	

taxa (*Paraethomys*, *Ellobius*) was anagenetic, and Jaeger (1975) was the first to conclude that Tighennif is the earliest of them. The other rodent taxa are consistent with this interpretation, although they do not firmly support it.

In summary, although all faunal indications are not fully convergent, we may conclude that, leaving aside the poorly documented ThI-L, Tighennif is almost certainly the oldest site. Still, it is clear that the whole Th-OH faunal unit belongs to the early part of the Middle Pleistocene, at more than 0.5 Ma. Within this unit, the biochronology suggests a succession that the stratigraphy is at present unable to confirm or reject. The rodent assemblage from GDR slightly differs from the one from "Thomas I" described by Jaeger (1975, 1988) and Tong (1989), which is probably what we called ThI-ABCE, but nothing suggests that GDR is of later age, so that we may assume that it is slightly earlier (Geraads, 2002, 2010a). By contrast, the ThI-Hom rodent assemblage might be earlier because of some metric differences in rodent teeth (Geraads, 2002, 2010a).

Taphonomy of Small and Large Mammals

A taphonomic study was carried out on the small and large mammal remains recovered from ThI-Hom and GDR since 2005. Nearly 3000 and 4000 remains, respectively, were studied for the two sites. Table 39.2 provides the abundance data for each taxon. For each faunal assemblage, we determined the number of total remains (NRT), the number of identified specimens (NISP), the number of anatomically identified specimens (NISPa), and the minimum number of individuals (MNI; Lyman, 1994).

Faunal Spectrum

As highlighted above, the two sites have almost the same faunal lists but the abundance of the various taxa differs. At ThI-Hom, bovids are dominant among herbivores, especially the gazelles (*Gazella* cf. *atlantica*) and Alcelaphini, mainly represented by the blesbok genus *Damaliscus*. At GDR, gazelles and Alcelaphini rates are roughly equivalent, but the white rhinoceros (*Ceratotherium*) comes right after and the zebras are more numerous. Carnivores are more abundant and diverse at ThI-Hom than at GDR. In both sites, the jackal *Lupulella mohibi* dominates, especially at ThI-Hom, whereas at GDR hyenids are more common. The primates *Homo* sp. and *Theropithecus oswaldi* are more frequent at ThI-Hom; smaller mammals (porcupines and lagomorphs) have about the same rates.

Bone Preservation and Fragmentation

As shown by bone destruction and ratios of unreadable bone surfaces (mainly encrusted remains), bone preservation is better at GDR than at ThI-Hom. Even though complete, small articular bones are more numerous in the latter, long bone fragmentation is more intensive at ThI-Hom (Daujeard et al., 2012). Very few ungulate long bones are complete in the two series. Green bone fractures are the most significant fracture category, and these are mostly associated with carnivore tooth-marks. The articular portions of long bones have been more spared at ThI-Hom than at GDR. The epiphysis/diaphysis ratios are low in the two sites and are a priori consistent with carnivore feeding damage (Blumenschine, 1988).

Age and Skeletal Profiles

For both series, the dominant Antilopini and cf. ?*Damaliscus* are equally distributed among all age-classes, attesting to a non-selective predation. In contrast, for other taxa, young and old individuals dominate, either derived from selective hunting (among the most vulnerable individuals) or scavenging on animals that died of natural causes.

For carnivores, age profiles are different and indicate the dominance of adults, with some old individuals, which seem

Table 39.2 Relative abundance and bone indices for the large fauna at GDR and ThI-Hom (NISP; NISPa; NRT; MNI; identification index: NISPa/NRT; bone destruction index: isolated teeth/NISPa; S1–S4: bovid sizes modified from Brain, 1981).

Taxa	NISP GDR		MNI GDR		NISP ThI-Hom		MNI ThIHom	
Felis cf. *silvestris*	6	0.60%	1	1.80%	1	0.10%	1	1.40%
Lynx thomasi	–	–	–	–	1	0.10%	1	1.40%
Panthera sp.	1	0.10%	1	1.80%	4	0.30%	2	2.70%
Hyaena hyaena	2	0.20%	1	1.80%	3	0.20%	2	2.70%
Crocuta crocuta	9	0.90%	3	5.30%	2	0.20%	2	2.70%
Hyaenidae indet.	17	1.70%	–	–	9	0.70%	–	–
Lupulella mohibi	41	4.00%	5	8.80%	406	32.60%	8	11.00%
Vulpes spp.	–	–	–	–	33	2.60%	2	2.70%
Canidae indet.	13	1.30%	–	–	11	0.90%	–	–
Ursus bibersoni	4	0.40%	2	3.50%	30	2.40%	3	4.10%
Mellivora capensis	1	0.10%	1	1.80%	39	3.10%	1	1.40%
Mustelidae indet.	3	0.30%	–	–	1	0.10%	1	1.40%
Monachus sp.	–	–	–	–	3	0.20%	1	1.40%
Total CARNIVORA	97	9.50%	14	24.60%	543	43.50%	24	32.90%
Total PROBOSCIDEA	–	–	–	–	1	0.10%	1	1.40%

Table 39.2 (cont.)

Taxa	NISP GDR		MNI GDR		NISP ThI-Hom		MNI ThIHom	
Ceratotherium mauritanicum	165	16.10%	7	12.30%	13	1.00%	2	2.70%
Equus cf. *mauritanicus*	21	2.00%	3	5.30%	7	0.60%	2	2.70%
Total PERISSODACTYLA	186	18.10%	10	17.50%	20	1.60%	4	5.50%
Phacochoerus cf. *africanus*	1	0.10%	1	1.80%	5	0.40%	1	1.40%
Kolpochoerus maroccanus	–	–	–	–	1	0.10%	1	1.40%
Camelus cf. *thomasi*	5	0.50%	2	3.50%	–	–	–	–
Gazella cf. *atlantica* – S1–2	246	24.00%	8	14.00%	319	25.60%	16	21.90%
Redunca sp. – S2	1	0.10%	1	1.80%	3	0.20%	1	1.40%
Alcelaphini (cf. ?*Damaliscus*) – S2–3	247	24.10%	8	14.00%	147	11.80%	9	12.30%
Connochaetes taurinus – S3	6	0.60%	2	3.50%	1	0.10%	1	1.40%
Oryx sp. – S3	2	0.20%	1	1.80%	2	0.20%	1	1.40%
Bovini (cf. *Syncerus*) – S4	25	2.40%	3	5.30%	48	3.80%	5	6.80%
Bovidae indet. S2	105	10.20%	–	–	36	2.90%	–	–
Bovidae indet. S3	38	3.70%	–	–	40	3.20%	–	–
Bovidae indet. S3–4	12	1.20%	–	–	–	–	–	–
Total ARTIODACTYLA	688	67.10%	26	45.60%	602	48.30%	35	47.90%
Homo sp.	1	0.10%	1	1.80%	16	1.30%	2	2.70%
Theropithecus oswaldi	3	0.30%	1	1.80%	14	1.10%	2	2.70%
Total PRIMATES	4	0.40%	2	3.50%	30	2.40%	4	5.50%
Hystrix cf. *cristata*	35	3.40%	3	5.30%	41	3.30%	4	5.50%
Leporidae	15	1.50%	2	3.50%	10	0.80%	1	1.40%
Total NISP/MNI	1025	100.00%	57	100.00%	1247	100.00%	73	100.00%
NISPa	1142				1532			
NRT	3864				2692			
Identification index	29.60%				56.90%			
Isolated teeth	203				513			
Bone destruction	17.80%				33.50%			
Unreadable bone surface	3.50%				6.40%			
N coprolites	23				111			
Completeness index	19.80%				29.50%			
Ungulate long bone completeness index	3.30%				1.50%			

to result from intraguild competition rather than from natural mortality. Nevertheless, the presence of a few juveniles among hyenids, canids and mustelids indicates the temporary use of the caves as dens (Klein and Cruz-Uribe, 1984).

At GDR, we observe the same skeletal profiles for small- and medium-sized bovids, i.e., the predominance of cranial remains (without isolated teeth) and upper limb elements. The rhino profile is slightly different with the decrease of limb extremities whereas axial elements are more common. At ThI-Hom, the greater abundance of cranial remains of smaller bovids is consistent with fossil carnivore accumulations (Klein and Cruz-Uribe, 1984). In the two series, other herbivores are mostly represented by elements of the autopod and by some isolated teeth, which could be indicative of gathering activities over scavenged carcasses.

Bone Surface Modifications

At ThI-Hom, 19.5 percent of the bones whose surface is clean and legible bear carnivore tooth-marks, whereas this proportion is only of 7.5 percent at GDR. In the two series, although some large tooth-marks (length >4 mm), coprolites, and ingested bones indicate the involvement of large carnivores, the majority of the tooth-mark and coprolite measurements were left by the dominant middle-sized canid (Selvaggio and Wilder, 2001; Dominguez-Rodrigo and Piqueras, 2003), here *Lupulella mohibi*. Porcupine tooth-marks are also present in about 5 percent of the remains.

No cut-marks have been observed at ThI-Hom, in contrast to GDR where 1% of the readable bone elements, especially those of Alcelaphini, gazelles, and equids, were processed by hominins. Butchery marks are widespread along diaphyses whereas porcupine and carnivore tooth-marks are present on both shaft and articular portions. Numerous steps in the butchery process are evident, such as scraping or cutting of tendons, skin, or muscle attachments for skinning, defleshing, and dismembering. No obvious cut-marks have yet been identified on the rhinoceros remains.

Bone Depositional Histories and Their Effect on the Faunal Samples

In these two Middle Pleistocene faunal assemblages, the high percentage of carnivore remains (MNI), including some juveniles, and the presence of numerous coprolites and of digested or tooth-marked remains are characteristics of carnivore dens (e.g., Cruz-Uribe, 1991; Pickering, 2002).

At ThI-Hom, the larger number of carnivore remains and of their tooth-marks and the intensive bone fragmentation, associated with the absence of hominin modifications, prompt us to attribute the major part of the faunal accumulation, including that of hominin remains, to various carnivores, and mainly to the small jackals and hyenids (Daujeard et al., 2012, 2016). The predation of small- and medium-sized bovids by various types of predators and the scavenging of larger taxa are two possible causes of the accumulations. The absence of cut-marks raises the question of the role played by hominins in this cave. As the studied assemblage comes from deep inside the cave, any hominin occupation of the site may well have been concentrated closer to the entrance, which has not yet been excavated.

At GDR, the lower ratio of carnivores and the various surface modifications indicate that the accumulation and the processing of carcasses was undertaken by both carnivores and humans, perhaps in competition with each other. Among carnivores, small canids were less numerous than at ThI-Hom, in contrast to hyenids. Subsistence activities of humans clearly took place in the cave, including production of lithic artifacts and processing of carcass pieces gathered on scavenged or predated animals.

In conclusion, at ThI-Hom, a few artifacts and hominin remains are associated with a rich faunal assemblage that appears to reflect a carnivore accumulation. At GDR, the close association of a rich Acheulean industry and numerous faunal remains, including many rhinoceros, added to the cut-marked specimens, provide evidence for a stronger hominin impact.

These two scenarios are reflected in the relative abundance of the various taxa. First, carnivore diversity is higher in the carnivore den of ThI-Hom. At GDR, the greater frequency of ?*Damaliscus* and *Equus* could result from the selective bias by hominins, whereas the dominance of the gazelles at ThI-Hom could be explained by the strong impact of the jackal. The abundance of primates, both hominin and giant extinct geladas, also appears to depend on the context. In the strict carnivore den of ThI-Hom, they are more numerous than in the mixed deposit of GDR. In this latter site, the exceptional presence of rhinoceros, including heads, remains unexplained. Some animals may have fallen in a pit or through a collapsed cave roof (of which, however, there is no evidence at present), driven or not by humans, and then processed, but further geoarcheological and taphonomic studies are necessary to rule on this important question.

Taphonomy of Micromammals

Geraads (1994a) made some preliminary observations on GDR. The virtual lack of bats and digestion marks on rodent teeth and bones show that the assemblage was accumulated by predators. These marks are less common, and the bones less fragmented than would be expected in the case of a small carnivore, and they better fit a bird of prey, but no conclusion can be drawn as to its identity, because the anatomical composition does not satisfactorily match the pellets of any modern Strigiform bird, and because the faunal composition of their pellets reflects more that of the available resources than the nature of the predator, as shown for the barn owl (Ba et al., 2000). The only potential accumulator whose remains have been found in the cave is *Strix aluco*, the tawny owl.

Paleoecology

We have seen above that all faunal assemblages from the various levels of the Th-OH Quarries are biased samples of the biocenoses, as most of the remains were brought into the caves and fissures by hominins and/or carnivores. Still, the ecological indications that they provide are so unambiguous that it is unlikely that the actual environment much differed from the one that they suggest.

As shown by Table 39.3, the Gerbillidae (*Meriones* and *Gerbillus* s.l., including *Dipodillus*) largely predominate among rodents; even though these numbers should not be taken at face value because of predatory preferences or sampling biases (due, e.g., to size of the teeth), they clearly indicate an open, dry environment. The abundance of the arvicolid *Ellobius*, a group unknown in more southern regions, is probably underestimated because of its large, fragile teeth that do not resist acid treatment and sieving; it attests to a mild climate, perhaps with marked seasonality.

On the whole, even though they were probably mostly introduced into the caves by hominins or carnivores, the large mammals confirm these conclusions. *Theropithecus oswaldi* might have preferred environments more open than other

Table 39.3 Number of rodent m1s in the main levels of the Th-OH Quarries

	Mus	Praomys	Paraethomys	Eliomys	Gerbillus s.l.	Meriones	Ellobius
ThI-ABCE	4	1	31	2	123	23	24
OH1-GDR	15	5	59	9	402	108	70
ThI-Hom	7	1	3	1	21	9	5

species of the genus. Carnivores are not good ecological indicators, and many of them were probably cave-dwellers, but the virtual absence of the leopard argues against significant levels of tree cover. The zebra and white rhino were certainly grazers. The warthog is omnivorous, but mostly a grazer. Among bovids, the browsing tragelaphins and the wetland-dwellers reduncins are scarce, while the Antilopini and Alcelaphini, well-known to roam open savannas, together with *Oryx* found in deserts or semi-deserts, make up the bulk of the assemblage. This is confirmed by the indications provided by the non-mammalian fauna: C. Mourer-Chauviré identified the black-bellied sandgrouse, also an inhabitant of desert or semi-deserts, while the other birds and reptiles also inhabit dry or arid bushland.

Conclusion

In summary, the Th-OH Quarries site fauna differs from other sites, both regionally and across Africa. A remarkable feature of the mammalian fauna as a whole, as at Ahl al Oughlam, is its low diversity relative to that of Eastern Africa sites. It may be that, in contrast to this earlier site, which is richer and lacks hominins, the samples from the Th-OH quarries do not fully document the mammalian ecosystem because of human and/or carnivore selection, but the general picture is so clear that it is unlikely that this selection, if any, systematically acted against mesic or closed environment forms. We believe that, as at Ahl al Oughlam, this low diversity indicates a harsh environment, relatively cold and/or highly seasonal. Among rodents, it is a characteristic of the whole northwestern African Pleistocene, and this diversity even decreases again in the late Pleistocene (Stoetzel et al., 2011; Geraads et al., 2013b). If this is correct, it might explain why the peopling of this part of the continent, first documented at Aïn Hanech in Algeria (Arambourg, 1949), occurred only after that of East and South Africa and, in our opinion, even after the "Out of Africa" event (Geraads et al., 2004b).

Acknowledgments

We are most grateful to S. Reynolds and R. Bobe for inviting us to contribute this chapter, and for their editorial work. Thanks also to D. Reed for his review and comments on the manuscript. The study of Thomas Quarry is conducted by the Franco-Moroccan Préhistoire de Casablanca program and supported by the Institut National des Sciences de l'Archéologie et du Patrimoine (INSAP) of the Ministère de la Jeunesse, de la Culture et de la Communication/Département de la Culture of the Kingdom of Morocco, the Ministère de l'Europe et des Affaires Étrangères of France, the Laboratoire d'Excellence Archimède – Programme Investir l'Avenir ANR-11-LABX-0032–01 – within the framework of the "Origines" project and the Paul Valéry Montpellier 3 University (France). It is also financially supported by the Department of Human Evolution of the Max Planck Institute for Evolutionary Anthropology in Leipzig (Germany), the Collège de France, the Muséum National d'Histoire Naturelle in Paris, and the University of Bordeaux (France).

Volume References

Abbate, E., Albianelli, A., Azzaroli, A., et al. (1998). A one-million-year-old *Homo* cranium from the Danakil (Afar) Depression of Eritrea. *Nature* 393(6684), 458–460.

Abbate, E., Woldehaimanot, B., Bruni, P., et al. (2004). Geology of the *Homo*-bearing Pleistocene Dandiero Basin (Buia region, Eritrean Danakil Depression). *Rivista Italiana di Paleontologia e Stratigrafia* 10, 5–34.

Abbate, E., Albianelli, A., Awad, A., et al. (2010). Pleistocene environments and human presence in the middle Atbara valley (Khashm El Girba, Eastern Sudan). *Palaeogeography, Palaeoclimatology, Palaeoecology* 292, 12–34.

Abbate, E., Bruni, P., Landucci, F. and Pellicanò, G. (2012). Unusual ichnofossils in Homo erectus-bearing beds of the Pleistocene lake deposits in central-eastern Eritrea, East Africa. *Palaios* 27, 97–104.

Adams, J.W. (2012a). A revised listing of fossil mammals from the Haasgat cave system *ex-situ* deposits (HGD), South Africa. *Palaeontologia Electronica*, 15(3), 1–88.

Adams, J.W. (2012b). Stable carbon isotope analysis of fauna from the Gondolin GD 2 fossil assemblage, South Africa. *Annals of the Ditsong National Museum of Natural History*, 2(1), 1–5.

Adams, J.W. (2012c). Craniodental and postcranial remains of the extinct porcupine *Hystrix makapanensis* Greenwood, 1958 (Rodentia: Hystricidae) from Gondolin, South Africa. *Annals of the Ditsong National Museum of Natural History*, 2(1), 7–17.

Adams, J.W. and Rovinsky, D.S. (2018). Taphonomic interpretations of the Haasgat HGD assemblage: A case study in the impact of sampling and preparation methods on reconstructing South African karstic assemblage formation. *Quaternary International*, 495, 4–18.

Adams, J.W., Hemingway, J., Kegley, A.D.T. and Thackeray, J.F. (2007). Luleche, a new paleontological site in the Cradle of Humankind, North-West Province, South Africa. *Journal of Human Evolution*, 53(6), 751–754.

Adams, J.W., Herries, A.I.R., Hemingway, J., et al (2010). Initial fossil discoveries from Hoogland, a new Pliocene primate-bearing karstic system in Gauteng Province, South Africa. *Journal of Human Evolution*, 59(6), 685.

Adams, J.W., Kegley, A.D. and Krigbaum, J. (2013). New faunal stable carbon isotope data from the Haasgat HGD assemblage, South Africa, including the first reported values for *Papio angusticeps* and *Cercopithecoides haasgati*. *Journal of Human Evolution*, 64(6), 693.

Adams, J.W., Olah, A., McCurry, M., et al. (2015). Newly discovered *in situ* primates and mammals from the early Pleistocene Haasgat deposits, South Africa. *American Journal of Physical Anthropology*, 156, 66.

Adams, J.W., Rovinsky, D.S., Herries, A.I. and Menter, C.G. (2016). Macromammalian faunas, biochronology and palaeoecology of the early Pleistocene Main Quarry hominin-bearing deposits of the Drimolen Palaeocave System, South Africa. *PeerJ*, 4, e1941.

Adelsberger, K.A., Wirth, K.R., Mabulla, A.Z.P. and Bowman, D.C. (2011). Geochemical and mineralogical characterization of Middle Stone Age tools of Laetoli, Tanzania and comparisons with possible source materials. In: T. Harrison (Ed.), *Paleontology and Geology of Laetoli, Tanzania: Human Evolution in Context. Volume 1: Geology, Geochronology, Paleoecology and Paleoenvironment*. Dordrecht: Springer, pp. 143–165.

Agnew, N. and Demas, M. (1998). Preserving the Laetoli footprints. *Scientific American* 279, 44–55.

Agnew, N., Demas, M. and Leakey, M.D. (1996). The Laetoli footprints. *Science* 271, 1651–1652.

Agrawal, R., Imieliński, T. and Swami, A. (1993). Mining association rules between sets of items in large databases. In: *Proceedings of the 1993 ACM SIGMOD International Conference on Management of Data*. New York: ACM, pp. 207–216.

Aguirre, E. and Leakey, P. (1974). Nakali: nueva fauna de Hipparion del Rift Valley de Kenya. *Estudios Geológicos* 30, 219–227.

Agustí, J., Garcés, M. and Krijgsman, W. (2006). Evidence for African–Iberian exchanges during the Messinian in the Spanish mammalian record. *Palaeogeography, Palaeoclimatology, Palaeoecology*, 238(1), 5–14.

Agustí, J., Cabrera, L. and Garcés, M. (2013). The Vallesian mammal turnover: A late Miocene record of decoupled land-ocean evolution. *Geobios*, 46(1), 151–157.

Aiello, L.C. and Wheeler, P. (1995). The expensive-tissue hypothesis: the brain and the digestive system in human and primate evolution. *Current Anthropology* 36, 199–221.

Alba, D.M., Delson, E., Carnevale, G., et al. (2014). First joint record of *Mesopithecus* and cf. *Macaca* in the Miocene of Europe. *Journal of Human Evolution* 67, 1–18.

Albert, R.M. and Bamford, M.K. (2012). Vegetation during UMBI and deposition of Tuff IF at Olduvai Gorge, Tanzania (ca. 1.8 Ma), based on phytoliths and plant remains. *Journal of Human Evolution* 63, 342–350.

Albert, R.M., Bamford, M.K., Stanistreet, I., et al. (2015). Vegetation landscape at DK locality, Olduvai Gorge, Tanzania. *Palaeogeography, Palaeoclimatology, Palaeoecology* 426, 34–45.

Alemseged, Z. (1998). L'hominidé Omo-323: sa position phylétique et son environnement dans le cadre de l'évolution des communautés de mammifères du Plio-Pléistocène dans la basse vallée de l'Omo (Ethiopie). PhD dissertation, Anthropologie, Muséum National d'Histoire Naturelle, Paris.

Alemseged, Z. (2003). An integrated approach to taphonomy and faunal change in the Shungura Formation (Ethiopia) and its implication for hominid evolution. *Journal of Human Evolution* 44(4), 451–478.

Alemseged, and Geraads, D. (1998). *Theropithecus atlanticus* (Cercopithecidae, Mammalia) from the late Pliocene of Ahl al Oughlam, Casablanca, Morocco. *Journal of Human Evolution* 34, 609–621.

Alemseged, Z. and Geraads, D. (2000). A new Middle Pleistocene fauna from the Busidima-Telalak region of the Afar, Ethiopia. *Comptes Rendu de l'Académie des Sciences Paris* 331, 459–556.

Alemseged, Z., Coppens, Y. and Geraads, D. (2002). Hominid cranium from Omo: description and taxonomy of Omo-323-1976-896. *American Journal of Physical Anthropology*, 117, 103–112.

Alemseged, Z., Wynn, J. G., Kimbel, W. H., et al. (2005). A new hominin from the Basal Member of the Hadar Formation, Dikika,

Ethiopia, and its geological context. *Journal of Human Evolution* 49(4), 499–514.

Alemseged, Z., Spoor, F., Kimbel, W.H., et al. (2006). A juvenile early hominin skeleton from Dikika, Ethiopia. *Nature* 443, 296–301.

Alemseged, Z., Bobe, R. and Geraads, D. (2007). Comparability of fossil data and its significance for the interpretation of hominin environments. A case study in the lower Omo Valley, Ethiopia. In: A.K. Behrensmeyer, R. Bobe and Z. Alemseged (Eds.), *Hominin Environments in the East African Pliocene: An Assessment of the Faunal Evidence*. Dordrecht: Springer, pp. 159–181.

Alemseged, Z., Wynn, J.G., Geraads, D., et al. (2020). Fossils from Mille-Logya, Afar, Ethiopia, elucidate the link between Pliocene environmental changes and Homo origins. *Nature Communications* 11, 2480.

Albianelli, A. and Napoleone, G. (2004). Magnetostratigraphy of the Homo-bearing Pleistocene Dandiero Basin (Danakil Depression, Eritrea). *Rivista Italiana di Stratigrafia e Paleontologia* 110(Supplement), 35–44.

Alroy, J. (1998). Equilibrial diversity dynamics in North American mammals. In: M.L. McKinney and J. Drake (Eds.), *Biodiversity Dynamics: Turnover of Populations, Taxa, and Communities*. New York: Columbia University Press, pp. 232–287.

Alroy, J. (2000). New methods for quantifying macroevolutionary patterns and processes. *Paleobiology* 26, 707–733.

Almécija, S., Tallman, M., Alba, D.M., et al. (2013) The femur of *Orrorin tugenensis* exhibits morphometric affinities with both Miocene apes and later hominins. *Nature Communications*, 4(1), 1–12.

Altamura, F., Gaudzinski-Windeuser, S., Melis, R.T. and Mussi, M. (2019). Reassessing hominin skills at an early middle Pleistocene hippo butchery site: Gombore II-2 (Melka Kunture, Upper Awash valley, Ethiopia). *Journal of Paleolithic Archaeology* 3, 1–32. https://doi.org/10.1007/s41982-019-00046-0

Altamura, F., Bennett, M.R., Marchetti, L., et al. (2020). Ichnological and archaeological evidence from Gombore II OAM, Melka Kunture, Ethiopia: an integrated approach to reconstruct local environments and biological presences between 1.2–0.85 Ma. *Quaternary Science Reviews* 244, 106506. https://doi.org/10.1016/j.quascirev.2020.106506

Amani, F. and Geraads, D. (1993). Le gisement moustérien du Djebel Irhoud, Maroc: précisions sur la faune et la biochronologie, et description d'un nouveau reste humain. *Comptes Rendu de l'Académie des Sciences Paris* 316, 847–852.

Amani, F. and Geraads, D. (1998). Le gisement Moustérien du Djebel Irhoud, Maroc: précisions sur la faune et la paléoecologie. *Bulletin d'Archéologie Marocaine* 18, 11–17.

Ambrose, S.H. (1998). Chronology of the Later Stone Age and food production in East Africa. *Journal of Archaeological Science* 25, 377–392.

Ambrose, S.H., Hlusko, L.J., Kyule, D., Deino, A. and Williams, M. (2003). Lemudong'o: a new 6 Ma paleontological site near Narok, Kenya Rift Valley. *Journal of Human Evolution* 44, 737–742.

Ambrose, S.H., Bell, C.J., Bernor, R.L., et al. (2007a). The paleoecology and paleogeographic context of Lemudong'o Locality 1, a late Miocene terrestrial fossil site in southern Kenya. *Kirtlandia* 56, 38–52.

Ambrose, S.H., Nyamai, C.M., Mathu, E.M. and Williams, M.A. (2007b). Geology, geochemistry, and stratigraphy of the Lemudong'o Formation, Kenya Rift Valley. *Kirtlandia* 56, 53–64.

Ambrose, S.H., WoldeGabriel, G., White, T.D. and Suwa, G. (2011). The role of paleosol carbon isotopes in reconstructing the Aramis Ardipithecus ramidus habitat: woodland or grassland. *PaleoAnthropology* 2011, A1.

Ameur, R., Jaeger, J.-J. and Michaux, J. (1976). Radiometric age of early *Hipparion* in North-West Africa. *Nature* 261, 38–39.

Andrews, P. (1983). Small faunal diversity at Olduvai Gorge. In: J. Clutton-Brock and C. Grigson (Eds.), *Animals and Archaeology: 1. Hunters and their Prey*. Oxford: BAR International Series 163.

Andrews, P. (1989). Palaeoecology of Laetoli. *Journal of Human Evolution* 18, 173–181.

Andrews, P. (1990). *Owls, Caves, and Fossils*. London: Natural History Museum.

Andrews, P. (2006). Taphonomic effects of faunal impoverishment and faunal mixing. *Palaeogeography, Palaeoclimatology, Palaeoecology* 241, 572–589.

Andrews, P. and Bamford, M. (2008). Past and present ecology of Laetoli, Tanzania. *Journal of Human Evolution* 58, 78–98.

Andrews, P. and Evans, E.N. (1979). The environment of *Ramapithecus* in Africa. *Paleobiology* 5(1), 22–30.

Andrews, P. and Hixson, S. (2014). Taxon-free methods of palaeoecology. *Annales Zoologici Fennici* 51(1–2), 269–284.

Andrews, P.J. and Humphrey, L. (1999). African Miocene environments and the transition to early hominines. In: T. Bromage and F. Schrenk (Eds.), *African Biogeography, Climate Change and Human Evolution*. Oxford: Oxford University Press, pp. 282–315.

Andrews, P. and O'Brien, E. (2000). Climate, vegetation, and predictable gradients in mammal species richness in southern Africa. *Journal of Zoology* 251, 205–231.

Andrews, P. and O'Brien, E. (2010). Mammal species richness in Africa. In L. Werdelin and W. Sanders (Eds.), *Cenozoic Mammals of Africa*. New York: Columbia University Press, pp. 929–947.

Andrews, P., Lord, J.M. and Evans, E.M.N. (1979). Patterns of ecological diversity in fossil and modern mammalian faunas. *Biological Journal of the Linnean Society* 11, 177–205.

Andrews, P., Bamford, M.K., Njau, E.-F. and Leliyo, G. (2011). The ecology and biogeography of the Endulen–Laetoli area in northern Tanzania. In: T. Harrison (Ed.), *Paleontology and Geology of Laetoli: Human Evolution in Context: Volume 1: Geology, Geochronology, Paleoecology and Paleoenvironment*. Dordrecht: Springer, pp. 167–200.

Antón, S.C. (2012). Early *Homo*: who, when, and where. *Current Anthropology* 53(S6), S278–S298.

Antón, S.C. (2013). *Homo erectus* and related taxa. In: D.R. Begun (Ed.), *A Companion to Paleoanthropology*. Pondicherry: Blackwell Publishing Ltd, pp. 497–516.

Antón, S.C., Potts, R. and Aiello, L.C. (2014). Evolution of early *Homo*: an integrated biological perspective. *Science* 345(6192), 1236828.

Aouadi, N., Dridi, Y. and Dhia, W.B. (2014). Holocene environment and subsistence patterns from Capsian and Neolithic sites in Tunisia. *Quaternary International* 320, 3–14.

Aouraghe, H. (2000). Les carnivores fossiles d'El Harhoura 1, Temara, Maroc. *L'anthropologie* 104, 147–171.

Aouraghe, H. (2004). Les populations de mammifères atériens d'El Harhoura 1 (Témara, Maroc). *Bulletin d'Archéologie Marocaine* 20, 83–104.

Arambourg, C. (1947). *Contribution à l'étude géologique et paléontologique du bassin du lac Rodolphe et de la basse vallée de l'Omo. 2. ptie. Paléontologie*. Paris: Éditions du Muséum.

Arambourg, C. (1948). *Contribution à l'étude géologique et paléontologique du bassin du lac Rudolphe et de la basse vallée de l'Omo. Paléontologie. Mission scientifique de l'Omo, Fasc. 3 (Géologie)*. Paris: Éditions du Muséum, pp. 231–562.

Arambourg, C. (1949). Sur la présence, dans le Villafranchien d'Algérie, de vestiges éventuels d'industrie humaine. *Comptes-rendus de l'Académie des Sciences* 229, 66–67.

Arambourg, C. (1954). L'Hominien fossile de Ternifine (Algérie). *Comptes-rendus de l'Académie des Sciences* 239, 893–895.

Arambourg, C. (1959). Vertébrés continentaux du Miocène supérieur de l'Afrique du Nord. *Publications du Service Géologique de l'Algérie, NS, Paléontologie* 4, 1–159.

Volume References

Arambourg, C. (1961). Note préliminaire sur quelques Vertébrés nouveaux du Burdigalien de Libye. *Comptes rendus sommaires des séances de la Société géologique de France* 4, 107–109.

Arambourg, C. (1963a). Le gisement de Ternifine. L'*Atlanthropus mauritanicus*. *Archives de l'Institut de Paléontologie Humaine* 32, 37–190.

Arambourg, C. (1963b). Continental vertebrate faunas of the Tertiary of North Africa. *African Ecology and Human Evolution* 36, 55.

Arambourg, C. (1967). Appendix A. Observations sur la faune des Grottes d'Hercule près de Tanger, Maroc. In: B. Howe (Ed.), *The Palaeolithic of Tangier, Morocco: Excavations at Cape Ashakara, 1939-1947*. Cambridge, MA: The Peabody Museum, pp. 181–186.

Arambourg, C. (1970). Les vertébrés du Pléistocène de l'Afrique du Nord. *Archives du Muséum National d'Histoire Naturelle, ser. 7*, 10, 1–126.

Arambourg, C. (1979). *Vertébrés villafranchiens d'Afrique du Nord (Artiodactyles, Carnivores, Primates, Reptiles, Oiseaux)*. Paris: Fondation Singer-Polignac, 141 pp.

Arambourg, C. and Biberson, P. (1955). Découverte de vestiges humains acheuléens dans la carrière de Sidi Abderrahman, près Casablanca. *Comptes-rendus de l'Académie des Sciences* 240, 1661–1663.

Arambourg, C. and Coppens, Y. (1968). Découverte d'un australopithécien nouveau dans les gisements de l'Omo (Éthiopie). *South African Journal of Science*, 64, 58–59.

Arambourg, C. and Hoffstetter, R. (1963). Le gisement de Ternifine. Historique et géologie. *Archives de l'Institut de Paléontogie Humaine*, 32, 9–36.

Archer, W., Aldeias, V. and McPherron, S.P. (2020). What is '*in situ*'? A reply to Harmand et al. (2015). *Journal of Human Evolution* 142, 102740.

Arènes, J. and Depape, G. (1953). Etude paléobotanique. Contribution à l'étude des flores fossiles de l'Afrique du Nord. *Archives du Muséum National d'Histoire Naturelle, ser. 7* 2, 1–85.

Armour-Chelu, M. and Bernor, R.L. (2011). Equidae. In: T. Harrison (Ed.), *Paleontology and Geology of Laetoli: Human Evolution in Context. Vol. 2: Fossil Hominins and the Associated Fauna*. Dordrecht: Springer, pp. 295–326.

Armour-Chelu, M., Bernor, R.L. and Mittman, H.-W. (2006). Hooijer's hypodigm for "*Hipparion*" cf. *ethiopicum* (Equidae, Hipparioninae) from Olduvai, Tanzania and comparative material from the East African Plio-Pleistocene. *Beiträge zur Paläontologie* 30, 15–24.

Arnason, U. and Janke, A. (2002). Mitogenomic analyses of eutherian relationships. *Cytogenetic and Genome Research* 96(1–4), 20–32.

Aronson, J.L. and Hailemichael, M. (2010). Reply to "Is the Pliocene Ethiopian Monsoon extinct? A comment on Aronson et al. (2008)". *Journal of Human Evolution* 59, 139–142.

Aronson, J.L. and Taieb, M. (1981). Geology and paleogeography of the Hadar hominid site, Ethiopia. In: G. Rapp and C.F. Vondra (Eds.), *Hominid Sites: Their Geologic Setting*. Boulder: Westview Press, pp. 165–195.

Aronson, J.L., Hailemichael, M. and Savin, S.M. (2008). Hominid environments at Hadar from paleosol studies in a framework of Ethiopian climate change. *Journal of Human Evolution* 55, 532–550.

Asfaw, B. (1987). The Belohdelie frontal: new evidence of early hominid cranial morphology from the Afar of Ethiopia. *Journal of Human Evolution* 16(7–8), 611–624.

Asfaw, B., Beyene, Y., Semaw, S., et al. (1991). Fejej: a new paleoanthropological research area in Ethiopia. *Journal of Human Evolution* 21, 137–143.

Asfaw, B., Beyene, Y., Suwa, G., et al. (1992). The earliest Acheulean from Konso-Gardula. *Nature* 360, 732–735.

Asfaw, B., Beyene, Y., Semaw, S., et al. (1993). Tephra from Fejej, Ethiopia – a reply. *Journal of Human Evolution* 25, 519–521.

Asfaw, B., White, T., Lovejoy, O., et al. (1999). *Australopithecus garhi*: a new species of early hominid from Ethiopia. *Science* 284(5414), 629–635.

Asfaw, B., Gilbert, W.H., Beyene, Y., et al. (2002). Remains of *Homo erectus* from Bouri, Middle Awash, Ethiopia. *Nature* 416(6878), 317–320.

Ashley, G.M. (2020). Paleo-Critical Zones, windows into the changing life and landscapes during the Quaternary Period. *Quaternary Research* 96, 53–65.

Ashley, G. and Hay, R.L. (2002). Sedimentation patterns in a Plio-Pleistocene volcaniclastic rift-platform basin, Olduvai Gorge, Tanzania. In: R.W. Renaut and G.M. Ashley (Eds.), *Sedimentation in Continental Rifts*. Tulsa: SEPM (Society for Sedimentary Geology), pp. 107–122.

Ashley, G.M. and Liutkus, C.M. (2002). Tracks, trails and trampling by large vertebrates in a rift valley paleo-wetland, lowermost Bed II, Olduvai Gorge, Tanzania. *Ichnos* 9(1–2), 23–32.

Ashley, G.M., Tactikos, J.C. and Owen, R.B. (2009). Hominin use of springs and wetlands: paleoclimate and archaeological records from Olduvai Gorge (1.79–1.74 Ma). *Palaeogeography, Palaeoclimatology, Palaeoecology* 272, 1–16.

Ashley, G.M., Barboni, D., Dominguez-Rodrigo, M., et al. (2010). A spring and wooded habitat at FLK Zinj and their relevance to origins of human behavior. *Quaternary Research* 74, 304–314.

Ashley, G.M., Bunn, H.T., Delaney, J.S., et al. (2014). Paleoclimatic and paleoenvironmental framework of FLK North archaeological site, Olduvai Gorge, Tanzania. *Quaternary International* 322–323, 54–65.

Ashley, G.M., de Wet, C.B., Barboni, D. and Magill, C.R. (2016). Subtle signatures of seeps: record of groundwater in a Dryland, DK, Olduvai Gorge, Tanzania. *The Depositional Record* 2, 4–21.

Ashley, G.M., Barboni, D., Dominguez-Rodrigo, M., et al. (2017). Paleoenvironmental and paleoecological reconstruction of a freshwater oasis in savannah grassland at FLK North, Olduvai Gorge, Tanzania. *Quaternary Research* 74, 333–343.

Assefa, Z. (2006). Faunal remains from Porc-Epic: paleoecological and zooarchaeological investigations from a Middle Stone Age site in southeastern Ethiopia. *Journal of Human Evolution* 51, 50–75.

Assefa, Z., Yirga, S. and Reed, K.E. (2008). The large-mammal fauna from the Kibish Formation. *Journal of Human Evolution* 55, 501–512.

Auffenberg, W. (1981). The fossil turtles of Olduvai Gorge, Tanzania, Africa. *Copeia* 1981, 509–522.

Avery, D.M. (1981). Holocene micromammalian faunas from the Northern Cape, South Africa. *South African Journal of Science* 77, 265–273.

Avery, D.M. (1982a). Micromammals as palaeoenvironmental indicators and an interpretation of the late quaternary in the Southern Cape Province, South Africa. *Annals of the South African Museum* 85, 183–374.

Avery, D.M. (1982b). The micromammalian fauna from Border Cave, Kwazulu, South Africa. *Journal of Archaeological Science* 9(2), 187–204.

Avery, D.M. (1987a). Micromammalian evidence for natural vegetation and the introduction of farming during the Holocene in the Magaliesberg, Transvaal. *South African Journal of Science* 83, 221–225.

Avery, D.M. (1987b). Late Pleistocene coastal environment of the Southern Cape province of South Africa: micromammals from Klasies river mouth. *Journal of Archaeological Science* 14(4), 405–421.

Avery, D.M. (1990). Holocene climatic change in Southern Africa: the contribution of micromammals to its study. *South African Journal of Science* 86, 407–412.

Avery, D.M. (1991). Micromammals, owls and vegetation change in the Eastern Cape Midlands, South Africa, during the last millennium. *Journal of Arid Environments* 20, 357–369.

Avery, D.M. (1992). The environment of early modern humans at Border Cave, South Africa: micromammalian evidence. *Palaeogeography, Palaeoclimatology, Palaeoecology* 91, 71–87.

Avery, D.M. (1995a). Southern savannahs and Pleistocene hominid adaptations: the micromammalian perspective. In: E. Vrba, G. Denton, T. Partridge and L. Burckle (Eds.), *Paleoclimate and Evolution with Emphasis on Human Origins*. New Haven: Yale University Press, pp. 459–478.

Avery, D.M. (1995b). A preliminary assessment of the micromammalian remains from Gladysvale Cave, South Africa. *Palaeontologia Africana* 32, 1–10.

Avery, D.M. (1997). Micromammals and the Holocene environment of Rose Cottage Cave. *South African Journal of Science* 93, 445–448.

Avery, D.M. (1998). An assessment of the lower Pleistocene micromammalian fauna from Swartkrans Members 1–3, Gauteng, South Africa. *Geobios* 31, 393–414.

Avery, D.M. (2001). The Plio-Pleistocene vegetation and climate of Sterkfontein and Swartkrans, South Africa, based on micromammals. *Journal of Human Evolution* 41, 113–132.

Avery, D.M. (2007). Pleistocene micromammals from Wonderwerk Cave, South Africa: practical issues. *Journal of Archaeological Science* 34, 613–625.

Avery, D.M. (2019). *A Fossil History of Southern African Land Mammals*. Cambridge: Cambridge University Press.

Avery, D.M. (2022). Rodents and other micromammals from the Pleistocene strata in Excavation 1 at Wonderwerk Cave, South Africa: a work in progress. *Quaternary International* 614, 23–36.

Avery, D.M. and Avery, G. (2011). Micromammals in the Northern Cape Province of South Africa, past and present. *African Natural History* 7, 3–39.

Avery, S.T. and Tebbs, E.J. (2018). Lake Turkana, major Omo River developments, associated hydrological cycle change and consequent lake physical and ecological change. *Journal of Great Lakes Research* 44, 1164–1182.

Avery, D.M., Stratford, D.J. and Sénégas, F. (2010). Micromammals and the formation of the Name Chamber, at Sterkfontein, South Africa. *Geobios*, 43(4), 379–387.

Avery, G., Kandel, A.W., Klein, R.G., Conard, N.J. and Cruz-Uribe, K. (2004). Tortoises as food and taphonomic elements in palaeo 'landscapes'. In: J.-P. Brugal and J. Desse (Eds.), *Petits animaux et sociétés humaines: du complément alimentaire aux ressources utilitaires*. Antibes: Editions APDCA, pp. 147–161.

Azaïs, F.B. and Chambard, R. (1931). *Cinq années de recherches archéologiques en Ethiopie*. Paris: Librairie Orientaliste Paul Geuthner.

Ba, K., Granjon, L., Hutterer, R., and Duplantier, J.-M. (2000). Les micromammifères du Djoudj (Delta du Sénégal) par l'analyse du régime alimentaire de la chouette effraie, Tyto alba. *Bonner zoologische Beiträge* 49, 31–38.

Bache, F., Popescu, S.M., Rabineau, M., et al. (2012). A two-step process for the reflooding of the Mediterranean after the Messinian Salinity Crisis. *Basin Research* 24(2), 125–153.

Bachiri Taoufiq, N., Barhoun, N. and Suc, J.-P. (2008). Les environnements continentaux du corridor rifain (Maroc) au Miocène supérieur d'après la palynologie. *Geodiversitas* 30, 41–58.

Backwell, L.R. and d'Errico, F. (2001). Evidence of termite foraging by Swartkrans early hominids. *Proceedings of the National Academy of Sciences* 98(4), 1358–1363.

Backwell, L.R. and d'Errico, F. (2004). Swartkrans; a cave's chronicle of early man. Additional evidence of early hominid bone tools from Swartkrans. *Transvaal Museum Monographs* 8(1).

Backwell, L. and d'Errico, F. (2008). Early hominid bone tools from Drimolen, South Africa. *Journal of Archaeological Science* 35(11), 2880–2894.

Backwell, L., Pickering, R., Brothwell, D., et al. (2009). Probable human hair found in a fossil hyaena coprolite from Gladysvale cave, South Africa. *Journal of Archaeological Science* 36(6), 1269–1276.

Backwell, L.R., Parkinson A.H., Roberts E.M., d'Errico F. and Huchet J.-B. (2012). Criteria for identifying bone modification by termites in the fossil record. *Paleogeography, Paleoclimatology, Paleoecology* 337–338, 72–87.

Backwell, L., Huchet, J.B., Jashashvili, T., Dirks, P.H. and Berger, L.R. (2020). Termites and necrophagous insects associated with early Pleistocene (Gelasian) *Australopithecus sediba* at Malapa, South Africa. *Palaeogeography, Palaeoclimatology, Palaeoecology* 560, 109989.

Badenhorst, S. and Plug, I. (2012). The faunal remains from the Middle Stone Age levels of Bushman Rock Shelter in South Africa. *South African Archaeological Bulletin* 67, 16–31.

Badenhorst, S. and Steininger, C.M. (2019). The Equidae from Cooper's D, an early Pleistocene fossil locality in Gauteng, South Africa. *PeerJ* 7, e6909.

Badenhorst, S., Senegas, F., Gommery, D., et al. (2011). Pleistocene faunal remains from Garage Ravine Cave on Bolt's Farm in the Cradle of Humankind, South Africa. *Annals of the Ditsong National Museum of Natural History* 1(1), 33–40.

Badenhorst, S., van Niekerk, K.L. and Henshilwood, C.S. (2014). Rock hyraxes (*Procavia capensis*) from Middle Stone Age levels at Blombos Cave, South Africa. *African Archaeological Review* 31(1), 25–43.

Bagley, B. and Nyblade, A.A. (2013). Seismic anisotropy in eastern Africa, mantle flow, and the African superplume. *Geophysical Research Letters* 40, 1500–1505.

Badgley, C. (1986). Taphonomy of mammalian fossil remains from Siwalik rocks of Pakistan. *Paleobiology* 12, 119–142.

Bagtache, B., Hadjouis, D. and Eisenmann, V. (1984). Présence d'un *Equus caballin* (*E. algericus* n. sp.) et d'une autre espèce nouvelle d'*Equus* (*E. melkiensis* n. sp.) dans l'Atérien des Allobroges, Algérie. *Comptes Rendus de l'Académie des Sciences* 14, 609–612.

Bailey, G.N. and King, G.C.P. (2011). Dynamic landscapes and human dispersal patterns: tectonics, coastlines, and the reconstruction of human habitats. *Quaternary Science Review* 30, 1533–1553.

Bailey, G.N., Reynolds, S.C. and King, G.C. (2011). Landscapes of human evoln: models and methods of tectonic geomorphology and the reconstruction of hominin landscapes. *Journal of Human Evolution* 60(3), 257–280.

Bailloud, G. (1965). Les gisements paléolithiques de Melka-Konture. *Cahiers de l'Institut éthiopien d'archéologie* 1, 1–37.

Bailón, S. (2000). Amphibiens et reptiles du Pliocène terminal d'Ahl al Oughlam (Casablanca, Maroc). *Geodiversitas* 22(4), 539–558.

Bailón, S. (2016). Les Squamates. In: J.-P. Raynal and A. Mohib (Eds.), *Préhistoire de Casablanca. 1 - La Grotte des Rhinocéros (fouilles 1991 et 1996). Villes et Sites Archéologiques du Maroc, volume 6*. Rabat: Ministère de la Culture, INSAP, p. 87.

Bajo, P., Drysdale, R.N., Woodhead, J.D., et al. (2020). Persistent influence of obliquity on ice age terminations since the Middle Pleistocene transition. *Science* 367, 1235.

Baker, B.H. (1958). Geology of the Magadi area. Report No. 42, Geological Survey of Kenya.

Volume References

Baker, B.H. (1963). Geology of the area south of Magadi. Degree Sheet 58, N.W. Quarter. Report No. 61, Geological Survey of Kenya.

Bakker, E.M.V.Z. and Mercer, J.H. (1986). Major late Cainozoic climatic events and palaeoenvironmental changes in Africa viewed in a world wide context. *Palaeogeography, Palaeoclimatology, Palaeoecology* 56(3), 217–235.

Bamford, M. (1999). Pliocene fossil woods from an early hominid cave deposit, Sterkfontein, South Africa. *South African Journal of Science* 95, 231–237.

Bamford, M.K. (2000). Cenozoic macro-plants. In: T.C. Partridge and R.R. Maud (Eds.), *The Cenozoic of Southern Africa*. Oxford: Oxford Monographs on Geology and Geophysics, 40, pp. 351–356.

Bamford, M.K. (2005). Early Pleistocene fossil wood from Olduvai Gorge, Tanzania. *Quaternary International* 129, 15–22.

Bamford, M. (2011a). Fossil woods. In: T. Harrison (Ed.), *Paleontology and Geology of Laetoli: Human Evolution in Context. Vol. 1: Geology, Geochronology, Paleoecology, and Paleoenvironment*. Dordrecht: Springer, pp. 217–233.

Bamford, M. (2011b). Fossil leaves, fruits and seeds. In: T. Harrison (Ed.), *Paleontology and Geology of Laetoli: Human Evolution in Context. Vol. 1: Geology, Geochronology, Paleoecology, and Paleoenvironment*. Dordrecht: Springer, pp. 235–252.

Bamford, M.K. (2012). Fossil sedges, macroplants and roots from Olduvai Gorge, Tanzania. *Journal of Human Evolution* 63, 351–363.

Bamford, M.K. (2015a). Macrobotanical remains from Wonderwerk Cave (Excavation 1), Oldowan to Late Pleistocene (2 Ma to 14ka BP), South Africa. *African Archaeological Review* 32, 813–838.

Bamford, M.K. (2015b). Charcoal from pre-Holocene Stratum 5, Wonderwerk Cave, South Africa. *Palaeoecology of Africa* 33, 153–174.

Bamford, M. (2017). Pleistocene fossil woods from the Okote Member, site FwJj 14 in the Ileret region, Koobi Fora Formation, northern Kenya. *Journal of Human Evolution* 112, 134–147.

Bamford, M.K. and Henderson, Z.L. (2003). A reassessment of the wooden fragment from Florisbad, South Africa. *Journal of Archaeological Science* 30(6), 637–650.

Bamford, M., Albert, R.M. and Cabanes, D. (2006). Plio-Pleistocene macroplant fossil remains and phytoliths from lowermost Bed II in the eastern palaeolake margin of Olduvai Gorge, Tanzania. *Quaternary International* 148, 95–112.

Bamford, M.K., Stanistreet, I. G., Stollhofen, H. and Albert, R.M. (2008). Late Pliocene grassland from Olduvai Gorge, Tanzania. *Palaeogeography, Palaeoclimatology, Palaeoecology* 257, 280–293.

Bamford, M.K., Neumann, F.H., Pereira, L.M., et al. (2010). Botanical remains from a coprolite from the Pleistocene hominin site of Malapa, Sterkfontein Valley, South Africa. *Palaeontologica Africana* 45, 23–28.

Bamford, M.K., Senut, B. and Pickford, M. (2013). Fossil leaves from Lukeino, a 6-million-year-old formation in the Baringo Basin, Kenya. *Geobios* 46(4), 253–272.

Barboni, D. (2014). Vegetation of northern Tanzania during the Plio-Pleistocene: a synthesis of the paleobotanical evidences from Laetoli, Olduvai, and Peninj hominin sites. *Quaternary International* 322–323, 264–276.

Barboni, D., Ashley, G.M., Dominguez-Rodrigo, M., et al. (2010). Phytoliths infer locally dense and heterogeneous paleovegetation at FLK North and surrounding localities during upper Bed I time, Olduvai Gorge, Tanzania. *Quaternary Research* 74, 344–354.

Barbour, G.B. (1949a). Makapansgat. *Science Monthly* 69, 141–147.

Barbour, G.B. (1949b). Ape or man? An incomplete chapter of human ancestry from South Africa. *Ohio Journal of Science* 49, 129–145.

Bardin, G., Raynal, J.-P. and Kieffer, G. (2004). Drainage patterns and regional morphostructure at Melka Kunture (Upper Awash, Ethiopia). In: J. Chavaillon and M. Piperno (Eds.), *Studies on the Early Paleolithic site of Melka Kunture, Ethiopia – 2004*. Florence: Istituto Italiano di Preistoria e Protostoria, pp. 83–92.

Barker, D.S. and Milliken, K.L. (2008). Cementation of the Footprint Tuff, Laetoli, Tanzania. *The Canadian Mineralogist* 46, 831–841.

Bar-Matthews, M., Marean, C.W., Jacobs, Z., et al. (2010). A high resolution and continuous isotopic speleothem record of paleoclimate and paleoenvironment from 90 to 53 ka from Pinnacle Point on the south coast of South Africa. *Quaternary Science Reviews* 29(17–18), 2131–2145.

Barnosky, A.D. (2001). Distinguishing the effects of the red queen and court jester on Miocene mammal evolution in the northern Rocky Mountains. *Journal of Vertebrate Paleontology* 21, 172–185.

Barnosky, A. (2005). Effects of Quaternary climatic change on speciation in mammals. *Journal of Mammalian Evolution* 12(1), 247–264. doi: 10.1007/s10914-005-4858-8

Barnosky, A.D., Matzke, N., Tomiya, S., et al. (2011). Has the earth's sixth mass extinction already arrived? *Nature* 471, 51–57.

Barr, W.A. (2015). Paleoenvironments of the Shungura Formation (Plio-Pleistocene: Ethiopia) based on ecomorphology of the bovid *Astragalus*. *Journal of Human Evolution* 88, 97–107.

Barr, W.A. (2017). Bovid locomotor functional trait distributions reflect land cover and annual precipitation in sub-Saharan Africa. *Evolutionary Ecology Research* 18(3), 253–269.

Barrett, L., Gaynor, D., Rendall, D., Mitchell, D. and Henzi, S.P. (2004). Habitual cave use and thermoregulation in chacma baboons (*Papio hamadryas ursinus*). *Journal of Human Evolution* 46(2), 215–222.

Barsky, D., Chapon-Sao, C., Bahain, J.-J., et al. (2011). The early Oldowan stone-tool assemblage from Fejej FJ-1A, Ethiopia. *Journal of African Archaeology* 9, 207–224.

Barthelme, J. (1991). Lenderut: a new Acheulian site in the southern Kenya rift. *Nyame Akuma* 35, 21–24.

Basu, C., Falkingham, P.L. and Hutchinson, J.R. (2016). The extinct, giant giraffid *Sivatherium giganteum*: skeletal reconstruction and body mass estimation. *Biology Letters* 12.

Beadle, L.C. (1974). *The Inland Waters of Tropical Africa*. London: Longman.

Beaumont, P.B. (1982). Aspects of the Northern Cape Pleistocene project. In: J.A. Coetzee and E.M. van Zinderen Bakker (Eds.), *Palaeoecology of Africa and the Surrounding Islands vol. 15*. Cape Town: A.A. Balkema, pp. 41–44.

Beaumont, P.B. (1990). Wonderwerk Cave. In: P. Beaumont and D. Morris (Eds.), *Guide to Archaeological Sites in the Northern Cape*. Kimberly: McGregor Museum, pp. 101–134.

Beaumont, P.B. (2004). Wonderwerk Cave. In: P. Beaumont and D. Morris (Eds.), *Archaeology in the Northern Cape: Some Key Sites*. Kimberly: McGregor Museum, pp. 31–36.

Beaumont, P.B. (2011). The edge: more on fire-making by about 1.7 million years ago at Wonderwerk Cave in South Africa. *Current Anthropology* 52(4), 585–595.

Beaumont, P.B. and Vogel, J.C. (2006). On a timescale for the past million years of human history in central South Africa. *South African Journal of Science* 102, 217–228.

Beauvilain, A. (2008). The contexts of discovery of *Australopithecus bahrelghazali* (Abel) and of *Sahelanthropus tchadensis* (Tounami): unearthed, embedded in sandstone, or surface collected? *South African Journal of Science* 104, 165–168.

Beauvilain, A. and Le Guellec, Y. (2004). Further details concerning fossils attributed to *Sahelanthropus tchadensis* (Toumaï). *South African Journal of Science* 100, 142–144.

Beck, C.C., Feibel, C.S., Wright, J.D. and Mortlock, R.A. (2019). Onset of the African Humid Period by 13.9 kyr BP at Kabua Gorge, Turkana Basin, Kenya. *The Holocene* 29, 1011–1019.

Bedaso, Z.K. (2011). Stable isotope studies of paleoenvironment and paleoclimate from Afar, Ethiopia. PhD dissertation, University of South Florida.

Bedaso, Z.K., Wynn, J.G., Alemseged, Z. and Geraads, D. (2010). Paleoenvironmental reconstruction of the Asbole fauna (Busidima Formation, Afar, Ethiopia) using stable isotopes. *Geobios* 43, 165–177.

Bedaso, Z.K., Wynn, J.G., Alemseged, Z. and Geraads, D. (2013). Dietary and paleoenvironmental reconstruction using stable isotopes of herbivore tooth enamel from middle Pliocene Dikika, Ethiopia: implication for *Australopithecus afarensis* habitat and food resources. *Journal of Human Evolution* 64, 21–38.

Beden, M. (1976). Proboscideans from Omo group deposits. In: Y. Coppens, F.C. Howell, G.L.I. Isaac and R.E.F. Leakey (Eds.), *Earliest Man and Environments in the Lake Rudolf Basin*. Chicago: University of Chicago Press, 193–208.

Beden, M. (1979). Les éléphants (*Loxodonta* et *Elephas*) d'Afrique Orientale: systématique, phylogénie, intérêt biochronologique. Thèse, Université de Poitiers, France.

Beden, M. (1987). *Les faunes Plio-Pléistocène de la basse vallée de l'omo (Éthiopie) Tome 2, Les éléphantidés (Mammalia: Proboscidea)*. Cahiers de paléontologie. Paris: Editions du CNRS.

Begon, M., Townsend, C.R. and Harper, J.L. (2006). *Ecology: From Individuals to Ecosystems*, 4th ed. Oxford: Blackwell.

Begun, D.R. (2015). *The Real Planet of the Apes: A New Story of Human Origins*. Princeton: Princeton University Press.

Behrensmeyer, A.K. (1975). The taphonomy and paleoecology of Plio-Pleistocene vertebrate assemblages East of Lake Rudolf, Kenya. *Bulletin of the Museum of Comparative Zoology* 146, 473–578.

Behrensmeyer, A.K. (1976). Lothagam Hill, Kanapoi, and Ekora: A general summary of stratigraphy and faunas. In: Y. Coppens, F.C. Howell, G.L. Isaac and R.E. Leakey (Eds.), *Earliest Man and Environments in the Lake Rudolf Basin*. Chicago: University of Chicago Press, pp. 163–170.

Behrensmeyer, A.K. (1978a). The habitat of Plio-Pleistocene hominids in East Africa: taphonomic and microstratigraphic evidence. In: C.J. Jolly (Ed.), *Early Hominids of Africa*. London: Duckworth, pp. 165–189.

Behrensmeyer, A.K. (1978b). Taphonomic and ecologic information from bone weathering. *Paleobiology* 4, 150–162.

Behrensmeyer, A.K. (1982). Time resolution in fluvial vertebrate assemblages. *Paleobiology* 8(3), 211–227.

Behrensmeyer, A.K. (1985). Taphonomy and the paleoecologic reconstruction of hominid habitats in the Koobi Fora Formation. In: Y. Coppens (Ed.), *L'Environnement des Hominidés au Plio-Pléistocène*. Paris: Masson, pp. 309–324.

Behrensmeyer, A.K. (1988). Vertebrate preservation in fluvial channels. *Palaeogeography, Palaeoclimatolology, Palaeoecology* 63(1–3), 183–199.

Behrensmeyer, A.K. (1991). Terrestrial vertebrate accumulations. In: P. Allison and D.E.G. Briggs (Eds.), *Taphonomy: Releasing the Data Locked in the Fossil Record*. New York: Plenum, pp. 291–335.

Behrensmeyer, A.K. (2006). Climate change and human evolution. *Science* 311, 476–478.

Behrensmeyer, A.K. and Barry, J.C. (2005). Biostratigraphic surveys in the Siwaliks of Pakistan: a method for standardized surface sampling of the vertebrate fossil record. *Palaeontologia Electronica* 8, 1–24.

Behrensmeyer, A.K. and Boaz, D.E.D. (1980). The recent bones of Amboseli Park, Kenya in relation to East African paleoecology. In: A.K. Behrensmeyer and A. Hill (Eds.), *Fossils in the Making: Vertebrate Taphonomy and Paleoecology*. Chicago: University of Chicago Press, pp. 72–93.

Behrensmeyer, A.K. and Boaz, D.E.D. (1981). Late Pleistocene geology and paleontology of Amboseli National Park, Kenya. In: J.A. Coetzee (Ed.), *Palaeoecology of Africa and the Surrounding Islands* Vol. 13. Rotterdam: Balkema, pp. 175–188.

Behrensmeyer, A.K. and Cooke, H.B.S. (1985). Paleoenvironments, stratigraphy, and taphonomy in the African Pliocene and early Pleistocene. In: E. Delson (Ed.), *Ancestors: The Hard Evidence*. New York: Alan R. Liss, pp. 60–62.

Behrensmeyer, A.K. and Isaac, G.L. (1997). Geological context and paleoenvironments. In: G.L. Isaac (Ed.), *Koobi Fora Research Project Volume 5: Plio-Pleistocene Archaeology*. Oxford: Clarendon Press, pp. 12–70.

Behrensmeyer, A.K. and Kidwell, S.M. (1985). Taphonomy's contributions to paleobiology. *Paleobiology*, 11(1), 105–119.

Behrensmeyer, A.K. and Laporte, L.F. (1981). Footprints of a Pleistocene hominid in northern Kenya. *Nature* 289(5794), 167–169.

Behrensmeyer, A.K. and Reed, K.E. (2013). Reconstructing the habitats of *Australopithecus*: Paleoenvironments, site taphonomy, and faunas. In: K. Reed, J. Fleagle and R. Leakey (Eds.), *The Paleobiology of Australopithecus*. New York: Springer, pp. 41–60.

Behrensmeyer, A.K. and Western, D. (2009). Bone burial in land surface assemblages and its impact on the vertebrate fossil record. *Journal of Vertebrate Paleontology* 29(Supplement to #3), 61.

Behrensmeyer, A.K., Western, D. and Boaz, D.E.D. (1979). New perspectives in vertebrate paleoecology from a recent bone assemblage. *Paleobiology* 5, 12–21.

Behrensmeyer, A.K., Damuth, J.D., DiMichele, W.A., et al. (1992). *Terrestrial Ecosystems through Time: Evolutionary Paleoecology of Terrestrial Plants and Animals*. Chicago: University of Chicago Press.

Behrensmeyer, A.K., Potts, R., Plummer, T., et al. (1995). The Pleistocene locality of Kanjera, Western Kenya: stratigraphy, chronology and paleoenvironments. *Journal of Human Evolution*, 29, 247–274.

Behrensmeyer, A.K., Todd, N.E., Potts, R. and McBrinn, G.E. (1997). Late Pliocene faunal turnover in the Turkana Basin, Kenya. *Science* 278: 1589–1594.

Behrensmeyer, A.K., Kidwell, S.M. and Gastaldo, R.A. (2000). Taphonomy and paleobiology. *Paleobiology* 26(S4), 103–147.

Behrensmeyer, A.K., Potts, R., Deino, A. and Ditchfield, P. (2002). Olorgesailie, Kenya: a million years in the life of a rift basin. In: R.W. Renaut and G.M. Ashley (Eds.), *Sedimentation in Continental Rifts*, SEPM Special Publication 73. Broken Arrow, OK: Society for Sedimentary Geology, pp. 97–106.

Behrensmeyer, A.K., Harmon, E.H. and Kimbel, W.H. (2003). Environmental context and taphonomy of the A.L. 333 Locality, Hadar, Ethiopia. *PaleoAnthropology PAS 2003 abstracts*, A2.

Behrensmeyer, A.K., Bobe, R. and Alemseged, Z. (2007a). Approaches to the analysis of faunal change during the East African Pliocene. In: R. Bobe, Z. Alemseged and A.K. Behrensmeyer (Eds.), *Hominin Environments in the East African Pliocene: An Assessment of the Faunal Evidence*. Berlin: Springer, 1–24.

Behrensmeyer A.K., Alemseged Z., Bobe R. (2007b). Finale and future. Investigating faunal evidence for hominin paleoecology in East Africa. In: R. Bobe, Z. Alemseged and A.K. Behrensmeyer (Eds.), *Hominin Environments in the East African Pliocene: An Assessment of the Faunal Evidence*. Berlin: Springer Verlag, pp. 333–345.

Behrensmeyer, A.K., Potts, R. and Deino, A. (2018). The Oltulelei Formation of the southern Kenyan Rift Valley: a chronicle of rapid landscape transformation over the last 500 ky. *Bulletin of the Geological Society of America*, 130(9–10), 1474–1492.

Belmaker, M. (2006). Large mammalian community structure through time: 'Ubeidiya' as a case study. PhD dissertation, The Hebrew University of Jerusalem, Jerusalem, Israel.

Belmaker, M. (2010). Early Pleistocene faunal connections between Africa and Eurasia: an ecological perspective. In: J.G. Fleagle, J.J. Shea, F.E. Grine, A.L. Baden and R.E. Leakey (Eds.), *Out of Africa I*. Dordrecht: Springer, pp. 183–205.

Belmaker, M. (2018). Insight from carnivore community composition on the paleoecology of early Pleistocene Eurasian sites: implications for the dispersal of hominins out of Africa. *Quaternary International* 464(A), 3–17. DOI: 10.1016/j.quaint.2017.02.017

Belyea, L.R. and Lancaster, J. (1999). Assembly rules within a contingent ecology. *Oikos* 86, 402–416.

Ben Moktar, N. and Mannaï-Tayech, B. (2015). Palynological reconstruction of climate and paleoenvironment during the lower to middle Miocene in northeast Tunisia. *Arabian Journal of Geosciences* 8, 11149–11159.

Benammi, M., Calvo, M., Prévot, M. and Jaeger, J.-J. (1996). Magnetostratigraphy and paleontology of Aït Kandoula basin (High Atlas, Morocco) and the African-European late Miocene terrestrial fauna exchanges. *Earth and Planetary Science Letters* 145(1), 15–29.

Bender, P.A. (1990). A reconsideration of the fossil Suidae of the Makapansgat Limeworks, Potgietersrus, Northern Transvaal. Unpublished MSc dissertation. University of the Witwatersrand, Johannesburg.

Bender, P.A. (1992). A reconsideration of the fossil Suid, Potamochoeroides shawi, from the Makapansgat Limeworks, Potgietersrus, Northern Transvaal. *Navorsinge van die Nasionale Museum, Bloemfontein* 8, 1–67.

Bender, P.A. and Brink, J.S. (1992). A preliminary report on new large mammal fossil finds from the Cornelia-Uitzoek site. *South African Journal of Science* 88, 512–515.

Benefit, B.R. and McCrossin, M.L. (1990). Diet, species diversity, and distribution of African fossil baboons. *Kroeber Anthropological Society Papers* 71-72, 79–93.

Benefit, B.R. and Pickford, M. (1986). Miocene fossil cercopithecoids from Kenya. *American Journal of Physical Anthropology* 69, 441–464.

Benito-Calvo, A. and de la Torre, I. (2011). Analysis of orientation patterns in Olduvai Bed I assemblages using GIS techniques: Implications for site formation processes. *Journal of Human Evolution* 61, 50–60.

Bennett, K.D. (1997). *Evolution and Ecology: The Pace of Life*. Cambridge: Cambridge University Press.

Bennett, M.R. and Reynolds, S.C. (2021). Inferences from footprints: archaeological best practice. In: A. Pastoors and T. Lenssen-Erz (Eds.), *Reading Prehistoric Human Tracks*. Cham: Springer, pp. 15–39.

Bennett, M.R., Harris, J.W.K., Richmond, B.G., et al. (2009). Early hominin foot morphology based on 1.5-million-year-old footprints from Ileret, Kenya. *Science* 323, 1197–1201.

Bennington, J.B., Dimichele, W.A., Badgley, C., et al. (2009). Critical Issues of scale in paleoecology. *Palaios* 24(1), 1–4.

Benton, M.J. and Storrs, G.W. (1994). Testing the quality of the fossil record: paleontological knowledge is improving. *Geology* 22(2), 111–114.

Berge, C., Penin, X. and Pellé, É. (2006). New interpretation of Laetoli footprints using an experimental approach and Procrustes analysis: preliminary results. *Comptes Rendus Palevol* 5, 561–569.

Berger, L.R. (2006). Brief communication: Predatory bird damage to the Taung type-skull of *Australopithecus africanus* Dart 1925. *American Journal of Physical Anthropology* 131, 166–168.

Berger, L. and Brink, J. (2007). An atlas of Southern African mammalian fossil bearing sites – Late Miocene to Late Pleistocene. Online at: www.profleeberger.com/files/An_Atlas_of_southern_African_Fossil_Bearing_Sites.pdf.

Berger, L.R. and Clarke, R.J. (1995). Eagle involvement in accumulation of the Taung child fauna. *Journal of Human Evolution* 29, 275–299.

Berger, L.R. and Lacruz, R. (2003). Preliminary report on the first excavations at the new fossil site of Motsetse, Gauteng, South Africa. *South African Journal of Science*, 99, 279–282.

Berger, L.R. and McGraw, W.S. (2007). Further evidence for eagle predation of, and feeding damage on, the Taung child. *South African Journal of Science* 103, 496–498.

Berger, L.R. and Parkington, J.E. (1995). A new Pleistocene hominid-bearing locality at Hoedjiespunt, South Africa. *American Journal of Physical Anthropology* 98(4), 601–609.

Berger, L.R. and Tobias, P.V. (1994). New discoveries at the early hominid site of Gladysvale, South Africa. *South African Journal of Science*, 90(4), 223–226.

Berger, L.R., Keyser, A.W. and Tobias, P.V. (1993). Gladysvale: first early hominid site discovered in South Africa since 1948. *American Journal of Physical Anthropology* 92(1), 107–111.

Berger, L.R., Pickford, M. and Thackeray, J.F. (1995). A Plio-Pleistocene hominin upper central incisor from the Cooper's site, South Africa. *South African Journal of Science* 91, 341–342.

Berger, L.R., Lacruz, R. and de Ruiter, D.J. (2002). Brief communication: Revised age estimates of *Australopithecus*-bearing deposits at Sterkfontein, South Africa. *American Journal of Physical Anthropology* 119, 192–197.

Berger, L.R., de Ruiter, D.J., Steininger, C.M. and Hancox, P.J. (2003). Preliminary results of excavations at the newly investigated Coopers D deposit, Gauteng, South Africa. *South African Journal of Science* 99, 276–278.

Berger, L.R., Lacruz, R., Hall, G., et al. (2006). An Acheulean handaxe from Gladysvale Cave Site, Gauteng, South Africa: research in action. *South African Journal of Science* 102(3), 103–105.

Berger, L.R., Pickering, R., Kuhn, B., et al. (2009). A Mid-Pleistocene in situ fossil brown hyaena (*Parahyaena brunnea*) latrine from Gladysvale Cave, South Africa. *Palaeogeography, Palaeoclimatology, Palaeoecology* 279(3–4), 131–136.

Berger, L.R., de Ruiter, D.J., Churchill, S.E., et al. (2010). *Australopithecus sediba*: a new species of *Homo*-like australopith from South Africa. *Science* 328, 195–204.

Berger, L.R., Hawks, J., de Ruiter, D.J., et al. (2015). *Homo naledi*, a new species of the genus *Homo* from the Dinaledi Chamber, South Africa. *elife* 4, e09560.

Berna, F., Goldberg, P., Horwitz, L.K., et al. (2012). Microstratigraphic evidence of in situ fire in the Acheulean strata of Wonderwerk Cave, Northern Cape province, South Africa. *Proceedings of the National Academy of Sciences* 109(20), E1215–E1220.

Bernor, R.L. (2007). The latest Miocene hipparionine (Equidae) from Lemudong'o, Kenya. *Kirtlandia* 56, 148–151.

Bernor, R.L. and Harris, J.M. (2003). Systematics and evolutionary biology of the late Miocene and early Pliocene hipparionine equids from Lothagam, Kenya. In: M.G. Leakey and J.M. Harris (Eds.), *Lothagam: The Dawn of Humanity in Eastern Africa*. New York: Columbia University Press, pp. 387–438.

Bernor, R.L. and Kaiser, T.M. (2006). Systematics and paleoecology of the earliest Pliocene equid, *Eurygnathohippus hooijeri* n. sp. from Langebaanweg, South Africa. *Mitteilungen aus dem Hamburgischen zoologischen Museum und Institut* 103, 149–186.

Bernor, R.L. and Sanders, W.J. (1990). Fossil Equidae from Plio-Pleistocene strata of the upper Semliki, Zaire. In: N.T. Boaz (Ed.), *Evolution of Environments and Hominidae in the African Western*

Rift Valley. Martinsville: Virginia Museum of Natural History, pp. 189–196.

Bernor, R.L., Kaiser, T.M. and Nelson, S.V. (2004). The Oldest Ethiopian Hipparion (Equinae, Perissodactyl from Chorora: Systematics, Paleodiet and Paleoclimate. *Courier-Forschungsinstitut Senckenberg*, 246, 213–226.

Bernor, R.L., Scott, R.S. and Haile-Selassie, Y. (2005). A contribution to the evolutionary history of Ethiopian hipparionine horses (Mammalia, Equidae): morphometric evidence from the postcranial skeleton. *Geodiversitas* 27, 133–158.

Bernor, R., Rook, L. and Haile-Selassie, Y. (2009). *Paleobiogeography. Ardipithecus kadabba: Late Miocene Evidence from the Middle Awash, Ethiopia*. Berkeley: University of California Press, pp. 549–563.

Bernor, R.L., Armour-Chelu, M., Gilbert, W.H., Kaiser, T.M. and Schulz, E. (2010). Equidae. In: L. Werdelin and W.J. Sanders (Eds.), *Cenozoic Mammals of Africa*. Berkeley: University of California Press, pp. 685–721.

Bernor, R.L., Gilbert, H., Semprebon, G.M., Simpson, S. and Semaw, S. (2013). *Eurygnathohippus woldegabrieli*, sp. nov. (Perissodactyla, Mammalia), from the Middle Pliocene of Aramis, Ethiopia. *Journal of Vertebrate Paleontology* 33, 1472–1485.

Bernoussi, R. (1997). Contribution à l'étude paléontologique et observations archéozoologiques pour deux sites du Pléistocène moyen du Maroc atlantique, la grotte à Hominidés de la carrière Thomas I et la Grotte des Rhinocéros de la carrière Oulad Hamida 1 (Casablanca, Maroc). Thèse Univ. Bordeaux I, no. 1711, 265 pp.

Besse, J. and Courtillot, V. (2002). Apparent and true polar wander and the geometry of the geomagnetic field over the last 200 Myr. *Journal of Geophysical Research: Solid Earth* 107(B11), EPM-6.

Betzler, C. and Ring, U. (1995). Sedimentology of the Malawi Rift: facies and stratigraphy of the Chiwondo Beds, northern Malawi. *Journal of Human Evolution* 28(1), 23–35.

Betzler, C., Eberli, G. P., Kroon, D., et al. (2016). The abrupt onset of the modern South Asian Monsoon winds. *Scientific Reports* 6, 29838.

Beyene, Y., Katoh, S., WoldeGabriel, G., et al. (2013). The characteristics and chronology of the earliest Acheulean at Konso, Ethiopia. *Proceedings of the National Academy of Sciences of the USA*, 110, 1584–1591.

Beyene, Y., Asfaw, B., Sano, K. and Suwa, G. (2015). *The Konso-Gardula Research Project, Volume 2. Archaeological Collections: Background and the Early Acheulean Assemblages*. Bulletin 48. Tokyo: The University Museum, The University of Tokyo, pp. 1–103.

Biberson, P. (1961a). Le cadre paléogéographique de la préhistoire du Maroc atlantique. *Publications du Service des Antiquités du Maroc* 16, 1–235.

Biberson, P. (1961b). Le paléolithique inférieur du Maroc atlantique. *Publications du Service des Antiquités du Maroc* 17, 1–544.

Bibi, F. (2011a). *Tragelaphus nakuae*: evolutionary change, biochronology, and turnover in the African Plio-Pleistocene. *Zoological Journal of the Linnean Society London*, 162, 699–711.

Bibi, F. (2011b). Mio-Pliocene faunal exchanges and african biogeography: the record of fossil bovids. *PLoS ONE*, 6(2), e16688.

Bibi, F. and Kiessling, W. (2015). Continuous evolutionary change in Plio-Pleistocene mammals of eastern Africa. *Proceedings of the National Academy of Sciences of the USA* 112, 10623–10628.

Bibi, F., Hill, A., Beech, M. and Yasin, W. (2008). A river fauna from the Arabian desert: late Miocene fossils from the United Arab Emirates. *Journal of Vertebrate Paleontology* 28(3), 53A–53A.

Bibi, F., Souron, A., Bocherens, H., Uno, K. and Boisserie, J.-R. (2013). Ecological change in the lower Omo Valley around 2.8 Ma. *Biology Letters* 9: 20120890.

Bibi, F., Rowan, J. and Reed, K. (2017). Late Pliocene Bovidae from Ledi-Geraru (Lower Awash Valley, Ethiopia) and their implications for Afar paleoecology. *Journal of Vertebrate Paleontology*, 37, e1337639.

Bibi, F., Pante, M., Souron, A., et al. (2018). Paleoecology of the Serengeti during the Oldowan–Acheulean transition at Olduvai Gorge, Tanzania: the mammal and fish evidence. *Journal of Human Evolution* 120, 48–75.

Bigazzi, G., Balestrieri, M.L., Norelli, P. and Oddone, M. (2004). Fission-track dating of a tephra layer in the Alat Formation of the Dandero Group (Danakil Depression, Eritrea). *Rivista Italiana di Stratigrafia e Paleontologia* 110(Supplement), 45–49.

Binford, L.R. (1981). *Bones, Ancient Men and Modern Myths*. New York: New York Academic Press.

Binford, L.R. (1983). *In Pursuit of the Past*. New York: Thames and Hudson.

Binford, L.R. (1986). Comment on "Systematic butchery by Plio-Pleistocene hominids at Olduvai Gorge." *Current Anthropology* 27, 444–446.

Binford, L.R., Bunn, H.T. and Kroll, E.M. (1988a). Fact and fiction about the *Zinjanthropus* floor: data, arguments, and interpretations. *Current Anthropology* 29, 123–135.

Binford, L.R., Mills, M. and Stone, N.M. (1988b). Hyena scavenging behavior and its implications for the interpretation of faunal assemblages from FLK 22 (the Zinj floor) at Olduvai Gorge. *Journal of Anthropological Archaeology* 7, 99–135.

Binetti, K.M. (2011). Early Pliocene hominid paleoenvironments in the Tugen Hills, Kenya. PhD dissertation, Yale University.

Birchette, M. (1981). Postcranial remains of *Cercopithecoides*. *American Journal of Physical Anthropology* 54, 201.

Birkenfeld, M., Avery, D.M. and Horwitz, L.K. (2015). GIS virtual reconstructions of the temporal and spatial relations of fossil deposits at Wonderwerk Cave (South Africa). *African Archaeological Review* 32, 857–876.

Bishop, L.C. (1994). Pigs and the ancestors: hominids, suids and environments during the Plio-Pleistocene of East Africa. PhD dissertation, Yale University. Ann Arbor, MI: University Microforms International. ProQuest publication number 9430258.

Bishop, L.C. (1997). Fossil suids from the Manonga Valley, Tanzania. In: T. Harrison (Ed.), *Neogene Paleontology of the Manonga Valley, Tanzania: A Window into the Evolutionary History of East Africa*. New York: Springer, pp. 191–217.

Bishop, L.C. (1999). Suid paleoecology and habitat preferences at African Pliocene and Pleistocene hominid localities. In: T.G. Bromage and F. Schrenk (Eds.), *African Biogeography, Climate Change, and Human Evolution*. Oxford: Oxford University Press, pp. 216–225.

Bishop, L.C. (2010). Suoidea. In: L. Werdelin and W.J. Sanders (Eds.), *Cenozoic Mammals of Africa*. Berkeley: University of California Press, pp. 821–842.

Bishop, L.C. (2011). Suidae. In: T. Harrison (Ed.), *Paleontology and Geology of Laetoli: Human Evolution in Context. Vol. 2: Fossil Hominins and the Associated Fauna*. Dordrecht: Springer, pp. 327–337.

Bishop, L. and Hill, A. (1999). Fossil Suidae from the Baynunah Formation, Emirate of Abu Dhabi, United Arab Emirates. In: P.J. Whybrow and A.P. Hill (Eds.), *Fossil Vertebrates of Arabia, with Emphasis on the Late Miocene Faunas, Geology, and Palaeoenvironments of the Emirate of Abu Dhabi, United Arab Emirates*. New Haven: Yale University Press, pp. 254–270

Bishop, L.C. and Reynolds, S.C. (2000). Fauna from Twin Rivers. In: L. Barham (Ed.), *The Middle Stone Age of Zambia, South Central Africa*. Bristol: Western Academic & Specialist Press, pp. 217–222.

Bishop, L.C., Hill, A. and Kingston, J.D. (1999a). Palaeoecology of Suidae from the Tugen Hills, Baringo, Kenya. In: P. Andrews and P. Banham (Eds.), *Late Cenozoic Environments and Hominid Evolution: A tribute to Bill Bishop*. London: Geological Society of London, pp. 99–111.

Bishop, L.C., Pickering, T.R., Plummer, T. and Thackeray, J.F. (1999b). Paleoenvironment setting for the Oldowan Industry at Sterkfontein (abstract). Paper for presentation at the XV International Union for Quaternary Research, 3–11 August 1999, Durban, South Africa.

Bishop, L.C., King, T., Hill, A. and Wood, B. (2006a). Palaeoecology of *Kolpochoerus heseloni* (= *K. limnetes*): a multiproxy approach. *Proceedings of the Royal Society of South Africa* 61, 81–88.

Bishop, L.C., Plummer, T.W., Ferraro, J.V., et al. (2006b). Recent research into oldowan hominin activities at Kanjera South, Western Kenya. *African Archaeological Review* 23, 31.

Bishop, L.C., Plummer, T.W., Hertel, F. and Kovarovic, K. (2011). Paleoenvironments of Laetoli, Tanzania as determined by antelope habitat preferences. In: T. Harrison (Ed.), *Paleontology and Geology of Laetoli: Human Evolution in Context. Vol. 1: Geology, Geochronology, Paleoecology, and Paleoenvironment*. Dordrecht: Springer, pp. 355–366.

Bishop, W.W. (1968). The evolution of fossil environments in East Africa. *Transactions of the Leicester Literary and Philosophical Society* 62, 22–44.

Bishop, W.W. (1971). The late Cenozoic history of East Afrca in relation to hominoid evolution. In: K.K. Turekian (Ed.), *The Late Cenozoic Glacial Ages*. New Haven: Yale University Press, pp. 493–527.

Bishop, W.W. and Chapman, G.R. (1970). Early Pliocene sediments and fossils from the northern Kenya Rift Valley. *Nature* 226, 914–918.

Bishop, W.W. and Pickford, M.H.L. (1975). Geology, fauna and palaeoenvironments of the Ngorora Formation, Kenya Rift Valley. *Nature* 254, 185–192.

Bishop, W.W. and Whyte, F. (1962). Tertiary mammalian faunas and sediments in Karamoja and Kavirondo, East Africa. *Nature* 4861, 1283–1287.

Bishop, W.W., Chapman, G.R., Hill, A. and Miller, J.A. (1971). Succession of Cainozoic vertebrate assemblages from Northern Kenya Rift Valley. *Nature* 233(5319), 389–394.

Bishop, W., Hill, A. and Pickford, M. (1978). Chesowanja: a revised geological interpretation. In: W.W. Bishop (Ed.), *Geological Background to Fossil Man*. Edinburgh: Scottish Academic Press, pp. 309–327.

Black, C.C. and Krishtalka, L. (1986). Rodents, bats, and insectivores from the Plio-Pleistocene sediments to the east of Lake Turkana, Kenya. *Contributions in Science* 372, 1–15.

Blois, J.L. and Hadly, E.A. (2009). Mammalian responses to Cenozoic climatic change. *Annual Review of Earth and Planetary Sciences* 37, 181–208.

Blondel, C., Merceron, G., Andossa, L., et al. (2010). Dental mesowear analysis of the late Miocene Bovidae from Toros-Menalla (Chad) and early hominid habitats in Central Africa. *Palaeogeography, Palaeoclimatology, Palaeoecology* 292, 184–191.

Blondel, C., Rowan, J., Merceron, G., et al. (2018). Feeding ecology of Tragelaphini (Bovidae) from the Shungura Formation, Omo Valley, Ethiopia: contribution of dental wear analyses. *Palaeogeography, Palaeoclimatology, Palaeoecology* 496, 103–120.

Blome, M.W., Cohen, A.S., Tryon, C.A., Brooks, A.S. and Russell, J. (2012). The environmental context for the origins of modern human diversity: a synthesis of regional variability in African climate 150,000–30,000 years ago. *Journal of Human Evolution* 62, 563–592.

Blum, M.G.B. and Jakobsson, M. (2010). Deep divergences of human gene trees and models of human origins. *Molecular Biology and Evolution* 28, 889–898.

Blumenschine, R.J. (1986). *Early Hominid Scavenging Opportunities: Implications of Carcass Availability in the Serengeti and Ngorongoro Ecosystems*. British Archaeological Reports International Series 283.

Blumenschine, R.J. (1987). Characteristics of an early hominid scavenging niche. *Current Anthropology* 29, 382–407.

Blumenschine, R.J. (1988). An experimental model of the timing of hominid and carnivore influence on archaeological bone assemblages. *Journal of Archaeological Science* 15, 483–502.

Blumenschine, R.J. (1995). Percussion marks, tooth marks, and experimental determinations of the timing of hominid and carnivore access to long bones at FLK Zinjanthropus, Olduvai Gorge, Tanzania. *Journal of Human Evolution* 29, 21–51.

Blumenschine, R.J. and Masao, F.T. (1991). Living sites at Olduvai Gorge, Tanzania? Preliminary landscape archaeology results in the basal Bed II lake margin zone. *Journal of Human Evolution* 21, 451–462.

Blumenschine, R.J. and Peters, C.R. (1998). Archaeological predictions for hominid land use in the paleo-Olduvai Basin, Tanzania, during lowermost Bed II times. *Journal of Human Evolution* 34, 565–607.

Blumenschine, R.J. and Pobiner, B.L. (2007). Zooarchaeology and the ecology of Oldowan hominin carnivory. In: P.S. Ungar (Ed.), *Evolution of the Human Diet*. New York: Oxford University Press, pp. 167–190.

Blumenschine, R.J., Marean, C.W. and Capaldo, S.D. (1996). Blind tests of inter-analyst correspondence and accuracy in the identification of cut marks, percussion marks, and carnivore tooth marks on bone surfaces. *Journal of Archaeological Science* 23, 493–507.

Blumenschine, R.J., Peters, C.R., Masao, F.T., et al. (2003). Late Pliocene *Homo* and hominid land use from Western Olduvai Gorge, Tanzania. *Science* 299(5610), 1217–1221.

Blumenschine, R.J., Stanistreet, I.G. and Masao, F.T. (2012a). Olduvai Gorge and the Olduvai Landscape Paleoanthropology Project. *Journal of Human Evolution* 63, 247–250.

Blumenschine, R.J., Stanistreet, I.G., Njau, J.K., et al. (2012b). Environments and hominin activities across the FLK Peninsula during Zinjanthropus times (1.84 Ma), Olduvai Gorge, Tanzania. *Journal of Human Evolution* 63, 364–383.

Blumenthal, S.A., Levin, N.E., Brown, F.H., et al. (2017). Aridity and hominin environments. *Proceedings of the National Academy of Sciences* 114, 7331–7336.

Boaz, N.T. (1990). *Evolution of Environments and Hominidae in the African Western Rift Valley*. Memoir Number 1. Martinsville: Virginia Museum of Natural History, p. 356.

Boaz, N.T., El-Arnauti, A., Gaziry, A.W., de Heinzelin, J. and Boaz, D.D. (Eds.) (1987). *Neogene Paleontology and Geology of As Sahabi*. New York: Alan R. Liss.

Boaz, N.T., El-Arnauti, A., Pavlakis, P., Salem, M.J. (Eds.) (2008a). *Circum-Mediterranean Geology and Biotic Evolution During the Neogene Period: The Perspective from Libya*. Garyounis Scientific Bulletin, Special Issue 5. Benghazi: University of Garyounis. 308 pp.

Boaz, N., El-Arnauti, A., Agustí, J., et al. (2008b). Temporal, lithostratigraphic, and biochronologic setting of the Sahabi Formation, North-Central Libya. *Geology of East Libya* 3, 959–972.

Bobe, R. (1997). Hominid environments in the Pliocene: an analysis of fossil mammals from the lower Omo valley, Ethiopia. PhD dissertation, Anthropology, University of Washington.

Bobe, R. (2006). The evolution of arid ecosystems in eastern Africa. *Journal of Arid Environments* 66(3), 564–584.

Bobe, R. (2011). Fossil mammals and paleoenvironments in the Omo-Turkana Basin. *Evolutionary Anthropology* 20, 254–263.

Bobe, R. and Behrensmeyer, A.K. (2004). The expansion of grassland ecosystems in Africa in relation to mammalian evolution and the origin of the genus *Homo*. *Palaeogeography, Palaeoclimatology, Palaeoecology* 207, 399–420.

Bobe, R. and Carvalho, S. (2019). Hominin diversity and high environmental variability in the Okote Member, Koobi Fora Formation, Kenya. *Journal of Human Evolution* 126, 91–105.

Bobe, R. and Eck, G.G. (2001). Responses of African bovids to Pliocene climatic change. *Paleobiology* 27, 1–47.

Bobe, R. and Leakey, M.G. (2009). Ecology of Plio-Pleistocene mammals in the Omo – Turkana Basin and the emergence of *Homo*. In: F.E. Grine, J.G. Fleagle and R.E. Leakey (Eds.), *The First Humans – Origin and Early Evolution of the Genus Homo*. Dordrecht, Springer, pp. 173–184.

Bobe, R., Behrensmeyer, A.K. and Chapman, R.E. (2002). Faunal change, environmental variability, and late Pliocene hominin evolution. *Journal of Human Evolution* 42, 475–497.

Bobe, R., Alemseged, Z. and Behrensmeyer, A.K. (Eds.) (2007a). *Hominin Environments in the East African Pliocene: An Assessment of the Faunal Evidences*. Dordrecht: Springer.

Bobe, R., Behrensmeyer, A.K., Eck, G. and Harris, J.M. (2007b). Patterns of abundance and diversity in late Cenozoic bovids from the Turkana and Hadar Basins, Kenya and Ethiopia. In: R. Bobe, Z. Alemseged and A.K. Behrensmeyer (Eds.), *Hominin Environments in the East African Pliocene: An Assessment of the Faunal Evidence*. Dordrecht: Springer, pp. 129–157.

Bobe, R., Assefa, Z., and Lepre, C.J. (2009). *The Akaki-Fanta prehistoric site, Addis Ababa, Ethiopia*. Report to the National Geographic Society. Washington, DC: National Geographic Society, p. 12.

Bobe, R., Manthi, F.K., Ward, C.V., Plavcan, J.M., and Carvalho, S. (2020a). The ecology of *Australopithecus anamensis* in the early Pliocene of Kanapoi, Kenya. *Journal of Human Evolution* 140, 102717.

Bobe, R., Martínez, F.I. and Carvalho, S. (2020b). Primate adaptations and evolution in the southern African Rift Valley. *Evolutionary Anthropology* 29, 94–101.

Bocherens, H., Koch, P., Mariotti, A., Geraads, D. and Jaeger, J.-J. (1996). Isotopic biogeochemistry (13C, 18O) of mammalian enamel from African Pleistocene Hominid sites. *Palaios* 11, 306–318.

Boisserie, J.R. (2005). The phylogeny and taxonomy of Hippopotamidae (Mammalia: Artiodactyla): a review based on morphology and cladistic analysis. *Zoological Journal of the Linnean Society* 143(1), 1–26.

Boisserie, J.-R. (2020). Hippopotamidae (Cetartiodactyla, Hippopotamoidea) from Kanapoi, Kenya, and the taxonomic status of the late early Pliocene hippopotamids from the Turkana Basin. *Journal of Human Evolution* 140, 102377.

Boisserie, J.R. and Merceron, G. (2011). Correlating the success of Hippopotaminae with the C_4 grass expansion in Africa: relationship and diet of early Pliocene hippopotamids from Langebaanweg, South Africa. *Palaeogeography, Palaeoclimatology, Palaeoecology* 308(3–4), 350–361.

Boisserie, J.-R. and White, T.D. (2004). A new species of Pliocene Hippopotamidae from the Middle Awash, Ethiopia. *Journal of Vertebrate Paleontology* 24, 464–473.

Boisserie, J.-R., Brunet, M., Andossa, L. and Vignaud, P. (2003). Hippopotamids from the Djurab Pliocene faunas, Chad, Central Africa. *Journal of African Earth Sciences* 36, 15–27.

Boisserie, J.R., Zazzo, A., Merceron, G., et al. (2005a). Diets of modern and late Miocene hippopotamids: evidence from carbon isotope composition and micro-wear of tooth enamel. *Palaeogeography, Palaeoclimatology, Palaeoecology*, 221(1–2), 153–174. doi:10.1016/j.palaeo.2005.02.010

Boisserie, J.-R., Likius, A., Vignaud, P. and Brunet, M. (2005b) A new late Miocene hippopotamid from Toros-Menalla, Chad. *Journal of Vertebrate Paleontology* 25(3), 665–673.

Boisserie, J.R., Guy, F., Delagnes, A., et al. (2008). New palaeoanthropological research in the Plio-Pleistocene Omo Group, Lower Omo Valley, SNNPR (Southern Nations, Nationalities and People Regions), Ethiopia. *Comptes Rendus Palevol* 7(7), 429–439.

Boisserie, J.-R., Souron, A., Mackaye, H.T., et al. (2014). A new species of *Nyanzachoerus* (Cetartiodactyla: Suidae) from the Late Miocene Toros-Ménalla, Chad, Central Africa. *PLoS ONE* 9, e103221.

Boisserie, J.-R., Suwa, G., Asfaw, B., et al. (2017). Basal hippopotamines from the upper Miocene of Chorora, Ethiopia. *Journal of Vertebrate Paleontology* 37, e1297718.

Bolter, D.R., Elliott, M.C., Hawks, J. and Berger, L.R. (2020). Immature remains and the first partial skeleton of a juvenile *Homo naledi*, a late Middle Pleistocene hominin from South Africa. *PLoS ONE* 15(4), e0230440.

Bondioli, L., Coppa, A., Frayer, D.W., et al. (2006). A one million year old human pubic symphysis. *Journal of Human Evolution* 50, 479–483.

Boné, E.L. and Dart, R.A. (1955). A catalog of the Australopithecine fossils found at the Limeworks, Makapansgat. *American Journal of Physical Anthropology* 13, 621–624.

Bonnefille, R. (1968). Contribution à l'étude de la flore d'un niveau pléistocène de la haute vallée de l'Aouache (Ethiopie). *Comptes Rendu de l'Académie des Sciences Paris* 266, 1229–1232.

Bonnefille, R. (1969). Indication sur la paléoflore d'un niveau du Quaternaire moyen du site de Melka Kontouré (Ethiopie). *Comptes rendu sommaire des Séances de la Société géologique de France* 7, 238–239.

Bonnefille, R. (1971). Atlas des pollens d'Ethiopie. Principales espèces des forêts de montagne. *Pollens et spores* 13, 15–72.

Bonnefille, R. (1972). Associations polliniques actuelles et quaternaires en Ethiopie (Vallées de l'Awash et de l'Omo). Thèse de Doctorat ès Sciences, Université Paris VI, France.

Bonnefille, R. (1983). Evidence for a cooler and drier climate in the Ethiopian uplands towards 2.5 Myr ago. *Nature* 303, 487–491.

Bonnefille, R. (1984a). Palynological research at Olduvai Gorge. *National Geographic Society Research Papers* 17, 227–243.

Bonnefille, R. (1984b). Cenozoic vegetation and environments of early hominids in East Africa. In: R.O. White (Ed.), *The Evolution of the East Asian Environment*. Hong Kong: University of Hong Kong, pp.579–612.

Bonnefille, R. (2010). Cenozoic vegetation, climate changes and hominid evolution in tropical Africa. *Global and Planetary Change* 72, 390–411.

Bonnefille, R. and Dechamps, R. (1983). Data on fossil flora. In: J. de Heinzelin (Ed.), *The Omo Group*. Tervuren: Musée Royale de l'Afrique Central, pp. 191–207.

Bonnefille, R. and Letouzey, R. (1976). Fruits fossiles d'*Antrocaryon* dans la vallée de l'Omo (Éthiopie). *Adansonia, Ser. 2*, 16, 65–82.

Bonnefille, R. and Riollet, G. (1980). Palynologie, vegetation et climats de Bed I et Bed II à Olduvai, Tanzanie. In: R.E. Leakey and B.A. Ogot (Eds.), *Proceedings of the Eighth Pan-African Congress of Prehistory and Quaternary Studies*. Nairobi: The International Louis Leakey Memorial Institute for African Prehistory, pp. 123–127.

Bonnefille, R. and Riollet, G. (1987). Palynological spectra from the Upper Laetolil Beds. In: M.D. Leakey and J.M. Harris (Eds.), *Laetoli: A Pliocene Site in Northern Tanzania*. Oxford: Clarendon Press, pp. 23–47.

Volume References

Bonnefille, R., Vincens, A. and Buchet, G. (1987). Palynology, stratigraphy, and paleoenvironments of a Pliocene hominid site (2.9–3.3 M.Y.) at Hadar, Ethiopia. *Palaeogeography, Palaeoclimatology, Palaeoecology* 60, 249–281.

Bonnefille, R., Potts, R., Chalié, F., Jolly, D. and Peyron, O. (2004). High-resolution vegetation and climate change associated with Pliocene *Australopithecus afarensis*. *Proceedings of the National Academy of Sciences*, 101, 12125–12129.

Bonnefille, R., Melis, R.T. and Mussi, M. (2018). Variability in the mountain environment at Melka Kunture archaeological site, Ethiopia, during the Early Pleistocene (~1.7 Ma) and the Middle Pleistocene transition (0.9–0.6 Ma). In: R. Gallotti and M. Mussi (Eds.), *The Emergence of the Acheulean in East Africa and Beyond: Contributions in Honor of Jean Chavaillon*. Cham: Springer International Publishing, pp. 93–114.

Boshoff, A.F. and Kerley, G.I.H. (2001). Potential distributions of the medium- to large sized mammals in the Cape Floristic Region, based on historical accounts and habitat requirements. *African Zoology* 36, 245e273.

Boshoff, A., Landman, M. and Kerley, G. (2016). Filling the gaps on the maps: historical distribution patterns of some larger mammals in part of southern Africa. *Transactions of the Royal Society of South Africa* 71, 23–87.

Boswell, P.G.H. (1935). Human remains from Kanam and Kanjera, Kenya Colony. *Nature* 135, 371–371.

Bougariane, B., Zouhri, S., Ouchaou, B., Oujaa, A. and Boudad, L. (2010). Large mammals from the Upper Pleistocene at Tamaris I 'Grotte des gazelles' (Casablanca, Morocco): paleoecological and biochronological implications. *Historical Biology* 22, 295–302.

Boulton, S.J., Van De Velde, J.H., and Grimes, S.T. (2019). Palaeoenvironmental and tectonic significance ofMiocene lacustrine and palustrine carbonates (Aït Kandoula Formation) in the Ouarzazate Foreland Basin, Morocco. *Sedimentary Geology* 383, 195–215.

Bowen, B.E. and Von dra, C.F. (1973). Stratigraphical relationships of the Plio-Pleistocene deposits, East Rudolf, Kenya. *Nature* 242, 391–393.

Brachert, T.C., Brügmann, G.B., Mertz, D.F., et al. (2010). Stable isotope variation in tooth enamel from Neogene hippopotamids: monitor of meso and global climate and rift dynamics on the Albertine Rift, Uganda. *International Journal of Earth Sciences* 99, 1663–1675.

Bradley, B.J. (2008). Reconstructing phylogenies and phenotypes: a molecular view of human evolution. *Journal of Anatomy* 212(4), 337–353.

Braga, J. and Thackeray, J.F. (2003). Early *Homo* at Kromdraai B: probabilistic and morphological analysis of the lower dentition. *Comptes Rendu Palevol* 2, 269–279.

Braga, J. and Thackeray, J.F. (2016). *Kromdraai, a Birthplace of Paranthropus in the Cradle of Humankind*. Stellenbosch: African Sun Media Metro, 113 pp.

Braga, J., Thackeray, J.F., Dumoncel, J., et al. (2013). A new partial temporal bone of a juvenile hominin from the site of Kromdraai B (South Africa). *Journal of Human Evolution* 65, 447–456.

Braga, J., Thackeray, J.F., Bruxelles, L., Dumoncel, J. and Fourvel, J.-B. (2017). Stretching the time span of hominin evolution at Kromdraai (Gauteng, South Africa): recent discoveries. *Comptes Rendu Palevol* 16(1), 58–70.

Brain, C.K. (1958). *The Transvaal Ape-man-bearing Cave Deposits*. Transvaal Museum Memoir No. 11. Pretoria: Transvaal Museum.

Brain, C.K. (1967). Hottentot food remains and their bearing on the interpretation of fossil bone assemblages. *Scientific Papers of theNamib Desert Research Station* 32, 1–11.

Brain, C.K. (1969a). The contribution of Namib Desert Hottentots to an understanding of australopithecine bone accumulations. *Scientific Papers of the Namib Desert Research Station* 39, 13–22.

Brain, C.K. (1969b). Faunal remains from the Bushman Rock Shelter, Eastern Transvaal. *South African Archaeological Bulletin* 24, 52–55.

Brain, C.K. (1970). New finds at the Swartkrans australopithecine site. *Nature* 225, 1112–1119.

Brain, C.K. (1972). An attempt to reconstruct the behaviour of australopithecines: the evidence for interpersonal violence. *Zoologica Africana* 7, 379–401.

Brain, C.K. (1974). Some suggested procedures in the analysis of bone accumulations from southern African Quaternary sites. *Annals of the Transvaal Museum* 29, 1–8.

Brain, C.K. (1975a). An introduction to the South African australopithecine bone accumulations. In: A.T. Clason (Ed.), *Archaeological Studies*. Amsterdam: North Holland, pp. 109–119.

Brain, C.K. (1975b). An interpretation of the bone assemblage from the Kromdraai australopithecine site, South Africa. In: R.H. Tuttle (Ed.), *Palaeontology, Morphology and Palaeoecology*. The Hague: Mouton, pp. 225–243.

Brain, C.K. (1976). A re-interpretation of the Swartkrans site and its remains. *South African Journal of Science* 72, 141–146.

Brain, C.K. (1978). Some aspects of the South African australopithecine sites and their bone accumulations. In: C. Jolly (Ed.), *African Hominidae of the Plio-Pleistocene*. London: Duckworth, pp. 131–161.

Brain, C.K. (1980). Some criteria for the recognition of bone-collecting agencies in African caves. In:A.K. Behrensmeyer and A.P. Hill (Eds.), *Fossils in the Making*. Chicago: University of Chicago Press, pp. 107–130.

Brain, C.K. (1981). *The Hunters or the Hunted? An Introduction to African Cave Taphonomy*. Chicago: The University of Chicago Press.

Brain, C.K. (1993a). Structure and stratigraphy of the Swartkrans Cave in the light of the new excavations. In: C.K. Brain (Ed.), *Swartkrans: A Cave's Chronicle of Early Man*. Transvaal Museum Monograph No. 8. Pretoria: Transvaal Museum, pp.7–22.

Brain, C.K. (1993b). A taphonomic overview of the Swartkrans fossil assemblages. In: C.K. Brain (Ed.), *Swartkrans: A Cave's Chronicle of Early Man*. Transvaal Museum Monograph No. 8. Pretoria: Transvaal Museum, pp.257–264.

Brain, C.K. (1993c). The occurrence of burnt bones at Swartkrans and their implications for the control of fire by early hominids. In: C.K. Brain (Ed.), *Swartkrans: A Cave's Chronicle of Early Man*. Transvaal Museum Monograph No. 8. Pretoria: Transvaal Museum, pp.229–242.

Brain, C.K. (1994). *Swartkrans: A Cave's Chronicle of Early Man*. Transvaal Museum Monograph. Pretoria: Transvaal Museum.

Brain, C.K. and Shipman, P. (1993). The Swartkrans bone tools. In: C.K. Brain (Ed.), *Swartkrans: A Cave's Chronicle of Early Man*. Transvaal Museum Monograph No. 8. Pretoria: Transvaal Museum, pp.195–215.

Brain, C.K. and Sillen, A. (1988). Evidence from the Swartkrans cave for the earliest use of fire. *Nature* 336, 464–466.

Brain, C.K., Lowe, C.V.R. and Dart, R.A. (1955). Kafuan stone artefacts in the post-australopithecine breccia at Makapansgat. *Nature* 175(4444), 16–18.

Brain, C.K., Churcher, R.S., Clark, J.D., et al. (1988). New evidence of early hominids, their culture and environment from the Swartkrans Cave, South Africa. *South African Journal of Science* 84, 828–835.

Bramble, D.M. and Lieberman, D.E. (2004). Endurance running and the evolution of *Homo*. *Nature* 432(7015), 345–352.

Brandy, L.-D., Sabatier, M. and Jaeger, J.-J. (1980). Implications phylogénétiques et biogéographiques des dernières découvertes de Muridae en Afghanistan, au Pakistan et en Ethiopie. *Geobios* 13, 639–643.

Brantingham, P.J. (2003). A neutral model of stone raw material procurement. *American Antiquity* 68(3), 487–509.

Braun, D.R. (2006). The ecology of Oldowan technology: perspectives from Koobi Fora and Kanjera South. Doctoral dissertation, Rutgers University.

Braun, D. and Harris, J.W.K. (2009). Plio-Pleistocene technological variation: a view from the KBS Mb., Koobi Fora Formation. In: K. Schick and N. Toth (Eds.), *The Cutting Edge: New Approaches to the Archaeology of Human Origins*. Gosport, IN: The Stone Age Institute, pp. 17–31.

Braun, D., Plummer, T.W., Ditchfield, P., et al. (2008). Oldowan behavior and raw material transport: perspectives from the Kanjera Formation. *Journal of Archaeological Science* 35, 2329–2345.

Braun, D.R., Plummer, T., Ferraro, J.V., Ditchfield, P. and Bishop, L.C. (2009). Raw material quality and Oldowan hominin toolstone preferences: evidence from Kanjera South, Kenya. *Journal of Archaeological Science* 36, 1605–1614.

Braun, D.R., Harris, J.W.K., Levin, N.E., et al. (2010). Early hominin diet included diverse terrestrial and aquatic animals 1.95 Ma in East Turkana, Kenya. *Proceedings of the National Academy of Sciences*, 107(22), 10002–10007.

Braun, D.R., Levin, N.E., Stynder, D., et al. (2013). Mid-Pleistocene Hominin occupation at Elandsfontein, Western Cape, South Africa. *Quaternary Science Reviews* 82, 145–166.

Braun, K., Bar-Matthews, M., Matthews, A., et al. (2019a). Late Pleistocene records of speleothem stable isotopic compositions from Pinnacle Point on the South African south coast. *Quaternary Research*, 91, 265–288.

Braun, D.R., Aldeias, V., Archer, W., et al. (2019b). Earliest known Oldowan artifacts at >2.58 Ma from Ledi-Geraru, Ethiopia, highlight early technological diversity. *Proceedings of the National Academy of Sciences* 116, 11712.

Brickhill, J.A.J. (1976). Some fossil felids from Makapansgat Limeworks. Unpublished BSc dissertation, University of the Witwatersrand.

Brink, J.S. (1987). The archaeozoology of Florisbad, Orange Free State. *Memoirs of the National Museum, Bloemfontein* 24, 1–151.

Brink J.S. (1988). The taphonomy and palaeoecology of the Florisbad spring fauna. *Palaeoecology of Africa* 19, 169–179.

Brink, J.S. (1994). An ass, *Equus* (*Asinus*) sp., from the late Quaternary mammalian assemblages of Florisbad and Vlakkraal, central southern Africa. *South African Journal of Science* 90, 497–500.

Brink, J.S. (1999). Preliminary report on a caprine from the Cape mountains, South Africa. *Archaeozoologia* 10, 11–26.

Brink, J.S. (2004). The taphonomy of an early/middle Pleistocene hyaena burrow at Cornelia-Uitzoek, South Africa. *Revue de Palaéobiologie*, 23, 731–740.

Brink, J.S. (2005). The evolution of the black wildebeest, *Connochaetes gnou*, and modern large mammal faunas in central South Africa. PhD thesis, University of Stellenbosch, South Africa.

Brink, J.S. (2016). Faunal evidence for mid- and late Quaternary environmental change in southern Africa. In: J. Knight and S.W. Grab (Eds.), *Quaternary Environmental Change in Southern Africa: Physical and Human Dimensions*. Cambridge: Cambridge University Press.

Brink, J.S. and Deacon, H.J. (1982). A study of a Last Interglacial shell midden and bone accumulation at Herolds Bay, Cape Province, South Africa. *Palaeoecology of Africa* 15, 31–39.

Brink, J.S. and Lee-Thorp, J.A. (1992). The feeding niche of an extinct springbok, *Antidorcas bondi* (Antelopini, Bovidae), and its paleoenvironmental meaning. *South African Journal of Science* 88, 227–229.

Brink, J.S. and Rossouw, L. (2000). New trial excavations at the Cornelia-Uitzoek type locality. *Navorsinge van die Nasionale Museum* 16, 141–156.

Brink, J.S., Herries, A.I.R., Moggi-Cecchi, J., et al. (2012). First hominine remains from a ~1.0 million year old bone bed at Cornelia-Uitzoek, Free State Province, South Africa. *Journal of Human Evolution* 63, 527–535.

Brink, J.S., de Beer, F.C., Hoffman, J. and Bam, L. (2013). The evolutionary meaning of *Raphicerus*-like morphology in the dentitions and postcrania of *Antidorcas bondi* (Antilopini). *Zitteliana* 31, 21.

Brink, J.S., Bousman C.B. and Grün R. (2015a). A reconstruction of the skull of *Megalotragus priscus* (Broom, 1909), based on a find from Erfkroon, Modder River, South Africa, with notes on the chronology and biogeography of the species. *Palaeoecology of Africa* 33, 71–94.

Brink, J., Holt, S. and Horwitz, L.K. (2015b). Preliminary findings on macro-faunal taxonomy, taphonomy, biochronology and palaeoecology from the basal layers of Wonderwerk Cave, South Africa. In: I. Thiaw and H. Bocoum (Eds.), *Preserving African Cultural Heritage. (Proceedings of the 13th Congress of the Panafrican Archaeological Association for Prehistory and Related Studies – PAA and of the 20th Meeting of the Society of Africanist Archaeologists – Safa)*. Dakar: Memoires de IIFAN – C. A. DIOP, no. 93, pp. 137–147.

Brink, J.S., Holt, S. and Horwitz, L.K. (2016). The Oldowan and early Acheulean mammalian fauna of Wonderwerk Cave (Northern Cape Province, South Africa). *African Archaeological Review* 33, 223–250.

Broadley, D.G. (1962). Some fossil chelonian fragments from Makapansgat. *Nature* 194(4830), 791.

Broadley, D.G. (1997). A new species of *Psammobates* (Reptilia: Testudinidae) from the early Pleistocene of South Africa. *Palaeontologica Africana* 34, 111–114.

Broccoli, A.J., Dahl, K.A. and Stouffer, R.J. (2006). Response of the ITCZ to Northern Hemisphere cooling. *Geophysical Research Letters* 33(1).

Brochu, C.A. (2020). Pliocene crocodiles from Kanapoi, Turkana Basin, Kenya. *Journal of Human Evolution* 140, 102410.

Brochu, C.A. and Storrs, G.W. (2012). A giant crocodile from the Plio-Pleistocene of Kenya, the phylogenetic relationships of Neogene African crocodylines, and the antiquity of *Crocodylus* in Africa. *Journal of Vertebrate Paleontology* 32, 587–602.

Brochu, C.A., Njau, J., Blumenschine, R.J. and Densmore, Ll.D. (2010). New horned crocodile from the Plio-Pleistocene hominid sites at Olduvai Gorge, Tanzania. *PLoS ONE* 5(2), e9333. doi:10.1371/journal.pone.0009333

Brock, A., McFadden, P.L. and Partridge, T.C. (1977). Preliminary palaeomagnetic results from Makapansgat and Swartkrans. *Nature* 266(5599), 249–250.

Brocklehurst, N., Upchurch, P., Mannion, P.D. and O'Connor, J. (2012). The completeness of the fossil record of Mesozoic birds: implications for early avian evolution. *PLoS ONE* 7(6), e30956.

Bromage, T.G. and Schrenk, F. (1987). A cercopithecoid tooth from the Pliocene in Malawi. *Journal of Human Evolution* 16, 497–500.

Bromage, T.G., Schrenk, F. and Kaufulu, Z. (1985). Plio-Pleistocene deposits in Malawi's hominid corridor. *National Geographic Society Research Report* 21, 51–52.

Bromage, T.G., Schrenk, F. and Juwayeyi, Y.M. (1995). Paleobiogeography of the Malawi Rift: age and vertebrate paleontology of the Chiwondo Beds, northern Malawi. *Journal of Human Evolution* 28, 37–57.

Brooks, A.C. (1961). *A study of the Thomson's gazelle (Gazella thomsonii Gunther) in Tanganyika*. London: Colonial Research Publications (25).

Brooks, A.S. and Yellen, J.E. (1987). The preservation of activity areas in the archaeological record: ethnoarchaeological and archaeological work in northwest Ngamiland, Botswana. In: S. Kent (Ed.), *Method and Theory of Activity Area Research: An Ethnoarchaeologial Approach*. New York: Columbia University Press, pp. 63–106.

Brooks, A.S., Nevell, L., Yellen, J.E. and Hartman, G. (2006). Projectile technologies of the African MSA. In: E. Hovers and S.L. Kuhn (Eds.), *Transitions Before the Transition: Evolution and Stability in the Middle Paleolithic and Middle Stone Age*. New York: Springer, pp. 233–256.

Brooks, A.S., Yellen, J.E., Potts, R., et al. (2018). Long-distance stone transport and pigment use in the earliest Middle Stone Age. *Science* 360, 90–94.

Brooks, T., Balmford, A., Burgess, N., et al. (2001). Toward a blueprint for conservation in Africa. *Bioscience* 51, 613–624.

Broom, R. (1913). Man contemporaenous with extinct animals in South Africa. *Annals of the South African Museum* XII, 13–16.

Broom, R. (1925a). Some notes on the Taungs skull. *Nature* 115, 569.

Broom, R. (1925b). On the newly discovered South African man-ape. *Natural History* 25, 409–418.

Broom, R. (1929). Note on the milk dentition of Australopithecus. *Proceedings of the Zoological Society of London* 99, 85–88.

Broom, R. (1930). The age of *Australopithecus*. *Nature* 125, 814.

Broom, R. (1934). On the fossil remains associated with *Australopithecus africanus*. *South African Journal of Science* 31, 471–480.

Broom, R. (1936). New fossil anthropoid skull from South Africa. *Nature* 138, 486–488.

Broom, R. (1937). Notices of a few more new fossil mammals from the caves of the Transvaal. *Annals of the Transvaal Museum* 20(10), 509–514.

Broom, R. (1938a). The Pleistocene anthropoid apes of South Africa. *Nature* 142, 377–379.

Broom, R. (1938b). Further evidence on the structure of the South African Pleistocene anthropoids. *Nature* 142(3603), 897–899.

Broom, R. (1939). The fossil rodents of the limestone cave at Taungs. *Annals of the Transvaal Museum* 19, 315–317.

Broom, R. (1941). Mandible of a young *Paranthropus* child. *Nature* 147, 607–608.

Broom, R. (1942). The hand of the ape-man, *Paranthropus robustus*. *Nature* 149, 513–514.

Broom, R. (1943). An ankle-bone of the Ape-man, *Paranthropus robustus*. *Nature* 152, 689–690.

Broom, R. (1943). South Africa's part in the solution of the problem of the origin of man. *South African Journal of Science* 40, 68–80.

Broom, R. (1945). Age of the South African ape-man. *Nature* 155, 389–390.

Broom, R. (1946). The occurrence and general structure of the South African ape-men. *Transvaal Museum Memoirs* 2, 7–153.

Broom, R. (1948a). Some South African Pliocene and Pleistocene mammals. *Annals of the Transvaal Museum* 21, 1–38.

Broom, R. (1948b). The giant rodent mole, *Gypsorhychus*. *Annals of the Transvaal Museum* 21, 47–49.

Broom, R. (1949). Jaw of the ape-man *Paranthropus crassidens*. *Nature* 163, 903.

Broom, R. (1950). The genera and species of the South African fossil ape-men. *American Journal of Physical Anthropology* 8(1), 1–14.

Broom, R. and Robinson, J.T. (1949). A new type of fossil man. *Nature* 164(4164), 322–323.

Broom, R. and Robinson, J.T. (1952). Swartkrans Ape-Man, '*Paranthropus crassidens*'. *Transvaal Museum Memoire* 2, Pretoria.

Broom, R. and Schepers, G.W.H. (1946). The South African Fossil Ape-Men: The Australopithecinae. Transvaal Museum Memoir No. 2. Pretoria: Transvaal Museum,

Broom, R., Robinson, J.T. and Schepers, G.W.H. (1950). *Sterkfontein Ape-Man Plesianthropus (Transvaalensis)*. Transvaal Museum Memoir No. 4. Pretoria: Transvaal Museum.

Brophy, J.K. (2011). Reconstructing the habitat mosaic associated with *Australopithecus robustus*: evidence from quantitative morphological analysis of bovid teeth. Doctoral dissertation, Texas A&M University.

Brophy, J.K., de Ruiter, D.J., Athreya, S. and DeWitt, T.J. (2014). Quantitative morphological analysis of bovid teeth and implications for paleoenvironmental reconstruction of Plovers Lake, Gauteng Province, South Africa. *Journal of Archaeological Science* 41, 376–388.

Brown, A. and Verhagen, B. (1985). Two *Antidorcas bondi* individuals from the Late Stone Age site of Kruger Cave 35/83, Olifantshoek, Rustenburg District, South Africa. *South African Journal of Science* 81, 102.

Brown, B., Brown, F.H. and Walker, A. (2001). New hominids from the Lake Turkana Basin, Kenya. *Journal of Human Evolution* 41, 29–44.

Brown, F.H. (1969). Observations of the stratigraphy and radiometric age of the 'Omo Beds', lower Omo basin, southern Ethiopia. *Quaternaria* 11, 7–14.

Brown, F.H. (1982). Tulu Bor Tuff at Koobi Fora correlated with the Sidi Hakoma Tuff at Hadar. *Nature* 300, 631–633.

Brown, F.H. (1995). The potential of the Turkana Basin for paleoclimatic reconstruction in east Africa. In: E.S. Vrba, G.H. Denton, T.C. Partridge and L.H. Burkle (Ed.), *Paleoclimate and Evolution with Emphasis on Human Origins*. New Haven: Yale University Press, pp. 319–330.

Brown, F.H. and Cerling, T.E. (1982). The stratigraphic significance of the Tulu Bor Tuff of the Koobi Fora Formation. *Nature* 299, 212–215.

Brown, F.H. and de Heinzelin, J. (1983). The lower Omo Basin. In: J. de Heinzelin (Ed.), *The Omo Group*. Tervuren: Musee Royale de l'Afrique Centrale, pp. 7–24.

Brown, F.H. and Feibel, C.S. (1986). Revision of lithostratigraphic nomenclature in the Koobi Fora region, Kenya. *Journal of the Geological Society of London* 143, 297–310.

Brown, F.H. and Feibel, C.S. (1991). Stratigraphy, depositional environments and palaeogeography of the Koobi Fora Formation. In: J.M. Harris (Ed.), *Koobi Fora Research Project, Volume 3: The Fossil Ungulates: Geology, Fossil Artiodactyls, and Paleoenvironments*. Oxford: Clarendon Press, pp. 1–30.

Brown, F.H. and Fuller, C.R. (2008). Stratigraphy and tephra of the Kibish Formation, southwestern Ethiopia. *Journal of Human Evolution* 55, 366–403.

Brown, F.H. and McDougall, I. (2011). Geochronology of the Turkana Depression of Northern Kenya and Southern Ethiopia. *Evolutionary Anthropology* 20, 217–227.

Brown, F.H. and Nash, W.P. (1976). Radiometric dating and tuff mineralogy of Omo Group deposits. In: Y. Coppens, F.C. Howell, G.L.I. Isaac and R.E.F. Leakey (Eds.), *Earliest Man and Environments in the Lake Rudolf Basin*. Chicago: University of Chicago Press, pp. 50–63.

Brown, F.H., de Heinzelin, J. and Howell, F.C. (1970). Plio/Pleistocene formations in the lower Omo Basin, southern Ethiopia. *Quaternaria* 8, 247–268.

Brown, F.H., Shuey, R.T. and Croes, M.K. (1978). Magnetostratigraphy of the Shungura and Usno Formations, southwestern Ethiopia: new data and comprehensive reanalysis. *Geophysical Journal International* 54(3), 519–538.

Brown, F.H., McDougall, I., Davies, T. and Maier, R. (1985). An integrated Plio-Pleistocene chronology for the Turkana Basin. In: E. Delson (Ed.), *Ancestors: The Hard Evidence*. New York: Alan R. Liss, pp. 82–90.

Brown, F.H., Haileab, B. and McDougall, I. (2006). Sequence of tuffs between the KBS Tuff and the Chari Tuff in the Turkana Basin, Kenya and Ethiopia. *Journal of the Geological Society of London* 163, 185–204.

Brown, K.S., Marean, C.W., Herries, A.I.R., et al. (2009). Fire as an engineering tool of early modern humans. *Science* 325, 859–862.

Bruch, A.A., Sievers, C. and Wadley, L. (2012). Quantification of climate and vegetation from southern African Middle Stone Age sites – an application using Late Pleistocene plant material from Sibudu, South Africa. *Quaternary Science Reviews*, 45, 7–17.

Brugal, J.P. (Ed.) (2017). Classes de taille chez les grands mammifères. In: *Taphonomies*. Paris: Edition des Archives Contemporaines, Coll. Sciences Archéologiques, pp. 472–476.

Brugal, J.-P. and Denys, C. (1989). Vertébrés du site acheuléen d'Isenya (Kenya, district de Kajiado). Implications paléoécologiques et paléobiogéographiques. *Comptes Rendu de l'Académie des Sciences Paris* 308, 1503–1508.

Brugal, J.P., Roche, H. and Kibunjia, M. (2003). Faunes et paléoenvironnements des principaux sites archéologiques plio-pléistocènes de la formation de Nachukui (Ouest-Turkana, Kenya). *Comptes Rendus Palevol* 2(8), 675–684.

Bruhn, R.L., Brown, F.H., Gathogo, P.N. and Haileab, B. (2011). Pliocene volcano-tectonics and paleogeography of the Turkana Basin, Kenya and Ethiopia. *Journal of African Earth Sciences* 59, 295–312.

Brumfitt, I.M., Chinsamy, A. and Compton, J.S. (2013). Depositional environment and bone diagenesis of the Mio/Pliocene Langebaanweg bonebed, South Africa. *South African Journal of Geology* 116(2), 241–258.

Brun, A., Guerin, C., Levy, A., Riser, J. and Rognon, P. (1988). Steppic environments at the end of the Upper Pleistocene in southern Tunisia (Oued el Akarit). *Journal of African Earth Sciences* 7, 969–980.

Bruner, E., Bondioli, L., Coppa, A., et al. (2011a). A preliminary paleoneurological survey of the endocast from Buia (UA-31). *PaleoAnthropology Journal* 2011, 5 (abstract).

Bruner, E., de la Cuétara, J.M. and Holloway, R.L. (2011b). A bivariate approach to the variation of the parietal curvature in the genus *Homo*. *Anatomic Record* 294, 1548–1556.

Bruner, E., Bondioli, L., Coppa, A., et al. (2016). The endocast of the one-million-year-old human cranium from Buia (UA 31), Danakil Eritrea. *American Journal of Physical Anthropology* 160, 458–468.

Brunet, M. (2010). Two new Mio-Pliocene Chadian hominids enlighten Charles Darwin's 1871 prediction. *Philosophical Transactions of the Royal Society B: Biological Sciences* 365(1556), 3315–3321.

Brunet, M. and White, T.D. (2001). Deux nouvelles espèces de Suini (Mammalia, Suidae) du continent Africain (Ethiopie; Tchad). *Comptes Rendus de l'Academie des Sciences, Paris* 332, 51–57.

Brunet, M., Beauvilain, A., Coppens, Y., et al. (1995). The first australopithecine 2,500 kilometres west of the Rift Valley (Chad). *Nature* 378(6554), 273–275.

Brunet, M., Beauvilain, A., Coppens, Y., et al. (1996). *Australopithecus bahrelghazali*, une nouvelle espèce d'Hominidé ancien de la région de Koro Toro (Tchad). *Comptes Rendus de l'Académie des Sciences* 322, 907–913.

Brunet, M., Beauvilain, A., Geraads, D., et al. (1998). Tchad: découverte d'une faune de mammifères du Pliocène inférieur. *Comptes Rendus de l'Académie des Sciences – Series IIA – Earth and Planetary Science* 326, 153–158.

Brunet, M., Beauvilain, A., Billiou, D., et al. (2000). Chad: discovery of a vertebrate fauna close to the Mio-Pliocene boundary. *Journal of Vertebrate Paleontology* 20, 205–209.

Brunet, M., Guy, F., Pilbeam, D., et al. (2002). A new hominid from the Upper Miocene of Chad, Central Africa. *Nature* 418(6894), 145–151.

Brunet, M., Guy, F., Pilbeam, D., et al. (2005). New material of the earliest hominid from the Upper Miocene of Chad. *Nature* 434, 752–755.

Bruxelles, L., Clarke, R.J., Maire, R., Ortega, R. and Stratford, D. (2014). Stratigraphic analysis of the Sterkfontein StW 573 *Australopithecus* skeleton and implications for its age. *Journal of Human Evolution* 70, 36–48.

Bryant, J.D. and Froelich, P.N. (1995). A model of oxygen isotope fractionation in body water of large mammals. *Geochimica et Cosmochimica Acta* 59(21), 4523–4537.

Bulpin, T.V. (1980). *Discovering South Africa* (2nd ed.). Cape Town: T.V. Bulpin Publications (Pty) Ltd.

Bunn, H.T. (1981). Archaeological evidence for meat-eating by Plio-Pleistocene hominids from Koobi Fora and Olduvai Gorge. *Nature* 291, 574–577.

Bunn, H. (1982). Meat-eating and human evolution: studies on the diet and subsistence patterns of Plio-Pleistocene hominids in East Africa. Doctoral Dissertation, University of California, Berkeley.

Bunn, H.T. (1997). The bone assemblages from the excavated sites. In: G.L. Isaac (Ed.), *Koobi Fora Research Project Volume 5: Plio-Pleistocene Archaeology*. Oxford: Clarendon Press, pp. 402–458.

Bunn, H.T. (2007). Meat made us human. In: P.S. Ungar (Ed.), *Evolution of the Human Diet*. New York: Oxford University Press, pp. 191–211.

Bunn, H.T. and Kroll, E.M. (1986). Systematic butchery by Plio/Pleistocene hominids at Olduvai Gorge, Tanzania. *Current Anthropology* 27, 431–451.

Bunn, H.T. and Kroll, E.M. (1988). Fact and fiction about the *Zinjanthropus* floor: data, arguments, and interpretations. *Current Anthropology* 29, 135–149.

Bunn, H.T. and Pickering, T.R. (2010). Bovid mortality profiles in paleoecological context falsify hypotheses of endurance running–hunting and passive scavenging by early Pleistocene hominins. *Quaternary Research* 74(3), 395–404.

Bush, A.M., Powell, M.G., Arnold, W.S., Bert, T.M. and Daley, G.M. (2002). Time-averaging, evolution, and morphologic variation. *Paleobiology* 28(1), 9–25.

Bush, A.M., Markey, M.J. and Marshall, C.R. (2004). Removing bias from diversity curves: the effects of spatially organized biodiversity on sampling-standardization. *Paleobiology* 30(4), 666–686.

Butler, P. (1952). The milk molars of Perissodactyla, with remarks on molar occlusion. *Proceedings of the Zoological Society of London* 121, 777–817.

Butler, P.M. and Greenwood, M. (1976). Elephant-shrews (Macroscelididae) from Olduvai and Makapansgat. In: R.J.G. Savage and S.C. Coryndon (Eds.), *Fossil Vertebrates of Africa*. London: Academic Press, pp. 1–55.

Butler, R.J., Benson, R.B.J., Carrano, M.T., Mannion, P.D. and Upchurch, P. (2011). Sea level, dinosaur diversity and sampling biases: investigating the 'common cause' hypothesis in the terrestrial realm. *Proceedings of the Royal Society B: Biological Sciences* 278(1709), 1165–1170.

Butzer, K.W. (1971). Another look at the australopithecine cave breccias of the Transvaal 1. *American Anthropologist* 73(5), 1197–1201.

Volume References

Butzer, K.W. (1974). Geology of the Cornelia Beds. *Memoir – Nasionale Museum, Bloemfontein* 9, 7–32.

Butzer, K.W. (1976). The Mursi, Nkalabong, and Kibish formations, lower Omo Basin, Ethiopia. In: Y. Coppens, F.C. Howell, G.L. Isaac and R.E.F. Leakey (Eds.), *Earliest Man and Environments in the Lake Rudolf Basin*. Chicago: University of Chicago Press, pp. 24–49.

Butzer, K.W. (1980). Palaeoecology of the South African Australopithecines. In R. Leakey and B. Ogot (Eds.), *Proceedings of the Pan-African Congress of Prehistory and Quaternary Studies, Nairobi, 1977*. Nairobi, pp. 131–132.

Butzer, K.W. (1984a). Archaeology and Quaternary environment in the interior of southern Africa. In: R.G. Klein (Ed.), *Southern African Prehistory and Paleoenvironments*. Rotterdam: Balkema, pp. 1–64.

Butzer, K.W. (1984b). Late Quaternary environments in South Africa. In: J.C. Vogel (Ed.), *Late Cenozoic Palaeoclimates of the Southern Hemisphere*. Rotterdam: Balkema, pp. 235–264.

Butzer, K.W. and Thurber, D.L. (1969). Some late Cenozoic sedimentary formations of the Lower Omo Basin. *Nature* 222, 1138–1143.

Butzer, K.W., Beaumont, P.B. and Vogel, J.C. (1978a). Lithostratigraphy of Border cave, KwaZulu, south Africa: a middle stone age sequence beginning c. 195,000 BP. *Journal of Archaeological Science* 5(4), 317–341.

Butzer, K.W., Stuckenrath, R., Bruzewicz, A.J. and Helgren, D.M. (1978b). Late Cenozoic paleoclimates of the Gaap Escarpment, Kalahari margin, South Africa. *Quaternary Research* 10(3), 310–339.

Butzer, K.W., Stuckenrath, R. and Vogel, J.C. (1979, April). The geo-archaeological sequence of Wonderwerk Cave, South Africa. In: Society of Africanist Archaeologists Meeting Calgary Abstracts.

Cabanes, D., Shahack-Gross, R. (2015). Understanding fossil phytolith preservation: the role of partial dissolution in paleoecology and archaeology. *PLoS ONE* 10, e0125532.

Cabido, M., Pons, E., Cantero, J.J., Lewis, J.P. and Anton, A. (2008). Photosynthetic pathway variation among C_4 grasses along a precipitation gradient in Argentina. *Journal of Biogeography* 35, 131–140.

Cadman, A. and Rayner, R.J. (1989). Climatic change and the appearance of *Australopithecus africanus* in the Makapansgat sediments. *Journal of Human Evolution* 18(2), 107–113.

Calandra, I. and Merceron, G. (2016). Dental microwear texture analysis in mammalian ecology. *Mammal Review* 46(3), 215–228.

Caley, T., Extier, T., Collins, J.A., et al. (2018). A two-million-year-long hydroclimatic context for hominin evolution in southeastern Africa. *Nature*, 560(7716), 76–79.

Callaway, E. (2018). Femur findings remain a secret. *Nature* 553, 391–392.

Calow, P.P. (Ed.). (1999). *Blackwell's Concise Encyclopedia of Ecology*. Oxford: Blackwell.

Camp, C.L. (1948). University of California African expedition – southern section. *Science* 108, 550–552.

Campbell, T.L., Lewis, P.J. and Williams, J.K. (2011). Analysis of the modern distribution of South African *Gerbilliscus* (Rodentia: Gerbillinae) with implications for Plio-Pleistocene palaeoenvironmental reconstruction. *South African Journal of Science* 107(1/2), Art. #497.

Campbell, M.C. and Tishkoff, S.A. (2010). The evolution of human genetic and phenotypic variation in Africa. *Current Biology* 20, R166–R173.

Campisano, C.J. (2007). Tephrostratigraphy and hominin paleoenvironments of the Hadar Formation, Afar depression, Ethiopia. PhD dissertation, Rutgers University.

Campisano, C.J. (2012). Geological summary of the Busidima Formation (Plio-Pleistocene) at the Hadar paleoanthropological site, Afar Depression, Ethiopia. *Journal of Human Evolution* 62, 338–352.

Campisano, C.J. and Feibel, C.S. (2007). Connecting local environmental sequences to global climate patterns: evidence from the hominin-bearing Hadar Formation, Ethiopia. *Journal of Human Evolution* 53(5), 515–527.

Campisano, C.J. and Feibel, C.S. (2008). Depositional environments and stratigraphic summary of the Pliocene Hadar formation at Hadar, Afar depression, Ethiopia. In: J. Quade and J. Wynn (Eds.), *The Geology of Early Humans in the Horn of Africa*. Boulder: The Geological Society of America, pp.179–201.

Campisano, C.J. and Reed, K.E. (2007). Spatial and temporal patterns of *Australopithecus afarensis* habitats at Hadar, Ethiopia. *PaleoAnthropology PAS 2007 abstracts*, A6.

Campisano, C. J., Cohen, A. S., Arrowsmith, J. R., et al. (2017). The Hominin Sites and Paleolakes Drilling Project: high-resolution paleoclimate records from the East African Rift System and their implications for understanding the environmental context of hominin evolution. *Paleoanthropology* 1–43.

Cande, S.C. and Kent, D.V. (1995). Revised calibration of the geomagnetic polarity time scale for the Late Cretaceous and Cenozoic. *Journal of Geophysical Research* 100, 6093–6095.

Cane, M.A. and Molnar, P. (2001). Closing the Indonesian seaway as a precursor to east African aridification around 3–4 million years ago. *Nature* 411, 157–162.

Cannon, M.D. (2001). Archaeofaunal relative abundance, sample size, and statistical methods. *Journal of Archaeological Science* 28(2), 185–195.

Capaldo, S.D. (1997). Experimental determinations of carcass processing by Plio-Pleistocene hominids and carnivores at FLK 22 (*Zinjanthropus*), Olduvai Gorge, Tanzania. *Journal of Human Evolution* 33, 555–597.

Capaldo, S.D. and Peters, C.R. (1995). Skeletal inventories from wildebeest drownings at lakes Masek and Ndutu in the Serengeti ecosystem. *Journal of Archaeological Science* 22, 385–408.

Carney, J., Hill, A., Miller, J.A. and Walker, A. (1971). Late australopithecine from Baringo District, Kenya. *Nature* 230, 509–514.

Carrión, J.S. and Scott, L. (1999). The challenge of pollen analysis in palaeoenvironmental studies of hominid beds: the record from Sterkfontein caves. *Journal of Human Evolution* 36(4), 401–408.

Cartwright, C.R. (2013). Identifying the woody resources of Diepkloof Rock Shelter (South Africa) using scanning electron microscopy of the MSA wood charcoal assemblages. *Journal of Archaeological Science* 40(9), 3463–3474.

Cartwright, C. and Parkington, J. (1997). The wood charcoal assemblages from Elands Bay Cave, southwestern Cape: principles, procedures and preliminary interpretation. *The South African Archaeological Bulletin* 52, 59–72.

Caruana, M.V. (2017). Lithic production strategies in the Oldowan assemblages from Sterkfontein Member 5 and Swartkrans Member 1, Gauteng Province, South Africa. *Journal of African Archaeology* 15(1), 1–19.

Castañeda, I.S., Mulitza, S., Schefuß, E., et al. (2009). Wet phases in the Sahara/Sahel region and human migration patterns in North Africa. *Proceedings of the National Academy of Sciences of the USA* 106, 20159–20163.

Cerdeño, E. (1998). Diversity and evolutionary trends of the Family Rhinocerotidae (Perissodactyla). *Palaeogeography, Palaeoclimatology, Palaeoecology*, 141(1), 13–34.

Cerling, T.E. (1992). Development of grasslands and savannas in East Africa during the Neogene. *Palaeogeography, Palaeoclimatology, Palaeoecology (Global and Planetary Change Section)* 97, 241–247.

Cerling, T.E. (2003). Diets of east African bovidae based on stable isotope analysis. *Journal of Mammalogy* 84(2), 456–470.

Cerling, T.E. and Hay, R.L. (1986). An isotopic study of paleosol carbonates from Olduvai Gorge. *Quaternary Research* 25, 63–78.

Cerling, T.E. and Viehl, K. (2004). Seasonal diet changes of the forest hog (*Hylochoerus meinertzhageni* Thomas) based on the carbon isotopic composition of hair. *African Journal of Ecology* 42(2), 88–92.

Cerling, T.E., Bowman, J.R. and O'Neil, J.R. (1988). An isotopic study of a fluvial–lacustrine sequence: the Plio-Pleistocene Koobi For a Formation, East Africa. *Palaeogeography, Palaeoclimatology, Palaeoecology* 63, 335–356.

Cerling, T.E., Quade, J., Wang, Y. and Bowman, J.R. (1989). Carbon isotopes in soils and palaeosols as ecology and palaeoecology indicators. *Nature*, 341, 138–139.

Cerling, T.E., Wang, Y. and Quade, J. (1993). Expansion of C_4 ecosystems as an indicator of global ecological change in the Late Miocene. *Nature* 361, 344–345.

Cerling, T.E., Harris, J.M., MacFadden, B.J., et al. (1997). Global vegetation change through the Miocene–Pliocene boundary. *Nature* 389, 153–158.

Cerling, T.E., Harris, J.M. and Leakey, M.G. (1999). Browsing and grazing in elephants: the isotope record of modern and fossil proboscideans. *Oecologia* 120, 364–374.

Cerling, T.E., Harris, J.M., Leakey, M.G. and Mudida, N. (2003a). Stable isotope ecology of Northern Kenya, with emphasis on the Turkana Basin, Kenya. In: M.G. Leakey and J.M. Harris (Eds.), *Lothagam: the Dawn of Humanity in Africa*. New York: Columbia University Press, pp. 583–603.

Cerling, T., Harris, J. and Leakey, M. (2003b). Isotope paleoecology of the Nawata and Nachukui Formations at Lothagam, Turkana Basin, Kenya. In: M.G. Leakey and J.M. Harris (Eds.), *Lothagam: the Dawn of Humanity in Africa*. New York: Columbia University Press, pp. 605–624.

Cerling, T.E., Harris, J.M. and Passey, B. H. (2003c). Diets of east African bovidae based on stable isotope analysis. *Journal of Mammalogy* 84, 456–470.

Cerling, T., Harris, J.M. and Leakey, M. (2005). Environmentally driven dietary adaptations in African mammals. In: I.T. Baldwin, M.M. Caldwell, G. Heldmaier, et al. (Eds.), *A History of Atmospheric CO2; and Its Effects on Plants, Animals, and Ecosystems*. New York: Springer, Vol. 177, pp. 258–272.

Cerling, T.E., Levin, N.E., Quade, J., et al. (2010). Comment on the paleoenvironment of *Ardipithecus ramidus*. *Science* 328, 1105-d.

Cerling, T.E., Mbua, E., Kirera, F.M., et al. (2011a). Diet of *Paranthropus boisei* in the early Pleistocene of East Africa. *Proceedings of the National Academy of Sciences* 108, 9337–9341.

Cerling, T.E., Wynn, J.G., Andanje, S.A., et al. (2011b). Woody cover and hominin environments in the past 6 million years. *Nature* 476(7358), 51–56.

Cerling, T.E., Manthi, F.K., Mbua, E.N., et al. (2013a). Stable isotope-based diet reconstructions of Turkana Basin hominins. *Proceedings of the National Academy of Sciences* 110(26), 10501–10506.

Cerling, T.E., Chritz, K.L., Jablonski, N.G., Leakey, M.G. and Manthi, F.K. (2013b). Diet of *Theropithecus* from 4 to 1 Ma in Kenya. *Proceedings of the National Academy of Sciences of the United States of America* 110, 10507–10512.

Cerling, T.E., Brown, F.H. and Wynn, J.G. (2014). On the environment of Aramis. *Current Anthropology* 55, 469–470.

Cerling, T.E., Andanje, S.A., Blumenthal, S.A., et al. (2015a). Dietary changes of large herbivores in the Turkana Basin, Kenya from 4 to 1 Ma. *Proceedings of the National Academy of Sciences* 112, 11467–11472.

Cerling, T.E., Brown, F.H. and Wynn, J.G. (2015b). On the environment of Aramis: concerning comment and replies of August 2014. *Current Anthropology* 56, 445–446.

Chaïd-Saoudi, Y., Geraads, D. and Raynal, J.-P. (2006). The fauna and associated artefacts from the Lower Pleistocene site of Mansourah (Constantine, Algeria). *Comptes-Rendus Palevol* 5, 963–971.

Chao, A. and Jost, L. (2012). Coverage-based rarefaction and extrapolation: standardizing samples by completeness rather than size. *Ecology* 93(12), 2533–2547.

Chao, A., Gotelli, N.J., Hsieh, T.C., et al. (2014). Rarefaction and extrapolation with Hill numbers: a framework for sampling and estimation in species diversity studies. *Ecological Monographs* 84(1), 45–67.

Chapman, C.A., Gautier-Hion, A., Oates, J.F. and Onderdonk, P.A. (1999). African primate communities: determinants of structure and threats to survival. In: J.G. Fleagle, C.H. Janson and K.E. Reed (Eds.), *Primate Communities*. Cambridge: Cambridge University Press, pp. 1–37.

Chapman, G.R. (1971). The geological evolution of the Northern Kamasia Hills Baringo District, Kenya. PhD dissertation, University of London.

Chapman, G.R. and Brook, M. (1978). Chronostratigraphy of the Baringo Basin, Kenya. In: W.W. Bishop (Ed.), *Geological Background to Fossil Man*. Edinburgh: Scottish Academic Press, pp. 207–223.

Chapman, G.R., Lippard, S.J. and Martyn, J.E. (1978). The stratigraphy and structure of the Kamasia Range, Kenya Rift Valley. *Journal of the Geologicical Society of London* 135, 265–281.

Chapon, C., Bahain, J.-J., de Lumley, H., Perrenoud, C. and Van Damme, D. (2005). Stratigraphie, sédimentologie et magnétostratigraphie du site oldowayen de Fejej FJ-1, sud-Omo, Ethiopie: premiers résultats. *Quaternaire* 16, 143–152.

Chapon, C., Bahain, J.-J., Beyene, Y., et al. (2011). Geochemistry of the Fejej tuffs (South Omo, Ethiopia), their tephrostratigraphical correlation with Plio-Pleistocene formations in the Omo-Turkana Basin. *Comptes Rendus Palevol* 10, 251–258.

Charles-Dominique, T., Davies, T.J., Hempson, G.P., et al. (2016). Spiny plants, mammal browsers, and the origin of African savannas. *Proceedings of the National Academy of Sciences* 113(38), E5572–E5579.

Charteris, J., Wall, J.C. and Nottrodt, J.W. (1981). Functional reconstruction of gait from the Pliocene hominid footprints at Laetoli, northern Tanzania. *Nature* 290, 496–498.

Charteris, J., Wall, J.C. and Nottrodt, J.W. (1982). Pliocene hominid gait: new interpretations based on available footprint data from Laetoli. *American Journal of Physical Anthropology* 58, 133–144.

Chase, B.M. and Meadows, M.E. (2007). Late Quaternary dynamics of southern Africa's winter rainfall zone. *Earth Science Reviews* 84, 103–138.

Chavaillon, J. (1973). Chronologie des niveaux paléolithiques de Melka-Kunturé. *Comptes Rendu de l'Académie des Sciences (D)* 276, 1533–1536.

Chavaillon, J. (1976). Evidence for the technical practices of early pleistocene hominids, Shungura Formation, Lower Omo Valley, Ethiopia. In: Y. Coppens, F.C. Howell, G.L. Isaac and R.E.F. Leakey (Eds.), *Earliest Man and Environments in the Lake Rudolf Basin*. Chicago: University of Chicago Press, pp. 565–573.

Chavaillon, J. (1979). Stratigraphie du site archéologique de Melka-Kunturé (Ethiopie). *Bulletin de la Société géologique de France (sér. 7)* 21, 227–232.

Chavaillon, J. (1980). Chronologie archéologique de Melka-Kunturé (Ethiopie). In: R.E. Leakey and B.A. Ogot (Eds.), *Proceedings of the 8th Panafrican Congress of Prehistory and Quaternary Studies, 1977*. Nairobi: The International Louis Leakey Memorial Institute for African Prehistory, pp. 200–201.

Chavaillon, J. (1982). Les habitats paléolithiques de Melka-Kunturé. *Proceedings of the Xth IUSPP*, Mexico, 19–24 October 1981, pp. 149–168.

Volume References

Chavaillon, J. and Berthelet, A. (2004). The archaeological sites of Melka Kunture. In: J. Chavaillon and M. Piperno (Eds.), *Studies on the Early Paleolithic site of Melka Kunture, Ethiopia*. Florence: Istituto Italiano di Preistoria e Protostoria, pp. 25–80.

Chavaillon, J. and Chavaillon, N. (1971). Présence éventuelle d'un abri oldowayen dans le gisement de Melka-Kunturé (Ethiopie). *Comptes rendus de l'Académie des Sciences* 273, 623–625.

Chavaillon, J. and Coppens, Y. (1975). Découverte d'Hominidé dans un site acheuléen de Melka-Kunturé. *Bulletins et mémoires de la Société d'anthropologie Paris* 2, 125–128.

Chavaillon, J. and Coppens, Y. (1986). Nouvelle découverte d'*Homo erectus* à Melka-Kunturé. *Comptes Rendu de l'Académie des Sciences (II)* 1, 99–104.

Chavaillon, J. and Piperno, M. (2004a). History of excavations at Melka Kunture. In: J. Chavaillon and M. Piperno (Eds.), *Studies on the Early Paleolithic site of Melka Kunture, Ethiopia*. Florence: Istituto Italiano di Preistoria e Protostoria, pp. 3–23.

Chavaillon, J. and Piperno, M. (Eds.) (2004b). *Studies on the Early Paleolithic site of Melka Kunture, Ethiopia*. Florence: Istituto Italiano di Preistoria e Protostoria.

Chavaillon, J. and Taieb, M. (1968). Stratigraphie du Quaternaire de Melka-Kunturé, vallée de l'Awash, Ethiopie. Premiers résultats. *Comptes Rendu de l'Académie des Sciences (D)* 266, 1210–1212.

Chavaillon, J., Brahimi, C. and Coppens, Y. (1974). Première découverte d'Hominidé dans l'un des sites acheuléens de Melka-Kunturé (Ethiopie), *Comptes Rendu de l'Académie des Sciences (D)* 278, 3299–3302.

Chavaillon, J., Chavaillon, N., Coppens, Y. and Senut, B. (1977). Présence d'Hominidé dans le site oldowayen de Gomboré I à Melka-Kunturé. *Comptes Rendu de l'Académie des Sciences (D)* 285, 961–963.

Chavaillon, J., Chavaillon, N., Hours, F. and Piperno, M. (1979). From the Oldowan to the Middle Stone Age at Melka Kunture (Ethiopia). Understanding cultural changes. *Quaternaria* 21, 1–26.

Chavaillon, J., Hours, F. and Coppens, Y. (1987). Découverte de restes humains fossiles associés à un outillage acheuléen final à Melka-Kunturé (Ethiopie). *Comptes Rendu de l'Académie des Sciences II* 10, 539–542.

Chazan, M. (2015a). The Earlier Stone Age lithic assemblage from Wonderwerk Cave, Northern Cape Province, South Africa. In: I. Thiaw and H. Bocoum (Eds.), *Preserving African Cultural Heritage. Proceedings of the 13th Congress of the Panafrican Archaeological Association for Prehistory and Related Studies – PAA and of the 20th Meeting of the Society of Africanist Archaeologists – Safa*. Dakar: Memoires de IIFAN – C. A. DIOP, no. 93, pp. 247–252.

Chazan, M. (2015b). Technological trends in the Acheulean of Wonderwerk Cave, South Africa. *African Archaeological Review* 32, 701–728.

Chazan, M. and Horwitz, L.K. (2015). An overview of recent research at Wonderwerk Cave, South Africa. In: I. Thiaw and H. Bocoum (Eds.), *Preserving African Cultural Heritage. Proceedings of the 13th Congress of the Panafrican Archaeological Association for Prehistory and Related Studies – PAA and of the 20th Meeting of the Society of Africanist Archaeologists – Safa*. Dakar: Memoires de IIFAN – C. A. DIOP, no. 93, pp. 253–261.

Chazan, M., Ron, H., Matmon, A., et al. (2008). Radiometric dating of the Earlier Stone Age sequence in Excavation I at Wonderwerk Cave, South Africa: preliminary results. *Journal of Human Evolution* 55(1), 1–11.

Chazan, M., Avery, M.D., Bamford, M.K., et al. (2012). The Oldowan horizon in Wonderwerk Cave (South Africa): archaeological, geological, paleontological and paleoclimatic evidence. *Journal of Human Evolution* 63, 859–866.

Chazan, M., Porat, N., Sumner, T.A. and Horwitz, L.K. (2013). The use of OSL dating in unstructured sands: the archaeology and chronology of the Hutton Sands at Canteen Kopje (Northern Cape Province, South Africa). *Archaeological and Anthropological Sciences* 5(4), 351–363.

Chazan, M., Horwitz, L.K., Ecker, M., et al. (2017). Renewed excavations at Wonderwerk Cave, South Africa. *Evolutionary Anthropology* 26(6), 258–260.

Chazan, M., Berna, F., Brink, J., et al. (2020). Archeology, environment, and chronology of the early middle stone age component of Wonderwerk cave. *Journal of Paleolithic Archaeology* 3(3), 302–335.

Chen, F.-C. and Li, W.-H. (2001). Genomic divergences between humans and other hominoids and the effective population size of the common ancestor of humans and chimpanzees. *The American Journal of Human Genetics* 68(2), 444–456.

Cheney, D.L. and Seyfarth, R.M. (1981). Selective forces affecting the predator alarm calls of vervet monkeys. *Behaviour* 76, 25–61.

Chernet, T., Hart, W.K., Aronson, J.L. and Walter, R.C. (1998). New age constraints on the timing of volcanism and tectonism in the northern Main Ethiopian Rift–southern Afar transition zone (Ethiopia). *Journal of Volcanology and Geothermal Research* 80, 267–280.

Chorowicz, J. (2005). The East African rift system. *Journal of African Earth Sciences*, 43, 379–410.

Churcher, C.S. (1956). The fossil Hyracoidea of the Transvaal and Taungs deposits. *Annals of the Transvaal Museum* 22, 477–501.

Churcher, C.S. (2000). Extinct equids from Limeworks Cave and Cave of Hearths, Makapansgat, Northern Province, and a consideration of variation in the cheek teeth of *Equus capensis* Broom. *Palaeontologica Africana* 36, 97–117.

Churcher, C.S. (2006). Distribution and history of the Cape zebra (*Equus capensis*) in the Quaternary of Africa. *Transactions of the Royal Society of South Africa* 61, 89–95.

Churcher, C.S. and Hooijer, D.A. (1980). The Olduvai zebra (*Equus oldowayensis*) from the later Omo beds, Ethiopia. *Zoologische Mededelingen* 55(22), 265–281.

Churcher, C.S., Kleindienst, M.R. and Schwarcz, H.P. (1999). Faunal remains from a Middle Pleistocene lacustrine marl in Dakhleh Oasis, Egypt: palaeoenvironmental reconstructions. *Palaeogeography, Palaeoclimatology, Palaeoecology* 154, 301–312.

Churcher, C.S., Kleindienst, M.R., Wiseman, M.F. and McDonald, M.M.A. (2008). The Quaternary faunas of Dakhleh Oasis, Western Desert of Egypt. In: M.F. Wiseman (Ed.), *The Oasis Papers 2. Proceedings of the Second International Conference on the Dakhleh Oasis Project*. Oxford: Oxbow Books, pp. 3–24.

Churchill, S.E., Brink, J.S., Berger, L.R., et al. (2000a). Erfkroon: a new Florisian fossil locality from fluvial contexts in the western Free State, South Africa. *South African Journal of Science* 96, 161–163.

Churchill, S.E., Berger, L.R. and Parkington, J.E. (2000b). A Middle Pleistocene human tibia from Hoedjiespunt, Western Cape, South Africa. *South African Journal of Science* 96(7), 367–369.

Cipriani, L. (1928). Skull "*Australopithecus africanus*" Dart. *Archivio per l'antropologia e la etnologia* LVII, 1–29.

Clark, J.D. (1974). The stone artefacts from Cornelia, O.F.S., South Africa. *Memoir – Nasionale Museum, Bloemfontein* 9, 33–62.

Clark, J.D. (1979). Hominid occupation of the East-Central Highlands of Ethiopia in the Plio-Pleistocene. *Nature* 282, 33–39.

Clark, J.D. (1987). Transitions: *Homo erectus* and the Acheulian: the Ethiopian sites of Gadeb and the Middle Awash. *Journal of Human Evolution* 16, 809–826.

Clark, J.D. (1993). Stone artefact assemblages from Members 1–3, Swartkrans Cave. In: C.K. Brain (Ed.), *Swartkrans: A Cave's Chronicle of Early Man*. Transvaal Museum Monograph No. 8. Pretoria: Transvaal Museum, pp. 167–194.

Clark, J.D. and Haynes, C.V. (1970). An elephant butchery site at Mwanganda's Village, Karonga, Malawi and its relevance to palaeolithic archaeology. *World Archaeology* I, 390–411.

Clark, J.D., Oakley, K.P., Wells, L.H. and McCleland, J.A.C. (1947). New studies on Rhodesian Man. *Journal of the Royal Anthropological Institute of Great Britain and Ireland* 77, 7–32.

Clark, J.D., Stephens, E.A. and Coryndon, S.C. (1966). Pleistocene fossiliferous lake beds of the Malawi (Nyasa) Rift: a preliminary report. *American Anthropologist* 68, 46–49.

Clark, J.D., Haynes, C.V., Mawby, F.E. and Gauthier, A. (1970). Interim report on palaeo-anthropological investigations in the Lake Malawi Rift. *Quaternaria* 13, 305–354.

Clark, J.D., Asfaw, B., Assefa, G., et al. (1984). Palaeoanthropological discoveries in the Middle Awash Valley, Ethiopia. *Nature* 307(5950), 423–428.

Clark, J.D., de Heinzelin, J., Schick, D., et al. (1994). African *Homo erectus*: old radiometric ages and young Oldowan assemblages in the Middle Awash Valley, Ethiopia. *Science* 264, 1907–1910.

Clark, J.D., Beyene, Y., WoldeGabriel, G., et al. (2003). Stratigraphic, chronological and behavioural contexts of Pleistocene *Homo sapiens* from Middle Awash, Ethiopia. *Nature* 423(6941), 747.

Clark, J.L. and Plug, I. (2008). Animal exploitation strategies during the South African Middle Stone Age: Howiesons Poort and post-Howiesons Poort fauna from Sibudu Cave. *Journal of Human Evolution* 54, 886–898.

Clarke, R.J. (1977). The cranium of the Swartkrans hominid, SK 847 and its relevance to human origins. PhD thesis, University of the Witwatersrand, Johannesburg.

Clarke, R.J. (1985). *Australopithecus* and early *Homo* in southern Africa. In: E. Delson (Ed.), *Ancestors: the Hard Evidence*. New York: Alan R. Liss, pp. 171–177.

Clarke, R.J. (1988). A new *Australopithecus* cranium from Sterkfontein and its bearing on the ancestry of *Paranthropus*. In: F.E. Grine (Ed.), *Evolutionary History of the 'Robust' Australopithecines*. New York: Routledge, pp.285–292.

Clarke, R.J. (1994). On some new interpretations of Sterkfontein stratigraphy. *South African Journal of Science* 90, 211–214.

Clarke, R.J. (1998). The first ever discovery of a well-preserved skull and associated skeleton of *Australopithecus*. *South African Journal of Science* 94, 460–463.

Clarke, R.J. (1999). Discovery of complete arm and hand of the 3.3 million-year-old *Australopithecus* skeleton from Sterkfontein. *South African Journal of Science* 95, 477–480.

Clarke, R.J. (2002a). Newly revealed information on the Sterkfontein Member 2 *Australopithecus* skeleton. *South African Journal of Science* 98, 523–526.

Clarke, R.J. (2002b). On the unrealistic 'revised age estimates' for Sterkfontein. *South African Journal of Science* 98, 415–419.

Clarke, R.J. (2006). A deeper understanding of the stratigraphy of the Sterkfontein fossil hominid site. *Transactions of the Royal Society of Africa* 61, 111–120.

Clarke, R.J. (2012). A brief review of history and results of 40 years of Sterkfontein excavations. *African Genesis: Perspectives on Hominin Evolution*, 62, 120.

Clarke, R.J. and Howell, F.C. (1972). Affinities of the Swartkrans 847 hominin cranium. *American Journal of Physical Anthropologie* 37, 319–336.

Clarke, R.J. and Kuman, K. (2019). The skull of StW 573, a 3.67 Ma *Australopithecus prometheus* skeleton from Sterkfontein caves, South Africa. *Journal of Human Evolution* 134, 102634.

Clarke, R.J., Howell, F.C. and Brain, C.K. (1970). More evidence of an advanced hominid at Swartkrans. *Nature* 225, 1219–1222.

Clauzon, G., Suc, J.-P., Gautier, F., Berger, A. and Loutre, M.-F. (1996). Alternate interpretation of the Messinian salinity crisis: controversy resolved? *Geology* 24(4), 363–366.

Clementz, M.T. and Koch, P.L. (2001). Differentiating aquatic mammal habitat and foraging ecology with stable isotopes in tooth enamel. *Oecologia* 129(3), 461–472.

Clementz, M.T., Holroyd, P.A. and Koch, P.L. (2008). Identifying aquatic habits of herbivorous mammals through stable isotope analysis. *Palaios* 23(9), 574–585.

Close, R.A., Evers, S.W., Alroy, J. and Butler, R.J. (2018). How should we estimate diversity in the fossil record? Testing richness estimators using sampling-standardised discovery curves. *Methods in Ecology and Evolution* 9(6), 1386–1400.

Codron, D., Codron, J., Lee-Thorp, J., et al. (2007). Stable isotope characterization of mammalian predator–prey relationships in a South African savanna. *European Journal of Wildlife Research* 53(3), 161–170.

Codron, D., Brink, J.S., Rossouw, L. and Clauss, M. (2008). The evolution of ecological specialization in southern African ungulates: competition or physical environmental turnover? *Oikos* 117(3), 344–353.

Coe, M. (1980). The role of modern ecological studies in the reconstruction of paleoenvironments in sub-Saharan Africa. In: A.K. Behrensmeyer and A.P. Hill (Eds.), *Fossils in the Making: Vertebrate Taphonomy and Paleoecology*. Chicago: The University of Chicago Press, pp. 55–67.

Coetzee, J.A. (1993). African flora since the terminal Jurassic. In: P. Goldblatt (Ed.), *Biological Relationships between Africa and South America*. New Haven: Yale University Press.

Coetzee, L. and Brink, J.S. (2003). Fossil oribatid mites (Acari, Oribatida) from the Florisbad Quaternary deposits, South Africa. *Quaternary Research* 59(2), 246–254.

Coffing, K., Feibel, C.S., Leakey, M.G. and Walker, A. (1994). Four-million-year old hominids from East Lake Turkana, Kenya. *American Journal of Physical Anthropology* 93, 55–65.

Cohen, A., Arrowsmith, R., Behrensmeyer, A.K., et al. (2009). Understanding paleoclimate and human evolution through the Hominin Sites and Paleolakes Drilling Project. *Scientific Drilling* 8, 60–65.

Cohen, B., O'Regan, H. and Steininger, C. (2019). Mongoose manor: Herpestidae remains from the Early Pleistocene Cooper's D locality in the Cradle of Humankind, Gauteng, South Africa. *Palaeontologia Africana*, 53.

Cohen, K.M. and Gibbard, P. (2011). *Global Chronostratigraphical Correlation Table for the last 2.7 Million Years*. Cambridge: Subcommission on Quaternary Stratigraphy (International Commission on Stratigraphy).

Colcord, D.E., Shilling, A.M., Sauer, P.E., et al. (2018). Sub-Milankovitch paleoclimatic and paleoenvironmental variability in East Africa recorded by Pleistocene lacustrine sediments from Olduvai Gorge, Tanzania. *Palaeogeography, Palaeoclimatology, Palaeoecology* 495, 284–291.

Colin, C., Siani, G., Segueni, F., et al. (2008). Restitution de l'histoire de la mousson nord-africaine entre 6,2 et 4,9 Ma et relations possibles avec les èvènements tardi-Miocène. *Comptes Rendus Geoscience* 340, 749–760.

Colin, C., Siani, G., Liu, Z., et al. (2014). Late Miocene to early Pliocene climate variability off NW Africa (ODP Site 659). *Palaeogeography, Palaeoclimatology, Palaeoecology* 401, 81–95.

Collins, J.A., Carr, A.S., Schefuß, E., Boom, A. and Sealy, J. (2017). Investigation of organic matter and biomarkers from Diepkloof Rock Shelter, South Africa: insights into Middle Stone Age site usage and palaeoclimate. *Journal of Archaeological Science* 85, 51–65.

Collinson, M.E. and Hooker, J.J. (1991). Fossil evidence of interactions between plants and plant-eating mammals. *Philosophical Transactions of the Royal Society of London* 333, 197–208.

Collinson, M.E. and Hooker, J.J. (2003). Paleogene vegetation of Eurasia: framework for mammalian faunas. *Deinsea* 10, 41–83.

Compton, J.S. (2011). Pleistocene sea-level fluctuations and human evolution on the southern coastal plain of South Africa. *Quaternary Science Reviews* 30, 506–527.

Conroy, G.C. (1996). The cave breccias of Berg Aukas, Namibia: a clustering approach to mine dump paleontology. *Journal of Human Evolution* 30(4), 349–355.

Conroy, G.C., Jolly, C.J., Cramer, D. and Kalb, J.E. (1978). Newly discovered fossil hominid skull from the Afar depression, Ethiopia. *Nature* 276, 67–70.

Conroy, G.C., Senut, B., Van Couvering, J. and Mein, P. (1992). *Otavipithecus namibiensis*, first Miocene hominoid from southern Africa. *Nature*, 356(6365), 144–148.

Conroy, G.C., Pickford, M., Senut, B. and Mein, P. (1993). Diamonds in the desert: the discovery of *Otavipithecus namibiensis*. *Evolutionary Anthropology: Issues, News, and Reviews* 2(2), 46–52.

Conroy, G.C., Senut, B., Gommery, D., Pickford, M. and Mein, P. (1996). Brief communication: new primate remains from the Miocene of Namibia, southern Africa. *American Journal of Physical Anthropology* 99(3), 487–492.

Cooke, H.B.S. (1963). Pleistocene mammal faunas of Africa, with particular reference to southern Africa. In: F.C. Howell and F. Bourlière (Eds.), *African Ecology and Human Evolution*. Chicago: Aldine, pp. 65–116.

Cooke, H.B.S. (1967). The Pleistocene sequence in South Africa and problems of correlation. In: W.W. Bishop and J.D. Clark (Eds.), *Background to Evolution in Africa*. Chicago: University of Chicago Press, pp. 175–184.

Cooke, H.B.S. (1974). The fossil mammals of Cornelia, OFS, South Africa. *Memoires of the National Museum, Bloemfontein* 9, 63–84.

Cooke, H.B.S. (1976). Suidae from Plio-Pleistocene strata of the Rudolf Basin. In: Y. Coppens, F.C. Howell, G.L. Isaac and R.E.F. Leakey (Eds.), *Earliest Man and Environments in the Lake Rudolf Basin*. Chicago: University of Chicago Press, pp. 251–263.

Cooke, H.B.S. (1978a). Suid evolution and correlation of African hominid localities: an alternative taxonomy. *Science* 201, 460–463.

Cooke, H.B.S. (1978b). Plio-Pleistocene Suidae from Hadar, Ethiopia. *Kirtlandia* 29, 1–63.

Cooke, H.B.S. (1978c). Faunal evidence for the biotic setting of early African hominids. In C.J. Jolly (Ed.), *Early Hominids of Africa*. New York: St. Martin's Press, pp. 267–284.

Cooke, H.B.S. (1982). *Phacochoerus modestus* from Bed I, Olduvai Gorge, Tanzania. *Zeitschrift der Geologischen Wissenschaften* 10, 899–908.

Cooke, H.B.S. (1983). Human evolution: the geological framework. *Canadian Journal of Anthropology* 3, 143–161.

Cooke, H.B.S. (1988). The larger mammals from Cave of Hearths. In: R. Mason (Ed.), *Cave of Hearths, Makapansgat, Transvaal*. Johannesburg: University of the Witwatersrand Archaeological Research Unit, pp. 507–534.

Cooke, H.B.S. (1990a). Taung fossils in the University of California collections. In G.H. Sperber (Ed.), *From Apes to Angels*. New York: Wiley-Liss, pp. 119–134.

Cooke, H.B.S. (1990b). Suid remains from the upper Semliki area, Zaire. In: N.T. Boaz (Ed.), *Evolution of Environments and Hominidae in the African Western Rift Valley*. Martinsville: Virginia Museum of Natural History, pp. 197–201.

Cooke, H.B.S. (1994). *Phacochoerus modestus* from Sterkfontein Member 5. *South African Journal of Science* 90, 99–100.

Cooke, H.B.S. (1997). The status of the African fossil suids *Kolpochoerus limnetes* (Hopwood, 1926), *K. phacochoeroides* (Thomas, 1884) and *K. afarensis* (Cooke, 1978). *Geobios* 30, 121–126.

Cooke, H.B.S. (2005). Makapansgat suids and *Metridiochoerus*. *Paleontologica Africana* 41, 131–140.

Cooke, H.B.S. (2007). Stratigraphic variation in Suidae from the Shungura Formation and some coeval deposits. In: R. Bobe, Z. Alemseged and A.K. Behrensmeyer (Eds.), *Hominin Environments in the East African Pliocene: An Assessment of the Faunal Evidence*. New York: Springer, pp. 107–127.

Cooke, H.B.S. and Ewer, R.F. (1972). Fossil Suidae from Kanapoi and Lothagam, northwestern Kenya. *Bulletin of the Museum of Comparative Zoology* 143, 149–296.

Cooke, H.B.S. and Wells, L.W. (1951). Fossil remains from Chelmer, near Bulawayo, Southern Rhodesia. *South African Journal of Science* 57, 205–209.

Cooke, H.B.S. and Wilkinson A.F. (1978). Suidae and Tayassuidae. In: V.J. Maglio and H.B.S. Cooke (Eds.,) *Evolution of African Mammals*. Cambridge, MA: Harvard University Press, pp. 435–482.

Cooke, H.B.S., Malan, B.D. and Wells, L.H. (1945). 3. Fossil man in the Lebombo Mountains, South Africa: the 'Border Cave', Ingwavuma District, Zululand. *Man*, 45, 6–13.

Coombs, M.C. and Cote, S.M. (2010). Chalicotheriidae. In: L. Werdelin and W.J. Sanders (Eds.), *Cenozoic Mammals of Africa*. Berkeley: University of California Press, pp. 659–667.

Copeland, S.R., Sponheimer, M., Spinage, C.A., et al. (2009). Stable isotope evidence for impala *Aepyceros melampus* diets at Akagera National Park, Rwanda. *African Journal of Ecology* 47(4), 490–501.

Copeland, S.R., Sponheimer, M., Lee-Thorp, J.A., et al. (2010). Using strontium isotopes to study site accumulation processes. *Journal of Taphonomy* 8, 115–127.

Copeland, S.R., Sponheimer, M., de Ruiter, D.J., et al. (2011). Strontium isotope evidence for landscape use by early hominins. *Nature* 474, 76–79.

Coppa, A., Abbate, E., Bondioli, L., et al. (2012). Mulhuli-Amo, a new late Early Pleistocene paleoanthropological site in the northern Danakil Depression, Eritrea. *Proceedings of the ESHE Meetings* 1, 58–59 (abstract).

Coppa, A., Bondioli, L., Candilio, F., et al. (2014). New 1 Ma old human cranial remains from Mulhuli-Amo, near Uadi Aalad, Danakil (Afar) depression of Eritrea. *American Journal of Physical Anthropology* 153(S58), 97.

Coppens, Y. (1966). An early hominid from Chad. *Current Anthropology* 7, 584–585.

Coppens, Y. (1975). Evolution des hominidés et de leur environnement au cours du Plio-Pléistocène dans la basse vallée de l'Omo en Ethiopie. *Comptes Rendu de l'Académie des Sciences Paris, Série D, Sciences Naturelles* 281, 1693–1696.

Coppens, Y. (1977). Hominid remains from the Plio/Pleistocene formations of the Omo Basin, Ethiopia. *Journal of Human Evolution* 6, 169–173.

Coppens, Y. (1978). Evolution of the hominids and their environment during the Plio-Pleistocene in the lower Omo Valley, Ethiopia. In: W.W. Bishop (Ed.), *Geological Background to Fossil Man*. Edinburgh: Scottish Academic Press, pp. 499–506.

Coppens, Y., Howell, F.C., Isaac, G.L. and Leakey, R.E. (1976). *Earliest Man and Environments in the Lake Rudolf Basin: Stratigraphy, Paleoecology, and Evolution*. Chicago: University of Chicago Press, p. 615.

Cordova, C. and Avery, G. (2017). African savanna elephants and their vegetation associations in the Cape Region, South Africa: opal phytoliths from dental calculus on prehistoric, historic and reserve elephants. *Quaternary International* 443, 189–211.

Cordova, C.E. and Scott, L. (2011). The potential of Poaceae, Cyperaceae, and Restionaceae phytoliths to reflect past environmental conditions in South Africa. In: J. Runge (Ed.), *African Palaeoenviornments and Geomorphic Landscape Evolution*. London: CRC Press, pp. 107–133.

Corfield, T.F. (1973). Elephant mortality in Tsavo National Park, Kenya. *African Journal of Ecology* 11, 339–368.

Cornelissen, E., Boven, A., Dabi, A., et al. (1990). The Kapthurin Formation revisited. *African Archaeological Review* 8, 23–75.

Coryndon, S.C. (1966). Preliminary report on some fossils from the Chiwondo Beds of the Karonga District, Malawi. *American Anthropologist* 68, 59–66.

Coryndon, S.C. (1970). Evolutionary trends in East African Hippopotamidae. *Bulletin de Liaison de l'Association Sénégalaise pour l'Etude du Quaternaire de l'Ouest africain (ASEQUA), Dakar* 25, 107–116.

Coryndon, S.C. and Coppens, Y. (1973). Preliminary report on Hippopotamidae (Mammalia, Artiodactyla) from the Plio/Pleistocene of the lower Omo basin, Ethiopia. *Fossil Vertebrates of Africa* 3, 139–157.

Cote, S.M. (2004). Origins of the African hominoids: an assessment of the palaeobiogeographical evidence. *Comptes Rendus Palevol* 3(4), 323–340.

Cote, S. (2018). Savannah savvy. *Nature Ecology & Evolution* 2, 210–211.

Coutros, P. (2016). *All Climates are Local Climates: Palaeoenvironmental Perspectives from the Diallowali Site System*. Society of Africanist Archaeologists, 23. Toulouse: Université Toulouse Jean Jaurès.

Couvreur, T.L.P., Chatrou, L.W., Sosef, M.S.M. and Richardson, J.E. (2008) Molecular phylogenetics reveal multiple tertiary vicariance origins of African rain forest trees. *BMC Biology* 6, 54.

Cowling, R.M., Cartwright, C.R., Parkington, J.E. and Allsopp, J.C. (1999). Fossil wood charcoal assemblages from Elands Bay Cave, South Africa: implications for Late Quaternary vegetation and climates in the winter-rainfall fynbos biome. Journal of Biogeography 26(2), 367–378.

Cowling, R.M., Proches, Ș., Vlok, J.H.J. and van Staden, J. (2005). On the origin of southern African subtropical thicket vegetation. *South African Journal of Botany* 71(1), 1–23.

Cowling, S.A., Cox, P.M., Jones, C.D., et al. (2008). Simulated glacial and interglacial vegetation across Africa: implications for species phylogenies and trans-African migration of plants and animals. *Global Change Biology* 14, 827–840.

Crader, D.C. (1974). The effects of scavengers on bone material from a large mammal: an experiment conducted among the Bisa of the Luangwa Valley, Zambia. In: C.B. Donnan and C.W. Clewlow (Eds.), *Ethnoarchaeology: Archaeology Survey Monograph 4*. Los Angeles: Institute of Archaeology, University of California, pp. 161–173.

Crawford, T., McKee, J., Kuykendall, K., Latham, A. and Conroy, G.C. (2004). Recent paleoanthropological excavations of *in situ* deposits at Makapansgat, South Africa – a first report. *Collegium Antropologicum* 28(2), 43–57.

Crevecoeur, I., Rougier, H., Grine, F. and Froment, A. (2009). Modern human cranial diversity in the late Pleistocene of Africa and Eurasia: evidence from Nazlet Khater, Pestera cu Oase, and Hofmeyr. *American Journal of Physical Anthropology* 140, 347–358.

Crevecoeur, I., Skinner, M.M., Bailey, S.E., et al. (2014). First early hominin from central Africa (Ishango, Democratic Republic of Congo). *PLoS ONE* 9, e84652.

Cressier, P. (1980). Magnétostratigraphie du gisement pléistocène de Melka-Kunturé (Ethiopie). Datation des niveaux oldowayens et acheuléens. Thèse, University Louis Pasteur, Strasbourg, France.

Crompton, R.H., Pataky, T.C., Savage, R., et al. (2012). Human-like external function of the foot, and fully upright gait, confirmed in the 3.66 million year old Laetoli hominin footprints by topographic statistics, experimental footprint formation and computer simulation. *Journal of the Royal Society Interface* 9, 707–719.

Crusafont-Pairó, M. (1979). Les Giraffidés des gisements du Bled Douarah (W. de Gafsa, Tunisie). *Notes du Service géologique de Tunisie* 44, 7–41.

Cruz-Uribe, K. (1983). The mammalian fauna from Redcliff Cave, Zimbabwe. *South African Archaeological Bulletin* 38, 7–16.

Cruz-Uribe, K. (1991). Distinguishing hyena from hominid bone accumulations. *Journal of Field Archaeology* 18, 467–486.

Cruz-Uribe, K., Klein, R.G., Avery, G., et al. (2003). Excavation of buried Late Acheulean (Mid-Quaternary) land surfaces at Duinefontein 2, Western Cape Province, South Africa. *Journal of Archaeological Science* 30(5), 559–575.

Csermely, D. (1996). Antipredator behavior in lemurs: evidence of an extinct eagle on Madagascar or something else? *International Journal of Primatology* 17: 349–354.

Cumming, D.H.M. (1975). *A Field Study of the Ecology and Behavior of Warthog*. Salisbury, Rhodesia: The Trustees of the National Museums and Monuments of Rhodesia.

Curnoe, D. (2010). A review of early *Homo* in southern Africa focusing on cranial, mandibular and dental remains, with the description of a new species (*Homo gautengensis* sp. nov.). *Homo* 61, 151–177.

Curnoe, D., Herries, A.I.R., Brink, J., et al. (2006). Discovery of Middle Pleistocene fossil and stone tool-bearing deposits at Groot Kloof, Ghaap Escarpment, Northern Cape Province. *South African Journal of Science* 102, 180–184.

Curran, S. and Haile-Selassie, Y. (2016). Paleoecological reconstruction of hominin-bearing Middle Pliocene Localities at Woranso-Mille, Ethiopia. *Journal of Human Evolution* 96, 97–112.

Cuthbert, M.O., Gleeson, T., Reynolds, S.C., et al. (2017). Modelling the role of groundwater hydro-refugia in East African hominin evolution and dispersal. *Nature Communications* 8, 15696.

Cutler, A.H., Behrensmeyer, A.K. and Chapman, R.E. (1999). Environmental information in a recent bone assemblage: roles of taphonomic processes and ecological change. *Palaeogeography, Palaeoclimatology, Palaeoecology* 149, 359–372.

Daly, A.J., Baetens, J.M. and De Baets, B. (2018). Ecological diversity: measuring the unmeasurable. *Mathematics*, 6(7), 119.

Damuth, J. and Janis, C. (2011). On the relationship between hypsodonty and feeding ecology in ungulate mammals, and its utility in palaeoecology. *Biological Reviews* 86, 733–758.

Damuth, J.D., DiMichele, W.A., Potts, R., Sues, H.D. and Wing, S.L. (1992). *Terrestrial Ecosystems Through Time: Evolutionary Paleoecology of Terrestrial Plants and Animals (No. 2)*. Chicago: University of Chicago Press.

Darlington, J.P.E.C. (2005). Distinctive fossilized termite nests at Laetoli, Tanzania. *Insectes Sociaux* 52, 408–409.

Darlington, J.P.E.C. (2011). Trace fossils interpreted in relation to the extant termite fauna at Laetoli, Tanzania. In: T. Harrison (Ed.), *Paleontology and Geology of Laetoli: Human Evolution in Context. Vol. 2: Fossil Hominins and the Associated Fauna*. Dordrecht: Springer, pp. 555–565.

Dart, R.A. (1925a). *Australopithecus africanus*: the man-ape of South Africa. *Nature* 115, 195–199.

Dart, R.A. (1925b). A note on Makapansgat: a site of early human occupation. *South African Journal of Science* 22, 454.

Dart, R.A. (1926). Taungs and its significance. *Natural History* 26, 315–327.

Dart, R.A. (1929). A note on the Taungs skull. *South African Journal of Science* 26, 648–658.

Dart, R.A. (1948). The Makapansgat proto-human *Australopithecus prometheus*. *American Journal of Physical Anthropology* 6, 259–281.

Dart, R.A. (1950). A note on the limestone caverns of Leba, near Humpata, Angola. *The South African Archaeological Bulletin* 5(20), 149–151.

Dart, R.A. (1952). Faunal and climatic fluctuations in Makapansgat Valley: their relation to the geologic age and Promethean status of Australopithecus. In L.S.B. Leakey and S. Cole (Eds.), *Proceedings of the 1st Pan African Congress on Prehistory, Nairobi, 1947*. Oxford: Blackwell, pp. 96–106.

Dart, R.A. (1955). The first australopithecine fragment from the Makapansgat pebble culture stratum. *Nature* 176(4473), 170–171.

Dart, R.A. (1956). Cultural status of the South African man-apes. Smithsonian Report no. 4240, pp. 317–338.

Dart, R.A. (1957). *The Osteodontokeratic Culture of Australopithecus prometheus*. Transvaal Museum Memoir No. 11. Pretoria: Transvaal Museum.

Dart, R.A. (1959). The first Australopithecus cranium from the pink breccia at Makapansgat. *American Journal of Physical Anthropology* 17, 77–82.

Dart, R.A. (1960). The bone tool-manufacturing ability of *Australopithecus prometheus*. *American Anthropologist* 62, 134–143.

Dart, R.A. (1962). The gradual appraisal of *Australopithecus*. In: G. Kurth (Ed.), *Evolution und Hominisation*. Stuttgart: Gustav Fischer Verlag, pp. 141–156.

Dart, R.A. and Craig, D. (1959). *Adventures with the Missing Link*. London: Hamish Hamilton.

Darwent, C.M. (2007). Lagomorphs (Mammalia) from the late Miocene deposits at Lemudong'o, southern Kenya. *Kirtlandia* 56, 112–120.

Darwin, C. (1859). *Origin of Species by Natural Selection*.

Database for Hydrological Time Series of Inland Waters (DAHITI) – Victoria, Lake, retrieved 21 Nov 2017.

Daujeard, C., Geraads, D., Gallotti, R., Mohib, A. and Raynal, J.-P. (2012). Carcass acquisition and consumption by carnivores and hominins in Middle Pleistocene sites of Casablanca (Morocco). *Journal of Taphonomy* 10, 339–363.

Daujeard, C., Geraads, D., Gallotti, R., et al. (2016). Pleistocene hominins as a resource for carnivores: a c.500,000-year-old human femur bearing tooth-marks in North Africa (Thomas Quarry I, Morocco). *PLoS ONE* 11(4), e0152284. doi:10.1371/journal.pone.0152284

Daujeard, C., Falguères, C., Shao, Q., Geraads, D., Hublin, J.-J., Lefèvre, D., El Graoui, M., Rué, M., Gallotti, R., Delvigne, V., Queffelec, A., Ben Arous, E., Tombret, O., Mohib, A. and Raynal, J.-P. (2020). Earliest African evidence of carcass processing and consumption in cave at 700ka, Casablanca, Morocco. *Scientific Reports* 10: 4761.

Dauphin, Y., Kowalski, C. and Denys, C. (1994). Assemblage data and bone and teeth modifications as an aid to paleoenvironmental interpretations of the open-air Pleistocene site of Tighenif (Algeria). *Quaternary Research* 42, 340–349.

Davenport, T.R.B., Stanley, W.T., Sargis, E.J., et al. (2006). A new genus of African monkey, Rungwecebus: morphology, ecology, and molecular phylogenetics. *Science* 312, 1378–1381.

Davidson, A. (1983). *The Omo River Project. Reconnaissance of Geology and Geochemistry of Parts of Ilubabor, Kefa, Gemu Gofa and Sidamo, Ethiopia*. Ethipia: Ministry of Mines and Energy, Ethiopian Institute of Geological Surveys.

Davidson, A., Shiferaw, A., Leul, E.G., Davis, J.C. and Moore, J.M. (1973). Preliminary report on the geology and geochemistry of parts of Sidamo, Gemu Gofa, and Kefa Provinces, Ethiopia. Omo River Project report, no. 1. Imperial Ethiopian Government, Ministry of Mines.

Davidson, I. and Solomon, S. (1990). Was OH 7 the victim of a crocodile attack? In: S. Solomon, I. Davidson and D. Watson (Eds.), *Problem Solving in Taphonomy: Archaeological and Palaeontological Studies from Europe, Africa and Oceania*, Vol. 2. St. Lucia, Queensland: Tempus, pp. 197–206.

Dawkins, R. (1986). *The Blind Watchmaker*. London: Longman.

Dawson, J.B. (2008). *The Gregory Rift Valley and Neogene – Recent Volcanoes of Northern Tanzania*. London: Geological Society of London.

Day, M.H. (1971). Postcranial remains of *Homo erectus* from bed IV, Olduvai Gorge, Tanzania. *Nature* 232, 383–387.

Day, M.H. (1986). *Guide to Fossil Man*, 4th ed. Chicago: Chicago University Press.

Day, M.H. and Napier, J.R. (1964). Hominid fossils from Bed I, Olduvai Gorge, Tanganyika: fossil foot bones. *Nature* 201, 969–970.

Day, M.H. and Wickens, E.H. (1980). Laetoli Pliocene hominid footprints and bipedalism. *Nature* 286, 385–387.

Day, M., Leakey, R., Walker, A. and Wood, B. (1976). New hominids from East Turkana, Kenya. *American Journal of Physical Anthropology* 45, 369–435.

Day, M.H., Leakey, M.D. and Magori, C. (1980). A new hominid fossil skull (L.H. 18) from the Ngaloba Beds, Laetoli, northern Tanzania. *Nature* 284, 55–56.

d'Huart, J.-P. (1978). *Ecologie de l'hylochere (Hylochoerus meinertzhageni Thomas) au Parc National des Virunga*. Exploration du Parc National des Virunga, Deuxieme Serie, Fascicule 25. Brussels: Fondation pour Favoriser les Recherches scientifiques en Afrique.

de Bonis, L., Peigné, S., Likius, A., et al. (2007). The oldest African fox (*Vulpes riffautae* n. sp., Canidae, Carnivora) recovered in late Miocene deposits of the Djurab desert, Chad. *Naturwissenschaften* 94, 575.

de Bonis, L., Peigné, S., Mackaye, H.T., et al. (2008). The fossil vertebrate locality Kossom Bougoudi, Djurab desert, Chad: a window in the distribution of the carnivoran faunas at the Mio-Pliocene boundary in Africa. *Comptes Rendus Palevol* 7, 571–581.

de Bonis, L., Peigné, S., Taisso Mackaye, H., et al. (2010). New sabre-toothed cats in the Late Miocene of Toros Menalla (Chad). *Comptes Rendus Palevol* 9, 221–227.

De Bruijn, H. (1973) Analysis of the data bearing upon the correlation of the Messinian with the succession of land mammals. *Messinian Events in the Mediterranean: Proceedings, Koninklijke Nederlandse Akademie van Wetenschappen*, 76, 260–262.

De Franceschi, D., Bamford, M., Pickford, M. and Senut, B. (2016). Fossil wood from the upper Miocene Mpesida Beds at Cheparain (Baringo District, Kenya): botanical affinities and palaeoenvironmental implications. *Journal of African Earth Sciences* 115, 271–280.

De Graaff, G. (1957). A new chrysochlorid from Makapansgat. *Palaeontologica Africana* 5, 21–27.

De Graaf, G. (1960). A preliminary investigation of the mammalian microfauna in Pleistocene deposits in the Transvaal System. *Palaeontologia Africana* 7, 59–118.

de Heinzelin, J. (1962). Les formations du Western Rift et de la cuvette congolaise. *Annales du Musée Royal de l'Afrique Centrale* 40, 129–243.

de Heinzelin, J. (1983a). Paleoenvironments. In: J. de Heinzelin (Ed.), *The Omo Group*. Tervuren: Musée Royal de l'Afrique Centrale, pp. 209–218.

de Heinzelin, J. (Ed.) (1983b). *The Omo Group. Annales, Sciences Géologiques*, Vol. 85. Tervuren: Musée Royal de l'Afrique Centrale.

de Heinzelin, J. and Haesaerts, P. (1983a) The Shungura Formation. In: J. de Heinzelin (Ed.), *The Omo Group*. Tervuren: Musée Royal de l'Afrique Centrale, pp. 25–127.

de Heinzelin, J. and Haesaerts, P. (1983b). The Usno Formation. In: J. de Heinzelin (Ed.), *The Omo Group*. Tervuren: Musée Royal de l'Afrique Centrale, pp. 129–139.

de Heinzelin, J. and Haesaerts, P. (1983c). The Mursi Formation. In: J. de Heinzelin (Ed.), *The Omo Group*. Tervuren: Musée Royal de l'Afrique Centrale, pp. 141–143.

de Heinzelin, J., Haesaerts, P. and Howell, F.C. (1976). Plio-Pleistocene formations of the lower Omo basin with particular reference to the Shungura Formation. In: Y. Coppens, F.C. Howell, G.L. Isaac and R.E. Leakey (Eds.), *Earliest Man and Environments in the Lake Rudolf Basin*. Chicago: University of Chicago Press, pp. 24–49.

de Heinzelin, J., Clark, J.D., White, T.D., et al. (1999). Environment and behavior of 2.5-million-year-old Bouri hominids. *Science* 284, 625–629.

de Heinzelin, J., Clark, J.D. and Gilbert, W.H. (2000). *The Acheulean and Plio-Pleistocene deposits of the Middle Awash valley, Ethiopia, Annales – Sciences Géologiques* Vol. 104. Tervuren: Musée Royale de l'Afrique Central.

de la Torre, I. (2006). *Estrategias tecnológicas en el Pleistoceno inferior de África oriental (Olduvai y Peninj, norte de Tanzania)*. Madrid: Servicio de Publicaciones Universidad Complutense de Madrid.

de la Torre, I. (2009). Technological strategies in the Lower Pleistocene at Peninj (West of Lake Natron, Tanzania). In: K. Schick and N. Toth (Eds.), *The Cutting Edge: New Approaches to the Archaeology of Human Origins*. Bloomington: Stone Age Institute Press, pp. 93–113.

de la Torre, I. (2011). The Early Stone Age lithic assemblages of Gadeb (Ethiopia) and the developed Oldowan/early Acheulean in East Africa. *Journal of Human Evolution* 60, 768–812.

de la Torre, I. and Benito-Calvo, A. (2013). Application of GIS methods to retrieve orientation patterns from imagery; a case study from Beds I and II, Olduvai Gorge (Tanzania). *Journal of Archaeological Science* 40, 2446–2457.

de la Torre, I. and Mora, R. (2004). *El Olduvayense de la Sección Tipo de Peninj (Lago Natron, Tanzania)*, vol. 1. Barcelona: CEPAP.

de la Torre, I., Mora, R., Domínguez-Rodrigo, M., Luque, L. and Alcalá, L. (2003). The Oldowan industry of Peninj and its bearing on the reconstruction of the technological skills of Lower Pleistocene hominids. *Journal of Human Evolution* 44, 203–224.

de la Torre, I., deBeaune, S., Davidson, I., et al. (2004). Omo revisited: evaluating the technological skills of Pliocene hominids. *Current Anthropology* 45(4), 439–465.

de la Torre, I., Mora, R. and Martínez-Moreno, J. (2008). The early Acheulean in Peninj (Lake Natron, Tanzania). *Journal of Anthropological Archaeology* 27(2), 244–264.

de la Torre, I., McHenry, L. and Njau, J. (2018). From the Oldowan to the Acheulean at Olduvai Gorge, Tanzania – an introduction to the special issue. *Journal of Human Evolution* 120, 1–6.

de Lapparent de Broin, F. (2000). African chelonians from the Jurassic to the present: phases of development and preliminary catalogue of the fossil record. *Palaeontologia Africana* 36, 43–82.

de Lumley, M.-A. and Marchal, F. (2004). Les restes d'hominidés du site de FJ-1. In: H. de Lumley and Y. Beyene (Eds.), *Les sites préhistoriques de la région de Fejej, Sud-Omo, Éthiopie, dans leur contexte stratigraphique et paléontologique*. Paris: Éditions Recherche sur les Civilisations, pp. 203–340.

de Ruiter, D.J. (2001). A methodological analysis of the relative abundance of hominids and other macromammals from the site of Swartkrans, South Africa. PhD thesis, Faculty of Science, University of the Witwatersrand, Johannesburg.

de Ruiter, D.J. (2003). Revised faunal lists for Members 1–3 of Swartkrans, South Africa. *Annals of the Transvaal Museum* 40, 29–41.

de Ruiter, D.J. (2004). Relative abundance, skeletal part representation and accumulating agents of macromammals at Swartkrans. In: C. Brain (Ed.), *Swartkrans: A Cave's Chronicle of Early Man*, 2nd ed. Pretoria: Transvaal Museum Press, pp. 265–278.

de Ruiter, D.J. and Berger, L.R. (2000). Leopards as taphonomic agents in dolomitic caves – implications for bone accumulations in the hominid-bearing deposits of South Africa. *Journal of Archaeological Science* 27(8), 665–684.

de Ruiter, D.J., Sponheimer, M. and Lee-Thorp, J.A. (2008a). Indications of habitat association of *Australopithecus robustus* in the Bloubank Valley, South Africa. *Journal of Human Evolution* 55, 1015–1030.

de Ruiter, D., Brophy, J.K., Lewis, P.J., Churchill, S.E. and Berger, L.R. (2008b). Faunal assemblage composition and paleoenvironment of Plovers Lake, a Middle Stone Age locality in Gauteng Province, South Africa. *Journal of Human Evolution* 55, 1102–1117.

de Ruiter, D.J., Pickering, R., Steininger, C.M., et al. (2009). New *Australopithecus robustus* fossils and associated U–Pb dates from Cooper's Cave (Gauteng, South Africa). *Journal of Human Evolution* 56, 497–513.

de Ruiter, D.J., Copeland, S.R., Lee-Thorp, J.A. and Sponheimer, M. (2010a). Investigating the role of eagles as accumulating agents in the dolomitic cave infills of South Africa. *Journal of Taphonomy* 8, 129–154.

de Ruiter, D.J., Brophy, J.K., Lewis, P.J., et al. (2010b). Preliminary investigation of Matjhabeng, a Pliocene fossil locality in the Free State of South Africa. *Palaeontologica Africana*, 45, 11–22.

de Ruiter, D.J., Churchill, S.E. and Berger, L.R. (2013). *Australopithecus sediba* from Malapa, South Africa. In: K.E. Reed, J.G. Fleagle and R.E.F. Leakey (Eds.), *The Paleobiology of Australopithecus*. Dordrecht: Springer, pp. 147–160.

d'Errico, F., Backwell, L., Villa, P., et al. (2012a). Early evidence of San material culture represented by organic artifacts from Border Cave, South Africa. *Proceedings of the National Academy of Sciences* 109(33), 13214–13219.

d'Errico, F., Moreno, R.G. and Rifkin, R.F. (2012b). Technological, elemental and colorimetric analysis of an engraved ochre fragment from the Middle Stone Age levels of Klasies River Cave 1, South Africa. *Journal of Archaeological Science* 39(4), 942–952.

Deacon, H.J. (1970). The Acheulian occupation at Amanzi Springs, Uitenhage District, Cape Province. *Annals of the Cape Provincial Museums* 8, 89–189.

Deacon, H.J. (1979). Excavations at Boomplaas cave – a sequence through the upper Pleistocene and Holocene in South Africa. *World Archaeology*, 10(3), 241–257.

Deacon, H.J. (1995). Two late Pleistocene–Holocene archaeological depositories from the southern Cape, South Africa. *The South African Archaeological Bulletin* 50, 121–131.

Deacon, H.J. and Geleijnse, V.B. (1988). The stratigraphy and sedimentology of the main site sequence, Klasies River, South Africa. *The South African Archaeological Bulletin*, 43, 5–14.

Deacon, H.J., Deacon, J., Scholtz, A., et al. (1984). Correlation of palaeoenvironmental data from the Late Pleistocene and Holocene deposits at Boomplaas Cave, Southern Cape. In: J.C. Vogel (Ed.), *Late Cainozoic Palaeoclimates of the Southern Hemisphere*. Rotterdam: Balkema, pp. 339–352.

Deacon, J. (1984). *The Later Stone Age of southernmost Africa*. International Series 213. Oxford: British Archaeological Reports.

Deane, A.S. (2009). Early Miocene catarrhine dietary behaviour: the influence of the Red Queen effect on incisor shape and curvature. *Journal of Human Evolution* 56, 275–285.

Dechamps, R. and Maes, F. (1985). Essai de reconstitution des climats et des végétations de la basse vallée de l'Omo au Plio-Pléistocène à l'aide de bois fossils. In: Y. Coppens (Ed.), *L'Environnement des Hominidés au Plio-Pléistocène*. Paris: Masson, pp. 175–222.

Dechamps, R. and Maes, F. (1990). Woody plant communities and climate in the Pliocene of the Semliki Valley, Zaire. In: N.T. Boaz

(Ed.), *Evolution of Environments and Hominidae in the African Western Rift Valley.* Martinsville: Virginia Museum of Natural History, pp. 71–94.

Dechamps, R., Senut, B. and Pickford, M. (1992). Fruits fossiles pliocènes et pléistocènes du Rift occidental ougandais. Signification paléoenvironnementale. *Comptes rendus de l'Académie des sciences. Série 2, Mécanique, Physique, Chimie, Sciences de l'univers, Sciences de la Terre* 314(3), 325–331.

DeGusta, D. and Vrba, E. (2003). A method for inferring paleohabitats from the functional morphology of bovid astragali. *Journal of Archaeological Science* 30, 1009–1022.

DeGusta, D. and Vrba, E. (2005). Methods for inferring paleohabitats from the functional morphology of bovid phalanges. *Journal of Archaeological Science* 32, 1099–1113.

Dehghani, R., Wanntorp, L., Pagani, M., et al. (2008). Phylogeography of the white-tailed mongoose (Herpestidae, Carnivora, Mammalia) based on partial sequences of the mtDNA control region. *Journal of Zoology* 276, 385–393.

Deino, A.L. (2011). ^{40}Ar/^{39}Ar dating of Laetoli, Tanzania. In: T. Harrison (Ed.), *Paleontology and Geology of Laetoli: Human Evolution in Context. Volume 1: Geology, Geochronology, Paleoecology and Paleoenvironment.* Dordrecht: Springer, pp. 77–97.

Deino, A.L. (2012). ^{40}Ar/^{39}Ar dating of Bed I, Olduvai Gorge, Tanzania, and the chronology of early Pleistocene climate change. *Journal of Human Evolution* 63(2), 251–273.

Deino, A.L. and Ambrose, S.H. (2007). ^{40}Ar/^{39}Ar dating of the Lemudong'o late Miocene fossil assemblages, southern Kenya Rift. *Kirtlandia* 56, 65–71.

Deino, A.L. and Hill, A. (2002). Ar-40/Ar-39 dating of Chemeron Formation strata encompassingthe site of hominid KNM-BC 1, Tugen Hills, Kenya. *Journal of Human Evolution*, 42(1–2), 141–151.

Deino, A. and McBrearty, S. (2002). ^{40}Ar/^{39}Ar dating of the Kapthurin Formation, Baringo, Kenya. *Journal of Human Evolution* 42, 185–210.

Deino, A. and Potts, R. (1990). Single crystal ^{40}Ar/^{39}Ar dating of the Olorgesailie Formation, southern Kenya rift. *Journal of Geophysical Research* 95(B6), 8453–8470.

Deino, A.L., Tauxe, L., Hill, A. and Monaghan, M. (2002). ^{40}Ar/^{39}Ar geochronology and paleomagnetic stratigraphy of the Lukeino and lower Chemeron succession at Tabarin and Kapcheberek, Tugen Hills, Kenya. *Journal of Human Evolution* 42, 117–140.

Deino, A.L., Kingston, J.D., Glen, J.M., Edgar, R.K. and Hill, A. (2006a). Precessional forcing of lacustrine sedimentation in the late Cenozoic Chemeron Basin, Central Kenya Rift, and calibration of the Gauss/Matuyama boundary. *Earth and Planetary Science Letters* 247(1–2), 41–60.

Deino, A.L., Domínguez-Rodrigo, M. and Luque, L. (2006b). ^{40}Ar/^{39}Ar dating of the Pleistocene Peninj group, lake Natron, Tanzania. *AGU Fall Meeting Abstracts*, pp. V53C-1771.

Deino, A.L., Scott, G.R., Saylor, B., et al. (2010). ^{40}Ar/^{39}Ar dating, paleomagnetism, and tephrochemistry of Pliocene strata of the hominid-bearing Woranso-Mille area, west-central Afar Rift, Ethiopia. *Journal of Human Evolution*, 58, 111–126.

Deino, A.L., Behrensmeyer, A.K., Brooks, A.S., et al. (2018). Chronology of the Acheulean to Middle Stone Age transition in Eastern Africa. *Science* 360, 95–98.

Deino, A.L., Sier, M.J., Garello, D.I., et al. (2019). Chronostratigraphy of the Baringo–Tugen Hills–Barsemoi (HSPDP-BTB13-1A) core – ^{40}Ar/^{39}Ar dating, magnetostratigraphy, tephrostratigraphy, sequence stratigraphy and Bayesian age modeling. *Palaeogeography, Palaeoclimatology, Palaeoecology* 570, 109519.

Delagnes, A. and Roche, H. (2005). Late pliocene hominid knapping skills: the case of Lokalalei 2 C, West Turkana, Kenya. *Journal of Human Evolution* 48, 435–472.

Delagnes, A., Boisserie, J.R., Beyene, Y., et al. (2011). Archaeological investigations in the Lower Omo Valley (Shungura Formation, Ethiopia): new data and perspectives. *Journal of Human Evolution* 61(2), 215–222.

Delfino, M. (2020). Early Pliocene anuran fossils from Kanapoi, Kenya, and the first fossil record for the African burrowing frog *Hemisus* (Neobatrachia: Hemisotidae). *Journal of Human Evolution* 140, 102353.

Delfino, M., Segid, A., Yosief, D., et al. (2004). Fossil reptiles from the Pleistocene *Homo*-bearing locality of Buia (Eritrea, Northern Danakil Depression). *Rivista Italiana di Stratigrafia e Paleontologia* 110(Supplement), 51–60.

Delson, E. (1984). Cercopithecid biochronology of the African Plio-Pleistocene: correlation among eastern and southern hominid-bearing localities. *Courier Forschungsinstitut Senckenberg* 69, 199–218.

Delson, E. (1988). Chronology of South African australopiths site units. In: F.E. Grine (Ed.), *Evolutionary History of the Robust Australopithecines.* New York: Aldine de Gruyter, pp. 317–325.

Delson, E. and Hoffstetter, R. (1993). *Theropithecus* from Ternifine, Algeria. In: N.G. Jablonski (Ed.), *Theropithecus: The Rise and Fall of a Primate Genus.* Cambridge: Cambridge University Press, pp. 191–208.

Delson, E., Eck, G.G., Leakey, M.G. and Jablonski, N.G. (1993). A partial catalogue of fossil remains of *Theropithecus.* In: N.G. Jablonski (Ed.), *Theropithecus: The Rise and Fall of a Primate Genus.* Cambridge: Cambridge University Press, pp. 499–525.

Dembo, M., Matzke, N.J., Mooers, A.O. and Collard, M. (2015). Bayesian analysis of a morphological supermatrix sheds light on controversial fossil hominin relationships. *Proceedings of the Royal Society B* 282, 20150943.

deMenocal, P.B. (1995). Plio-Pleistocene African climate. *Science* 270, 53–59.

deMenocal, P.B. (2004). African climate change and faunal evolution during the Pliocene–Pleistocene. *Earth and Planetary Science Letters* 220, 3–24.

deMenocal, P.B. (2011). Climate and human evolution. *Science* 331, 540–542.

deMenocal, P.B. and Brown, F.H. (1999). Pliocene tephra correlations between East African hominid localities, the Gulf of Aden, and the Arabian Sea. In: J. Agustí, L. Rook and P. Andrews (Eds.), *Evolution of Neogene Terrestrial Ecosystems in Europe.* Cambridge: Cambridge University Press, pp. 23–54.

deMenocal, P., Ortiz, J., Guilderson, T., et al. (2000). Abrupt onset and termination of the African Humid Period: rapid climate responses to gradual insolation forcing. *Quaternary Science Reviews* 19, 347–361.

Deocampo, D.M. (2002). Sedimentary structures generated by *Hippopotamus amphibius* in a lake-margin wetland, Ngorongoro Crater, Tanzania. *PALAIOS* 17, 212–217.

Denys, C. (1987a). Fossil rodents (other than Pedetidae) from Laetoli. In: M.D. Leakey and J.M. Harris (Eds.), *Laetoli: A Pliocene Site in Northern Tanzania.* Oxford: Clarendon Press, pp. 118–170.

Denys, C. (1987b). Micromammals from the west Natron Pleistocene deposits (Tanzania): biostratigraphy and paleoecology. *Sciences géologiques. Bulletin* 40, 185–201.

Denys, C. (1990a). Deux nouvelles espèces d'*Aethomys* (Rodentia, Muridae) à Langebaanweg (Pliocène, Afrique du Sud): implications phylogénétiques et paléoécologiques. *Annales de Paléontologie* 76, 41–69.

Denys, C. (1990b). The oldest *Acomys* (Rodentia, Muridae) from the Lower Pliocene of South Africa and the problem of its murid affinities. *Palaeontographica Abteilung A, Palaozoologie-stratigraphie* 210, 79–91.

Denys, C. (1992). Présence de *Saccostomus* (Rodentia, Mammalia) a Olduvai Bed I (Tanzanie, Pléistocčne inférieur). Implications phylétiques et paléobiogéographiques. *Geobios*, 25(1), 145–154.

Denys, C. (1997). Rodent faunal lists in karstic and open-air sites of Africa: an attempt to evaluate predation and fossilisation biases on paleodiversity [Listas faunísticas de roedores en yacimientos kársticos y al aire libre de África: un intento para evaluar los sesgos de predación y fosilización sobre la paleodiversidad]. *Journal of Iberian Geology [Cuadernos de geología ibérica]* 23, 73–94.

Denys, C. (1999). Of mice and men. Evolution in East and South Africa during Plio-Pleistocene times. In: T.G. Bromage and F. Schrenk (Eds.), *African Biogeography, Climate Change and Human Evolution*. New York: Oxford University Press, pp.226–252.

Denys, C. (2011). Rodents. In: T. Harrison (Ed.), *Paleontology and Geology of Laetoli: Human Evolution in Context. Vol. 2: Fossil Hominins and the Associated Fauna*. Dordrecht: Springer, pp. 15–53.

Denys, C., Patou, M. and Djemmali, N. (1984). Tighennif (Ternifinne, Algérie). Premiers résultats concernant l'origine de l'accumulation du matériel osseux de ce gisement Pléistocène *Comptes Rendu de l'Académie des Sciences Paris II* 299, 481–486.

Denys, C., Geraads, D., Hublin, J.-J. and Tong, H. (1987). Méthode d'étude taphonomique des microvertébrés. Application au site pléistocène de Tighenif (Ternifine, Algérie). *Archeozoologia* 1, 53–82.

Denys, C., Williams, C., Dauphin, Y., Andrews, P. and Fernandez-Jalvo, Y. (1996). Diagenetical changes in Pleistocene small mammal bones from Olduvai Bed I. *Palaeogeography, Palaeoclimatology, Palaeoecology* 126, 121–134.

Denys, C., Chitaukali, W., Mfune, J.K., Combrexelle, M. and Cacciani, F. (1999). Diversity of small mammals in owl pellet assemblages of Karonga district, northern Malawi. *Acta Zoologica Cracoviensia*, 42, 393–396.

DeSilva, J.M., Steininger, C.M. and Patel, B.A. (2013). Cercopithecoid primate postcranial fossils from Cooper's D, South Africa. *Geobios* 46, 381–394.

DeSilva, J.M., Gill, C.M., Prang, T.C., Bredella, M.A. and Alemseged, Z. (2018). A nearly complete foot from Dikika, Ethiopia and its implications for the ontogeny and function of *Australopithecus afarensis*. *Science Advances* 4, eaar7723.

Desio, A. (1935). Studi geologici sulla Cirenaica, sul deserto Libico, sulla Tripolitania, et sulla Fezzan orientali. In: *Missione scientifica della reale Accademia d'Italia a Cufra 1*. Roma: Reale Accademia d'Italia.

D'Huart, J., de Jong, Y.A. and Butynski, T. (2016). *Phacochoerus aethiopicus*. The IUCN Red List of Threatened Species 2016: e.T41767A44140316.

Dibble, H.L., Aldeias, V., Alvarez-Fernandez, E., et al. (2012). New excavations at the site of Contrebandiers Cave, Morocco. *PaleoAnthropology* 2012, 145–201.

Dice, L.R. (1945). Measures of the amount of ecologic association between species. *Ecology* 26, 297–302.

Diekmann, B. and Kuhn, G. (2002). Sedimentary record of the mid-Pleistocene climate transition in the southeastern South Atlantic (ODP Site 1090). *Palaeogeography, Palaeoclimatology, Palaeoecology* 182(3–4), 241–258.

Dietl, G.P. and Flessa, K.W. (2009). Conservation paleobiology: using the past to manage the future. *The Paleontological Society Papers*, Vol. 15, Paleontological Society.

Dietrich, W.O. (1941). Die säugetierpaläontologischen Ergebnisse der Kohl-Larsen'schen Expedition 1937–1939 im nördlichen Deutsch-Ostafrika. *Zentralblatt für Mineralogie, Geologie und Paläontologie, Abt. B, Stuttgart*, 217–223.

Dietrich, W.O. (1942a). Ältestquartäre Säugetiere aus der südlichen Serengeti, Deutsch-Ostafrika. *Palaeontographica* 94A, 43–133.

Dietrich, W.O. (1942b). Zur Entwicklungsmechanik des Gebisses der afrikanischen Nashörner. *Zentralblatt für Mineralogie, Geologie und Paläontologie, Abt. B, Stuttgart*, 297–300.

Dietrich, W.O. (1945). Nashornreste aus dem Quartär Deutsch-Ostafrikas. *Palaeontographica* 96A, 46–90.

Dietrich, W.O. (1950). Fossile Antilopen und Rinder Äquatorialafrikas (Material der Kohl-Larsen'schen Expeditionen). *Palaeontographica* 99A, 1–62.

Dietrich, W.O. (1951). Daten zu den fossilen Elefanten Afrikas und Ursprung der Gattung *Loxodonta*. *Neues Jahrbuch für Mineralogie, Geologie und Paläontologie, Stuttgart*, 93, 325–378.

DiMaggio, E.N., Campisano, C.J., Arrowsmith, J.R., et al. (2008). Correlation and stratigraphy of the BKT-2 volcanic complex in west-central Afar, Ethiopia. In: J. Quade and J.G. Wynn (Eds.), *The Geology of Early Humans in the Horn of Africa*. Boulder: Geological Society of America, pp. 163–178.

DiMaggio, E.N., Campisano, C.J., Rowan, J., et al. (2015a). Late Pliocene fossiliferous sedimentary record and the environmental context of early *Homo* from Afar, Ethiopia. *Science* 347, 1355–1359.

DiMaggio, E.N., Arrowsmith, J.R., Campisano, C.J., et al. (2015b). Tephrostratigraphy and depositional environment of young (<2.94 Ma) Hadar Formation deposits at Ledi-Geraru, Afar, Ethiopia. *Journal of African Earth Sciences* 112, 234–250.

Di Vincenzo, F., Rodriguez, L., Carretero, J.M., et al. (2015). The massive fossil humerus from the Oldowan horizon of Gombore I, Melka Kunture (Ethiopia, >1.39 Ma). *Quaternary Science Reviews* 122, 207–221.

Dirks, P.H. and Berger, L.R. (2013). Hominin-bearing caves and landscape dynamics in the Cradle of Humankind, South Africa. *Journal of African Earth Sciences* 78, 109–131.

Dirks, P.H., Kibii, J.M., Kuhn, B.F., et al. (2010). Geological setting and age of *Australopithecus sediba* from southern Africa. *Science*, 328(5975), 205–208.

Dirks, P.H., Berger, L.R., Roberts, E.M., et al. (2015). Geological and taphonomic context for the new hominin species Homo naledi from the Dinaledi Chamber, South Africa. *Elife*, 4, e09561.

Dirks, P.H., Roberts, E.M., Hilbert-Wolf, H., et al. (2017). The age of Homo naledi and associated sediments in the Rising Star Cave, South Africa. *Elife*, 6, e24231.

Disotell, T.R. (2006). 'Chumanzee' evolution: the urge to diverge and merge. *Genome Biology* 7(11), 1.

Disotell, T.R. (2013). Genetic perspectives on ape and human evolution. In: D.R. Begun (Ed.), *A Companion to Paleoanthropology*. Chichester: Wiley-Blackwell, pp. 290–305.

Ditchfield, P. and Harrison, T. (2011). Sedimentology, lithostratigraphy and depositional history of the Laetoli area. In: T. Harrison (Ed.), *Paleontology and Geology of Laetoli: Human Evolution in Context. Vol. 1: Geology, Geochronology, Paleoecology, and Paleoenvironment*. Dordrecht: Springer, pp. 47–76.

Ditchfield, P., Hicks, J., Plummer, T., Bishop, L.C. and Potts, R. (1999). Current research on the Late Pliocene and Pleistocene deposits north of Homa Mountain, southwestern Kenya. *Journal of Human Evolution* 36(2), 123–150.

Ditchfield, P.W., Kingston, J.D., Plummer, T., et al. (2006). Tooth enamel oxygen isotope analysis to investigate seasonality at the late Pliocene Oldowan site Kanjera South, Kenya. *PaleoAnthropology* 2006:A16.

Ditchfield, P.W., Whitfield, E., Vincent, T., et al. (2019). Geochronology and physical context of Oldowan site formation at Kanjera South, Kenya. *Geological Magazine* 156(7), 1190–1200.

Dixey, F. (1927). The Tertiary and post-Tertiary lacustrine sediments of the Nyasan Rift-Valley. *Quarterly Journal of the Geological Society* 83(1–5), 432–442.

Djemmali, N.-E. (1985). L'industrie lithique acheuléenne du gisement de Tighennif (Ternifine), Algérie. Thèse doctorat 3ème cycle, Université P. et M. Curie, Paris.

Dobson, M. (2004). Freshwater crabs in Africa. *Freshwater Forum* 21, 3–26.

Volume References

Dodson, P. (1973). The significance of small bones in paleoecological interpretation. *Contributions to Geology* 12, 15–19.

Dodson, P. and Wexlar, D. (1979). Taphonomic investigations of owl pellets. *Paleobiology* 5, 275–284.

Dollion, A.Y., Cornette, R., Tolley, K.A., et al. (2015). Morphometric analysis of chameleon fossil fragments from the Early Pliocene of South Africa: a new piece of the chamaeleonid history. *The Science of Nature* 102(1–2), 2.

Doman, J.H. (2017). The Paleontology and Paleoecology of the Late Miocene Mpesida Beds and Lukeino Formation, Tugen Hills succession, Baringo, Kenya, Anthropology. Thesis, Department of Anthropology, Yale University, p. 202.

Doman, J. and Coutros, P. (2015). Environmental heterogeneity of a late Miocene east African landscape: introducing new mammalian fauna and integrating multiple paleoecological methods and modern forest ecology techniques in the Mpesida Beds, Baringo, Kenya. *Journal of Vertebrate Paleontology, SVP Program and Abstracts Book* (75).

Domínguez-Rodrigo, M. (1997). Meat-eating by early hominids at the FLK 22 *Zinjanthropus* site, Olduvai Gorge (Tanzania): an experimental approach using cut-mark data. *Journal of Human Evolution* 33, 669–690.

Dominguez-Rodrigo, M.C. (2014). Is the 'Savanna Hypothesis' a dead concept for explaining the emergence of the earliest hominins? *Current Anthropology* 55(1), 59–81.

Dominguez-Rodrigo, M. and Piqueras, A. (2003). The use of tooth pits to identify carnivore taxa in tooth-marked archaeofaunas and their relevance to reconstruct hominid carcass processing behaviours. *Journal of Archaeological Science* 30, 1385–1391.

Domínguez-Rodrigo, M., de la Torre, I., de Luque, L., et al. (2002). The ST site complex at Peninj, west Lake Natron, Tanzania: implications for early hominid behavioural models. *Journal of Archaeological Science* 29, 639–665.

Domínguez-Rodrigo, M., Barba, R. and Egeland, C.P. (2007). *Deconstructing Olduvai: A Taphonomic Study of the Bed I Sites*. Dordrecht: Springer.

Domínguez-Rodrigo, M., Mabulla, A., Luque, L., et al. (2008). A new archaic Homo sapiens fossil from Lake Eyasi, Tanzania. *Journal of Human Evolution* 54, 899–903.

Domínguez-Rodrigo, M., de Juana, S., Gala, A.B. and Rodríguez, M. (2009a). A new protocol to differentiate trampling marks from butchery cut marks. *Journal of Archaeological Science* 36, 2643–2654.

Domínguez-Rodrigo, M., Alcalá, L. and Luque, L. (Eds.) (2009b). *Peninj: A Research Project on Human Origins 1995–2005*. Oxford: Oxbow Books.

Domínguez-Rodrigo, M., Bunn, H.T., Mabulla, A., Baquedano, E. and Pickering, T.R. (2010a). Paleoecology and hominin behavior during Bed I at Olduvai Gorge (Tanzania). *Quaternary Research* 74, 301–303.

Domínguez-Rodrigo, M., Pickering, T.R., Bunn, H.T. (2010b). Configurational approach to identifying the earliest hominin butchers. *Proceedings of the National Academy of Sciences* 107, 20929–20934.

Domínguez-Rodrigo, M., Bunn, H.T., Pickering, T.R., et al. (2012). Autochthony and orientation patterns in Olduvai Bed I: a re-examination of the status of post-depositional biasing of archaeological assemblages from FLK North (FLKN). *Journal of Archaeological Science* 39, 2116–2127.

Dominguez-Rodrigo, M., Pickering, T. R., Baquedano, E., et al. (2013). First partial skeleton of a 1.34-million-year-old *Paranthropus boisei* from Bed II, Olduvai Gorge, Tanzania. *PLoS ONE* 8(12), e80347.

Domínguez-Rodrigo, M., Uribelarrea, D., Santonja, M., et al. (2014a). Autochthonous anisotropy of archaeological materials by the action of water: experimental and archaeological reassessment of the orientation patterns at the Olduvai sites. *Journal of Archaeological Science* 41, 44–68.

Domínguez-Rodrigo, M., Diez-Martín, F., Mabulla, A., et al. (2014b). The evolution of hominin behavior during the Oldowan–Acheulean transition: recent evidence from Olduvai Gorge and Peninj (Tanzania). *Quaternary International*, 322, 1–6.

Domínguez-Rodrigo, M., Baquedano, E., Mabulla, A., Mercader, J. and Egeland, C.P. (2017). Paleoecological reconstructions of the Bed I and Bed II lacustrine basins of Olduvai Gorge (Tanzania) and insights into early human behavior. *Palaeogeography, Palaeoclimatology, Palaeoecology* 488, 1–8.

Dongmann, G., Nurnberg, H.W., Forstel, H. and Wagener, K. (1974). On the enrichment of $H_2{}^{18}O$ in the leaves of transpiring plants. *Radiation and Environmental Biophysics* 11, 41–52.

Dorale, J.A., Edwards, R.L., Alexander Jr, C.A., et al. (2004). Uranium-series dating of speleothems: current techniques, limits, & applications. In: I.D. Sasowsky and J.E. Mylroie (Eds.), *Studies of Cave Sediments: Physical and Chemical Records of Paleoclimate*. New York: Kluwer Academic/Plenum Publishers, pp. 177–197.

Doran, T.L., Herries, A.I., Hopley, P.J., et al. (2015). Assessing the paleoenvironmental potential of Pliocene to Holocene tufa deposits along the Ghaap Plateau escarpment (South Africa) using stable isotopes. *Quaternary Research* 84(1), 133–143.

Douady, C.J., Catzeflis, F., Raman, J., Springer, M.S. and Stanhope, M.J. (2003). The Sahara as a vicariant agent, and the role of Miocene climatic events, in the diversification of the mammalian order Macroscelidea (elephant shrews). *Proceedings of the National Academy of Sciences*, 100(14), 8325–8330.

Drake, R. and Curtis, G.H. (1987). K–Ar geochronology of the Laetoli fossil localities. In: M.D. Leakey and J.M. Harris (Eds.), *Laetoli: A Pliocene Site in Northern Tanzania*. Oxford: Clarendon Press, pp. 48–52.

Drapeau, M.S.M., Bobe, R., Wynn, J.G., et al. (2014). The Omo Mursi Formation: a window into the East African Pliocene. *Journal of Human Evolution*, 75, 64–79. doi: 10.1016/j.jhevol.2014.07.001.

Drapeau, M.S.M, Wynn, J.G., Geraads, D., et al. (2016). Where they were not: What can the Mursi Formation tell us about early hominins habitat preferences? *Program of the 44th annual meeting of the Canadian Association of Physical Anthropology*, 27. https://caba-acab.net/sites/default/files/basic-page/capa_2016_program_final.pdf

Dreyer, T.F. (1938). The archaeology of the Florisbad deposits. *Argeologiese Navorsing van die Nasionale Museum, Bloemfontein* 1, 183–190.

Du, A. and Alemseged, Z. (2018). Diversity analysis of Plio-Pleistocene large mammal communities in the Omo-Turkana Basin, eastern Africa. *Journal of Human Evolution* 124, 25–39.

Du, A., Robinson, J.R., Rowan, J., Lazagabaster, I.A. and Behrensmeyer, A.K. (2019). Stable carbon isotopes from paleosol carbonate and herbivore enamel document differing paleovegetation signals in the eastern African Plio-Pleistocene. *Review of Palaeobotany and Palynology* 261, 41–52.

Du, A., Rowan, J., Wang, S.C., Wood, B.A. and Alemseged, Z. (2020). Statistical estimates of hominin origination and extinction dates: a case study examining the *Australopithecus anamensis–afarensis* lineage. *Journal of Human Evolution* 138, 102688.

Dubois, C., Quinif, Y., Baele, J.M., et al. (2014). The process of ghost-rock karstification and its role in the formation of cave systems. *Earth-Science Reviews* 131, 116–148.

Du Toit, J.T. and Owen-Smith, N. (1989). Body size, population metabolism, and habitat specialization among large African herbivores. *The American Naturalist*, 133(5), 736–740.

Dumouchel, L. (2017). Australopithecus anamensis paleoenvironments in the Omo-Turkana basin using stable isotope analysis of tooth enamel from mixed feeding taxa. *PaleoAnthropology*, A10.

Dumouchel, L. (2018). A multi-proxi analysis of Australopithecus anamensis paleoecology in the Omo-Turkana Basin. PhD dissertation, George Washington University, p. 171.

Dunbar, R.I.M. (1983). Theropithecines and hominids: contrasting solutions to the same ecological problem. *Journal of Human Evolution* 12, 647–658.

Dunhill, A.M., Benton, M.J., Twitchett, R.J. and Newell, A.J. (2012). Completeness of the fossil record and validity of sampling proxies at outcrop level. *Palaeontology* 55(6), 1155–1175.

Dunhill, A.M., Hannisdal, B. and Benton, M. J. (2014). Disentangling rock record bias and common-cause from redundancy in the British fossil record. *Nature Communications* 5, 4818.

Dupont, L. and Leroy, S. (1995). Steps toward drier climatic conditions in Northwestern Africa during the Upper Pliocene. In: E.S. Vrba, G. Denton, T. Partridge and L. Burckle (Eds.), *Paleoclimate and Evolution*. New Haven: Yale University Press, pp. 289–298.

Dupont-Nivet, G., Sier, M., Campisano, C.J., et al. (2008). Magnetostratigraphy of the eastern Hadar Basin (Ledi-Geraru research area, Ethiopia) and implications for hominin paleoenvironments. In: J. Quade and J.G. Wynn (Eds.), *The Geology of Early Humans in the Horn of Africa*. Boulder: The Geological Society of America, pp. 67–85.

Duringer, P., Schuster, M., Genise, J.F., et al. (2006). The first fossil fungus gardens of Isoptera: oldest evidence of symbiotic termite fungiculture (Miocene, Chad basin). *Naturwissenschaften* 93, 610–615.

Duringer, P., Schuster, M., Genise, J.F., et al. (2007). New termite trace fossils: galleries, nests and fungus combs from the Chad basin of Africa (Upper Miocene–Lower Pliocene). *Palaeogeography, Palaeoclimatology, Palaeoecology* 251, 323–353.

Durkee, H. and Brown, F. H. (2014). Correlation of volcanic ash layers between the Early Pleistocene Acheulean sites of Isinya, Kariandusi, and Olorgesailie, Kenya. *Journal of Archaeological Science* 49, 510–517.

Dusseldorp, G., Lombard, M. and Wurz, S. (2013). Pleistocene *Homo* and the updated Stone Age sequence of South Africa. *South African Journal of Science* 109(5/6), Art.#0042.

Duvernoy, G.L. (1851). Note sur une espèce de buffle fossile (*Bubalus* (*Arni*) *antiquus*), découverte en Algérie. *Comptes Rendus de l'Académie des Sciences* 33, 595–597.

Dynesius, M. and Jansson, R. (2000). Evolutionary consequences of changes in species' geographical distributions driven by Milankovitch climate oscillations. *Proceedings of the National Academy of Sciences of the United States of America* 97(16), 9115–9120.

Eberz, G.W., Williams, F.M. and Williams, M.A.J. (1988). Plio-Pleistocene volcanism and sedimentary facies changes at Gadeb prehistoric site, Ethiopia. *Geologische Rundschau* 77, 513–527.

Ebinger, C.J., 1989. Tectonic development of the western branch of the East African rift system. *Geological Society of America Bulletin* 101, 885–903.

Ebinger, C. and Scholz, C.A. (2012). Continental rift basins: the East African perspective. In: C. Busby and A. Azor (Eds.), *Tectonics of Sedimentary Basins: Recent Advances*. Oxford: Wiley-Blackwell, pp. 183–208.

Ebinger, C.J., Deino, A.L., Drake, R.E. and Tesha, A.L. (1989). Chronology of volcanism and rift basin propagation: Rungwe volcanic province, East Africa. *Journal of Geophysical Research* 94, 15785–15803.

Ebinger, C.J., Deino, A.L., Tesha, A.L. and Ring, U. (1993). Regional tectonic controls on rift basin geometry: evolution of an East African lake basin. *Journal of Geophysical Research* B98, 17821–17836.

Ebinger, C.J., Yemane, T., Harding, D.J., et al. (2000). Rift deflection, migration, and propagation: linkage of the Ethiopian and Eastern rifts, Africa. *Geological Society of America Bulletin* 112, 163–176.

Echassoux, A., Moullé, P.-É., Desclaux, E. and Alemseged, Z. (2004). Les faunes Plio-Pléistocène du site de Fejej FJ1. In: H. de Lumley and Y. Beyene (Eds.), *Les sites préhistoriques de la région de Fejej, Sud-Omo, Éthiopie, dans leur contexte stratigraphique et paléontologique*. Paris: Éditions Recherche sur les Civilisations, pp. 203–340.

Eck, G.G. (1993). *Theropithecus darti* from the Hadar Formation, Ethiopia. In: N.G. Jablonski (Ed.), Theropithecus: The Rise and Fall of a Primate Genus. Cambridge: Cambridge University Press, pp. 15–83.

Eck, G.G. (2007). The effects of collection strategy and effort on faunal recovery. A case study of the American and French collections from the Shungura Formation, Ethiopia. In: A.K. Behrensmeyer, R. Bobe and Z. Alemseged (Eds.), *Hominin Environments in the East African Pliocene: An Assessment of the Faunal Evidence*. Dordrecht: Springer, pp. 183–215.

Ecker, M. (2016). Two million years of environmental change: a case study from Wonderwerk Cave, Northern Cape, South Africa. DPhil dissertation, University of Oxford.

Ecker, M. and Lee-Thorp, J.A. (2018). The dietary ecology of the extinct springbok *Antidorcas bondi*. *Quaternary international* 495, 136–143.

Ecker, M., Botha-Brink, J., Lee-Thorp, J., Piuz, A. and Horwitz, L. (2015a). Ostrich eggshell as a source of palaeoenvironmental information in the arid interior of South Africa: a case study from Wonderwerk Cave. In J. Runge (Ed.), *Changing Climates, Ecosystems and Environments within Arid Southern Africa and Adjoining Regions*. Palaeoecology of Africa, 33. Boca Raton: CRC Press, pp. 95–115.

Ecker M., Brink J., Scott L., et al. (2015b). New isotopic insights into palaeoecology and palaeoenvironment over 2 million years from Wonderwerk Cave, South Africa. Poster Session 2, Poster 75, 5th Annual meeting of ESHE, London, 10–12 September. Abstract p. 84.

Ecker, M., Brink, J., Horwitz, L.K., Scott, L. and Lee-Thorp, J.A. (2018a). A 12,000 year record of changes in herbivore niche separation and palaeoclimate (Wonderwerk Cave, South Africa). *Quaternary Science Reviews* 180, 132–144.

Ecker, M., Brink, J.S., Rossouw, L., et al. (2018b). The palaeoecological context of the Oldowan–Acheulean in southern Africa. *Nature Ecology & Evolution* 2(7), 1080–1086.

Edwards, E.J., Osborne, C.P., Strömberg, C.A., et al. (2010). The origins of C_4 grasslands: integrating evolutionary and ecosystem science. *Science* 328, 587–591.

Efremov, J.A. (1940). Taphonomy: new branch of paleontology. *Pan-American Geologist* 74, 81–93.

Egeland, C.P. (2007). Zooarchaeology and taphonomy of the DK site. In: M. Domínguez-Rodrigo, R. Barba and C. Egeland (Eds.), *Deconstructing Olduvai: A Taphonomic Study of the Bed I Sites*. Dordrecht: Springer, pp. 253–268.

Ehleringer, J.R., Cerling, T.E. and Helliker, B.R. (1997). C_4 photosynthesis, atmospheric CO2, and climate. *Oecologia* 112(3), 285–299.

Eisenhart, W.L. (1974). The fossil Cercopithecoids of Makapansgat and Sterkfontein. BA thesis, Harvard College.

Eisenmann, V. (1976a). Le protostylide: Valeur systématique et signification phylétique chez les espèces actuelles et fossiles du genre *Equus* (Perissodactyla, Mammalia). *Zeitschrift für Säugetierkunde* 41, 349–365.

Eisenmann, V. (1976b). Equidae from the Shungura Formation. In: Y. Coppens, F.C. Howell, G.L. Isaac, and R.E. Leakey, R.E. (Eds.), *Earliest Man and Environments in the Lake Rudolf Basin*. Chicago: University of Chicago Press, pp. 225–233.

Eisenmann, V. (1979a). Etude des cornets des dents incisives inférieures des *Equus* (Mammalia, Perissodactyla) actuels et fossiles. *Palaeontographia Italica* 71, 55–75.

Eisenmann, V. (1979b). Les métapodes d' *Equus* sensu lato (Mammalia, Perissodactyla). *Geobios* 12, 863–886.

Eisenmann, V. (1980). *Les chevaux (Equus sensu lato) fossiles et actuels: crânes et dents jugales supérieures. Cahiers de paléontologie*. Paris: Centre national de la recherche scientifique.

Eisenmann, V. (1981). Etude des dents jugales inférieures des *Equus* (Mammalia, Perissodactyla) actuels et fossiles. *Palaeovertebrata* 10, 127–226.

Eisenmann, V. (1984). Sur quelques caractères adaptatifs du squelette d'*Equus* (Mammalia, Perissodactyla) et leurs implications paléoécologiques. *Bulletin du Museum national d'histoire naturelle, C, 4ème séres* 6, 185–195.

Eisenmann, V. (1985). Indications paléoécologiques fournies par les *Equus* (Mammalia, Perissodactyla) plio-pléistocènes d'Afrique. In: *L'Environnement des Hominidés au Plio-Pléistocène*. Paris: Masson, pp. 57–79.

Eisenmann, V. (1994). Equidae of the Albertine Rift Valley, Uganda. In: B. Senut and M. Pickford (Eds.), *Geology and Palaeobiology of the Albertine Rift Valley, Uganda–Zaire, Vol. II, Palaeobiology*. Publication Occasionelle. Orléans: Centre International pour la Formation et les Echanges Géologiques – CIFEG, pp. 289–307.

Eisenmann, V. (1998). Folivores et tondeurs d'herbe: forme de la symphyse mandibulaire des Equidés et des Tapiridés (Perissodactyla, Mammalia). *Geobios* 31, 113–123.

Eisenmann, V. and Geraads, D. (2007). The hipparion from the late Pliocene of Ahl al Oughlam, Morocco, and a revision of the relationships of Pliocene and Pleistocene African hipparions. *Palaeontologica Africana* 42, 51–98.

Eizirik, E., Murphy, W.J., Springer, M.S. and O'Brien, S J. (2004). Molecular phylogeny and dating of early primate divergences. In: C.F. Ross and R.F. Kay (Eds.), *Anthropoid Origins. Developments in Primatology: Progress and Prospects*. Boston, MA: Springer, pp. 45–64.

El-Saadawi, W., Kamal-El-Din, M., Wheeler, E.A., et al. (2014). Early Miocene woods of Egypt. *IAWA Journal* 35, 35–50.

El-Shawaihdi, M.H., Mozley, P.S., Boaz, N.T., et al. (2016). Stratigraphy of the Neogene Sahabi units in the Sirt Basin, northeast Libya. *Journal of African Earth Sciences* 118, 87–106.

Eldredge, N. and Gould, S.J. (1972). Punctuated equilibria: an alternative to phyletic gradualism. In: T.J.M. Schopf (Ed.), *Models in Paleobiology*. San Francisco: Freeman, Cooper and Company, pp. 82–115.

Ellis, R.P. (1987). A review of comparative leaf blade anatomy in the systematics of the Poaceae: the past twenty five years. In: T.R. Soderstrom, K.W. Hilu, C.S. Campbell, and M.E. Barkworth (Eds.), *Grass Systematics and Evolution*. Washington, DC: Smithsonian Institution Press, pp. 3–10.

Ellison, A.M. (2010). Partitioning diversity 1. *Ecology* 91(7), 1962–1963.

Elton, S. (2001). Locomotor and habitat classification of cercopithecoid postcranial material from Sterkfontein Member 4, Bolt's Farm, and Swartkrans Member 1 and 2, South Africa. *Palaeontologica Africana* 37, 115–126.

Elton, S. (2006). Forty years on and still going strong: the use of hominin–cercopithecid comparisons in palaeoanthropology. *Journal of the Royal Anthropological Institute* 12, 19–38.

Engel, J., Woodhead, J., Hellstrom, J., et al. (2019). Corrections for initial isotopic disequilibrium in the speleothem U–Pb dating method. *Quaternary Geochronology* 54, 101009.

Ennouchi, E. (1962). Un Neanderthalien: l'homme du Jebel Irhoud (Maroc). *L'Anthropologie* 66, 279–299.

Ennouchi, E. (1968). Le deuxième crâne de l'homme d'Irhoud. *Annales de Paléontologie (Vertébrés)* 54, 117–128.

Ennouchi, E. (1969). Découverte d'un pithécanthropien au Maroc. *Comptes Rendus de l'Académie des Sciences D* 269, 763–765.

Ennouchi, E. (1970). Un nouvel archanthropien au Maroc. *Annales de Paléontologie* 56, 95–107.

Ennouchi, E. (1972). Nouvelle découverte d'un archanthropien au Maroc. *Comptes Rendus de l'Académie des Sciences Paris D* 274, 3088–3090.

Ennouchi, E. (1975). New discovery of an Archanthropian in Morocco. *Journal of Human Evolution* 4, 441–443.

Ennouchi, E. (1976). Un deuxième archanthropien à la carrière Thomas III (Maroc). *Bulletin du Museum national d'Histoire Naturelle., sciences des Terre, séries 3* 56, 273–296.

Erlanger, E.D., Granger, D.E., Gibbon, R.J. (2012). Rock uplift rates in South Africa from isochron burial dating of fluvial and marine terraces. *Geology* 40, 1019–1022.

Eriksson, P.G., Schweitzer, J.K., Bosch, P.J.A., et al. (1993). The Transvaal sequence: an overview. *Journal of African Earth Science* 16, 25–51.

Eronen, J.T., Ataabadi, M.M., Micheels, A., et al. (2009). Distribution history and climatic controls of the Late Miocene Pikermian chronofauna. *Proceedings of the National Academy of Sciences* 106(29), 11867–11871.

Eronen, J.T., Puolamäki, P., Liu, L., et al. (2010a). Precipitation and large herbivorous mammals I: estimates from present-day communities. *Evolutionary Ecology Research* 12, 217–233.

Eronen, J.T., Puolamäki, P., Liu, L., et al. (2010b). Precipitation and large herbivorous mammals II: application to fossil data. *Evolutionary Ecology Research* 12, 235–248.

Esau, K. (1960). *Anatomy of Seed Plants*. New York: John Wiley and Sons.

Esterhuysen, A.B., Sanders, V.M. and Smith, J.M. (2008). Human skeletal and mummified remains from the AD1854 siege of Mugombane, Limpopo, South Africa. *Journal of Archaeological Sciences* 36, 1038–1049.

Estes, R.D. (2012). *The Behavior Guide to African Mammals: Including Hoofed Mammals, Carnivores, Primates*. Berkeley: University of California Press.

Eugster, H.P. (1981). Lake Magadi, Kenya, and its precursors. In: A. Nissenbaum (Ed.), *Hypersaline Brines and Evaporitic Environments*. Amsterdam: Elsevier, pp. 195–232.

Evans, E.M.N., van Couvering, J.H. and Andrews, P. (1981). Palaeoecology of Miocene sites in Western Kenya. *Journal of Human Evolution* 10, 35–48.

Everett, M. (2010). The paleoecology of the Pleistocene Upper Busidima Formation, Gona, Afar Depression, Ethiopia. PhD thesis, University of Indiana.

Ewer, R.F. (1956). The dating of the Australopithecinae: faunal evidence. *South African Archaeological Bulletin* 11, 41–45.

Ewer, R.F. (1957a). Faunal evidence on the dating of the Australopithecinae. In: J.D. Clark and S. Cole (Eds.), *Proceedings of the Third Pan-African Congress on Prehistory, 1955*. London: Livingstone, pp. 135–142.

Ewer, R.F. (1957b). Some fossil carnivores from Makapansgat valley. *Palaeontologica Africana* 4, 57–67.

Ewer, R.F. (1958). The fossil Suidae of Makapansgat. *Proceedings of the Zoological Society of London* 1303, 329–372.

Ewer, R.F. (1967). The fossil hyaenids of Africa – a reappraisal. In W.W. Bishop and J.D. Clard (Eds.), *Background to Evolution in Africa*. Chicago: University of Chicago Press, pp. 109–123.

Faith, J.T. (2011). Ungulate community richness, grazer extinctions, and human subsistence behavior in southern Africa's Cape Floral Region. Palaeogeography, Palaeoclimatology, Palaeoecology 306, 219–227.

Faith, J.T. (2012a). Conservation implications of fossil roan antelope (*Hippotragus equinus*) in southern Africa's Cape Floristic Region. In: J. Louys (Ed.), *Paleontology in Ecology and Conservation*. Heidelberg: Springer, pp. 239–251.

Faith, J.T. (2012b). Palaeozoological insights into management options for a threatened mammal: southern Africa's Cape mountain zebra (*Equus zebra zebra*). Diversity and Distributions 18, 438–447.

Faith, J.T. (2013). Taphonomic and paleoecological change in the large mammal sequence from Boomplaas Cave, Western Cape, South Africa. Journal of Human Evolution 65, 715–730.

Faith, J.T. (2014). Late Pleistocene and Holocene mammal extinctions on continental Africa. Earth-Science Reviews 128, 105–121.

Faith, J.T. and Behrensmeyer, A.K. (2013). Climate change and faunal turnover: testing the mechanics of the turnover–pulse hypothesis with South African fossil data. Paleobiology 39, 609–627.

Faith, J.T. and O'Connell, J.F. (2011). Revisiting the late Pleistocene mammal extinction record at Tight Entrance Cave, southwestern Australia. Quaternary Research 76(3), 397–400.

Faith, J.T. and Thompson, J.C. (2013). Fossil evidence for seasonal calving and migration of extinct blue antelope (*Hippotragus leucophaeus*) in southern Africa. Journal of Biogeography 40(11), 2108–2118.

Faith, J.T., Choiniere, J.N., Tryon, C.A., Peppe, D.J. and Fox, D.L. (2011). Taxonomic status and paleoecology of *Rusingoryx atopocranion* (Mammalia, Artiodactyla), an extinct Pleistocene bovid from Rusinga Island, Kenya. Quaternary Research 75, 697–707.

Faith, J.T., Potts, R., Plummer, T.W., et al. (2012). New perspectives on middle Pleistocene change in the large mammal faunas of East Africa: *Damaliscus hypsodon* sp. nov. (Mammalia, Artiodactyla) from Lainyamok, Kenya. Palaeogeography, Palaeoclimatology, Palaeoecology 361–362, 84–93.

Faith, J.T., Tryon, C.A., Peppe, D.J. and Fox, D.L. (2013). The fossil history of Grévy's zebra (*Equus grevyi*) in equatorial East Africa. Journal of Biogeography 40, 359–369.

Faith, J.T., Tryon, C.A., Peppe, D.J., et al. (2015). Paleoenvironmental context of the Middle Stone Age record from Karungu, Lake Victoria Basin, Kenya, and its implications for human and fauna dispersals in East Africa. Journal of Human Evolution 83, 28–45.

Faith, J.T., Tryon, C.A. and Peppe, D.J. (2016). Environmental change, ungulate biogeography, and their implications for early human dispersals in equatorial East Africa. In: S.C. Jones and B.A. Stewart (Eds.), *Africa from MIS 6-2: Population Dynamics and Paleoenvironments*. Dordrecht: Springer, pp. 233–245.

Faith, J.T., Rowan, J., Du, A. and Koch, P.L. (2018). Plio-Pleistocene decline of African megaherbivores: no evidence for ancient hominin impacts. Science 362, 938.

Faith, J.T., Du, A. and Rowan, J. (2019a). Addressing the effects of sampling on ecometric-based paleoenvironmental reconstructions. Palaeogeography, Palaeoclimatology, Palaeoecology 528, 175–185.

Faith, J.T., Chase, B.M. and Avery, D.M. (2019b). Late Quaternary micromammals and the precipitation history of the southern Cape, South Africa. Quaternary Research 91(2), 848–860.

Fara, E., Likius, A., Mackaye, H.T., Vignaud, P. and Brunet, M. (2005). Pliocene large-mammal assemblages from northern Chad: sampling and ecological structure. Naturwissenschaften 92, 537–541.

Fauquette, S., Suc, J.-P., Bertini, A., et al. (2006). How much did climate force the Messinian salinity crisis? Quantified climatic conditions from pollen records in the Mediterranean region. Palaeogeography, Palaeoclimatology, Palaeoecology 238, 281–301.

Feakins, S.J. (2013). Pollen-corrected leaf wax D/H reconstructions of northeast African hydrological changes during the late Miocene. Palaeogeography, Palaeoclimatology, Palaeoecology 374, 62–71.

Feakins, S.J. and deMenocal, P.B. (2010). Global and African regional climate during the Cenozoic. In: L. Werdelin and W.J. Sanders (Eds.), *Cenozoic Mammals of Africa*. Berkeley: University of California Press, pp. 45–55.

Feakins, S.J., deMenocal, P.B. and Eglinton, T.J. (2005). Biomarker records of late Neogene changes in northeast African vegetation. Geology 33, 977–980.

Feakins, S.J., Levin, N.E., Liddy, H.M., et al. (2013). Northeast African vegetation change over 12 m.y. Geology 41(3), 295–298.

Feathers, J.K. (2002). Luminescence dating in less than ideal conditions: case studies from Klasies River main site and Duinefontein, South Africa. Journal of Archaeological Science 29(2), 177–194.

Feathers, J.K. and Bush, D.A. (2000). Luminescence dating of middle stone age deposits at Die Kelders. Journal of Human Evolution 38(1), 91–119.

Feddi, N., Fauquette, S. and Suc, J.-P. (2011). Histoire plio-pléistocène des écosystèmes végétaux de Méditerranée sud-occidentale: apport de l'analyse pollinique de deux sondages en mer d'Alboran. Geobios 44, 57–69.

Fedorov, A., Dekens, P., McCarthy, M., et al. (2006) The Pliocene paradox (mechanisms for a permanent El Niño). Science 312(5779), 1485–1489.

Fedorov, A.V., Brierley, C.M., Lawrence, K.T., et al. (2013). Patterns and mechanisms of early Pliocene warmth. Nature 496, 43–49.

Feibel, C.S. (1988). Paleoenvironments of the Koobi Fora Formation, northern Kenya. Thesis. University of Utah, p. 330.

Feibel, C.S. (1994). Freshwater stingrays from the Plio-Pleistocene of the Turkana Basin, Kenya and Ethiopia. Lethaia 26, 359–366.

Feibel, C.S. (1999a). Basin evolution, sedimentary dynamics, and hominid habitats in East Africa: an ecosystem approach. In: T.G. Bromage and F. Schrenk (Eds.), *African Biogeography, Climate Change, and Human Evolution*. Oxford: Oxford University Press, pp. 276–281.

Feibel, C.S. (1999b). Tephrostratigraphy and geological context in paleoanthropology. Evolutionary Anthropology 8, 87–100.

Feibel, C.S. (2003). Stratigraphy and depositional setting of the Pliocene Kanapoi Formation, lower Kerio valley, Kenya. In: J.M. Harris and M.G. Leakey (Eds.), *Geology and Vertebrate Paleontology of the Early Pliocene site of Kanapoi, Northern Kenya*. Los Angeles: Natural History Museum of Los Angeles County, pp. 9–20.

Feibel, C. (2011). A geological history of the Turkana Basin. Evolutionary Anthropology: Issues, News, and Reviews 20(6), 206–216.

Feibel, C.S., Brown, F.H. and McDougall, I. (1989). Stratigraphic context of fossil hominids from the Omo group deposits: Northern Turkana Basin, Kenya and Ethiopia. American Journal of Physical Anthropology 78(4), 595–622.

Feibel, C.S., Harris, J.M. and Brown, F.H. (1991). Palaeoenvironmental context for the late Neogene of the Turkana Basin. In: J.M. Harris (Ed.), *Koobi Fora Research Project, Volume 3: The Fossil Ungulates: Geology, Fossil Artiodactyls, and Paleoenvironments*. Oxford: Clarendon Press, pp. 321–370.

Volume References

Feibel, C.S., Agnew, N., Latimer, B., et al. (1996). The Laetoli hominid footprints – a preliminary report on the conservation and scientific restudy. *Evolutionary Anthropology* 4, 149–154.

Feibel, C.S., Lepre, C.J. and Quinn, R.L. (2009). Stratigraphy, correlation, and age estimates for fossils from Area 123, Koobi Fora. *Journal of Human Evolution* 57(2), 112–122.

Fernandez, P., Bouzouggar, A., Collina-Girard, J. and Coulon, M. (2015). The last occurrence of *Megaceroides algericus* Lyddekker, 1890 (Mammalia, Cervidae) during the middle Holocene in the cave of Bizmoune (Morocco, Essaouira region). *Quaternary International* 374, 154–167.

Fernández-Jalvo, Y. and Andrews, P. (2003). Experimental effects of water abrasion on bone fragments. *Journal of Taphonomy* 1, 147–163.

Fernández-Jalvo, Y. and Andrews, P. (2016). *Atlas of Taphonomic Identifications*. Dordrecht: SpringerScience and Business.

Fernández-Jalvo, Y. and Avery, D.M. (2015). Pleistocene micromammals and their predators at Wonderwerk Cave, South Africa. *African Archaeological Review* 32, 751–791.

Fernandez-Jalvo, Y., Denys, C., Andrews, P., et al. (1998). Taphonomy and palaeoecology of Olduvai Bed-I (Pleistocene, Tanzania). *Journal of Human Evolution* 34, 137–172.

Fernández-Jalvo, Y., Tormoa, L., Andrews, P. and Marin-Monfort, M.D. (2018). Taphonomy of burnt bones from Wonderwerk Cave (South Africa). *Quaternary International* 495, 19–29.

Ferraro, J.V., Plummer, T.W., Pobiner, B.L., et al. (2013). Earliest archaeological evidence of persistent hominin carnivory. *PLoS ONE* 8(4), e62174.

Ferretti, M.P., Torre, D. and Rook, L. (2001). The *Stegotetrabelodon* remains from Cessaniti (Calabria, Southern Italy) and their bearing on Late Miocene biogeography of the genus. In: G. Cavarretta et al. (Eds.), *Proceedings of the First International Congress of La Terra degli Elefanti, The World of Elephants*. Rome: Consiglio Nazionale delle Ricerche, pp. 633–636.

Ferretti, M.P., Ficcarelli, G., Libsekal, Y., Tecle, T.M. and Rook, L. (2003a). Fossil elephants from Buia (Northern Afar Depression, Eritrea) with remarks on the systematics of *Elephas recki* (Proboscidea, Elephantidae). *Journal of Vertebrate Paleontology* 23, 244–257.

Ferretti, M.P., Rook, L. and Torre, D. (2003b). *Stegotetrabelodon* (Proboscidea, Elephantidae) from the Late Miocene of Southern Italy. *Journal of Vertebrate Paleontology* 23, 659–666.

Fichtel, C., Perry, S. and Gros-Louis, J. (2005). Alarm calls of white-faced capuchin monkeys: an acoustic analysis. *Animal Behaviour* 70, 165–176.

Field, D.J. (2020). Preliminary paleoecological insights from the Pliocene avifauna of Kanapoi, Kenya: Implications for the ecology of *Australopithecus anamensis*. *Journal of Human Evolution* 140, 102384.

Fiore, I. and Tagliacozzo, A. (2004). Taphonomic analysis of the bone remains from the Oldowan site of Garba IV. In: J. Chavaillon and M. Piperno (Eds.), *Studies on the Early Paleolithic site of Melka Kunture, Ethiopia*. Florence: Istituto Italiano di Preistoria e Protostoria, pp. 639–682.

Fiorillo, A.R. (1988). Taphonomy of Hazard Homestead Quarry (Ogallala Group), Hitchcock County, Nebraska. *Rocky Mountain Geology* 26, 57–97.

Fleagle, J.G., Rasmussen, D.T., Yirga, S., Bown, T.M. and Grine, F.E. (1991). New hominid fossils from Fejej, Southern Ethiopia. *Journal of Human Evolution* 21(2), 145–152.

Flecker, R., Krijgsman, W., Capella, W., et al. (2015). Evolution of the Late Miocene Mediterranean–Atlantic gateways and their impact on regional and global environmental change. *Earth-Science Reviews* 150, 365–392.

Flowers, R.M. and Schoene, B. (2010). (U–Th)/He thermochronometry constraints on unroofing of the eastern Kaapvaal craton and significance for uplift of the southern African Plateau. *Geology* 38, 827–830.

Flügel, T.J., Eckardt, F.D. and Cotterill, F.P.D. (2015). The present day drainage patterns of the Congo River system and their Neogene evolution. In: M.J. de Wit, F. Guillocheau and M.C.J. de Wit (Eds.), *Geology and Resource Potential of the Congo Basin*. Heidelberg: Springer, pp. 315–337.

Flynn, L.J. and Maurice, S. (1984). A muroid rodent of Asian affinity from the Miocene of Kenya. *Journal of Vertebrate Paleontology* 3, 160–165.

Foley, R. (1993). African terrestrial primates: the comparative evolutionary biology of Theropithecus and the Hominidae. In: N.G. Jablonski (Ed.), *Theropithecus: The Rise and Fall of a Primate Genus*. Cambridge: Cambridge University Press, pp. 245–270.

Foley, R.A. (1994). Speciation, extinction and climatic change in hominid evolution. *Journal of Human Evolution* 26, 275–289.

Foley, R. (2005). Species diversity in human evolution: challenges and opportunities. *Transactions of the Royal Society of South Africa* 60, 67–72.

Folinsbee, K.E. and Reisz, R.R. (2013). New craniodental fossils of Papionin monkeys from Cooper's D, South Africa. *American Journal of Physical Anthropology* 151, 613–629.

Forbes, S.A. (1907). On the local distribution of certain Illinois fishes: an essay in statistical ecology. *Bulletin of the Illinois State Laboratory of Natural History* 7, 273–303.

Forrest, F.L. (2017). Zooarchaeological and palaeoenvironmental reconstruction of newly excavated Middle Pleistocene deposits from Elandsfontein, South Africa. Unpublished doctoral dissertation, City University of New York.

Forstén, A. (1972). *Hipparion primigenium* from Southern Tunisia. *Notes du Service géologique de Tunisie* 35, 7–28.

Fortelius, M. and Solounias, N. (2000). Functional characterization of ungulate molars using the abrasion-attrition wear gradient: a new method for reconstructing paleodiets. *American Museum Novitates* 3301, 1–36.

Fortelius, M., Andrews, P., Bernor, R., Viranta, S. and Werdelin, L. (1996). Preliminary analysis of taxonomic diversity, turnover and provinciality in a subsample of large land mammals from the later Miocene of western Eurasia. *Acta Zoologica Cracoviensia*, 39, 167–178.

Fortelius, M., Eronen, J.T., Jernvall, J., et al. (2002). Fossil mammals resolve regional patterns of Eurasian climate change over 20 million years. *Evolutionary Ecology Research* 4, 1005–1016.

Fortelius, M., Žliobaitė, I., Kaya, F., et al. (2016). An ecometric analysis of the fossil mammal record of the Turkana Basin. *Philosophical Transactions of the Royal Society of London B: Biological Sciences* 371, 20150232.

Foster, A., Ebinger, C., Mbede, E., Rex, D., 1997. Tectonic development of the northern Tanzanian sector of the East African Rift System. *Journal of the Geological Society of London* 154, 689–700.

Fourie, N.N., Lee-Thorp, J.A. and Ackermann, R.R. (2002). Biogeochemical and craniometric investigation of dietary ecology, niche separation, and taxonomy of Plio-Pleistocene Cercopithecoids from the Makapansgat Limeworks. *American Journal of Physical Anthropology* 135, 121–135.

Fourtau, R. (1920). *Contribution à l'étude des vertébrés miocènes de l'Egypte*. Cairo: Ministry of Finance, Survey Dept, 121 pp.

Fourvel, J.-B. (2018). *Civettictis braini* nov. sp. (Mammalia: Carnivora), a new viverrid from the hominin-bearing site of Kromdraai (Gauteng, South Africa). *Comptes Rendus Palevol* 17(6), 366–377.

Fourvel, J.-B., Brink, J., O'Regan, H., Beaudet, A., Pavia, M. (2016). Some preliminary interpretations of the oldest faunal assemblage from Kromdraai. In: J. Braga and J.F. Thackeray (Eds.), *Kromdraai, a Birthplace of Paranthropus in the Cradle of Humankind.* Stellenbosch: African Sun Media Metro, pp. 71–104.

Franz-Odendaal, T.A., Lee-Thorp, J.A. and Chinsamy, A. (2002). New evidence for the lack of C-4 grassland expansions during the early Pliocene at Langebaanweg, South Africa. *Paleobiology* 28(3), 378–388.

Fredieu, J., Levin, N., Melillo, S., Semaw, S. and Simpson, S. W. (2007). Dietary reconstruction of Early Pliocene bovids from the Gona Project Area, Ethiopia. *Journal of Human Evolution* S44, 110.

Freedman, L. (1957). The fossil Cercopithecoidea of South Africa. *Annals of the Transvaal Museum* 23, 121–262.

Freedman, L. (1960). Some new cercopithecoid specimens from Makapansgat, South Africa. *Palaeontologica Africana* 7, 7–45.

Freedman, L. (1976). South African fossil Cercopithecoidea: a reassessment including a description of new material from Makapansgat, Sterkfonein, and Taung. *Journal of Human Evolution* 5, 297–315.

Friis, I., Demissew, S. and van Breugel, P. (2011). *Atlas of the Potential Vegetation of Ethiopia.* Addis Ababa: Addis Ababa University Press and Shama Books.

Frost, S.R. (2001). New early Pliocene Cercopithecidae (Mammalia: Primates) from Aramis, Middle Awash Valley, Ethiopia. *American Museum Novitates* 3350, 1–36.

Frost, S.R. (2007). African Pliocene and Pleistocene cercopithecid evolution and global climate change. In: R. Bobe, Z. Alemseged and A.K. Behrensmeyer (Eds.), *Hominin Environments in the East African Pliocene: An Assessment of the Faunal Evidence.* Dordrecht: Springer, pp. 51–76.

Frost, S.R. (2014). Fossil Cercopithecidae of the Konso Formation. In: G. Suwa, Y. Beyene and B. Asfaw (Eds.), *The Konso-Gardula Research Project Volume 1. Paleonotological Collections: Background and Fossil Aves, Cercopithecidae, and Suidae.* Tokyo: The University Museum, The University of Tokyo, Bulletin 47, pp. 41–72.

Frost, S.R. and Alemseged, Z. (2007). Middle Pleistocene fossil Cercopithecidae from Asbole, Afar Region, Ethiopia. *Journal of Human Evolution* 53, 227–259.

Frost, S.R. and Delson, E. (2002). Fossil Cercopithecidae from the Hadar Formation and surrounding areas of the Afar Depression, Ethiopia. *Journal of Human Evolution* 43, 687–748.

Frost, S.R. and Kullmer, O. (2008). Cercopithecidae from the Pliocene Chiwondo Beds, Malawi-Rift. *Geobios* 41(6), 743–749.

Frost, S.R., Plummer, T., Bishop, L.C., et al. (2003). Partial cranium of *Cercopithecoides kimeui* Leakey, 1982 from Rawi Gully, Southwestern Kenya. *American Journal of Physical Anthropology* 122(3), 191–199.

Frost, S.R., Haile-Selassie, Y. and Hlusko, L. (2009). Cercopithecidae. In: Y. Haile-Selassie and G. WoldeGabriel (Eds.), *Ardipithecus kadabba: Late Miocene Evidence from the Middle Awash, Ethiopia.* Berkeley: University of California Press, pp. 135–158.

Frost, S.R., Schwartz, H.L., Giemsch, L., et al. (2012). Refined age estimates and paleoanthropological investigations of the Manyara Beds, Tanzania. *Journal of Anthropological Sciences* 90, 1–12.

Frost, S.R., Jablonski, N.G. and Haile-Selassie, Y. (2014). Early Pliocene Cercopithecidae from Woranso-Mille (Central Afar, Ethiopia) and the origins of the *Theropithecus oswaldi* lineage. *Journal of Human Evolution* 76, 39–53.

Frost, S.R., Gilbert, C.C., Pugh, K.D., Guthrie, E.H. and Delson, E. (2015). The hand of *Cercopithecoides williamsi* (Mammalia, Primates): earliest evidence for thumb reduction among colobine monkeys. *PLoS ONE* 10, e0125030.

Frost, S.R., Ward, C.V., Manthi, F.K. and Plavcan, J.M. (2020). Cercopithecid fossils from Kanapoi, West Turkana, Kenya (2007–2015). *Journal of Human Evolution* 140, 102642.

Fuchs, V.E. (1934). The geological work of the Cambridge Expedition to the East African Lakes, 1930–31. *Geological Magazine* 71, 145–166.

Fuchs, V.E. (1950). Pleistocene events in the Baringo basin, Kenya Colony. *Geological Magazine*, 87(3), 149–174.

Furstenburg, D. (2002). Springbok *Antidorcas marsupialis* (Zimmerman, 1780). *Wild & Jag/Game & Hunt* 8, 12–14.

Gagnon, M. and Chew, A. (2000). Dietary preferences in extant African Bovidae. *Journal of Mammology* 81, 490–511.

Gallotti, R. (2013). An older origin for the Acheulean at Melka Kunture (Upper Awash, Ethiopia): techno-economic behaviours at Garba IVD. *Journal of Human Evolution* 65, 594–620.

Gallotti, R. and Mussi, M. (2015). The unknown Oldowan: ~1.7-million-year-old standardized obsidian small tools from Garba IV, Melka Kunture, Ethiopia. *PLoS ONE* 10, e0145101.

Gallotti, R. and Mussi, M. (Eds.) (2018). Before, during, and after the early Acheulean at Melka Kunture (Upper Awash, Ethiopia): a technoeconomic comparative analysis. In: The Emergence of the Acheulean in East Africa and Beyond: Contributions in honor of Jean Chavaillon. Cham: Springer International Publishing, pp. 53–92.

Gallotti, R. and Piperno, M. (2003). Recent activities of the Italian Archaeological Mission at Melka Kunture: the Open Air Museum Project and the GIS application to the study of the Oldowan sites. In: J.M. Moreno, R.M. Torcal and I. de la Torre Sainz (Eds.), *Oldowan: Rather More Than Smashing Tools, First Hominid Technology Workshop.* Treballs d'Arqueologia, 9, Bellaterra. Barcelona: Universitat Autònoma de Barcelona, pp. 37–75.

Gallotti, R., Collina, C., Raynal, J.-P., et al. (2010). The Early Middle Pleistocene site of Gombore II (Melka Kunture, Upper Awash, Ethiopia) and the issue of Acheulean bifacial shaping strategies. *African Archaeological Review* 27, 291–322.

Gallotti, R., Raynal, J.-P., Geraads, D. and Mussi, M. (2014). Garba XIII (Melka Kunture, Upper Awash, Ethiopia): a new Acheulean site of the late Lower Pleistocene. *Quaternary International* 343, 17–27.

Gallotti, R., Mohib, A., Fernandes, P., Graoui, M., Lefèvre, D., Raynal, J.-P. (2020). Dedicated core-on-anvil production of bladelet-like flakes in the Acheulean at Thomas Quarry I—L1 (Casablanca, Morocco). Scientific Reports 10, 9225.

García-Alix, A., Minwer-Barakat, R., Martín Suarez, E., et al. (2016). Updating the Europe–Africa small mammal exchange during the late Messinian. *Journal of Biogeography* 43, 1336–1348.

Garcia-Castellanos, D. and Villaseñor, A. (2011). Messinian salinity crisis regulated by competing tectonics and erosion at the Gibraltar arc. *Nature* 480, 359.

Gargani, J. and Rigollet, C.C.L. (2007). Mediterranean Sea level variations during the Messinian salinity crisis. *Geophysical Research Letters* 34(10).

Gautier, A. (1976). Animal remains from archaeological sites of terminal Paleolithic to Old Kingdom age in the Fayum. In: F. Wendorf and R. Schild (Eds.), *Prehistory of the Nile Valley.* New York: Academic Press, pp. 369–381.

Gautier, A. (1993). The Middle Palaeolithic archaeofaunas from Bir Tarfawi (Western Desert, Egypt). In: F. Wendorf, R. Schild and A.E. Close (Eds.), *Egypt during the Last Interglacial.* New York: Plenum Press, pp. 121–143.

Gautier, A. and Van Neer, W. (1989). Animal remains from the late Palaeolithic sequence at Wadi Kubbaniya. In: F. Wendorf, R. Schild and A.E. Close (Eds.), *The Prehistory of Wadi Kubbanniya. Vol 2. Stratigraphy, Paleoeconomy and Environment.* Dallas: SMU Press, pp. 119–161.

Gautier, A., Ballmann, P. and Van Neer, W. (1980). Molluscs, fish, birds and mammals from the Late Paleolithic sites in Wadi Kubbaniya. In: F. Wendorf, R. Schild and A.E. Close (Eds.), *Loaves and Fishes: The Prehistory of Wadi Kubbaniya.* New Delhi: Pauls Press, pp. 281–295.

Gawthorpe, R.L. and Leeder, M.R. (2000). Tectono-sedimentary evolution of active extensional basins. *Basin Research*, 12, 195–218.

Ge, D., Zhang, Z., Xia, L., et al. (2012). Did the expansion of C 4 plants drive extinction and massive range contraction of micromammals? Inferences from food preference and historical biogeography of pikas. *Palaeogeography, Palaeoclimatology, Palaeoecology* 326, 160–171.

Genise, J.F. and Harrison, T. (2018). Walking on ashes: insect trace fossils from Laetoli indicate poor grass cover associated with early hominin environments. *Palaeontology* 61(4), 597–624.

Gentry, A.W. (1967). *Pelorovis oldowayensis* Reck, an extinct bovid from East Africa. *Bulletin of the British Museum (Natural History) Geology* 14, 245–299.

Gentry, A.W. (1970). Revised classification for Makapania broomi Wells and Cooke Bovidae, Mammalia. *Palaeontologica Africana* 13, 63–67.

Gentry, A.W. (1981). Notes on Bovidae (Mammalia) from the Hadar Formation, and from Amado and Geraru, Ethiopia. *Kirtlandia* 33, 1–30.

Gentry, A.W. (1985). The bovidae of the Omo group deposits, Ethiopia (French and American collections). In: Y. Coppens and F.C. Howell (Eds.), *Les faunes plio-pléistocènes de la basse vallée de l'Omo (Éthiopie) Tome 1 Périssodactyles, artiodactyles (bovidae)*. Paris: Éditions du CNRS, pp. 119–214.

Gentry, A.W. (1987). Pliocene Bovidae from Laetoli. In: M.D. Leakey and J.M Harris (Eds.), *Laetoli: A Pliocene Site in Northern Tanzania*. Oxford: Clarendon Press, pp. 378–408.

Gentry, A.W. (1990). The Semliki fossil bovids. In: N.T. Boaz (Ed.), *Evolution of Environments and Hominidae in the African Western Rift Valley*. Martinsville: Virginia Museum of Natural History, pp. 225–234.

Gentry, A.W. (1996). A fossil *Budorcas* (Mammalia, Bovidae) from Africa. In: K.M. Stewart and K.L. Seymour (Eds.), *Palaeoecology and Palaeoenvironments of Late Cenozoic Mammals*. Toronto: University of Toronto Press, pp. 571–587.

Gentry, A.W. (1997). Fossil ruminants (Mammalia) from the Manonga Valley, Tanzania. In: T. Harrison (Ed.), *Neogene Paleontology of the Manonga Valley, Tanzania*. New York: Plenum Press, pp. 107–135.

Gentry, A.W. (2006). A new bovine (Bovidae, Artiodactyla) from the Hadar Formation, Ethiopia. *Transactions of the Royal Society of South Africa* 61, 41–50.

Gentry, A.W. (2010). Bovidae. In: S. Werdelin and W.J. Sanders (Eds.), *Cenozoic Mammals of Africa*. Berkeley: University of California Press, pp. 741–796.

Gentry, A.W. (2011). Bovidae. In: T. Harrison (Ed.), *Paleontology and Geology of Laetoli: Human Evolution in Context. Vol. 2: Fossil Hominins and the Associated Fauna*. Dordrecht: Springer, pp. 363–465.

Gentry, A.W. and Gentry, A. (1978a). Fossil Bovidae (Mammalia) of Olduvai Gorge, Tanzania. Part I. *Bulletin of the British Museum (Natural History) Geology* 29, 289–446.

Gentry, A.W. and Gentry, A. (1978b). Fossil Bovidae (Mammalia) of Olduvai Gorge, Tanzania, Part II. *Bulletin of the British Museum (Natural History) Geology* 30, 1–83.

George, M. (1950). A chalicothere from the Limeworks quarry of the Makapan Valley, Potgietersrust District. *South African Journal of Science* 46, 241–242.

Geraads, D. (1979). La faune des gisements de Melka-Kunturé (Ethiopie): Artiodactyles, Primates. *Abbay* 10, 21–49.

Geraads, D. (1980a). La faune des sites à *Homo erectus* des carrières Thomas (Casablanca, Maroc). *Quaternaria* 22, 65–94.

Geraads, D. (1980b). Un nouveau Félidé (Fissipeda, Mamalia) du Pléistocène moyen du Maroc: *Lynx thomasi* n.sp. *Geobios* 13, 441–444.

Geraads, D. (1981). Bovidae et Giraffidae (Artiodactyla, Mammalia) du Pléistocène de Ternifine (Algérie). *Bulletin du Museum national d' Histoire naturelle, C, 4ème séries* 3, 47–86.

Geraads, D. (1985). La faune des gisements de Melka Kunturé (Ethiopie). In: L'environnement des Hominidés au Plio-Pléistocène. Fondation Singer-Polignac. Paris: Masson, pp. 165–174.

Geraads, D. (1986). Ruminants pléistocènes d'Oubeidiyeh. *Mémoires et Travaux du Centre Recherche Français de Jérusalem* 5, 93–105.

Geraads, D. (1987a). La faune des dépôts pléistocènes de l'Ouest du lac Natron (Tanzanie); interprétation biostratigraphique. *Sciences Géologiques, Bulletins et mémoires* 40, 167–184.

Geraads, D. (1987b). Dating the northern African cercopithecid fossil record. *Human Evolution* 2(1), 19–27.

Geraads, D. (1989) Vertébrés fossiles du miocène supérieur du Djebel Krechem el Artsouma (Tunisie centrale). Comparaisons biostratigraphiques. *Geobios* 22(6), 777–801.

Geraads, D. (1993a). Middle Pleistocene *Crocidura* (Mammalia, Insectivora) from Oulad Hamida I, Morocco, and their phylogenetic relationships. *Proceedings, Koninklijke Nederlandse Akademie van Wetenschappen* 96, 281–294.

Geraads, D. (1993b). *Kolpochoerus phacochoeroides* (Thomas, 1884) (Suidae, Mammalia), du Pliocène supérieur de Ahl al Oughlam (Casablanca, Maroc). *Geobios* 26, 731–743.

Geraads, D. (1994a). Rongeurs et Lagomorphes du Pléistocène moyen de la "Grotte des Rhinocéros", carrière Oulad Hamida 1, à Casablanca, Maroc. *Neues Jahrbuch für Geologie und Paläontologie - Abhandlungen* 191, 147–172.

Geraads, D. (1994b). Evolution of Bovid diversity in the Plio-Pleistocene of Africa. *Historical Biology* 7, 221–237.

Geraads, D. (1994c). Girafes fossiles d'Ouganda. In: B. Senut and M. Pickford (Eds.), *Geology and Palaeobiology of the Albertine Rift Valley, Uganda–Zaire*. Orléans: CIFEG – Centre International pour la Formation et les Echanges Géologiques, pp. 375–381.

Geraads, D. (1995). Rongeurs et insectivores du Pliocène final de Ahl al Oughlam, Casablanca, Maroc. *Geobios* 28, 99–115.

Geraads, D. (1996). Le *Sivatherium* (Giraffidae, Mammalia) du Pliocène final d'Ahl al Oughlam (Casablanca, Maroc) et l'évolution du genre en Afrique. *Paläontologische Zeitschrift* 70, 623–629.

Geraads, D. (1997). Carnivores du Pliocène terminal de Ahl al Oughlam (Casablanca, Maroc). *Geobios* 30, 127–164.

Geraads, D. (1998). Rongeurs du Mio-Pliocène de Lissasfa (Casablanca, Maroc). *Geobios* 31, 229–245.

Geraads, D. (2001). Rongeurs du Miocene supérieur de Chorora (Ethiopie): Dendromuridae, Muridae et conclusions. *Palaeovertebrata* 30, 89–109.

Geraads, D. (2002). Plio-Pleistocene Mammalian biostratigraphy of Atlantic Morocco. *Quaternaire* 13, 43–53.

Geraads, D. (2004a). First record of *Dinofelis* (Felidae, Mammalia) from North Africa. *Neues Jahrbuch fur Geologie und Palaontologie Monatshefte* 2004, 308–320.

Geraads, D. (2004b). New skulls of *Kolpochoerus phacochoeroides* (Suidae: Mammalia) from the late Pliocene of Ahl al Oughlam, Morocco. *Palaeontologica Africana* 40, 69–83.

Geraads, D. (2005). Pliocene Rhinocerotidae (Mammalia) from Hadar and Dikika (Lower Awash, Ethiopia), and a revision of the origin of modern African rhinos. *Journal of Vertebrate Paleontology* 25, 451–461.

Geraads, D. (2006). The late Pliocene locality of Ahl al Oughlam, Morocco: vertebrate fauna and interpretation. *Transactions of the Royal Society of South Africa* 61, 97–101.

Geraads, D. (2008). Plio-Pleistocene Carnivora of Northwestern Africa: a short review. *Comptes Rendus Palevol* 7, 591–599.

Geraads, D. (2010a). Biogeographic relationships of Pliocene and Pleistocene North-western African mammals. *Quaternary International* 212, 159–168.

Geraads, D. (2010b). Biochronologie mammalienne du Quaternaire du Maroc atlantique, dans son cadre régional. *L'Anthropologie* 114, 324–340.

Geraads, D. (2010c). Tragulidae. In: L. Werdelin and W.J. Sanders (Eds.), *Cenozoic Mammals of Africa*. Berkeley: University of California Press, pp. 723–729.

Geraads, D. (2010d). Rhinocerotidae. In: L. Werdelin and W.J. Sanders (Eds.), *Cenozoic Mammals of Africa*. Berkeley: University of California Press, pp. 675–689.

Geraads, D. (2011). A revision of the fossil Canidae (Mammalia) of North-western Africa. *Palaeontology* 54, 429–446.

Geraads, D. (2012). The faunal context of human evolution in the late Middle/Late Pleistocene of North-western Africa. In: J.-J. Hublin and S. McPherron (Eds.), *Modern Origins: A North African Perspective*. Dordrecht: Springer, pp. 49–60.

Geraads, D. (2014). How old is the cheetah skull shape? The case of *Acinonyx pardinensis* (Mammalia, Felidae). *Geobios* 47, 39–44.

Geraads, D. (2016a). Pleistocene Carnivora (Mammalia) from Tighennif (Ternifine), Algeria. *Geobios* 49, 445–445.

Geraads, D. (2016b). Rodentia et Lagomorpha. In: J.-P. Raynal and A. Mohib (Eds.), *Préhistoire de Casablanca. 1 – La Grotte des Rhinocéros (fouilles 1991 et 1996). Villes et Sites Archéologiques du Maroc, volume 6*. Rabat: Ministère de la Culture, INSAP, pp. 95–104.

Geraads, D. (2016c). Insectivores. In: J.-P. Raynal and A. Mohib (Eds.), *Préhistoire de Casablanca. 1 – La Grotte des Rhinocéros (fouilles 1991 et 1996). Villes et Sites Archéologiques du Maroc, volume 6*. Rabat: Ministère de la Culture, INSAP, pp. 105–110.

Geraads, D. (2020). Perissodactyla (Rhinocerotidae and Equidae) from Kanapoi. *Journal of Human Evolution* 140, 102373.

Geraads, D. and Alemseged, Z. (2016c). Cercopithecidae. In: J.-P. Raynal and A. Mohib (Eds.), *Préhistoire de Casablanca. 1 – La Grotte des Rhinocéros (fouilles 1991 et 1996). Villes et Sites Archéologiques du Maroc, volume 6*. Rabat: Ministère de la Culture, INSAP, pp. 91–93.

Geraads, D. and Amani, F. (1997). La faune du gisement à *Homo erectus* de l'Aïn Maarouf près de El Hajeb (Maroc). *L'Anthropologie* 101, 522–530.

Geraads, D. and Amani, F. (1998). Bovidae (Mammalia) du Pliocène final d'Ahl al Oughlam, Casablanca, Maroc. *Paläontologische Zeitschrift* 72, 191–205.

Geraads, D. and Amani, F. (2016). Bovidae. In: J.-P. Raynal and A. Mohib (Eds.), *Préhistoire de Casablanca. 1 – La Grotte des Rhinocéros (fouilles 1991 et 1996). Villes et Sites Archéologiques du Maroc, volume 6*. Rabat: Ministère de la Culture, INSAP, pp. 135–139.

Geraads, D. and Bernoussi, R. (2016a). Carnivora. In: J.-P. Raynal and A. Mohib (Eds.), *Préhistoire de Casablanca. 1 – La Grotte des Rhinocéros (fouilles 1991 et 1996). Villes et Sites Archéologiques du Maroc, volume 6*. Rabat: Ministère de la Culture, INSAP, pp. 111–119.

Geraads, D. and Bernoussi, R. (2016b). Rhinocerotidae. In: J.-P. Raynal and A. Mohib (Eds.), *Préhistoire de Casablanca. 1 – La Grotte des Rhinocéros (fouilles 1991 et 1996). Villes et Sites Archéologiques du Maroc, volume 6*. Rabat: Ministère de la Culture, INSAP, pp. 121–127.

Geraads, D. and Bernoussi, R. (2016c). Equidae. In: J.-P. Raynal and A. Mohib (Eds.), *Préhistoire de Casablanca. 1 – La Grotte des Rhinocéros (fouilles 1991 et 1996). Villes et Sites Archéologiques du Maroc, volume 6*. Rabat: Ministère de la Culture, INSAP, pp. 129–131.

Geraads, D. and Bernoussi, R. (2016d). Hippopotamidae, Suidae et Camelidae. In: J.-P. Raynal and A. Mohib (Eds.), *Préhistoire de Casablanca. 1 – La Grotte des Rhinocéros (fouilles 1991 et 1996). Villes et Sites Archéologiques du Maroc, volume 6*. Rabat: Ministère de la Culture, INSAP, pp. 133–134.

Geraads, D. and Bobe, R. (2020a). Ruminants (Giraffidae and Bovidae) from Kanapoi. *Journal of Human Evolution* 140, 102383.

Geraads, D. and Bobe, R. (2020b). Suidae from Kanapoi. *Journal of Human Evolution* 140, 102337.

Geraads, D. and Metz-Muller, F. (1999). Proboscidea (Mammalia) du Pliocène final d'Ahl al Oughlam (Casablanca, Maroc). *Neues Jahrbuch fur Geologie und Palaontologie Monatshefte* 1999, 52–64.

Geraads, D. and Thomas, H. (1994). Bovidés du Plio-Pléistocène d'Ouganda. In: B. Senut and M. Pickford (Eds.), *Geology and Palaeobiology of the Albertine Rift Valley, Uganda–Zaire*. Orléans: CIFEG – Centre International pour la Formation et les Echanges Géologiques, pp. 383–407.

Geraads, D., Zouhri, S. (2021). *Eoazara xerrii* n.gen. n.sp. (Mammalia, Rhinocerotidae, Elasmotheriinae) from the upper Miocene of Skoura, Ouarzazate, Morocco. *Acta Palaeontologica Polonica*. 66, 753–765.

Geraads, D., Beriro, P. and Roche, H. (1980). La faune et l'industrie des sites à *Homo erectus* des carrières Thomas (Casablanca, Maroc). Précisions sur l'âge de ces Hominidés. *Comptes Rendus de l'Académie des Sciences Paris D* 291, 195–198.

Geraads, D., Hublin, J.-J., Jaeger, J.-J., et al. (1986). The Pleistocene hominid site of Ternifine, Algeria: new results on the environment, age and human industries. *Quaternary Research* 25, 380–386.

Geraads, D., Amani, F. and Hublin, J.-J. (1992). Le gisement pléistocène moyen de l'Aïn Maarouf près de El Hajeb, Maroc: présence d'un Hominidé. *Comptes Rendus de l'Académie des Sciences Paris II* 314, 319–323.

Geraads, D., Amani, F., Raynal, J-P. and Sbihi-Alaoui, F.Z. (1998). La faune de mammifères du Pliocène terminal d'Ahl al Oughlam, Casablanca, Maroc. *Comptes Rendus de l'Académie des Sciences Series IIA – Earth and Planetary Science* 326, 671–676.

Geraads, D., Brunet, M., Mackaye, H.T. and Vignaud, P. (2001). Pliocene Bovidae (Mammalia) from the Koro Toro australopithecine sites, Chad. *Journal of Vertebrate Paleontology* 21, 335–346.

Geraads, D., Eisenmann, V. and Petter, G. (2004a). The large mammal fauna of the Oldowayan sites of Melka-Kunturé, Ethiopia. In: J. Chavaillon and M. Piperno (Eds.), *Studies on the Early Paleolithic site of Melka Kunture, Ethiopia*. Florence: Istituto Italiano di Preistoria e Protostoria, pp. 169–192.

Geraads, D., Raynal, J.-P. and Eisenmann, V. (2004b). The earliest human occupation of North Africa: a reply to Sahnouni et al. (2002). *Journal of Human Evolution* 46, 751–761.

Geraads, D., Alemseged, Z., Reed, D., Wynn, J. and Roman, D.C. (2004c). The Pleistocene fauna (other than Primates) from Asbole, lower Awash Valley, Ethiopia, and its environmental and biochronological implications. *Géobios* 37, 697–718.

Geraads, D., Blondel, C., Likius, A., et al. (2008). New Hippotragini (Bovidae, Mammalia) from the Late Miocene of Toros-Menalla (Chad). *Journal of Vertebrate Paleontology* 28, 231–242.

Geraads, D., Melillo, S. and Haile-Selassie, Y. (2009a). Middle Pliocene Bovidae from hominid-bearing sites in the Woranso-Mille area, Afar region, Ethiopia. *Palaeontologia Africana* 44, 59–70.

Geraads, D., Blondel, C., Mackaye, H.T., et al. (2009b). Bovidae (Mammalia) from the lower Pliocene of Chad. *Journal of Vertebrate Paleontology* 29, 923–933.

Geraads, D., Raynal, J.-P. and Sbihi-Alaoui, F.-Z. (2010a). Mammalian faunas from the Pliocene and Pleistocene of Casablanca (Morocco). *Historical Biology* 22, 275–285.

Geraads, D., Alemseged, Z., Bobe, R. and Reed, D. (2010b). *Nyctereutes lockwoodi*, n. sp., a new canid (Carnivora: Mammalia) from the middle Pliocene of Dikika, Lower Awash, Ethiopia. Journal of Vertebrate Paleontology 30, 981–987.

Geraads, D., Alemseged, Z., Bobe, R. and Reed, D. (2011). *Enhydriodon dikikae*, sp. nov. (Carnivora: Mammalia), a gigantic otter from the Pliocene of Dikika, Lower Awash, Ethiopia. *Journal of Vertebrate Paleontology* 31, 447–453.

Geraads, D., Bobe, R. and Reed, K. (2012a). Pliocene Bovidae (Mammalia) from the Hadar Formation of Hadar and Ledi-Geraru, Lower Awash, Ethiopia. *Journal of Vertebrate Paleontology* 32, 180–197.

Geraads, D., El Boughabi, S. and Zouhri, S. (2012b). *Skouraia helicoides* n.gen., n.sp., a new caprin bovid (Mammalia) from the late Miocene of Morocco. *Palaeontologia Africana* 47, 19–24.

Geraads, D., Bobe, R. and Reed, K. (2013a). Pliocene Giraffidae (Mammalia) from the Hadar Formation of Hadar and Ledi-Geraru, Lower Awash, Ethiopia. *Journal of Vertebrate Paleontology* 33, 470–481.

Geraads, D., Amani, F., Ben-Ncer, A., et al. (2013b). The rodents from the late Middle Pleistocene hominid-bearing site of J'bel Irhoud, Morocco, and their paleoclimatic significance. *Quaternary Research* 80, 552–561.

Geraads, D., Bobe, R. and Manthi, F.K. (2013c). New ruminants (Mammalia) from the Pliocene of Kanapoi, Kenya, and a revision of previous collections, with a note on the Suidae. *Journal of African Earth Sciences* 85: 53–61.

Geraads, D., Drapeau, M.S.M., Bobe, R. and Fleagle, J.G. (2015a). *Vulpes mathisoni*, sp. nov., a new fox from the Pliocene Mursi Formation of southern Ethiopia and its contribution to the origin of African foxes. *Journal of Vertebrate Paleontology* 34, e943765.

Geraads, D., Alemseged, Z., Bobe, R. and Reed, D. (2015b). Pliocene Carnivora (Mammalia) from the Hadar Formation at Dikika, lower Awash Valley, Ethiopia. *Journal of African Earth Sciences* 107, 28–35.

Geraads, D., Zouhri, S. and Markov, G.N. (2019). The first *Tetralophodon* (Mammalia, Proboscidea) cranium from Africa. *Journal of Vertebrate Paleontology* 39(3), e1632321.

Geraads, D., Barr, W.A., Reed, D., Laurin, M. and Alemseged, Z. (2021). New remains of Camelus grattardi (Mammalia, Camelidae) from the Plio-Pleistocene of Ethiopia and the phylogeny of the genus. *Journal of Mammalian Evolution* 28, 359–370.

Gereta, E. and Wolanski, E. (1998). Wildlife–water quality interactions in the Serengeti National Park, Tanzania. *African Journal of Ecology* 36, 1–14.

Gerlach, J. (2001). Tortoise phylogeny and the 'Geochelone' problem. *Phelsuma* 9, 1–24.

Gervais, P. (1869). *Zoologie et Paléontologie générales*. Paris: Arthus Bertrand.

Gèze, R. (1980). Les Hippopotamidae (Mammalia, Artiodactyla) du Plio-Pléistocène de l'Ethiopie (Afrique Orientale). PhD thesis, University Paris VI.

Gèze, R. (1985). Répartition paléoécologique et relations phylogénétiques des Hippopotamidae (Mammalia, Artiodactyla) du néogène d'Afrique Orientale. In: *L'environnement des Hominidés au Plio-Pléistocène*. Fondation Singer-Polignac. Paris: Masson, pp.81–100.

Ghinassi, M., Libsekal, Y., Papini, M. and Rook, L. (2009). Palaeoenvironments of the Buia *Homo* site: high-resolution facies analysis and non-marine sequence stratigraphy in the Alat formation (Pleistocene Dandiero Basin, Danakil depression, Eritrea). *Palaeogeography, Palaeoclimatology, Palaeoecology* 280(3-4), 415–431.

Ghinassi, M., Billi, P., Libsekal, Y., Papini, M. and Rook, L. (2013). Inferring fluvial morphodynamics and overbank flow control from 3D outcrop sections of a Pleistocene point bar, Dandiero Basin, Eritrea. *Journal of Sedimentary Research* 83, 1065–1083.

Ghinassi, M., Oms, O., Papini, M., et al. (2015). An integrated study of the *Homo*-bearing Aalat stratigraphic section (Eritrea): an expanded continental record at the Early–Middle Pleistocene transition. *Journal of African Earth Sciences* 112, 163–185.

Gibbard, P.L. and Head, M.J. (2009). IUGS ratification of the Quaternary System/Period and the Pleistocene Series/Epoch with a base at 2.58 Ma. *Quaternaire. Revue de l'Association française pour l'étude du Quaternaire* 20(4), 411–412.

Gibbon, R.J., Granger, D.E., Kuman, K. and Partridge, T.C. (2009). Early Acheulean technology in the Rietputs Formation, South Africa, dated with cosmogenic nuclides. *Journal of Human Evolution* 56(2), 152–160.

Gibbon, R.J., Pickering, T.R., Sutton, M.B., et al. (2014). Cosmogenic nuclide burial dating of hominin-bearing Pleistocene cave deposits at Swartkrans, South Africa. *Quaternary Geochronology* 24, 10–15.

Gibert, L., Scott, G.R., Scholz, D., et al. (2016). Chronology for the Cueva Victoria fossil site (SE Spain): evidence for early Pleistocene Afro-Iberian dispersals. *Journal of Human Evolution* 90, 183–197.

Gifford-Gonzalez, D. (2003). The fauna from Ele Bor: evidence for the persistence of foragers into the later Holocene of arid north Kenya. *African Archaeological Review* 20, 81–119.

Gilbert, C.C. (2007a). Craniomandibular morphology supporting the diphyletic origin of mangabeys and a new genus of the *Cercocebus/Mandrillus* clade, *Procercocebus*. *Journal of Human Evolution* 53, 69–102.

Gilbert, C.C. (2007b). Identification and description of the first *Theropithecus* (Primates: Cercopithecidae) material from Bolt's Farm, South Africa. *Annals of the Transvaal Museum* 44(1), 1–10.

Gilbert, C.C. (2013). Cladistic analysis of extant and fossil African papionins using craniodental data. *Journal of Human Evolution* 64(5), 399–433.

Gilbert, C.C., McGraw, W.S. and Delson, E. (2009). Brief communication: Plio-Pleistocene eagle predation on fossil cercopithecids from the Humpata Plateau, southern Angola. *American Journal of Physical Anthropology* 139, 421–429.

Gilbert, C., Goble, E. and Hill, A. (2010). Miocene Cercopithecoidea from the Tugen Hills, Kenya. *Journal of Human Evolution* 59, 465–483.

Gilbert, C.C., Goble, E.D., Kingston, J.D. and Hill, A. (2011). Partial skeleton of *Theropithecus brumpti* (Primates, Cercopithecidae) from the Chemeron Formation of the Tugen Hills, Kenya. *Journal of Human Evolution* 61, 347–362.

Gilbert, C.C., Steininger, C.M., Kibii, J.M. and Berger, L.R. (2015). *Papio* cranium from the hominin-bearing site of Malapa: implications for the evolution of modern baboon cranial morphology and South African Plio-Pleistocene biochronology. *PLoS ONE* 10(8), e0133361.

Gilbert, C.C., Frost, S.R. and Delson, E. (2016). Reassessment of Olduvai Bed I cercopithecoids: a new biochronological and biogeographical link to the South African fossil record. *Journal of Human Evolution* 92, 50–59.

Gilbert, W.H. (2008). Suidae. In: W. Gilbert and B. Asfaw (Eds.) *Homo erectus: Pleistocene Evidence from the Middle Awash, Ethiopia*. Berkeley: University of California Press, pp. 45–95.

Gilbert, W.H. and Asfaw, B. (Eds.) (2008). Homo erectus. Pleistocene Evidence from the Middle Awash, Ethiopia. Berkeley: University of California Press.

Ginsburg, L. (1977a). L'Hyracoïde (Mammifère subongulé) du Miocène de Beni Mellal (Maroc). *Géologie Méditerranéenne* 4, 241–254.

Ginsburg, L. (1977b). Listriodon juba, suidé nouveau du Miocène de Beni Mellal (Maroc). *Géologie Méditerranéenne* 4, 221–224.

Ginsburg, L. (1977c). Les carnivores du Miocène de Beni Mellal. *Géologie Méditerranéenne* 4, 225–240.

Giresse, P. (2005). Mesozoic–Cenozoic history of the Congo Basin. *Journal of African Earth Sciences* 43, 301–315.

Glazko, G.V. and Nei, M. (2003). Estimation of divergence times for major lineages of primate species. *Molecular Biology and Evolution* 20(3), 424–434.

Gmira, S., De Lapparent, F., Geraads, D., et al. (2013). Les Tortues d'Ahl Al Oughlam, et de ses environs au Pliocène supérieur du Maroc. *Geodiversitas* 35, 691–733.

Goble, E.D. (2011). Paleontology of the Chemeron Formation, Tugen Hills, Kenya with emphasis on faunal shifts and precessional climatic forcing. Doctoral dissertation, Yale University, New Haven.

Goble, E.D., Hill, A. and Kingston, J. (2008). Digital elevation models as heuristic tools. Paper presented at the The Paleoanthropology Society Meetings, Vancouver, CA.

Goldberg, P., Berna, F. and Chazan, M. (2015). Deposition and diagenesis in the Earlier Stone Age of Wonderwerk Cave, Excavation 1, South Africa. *African Archaeological Review* 32, 613–643.

Gommery, D., Thackeray, J.F., Sénégas, F., Potze, S. and Kgasi, L. (2008a). The earliest primate (*Parapapio* sp.) from the Cradle of Humankind World Heritage site (Waypoint 160, Bolt's Farm, South Africa). *South African Journal of Science* 104(9–10), 405–408.

Gommery, D., Thackeray, J.F., Potze, S. and Braga, J. (2008b). The first recorded occurrence of honey badger of the genus *Mellivora* (Carnivora: Mustelidae) at Kromdraai B, South Africa. *Annals of the Transvaal Museum* 45(1), 145–148.

Gommery, D., Senegas, F., Badenhorst, S., et al. (2012a). Preliminary results concerning the discovery of new fossiliferous sites at Bolt's Farm (Cradle of Humankind, South Africa). *Annals of the Ditsong National Museum of Natural History* 2(1), 33–45.

Gommery, D., Senegas, F., Badenhorst, S., Potze, S. and Kgasi, L. (2012b). Minnaar's Cave: a Plio-Pleistocene site in the Cradle of Humankind, South Africa: its history, location, and fauna. *Annals of the Ditsong National Museum of Natural History* 2(1), 19–31.

Gommery, D., Kgasi, L., Sénégas, F., et al. (2019). Waypoint 160, Bolt's Farm Cave System: first *in situ* primate remains. *Annals of the Ditsong National Museum of Natural History* 8(8), S1–5.

Goodman, S.M. (1994). The enigma of antipredator behavior in lemurs: evidence of a large extinct eagle on Madagascar. *International Journal of Primatology* 15, 129–134.

Goodwin, A.J.H. (1928). The archaeology of the Vaal River gravels. *Transactions of the Royal Society of South Africa* 16, 77–102.

Goodwin, D.H., Flessa, K.W., Tellez-Duarte, M.A., et al. (2004). Detecting time-averaging and spatial mixing using oxygen isotope variation: a case study. *Palaeogeography, Palaeoclimatology, Palaeoecology* 205(1–2), 1–21.

Gordon, C.C. and Buikstra, J.E. (1981). Soil pH, bone preservation, and sampling bias at mortuary sites. *American Antiquity* 46, 566–571.

Gordon, I. and Prins, H.H.T. (Eds.) (2008). *The Ecology of Browsing and Grazing*. Ecological studies vol. 195. Berlin: Springer.

Gordon, K.D. (1982). A study of microwear on chimpanzee molars: implications for dental microwear analysis. *American Journal of Physical Anthropology* 59, 195–215.

Gordon, K.D. (1988). A review of methodology and quantification in dental microwear analysis. *Scanning Microscopy* 2, 1139–1147.

Goren-Inbar, N., Alperson-Afil, N., Sharon, G. and Herzlinger, G. (2018). *The Acheulian Site of Gesher Benot Ya'aqov Volume IV: The Lithic Assemblages*. New York: Springer.

Gose, W.A. (2000). Palaeomagnetic studies of burned rocks. *Journal of Archaeological Science* 27, 409–421.

Goudie, A.S. (2005). The drainage of Africa since the Cretaceous. *Geomorphology* 67, 437–456.

Gouws, G. and Stewart, B.A. (2001). Potamonautid river crabs (Decapoda, Brachyura, Potamonautidae) of KwaZulu-Natal, South Africa. *Water SA* 27, 85–98.

Govender, R. (2015). Preliminary phylogenetics and biogeographic history of the Pliocene seal, *Homiphoca capensis* from Langebaanweg, South Africa. *Transactions of the Royal Society of South Africa* 70(1), 25–39.

Govender, R. and Chinsamy, A. (2013). Early Pliocene (5 Ma) shark–cetacean trophic interaction from Langebaanweg, western coast of South Africa. *Palaios* 28(5), 270–277.

Govender, R., Chinsamy, A. and Ackermann, R.R. (2012). Anatomical and landmark morphometric analysis of fossil phocid seal remains from Langebaanweg, West Coast of South Africa. *Transactions of the Royal Society of South Africa* 67(3), 135–149.

Gowlett, J.A.J. (1996). Rule systems in the artefacts of Homo erectus and early Homo sapiens: constrained or chosen? In: P. Mellars and K. Gibson (Eds.), *Modelling the Early Human Mind*. Cambridge: McDonald Institute, pp. 191–215.

Gowlett, J.A.J. and Crompton, R.H. (1994). Kariandusi: Acheulean morphology and the question of allometry. *African Archaeological Review* 12, 3–42.

Gowlett, J.A.J., Harris, J.W.K., Walton, D. and Wood, B.A. (1981). Early archaeological sites, hominid remains and traces of fire from Chesowanja, Kenya. *Nature* 294(5837), 125–129.

Gowlett, J.A.J., Brink, J.S., Herries, A.I.R., et al. (2015). At the heart of the African Acheulean: the physical, social and cognitive landscapes of Kilombe. In: F. Coward, R. Hosfield and F. WenbanSmith (Eds.), *Settlement, Society and Cognition in Human Evolution: Landscapes in Mind*. Cambridge: Cambridge University Press, pp. 75–93.

Graham, A. and Bell, R. (1969). Factors influencing the countability of animals. *East African Agrricultural and Forestry Journal* 34, 38–43.

Granger, D.E., Gibbon, R.J., Kuman, K., et al. (2015). Newcosmogenic burial ages for Sterkfontein Member 2 *Australopithecus* and Member 5 Oldowan. *Nature* 522(7554), 85–88.

Granjon, L. and Dempster, E.R. (2013). Genus *Gerbilliscus* gerbils. In: D. Happold (Ed.), *Mammals of Africa, Volume III: Rodents, Hares and Rabbits*. London: Bloomsbury, pp. 268–270.

Grant, K.M., Rohling, E.J., Westerhold, T., et al. (2017). 3 million year index for North African humidity/aridity and the implication of potential pan-African humid periods. *Quaternary Science Reviews* 171, 100–118.

Gray, B.T. (1980). Environmental reconstruction of the Hadar Formation (Afar, Ethiopia). PhD dissertation, Case Western Reserve University.

Grayson, D.K. (2005). A brief history of Great Basin pikas. *Journal of Biogeography* 32, 2103–2111.

Green, D.J. and Alemseged, Z. (2012). *Australopithecus afarensis* scapular ontogeny, function, and the role of climbing in human evolution. *Science* 338, 514–517.

Green, D.J., Spiewak, T.A., Seitelman, B. and Gunz, P. (2016). Scapular shape of extant hominoids and the African ape/modern human last common ancestor. *Journal of Human Evolution* 94, 1–12.

Greenacre, M.J. (1993). *Correspondence Analysis in Practice*. London: Academic Press.

Greenacre, M.J. (2007). *Correspondence Analysis in Practice*. 2nd ed. London: Chapman and Hall.

Greenacre, M.J. and Vrba, E.S. (1984). Graphical display and interpretation of antelope census data in African wildlife areas, using correspondence analysis. *Ecology* 65(3), 984–997.

Greenwood, M. (1955). Fossil Hystricoidea from the Makapan Valley, Transvaal. *Palaeontologica Africana* 3, 77–85.

Greenwood, M. (1958). Fossil Hystricoidea from the Makapan Valley, Transvaal. *Annals and Magazine of Natural History* 13, 365.

Gregory, J.W. (1921). *The Rift Valleys and Geology of East Africa*. London: London Seeley Service.

Griffin, D.L. (1999). The late Miocene climate of northeastern Africa: unravelling the signals in the sedimentary succession. *Journal of the Geological Society, London* 156, 817–826.

Volume References

Griffin, D.L. (2002). Aridity and humidity: two aspects of the late Miocene climate of North Africa and the Mediterranean. *Palaeogeography, Palaeoclimatology, Palaeoecology* 182(1–2), 65–91.

Griffin, D.L. (2006). The late Neogene Sahabi rivers of the Sahara and their climatic and environmental implications for the Chad Basin. *Journal of the Geological Society* 163(6), 905–921.

Griffiths, J.F. (1976). *Climate and the Environment*. Boulder: Westview Press.

Grine, F.E. (1981). Trophic differences between 'gracile' and 'robust' australopithecines: a scanning electron microscope analysis of occlusal events. *South African Journal of Science* 77, 203–230.

Grine, F.E. (1982). A new juvenile hominid (Mammalia; Primates) from Member 3, Kromdraai Formation, Transvaal, South Africa. *Annals of the Transvaal Museum* 33, 165–239.

Grine, F.E. (1986). Dental evidence for dietary differences in *Australopithecus* and *Paranthropus*: a quantitative analysis of permanent molar microwear. *Journal of Human Evolution* 15, 783–822.

Grine, F.E. (Ed.) (1988). New craniodental fossils of *Paranthropus* from the Swartkrans Formation and their significance in "robust" australopithecine evolution. In: *Evolutionary History of the "Robust" Australopithecines*. New York: Aldine de Gruyter, pp. 223–243.

Grine, F.E. (1989). New hominid fossils from the Swartkrans Formation (1979–1986 excavations): craniodental specimens. *American Journal of Physical Anthropology* 79, 409–449.

Grine, F.E. (2005). Early *Homo* at Swartkrans, South Africa: a review of the evidence and an evaluation of recently proposed morphs. *South African Journal of Science* 101, 43–52.

Grine, F.E. (2012). Observations on Middle Stone Age human teeth from Klasies River Main Site, South Africa. *Journal of Human Evolution* 63(5), 750–758.

Grine, F.E., Klein, R.G. and Volman, T.P. (1991). Dating, archaeology and human fossils from the Middle Stone Age levels of Die Kelders, South Africa. *Journal of Human Evolution*, 21(5), 363–395.

Grine, F.E., Jungers, W.L., Tobias, P.V. and Pearson, O.M. (1995). Fossil *Homo* femur from Berg Aukas, northern Namibia. *American Journal of Physical Anthropology* 97(2), 151–185.

Grine, F.E., Jungers, W.L. and Schultz, J. (1996). Phenetic affinities among early *Homo* crania from East and South Africa. *Journal of Human Evolution* 30, 189–225.

Grine, F.E., Leakey, M.G., Gathago, P.N., et al. (2019). Complete permanent mandibular dentition of early *Homo* from the upper Burgi Member of the Koobi Fora Formation, Ileret, Kenya. *Journal of Human Evolution* 131, 152–175.

Grove, M. (2012). Amplitudes of orbitally induced climatic cycles and patterns of hominin speciation. *Journal of Archaeological Science* 39, 3085–3094.

Grün, R. and Beaumont, P. (2001). Border Cave revisited: a revised ESR chronology. *Journal of Human Evolution* 40(6), 467–482.

Grün, R., Beaumont, P.B. and Stringer, C.B. (1990). ESR dating evidence for early modern humans at Border Cave in South Africa. *Nature* 344(6266), 537.

Grün, R., Brink, J.S., Spooner, N.A., et al. (1996). Direct dating of Florisbad hominid. *Nature* 382(6591), 500.

Guérin, C. (1976). Les restes de Rhinocéros du gisement Miocène de Beni Mellal, Maroc. *Géologie Méditerranéenne* 3, 105–108.

Guest, N.J. (1953). The geology and petrology of the Engaruka Oldoinyo Lengai-Lake Natron Area of Northern Tanganyka Territory. PhD thesis, Sheffield.

Guillocheau, F., Chelalou, R., Linol, B., et al. (2015). Cenozoic landscape evolution in and around the Congo Basin: constraints from sediments and planation surfaces. In: M.J. de Wit, F. Guillocheau and M.C.J. de Wit (Eds.), *Geology and Resource Potential of the Congo Basin*. Berlin: Springer, pp. 271–313.

Guillemot, C. (1997). Recherches paléoanthropologiques dans la basse vallée de l'Omo. *Bulletin de la maison des études éthiopiennes* 11, 69–78.

Gundling, T. and Hill, A. (2000). Geological context of fossil Cercopithecoidea from eastern Africa. In: P.F. Whitehead and C.J. Jolly (Eds.), *Old World Monkeys* Cambridge; New York: Cambridge University Press, pp. 180–213.

Gunnell, G.G., Eiting, T.P. and Geraads, D. (2011). New late Pliocene bats (Chiroptera) from Ahl al Oughlam, Morocco. *Neues Jahrbuch für Geologie und Paläontologie - Abhandlungen* 260, 55–71.

Gunz, P., Bookstein, F.L., Mitteroecker, P., et al. (2009). Early modern human diversity suggests subdivided population structure and a complex out-of-Africa scenario. *Proceedings of the National Academy of Sciences of the USA* 106, 6094–6098.

Gunz, P., Neubauer, S., Falk, D., et al. (2020). *Australopithecus afarensis* endocasts suggest ape-like brain organization and prolonged brain growth. *Science Advances* 6, eaaz4729.

Gutherz, X., Lesur, J., Cauliez, J., et al. (2015). New insights on the first Neolithic societies in the Horn of Africa: the site of Wakrita, Djibouti. *Journal of Field Archaeology* 40, 55–68.

Habermann, J.M., Stanistreet, I.G., Stollhofen, H., et al. (2016). *In situ* ~2.0 Ma trees discovered as fossil rooted stumps, lowermost Bed I, Olduvai Gorge, Tanzania. *Journal of Human Evolution* 90, 74–87.

Habermann, J.M., Alberti, M., Aldeias, V., et al. (2019). Gorongosa by the sea: first Miocene fossil sites from the Urema Rift, central Mozambique, and their coastal paleoenvironmental and paleoecological contexts. *Palaeogeography, Palaeoclimatology, Palaeoecology* 514, 723–738.

Hadjouis, D. (1985). Les Bovidés (Artiodactyla, Mammalia) du gisement Atérien des Phacochères (Alger, Algérie). Interprétations paléontologiques et phylogénétiques. *Comptes Rendu de l'Académie des Sciences Paris* 301, 1251–1254.

Hadjouis, D. (1990). *Megaceroides algericus* (Lydekker, 1890), du gisement des Phacochères (Alger, Algérie). Etude critique de la position systématique de Megaceroides. *Quaternaire* 1, 247–258.

Hadjouis, D. (2002). Un nouveau Bovini dans le faune du Pléistocène supérieur d'Algérie. *L'Anthropologie* 106, 377–386.

Hadjouis, D. (2010). The paleontology of North Africa vertebrates through Camille Arambourg's research: a report on vertebrates' faunae of the North Africa Neogene. *Historical Biology* 22, 200–214.

Haesaerts, P., Stoops, G. and Van Vliet-Lanoë, B. (1983). Data on sediments and fossil soils. In: J. de Heinzelin (Ed.), *The Omo Group*. Tervuren: Musée Royal de l'Afrique Centrale, pp. 149–185.

Hagemann, S.I. (2010). Paleoecology and taphonomy of a hominid-bearing site: Locality 261–1, Allia Bay, Kenya. Thesis, Rutgers University, p. 129.

Hahsler, M. (2017). arulesViz: Interactive Visualization of Association Rules with R. *The R Journal* 9, 163–175.

Hahsler, M. and Karpienko, R. (2017). Visualizing association rules in hierarchical groups. *Journal of Business Economics* 87, 317–335.

Hahsler, M., Grün, B. and Hornik, K. (2005). arules – a computational environment for mining association rules and frequent item sets. *Journal of Statistical Software* 14(15), 1–25.

Hahsler, M., Chelluboina, S., Hornik, K. and Buchta, C. (2011). The arules R-Package Ecosystem: analyzing interesting patterns from large transaction data sets. *Journal of Machine Learning Research* 12, 2021–2025.

Haile-Selassie, Y. (2001). Late Miocene hominids from the Middle Awash, Ethiopia. *Nature* 412, 178–181.

Haile-Selassie, Y. (2010). Phylogeny of early Australopithecus: new fossil evidence from the Woranso-Mille (central Afar, Ethiopia). *Philosophical Transactions of the Royal Society B* 365, 3323–3331.

Haile-Selassie, Y. and Asfaw B. (2000). A newly discovered Early Pliocene hominid bearing site in the Mulu Basin. *Journal of Physical Anthropology*, 111(Supp. 30). 170.

Haile-Selassie, Y. and Howell, F.C. (2009). Carnivora. In: Y. Haile-Selassie and G. WoldeGabriel (Eds.), *Ardipithecus kadabba: Late Miocene Evidence from the Middle Awash, Ethiopia*. Berkeley: University of California Press, pp. 237–276.

Haile-Selassie, Y. and Simpson, S.W. (2013). A new species of *Kolpochoerus* (Mammalia: Suidae) from the Pliocene of Central Afar, Ethiopia: its taxonomy and phylogenetic relationships. *Journal of Mammalian Evolution* 20, 115–127.

Haile-Selassie, Y. and WoldeGabriel, G. (Eds). (2009a) *Ardipithecus kadabba: Late Miocene Evidence from the Middle Awash, Ethiopia*. Berkeley: University of California Press.

Haile-Selassie, Y. and WoldeGabriel, G. (2009b). Introduction. In: *Ardipithecus kadabba: Late Miocene Evidence from the Middle Awash, Ethiopia*. Berkeley: University of California Press, pp. 1–25.

Haile-Selassie, Y., Suwa, G. and White, T.D. (2004a). Late Miocene teeth from Middle Awash, Ethiopia, and early hominid dental evolution. *Science* 303(5663), 1503–1505.

Haile-Selassie, Y., WoldeGabriel, G., White, T.D., et al. (2004b). Mio-Pliocene mammals from the Middle Awash, Ethiopia. *Geobios* 37(4), 536–552.

Haile-Selassie, Y., Deino, A., Saylor, B., Umer, M. and Latimer, B. (2007). Preliminary geology and paleontology of new hominid-bearing Pliocene localities in the central Afar region of Ethiopia. *Anthropological Sciences* 115, 215–222.

Haile-Selassie, Y., White, T., Bernor, R.L., Rook, L. and Vrba, E.S. (2009a) Biochronology, faunal turnover, and evolution. In: Y. Haile-Selassie and G. WoldeGabriel (Eds.), *Ardipithecus kadabba: Late Miocene Evidence from the Middle Awash, Ethiopia*. Berkeley: University of California Press, pp. 565–583.

Haile-Selassie, Y., Suwa, G. and White, T. (2009b). Hominidae. In Y. Haile-Selassie and G. WoldeGabriel (Eds.), *Ardipithecus kadabba: Late Miocene Evidence from the Middle Awash, Ethiopia*. Berkeley: University of California Press, pp. 159–236.

Haile-Selassie, Y., Vrba, E. and Bibi, F. (2009c). Bovidae. In: Y. Haile-Selassie and G. WoldeGabriel (Eds.), *Ardipithecus kadabba: Late Miocene Evidence from the Middle Awash, Ethiopia*. Berkeley: University of California Press, pp. 277–330.

Haile-Selassie, Y., Latimer, B.M., Alene, M., et al. (2010a). An early *Australopithecus afarensis* postcranium from Woranso-Mille, Ethiopia. *Proceedings of the National Academy of Sciences, USA* 107, 12121–12126.

Haile-Selassie, Y., Saylor, B.Z., Deino, A., Alene, M., and Latimer, B.M. (2010b). New hominid fossils from Woranso-Mille (Central Afar, Ethiopia) and taxonomy of early *Australopithecus*. *American Journal of Physical Anthropology* 141, 406–417.

Haile-Selassie, Y., Saylor, B.Z., Deino, A., et al. (2012). A new hominin foot from Ethiopia shows multiple Pliocene bipedal adaptations. *Nature* 483, 565–569.

Haile-Selassie Y., Gibert, L, Melillo S.M., et al. (2015). New species from Ethiopia further expands Middle Pliocene hominin diversity. *Nature* 521, 483–488.

Haile-Selassie, Y., Mellilo, S. and Su, D.F. (2016a). The Pliocene hominin conundrum: do more fossils mean less clarity? *Proceedings of the National Academy of Sciences, USA* 113, 6364–6371.

Haile-Selassie, Y., Melillo, S.M., Ryan, T.M., et al. (2016b). Dentognathic remains of *Australopithecus afarensis* from Nefuraytu (Woranso-Mille, Ethiopia): Comparative description, geology, and paleoecological context. *Journal of Human Evolution* 100, 35–53.

Haile-Selassie, Y., Melillo, S.M., Vazzana, A., Benazzi, S. and Ryan, T.M. (2019). A 3.8-million-year-old hominin cranium from Woranso-Mille, Ethiopia. *Nature* 573, 214–219.

Haileab, B. and Brown, F.H. (1994). Tephra correlations between the Gadeb prehistoric site and the Turkana Basin. *Journal of Human Evolution* 26, 167–173.

Haileab, B. and Feibel, C.S. (1993). Tephra from Fejej, Ethiopia. *Journal of Human Evolution* 25, 515–517.

Haileab, B., Brown, F.H., McDougall, I. and Gathogo, P.N. (2004). Gombe Group basalts and initiation of Pliocene deposition in the Turkana depression, northern Kenya and southern Ethiopia. *Geological Magazine* 141, 41–53.

Hailemichael, M. (2000). The Pliocene environment of Hadar, Ethiopia: a comparative isotopic study of paleosol carbonates and lacustrine mollusk shells of the Hadar Formation. PhD dissertation, Case Western Reserve University.

Hailemichael, M., Aronson, J.L., Savin, S., Tevesz, M.J.S. and Carter, J.G. (2002) $\delta^{18}O$ in mollusk shells from Pliocene Lake Hadar and modern Ethiopian lakes: implications for history of the Ethiopian monsoon. *Palaeogeography, Palaeoclimatology, Palaeoecology* 186, 81–99.

Haines, R.W. and Lye, K.A. (1983). *The Sedges and Rushes of East Africa*. Nairobi: East African Natural History Society.

Halkett, D., Hart, T., Yates, R., et al. (2003). First excavation of intact Middle Stone Age layers at Ysterfontein, Western Cape Province, South Africa: implications for Middle Stone Age ecology. *Journal of Archaeological Science* 30, 955–971.

Hallett-Desguez, E. (2012). Analyse Archéozoologique de la Macrofaune. In: M.A. El Hajraoui, R. Nespoulet, A. Debénath and H.L. Dibble (Eds.), *Préhistoire de la Région de Rabat-Témara. Villes et Sites Archéologiques du Maroc*. Rabat: Institut National des Sciences de l'Archéologie et du Patrimoine, pp. 239–248.

Hamdine, W., Thévenot, M., Michaux, J. (1998). Histoire récente de l'ours brun au Maghreb. *Comptes Rendus de l'Académie des Sciences Paris* 321, 565–570.

Hamilton, W.R. (1973a). North African lower Miocene rhinoceroses. *Bulletin of the British Museum (Natural History) Geology* 24, 349–395.

Hamilton, W.R. (1973b). The Lower Miocene ruminants of Gebel Zelten, Libya. *Bulletin of the British Museum (Natural History) Geology* 21, 75–150.

Hammer, Ø. and Harper, D.A.T. (2006). *Paleontological Data Anlalysis*. Oxford: Blackwell Publishing.

Hammer, Ø., Harper, D.A.T. and Ryan, P.D. (2001). PAST: paleontological statistics software package for education and data analysis. *Palaeontologia Electronica* 4(1), 9 pp.

Hammer, Ø., Harper, D.A. and Ryan, P.D. (2020). *PAST – Palaeontological Statistics*, version 4.0. Paleontological Museum, University of Oslo, Oslo.

Handa, N., Nakatsukasa, M., Kunimatsu, Y., Tsubamoto, T. and Nakaya, H. (2015). New specimens of *Chilotheridium* (Perissodactyla, Rhinocerotidae) from the upper Miocene Namurungule and Nakali Formations, northern Kenya. *Paleontological Research* 19, 181–194.

Handa, N., Nakatsukasa, M., Kunimatsu, Y. and Nakaya, H. (2017). A new Elasmotheriini (Perissodactyla, Rhinocerotidae) from the upper Miocene of Samburu Hills and Nakali, northern Kenya. *Geobios* 50, 197–209.

Handa, N., Nakatsukasa, M., Kunimatsu, Y. and Nakaya, H. (2019). Additional specimens of *Diceros* (Perissodactyla, Rhinocerotidae) from the upper Miocene Nakali Formation in Nakali, central Kenya. *Historical Biology* 31, 262–273.

Hanon, R., Péan, S. and Prat, S. (2018). Reassessment of anthropic modifications on the early Pleistocene hominin specimen Stw53 (Sterkfontein, South Africa). *Bulletins et Mémoires de la Société d'Anthropologie de Paris* 30(1–2), 49–58.

Happold, D. and Lock, J.M. (2013). The biotic zones of Africa. In: J. Kingdon, D.C. Happold, and T.M. Butynski (Eds.), *Mammals of Africa*. London: Bloomsbury, pp. 57–74.

Haq, B.U., Hardenbol, J. and Vail, P.R. (1987). Chronology of fluctuating sea levels since the Triassic. *Science* 235(4793), 1156–1167.

Haradon, C.M. (2010). The ecological context of the Acheulean to Middle Stone Age transition in Africa. PhD thesis, George Washington University.

Harcourt-Smith, W.E.H. (2015). Origin of bipedal locomotion. In: W. Henke and I. Tattersall (Eds.), *Handbook of Paleoanthropology*, 2nd ed. Berlin: Springer, pp. 1919–1959.

Harcourt-Smith, W.E.H. and Aiello, L.C. (2004). Fossils, feet and the evolution of bipedal locomotion. *Journal of Anatomy* 204, 403–416.

Hardenbol, J., Thierry, J., Farley, M.B., et al. (1998). Mesozoic and Cenozoic sequence chronostratigraphic framework of European basins. In: C.-P. Graciansky, J. Hardenbol, T. Jacquin and P.R. Vail (Eds.), *Mesozoic and Cenozoic Sequence Stratigraphy of European Basins*. SEPM, Special Publications, 60, 3–13.

Harding, R.M. and McVean, G. (2004). A structured ancestral population for the evolution of modern humans. *Current Opinion in Genetics and Development* 14, 667–674.

Hare, V. and Sealy, J. (2013). Middle Pleistocene dynamics of southern Africa's winter rainfall zone from δ13 C and δ18O values of Hoedjiespunt faunal enamel. *Palaeogeography, Palaeoclimatology, Palaeoecology* 374, 72–80.

Harmand, S. (2009). Raw material and economic behaviours at Oldowan and Acheulean in the West Turkana region, Kenya. In: B. Adams and B. Blades (Eds.), *Lithic Materials and Paleolithic Societies*. Oxford: Blackwell, pp. 3–14.

Harmand, S., Lewis, J.E., Feibel, C.S., et al. (2015). 3.3-million-year-old stone tools from Lomekwi 3, West Turkana, Kenya. *Nature* 521, 310–315.

Harris, J.M. (1976a). Pleistocene Giraffidae (Mammalia, Artiodactyla) from East Rudolf, Kenya. In: R.J.G. Savage and S.C. Coryndon (Eds.), *Fossil Vertebrates of Africa, vol. 4*. London: Academic Press, pp. 283–332.

Harris, J.M. (1976b). Cranial and dental remains of *Deinotherium bozasi* (Mammalia: Proboscidea) from East Rudolf, Kenya. *Journal of Zoology* 178, 57–75.

Harris, J.M. (1983a). Koobi Fora Research Project, Volume 2: the fossil ungulates: Proboscidea, Perissodactyla, and Suidae. In: R.E. Leakey and G.L. Isaac (Eds.), *Koobi Fora: Researches into Geology, Palaeontology, and Human Origins*. Oxford: Clarendon Press, p. 321.

Harris, J.M. (Ed.) (1983b). Family Suidae. In: *Koobi Fora Research Project. Vol. 2: The Fossil Ungulates: Proboscidea, Perissodactyla, and Suidae*. Oxford: Clarendon Press, pp. 215–302.

Harris, J.M. (1985). Age and paleoecology of the Upper Laetolil Beds, Laetoli, Tanzania. In: E. Delson (Ed.), *Ancestors: The Hard Evidence*. New York: Alan R. Liss, pp. 76–81.

Harris, J.M. (1987). Summary. In: M.D. Leakey and J.M. Harris (Eds.), *Laetoli: A Pliocene Site in Northern Tanzania*. Oxford: Clarendon Press, pp. 524–531.

Harris, J.M. (Ed.) (1991a). Family Bovidae. In: *Koobi Fora Research Project, Vol. 3: The Fossil Ungulates: Geology, Fossil Artiodactyls, and Palaeoenvironments*. Oxford: Clarendon Press, pp. 139–320.

Harris, J.M. (Ed.) (1991b). Family Hippopotamidae. In: *Koobi Fora Research Project, Vol. 3: The Fossil Ungulates: Geology, Fossil Artiodactyls, and Palaeoenvironments*. Oxford: Clarendon Press, pp. 31–85.

Harris, J.M. (Ed.) (1991c). *Koobi Fora Research Project, Vol. 3: The Fossil Ungulates: Geology, Fossil Artiodactyls, and Palaeoenvironments*. Oxford: Clarendon Press.

Harris, J.M. (Ed.) (1991d). Family Giraffidae. In: *Koobi Fora Research Project, Vol. 3: The Fossil Ungulates: Geology, Fossil Artiodactyls, and Palaeoenvironments*. Oxford: Clarendon Press, pp. 93–138.

Harris, J.M. (2003). Bovidae from the Lothagam succession. In: M.G. Leakey and J.M. Harris (Eds.), *Lothagam: The Dawn of Humanity in Eastern Africa*. New York: Columbia University Press, pp. 531–579.

Harris, J.M. and Cerling, T.E. (2002). Dietary adaptations of extant and Neogene African suids. *Journal of Zoology* 256, 45–54.

Harris, J.M. and Leakey, M.G. (2003a). *Geology and Vertebrate Paleontology of the Early Pliocene Site of Kanapoi, Northern Kenya, Contributions in Science*. Los Angeles: Natural History Museum of Los Angeles County, p. 132.

Harris, J.M. and Leakey, M.G. (2003b). Lothagam Suidae. In: M.G. Leakey, and J.M. Harris (Eds.), *Lothagam: The Dawn of Humanity in Eastern Africa*. New York: Columbia University Press, pp. 485–519.

Harris, J.M. and White, T.D. (1979). Evolution of the Plio-Pleistocene African Suidae. *Transactions of the American Philosophical Society* 69(2), 1–128.

Harris, J.M., Brown, F.H., Leakey, M.G., Walker, A.C. and Leakey, R.E. (1988a). Pliocene and Pleistocene Hominid-Bearing Sites from West of Lake Turkana, Kenya. *Science* 239(4835), 27–33.

Harris, J.M., Brown, F.H. and Leakey, M.G. (1988b). *Stratigraphy and Paleontology of Pliocene and Pleistocene Localities West of Lake Turkana, Kenya*. Los Angeles: Natural History Museum of Los Angeles County.

Harris, J.M., Leakey, M.G. and Cerling, T.E. (2003). Early Pliocene tetrapod remains from Kanapoi, Lake Turkana Basin, Kenya. In: J.M. Harris, and M.G. Leakey (Eds.), *Geology and Vertebrate Paleontology of the Early Pliocene Site of Kanapoi, Northern Kenya Contributions in Science*. Los Angeles: Natural History Museum of Los Angeles County, pp. 39–113.

Harris, J.M., Leakey, M.G. and Brown, F.H. (2006). A brief history of research at Koobi Fora, northern Kenya. *Ethnohistory* 53, 35–69.

Harris, J.M., Cerling, T.E., Leakey, M.G. and Passey, B.H. (2008). Stable isotope ecology of fossil hippopotamids from the Lake Turkana Basin of East Africa. *Journal of Zoology* 275(3), 323–331.

Harris, J.M., Geraads, D. and Solounias, N. (2010a). Camelidae. In: L. Werdelin and W.J. Sanders (Eds.), *Cenozoic Mammals of Africa*. Berkeley, University of California Press, pp. 815–820.

Harris, J.M., Solounias, N. and Geraads, D. (2010b). Giraffoidea. In: L. Werdelin and W.J. Sanders (Eds.), *Cenozoic Mammals of Africa*. Berkeley, University of California Press, pp. 797–811.

Harris, J.W.K. and Harris, K. (1981). A note on the archaeology at Laetoli. *Nyame Akuma* 18, 18–21.

Harris, J.W.K. and Isaac, G.L. (1976). The Karari Industry: Early Pleistocene archaeological evidence from the terrain east of Lake Turkana, Kenya. *Nature* 262, 102–107.

Harris, J.W.K., Williamson, P.G., Verniers, J., et al. (1987). Late Pliocene hominid occupation in Central Africa: the setting, context, and character of the Senga 5A site, Zaire. *Journal of Human Evolution* 16, 701–728.

Harris, J.W.K., Williamson, P.G., Morris, P.J., et al. (1990). Archaeology of the Lusso Beds. In: N.T. Boaz (Ed.), *Evolution of Environments and Hominidae in the African Western Rift Valley*. Martinsville: Virginia Museum of Natural History, pp. 237–272.

Harrison, J.L. (1962). The distribution of feeding habits among animals in a tropical rain forest. *Journal of Animal Ecology* 31, 53–64.

Harrison, T. (1997a). *Neogene Paleontology of the Manonga Valley, Tanzania: A Window into the Evolutionary History of East Africa*. New York: Springer.

Harrison, T. (Ed.) (1997b). Paleoecology and taphonomy of fossil localities in the Manonga Valley, Tanzania. In: *Neogene Paleontology of the Manonga Valley, Tanzania: A Window into the Evolutionary History of East Africa*. New York: Springer, pp. 79–105.

Harrison, T. (2002). First recorded hominins from the Ndolanya Beds, Laetoli, Tanzania. *American Journal of Physical Anthropolopy* 32(Suppl.), 83.

Harrison, T. (2005). Fossil bird eggs from Laetoli, Tanzania: their taxonomic and paleoecological implications. *Journal of African Earth Sciences* 41, 289–302.

Harrison, T. (2010a). Apes among the tangled branches of human origins. *Science* 327(5965), 532–534.

Harrison, T. (2010b). Dendropithecoidea, Proconsuloidea, and Hominoidea. In: L. Werdelin and W.J. Sanders (Eds.), *Cenozoic Mammals of Africa*. Berkeley: University of California Press, pp. 429–469.

Harrison, T. (2011a). *Paleontology and Geology of Laetoli: Human Evolution in Context, Vol. 1: Geology, Geochronology, Paleoecology and Paleoenvironment*. Dordrecht: Springer.

Harrison, T. (2011b). *Paleontology and Geology of Laetoli: Human Evolution in Context, Vol. 2: Fossil Hominins and the Associated Fauna*. Dordrecht: Springer.

Harrison, T. (Ed.) (2011c). Hominins from the Upper Laetolil and Upper Ndolanya Beds, Laetoli. In: *Paleontology and Geology of Laetoli: Human Evolution in Context, Vol. 2: Fossil Hominins and the Associated Fauna*. Dordrecht: Springer, pp. 141–188.

Harrison, T. (Ed.) (2011d). Introduction: the Laetoli hominins and associated fauna. In: *Paleontology and Geology of Laetoli: Human Evolution in Context, Vol. 2: Fossil Hominins and the Associated Fauna*. Dordrecht: Springer, pp. 1–14.

Harrison, T. (Ed.) (2011e). Laetoli revisited: Renewed paleontological and geological investigations at localities on the Eyasi Plateau in northern Tanzania. In: *Paleontology and Geology of Laetoli: Human Evolution in Context, Vol. 2: Fossil Hominins and the Associated Fauna*. Dordrecht: Springer, pp. 1–15.

Harrison, T. (Ed.) (2011f). Cercopithecids (Cercopithecidae, Primates). In: *Paleontology and Geology of Laetoli: Human Evolution in Context, Vol. 2: Fossil Hominins and the Associated Fauna*. Dordrecht: Springer, pp. 83–139.

Harrison, T. (Ed.) (2011g). Galagidae (Lorisoidea, Primates). In: *Paleontology and Geology of Laetoli: Human Evolution in Context, Vol. 2: Fossil Hominins and the Associated Fauna*. Dordrecht: Springer, pp. 75–81.

Harrison, T. (Ed.) (2011h). Tortoises (Chelonii, Testudinidae). In: *Paleontology and Geology of Laetoli: Human Evolution in Context, Vol. 2: Fossil Hominins and the Associated Fauna*. Dordrecht: Springer, pp. 479–503.

Harrison, T. (Ed.) (2011i). Coprolites: Taphonomic and paleoecological implications. In: *Paleontology and Geology of Laetoli: Human Evolution in Context, Vol. 1: Geology, Geochronology, Paleoecology and Paleoenvironment*. Dordrecht: Springer, pp. 279–292.

Harrison, T. (2017). The paleoecology of the Upper Ndolanya Beds, Laetoli, Tanzania, and its implications for hominin evolution. In: A. Marom and E. Hovers (Eds.), *Human Paleontology and Prehistory: Contributions in Honor of Yoel Rak*. Dordrecht: Springer, pp. 31–44.

Harrison, T. and Baker, E. (1997). Paleontology and biochronology of fossil localities in the Manonga Valley, Tanzania. In: T. Harrison (Ed.), *Neogene Paleontology of the Manonga Valley, Tanzania*. New York: Plenum, pp. 361–393.

Harrison, T. and Kweka, A. (2011). Paleontological localities on the Eyasi Plateau, including Laetoli. In: T. Harrison (Ed.), *Paleontology and Geology of Laetoli, Tanzania: Human Evolution in Context. Volume 1: Geology, Geochronology, Paleoecology and Paleoenvironment*. Dordrecht: Springer, pp. 17–45.

Harrison, T. and Mbago, M.L. (1997). Introduction: paleontological and geological research in the Manonga Valley, Tanzania. In: T. Harrison (Ed.), *Neogene Paleontology of the Manonga Valley, Tanzania: A Window into the Evolutionary History of East Africa*. New York: Springer, pp. 1–32.

Harrison, T. and Msuya, C.P. (2005). Fossil struthionid eggshells from Laetoli, Tanzania: their taxonomic and biostratigraphic significance. *Journal of African Earth Science* 41, 303–315.

Harrison, T. and Rein, T.R. (2016). The hands of fossil non-hominoid anthropoids. In: T.L. Kivell, P. Lemelin, B.G. Richmond and D. Schmitt (Eds.), *The Evolution of the Primate Hand: Anatomical, Developmental, Functional, and Paleontological Evidence*. New York: Springer, pp. 455–483.

Hartstone-Rose, A., de Ruiter, D.J., Berger, L.R. and Churchill, S.E. (2007). A sabre-tooth felid from Cooper's Cave (Gauteng, South Africa) and its implications for Megantereon (Felidae: Machairodontinae) taxonomy. *Palaeontologica Africana* 42, 99–108.

Hartstone-Rose, A., Werdelin, L., de Ruiter, D.J., Berger, L.R. and Churchill, S.E. (2010). The Plio-Pleistocene ancestor of wild dogs, *Lycaon sekowei* n. sp. *Journal of Paleontology* 84, 290–308.

Harvey, P.H. and Pagel, M.D. (1991). *The Comparative Method in Evolutionary Biology*. Oxford: Oxford University Press.

Hasegawa, M., Thorne, J.L. and Kishino, H. (2003). Time scale of eutherian evolution estimated without assuming a constant rate of molecular evolution. *Genes & Genetic Systems* 78(4), 267–283.

Hatala, K.G., Roach, N.T., Ostrofsky, K.R., et al. (2016). Footprints reveal direct evidence of group behavior and locomotion in *Homo erectus*. *Scientific Reports* 6, 28766.

Hatala, K.G., Roach, N.T., Ostrofsky, K.R., et al. (2017). Hominin track assemblages from Okote Member deposits near Ileret, Kenya, and their implications for understanding fossil hominin paleobiology at 1.5 Ma. *Journal of Human Evolution* 112, 93–104.

Haug, G.H. and Tiedemann, R. (1998). Effect of the formation of the Isthmus of Panama on Atlantic Ocean thermohaline circulation. *Nature* 393(6686), 673–676.

Harvati, K., Stringer, C., Grün, R., et al. (2013). The Later Stone Age calvaria from Iwo Eleru, Nigeria: morphology and chronology. *PLos ONE* 6, e24024.

Hay, R.L. (1976). *Geology of the Olduvai Gorge: A Study of Sedimentation in a Semiarid Basin*. Berkeley: University of California Press.

Hay, R.L. (1978). Melilitite–carbonatite tuffs in the Laetolil Beds of Tanzania. *Contributions in Mineralogy and Petrology* 17, 255–274.

Hay, R.L. (1981). Palaeoenvironment of the Laetolil Beds, northern Tanzania. In: G. Rapp and C.F. Vondra (Eds.), *Hominid Sites: Their Geological Settings*. American Association for the Advancement of Science, Selected Symposium 63. Boulder: Westview Press, pp. 7–24.

Hay, R.L. (1986). Role of tephra in the preservation of fossils in Cenozoic deposits of East Africa. In: L.E. Frostick, R.W. Renaut, I. Reid and J.J. Tiercelin (Eds.), *Sedimentation in the African Rifts*. Geological Society Special Publication No. 25. Oxford: Blackwell Scientific Publications, pp. 339–344.

Hay, R.L. (1987). Geology of the Laetoli area. In: M.D. Leakey and J.M. Harris (Eds.), *Laetoli: A Pliocene Site in Northern Tanzania*. Oxford: Oxford University Press, pp. 23–47.

Hay, R.L. (1990). Olduvai Gorge: a case history in the interpretation of hominid paleoenvironments in East Africa. *Geological Society of America Special Paper* 242, 23–37.

Hay, R.L. (1996). Stratigraphy and lake-margin paleoenvironments of lowermost Bed II in Olduvai Gorge. *Kaupia* 6, 223–230.

Hay, R.L. and Kyser, T.K. (2001). Chemical sedimentology and paleoenvironmental history of Lake Olduvai, a Pliocene lake in northern Tanzania. *Geological Society of America Bulletin* 113, 1505–1521.

Hay, R.L. and Leakey, M.D. (1982). The fossil footprints of Laetoli. *Scientific American* 246, 50–57.

Hay, R.L. and Reeder, R.J. (1978). Calcretes of Olduvai Gorge and the Ndolanya Beds of northern Tanzania. *Sedimentology* 25, 649–673.

Hays, J.D., Imbrie, J. and Shackleton, N.J. (1976). Variations in Earth's orbit: pacemaker of ice ages. *Science* 194, 1121–1132.

Hayward, M.W. (2006). Prey preferences of the spotted hyaena (*Crocuta crocuta*) and degree of dietary overlap with the lion (*Panthera leo*). *Journal of Zoology* 270(4), 606–614.

Head, J.J. and Bell, C.J. (2007). Snakes from Lemudong'o, Kenya Rift Valley. *Kirtlandia* 56, 177–179.

Head, J.J. and Müller, J. (2020). Squamate reptiles from Kanapoi: faunal evidence for hominin paleoenvironments. *Journal of Human Evolution* 140, 102451.

Head, M.J. and Gibbard, P.L. (Eds.) (2005). Early–Middle Pleistocene transitions: an overview and recommendation for the defining boundary. In: *Early–Middle Pleistocene Transitions: The Land-Ocean Evidence*. London: Geological Society of London, Special Publication 247, pp. 1–18.

Heaton, J.L. (2006). Taxonomy of the Sterkfontein fossil Cercopithecinae: the Papionini of Members 2 and 4 (Gauteng, South Africa). Unpublished PhD dissertation, Indiana University.

Hedges, R.E.M. (2002). Bone diagenesis: an overview of processes. *Archaeometry* 44, 319–328.

Heinrich, S., Zonneveld, K.A., Bickert, T. and Willems, H. (2011). The Benguela upwelling related to the Miocene cooling events and the development of the Antarctic Circumpolar Current: evidence from calcareous dinoflagellate cysts. *Paleoceanography* 26(3).

Heintz, E. (1973). Un nouveau bovidé du Miocène de Beni Mellal, Maroc: *Benicerus theobaldi* n.g. n.sp. (Bovidae, Artiodactyla, Mammalia). *Annales Scientifiques de l'Université de Besançon, Géologie* 3, 245–248.

Heintz, E. (1976). Les Giraffidae (Artiodactyla, Mammalia) du Miocène de Beni Mellal, Maroc. *Géologie Méditerranéenne* 3, 91–104.

Helgren, D.M. and Brooks, A.S. (1983). Geoarchaeology at Gi, a Middle Stone Age and Later Stone Age site in the northern Kalahari. *Journal of Archaeological Science* 10, 181–197.

Helm, C., Cawthra, H., Cowling, R., et al. (2018). Palaeoecology of giraffe tracks in Late Pleistocene aeolianites on the Cape south coast. *South African Journal of Science* 114(1–2), 1–8.

Helm, C.W., Cawthra, H.C., Cowling, R.M., et al. (2019a). Pleistocene vertebrate tracksites on the Cape south coast of South Africa and their potential palaeoecological implications. *Quaternary Science Reviews* 235, 105857.

Helm, C.W., Cawthra, H.C., de Vynck, J.C., et al. (2019b). The Pleistocene fauna of the Cape south coast revealed through ichnology at two localities. *South African Journal of Science* 115(1–2), 1–9.

Henderson, Z., Scott, L., Rossouw, L. and Jacob, Z. (2006). Dating, paleoenvironments, and archaeology: a progress report on the Sunnyside 1 Site, Clarens, South Africa. *Archeological Papers of the American Anthropological Association* 16, 139–149.

Hendey, Q.B. (1968). The Melkbos site: an Upper Pleistocene fossil occurrence in the south-western Cape Province. *Annals of the South African Museum* 52, 89–119.

Hendey, Q.B. (1970). The age of the fossiliferous deposits at Langebaanweg, Cape Province. *Annals of the South African Museum* 56(3), 119–131.

Hendey, Q.B. (1974). The late Cainozoic carnivora of the south-western Cape Province. *Annals of the South African Museum* 63(1), 112–116.

Hendey, Q.B. (1977). Fossil bear from South Africa. *South African Journal of Science* 73(4), 112.

Hendey, Q.B. (1981a). Geological succession at Langebaanweg, Cape Province, and global events of the late Tertiary. *South African Journal of Science* 77(1), 33–38.

Hendey, Q.B. (1981b). Palaeoecology of the late tertiary fossil occurrences in" E" Quarry, Langebaanweg, South Africa and a reinterpretation of their geological context. *Annals of the South African Museum* 84, 1–104.

Hendey, Q.B. and Cooke, H.B.S. (1985). *Kolpochoerus paiceae* (Mammalia, Suidae) from Skurwerug, near Saldanha, South Africa, and its palaeoenvironmental implications. *Annales of the South African Museum* 97, 9–56.

Hendey, Q.B. and Hendey, H. (1968). New Quaternary fossil sites near Swartklip, Cape Province. *Annals of the South African Museum* 52, 43–73.

Hennig, E. (1948). Quartärfaunen und Urgeschichte Ostafrikas. *Naturwissenschaftliche Rundschau* 1, 212–217.

Henry, A.G., Ungar, P.S., Passey, B.H., et al. (2012). The diet of Australopithecus sediba. *Nature* 487(7405), 90.

Henshilwood, C.S. (1997). Identifying the collector: evidence for human processing of the Cape Dune Mole-Rat, *Bathyergus suillus*, from Blombos Cave, southern Cape, South Africa. *Journal of Archaeological Science* 24(7), 659–662.

Henshilwood, C.S., Sealy, J.C., Yates, R., et al. (2001). Blombos Cave, Southern Cape, South Africa: preliminary report on the 1992–1999 excavations of the Middle Stone Age levels. *Journal of Archaeological Science* 28, 421–448.

Henshilwood, C.S., Errico, F., Yates, R., et al. (2002). Emergence of modern human behavior: Middle Stone Age engravings from South Africa. *Science* 295(5558), 1278–1280.

Henshilwood, C.S., d'Errico, F., Van Niekerk, K.L., et al. (2011). A 100,000-year-old ochre-processing workshop at Blombos Cave, South Africa. *Science* 334(6053), 219–222.

Hernandez Fernandez, M. and Vrba, E. (2006). Plio-Pleistcoene climatic change in the Turkana basin (East Africa): evidence from large mammal faunas. *Journal of Human Evolution* 50, 595–626.

Hernesniemi, E., Giaourtsakis, I.X., Evans, A.R. and Fortelius, M. (2011). Rhinoceroses. In: T. Harrison (Ed.), *Paleontology and Geology of Laetoli: Human Evolution in Context. Vol. 2: Fossil Hominins and the Associated Fauna*. Dordrecht: Springer, pp. 275–294.

Herries, A.I.R. (2003). Magnetostratigraphic seriation of the South African hominin paleocaves. PhD dissertation, University of Liverpool.

Herries, A.I. and Adams, J.W. (2013). Clarifying the context, dating and age range of the Gondolin hominins and *Paranthropus* in South Africa. *Journal of Human Evolution* 65(5), 676–681.

Herries, A.I.R. and Latham, A.G. (2009). Archaeomagnetic studies at the Cave of Hearths. The cave of hearths: Makapan middle Pleistocene research project. *University of Southampton Series in Archaeology* 1, 59–64.

Herries, A.I.R. and Shaw, J. (2011). Palaeomagnetic analysis of the Sterkfontein palaeocave deposits; age implications for the hominin fossils and stone tool industries. *Journal of Human Evolution* 60, 523–539.

Herries, A.I., Reed, K.E., Kuykendall, K.L. and Latham, A.G. (2006a). Speleology and magnetobiostratigraphic chronology of the Buffalo Cave fossil site, Makapansgat, South Africa. *Quaternary Research* 66(2), 233–245.

Herries, A.I., Adams, J.W., Kuykendall, K.L. and Shaw, J. (2006b). Speleology and magnetobiostratigraphic chronology of the GD 2 locality of the Gondolin hominin-bearing paleocave deposits, North West Province, South Africa. *Journal of Human Evolution* 51(6), 617–631.

Herries, A.I.R., Curnoe, D. and Adams, J.W. (2009). A multidisciplinary seriation of early *Homo* and Paranthropus bearing palaeocaves in southern Africa. *Quaternary International* 202(1–2), 14–28.

Herries, A.I., Hopley, P.J., Adams, J.W., Curnoe, D. and Maslin, M.A. (2010). Letter to the editor: Geochronology and palaeoenvironments of Southern African hominin-bearing localities – a reply to Wrangham et al., 2009."Shallow-water habitats as sources of fallback foods for hominins". *American Journal of Physical Anthropology* 143(4), 640–646.

Herries, A.I.R., Pickering, R., Adams, J.W., et al. (2013). A multidisciplinary perspective on the age of Australopithecus in southern Africa. In K.E. Reed, J.G. Fleagle and R.F. Leakey (Eds.), *The Paleobiology of Australopithecus*. Dordrecht: Springer, pp. 21–40.

Herries, A.I., Kappen, P., Kegley, A.D., et al. (2014). Palaeomagnetic and synchrotron analysis of > 1.95 Ma fossil-bearing palaeokarst at Haasgat, South Africa. *South African Journal of Science* 110(3–4), 1–12.

Herries, A.I., Murszewski, A., Pickering, R., et al. (2018). Geoarchaeological and 3D visualisation approaches for contextualising in-situ fossil bearing palaeokarst in South Africa: a case study from the ~2.61 Ma Drimolen Makondo. *Quaternary international* 483, 90–110.

Herries, A.I.R., Adams, J.W., Joannes-Boyau, R., et al. (2019). Integrating palaeocaves into palaeolandscapes: an analysis of cave levels and karstification history across the Gauteng Malmani dolomite, South Africa. *Quaternary Science Reviews* 220, 310–334.

Herries, A.I., Martin, J.M., Leece, A.B., et al. (2020). Contemporaneity of *Australopithecus*, *Paranthropus*, and early Homo erectus in South Africa. *Science* 368(6486).

Higgs, E.S. (1967). Environment and chronology: the evidence from mammalian fauna. In: C.B.M. McBurney (Ed.), *The Haua Fteah (Cyrenaica) and the Stone Age of the South-East Mediterranean*. Cambridge: Cambridge University Press, pp. 149–164.

Hilgen, F., Kuiper, K., Krijgsman, W., Snel, E. and van der Laan, E. (2007). Astronomical tuning as the basis for high resolution chronostratigraphy: the intricate history of the Messinian Salinity Crisis. *Stratigraphy* 4(2–3), 231–238.

Hilgen, F.J., Lourens, L.J., and Van Dam, J.A. (2012). The Neogene Period. In: F.M. Gradstein, J.G. Ogg, M.D. Schmitz and G.M. Ogg (Eds.), *The Geologic Time Scale 2012*. Oxford: Elsevier, pp. 923–978.

Hill, A. (1975). Taphonomy of contemporary and Late Cenozoic East African vertebrates. PhD dissertation, University of London.

Hill, A. (1979a). Disarticulation and scattering of mammal skeletons. *Paleobiology* 5, 261–274.

Hill, A. (1979b). Butchery and natural disarticulation: an investigatory technique. *American Antiquity* 44, 739–744.

Hill, A. (1980). Postmortem damage to the remains of contemporary East African mammals. In: A.K. Behrensmeyer and A.P. Hill (Eds.), *Fossils in the Making: Vertebrate Taphonomy and Paleoecology*. Chicago: The University of Chicago Press, pp. 131–152.

Hill, A. (1985). Early Hominid from Baringo, Kenya. *Nature* 315(6016), 222–224.

Hill, A. (1989). Bone modification by modern spotted hyenas. In: R. Bonnichsen and M.H. Sorg (Eds.), *Bone Modification*. Orono: Center for the Study of the First American, Institute for Quaternary Studies, University of Maine, pp. 169–178.

Hill, A. (1995) Faunal and environmental change in the Neogene of east Africa: evidence from the Tugen Hills sequence, Baringo District, Kenya. In: E.S. Vrba, G.H. Denton, T.C. Partridge and L.H. Burckle (Eds.), *Paleoclimate and Evolution, with Emphasis on Human Origins*. New Haven: Yale University Press, pp. 178–193.

Hill, A. (1999). The Baringo Basin, Kenya: from Bill Bishop to BPRP. In: P. Andrews and P. Banham (Eds.), *Late Cenozoic Environments and Hominid Evolution: a Tribute to Bill Bishop*. London: Geological Society of London, pp. 85–97.

Hill, A. (2002). Paleoanthropological research in the Tugen Hills, Kenya – introduction. *Journal of Human Evolution*, 42(1–2), 1–10. doi:10.1006/jhev.2001.0520

Hill, A. (2007). Preface. In: R. Bobe, Z. Alemseged and A.K. Behrensmeyer (Eds.), *Hominin Environments in the East African Pliocene: An Assessment of the Faunal Evidence*. Dordrecht: Springer, pp. xvii–xx.

Hill, A. and Behrensmeyer, A.K. (1984). Disarticulation patterns of some modern East African mammals. *Paleobiology* 10, 366–376.

Hill, A. and Ward, S. (1988). Origin of the Hominidae: the record of African large Hominoid evolution between 14 my and 4 my. *Yearbook of Physical Anthropology* 31, 49–83.

Hill, A., Drake, R., Tauxe, L., et al. (1985). Neogene palaeontology and geochronology of the Baringo Basin, Kenya. *Journal of Human Evolution* 14, 759–773.

Hill, A., Curtis, G. and Drake, R. (1986). Sedimentary stratigraphy of the Tugen Hills, Baringo, Kenya. In: L.E. Frostick, R.W. Renaut, I. Rein and J.J. Tiercelin (Eds.), *Sedimentation in the African Rifts*. Geological Society Special Publication No. 25. London: Geological Society of London, pp. 285–295.

Hill, A., Ward, S., Deino, A., Curtis, G., and Drake, R. (1992). Earliest *Homo*. *Nature* 355(6362), 719–722.

Hill, A., Leakey, M., Kingston, J.D. and Ward, S.C. (2002). New cercopithecoids and a hominoid from 12.5 Ma in the Tugen Hills succession, Kenya. *Journal of Human Evolution* 42, 75–93.

Hill, M.O. (1973). Diversity and evenness: a unifying notation and its consequences. *Ecology* 54(2), 427–432.

Hivernel-Guerre, F. (1976). Les industries du Late Stone Age dans la région de Melka-Kunturé. In: A. Berhanou, J. Chavaillon and R. Sutton (Eds.), *Proceedings of the 7th Congress of Prehistory and Quaternary Studies, 1971*. Addis-Abeba: Ministry of Culture, pp. 93–98.

Hlubik, S., Berna, F., Feibel, C., Braun, D. and Harris, J.W.K. (2017). Researching the nature of fire at 1.5 Mya on the site of FxJj20 AB, Koobi Fora, Kenya, using high-resolution spatial analysis and FTIR spectrometry. *Current Anthropology* 58, S243–S257.

Hlubik, S., Cutts, R., Braun, D.R., et al. (2019). Hominin fire use in the Okote Member at Koobi Fora, Kenya: new evidence for the old debate. *Journal of Human Evolution* 133, 214–229.

Hlusko, L.J. (2007a). Earliest evidence for *Atherurus* and *Xenohystrix* (Hystricidae, Rodentia) in Africa, from the late Miocene site of Lemudong'o, Kenya. *Kirtlandia* 56, 86–91.

Hlusko, L.J. (2007b). A new late Miocene species of *Paracolobus* and other Cercopithecoidea (Mammalia: Primates) fossils from Lemudong'o, Kenya. *Kirtlandia* 56, e85.

Hobolth, A., Christensen, O.F., Mailund, T. and Schierup, M.H. (2007). Genomic relationships and speciation times of human, chimpanzee, and gorilla inferred from a coalescent hidden Markov model. *PLoS Genetics* 3(2), e7.

Volume References

Hodell, D.A., Elmstrom, K.M. and Kennett, J.P. (1986). Latest Miocene benthic δ18O changes, global ice volume, sea level and the 'Messinian salinity crisis'. *Nature* 320, 411–414.

Hodell, D.A., Curtis, J.H., Sierro, F.J. and Raymo, M.E. (2001). Correlation of late Miocene to early Pliocene sequences between the Mediterranean and North Atlantic. *Paleoceanography* 16(2), 164–178.

Hodgkins, J., Marean, C.W., Venter, J.A., et al. (2020). An isotopic test of the seasonal migration hypothesis for large grazing ungulates inhabiting the Palaeo-Agulhas Plain. *Quaternary Science Reviews*, 235, 106221.

Hoetzel, S., Dupont, L.M. and Wefer, G. (2015). Miocene–Pliocene vegetation change in south-western Africa (ODP Site 1081, offshore Namibia). *Palaeogeography, Palaeoclimatology, Palaeoecology* 423, 102–108.

Holbourn, A.E., Kuhnt, W., Clemens, S.C., et al. (2018). Late Miocene climate cooling and intensification of southeast Asian winter monsoon. *Nature Communications* 9, 1584.

Holland, S.M. (2003). Confidence limits on fossil ranges that account for facies changes. *Paleobiology* 29(4), 468–479.

Holland, S.M. (2016). The non-uniformity of fossil preservation. *Philosophical Transactions: Biological Sciences* 371(1699), 1–11.

Holmgren, K., Lee-Thorp, J.A., Cooper, G.R.I., et al. (2003). Persistent millennial-scale climatic variability over the past 25,000 years in Southern Africa. *Quaternary Science Reviews* 22, 2311–2326.

Holt, S., Horwitz, L.K., Hoffman, J. and Codron, D. (2019). Structural density of the leopard tortoise (*Stigmochelys pardalis*) shell and its implications for taphonomic research. *Journal of Archaeological Science: Reports* 26, 101819.

Hönisch, B., Hemming, N.G., Archer, D., Siddal, M. and McManus, J.F. (2009). Atmospheric carbon dioxide concentration across the mid-Pleistocene transition. *Science* 324(5934), 1551–1554.

Hooijer, D.A. (1958). Fossil rhinoceroses from the Limeworks Cave, Makapansgat. *Palaeontologica Africana* 6, 1–13.

Hooijer, D.A. and Churcher, C.S. (1985). Perissodactyla of the Omo Group deposits, American collections. In: Y. Coppens and F.C. Howell (Eds.), *Les Faunes Plio-Pléistocènes de la Basse Vallée de l'Omo (Éthiopie): Tome 1: Périssodactyles – Artiodactyles (Bovidae)*. Paris: CNRS, pp. 97–117.

Hooijer, D.A. and Maglio, V.J. (1974). Hipparions from the Late Miocene and Pliocene of northwestern Kenya. *Zoologische Verhandelingen* 134, 1–34.

Hooijer, D.A. and Patterson, B. (1972). Rhinoceroses from the Pliocene of northwestern Kenya. *Bulletin of the Museum of Comparative Zoology* 144, 1–26.

Hooker, P.J. and Miller, J.A. (1979). K–Ar dating of the Pleistocene fossil hominid site at Chesowanja, North Kenya. *Nature* 282, 710–712.

Hopley, P.J. and Maslin, M.A. (2010). Climate-averaging of terrestrial faunas: an example from the Plio-Pleistocene of South Africa. *Paleobiology* 36(1), 32–50.

Hopley, P., Latham, A. and Marshall, J. (2006). Palaeoenvironments and palaeodiets of mid-Pliocene micromammals from Makapansgat Limeworks, South Africa: a stable isotope and dental microwear approach. *Paleogeography, Paleoclimatology, Paleoecology* 233, 235–251.

Hopley, P.J., Marshall, J.D., Weedon, G.P., et al. (2007a). Orbital forcing and the spread of C_4 grasses in the late Neogene: stable isotope evidence from South African speleothems. *Journal of Human Evolution* 53, 620–634.

Hopley, P., Weedon, G., Marshall, J., et al. (2007b). High- and low-latitude orbital forcing of early hominin habitats in South Africa. *Earth and Planetary Science Letters* 256, 419–432.

Hopley, P.J., Herries, A.I.R., Edwards Baker, S., Kuhn, B.F. and Menter, C.G. (2013). Brief communication: Beyond the South Africa cave paradigm – Australopithecus africanus from Plio-Pleistocene paleosol deposits at Taung. *American Journal of Physical Anthropology* 151, 316–324.

Hopley, P.J., Weedon, G.P., Brierley, C.M., et al. (2018). Orbital precession modulates interannual rainfall variability, as recorded in an Early Pleistocene speleothem. *Geology* 46, 731–734.

Hopley, P.J., Reade, H., Parrish, R., De Kock, M. and Adams, J.W. (2019). Speleothem evidence for C_3 dominated vegetation during the Late Miocene (Messinian) of South Africa. *Review of Palaeobotany and Palynology* 264, 75–89.

Hopley, P., Vermeesch, P., Parrish, R. and Latham, A. (2021). Clusters of flowstone ages are not supported by statistical evidence. *Nature* 594(7863), E10–E10.

Horwitz, L.K. and Chazan, M. (2015). Past and present at Wonderwerk Cave (Northern Cape Province, South Africa). *African Archaeological Review* 32, 595–612.

Hours, F. (1976). Le Middle Stone Age de Melka-Kunturé. In: Berhanou, A., Chavaillon, J. and Sutton, R. (Eds.), *Proceedings of the 7th Congress of Prehistory and Quaternary Studies, 1971*, Addis-Ababa: Ministry of Culture, pp. 99–104.

Hovers, E. (2003). Treading carefully; site formation processes and Pliocene lithic technology. In: J.M. Martinez-Moreno, R. Mora, and I. de la Torre (Eds.), *Oldowan: Rather More Than Smashing Stones*. Barcelona: Universitat Autonoma de Barcelona, pp. 145–164.

Howell, F.C. (1968). Omo research expedition. *Nature* 219, 567–572.

Howell, F.C. (1969). Remains of Hominidae from Pliocene/Pleistocene formations in the lower Omo Basin, Ethiopia. *Nature* 223, 1234–1239.

Howell, F.C. (1978a). Overview of the Pliocene and earlier Pleistocene of the lower Omo basin, southern Ethiopia. In: C.J. Jolly (Ed.), *Early Hominids of Africa*. London: Duckworth, pp. 85–130.

Howell, F.C. (1978b). Hominidae. In: V.J. Maglio and H.B.S. Cooke (Eds.), *Evolution of African Mammals*. Cambridge, MA: Harvard University Press, pp. 154–248.

Howell, F.C. (1987a). Preliminary observations on Carnivora from the Sahabi formation (Libya). In: N.T. Boaz, A. El-Arnauti, A.W. Gaziry, J. de Heinzelin and D.D. Boaz (Eds.), *Neogene Paleontology and Geology of As Sahabi*. New York: Alan R. Liss, pp. 153–181.

Howell, F.C. and Bourlière, F. (1963). *African Ecology and Human Evolution*. Chicago: Aldine Publishing.

Howell, F.C. and Coppens, Y. (1973). Deciduous teeth of Hominidae from the Pliocene/Pleistocene of the Lower Omo Basin, Ethiopia. *Journal of Human Evolution* 2, 461–472.

Howell, F.C. and Coppens, Y. (1974). Inventory of remains of Hominidae from Pliocene/Pleistocene formations of the lower Omo basin, Ethiopia (1967–1972). *American Journal of Physical Anthropology* 40, 1–16.

Howell, F.C. and Coppens, Y. (1976). An overview of Hominidae from the Omo Succession, Ethiopia. In: Y. Coppens, F.C. Howell, G.L. Isaac and R.E. Leakey (Eds.), *Earliest Man and Environments in the Lake Rudolf Basin*. Chicago: University of Chicago Press, pp. 522–532.

Howell, F.C. and Coppens, Y. (1983). Introduction. In: J. de Heinzelin (Ed.), *The Omo Group*. Tervuren: Musée Royal de l'Afrique Centrale, pp. 1–5.

Howell, F.C. and Garcia, N. (2007). Carnivora (Mammalia) from Lemudong'o (Late Miocene: Narok District, Kenya). *Kirtlandia* 56, 121–139.

Howell, F.C., Haesaerts, P. and de Heinzelin, J. (1987). Depositional environments, archeological occurrences and hominids from

Members E and F of the Shungura Formation (Omo basin, Ethiopia). *Journal of Human Evolution* 16, 665–700.

Hrdlička, A. (1925). The Taungs ape. *American Journal of Physical Anthropology* 8, 379–392.

Hsieh, T.C., Ma, K.H. and Chao, A. (2016). iNEXT: an R package for rarefaction and extrapolation of species diversity (Hill numbers). *Methods in Ecology and Evolution* 7(12), 1451–1456.

Hubbell, S.P. (2001). *The Unified Neutral Theory of Biodiversity and Biogeography. Monographs in Population Biology 32*. Princeton: Princeton University Press.

Hublin, J.-J. (1992). Le fémur humain du pléistocène moyen de l'Ain Maarouf près de El Hajeb (Maroc). *Comptes Rendus de l'Académie des Sciences sér. II* 314, 975–980.

Hublin, J.-J. (2001). North-western African Middle Pleistocene hominids and their bearing on the origin of *Homo sapiens*. In: L. Barham and K. Robson-Brown (Eds.), *Human Roots; Africa and Asia in the Middle Pleistocene*. Bristol: CHERUB, pp. 99–121.

Hublin, J.-J. Tillier, A.M. and Tixier, J. (1987). L'humérus d'enfant moustérien (*Homo* 4) du Djebel Irhoud (Maroc) dans son contexte archéologique. *Bulletins et Mémoires de la Société d'Anthropologie de Paris series 14*, 4, 115–141.

Hublin, J.-J., Ben-Ncer, A., Bailey, S.E., et al. (2017). New fossils from Jebel Irhoud, Morocco and the pan-African origin of *Homo sapiens*. *Nature* 546, 289–292.

Hughes, A.R. and Tobias, P.V. (1977). A fossil skull probably of the genus *Homo* from Sterkfontein, Transvaal. *Nature* 265(5592), 310.

Hughes, R.H. and Hughes, J.S. (1992). *A Directory of African Wetlands*. Gland: IUCN/Cambridge: UK/UNEP/Nairobi: WCMC.

Hujer, W., Kuiper, K., Viola, T.B., Wagreich, M. and Faupl, P. (2015). Lithostratigraphy of the Late Miocene to Early Pleistocene hominid-bearing Galili Formation, southern Afar Depression, Ethiopia. *Australian Journal of Earth Sciences* 108(2), 105–127.

Hull, P.M. and Norris, R.D. (2009). Evidence for abrupt speciation in a classic case of gradual evolution. *Proceedings of the National Academy of Sciences* 106(50), 21224–21229.

Humphreys, A.J.B. and Thackeray, A.I. (1983). Ghaap and Gariep; later stone age studies in the Northern Cape. *South African Archaeological Society Monograph Series* 2.

Hunter, J.P. and Fortelius, M. (1994). Comparative dental occlusal morphology, facet development and microwear in two sympatric species of *Listriodon* (Mammalia, Suidae) from the middle Miocene of western Anatolia (Turkey). *Journal of Vertebrate Paleontology* 14, 105–126.

Hurlbert, S.H. (1971). The nonconcept of species diversity: a critique and alternative parameters. *Ecology* 52, 577–586.

Hutchinson, G.E. and MacArthur, R.H. (1959). A theoretical ecological model of size distributions among species of animals. *The American Naturalist* 93, 117–125.

Hutson, J.M. (2012). Neotraphonomic measures of carnivore serial predation at Ngamo. *Pan* as an analog for interpreting open-air faunal assemblages. *Journal of Archaeological Science* 39, 440–457.

Hutson, J.M. (2018). The faunal remains from Bundu Farm and Pniel 6: examining the problematic Middle Stone Age archaeological record within the southern African interior. *Quaternary International* 466, 178–193.

Hutterer, R. (2010). The Middle Palaeolithic vertebrate fauna of Ifri n'Ammar. In: M. Nami and J. Moser (Eds.), *La Grotte d'Ifri n'Ammar, Le Paléolithique Moyen*. Boon: Kommission fur Archaologie Aubereuropaisher Kulturen, pp. 307–314.

Icole, M., Taieb, M., Perinet, G., Manega, P. and Robert, C. (1987). Minéralogie des sédiments du Groupe Peninj (Lac Natron, Tanzanie). Reconstitution des paléoenvironnements lacustres. *Sciences Géologiques, Bulletins et Memoires*, 40, 71–82.

Inizan, M.L., Reduron-Ballinger, M., Roche, H. and Tixier, J. (1999). *Technology and Terminology of Knapped Stone (Préhistoire de la Pierre taillée 5)*. Nanterre: CREP.

Inskeep, R.R. (1987). *Nelson Bay Cave. Cape Province, South Africa: The Holocene Levels*. Oxford: Archaeopress.

Isaac, G.L. (1965). The stratigraphy of the Peninj Beds and the provenance of the Natron australopithecine mandible. *Quaternaria* 7, 101–130.

Isaac, G.L. (1967). The stratigraphy of the Peninj Group – Early Middle Pleistocene formations west of Lake Natron, Tanzania. In: W.W. Bishop and J.D. Clark (Eds.), *Background to Evolution in Africa*. Chicago: University of Chicago Press, pp. 229–257.

Isaac, G.L. (1971). The diet of early man: aspects of archaeological evidence from Lower and Middle Pleistocene sites in Africa. *World Archaeology* 2, 278–299.

Isaac, G.L. (1977). *Olorgesailie: Archaeological Studies of a Middle Pleistocene Lake Basin in Kenya*. Chicago: Chicago University Press.

Isaac, G.L. (1978a). The food-sharing behavior of protohuman hominids. In: G. Isaac and R.E.F. Leakey (Eds.), *Human Ancestors: Readings from Scientific American*. San Francisco: W.H. Freeman and Company, pp. 110–123.

Isaac, G.L. (1978b). The Olorgesailie Formation: stratigraphy, tectonics and the palaeogeographic context of the middle Pleistocene archaeological sites. In: W.W. Bishop (Ed.), *Geological Background to Fossil Man*. Edinburgh: Scottish Academic Press, pp. 173–206.

Isaac, G.L. (1981–1982). Natron Site Notes. Unpublished manuscript, Smithsonian Institution Archives.

Isaac, G.L. (1997). Koobi Fora Research Project Volume 5: Plio-Pleistocene archaeology. In: R.E. Leakey (Ed.), *Koobi Fora: Researches into Geology, Palaeontology, and Human Origins*. Oxford: Clarendon Press, p. 596.

Isaacs, G.L. and Curtis, G.H. (1974). Age of early Acheulian industries from the Peninj Group, Tanzania. *Nature* 249(5458), 624–627.

Isaac, G.L. and Harris, J.W.K. (1978). Archaeology. In: M.G. Leakey and R.E. Leakey (Eds.), *Koobi Fora Research Project, Volume 1: The Fossil Hominids and an Introduction to Their Context, 1968–1974*. Oxford: Clarendon Press, pp. 64–85.

Isaac, G.L. and Harris, J.W.K. (1997). Sites stratified within the KBS tuff. In: G.L. Isaac (Ed.), *Koobi Fora Research Project Volume 5: Plio-Pleistocene Archaeology*. Oxford: Clarendon Press, pp. 71–99.

Ishida, H. and Pickford, M. (1997). A new Late Miocene hominoid from Kenya: *Samburupithecus kiptalami* gen. et sp. nov. *Comptes Rendus de l'Académie des Sciences – Series IIA – Earth and Planetary Science* 325(10), 823–829.

Ivanovic, R.F., Valdes, P.J., Flecker, R. and Gutjahr, M. (2014). Modelling global-scale climate impacts of the late Miocene Messinian Salinity Crisis. *Climate of the Past* 10, 607–622.

Jablonski, N.G. (Ed.) (1993). The phylogeny of *Theropithecus*. In: *Theropithecus: The Rise and Fall of a Primate Genus*. Cambridge: Cambridge University Press, pp. 209–224.

Jablonski, N.G. (1994). New fossil cercopithecid remains from the Humpata Plateau, southern Angola. *American Journal of Physical Anthropology* 94(4), 435–464.

Jablonski, N.G. (2002). Fossil Old World monkeys: the late Neogene radiation. In: W.C. Hartwig (Ed.), *The Primate Fossil Record (Vol. 33)*. Cambridge: Cambridge University Press, pp. 255–299.

Jablonski, N.G. and Frost, S. (2010). Cercopithecoidea. In: L. Werdelin and W. Sanders (Eds.), *Cenozoic Mammals of Africa*. Berkeley: University of California Press, pp. 393–428.

Jablonski, N.G. and Leakey, M.G. (2008). Koobi Fora Research Project: the fossil monkeys. In: R.E. Leakey (Ed.), *Koobi Fora: Researches into Geology, Paleontology, and Human Origins*. San Francisco: California Academy of Sciences, p. 469.

Jablonski, N.G., Leakey, M.G. and Antón, M. (2008). Systematic paleontology of the cercopithecines. In: N.G. Jablonski and M.G. Leakey (Eds.), *Koobi Fora Research Project: The Fossil Monkeys*. San Francisco: California Academy of Sciences, pp. 103–300.

Jackman, B. and Scott, J. (1983). *The Marsh Lions*. Boston, MA: David R. Godine.

Jackson, A.L., Inger, R., Parnell, A.C. and Bearhop, S. (2011). Comparing isotopic niche widths among and within communities: SIBER – Stable Isotope Bayesian Ellipses in R. *Journal of Animal Ecology* 80(3), 595–602.

Jacobs, B.F. (1999). Estimation of rainfall variables from leaf characters in tropical Africa. *Palaeogeography, Palaeoclimatology, Palaeoecology* 145, 231–250.

Jacobs, B.F. (2001). Estimation of low-latitude paleoclimates using fossil angiosperm leaves: examples from the Miocene Tugen Hills, Kenya. *Paleobiology* 28, 399–421.

Jacobs, B.F. and Deino, A.L. (1996). Test of climate-leaf physiognomy regression models, their application to two Miocene floras from Kenya, and $^{40}Ar/^{39}Ar$ dating of the Late Miocene Kapturo site. *Palaeogeography, Palaeoclimatology, Palaeoecology* 123, 259–271.

Jacobs, B.F. and Kabuye, C.H. (1987). A middle Miocene (12.2 my old) forest in the East African Rift Valley, Kenya. *Journal of Human Evolution* 16, 147–155.

Jacobs, B.F., Kingston, J.D. and Jacobs, L.L. (1999). The origin of grass-dominated ecosystems. *Annals of the Missouri Botanical Garden* 86, 590–643.

Jacobs, B.F., Pan, A.D. and Scotese, C.D. (2010). A review of the Cenozoic vegetation history of Africa. In: L. Werdelin and W.J. Sanders (Eds.), *Cenozoic Mammals of Africa*. Berkeley: University of California Press, pp. 57–72.

Jacobs, Z. (2010). An OSL chronology for the sedimentary deposits from Pinnacle Point Cave 13B – a punctuated presence. *Journal of Human Evolution* 59 (3–4), 289–305.

Jacobs, Z., Duller, G.A., Wintle, A.G. and Henshilwood, C.S. (2006). Extending the chronology of deposits at Blombos Cave, South Africa, back to 140 ka using optical dating of single and multiple grains of quartz. *Journal of Human Evolution* 51(3), 255–273.

Jaeger, J.-J. (1971). Les Micrommamifères du "Villafranchien" inférieur du Lac Ichkeul (Tunisie): données stratigraphiques et biogéographiques nouvelles. *Comptes rendus de l'Académie des Sciences D* 273, 562–565.

Jaeger, J.-J. (1973). Les faunes de Mammifères et les Hominidés fossiles du Pléistocène moyen du Maghreb. *Travaux de la R.C.P.* 29, 265–290.

Jaeger, J.-J. (1975). Les Muridae (Mammalia, Rodentia) du Pliocène et du Pléistocène du Maghreb. Origine, évolution, données biogéographiques et paléoclimatiques. Thèse, Université des Sciences et Techniques du Languedoc, Montpellier.

Jaeger, J.J. (1976). Les Rongeurs (Mammalia, Rodentia) du Pléistocène inférieur d'Olduvai Bed I (Tanzanie). 1ère partie: les Muridés. In: R.J.G. Savage and S.C. Coryndon (Eds.), *Fossil Vertebrates of Africa*. London: Academic Press, pp. 58–120.

Jaeger, J.J. (1977a). Les rongeurs du Miocène moyen et supérieur du Maghreb. *Paleovertebrata* 8, 1–164.

Jaeger, J.-J. (1977b). Rongeurs (Mammalia, Rodentia) du Miocène de Beni-Mellal. *Palaeovertebrata* 7, 91–132.

Jaeger, J.J. (1979). Les faunes de rongeurs et de lagomorphes du Pliocène et du Pléistocène d'Afrique orientale. *Bulletin du Société Géologique de France* 21(3), 301–308.

Jaeger, J.-J. (1981). Les hommes fossiles du Pléistocène moyen du Maghreb. In: B.A. Sigmon, and J.S. Cybulski (Eds.), *Homo erectus: Papers in Honor of Davidson Black*. Toronto: University of Toronto Press, pp. 159–187.

Jaeger, J.-J. (1988). Origine et évolution du genre *Ellobius* (Mammalia, Rodentia) en Afrique Nord-Occidentale. *Folia Quaternaria* 57, 3–50.

Janis, C.M. (1988). An estimation of tooth volume and hypsodonty indices in ungulate mammals, and the correlation of these factors with dietary preference. *Mémoires du Muséum national d'histoire naturelle, Paris* 53, 367–387.

Jarman, P.J. (1974). The social organization of antelope in relation to their ecology. *Behaviour* 48(3/4), 215–267.

Jerardino, A. (2012). Large shell middens and hunter-gatherer resource intensification along the West Coast of South Africa: the Elands Bay case study. *The Journal of Island and Coastal Archaeology* 7(1), 76–101.

Jerardino, A. (2016). On the origins and significance of Pleistocene coastal resource use in southern Africa with particular reference to shellfish gathering. *Journal of Anthropological Archaeology* 41, 213–230.

Jerardino, A. and Marean, C.W. (2010). Shellfish gathering, marine paleoecology and modern human behavior: perspectives from cave PP13B, Pinnacle Point, South Africa. *Journal of Human Evolution* 59 (3–4), 412–424.

Jernvall, J. and Fortelius, M. (2002). Common mammals drive the evolutionary increase of hypsodonty in the Neogene. *Nature* 417, 538–540.

Johanson, D. (2017). The paleoanthropology of Hadar, Ethiopia. *Comptes Rendus Palevol* 16, 140–154.

Johanson, D.C. (1976). Ethiopia yields first "family" of early man. *National Geographic* 150, 790–811.

Johanson, D.C. and Coppens, Y. (1976). A preliminary anatomical diagnosis of the first Plio-Pleistocene hominid discoveries in the central Afar, Ethiopia. *American Journal of Physical Anthropology* 45, 217–234.

Johanson, D.C. and Taieb, M. (1976). Plio-Pleistocene hominid discoveries in Hadar, Ethiopia. *Nature* 260, 293–297.

Johanson, D.C., Taieb, M., Gray, B.T. and Coppens, Y. (1978a). Geological framework of the Pliocene Hadar Formation (Afar, Ethiopia) with notes on paleontology including hominids. In: W.W. Bishop (Ed.), *Geological Background to Fossil Man*. Edinburgh: Scottish Academic Press, pp. 549–564.

Johanson, D.C., White, T.D. and Coppens, Y. (1978b). A new species of the genus *Australopithecus* (Primates: Hominidae) from the Pliocene of eastern Africa. *Kirtlandia* 28, 1–14.

Johanson, D.C., Taieb, M., and Coppens, Y. (1982a). Pliocene hominids from the Hadar Formation, Ethiopia (1973–1977): stratigraphic, chronologic, and paleoenvironmental contexts, with notes on hominid morphology and systematics. *American Journal of Physical Anthropology* 57, 373–402.

Johanson, D.C., Lovejoy, C.O., Kimbel, W.H., et al. (1982b). Morphology of the Pliocene partial hominid skeleton (A.L. 288-1) from the Hadar Formation, Ethiopia. *American Journal of Physical Anthropology* 57, 403–451.

Johanson, D.C., White, T.D. and Coppens, Y. (1982c). Dental remains from the Hadar Formation, Ethiopia: 1974–1977 collections. *American Journal of Physical Anthropology* 57, 545–603.

Johanson, D.C., Masao, F.T., Eck, G.G., et al. (1987). New partial skeleton of *Homo habilis* from Olduvai Gorge, Tanzania. *Nature* 327, 205–209.

Johnson, B.J., Miller, G.H., Fogel, M.L. and Beaumont, P.B. (1997). The determination of late Quaternary paleoenvironments at Equus Cave, South Africa, using stable isotopes and amino acid racemization in ostrich eggshell. *Palaeogeography, Palaeoclimatology, Palaeoecology* 136, 121–137.

Johnson, C.R. and McBrearty, S. (2012). Archaeology of middle Pleistocene lacustrine and spring paleoenvironments in the Kapthurin Formation, Kenya. *Journal of Anthropological Archaeology* 31(4), 485–499.

Jolly, C.J. (1970). The seed eaters: a new model for hominid differentiation based on a baboon analogy. *Man* 5, 5–26.

Jones, S.C. and Stewart, B.A. (Eds.) (2016). *Africa from MIS 6–2: Population Dynamics and Paleoenvironments.* Dordrecht: Springer.

Jones, T., Ehardt, C.L., Butynski, T.M., et al. (2005). The highland mangabey Lophocebus kipunji: a new species of African monkey. *Science* 308, 1161–1164.

Jost, L. (2006). Entropy and diversity. *Oikos* 113(2), 363–375.

Jost, L. (2007). Partitioning diversity into independent alpha and beta components. *Ecology* 88(10), 2427–2439.

Kadima, E., Delvaux, D., Sebagenzi, S.N., Tack, L. and Kabeya, S.M. (2011). Structure and geological history of the Congo Basin: an integrated interpretation of gravity, magnetic and reflection seismic data. *Basin Research* 23, 499–527.

Kaiser, T.M. (2000). Proposed fossil insect modification to fossil mammalian bone from Plio-Pleistocene hominid-bearing deposits of Laetoli (northern Tanzania). *Annals of theEntomological Society of America* 93, 693–700.

Kaiser, T.M. (2011). Feeding ecology and niche partitioning of the Laetoli ungulate faunas. In: T. Harrison (Ed.), *Paleontology and Geology of Laetoli, Tanzania: Human Evolution in Context. Vol. 1: Geology, Geochronology, Paleoecology and Paleoenvironment.* Dordrecht: Springer, pp. 329–354.

Kaiser, T.M. and Fortelius, M. (2003). Differential mesowear in occluding upper and lower molars: opening mesowear analysis for lower molars and premolars in hypsodont horses. *Journal of Morphology* 258, 67–83.

Kaiser, T., Bromage, T.G. and Schrenk, F. (1995). Hominid Corridor Research Project update: new Pliocene fossil localities at Lake Manyara and putative oldest Early Stone Age occurrences at Laetoli (Upper Ndolanya Beds), northern Tanzania. *Journal of Human Evolution* 28, 117–120.

Kaiser, T.M., Seiffert, C., Hertler, C., et al. (2010). Makuyuni, a new Lower Palaeolithic hominid site in Tanzania. *Mitteilungen aus dem Hamburgischen Zoologischen Museum und Institut* 106, 69–110.

Kalb, J.E. (1993). Refined stratigraphy of the hominid-bearing Awash Group, Middle Awash valley, Afar depression, Ethiopia. *Newsletters on Stratigraphy*, 29, 21–62.

Kalb, J.E. (1995). Fossil elephantoids, Awash paleolake basins, and the Afar triple junction, Ethiopia. *Palaeogeography, Palaeoclimatology, Palaeoecology* 114, 357–368.

Kalb, J.E. and Mebrate, A. (1993). Fossil elephantoids from the hominid-bearing Awash Group, Middle Awash Valley, Afar depression, Ethiopia. *Transactions of the American Philosophical Society* 83(1), 1–110.

Kalb, J.E., Wood, C.B., Smart, C., et al. (1980). Preliminary geology and palaeontology of the Bodo D'ar hominid Site, Afar, Ethiopia. *Palaeogeography, Palaeoclimatology, Palaeoecology* 30, 107–120.

Kalb, J.E., Jolly, C.J., Mebrate, A., et al. (1982a). Fossil mammals and artefacts from the Middle Awash Valley, Ethiopia. *Nature* 298, 25–29.

Kalb, J.E., Jolly, C.J., Tebedge, S., et al. (1982b). Vertebrate faunas from the Awash Group, Middle Awash Valley, Afar, Ethiopia. *Journal of Vertebrate Paleontology* 2, 237–258.

Kalb, J.E., Oswald, E.B., Mebrate, A., Tebedge, C., Jolly, C. (1982c). Stratigraphy of the Awash Group, Middle Awash Valley, Afar, Ethiopia. *Newsletters on Stratigraphy* 11, 95–127.

Kandel, A.W. and Conard, N.J. (2012). Settlement patterns during the earlier and Middle stone age around Langebaan Lagoon, western Cape (South Africa). *Quaternary International* 270, 15–29.

Kappelman, J. (1984). Plio-Pleistocene environments of Bed I and Lower Bed II, Olduvai Gorge, Tanzania. *Palaeogeography, Palaeoclimatology, Palaeoecology* 48, 171–196.

Kappelman, J. (1986). Plio-Pleistocene marine–continental correlation using habitat indicators from Olduvai Gorge, Tanzania. *Quaternary Research* 25, 141–149.

Kappelman, J. (1991). The paleoenvironment of Kenyapithecus at Fort Ternan. *Journal of Human Evolution* 20, 95–129.

Kappelman, J., Swisher, C.C., Fleagle, J.G., et al. (1996). Age of *Australopithecus afarensis* from Fejej, Ethiopia. *Journal of Human Evolution* 30, 139–146.

Kappelman, J., Plummer, T., Bishop, L., Duncan, A. and Appleton, S. (1997). Bovids as indicators of Plio-Pleistocene paleoenvironments in East Africa. *Journal of Human Evolution* 32, 229–256.

Karl, H.V. (2012). Human consumption of turtles of the *Homo rudolfensis* site Uraha (Malawi, East Africa). *Archaeofauna* 21, 267–279.

Kaszycka, K.A. (2002). *Status of Kromdraai. Cranial, Mandibular and Dental Morphology, Systematic Relationships, and Significance of the Kromdraai Hominids.* Paris: Editions du CNRS.

Katoh, S., Nagaoka, S., WoldeGabriel, G., et al. (2000). Chronostratigraphy and correlation of the Plio-Pleistocene tephra layers of the Konso Formation, southern Main Ethiopian Rift, Ethiopia. *Quaternary Science Reviews* 19, 1305–1317.

Katoh, S., Suwa, G., Nakaya, H. and Beyene, Y. (2014). Stratigraphic and chronological context of the Konso Formation paleontology. In: G. Suwa, Y. Beyene and B. Asfaw (Eds.), *The Konso-Gardula Research Project Volume 1. Paleonotological Collections: Background and Fossil Aves, Cercopithecidae, and Suidae.* Tokyo: The University Museum, The University of Tokyo, Bulletin, 47, 11–23.

Katoh, S., Beyene, Y., Itaya, T., et al. (2016). New geological and palaeontological age constraint for the gorilla–human lineage split. *Nature* 530, 215–218.

Kaufulu, Z.M., Vrba, E.S. and White, T.D. (1981). Age of the Chiwondo Beds, northern Malawi. *Annals of the Transvaal Museum* 33, 1–8.

Kent, P.E. (1941). The recent history and Pleistocene deposits of the plateau north of Lake Eyasi, Tanganyika. *Geological Magazine* 78, 173–184.

Kent, P.E. (1942). The Pleistocene beds of Kanam and Kanjera, Kavirondo, Kenya. *Geological Magazine* 79(2), 117–132.

Kerr, J.T. and Packer, L. (1997). Habitat heterogeneity as a determinant of mammal species richness in high-energy regions. *Nature* 385, 252–254.

Keyser, A.W. and Martini, J.E.J. (1991). Haasgat, a new Plio-Pleistocene fossil locality. *Palaeontologia Africana* 21, 119–129.

Keyser, A.W., Menter, C.G., Moggi-Cecchi, J., Pickering, T.R. and Berger, L.R. (2000). Drimolen: a new hominid-bearing site in Gauteng, South Africa. *South African Journal of Science* 96(4), 193–197.

Kiberd, P. (2006). Bundu farm: a report on archaeological and paleoenvironmental assemblages from a pan site in Bushmanland, Northern Cape, South Africa. *South African Archaeological Bulletin* 61, 189–201.

Kibii, J.M. (2000). The macrofauna from Jacovec Cavern, Sterkfontein. MSc thesis, University of the Witwatersand.

Kibii, J.M. (2004). Comparative taxonomic, taphonomic and palaeoenvironmental analysis of 4–2.3 million year old australopithecine cave infills at Sterkfontein. PhD thesis, University of the Witwatersrand, Johannesburg.

Kibunjia, M. (1994). Pliocene archaeological occurrences in the Lake Turkana basin. *Journal of Human Evolution* 27, 159–171.

Kidane, T., Platzman, E., Ebinger, C., Abebe, B. and Rochette, P. (2006). Paleomagnetic constraints on continental break-up processes: observations from the Main Ethiopian rift. In: G. Yirgu, C.J. Ebinger and P.K.H. Maguire (Eds.), *The Afar Volcanic Province within the East African Rift*. London: Geological Society Special Publication 259, 165–183.

Kidane, T., Brown, F.H. and Kidney, C. (2014). Magnetostratigraphy of the Fossil-Rich Shungura Formation, southwest Ethiopia. *Journal of African Earth Sciences* 97, 207–223.

Kieffer, G., Raynal, J.-P. and Bardin, G. (2002). Cadre structural et volcanologiques des sites du Paléolithique ancien de Melka Kunture (Awash, Ethiopie): Premiers résultats. In: J.-P. Raynal, C. Albore-Livadie and M. Piperno (Eds.), Hommes et Volcans. De l'éruption à l'objet. *Les Dossiers de l'Archéologie* 2, 77–92.

Kieffer, G., Raynal, J.-P. and Bardin, G. (2004). Volcanic markers in coarse alluvium at Melka Kunture (Upper Awash, Ethiopia). In: J. Chavaillon, and M. Piperno (Eds.), *Studies on the Early Paleolithic site of Melka Kunture, Ethiopia*. Florence: Istituto Italiano di Preistoria e Protostoria, pp. 93–101.

Kimbel, W.H. (1988). Identification of a partial cranium of *Australopithecus afarensis* from the Koobi Fora Formation, Kenya. *Journal of Human Evolution* 17, 647–656.

Kimbel, W.H. and Delezene, L.K. (2009). "Lucy" redux: a review of research on *Australopithecus afarensis*. *American Journal of Physical Anthropology* 140, 2–48.

Kimbel, W.H. and White, T.D. (1988). Variation, sexual dimorphism and the taxonomy of *Australopithecus*. In: F.E. Grine (Ed.), *Evolutionary History of the "Robust" Australopithecines*. New York: Aldine de Gruyter, pp. 175–192.

Kimbel, W.H., Johanson, D.C. and Coppens, Y. (1982). Pliocene hominid cranial remains from the Hadar Formation, Ethiopia. *American Journal of Physical Anthropology* 57, 453–499.

Kimbel, W.H., White, T.D. and Johanson, D.C. (1984). Cranial morphology of *Australopithecus afarensis*: a comparative study based on a composite reconstruction of the adult skull. *American Journal of Physical Anthropology* 64, 337–388.

Kimbel, W.H., Johanson, D.C. and Rak, Y. (1994). The first skull and other new discoveries of *Australopithecus afarensis* at Hadar, Ethiopia. *Nature* 368, 449–451.

Kimbel, W.H., Walter, R.C., Johanson, D.C., et al. (1996). Late Pliocene *Homo* and Oldowan tools from the Hadar Formation (Kada Hadar Member), Ethiopia. *Journal of Human Evolution* 31, 549–561.

Kimbel, W.H., Johanson, D.C. and Rak, Y. (1997). Systematic assessment of a maxilla of *Homo* from Hadar, Ethiopia. *American Journal of Physical Anthropology* 103, 235–262.

Kimbel, W.H., Rak, Y. and Johanson, D.C. (2004). *The Skull of Australopithecus afarensis*. New York: Oxford University Press.

Kimbel, W. H., Lockwood, C. A., Ward, C. V., et al. (2006). Was *Australopithecus anamensis* ancestral to *A. afarensis*? A case of anagenesis in the hominin fossil record. *Journal of Human Evolution* 51(2), 134–152.

King, L.C. (1951). The geology of Makapan and other caves. *Transactions of the Royal Society of South Africa* 33, 121–151.

Kingdon, J. (1990). *Island Africa: The Evolution of Africa's Rare Animals and Plants*. Princeton: Princeton University Press.

Kingdon, J. (2003). *Lowly Origin: When, Where, and Why Our Ancestors First Stood Up*. Princton: Princeton University Press.

Kingdon, J. (2015). *The Kingdon Field Guide to African Mammals*. London: Bloomsbury Publishing.

Kingdon, J. and Hoffmann, M. (2013). *Mammals of Africa. Volume VI: Pigs, Hippopotamuses, Chevrotain, Giraffes, Deer and Bovids*. London: Bloomsbury Publishing.

Kingdon, J., Happold, D., Butynski, T., et al. (2013). *Mammals of Africa, Vol. 3*. London: A&C Black.

Kingston, J.D. (1999). Environmental determinants in early hominid evolution; issues and evidence from the Tugen Hills, Kenya. In: P. Andrews and P. Banham (Eds.), *Late Cenozoic Environments and Hominid Evolution: a Tribute to Bill Bishop*. London: Geological Society of London, pp. 69–84.

Kingston, J.D. (2007). Shifting adaptive landscapes: progress and challenges in reconstructing early hominid environments. *American Journal of Physical Anthropology* 134(S45), 20–58.

Kingston, J. (2011). Stable isotopic analyses of Laetoli fossil herbivores. In: T. Harrison (Ed.), *Paleontology and Geology of Laetoli, Tanzania: Human Evolution in Context. Vol. 1: Geology, Geochronology, Paleoecology and Paleoenvironment*. Dordrecht: Springer, pp. 293–328.

Kingston, J.D. and Harrison, T. (2007). Isotopic dietary reconstructions of Pliocene herbivores at Laetoli: implications for early hominin paleoecology. *Palaeogeography, Palaeoclimatology, Palaeoecology* 243(3–4), 272–306.

Kingston, J. and Hill, A. (1999). Late Miocene palaeoenvironments in Arabia: a synthesis. In: P.J. Whybrow and A.P. Hill (Eds.), *Fossil Vertebrates of Arabia: With Emphasis on the Late Miocene Faunas, geology, and Palaeoenvironments of the Emirate of Abu Dhabi, United Arab Emirates*. New Haven: Yale University Press, pp. 389–407.

Kingston, J., Marino, B. and Hill, A. (1994). Isotopic evidence for Neogene hominins paleoenvironments in the Kenya Rift-Valley. *Science* 264, 955–959.

Kingston, J.D., Jacobs, B.F., Hill, A. and Deino, A.L. (2002). Stratigraphy, age and environments of the late Miocene Mpesida Beds, Tugen Hills, Kenya. *Journal of Human Evolution* 42, 95–116.

Kingston, J.D., Ditchfield, P.W., Plummer, T.W., et al. (2006). Isotopic approaches to paleoecological reconstruction at Olduvai Bed I (Tanzania) and Kanjera (Kenya). *American Journal of Physical Anthropology*, S42, 113–114.

Kingston, J.D., Deino, A.L., Edgar, R.K. and Hill, A. (2007). Astronomically forced climate change in the Kenyan Rift Valley 2.7–2.55 Ma: implications for the evolution of early hominin ecosystems. *Journal of Human Evolution* 53(5), 487–503.

Kingswood, S.C. and Kumamoto, A.T. (1997). *Madoqua kirkii*. *Mammalian Species* 569, 1–10.

Kirsanow, K.O. (2009). Animal physiology, biomineral diagenesis, and the isotopic reconstruction of palaeoenvironment. Unpublished PhD dissertation, Harvard University, Cambridge, MA.

Kitching, I.J. and Sadler, S. (2011). Lepidoptera, Insecta. In: T. Harrison (Ed.), *Paleontology and Geology of Laetoli: Human Evolution in Context. Vol. 2: Fossil Hominins and the Associated Fauna*. Dordrecht: Springer, pp. 549–554.

Kitching, J.W. (1951). A new species of hippopotamus from Potgietersrus. *South African Journal of Science* 477, 209–211.

Kitching, J.W. (1963). A fossil *Orycteropus* from the limeworks quarry, Makapanasgat, Potgietersrus. *Palaeontologica Africana* 8, 119–121.

Kitching, J.W. (1965). A new giant hyracoid from the limeworks quarry, Makapanasgat, Potgietersrus. *Palaeontologica Africana* 9, 91–96.

Kitching, J.W. (1980). On some fossil Arthropoda from the Limeworks, Makapansgat, Potgietersrus. *Palaeontologica Africana* 23, 63–68.

Klein, R.G. (1972). The late Quaternary mammalian fauna of Nelson Bay Cave (Cape Province, South Africa): its implications for megafaunal extinctions and environmental and cultural change. *Quaternary Research* 2, 135–142.

Klein, R.G. (1973). Geological antiquity of Rhodesian Man. *Nature* 244, 311–312.

Klein, R.G. (1975). Paleoanthropological implications of the nonarcheological bone assemblage from Swartklip I, southwestern Cape Province, South Africa. *Quaternary Research* 5, 275–288.

Klein, R.G. (1976). The mammalian fauna of the Klasies River Mouth sites, Southern Cape Province, South Africa. *South African Archaeological Bulletin* 31, 75–98.

Klein, R.G. (1977). The mammalian fauna from the Middle and Later Stone Age (Later Pleistocene) levels of Border Cave, Natal Province, South Africa. *South African Archaeological Bulletin* 34, 14–27.

Klein, R.G. (1978a). A preliminary report on the larger mammals from the Boomplaas stone age cave site, Cango Valley, Oudtshoorn District, South Africa. *South African Archaeological Bulletin* 33, 66–75.

Klein, R.G. (1978b). The fauna and overall interpretation of the "Cutting 10" Acheulean site at Elandsfontein (Hopefield), Southwestern Cape Province, South Africa. *Quaternary Research* 10, 69–83.

Klein, R.G. (1980). Environmental and ecological implications of large mammals from Upper Pleistocene and Holocene sites in southern Africa. *Annals of the South African Museum* 81, 223–283.

Klein, R.G. (1983). Palaeoenvironmental implications of Quaternary large mammals in the fynbos region. In: H.J. Deacon, Q.B. Hendey and J.J.N. Lambrechts (Eds.), *Fynbos Palaeoecology: A Preliminary Synthesis, South African National Scientific Programmes Report No 75*. Cape Town: Mills Litho, pp. 116–138.

Klein, R.G. (1984a). Later Stone Age faunal samples from Heuningneskrans Shelter (Transvaal) and Leopard's Hill Cave (Zambia). *South African Archaeological Bulletin* 39, 109–116.

Klein, R.G. (1984b). Mammalian extinctions and Stone Age people in Africa. In: P.S. Martin and R.G. Klein (Eds.), *Quaternary Extinctions: A Prehistoric Revolution*. Tucson: University of Arizona Press, pp. 553–573.

Klein, R.G. (Ed.) (1984c). The large mammals of southern Africa: Late Pliocene to recent. In: *Southern African Prehistory and Paleoenvironments*. Rotterdam: Balkema, pp. 107–146.

Klein, R.G. (1988). The archaeological significance of animal bones from Acheulian sites in southern Africa. *African Archaeological Review* 6, 3–26.

Klein, R.G. (1989). Why does skeletal part representation differ between smaller and larger bovids at Klasies River Mouth and other archeological sites? *Journal of Archaeological Science* 16(4), 363–381.

Klein, R.G. (1991). Size variation in the Cape dune molerat (*Bathyergus suillus*) and Late Quaternary climatic change in the southwestern Cape Province, South Africa. *Quaternary Research* 36(3), 243–256.

Klein, R.G. and Cruz-Uribe, K. (1984). *The Analysis of Animal Bones from Archaeological Sites*. Chicago: University of Chicago Press.

Klein, R.G. and Cruz-Uribe, K. (1987). Large mammal and tortoise bones from Eland's Bay Cave and nearby sites, Western Cape Province, South Africa. In: J.E. Parkington and M. Hall (Eds.), *Papers in the Prehistory of the Western Cape, South Africa*. Cambridge: BAR International Series 322, pp. 132–163.

Klein, R.G. and Cruz-Uribe, K. (1991). The bovids from Elandsfontein, South Africa, and their implications for the age, palaeoenvironment, and origins of the site. *African Archaeological Review* 9, 21–79.

Klein, R.G. and Cruz-Uribe, K. (2016). Large mammal and tortoise bones from Elands Bay Cave (South Africa): implications for Later Stone Age environment and ecology. *Southern African Humanities* 29(1), 259–282.

Klein, R.G. and Cruz-Uribe, K. (2000). Middle and Later Stone Age large mammal and tortoise remains from Die Kelders Cave 1, Western Cape Province, South Africa. *Journal of Human Evolution* 38, 169–195.

Klein, R.G. and Scott, K. (1986). Re-analysis of faunal assemblages from the Haua Fteah and other late Quaternary archaeological sites in Cyernaican Libya. *Journal of Archaeological Science* 13, 515–542.

Klein, R.G., Cruz-Uribe, K. and Beaumont, P.B. (1991). Environmental, ecological, and paleoanthropological implications of the Late Pleistocene mammalian fauna from Equus Cave, Northern Cape Province, South Africa. *Quaternary Research* 36, 94–119.

Klein, R.G., Avery, G., Cruz-Uribe, K., et al. (1999). Duinefontein 2: an Acheulean site in the western Cape province of South Africa. *Journal of Human Evolution* 37(2), 153–190.

Klein, R.G., Avery, G., Cruz-Uribe, K., et al. (2004). The Ysterfontein 1 Middle Stone Age site, South Africa, and early human exploitation of coastal resources. *Proceedings of the National Academy of Sciences* 101(16), 5708–5715.

Klein, R.G., Avery, G., Cruz-Uribe, K. and Steele, T.E. (2007). The mammalian fauna associated with an archaic hominin skullcap and later Acheulean artifacts at Elandsfontein, Western Cape Province, South Africa. *Journal of Human Evolution* 52, 164–186.

Kleindienst, M.R. (1962). Component of the East African Acheulean assemblage: an analytic approach. In: G. Mortelmans and J. Nenquin (Eds.), *Actes du IV Congrès Panafricain de Préhistoire et de l0 Etude du Quaternaire, Leopoldville, 1959*. Belgie Annalen, Musée Royal de l0 Afrique Centrale, Tervuren, pp. 81e108.

Kleinsasser, L.L., Quade, J., Mcintosh, W.C., et al. (2008). Stratigraphy and geochronology of the late Miocene Adu-Asa Formation at Gona, Ethiopia. In: J. Quade and J.G. Wynn (Eds.), *The Geology of Early Humans in the Horn of Africa*. Geological Society of America Special Paper 446. Boulder: Geological Society of America, pp. 33–65.

Koch, C.F. (1987). Prediction of sample size effects on the measured temporal and geographic distribution patterns of species. *Paleobiology* 3(1), 100–107.

Kohl-Larsen, L. (1943). Auf den Sporen des Vormenschen. Stuttgart: Strecker und Schröder.

Köhler, C.M., Heslop, D., Krijgsman, W. and Dekkers, M.J. (2010). Late Miocene paleoenvironmental changes in North Africa and the Mediterranean recorded by geochemical proxies (Monte Gibliscemi section, Sicily). *Palaeogeography, Palaeoclimatology, Palaeoecology* 285, 66–73.

Köhler, M. (1993). *Skeleton and Habitat of Recent and Fossil Ruminants*. Münchner geowissenschaftliche Abhandlungen Reihe A, Geologie und Paläontologie 25, pp. 1–88.

Kohn, M.J., Schoeninger, M.J. and Valley, J.W. (1996). Herbivore tooth oxygen isotope compositions: effects of diet and physiology. *Geochimica et Cosmochimica Acta* 60, 3889–3896.

Kovarovic, K. (2004). Bovids as palaeoenvironmental indicators. An ecomorphological analysis of bovid postcranial remains from Laetoli, Tanzania. Ph.D. Dissertation, University of London.

Kovarovic, K. and Andrews, P. (2007). Bovid postcranial ecomological survey of the Laetoli paleoenvironment. *Journal of Human Evolution* 52, 663–680.

Kovarovic, K. and Andrews, P. (2011). Environmental change within the Laetoli fossiliferous sequence: vegetation catenas and bovid ecomorphology. In: T. Harrison (Ed.), *Paleontology and Geology of Laetoli, Tanzania: Human Evolution in Context. Vol. 1: Geology, Geochronology, Paleoecology and Paleoenvironment*. Dordrecht: Springer, pp. 367–380.

Kovarovic, K., Andrews, P. and Aiello, L. (2002). The palaeoecology of the Upper Ndolanya Beds at Laetoli, Tanzania. *Journal of Human Evolution* 43, 395–418.

Kovarovic, K., Slepkov, R. and McNulty, K.P. (2013). Ecological continuity between Lower and Upper Bed II, Olduvai Gorge, Tanzania. *Journal of Human Evolution* 64, 538–555.

Krell, F.-T. and Schawaller, W. (2011). Beetles (Insecta: Coleoptera). In: T. Harrison (Ed.), *Paleontology and Geology of Laetoli: Human Evolution in Context. Vol. 2: Fossil Hominins and the Associated Fauna*. Dordrecht: Springer, pp. 535–554.

Krigbaum, J., Berger, M.H., Daegling, D.J. and McGraw, W.S. (2013). Stable isotope canopy effects for sympatric monkeys at Tai Forest, Cote d'Ivoire. *Biology Letters* 9, 20130466.

Krijgsman, W., Hilgen, F.J., Raffi, I., Sierro, F.J. and Wilson, D.S. (1999). Chronology, causes and progression of the Messinian salinity crisis. *Nature* 400, 652–655.

Kröpelin, S., Verschuren, D., Lézine, A.-M., et al. (2008). Climate-driven ecosystem succession in the Sahara: the past 6000 years. *Science* 320, 765–768.

Kruger, A. and Badenhorst, S. (2018). Remains of a barn owl (*Tyto alba*) from the Dinaledi Chamber, Rising Star Cave, South Africa. *South African Journal of Science* 114(11–12), 1–5.

Kruuk, H. (1972). *The Spotted Hyena*. Chicago: The University of Chicago Press.

Kruuk, H. and Turner, M. (1967). Comparative notes on predation by lion, leopard, cheetah and wild dog in the Serengeti area, East Africa. *Mammalia* 31, 1–27.

Ksepka, D.T. and Thomas, D.B. (2011). Multiple cenozoic invasions of Africa by penguins (Aves, Sphenisciformes). *Proceedings of the Royal Society B: Biological Sciences* 279(1730), 1027–1032.

Kuhn, B.F., Berger, L.R. and Skinner, J.D. (2008). Examining criteria for identifying and differentiating fossil faunal assemblages accumulated by hyenas and hominins using extant hyenid accumulations. *International Journal of Osteoarchaeology* 20, 15–35.

Kuhn, B.F., Werdelin, L., Hartstone-Rose, A., Lacruz, R.S. and Berger, L.R. (2011). Carnivoran remains from the Malapa hominin site, South Africa. *PLoS ONE*, 6(11), e26940.

Kuhn, B.F., Carlson, K., Hopley, P.J., Zipfel, B. and Berger, L.R. (2015). Identification of fossilized eggshells from the Taung hominin locality, Taung, Northwest Province, South Africa. *Palaeontologia Electronica* 18.1.12A, 1–16. paleo-electronica.org/content/2015/1026-identification-of-fossil-eggs

Kuhn, B.F., Herries, A.I.R., Pickering, R., et al. (2016). Renewed investigations at Taung; 90 years after *Australopithecus africanus*. *Palaeontologia Africana* 51, 1–17.

Kuhn, B.F., Werdelin, L. and Steininger, C. (2017). Fossil Hyaenidae from Cooper's Cave, South Africa, and the palaeoenvironmental implications. *Palaeobiodiversity and Palaeoenvironments* 97(2), 355–365.

Kullmer, O. (1999). Evolution of African Plio-Pleistocene suids (Suidae; Artiodactyla) based on tooth pattern analysis. *Kaupia* 9, 1–34.

Kullmer, O. (2008). The fossil suidae from the Plio-Pleistocene Chiwondo Beds of Northern Malawi. *African Journal of Vertebrate Paleontology* 208, 208–216.

Kullmer, O., Sandrock, O., Schrenk, F. and Bromage, T.G. (1999a). The Malawi Rift: biogeography, ecology and coexistence of *Homo* and *Paranthropus*. *Anthropologie* 37(3), 221–231.

Kullmer, O., Sandrock, O., Abel, R., et al. (1999b). The first *Paranthropus* from the Malawi Rift. *Journal of Human Evolution* 37, 121–127.

Kullmer, O., Sandrock, O., Viola, T.B., et al. (2008). Suids, elephantoids, paleochronology, and paleoecology of the Pliocene hominid site Galili, Somali region, Ethiopia. *Palaios* 23, 452–464.

Kullmer, O., Sandrock, O., Kupczik, K., et al. (2011). New primate remains from Mwenirondo, Chiwondo Beds in northern Malawi. *Journal of Human Evolution* 61, 617–623.

Kuman, K. (1994a). The archaeology of Sterkfontein: preliminary findings on site formation and cultural change. *South African Journal of Science* 90, 215–219.

Kuman, K. (1994b). The archaeology of Sterkfontein – past and present. *Journal of Human Evolution* 27, 471–495.

Kuman, K. (2003). Site formation in the early South African Stone Age sites and its influence on the archaeological record. *South African Journal of Science* 99, 251–254.

Kuman, K. and Clarke, R.J. (1986). Florisbad – new investigations at a Middle Stone Age hominid site in South Africa. *Geoarchaeology*, 1(2), 103–125.

Kuman, K. and Clarke, R.J. (2000). Stratigraphy, artefact industries and hominid associations for Sterkfontein Member 5. *Journal of Human Evolution* 38, 827–847.

Kuman, K., Field, A. and Thackeray, J.F. (1997). Discovery of new artefacts at Kromdraai. *South African Journal of Science* 93, 187–193.

Kuman K., Inbar, M. and Clarke, R.J. (1999). Palaeoenvironments and cultural sequence of the Florisbad Middle Stone Age hominid site, South Africa. *Journal of Archaeological Science* 26, 1409–1425.

Kumar, S., Filipski, A., Swarna, V., Walker, A. and Hedges, S. B. (2005). Placing confidence limits on the molecular age of the human–chimpanzee divergence. *Proceedings of the National Academy of Sciences of the United States of America* 102(52), 18842–18847.

Kunimatsu, Y., Nakatsukasa, M., Sawada, Y., et al. (2007). A new Late Miocene great ape from Kenya and its implications for the origins of African great apes and humans. *Proceedings of the National Academy of Sciences* 104(49), 19220–19225.

Kunimatsu, Y., Nakatsukasa, M., Sawada, Y., et al. (2016). A second hominoid species in the early Late Miocene fauna of Nakali (Kenya). *Anthropological Science* 124, 75–83.

Kunimatsu, Y., Nakatsukasa, M., Sakai, T., et al. (2017a). A newly discovered galagid fossil from Nakali, an early Late Miocene locality of East Africa. *Journal of Human Evolution* 105, 123–126.

Kunimatsu, Y., Sawada, Y., Sakai, T., et al. (2017b). The latest occurrence of the nyanzapithecines from the early Late Miocene Nakali Formation in Kenya, East Africa. *Anthropological Science* 125, 45–51.

Kunneriath, M. and Gaillard, C. (2010). Techno-typological analysis of lithic collections from Sheppard Island and Pniel, Vaal River Valley, South Africa. *Annali dell'Università di Ferrara, Museologia Scientifica e Naturalistica* 6, 111–116.

Kuper, R. and Kröpelin, S. (2006). Climate-controlled Holocene occupation in the Sahara: motor of Africa's evolution. *Science* 313, 803–807.

Kurashina, H. (1987). Comparison of Gadeb and other Early Stone Age assemblages from Africa south of the Sahara. *African Archaeological Review* 5, 19–28.

Kurtén, B. (1976). Fossil Carnivora from the late Tertiary of Bled Douarah and Cherichira, Tunisia. *Notes du Service Géologique de Tunisie* 42, 177–214.

Kuykendall, K.L. (2012). On the evolutionary development of early hominid molar teeth and the Gondolin *Paranthropus* molar. In: S.C. Reynolds and A. Gallagher (Eds.), *African Genesis: Perspectives on Hominin Evolution*. Cambridge: Cambridge University Press, pp. 280–297.

Kuykendall, K.L., Toich, C.A. and McKee, J.K. (1995). Preliminary analysis of the fauna from Buffalo Cave, northern Transvaal, South Africa. *Palaeontologia Africana* 32, 27–31.

Kyauka, P.S. (1994). A comparative study of the Laetoli Hominid 21 skeleton and its implications for the developmental biology of Australopithecus afarensis. PhD dissertation, University of California, Berkeley.

Kyauka, P.S. and Ndessokia, P. (1990). A new hominid tooth from Laetoli, Tanzania. *Journal of Human Evolution* 19, 747–750.

L'Abbé, E.N., Symes, S.A., Pokines, J.T., et al. (2015). Evidence of fatal skeletal injuries on Malapa Hominins 1 and 2. *Scientific Reports* 5, 15120.

Lacomba, J.I., Morales, J., Robles, F., Santiesteban, C. and Alberdi, M.T. (1986). Sedimentología y paleontología del yacimiento finimioceno de La Portera (Valencia). *Estudios geológicos* 42(2–3), 167–180.

Lacruz, R. (2007). Enamel microstructure of the hominid KB 5223 from Kromdraai, South Africa. *American Journal of Physical Anthropology* 132, 175–182.

Lacruz, R.S. and Maude, G. (2005). Bone accumulations at brown hyaena (*Parahyaena brunnea*) den sites in the Makgadikgadi Pans, northern Botswana: taphonomic, behavioral and palaeoecological implications. *Journal of Taphonomy* 3, 43–54.

Lacruz, R.S., Brink, J.S., Hancox, P.J., et al. (2002). Palaeontology and geological context of a middle Pleistocene faunal assemblage from Gladysvale Cave, South Africa. *Palaeontologia Africana* 38, 99–114.

Lague, M.R., Chirchir, H., Green, D.J., et al. (2019a). Cross-sectional properties of the humeral diaphysis of *Paranthropus boisei*: implications for upper limb function. *Journal of Human Evolution* 126, 51–70.

Lague, M.R., Chirchir, H., Green, D.J., et al. (2019b). Humeral anatomy of the KNM-ER 47000 upper limb skeleton from Ileret, Kenya: implications for taxonomic identification. *Journal of Human Evolution* 126, 24–38.

Lahr, M.M. and Foley, R. (1998). Toward a theory of modern human origins: geography, demography, and diversity in recent human evolution. *Yearbook of Physical Anthropology* 41, 137–176.

Lanzarone, P., Garrison, E., Bobe, R. and Getahun, A. (2016). Examining fluvial stratigraphic architecture using ground-penetrating radar at the Fanta Stream fossil and archaeological site, Central Ethiopia. *Geoarchaeology* 31, 577–591.

Laplace, G. (1956). Découverte de galets taillés (Pebble culture) dans le Quaternaire ancien de Mansourah (Constantine). *Comptes Rendus de l'Académie des Sciences* 247, 184–185.

Larbey, C., Mentzer, S.M., Ligouis, B., Wurz, S. and Jones, M.K. (2019). Cooked starchy food in hearths ca. 120 kya and 65 kya (MIS 5e and MIS 4) from Klasies River Cave, South Africa. *Journal of Human Evolution* 131, 210–227.

Larrasoaña, J., Roberts, A., Rohling, E., Winklhofer, M. and Wehausen, R. (2003). Three million years of monsoon variability over the northern Sahara. *Climate Dynamics* 21, 689–698.

Larrasoaña, J.C., Roberts, A.P. and Rohling, E.J. (2013). Dynamics of green Sahara periods and their role in hominin evolution. *PLoS ONE* 8(10), e76514.

Laskar, J., Robutel, P., Joutel, F., et al. (2004). A long-term numerical solution for the insolation quantities of the Earth. *Astronomy & Astrophysics* 428(1), 261–285.

Latham, A. and Warr, G. (2008). Makapansgat Limeworks stratigraphy and the singular case of Member X. *Palaeontologica Africana* 43, 45–50.

Latham, A.G, Herries, A.I.R., Quinney, P., Sinclair, A. and Kuykendall, K. (1999). The Makapansgat australopithecine site from a speleological perspective. In: A.M. Pollard (Ed.), *Geoarchaeology: Exploration, Environments, Resources*. Royal Geological Society Special Publications 165. London: Royal Geological Society, pp. 61–77.

Latham, A.G., Herries, A.I.R. and Kuykendall, K. (2003). The formation and sedimentary infilling of the Limeworks Cave, Makapansgat, South Africa. *Palaeontological Africana* 39, 69–82.

Latham, A.G., Herries, A.I. and Kuykendall, K.L. (2004). The formation and sedimentary infilling of the Limeworks Cave, Makapansgat, South Africa. *Geoarchaeology* 19, 323–342.

Latham, A.G., McKee, J.K. and Tobias, P.V. (2007). Bone breccias, bone dumps, and sedimentary sequences of the western Limeworks, Makapansgat, South Africa. *Journal of Human Evolution* 52, 388–400.

Latham, T.S., Sutton, P.A. and Verosub, K.L. (1992). Non-destructive XRF characterization of basaltic artifacts from Truckee, California. *Geoarchaeology* 7, 81–100.

Latimer, B. (1991). Locomotor adaptations in *Australopithecus afarensis*: the issue of arboreality. In: B. Senut and Y. Coppens (Eds), *Origine(s) de la Bipédie chez les Hominidés*. Paris: CNRS, pp. 169–176.

Latimer, B.M., Ohman, J.C. and Lovejoy, C.O. (1987). Talocrural joint in African hominoids. Implications for *Australopithecus afarensis*. *American Journal of Physical Anthropology* 74, 155–175.

Lavocat, R. (1952). Sur une faune de mammifères miocènes découverte à Beni Mellal (Atlas marocain). *Comptes Rendus de l'Académie des Sciences* 235, 189–191.

Lazagabaster, I.A., Brophy, J., Sanisidro, O., Pineda-Munoz, S. and Berger, L. (2018a). A new partial cranium of *Metridiochoerus* (Suidae, Mammalia) from Malapa, South Africa. *Journal of African Earth Sciences* 145, 49–52.

Lazagabaster, I.A., Souron, A., Rowan, J., et al. (2018b). Fossil Suidae (Mammalia, Artiodactyla) from Lee Adoyta, Ledi-Geraru, lower Awash Valley, Ethiopia: implications for late Pliocene turnover and paleoecology. *Palaeogeography, Palaeoclimatology, Palaeoecology* 504, 186–200.

Le Bas, M.J. (1977). *Carbonatite–Nephelinite Volcanism: An African Case History*. London: John Wiley & Sons.

Le Fur, S., Fara, E., Mackaye, H.T., Vignaud, P. and Brunet, M. (2009). The mammal assemblage of the hominid site TM266 (Late Miocene, Chad Basin): ecological structure and paleoenvironmental implications. *Naturwissenschaften* 96, 565–574.

Leakey, L.S.B. (1928). The Oldoway skull. *Nature* 121, 499–500.

Leakey, L.S.B. (1936). Fossil human remains from Kanam and Kanjera, Kenya Colony. *Nature* 138, 643–643.

Leakey, L.S.B. (1951). *Olduvai Gorge: A Report on the evolution of the Hand-Axe Culture in Beds I–IV*. Cambridge: Cambridge University Press.

Leakey, L.S.B. (1958). Some East African Pleistocene Suidae. *Fossil Mammals of Africa* 14, 1–133.

Leakey, L.S.B. (1959). A new fossil skull from Olduvai. *Nature* 189, 491–493.

Leakey, L.S.B. (1960). Recent discoveries at Olduvai Gorge. *Nature* 188, 1050–1052.

Leakey, L.S.B. (1961a). New finds at Olduvai Gorge. *Nature* 189, 649–650.

Leakey, L.S.B. (1961b). The juvenile mandible from Olduvai. *Nature* 191, 417–418.

Leakey, L.S.B. (1965). *Olduvai Gorge. Vol. 1, A Preliminary Report on the Geology and Fauna, 1951–1961*. London: Cambridge University Press.

Leakey, L.S.B. (1972). *Homo sapiens* in the Middle Pleistocene and the evidence of *Homo sapiens*' evolution. In: F. Bordes (Ed.), *The Origin of Homo sapiens*. Paris: UNESCO, pp. 25–29.

Leakey, L.S.B. and Leakey, M.D. (1963). *Archaeological Excavations at Olduvai Gorge, Tanzania*. Washington, DC: National Geographic Society Research Reports, pp. 179–182.

Leakey, L.S.B. and Leakey, M.D. (1964). Recent discoveries of fossil Hominids in Tanganyika: at Olduvai and near Lake Natron. *Nature* 202, 5–7.

Leakey, L.S.B., Hopwood, A.T. and Reck, H. (1931). New yields from the Oldoway Bone Beds, Tanganyika Territory. *Nature* 128, 1075–1075.

Leakey, L.S.B., Evernden, J.F. and Curtis, G.H. (1961). Age of Bed I, Olduvai Gorge, Tanganyika. *Nature* 191, 478–479.

Volume References

Leakey, L.S.B., Tobias, P.V. and Napier, J.R. (1964). A new species of the genus *Homo* from Olduvai Gorge. *Nature* 202, 7–9.

Leakey, L.S.B., Savage, R.J.G. and Coryndon, S.C. (1973). *Fossil Vertebrates of Africa*, Volume 3. London: Academic Press.

Leakey, M.D. (1966). A review of the Oldowan Culture from Olduvai Gorge, Tanzania. *Nature* 210, 462–466.

Leakey, M.D. (1969). Recent discoveries of hominid remains at Olduvai Gorge, Tanzania. *Nature* 223, 756–756.

Leakey, M.D. (1970). New hominid remains and early artefacts from northern Kenya: early artefacts from the Koobi Fora area. *Nature*, 226, 228–230.

Leakey, M.D. (1971). *Olduvai Gorge. Vol.3, Excavations in Beds 1 and 2, 1960-1963*. London: Cambridge University Press.

Leakey, M.D. (1978). Pliocene footprints at Laetoli, northern Tanzania. *Antiquity* 52, 133.

Leakey, M.D. (1979). 3.6 million years old footprints in the ashes of time. *National Geographic Magazine* 155, 446–457.

Leakey, M.D. (1981). Tracks and tools. *Philosophical Transactions of the Royal Society of London, B*, 292, 95–102.

Leakey, M.D. (1984). *Disclosing the Past. An Autobiography*. New York: Doubleday.

Leakey, M.D. (1987a). The hominid footprints: introduction. In: M.D. Leakey and J.M. Harris (Eds.), *Laetoli: A Pliocene Site in Northern Tanzania*. Oxford: Clarendon Press, pp. 490–496.

Leakey, M.D. (1987b). Introduction. In: M.D. Leakey and J.M. Harris (Eds.), *Laetoli: A Pliocene Site in Northern Tanzania*. Oxford: Clarendon Press, pp. 1–22.

Leakey, M.D. (1987c). The Laetoli hominid remains. In: M.D. Leakey and J.M. Harris (Eds.), *Laetoli: A Pliocene Site in Northern Tanzania*. Oxford: Clarendon Press, pp. 108–117.

Leakey, M.D. (1987d). Animal prints and trails. In: M.D. Leakey and J.M. Harris (Eds.), *Laetoli: A Pliocene Site in Northern Tanzania*. Oxford: Clarendon Press, pp. 451–489.

Leakey, M.D. (1994). *Olduvai Gorge. Volume 5, Excavations in Beds III and IV, and the Masek Beds, 1968-1971*. Cambridge: Cambridge University Press.

Leakey, M.D. and Harris, J.M. (Eds.) (1987). *Laetoli: A Pliocene Site in Northern Tanzania*. Oxford: Clarendon Press.

Leakey, M.D. and Hay, R.L. (1979). Pliocene footprints in the Laetolil Beds at Laetoli, northern Tanzania. *Nature* 278, 317–323.

Leakey, M.D. and Roe, D.A. (1994). *Olduvai Gorge: Geology and Dating of Beds III, IV and the Masek Beds, 1968-1971*. Cambridge: Cambridge University Press.

Leakey, M.D., Clarke, R.J. and Leakey, L.S.B. (1971). New hominid skull from Bed I, Olduvai Gorge, Tanzania. *Nature* 232, 308–312.

Leakey, M.D., Hay, R.L., Curtis, G.H., et al. (1976). Fossil hominids from the Laetolil Beds. *Nature* 262, 460–466.

Leakey, M.G. and Harris, J.M. (2003a). *Lothagam: The Dawn of Humanity In Eastern Africa*. New York: Columbia University Press.

Leakey, M.G. and Harris, J.M. (2003b). Lothagam: its significance and contributions. In:*Lothagam: The Dawn of Humanity in Eastern Africa*. New York: Columbia University Press, pp. 625–660.

Leakey, M.G. and Leakey, R.E.F. (1976). Further Cercopithecinae (Mammalia, Primates) from the Plio/Pleistocene of East Africa. In: R.J.G. Savage and S.C. Coryndon (Eds.), *Fossil Vertebrates of Africa*, vol. 4. London: Academic Press, pp. 121–146.

Leakey, M.G. and Leakey, R.E. (1978). Koobi Fora Research Project, Volume 1: The fossil hominids and an introduction to their context, 1968-1974. In: R.E. Leakey and G.L. Isaac (Eds.), *Koobi Fora: Researches into Geology, Palaeontology, and Human Origins*. Oxford: Clarendon Press, p. 191.

Leakey, M.G. and Walker, A. (2003). The Lothagam hominids. In:*Lothagam: The Dawn of Humanity in Eastern Africa*. New York: Columbia University Press, pp. 249–260.

Leakey, M.G. and Werdelin, L. (2010). Early Pleistocene mammals of Africa: background to dispersal. In J.G. Fleagle, J.J. Shea, F.E. Grine, A.L. Baden and R.E. Leakey (Eds.), *Out of Africa I*. Dordrecht: Springer, pp. 3–11.

Leakey, M.G., Feibel, C.S., McDougall, I. and Walker, A. (1995). New four-million-year-old hominid species from Kanapoi and Allia Bay, Kenya. *Nature* 376, 565–571.

Leakey, M.G., Feibel, C.S., Bernor, R.L., et al. (1996). Lothagam: a record of faunal change in the Late Miocene of East Africa. *Journal of Vertebrate Paleontology* 16(3), 556–570.

Leakey, M.G., Feibel, C.S., McDougall, I., Ward, C.V. and Walker, A. (1998). New specimens and confirmation of an early age for *Australopithecus anamensis*. *Nature* 393, 62–66.

Leakey, M.G., Spoor, F., Brown, F.H., et al. (2001). New hominin genus from eastern Africa shows diverse middle Pliocene lineages. *Nature* 410, 433–440.

Leakey, M.G., Teaford, M.F. and Ward, C.V. (2003). Cercopithecidae from Lothagam. In:*Lothagam: The Dawn of Humanity in Eastern Africa*. New York: Columbia University Press, pp. 201–248.

Leakey, M.G., Spoor, F., Dean, M.C., et al. (2012). New fossils from Koobi Fora in northern Kenya confirm taxonomic diversity in early *Homo*. *Nature* 488, 201–204.

Leakey, R.E.F. (1969). Early *Homo sapiens* remains from the Omo River region of south-west Ethiopia: faunal remains from the Omo Valley. *Nature*, 222, 1132–1133.

Leakey, R.E.F. (1970). New hominid remains and early artefacts from northern Kenya: fauna and artefacts from a new Plio-Pleistocene locality near Lake Rudolf in Kenya. *Nature* 226, 223–224.

Leakey, R.E. (1973). Evidence for an advanced Plio-Pleistocene hominid from East Rudolf, Kenya. *Nature* 242, 447–450.

Leakey, R.E.F. (1976). New hominid fossils from the Koobi Fora Formation in Northern Kenya. *Nature* 261, 574–576.

Lebatard, A.-E., Bourlès, D.L., Duringer, P., et al. (2008). Cosmogenic nuclide dating of *Sahelanthropus tchadensis* and *Australopithecus bahrelghazali*: Mio-Pliocene hominids from Chad. *Proceedings of the National Academy of Sciences* 105, 3226–3231.

Lebatard, A.E., Bourlès, D.L., Braucher, R., et al. (2010). Application of the authigenic 10Be/9Be dating method to continental sediments: reconstruction of the Mio-Pleistocene sedimentary sequence in the early hominid fossiliferous areas of the northern Chad Basin. *Earth and Planetary Science Letters* 297(1–2), 57–70.

Leblanc, M., Favreau, G., Tweed, S., et al. (2007). Remote sensing for groundwater modelling in large semiarid areas: Lake Chad Basin, Africa. *Hydrogeology Journal*, 15(1), 97–100.

Le Cabec, A., Colard, T., Charabidze, D. et al. (2021). Insights into the palaeobiology of an early Homo infant: multidisciplinary investigation of the GAR IVE hemi-mandible, Melka Kunture, Ethiopia. Scientific Reports, 11, 23087.

Lee, R. and Roberts, D. (1997). Last interglacial (c. 117 kyr) human footprints from South Africa. *South African Journal of Science*, 93(8), 349–350.

Leece, A.B., Kegley, A.D., Lacruz, R.S., et al. (2016). The first hominin from the early Pleistocene paleocave of Haasgat, South Africa. *PeerJ*, 4, e2024.

Lee-Thorp, J.A. and Beaumont, P.B. (1995). Vegetation and seasonality shifts during the Late Quaternary deduced from 13C/12C ratios of grazers at Equus Cave, South Africa. *Quaternary Research* 43(3), 426–432.

Lee-Thorp, J. and Ecker, M. (2015). Holocene environmental change at Wonderwerk Cave, South Africa: insights from stable light isotopes in ostrich egg shell. *African Archaeological Review* 32, 793–811.

Lee-Thorp, J. and Sponheimer, M. (2003). Three case studies used to reassess the reliability of fossil bone and enamel isotope signals for paleodietary studies. *Journal of Anthropological Archaeology*, 22(3), 208–216.

Lee-Thorp, J.A. and Sponheimer, M. (2013). Hominin ecology from hard-tissue biogeochemistry. In: P. Ungar, E. Kaye, J.A. Lee-Thorp and M. Sponheimer (Eds.), *Early Hominin Paleoecology*. Boulder: University Press of Colorado, pp. 281–324.

Lee-Thorp, J.A. and Talma, A.S. (2000). Stable light isotopes and environments in the southern African Quaternary and Late Pliocene. *Oxford Monographs on Geology and Geophysics* 40, 236–251.

Lee-Thorp, J.A. and van der Merwe, N.J. (1993). Stable carbon isotope studies of Swartkrans fossils. In: C.K. Brain (Ed.), *Swartkrans: A Cave's Chronicle of Early Man*. Transvaal Museum Monograph No. 8. Pretoria: Transvaal Museum, pp. 251–256.

Lee-Thorp, J.A., van der Merwe, N.J. and Brain, C.K. (1989). Isotopic evidence for dietary differences between two extinct baboon species from Swartkrans. *Journal of Human Evolution* 18, 183–190.

Lee-Thorp, J., van der Merwe, N. and Brain, C. (1994). Diet of *Australopithecus robustus* at Swartkrans from stable carbon isotope analysis. *Journal of Human Evolution* 27, 361–372.

Lee-Thorp, J.A., Manning, L. and Sponheimer, M. (1997). Problems and prospects for carbon isotope analysis of very small samples of fossil tooth enamel. *Bulletin de la Société géologique de France* 168, 767–773.

Lee-Thorp, J.A., Thackeray, J.F. and van der Merwe, N. (2000). The hunters and the hunted revisited. *Journal of Human Evolution* 39, 565–576.

Lee-Thorp, J.A., Sponheimer, M. and Van der Merwe, N.J. (2003). What do stable isotopes tell us about Hominid dietary and ecological niches in the Pliocene? *International Journal of Osteoarchaeology* 13, 104–113.

Lee-Thorp, J.A., Sponheimer, M. and Luyt, J. (2007). Tracking changing environments using stable carbon isotopes in fossil tooth enamel: an example from the South African hominin sites. *Journal of Human Evolution* 53(5), 595–601.

Lee-Thorp, J., Likius, A., Mackaye, H.T., et al. (2012). Isotopic evidence for an early shift to C_4 resources by Pliocene hominins in Chad. *Proceedings of the National Academy of Sciences* 109, 20369–20372.

Lefèvre, D. (2000). Du continent à l'océan. Morphostratigraphie et paléogéographie du Quaternaire du Maroc atlantique. Le modèle casablancais. *Thèse HDR*, vol. 3(2), pp. 100–308, Univ. Montpellier 3.

Lefèvre, D. and Raynal, J.P. (2002). Les formations plio-pléistocènes de Casablanca et la chronostratigraphie du Quaternaire marin du Maroc revisitées. *Quaternaire* 13, 9–21.

Lefèvre, D., Raynal, J.-R. and El Graoui, M. (2016). Le Quaternaire d'Oulad Hamida. In: J.-P. Raynal and A. Mohib (Eds.), *Préhistoire de Casablanca. 1 - La Grotte des Rhinocéros (fouilles 1991 et 1996)*. Villes et Sites Archéologiques du Maroc, volume 6. Rabat: Ministère de la Culture, INSAP, pp. 45–59.

Lefèvre, D., Texier, J.P., Raynal, J.P., Occhietti, S. and Evin, J. (1994). Enregistrements-réponses des variations climatiques du Pléistocène supérieur et de l'Holocène sur le littoral de Casablanca (Maroc). Quaternaire 5, 173–180.

Legendre, P. and De Cáceres, M. (2013). Beta diversity as the variance of community data: dissimilarity coefficients and partitioning. *Ecology Letters* 16(8), 951–963.

Legendre, P. and Gallagher, E. D. (2001). Ecologically meaningful transformations for ordination of species data. *Oecologia* 129(2), 271–280.

Legendre, S. (1989). Les communautés de mammifères du Paléogène (Eocène supérieur et Oligocène) d'Europe occidentale: structures, milieux et evolution. *Münchner Geowissenschaftliche Abhandlungen (A)* 16, 1–110.

Lehmann, S.B., Braun, D.R., Dennis, K.J., et al. (2016). Stable isotopic composition of fossil mammal teeth and environmental change in southwestern South Africa during the Pliocene and Pleistocene. *Palaeogeography, Palaeoclimatology, Palaeoecology*, 457, 396–408.

Lehmann, T. (2004). Fossil aardvark (*Orycteropus*) from Swartkrans Cave, South Africa. *South African Journal of Science*, 100(5), 311–314.

Lehmann, T., Vignaud, P., Mackaye, H.T. and Brunet, M. (2004). A fossil aardvark (Mammalia, Tubulidentata) from the lower Pliocene of Chad. *Journal of African Earth Sciences* 40, 201–217.

Lehmann, T., Vignaud, P., Likius, A. and Brunet, M. (2005). A new species of Orycteropodidae (Mammalia, Tubulidentata) in the Mio-Pliocene of northern Chad. *Zoological Journal of the Linnean Society* 143, 109–131.

Leichliter, J.N. (2018). Early Hominin environments in Southern Africa: a micromammalian perspective. Doctoral dissertation, University of Colorado at Boulder.

Leichliter, J.N., Sponheimer, M., Avenant, N.L., et al. (2016). Small mammal insectivore stable carbon isotope compositions as habitat proxies in a South African savanna ecosystem. *Journal of Archaeological Science: Reports* 8, 335–345.

Leichliter, J., Sandberg, P., Passey, B., et al. (2017). Stable carbon isotope ecology of small mammals from the Sterkfontein Valley: implications for habitat reconstruction. *Palaeogeography, Palaeoclimatology, Palaeoecology*, 485, 57–67.

Lemorini, C., Plummer, T.W., Braun, D.R., et al. (2014). Old stones' song: use-wear experiments and analysis of the Oldowan quartz and quartzite assemblage from Kanjera South (Kenya). *Journal of Human Evolution* 72, 10–25.

Lemorini, C., Plummer, T.W., Braun, D.R., et al. (2019). Old stones' song: use-wear experiments and analysis of the Oldowan quartz and quartzite assemblage from Kanjera South (Kenya). *Archaeological and Anthropological Sciences* 11, 4729–4754.

Lennox, S.J. and Bamford, M. (2015). Use of wood anatomy to identify poisonous plants: charcoal of *Spirostachys africana*. *South African Journal of Science*, 111(3–4), 1–9.

Lennox, S.J. and Wadley, L. (2019). A charcoal study from the Middle Stone Age, 77,000 to 65,000 years ago, at Sibudu, KwaZulu-Natal. *Transactions of the Royal Society of South Africa*, 74(1), 38–54.

Lepre, C.J. (2014). Early Pleistocene lake formation and hominin origins in the Turkana–Omo rift. *Quaternary Science Reviews* 102, 181–191.

Lepre, C.J., Roche, H., Kent, D.V., et al. (2011). An earlier origin for the Acheulian. *Nature* 477, 82–85.

Leroy, S. and Dupont, L. (1994). Development of vegetation and continental aridity in northwestern Africa during the Late Pliocene: the pollen record of ODP site 658. *Palaeogeography, Palaeoclimatology, Palaeoecology* 109, 295–316.

Leroy, S.A.G. and Dupont, L.M. (1997). Marine palynology of the ODP 658 (N-W Africa) and its contribution to the stratigraphy of Late Pliocene. *Geobios* 30, 351–359.

Lesur, J., Vigne, J.-D. and Gutherz, X. (2007). Exploitation of wild mammals in South-west Ethiopia during the Holocene (4000 BC–500 AD): the finds from Moche Borago shelter (Wolayta). *Environmental Archaeology* 12, 139–159.

Lesur, J., Faith, J.T., Bon, F., et al. (2016). Paleoenvironmental and biogeographic implications of terminal Pleistocene large mammals from the Ziway-Shala Basin, Main Ethiopian Rift, Ethiopia. *Palaeogeography, Palaeoclimatology, Palaeoecology* 449, 567–579.

Levin, N.E. (2013). Compilation of East Africa Soil Carbonate Stable Isotope Data. Integrated Earth Data Applications. doi:10.1594/IEDA/100231.

Levin, N.E. (2015). Environment and climate of early human evolution. *Annual Review of Earth and Planetary Sciences* 43, 405–429.

Levin, N.E., Quade, J., Simpson, S.W., Semaw, S. and Rogers, M. (2004). Isotopic evidence for Plio-Pleistocene environmental change at Gona, Ethiopia. *Earth and Planetary Science Letters* 219, 93–110.

Levin, N.E., Cerling, T.E., Passey, B., Harris, J. and Ehleringer, J. (2006). A stable isotope aridity index for terrestrial environments. *Proceedings of the National Academy of Science* 103, 11201–11205.

Levin, N.E., Simpson, S.W., Quade, J., Cerling, T.E. and Frost, S.R. (2008). Herbivore enamel carbon isotopic composition and the environmental context of *Ardipithecus* at Gona, Ethiopia. In: J. Quade and J.G. Wynn (Eds.), *The Geology of Early Humans in the Horn of Africa*. Geological Society of America Special Paper 446. Boulder: Geological Society of America, pp. 215–234.

Levin, N.E., Brown, F.H., Behrensmeyer, A.K., Bobe, R. and Cerling, T.E. (2011). Paleosol carbonates from the Omo Group: isotopic records of local and regional environmental change in East Africa. *Palaeogeography, Palaeoclimatology, Palaeoecology* 307, 75–89.

Levin, N.E., Haile-Selassie, Y., Frost, S.R. and Saylor, B.Z. (2015). Dietary change among hominins and cercopithecids in Ethiopia during the early Pliocene. *Proceedings of the National Academy of Sciences of the United States of America* 117, 12304–1230.

Levin, S.A., Carpenter, S.R., Godfray, H.C.J., et al. (2009). *The Princeton Guide to Ecology*. Princeton: Princeton University Press, p. 848.

Levinson, M. (1985). Are fossil rodents useful in palaeo-ecological interpretations. *Annals of the Geological Survey of South Africa* 19, 53–64.

Lewin, R. (1983). Ethiopia halts prehistoric research. *Science* 219, 147–149.

Lewis, A.R., Marchant, D.R., Ashworth, A.C., Hemming, S.R. and Machlus, M.L. (2007). Major middle Miocene global climate change: evidence from East Antarctica and the Transantarctic Mountains. *Geological Society of America Bulletin* 119, 1449–1461.

Lewis, M.E. (1997). Carnivoran paleoguilds of Africa: implications for hominid food procurement strategies. *Journal of Human Evolution* 32(2–3), 257–288.

Lézine, A.-M. (1989). Late Quaternary vegetation and climate of the Sahel. *Quaternary Research* 32, 317–334.

Lézine, A.-M., Casanova, J. and Hillaire-Marce, C. (1990). Across an early Holocene humid phase in western Sahara: pollen and isotope stratigraphy. *Geology* 18, 264–267.

Lihoreau, F., Boisserie, J.-R., Viriot, L., et al. (2006). Anthracothere dental anatomy reveals a late Miocene Chado-Libyan bioprovince. *Proceedings of the National Academy of Sciences*, 103(23), 8763–8767.

Lihoreau, F., Boisserie, J.R., Blondel, C., et al. (2014). Description and palaeobiology of a new species of *Libycosaurus* (Cetartiodactyla, Anthracotheriidae) from the Late Miocene of Toros-Menalla, northern Chad. *Journal of Systematic Palaeontology* 12, 761–798.

Lihoreau, F., Sarr, R., Chardon, D., et al. (2021). A fossil terrestrial fauna from Tobène (Senegal) provides a unique early Pliocene window in western Africa. *Gondwana Research* 99, 21–35.

Linseele, V., Van Neer, W., Thys, S., et al. (2014). New archaeozoological data from the Fayum "Neolithic" with a critical assessment of the evidence for early stock keeping in Egypt. *PLoS ONE* 9, e108517.

Lisiecki, L.E. and Raymo, M.E. (2007). Plio-Pleistocene climate evolution: trends and transitions in glacial cycle dynamics. *Quaternary Science Reviews* 26, 56–69.

Livingston, D. and Kingdon, J. (2013). The evolution of a continent: geography and geology. In: J. Kingdon, D.C. Happold, T.M. Butynski, et al. (Eds.), *Mammals of Africa*. London: Bloomsbury Publishing, pp. 27–42.

Lockwood, C.A. and Tobias, P.V. (1999). A large male hominin cranium from Sterkfontein, South Africa, and the status of *Australopithecus*. *Journal of Human Evolution* 36, 637–685.

Lockwood, C.A., Kimbel, W.H. and Johanson, D.C. (2000). Temporal trends and metric variation in the mandibles and dentition of *Australopithecus afarensis*. *Journal of Human Evolution* 39, 23–55.

Loftus, E., Roberts, P. and Lee-Thorp, J.A. (2016). An isotopic generation: four decades of stable isotope analysis in African archaeology. *Azania: Archaeological Research in Africa* 51(1), 88–114.

Loget, N., Driessche, J.V.D. and Davy, P. (2005). How did the Messinian salinity crisis end? *Terra Nova*, 17(5), 414–419.

Lombard, M., Malmström, H., Schlebusch, C., et al. (2019). Genetic data and radiocarbon dating question Plovers Lake as a Middle Stone Age hominin-bearing site. *Journal of Human Evolution* 131, 203–209.

Longinelli, A. (1984). Oxygen isotopes in mammal bone phosphate: a new tool for paleohydrological and paleoclimatological research. *Geochimica et Cosmochimica Acta* 48, 385–390.

López-Martínez, N., Likius, A., Mackaye, H.T., Vignaud, P. and Brunet, M. (2007). A new Lagomorph from the Late Miocene of Chad (Central Africa). [Un nuevo Lagomorfo del Mioceno superior de Chad (África central).] *Revista Española de Paleontología* 22(1), 1–20.

López-Sáez, J.-A. and Domínguez-Rodrigo, M. (2009). Palynology of OGS-6a and OGS-7, two new 2.6 Ma archaeological sites from Gona, Afar, Ethiopia: insights on aspects of Late Pliocene habitats and the beginnings of stone-tool use. *Geobios* 42, 503–511.

Lorenzen, E.D., Heller, R. and Siegismund, H.R. (2012). Comparative phylogeography of African savannah ungulates. *Molecular Ecology* 21, 3656–3670.

Lotter, M.G. and Kuman, K. (2018). The Acheulean in South Africa, with announcement of a new site (Penhill Farm) in the lower Sundays River Valley, Eastern Cape Province, South Africa. *Quaternary International* 480, 43–65.

Lotter, M.G., Gibbon, R.J., Kuman, K., et al. (2016). A geoarchaeological study of the middle and upper Pleistocene levels at Canteen Kopje, Northern Cape Province, South Africa. *Geoarchaeology* 31(4), 304–323.

Louchart, A. (2011). Aves. In: T. Harrison (Ed.), *Paleontology and Geology of Laetoli: Human Evolution in Context. Vol. 2: Fossil Hominins and the Associated Fauna*. Dordrecht: Springer, pp. 505–533.

Louchart, A. (2014). Fossil birds of the Konso Formation. In: G. Suwa, Y. Beyene and B. Asfaw (Eds.), *The Konso-Gardula Research Project Volume 1. Paleonotological Collections: Background and Fossil Aves, Cercopithecidae, and Suidae*. Tokyo: The University Museum, The University of Tokyo, Bulletin, 47, 25–39.

Louchart, A., Mourer-Chauviré, C., Vignaud, P., Taisso MacKaye, H. and Brunet, M. (2005a). A finfoot from the Late Miocene of Toros Menalla (Chad, Africa): palaeobiogeographical and palaeoecological implications. *Palaeogeography, Palaeoclimatology, Palaeoecology* 222, 1–9.

Louchart, A., Vignaud, P., Mackaye, H.T. and Brunet, M. (2005b). A new swan (Aves: Anatidae) in Africa, from the latest Miocene of Chad and Libya. *Journal of Vertebrate Paleontology* 25, 384–392.

Louchart, A., Haile-Selassie, Y., Vignaud, P., Likius, A. and Brunet, M. (2008). Fossil birds from the late Miocene of Chad and Ethiopia and zoogeographical implications. *Oryctos* 7, 147–167.

Louchart, A., Wesselman, H., Blumenschine, R.J., et al. (2009). Taphonomic, avian, and small-vertebrate indicators of *Ardipithecus ramidus* habitat. *Science*, 326, 66.

Louys, J. (2012). *Paleontology in Ecology and Conservation*. New York: Springer.

Louys, J., Meloro, C., Elton, S., Ditchfield, P. and Bishop, L.C. (2015). Analytical framework for reconstructing heterogeneous environmental variables from mammal community structure. *Journal of Human Evolution* 78, 1–11.

Lovejoy, C. (2009). Reexamining human origins in light of *Ardipithecus ramidus*. *Science* 326(5949), 74.

Lovejoy, C.O., Meindl, R.S., Ohman, J.C., Heiple, K.G. and White, T.D. (2002). The Maka femur and its bearing on the antiquity of human walking: applying contemporary concepts of morphogenesis to the human fossil record. *American Journal of Physical Anthropology* 119, 97–133.

Lucas, P.W., Omar, R., Al-Fadhalah, K., et al. (2013). Mechanisms and causes of wear in tooth enamel: implications for hominin diets. *Journal of the Royal Society Interface* 10: 20120923.

Lüdecke T., Schrenk F., Thiemeyer H., et al. (2016a). Persistent C_3 vegetation accompanied Plio-Pleistocene hominin evolution in the Malawi Rift (Chiwondo Beds, Karonga Basin, East African Rift System). *Journal of Human Evolution* 90, 163–175.

Lüdecke T., Mulch A., Kullmer O., et al. (2016b). Stable isotope dietary reconstructions of herbivore enamel reveal heterogenous savanna ecosystems in the Plio-Pleistocene Malawi Rift. *Paleogeography, Paleoclimatology, Paleoecology* 459, 170–181.

Lüdecke, T., Kullmer, O., Wacker, U., et al. (2018). Dietary versatility of Early Pleistocene hominins. *Proceedings of the National Academy of Sciences* 115(52), 13330–13335.

Ludwig, A.J. and Reynolds, J.F. (1988). *Statistical Ecology: A Primer on Methods and Computing*. New York: Wiley.

Luiselli, L., Politano, E. and Angelici, F.M. (2000). Ecological correlates of the distribution of terrestrial and freshwater Chelonians in the Niger Delta, Nigeria: a biodiversity assessment with conservation implications. *Revue D'Ecologie – La Terre et la Vie* 55, 3–23.

Luiselli, L., Akani, G.C., Ebere, N., et al. (2011). Food habits of a pelomedusid turtle, *Pelomedusa subrufa*, in tropical Africa (Nigeria): the effects of sex, body size, season, and site. *Chelonian Conservation and Biology* 10, 138–144.

Lukich, V., Porat, N., Faershtein, G., Cowling, S. and Chazan, M. (2019). New chronology and stratigraphy for Kathu Pan 6, South Africa. *Journal of Paleolithic Archaeology* 2(3), 235–257.

Lukich, V., Cowling, S. and Chazan, M. (2020). Palaeoenvironmental reconstruction of Kathu Pan, South Africa, based on sedimentological data. *Quaternary Science Reviews* 230, 106153.

Lupien, R.L., Russell, J.M., Yost, C.L., et al. (2019). Vegetation change in the Baringo Basin, East Africa across the onset of Northern Hemisphere glaciation 3.3–2.6 Ma. *Palaeogeography, Palaeoclimatology, Palaeoecology* 570, 109426.

Luque, L., Alcalá, L. and Domínguez-Rodrigo, M. (2009). The Peninj Group: tectonics, volcanism, and sedimentary paleoenvironments during the Lower Pleistocene in the Lake Natron Basin (Tanzania). In: M. Domínguez-Rodrigo, L. Alcalá and L. Luque (Eds.), *Peninj. A Research Project on Human Origins (1995–2005)*. Oxford: Oxbow, pp. 15–48.

Luyt, C.J. (2001). Revisiting palaeoenvironments from the hominid-bearing Plio-Pleistocene sites: new isotopic evidence from Sterkfontein. Unpublished masters thesis. University of Cape Town.

Luyt, C.J. and Lee-Thorp, J.A. (2003). Carbon isotope ratios of Sterkfontein fossils indicate a marked shift to open environments c. 1.7 Myr ago. *South African Journal of Science* 99, 271–273.

Luz, B., Kolodny, Y. and Horowitz, M. (1984). Fractionation of oxygen isotopes between mammalian bone phosphate and environmental drinking water. *Geochimica et Cosmochimica Acta* 48, 1689–1693.

Lyman, R.L. (1994). *Vertebrate Taphonomy*. New York: Cambridge University Press.

Lyman, R.L. (2006). Paleozoology in the service of conservation biology. *Evolutionary Anthropology* 15, 11–19.

Lyman, R.L. (2010). What taphonomy is, what it isn't, and why taphonomists should care about the difference. *Journal of Taphonomy* 8, 1–16.

Lyman, R.L. and O'Brien, M.J. (1987). Plow-zone zooarchaeology: fragmentation and identifiability. *Journal of Field Archaeology* 14, 493–498.

Macchiarelli, R., Bondioli, L., Coppa, A., et al. (2002). The one-million-year-old human remains from the Danakil (Afar) depression of Eritrea. *American Journal of Physical Anthropology* Supplement 34, 104 (abstract).

Macchiarelli, R., Bondioli, L., Falk, D., et al. (2004a). Early Pliocene hominid tooth from Galili, Somali Region, Ethiopia. *Collegium Anthropologicum* 28, 65–76.

Macchiarelli, R., Bondioli, L., Chech, M., et al. (2004b). The late Early Pleistocene Human Remains from Buia Danakil Depression, Eritrea. *Rivista Italiana di Stratigrafia e Paleontologia* 110 (Supplement), 133–144.

Macchiarelli, R., Bondioli, L., Coppa, A., et al. (2007). Extensive variation in the east African Early Pleistocene human fossil record: additional evidence from Uadi Aalad, Eritrea. *Bulletins et Memoires de la Société d'Anthropologie de Paris* 19, 279–280 (abstract).

Macchiarelli, R., Bondioli, L., Bruner, E., et al. (2014). The 1 Ma old human assemblage from the Homo site at Uadi Aalad, Buia (Danakil Depression of Eritrea): an updated record. *The African Human Fossil Record* (Toulouse, 26–27 September).

MacFadden, B.J. (1998). Tale of two rhinos: isotopic ecology, paleodiet, and niche differentiation of *Aphelops* and *Teleoceras* from the Florida Neogene. *Paleobiology* 24(2), 274–286.

MacFadden, B.J. (2005). Diet and habitat of toxodont megaherbivores (Mammalia, Notoungulata) from the late Quaternary of South and Central America. *Quaternary Research* 64(2), 113–124.

MacGregor, D. (2015). History of the development of the East African Rift System: a series of interpreted maps through time. *Journal of African Earth Sciences* 101, 232–252.

Macho, G.A. (2014). An ecological and behavioral approach to hominin evolution during the Pliocene. *Quaternary Science Reviews* 96, 23–31.

MacIntyre, R.M., Mitchell, J.G. and Dawson, J.B. (1974). Age of fault movements in Tanzanian sector of East African Rift System. *Nature* 247, 354–356.

MacLatchy, L., DeSilva, J., Sanders, W.J. and Wood, B. (2010). Hominini. In: L. Werdelin and W.J. Sanders (Eds.), *Cenozoic Mammals of Africa*. Berkeley: University of California Press, pp. 471–540.

Madella, M., Alexandre, A. and Ball, T. (2005). International code for phytolith nomenclature 1.0. *Annals of Botany* 96, 253–260.

Madden, R.H. (2014). *Hypsodonty in Mammals: Evolution, Geomorphology, and the Role of Earth Surface Processes*. Cambridge: Cambridge University Press.

Maddock, L. (1979). The migration and grazing succession. In: A.R.E. Sinclair and M. Norton-Griffiths (Eds.), *Serengeti*. Chicago: Chicago University Press.

Magill, C.R., Ashley, G.M. and Freeman, K.H. (2013a). Ecosystem variability and early human habitats in eastern Africa. *Proceedings of the National Academy of Sciences* 110, 1167–1174.

Magill, C.R., Ashley, G.M. and Freeman, K.H. (2013b). Water, plants, and early human habitats in eastern Africa. *Proceedings of the National Academy of Sciences* 110, 1175–1180.

Maglio, V.J. (1970). Four new species of Elephantidae from the Plio-Pleistocene of northwestern Kenya. *Breviora* 341, 1–43.

Maglio, V.J. (1973). Origin and evolution of the Elephantidae. *Transactions of the American Philosophical Society* 63, 1–149.

Magori, C.C. and Day, M.H. (1983). Laetoli Hominid 18: an early *Homo sapiens* skull. *Journal of Human Evolution* 12, 747–753.

Maguire, J.M. (1979). A taxonomic and ecological study of the living and fossil Hystricidae with particular reference to southern Africa. PhD thesis, University of the Witwatersrand.

Maguire, J.M. (1985). Recent geological, stratigraphic and palaeontological studies at Makapansgat Limeworks. In: P.V. Tobias (Ed.), *Hominid Evolution: Past, Present and Future*. New York: Alan R. Liss, pp. 151–164.

Maguire, J.M., Pemberton, D. and Collett, M.H. (1980). The Makapansgat Limeworks grey breccia: Hominids, hyenas or hillwash? *Palaeontologica Africana* 23, 75–98.

Maguire, J.M., Schrenk, F. and Stanistreet, I.G. (1985). The lithostratigraphy of the Makapansgat Limeworks Australopithecine site: some matters arising. *Annals of the Geological Survey of South Africa* 19, 37–51.

Magurran, A.E. (1988). *Ecological Diversity and its Measurement*. Princeton: Princeton University Press.

Maier, W. (1970). New fossil Cercopithecoidea from the Pleistocene cave deposits of the Makapansgat limeworks, South Africa. *Palaeontologica Africana* 12, 69–107.

Maier, W. (1972). The first complete skull of Simopithecus [Theropithecus] darti from Makapansgat, SA, and its systematic position. *Journal of Human Evolution* 1, 395–405.

Maitima, J.M. (1991). Vegetation response to climatic change in the Central Rift Valley, Kenya. *Quaternary Research* 35, 234–245.

Makinouchi, T., Ishida, S., Sawada, Y., et al. (1992). Geology of the Sinda-Mohari Region, Haut-Zaïre Province, Eastern Zaïre. *African Studies, Monographs* 17, 3–18.

Malan, B.D. and Cooke, H.B.S. (1941). A preliminary account of the Wonderwerk Cave, Kuruman. *South African Journal of Science* 37, 300–312.

Malan, B.D. and Wells, L.H. (1943). A further report on the Wonderwerk Cave, Kuruman. *South African Journal of Science* 40, 258–270.

Mallon, J.C., Henderson, D.M., McDonough, C.M. and Loughry, W.J. (2018). A 'bloat-and-float' taphonomic model best explains the upside-down preservation of ankylosaurs. *Palaeogeography, Palaeoclimatology, Palaeoecology* 497, 117–127.

Maloiy, G.M.O., Rugangazi, B.M. and Clemens, E.T. (1988). Physiology of the dik-dik antelope. *Comparative Biochemistry and Physiology* 91A, 1–8.

Manega, P.C. (1993). Geochronology, geochemistry and isotopic study of the Plio-Pleistocene hominid sites and the Ngorongoro volcanic highland in northern Tanzania. Unpublished PhD, University of Chicago, Boulder.

Manegold, A. (2013). Two new parrot species (Psittaciformes) from the early Pliocene of Langebaanweg, South Africa, and their palaeoecological implications. *Ibis* 155(1), 127–139.

Manegold, A. and Louchart, A. (2012). Biogeographic and paleoenvironmental implications of a new woodpecker species (Aves, Picidae) from the early Pliocene of South Africa. *Journal of Vertebrate Paleontology* 32(4), 926–938.

Manegold, A., Pavia, M. and Haarhoff, P. (2014). A new species of *Aegypius* vulture (Aegypiinae, Accipitridae) from the early Pliocene of South Africa. *Journal of Vertebrate Paleontology* 34(6), 1394–1407.

Mannion, P.D., Upchurch, P., Carrano, M.T. and Barrett, P.M. (2011). Testing the effect of the rock record on diversity: a multidisciplinary approach to elucidating the generic richness of sauropodomorph dinosaurs through time. *Biological Reviews* 86(1), 157–181.

Manthi, F.K. and Winkler, A.J. (2020). Rodents and other terrestrial small mammals from Kanapoi, north-western Kenya. *Journal of Human Evolution* 140, 102694.

Manthi, F.K., Brown, F.H., Plavcan, M.J. and Werdelin, L. (2018). Gigantic lion, *Panthera leo*, from the Pleistocene of Natodomeri, eastern Africa. *Journal of Paleontology* 92, 305–312.

Manthi, F.K., Cerling, T.E., Chritz, K.L. and Blumenthal, S.A. (2020a). Diets of mammalian fossil fauna from Kanapoi, northwestern Kenya. *Journal of Human Evolution* 140, 102338.

Manthi, F.K., Plavcan, J.M. and Ward, C.V. (2020b). Introduction to special issue Kanapoi: Paleobiology of a Pliocene Hominin Site in Kenya. *Journal of Human Evolution* 140, 102718.

Marçais, J. (1934). Découverte de restes humains fossiles dans les grès quaternaires de Rabat (Maroc). *L'Anthropologie* 44, 579–583.

Marean, C.W. (1991). Measuring the post-depositional destruction of bone in archaeological assemblages. *Journal of Archeological Science* 18, 677–694.

Marean, C.W. (1992a). Hunter to herder: the large mammal remains from Enkapune Ya Muto rockshelter (Central Rift, Kenya). *African Archaeological Review* 10, 65–127.

Marean, C.W. (1992b). Implications of late Quaternary mammalian fauna from Lukenya Hill (south-central Kenya) for paleoenvironmental change and faunal extinctions. *Quaternary Research* 37, 239–255.

Marean, C.W. (1997). Hunter-gatherer foraging strategies in tropical grasslands: model building and testing in the East African Middle and Later Stone Age. *Journal of Anthropological Archaeology* 16, 189–225.

Marean, C.W. (2010). Pinnacle Point Cave 13B (Western Cape Province, South Africa) in context: the Cape floral kingdom, shellfish, and modern human origins. *Journal of Human Evolution* 59(3–4), 425–443.

Marean, C.W. and Assefa, Z. (2005). The Middle and Upper Pleistocene African record for the biological and behavioral origins of modern humans. In: A. Stahl (Ed.), *African Archaeology: A Critical Introduction*. Malden: Blackwell, pp. 93–129.

Marean, C.W. and Gifford-Gonzalez, D. (1991). Late Quaternary extinct ungulates of East Africa and palaeoenvironmental implications. *Nature* 350, 418–420.

Marean, C.W., Nilssen, P.J., Brown, K., Jerardino, A. and Stynder, D. (2004). Paleoanthropological investigations of Middle Stone Age sites at Pinnacle Point, Mossel Bay (South Africa): archaeology and hominid remains from the 2000 field season. *Paleoanthropology*, 2(1).

Marean, C.W., Bar-Matthews, M., Bernatchez, J., et al. (2007). Early human use of marine resources and pigment in South Africa during the Middle Pleistocene. *Nature* 449(7164), 905–908.

Marean, C.W., Anderson, R.J., Bar-Matthews, M., et al. (2015). A new research strategy for integrating studies of paleoclimate, paleoenvironment, and paleoanthropology. *Evolutionary Anthropology: Issues, News, and Reviews* 24(2), 62–72.

Mares, M.A. (1992). Neotropical mammals and the myth of Amazonian biodiversity. *Science* 255, 976–979.

Marin-Monfort, M.D., García-Morato, S., Andrews, P., et al. (2022). The owl that never left! Taphonomy of Earlier Stone Age small mammal assemblages from Wonderwerk Cave (South Africa). *Quaternary International* 614, 111–125.

Marker, M.E. and Gamble, F.M. (1987). Karst in southern Africa. *Endins: publicació d'espeleologia* 13, 93–98.

Marks, A.E., Peters, J. and Van Neer, W. (1987). Late Pleistocene and early Holocene occupations in the Upper Atbara River Valley, Sudan. In: A.E. Close (Ed.), *Prehistory of Arid North Africa: Essays in Honor of Fred Wendorf*. Dallas: Southern Methodist University Press, pp. 137–162.

Marshall, C.R. (1990). Confidence intervals on stratigraphic ranges. *Paleobiology* 16, 1–10.

Marshall, C.R. (1994). Confidence intervals on stratigraphic ranges: partial relaxation of the assumption of randomly distributed fossil horizons. *Paleobiology* 20(4), 459–469.

Marshall, C.R. (1997). Confidence intervals on stratigraphic ranges with nonrandom distributions of fossil horizons. *Paleobiology* 23(2), 165–173.

Martin, F., Plastiras, C.A., Merceron, G., Souron, A. and Boisserie, J.R. (2018). Dietary niches of terrestrial cercopithecines from the Plio-Pleistocene Shungura Formation, Ethiopia: evidence from dental microwear texture analysis. *Scientific Reports* 8(1), 1–13.

Martin, J.W. and Trautwein, S. (2003). Fossil crabs (Crustacea, Decapoda, Brachyura) from Lothagam. In: M.G. Leakey and J.M. Harris (Eds.), *Lothagam: The Dawn of Humanity in Eastern Africa*. New York: Columbia University Press, pp. 67–74.

Martínez-Navarro, B. (2010). Early Pleistocene faunas of Eurasia and hominin dispersals. In: J.G. Fleagle, J.J. Shea, F.E. Grine, A.L. Baden and R.E. Leakey (Eds.), *Out of Africa I: The First Hominin Colonization of Eurasia*. Dordrecht: Springer, pp. 207–224.

Martínez-Navarro, B., Rook, L., Segid, A., et al. (2004). The large fossil mammals from Buia (Eritrea): systematics, biochronology and paleoenvironments. *Rivista Italiana di Paleontologia e Stratigrafia* 110, 61–88.

Martínez-Navarro, B., Rook, L., Papini, M. and Libsekal, Y. (2010). A new species of bull from the Early Pleistocene paleoanthropological site of Buia (Eritrea): parallelism on the dispersal of the genus *Bos* and the Acheulian culture. *Quaternary International* 212, 169–175.

Martínez-Navarro, B., Karoui-Yaakoub, N., Oms, O., et al. (2014). The early Middle Pleistocene archeopaleontological site of Wadi Sarrat (Tunisia) and the earliest record of *Bos primigenius*. *Quaternary Science Reviews* 90, 37–46.

Martini, F., Libsekal, Y., Filippi, O., et al. (2004). Characterization of lithic complexes from Buia (Dandiero Basin, Danakil Depression, Eritrea). *Rivista Italiana di Paleontologia e Stratigrafia* 110 (Supplement), 99–132.

Martyn, J. (1967). Pleistocene deposits and new fossil localities in Kenya. *Nature* 215(5100), 476.

Marzocchi, A., Lunt, D.J., Flecker, R., et al. (2015). Orbital control on late Miocene climate and the North African monsoon: insight from an ensemble of sub-precessional simulations. *Climate of the Past* 11, 1271–1295.

Masao, F.T., Anton, S.C. and Njau, J.K. (2013). Results of recent investigations of the Oldowan and associated hominid remains at the DK site, Olduvai Gorge: a conservation exercise. *Proceedings of the 22 International Symposium Africa, Cradle of Humanity: Recent Discoveries, Travaux du Centre National de Recherches Préhistoriques, Anthropologiques et Historiques* 18, 147–168.

Maslin, M.A. and Christensen, B. (2007). Tectonics, orbital forcing, global climate change, and human evolution in Africa: introduction to the African paleoclimate special volume. *Journal of Human Evolution* 53(5), 443–464.

Maslin, M.A. and Trauth, M.H. (2009). Plio-Pleistocene East African pulsed climate variability and its influence on early human evolution. In: F.E. Grine, J.G. Fleagle and R.E. Leakey (Eds.), *The First Humans: Origin and Early Evolution of the Genus Homo*. Dordrecht: Springer, pp. 151–158.

Maslin, M.A., Brierley, C., Milner, A., et al. (2014). East African climate pulses and early human evolution. *Quaternary Science Reviews* 101, 1–17.

Maslin, M.A., Shultz, S. and Trauth, M.H. (2015). A synthesis of the theories and concepts of early human evolution. *Philosophical Transactions of the Royal Society B* 370, 2014.0064.

Mason, R.J. (1962). *Prehistory of the Transvaal*. Johannesburg: Witwatersrand University Press.

Mason, R.J. (1988a). A Middle Stone Age faunal site at Kalkbank, northerrn Transvaal: archaeology and interpretation. *Paleoecology of Africa* 19, 201–203.

Mason, R.J. (1988b). *Cave of Hearths, Makapansgat Transvaal*. Occasional Paper No. 21. Johannesburg: Archaeological Research Unit, University of the Witwatersrand.

Masters, J.C. and Rayner, R.J. (1993). Competition and macroevolution: the ghost of competition yet to come? *Biological Journal of the Linnean Society* 49, 87–98.

Matthews, T. (1999). Taphonomy and the micromammals from Elands Bay Cave. *The South African Archaeological Bulletin* 54(170), pp.133–140.

Matthews, T., Parkington, J.E. and Denys, C. (2006a). The taphonomy of the micromammals from the late Middle Pleistocene site of Hoedjiespunt 1 (Cape Province, South Africa). *Journal of Taphonomy* 4(1), 11–26.

Matthews, T., Denys, C. and Parkington, J.E. (2006b). An analysis of the mole rats (Mammalia: Rodentia) from Langebaanweg (Mio-Pliocene, South Africa). *Geobios* 39(6), 853–864.

Matthews, T., Rector, A., Jacobs, Z., Herries, A.I. and Marean, C.W. (2011). Environmental implications of micromammals accumulated close to the MIS 6 to MIS 5 transition at Pinnacle Point Cave 9 (Mossel Bay, Western Cape Province, South Africa). *Palaeogeography, Palaeoclimatology, Palaeoecology* 302(3–4), 213–229.

Matthews, T., van Dijk, E., Roberts, D.L. and Smith, R.M. (2015). An early Pliocene (5.1 Ma) fossil frog community from Langebaanweg, south-western Cape, South Africa. *African Journal of Herpetology* 64(1), 39–53.

Matthews, T., John Measey, G. and Roberts, D.L. (2016). Implications of summer breeding frogs from Langebaanweg, South Africa: regional climate evolution at 5.1 mya. *South African Journal of Science* 112(9–10), 1–7.

Matthews, T., Marean, C.W. and Cleghorn, N. (2019). Past and present distributions and community evolution of Muridae and Soricidae from MIS 9 to MIS 1 on the edge of the Palaeo-Agulhas Plain (south coast, South Africa). *Quaternary Science Reviews* 235, 105774.

Matmon, A., Ron, H., Chazan, M., Porat, N. and Horwitz, L.K. (2012). Reconstructing the history of sediment deposition in caves: a case study from Wonderwerk Cave. *Geological Society of America Bulletin* 124, 611–625.

Matmon, A., Hidy, A.J., Vainer, S., et al. (2015). New chronology for the southern Kalahari Group sediments with implications for sediment-cycle dynamics and early hominin occupation. *Quaternary Research* 84, 118–132.

Mawby, I.E. (1970). Fossil vertebrates from northern Malawi: preliminary report. *Quaternaria* 13, 319–323.

Maxwell, S.J. (2018). The quality of the early hominin fossil record: implications for evolutionary analyses. PhD thesis, Department of Earth and Planetary Sciences, Birkbeck, University of London.

Maxwell, S.J., Hopley, P.J., Upchurch, P. and Soligo, C. (2018). Sporadic sampling, not climatic forcing, drives observed early hominin diversity. *Proceedings of the National Academy of Sciences* 115(19), 4891–4896.

Mayr, E. (1942). *Systematics and the Origin of Species*. New York: Columbia University Press.

Mayr, E. (1963). *Animal Species and Evolution*. Cambridge, MA: Harvard University Press.

Mayr, E. (1970). *Populations, Species, and Evolution*. Cambridge, MA: Harvard University Press.

Mbua, E., Kusaka, S., Kunimatsu, Y., et al. (2016). Kantis: a new *Australopithecus* site on the shoulders of the Rift Valley near Nairobi, Kenya. *Journal of Human Evolution* 94, 28–44.

McBrearty, S. and Brooks, A.S. (2000). The revolution that wasn't: a new interpretation of the origin of modern human behavior. *Journal of Human Evolution* 39, 453–463.

McBrearty, S. and Jablonski, N.G. (2005). First fossil chimpanzee. *Nature* 437, 105–108.

McBrearty, S., Tryon, C. (2006). From Acheulean to Middle Stone Age in the Kapthurin Formation, Kenya. In: E. Hovers and S.L. Kuhn (Eds.), *Transitions before the Transition*. New York: Springer, pp. 257–277.

McBrearty, S., Bishop, L. and Kingston, J.D. (1996). Variability in traces of Middle Pleistocene hominid behavior in the Kapthurin Formation, Baringo, Kenya. *Journal of Human Evolution* 30, 563–580.

McCall, G.J.H., Baker, B.H. and Walsh, J. (1967). Late Tertiary and Quaternary sediments of the Kenya Rift Valley. In: W.W. Bishop and J.D. Clark (Eds.), *Background to Evolution in Africa*. Chicago: Chicago University Press, pp. 191–220.

McCarthy, T.C. and Hancox, P.J. (2000). Wetlands. In: T.C. Partridge and R.R. Maud (Eds.), *Cenozoic of Southern Africa*. Oxford: Oxford University Press, pp. 218–235.

McDougall, I. (1985). K–Ar and $^{40}Ar/^{39}Ar$ dating of the hominid-bearing Pliocene–Pleistocene sequence at Koobi Fora, Lake Turkana, northern Kenya. *Geological Society of America Bulletin* 96, 159–175.

McDougall, I. and Brown, F.H. (2006). Precise 40Ar/39Ar geochronology for the upper Koobi Fora Formation, Turkana Basin, northern Kenya. *Journal of the Geological Society of London* 163, 205–220.

McDougall, I. and Brown, F.H. (2008). Geochronology of the pre-KBS Tuff sequence, Omo Group, Turkana Basin. *Journal of the Geological Society* 165, 549–562.

McDougall, I. and Feibel, C.S. (1999). Numerical age control for the Miocene–Pliocene succession at Lothagam, a hominoid-bearing sequence in the northern Kenya Rift. *Journal of the Geological Society* 156(4), 731–745.

McDougall, I., Davies, T., Maier, R. and Rudowski, R. (1985). Age of the Okote Tuff Complex at Koobi Fora, Kenya. *Nature* 316, 792–794.

McDougall, I., Brown, F.H. and Fleagle, J.G. (2008). Sapropels and the age of hominins Omo I and II, Kibish, Ethiopia. *Journal of Human Evolution* 55, 409–420.

McDougall, I., Brown, F.H., Vasconcelos, P.M., et al. (2012). New single crystal $^{40}Ar/^{39}Ar$ ages improve time scale for deposition of the Omo Group, Omo–Turkana Basin, East Africa. *Journal of the Geological Society* 169, 213–226.

McFadden, P.L., Brock, A. and Partridge, T.C. (1979). Paleomagnetism and the age of the Makapansgat hominid site. *Earth and Planetary Science Letters* 44, 411–415.

McGraw, W.S., Cooke, C. and Shultz, S. (2006). Primate remains from African crowned eagle *Stephanoaetus coronatus* nests in Ivory Coast's Tai Forest: implications for primate predation and early hominid taphonomy in South Africa. *American Journal of Physical Anthropology* 131, 151–165.

McHenry, H.M. (1986). The first bipeds: a comparison of the *Australopithecus afarensis* and *Australopithecus africanus* postcranium and implications for the evolution of bipedalism. *Journal of Human Evolution* 15, 177–191.

McHenry, H.M. (1991). First steps? Analyses of the postcranium of early hominids. In: B. Senut and Y. Coppens (Eds.), *Origine(s) de la Bipédie chez les Hominidés*. Paris: CNRS, pp. 133–142.

McHenry, H.M. (1994). Early hominid postcrania: phylogeny and function. In: R.S. Corruccini and R.L. Ciochon (Eds.), *Integrative Paths to the Past: Paleoanthropological Advances in Honor of F. Clark Howell*. Englewood Cliffs: Prentice Hall, pp. 251–268.

McHenry, L.J. (2005). Phenocryst composition as a tool for correlating fresh and altered tephra, Bed I, Olduvai Gorge, Tanzania. *Stratigraphy* 2, 101–115.

McHenry, L.J. (2011). Geochemistry and mineralogy of the Laetoli area tuffs: Lower Laetolil through Naibadad Beds. In: T. Harrison (Ed.), *Paleontology and Geology of Laetoli, Tanzania: Human Evolution in Context. Volume 1: Geology, Geochronology, Paleoecology and Paleoenvironment*. Dordrecht: Springer, pp. 121–141.

McHenry, L.J. (2012). A revised stratigraphic framework for Olduvai Gorge Bed I based on tuff geochemistry. *Journal of Human Evolution* 63, 284–299.

McHenry, L.J. and Stanistreet, I.G. (2018). Tephrochronology of Bed II, Olduvai Gorge, Tanzania, and placement of the Oldowan–Acheulean transition. *Journal of Human Evolution* 120, 7–18.

McHenry, L.J., Mollel, G.F. and Swisher, C.C. (2008). Compositional and textural correlations between Olduvai Gorge Bed I tephra and volcanic sources in the Ngorongoro Volcanic Highlands, Tanzania. *Quaternary International* 178, 306–319.

McHenry, L.J., Luque, L., Gómez, J.Á. and Diez-Martín, F. (2011). Promise and pitfalls for characterizing and correlating the zeolitically altered tephra of the Pleistocene Peninj Group, Tanzania. *Quaternary Research* 75, 708–720.

McHenry, L.J., Stollhofen, H. and Stanistreet, I.G. (2013). Use of single-grain geochemistry of cryptic tuffs and volcaniclastic sandstones improves the tephrostratigraphic framework of Olduvai Gorge, Tanzania. *Quaternary Research* 80, 235–249.

McHenry, L.J., Njau, J.K., de la Torre, I. and Pante, M.C. (2016). Geochemical "fingerprints" for Olduvai Gorge Bed II tuffs and implications for the Oldowan–Acheulean transition. *Quaternary Research* 85, 147–158.

McKee, J.K. (1991). Palaeo-ecology of the Sterkfontein hominids: a review and synthesis. *Palaeontologia Africana* 28, 41–51.

McKee, J.K. (1993a). The faunal age of the Taung hominid deposit. *Journal of Human Evolution* 14, 252–265.

McKee, J.K. (1993b). Formation and geomorphology of caves in calcareous tufas and implications for the study of Taung fossil deposits. *Transactions of the Royal Society of South Africa* 48, 307–322.

McKee, J.K. (1994). Catalogue of fossil sites at the Buxton Limeworks, Taung. *Palaeontologia Africana* 31, 73–81.

McKee, J.K. (1996). Faunal turnover patterns in the Pliocene and Pleistocene of southern Africa. *South African Journal of Science* 92(3), 111–113.

McKee, J.K. (2001). Faunal turnover rates and mammalian biodiversity of the late Pliocene and Pleistocene of eastern Africa. *Paleobiology* 27, 500–511.

McKee, J.K. (2010). Taphonomic processes of bone distribution and deposition in the tufa caves of Taung, South Africa. *Journal of Taphonomy* 8, 203–213.

McKee, J.K. (2016). Return to the Taung cave paradigm. *American Journal of Physical Anthropology* 159(2), 348–351.

McKee, J.K. and Keyser, A.W. (1994). Craniodental remains of *Papio angusticeps* from the Haasgat cave site, South Africa. *International Journal of Primatology* 15(6), 823–841.

McKee, J.K. and Kuykendall, K.L. (2016). The Dart deposits of the Buxton Limeworks, Taung, South Africa, and the context of the Taung *Australopithecus* fossil. *Journal of Vertebrate Paleontology* 36(2), e1054937.

McKee, J.K. and Tobias, P.V. (1990). New fieldwork at the Taung Hominid Site: 1988–1989. *American Journal of Physical Anthropology* 81, 266–267.

McKee, J.K. and Tobias, P.V. (1994). Taung stratigraphy and taphonomy: preliminary results based on the 1988–89 excavations. *South African Journal of Science* 90, 233–235.

McKee, J.K., Thackeray, J.F. and Berger, L.R. (1995). Faunal assemblage seriation of Southern African Pliocene and Pleistocene fossil deposits. *American Journal of Physical Anthropology* 106, 235–250.

McKee, J.K., von Mayer, A. and Kuykendall, K.L. (2011). New species of *Cercopithecoides* from Haasgat, North West Province, South Africa. *Journal of Human Evolution* 60(1), 83–93.

McKenzie, D.P., Davies, D. and Molnar, P. (1970). Plate tectonics of the Red Sea and East Africa. *Nature* 226, 243–248.

McNabb, J. and Beaumont, P. (2011). *A Report on the Archaeological Assemblages from Excavations by Peter Beaumont at Canteen Koppie, Northern Cape, South Africa*. Southampton Series in Archaeology 4. Oxford: Archaeopress.

McPherron, S.P., Alemseged, Z., Marean, C.W., et al. (2010). Evidence for stone-tool-assisted consumption of animal tissues before 3.39 million years ago at Dikika, Ethiopia. *Nature* 466, 857–860.

Meadows, M.E. and Baxter, A.J. (1999). Late Quaternary palaeoenvironments of the southwestern Cape, South Africa: a regional synthesis. *Quaternary International* 57, 193–206.

Medin, T., Martínez-Navarro, B., Rivals, F., Libsekal, Y. and Rook, L. (2015). The late Early Pleistocene suid remains from the paleoanthropological site of Buia (Eritrea): systematics, biochronology and eco-geographical context. *Palaeogeography, Palaeoclimatology, Palaeoecology* 431, 26–42.

Mehlman, M.J. (1987). Provenience, age and associations of archaic *Homo sapiens* crania from Lake Eyasi, Tanzania. *Journal of Archaeological Science* 14, 133–162.

Mehlman, M.J. (1989). Later Quaternary archaeological sequences in northern Tanzania. PhD thesis, University of Illinois, Urbana-Champaign.

Meijaard, E., Oliver, W.L.R. and d'Huart, J.-P. (2011). Suidae. In: D.E. Wilson and R. Mittermeier (Eds.), *Handbook of the Mammals of the World. Vol. 2. Hoofed Mammals*. Paris: Lynx Edicions, pp. 248–291.

Meldrum, D.J. (2004). Fossilized Hawaiian footprints compared with Laetoli hominid footprints. In: D.J. Meldrum and C.E. Hilton (Eds.), *From Biped to Strider: The Emergence of Modern Human Walking, Running, and Resource Transport*. New York: Kluwer Academic, pp. 63–83.

Meldrum, D.J., Lockley, M.G., Lucas, S.G. and Musiba, C. (2011). Ichnotaxonomy of the Laetoli trackways: the earliest hominin footprints. *Journal of African Earth Sciences* 60, 1–12.

Melson, W.G. and Potts, R. (2002). Origin of reddened and melted zones in Pleistocene sediments of the Olorgesailie basin, southern Kenya rift. *Journal of Archaeological Science* 29, 307–316.

Menter, C.G., Kuykendall, K.L., Keyser, A.W. and Conroy, G.C. (1999). First record of hominid teeth from the Plio-Pleistocene site of Gondolin, South Africa. *Journal of Human Evolution* 37, 299–307.

Merceron, G. and Ungar, P. (2005). Dental microwear and palaeoecology of bovids from the Early Pliocene of Langebaanweg, Western Cape Province, South Africa. *South African Journal of Science* 101(7), 365–370.

Merrick, H.V., Brown, F.H. and Nash, W.P. (1994). Use and movement of obsidian in the Early and Middle Stone Ages of Kenya and Northern Tanzania. In: S.T. Childs (Ed.), *Society, Culture, and Technology in Africa*, vol. 11. Philadelphia: University of Pennsylvania Press, pp. 29–44.

Merritt, S.R. (2017). Investigating hominin carnivory in the Okote Member of Koobi Fora, Kenya with an actualistic model of carcass consumption and traces of butchery on the elbow. *Journal of Human Evolution* 112, 105–133.

Merzoug, S. and Sari, L. (2008). Re-examination of the Zone I material from Tamar Hat (Algeria): zooarchaeological and technofunctional analyses. *African Archaeological Review* 25, 57–73.

Metcalfe, C.R. (1971). *Anatomy of the Monocotyledons: Volume V, Cyperaceae*. Oxford: Clarendon Press.

Meyer, A., Kocher, T.D., Basasibwaki, P. and Wilson, A.C. (1990). Monophyletic origin of Lake Victoria cichlid fishes suggested by mitochondrial DNA sequences. *Nature* 347(6293), 550–553.

Meylan, P. (1990). Fossil turtles from the upper Semliki, Zaire. In: N.T. Boaz (Ed.), *Evolution of Environments and Hominidae in the African Western Rift Valley*. Martinsville: Virginia Museum of Natural History, pp. 163–170.

Miall, D. (1996). *The Geology of Fluvial Deposits. Sedimentary Facies, Basin Analysis, and Petroleum Geology*. Berlin: Springer.

Michel, P. (1992). Pour une meilleure connaissance du Quaternaire Continental Marocain: les vertébrés fossiles du Maroc Atlantique, Central et Oriental. *L'Anthropologie* 96, 643–656.

Michel, P. and Wengler, L. (1993). Le site paléontologique et archéologique de Doukkala II (Maroc, Pléistocène moyen et supérieur): Premier jalon en Afrique du Nord d'un comportement humain assimilable à "charognage contrôlé et actif". *Comptes Rendu de l'Académie des Sciences Paris* 317, 557–562.

Michel, P., Campmas, E., Stoetzel, E., et al. (2009). La macrofaune du Pléistocène supérieur d'El Harhoura 2 (Témara, Maroc): données préliminaires. *L'Anthropologie* 113, 283–312.

Michel, P., Campmas, E., Stoetzel, E., et al. (2010). Upper Palaeolithic (layer 2) and Middle Palaeolithic (layer 3) large faunas from El Harhoura 2 Cave (Témara, Morocco): paleontological, paleoecological and paleoclimatic data. *Historical Biology* 22, 327–340.

Mihlbachler, M.C., Rivals, F., Solounias, N. and Semprebon, G.M. (2011). Dietary change and evolution of horses in North America. *Science* 331(6021), 1178–1181.

Miller, D.G.M. (1979). Daily basking patterns of the fresh-water turtle. *South African Journal of Zoology* 14, 139–142.

Miller, E.R., Benefit, B.R., McCrossin, M.L., et al. (2009). Systematics of early and middle Miocene Old World monkeys. *Journal of Human Evolution* 57, 195–211.

Miller, E.R., Gunnell, G.F., Abdel Gawad, M.K., et al. (2014). Anthracotheres from Wadi Moghra, Early Miocene, Egypt. *Journal of Paleontology* 88, 967–981.

Miller, J.H., Behrensmeyer, A.K., Du, A., et al. (2014). Ecological fidelity of functional traits based on species presence–absence in a modern mammalian bone assemblage (Amboseli, Kenya). *Paleobiology* 40, 560–583.

Miller, J.M., Hallager, S., Monfort, S.L., et al. (2011). Phylogeographic analysis of nuclear and mtDNA supports subspecies designations in the ostrich (*Struthio camelus*). *Conservation Genetics* 12, 423–431.

Miller, K.G., Fairbanks, R.G. and Mountain, G.S. (1987) Tertiary oxygen isotope synthesis, sea level history, and continental margin erosion. *Paleoceanography* 2(1), 1–19.

Milne, G. (1935). Some suggested units of classification and mapping, particularly for East African soils. *Soil Research* 4, 183–198.

Milne, G. (1947). A soil reconnaissance journey through parts of Tanganyika Territory December 1935 to February 1936. *Journal of Ecology* 35, 192–265.

Mitchell, P. (2002). *The Archaeology of Southern Africa*. Cambridge: Cambridge University Press.

Moehlman, P.D., Kebede, F. and Yohannes, H. (2015). Equus africanus. The IUCN Red List of Threatened Species 2015, e.T7949A451070994.

Moggi-Cecchi, J. (2003). The elusive'second species' in Sterkfontein Member 4: the dental metrical evidence: research articles: human origins research in South Africa. *South African Journal of Science* 99(5–6), 268–270.

Moggi-Cecchi, J., Menter, C., Boccone, S. and Keyser, A. (2010). Early hominin dental remains from the Plio-Pleistocene site of Drimolen, South Africa. *Journal of Human Evolution* 58, 374–405.

Mohr, P. (1999). Le système des rifts Africains. Environnement géologique et géographique. In: A. Gallay (Ed.), *Comment l'Homme? A la découverte des premiers hominidés d'Afrique de l'Est*. Paris: Errance, pp. 231–288.

Mokokwe, W.D. (2006). Goldsmith's: Preliminary Study of a newly discovered Pleistocene site near Sterkfontein. Unpublished PhD thesis, University of the Witwatersrand.

Mokokwe, D.W. (2016). Taxonomy, taphonomy and spatial distribution of the cercopithecoid postcranial fossils from Sterkfontein caves. Doctoral dissertation, University of the Witwatersrand.

Moleón, M., Sánchez-Zapata, J.A., Margalida, A., et al. (2014). Humans and scavengers: the evolution of interactions and ecosystem services. *BioScience* 64, 394–403.

Mollel, G.F. (2007). Petrochemistry and geochemistry of Ngorongoro volcanic highland complex (NVHC) and its relationship to Laetoli and Olduvai Gorge, Tanzania. PhD dissertation, Rutgers University, New Brunswick, NJ.

Mollel, G.F. and Swisher III, C.C. (2012). The Ngorongoro Volcanic Highland and its relationships to volcanic deposits at Olduvai Gorge and East African Rift volcanism. *Journal of Human Evolution* 63, 274–283.

Mollel, G., Swisher, C., Feigenson, M. and Carr, M.J. (2008). Geochemical evolution of Ngorongoro Caldera, Northern Tanzania: implications for crust–magma interaction. *Earth and Planetary Science Letters* 271, 337–347.

Mollel, G., Swisher, C., Feigenson, M. and Carr, M.J. (2009). Petrogenesis of basalt-trachyte lavas from Olmoti crater, Tanzania. *Journal of African Earth Sciences* 54, 127–143.

Mollel, G.F., Swisher III, C.C., McHenry, L.J., Feigenson, M.D. and Carr, M.J. (2011). Petrology, geochemistry and age of Satiman, Lemagurut and Oldeani: sources of the volcanic deposits of the Laetoli area. In: T. Harrison (Ed.), *Paleontology and Geology of Laetoli, Tanzania: Human Evolution in Context. Volume 1: Geology, Geochronology, Paleoecology and Paleoenvironment*. Dordrecht: Springer, pp. 99–119.

Molnar, P., England, P. and Martinod, J. (1993). Mantle dynamics, uplift of the Tibetan Plateau, and the Indian Monsoon. *Reviews of Geophysics* 31, 357–396.

Molnar, P., Boos, W.R. and Battisti, D.S. (2010). Orographic controls on climate and paleoclimate of Asia: thermal and mechanical roles for the Tibetan Plateau. *Annual Review of Earth and Planetary Sciences* 38, 77–102.

Monchot, H. and Aouraghe, H. (2009). Deciphering the taphonomic history of an Upper Paleolithic faunal assemblage from Zouhrah Cave/El Harhoura 1, Morocco. *Quaternaire* 20, 239–253.

Monson, T.A., Brasil, M.F. and Hlusko, L.J. (2015). Materials collected by the southern branch of the UC Africa Expedition with a report on previously unpublished Plio-Pleistocene fossil localities. *Paleobios* 32(1).

Moore, T., Loutit, T. and Greenlee, S. (1987). Estimating short-term changes in Eustatic sea level. *Paleoceanography* 2(6), 625–637.

Moorjani, P., Amorim, C.E.G., Arndt, P.F. and Przeworski, M. (2016). Variation in the molecular clock of primates. *Proceedings of the National Academy of Sciences* 113(38), 10607–10612.

Mora, R., Domínguez-Rodrigo, M., de la Torre, I., Luque, L. and Alcalá, L. (2003). The archaeology of the Peninj "ST Complex" (Lake Natron, Tanzania). In: J. Martínez-Moreno, R. Mora and I. de la Torre (Eds.), *Oldowan: Rather More than Smashing Stones. First Hominid Technology Workshop*. Bellaterra, December 2001. Barcelona: Treballs d'Arqueologia, 9, 77–116.

Morales, J. and Pickford, M. (2005). Carnivores from the Middle Miocene Ngorora Formation (13–12 Ma), Kenya. *Estudios Geológicos* 61, 271–284.

Morales, J. and Pickford, M. (2006). A large percrocutid carnivore from the Late Miocene (ca. 10–9 Ma) of Nakali, Kenya. *Annales de Paléontologie* 92, 359–366.

Morales, J., Brewer, P. and Pickford, M. (2010). Carnivores (Creodonta and Carnivora) from the basal middle Miocene of Gebel Zelten, Libya, with a note on a large amphicyonid from the middle Miocene of Ngorora, Kenya. *Bulletin of the Tethys Geological Society* 5, 43–54.

Morales, J., Cantalapiedra, J. L., Valenciano, A., et al. (2015). The fossil record of the Neogene carnivore mammals from Spain. *Palaeobiodiversity and Palaeoenvironments* 95(3), 373–386.

Morgan, L.E., Renne, P.R., Kieffer, G., et al. (2012). A chronological framework for a long and persistent archaeological record: Melka Kunture, Ethiopia. *Journal of Human Evolution* 62, 104–115.

Morgan, M.E., Kingston, J.D. and Marino, B.D. (1994). Carbon isotopic evidence for the emergence of C_4 plants in the Neogene from Pakistan and Kenya. *Nature* 367(6459), 162–165.

Morison, C.G.T., Hoyle, A.C. and Hope-Simpson, J.F. (1948). Tropical soil–vegetation catenas and mosaics: a study in the south-western part of the Anglo-Egyptian Sudan. *Journal of Ecology* 36(1), 1–84.

Morley, R.J. (2000). *Origin and Evolution of Tropical Rain Forests*. New York: John Wiley & Sons.

Morley, R.J. and Kingdon, J. (2013). Africa's environmental and climatic past. In: J. Kingdon, D. Happold, M. Hoffmann, et al. (Eds.) *Mammals of Africa. Volume I: Introductory Chapters and Afrotheria*. London: Bloomsbury Publishing, pp. 43–56.

Morley, R.J. and Richards, K. (1993). Gramineae cuticle: a key indicator of Late Cenozoic climatic change in the Niger Delta. *Review of Paleobotany and Palynology* 77, 119–127.

Morlo, M., Miller, E.R. and El-Barkooky, A.N. (2007). Creodonta and Carnivora from Wadi Moghra, Egypt. *Journal of Vertebrate Paleontology* 27, 145–159.

Morlo, M., Miller, E.R., Bastl, K., et al. (2019). New Amphicyonids (Mammalia, Carnivora) from Moghra, Early Miocene, Egypt. *Geodiversitas* 41, 731–745.

Morris, S.F. (1976). A new fossil freshwater crab from the Ngorora Formation (Miocene) of Kenya. *Bulletin of the British Museum (Natural History) Geology* 27, 295–300.

Morton, W.H., Rex, D.C., Mitchell, J.G. and Mohr, P. (1979). Riftward younging of volcanic units in the Addis Ababa region, Ethiopian rift valley. *Nature* 280, 284–288.

Mourer-Chauviré, C. (2016). Les Oiseaux. In: J.-P. Raynal and A. Mohib (Eds.), *Préhistoire de Casablanca. 1 – La Grotte des Rhinocéros (fouilles 1991 et 1996). Villes et Sites Archéologiques du Maroc, volume 6*. Rabat: Ministère de la Culture, INSAP, pp. 89–90.

Mourer-Chauviré, C. and Geraads, D. (2008). The Struthionidae and Pelagornithidae (Aves: Struthioniformes, Odontopterygiformes) from the late Pliocene of Ahl Al Oughlam, Morocco. *Oryctos* 7, 169–194.

Mourer-Chauviré, C. and Geraads, D. (2010). The upper Pliocene avifauna of Ahl al Oughlam, Morocco. Systematics and biogeography. *Records of the Australian Museum* 62(1), 157–184.

Moussa, A., Novello, A., Lebatard, A.-E., et al. (2016). Lake Chad sedimentation and environments during the late Miocene and Pliocene: new evidence from mineralogy and chemistry of the Bol core sediments. *Journal of African Earth Sciences* 118, 192–204.

Moyà-Solà, S., Agustí, J. and Pons, J. (1984). The Mio-Pliocene insular faunas from the west Mediterranean origin and distribution factors. *Paléobiologie continentale* 14(2), 347–357.

Mucina, L. and Rutherford, M.C. (2006). *The Vegetation of South Africa, Lesotho and Swaziland. Strelitzia, vol. 19*. Pretoria: South African National Biodiversity Institute.

Mucina, L., Rutherford, M.C. and Powrie, L.W. (2006). Vegetation atlas of South Africa, Lesotho and Swaziland. In: L. Mucina and M.C. Rutherford (Eds.), *The Vegetation of South Africa, Lesotho and Swaziland*. Pretoria: South African National Biodiversity Institute, pp. 748–789.

Mulholland, S.C. (1989). Phytolith shape frequencies in North Dakota grasses: a comparison to general patterns. *Journal of Archaeological Science* 16, 489–511.

Mullin, S.K., Pillay, N. and Taylor, P.J. (2005). The distribution of the water rat *Dasymys* (Muridae) in Africa: a review. *South African Journal of Science* 101(3), 117–124.

Musiba, C.M. (1999). Laetoli Pliocene paleoecology: a reanalysis via morphological and behavioral approaches. PhD dissertation, University of Chicago, Chicago.

Musiba, C., Magori, C., Stoller, M., et al. (2007). Taphonomy and paleoecological context of the Upper Laetolil Beds (Localities 8 and 9), Laetoli in northern Tanzania. In: R. Bobe, Z. Alemseged and A.K. Behrensmeyer (Eds.), *Hominin Environments in the East African Pliocene: An Assessment of the Faunal Evidence*. Dordrecht: Springer, pp. 257–278.

Musiba, C.M., Mabulla, A., Selvaggio, M. and Magori, C.C. (2008). Pliocene animal trackways at Laetoli: research and conservation potential. *Ichnos* 15, 166–178.

Mussi, M., Altamura, F., Macchiarelli, R., Melis, R.T. and Spinapolice, E. (2014). Garba III (Melka Kunture, Ethiopia): a MSA site with archaic *Homo sapiens* remains revisited. *Quaternary International* 343, 28–39.

Mussi, M., Altamura, F., Di Bianco, L., et al. (2021). After the emergence of the Acheulean at Melka Kunture (Upper Awash, Ethiopia): from Gombore IB (1.6 Ma) to Gombore Iγ (1.4 Ma), Gombore Iδ (1.3 Ma) and Gombore II OAM Test Pit C (1.2 Ma). *Quaternary International*. DOI 10.1016/j.quaint.2021.02.031

Mutakyahwa, M. (1997). Mineralogy of the Wembere-Manonga Formation, Manonga Valley, Tanzania, and the possible provenance of the sediments. In: T. Harrison (Ed.), *Neogene Paleontology of the Manonga Valley, Tanzania*. New York: Plenum, pp. 67–78.

Myers, N., Mittermeier, R.A., Mittermeier, C.G., de Fonesca, G.A.B. and Kent, J. (2000). Biodiversity hotspots for conservation priorities. *Nature* 403, 853–858.

Nagaoka, S., Katoh, S., WoldeGabriel, G., et al. (2005). Lithostratigraphy and sedimentary environments of the hominid-bearing Pliocene–Pleistocene Konso Formation in the southern Main Ethiopian Rift, Ethiopia. *Palaeogeography, Palaeoclimatology, Palaeoecology* 216, 333–457.

Naidoo, J. (1987). The siege of Makapansgat: a massacre? And a Trekker victory? *History in Africa* 14, 173–187.

Nakatsukasa, M., Mbua, E., Sawada, Y., et al. (2010). Earliest colobine skeletons from Nakali, Kenya. *American Journal of Physical Anthropology* 143, 365–382.

Nakaya, H., Pickford, M., Yasui, K. and Nakano, Y. (1987). Additional large mammalian fauna from the Namurungule Formation, Samburu Hills, northern Kenya. *African Study Monographs, Supplementary Issue* 5, 47–98.

Nami, H.G., de la Peña, P., Vásquez, C.A., Feathers, J. and Wurz, S. (2016). Palaeomagnetic results and new dates of sedimentary deposits from Klasies River Cave 1, South Africa. *South African Journal of Science*, 112(11–12), 1–12.

NASA Earth Observatory (2004). Topography of Olduvai Gorge, East Africa. http://earthobservatory.nasa.gov/IOTD/view.php?id=4705.

Nash, D.J. and Endfield, G.H. (2002). A 19th century climate chronology for the Kalahari region of central southern Africa derived from missionary correspondence. *International Journal of Climatology* 22, 821–841.

Ndessokia, P.N.S. (1987). Paleofauna composition and paleoenvironment of Peninj (Marita-Nane site) in West Lake Natron basin, Northern Tanzania. *Sciences Géologiques, Bulletins et Memoires* 40, 203–208.

Ndessokia, P.N.S. (1990). The mammalian fauna and archaeology of the Ndolanya and Olpiro Beds, Laetoli, Tanzania. PhD dissertation, University of California, Berkeley.

Negash, E.W., Alemseged, Z., Wynn, J.G. and Bedaso, Z.K. (2015). Paleodietary reconstruction using stable isotopes and abundance analysis of bovids from the Shungura Formation of South Omo, Ethiopia. *Journal of Human Evolution* 88, 127–136.

Negash, E.W., Alemseged Z., Bobe R., et al. (2020). Dietary trends in herbivores from the Shungura Formation, southwestern Ethiopia. *Proceedings of the National Academy of Science* 117(36), 21921–21927.

Nel, T.H. and Henshilwood, C.S. (2016). The small mammal sequence from the c. 76–72 ka still bay levels at Blombos Cave, South Africa – Taphonomic and Palaeoecological implications for human behaviour. *PLoS ONE* 11(8).

Nel, T.H., Wurz, S. and Henshilwood, C.S. (2018). Small mammals from marine isotope stage 5 at Klasies River, South Africa – reconstructing the local palaeoenvironment. *Quaternary International* 471, 6–20.

Nespoulet, R., El Hajraoui, M.A., Amani, F., et al. (2008). Palaeolithic and Neolithic occupations in the Temara region (Rabat, Morocco): recent data on hominin contexts and behavior. *African Archaeological Review* 25, 21–39.

Neukirchen, F., Finkenbein, T. and Keller, J. (2010). The lava sequence of the East African Rift escarpment in the Oldoinyo Lengai–Lake Natron sector, Tanzania. *Journal of African Earth Sciences* 58, 734–751.

Newham, E., Benson, R., Upchurch, P., Goswami, A. (2014). Mesozoic mammaliaform diversity: the effect of sampling corrections on reconstructions of evolutionary dynamics. *Palaeogeography, Palaeoclimatology, Palaeoecology* 412, 32–44.

Nicholson, K.E. (2003). Palaeoenvironment and palaeoecology at Kanjera North: the isotopic evidence. MSc thesis (unpublished), University of Oxford.

Nicholson, S.E. (2000). The nature of rainfall variability over Africa on time scales of decades to millennia. *Global and Planetary Change* 26(1–3), 137–158.

Nicholson, S.E., Kim, J., Ba, M.B. and Lare, A.R. (1997). The mean surface water balance over Africa and its interannual variability. *Journal of Climate* 10, 2981–3002.

Nigro, J.D., Ungar, P.S. de Ruiter, D.J. and Berger, L.R. (2003). Developing a geographic information system (GIS) for mapping and analyzing fossil deposits at Swartkrans, Gauteng Province, South Africa. *Journal of Archeological Science* 30, 317–324.

Njau, J.K. (2006). The relevance of crocodile to Oldowan hominin paleoecology at Olduvai Gorge, Tanzania. Doctoral dissertation, Rutgers, the State University of New Jersey, New Brunswick.

Njau, J.K. (2012a). *Crocodile Predation and Hominin Evolution: Landscape Paleoanthropology at Olduvai Gorge*. Saarbrücken: Lambert Academic Publishing.

Njau, J.K. (2012b). Reading Pliocene bones. *Science* 336, 46–47.

Njau, J.K. and Blumenschine, R.J. (2006). A diagnosis of crocodile feeding traces on larger mammal bone, with fossil examples from the Plio-Pleistocene Olduvai Basin, Tanzania. *Journal of Human Evolution* 50, 142–162.

Njau, J.K. and Blumenschine, R.J. (2012). Crocodylian and mammalian carnivore feeding traces on hominid fossils from FLK 22 and FLK NN 3, Plio-Pleistocene, Olduvai Gorge, Tanzania. *Journal of Human Evolution* 63, 408–417.

Njau, J.K., Stanistreet, I., McHenry, L.J., et al. (2015). *New Investigations on Hominin Paleolandscapes, Paleoenvironments and Paleoclimates through Scientific Drilling at Olduvai Gorge, Tanzania*. Baltimore, MD: Geological Society of America (GSA).

Norton-Griffiths, M., Herlocker, D. and Pennycuick, L. (1975). The patterns of rainfall in the Serengeti Ecosystem, Tanzania. *African Journal of Ecology* 13, 347–374.

Novello, A., Barboni, D., Sylvestre, F., et al. (2017). Phytoliths indicate significant arboreal cover at *Sahelanthropus* type locality TM266 in northern Chad and a decrease in later sites. *Journal of Human Evolution* 106, 66–83.

Oakley, K.P., Campbell, B.G. and Molleson, T.I. (1975). *Catalogue of Fossil Hominids (Vol. 2)*. London: British Museum (Natural History).

Occhietti, S., Raynal, J.-P., Pichet, P. and Lefèvre, D. (2002). Aminostratigraphie des formations littorales pléistocènes et holocènes de la région de Casablanca, Maroc. *Quaternaire* 13, 55–63.

Odes, E.J., Parkinson, A.H., Randolph-Quinney, P.S., et al. (2017). Osteopathology and insect traces in the *Australopithecus africanus* skeleton StW 431. *South African Journal of Science* 113(1–2), 1–7.

Ogola, C.A. (2009). The Sterkfontein western breccias: statigraphy, fauna and artefacts. Doctoral dissertation, University of the Witwatersrand.

O'Leary, M.H. (1988). Carbon isotopes in photosynthesis. *Bioscience* 38(5), 328–336.

Oliver, J.S. (1994). Estimates of hominid and carnivore involvement in the FLK-Zinjanthropus fossil assemblage: some socioecological implications. *Journal of Human Evolution* 27, 267–294.

Oliver, J.S., Plummer, T.W., Hertel, F. and Bishop, L.C. (2019). Bovid mortality patterns from Kanjera South, Homa Peninsula, Kenya and FLK-Zinj, Olduvai Gorge, Tanzania: evidence for habitat mediated variability in Oldowan hominin hunting and scavenging behavior. *Journal of Human Evolution* 131, 61–75.

Opperman, H. (1978). Excavations in the Buffelskloof rock shelter near Calitzdorp, Southern Cape. *South African Archaeological Bulletin* 33, 18–38.

O'Regan, H.J. and Reynolds, S.C. (2009). An ecological reassessment of the southern Africa carnivore guild: a case study from Member 4, Sterkfontein, South Africa. *Journal of Human Evolution* 57, 212–222.

O'Regan, H.J., Bishop, L.C., Lamb, A., Elton, S. and Turner, A. (2005). Large mammal turnover in Africa and the Levant between 1.0 and 0.5 Ma. In: M.J. Head and P.L. Gibbard (Eds.), *Early–Middle Pleistocene Transitions: The Land–Ocean Evidence*. Geological Society Special Publications, 247. London: Royal Geological Society, pp. 231–349.

O'Regan, H.J., Kuman, K. and Clarke, R.J. (2011a). The likely accumulators of bones: five Cape porcupine den assemblages and the role of porcupines in the Post-Member 6 Infill at Sterkfontein, South Africa. *Journal of Taphonomy* 9(2), 69–87.

O'Regan, H.J., Turner, A., Bishop, L.C., Elton, S. and Lamb, A.L. (2011b). Hominins without fellow travellers? First appearances and inferred dispersals of Afro-Eurasian large-mammals in the Plio-Pleistocene. *Quaternary Science Review* 30, 1343–1352.

O'Regan, H.J., Cohen, B.F. and Steininger, C.M. (2013). Mustelid and viverrid remains from the Pleistocene site of Cooper's D, Gauteng, South Africa. *Palaeontologica Africana* 48, 19–23.

Otero, O., Pinton, A., Mackaye, H.T., et al. (2009). Fishes and palaeogeography of the African drainage basins: relationships between Chad and neighbouring basins throughout the Mio-Pliocene. *Palaeogeography, Palaeoclimatology, Palaeoecology* 274, 134–139.

Otero, O., Pinton, A., Mackaye, H.T., et al. (2010). The early/late Pliocene ichthyofauna from Koro-Toro, Eastern Djurab, Chad. *Geobios* 43, 241–251.

Otero, O., Lécuyer, C., Fourel, F., et al. (2011) Freshwater fish $\delta 18O$ indicates a Messinian change of the precipitation regime in Central Africa. *Geology* 39(5), 435–438.

Owen, D.F. (1965). A populational study of an Equatorial land snail, *Limicolaria martensiana* (Achatinidae). *Proceedings of the Zoological Society of London* 144, 361–382.

Owen, R.B. and Renaut, R.W. (1986). Sedimentology, stratigraphy and palaeoenvironments of the Holocene Galana Boi Formation, NE Lake Turkana, Kenya. *Geological Society, London, Special Publications* 25, 311.

Owen, R.B., Potts, R., Behrensmeyer, A.K., Ditchfield, P. (2008). Diatomaceous sediments and environmental change in the Pleistocene Olorgesailie Formation, southern Kenya Rift Valley. *Palaeogeography, Palaeoclimatology, Palaeoecology* 269, 17–37.

Owen, R.B., Renaut, R.W., Scott, J.J., Potts, R. and Behrensmeyer, A.K. (2009). Wetland sedimentation and associated diatoms in the Pleistocene Olorgesailie Basin, southern Kenya Rift Valley. *Sedimentary Geology* 222, 124–137.

Owen-Smith, R.N. (1988). *Megaherbivores: The Influence of Very Large Body Size on Ecology*. Cambridge: Cambridge University Press.

Pallas, L., Daver, G., Mackaye, H.T., et al. (2019). A window into the early evolutionary history of Cercopithecidae: Late Miocene evidence from Chad, Central Africa. *Journal of Human Evolution* 132, 61–79.

Palmqvist, P., Pérez-Claros, J.A., Janis, C.M. and Gröcke, D.R. (2008). Tracing the ecophysilogy of ungulates and predator–prey relationships in an early Pleistocene large mammal community. *Palaeogeography, Palaeoclimatology, Palaeoecology* 266, 95–111.

Paquet, H. (1970). Evolution géochimique des minéraux argileux dans les altérations et les sols des climats méditérranéens et tropicaux à saisons contrastées. *Bulletin et Memoires du Service de la Carte Geologique d'Alsace et de Lorraine* 30, 1–210.

Pante, M.C. and Blumenschine, R.J. (2010). Fluvial transport of bovid long bones fragmented by the feeding activities of hominins and carnivores. *Journal of Archaeological Science* 37, 846–854.

Pante, M.C., Blumenschine, R.J., Capaldo, S.D. and Scott, R.S. (2012). Validation of bone surface modification models for inferring fossil hominin and carnivore feeding interactions, with reapplication to FLK 22, Olduvai Gorge, Tanzania. *Journal of Human Evolution* 63, 395–407.

Pante, M.C., Blumenschine, R.J., Capaldo, S.D. and Scott, R.S. (2015). Revalidation of bone surface modification models for inferring fossil hominin and carnivore feeding interactions. *Quaternary International* 355, 164–168.

Parker, J., Hopley, P.J. and Kuhn, B.F. (2016). Fossil carder bee's nest from the hominin locality of Taung, South Africa. *PLoS ONE* 11(9), e0161198.

Parkington, J.E. (1972). Seasonal mobility in the late Stone Age. *African Studies* 31, 223–44.

Parkington, J.E. (1976). Coastal settlement between the mouths of the Berg and the Olifants rivers, Cape Province. *South African Archaeological Bulletin* 31, 127–140.

Parkington, J.E. (1980). The Elands Bay cave sequence: cultural stratigraphy and subsistence strategies. In *Proceedings of the 8th Pan-African Congress of Prehistory and Quaternary Studies*. Nairobi: International Louis Leakey Memorial Institute for African Prehistory, pp. 315–320.

Parkington, J.E. (1981). The effects of environmental change on the scheduling of visits to the Elands Bay Cave, Cape Province, South Africa. In: I. Hodder, G. Isaac and N. Hammond (Eds.), *Pattern of the Past: Studies in Honour of David Clarke*. Cambridge: Cambridge University Press, pp. 341–359.

Parkington, J.E. (1987). Changing views of prehistoric settlement in the western Cape. In: *Papers in the Prehistory of the Western Cape, South Africa*, Vol. 322. Oxford: British Archaeological Reports, pp. 4–23.

Parkington, J.E. and Poggenpoel, C. (1987). Diepkloof rock shelter. In: J.E. Parkington and M. Hall, (Eds.), *Papers in the Prehistory of the Western Cape, South Africa*, Vol. 332. Oxford: British Archaeological Reports, pp. 269–293.

Parkington, J., Cartwright, C., Cowling, R.M. and Baxter, A. (2000). Africa: wood charcoal and pollen TS evidence from Elands Bay Cave. *South African Journal of Science* 96, 543.

Parkinson, A.H. (2016). Traces of insect activity at Cooper's D fossil site (Cradle of Humankind, South Africa). *Ichnos* 23(3–4), 322–339.

Parkinson, J. (2013). A GIS Image analysis approach to documenting Oldowan hominin carcass acquisition: evidence from Kanjera South, FLK Zinj, and neotaphonomic models of carnivore bone destruction. PhD dissertation, City University of New York.

Parravicini, A. and Pievani, T. (2016). Multi-level human evolution: ecological patterns in hominin phylogeny. *Journal of Anthropological Sciences* 94, 1–16.

Partridge, T.C. (1973). Geomorphological dating of cave openings at Makapansgat, Sterkfontein, Swartkrans and Taung. *Nature* 246, 75–79.

Partridge, T.C. (1975). Stratigraphic, geomorphological and palaeoenvironmental studies of the Makapansgat Limeworks and Sterkfontein hominid sites: a progress report on research carried out between 1965 and 1975. In: Conference Report on Recent Progress in Later Cenozoic Studies in Southern Africa, Cape Town.

Partridge, T.C. (1978). Re-appraisal of lithostratigraphy of Sterkfontein hominid site. *Nature* 275(5678), 282–287.

Partridge, T.C. (1979). Re-appraisal of lithostratigraphy of Makapansgat Limeworks hominid site. *Nature* 279(5713), 484–488.

Partridge, T.C. (1982). Some preliminary observations on the stratigraphy and sedimentology of the Kromdraai B hominid site. In: J.A. Coetzee and E.M. Van Zinderen Bakker (Eds.), *Palaeoecology of Africa and the Surrounding Islands*, Vol. 15. Rotterdam: Balkema, pp. 3–12.

Partridge, T.C. (1985). Spring flow and tufa accretion at Taung. In: P.V. Tobias (Ed.), *Hominid Evolution Past, Present and Future*. New York: Alan R. Liss, pp. 171–187.

Partridge, T.C. (2000). Hominid-bearing cave and tufa deposits. In: T.C. Partridge and R.R. Maud (Eds.), *The Cenozoic of Southern Africa*. Oxford: Oxford University Press, pp. 100–130.

Partridge, T.C. (2005). Dating of the Sterkfontein hominids: progress and possibilities. *Transactions of the Royal Society of South Africa* 60(2), 107–110.

Partridge, T.C. (2010). Tectonics and geomorphology of Africa during the Phanerozoic. In: L. Werdelin and W.J. Sanders (Eds.), *Cenozoic Mammals of Africa*. Berkeley: University of California Press, pp. 3–17.

Partridge, T.C. and Maud, R.R. (1987). Geomorphic evolution of southern Africa since the Mesozoic. *South African Journal of Geology* 90, 179–208.

Partridge, T.C., Bollen, J., Tobias, P.V. and McKee, J.K. (1991). New light on the provenance of the Taung Skull. *South African Journal of Science* 87, 80–83.

Partridge, T.C., deMenocal, P.B., Lorentz, S., Paiker, M.J. and Vogel, J.C. (1997). Orbital forcing of climate over South Africa: a 200,000-year rainfall record from the Pretoria Saltpan. *Quaternary Science Reviews* 16, 1125–1133.

Partridge, T.C., Shaw, J., Heslop, D. and Clarke, R.J. (1999). The new hominid skeleton from Sterkfontein, South Africa: age and preliminary assessment. *Journal of Quaternary Science* 14(4), 293–298.

Partridge, T.C., Granger, D.E., Caffee, M.W. and Clarke, R.J. (2003). Lower Pliocene hominid remains from Sterkfontein. *Science* 300, 607–612.

Passey, B.H., Cerling, T.E., Perkins, M.E., et al. (2002). Environmental change in the Great Plains: an isotopic record from fossil horses. *Journal of Geology* 110, 123–140.

Passey, B.H., Robinson, T.F., Ayliffe, L.K., et al. (2005). Carbon isotope fractionation between diet, breath CO_2, and bioapatite in different mammals. *Journal of Archaeological Science* 32, 1459–1470.

Passey, B.H., Levin, N.E., Cerling, T.E., Brown, F.H. and Eiler, J.M. (2010). High-temperature environments of human evolution in East Africa based on bond ordering in paleosol carbonates. *Proceedings of the National Academy of Sciences* 107, 11245–11249. doi:10.1073/pnas.1001824107.

Patterson, B. (1966). A new locality for early Pleistocene fossils in north-western Kenya. *Nature* 212, 577–581.

Patterson, B. and Howells, W.W. (1967). Hominid humeral fragment from early Pleistocene of northwestern Kenya. *Science* 156, 64–66.

Patterson, B., Behrensmeyer, A.K. and Sill, W.D. (1970). Geology of a new Pliocene locality in northwestern Kenya. *Nature* 256, 279–284.

Patterson, D.B., Faith, J.T., Bobe, R. and Wood, B. (2014). Regional diversity patterns in African bovids, hyaenids, and felids during the past 3 million years: the role of taphonomic bias and implication for the evolution of *Paranthropus*. *Quaternary Science Reviews* 96, 9–22.

Patterson, D.B., Lehmann, S.B., Matthews, T., et al. (2016). Stable isotope ecology of Cape dune mole-rats (*Bathyergus suillus*) from Elandsfontein, South Africa: Implications for C 4 vegetation and hominin paleobiology in the Cape Floral Region. *Palaeogeography, Palaeoclimatology, Palaeoecology* 457, 409–421.

Patterson, D.B., Braun, D.R., Behrensmeyer, A.K., et al. (2017a). Landscape scale heterogeneity in the East Turkana ecosystem during the Okote Member (1.56–1.38 Ma). *Journal of Human Evolution* 112, 148–161.

Patterson, D.B., Braun, D.R., Behrensmeyer, A.K., et al. (2017b). Ecosystem evolution and hominin paleobiology at East Turkana, northern Kenya between 2.0 and 1.4 Ma. *Palaeogeography, Palaeoclimatology, Palaeoecology* 481, 1–13.

Patterson, D.B., Braun, D.R., Allen, K., et al. (2019). Comparative isotopic evidence from East Turkana supports a dietary shift within the genus *Homo*. *Nature Ecology & Evolution* 3, 1048–1056.

Patterson, N., Richter, D.J., Gnerre, S., Lander, E.S. and Reich, D. (2006). Genetic evidence for complex speciation of humans and chimpanzees. *Nature* 441(7097), 1103–1108.

Pavia, M. (2019). *Geronticus thackerayi*, sp. nov. (Aves, Threskiornithidae), a new ibis from the hominin-bearing locality of Kromdraai (Cradle of Humankind, Gauteng, South Africa). *Journal of Vertebrate Paleontology*, 39(3), e1647433.

Pavia, M., Davies, G.B., Gommery, D. and Kgasi, L. (2017). Mid-Pliocene bald ibis (*Geronticus* cf. *calvus*; Aves: Threskiornithidae) from the Cradle of Humankind, Gauteng, South Africa and its environmental and evolutionary implications. *PalZ*, 91(2), 237–243.

Pavlakis, P.P. (1990). Plio-Pleistocene Hippopotamidae from the upper Semliki. In: N.T. Boaz (Ed.), *Evolution of Environments and Hominidae in the African Western Rift Valley*. Martinsville: Virginia Museum of Natural History.

Payne, S. (1972). Partial recovery and sample bias: the results of some sieving experiments. In: T.S. Higgs (Ed.), *Papers in Economic Prehistory*. Cambridge: Cambridge University Press, pp. 49–64.

Payne, S. (1975). Partial recovery and sample bias. In: A.T. Clason (Ed.), *Archaeozoological Studies*. Amsterdam: North-Holland Publishing Company, pp. 7–17.

Peabody, F.E. (1954). Travertines and cave deposits of the Kaap Escarpment of South Africa, and the type locality of *Australopithecus africanus* Dart. *Bulletin of the Geological Society of America* 65, 671–706.

Peet, R.K. (1974). The measurement of species diversity. *Annual Review of Ecology and Systematics* 5, 285–307.

Peigné, S., de Bonis, L., Likius, A., et al. (2005a). The earliest modern mongoose (Carnivora, Herpestidae) from Africa (late Miocene of Chad). *Naturwissenschaften* 92, 287–292.

Peigné, S., de Bonis, L., Likius, A., et al. (2005b). A new machairodontine (Carnivora, Felidae) from the Late Miocene

hominid locality of TM 266, Toros-Menalla, Chad. *Comptes Rendus Palevol* 4, 243–253.
Peigné, S., de Bonis, L., Mackaye, H.T., et al. (2008). Late Miocene Carnivora from Chad: Herpestidae, Viverridae and small-sized Felidae. Comptes Rendus Palevol 7, 499–527.
Pennycuick, C.J. and Western, D. (1972). An investigation of some sources of bias in aerial transect sampling of large mammal populations. *African Journal of Ecology* 10, 175–191.
Péringuey L. (1911). The Stone Ages of South Africa as represented in the collections of the South African Museum. *Annals of the South African Museum* 8, 1–218.
Perini, S., Muttoni, G., Monesi, E., Melis, R.T., Mussi, M. (2021). Magnetochronology and age models of deposition of the Melka Kunture stratigraphic sequence (Upper Awash, Ethiopia) and age assessments of the main archeological levels therein contained. *Quaternary Science Reviews* 274, 107259.
Peters, C.R. (1999). African wild plants with rootstocks reported to be eaten raw: the monocotyledons, Part IV. In: J. Timberlake and S. Kativu (Eds.), *African Plants: Biodiversity, Taxonomy and Uses*. Kew: Royal Botanic Gardens, pp. 483–503.
Peters, C.R. (2007). Theoretical and actualistic ecobotanical perspectives on early hominin diets and paleoecology. In: P.S. Ungar (Ed.), *Evolution of the Human Diet*. New York: Oxford University Press, pp. 233–261.
Peters, C.R. and Blumenschine, R.J. (1995). Landscape perspectives on possible land use patterns for Early Pleistocene hominids in the Olduvai Basin, Tanzania. *Journal of Human Evolution* 29, 321–362.
Peters, C.R. and Blumenschine, R.J. (1996). Landscape perspectives on possible land use patterns for early Pleistocene hominids in the Olduvai basin, Tanzania: Part II, expanding the landscape models. *Kaupia* 6, 175–221.
Peters, C.R. and O'Brien, E.M. (2001). Palaeo-Lake Congo: implications for Africa's late Cenozoic climate – some unanswered questions. In: K. Heine and J. Runge (Eds.), *Palaeoecology of Africa and the Surrounding Islands*. Rotterdam: Balkema, pp. 11–18.
Peters, C.R. and Vogel, J.C. (2005). Africa's wild C_4 plant foods and possible early hominid diets. *Journal of Human Evolution* 48, 219–236.
Peters, C.R., Blumenschine, R.J., Hay, R.L., et al. (2008). Paleoecology of the Serengeti–Mara ecosystem. In: A.R.E. Sinclair, C. Packer, S.A.R. Mduma and J.M. Fryxell (Eds.), *Serengeti III: Human Impacts on Ecosystem Dynamics*. Chicago: University of Chicago Press, pp. 47–94.
Peters, J. (1990a). Late Palaeolithic ungulate fauna and landscape in the plain of Kom Ombo. *Sahara* 3, 45–52.
Peters, J. (1990b). Late Pleistocene hunter-gatherers at Ishango (Eastern Zaire): the faunal evidence. *Revue de Paléobiologie* 9, 73–112.
Peters, R.H. and Raelson, J.V. (1984). Relations between individual size and mammalian population density. *The American Naturalist* 124, 498–571.
Petrocchi, C. (1934). I ritrovamenti faunistici di es-Sahabi. *Rivista delle Colonie Italiane* 7, 733–742.
Petter, G. (1963). Étude quelques Viverridés (Mammifères, Carnivores) du Pléistocène inférieur du Tanganyika (Afrique orientale). *Bulletins du Société Géologiques de France, Series 7* 5, 265–274.
Petter, G. (1973). Carnivores pléistocènes du ravin d'Olduvai (Tanzanie). In: L.S.B. Leakey, R.J.G. Savage and S.C. Coryndon (Eds.), *Fossil Vertebrates of Africa*, vol. 3. London: Academic Press, pp. 44–100.
Petter, G. and Howell, F.C. (1988). Nouveau félidé machairodonte (Mammalia, Carnivora) de la faune pliocène de l'Afar (Éthiopie): *Homotherium hadarensis* n. sp. *Comptes Rendus de l'Académie de Sciences, Paris, Série II* 306, 731–738.
Petter, G., Pickford, M. and Senut, B. (1994). Presence of the genus *Agriotherium* (Mammalia, Carnivora, Ursidae) in the Late Miocene of the Nkondo Formation (Uganda, East Africa). *Comptes Rendus de l'Académie de Sciences* 319, 713–717.
Peypouquet, J.P., Carbonel, P., Taieb, M., Tiercelin, J.J. and Perinet, G. (1983). Ostracoda and evolution process of paleohydrologic environments in the Hadar Formation (the Afar depression, Ethiopia). In: R.F. Maddocks (Ed.), *Applications of Ostracoda*. Houston: University of Houston Geosciences, pp. 277–285.
Philander, S.G. and Fedorov, A.V. (2003). Role of tropics in changing the response to Milankovich forcing some three million years ago. *Paleoceanography* 18, 1–12.
Pickering, R. (1969). Regional mapping. 1. The geology of the country around Endulen. *Records of the Geological Survey of Tanganyika* 11, 1–9.
Pickering, R. (2015). U–Pb dating small buried stalagmites from Wonderwerk Cave, South Africa: a new chronometer for earlier Stone Age cave deposits. *The African Archaeological Review* 32(4), 645–668.
Pickering, R. and Kramers, J.D. (2010). Re-appraisal of the stratigraphy and determination of new U–Pb dates for the Sterkfontein hominin site, South Africa. *Journal of Human Evolution* 59(1), 70–86.
Pickering, R., Hancox, P.J., Lee-Thorp, J.A., et al. (2007). Stratigraphy, U–Th chronology, and paleoenvironments at Gladysvale Cave: insights into the climatic control of South African hominin-bearing cave deposits. *Journal of Human Evolution* 53(5), 602–619.
Pickering, R., Kramers, J.D., Partridge, T., Kodolanyi, J. and Pettke, T. (2010). U–Pb dating of calcite–aragonite layers in speleothems from hominin sites in South Africa by MC-ICP-MS. *Quaternary Geochronology* 5, 544–558.
Pickering, R., Kramers, J.D., Hancox, J.P., de Ruiter, D.J. and Woodhead, J.D. (2011). Contemporary flowstone development links early hominin bearing cave deposits in South Africa. *Earth and Planetary Science Letters* 306, 23–32.
Pickering, R., Herries, A.I., Woodhead, J.D., et al. (2019). U–Pb-dated flowstones restrict South African early hominin record to dry climate phases. *Nature* 565(7738), 226.
Pickering, T.R. (1999). Taphonomic interpretations of the Sterkfontein early hominid site (Gauteng, South Africa) reconsidered in light of recent evidence. PhD thesis, Department of Anthropology, University of Wisconsin.
Pickering, T.R. (2002). Reconsideration of criteria for differentiating faunal assemblages accumulated by hyaenas and hominids. *International Journal of Osteoarchaeology* 12, 127–141.
Pickering, T.R. and Egeland, C.P. (2006). Experimental patterns of hammerstone percussion damage on bones: implications for inferences of carcass processing by humans. *Journal of Archaeological Science* 33, 459–469.
Pickering, T.R., White, T.D. and Toth, N. (2000). Cutmarks on a Plio-Pleistocene hominid from Sterkfontein, South Africa. *American Journal of Physical Anthropology* 111, 579–584.
Pickering, T.R., Clarke, R.J. and Heaton, J.L. (2004a). The context of Stw 573, an early hominid skull and skeleton from Sterkfontein Member 2: taphonomy and palaeoenvironment. *Journal of Human Evolution* 46, 277–295.
Pickering, T.R., Clarke, R.J. and Moggi-Cecchi, J. (2004b). The role of carnivores in the accumulation of the Sterkfontein Member 4 hominid fossil assemblage: a taphonomic reassessment of the complete hominid fossil sample (1936–1999). *American Journal of Physical Anthropology* 125, 1–15.
Pickering, T.R., Dominguez-Rodrigo, M., Egeland, C.P. and Brain, C.K. (2005). The contribution of limb bone fracture patterns to reconstructing early hominid behaviour at Swartkrans

Cave (South Africa): archaeological application of a new analytical method. *International Journal of Osteoarchaeology* 14, 247–260.

Pickering, T.R., Egeland, C.P., Dominguez-Rodrigo, M., Brain, C.K. and Schnell, A.G. (2007). Testing the "shift in the balance of power" hypothesis at Swartkrans, South Africa: hominid cave use and subsistence behavior in the early Pleistocene. *Journal of Anthropological Archaeology* 27, 30–45.

Pickering, T.R., Heaton, J.L., Clarke, R.J., et al. (2012). New hominid fossils from Member 1 of the Swartkrans Formation, South Africa. *Journal of Human Evolution* 62, 618–628.

Pickering, T.R., Heaton, J.L., Sutton, M.B., et al. (2016). New early Pleistocene hominin teeth from the Swartkrans formation, South Africa. *Journal of Human Evolution* 100, 1–15.

Pickering, T.R., Heaton, J.L., Throckmorton, Z.J., Prang, T.C. and Brain, C.K. (2017). A burned primate cuboid from Swartkrans Cave, South Africa. *Annals of the Ditsong National Museum of Natural History* 7(1), 1–7.

Pickett, S.T.A., Kolasa, J. and Jones, C.G. (1994). *Ecological Understanding*. San Diego: Academic Press.

Pickford, M.H.L. (1978). Geology, palaeoenvironments and vertebrate faunas of the mid-Miocene Ngorora Formation, Kenya. In: W.W. Bishop (Ed.), *Geological Background to Fossil Man*. Special Publications. Edinburgh: Geological Society of London and Scottish Academic Press, pp. 237–262.

Pickford, M. (1984). *Kenya Palaeontology Gazetteer, Volume 1: Western Kenya*. Nairobi: National Museums of Kenya.

Pickford, M. (1987). The geology and palaeontology of the Kanam erosion gullies (Kenya). *Mainzer Geowissenschaftliche Mitteilungen* 6, 209–226.

Pickford, M. (1990). Révision des Suidés de la Formation Beglia (Tunisie). *Annales de Paléontologie* 76, 133–142.

Pickford, M. (1993). Climate change, biogeography and *Theropithecus*. In: N.G. Jablonski (Ed.), *Theropithecus: The Rise and Fall of a Primate Genus*. Cambridge: Cambridge University Press, pp 227–243.

Pickford, M. (1994a). Patterns of sedimentation and fossil distribution in the Kenya Rift Valleys. *Journal of African Earth Sciences* 18, 51–60.

Pickford, M. (1994b). Fossil Suidae of the Albertine Rift Valley, Uganda–Zaire. In: B. Senut and M. Pickford (Eds.), *Geology and Palaeobiology of the Albertine Rift Valley, Uganda–Zaire*. Palaeobiology-Paléobiologie vol. 2. Occasional Publication. Orléans: CIFEG, pp. 339–373.

Pickford, M. (1994c). A new species of *Prohyrax* (Mammalia, Hyracoidea) from the middle Miocene of Arrisdrift, Namibia. *Communications of the Geological Survey of Namibia* 9, 43–62.

Pickford, M. (1995). Fossil land snails of East Africa and their palaeoecological significance. *Journal of African Earth Sciences* 20, 167–226.

Pickford, M. (2000). Crocodiles from the Beglia Formation, Middle/Late Miocene boundary, Tunisia, and their significance for Saharan palaeoclimatology. *Annales de Paléontologie* 86(1), 59–67.

Pickford, M. (2001a). Equidae in the Ngorora Formation, Kenya, and the first appearance of the family in East Africa. *Revista Española de Paleontología* 16, 339–345.

Pickford, M. (2001b). New species of *Listriodon* (Suidae, Mammalia) from Bartule, Member A, Ngorora Formation (ca 13 Ma), Tugen Hills, Kenya. *Annales de Paléontologie* 87, 207–221.

Pickford, M. (2004). Paleoenvironments of early Miocene hominoid-bearing deposits at Napak, Uganda, based on terrestrial molluscs. *Annals of Paleontology* 90, 1–12.

Pickford, M. (2006). New suoid specimens from Gebel Zelten, Libya. *Estudios Geológicos* 62, 499–514.

Pickford, M. (2008). *Libycosaurus petrocchii* Bonarelli, 1947, and *Libycosaurus anisae* (Black, 1972) (Anthracotheriidae, Mammalia): nomenclatural and geochronological implications. *Annales de Paléontologie* 94, 39–55.

Pickford, M. (2009). Land snails from the early Miocene Legetet Formation, Koru, Kenya. *Geo-Pal Kenya* 2, 1–88.

Pickford, M. (2013a). The diversity, age, biogeographic and phylogenetic relationships of Plio-Pleistocene suids from Kromdraai, South Africa. *Annals of the Ditsong National Museum of Natural History* 3, 11–32.

Pickford, M. (2013b). Locomotion, diet, body weight, origin and geochronology of *Metridiochoerus andrewsi* from the Gondolin karst deposits, Gauteng, South Africa. *Annals of the Ditsong National Museum of Natural History* 3, 33–47.

Pickford, M. (2013c). *Gorongosa Palaeontology Survey*. Gorongosa: Gorongosa National Park, p. 13.

Pickford, M. (2020). The Fossil Suidae (Mammalia, Artiodactyla) from Ternifine (Tighenif) Algeria. *Münchner Geowissenschaftliche Abhandlungen* A 50, 1–66.

Pickford, M. and Fischer, M.S. (1987). *Parapliohyrax ngororaensis*, a new hyracoid from the Miocene of Kenya, with an outline of the classification of Neogene Hyracoidea. *Neues Jahrbuch für Geologie und Paläontologie, Abhandlungen* 175, 207–234.

Pickford, M. and Gommery, D. (2016). Fossil Suidae (Artiodactyla, Mammalia) from Aves Cave I and nearby sites in Bolt's Farm Palaeokarst System, South Africa. *Estudios Geologicos-Madrid* 72(2), e059.

Pickford, M. and Gommery, D. (2020). Fossil suids from Bolt's Farm Palaeokarst System, South Africa: implications for the taxonomy of *Potamochoeroides* and *Notochoerus* and for biochronology. *Estudios Geologicos-Madrid* 76(1), 127.

Pickford, M. and Morales, J. (1994). Biostratigraphy and palaeobiogeography of East Africa and the Iberian Peninsula. *Palaeogeography, Palaeoclimatology, Palaeoecology* 112(3–4), 297–322.

Pickford, M. and Senut, B. (1994). Palaeobiology of the Albertine Rift Valley: general conclusions and synthesis. In: B. Senut and M. Pickford (Eds.), *Geology and Palaeobiology of the Albertine Rift Valley, Uganda-Zaire, Vol. II, Palaeobiology*. Publication Occasionelle. Orléans: Centre International pour la Formation et les Echanges Géologiques – CIFEG, pp. 409–423.

Pickford, M. and Senut, B. (1997). Cainozoic mammals from coastal Namaqualand, South Africa. *Palaeontologia Africana* 34, 199–217.

Pickford, M. and Senut, B. (2001a). 'Millennium Ancestor', a 6-million-year-old bipedal hominid from Kenya – recent discoveries push back human origins by 1.5 million years. *South African Journal of Science*, 97(1–2), 22–22.

Pickford, M. and Senut, B. (2001b). The geological and faunal context of Late Miocene hominid remains from Lukeino, Kenya. *Comptes Rendus de l'Académie des Sciences-Series IIA – Earth and Planetary Science* 332(2), 145–152.

Pickford, M. and Senut, B. (2005). Hominoid teeth with chimpanzee- and gorilla-like features from the Miocene of Kenya: implications for the chronology of ape-human divergence and biogeography of Miocene hominoids. *Anthropological Science* 113(1), 95–102.

Pickford, M., Johanson, D.C., Lovejoy, C.O., White, T.D. and Aronson, J.L. (1983). A hominoid humeral fragment from the Pliocene of Kenya. *American Journal of Physical Anthropology* 60, 337–346.

Pickford, M., Ishida, H., Nakano, Y. and Yasui, K. (1987). Fossil terrestrial gastropods from the Namurungule Formation, Kenya. *African Study Monographs, Supplementary Issue* 5, 155–156.

Pickford, M., Mein, P. and Senut, B. (1992). Primate bearing Plio-Pleistocene cave deposits of Humpata, southern Angola. *Human Evolution* 7(1), 17–33.

Pickford, M., Senut, B. and Hadoto, D. (1993). *Geology and palaeobiology of the Albertine Rift Valley, Uganda-Zaire, Vol. I, Geology*. Publication Occasionelle. Orléans: Centre International pour la Formation et les Echanges Géologiques – CIFEG, p. 190.

Pickford, M., Mein, P. and Senut, B. (1994). Fossiliferous Neogene karst fillings in Angola, Botswana and Namibia. *South African Journal of Science* 90, 227–227.

Pickford, M., Senut, B. and Mourer-Chauvire, C. (2004). Early Pliocene Tragulidae and peafowls in the Rift Valley, Kenya: evidence for rainforest in East Africa. *Comptes Rendus Palevol* 3, 179–189.

Pickford, M., Wanas, H. and Soliman, H. (2006). Indications for a humid climate in the Western Desert of Egypt 11–10 Myr ago: evidence from Galagidae (Primates, Mammalia). *Comptes Rendus Palevol* 5(8), 935–943.

Pickford, M., Coppens, Y., Senut, B., Morales, J. and Braga, J. (2009). Late Miocene hominoid from Niger. *Comptes Rendus Palevol* 8, 413–425.

Pickford, M., Miller, E.R. and El-Barkooky, A.N. (2010). Suidae and Sanitheriidae from Wadi Moghra, early Miocene, Egypt. *Acta Palaeontologica Polonica* 55, 1–11.

Pik, R., Marty, B., Carignan, J. and Lavé, J. (2003). Stability of the Upper Nile drainage network (Ethiopia) deduced from (U–Th)/He thermochronometry: implications for uplift and erosion of the Afar plume dome. *Earth and Planetary Science Letters* 215(1), 73–88.

Pilbeam, D. (1974). Hominid-bearing deposits at Kanjera, Nyanza Province, Kenya. Unpublished report.

Pilger, A. and Rösler, A. (Eds.) (1976). Temporal relationships in the tectonic evolution of the Afar Depression (Ethiopia) and the adjacent Afro-Arabian rift system In: *Afar Between Continental and Oceanic Rifting: Inter-Union Commission on Geodynamics, Scientific Report No. 16*. Stuttgart: Schweizerbart'sche Verlagsbuchhandlung, pp. 1–25.

Piperno, M. and Bulgarelli-Piperno, G. (1975). First approach to the ecological and cultural significance of the early palaeolithic occupation site of Garba IV at Melka-Kunturé (Ethiopia). *Quaternaria* 18, 347–382.

Piperno, M., Collina, C., Gallotti, R., et al. (2009). Obsidian exploitation and utilization during the Oldowan at Melka Kunture (Ethiopia). In: E. Hovers and D.R. Braun (Eds.), *Interdisciplinary Approaches to the Oldowan*. Dordrecht: Springer, pp. 111–128.

Pirrone, C.A., Buatois, L.A. and Bromley, R.G. (2014). Ichnotaxobases for bioerosion trace fossils in bones. *Journal of Paleontology* 88, 195–203.

Pisias, N.G. and Moore Jr., T. (1981). The evolution of Pleistocene climate: a time series approach. *Earth and Planetary Science Letters* 52, 450–458.

Plana, V. (2004). Mechanisms and tempo of evolution in the African Guineo-Congolian rainforest. *Philosophical Transactions: Biological Sciences* 359, 1585–1594.

Plint, T. and Magill, C.R. (2021). Large mammal tracks in 1.8-million-year-old volcanic ash (Tuff IF, Bed I) at Olduvai Gorge, Tanzania. *Ichnos* 28, 114–124.

Plug, I. (1981). Some research results on the late Pleistocene and early Holocene deposits of Bushman Rock Shelter, eastern Transvaal. *The South African Archaeological Bulletin* 36, 14–21.

Plug, I. (1997). Late Pleistocene and Holocene hunter-gatherers in the eastern highlands of South African and Lesotho: a faunal interpretation. *Journal of Archaeological Science* 24, 715–727.

Plug, I. (2004). Resource exploitation: animal use during the Middle Stone Age at Sibudu cave, KwaZulu-Natal: Sibudu cave. *South African Journal of Science* 100(3–4), 151–158.

Plug, I. (2006). Aquatic animals and their associates from the Middle Stone Age levels at Sibudu. *Southern African Humanities* 18(1), 289–299.

Plug, I. and Badenhorst, S. (2001). The distribution of macromammals in southern Africa over the past 30,000 years as reflected in animal remains from archaeological sites. *Transvaal Museum Monograph* 12, 1–234.

Plug, I. and Clark, J.L. (2008). The air: a preliminary report on the birds from Sibudu Cave, KwaZulu-Natal, South Africa. *Goodwin Series* 10, 133–142.

Plug, I. and Engela, R. (1992). The macrofaunal remains from recent excavations at Rose Cottage Cave, Orange Free State. *The South African Archaeological Bulletin* 47, 16–25.

Plug, I. and Keyser, A.W. (1994). Haasgat Cave, a Pleistocene site in the central Transvaal: geomorphological, faunal and taphonomic considerations. *Annals of the Transvaal Museum* 36(9), 139–145.

Plummer, T.W. (1992). Site formation and paleoecology at the early to middle Pleistocene locality of Kanjera. PhD thesis, Yale University.

Plummer, T.W. (2004). Flaked stones and old bones: biological and cultural evolution at the dawn of technology. *Yearbook of Physical Anthropology* 47, 118–164.

Plummer, T. and Bishop, L. (1994). Hominid paleoecology at Olduvai Gorge, Tanzania as indicated by antelope remains. *Journal of Human Evolution* 27, 47–75.

Plummer, T.W. and Bishop, L.C. (2016). Oldowan hominin behavior and ecology at Kanjera South, Kenya. *Journal of Anthropological Sciences* 94, 29–40.

Plummer, T.W. and Potts, R. (1989). Excavations and new findings at Kanjera, Kenya. *Journal of Human Evolution* 18(3), 269–276.

Plummer, T. and Potts, R. (1995). Hominid fossil sample from Kanjera, Kenya: description, provenance, and implications of new and earlier discoveries. *American Journal of Physical Anthropology* 96(1), 7–23.

Plummer, T.W. and Stanford, C.B. (2000). Analysis of a bone assemblage made by chimpanzees at Gombe National Park, Tanzania. *Journal of Human Evolution* 39, 345–365.

Plummer, T.W., Kinyua, A.M. and Potts, R. (1994). Provenancing of hominid and mammalian fossils from Kanjera, Kenya, using EDXRF. *Journal of Archaeological Science* 21(4), 553–563.

Plummer, T., Bishop, L.C., Ditchfield, P. and Hicks, J. (1999). Research on late Pliocene Oldowan sites at Kanjera South, Kenya. *Journal of Human Evolution*, 36(2), 151–170.

Plummer, T.W., Bishop, L.C., Ditchfield, P.W., Kingston, J.D. and Hertel, F. (2006). Consensus approach to reconstructing Oldowan hominin paleoecology at Kanjera (Kenya) and Olduvai Gorge Bed I (Tanzania). Presented at the annual meetings of the Society for American Archaeology, held in San Juan, Puerto Rico, 26–30 April.

Plummer, T.W., Bishop, L.C., Ditchfield, P.W., et al. (2009a). The environmental context of Oldowan hominin activities at Kanjera South, Kenya. In: E. Hovers and D. Braun (Eds.), *Interdisciplinary Approaches to the Oldowan*. Dordrecht: Springer, pp. 149–160.

Plummer, T.W., Ditchfield, P.W., Bishop, L.C., et al. (2009b). Oldest evidence of toolmaking hominins in a grassland-dominated ecosystem. *PLoS One*, 4 (9), e7199.

Plummer, T.W., Ferraro, J.V., Louys, J., et al. (2015). Bovid ecomorphology and hominin paleoenvironments of the Shungura Formation, lower Omo River Valley, Ethiopia. *Journal of Human Evolution* 88, 108–126.

Plummer, T.W., Oliver, J.S., Bishop, L.C. and Hertel, F. (2018). Habitat-related variation in Oldowan prey acquisition: comparison of Kanjera South and FLK-Zinj. Presented at the 15th Congress of PanAfrican Archaeological Association, held in Rabat, Morocco, 10–14 September.

Pocock, T.N. (1969). Pleistocene bird fossils from Kromdraai and Sterkfontein. *Ostrich* 40(S1), 1–6.

Pocock, T.N. (1985). Plio-Pleistocene mammalian microfauna in southern Africa. *Annals of the Geological Survey of South Africa* 19, 65–67.

Pocock, T.N. (1987). Plio-Pleistocene fossil mammalian microfauna of Southern Africa – a preliminary report including description of two new fossil muroid genera (Mammalia: Rodentia). *Palaeontologica Africana* 26, 69–91.

Pomel, A. (1879). Ossements d'éléphants et d'hippopotames découverts dans une station préhistorique de la plaine d'Eghis (province d'Oran). *Bulletin de la Société géologique de France, 3ème sér* 7, 44–51.

Pomel, A. (1886). Sur la station préhistorique de Ternifine près Mascara. *Comptes rendus de l'Association Française pour l'Avancement des Sciences* 14, 128.

Pomel, A. (1893–1897). *Paléontologie, Monographies (8 fascicles:* 1893 – *Caméliens et cervidés;* 1894 – *Les boséláphes Ray;* 1895a – *Les antilopes Pallas;* 1895b – *Les éléphants quaternaires;* 1896a – *Les rhinocéros quaternaires;* 1896b – *Les hippopotames;* 1897a – *Les équidés;* 1897b – *Les carnassiers).* Service de la carte géologique de l'Algérie.

Poole, D.F.G. (1961). Notes on tooth replacement in the Nile crocodile (*Crocodilus niloticus*). *Proceedings of the Zoological Society of London* 136, 131–140.

Porat, N., Chazan, M., Grün, R. and Horwitz, L.K. (2010). New radiometric ages for the Fauresmith industry from Kathu Pan, southern Africa: implications for the Earlier to Middle Stone Age transition. *Journal of Archaeological Science* 37, 269–283.

Porraz, G., Val, A., Dayet, L., et al. (2015). Bushman Rock Shelter (Limpopo, South Africa): a perspective from the edge of the Highveld. *The South African Archaeological Bulletin* 70, 166–179.

Porraz, G., Schmid, V.C., Miller, C.E., et al. (2016). Update on the 2011 excavation at Elands Bay Cave (South Africa) and the Verlorenvlei stone age. *Southern African Humanities* 29(1), 33–68.

Potts, R. (1984). Home bases and early hominids: reevaluation of the fossil record at Olduvai Gorge suggests that the concentrations of bones and stone tools do not represent fully formed campsites but an antecedent to them. *American Scientist* 72, 338–347.

Potts, R. (1988). *Early Hominin Activities at Olduvai*. New York: Aldine de Gruyter.

Potts, R. (1989). Olorgesailie: new excavations and findings in Early and Middle Pleistocene contexts, southern Kenya rift valley. *Journal of Human Evolution* 18, 477–484.

Potts, R. (1991). Why the Oldowan? Plio-Pleistocene toolmaking and the transport of resources. *Journal of Anthropological Research* 47, 153–176.

Potts, R. (1994). Variables vs. models of early Pleistocene hominid land use. *Journal of Human Evolution* 27, 7–24.

Potts, R. (1996). Evolution and climate variability. *Science* 273, 922–923.

Potts, R. (1998a). Variability selection in hominid evolution. *Evolutionary Anthropology* 7, 81–96.

Potts, R. (1998b). Environmental hypothesis of hominin evolution. *Yearbook of Physical Anthropology* 41, 93–136.

Potts, R. (2007). Environmental hypotheses of Pliocene human evolution. In: R. Bobe, Z. Alemseged and A.K. Behrensmeyer (Eds.), *Hominin Environments in the East African Pliocene: An Assessment of the Faunal Evidence*. Dordrecht, Springer: pp. 25–49.

Potts, R. (2013). Hominin evolution in settings of strong environmental variability. *Quaternary Science Reviews* 73, 1–13.

Potts, R. and Behrensmeyer, A.K. (1992). Late Cenozoic terrestrial ecosystems. In: A.K. Behrensmeyer, J.D. Damuth, W.A. DiMichele, et al. (Eds.), *Terrestrial Ecosystems Through Time: Evolutionary Paleoecology of Terrestrial Plants and Animals*. Chicago: University of Chicago Press, pp. 419–541.

Potts, R. and Deino, A. (1995). Mid-Pleistocene change in large mammal faunas of the southern Kenya rift. *Quaternary Research* 43, 106–113.

Potts, R. and Faith, J.T. (2015). Alternating high and low climate variability: the context of natural selection and speciation in Plio-Pleistocene hominin evolution. *Journal of Human Evolution* 87, 5–20.

Potts, R. and Shipman, P. (1981). Cutmarks made by stone tools on bones from Olduvai Gorge, Tanzania. *Nature* 291, 577–580.

Potts, R., Shipman, P. and Ingall, E. (1988). Taphonomy, paleoecology and hominids of Lainyamok, Kenya. *Journal of Human Evolution* 17, 597–614.

Potts, R., Ditchfield, P., Hicks, J. and Deino, A. (1997). Paleoenvironments of late Miocene and early Pliocene strata of Kanam, western Kenya. *American Journal of Physical Anthropology Supplement* 24, 188–189.

Potts, R., Behrensmeyer, A.K. and Ditchfield, P. (1999). Paleolandscape variation in early Pleistocene hominid activities: Members 1 and 7, Olorgesailie Formation, Kenya. *Journal of Human Evolution* 37, 747–788.

Potts, R., Behrensmeyer, A.K., Deino, A., Ditchfield, P. and Clark, J. (2004). Small mid-Pleistocene hominin associated with East African Acheulean technology. *Science* 305, 75–78.

Potts, R., Behrensmeyer, A.K., Faith, J.T., et al. (2018). Environmental dynamics during the onset of the Middle Stone Age in eastern Africa. *Science* 360, 86–90.

Pound, M.J., Haywood, A.M., Salzmann, U., et al. (2011). A Tortonian (Late Miocene, 11.61–7.25 Ma) global vegetation reconstruction. *Palaeogeography, Palaeoclimatology, Palaeoecology* 300, 29–45.

Powers, D.W. (1980). Geology of Mio-Pliocene sediments of the lower Kerio river valley, Kenya. PhD thesis, Department of Geological and Geophysical Sciences, Princeton University, Princeton.

Prat, S., Brugal, J.-P., Roche, H. and Texier, P.-J. (2003). Nouvelles découvertes de dents d'hominidés dans le membre Kaitio de la Formation de Nachukui (1,65–1,9 million d'années) à l'Ouest du Lac Turkana (Kenya). *Comptes Rendus Palévol* 2(8), 685–693.

Prat, S, Brugal, J.-P., Tiercelin, J.-J., et al. (2005). First occurrence of early *Homo* in the Nachukui Formation (West Turkana, Kenya) at 2.3–2.4 Myr. *Journal of Human Evolution*, 49, 230–240.

Prendergast, M., Luque, L., Domínguez-Rodrigo, M., et al. (2007). New excavations at Mumba Rockshelter, Tanzania. *Journal of African Archaeology* 5, 217–243.

Presnyakova, D., Braun, D.R., Conard, N.J., et al. (2018). Site fragmentation, hominin mobility and LCT variability reflected in the early Acheulean record of the Okote Member, at Koobi Fora, Kenya. *Journal of Human Evolution* 125, 159–180.

Profico, A., Di Vincenzo, F., Gagliardi, L., Piperno, M. and Manzi, G. (2016). Filling the gap. Human cranial remains from Gombore II (Melka Kunture, Ethiopia; ca. 850 ka) and the origin of *Homo heidelbergensis*. *Journal of Anthropological Science* 94, 1–24.

Pruetz, J.D. (2007). Evidence of cave use by savanna chimpanzees (*Pan troglodytes verus*) at Fongoli, Senegal: implications for thermoregulatory behavior. *Primates* 48, 316–319.

Püschel, H.P., Bertrand, O.C., O'Reilly, J.E., Bobe, R. and Püschel, T.A. (2021). Divergence-time estimates for hominins provide insight into encephalization and body mass trends in human evolution. *Nature Ecology & Evolution* 5, 808–819.

Quade, J. and Wynn, J.G. (Eds.) (2008). *The Geology of Early Humans in the Horn of Africa*. Geological Society of America Special Paper 446. Boulder: The Geological Society of America.

Quade, J., Levin, N., Semaw, S., et al. (2004). Paleoenvironments of the earliest stone toolmakers, Gona, Ethiopia. *Geological Society of America Bulletin* 116, 1529–1544.

Quade, J., Levin, N.E., Simpson, S.W., et al. (2008). The geology of Gona, Afar, Ethiopia. In: J. Quade and J.G. Wynn (Eds.). *The*

Geology of Early Humans in the Horn of Africa. Geological Society of America Special Paper 446. Boulder: The Geological Society of America, pp. 1–31.

Quick, L. (2013). Late Quaternary palaeoenvironments of the southern Cape, South Africa palynological evidence from three coastal wetlands. Doctoral dissertation, University of Cape Town.

Quick, L.J., Carr, A.S., Meadows, M.E., et al. (2015). A late Pleistocene–Holocene multi-proxy record of palaeoenvironmental change from Still Bay, southern Cape Coast, South Africa. *Journal of Quaternary Science* 30(8), 870–885.

Quinn, R.L. and Lepre, C.J. (2020). Revisiting the pedogenic carbonate isotopes and paleoenvironmental interpretation of Kanapoi. *Journal of Human Evolution* 140, 102549.

Quinn, R.L., Lepre, C.J., Wright, J.D. and Feibel, C.S. (2007). Paleogeographic variations of pedogenic carbonate δ13C values from Koobi Fora, Kenya: implications for floral compositions of Plio-Pleistocene hominin environments. *Journal of Human Evolution* 53, 560–573.

Quinn, R.L., Lepre, C.J., Feibel, C.S., et al. (2013). Pedogenic carbonate stable isotopic evidence for wooded habitat preference of early Pleistocene tool makers in the Turkana Basin. *Journal of Human Evolution* 65(1), 65–78.

Quinn, R.L., Lewis, J., Brugal, J.P., et al. (2020). Pliocene environmental change, hominin dietary niche expansion, and the origins of stone tools. *Palaeogeography, Palaeoclimatology, Palaeoecology* 562, 110074.

R Development Core Team. (2011). *R: A Language and Environment for Statistical Computing.* Vienna: R Foundation for Statistical Computing.

R Development Core Team. (2019). *R: A Language and Environment for Statistical Computing.* Vienna: R Foundation for Statistical Computing.

Raaum, R.L., Sterner, K.N., Noviello, C.M., Stewart, C.B. and Disotell, T.R. (2005). Catarrhine primate divergence dates estimated from complete mitochondrial genomes: concordance with fossil and nuclear DNA evidence. *Journal of Human Evolution* 48(3), 237–257.

Rage, J.C. and Bailon, S. (2011). Amphibia and Squamata. In: T. Harrison (Ed.), *Paleontology and Geology of Laetoli: Human Evolution in Context. Vol. 2: Fossil Hominins and the Associated Fauna.* Dordrecht: Springer, pp. 467–478.

Raia, P., Piras, P. and Kotsakis, T. (2005). Turnover pulse or Red Queen? Evidence from the large mammal communities during the Plio-Pleistocene of Italy. *Palaeogeography, Palaeoclimatology, Palaeoecology* 221, 293–312.

Raichlen, D.A., Pontzer, H. and Sockol, M.D. (2008). The Laetoli footprints and early hominin locomotor kinematics. *Journal Human Evolution* 54, 112–117.

Raichlen, D.A., Gordon, A.D., Harcourt-Smith, W.E.H., Foster, A.D. and Haas, W.R. (2010). Laetoli footprints preserve earliest direct evidence of human-like bipedal biomechanics. *PLoS ONE* 5(3), e9769.

Randall, R.M. (1972). The Hyaenidae of the Limeworks Site Makapansgat. Unpublished BSc dissertation, University of the Witwatersrand.

Randall, R.M. (1981). Fossil Hyaenidae from the Makapansgat Limeworks Deposit, South Africa. *Palaeontologica Africana* 24, 75–85.

Rasmussen, C., Reichenbacher, B., Lenz, O., et al. (2017). Middle–late Miocene palaeoenvironments, palynological data and a fossil fish Lagerstätte from the Central Kenya Rift (East Africa). *Geological Magazine* 154, 24–56.

Rasmussen, D.T., Pickford, M., Mein, P., Senut, B. and Conroy, G.C. (1996). Earliest known procaviid hyracoid from the Late Miocene of Namibia. *Journal of Mammalogy* 77(3), 745–754.

Raup, D.M. (1977). Systematists follow the fossils. *Paleobiology* 3(3), 328–329.

Ravelo, A.C., Andreasen, D.H., Lyle, M., Olivarez Lyle, A. and Wara, M.W. (2004). Regional climate shifts caused by gradual global cooling in the Pliocene epoch. *Nature* 429, 263–267.

Ravelo, A.C., Dekens, P.S. and McCarthy, M. (2006). Evidence for El Niño-like conditions during the Pliocene. *GSA Today* 16, 4–11.

Raymo, M.E. and Huybers, P. (2008). Unlocking the mysteries of the ice ages. *Nature* 451, 284–285.

Raynal, J.-P. and Kieffer, G. (2004). Lithology, dynamism and volcanic successions at Melka Kunture (Upper Awash, Ethiopia). In: J. Chavaillon and M. Piperno (Eds.), *Studies on the Early Paleolithic site of Melka Kunture, Ethiopia.* Florence: Istituto Italiano di Preistoria e Protostoria, pp. 111–135.

Raynal, J.-P. and Texier, J.-P. (1989). Découverte d'Acheuléen ancien dans la carrière Thomas 1 à Casablanca, et problème de l'ancienneté de la présence humaine au Maroc. *Comptes Rendus de l'Académie des Sciences* 308, 1743–1749.

Raynal, J.-P., Texier, J.-P., Geraads, D. and Sbihi-Alaoui, F.-Z. (1990). Un nouveau gisement paléontologique plio–pléistocène Afrique du Nord: Ahl Al Oughlam (ancienne carrière Deprez) à Casablanca (Maroc). *Comptes Rendus de l'Académie des Sciences Paris II* 310, 315–320.

Raynal, J.-P., Geraads, D., Magoga, L., et al. (1993). La grotte des Rhinocéros (Carrière Oulad Hamida 1, anciennement Thomas III, Casablanca), nouveau site acheuléen du Maroc atlantique. *Comptes Rendu de l'Académie des Sciences Paris* 316, 1477–1483.

Raynal, J.-P., Magoga, L., Sbihi-Alaoui, F.Z. and Geraads, D. (1995). The earliest occupation of Atlantic Morocco: the Casablanca evidence. In: W. Roebroeks, and T. van Kolfschoten (Eds.), *The Earliest Occupation of Europe.* Leiden: University of Leiden, pp. 255–262.

Raynal, J.-P., Lefèvre, D., Geraads, D. and El Graoui, M. (1999). Contribution du site paléontologique de Lissasfa (Casablanca, Maroc) à une nouvelle interprétation du Mio-Pliocène de la Meseta. *Comptes Rendus de l'Académie des Sciences, Sciences de la Terre et des Planètes* 329, 617–622.

Raynal, J.-P., Sbihi-Alaoui, F.Z., Geraads, D., Magoga, L. and Mohib, A. (2001). The earliest occupation of North-Africa: the Moroccan perspective. *Quaternary International* 75, 65–75.

Raynal, J.P., Sbihi-Alaoui, F.Z., Magoga, L., Mohib, A. and Zouak, M. (2002). Casablanca and the early occupation of north-atlantic Morocco. *Quaternaire* 13, 65–77.

Raynal, J.-P., Kieffer, G. and Bardin, G. (2004). Garba IV and the Melka Kunture Formation. A preliminary lithostratigraphic approach. In: J. Chavaillon and M. Piperno (Eds.), *Studies on the Early Paleolithic site of Melka Kunture, Ethiopia.* Florence: Istituto Italiano di Preistoria e Protostoria, pp. 137–166.

Raynal, J.-P., Amani, F., Geraads, D., et al. (2008). Felids Cave, a new Upper Pleistocene Palaeolithic site at Casablanca (Morocco). *L'Anthropologie* 112, 182–200.

Raynal, J.P., Sbihi-Alaoui, F.Z., Mohib, A. and Geraads, D. (2009). Préhistoire ancienne au Maroc atlantique: bilan et perspectives régionales. *Bulletin d'Archéologie marocaine* 21, 9–54.

Raynal, J.-P., Sbihi-Alaoui, F.Z., Mohib, A., et al. (2010). Hominid cave at Thomas Quarry I (Casablanca, Morroco): recent findings and their context. *Quaternary International* 223–224, 369–382.

Raynal, J.-P., Sbihi-Alaoui, F.Z., Mohib, A., et al. (2011). Contextes et âge des nouveaux restes dentaires humains du Pléistocène moyen de la carrière Thomas 1 à Casablanca (Maroc). *Bulletin de la Société préhistorique Française* 108, 645–669.

Raynal, J.-P., Mohib, A. and Lefèvre, D. (2016a). Casablanca des origins. In: J.-P. Raynal and A. Mohib (Eds.), *Préhistoire de Casablanca. 1 – La Grotte des Rhinocéros (fouilles 1991 et 1996).*

Raynal, J.-P., Sbihi-Alaoui, F.Z., Mohib, A., et al. (2016a). *Villes et Sites archéologiques du Maroc, volume 6*. Rabat: Ministère de la Culture, INSAP, pp. 11–33.

Raynal, J.-P., Sbihi-Alaoui, F.Z., Mohib, A., et al. (2016b). Nouveaux restes dentaires humains dans la Grotte à Hominidés de la carrière Thomas I à Casablanca (Maroc): contexte et datation directe par ablation laser ICP-MS. In: A. Akerraz, A.S. Ettahiri, and M. Kbiri-Alaoui (Eds.), *Hommage à Joudia Hassar-Benslimane*. Rabat: INSAP, Tome 1, pp. 59–71.

Raynal, J.-P., Lefèvre, D., Geraads, D., El Graoui, M. and Rué, M. (2016c). La Grotte des Rhinocéros (Casablanca, Maroc): le remplissage et son âge. In: J.-P. Raynal and A. Mohib (Eds.), *Préhistoire de Casablanca. 1 – La Grotte des Rhinocéros (fouilles 1991 et 1996). Villes et Sites Archéologiques du Maroc, volume 6*. Rabat: Ministère de la Culture, Rabat: INSAP, Tome 1, pp. 79–86.

Raynal, J.-P., Gallotti, R., Mohib, A., Fernandes, P. and Lefèvre, D. (2017). The western quest, first and second regional Acheuleans at Thomas-Oulad Hamida quarries (Casablanca, Morocco). In: D. Wojtczak et al. (Eds.), *Vocation Préhistoire. Hommage à Jean-Marie Le Tensorer*. Liège: ERAUL, pp. 309–322.

Rayner, R.J., Moon, B. and Masters, J.C. (1993). The Makapansgat australopithecine environment. *Journal of Human Evolution* 24, 219–231.

Reck, H. (1914). Erste vorläufige Mitteilung über den Fund eines fossilen Menschenskeletts aus Zentralafrika. *Sitzungsberichte der Gesellschaft Naturforschender Freunde zu Berlin* 3, 81e95.

Rector, A.L. and Reed, K.E. (2010). Middle and Late Pleistocene faunas of Pinnacle Point and their paleoecological implications. *Journal of Human Evolution* 59, 340–357.

Rector, A.L. and Verrelli, B.C. (2010). Glacial cycling, large mammal community composition, and trophic adaptations in the Western Cape, South Africa. *Journal of Human Evolution* 58, 90–102.

Rector, A.L., Reed, K.E., Meacham, S. and Steininger, C. (2016). The large mammal community from Cooper's D and its significance for *Paranthropus robustus* ecology. *American Journal of Physical Anthropology* 159(S62), 264.

Reda, H.G., Lazagabaster, I.A. and Haile-Selassie, Y. (2019). Newly discovered crania of *Nyanzachoerus jaegeri* (Tetraconodontinae, Suidae, Mammalia) from the Woranso-Mille (Ethiopia) and reappraisal of its generic status. *Journal of Mammalian Evolution*, 26(2), 179–199.

Reed, D. (2007). Serengeti micromammals and their implications for Olduvai paleoenvironments. In: R. Bobe, Z. Alemseged and A.K. Behrensmeyer (Eds.), *Hominin Environments in the East African Pliocene: An Assessment of the Faunal Evidence*. Dordrecht: Springer, pp. 217–255.

Reed, D. (2011a). Serengeti micromammal communities and the paleoecology of Laetoli, Tanzania. In: T. Harrison (Ed.), *Paleontology and Geology of Laetoli: Human Evolution in Context. Vol. 1: Geology, Geochronology, Paleoecology, and Paleoenvironment*. Dordrecht: Springer, pp. 253–263.

Reed, D.N. (2011b). New murid (Mammalia, Rodentia) fossils from a late Pliocene (2.4 Ma) locality, Hadar AL 894, Afar Region, Ethiopia. *Journal of Vertebrate Paleontology* 31, 1326–1337.

Reed, D. and Denys, C. (2011). The taphonomy and paleoenvironmental implications of the Laetoli micromammals. In: T. Harrison (Ed.), *Paleontology and Geology of Laetoli: Human Evolution in Context. Vol. 1: Geology, Geochronology, Paleoecology, and Paleoenvironment*. Dordrecht: Springer, pp. 265–278.

Reed, D.N. and Geraads, D. (2012). Evidence for a late Pliocene faunal transition based on a new rodent assemblage from Oldowan locality Hadar AL 894, Afar Region, Ethiopia. *Journal of Human Evolution* 62, 328–337.

Reed, D., Barr, W.A., McPherron, S.P., et al. (2015). Digital data collection in paleoanthropology. *Evolutionary Anthropology* 24, 238–249.

Reed, K.E. (1996). The paleoecology of Makapansgat and other African Plio-Pleistocene hominid localities. PhD thesis, Anthropological Sciences. State University of New York, Stony Brook.

Reed, K.E. (1997). Early hominid evolution and ecological change through the African Plio-Pleistocene. *Journal of Human Evolution* 32, 289–322.

Reed, K.E. (1998). Using large mammal communities to examine ecological and taxonomic structure and predict vegetation in extant and extinct assemblages. *Paleobiology* 24, 384–408.

Reed, K.E. (2008). Paleoecological patterns at the Hadar hominin site, Afar Regional State, Ethiopia. *Journal of Human Evolution* 54, 743–768.

Reed, K.E. (2013). Multiproxy paleoecology: reconstructing evolutionary context in paleoanthropology. In: D.R. Begun (Ed.), *A Companion to Paleoanthropology*. Oxford: Wiley Blackwell, pp. 203–225.

Reed, K.E. and Bibi, F. (2010). Fossil Tragelaphini (Artiodactyla: Bovidae) from the Late Pliocene Hadar Formation, Afar Regional State, Ethiopia. *Journal of Mammalian Evolution* 18, 57–69.

Reed, K.E. and Bidner, L.R. (2004). Primate communities: past, present, and possible future. *Yearbook of Physical Anthropology* 47, 2–39.

Reed, K.E. and Fish, J.L. (2005). Tropical and temperate seasonal influences on human evolution. In: D.K. Brockman and C.P. van Schaik (Eds.), *Seasonality in Primates: Studies of Living and Extinct Human and Non-Human Primates*. Cambridge: Cambridge University Press, pp. 489–518.

Reed, K.E. and Rector, A.L. (2006). African Pliocene paleoecology: hominin habitats, resources, and diets. In: P. Ungar (Ed.), *Evolution of the Human Diet: The Known, the Unknown, and the Unknowable*. Oxford: Oxford University Press, pp. 262–288.

Reed, K. and Russack, S.M. (2009). Tracking ecological change in relation to the emergence of *Homo* near the Plio-Pleistocene boundary. In: F.E. Grine, J.G. Fleagle and R.E. Leakey (Eds.), *The First Humans: Origin and Early Evolution of the Genus Homo*. Dordrecht: Springer, pp. 159–171.

Rein, T. (2010). Locomotor function and phylogeny: implications for interpreting the hominoid fossil record. PhD thesis, New York University.

Remane, A. (1950). Die Zähne des *Meganthropus africanus*. *Zeitschrift für Morphologie und Anthropologie* 42, 311–329.

Remane, A. (1954). Structure and relationships of *Meganthropus africanus*. *American Journal of Physical Anthropology* 12, 123–126.

Rémy, J.A. (1976). Présence de *Deinotherium* sp. Kaup (Proboscidea, Mammalia) dans la faune miocène de Beni Mellal, Maroc. *Géologie Méditerranéenne* 3, 109–114.

Renne, P., Walter, R., Verosub, K., Sweitzer, M. and Aronson, J. (1993). New data from Hadar (Ethiopia) support orbitally tuned time-scale to 3.3 Ma. *Geophysical Research Letters* 20, 1067–1070.

Renne, P.R., Swisher, C.C., Deino, A.L., et al. (1998). Intercalibration of standards, absolute ages and uncertainties in $^{40}Ar/^{39}Ar$ dating. *Chemical Geology* 145, 117–152.

Renne, P.R., WoldeGabriel, G., Hart, W.K., Heiken, G. and White, T. D. (1999). Chronostratigraphy of the Miocene–Pliocene Sagantole Formation, Middle Awash Valley, Afar rift, Ethiopia. *Geological Society of America Bulletin* 111(6), 869–885.

Retallack, G.J. (1991). Untangling the effects of burial alteration and ancient soil formation. *Annual Review of Earth and Planetary Sciences* 19(1), 183–206.

Retallack, G.J. (2001). *Soils of the Past: An Introduction to Paleopedology*. Oxford: Blackwell Science.

Retallack, G.J., Bestland, E.A. and Dugas, D.P. (1995). Miocene paleosols and habitats of Proconsul on Rusinga Island, Kenya. *Journal of Human Evolution* 29(1), 53–91.

Reti, J.S. (2016). Quantifying Oldowan stone tool production at Olduvai Gorge, Tanzania. *PLoS ONE* 11, e0147352.

Reynard, J.P. and Wurz, S. (2020). The palaeoecology of Klasies River, South Africa: an analysis of the large mammal remains from the 1984–1995 excavations of Cave 1 and 1A. *Quaternary Science Reviews*, 237, 106301.

Reynolds, S.C. (2006). Temporal changes in vegetation and mammalian communities during Oxygen Isotope Stage 3 at Sibudu Cave. *Southern African Humanities* 18(1), 301–314.

Reynolds, S.C. (2007a). Temporal variation in Plio-Pleistocene *Antidorcas* (Mammalia: Bovidae) horncores: the case from Bolt's Farm and why size matters. *South African Journal of Science*, 103(1–2), 47–50.

Reynolds, S.C. (2007b). Mammalian body size changes and Plio-Pleistocene environmental shifts: implications for understanding hominin evolution in eastern and southern Africa. *Journal of Human Evolution* 53, 528–548.

Reynolds, S.C. (2010). Where the wild things were: spatial and temporal distribution of carnivores in the Sterkfontein Valley in relation to the accumulation of mammalian assemblages. *Journal of Taphonomy* 8(2–3), 233–257.

Reynolds, S. and Kibii, J. (2011). Sterkfontein at 75: review of palaeoenvironments, fauna and archaeology from the hominin site of Sterkfontein (Gauteng Province, South Africa). *Palaeontologica Africana* 46, 59–88.

Reynolds, S.C., Vogel, J.C., Clarke, R.J. and Kuman, K.A. (2003). Preliminary results of excavations at Lincoln Cave, Sterkfontein. *South African Journal of Science* 99, 286–288.

Reynolds, S.C., Clark, R.J. and Kuman, K.A. (2007). The view from Lincoln Cave: mid- to late Pleistocene fossil deposits from Sterkfontein hominid site, South Africa. *Journal of Human Evolution* 53, 260–271.

Reynolds, S., Bailey, G. and King, G. (2011). Landscapes and their relation to hominin habitats: case studies from *Australopithecus* sites in eastern and southern Africa. *Journal of Human Evolution* 60, 281–298.

Reynolds, S.C., Wilkinson, D.M., Marston, C.G. and O'Regan, H.J. (2015). The 'mosaic habitat' concept in human evolution: past and present. *Transactions of the Royal Society of South Africa* 70(1), 57–69.

Reynolds, S.C., Marston, C.G., Hassani, H., King, G.C. and Bennett, M.R. (2016). Environmental hydro-refugia demonstrated by vegetation vigour in the Okavango Delta, Botswana. *Scientific Reports*, 6.

Rhodes, E.J., Raynal, J.-P., Geraads, D. and Sbihi-Alaoui, F.Z. (1994). Premières dates RPE pour l'Acheuléen du Maroc atlantique (Grotte des Rhinocéros, Casablanca). *Comptes rendus de l'Académie de Sciences, Paris (II)* 319, 1109–1115.

Rhodes, E.J., Singarayer, J.S., Raynal, J.-P., Westaway, K.E. and Sbihi-Alaoui, F.Z. (2006). New age estimations for the Palaeolithic assemblages and Pleistocene succession of Casablanca, Morocco. *Quaternary Science Reviews* 25, 2569–2585.

Rich, P.V. (1980). Preliminary report on the fossil avian remains from late Tertiary sediments at Langebaanweg (Cape Province), South Africa. *South African Journal of Science* 76(4), 166–170.

Richard, M., Chazan, M. and Porat, N. (2022). Single grain TT-OSL ages for the Earlier Stone Age site of Bestwood 1 (Northern Cape Province, South Africa). Quaternary International 614, 16–22.

Richmond, B.G. and Jungers, W. L. (2008). *Orrorin tugenensis* femoral morphology and the evolution of hominin bipedalism. *Science*, 319(5870),1662–1665.

Richmond, B.G., Green, D.J., Lague, M.R., et al. (2020). The upper limb of *Paranthropus boisei* from Ileret, Kenya. *Journal of Human Evolution* 141, 102727.

Richter, D., Grün, R., Joannes-Boyau, R., et al. (2017). The age of the *Homo sapiens* fossils from Jebel Irhoud (Morocco) and the origins of the Middle Stone Age. *Nature* 546, 293–296.

Rieux, A., Eriksson, A., Li, M., et al. (2014). Improved calibration of the human mitochondrial clock using ancient genomes. *Molecular Biology and Evolution*, 31(10), 2780–2792.

Riga, A., Mori, T., Pickering, T.R., Moggi-Cecchi, J. and Menter, C.G. (2019). Ages-at-death distribution of the early Pleistocene hominin fossil assemblage from Drimolen (South Africa). *American Journal of Physical Anthropology* 168(3), 632–636.

Rightmire, G.P. (1979). Cranial remains of *Homo erectus* from Beds II and IV, Olduvai Gorge, Tanzania. *American Journal of Physical Anthropology* 51, 99–115.

Rightmire, G.P. (1998). Human evolution in the middle Pleistocene: the role of *Homo heidelbergensis*. *Evolutionary Anthropology* 6, 218–227.

Rightmire, G.P. (2013). *Homo erectus* and Middle Pleistocene hominins: brain size, skull form, and species recognition. *Journal of Human Evolution* 65, 223–252.

Rightmire, G.P. and Deacon, H.J. (1991). Comparative studies of late Pleistocene human remains from Klasies River mouth, South Africa. *Journal of Human Evolution* 20(2), 131–156.

Ring, U. and Betzler, C. (1995). Geology of the Malawi Rift: kinematic and tectonosedimentary background to the Chiwondo Beds, northern Malawi. *Journal of Human Evolution* 28, 7–21.

Ring, U., Albrecht, C. and Schrenk, F. (2018). The East African Rift System: tectonics, climate, and biodiversity. In: C. Hoorn, A. Perrigo and A. Antonelli (Eds.), *Mountains, Climate and Biodiversity*. Hoboken: Wiley Blackwell.

Ritchie, M.E. (2008). Global environmental changes and their impact on the Serengeti. In: A.R.E. Sinclair, C. Packer, S.A.R. Mduma and J.M. Fryxell (Eds.), *Serengeti III: Human Impacts on Ecosystem Dynamics*. Chicago: University of Chicago Press, pp. 183–208.

Rito, T., Richards, M.B., Fernandes, V., et al. (2013). The first modern human dispersals across Africa. *PLoS ONE* 8, e80031.

Robbins, L.M. (1987). Hominid footprints from Site G. In: M.D. Leakey and J.M. Harris (Eds.), *Laetoli: A Pliocene Site in Northern Tanzania*. Oxford: Clarendon Press, pp. 497–502.

Roberts, D.L. (2003). Vertebrate trackways in Pleistocene coastal calcareous aeolianites South Africa. *Abstract, XVI Inqua Congess*. Reno, Nevada: Desert Research Institute, p. 96.

Roberts, D.L., Bateman, M.D., Murray-Wallace, C.V., Carr, A.S. and Holmes, P.J. (2008). Last interglacial fossil elephant trackways dated by OSL/AAR in coastal aeolianites, Still Bay, South Africa. *Palaeogeography, Palaeoclimatology, Palaeoecology* 257(3), 261–279.

Roberts, D.L., Bateman, M.D., Murray-Wallace, C.V., Carr, A.S. and Holmes, P.J. (2009). West coast dune plumes: climate driven contrasts in dunefield morphogenesis along the western and southern South African coasts. *Palaeogeography, Palaeoclimatology, Palaeoecology* 271(1–2), 24–38.

Roberts, D.L., Matthews, T., Herries, A.I., et al. (2011). Regional and global context of the Late Cenozoic Langebaanweg (LBW) palaeontological site: West Coast of South Africa. *Earth-Science Reviews* 106(3–4), 191–214.

Robinson, C. (2011). Giraffidae. In: T. Harrison (Ed.), *Paleontology and Geology of Laetoli: Human Evolution in Context. Vol. 2: Fossil Hominins and the Associated Fauna*. Dordrecht: Springer, pp. 339–362.

Robinson, J.R. and Wadley, L. (2018). Stable isotope evidence for (mostly) stable local environments during the South African Middle Stone Age from Sibudu, KwaZulu-Natal. *Journal of Archaeological Science* 100, 32–44.

Robinson, J.R., Rowan, J., Campisano, C.J., Wynn, J.G. and Reed, K.E. (2017). Late Pliocene environmental change during the transition from *Australopithecus* to *Homo*. *Nature Ecology & Evolution* 1, 0159.

Robinson, J.T. (1952). The australopithecine-bearing deposits of the Sterkfontein area. *Annals of the Transvaal Museum* 22(1), 1–19.

Robinson, J.T. (1953a). *Meganthropus*, australopithecines and hominids. *American Journal of Physical Anthropology* 11, 1–38.

Robinson, J.T. (1953b). *Telanthropus* and its phylogenetic significance. *American Journal of Physical Anthropology* 11, 445–501.

Robinson, J.T. (1954). The genera and species of the Australopithecinae. *American Journal of Physical Anthropology* 12, 181–200.

Robinson, J.T. (1955). Further remarks on the relationship between "*Meganthropus*" and australopithecines. *American Journal of Physical Anthropology* 13, 429–445.

Robinson, J.T. (1956). *The Dentition of the Australopithecinae*. Transvaal Museum Memoir No. 9. Pretoria: Transvaal Museum.

Robinson, J.T. (1961). The australopithecines and their bearing on the origin of man and tool-making. *South African Journal of Science* 57, 3–13.

Robinson, J.T. (1962). Sterkfontein stratigraphy and the significance of the Extension Site. *South African Archaeological Bulletin* 17, 87–107.

Robinson, J.T. (1963). Adaptive radiation in the australopithecines and the origin of man. In: F.C. Howell and F. Bourlière (Eds.), *African Ecology and Human Evolution*. Chicago: Aldine, pp.385–416.

Robinson, P. (1972). *Pachytragus solignaci*, a new species of caprine bovid from the late Miocene Beglia Formation of Tunisia. *Notes du Service géologique de Tunisie* 37, 73–94.

Robinson, P. (1986) Very hypsodont antelopes from the Beglia Formation (central Tunisia), with a discussion of the Rupicaprinae. *Rocky Mountain Geology* 24(special paper 3), 305–315.

Robinson, P. and Black, C.C. (1974). Vertebrate faunas from the Neogene of Tunisia. *Annals of the Geological Survey of Egypt* 4, 319–332.

Robinson, P., Black, C. and Craig, C. (1969). Note préliminaire sur les vertébrés fossiles du Vindobonien (formation Beglia) du Bled Douarah, Gouvernorat de Gafsa, Tunisie. *Notes du Service géologique de Tunisie* 31, 67–70.

Roche, C. (2004). 'The Springbok … Drink the Rain's Blood': indigenous knowledge and its use in environmental history – the case of the /Xam and an understanding of Springbok Treks. *South African Historical Journal* 53, 1–22.

Roche, H. (2005). From simple flaking to shaping: stone knapping evolution among early Hominids. In: V. Roux and B. Bril (Eds.), *Stone Knapping: The Necessary Conditions for a Uniquely Hominid Behaviour*. Cambridge: Mc Donald Institute Monograph Series, pp. 35–48.

Roche, H. (2011). The archaeology of human origins: the contribution of West Turkana, Kenya. In: J. Sept and D. Pilbeam (Eds.), *Casting the Net Wide, Papers in Honor of Glynn Isaac*. American School of Prehistoric Research Monograph series. Cambridge, MA: Oxbow Books, pp. 75–92.

Roche, H. and Kibunjia, M. (1996). Contribution of the West Turkana plio-pleistocene to the archaeology of the Lower Omo/Turkana Basin. *Kaupia* 6, 27–30.

Roche, H., Delagnes, A., Brugal, J.-P., et al. (1999). Evidence for early hominids lithic production and technical skill at 2.3 Myr, West Turkana, Kenya. *Nature* 399, 57–60.

Roche, H., Brugal, J.-P., Delagnes, A., et al. (2003). Les sites archéologiques plio-pléistocènes de la Formation de Nachukui (Ouest Turkana, Kenya): bilan préliminaire 1996–2000. *Comptes Rendus Palévol* 2(8), 663–673.

Roche, D., Ségalen, L., Senut, B. and Pickford, M. (2013). Stable isotope analyses of tooth enamel carbonate of large herbivores from the Tugen Hills deposits: palaeoenvironmental context of the earliest Kenyan hominids. *Earth and Planetary Science Letters* 381, 39–51.

Rodriguez, J. (1999). Use of cenograms in mammalian palaeoecology. A critical review. *Lethaia* 32(4), 331–347.

Rogers, M.J. and Semaw, S. (2009). From nothing to something: the appearance and context of the earliest archaeological record. In: M. Camps and P. Chauhan (Eds.), *Sourcebook of Paleolithic Transitions*. New York: Springer, pp. 155–171.

Rogers, M.J., Harris, J.W.K. and Feibel, C.S. (1994). Changing patterns of land use by Plio-Pleistocene hominids in the Lake Turkana Basin. *Journal of Human Evolution* 27, 139–158.

Roman, D., Campisano, C., Quade, J., et al. (2008). Composite tephrostratigraphy of the Dikika, Gona, Hadar, and Ledi-Geraru project areas, northern Awash, Ethiopia. *Geological Society of America Special Papers* 446, 119–134.

Rook, L. (2008). The discovery of the Sahabi Site: Ardito Desio or Carlo Petrocchi? *Garyounis Scientific Bulletin* 2008, 13–21.

Rook, L., Ghinassi, M., Libsekal, Y., et al. (2010). Stratigraphic context and taxonomic assessment of the large cercopithecoid (Primates, Mammalia) from the late Early Pleistocene palaeoanthropological site of Buia (Eritrea). *Journal of Human Evolution* 59, 692–697.

Rook, L., Ghinassi, M., Carnevale, G., et al. (2013). Stratigraphic context and paleoenvironmental significance of minor taxa (Pisces, Reptilia, Aves, Rodentia) from the late Early Pleistocene paleoanthropological site of Buia (Eritrea). *Journal of Human Evolution* 64, 83–92.

Rook, L., Abbate, E., Bondioli, L., et al. (2014). The Homo-bearing late Early Pleistocene site of Mulhuli-Amo, northern Danakil Depression of Eritrea. Geochronological setting, paleoenvironmental reconstruction and paleoanthropological findings. International Symposium on The African Human Fossil Record, pp. 17–18 (abstract).

Rosenzweig, M.L. (1995). *Species Diversity in Space and Time*. Cambridge: Cambridge University Press.

Rossie, J.B. and Hill, A. (2018). A new species of Simiolus from the Middle Miocene of the Tugen Hills, Kenya. *Journal of Human Evolution* 125, 50–58.

Rossignol-Strick, M. (1985). Mediterranean Quaternary sapropels, an immediate response of the African monsoon to variation of insolation. *Paleogeography, Paleoclimatology, Paleoecology* 49, 237–263.

Rossouw, L. (2009). The application of fossil grass-phytolith analysis in the reconstruction of Cainozoic environments in the South African interior. Doctoral dissertation, University of the Free State.

Rossouw, L. (2016). An Early Pleistocene phytolith record from Wonderwerk Cave, Northern Cape, South Africa. *African Archaeological Review* 33, 251–263.

Rossouw, L. and Scott, L. (2011). Phytoliths and pollen, the microscopic plant remains in Pliocene volcanic sediments around Laetoli, Tanzania. In: T. Harrison (Ed.), *Paleontology and Geology of Laetoli, Tanzania: Human Evolution in Context. Vol. 1: Geology, Geochronology, Paleoecology and Paleoenvironment*. Dordrecht: Springer, pp. 201–215.

Rossouw, L., Stynder, D.D. and Haarhof, P. (2009). Evidence for opal phytolith preservation in the Langebaanweg 'E' Quarry Varswater Formation and its potential for palaeohabitat reconstruction. *South African Journal of Science* 105(5–6), 223–227.

Rowan, J., Faith, J.T., Gebru, Y. and Fleagle, J.G. (2015). Taxonomy and paleoecology of fossil Bovidae (Mammalia, Artiodactyla) from the Kibish Formation, southern Ethiopia: implications for dietary change, biogeography, and the structure of living bovid faunas of East Africa. *Palaeogeography, Palaeoclimatology, Palaeoecology* 420, 210–222.

Rowan, J., Kamilar, J.M., Beaudrot, L. and Reed, K.E. (2016). Strong influence of palaeoclimate on the structure of modern African mammal communities. *Proceedings of the Royal Society B: Biological Sciences* 283(1840), 20161207.

Rowan, J., Locke, E.M., Robinson, J.R., et al. (2017). Fossil Giraffidae (Mammalia, Artiodactyla) from Lee Adoyta, Ledi-Geraru, and

Late Pliocene dietary evolution in giraffids from the Lower Awash Valley, Ethiopia. *Journal of Mammalian Evolution* 24, 359–371.

Rovinsky, D.S., Herries, A.I., Menter, C.G. and Adams, J.W. (2015). First description of *in situ* primate and faunal remains from the Plio-Pleistocene Drimolen Makondo palaeocave infill, Gauteng, South Africa. *Palaeontologia Electronica* 18(2), 1–21.

Rubenstein, D., Low Mackey, B., Davidson, Z.D., Kebede, F. and King, S.R.B. (2016). *Equus grevyi*. The IUCN Red List of Threatened Species 2016, e.T7950A89624491

Ruth, A.A., Raghanti, M.A., Meindl, R.S. and Lovejoy, C.O. (2016). Locomotor pattern fails to predict foramen magnum angle in rodents, strepsirrhine primates, and marsupials. *Journal of Human Evolution* 94, 45–52.

Rüther, H., Chazan, M., Schroeder, R., et al. (2009). Laser scanning for conservation and research of African cultural heritage sites: the case study of Wonderwerk Cave, South Africa. *Journal of Archaeological Science* 36, 1847–1856.

Rutherford, M.C. and Westfall, R.H. (1986). Biomes of southern Africa – an objective categorization. *Memoires of the Botanical Survey of South Africa* 54, 1–98.

Sabatier, M. (1978). Un nouveau *Tachyoryctes* (Mammalia, Rodentia) du basin Pliocène de Hadar (Éthiopie). *Géobios* 11, 95–99.

Sabatier, M. (1979). Les rongeurs des sites à Hominidés de Hadar et Melka-Kunture (Ethiopie). Thèse USTL, Montpellier, France.

Sabatier, M. (1982). Les rongeurs du site Pliocène à hominidés de Hadar (Ethiopie). *Paleovertebrata* 12, 1–56.

Saegusa, H. and Haile-Selassie, Y. (2009). Proboscidea. In: Y. Haile-Selassie and G. WoldeGabriel (Eds.), *Ardipithecus kadabba: Late Miocene Evidence from the Middle Awash, Ethiopia*. Berkeley: University of California Press, pp. 469–516.

Sahle, Y., El Zaatari, S. and White, T.D. (2017). Hominid butchers and biting crocodiles in the African Plio–Pleistocene. *Proceedings of the National Academy of Sciences* 114(50), 13164–13169.

Sahnouni, M. (2006). Les plus vieilles traces d'occupation humaine en Afrique du Nord: perspective de l'Ain Hanech, Algérie. *Comptes Rendus Palevol* 5, 243–254.

Sahnouni, M., Hadjouis, D., van der Made, J., et al. (2002). Further research at the Oldowan site of Ain Hanech, North-Eastern Algeria. *Journal of Human Evolution* 43, 925–937.

Sahnouni, M., Rosell, J., Van der Made, J., et al. (2013). The first evidence of cut marks and usewear traces from the Plio-Pleistocene locality of El-Kherba (Ain Hanech), Algeria: implications for early hominin subsistence activities circa 1.8 Ma. *Journal of Human Evolution* 64, 137–150.

Sahnouni, M., Parés, J.M., Duval, M., et al. (2018). 1.9-million- and 2.4-million-year-old artifacts and stone tool–cutmarked bones from Ain Boucherit, Algeria. *Science* 362, 1297–1301. 10.1126/science.aau0008

Sakai, T., Saneyoshi, M., Tanaka, S., et al. (2010). Climate shift recorded at around 10 Ma in Miocene succession of Samburu Hills, northern Kenya Rift, and its significance. *Geological Society, London, Special Publications* 342(1), 109–127.

Salzburger, W., Van Bocxlaer, B. and Cohen, A.S. (2014). Ecology and evolution of the African Great Lakes and their faunas. *Annual Review of Ecology, Evolution, and Systematics* 45, 519–545.

Salzmann, U., Williams, M., Haywood, A.M., et al. (2011). Climate and environment of a Pliocene warm world. *Palaeogeography, Palaeoclimatology, Palaeoecology* 309, 1–8.

Sampson, C.G. (2003). Amphibians from the Acheulean site at Duinefontein 2 (Western Cape, South Africa). *Journal of Archaeological Science* 30(5), 547–557.

Sanders, H.L. (1968). Marine benthic diversity: a comparative study. *The American Naturalist* 102(925), 243–282.

Sanders, W.J. (1990). Fossil Proboscidea from the Pliocene Lusso Beds of the Western Rift, Zaire. In: N.T. Boaz (Ed.), *Evolution of Environments and Hominidae in the African Western Rift Valley*. Martinsville: Virginia Museum of Natural History.

Sanders, W.J. (1997). Fossil Proboscidea from the Wembere–Manonga Formation, Manonga Valley, Tanzania. In: T. Harrison (Ed.), *Neogene Paleontology of the Manonga Valley, Tanzania*. New York: Plenum Press, pp. 265–310.

Sanders, W.J. (2007). Taxonomic review of fossil Proboscidea (Mammalia) from Langebaanweg, South Africa. *Transactions of the Royal Society of South Africa* 62, 1–16.

Sanders, W.J. (2011). Proboscidea. In: T. Harrison (Ed.), *Paleontology and Geology of Laetoli: Human Evolution in Context*. Dordrecht: Springer, pp. 233–262.

Sanders, W.J. (2020). Proboscidea from Kanapoi, Kenya. *Journal of Human Evolution* 140, 102547.

Sanders, W. and Haile-Selassie, Y. (2012). A new assemblage of mid-Pliocene proboscideans from the Woranso-Mille area, Afar Region, Ethiopia: taxonomic, evolutionary, and paleoecological considerations. *Journal of Mammalian Evolution* 19, 105–128.

Sanders, W.J. and Miller, E.R. (2002). New proboscideans from the Early Miocene of Wadi Moghra, Egypt. *Journal of Vertebrate Paleontology* 22, 388–404.

Sanders, W.J., Trapani, J. and Mitani, J.C. (2003). Taphonomic aspects of crowned hawk-eagle predation on monkeys. *Journal of Human Evolution* 44, 87–105.

Sanders, W.J., Gheerbrant, E., Harris, J.M., Saegusa, H. and Delmer, C. (2010). Proboscidea. In: L. Werdelin and W.J. Sanders (Eds.), *Cenozoic Mammals of Africa*. Berkeley: University of California Press, pp. 161–251.

Sandrock, O., Kullmer, O., Schrenk, F., Yuwayeyi, Y.M. and Bromage, T.G. (2007). Fauna, taphonomy and ecology of the Plio-Pleistocene Chiwondo Beds, Northern Malawi. In: R. Bobe, Z. Alemseged and A.K. Behrensmeyer (Eds.), *Hominin Environments in the East African Pliocene: an Assessment of the Faunal Evidence*. Dordrecht: Springer, pp. 315–332.

Sands, W.A. (1987). Ichnocoenoses of probable termite origin from Laetoli. In: M.D. Leakey and J.M. Harris (Eds.), *Laetoli: A Pliocene Site in Northern Tanzania*. Oxford: Clarendon Press, pp. 409–433.

Saneyoshi, M., Nakayama, K., Sakai, T., Sawada, Y. and Ishida, H. (2006). Half graben filling processes in the early phase of continental rifting: the Miocene Namurungule Formation of the Kenya Rift. *Sedimentary Geology* 186, 111–131.

Sankaran, M., Hanan, N.P., Scholes, R.J., et al. (2005). Determinants of woody cover in African savannas. *Nature* 438, 846–849.

Sarna-Wojcicki, A.M., Meyer, C.E., Roth, P.H. and Brown, F.H. (1985). Ages of tuff beds at East African early hominid sites and sediments in the Gulf of Aden. *Nature* 313, 306–308.

Sarnthein, M., Thiede, J., Pflaumann, U., et al. (1982). Atmospheric and oceanic circulation patterns off Northwest Africa during the past 25 million years. In: U. Rad, K. Hinz, M. Sarnthein and E. Seibold (Eds.), *Geology of the Northwest African Continental Margin*. New York: Springer Science & Business Media, pp. 545–604.

Sausse, F. (1975). La mandibule atlanthropienne de la carrière Thomas I (Casablanca). *L'Anthropologie* 79, 81–112.

Savage, R.J.G. and Hamilton, W.R. (1973). Introduction to the Miocene mammal faunas of Gebel Zelten, Libya. *Bulletin of the British Museum (Natural History) Geology* 22, 513–527.

Sawada, Y., Pickford, M., Itaya, T., et al. (1998). K–Ar ages of Miocene Hominoidea (*Kenyapithecus* and *Samburupithecus*) from Samburu Hills, northern Kenya. *Comptes Rendus de l'Académie des Sciences – Series IIA – Earth and Planetary Science* 326, 445–451.

Sawada, Y., Pickford, M., Senut, B., et al. (2002). The age of *Orrorin tugenensis*, an early hominid from the Tugen Hills, Kenya. *Comptes Rendus Palevol* 1, 293–303.

Sawada, Y., Saneyoshi, M., Nakayama, K., et al. (2006). The ages and geological backgrounds of Miocene hominoids *Nacholapithecus*, *Samburupithecus*, and *Orrorin* from Kenya. In: H. Ishida, R. Tuttle, M. Pickford, N. Ogihara and M. Nakatsukasa (Eds.), *Human Origins and Environmental Backgrounds*. Boston, MA: Springer US, pp. 71–96.

Saylor, B.Z., Angelini, J., Deino, A., et al. (2016). Tephrostratigraphy of the Waki-Mille area of the Woranso-Mille paleoanthropological research project, Afar, Ethiopia. *Journal of Human Evolution* 93, 25–45.

Schefuß, E., Schouten, S., Jansen, J.F. and Damsté, J.S.S. (2003). African vegetation controlled by tropical sea surface temperatures in the mid-Pleistocene period. *Nature* 422, 418–421.

Schick, K.D. (1987). Modeling the formation of Early Stone Age artifact concentrations. *Journal of Human Evolution* 16, 789–807.

Schmid, P. (2004). Functional interpretation of the Laetoli footprints. In: D.J. Meldrum and C.E. Hilton (Eds.), *From Biped to Strider: The Emergence of Modern Human Walking, Running, and Resource Transport*. New York: Kluwer Academic, pp. 49–62.

Schmid, P. and Berger, L.R. (1997). Middle Pleistocene hominid carpal proximal phalanx from the Gladysvale site, South Africa. *South African Journal of Science* 93(10), 430–431.

Schmitt, J.-J., Wempler, J.-M., Chavaillon, J. and Andrews, M.C. (1977). Initial K/Ar and paleomagnetic results of the Melka-Kunturé early-man sites, Ethiopia. In: *Proceedings 8th Panafrican Congress of Prehistory and Quaternary Studies*. Nairobi: International Louis Leakey Memorial Institute for African Prehistory.

Schmitt, T.J. and Nairn, A.E.M. (1984). Interpretations of the magnetostratigraphy of the Hadar hominid site, Ethiopia. *Nature* 309, 704–706.

Schneider, S., Hornung, J. and Hinderer, M. (2017). Evolution of the northern Albertine Rift reflected in the provenance of synrift sediments (Nkondo-Kaiso area, Uganda). *Journal of African Earth Sciences* 131, 183–197.

Schoeninger, M.J., Reeser, H. and Hallin, K. (2003). Paleoenvironment of *Australopithecus anamensis* at Allia Bay, East Turkana, Kenya: evidence from mammalian herbivore enamel stable isotopes. *Journal of Anthropological Archaeology* 22(3), 200–207.

Scholz, C.A., Cohen, A.S., Johnson, T.C., et al. (2011). Scientific drilling in the Great Rift Valley: the 2005 Lake Malawi Scientific Drilling Project – an overview of the past 145,000 years of climate variability in Southern Hemisphere East Africa. *Palaeogeography, Palaeoclimatology, Palaeoecology* 303(1–4), 3–19.

Schrenk, F., Bromage, T.G., Betzler, C.G., Ring, U. and Juwayeyi, Y.M. (1993). Oldest *Homo* and Pliocene biogeography of the Malawi Rift. *Nature* 365, 833–836.

Schrenk, F., Bromage, T.G., Gorthner, A. and Sandrock, O. (1995). Paleoecology of the Malawi Rift: vertebrate and invertebrate faunal contexts of the Chiwondo Beds, northern Malawi. *Journal of Human Evolution* 28, 59–70.

Schroeder, L., Scott, J.E., Garvin, H.M., et al. (2017). Skull diversity in the *Homo* lineage and the relative position of *Homo naledi*. *Journal of Human Evolution* 104, 124–135.

Schubert, B.W. (2007). Dental mesowear and the palaeodiets of bovids from Makapansgat Limeworks Cave, South Africa. *Palaeontologica Africana* 42, 43–50.

Schubert, B.W., Ungar, P.S., Sponheimer, M. and Reed, K.E. (2006). Microwear evidence for Plio-Pleistocene bovid diets from Makapansgat Limeworks Cave, South Africa. *Palaeogeography, Palaeoclimatology, Palaeoecology* 241, 301–319.

Schulze, R.E. (1997). *South African Atlas of Agrohydrology and Climatology*. Report TT82/96 ACRU Report 46. Pretoria: South African Water Research Commission, pp. 276.2.

Schuster, M., Duringer, P., Ghienne, J.-F., et al. (2006). The age of the Sahara desert. *Science*, 311(5762), 821–821.

Schwarcz, H.P., Grün, R. and Tobias, P.V. (1994). ESR dating studies of the australopithecine site of Sterkfontein, South Africa. *Journal of Human Evolution* 26, 175–181.

Schwartz, J.H. and Tattersall, I. (2003). *The Human Fossil Record, Vol. 2. The Craniodental Morphology of Genus Homo (African and Asia)*. New York: Wiley-Liss.

Schweitzer, F.R. and Wilson, M.L. (1982). Byneskranskop 1, a late Quaternary living site in the southern Cape Province, South Africa. *Annals of the South African Museum* 88, 1–203.

Scott, J.R. (2012). Dental microwear texture analysis of Pliocene bovids from four early hominin fossil sites in eastern Africa: implications for paleoenvironmental dynamics and human evolution. PhD dissertation, University of Arkansas.

Scott, L. (1987). Pollen analysis of hyena coprolites and sediments from Equus Cave, Taung, Southern Kalahari (South Africa). *Quaternary Research* 28(1), 144–156.

Scott, L. and Neumann, F.H. (2018). Pollen-interpreted palaeoenvironments associated with the Middle and Late Pleistocene peopling of Southern Africa. *Quaternary International* 495, 169–184.

Scott, L. and Nyakale, M. (2002). Pollen indications of Holocene palaeoenvironments at Florisbad spring in the central Free State, South Africa. *The Holocene* 12(4), 497–503.

Scott, L. and Rossouw, L. (2005). Reassessment of botanical evidence for palaeoenvironments at Florisbad, South Africa. *South African Archaeological Bulletin* 60(182), 96.

Scott, L. and Thackeray, J.F. (2015). Palynology of Holocene deposits in Excavation 1 at Wonderwerk Cave, Northern Cape (South Africa). *African Archaeological Review* 32, 839–855.

Scott, L., Fernández-Jalvo, Y., Carrión, J. and Brink, J. (2003). Preservation and interpretation of pollen in hyaena coprolites: taphonomic observations from Spain and southern Africa. *Palaeontologia Africana* 39, 83–91.

Scott, L., Neumann, F.H., Brook, G.A., et al. (2012). Terrestrial fossil-pollen evidence of climate change during the last 26 thousand years in Southern Africa. *Quaternary Science Reviews* 32, 100–118.

Scott, R.S., Ungar, P.S., Bergstrom, T.S., et al. (2006). Dental microwear texture analysis: technical considerations. *Journal of Human Evolution* 51(4), 339–349.

Sealy, J., Naidoo, N., Hare, V.J., Brunton, S. and Faith, J.T. (2020). Climate and ecology of the palaeo-Agulhas Plain from stable carbon and oxygen isotopes in bovid tooth enamel from Nelson Bay Cave, South Africa. *Quaternary Science Reviews* 235, 105974.

Seiffert, E.R., Perry, J.M., Simons, E.L. and Boyer, D.M. (2009). Convergent evolution of anthropoid-like adaptations in Eocene adapiform primates. *Nature* 461(7267), 1118–1121.

Sellers, W.I., Cain, G.M., Wang, W. and Crompton, R.H. (2005). Stride lengths, speed and energy costs in walking of *Australopithecus afarensis*: using evolutionary robotics to predict locomotion of early human ancestors. *Journal of the Royal Society Interface* 2, 431–441.

Selvaggio, M.M. (1998). Evidence for a three-stage sequence of hominid and carnivore involvement with long bones at FLK Zinjanthropus, Olduvai Gorge, Tanzania. *Journal of Archaeological Science* 25, 191–202.

Selvaggio, M.M. and Wilder, J. (2001). Identifying the involvement of multiple carnivore taxa with archaeological bone assemblages. *Journal of Archaeological Science* 28, 465–470.

Semaw, S., Renne, P., Harris, J.W.K., et al. (1997). 2.5-million-year-old stone tools from Gona, Ethiopia. *Nature* 385, 333–336.

Semaw, S., Schick, K., Toth, N., et al. (2001). Further 2.5–2.6 million year old artifacts, new Plio-Pleistocene archaeological sites and hominid discoveries of 1999 from Gona Ethiopia. *Journal of Human Evolution* 40, A20.

Semaw, S., Rogers, M.J., Quade, J., et al. (2003). 2.6-Million-year-old stone tools and associated bones from OGS-6 and OGS-7, Gona, Afar, Ethiopia. *Journal of Human Evolution* 45, 169–177.

Semaw, S., Simpson, S.W., Quade, J., et al. (2005). Early Pliocene hominids from Gona, Ethiopia. *Nature* 433, 301–305.

Semaw, S., Rogers, M.J. and Stout, D. (2009). The Oldowan–Acheulian transition: is there a "developed Oldowan" artifact tradition? In: M. Camps and P. Chauhan (Eds.), *Sourcebook of Paleolithic Transitions*. New York, Springer, pp. 173–193.

Semaw, S., Rogers, M.J., Simpson, S.W., et al. (2020). Co-occurrence of Acheulian and Oldowan artifacts with *Homo erectus* cranial fossils from Gona, Afar, Ethiopia. *Science Advances* 6, eaaw4694.

Semprebon, G.M. and Rivals, F. (2007). Was grass more prevalent in the pronghorn past? An assessment of the dietary adaptations of Miocene to recent Antilocapridae (Mammalia: Artiodactyla). *Palaeogeography, Palaeoclimatology, Palaeoecology* 253(3–4), 332–347.

Semprebon, G.M. and Rivals, F. (2010). Trends in the paleodietary habits of fossil camels from the Tertiary and Quaternary of North America. *Palaeogeography, Palaeoclimatology, Palaeoecology* 295(1–2), 131–145.

Sen, S. (1990). *Hipparion* datum and its chronologic evidence in the Mediterranean area. In: E.H. Lindsay, V. Fahlbusch and P. Mein (Eds.), *European Neogene Mammal Chronology*. New York: Springer Science & Business Media, pp. 495–505.

Sénégas, F., Thackeray, J.F., Gommery, D. and Braga, J. (2002). Palaeontological sites on 'Bolt's Farm', Sterkfontein Valley, South Africa. *Annals of the Transvaal Museum* 39(1), 65–67.

Sénégas, F., Paradis, E. and Michaux, J. (2005). Homogeneity of fossil assemblages extracted from mine dumps: an analysis of Plio-Pleistocene fauna from South African caves. *Lethaia* 38(4), 315–322.

Senut, B. and Gommery, D. (1997). Squelette postcrânien d'*Otavipithecus*, Hominoidea du Miocène moyen de Namibie. *Annales de Paléontologie* 83, 267–284.

Senut, B. and Pickford, M. (Eds.) (1994). *Geology and Palaeobiology of the Albertine Rift Valley, Uganda-Zaire, Vol. II, Palaeobiology*. Publication Occasionelle. Orléans: Centre International pour la Formation et les Echanges Géologiques – CIFEG, p. 423.

Senut, B., Pickford, M., Gommery, D., et al. (2001). First hominid from the Miocene (Lukeino Formation, Kenya). *Comptes Rendus de l'Academie des Sciences, Serie II: Sciences de la Terre et des Planetes* 332, 137–144.

Senut, B., Pickford, M. and Ségalen, L. (2009). Neogene desertification of Africa. *Comptes Rendus Geoscience* 341(8–9), 591–602.

Şenyürek, M. (1955). A note on the teeth of *Meganthropus africanus* Weinert from Tanganyika Territory. *Belleten* 19, 1–55.

Sepkoski Jr, J.J. (1988). Alpha, beta, or gamma: where does all the diversity go? *Paleobiology* 14, 221–234.

Sepulchre, P., Ramstein, G., Fluteau, F., et al. (2006). Tectonic uplift and eastern African aridification. *Science* 313, 1419–1423.

Sewell, L. (2019). Using a multiproxy analysis of springbok fossils to track two million years of vegetation changes as experienced by our hominin ancestors. Unpublished PhD thesis. Department of Archaeology, Anthropology and Forensic Science, Bournemouth University.

Sewell, L., Merceron, G., Hopley, P.J., Zipfel, B. and Reynolds, S.C. (2019). Using springbok (*Antidorcas*) dietary proxies to reconstruct inferred palaeovegetational changes over 2 million years in Southern Africa. *Journal of Archaeological Science: Reports* 23, 1014–1028.

Shaar, R., Matmon, A., Horwitz, L.K., et al. (2021). Magnetostratigraphy and cosmogenic dating of Wonderwerk Cave: new constraints for the chronology of the South African Earlier Stone Age. *Quaternary Science Reviews* 259, 106907.

Shackleton, N.J. (2000). The 100,000-year ice-age cycle identified and found to lag temperature, carbon dioxide, and orbital eccentricity. *Science* 289, 1897–1902.

Shackleton, N.J. and Kennett, J.P. (1975). Paleotemperature history of the Cenozoic and the initiation of Antarctic glaciation: oxygen and carbon isotope analyses in DSDP Sites 277, 279, and 281. *Initial Reports of the Deep Sea Drilling Project* 29, 743–755.

Shackleton, N.J., Backman, J., Zimmerman, H., et al. (1984). Oxygen isotope calibration of the onset of ice-rafting and history of glaciation in the North Atlantic region. *Nature* 307, 620–623.

Shackleton, N.J., Berger, A. and Peltier, W.R. (1990). An alternative astronomical calibration of the lower Pleistocene timescale based on ODP Site 677. *Earth and Environmental Science Transactions of the Royal Society of Edinburgh* 81(4), 251–261.

Shackleton, R.M. (1978). Geological map of the Olorgesailie area. In: W.W. Bishop (Ed.), *Geological Background to Fossil Man*. Edinburgh: Scottish Academic Press, pp. 171–172.

Shaffer, B.S. (1992). Quarter-inch screening: understanding biases in recovery of vertebrate faunal remains. *American Antiquity* 57, 129–136.

Shaffer, B.S. and Sanchez, J.L.J. (1994). Comparison of 1/8″- and 1/4″-mesh recovery of controlled samples of small-to-medium sized mammals. *American Antiquity* 59, 525–530.

Shaw, J.C.M. (1939). Further remains of a Sterkfontein ape. *Nature* 143, 117.

Shaw, J.C.M. (1940). Concerning some remains of a new Sterkfontein primate. *Annals of the Transvaal Museum* 20, 145–156.

Sheehan, P.M., Fastovsky, D.E., Hoffman, R.G., Berghaus, C.B. and Gabriel, D.L. (1991). Sudden extinction of the dinosaurs: latest Cretaceous, Upper Great Plains, U.S.A. *Science* 254, 835–839.

Shipman, P. (1986). Studies of hominid–faunal interactions at Olduvai Gorge. *Journal of Human Evolution* 15, 691–706.

Shipman, P. and Harris, J. (1988). Habitat preference and paleoecology of *Australopithecus boisei* in Eastern Africa. In: F. Grine (Ed.), *Evolutionary History of the Robust Australopithecines*. New York: De Gruyter, pp. 343–381.

Shipman, Bosler, W., Davis, K.L., et al. (1981). Butchering of giant geladas at an Acheulian site. *Current Anthropology* 22, 257–268.

Shipman, P., Potts, R. and Pickford, M. (1983). Lainyamok: a new middle Pleistocene hominid site. *Nature* 306, 365–368.

Shorrocks, B. (2007). *The Biology of African Savannahs*. Oxford: Oxford University Press.

Shultz, S. and Maslin, M.A. (2013). Early human speciation, brain expansion and dispersal influenced by African climate pulses. *PLoS ONE* 8, e76750.

Sievers, C. (2006). Seeds from the middle stone age layers at Sibudu Cave. *Southern African Humanities* 18(1), 203–222.

Sievers, C. (2011). Sedges from Sibudu, South Africa: evidence for their use. In: A.G. Fahmy et al. (Eds.), *Windows on the African Past: Current Approaches to African Archaeobotany. Reports in African Archaeology 3*. Frankfut am Main: Africa Magna Verlag, pp. 9–18.

Signor, P.W. and Lipps, J.H. (1982). Sampling bias, gradual extinction patterns, and catastrophes in the fossil record. In: L.T. Silver and P.H. Schultz (Eds.), *Geological Implications of Impacts of Large Asteroids and Comets on the Earth*. Boulder: Geological Society of America, vol. 190, pp. 291–296.

Sikes, N. (1994). Early hominin habitat preferences in East Africa: paleosol carbon isotopic evidence. *Journal of Human Evolution* 27, 25–45.

Sikes, N.E., Potts, R. and Behrensmeyer, A.K. (1999). Early Pleistocene habitat in Member 1 Olorgesailie based on paleosol stable isotopes. *Journal of Human Evolution* 37, 721–746.

Sillen, A. and Hoering, T. (1993). Chemical characterization of burnt bones from Swartkrans. In: C.K. Brain (Ed.), *Swartkrans: A Cave's Chronicle of Early Man*. Transvaal Museum Monograph No. 8. Pretoria: Transvaal Museum, pp. 243–249.

Sillen, A., Hall, G., Richardson, S. and Armstrong, R. (1998). $^{87}Sr/^{86}Sr$ ratios in modern and fossil food-webs of the Sterkfontein Valley: implications for early hominid habitat preference. *Geochimica et Cosmochimica Acta* 62(14), 2463–2473.

Simberloff, D. (1972). Properties of the rarefaction diversity measurement. *The American Naturalist* 106, 414–418.

Simpson, E.H. (1949). Measurement of diversity. *Nature* 163, 688.

Simpson, G.G. (1964). Species diversity of North American recent mammals. *Systematic Zoology* 13, 57–73.

Simpson, G.G. (1965). Family: Galagidae. In: L.S.B. Leakey (Ed.), *Olduvai Gorge 1951–61: Volume 1. A Preliminary Report on the Geology and Fauna*. Cambridge: Cambridge University Press, pp. 15–16.

Simpson, S.W., Quade, J., Levin, N.E., et al. (2008). A female *Homo erectus* pelvis from Gona, Ethiopia. *Science* 322, 1089–1092.

Simpson, S.W., Kleinsasser, L., Quade, J., et al. (2015). Late Miocene hominin teeth from the Gona Paleoanthropological Research Project area, Afar, Ethiopia. *Journal of Human Evolution* 81, 68–82.

Simpson, S.W., Levin, N.E., Quade, J., Rogers, M.J. and Semaw, S. (2019). *Ardipithecus ramidus* postcrania from the Gona Project area, Afar Regional State, Ethiopia. *Journal of Human Evolution* 129, 1–45.

Sinclair, A.R.E. (1979a). The eruption of the ruminants. In: A.R.E. Sinclair and M. Norton-Griffiths (Eds.), *Serengeti, Dynamics of an Ecosystem*. Chicago: University of Chicago Press, pp. 82–103.

Sinclair, A.R.E. (1979b). Serengeti, dynamics of an ecosystem. In: A.R.E. Sinclair and M. Norton-Griffiths (Eds.), *Serengeti, Dynamics of an Ecosystem*. Chicago: University of Chicago Press, pp. 82–103.

Sinclair, A.R.E., Mduma, S.A.R. and Arcese, P. (2000). What determines phenology and synchrony of ungulate breeding in the Serengeti? *Ecology* 81(8), 2100–2111.

Singer, B.S. (2014). A Quaternary geomagnetic instability time scale. *Quaternary Geochronology* 21(c), 29–52.

Singer, R. and Wymer, J. (1968). Archaeological investigations at the Saldanha skull site in South Africa. *The South African Archaeological Bulletin* 23(91), 63–74.

Singer, R. and Wymer, J. (1982). *The Middle Stone Age at Klasies River Mouth in South Africa*. Chicago: University of Chicago Press.

Skinner, J.D. and Amithers, R.H.N. (1990). *The Mammals of the Southern African Subregion* (2nd ed.). Pretoria: University of Pretoria.

Skinner, M.M., Kivell, T.L., Potze, S. and Hublin J.-J. (2013). Microtomographic archive of fossil hominin specimens from Kromdraai B, South Africa. *Journal of Human Evolution* 64, 434–447.

Smit, H.A., Robinson, T.J., Watson, J.E.M. and Jansen van Vuren, B. (2008). A new species of elephant-shrew (Afrotheria: Macroscelidea: *Elephantulus*) from South Africa. *Journal of Mammalogy* 89, 1257–1269.

Smith, A.B. (1994). *Systematics and the Fossil Record*. Oxford: Blackwell Scientific.

Smith, C.C., Morgan, M.E. and Pilbeam, D. (2010). Isotopic ecology and dietary profiles of Liberian chimpanzees. *Journal of Human Evolution* 58, 43–55.

Smith, G.M., Ruebens, K., Gaudzinski-Windheuser, S. and Steele, T.E. (2019). Subsistence strategies throughout the African Middle Pleistocene: faunal evidence for behavioral change and continuity across the Earlier to Middle Stone Age transition. *Journal of Human Evolution* 127, 1–20.

Smith, P., Nshimirimana, R., de Beer, F.C., et al. (2012). Canteen Kopje: a new look at an old skull. *South African Journal of Science* 108(1/2), 1–9.

Smith, R.J. (2016). Explanations for adaptations, just-so stories, and limitations on evidence in evolutionary biology. *Evolutionary Anthropology* 25(6), 276–287.

Smith, S.M., Sprain, C.J., Clemens, W.A., et al. (2018). Early mammalian recovery after the end-Cretaceous mass extinction: a high-resolution view from McGuire Creek area, Montana, USA. *GSA Bulletin* 130, 2000–2014.

Smithers, R.H.N. (1983). *The Mammals of the Southern African Subregion*. Pretoria: University of Pretoria.

Soares, P., Alshamali, F., Pereira, J.B., et al. (2012). The expansion of mtDNA haplogroup L3 within and out of Africa. *Molecular Biology and Evolution* 29, 915–927.

Soligo, C. and Andrews, P. (2005). Taphonomic bias, taxonomic bias and historical non-equivalence of faunal structure in early hominin localities. *Journal of Human Evolution* 49, 206–229.

Solounias, N. and Semprebon, G.M. (2002). Advances in the reconstruction of ungulate ecomorphology with application to early fossil equids. *American Museum Novitates* 3366, 1–49.

Solounias, N., McGraw, W.S., Hayek, L.A.C. and Werdelin, L. (2000). The paleodiet of the Giraffidae. In E.S. Vrba and G.B. Schaller (Eds.), *Antelopes, Deer, and Relatives*. New Haven: Yale University Press, pp. 84–95.

Souron, A. (2012). Histoire évolutive du genre *Kolpochoerus* (Cetartiodactyla: Suidae) au Plio-Pléistocène en Afrique Orientale. Thesis, University of Poitiers, France.

Souron, A. (2017). Diet and ecology of extant and fossil wild pigs. In: M. Melletti and E. Meijaard (Eds.), *Ecology, Conservation and Management of Wild Pigs and Peccaries*. Cambridge: Cambridge University Press, pp. 29–38.

Souron, A., Boisserie, J.R. and White, T.D. (2013). A new species of the suid genus *Kolpochoerus* from Ethiopia. *Acta Palaeontologica Polonica* 60(1), 79–96.

Souron, A., Boisserie, J.-R. and White, T.D. (2015). A new species of *Kolpochoerus* from Ethiopia. *Acta Paleontologica Polonica* 60, 79–96.

South African Rain Atlas, online resource http://134.76.173.220/rainfall/index.html, accessed 20/08/2013.

Spencer, L. (1995a). Antelopes and grasslands: reconstructing African hominid environments. PhD thesis, Anthropological Sciences. State University of New York, Stony Brook.

Spencer, L. (1995b). Morphological correlates of dietary resource partitioning in the African bovidae. *Journal of Mammology* 76, 448–471.

Sponheimer, M. and Lee-Thorp, J.A. (1999). Isotopic evidence for the diet of an early hominid, *Australopithecus africanus*. *Science* 283, 368–370.

Sponheimer, M. and Lee-Thorp, J.A. (2003). Using carbon isotope data of fossil bovid communities for palaeoenvironmental reconstruction. *South African Journal of Science* 99(5–6), 273–275.

Sponheimer, M. and Lee-Thorp, J.A. (2009). Biogeochemical evidence for the environments of early *Homo* in South Africa. In: F.E. Grine., J.G. Fleagle and R.E. Leakey (Eds.), *The First Humans: Origin and Early Evolution of the Genus Homo. Vertebrate Paleobiology and Paleoanthropology*. New York: Springer Science, pp. 185–194.

Sponheimer, M., Reed, K.E. and Lee-Thorp, J. (1999). Combining isotopic and ecomorphological data to refine bovid paleodietary reconstruction: a case study from the Makapansgat Limeworks hominin locality. *Journal of Human Evolution* 36, 705–718.

Sponheimer, M., Reed, K. and Lee-Thorp, J.A. (2001). Isotopic palaeoecology of Makapansgat Limeworks perissodactyla. *South African Journal of Science* 97(7–8), 327–329.

Sponheimer, M., Lee-Thorp, J.A., de Ruiter, D.J., et al. (2005a). Hominins, sedges, and termites: new carbon isotope data from the Sterkfontein Valley and Kruger National Park. *Journal of Human Evolution* 418, 301–312.

Sponheimer, M., de Ruiter, D.J., Lee-Thorp, J. and Späth, A. (2005b). Sr/Ca and early hominin diets revisited: new data from modern and fossil enamel. *Journal of Human Evolution* 48, 147–156.

Sponheimer, M., Loudon, J. E., Codron, D., et al. (2006a). Do "savanna" chimpanzees consume C_4 resources? *Journal of Human Evolution* 51, 128–133.

Sponheimer, M., Passey, B.H., de Ruiter, D.J., et al. (2006b). Isotope evidence for dietary variability in the early hominin *Paranthropus robustus*. *Science* 314, 980–982.

Sponheimer, M., Lee-Thorp, J.A. and de Ruiter, D.J. (2007). Icarus, isotopes, and australopith diets. In: P.S. Ungar (Ed.), *Evolution of the Human Diet: The Known, The Unknown, and The Unknowable*. Oxford: Oxford University Press, pp. 132–149.

Sponheimer, M., Alemseged, Z., Cerling, T. E., et al. (2013). Isotopic evidence of early hominin diets. *Proceedings of the National Academy of Sciences of the United States of America* 110, 10513–10518.

Spoor, F., Leakey, M.G., Gathogo, P.N., et al. (2007). Implications of new early *Homo* fossils from Ileret, east of Lake Turkana, Kenya. *Nature* 448, 688–691.

Spoor, F., Leakey, M.G. and Leakey, L.N. (2010). Hominin diversity in the Middle Pliocene of eastern Africa: the maxilla of KNM-WT 40000. *Philosophical Transactions of the Royal Society B: Biological Sciences* 365, 3377–3388.

Stammers, R.C., Caruana, M.V. and Herries, A.I. (2018). The first bone tools from Kromdraai and stone tools from Drimolen, and the place of bone tools in the South African Earlier Stone Age. *Quaternary International* 495, 87–101.

Stanistreet, I.G. (2012). Fine resolution of early hominin time, Beds I and II, Olduvai Gorge, Tanzania. *Journal of Human Evolution* 63, 300–308.

Stanistreet, I.G., Stollhofen, H., Njau, J.K., et al. (2018). Lahar inundated, modified and preserved 1.88 Ma early hominin (OH24 and OH56) Olduvai DK site. *Journal of Human Evolution* 116, 27–42.

Stankiewicz, J. and de Wit, M.J. (2006). A proposed drainage evolution model for Central Africa – did the Congo flow east? *Journal of African Earth Sciences* 44, 75–84.

Stauffer, R.L., Walker, A., Ryder, O., Lyons-Weiler, M. and Hedges, S.B. (2001). Human and ape molecular clocks and constraints on paleontological hypotheses. *Journal of Heredity* 92(6), 469–474.

Steele, T.E. (2012). Late Pleistocene human subsistence in Northern Africa: the state of our knowledge and placement in a continental context. In: J.-J. Hublin and S.P. McPherron (Eds.), *Modern Origins: A North African Perspective*. Dordrecht: Springer, pp. 107–125.

Steele, T.E. and Klein, R.G. (2013). The Middle and later Stone Age faunal remains from Diepkloof Rock Shelter, Western Cape, South Africa. *Journal of Archaeological Science* 40, 3453–3462.

Stearns, C.E. (1978). Pliocene–Pleistocene emergence of the Moroccan Meseta. *Geological Society of America Bulletin* 89, 1630–1644.

Stein, R. and Sarnthein, M. (1984). Late Neogene oxygen isotope stratigraphy and terrigenous flux rates at Site 544B off Morocco. *Initial Reports DSDP* 79, 385–394.

Steininger, C. (2011). The dietary behaviour of early Pleistocene bovids from Cooper's Cave and Swartkrans, South Africa. Unpublished PhD thesis, University of the Witwatersrand, Johannesburg.

Steininger, C., Berger, L.R. and Kuhn, B.F. (2008). A partial skull of *Paranthropus robustus* from Cooper's Cave, South Africa. *South African Journal of Science* 104, 1–4.

Steininger, F.F., Rabeder, G. and Rögl, F. (1985). Land mammal distribution in the Mediterranean Neogene: a consequence of geokinematic and climatic events. In: D.J. Stanley and F.C. Wezel (Eds.), *Geological Evolution of the Mediterranean Basin*. New York: Springer, pp. 559–571.

Steiper, M. and Young, N. (2006). Primate molecular divergence dates. *Molecular Phylogenetics and Evolution* 41(2), 384–394.

Stern, J.T. (2000). Climbing to the top: a personal memoir of *Australopithecus afarensis*. *Evolutionary Anthropology* 9, 113–133.

Stern, J.T. and Susman, R.L. (1983). The locomotor anatomy of *Australopithecus afarensis*. *American Journal of Physical Anthropology* 60, 279–317.

Stern, N. (1994). The implications of time-averaging for reconstructing the land-use patterns of early tool-using hominids. *Journal of Human Evolution* 27(1–3), 89–105.

Stern, N., Porch, N. and McDougall, I. (2002). FxJj43: a window into a 1.5 million-year-old palaeolandscape in the Okote Member of the Koobi Fora Formation, Northern Kenya. *Geoarchaeology* 17, 349–392.

Stewart, B.A. and Mitchell, P.J. (2018). Late Quaternary palaeoclimates and human-environment dynamics of the Maloti–Drakensberg region, southern Africa. *Quaternary Science Reviews* 196, 1–20.

Stewart, K.M. (1990). Fossil fish from the upper Semliki. In: N.T. Boaz (Ed.), *Evolution of Environments and Hominidae in the African Western Rift Valley*. Martinsville: Virginia Museum of Natural History, pp. 141–163.

Stewart, K.M. (1997). Fossil fish from the Manonga Valley, Tanzania: description, paleoecology, and biogeographic relationships. In: T. Harrison (Ed.), *Neogene Paleontology of the Manonga Valley, Tanzania: A Window into the Evolutionary History of East Africa*. New York: Springer, pp. 333–349.

Stewart, K.M. (2001). The freshwater fish of Neogene Africa (Miocene–Pleistocene): systematics and biogeography. *Fish and Fisheries* 2, 177–230.

Stewart, K. (2003). Fossil fish remains from Mio-Pliocene deposits at Lothagam, Kenya. In: M.G. Leakey and J.M. Harris (Eds.), *Lothagam: The Dawn of Humanity in Eastern Africa*. New York: Columbia University Press, pp. 75–111.

Stewart, K.M. and Murray, A.M. (2013). Earliest fish remains from the Lake Malawi Basin, Malawi, and biogeographical implications. *Journal of Vertebrate Paleontology* 33, 532–539.

Stewart, K.M. and Rufolo, S.J. (2020). Kanapoi revisited: paleoecological and biogeographical inferences from the fossil fish. *Journal of Human Evolution* 140, 102452.

Stidham, T.A. (2007). Preliminary assessment of the late Miocene avifauna from Lemudong'o, Kenya. *Kirtlandia* 56, 173–176.

Stidham, T.A. (2009). A lovebird (Psittaciformes: *Agapornis*) from the Plio-Pleistocene Kromdraai B locality, South Africa. *South African Journal of Science* 105(3–4), 155–157.

Stidham, T.A. (2010). A small Pleistocene lovebird (Psittacidae: *Agapornis*) from Plovers Lake, South Africa. *Neues Jahrbuch für Geologie und Paläontologie-Abhandlungen* 256(1), 123–128.

Stoetzel, E., Marion, L., Nespoulet, R., El Hajraoui, M.A. and Denys, C. (2011). Taphonomy and palaeoecology of the late Pleistocene to middle Holocene small mammal succession of El Harhoura 2 cave (Rabat – Témara, Morocco). *Journal of Human Evolution* 60, 1–33.

Stollhofen, H. and Stanistreet, I.G. (2012). Plio-Pleistocene synsedimentary fault compartments, foundation for the eastern

Olduvai Basin palaeoenvironmental mosaic, Tanzania. *Journal of Human Evolution* 63, 309–327.

Stout, D., Quade, J., Semaw, S., Rogers, M.J. and Levin, N.E. (2005). Raw material selectivity of the earliest stone toolmakers at Gona, Afar, Ethiopia. *Journal of Human Evolution* 48, 365–380.

Stout, D., Semaw, S., Rogers, M.J. and Cauche, D. (2010). Technological variation in the earliest Oldowan from Gona, Afar, Ethiopia. *Journal of Human Evolution* 58, 474–491.

Stratford, D.J. (2011). The underground central deposits of the Sterkfontein caves, South Africa. Unpublished PhD thesis, University of the Witwatersrand, Johannesburg.

Stratford, D. (2015). The sterkfontein caves: geomorphology and hominin-bearing deposits. In: S. Grab and J. Knight (Eds.), *Landscapes and Landforms of South Africa. World Geomorphological Landscapes*. Cham: Springer International Publishing, pp. 147–153.

Stratford, D. (2017). A review of the geomorphological context and stratigraphy of the Sterkfontein caves, South Africa. In: A.N. Klimchouk, A. Palmer, J.S. De Waele, A. Auler and P. Audra (Eds.), *Hypogene Karst Regions and Caves of the World Cave and Karst Systems of the World*. Cham: Springer, pp. 879–891.

Stratford, D.J. (2018). The Sterkfontein Caves after eighty years of paleoanthropological research: the journey continues. *American Anthropologist* 120(1), 39–54.

Stratford, D.J., Bruxelles, L., Clarke, R.J. and Kuman, K. (2012). New stratigraphic interpretations of the fossil and artefact-bearing deposits of the Name Chamber, Sterkfontein. *The South African Archaeological Bulletin* 67(196), 159–167.

Stratford, D., Grab, S. and Pickering, T.R. (2014). The stratigraphy and formation history of fossil- and artefact-bearing sediments in the Milner Hall, Sterkfontein Cave, South Africa: new interpretations and implications for palaeoanthropology and archaeology. *Journal of African Earth Sciences* 96, 155–167.

Stratford, D., Bruxelles, L., Thackeray, J.F., Pickering, T.R. and Verheyden, S. (2020). Comments on 'U–Pb dated flowstones restrict South African early hominin record to dry climate phases' (Pickering et al. *Nature* 2018; 565: 226–229). *South African Journal of Science* 116(3–4), 1–2.

Strauss, D. and Sadler, P.M. (1989). Classical confidence intervals and Bayesian probability estimates for ends of local taxon ranges. *Mathematical Geology* 21(4), 411–427.

Street-Perrot, F.A. and Perrott, R. (1993). A Holocene vegetation, lake levels and climate of Africa. In: H.E. Wright Jr., J.E. Kutz bach, T. Webb III, et al. (Eds.), *Global Climates since the Last Glacial Maximum*. Minneapolis: University of Minnesota Press, pp. 318–356.

Stringer, C. (2012). The status of *Homo heidelbergensis* (Schoetensack, 1908). *Evolutionary Anthropology* 21, 101–107.

Stromer, E. (1902). Wirbeltierreste aus dem mittlerem Pliozän des Natrontales und einige subfossile und rezenten Säugetiereste aus Agypten. *Zeitschrift der Deutschen Geologischen Gesellschaft* 54, 108–115.

Struhsaker, T.T. (1967). Auditory communication among vervet monkeys (*Cercopithecus aethiops*). In: S.A. Altmann (Ed.), *Social Communication Among Primates*. Chicago: University of Chicago Press, pp. 281–324.

Stuut, J.-B.W., Crosta, X., van der Borg, K. and Schneider, R.R. (2004). On the relationship between Antactic sea ice and southwestern African climate during the late Quaternary. *Geology* 32, 909–912.

Stynder, D.D. (1997). The use of faunal evidence to reconstruct site history and Hoedjiespunt 1 (HDP1), Western Cape. Doctoral dissertation, University of Cape Town.

Stynder, D.D. (2009). The diets of ungulates from the hominid fossil-bearing site of Elandsfontein, Western Cape, South Africa. *Quaternary Research* 71(1), 62–70.

Stynder, D.D. (2011). Fossil bovid diets indicate a scarcity of grass in the Langebaanweg E Quarry (South Africa) late Miocene/early Pliocene environment. *Paleobiology* 37(1), 126–139.

Su, D. (2005). The Paleoecology of Laetoli, Tanzania: evidence from the mammalian fauna of the Upper Laetolil Beds. PhD dissertation, New York University.

Su, D.F. (2011). Large mammal evidence for the paleoenvironment of the Upper Laetolil and Upper Ndolanya Beds of Laetoli, Tanzania. In: T. Harrison (Ed.), *Paleontology and Geology of Laetoli: Human Evolution in Context. Vol. 1: Geology, Geochronology, Paleoecology, and Paleoenvironment*. Dordrecht: Springer, pp. 381–392.

Su, D.E. and Harrison, T. (2007). The paleoecology of the Upper Laetolil Beds at Laetoli – A reconsideration of the large mammal evidence. In: R. Bobe, Z. Alemseged and A.K. Behrensmeyer (Eds.), *Hominin Environments in the East African Pliocene: An Assessment of the Faunal Evidence*. Berlin: Springer, pp. 279–313.

Su, D. and Harrison, T. (2008). Ecological implications of the relative rarity of fossil hominins at Laetoli. *Journal of Human Evolution* 55, 672–681.

Su, D.F. and Harrison, T. (2015). The paleoecology of the Upper Laetolil Beds, Laetoli, Tanzania. A review and synthesis. *Journal of African Earth Sciences* 101, 405–419.

Su, D.F., Ambrose, S.H., DeGusta, D. and Haile-Selassie, Y. (2009). Paleoenvironment. In: Y. Haile-Selassie and G. WoldeGabriel (Eds.), *Ardipithecus kadabba: Late Miocene Evidence from the Middle Awash*. Berkeley: University of California Press, pp. 521–547.

Suc, J.-P., Popescu, S.-M., Fauquette, S., et al. (2018). Reconstruction of Mediterranean flora, vegetation and climate for the last 23 million years based on an extensive pollen dataset. *Ecologia Mediterranea* 44, 53–85.

Sudre, J. and Hartenberger, J.L. (1992). Oued Mya 1, nouveau gisement demammifères du Miocène supérieur dans le sud Algérien. *Geobios* 25(4), 553–565.

Surovell, T.A., Finley, J.B., Smith, G.M., Brantingham, P.J. and Kelly, R. (2009). Correcting temporal frequency distributions for taphonomic bias. *Journal of Archaeological Science* 36, 1715–1724.

Susman, R.L. and Stern, J.T. (1991). Locomotor behavior of early hominids: epistemology and fossil evidence. In: Y. Coppens and B. Senut (Eds.), *Origine(s) de la Bipédie chez les Hominidés*. Paris: Cahiers de Paléoanthropologie, CNRS, pp. 121–132.

Susman, R.L., Stern, J.T. and Jungers, W.L. (1984). Arboreality and bipedality in the Hadar hominids. *Folia Primatologia* 43, 113–156.

Susman, R.L., Stern, J.T. and Jungers, W.L. (1985). Locomotor adaptations in the Hadar hominids. In: E. Delson (Ed.), *Ancestors: The Hard Evidence*. New York: Alan R. Liss, pp. 184–192.

Sutton, M.B., Pickering, T.R., Pickering, R., et al. (2009). Newly discovered fossil- and artifact-bearing deposits, uranium-series ages, and Plio-Pleistocene hominids at Swartkrans Cave, South Africa. *Journal of Human Evolution* 57, 688–696.

Sutton, M.B., Kuman, K. and Steininger, C. (2017). Early Pleistocene stone artefacts from Cooper's Cave, South Africa. *The South African Archaeological Bulletin* 72(206), 156–161.

Suwa, G. (1990). A comparative analysis of hominid dental remains from the Shungura and Usno Formations, Omo Valley, Ethiopia. Unpublished PhD dissertation, University of California, Berkeley.

Suwa, G. and Ambrose, S.H. (2014). Reply to Cerling et al. *Current Anthropology* 55, 473–474.

Suwa, G., White, T.D. and Howell, F.C. (1996). Mandibular postcanine dentition from the Shungura Formation, Ethiopia: crown morphology, taxonomic allocations, and Plio-Pleistocene hominid evolution. *American Journal of Physical Anthropology* 101, 247–282.

Suwa, G., Asfaw, B., Beyene, Y., et al. (1997). The first skull of *Australopithecus boisei*. *Nature* 389, 489–492.

Suwa, G., Nakaya, H., Asfaw, B., et al. (2003). Plio-Pleistocene terrestrial mammal assemblage from Konso, Southern Ethiopia. *Journal of Vertebrate Paleontology* 23, 901–916.

Suwa, G., Asfaw, B., Haile-Selassie, Y., et al. (2007a). Early Pleistocene *Homo erectus* fossils from Konso, southern Ethiopia. *Anthropological Science* 115, 133–151.

Suwa, G., Kono, R.T., Katoh, S., Asfaw, B. and Beyene, Y. (2007b). A new species of great ape from the late Miocene epoch in Ethiopia. *Nature* 448(7156), 921–924.

Suwa, G., Nakaya, H. and Asfaw, B. (2014a). The Konso Formation paleontological assemblages: collecting and documentation methodologies. In: G. Suwa, Y. Beyene and B. Asfaw (Eds.), *The Konso-Gardula Research Project Volume 1. Paleonotological Collections: Background and Fossil Aves, Cercopithecidae, and Suidae*. Tokyo: The University Museum, The University of Tokyo, Bulletin, 47, 5–9.

Suwa, G., Souron, A. and Asfaw, B. (2014b). Fossil Suidae of the Konso Formation. In: G. Suwa, Y. Beyene and B. Asfaw (Eds.), *The Konso-Gardula Research Project Volume 1. Paleonotological Collections: Background and Fossil Aves, Cercopithecidae, and Suidae*, Tokyo: The University Museum, The University of Tokyo, Bulletin, 47, 73–88.

Suwa, G., Beyene, Y., Nakaya, H., et al. (2015). Newly discovered cercopithecid, equid and other mammalian fossils from the Chorora Formation, Ethiopia. *Anthropological Science* 123, 19–39.

Szalay, F.S. and Delson, E. (1979). *Evolutionary History of the Primates*. New York: Academic Press.

Taieb, M. (1971). Les dépôts quaternaires sédimentaires de la vallée de l'Aouache et leurs relations avec la néotectonique cassante du rift. *Quaternaria* 15, 351–365.

Taieb, M. (1974). Evolution Quaternarie du Bassin de l'Awash (Rift Éthiopien et Afar). PhD dissertation, Universite Paris VI.

Taieb, M. and Fritz, B. (Eds.) (1987). *Lake Natron: géologie, géochimie et paléontologie d'un bassin évaporatique du rift est-africain*. Sciences Géologiques Bulletin 40.

Taieb, M. and Tiercelin, J.J. (1979). Sédimentation Pliocène et paléoenvironments de rift: Exemple de la formation à Hominidés d'Hadar (Afar, Éthiopie). *Bulletin du Société Géologiques de France* 21, 243–253.

Taieb, M. and Tiercelin, J.J. (1980). La stratigraphie et paléoenvironnements sédimentaires de la formation d'Hadar, depression de l'Afar, Éthiopie. In: R.E. Leakey and B.A. Ogot (Eds.), *Proceedings of the 8th Panafrican Congress on Prehistory and Quaternary Studies, Nairobi, 1977*. Nairobi: TILLMIAP, pp. 109–114.

Taieb, M., Coppens, Y., Johanson, D.C., Kalb, J.E. (1972). Dépôts Sédimentaires et faunes du Plio-Pléistocène de la Basse Vallée de l'Awash (Afar Central, Éthiopie). *CComptes Rendu de l'Académie des Sciences Paris, Série D* 275, 819–822.

Taieb, M., Johanson, D.C., Coppens, Y., Bonnefille, R. and Kalb, J.E. (1974). Découverte d'Hominidés dans les séries Plio-pléistocènes d'Hadar (Bassin de l'Awash; Afar, Ethiopie). *Comptes Rendus de l'Académie des Sciences, Série D* 279, 735–738.

Taieb, M., Johanson, D.C., Coppens, Y. and Aronson, J.L. (1976). Geological and palaeontological background of Hadar hominid site, Afar, Ethiopia. *Nature* 260, 289–293.

Takemoto, H., Kawamoto, Y. and Furuichi, T. (2015). How did bonobos come to range south of the congo river? Reconsideration of the divergence of *Pan paniscus* from other *Pan* populations. *Evolutionary Anthropology: Issues, News, and Reviews* 24, 170–184.

Tamrat, E., Thouveny, N., Taieb, M. and Opdyke, N.D. (1995). Revised magnetostratigraphy of the Plio-Pleistocene sedimentary sequence of the Olduvai Formation (Tanzania). *Palaeogeography, Palaeoclimatology, Palaeoecology* 114, 273–283.

Tamrat, E., Thouveny, N., Taieb, M. and Brugal, J.P. (2014). Magnetostratigraphic study of the Melka Kunture archaeological site (Ethiopia) and its chronological implications. *Quaternary International* 343, 5–16.

Tarver, J.E., Donoghue, P.C.J. and Benton, M.J. (2011). Is evolutionary history repeatedly rewritten in light of new fossil discoveries? *Proceedings of the Royal Society B: Biological Sciences* 278, 599–604.

Tassy, P. (1994). Les proboscideans fossiles (Mammalia) du Rift Occidental, Ouganda. In: B. Senut and M. Pickford (Eds.), *Geology and Palaeobiology of the Albertine Rift Valley, Uganda-Zaire, Vol. II, Palaeobiology*. Publication Occasionelle. Orléans: Centre International pour la Formation et les Echanges Géologiques – CIFEG, pp. 217–257.

Tattersfield, P. (2011). Terrestrial Mollusca. In: T. Harrison (Ed.), *Paleontology and Geology of Laetoli: Human Evolution in Context. Vol. 2: Fossil Hominins and the Associated Fauna*. Dordrecht: Springer, pp. 567–587.

Taub, D.R. (2000). Climate and the U.S. distribution of C_4 grass subfamilies and decarboxylation variants of C_4 photosynthesis. *American Journal of Botany* 87, 1211–1125.

Tauxe, L., Deino, A., Behrensmeyer, A.K. and Potts, R. (1992). Pinning down the Brunhes/Matuyama and upper Jaramillo boundaries: a reconciliation of orbital and isotopic time scales. *Earth and Planetary Science Letters* 109, 561–572.

Tchernov, E., Horwitz, L.K., Ronen, A. and Lister, A. (1994). The faunal remains from Evron Quarry in relation to other Lower Paleolithic hominid sites in the southern Levant. *Quaternary Research* 42(3), 328–339.

Teaford, M.F. (1994). Dental microwear and dental function. *Evolutionary Anthropology* 3, 17–30.

Teaford, M.F. and Ungar, P.S. (2000). Diet and the evolution of the earliest human ancestors. *Proceedings of the National Academy of Sciences* 97(25), 13506–13511.

Teague, R.L. (2009). The ecological context of the Early Pleistocene hominin dispersal to Asia. PhD dissertation, The George Washington University.

Tennant, J.P., Mannion, P.D. and Upchurch, P. (2016). Sea level regulated tetrapod diversity dynamics through the Jurassic/Cretaceous interval. *Nature Communications* 7, 12737.

Texier, J.-P., Lefèvre, D. and Raynal, J.-P. (1994). Contribution pour un nouveau cadre stratigraphique des formations littorales quaternaires de la région de Casablanca. *Comptes rendus de l'Académie de Sciences Paris (II)* 318, 1247–1253.

Texier, J.-P., Lefèvre, D., Raynal, J.-P. and El Graoui, M. (2002). Lithostratigraphy of the littoral deposits of the last one million years in Casablanca region (Maroc). *Quaternaire* 13, 23–41.

Texier, P.J., Roche, H. and Harmand, S. (2006). Kokiselei 5, Formation de Nachukui (Kenya): un témoignage de la variabilité ou de l'évolution des comportements techniques au Pléistocène ancien? *BAR International Series* 1522, 11–22.

Texier, P.J., Porraz, G., Parkington, J., et al. (2010). A Howiesons Poort tradition of engraving ostrich eggshell containers dated to 60,000 years ago at Diepkloof Rock Shelter, South Africa. *Proceedings of the National Academy of Sciences* 107(14), 6180–6185.

Tfwala, C.M., van Rensburg, L.D., Schall, R., Mosia, S.M. and Dlamini P. (2017). Precipitation intensity–duration–frequency curves and their uncertainties for Ghaap plateau. *Climate Risk Management* 16, 1–9.

Thackeray, A.I., Thackeray, J.F., Beaumont, P.B. and Vogel, J.C. (1981). Dated rock engravings from Wonderwerk Cave, South Africa. *Science* 214, 64–67.

Thackeray, J.F. (1979). An analysis of faunal remains from archaeological sites in southern south west Africa (Namibia). *South African Archaeological Bulletin* 34, 18–33.

Thackeray, J.F. (1983). Man, animals and extinctions: the analysis of Holocene faunal remains from Wonderwerk Cave, South Africa. PhD thesis, Yale University.

Thackeray, J.F. (1984). Climate change and mammalian fauna from the Holocene deposits at Wonderwerk Cave, northern Cape. In: J.C. Vogel (Ed.), *Late Cainozoic Paleoclimates of the Southern Hemisphere*. Rotterdam: A.A. Balkema, pp. 371–374.

Thackeray, J.F. (2015). Analysis of faunal remains from Holocene deposits, Excavation 1, Wonderwerk Cave, South Africa. *African Archaeological Review* 32, 729–750.

Thackeray, J.F. (2016). A history of research on human evolution in South Africa from 1924 to 2016. *Revue de primatologie* 7(7).

Thackeray, J.F. and Brink, J.S. (2004). *Damaliscus niro* horns from Wonderwerk Cave and other Pleistocene sites: morphological and chronological considerations. *Palaeontologica Africana* 40, 89–93.

Thackeray, J.F. and Lee-Thorp, J.A. (1992). Isotopic analysis of equid teeth from Wonderwerk Cave, northern Cape Province, South Africa. *Palaeogeography, Palaeoclimatology, Palaeoecology* 99(1–2), 141–150.

Thackeray, J.F. and Watson, V. (1994). A preliminary account of faunal remains from Plovers Lake. *South African Journal of Science* 90, 231–232.

Thackeray, J.F., Van de Venter, A., Van Heerden, J., Chimimba, C.T. and Lee-Thorp, J.A. (1999). Stable carbon isotope ratios in four subspecies of modern *Aethomys namaquensis*: spatial variability as a possible analogue of temporal variability. In: J.A. Lee-Thorp and H. Clift (Eds.), *The Environmental Background to Hominid Evolution in Africa. Abstracts of the XV International Union for Quaternary Research Congress: 177*. Cape Town: University of Cape Town.

Thackeray, J.F., de Ruiter, D.J., Berger, L.R. and van der Merwe, N.J. (2001). Hominid fossils from Kromdraai: a revised list of specimens discovered since 1938. *Annals of the Transvaail Museum* 38, 43–56.

Thackeray, J.F., Kirschvink, J.L. and Raub, T.D. (2002). Palaeomagnetic analyses of calcified deposits from the Plio-Pleistocene hominid site of Kromdraai, South Africa. *South African Journal of Science* 98, 537–540.

Thackeray, J.F., McBride, V.A., Segonyane, S.P. and Franklyn, C.B. (2003). Trace element analysis of breccias associated with the type specimen of *Australopithecus* (*Paranthropus*) *robustus* from Kromdraai. *Annals of the Transvaal Museum* 40, 147–150.

Thackeray, J.F., Braga, J., Sénégas, F., et al. (2005). Discovery of a humerus shaft from Kromdraai B: part of the skeleton of the type specimen of *Paranthropus robustus* (Broom, 1938)? *Annals of the Transvaal Museum* 42, 92–93.

Thackeray, J.F., Gommery, D., Sénégas, F., et al. (2008). A survey of past and present work on Plio-Pleistocene deposits on Bolt's Farm, Cradle of Humankind, South Africa. *Annals of the Transvaal Museum* 45(1), 83–89.

Thomas, D.S.G. and Shaw, P.A. (1991). *The Kalahari Environment*. Cambridge: Cambridge University Press.

Thomas, H. (1981a). Le fauna de la Grotte à Néandertaliens du Jebel Irhoud (Maroc). *Quaternaria* 23, 191–217.

Thomas, H. (1981b). Les Bovidés miocènes de la formation de Ngorora du bassin de Baringo (Rift valley, Kenya). *Proceedings of the Koninklijke Nederlandse Akademie van Wetenschappen* 84, 335–410.

Thomas, H. and Petter, G. (1986). Révision de la faune de mammifères du Miocène supérieurde Menacer (ex-Marceau), Algérie: Discussion sur l'âge du gisement. *Geobios* 19(3), 357–373.

Thomas, P. (1884). Recherches stratigraphiques et paléontologiques sur quelques formations d'eau douce de l'Algérie. *Mémoires de la Société Géologique de France, series 3*, 3, 1–51.

Thompson, J.C. (2010). Taphonomic analysis of the middle stone age faunal assemblage from Pinnacle Point Cave 13B, Western Cape, South Africa. *Journal of Human Evolution* 59(3–4), 321–339.

Thompson, J.C. and Henshilwood, C.S. (2011). Taphonomic analysis of the Middle Stone Age larger mammal faunal assemblage from Blombos Cave, southern Cape, South Africa. *Journal of Human Evolution* 60(6), 746–767.

Thompson, J.C. and Henshilwood, C.S. (2014). Tortoise taphonomy and tortoise butchery patterns at Blombos Cave, South Africa. *Journal of Archaeological Science* 41, 214–229.

Thompson, J.C., McPherron, S.P., Bobe, R., et al. (2015). Taphonomy of fossils from the hominin-bearing deposits at Dikika, Ethiopia. *Journal of Human Evolution* 86, 112–135.

Thompson, J.C., Kimbel, W.H., Hovers, E. and Marean, C.W. (2016). New approaches to taphonomy and field survey of fossisl across the Hadar paleo-landscape at 3.3 Ma. *PaleoAnthropology PAS 2016 abstracts*, A31.

Thouveny, N. and Taieb, M. (1986). Preliminary magnetostratigraphic record of Pleistocene deposits, Lake Natron Basin, Tanzania. In: L.E. Frostick, R.W. Renaut, I. Reid and J.-J. Tiercelin (Eds.), *Sedimentation in the African Rifts*. Geological Society Special Publication 25. Washington, DC: Geological Society, pp. 331–336.

Thouveny, N. and Taieb, M. (1987). Étude paléomagnétique des formations du Plio-Pléistocène de la région de la Peninj (Ouest du Lac Natron, Tanzanie). Limites de l'interprétation magnétostratigraphique. *Strasbourg: Sciences et Géologie Bulletin* 40, 57–70.

Tiedemann, R., Sarnthein, M. and Shackleton, N.J. (1994). Astronomic timescale for the Pliocene Atlantic delta18O and dust flux records of Ocean Drilling Program site 659. *Paleoceanography* 9, 619–638.

Tiercelin, J.J. (1986). The Pliocene Hadar Formation, Afar depression of Ethiopia. In: L.E. Frostick, R.W. Renaut, I. Reid and J.J. Tiercelin (Eds.), *Sedimentation in the African Rifts*. Oxford: Blackwell Scientific, pp. 221–240.

Tiercelin, J.-J., Schuster, M., Roche, H., et al. (2010). New considerations on the stratigraphy and environmental context of the oldest (2.34 Ma) Lokalalei archaeological site complex of the Nachukui Formation, West Turkana, northern Kenya Rift. *Journal of African Earth Sciences* 58(2), 157–184.

Timmermann, A. and Friedrich, T. (2016). Late Pleistocene climate drivers of early human migration. *Nature* 538, 92–95.

Tipper, J.C. (1979). Rarefaction and rarefiction – the use and abuse of a method in paleoecology. *Paleobiology* 5(4), 423–434.

Tipple, B.J. (2013). Capturing climate variability during our ancestors' earliest days. *Proceedings of the National Academy of Sciences* 110(4), 1144–1145.

Tobias, P.V. (1967a). *Olduvai Gorge. Volume 2, The cranium of Australopithecus (Zinjanthropus) boisei*. Cambridge: Cambridge University Press.

Tobias, P.V. (1967b). Pleistocene deposits and new fossil localities in Kenya. *Nature* 215(5100), 476.

Tobias, P.V. (1971). Human skeletal remains from the Cave of Hearths, Makapansgat, Northern Transvaal. *American Journal of Physical Anthropology* 34, 335–368.

Tobias, P.V. (1979). Men, minds and hands: cultural awakenings over two million years of humanity. *The South African Archaeological Bulletin* 34(130), 85–92.

Tobias, P.V. (Ed.) (1985). The former Taung cave system in light of contemporary reports and its bearing on the skull's provenance: early deterrents to the acceptance of *Australopithecus*. In: *Hominid Evolution: Past, Present and Future Proceedings of the Taung Diamond Jubilee, Johannesburg and Mmabatho, South Africa*, pp. 25–40.

Tobias, P.V. (1988). Numerous apparently synapomorphic features in *Australopithecus robustus*, *Australopithecus boisei* and *Homo habilis*: support for the Skelton–McHenry–Drawhorn hypothesis. In: Grine FE (Ed.), *Evolutionary History of the "Robust" Australopithecines*. pp. 293–308. Adline de Gruyter: New York.

Tobias, P.V. (1991). *Olduvai Gorge. Volume 4, The Skulls, Endocasts and Teeth of Homo habilis*. Cambridge: Cambridge University Press.

Tobias, P.V. (2000). The fossil hominids. In: T.C. Partridge, R.R. Maud (Eds.), *The Cenozoic of Southern Africa*. Oxford Monograph on Geology and Geophysics. Oxford: Oxford University Press, pp. 252–276.

Tobias, P.V. and Hughes, A.R. (1969). The new Witwatersrand University excavation at Sterkfontein: progress report, some problems and first results. *The South African Archaeological Bulletin* 24(95/96), 158–169.

Tobias, P.V. and von Koenigswald, G.H.R. (1964). A comparison between the Olduvai hominines and those of Java and some implications for hominid phylogeny. *Nature* 204, 515–518.

Tobias, P.V., Vogel, J.C., Oschadleus, H.-D., Partridge, T.C. and McKee, J.K. (1993). New isotopic and sedimentological measurements of the Thabaseek deposits (South Africa) and the dating of the Taung hominid. *Quaternary Research* 40, 360–367.

Todd, N.E. (2006). Trends in proboscidean diversity in the African Cenozoic. *Journal of Mammalian Evolution* 13(1), 1–10.

Todd, N.E. (2010). New phylogenetic analysis of the family Elephantidae based on cranial–dental morphology. *Anatomical Record* 293, 74–90.

Toerien, M.J. (1952). The fossil hyaenids of the Makapansgat Valley. *South African Journal of Science* 489, 293–300.

Toerien, M.J. (1955). A sabre-tooth cat from the Makapangat Valley. *Palaeontologica Africana* 3, 43–46.

Toffolo, M.B., Brink, J.S. and Berna, F. (2015). Bone diagenesis at the Florisbad spring site, Free State Province (South Africa): implications for the taphonomy the Middle and Late Pleistocene faunal assemblages. *Journal of Archaeological Science: Reports* 4, 152–163.

Toffolo, M.B., Brink, J.S. and Berna, F. (2019). Microstratigraphic reconstruction of formation processes and paleoenvironments at the Early Pleistocene Cornelia-Uitzoek hominin site, Free State Province, South Africa. *Journal of Archaeological Science: Reports* 25, 25–39.

Tommasini, P. (1886). La sablière de Ternifine. *Bulletin de la Société Géographique de Oran* 6, 51–52.

Tong, H. (1986). The Gerbillinae (Rodentia) from Tighennif (Pleistocene of Algeria) and their significance. *Modern Geology* 10, 197–214.

Tong, H. (1989). Origine et evolution des Gerbillidae (Mammalia, Rodentia) en Afrique du Nord. *Mémoires de la Société géologique de France* NS 155, 1–118.

Tooth, S., McCarthy, T.S., Brandt, D., Hancox, P.J. and Morris, R. (2002). Geological controls on the formation of alluvial meanders and floodplain wetlands: the example of the Klip River, eastern Free State, South Africa. *Earth Surface Processes and Landforms* 27, 797–815.

Tooth, S., Brandt, D., Hancox, P.J. and McCarthy, T.S. (2004). Geological controls on alluvial river behaviour: a comparative study of three rivers on the South African Highveld. *Journal of African Earth Sciences* 38(1), 79–97.

Toots, H. (1965). Sequence of disarticulation in mammalian skeletons. *Rocky Mountain Geology* 4, 37–39.

Trapani, J., Sanders, W.J., Mitcani, J.C. and Heard, A. (2006). Precision and consistency of the taphonomic signature by crowned hawk-eagles (*Stephanoaetus coronatus*) in Kibale National Park, Uganda. *Palaios* 21, 114–131.

Trauth, M.H., Deino, A.L., Bergner, A.G.N. and Strecker, M.R. (2003). East African climate change and orbital forcing during the last 175 kyr BP. *Earth and Planetary Science Letters* 206, 297–313.

Trauth, M.H., Maslin, M.A., Deino, A. and Strecker, M.R. (2005). Late Cenozoic moisture history of East Africa. *Science* 309(5743), 2051–2053.

Trauth, M.H., Maslin, M.A., Deino, A.L., et al. (2007). High- and low-latitude forcing of Plio-Pleistocene East African climate and human evolution. *Journal of Human Evolution* 53, 475–486.

Trauth, M.H., Larrasoaña, J.C. and Mudelsee, M. (2009). Trends, rhythms and events in Plio-Pleistocene African climate. *Quaternary Science Reviews* 28, 399–411.

Trauth, M.H., Maslin, M.A., Deino, A.L., et al. (2010). Human evolution in a variable environment: the amplifier lakes of Eastern Africa. *Quaternary Science Reviews* 29, 2981–2988.

Treydte, A.C., Bernasconi, S.M., Kreuzer, M. and Edwards, P.J. (2006). Diet of the common warthog (*Phacochoerus africanus*) on former cattle grounds in a Tanzanian savanna. *Journal of Mammalogy* 87, 889–898.

Tribolo, C., Mercier, N., Douville, E., et al. (2013). OSL and TL dating of the Middle Stone Age sequence at Diepkloof Rock Shelter (South Africa): a clarification. *Journal of Archaeological Science* 40(9), 3401–3411.

Trueman, C.N. and Martill, D.M. (2002). The long-term survival of bone: the role of bioerosion. *Archaeometry* 44, 371–382.

Tryon, C.A. and Faith, J.T. (2013). Variability in the Middle Stone Age of Eastern Africa. *Current Anthropology* 54, S234–S254.

Tryon, C.A. and McBrearty, S. (2002). Tephrostratigraphy and the Acheulian to Middle Stone Age transition in the Kapthurin Formation, Kenya. *Journal of Human Evolution* 42, 211–235.

Tryon, C.A., Faith, J.T., Peppe, D.J., et al. (2010). The Pleistocene archaeology and environments of the Wasiriya Beds, Rusinga Island, Kenya. *Journal of Human Evolution* 59, 657–671.

Tryon, C.A., Peppe, D.J., Faith, J.T., et al. (2012). Late Pleistocene artefacts and fauna from Rusinga and Mfangano islands, Lake Victoria, Kenya. *Azania: Archaeological Research in Africa* 47, 14–38.

Tryon, C.A., Crevecoeur, I., Faith, J.T., et al. (2015). Late Pleistocene age and archaeological context for the hominin calvaria from GvJm-22 (Lukenya Hill, Kenya). *Proceedings of the National Academy of Sciences of the USA* 112, 2682–2687.

Tsubamoto, T., Yutaka, K., Nakaya, H., et al. (2015). New specimens of a primitive hippopotamus, *Kenyapotamus coryndonae*, from the Upper Miocene Nakali Formation, Kenya. *Journal of the Geological Society of Japan* 121, 153–159.

Tsubamoto, T., Kunimatsu, Y., Sakai, T., et al. (2017). Listriodontine suid and tragulid artiodactyls (Mammalia) from the Upper Miocene Nakali Formation, Kenya. *Paleontological Research* 21, 347–357.

Tsubamoto, T., Kunimatsu, Y., Sakai, T., et al. (2020). A new species of *Nyanzachoerus* (Mammalia, Artiodactyla, Suidae, Tetraconodontinae) from the Upper Miocene Nakali Formation, Kenya. *Paleontological Research* 24, 41–63.

Tsujikawa, H. (2005a). The palaeoenvironment of *Samburupithecus kiptalami* based on its associated fauna. *African Study Monographs* 32, 51–62.

Tsujikawa, H. (2005b). The updated Late Miocene large mammal fauna from Samburu Hills, northern Kenya. *African Study Monographs* 32, 1–50.

Tuomisto, H. (2012). An updated consumer's guide to evenness and related indices. *Oikos*, 121(8), 1203–1218.

Turner, A. (1984). Hominids and fellow travellers: human migration into high latitudes as part of a large mammal community. In: R.A.

Foley (Ed.), *Hominid Evolution and Community Ecology*. London: Academic Press, pp. 193–217.

Turner, A. (1989). Sample selection, schlepp effects and scavenging: the implications of partial recovery for interpretations of the terrestrial mammal assemblage from Klasies River Mouth. *Journal of Archaeological Science* 16(1), 1–11.

Turner, A. (1990). The evolution of the guild of larger terrestrial carnivores during the Plio-Pleistocene in Africa. *Geobios* 23(3), 349–368.

Turner, A. and Wood, B. (1993). Taxonomic and geographic diversity in robust australopithecines and other Plio-Pleistocene larger mammals. *Journal of Human Evolution* 24, 147–168.

Turner, A. and O'Regan, H. (2015). Zoogeography: primate and early hominin distribution and migration patterns. In: W. Henke and I. Tattersall (Eds.), *Handbook of Paleoanthropology*. Berlin: Springer-Verlag, pp. 623–642.

Turner, B.R. (1980). Sedimentological characteristics of the "red muds" at Makapansgat limeworks. *Palaeontologia Africana* 23, 51–58.

Tuttle, R.H. (1985). Ape footprints and Laetoli impressions: a response to the SUNY claims. In: P.V. Tobias (Ed.), *Hominid Evolution: Past, Present and Future*. New York: Alan R. Liss, pp. 129–133.

Tuttle, R.H. (1987). Kinesiological inference and evolutionary implications from Laetoli bipedal trails G-1, G-2/3 and A. In: M.D. Leakey and J.M. Harris (Eds.), *Laetoli: A Pliocene Site in Northern Tanzania*. Oxford: Clarendon Press, pp. 503–523.

Tuttle, R.H. (1990). The pitted pattern of Laetoli feet. *Natural History* 90, 60–65.

Tuttle, R.H. (1994). Up from electromyography: primate energetics and the evolution of human bipedalism. In: R.S. Corruccini and R.L. Ciochon (Eds.), *Integrative Paths to the Past*. Engelwood Cliffs: Prentice Hall, pp. 251–268.

Tuttle, R.H. (2008). Footprint clues in hominid evolution and forensics: lessons and limitations. *Ichnos* 15, 158–165.

Tuttle, R.H., Webb, D.M., Weidl, E. and Baksh, M. (1990). Further progress on the Laetoli trails. *Journal of Archaeological Science* 17, 347–362.

Tuttle, R.H., Webb, D. and Tuttle, N. (1991). Laetoli footprint trails and the evolution of hominid bipedalism. In: Y. Coppens and B. Senut (Eds.), *Origine(s) de la Bipédie chez les Hominidés*. Paris: Cahiers de Paléoanthropologie, CNRS, pp. 203–218.

Tuttle, R.H., Webb, D.M., Tuttle, N.I. and Baksh, M. (1992). Footprints and gaits of bipedal apes, bears, and barefoot people: perspective on Pliocene tracks. In: S. Matano, R.H. Tuttle, H. Ishida and M. Goodman (Eds.) *Topics in Primatology, Vol. 3: Evolutionary Biology, Reproductive Endocrinology, and Virology*. Tokyo: University of Tokyo Press, pp. 221–242.

Twiss, P.C., Suess, E. and Smith, R.M. (1969). Morphological classification of grass phytoliths. *Soil Science Society of America Journal* 33(1), 109–115.

Ullrich, H. (2001). Garusi Hominid 4 – Ein Australopithecinenzahn aus der Sammlung Kohl-Larsen. In: M. Schultz, K. Atzwanger, G. Bräuer, et al. (Eds.), *Homo – Unsere Herkunft und Zukunft. Proceedings 4. Kongress der Gesellschaft für Anthropologie e. V.* Göttingen: Cuvillier Verlag.

Ungar, P.S. (1994). Incisor microwear of Sumatran anthropoid primates. *American Journal of Physical Anthropology* 94, 339–363.

Ungar, P.S. (2005). Dental evidence for the diets of fossil primates from Rudabánya, Northeastern Hungary with comments on extant primate analogs and "noncompetitive" sympatry. *Palaeontologia Italia* 90, 97–112.

Ungar, P.S. (Ed.) (2007). *Evolution of the Human Diet*. Oxford: Oxford University Press.

Ungar, P. and Sponheimer, M. (2011). The diets of early hominins. *Science* 334, 190–193.

Ungar, P.S., Grine, F.E. and Teaford, M.F. (2006). Diet in early *Homo*: a review of the evidence and a new model of adaptive versatility. *Annual Review of Anthropology*, 35, 209–228.

Ungar, P.S., Merceron, G. and Scott, R.S. (2007). Dental microwear texture analysis of Varswater bovids and early Pliocene paleoenvironments of Langebaanweg, Western Cape Province, South Africa. *Journal of Mammalian Evolution* 14(3), 163–181.

Ungar, P.S., Scott, R.S., Scott, J.R. and Teaford, M. (2008). Dental microwear analysis: historical perspectives and new approaches. In: J.D. Irish and G.C. Nelson (Eds.), *Technique and Application in Dental Anthropology*. Cambridge: Cambridge University Press, pp. 389–425.

Uno, K.T., Cerling, T.E., Harris, J.M., et al. (2011). Late Miocene to Pliocene carbon isotope record of differential diet change among East African herbivores. *Proceedings of the National Academy of Sciences of the United States of America* 108, 6509–6514.

Uno, K.T., Polissar, P.J., Kahle, E., et al. (2016a). A Pleistocene palaeovegetation record from plant wax biomarkers from the Nachukui Formation, West Turkana, Kenya. *Philosophical Transactions of the Royal Society of London B: Biological Sciences* 371(1698).

Uno, K.T., Polissar, P.J., Jackson, K.E. and deMenocal, P.B. (2016b). Neogene biomarker record of vegetation change in eastern Africa. *Proceedings of the National Academy of Sciences* 113(23), 6355–6363.

Uno, K.T., Rivals, F., Bibi, F., et al. (2018). Large mammal diets and paleoecology across the Oldowan–Acheulean transition at Olduvai Gorge, Tanzania from stable isotope and tooth wear analyses. *Journal of Human Evolution* 120, 76–91.

Upchurch, P., Mannion, P.D., Benson, R.B.J., Butler, R.J. and Carrano, M.T. (2011). Geological and anthropogenic controls on the sampling of the terrestrial fossil record: a case study from the Dinosauria. In: A.J. McGowan and A.B. Smith (Eds.), *Comparing the Geological and Fossil Records: Implications for Biodiversity Studies*. Geological Society of London Special Publications, 358. London: Geological Society, pp. 209–240.

Urbanek, C., Faupl, P., Hujer, W., et al. (2005). Geology, paleontology and paleoanthropology of the Mount Galili Formation in the southern Afar Depression, Ethiopia – preliminary results. *Joannea Geologie und Paläontologie* 6, 29–43.

Vaks, A., Bar-Matthews, M., Ayalon, A., et al. (2007). Desert speleothems reveal climatic window for African exodus of early modern humans. *Geology* 35, 831–834.

Val, A. (2019). New data on avifaunal remains associated with the Middle Stone Age layers from Diepkloof Rock Shelter, Western Cape, South Africa. *Journal of Archaeological Science: Reports* 26, 101880.

Val, A. and Stratford, D.J. (2015). The macrovertebrate fossil assemblage from the Name Chamber, Sterkfontein: taxonomy, taphonomy and implications for site formation processes. *Palaeontologia Africana* 50, 1–17.

Val, A., Carlson, K.J., Steininger, C., et al. (2011). 3D techniques and fossil identification: an elephant shrew hemi-mandible from the Malapa site. *South African Journal of Science* 107(11–12), 1–5.

Val, A., Taru, P. and Steininger, C. (2014). New taphonomic analysis of large-bodied primate assemblage from Cooper's D, Bloubank Valley, South Africa. *South African Archeology Bulletin* 69, 49–58.

Val, A., de la Peña, P. and Wadley, L. (2016). Direct evidence for human exploitation of birds in the Middle Stone Age of South Africa: the example of Sibudu Cave, KwaZulu-Natal. *Journal of Human Evolution* 99, 107–123.

Volume References

Vallé, F., Dupont, L.M., Leroy, S.A.G., Schefuß, E. and Wefer, G. (2014). Pliocene environmental change in West Africa and the onset of strong NE trade winds (ODP Sites 659 and 658). *Palaeogeography, Palaeoclimatology, Palaeoecology* 414, 403–414.

Van Bocxlaer, B. (2020). Paleoecological insights from fossil freshwater mollusks of the Kanapoi Formation (Omo-Turkana Basin, Kenya). *Journal of Human Evolution* 140, 102341.

Van Bruggen, A.C. (1978). Land molluscs. In: M.J.A. Werger (Ed.), *Biogeography and Ecology of Southern Africa*. The Hague: W. Junk, pp. 877–923.

Van Couvering, J.A.H. (1980). Community evolution in East Africa during the late Cenozoic. In: A.K. Behrensmeyer and A.P. Hill (Eds.), *Fossils in the Making*. Chicago: University of Chicago Press, pp.272–298.

van Dam, J.A., Abdul Aziz, H., Sierra, M.A.A., et al. (2006). Long-period astronomical forcing of mammal turnover. *Nature* 443, 687–691.

Van Damme, D. and Pickford, M. (1999). The late Cenozoic Viviparidae (Mollusca, Gastropoda) of the Albertine Rift Valley (Uganda–Congo). *Hydrobiologia* 390, 171–217.

Van Damme, D. and Pickford, M. (2003). The late Cenozoic Thiaridae (Mollusca, Gastropoda, Cerithioidea) of the Albertine Rift Valley (Uganda–Congo) and their bearing on the origin and evolution of the Tanganyikan thalassoid malacofauna. *Hydrobiologia* 498, 1–83.

Van Damme, D. and Van Bocxlaer, B. (2009). Freshwater molluscs of the Nile Basin, past and present. In H.J. Dumont (Ed.), *The Nile. Monographiae Biologicae*, 89. Dordrecht: Springer, pp. 585–629.

van der Laan, E., Hilgen, F.J., Lourens, L.J., et al. (2012). Astronomical forcing of Northwest African climate and glacial history during the late Messinian (6.5–5.5 Ma). *Palaeogeography, Palaeoclimatology, Palaeoecology* 313–314, 107–126.

van der Made, J. (1998) Biometrical trends in the Tetraconodontinae, a subfamily of pigs. *Earth and Environmental Science Transactions of the Royal Society of Edinburgh* 89(3), 199–225.

Van der Made, J., Morales, J. and Montoya, P. (2006). Late Miocene turnover in the Spanish mammal record in relation to palaeoclimate and the Messinian Salinity Crisis. *Palaeogeography, Palaeoclimatology, Palaeoecology* 238(1), 228–246.

van der Merwe, N.J. (2013). Isotopic ecology of fossil fauna from Olduvai Gorge at ca 1.8 Ma, compared with modern fauna. *South African Journal of Science* 109(11–12), 1–14.

van der Merwe, N., Thackeray, F., Lee-Thorp, J.A. and Luyt, J. (2003). The carbon isotope ecology and diet of *Australopithecus africanus* at Sterkfontein, South Africa. *Journal of Human Evolution* 44, 581–597.

van der Merwe, N.J., Masao, F.T. and Bamford, M.K. (2008). Isotopic evidence for contrasting diets of early hominins *Homo habilis* and *Australopithecus boisei* of Tanzania. *South African Journal of Science* 104, 153–155.

Van der Meulen, A.J. and Daams, R. (1992). Evolution of early–middle Miocene rodent faunas in relation to long-term palaeoenvironmental changes. *Palaeogeography, Palaeoclimatology, Palaeoecology* 93, 227–253.

Van Dijk, D.E. (2003). Pliocene frogs from Langebaanweg, Western Cape Province, South Africa: news & views. *South African Journal of Science* 99(3), 123–124.

Van Dijk, D.E. (2006a). Langebaanweg anuran bones and associated biology. *African Natural History* 2, 184.

Van Dijk, D.E. (2006b). Anura from the Late Pleistocene at Klasies River main site, South Africa. *African Natural History* 2(1), 167–171.

Van Hoepen, E.C.N. (1930). Fossiele perde van Cornelia, O.V.S. *Paleontology Navorsinge van die Nasionale Museum, Bloemfontein* 2, 1–24.

Van Hoepen, E.C.N. (1932a). Die stamlyn van die sebras. *Paleontology Navorsinge van die Nasionale Museum, Bloemfontein* 2, 25–37.

Van Hoepen, E.C.N. (1932b). Voorlopige beskrywing van Vrystaatse soogdiere. *Paleontology Navorsinge van die Nasionale Museum, Bloemfontein* 2, 63–65.

Van Hoepen, E.C.N. (1947). A preliminary description of new Pleistocene mammals of South Africa. *Paleontology Navorsinge van die Nasionale Museum, Bloemfontein* 2, 103–106.

Van Neer, W. and Uerpmann, H.-P. (1989). Paleoecological significance of the Holocene faunal remains of the B.O.S. missions. In: R. Kuper (Ed.), *Forschungen zur Umweltgeschichte der Ostsahara*. Köln: Heinrich-Barth-Institut, pp. 307–341.

Van Pletzen, L. (2000). The large mammal fauna from Klasies River. Doctoral dissertation, Stellenbosch, Stellenbosch University..

Van Riet Lowe, C. (1938). The Makapan caves. An archaeological note. *South African Journal of Science* 35(12), 371–381.

van Riet Lowe, C. (1954). The Cave of Hearths. *The South African Archaeological Bulletin* 9, 25–29.

Van Valen, L. (1973). A new evolutionary law. *Evolutionary Theory* 1, 1–30.

Van Valkenburgh, B. (1988). Trophic diversity in past and present guilds of large predatory mammals. *Paleobiology* 14, 155–173.

van Zinderen Bakker, E.M. (1976). The evolution of late Quaternary paleoclimates of southern Africa. *Palaeoecology of Africa* 9, 160–202.

Van Zinderen Bakker, E.M. (1982). Pollen analytical studies of the Wonderwerk Cave, South Africa. *Pollen et Spores* 24, 235–250.

Van Zyl, W., Brink, J.S. and Badenhorst, S. (2016). Pleistocene Bovidae from X Cave on Bolt's Farm in the Cradle of Humankind in South Africa. *Annals of the Ditsong National Museum of Natural History* 6(7), 39–73.

Vainer, S., Erel, Y. and Matmon, A. (2018). Provenance and depositional environments of Quaternary sediments in the southern Kalahari Basin. *Chemical Geology* 476, 352–369.

Varnham, G.L., Mannion, P.D. and Kammerer, C.F. (2021). Spatiotemporal variation in completeness of the early cynodont fossil record and its implications for mammalian evolutionary history. *Palaeontology* 64(2), 307–333.

Vercammen, P. and Mason, D.R. (1993). The warthogs (*Phacochoerus africanus* and *P. aethiopicus*). In: W.L.R. Oliver (Ed.), *Pigs, Peccaries and Hippos: Status Survey and Action Plan*. Gland: World Conservation Union/Species Survival Commission, pp. 75–84.

Verdcourt, B. (1963). The Miocene non-marine Mollusca of Rusinga Island, Lake Victoria and other localities in Kenya. *Palaeontographica* 121(A), 1–37.

Verdcourt, B. (1987). Mollusca from the Laetolil and Upper Ndolanya Beds. In: M.D. Leakey and J.M. Harris (Eds.), *Laetoli: A Pliocene Site in Northern Tanzania*. Oxford: Clarendon Press, pp. 438–450.

Verna, C., Texier, P.J., Rigaud, J.P., Poggenpoel, C. and Parkington, J. (2013). The middle stone age human remains from Diepkloof rock shelter (Western cape, South Africa). *Journal of Archaeological Science* 40(9), 3532–3541.

Verheyen, E., Salzburger, W., Snoeks, J. and Meyer, A. (2003). Origin of the superflock of cichlid fishes from Lake Victoria, East Africa. *Science* 300(5617), 325–329.

Vermeersch, P.M. (2000). *Palaeolithic Living Sites in Upper and Middle Egypt*. Leuven: Leuven University Press.

Verniers, J. (1997). Detailed stratigraphy of the Neogene sediments at Tinde and other localities in the central Manonga Basin. In: T. Harrison (Ed.), *Neogene Paleontology of the Manonga Valley, Tanzania: A Window into the Evolutionary History of East Africa*. New York: Springer, pp. 33–65.

Verschuren, D., Sinninghe Damsté, J.S., Moernaut, J., et al. (2009). Half-precessional dynamics of monsoon rainfall near the East African equator. *Nature* 462, 637–641.

Viehl, K. (2003). Untersuchungen zur Nahrungsökologie des Afrikanischen Riesenwaldschweins (*Hylochoerus meinertzhageni* Thomas) im Queen Elizabeth National Park, Uganda. Doctoral dissertation, Universität Hannover.

Vilakazi, N., Gommery, D. and Kgasi, L. (2018). First fossil record of the spitting Elapidae in the cradle of humankind, South Africa. *South African Archaeological Bulletin* 73(207),35.

Villa, P. and Mahieu, E. (1991). Breakage patterns of human long bones. *Journal of Human Evolution* 21, 27–48.

Villa, P., Soriano, S., Tsanova, T., et al. (2012). Border Cave and the beginning of the Later Stone Age in South Africa. *Proceedings of the National Academy of Sciences of the USA* 109, 13208–13213.

Villaseñor, A. (2017). Diversity in the middle Pliocene: a multi-proxy analysis of climate's effect on vegetation and mammalian community structure with implications for human evolution. Thesis, George Washington University, p. 135.

Vignaud, P., Duringer, P., Mackaye, H.T., et al. (2002). Geology and palaeontology of the upper Miocene Toros-Menalla hominid locality, Chad. *Nature* 418, 152–155.

von den Driesch, A. (2004). The Middle Stone Age fish fauna from the Klasies river main site, South Africa. *Anthropozoologica* 39(2), 33–59.

Villmoare, B., Kimbel, W.H., Seyoum, C., et al. (2015). Early *Homo* at 2.8 Ma from Ledi-Geraru, Afar, Ethiopia. *Science*, 347(6228), 1352–1355.

Vincens, A. and Casanova, J. (1987). Modern background of Natron–Magadi basin (Tanzania–Kenya): physiography, climate, hydrology and vegetation. *Sciences Géologique Bulletin* 40, 9–21.

Viola, B., Kullmer, O., Sandrock, O., Hujer, W. and Seidler, H. (2008). An early australopithecine femur from Galili, Ethiopia. *Journal of Vertebrate Paleontology* 28(3), 156–157.

Viriot, L., Vignaud, P., Boisserie, J.-R., et al. (2008). Late Miocene to Early Pliocene Chadian vertebrate faunas: palaeoenvironmental and palaeobiogeographical implications. In: M.J. Salem, A. El-Arnauti and A. El Soher Sale (Eds.), *Geology of East Libya: Third Symposium on the Sedimentary Basins of Libya*. Benghazi: Earth Science Society of Libya, pp. 303–308.

Vogel, J.C. (1985). Further attempts at dating the Taung tufas. In: P.V. Tobias (Ed.), *Hominid Evolution: Past, Present and Future*. New York: Alan R. Liss, pp. 189–194.

Vogel, J.C. and Partridge, T.C. (1983). Preliminary radiometric ages for the Taung tufas. In J.C. Vogel (Ed.), *Late Cainozoic Palaeoclimates of the Southern Hemisphere*. Balkema: Rotterdam, pp. 507–514.

Vogel, J.C., Fuls, A. and Ellis, R. (1978). The geographical distribution of Kranz grasses in South Africa. *South African Journal of Science* 74, 209–219.

Von Endt, D.W. and Ortner, D.J. (1984). Experimental effects of bone size and temperature on bone diagensis. *Journal of Archaeological Science* 11, 247–253.

Voorhies, M.R. (1969). Taphonomy and population dynamics of an early Pliocene vertebrate fauna, Knox County, Nebraska. *Contributions to Geology, University of Wyoming Special Paper* 1, 1–69.

Vrba, E.S. (1974). Chronological and ecological implications of the fossil Bovidae at the Sterkfontein Australopithecine site. *Nature* 250, 19–23.

Vrba, E. (1975). Some evidence of the chronology and paleoecology of Sterkfontein, Swartkrans and Kromdraai from the fossil Bovidae. *Natur, e* 254, 301–304.

Vrba, E. (1976). *The Fossil Bovidae of Sterkfontein, Swartkrans and Kromdraai*. Transvaal Museum Memoir no. 21. Pretoria: Heer.

Vrba, E.S. (1980). The significance of bovid remains as indicators of environment and predation patterns. In: A.K. Behrensmeyer and A.P. Hill (Eds.), *Fossils in the Making*. Chicago: University of Chicago Press, pp. 247–271.

Vrba, E.S. (1981). The Kromdraai australopithecine site revisited in 1980: recent investigations and results. *Annals of the Transvaal Museum* 33, 17–60.

Vrba, E. (1982a). *Progress Report: Gondolin Site, Broederstroom Permit 3/102*. Pretoria: Transvaal Museum, p. 1.

Vrba, E.S. (1982b). Biostratigraphy and chronology, based particularly on Bovidae, of southern hominid-associated assemblages: Makapansgat, Sterkfontein, Taung, Kromdraai, Swartkrans; also Elandsfontein (Saldanha), Broken Hill (now Kabwe) and Cave of Hearths. Premier Congres Int de Paleontologie Humaine, 707e752.

Vrba, E. (1985a). Ecological and adaptive changes assoicated with early hominid evolution. In: E. Delson (Ed.), *Ancestors: The Hard Evidence*. New York: Alan R. Liss, pp. 63–71.

Vrba, E. (1985b). Environment and evolution: alternative causes of the temporal distribution of evolutionary events. *South African Journal of Science* 81, 229–236.

Vrba, E.S. (1985c). Early hominids in southern Africa: updated observations on chronological and ecological background. In: P.V. Tobias (Ed.), *Hominid Evolution: Past, Present and Future*. New York: Alan R Liss, pp. 195–200.

Vrba, E.S. (1987a). A revision of the Bovini Bovidae and a preliminary revised checklist of Bovidae from Makapansgat. *Palaeontologica Africana* 26, 33–46.

Vrba, E.S. (1987b). New species and a new genus of Hippotragini Bovidae from Makapansgat Limeworks. *Palaeontologica Africana* 26, 47–58.

Vrba, E.S. (1988). Late Pliocene climatic events and hominid evolution. In: F.E. Grine (Ed.), *Evolutionary History of the "Robust" Australopiths*. New York: Aldine de Gruyter, pp. 405–426.

Vrba, E.S. (1992). Mammals as a key to evolutionary theory. *Journal of Mammalogy* 73, 1–28.

Vrba, E.S. (1993). Turnover-pulses, the Red Queen, and related topics. *American Journal of Science* 293A, 418–452.

Vrba, E.S. (1995a). On the connections between paleoclimate and evolution. In: E.S. Vrba, G.H. Denton, T.C. Partridge and L.H. Burckle (Eds.), *Paleoclimate and Evolution, with Emphasis on Human Origins*. New Haven: Yale University Press, pp. 24–45.

Vrba, E. (1995b). The fossil record of African antelopes (Mammalia, Bovidae) in relation to human evolution and paleoclimate. In: E. Vrba, G. Denton, T.C. Partridge and L. Burckle (Eds.), *Paleoclimate and Evolution with Emphasis on Human Origins*. New Haven: Yale University Press, pp. 385–424.

Vrba, E.S. (1997). New fossils of Alcelaphini and Caprinae (Bovidae, Mammalia) from Awash, Ethiopia, and phylogenetic analysis of Alcelaphini. *Palaeontologica Africana* 34, 127–198.

Vrba, E.S. (2015). Role of environmental stimuli in hominid origins. In: W. Henke and I. Tattersall (Eds.), *Handbook of Paleoanthropology (1837–1886)*. Berlin: Springer-Verlag.

Vrba, E. and Gatesy, J. (1994). New antelope fossils from Awash, Ethiopia, and phylogenetic analysis of Hippotragini (Bovidae, Mammalia). *Palaeontologia Africana* 31, 55–72.

Vrba, E. and Panagos, D.C. (1982). New perspectives on taphonomy, palaeoecology and chronology of the Kromdraai apeman. *Palaeontologia Africana* 15, 13–26.

Wadley, L. (1987). *Later Stone Age Hunters and Gatherers of the Southern Transvaal: Social and Ecological Interpretation*. British Archaeological Reports Vol. 25. Oxford: B.A.R. International Series.

Wadley, L. (1997). Rose Cottage Cave: archaeological work 1987 to 1997. *South African Journal of Science* 93(10), 439–444.

Wadley, L. (2004). Vegetation changes between 61 500 and 26 000 years ago: the evidence from seeds in Sibudu Cave, KwaZulu-Natal: Sibudu Cave. *South African Journal of Science* 100(3), 167–173.

Wadley, L. (2006). Partners in grime: results of multi-disciplinary archaeology at Sibudu Cave. *Southern African Humanities* 18(1), 315–341.

Wadley, L. (2010). Were snares and traps used in the Middle Stone Age and does it matter? A review and case study from Sibudu, South Africa. *Journal of Human Evolution* 58, 179–192.

Wadley, L. and Jacobs, Z. (2006). Sibudu Cave: background to the excavations, stratigraphy and dating. *Southern African Humanities* 18(1), 1–26.

Wadley, L., Hodgskiss, T. and Grant, M. (2009). Implications for complex cognition from the hafting of tools with compound adhesives in the Middle Stone Age, South Africa. *Proceedings of the National Academy of Sciences of the USA* 106, 9590–9594.

Walker, A. (1981). Dietary hypotheses and human evolution. *Philosophical Transactions of the Royal Society, London* 292, 57–64.

Walker, A. and Leakey, R.E. (1993). *The Nariokotome Homo erectus Skeleton*. Cambridge, MA: Harvard University Press, p. 457.

Walker, A. and Teaford, M. (1988). The hunt for *Proconsul*. *Scientific American* 260, 76–82.

Walker, A., Leakey, R.E., Harris, J.M. and Brown, F.H. (1986). 2.5-Myr *Australopithecus boisei* from west of Lake Turkana, Kenya. *Nature* 322, 517–522.

Walker, J., Cliff, R.A. and Latham, A.G. (2006). U–Pb isotopic age of the StW 573 hominid from Sterkfontein, South Africa. *Science* 314, 1592–1594.

Walker, S.J., Lukich, V. and Chazan, M. (2014). Kathu Townlands: a high density Earlier Stone Age locality in the interior of South Africa. *PLoS One* 9(7), e103436.

Walsh, J. (1969). Geology of the Eldama Ravine – Kabarnet area. Report of the Geological Survey Kenya, 83.

Walter, R.C. (1994). The age of Lucy and the first family: single-crystal $^{40}Ar/^{39}Ar$ dating of the Denen Dora and lower Kada Hadar members of the Hadar Formation, Ethiopia. *Geology* 22, 6–10.

Walter, R.C. and Aronson, J.L. (1993). Age and source of the Sidi Hakoma Tuff, Hadar Formation, Ethiopia. *Journal of Human Evolution* 25, 229–240.

Walter, R.C., Manega, P.C., Hay, R.L., Drake, R.E. and Curtis, G.H. (1991). Laser-fusion $^{40}Ar/^{39}Ar$ dating of Bed I, Olduvai Gorge, Tanzania. *Nature* 354, 145–149.

Wara, M.W., Ravelo, A.C. and Delaney, M.L. (2005). Permanent El Nino-like conditions during the Pliocene Warm Period. *Science* 309, 758–761.

Ward, C.V. (2002). Interpreting the posture and locomotion of *Australopithecus afarensis*: where do we stand? *Yearbook of Physical Anthropology* 45, 185–215.

Ward, C.V. (2014). Taxonomic affinity of the Pliocene hominin fossils from Fejej, Ethiopia. *Journal of Human Evolution* 73, 98–102.

Ward, S. and Hill, A. (1987). Pliocene hominid partial mandible from Tabarin, Baringo, Kenya. *American Journal of Physical Anthropology* 72, 21–37.

Ward, C., Leakey, M. and Walker, A. (1999a). The new hominid species *Australopithecus anamensis*. *Evolutionary Anthropology* 7, 197–205.

Ward, C.V., Leakey, M.G., Brown, F.H., Harris, J.M. and Walker, A. (1999b). South Turkwel: a new Pliocene hominid site in Kenya. *Journal of Human Evolution* 36, 69–95.

Ward, C.V., Leakey, M.G. and Walker, A. (2001). Morphology of *Australopithecus anamensis* from Kanapoi and Allia Bay, Kenya. *Journal of Human Evolution* 41, 255–368.

Ward, C.V., Plavcan, J.M. and Manthi, F.K. (2010). Anterior dental evolution in the *Australopithecus anamensis-afarensis* lineage. *Philosophical Transactions of the Royal Society B* 365, 3333–3344.

Ward, C.V., Plavcan, J.M. and Manthi, F.K. (2020). New fossils of *Australopithecus anamensis* from Kanapoi, West Turkana, Kenya (2012–2015). *Journal of Human Evolution* 140, 102368.

Watson, V. (1991). Form, function and fibres: a preliminary study of the Swartkrans fossil birds. *Koedoe* 34, 23–29.

Watson, V. (1993a). Composition of the Swartkrans bone accumulations, in terms of skeletal parts and animals represented. In: C. Brain (Ed.), *Swartkrans: A Cave's Chronicle of Early Man*. Pretoria: Transvaal Museum, pp. 35–74.

Watson, V. (1993b). Glimpses from Gondolin: a faunal analysis of a fossil site near Broederstroom, Transvaal, South Africa. *Palaeontologica Africana* 30, 35–42.

Weigelt, E., Dupont, L. and Uenzelmann-Neben, G. (2008). Late Pliocene climate changes documented in seismic and palynology data at the southwest African Margin. *Global and Planetary Change* 63(1), 31–39.

Weigelt, J. (1927). *Rezente Wirbeltierleichen und ihre palaobio-logische Bedeutung*. Leipzig: Max Weg Verlag.

Weigelt, J. (1989). *Recent Vertebrate Carcasses and Their Paleobiological Implications* (translated by J. Schaefer). Chicago: The University of Chicago Press.

Weinert, H. (1950). Über die neuen Vor- und Frühmenschenfunde aus Afrika, Java, China und Frankreich. *Zeitschrift für Morphologie und Anthropologie* 42, 113–145.

Weiss, R.E. and Marshall, C.R. (1999). The uncertainty in the true end point of a fossil's stratigraphic range when stratigraphic sections are sampled discretely. *Mathematical Geology* 31(4), 435–453.

Wells, L.H. (1967). Antelopes in the Pleistocene of southern Africa. In: W.W. Bishop and J.D. Clark (Eds.), *Background to Evolution in Africa*. Chicago: Chicago University Press, pp 99–107.

Wells, L.H. (1969). Faunal subdivision of the Quaternary in southern Africa. *South African Archaeological Bulletin* 24, 93–95.

Wells, L.H. and Cooke, H.S.B. (1956). Fossil Bovidae from the Limeworks quarry, Makapansgat, Potgietersrust. *Palaeontologica Africana* 4, 1–55.

Wells, L.H., Cooke, H.B.S. and Malan, B.D. (1942). The associated fauna and culture of the Vlakkraal thermal springs, O.F.S. *Transactions of the Royal Society of South Africa* 29, 203–233.

Wendorf, F. and Schild, R. (1976). *Prehistory of the Nile Valley*. New York: Academic Press.

Wendorf, F., Schild, R. and Close, A.E. (1993). *Egypt During the Last Interglacial: The Middle Plaeolithic of Bir Tarfawi and Bir Sahara East*. New York: Plenum Press.

Wengler, L., Weisrock, A., Brochier, J.-E., et al. (2002). Enregistrement fluviatile et paléoenvironnements au Pléistocène supérieur sur la bordure méridionale atlantique de l'Anti-Atlas (Oued Assaka, SO Marocain). *Quaternaire* 13, 179–192.

Werdelin, L. and Barthelme, J. (1997). Brown hyena (*Parahyaena brunnea*) from the Pleistocene of Kenya. *Journal of Vertebrate Paleontology* 17, 758–761.

Werdelin, L. and Dehghani, R. (2011). Carnivora. In: T. Harrison (Ed.), *Paleontology and Geology of Laetoli: Human Evolution in Context. Vol. 2: Fossil Hominins and the Associated Fauna*. Dordrecht: Springer, pp. 189–232.

Werdelin, L. and Lewis, M.E. (2001). A revision of the genus *Dinofelis* (Mammalia, Felidae). *Zoological Journal of the Linnean Society* 132, 147–258.

Werdelin, L. and Lewis, M.E. (2013a). Temporal change in functional richness and evenness in the eastern African Plio-Pleistocene carnivoran guild. *PLoS ONE* 8(8), 1–11.

Werdelin, L. and Lewis, M.E. (2013b). Koobi Fora Research Project Volume 7, The: Carnivora. In: R.E. Leakey (Ed.), *Koobi Fora: Researches into Geology, Paleontology, and Human Origins*. San Francisco: California Academy of Sciences, p. 333.

Werdelin, L. and Peigné, S. (2010). Carnivora. In: L. Werdelin and W.J. Sanders (Eds.), *Cenozoic Mammals of Africa*. Berkeley: University of California Press, pp. 603–657.

Werdelin, L. and Sanders, W.J. (2010). *Cenozoic Mammals of Africa*. Berkeley: University of California Press.

Werdelin, L. and Simpson, S.W. (2009). The last amphicyonid (Mammalia, Carnivora) in Africa. *Geodiversitas* 31, 775–787.

Werdelin, L., Lewis, M. and Haile-Selassie, Y. (2014). Mid-Pliocene Carnivora from the Woranso-Mille Area, Afar Region, Ethiopia. *Journal of Mammalian Evolution* 21, 331–347.

Wesselman, H.B. (1984). The Omo micromammals: systematics and paleoecology of early man sites from Ethiopia. *Contributions to Vertebrate Evolution* 7, 1–219.

Wesselman, H.B. (1995). Of mice and almost-men: regional paleoecology and human evolution in the Turkana Basin. In: E.S. Vrba, G.H. Denton, T.C. Partridge and L.H. Burckle (Eds.), *Paleoclimate and Evolution with Emphasis on Human Origins*. New Haven: Yale University Press, pp. 356–368.

Wesselman, H.B., Black, M.T. and Asnake, M. (2009). Small mammals. In: Y. Haile-Selassie and G. WoldeGabriel (Eds.), *Ardipithecus kadabba: Late Miocene Evidence from the Middle Awash, Ethiopia*. Berkeley: University of California Press, pp. 105–133.

Wessels, W., Fejfar, O., Peláez-Campomanes, P., Van der Meulen, A., and De Bruijn, H. (2003). Miocene small mammals from Jebel Zelten, Libya. *Coloquios de Paleontología*, Volumen Extraordinario 1, 699–715.

Western, D. (1980). Linking the ecology of past and present mammal communities. In: A.K. Behrensmeyer and A.P. Hill (Eds.), *Fossils in the Making: Vertebrate Taphonomy and Paleoecology*. Chicago: The University of Chicago Press, pp. 41–54.

Western, D. (1989). The ecological role of elephants in Africa. *Pachyderm* 12, 42–45.

Western, D. (1997). *In the Dust of Kilimanjaro*. Washington, DC: Island Press.

Western, D. and Behrensmeyer, A.K. (2009). Bone assemblages track animal community structure over 40 years in an African savanna ecosystem. *Science* 324, 1061–1064.

Weston, E.M. (2003). Fossil Hippopotamidae from Lothagam. In: M.G. Leakey and J.M. Harris (Eds.), *Lothagam: The Dawn of Humanity in Eastern Africa*. New York: Columbia University Press, pp. 441–483.

Weston, E.M. and Boisserie, J.R. (2010). Hippopotamidae. In: L. Werdelin and W. Sanders (Eds.), *Cenozoic Mammals of Africa*. Berkeley: University of California Press, pp. 853–871.

Wheeler, P.E. (1991). The thermoregulatory advantages of hominid bipedalism in open equatorial environments: the contribution of increased convective heat loss and cutaneous evaporative cooling. *Journal of Human Evolution* 21(2), 107–115.

White, E.M. and Hannus, L.A. (1983). Chemical weathering of bone in archaeological soils. *American Antiquity* 48, 316–322.

White, F. (1983). *The Vegetation of Africa, a Descriptive Memoir to Accompany the UNESCO/AETFAT/UNSO Vegetation Map of Africa (3 Plates, Northwestern Africa, Northeastern Africa, and Southern Africa, 1: 5,000,000)*. Paris: UNESCO.

White, S.E. (1915). *The Rediscovered Country*. New York: Doubleday.

White, T.D. (1977). New fossil hominids from Laetolil, Tanzania. *American Journal of Physical Anthropology* 46, 197–230.

White, T.D. (1980a). Evolutionary implications of Pliocene hominid footprints. *Science* 208, 175–176.

White, T.D. (1980b). Additional fossil hominids from Laetoli, Tanzania: 1976–1979 specimens. *American Journal of Physical Anthropology* 53, 487–504.

White, T.D. (1981). Primitive hominid canine from Tanzania. *Science* 213, 348–349.

White, T.D. (1984). Pliocene hominids from the Middle Awash, Ethiopia. *Courier Forschungsinstitut Senckenberg* 69, 57–68.

White, T.D. (1985). The hominids of Hadar and Laetoli: An element-by-element comparison of the dental samples. In: E. Delson (Ed.), *Ancestors: The Hard Evidence*. New York: Alan R. Liss, pp. 138–152.

White, T.D. (1986). Cut marks on the Bodo cranium: a case of prehistoric defleshing. *American Journal of Physical Anthropology* 69(4), 503–509.

White, T.D. (1988). The comparative biology of "Robust" Australopithecus: clues from context. In: F.E. Grine (Ed.), *The Evolutionary History of the "Robust" Australopithecines*. New York: Aldine de Gruyter, pp. 449–483.

White, T.D. (1995). African omnivores: global climatic change and Plio-Pleistocene hominids and suids. In E.S. Vrba, G.H. Denton, T.C. Partridge and L.H. Burckle (Eds.), *Paleoclimate and Evolution, with Emphasis on Human Origins*. New Haven: Yale University Press, pp. 369–384.

White, T.D. (2002). Earliest hominids. In: W.C. Hartwig (Ed.), *The Primate Fossil Record*. Cambridge: Cambridge University Press, pp. 407–417.

White, T.D. (2004). Managing paleoanthropology's nonrenewable resources: a view from Afar. *Comptes Rendus Palevol* 3, 341–351.

White, T.D. and Harris, J.M. (1977). Suid evolution and correlation of African hominid localities. *Science* 198, 13–21.

White, T.D. and Suwa, G. (1987). Hominid footprints at Laetoli: facts and interpretations. *American Journal of Physical Anthropology* 72, 485–514.

White, T.D. and Suwa, G. (2004). A new species of *Notochoerus* (Artiodactyla, Suidae) from the Pliocene of Ethiopia. *Journal of Vertebrate Paleontology* 24, 474–480.

White, T.D., Moore, R.V. and Suwa, G. (1984). Hadar biostratigraphy and hominid evolution. *Journal of Vertebrate Paleontology* 4, 575–583.

White, T.D., Suwa, G., Hart, W.K., et al. (1993). New discoveries of *Australopithecus* at Maka in Ethiopia. *Nature* 366, 261–265.

White, T.D., Suwa, G. and Asfaw, B. (1994). *Australopithecus ramidus*, a new species of early hominid from Aramis, Ethiopia. *Nature* 371, 306–312.

White, T.D., Suwa, G. and Asfaw, B. (1996). Ardipithecus ramidus, a root species for Australopithecus. In: F. Facchini (Ed.), *The First Humans and Their Cultural Manifestations*. Proceedings of the Colloquia of the XIII International Congress of Prehistoric and Protohistoric Sciences, Forli, pp. *15–23*.

White, T.D., Suwa, G., Simpson, S. and Asfaw, B. (2000). Jaws and teeth of Australopithecus afarensis from Maka, Middle Awash, Ethiopia. *American Journal of Physical Anthropology* 111, 45–68.

White, T.D., Asfaw, B., DeGusta, D., et al. (2003). Pleistocene Homo sapiens from Middle Awash, Ethiopia. *Nature* 423, 742–747.

White, T.D., Asfaw, B. and Suwa, G. (2005). Pliocene hominid fossils from Gamedah, Middle Awash, Ethiopia. *Transactions of the Royal Society of South Africa* 60, 79–83.

White, T.D., WoldeGabriel, G., Asfaw, B., et al. (2006). Asa Issie, Aramis and the origin of *Australopithecus*. *Nature*, 440, 883–889.

White, T.D., Ambrose, S.H., Suwa, G., et al. (2009a). Macrovertebrate paleontology and the Pliocene habitat of *Ardipithecus ramidus*. *Science*, 326, 67.

White, T.D., Asfaw, B., Beyene, Y., et al. (2009b). *Ardipithecus ramidus* and the paleobiology of early hominids. *Science*, 326(5949), 64–86.

White, T.D., Ambrose, S.H., Suwa, G. and WoldeGabriel, G. (2010). Response to comment on the paleoenvironment of *Ardipithecus ramidus*. *Science* 328, 1105.

Whittaker, R.H. (1960). Vegetation of the Siskiyou mountains, Oregon and California. *Ecological Monographs* 30(3), 279–338.

Whittaker, R.H. (1972). Evolution and measurement of species diversity. *Taxon* 21(2–3), 213–251.

Wildman, D.E., Uddin, M., Liu, G., Grossman, L.I. and Goodman, M. (2003). Implications of natural selection in shaping 99.4%

nonsynonymous DNA identity between humans and chimpanzees: enlarging genus *Homo*. *Proceedings of the National Academy of Sciences* 100(12), 7181–7188.

Wilkins, J. and Chazan, M. (2012). Blade production ~500 thousand years ago at Kathu Pan 1, South Africa: support for a multiple origins hypothesis for early Middle Pleistocene blade technologies. *Journal of Archaeological Science* 39(6), 1883–1900.

Wilkins, J., Pollarolo, L. and Kuman, K. (2010). Prepared core reduction at the site of Kudu Koppie in northern South Africa: temporal patterns across the earlier and Middle Stone Age boundary. *Journal of Archaeological Science* 37, 1279–1292.

Wilkins, J., Schoville, B.J., Brown, K.S. and Chazan, M. (2012). Evidence for early hafted hunting technology. *Science* 338(2012), 942–946.

Will, M., Krapp, M., Stock, J.T. and Manica, A. (2021). Different environmental variables predict body and brain size evolution in *Homo*. *Nature Communications* 12(1), 1–12.

Williams, F.L. (2013). Dietary reconstruction of Pliocene Parapapio whitei from Makapansgat, South Africa, using dental microwear texture analysis. *Folia Primatologia* 85, 21–37.

Williams, F.L.E. and Geissler, E. (2014). Reconstructing the diet and paleoecology of Plio-Pleistocene *Cercopithecoides williamsi* from Sterkfontein, South Africa diet and paleoecology in *C. williamsi*. *Palaios* 29(9), 483–494.

Williams, F.L. and Patterson, J.W. (2010). Reconstructing the paleoecology of Taung, South Africa from low magnification of dental microwear features in fossil primates. *Palaios* 25, 439–448.

Williams, L.A.J. and Chapman, G.R. (1986). Relationships between major structures, salic volcanism and sedimentation in the Kenya Rift from the equator northwards to Lake Turkana. In: L.E. Frostick, R.W. Renaut, I. Rein and J.J. Tiercelin (Eds.), *Sedimentation in the African Rifts*. Geological Society Special Publication No. 25. London: Geological Society of London, pp. 59–74.

Williams, M.A., Williams, F.H., Gasse, F., Curtis, G.H. and Adamson, D.A. (1979). Pleistocene environments at Gadeb prehistoric site, Ethiopia. *Nature* 282, 29–33.

Williamson, P.G. (1990). Late Cenozoic mollusc faunas from the north west African rift (Uganda–Zaire). In: N.T. Boaz (Ed.), *Evolution of Environments and Hominidae in the African Western Rift Valley*. Martinsville: Virginia Museum of Natural History, pp. 125–139.

Willig, M.R. and Scheiner, S.M. (2011). The state of theory in ecology. In: S.M. Scheiner and M.R. Willig (Eds.), *The Theory of Ecology*. Chicago: University of Chicago Press, pp. 333–347.

Willig, M.R., Kaufman, D.M. and Stevens, R.D. (2003). Latitudinal gradients of biodiversity: pattern, process, scale, and synthesis. *Annual Review of Eecology, Evolution, and Systematics* 34(1), 273–309.

Wilkinson, M.J., Schoville, B.J., Brown, K.S. and Chazan, M. (2012). Evidence for early hafted hunting technology. *Science* 338, 942–946.

Wilkinson, R.D., Steiper, M.E., Soligo, C., et al. (2011). Dating primate divergences through an integrated analysis of palaeontological and molecular data. *Systematic Biology* 60, 16–31.

Winkler, A.J. (2002). Neogene paleobiogeography and East African paleoenvironments: contributions from the Tugen Hills rodents and lagomorphs. *Journal of Human Evolution* 42(1–2), 237–56.

Winkler, A.J., Denys, C. and Avery, D.M. (2010). Rodentia. In: L. Werdelin and W.J. Sanders (Eds.), *Cenozoic Mammals of Africa*. Berkeley: University of California Press, pp. 263–304.

WoldeGabriel, G., White, T., Suwa, G., et al. (1992). Kesem-Kebena: a newly discovered paleoanthropological research area in Ethiopia. *Journal of Field Archaeology* 19, 471–493.

WoldeGabriel, G., White, T.D., Suwa, G., et al. (1994). Ecological and temporal placement of early Pliocene hominids at Aramis, Ethiopia. *Nature* 371, 330–333.

WoldeGabriel, G., Haile-Selassie, Y., Renne, P.R., et al. (2001). Geology and paleontology of the Late Miocene Middle Awash Valley, Afar rift, Ethiopia. *Nature* 412, 175–178.

WoldeGabriel, G., Gilbert, W.H., Hart, W.K., Renne, P.R. and Ambrose, S. (2008). Geology and geochronology. In: W.H. Gilbert and B. Asfaw (Eds.), *Homo erectus: Pleistocene Evidence from the Middle Awash, Ethiopia*. Berkeley: University of California Press, pp. 13–43.

WoldeGabriel, G., Ambrose, S. H., Barboni, D., et al. (2009a). The geological, isotopic, botanical, invertebrate, and lower vertebrate surroundings of *Ardipithecus ramidus*. *Science* 326, 65–655.

WoldeGabriel, G., Hart, W.K., Renne, P.R., Haile-Selassie, Y. and White, T. (2009b). Stratigraphy of the Adu-Asa Formation. In: Y. Haile-Selassie and G. WoldeGabriel (Eds.), *Ardipithecus kadabba: Late Miocene Evidence from the Middle Awash, Ethiopia*. Berkeley: University of California Press, pp. 27–62.

WoldeGabriel, G., Endale, T., White, T.D., et al. (2013). The role of tephra studies in African paleoanthropology as exemplified by the Sidi Hakoma Tuff. *Journal of African Earth Sciences* 77, 41–58.

Wolfenden, E., Ebinger, C., Yirgu, G., Renne, P.R. and Kelley, S.P. (2005). Evolution of a volcanic rifted margin: Southern Red Sea, Ethiopia. *Geological Society of America Bulletin* 117, 846–864.

Wolff, R.G. (1975). Sampling and sample size in ecological analyses of fossil mammals. *Paleobiology* 1, 195–204.

Wolpoff, M.H., Senut, B., Pickford, M. and Hawks, J. (2002). Sahelanthropus or 'Sahelpithecus'? *Nature* 419, 581–582.

Wolverton, S. and Lyman, R.L. (2012). *Conservation Biology and Applied Zooarchaeology*. Tucson: University of Arizona Press.

Wood, B.A. (1991). *Koobi Fora Research Project Volume 4: Hominid Cranial Remains*. Oxford: Clarendon Press.

Wood, B. and Boyle, E.K. (2016). Hominin taxic diversity: fact or fantasy? *American Journal of Physical Anthropology* 159, 37–78

Wood, B. and Constantino, P. (2007). *Paranthropus boisei*: fifty years of evidence and analysis. *Yearbook of Physical Anthropology* 50, 106–132.

Wood, B. and Leakey, M. (2011). The Omo-Turkana Basin fossil hominins and their contribution to our understanding of human evolution in Africa. *Evolutionary Anthropology* 20, 264–292.

Wood, B. and Richmond, B.G. (2000). Human evolution: taxonomy and paleobiology. *Journal of Anatomy* 196, 19–60.

Wood, P.C. (2003). Fossil turtles from Lothagam. In: M. G. Leakey and J. M. Harris (Eds.), *Lothagam: The Dawn of Humanity in Eastern Africa*. New York: Columbia University Press, pp. 115–136.

Wood, R.C. (1973). A possible correlation between the ecology of living African pelomedusid turtles and their relative abundance in the fossil record. *Copeia* 1973, 627–629.

Woodborne, S., Hall, G., Robertson, I., et al. (2015). A 1000-year carbon isotope rainfall proxy record from South African baobab trees (*Adansonia digitate* L.). *PLoS ONE* 10, e0124202.

Woodhead, J., Hellstrom, J., Maas, R., et al. (2006). U–Pb geochronology of speleothems by MC-ICPMS. *Quaternary Geochronology* 1(3), 208–221.

Woodward, A.S. (1921). A new cave man from Rhodesia, South Africa. *Nature* 108, 371–372.

Wrangham, R.W. (1980). Bipedal locomotion as a feeding adaptation in gelada baboons, and its implications for hominid evolution. *Journal of Human Evolution* 9, 329–331.

Wronski, T. and Hausdorf, B. (2008). Distribution patterns of land snails in Ugandan rain forests support the existence of

Pleistocene forest refugia. *Journal of Biogeography* 35, 1759–1768.

Wurz, S. (1999). The Howiesons Poort backed artefacts from Klasies River: an argument for symbolic behaviour. *The South African Archaeological Bulletin* 54(169), 38–50.

Wurz, S. (2002). Variability in the middle stone age lithic sequence, 115,000–60,000 years ago at Klasies river, South Africa. *Journal of Archaeological Science* 29(9), 1001–1015.

Wurz, S., Bentsen, S.E., Reynard, J., et al. (2018). Connections, culture and environments around 100 000 years ago at Klasies River main site. *Quaternary International* 495, 102–115.

Wynn, J.G. (2000). Paleosols, stable carbon isotopes, and paleoenvironmental interpretation of Kanapoi, Northern Kenya. *Journal of Human Evolution* 39, 411–432.

Wynn, J.G. (2004). Influence of Plio-Pleistocene aridification on human evolution: evidence from paleosols of the Turkana Basin, Kenya. *American Journal of Physical Anthropology* 123, 106–118.

Wynn, J.G. and Bedaso, Z.K. (2010). Is the Pliocene Ethiopian monsoon extinct? A comment on Aronson et al. (2008). *Journal of Human Evolution* 59, 133–138.

Wynn, J.G., Alemseged, Z., Bobe, R., et al. (2006). Geological and palaeontological context of a Pliocene juvenile hominin at Dikika, Ethiopia. *Nature* 443, 332–336.

Wynn, J.G., Roman, D.C., Alemseged, Z., et al. (2008). Stratigraphy, depositional environments, and basin strcuture of the Hadar and Busidima Formations at Dikika, Ethiopia. In: J. Quade and J.G. Wynn (Eds.), *The Geology of Early Humans in the Horn of Africa*. Boulder: Geological Society of America, pp. 87–118.

Wynn, J.G., Sponheimer, M., Kimbel, W.H., et al. (2013). Diet of *Australopithecus afarensis* from the Pliocene Hadar Formation, Ethiopia. *Proceedings of the National Academy of Sciences* 110, 10495–10500.

Wynn, J.G., Reed, K.E., Sponheimer, M., et al. (2016). Dietary flexibility of *Australopithecus afarensis* in the face of paleoecological change during the middle Pliocene: faunal evidence from Hadar, Ethiopia. *Journal of Human Evolution* 99, 93–106.

Wynn, J.G., Alemseged, Z., Bobe, R., et al. (2020). Isotopic evidence for the timing of the dietary shift toward C_4 foods in eastern African *Paranthropus*. *Proceedings of the National Academy of Sciences* 117(36), 21978–21984.

Yalden, D.W., Largen, M.J., Kock, D. and Hillman, J.C. (1996). Catalogue of the mammals of Ethiopia and Eritrea. 7. Revised checklist, zoogeography and conservation. *Tropical Zoology* 9, 73–164.

Yasui, K., Kunimatsu, Y., Kuga, N., Bajope, B. and Ishida, H. (1992). Fossil mammals from the Neogene strata in the Sinda Basin, eastern Zaire. *African Study Monographs* 17, 87–107.

Yemane, T. (1997). Stratigraphy and sedimentology of the Hadar Formation. PhD dissertation, Iowa State University.

Yoder, A.D. and Yang, Z. (2000). Estimation of primate speciation dates using local molecular clocks. *Molecular Biology and Evolution* 17(7), 1081–1090.

Yost, C.L., Ivory, S.J., Deino, A.L., et al. (2021). Phytoliths, pollen, and microcharcoal from the Baringo Basin, Kenya reveal savanna dynamics during the Plio-Pleistocene transition. *Palaeogeography, Palaeoclimatology, Palaeoecology* 570, 109779.

Young, R.B. (1925). The calcareous tufa deposits of the Campbell Rand, from Boetsap to Taungs Native Reserve. *Transvaal Geological Society of South Africa* 28, 55–67.

Zachos, J., Pagani, M., Sloan, L., Thomas, E. and Billups, K. (2001). Trends, rhythms, and aberrations in global climate 65 Ma to present. *Science* 292, 686–693.

Zaitsev, A.N., Wenzel, T., Spratt, J., et al. (2011). Was Sadiman volcano a source for the Laetoli Footprint Tuff? *Journal of Human Evolution* 61, 121–124.

Zaitsev, A.N., Marks, M.A.W., Wenzel, T., et al. (2012). Mineralogy, geochemistry and petrology of the phonolitic to nephelinitic Sadiman volcano, Crater Highlands, Tanzania. *Lithos* 152, 66–83.

Zaitsev, A.N., Spratt, J., Sharygin, V.V., et al. (2015). Mineralogy of the Laetoli Footprint Tuff: a comparison with possible volcanic sources from the Crater Highlands and Gregory Rift. *Journal of African Earth Sciences* 111, 214–221.

Zanolli, C., Bondioli, L., Candilio, F., et al. (2013). Endostructural morphology of the late Early Pleistocene human dental remains from Uadi Aalad and Mulhuli-Amo, Danakil (Afar) depression of Eritrea. *American Journal of Physical Anthropology* 150(S56), 298 (abstract).

Zanolli, C., Bondioli, L., Coppa, A., et al. (2014). The late Early Pleistocene human dental remains from Uadi Aalad and Mulhuli-Amo (Buia), Eritrean Danakil: macromorphology and microstructure. *Journal of Human Evolution* 74, 96–113.

Zavada, M.S. and Cadman, A. (1993). Palynological investigations at the Makapansgat Limeworks: an australopithecine site. *Journal of Human Evolution* 25, 337–350.

Zazzo, A., Bocherens, H., Brunet, M., et al. (2000). Herbivore paleodiet and paleoenvironmental changes in Chad during the Pliocene using stable isotope ratios of tooth enamel carbonate. *Paleobiology* 26(2), 294–309.

Zhang, Z., Ramstein, G., Schuster, M., et al. (2014). Aridification of the Sahara desert caused by Tethys Sea shrinkage during the Late Miocene. *Nature* 513(7518), 401–404.

Ziegler, M., Simon, M.H., Hall, I.R., et al. (2013). Development of Middle Stone Age innovation linked to rapid climate change. *Nature Communications* 4, 1905.

Zilberman, U., Smith, P., Piperno, M. and Condemi, S. (2004). Evidence of amelogenesis imperfecta in an early African *Homo erectus*. *Journal of Human Evolution* 46(6), 647–653.

Zinke, J., Dullo, W.-C., Heiss, G.A. and Eisenhauer, A. (2004). ENSO and Indian Ocean subtropical dipole variability is recorded in a coral record off southwest Madagascar for the period 1659 to 1995. *Earth and Planetary Science Letters* 228, 177–194.

Zollikofer, C.P.E., Ponce de León, M.S., Lieberman, D.E., et al. (2005). Virtual cranial reconstruction of *Sahelanthropus tchadensis*. *Nature* 434, 755–759.

Zouhri, S., Geraads, D., El Boughabi, S. and El Harfi, A. (2012). Discovery of an Upper Miocene vertebrate fauna near Tizi N'Tadderht, Skoura, Ouarzazate Basin (Central High Atlas, Morocco). *Comptes Rendus Palevol* 11, 455–461.

Zouhri, S., Benammi, M., Geraads, D. and El Boughabi, S. (2017). Mammifères du Néogène continental du Maroc: Faunes, biochronologie et paléobiogéographie. *Mémoires de la Société Géologique de France* 180, 527–588.

Zuberbühler, K. (2001). Predator-specific alarm calls in Campbell's monkeys, Cercopithecus campbelli. *Behavioral Ecology and Sociobiology* 50, 414–422.

Zuberbühler, K., Noë, R. and Seyfarth, R.M. (1997). Diana monkey long-distance calls: messages for conspecifics and predators. *Animal Behaviour* 53, 589–604.

Zwane, B. (2018). A reconstruction of the Late Holocene environment using archaeological charcoal from Klasies River main site cave 1, southern Cape. Unpublished MSc dissertation, University of the Witwatersrand.

Index

A.L. 288–1 "Lucy", 214, 229
A.L. 333 "First Family", 214
Aalat Formation, 187
   vertebrates, non-mammalian, 187
Abundu Formation, 361, 365
   vertebrates, mammalian, 365
Acheulean industry, 33, 53, 55, 58, 60, 62, 82, 92, 94, 95, 96, 100, 101, 120, 122, 127, 128, 130, 145, 148, 162, 167, 168, 169, 171, 177, 178, 179, 187, 191, 197, 207, 257, 259, 266, 277, 298, 326, 331, 367, 374, 377, 378, 382, 383, 384, 387, 395, 461, 466, 476, 481, 483, 484, 537, 549, 555
   transition to Middle Stone Age, 176
Addai Formation, 187
Adu-Asa Formation, 31, 200, 246
   vertebrates, mammalian, 201
   vertebrates, non-mammalian, 201
Afar Rift, 161, 214, 245, 248, 376
African Humid Period, 36, 43, 45
African monsoon, 218, 277
African–Iberian mammal exchange, 31
Aguirre, Emiliano, 173
Ahl al Oughlam, 461, 465, 468, 480, 491
   micromammals, 471
   paleoenvironmental reconstruction, 473
   vertebrates, mammalian, 469
   vertebrates, non-mammalian, 471
Aïn Boucherit, 461, 465
Aïn Brimba, 461, 465
Aïn Hanech, 461, 465, 491
Aïn Maarouf, 466
Aka Aiteputh Formation, 173
Albertine Rift Valley, 180
Alcelaphini and Antilopini Criterion, 55
Allia Bay, 278
alpha (α-)diversity, 13
Amboseli, 339
Amplifier Lakes Hypothesis, 161
Andalee Ridge, 232
Anfa Formation, 481
anthropogenic biases
   in fossil prospection, 18
Apoko Formation, 361, 367

Arambourg, Camille, 278, 289, 311, 461, 463, 465, 466, 475
Aramis, 278, 454
   paleoenvironments, 167, 204
   vertebrates, mammalian, 204
Ardipithecus kadabba, 1, 30, 166, 167, 185, 197, 201, 202, 560
Ardipithecus ramidus, 21, 31, 32, 166, 167, 168, 175, 176, 197, 203, 206, 212, 213, 255, 332
   habitats, 203
   paleoenvironments, 32
Ardipithecus sp, 248
Aro Formation, 187
Asa Issie, 278
Asbole, 166
Atlanthropus mauritanicus, 466, 475, 481
   See *Homo heidelbergensis*
Atlantic meridional overturning circulation, 33
Atlas Range, 472
Australopithecus, 235, 278
   cf. *afarensis*, 242
   genus, origins of, 241, 278
   geographic range, 1
   paleoenvironments, 51
Australopithecus afarensis, 165, 167, 170, 171, 176, 179, 214, 222, 255, 311, 324, 330, 343, 435, 436
   dietary shifts, 241
   habitat preferences, 241
   isotopic dietary data, 19
   juvenile skeleton at Dikika, 229
Australopithecus africanus, 53, 135, 137
Australopithecus anamensis, 167, 171, 173, 255, 278, 311, 323, 330
   dietary shifts, 241
Australopithecus bahrelghazali, 184, 241
Australopithecus deyiremeda, 165, 237, 249
Australopithecus garhi, 167
Australopithecus prometheus, 67
Australopithecus sediba, 52
Awash River, 212, 214, 216, 229
Awash Valley, 231

Bahariya-Farafra, 464
Balchit, 257
Baringo Basin, 343
basal hominin, 29
Baynunah, 29

Beglia Formation, 26, 464
Behrensmeyer, Anna K., 1, 312
Benguela upwelling, 51
Beni Mellal, 463
Berg Aukas, 26, 51
   paleoenvironmental reconstruction, 51
Bestwood 1, 148
beta (β) diversity, 13
Biberson, P., 481
Biome, definition of, 7
Bishop, W.W. "Bill", 1, 334, 341, 342, 343, 531
Bled Douarah, 26
Blombos Cave, 62
   vertebrates, mammalian, 63
Bloubank stream, 82
Blumenschine, Robert, 394
Bodele Dora, 201
Bolt's Farm, 56
   paleoenvironmental reconstruction, 57
   vertebrates, mammalian, 56
   vertebrates, non-mammalian, 57
bonanza effect
   defininition of, 17
Boomplaas Cave, 63
   micromammals, 63
   vertebrates, mammalian, 63
Border Cave, 58
   micromammals, 58
   vertebrates, mammalian, 58
Bou Hanifia, 26, 461, 464
Bourlière, François, 1
Brain, Charles "Bob", 56, 82, 86, 102, 105, 137
Broom, Robert, 51, 52, 54, 55, 56, 82, 86, 92, 96, 102, 107, 115, 135, 137, 138
Brown, Frank, 1, 278, 279, 312, 314, 320, 330
Bruhnes Chron,
Bruhnes/Matuyama reversal, 262
Buffalo Cave, 51
Buia-Dandiero Basin, 187
   aquatic taxa, 192
   micromammals, 189
   paleoenvironmental reconstructions, 194
   vertebrates, mammalian, 189, 192
   vertebrates, non-mammalian, 189, 192
Bukra Formation, 187
Bushland, definition of, 3

Bushman Rock Shelter, 58
   invertebrates, 58
   vertbrates, non-mammalian, 58
   vertebrates, mammalian, 58
Busidima Formation, 231
   at Gona, 207
   paleosols, 199
   pollen, 208
Busidima River, 200
Butzer, Karl, 104, 120, 135, 140, 145, 278, 279
Buxton-Norlim Limeworks, 135, See Taung

C_3 plants, definition of, 10
C_4 plants, definition of, 10
Cameroon, 30
Cangalongue, 50
Canteen Kopje, 148
carrières Thomas. See Thomas Quarries
catena, definition of, 7
Cave of Hearths, 51, 66, See Makapansgat
Chado-Libyan biogeographical province, 29
Chavaillon, Jean, 257, 263
Chemeron Formation, 175
   paleoenvironmental reconstruction, 347, 353
   diatomites, 344
   vertebrates, mammalian, 347
Chemoigut Formation, 176
   vertebrates, mammalian, 176
   vertebrates, non-mammalian, 176
Chesowanja
   evidence for controlled use of fire, 176
Chew Bahir rift, 269
chimpanzee
   meat-eating, 10
Chitimwe Beds, 453
Chiwondo Beds, 140, 182, 453
   paleosols, 182
   vertebrates, mammalian, 182, 456
   paleoenvironmental reconstruction, 459
   vertebrates, mammalian, 182, 456
   vertebrates, non-mammalian, 182
Chorora Formation, 29, 168
   vertebrates, mammalian, 169
Chororapithecus, 25, 29

Index

Chororapithecus abyssinicus, 168
Chyulu Hills, 263
Clark, J. Desmond, 169
Clarke, Ronald, 114
climate archives
  continental drilling, 16
climate-averaging, 19
closed canopy effect, 79
Cold Air Cave, 51
Collapsed Cone, 80
common-cause effects, 16
community
  definition of, 6
  paleoecology, definition of, 13
Congo Basin, 184
Congo River, 184
convergent evolution
  definition of, 14
Cooke, H. B. S. (Basil), 120, 148
Cooper's Cave, 55, 86, 91, 92
  invertebrate traces, 55
  paleoenvironments, 55
  vertebrates, mammalian, 55, 89
  vertebrates, non-mammalian, 55
Cooper's B, 86
Cooper's D, 86
  paleoenvironmental reconstruction,
Coppens, Yves, 214, 278, 289
Cornelian Land Mammal Age, 120
Cornelia-Uitzoek, 58, 120, 133, 148, 503
  phytoliths, 124, 126, 131
  vertebrates, mammalian, 123
Cradle of Humankind World Heritage Site, 92

Danakil Depression, 187
Dandiero
  gastropods, 189
Dar Bou Azza Formation, 481
Dart, Raymond, 51, 58, 66, 135
  Savannah Hypothesis,
Darwin, Charles, 14
de Bozas, Bourg, 278, 289, 311
de Heinzelin, Jean, 1, 279
Deacon, Hilary, 63, 64
depositional environments
  eastern Africa, 16
  northern Africa, 18
  southern Africa, 17
Die Kelders, 62
  vertebrates, mammalian, 62
  vertebrates, non-mammalian, 62
Diepkloof rock shelter, 60
  micromammals, 60
  vertebrates, mammalian, 60
  vertebrates, non-mammalian, 60
Dikika, 166, 229, 231
  Australopithecus afarensis, 236
Dikika juvenile, DIK-1-1 ("Selam"), 236
  micromammals, 237

vertebrates, mammalian, 232, 236
vertebrates, non-mammalian, 239
Ditsong National Museum of Natural History, 138
diversity gradients, 14
Djurab Desert, 29
Drimolen
  bone tools, 54
  Main Quarry, 54
  Makondo site, 54
  micromammals, 54
  paleoenvironments, 54
  vertebrates, mammalian, 54
  vertebrates, non-mammalian, 54
Duinefontein 2, 62
  coprolites, 62
  micromammals, 62
  vertebrates, mammalian, 62

early *Homo*, 55, 114
  role of aridity in emergence of, 15
East African Rift System
  origins of, 161
East Rudolf. See East Turkana
ecomorphology
  definition of, 12
ecosystem, definition of, 6
Ekora, 172
  vertebrates, mammalian, 172
El Niño Southern Oscillation, 136
Elands Bay Cave, 59
  micromammals, 60
  vertebrates, mammalian, 59
  vertebrates, non-mammalian, 60
Elandsfontein, 9, 60, 193, 486, 503, 537
  pollen, 60
  vertebrates, mammalian, 60
endurance running, 119
Engare Nyiro river, 385
Engare Sero river, 385
environment, definition of, 6
Eonile, 462, 465
Eosahabi rivers, 31
Epipaleolithic, 257
Equid Tooth Site, 362
equitability, 13
eurytopy, 32

Fanta Stream, 169
faunal turnover, 36, 43
  definition of, 36
  pulses, 15
Fauresmith industry, 145, 148
Fayum, 472
Fejej, 171, 278
  vertebrates, mammalian, 171
  vertebrates, non-mammalian, 171
Felid Hill, 362, 367
  vertebrates, mammalian, 367

First Appearance Datum (FAD)
  definition, 19
Fish Cliffs, 365
Florisbad, 59, 121
  fossil wood, 59
  invertebrates, 59
  vertebrates, mammalian, 59
Forests
  afromontane, 3
  definition of, 3
  dry, 3
  gallery, 3
  rain, 3
fossil burrows, definition of, 10, 141, 377
Fossil Recovery Potential, 17, 22
fossil tooth morphology
  use in community reconstruction, 14
Fuchs, Vivian E., 343
Fynbos biome, 159

Gadeb, 169
Galana Boi Formation, 312
Galili, 242
Galili Formation, 168, 242
  Caashacado Member, 247
  Dhagax Member, 242, 247
  Dhidinley Member, 242, 246
  Godiray Member, 242, 246
  Lasdanan Member, micromammals, 249
  paleoenvironmental reconstruction, 249
  Shabeley Laag Member, 242, 247
  vertebrates, mammalian, 249
  vertebrates, non-mammalian, 249
  Lasdanan Member, 242, 245
gamma (γ-) diversity, 13
Gauss–Matuyama magnetic reversal, 69
Gentry, Alan, 286, 351
geomorphology
  Laetoli region, 9
Gerbil Event, 31
Getharkulle, 246
Ghaap Group dolomites, 145
Ghaap Plateau, 135
Gibraltar straits, 467
Gladysvale, 53
  coprolite, 53
  micromammals, 53
  paleobotanical remains, 53
  vertebrates, mammalian, 53
Goldsmith's Farm, 57
  paleoenvironmental reconstruction, 57
  vertebrates, mammalian, 57
Gombore, 266
Gona, 166, 197
  micromammals, 208, 212
  paleoenvironmental reconstruction, 202, 206, 209, 212
  paleoenvironments, 202, 206

vertebrates, mammalian, 201, 212
vertebrates, non-mammalian, 202, 205, 206, 208
Gondolin, 52
  micromammals, 52
  paleoenvironmental reconstruction, 52
  vertebrates, non-mammalian, 52
Goreya Formation, 187
Gorongosa National Park, 182
Grasslands
  definition of, 6
  edaphic, 56, 117
Green Sahara Periods
  definition of, 462
Green Sahara phases, 36
Gregory Rift, 360, 385
Gregory, John Walter, 332
Grotte des Rhinocéros, 481
Grumeti River, 410, 411
Gulf of Aden, 27, 28, 29, 30, 214, 229, 324, 325, 328
Gulf of Aden Rift, 231

Haasgat, 53, 79
  micromammals, 53
  vertebrates, mammalian, 53
  vertebrates, non-mammalian, 53
habitat, definition of, 6
habitat heterogeneity, 7
habitat spectra
  use in paleoenvironmental reconstructions, 12
Hadar Formation, 166, 214, 216, 231
  Basal Member, 216, 225, 231
  Denen Dora Member, 216, 231
  invertebrates, 218
  Kada Hadar Member, 216, 231
  micromammal, 220, 222
  mollusks, 218
  ostracods, 218
  paleosols, 216, 217
  pedogenic carbonates, 232
  pollen record, 218
  Sidi Hakoma Member, 216, 231, 232
  vertebrates, mammalian, 218, 222
  vertebrates, non-mammalian, 220, 222
Hadza, 373
Hamadi Das, 201
Harasib, 26
Harasib 3
  paleoenvironmental reconstruction, 51
Hay, Richard, 1, 395
Heinrich Events, 33
herbivores
  abrasive diets, 13
  browsing, use in paleohabitats, 13
  grazing, use in paleohabitats, 13

577

Index

Hill, Andrew, 343, 345, 351
Hoedjiespunt, 61
    micromammals, 61
    vertebrates, mammalian, 61
    vertebrates, non-mammalian, 61
Hoffman, A.C., 120
Hoffstetter, Robert, 475
Homa Formation, 177, 361
    vertebrates, mammalian, 362
Homa Peninsula, 177, 360
hominin foraging
    landscape models, 428
    marginal scavenging, 429
    passive scavenging, 429
    power scavenging, 429
hominin habitat types
    affected by rifting, 213
    mosaic environments, 19
hominin land use
    Olduvai Gorge, 9
hominin taxic diversity, 17, 21
hominin-climate interactions
    critique, 15
Hominini, 21, 24, 25, 161, 170, 324
Homo, 164, 176
    genus, 324
    genus origins of, 278
    geographic range, 1
    oldest specimen, 165
Homo erectus, 54, 114, 167, 169, 171, 179, 197, 208, 259, 277, 311, 326, 395, 412
    appearance of, 298, 310
    trackways, 327
Homo habilis, 10, 114, 171, 178, 311, 325, 394, 395, 409, 411, 430
Homo heidelbergensis, 167, 259, 484
Homo naledi, 56
Homo rhodesiensis, 475
Homo rudolfensis, 171, 182, 311, 325, 453
Homo sapiens, 33, 259, 278, 412, 435
    emergence of, 47
Homo sapiens idaltu, 167, 168
Homo sp, 127
Hoogland, 52
    paleoenvironmental reconstruction, 52
Horse Mandible Cave, 69, 80
Howell, F. Clark, 1, 213, 278, 289, 546
Howieson's Poort tool industry, 64
Hrdlička, Ales, 135
Humbu Formation, 178
Humpata Plateau, 50, 138

Iberian Peninsula, 31
Incisor morphology
    use in dietary reconstruction, 13
Indian Ocean Dipole, 136
indicator species
    use in paleoenvironmental reconstructions, 11
Intertropical Convergence Zone, 2, 28, 33, 136, 344
invertebrates
    use in paleoenvironmental reconstruction, 11
Isaac, Glynn, 312, 378, 384

Jebel Irhoud, 466
Jebel Zelten, 461, 463
Johanson, Donald, 214, 394

Kaiso Village Formation, 180
    vertebrates, mammalian, 180
Kalahari desert, 135, 147
Kalb, Jon, 214
Kamasia Range. See Tugen Hills
Kanam Formation, 361
    vertebrates, mammalian, 362
Kanapoi, 172, 241, 278, 312
    micromammals, 173
    vertebrates, mammalian, 173
    vertebrates, non-mammalian, 173
Kanjera, 361
    hominin foraging strategies, 370
    hominin habitats, 370
    vertebrates, mammalian, 178
Kanjera North Member, 367
    gastropods, 369
    vertebrates, mammalian, 368
Kanjera South Member, 79, 367
    hominin activities, 375
    gastropods, 369
    tool use, 373
    vertebrates, mammalian, 367
    vertebrates, non-mammalian, 369
Kantis, 176, 241
    vertebrates, mammalian, 176
Kapthurin, 486
Kapthurin Formation, 176
    gastropods, 176
    vertebrates, mammalian, 176
    vertebrates, non-mammalian, 176
Kapthurin River, 348
Karonga Basin, 453
Karre, 266
Kasibos Formation, 361, 365
    vertebrates, mammalian, 365
Kathu Pan 1, 148
Kef Haroun Formation, 481
Kenyanthropus platyops, 236, 324, 330
Kerio River, 311
Kesem-Kebena, 168
    vertebrates, mammalian, 168
    vertebrates, non-mammalian, 168
Kibish Formation, 278, 280
Kisegi-Nyabusosi, 180
Klasies River Cave, 64
    charcoal remains, 64
    vertebrates, mammalian, 64
    vertebrates, non-mammalian, 64
Klein, Richard, 62, 63
Kohl-Larsen, Ludwig, 436
Kollé, 183
    vertebrates, mammalian, 184
Konso
    micromammals, 273
    paleoenvironments, 273
    vertebrates, mammalian, 169, 271
    vertebrate, non-mammalian, 169, 271
Konso Formation, 169, 269
Konso-Gardula, 169
Koobi Fora Formation, 171, 300, 311
    Burgi Member, 325
    Chari Member, 327
    invertebrates, 328
    KBS Member, 325
    Lokochot Member, 324
    Lonyumun Member, 321
    micromammals, 316
    Moiti Member, 324
    Okote Member, 326
    Tulu Bor Member, 324
    vertebrates, mammalian, 315
    vertebrates, non-mammalian, 323, 328
    fossil wood, 327
    paleosols, 321
Koro Toro, 182, 183, 184, 222, 240, 241
    phytoliths, 184
    vertebrates, mammalian, 184
Kossom Bougoudi, 183
    vertebrates, mammalian, 183
    vertebrates, non-mammalian, 183
Kromdraai, 55, 82, 83, 84, 85, 86, 92, 502, 520, 571
    Member 3, 83
    paleoenvironments, 55
    paleohabitat reconstruction, 85
    vertebrates, mammalian, 55
    vertebrates, non-mammalian, 55
Kromdraai B, 55, 83, 84
Kyeoro Formation, 180

Laetoli, 140, 179, 435
    catenas, 7
    coprolites, 10
    footprints, 10
    fossil wood, 448
    gastropods, 442, 443
    hominin trackway, 435
    invertebrates, 448
    macrobotanical remains, 442, 443
    micromammals, 443, 450
    Naibadad Beds, 439
    Ngaloba Beds, 439
    Olpiro Beds, 439
    paleoenvironmental reconstruction, 448
    pollen, 449
    termite nests, 9
    Upper Laetolil Beds, 435
    Upper Ndolanya Beds, 435
    Upper Ngaloba Beds, 435
    vertebrates, mammalian, 443, 448
    vertebrates, non-mammalian, 442, 443
Lainyamok, 376
    vertebrates, mammalian, 381
Lake Abhe, 229
Lake Albert, 30, 161, 180
Lake Baringo, 332, 343
Lake Chad, 30, 182
Lake Chamo, 269
Lake Edward, 180, 181
Lake Eyasi, 436
Lake Gadeb
    pollen records, 169
Lake Hadar, 218
Lake Ichkeul, 461, 465
Lake Magadi, 376, 382, 384, 410
Lake Masek, 395
Lake Natron, 384, 385
Lake Ndutu, 395
Lake Rudolf. See Lake Turkana
Lake Tana, 161
Lake Turkana, 298, 311
Lake Victoria, 161, 360
Langebaanweg, 9, 61, 177, 349, 454, 514, 569
    vertebrates, mammalian, 61
    vertebrates, non-mammalian, 61
large cutting tool, 259
Lasdanan Member, 245
Last Appearance Datum (LAD)
    definition, 19, 46
Last Glacial Maximum, 33, 45
Later Stone Age, 33, 57, 145, 148, 169, 257
leaf morphology
    use in paleoenvironmental reconstruction, 11
leaf physiognomy, 28, 174, 534
Leakey, Louis, 362, 365, 394, 436
Leakey, Mary, 179, 394, 397, 435, 436
Leakey, Maeve, 172, 312
Leakey, Richard, 278, 299, 312, 384
Ledi-Geraru, 165
Lemagurut, 436
Lemudong'o, 176
    vertebrates, mammalian, 177
    vertebrates, non-mammalian, 177
Lenderut, 376, 382
Levallois
    cores, 128
    technique, 120, 130
Lissasfa, 464
Lokalalei, 372
Lomekwian industry, 298
Lonyumun Lake, 173
Lorenyang Lake, 325
Lothagam, 29, 30, 31, 100, 140, 172, 177, 312, 573

vertebrates, mammalian, 172
vertebrates, non-mammalian, 172
Lower Laetolil Beds, 241
lower Omo Valley, 289
Lukeino Formation, 30, 174
   paleoenvironmental reconstruction, 30
   vertebrates, mammalian, 175
   vertebrates, non-mammalian, 175
Luleche, 53
Lusso Beds, 181
   vertebrates, mammalian, 181
   vertebrates, non-mammalian, 181
   invertebrates, 181

Main Ethiopian Rift, 231, 257, 289
Maka, 241
Makapansgat, 51, 57, 66, 67, 74, 78, 79, 95, 506, 530
   Buffalo Cave
      paleoenvironments, 51
   coprolites, 77
   Exit Quarry, 51, 81
   Member 3, 51, 69, 77
   Member 4, 80
   Member 5, 80
   micromammals, 51, 76, 81
   paleoenvironmental reconstructions, 78, 80
   pebble, 51
   pollen, 51
   Rodent Corner, 51, 81
   taphonomic agents, 79
   vertebrates, mammalian, 71
Malan, B. D.,, 59, 145
Malapa, 52
   coprolite, 52
   micromammals, 52
   paleoenvironmental reconstructions, 52
   phytoliths, 52
Mamatwan Mine, 158
mammal species
   arboreal, as vegetation indicators, 340
Manonga Valley, 179, 437
Mansoura, 466
Maragheh, 28
Masai Mara, 429
Mason, Revil, 51, 66, 120
Matjhabeng, 58
   vertebrates, mammalian, 58
   vertebrates, non-mammalian, 58
Mazamba Formation, 182
megaherbivore
   definition of, 321
Melka Kunture Formation, 169, 257
   Melka Kunture, 169
      Garba I, 262
      Gombore, 257
      paleoenvironmental reconstruction, 268

Garba, 257
Garba IV, 262
Karre I, 257
Kella, 262
micromammals, 267
pollen assemblages, 259
Simbiro, 257
vertebrates, mammalian, 265
vertebrates, non-mammalian, 265
Wofi, 257
Menacer, 464
Mesgid Dora, 240
mesowear
   definition of, 13
Messinian salinity crisis, 1, 31, 467, 521, 532
microwear, dental
   definition of, 13
Middle Awash, 167, 231
   Adu-Asa Formation, 167
   Belohdelie, 167
   Bodo, 167
   Bouri Formation, 168
   Maka, 167
   Sagantole Formation, 167
Middle Stone Age, 33, 55, 57, 145, 168, 257, 259, 377, 378, 439
Middleton Shaw, J.C., 55
Mid-Miocene Climatic Optimum, 1
Milankovitch cycles, 2, 344, 345
   definition of, 344
Mille-Logya, 164
   vertebrates, mammalian, 164
Minaars, 54
   vertebrates, mammalian, 54
Moghara. See Wadi Moghra
molar hypsodonty, 13
Moncucco Torinese, 31
Moquorbashi, 245
mosaic vegetation, definition of, 7
Motsetse, 53
   micromammals, 54
   vertebrates, mammalian, 54
Mpesida Beds, 30, 174
   vertebrates, mammalian, 174
   vertebrates, non-mammalian, 174
Mt. Aalat, 187
Mt. Olmoti, 413, 428
Mt. Olorgesailie, 378
Mullu basin, 242
Mursi Formation, 170, 241, 278, 280, 312
   paleoenvironmental reconstruction, 287
   fossil wood, 288
   paleosols, 282
   vertebrates, mammalian, 284
   vertebrates, non-mammalian, 285, 287
   yellow sands, 279, 280

N 885, 184
Nachola Formation, 173

Nachukui Formation, 171, 298
   Kaitio Member, 300
   Kalochoro Member, 300
   Lokalalei Member, 300
Naiyena Engol, 301
Nasura 2, 300
   ostrich eggshell, 304
   paleoenvironmental reconstruction, 305, 308
   vertebrates, mammalian, 304
   vertebrates, non-mammalian, 304
Naiyena Engol river, 300
Nakali, 28, 173, 185
Nakalipithecus, 25, 173
Nakalipithecus nakayamai, 25, 28, 173
Nama-Karoo grassland, 159
Namurungule Formation, 28, 173
   vertebrates, mammalian, 173
Nawata Formation, 30, 172, 177
Nelson Bay Cave, 63
   micromammals, 64
   vertebrates, mammalian, 63
   vertebrates, non-mammalian, 64
Ngorongoro, 401, 436
Ngorongoro Volcanic Highlands, 395
Ngorora Formation, 174
   pollen, 174
   vertebrates, mammalian, 174
Niger Delta, 184
Niger Forest Phase, 29
Nile River
   drainage, 312
Nkalabong Formation, 278, 312
Nkalabong range, 280
Nkondo Formation, 180
   invertebrates, 180
   vertebrates, mammalian, 180
   vertebrates, non-mammalian, 180
Nkondo-Kaiso, 180
Northern Hemisphere Glaciation, 344
Nyaburogo Formation, 180
Nyabusosi Formation, 180
Nyakabingo Formation, 180
Nyokie, 382
   vertebrates, non-mammalian, 382

obsidian, raw material, 259
Ocean Drilling Program, 184
Okavango Delta, 30, 32, 78, 223, 416
Oldeani, 436
Oldoinyo Lengai, 385
Oldonyo Nyokie, 376
Oldowan industry, 55, 82, 92, 94, 95, 99, 100, 101, 148, 158, 162, 166, 169, 171, 172, 176, 179, 187, 191, 197, 207, 213, 214, 216, 256, 259, 298, 331, 369, 372, 373, 374, 387, 395, 397, 411, 439, 465, 500, 503

Olduvai event, 269
Olduvai Gorge, 127, 178, 413
   Bed I, 178, 372
   Bed II, 179, 277
   Bed III, 179
   Bed IV, 179
   home bases, 394
   hominin landuse, 394
   invertebrates, 397
   landscape reconstruction, 9
   Lower Bed II, 413, 428
   micromammals, 10, 401
   paleo-lake, 413
   paleo-wetland, 427
   phytoliths, 409, 414
   plant macrofossils, 397, 413
   pollen, 11
   stone circle, 399, 411
   vertebrates, mammalian, 402, 414
   vertebrates, non-mammalian, 404, 409, 414
Olduvai Gorge DK
   paleoenvironments, 410
   phytoliths, 410
   vertebrates, mammalian, 404
   vertebrates, non-mammalian, 410
Olkesiteti Member
   vertebrates, mammalian, 382
Olmoti, 436
Olorgesailie Basin, 376
   Member 1, 377
   Member 10, 378
   Member 11, 378
   Member 7, 377
   Olkesiteti Member, 378
   Olorgesailie Formation, 177, 377
   Oloronga Beds, 382
   vertebrates, mammalian, 378
Oltulelei Formation, 377
Oluka Formation, 180
Omo River, 279, 280, 289, 311
Omo Valley, 278
Omo-Turkana Basin, 272, 275, 283, 298, 307, 309, 312, 330
   refugium, 171
oncolites, 30
Orrorin, 1, 174, 185
   humerus morphology, 30
Orrorin tugenensis, 1, 30, 175, 185
Osteodontokeratic Culture model, 67
Otavi Mountains, 25
Otavipithecus, 26
Otavipithecus namibiensis, 51
Oued el Hammam. See Bou Hanifia
Oued Mya 1, 26
Oulad Hamida Formation, 481
Ouranopithecus, 28

paleo-lakes, 9
   Chad, 184
   Hadar, 9

Index

paleo-lakes (cont.)
  Kaiso, 180
  Konso, 9
  Lokochot, 324
  Lorenyang, 309
  Malawi, 459
  Obweruka, 180
  Olduvai, 9
  Olorgesailie, 9
  Turkana, 282
paleorivers
  Awash, 166, 169, 267
  Kerio, 312
  Lusso, 180
  Omo, 289, 309, 312
  Peninj, 384
  Thabaseek, 141
  Turkwel, 312
paleosols
  definition of, 8
  Taung, 9
PaleoTurkana Database, 315
Pan, 176
Pan–Homo
  divergence, 24
Paranthropus, 52
  appearance of, 298
  early, 343
  extinction, 310, 328
  genus, 324
  geographic range, 1
Paranthropus aethiopicus, 20, 290, 435, 436
Paranthropus boisei, 20, 169, 171, 182, 311, 326, 327, 384, 394
Paranthropus robustus, 54, 55, 56, 102, 108, 114
Partridge, Timothy, 67
Patterson, Bryan, 172, 311
Peabody, Frank, 145
pedogenesis, 245, 246, 377, 378, 482
Peninj, 178
  micromammals, 178, 388, 390
  paleoenvironmental reconstruction, 391
  pollen, 178
  vertebrates, mammalian, 178, 387
  vertebrates, non-mammalian, 388
phytoliths, 146, 159, 450
Pikermi, 28
Pilbeam, David, 362
Pinnacle Point, 63
  invertebrates, 63
  micromammals, 63
  vertebrates, mammalian, 63
plant physiognomy, definition of, 7
Plovers Lake, 54
  micromammals, 54
  paleoenvironments, 54
  pollen, use in paleoenvironmental reconstruction, 11

vertebrates, mammalian, 54
vertebrates, non-mammalian, 54
African Humid period, 36
Praeanthropus, 435, 439
punctuated equilibrium, 15

Rawi Formation, 177, 361, 365
  vertebrates, mammalian, 365
Reck, Hans, 395
Red Sea Rift, 231
refugia, 25, 32
refugium. See refugia
Rhinos Cave. See Grotte des Rhinocéros
  Acheulean industry, 490
  micromammals, 485
  vertebrates, mammalian, 485
  vertebrates, non-mammalian, 486
Rising Star Cave, 56
  vertebrates, non-mammalian, 56
Robinson, John, 56, 102, 107
Rose Cottage Cave, 59
  micromammals, 59
  vertebrates, mammalian, 59
  vertebrates, non-mammalian, 59
Rusinga Island, 10, 360

Sagantole Formation, 203, 231
Sahabi, 461
Sahara Desert, 29, 36, 185
Sahelanthropus tchadensis, 1, 4, 20, 29, 182, 183
Salé, 466
Samburu Hills, 28, 173
Samburupithecus kiptalami, 25, 28, 173
Samos, 28
sampling biases, 45
sand dunes, fossil, 9
Sangatole Formation
  As Duma member, 203
  Segala Noumou member, 203
Satiman, 436
Savanna Biome, 156, 159
  definition of, 6
Schoonspruit valley, 120
Schurveberg mountains, 52
Semliki River, 180
Serengeti, 11, 59, 80, 178, 237, 370, 373, 395, 411, 413, 428, 436, 443, 448, 450, 515
Shabeley Laag Member, 249
Shackleton, Robert, M., 343
Shaw, J.C. Middleton, 86
Shiangoro River, 280
Shungura Formation, 170, 278, 289, 300, 312, 456
  Kalam locality, 290
  micromammals, 291
  paleobotanical remains, 291
  paleoenvironmental reconstructions, 296

paleosols, 171, 291
"Type Locality", 290
species richness, 292
Sibudu Cave, 64
  paleobotanical remains, 64
  paleoenvironments, 64
  vertebrates, mammalian, 64
  vertebrates, non-mammalian, 64
Sidi Abdallah, 480
Sidi Abderrahmane, 466, 481
Sidi Hakoma Member, 234
  pollen, 218
Simbiro, 266
Sinda Beds, 180
  vertebrates, mammalian, 180
  vertebrates, non-mammalian, 180
Singer, Ronald, 64
Siwaliks, 28
Skoura, 464
Skurweberg Mountains, 53
southern Kenya rift, 378
species abundances
  use in paleoenvironmental reconstruction, 11
species richness
  estimates of, 14
speleothems
  use in dating studies, 18
Sterkfontein, 55, 56, 67, 86, 92, 93, 94, 95, 96, 97, 98, 99, 100, 101, 137, 498, 506, 530, 535, 547, 570, 571, 574
  formation, 93
  fossil wood, 98, 99
  invertebrate traces, 55
  Jacovec Cavern, 98
  Lincoln Cave, 100
  Member 2, 98
  Member 4, 98
  Member 5Stw53, 100East (Oldowan), 100West (Acheulean), 100
  micromammals, 99
  Name Chamber, 55
  paleoenvironmental reconstruction, 55
  Silberberg Grotto, 55
  vertebrates, mammalian, 100
  vertebrates, non-mammalian, 55
Still Bay tool industry, 9, 63, 64
Swartkrans, 56, 91, 92, 96, 98, 99, 102, 114, 115, 502, 571
  accumulating agents, 109
  bone tools, 106
  burnt bones, 56
  coprolites, 109
  ecologically sensitive taxa, 108
  gastropods, 116
  Hanging Remnant, 109
  Lower Bank Member 1, 109
  micromammals, 56, 116
  paleoenvironments, 105, 117

vertebrates, mammalian, 56, 105, 109
vertebrates, non-mammalian, 116

Taï Forest, 10
Taieb, Maurice, 1, 162, 166, 167, 214, 228, 229, 384
taphonomic bias
  definition of, 18
Taung, 57, 135, 136, 139, 141, 498
  aquatic fauna, 140
  child, *Australopithecus africanus*, 57
  Crustacea, 141
  invertebrates, 57
  micromammals, 138
  paleoenvironments, 140
  pollen records, 137
  taphonomic agents, 137
  vertebrates, mammalian, 57, 138
  vertebrates, non-mammalian, 57, 140
taxonomic composition
  use in paleoenvironmental reconstruction, 11
taxonomic habitat index
  use in paleoenvironmental reconstruction, 12
Tchiua, 50
Ternifine. See Tighenif
Th-OH quarries
  paleoenvironments, 491
Thabaseek Tufa, 137, 138
Thabasikwa River, 136
Thackeray, J. Francis, 145
Thomas Quarries, 466
Thomas Quarry I
  Grotte à Hominidés, 481, 482
Tibesti mountains, 262
Tighennif, 466, 475
  micromammals, 478, 479
  paleoenvironments, 480
  paleo-lake, 479
  vertebrates, mammalian, 477
  vertebrates, non-mammalian, 478
Tobène, 185
Tobias, Phillip, 67, 135, 138, 344
topographic heterogeneity, 30
Toros-Menalla, 20, 29, 30, 177, 182, 183, 501, 523
  insect traces, 183
  phytoliths, 183
  vertebrates, mammalian, 183
  vertebrates, non-mammalian, 183
Total-Evidence Dating
  definition of, 20
trace fossils, definition of, 10
Tugen Hills, 28, 174, 332
  body size effects, 340
  Chemeron Formation, 332
  Kapthurin Formation, 332

Lukeino Formation, 332
Mpesida beds, 31, 332
Muruyur Formation, 332
Ngorora Formation, 332
Sagatia, 333
vertebrates, mammalian, 337
Turnover Pulse Hypothesis, 36, 344

Ufefua, 50
Uhlig, Carl, 384
Upper Awash river, 256
Upper Awash Valley, 257
Upper Laetolil Beds, 240, 241
Uraha Hill, 453
Usno Formation, 170, 278, 312

Vaal River, 120
van Hoepen, E.C.N., 120, 127
van Riet Lowe, Clarence, 51, 66
Variability Selection Hypothesis, 15
vegetation
  associations, definition of, 7
  formation, definition of, 7
Vrba, Elisabeth, 15, 52, 55, 97, 105, 291

Wadi Moghra
Wadi Natrun, 461, 465
Wara Formation, 187
Warwire Formation, 180
Webi Shebele River, 169
Wembere-Manonga
  paleo-lake, 179
  vertebrates, mammalian, 179
  vertebrates, non-mammalian, 179
West African
  pollen records, 184
White, Frank, 3
White, Tim, 394
Winam Gulf, 360
Wochacha volcano, 262
Wonderwerk Cave, 58, 92, 101, 133, 142, 151, 155, 156, 158, 548, 559
  charcoal fragments, 149
  controlled use of fire, 59
  micromammals, 59, 148
  paleoenvironments, 160
  phytoliths, 156
  plant remains, 156
  vertebrates, mammalian, 59, 148
  vertebrates, non-mammalian, 59

Wonranso-Mille
  vertebrates, mammalian, 165
Wooded grasslands, definition of, 6
Woodlands, definition of, 3
Woranso-Mille, 165, 240, 278
Wymer, John, 64

Ysterfontein, 61
  vertebrates, mammalian, 62
  vertebrates, non-mammalian, 62

Zanclean Deluge, 31
Zaïre Air Boundary, 136
Zeit Wet phase, 31, 462
Zinjanthropus. See *Paranthropus*